COMPANION TO
CONTEMPORARY
ARCHITECTURAL
THOUGHT

COMPANION TO CONTEMPORARY ARCHITECTURAL THOUGHT

Edited by Ben Farmer
and Hentie Louw

LONDON and NEW YORK

First published in 1993
by Routledge
11 New Fetter Lane, London EC4P 4EE

Simultaneously published in the USA and Canada
by Routledge Inc.
29 West 35th Street, New York, NY 10001

Selection and editorial matter
© 1993 Ben Farmer and Hentie Louw
The chapters © 1993 Routledge

Typeset in 9¹/₂/12 Palatino, Scantext
by Leaper & Gard Ltd, Bristol
Printed in England by Clays Ltd, St. Ives plc
Printed on acid free paper

Acknowledgements

The following chapters have been reprinted with
permission of Rizzoli International Publications Inc.:
Chapter 44 (pp. 254–9) 'Structural theories and their
architectural expression: a review of possibilities', from
The Chicago Architectural Journal, Vol. 1.
Chapter 57 (pp. 342–9) 'Space, knowledge and power',
from *Skyline* (March 1982).

Chapter 54 (pp. 318–24) 'Architectural form and light' has
been reprinted with the permission of Macmillan Publishing
Company from *Descriptive art and modern interiors:
environments for people*, Vol. 69, ed. Maria Schofield,
copyright 1980. Originally published by Studio Vista
Publishers, Ltd.

British Library Cataloguing in Publication Data
Companion to Contemporary Architectural Thought
   I. Farmer, Ben II. Louw, Hentie
   720

Library of Congress Cataloging-in-Publication Data
Companion to contemporary architectural thought / edited by
   Ben Farmer and Hentie Louw ; consultant editor,
   Adrian Napper.
     p.   cm.
   Includes bibliographical references and index.
   1. Architectural criticism—History—20th century.   I. Farmer,
Ben, 1930–   .   II. Louw, H. J. (Hentie J.)   III. Napper,
Adrian. NA2599.C66   1992
720'. 1—dc20   92–12839

ISBN 0 415 01022 5

Contents

Preface

When one speaks of the art of building, the chaotic mess of clumsy debris, immense piles of shapeless materials, a dreadful noise of hammers, perilous scaffolding, a fearful grinding of machines and an army of dirty and mudcovered workmen – all this comes to the mind of ordinary people, the unpleasant outer cover of an art whose intriguing mysteries, noticed by few people, excite the admiration of all those who penetrate them. There they discover inventions of a boldness that proclaims a great and fertile genius, proportions of a stringency that indicates severe and systematic precision, and ornaments of an elegance that tells of a delicate and exquisite feeling. Whoever is able to grasp true beauty to this extent will, far from confounding architecture with the lesser arts, be inclined to range it among the more profound sciences. The sight of a building, perfect as a work of art, causes a delightful pleasure which is irresistible. It stirs in us noble and moving ideas and that sweet emotion and enchantment which works of art carrying the imprint of a superior mind arouse in us. A beautiful building speaks eloquently for its architect.

(Laugier 1753: 7–8)

A previous title of this book, *The Nature of Architecture,* perhaps best conveys the aims and scope of the project: it is an attempt to bring together, under one cover, a series of writings on architecture that will introduce the reader in a catholic way to the essential qualities of this important human activity as it has revealed itself through history.

Most fields that touch on architecture have undergone significant changes in the course of this century, which means that the perspective from which we view the subject and its role within society is very different now from what it was, say, a hundred years ago. However, while globally public attention is increasingly attracted to architecture in recognition of its cultural significance and because of concern over the performance and resource implications of buildings, very few people have a real grasp of the true purpose of the discipline itself.

This is partly due to its complexity and scale, but the fragmented form in which architecture is presented in the media must be an important contributing factor. Major scholarly works like Sigfried Giedion's *Space, Time and Architecture* (1941), which offer an overview of the subject, are rare these days – it is specialist studies and narrowly drawn general expositions which proliferate.

Although an understandable reaction to the uncertainties of a period of transition, we believe this trend to be detrimental to architectural development in the long run because it distorts the way in which the subject is conceived by professionals and lay people alike. Whatever other characteristics architecture might have, the one feature that stands out throughout history as being intrinsic to its nature is its tendency towards forming wholes. And it is this aspect of the discipline that seems to be most under threat.

The time therefore is ripe and the need manifest for a synoptic collaborative work – one that will bring the topic into focus as comprehensively as possible and provide an appreciation of the general state of the architectural world as it appears at the close of the twentieth century.

Essentially the book is theoretical in approach with the emphasis on timeless and universal considerations, although necessarily exemplified in a manner characteristic of our time. By seeking answers to such basic architectural questions as why, what, where, when, how and for whom buildings are built, we hope to give the reader some insights into the scope and richness of a discipline that has always drawn inspiration in equal measure from those two great founts of human knowledge: art and science.

The subject is examined through a series of individual essays written from different viewpoints (a 'plurality of voices' seemed a prudent response in view of the scale of the undertaking). Over one hundred authors, most of whom are architects and scholars of international standing, have contributed, but even this attempt at making the work wide-ranging and international through the co-ordination of expertise in the field has natural limitations.

First, it has to be accepted that, ultimately, the views expressed and the subject matter dealt with most closely reflect the values and interests of what is loosely known as 'Western civilization'. It is a condition that is unavoidable, but we trust that, with authors recruited on a world-wide basis, the end-product is sufficiently open-ended and objective to have relevance outside these cultural boundaries.

Second, it must be acknowledged that, despite our best efforts in getting a comprehensive coverage of the subject, gaps remain. It would be foolish to think that it could be otherwise with anything as broad-based and ancient as architecture. A certain arbitrariness in selection is endemic to any exercise of this kind. Another set of circumstances, someone else collecting and collating the material, might have produced a different – not necessarily any less viable – end-result.

In a sense this only confirms a central theme of the book, namely that architecture is a holistic entity whose constituents are organically interrelated, mutually supportive and, to an extent, interchangeable. If an overall picture or 'story' emerges from an enquiry into its nature, it does so in a manner analogous to a kaleidoscope.

This, of course, presupposes a coherent arrangement of the elements to begin with or, to put it in a more architectural way, a 'design' that would suggest a preferred order of reading the contents without precluding other partial samplings. In order to achieve this objective we have imposed a definite format on the volume: the essays focus on particular aspects of the subject; the book's structure gives them collective and cumulative significance. In this way a broad theme could be addressed while the specific selection within the various sub-sections allows the book to be read either sequentially or selectively. Another distinctive feature of the work is that it is richly illustrated in a variety of visual media. The pictorial record is meant not only to exemplify argument carried in the text in an architectural manner, but also to form a parallel reinforcing and extending narrative.

The essays themselves range from about 2,000 to 5,000 words in length. Most (over 90 per cent) were commissioned especially for the book; some of these were translated from the original languages of the authors. The rest feature because they have a pertinent message which has contemporary relevance. In each case the brief was that the paper should give an overview of a particular architectural issue, that it should introduce the reader to noteworthy results of scholarly investigations, but not to attempt exhaustive treatment nor to exclude the fruits of personal experience and wisdom.

An early editorial decision had been to try and maintain as much as possible of the individual qualities of each submission. Architecture is a broad church which has to accommodate many different approaches with numerous interpretations. We felt that it would be against the spirit of the subject matter to strive too rigorously for consistency of style and format. This also applies to the way in which the material was compiled. The book was prepared by a team of three editors, each being responsible for the selection of the contributors and the processing of the submitted material for a number of sub-sections.

We can only hope that whatever qualities may have been lost as a consequence of this policy are more than made up for by the greater variety of expression obtained. It has been the intention throughout, on the part of both publisher and editors, to produce a book that would be accessible to a wide audience; students and teachers of architecture and related subject areas, professionals and interested lay readers should all find something of value among its pages. To purists who object in principle to such an approach – who argue that this is an over-ambitious goal doomed to failure from the start because academic standards and popular appeal do not mix, that scope inevitably defeats depth of enquiry – we have only this answer: it is no different from the task that faces those involved in the creation of architecture every day.

B.F. and H.L.

REFERENCES

Giedion, S. (1941) *Space, Time and Architecture*, Cambridge, Mass.: Harvard University Press, 1967.

Laugier, M.-A. (1753) *Essai sur l'architecture*, Paris; trans. 1977, W. and A. Herrmann, *An Essay on Architecture*, Los Angeles: Hennessey & Ingalls.

Acknowledgements

The task of acknowledging the help we have received in the preparation of this encyclopedia is indeed a pleasant one. We owe particular thanks to our commissioning editor, Jonathan Price, for his vision and confidence in commissioning the work and for his support throughout.

We are indebted to the rest of the Routledge team for their help and co-operation: Shân Millie for so much of the detailed management; Emma Waghorn for leading and directing the copy-editing team; Graham Painting for his painstaking work in vetting typescripts and pursuing references; Nigel Marsh for co-ordinating all the visual material; Richard Raper for the onerous task of indexing; Judith Watts, the promotion manager, and finally, Michelle Darraugh for managing the final stages of the project so efficiently.

We owe a great debt for the help received from our home institutions. At Heriot Watt University, our thanks to Rosemary Hall for secretarial help. At the university of Newcastle upon Tyne, grateful thanks to Alison Tate for her work in setting up the project and in the production of the initial brochure; to Dr Margaret Wills, Librarian, Department of Architecture, for her invaluable help and knowledge of the material in the Seminar Library most germane to the project; to Margaret Davison for most of the secretarial work, and to Fausto Perrero, B.Arch. student, for Portuguese translations.

We would like to record our thanks to the Audio Visual Centre for advice and high-quality photographic service, particularly with respect to transforming illustrative materials; and to The Robinson Library (The University's main library) for access to reference books and special collections for illustrations.

A final personal note of thanks to Maureen Farmer for helping to test ideas over many years and for advice on sociological issues.

PART 1

INTRODUCTION

Introduction

The basic human needs of shelter from climate and safety from attack (the first purposes of buildings) have over the centuries been transformed into the provision of architecture as a manifestation of the human spirit.

The story of architecture begins when the struggle for survival had been won and investment could be made in work that had spiritual, symbolic or enriching significance. If the history of building started when we adopted shelter that was heavy and durable, an important intellectual stage was reached when buildings became assemblages of shaped parts; but temples and burial places are generally accepted as the first true works of architecture.

If it is to take root, architecture must relate to the needs of society – dynamic and confident architecture being produced by dynamic and confident societies, whereas uncertain or decadent societies have their characteristics reflected in what they build.

It is because architecture requires serious investment of all kinds (effort, skill, materials, wealth, risk) that it provides such a telling trace of human endeavour and social structure. Architecture as 'Mistress of the Arts' has always doubled as witness to culture.

As will be argued, architecture must respond to *people* in context and as they interact within and between societies. In these respects, *place* and *routes* are important, as are the building patterns and codes that have evolved over time.

Traditionally architecture can be seen to be place-, time- and culture-specific, with logic, practicality and purpose being of central importance, and with resource, vision, organizational ability, talent and available technology as the ultimate limitations. Now that we have the wealth, technology, means of communication and transport to build almost anything almost anywhere – not an entirely beneficial state of affairs – perhaps the major challenge facing architecture at the turn of the century is one of identity. The first four essays outline the nature of architecture, key developments within it, its significances, its challenges and its limitations. Hugh Casson's essay concludes the section by pointing up the excellence of anonymous architecture, but the rapid and continuous expansion of the world's population may require things to be done more deliberately in future – either great opportunity or awesome responsibility lies ahead.

B.F.

RECOMMENDED READING

Alexander, C. (1979) *The Timeless Way of Building*, New York: Oxford University Press.

Collins, P. (1965) *Changing Ideals in Modern Architecture 1750–1950*, London: Faber.

Cook, J.W. and Klotz, H. (eds) (1973) *Conversations with Architects*, London: Lund Humphries.

Creswell, H.B. (1986) *The Honeywood File and Honeywood Settlement*, London: Architectural Press.

Frampton, K. (1980) *Modern Architecture, A Critical History*, London: Thames & Hudson.

Giedion, S. (1967) *Space, Time and Architecture*, Cambridge, Mass.: Harvard University Press.

Hughes, R. (1991) *The Shock of the New: Art and the Century of Change*, London: Thames & Hudson.

Kostof, S. (ed.) (1977) *The Architect: Chapters in the History of a Profession*, New York: Oxford University Press.

Mumford, L. (1952) *Art and Technics*, London: Oxford University Press.

—— (1955) *Sticks and Stones: A Study of American Architecture and Civilization*, New York: Dover.

Pevsner, N. (1963) *An Outline of European Architecture*, 7th edn, Harmondsworth: Penguin.

Saint, A. (1983) *The Image of the Architect*, New Haven: Yale University Press.

Scully, V. (1961) *Modern Architecture: The Architecture of Democracy*, New York: George Braziller.

Vitruvius Pollio, M. (before AD 27) *De Architectura*; trans. M.J. Morgan 1914, *The Ten Books on Architecture*, Cambridge, Mass.: Harvard University Press; facsimile edn 1960, New York: Dover Publications.

1   The nature of architecture

Patrick Nuttgens

Architecture is not just an activity or an event or a collection of artefacts. It is not even simply an art. Architecture is fundamental to all human affairs; it stands at the very beginning of civilization, for without it there would be no possibility of civilization or culture. Architecture is inescapable, universal, endless and continuous. It is also elementary. It spans between the crudest form of accommodation in a cave to the most complex kind of sophisticated, artificial environment. But whatever its scale and whatever its complexity, for the most part it means shelter.

The beginning of architecture can therefore be taken as the provision of shelter – shelter not for a few but for everyone. And the most elementary form of that is the basic house, the dwelling for the ordinary man and woman – that is, for all people, in every part of the world. The nature of architecture is best understood if the study of it starts with common artefacts made by necessity and moves to the achievements created by choice and imagination.

From the beginning, as far as is known, there have been only two ways of providing that basic shelter. On the one hand, you could make a frame or skeleton and cover it with skin; on the other, you could make walls by placing one block upon another.

The skeleton-and-skin structure was developed in many parts of the world simply because it was so obviously a sensible idea. Of such structures the best-known is the North American tepee, with its poles leaning against one another and bound at the top with their ends overlapping, the whole structure wrapped round with animal skin. This simple structure became famous when the European settlers in North America encountered the native Indians. But it was not the only type. Other variations included the skin tents of Lapland, structures made of brushwood, clay and reed, and the wood and paper houses of the Japanese. These did not spread as widely as the other basic type, but they were the precursors of the framed structures of glass and iron of the nineteenth century, and of the steel and glass structures of the present day; they can be seen now also as precursors of modern spatial structures using synthetic materials.

The other basic type of shelter was more widespread. Almost everywhere in the world people have built by assembling blocks – of dried mud, clay, bricks or stones. Early structures were created simply by piling one block upon another; the problems solved in different ways in different parts of the world included finding ways of turning corners, and of leaving holes for people to get in or out, or to let light in and smoke out. The final problem was how to finish the house at the top – with either a sloping roof or a flat one. The materials could be almost anything: blocks made of alluvial mud sometimes bound with straw to make it more cohesive and lasting; or kiln-dried bricks; or even ice, as in the Eskimo igloos of the Arctic regions. But of all such materials, the most adaptable, permanent and expressive was stone. And stone in almost every part of the world has been exploited to make architecture of every kind, humble and grand.

For the moment we must look at the basic house. Of fundamental importance was the way the necessary spaces for living were assembled. As soon as humans began to look beyond the single unit for dwelling they had two ways of grouping the component rooms. The first method was the multiple dwelling, that is, one made up of a number of separate units, each with its own roof system, grouped together closely or freely. The *trullo* at Alberobello in southern Italy (Figure 1) is the best surviving example of that type. The vaulted stone rooms could be grouped together in twos, threes or fours and ultimately made into an elaborate and fascinating complex. Tents, as in Arab desert settlements, could be similarly grouped together.

Figure 1 *The* trulli *at Alberobello, southern Italy.*

Figure 2 *Skara Brae, Orkney.*

Especially fascinating is Skara Brae in Orkney (Figure 2). In 1850 a violent storm undid the work of another storm about 3,000 years earlier, and uncovered a Stone Age village of stone houses connected by passageways, with walls corbelled inwards to end in smoke-holes. They were probably originally covered by turfs. The houses had stone hearths, stone beds and even a stone dresser.

Alternatively, people could make a single compact dwelling, with all the rooms under one roof. Originally that entailed the housing of animals and humans under the same covering. The early houses of the Scottish Highlands were of this type; they housed people on one side of the fireplace, and cattle on the other. Once the animals had been moved out and given a separate shelter, this type of dwelling developed into the cottage of two rooms, the butt and ben – one room for living and one for sleeping.

It was a pattern that became more sophisticated when one room was assigned more importance than the other. The classic pattern was the Greek *megaron*, – a hall with a room opening off it – which started on the Mycenaean mainland. That simple pattern was, in due course, to become the basic component of any great house or any castle. Then the houses expanded upwards – the addition of an upper floor or a balcony required the construction of a stair, at first external, then internal.

Further refinements came with the development of ways of regulating temperature. For the sake of cool-

ness, houses in the East might be grouped around a courtyard. That was found so convenient that it spread by way of European monastic establishments to academic institutions such as the universities. But in harsher climates – most of Europe, especially the northern parts – the most important development was the making of a fireplace.

In the earliest houses the fire was in the centre of the floor, the smoke escaping through a hole in the roof with or without a lid to keep the rain out at other times. It was the moving of the fireplace to the wall, usually the outer wall in a rectangular house, and the gradual development of a chimney, at first of timber and then of stone, which created the house form. The movement of the fireplace to an outer wall can be considered the first architectural exercise of putting comfort before technical efficiency – a process which has continued ever since. Of equally fundamental, and ultimately definitive, importance was the separation of the uses – and therefore the users – of a building.

That basic architecture was what came to be classified in the nineteenth century as the vernacular. The Latin word *verna* means a home-born slave and vernacular architecture, like vernacular language, art and music, is thus the work of the underprivileged, the common people. The argument must now be taken further. If the key to vernacular architecture is the ordinary house, the key to *great* architecture is the tomb and the temple.

No better region exists to see this development than the 'fertile crescent' of the Middle East, the location of the first civilizations. There were tombs in the form of pyramids in ancient Egypt, and temples in Egypt and Mesopotamia. As with the vernacular, their origin can be seen as a response to challenge and demand, but from the very beginning, the great architecture of the tomb or the temple had an additional meaning or dimension.

The need of the people was no longer simply for shelter; there was a requirement for something more permanent, more lasting and more emotionally significant. In that sense the story of great architecture can be seen as the astonishing story of how individuals and groups have taken the structures, groupings, plans, access and service arrangements originally evolved to satisfy basic human needs, and transformed them into one of the greatest manifestations of the human spirit.

In that transformation – the beginning of architecture as an art – is it possible to identify the specifically architectural factors that make it distinct from all other arts and most other functions? Is it possible to search for an architectural meaning, that is, a meaning inherent in the building, not something extra or added in the form of decoration? If it is, how could such an architectural meaning be created in the first place, and how could it be made manifest?

There are two major structural forms which have throughout history made possible an architecture capable of being evocative and expressive. The first is the post and lintel. The lintel can be either flat, with one horizontal stone lying on top of two vertical stones as in Stonehenge, or triangular, in the form of a crudely carved pediment, also propped on two vertical stones. The second form is the arch, also of two basic types. The first was the corbelled arch, a system whereby stones or bricks are laid one on top of the other projecting inwards until, in the end, they join each other on the top without the need of a capstone or lintel. The corbelled arch was developed in many parts of the world, notably in the brickwork cisterns of Mohenjo-Daro in India's earliest civilization, in the Chinese vaulted tombs of the third century BC, and in the arches supporting the waterways that fed the hanging gardens of Babylon. The *true arch*, built of radiating wedge-shaped stones arranged to form a semi-circle, was an act of the imagination that released unprecedented architectural possibilities and, again, could take several forms. It could be a round arch as in Roman or Norman architecture, a pointed arch as in Gothic, or a stilted arch (rising vertically for a distance before turning inward, so that it could meet in a point at the top) as in much Moorish and Islamic architecture.

Both types were modified and refined until they almost achieved perfection. The most perfect post-and-lintel structure is the Greek temple, of which the climax was the Parthenon (Figure 3), erected on the Acropolis in Athens in the fourth century BC. The most perfect example of Gothic architecture was probably the cathedral of Chartres, dating from the twelfth, thirteenth and fourteenth centuries. With the cathedral at Beauvais, the masons took the refinement so far that part of the structure came crashing down. Of all adventurous structures, one of the most memorable and expressive is the Roman aqueduct, the Pont du Gard, at Nimes.

Such basic and influential structures have been changed, adapted and modified throughout the world. Because of the cultural triumph of the West for several centuries, other parts of the world have a greater

Figure 4 *The Buddhist temple at Borobudur.* (Photograph: *Douglas Dickens*)

knowledge of Western architecture than, until recently, we did of theirs. But in recent years our knowledge of Middle Eastern architecture, of Asian architecture and of that of the Far East, has become so much greater that it has modified and transformed the history of architecture – and made it considerably more fascinating. It has thus enlarged for everyone the meaning of architecture.

In many architectural styles, especially those once considered remote and exotic, decor or decoration can be seen as the key to design, particularly in regions where representation was, for religious reasons, forbidden and decoration had to be abstract. That applied for many centuries to much of the Middle East. In other regions the most elaborate sculptures were indicators of grand buildings rather than, as in Western Europe, the formal organization of the monument itself. Examples of such elaborate sculptures are to be found in the Dravidian temples of India, in the Angkor Wat in Cambodia and, notably, in Borobudur, Java (Figure 4) – the Buddhist temple of about AD 800, with a series of terraces topped with seventy-two bell-stupas with no fewer than seventy-two Buddhas hiding inside them. But Borobudur was also an example of a sophisticated geometry in the organization of the plan – and that introduces another essential component in the nature of architecture.

The plan is, after all, the essential factor in the creation of a work of architecture; it is the organization of areas and spaces to accommodate and link together the needs – or functions – for which the building is erected. The plan is thus the key to understanding the form of the building, for all architecture is concerned with utility as well as beauty, with the satisfaction of needs as well as the expression of individuality.

So widely spread and so various are the products of architecture that it has always been necessary to divide and subdivide them in categories so as to facilitate their understanding. For most of history, the easiest way has been to group or divide architecture into periods identified by architectural 'styles', and also by chronological eras. Such are the architectures of the first civilizations

Figure 3 *The Parthenon, Acropolis.*

in Mesopotamia and the Middle East, the architecture of Egypt, the architecture of Greece and Rome, Islamic architecture, Gothic architecture, the Renaissance and the baroque. But the pattern becomes more complicated and the system of classification less satisfactory with the Industrial Revolution of the late eighteenth and nineteenth centuries and the development of a modern architecture, now itself being re-examined and redefined.

It is necessary to emphasize that break because there are two major factors that separate the understanding of the nature of architecture today from that of almost any earlier period. The first is technical. The materials that characterize and are basic to modern architecture are fabricated materials such as steel, concrete and a range of plastics. And more than that: not only the materials but also the structures are original. Architecture is now able to create spatial structures based on concrete or plastics or tensile materials such as steel, which makes possible many forms which were unknown before.

The second factor is the social revolution of our time which has encouraged designers to identify important architecture as the architecture of the common people. For the first time in the history of architecture the housing of the ordinary person was seen in the twentieth century as being potentially the stuff of great architecture. That in itself led to certain inevitable conclusions. For example, modern architecture would be opposed to ornament, because ornament would not be relevant, it was thought, to the housing of the ordinary person. It was a theory almost certainly wrong but easily explicable.

Both of these factors raise major questions about the nature of architecture. Modern architecture has created unprecedented forms, such as the Sydney Opera House. It has made it more difficult to recognize the difference between good and bad architecture, or to distinguish great architecture from insignificant architecture. And it is no longer easy to classify architecture by styles, or even by periods.

One of the factors making that difficult was the development in the 1960s, as happened earlier at the turn of the century, of conservation – the practice of preserving and modifying and giving a new life to whole complexes as well as to individual buildings. It became increasingly unclear to which period or style the restored or renewed building belonged. It could therefore be argued that the only possible schema on the basis of which it is possible to have an understanding of architecture is to divide the corpus of work into building types rather than traditional styles. Such building types might be as follows: the architecture of government, of religion, of education, of day-to-day living, of leisure, of transport, of learning, of culture, of entertainment, of commerce, of industry, and of defence. Sir John Summerson, the eminent architectural historian, in a major paper delivered to the Royal Institute of British

Architects (Summerson 1957), considered that the programme of work was the only possible source for unity and therefore the key to modern design.

To elaborate that principle and apply it to the definition of the nature of architecture in the twentieth century, it might be argued that it is from the programme, the stated needs of the users of the building, that any idea is developed. That idea can give unity to the diversity of the programme; and that of course is the reason for the architecture being created in the first place. It therefore follows that any revelation of modern architecture must look back to the programme of work which it is attempting to satisfy. Does that mean that each work of architecture will be different, that there will be more styles and more types of building? That would appear to be a logical conclusion. In practice, however, it rarely happens, for the programmes are remarkably similar. Modern architecture reveals its similarity in almost every part of the world.

That sameness has provoked a widespread reaction to what is commonly seen as typical modern design. The present crisis in the definition of the nature of architecture arises from arguments about the personal and impersonal, and the reaction against the general anonymity which seems to be characteristic of the Modern Movement. It emphasizes the difference between the International Style (at first seen as the mainstream of the Modern Movement) and the regional styles which have more of history (and of nostalgia) about them.

Above all, certain basic factors in contemporary architecture make it difficult to relate to the history of recognized styles. The first has to do with scale. There appears to be no end to the possibilities of the height and general size of complexes, of the number of levels it is possible to create and the height to which they may go. The identification therefore of modern architecture with the satisfaction of conventional human needs is less obvious. The second factor is the development of technical services, which is increasingly recognized as the major development of the last fifty, or possibly hundred, years. Heating, lighting and acoustics, and services such as lifts, which have transformed the possibilities of building high, have been particularly important. It is clear that the technical services must work efficiently to make modern architecture a practical possibility. Their failure therefore becomes a significant factor in condemning a building as bad architecture.

Ultimately all modern architecture has to be multi-purpose and multi-level. It covers every scale from the tiny to the monstrous. Against such a background, is it possible to establish what is ultimately distinctive about architecture? What does it deal with which is different from any similar activity – from engineering and building and the visual arts? What, ultimately, architecture does – and does alone – is to create space. Not just space as in sculpture, but space for the accommodation and satisfaction of people's needs.

In one of the most influential, as well as elegant, of all studies of the theory of architecture, Geoffrey Scott emphasizes in his concluding chapter the inescapable significance of space in architecture:

> Even from a utilitarian point of view, space is logically our end. To enclose a space is the object of building; when we build we do but detach a convenient quantity of space, seclude it and protect it, and all architecture springs from that necessity. But aesthetically space is even more supreme. The architect models in space as a sculptor in clay. He designs his space as a work of art; that is, he attempts through its means to excite a certain mood in those who enter it.
>
> (Scott 1914: 227)

To make a space expressive – and a complex of spaces fascinating and memorable – is ultimately the purpose of architecture. In that sense, architecture is the most distinctive as well as the most fundamental of all the arts.

But what kind of art? It may be art considered as skill, which was the way ancient Greeks saw it, or art considered as a demonstration of authority, as in Rome and in the Renaissance, or art which has a spiritual meaning – the metaphysics of architecture as in the Gothic period of the Middle Ages – or art which expresses something romantic or poetic, as in the nineteenth century. What is clear is that architecture is always capable of making more than a simple statement about its use. It is more capable of expression than any other art-form, both because it is so elementary and basic and because it is so much more complex.

In the early years of the twentieth century, the Italian philosopher Benedetto Croce defined art as 'expression' (Croce 1900: 8). Without examining his theory in detail, it is clear that architecture is by far the richest and most complete of all the means of carrying out such expression. It expresses human needs and it finds out about those needs by examining the history of peoples' experience. It creates spaces which are not just decorative but are capable of being used. As such, architecture can be defined as an expression of human experience in the form of usable space.

Architecture involves more people than any other art-form. It involves the designer, the user and the observer. It has more requirements than any other art; it must function and it must look good. All of these factors and all of these agents change from time to time. No great building today is used as it was first intended, whether it was a house, a temple, a tomb or a palace. There is no end to the story of change in every kind of architecture. And no end to the study of its meaning.

In the final analysis, all architecture reveals the application of human ingenuity to the satisfaction of human needs. And among those needs are not only shelter, warmth and accommodation, but also the needs, felt at every moment in every part of the world in endlessly different ways, for something more profound, evocative and universal; for beauty, for permanence, for immortality.

REFERENCES

Croce, B. (1900) *Aesthetic*, 1920 edn, London: Vision Press/ Peter Owen, ch. 1, 'Intuition and expression'.

Scott, J. (1914) *The Architecture of Humanism*, 1980 edn, London: Architectural Press.

Summerson, J. (1957) *The Case for a Theory of Modern Architecture*, London: RIBA.

2 The temple or the cathedral: the search for spirituality in architecture, from the Renaissance to the present day.

Mark Dudek

> This is not simply a matter of ornament ... this quest is, in fact, curiously independent of stylistic development. It is more radical than all this; it is something resulting from a profound desire to dissolve the heavy prose of building into religious poetry; a desire to transform the heavy man-made temple into a multiple, imponderable pile of heavenly mansions.
>
> (Summerson 1963: 9)

Recently there has been an awakening of interest in architecture amongst those outside the profession. Contemporary architecture and urban issues have become the subject of mainstream media interest, which has brought with it astonishing levels of mostly negative criticism. The reasons for this are of course complex, but there is a common concern with the effects of modern architecture on our towns and cities, and on the environment in general.

Architecture perhaps does not reflect the spiritual needs of the age in the ways it did historically, or at least this is how it appears to many people who compare the architecture of this century to previous epochs. Inevitably, the increasingly secular nature of the Western world tends to limit the provision of those ritualistic buildings of the past, which give spirituality to the heart of our towns and cities today. But, perhaps more importantly, the overriding philosophy of logical positivism,[1] a philosophy which excludes all but that which is recognizable and observable, tends to inhibit architects in their quest for a contemporary architecture which satisfies our souls as well as our minds.[2] The notion of 'religious poetry' seems to be an inconceivable quest to the modern architect.

During the 1980s, much mainstream architecture became subject to merely stylistic considerations. There was widespread disillusionment with this approach towards the end of the decade, and the notion of a middle ground in architecture came to be tainted by the term 'Post-Modernism'. The consequence of this is an attempt now by many architects and critics to return to the ideologically extreme philosophies of High Modernism – minimalist interiors and flat roofs – or neo-classicism. Since classical architecture and High Modernism hold at their core a common obsession with scientific purity and mathematics, one suspects there is

much common ground linking the two. As in the resuscitation of classical concepts in art at the end of the eighteenth century, one senses a similar desire to combat the threat of chaos at the root of this movement towards Neo-Modernism[3] and neo-classicism.

However, the use of historical styles in the late twentieth century is highly inappropriate on a number of levels. For instance, proponents of the adoption of modernist ideology and all its rationalist baggage fail to recognize that if a whole generation of theory has brought us cities that are diagrammatic and unrefined, then perhaps the theory itself is diagrammatic and unrefined.[4] None the less, the suspicion persists that if design becomes compromised or less ideologically extreme than this, it will become mediocre or unrepresentative of the spirit of the modern world. This is the legacy of 1980s Post-Modernism. Now there is a real reluctance within the critical dialectic of architecture to accept that there is a valid 'middle ground', which is neither alienating for ordinary people, nor represents a false nostalgia for the past. Modernist urban architecture of the last forty years has created areas of our towns and cities which are often profoundly anti-urban.

What is this middle ground and what differentiates it from contemporary approaches to architectural design? In her essay 'Mannerist Rome', Caroline Constant describes how the experience of architecture, like any art, is subject to the sensual realm of perception, experienced subjectively, and to the abstract intellectual realm of cognition, understood objectively (Constant 1979: 19). Architecture can appeal to our emotions as well as our intellect. In a similar vein Summerson, writing in 1941, stated that the most successful buildings of the Modernist (pre-1939) period were buildings of an almost wholly diagrammatic nature (Summerson 1963: 200). Their success lay in their relationship with everything around them, rather than any inherent, self-generated qualities, and the consequence of this obsession with intellectual statements was that these buildings appeared to be like 'a neat prose account of this or that situation – a correct answer to a rather complicated examination question' (Summerson 1963: 200), but lacking the conviction to synthesize the subjective and the objective.

Most Modernist architecture continues to take its

impulses from the early ideologies of the heroic Modernists in its mirroring of a society which is mainly concerned with consumerism. In this respect, the failure of modern architecture does not lie in the lack of wit, sensibility and commitment of the modern architect, but rather in his or her inheritance of a tradition which fails to validate an architecture which appeals to the emotions as well as the intellect.

One can illustrate this idea by referring to a number of historic models. Architecture, unlike most other forms of art, is an experiential medium, and drawings or models can go only so far to clarify the nature of space.

Throughout the history of architecture there have been periods of great clarity and precise definition, often followed by epoques of less sure, more ambiguous tendencies. In Italian art and architecture of the quattrocento, for example, the whole art of building underwent profound change. The humanistic principles which brought about the Renaissance formalized for the first time beliefs which positioned humanity rather than God at the centre of the universe. In the plan form of the circular church, for example, an archetypically Renaissance form, this symbolism is very clear. However, the form also exemplifies an emphasis on plan organization, and the ability to see buildings in abstract compositional terms. It was at this stage that the notion of a secular building form, which could appeal to the scholarly aspirations of the *cognoscenti*, was first validated.

The Palladian villa, of which the Villa Capra, better known as the Villa Rotonda, would be the prime example, illustrates this point well. The Rotonda was built in 1567 for the prelate Paulo Almerico. It was a building primarily intended for the staging of entertainments, whilst enjoying views of the surrounding countryside. The appearance of the portico on all four sides enables the central drum space to act as the climax of the hierarchy (with humanity again at the centre), while the surrounding countryside is seemingly controlled and civilized by the four vistas. The notion of mathematical purity underlines the proportions of the whole building and the individual spaces and components of the piece. Its simple appearance belies its astonishing complexity. For instance, the unfluted columns of the portico play up the atmospheric effect of light on the solid surface. The ceiling of the portico is very slightly curved and lowered to prevent the effect of too deep a shadow above, and light penetrates the porch and gently dissolves into shadow. One of the themes of the building is the interpenetration of art and nature, and this is expressed by the horizontal effect of the porticoes. At the ends of each of the porticoes are two arched end walls, which subtly stop the form, and link the columns of the portico back into the building. The imperceptibly tapered verticals of the arches echo the entasis common to all classical columns, giving the effect of elasticity and mediating the rhythm of the columns into the bulk of the building.[5]

It is at every level the ideal villa, and whilst no one would deny that the piece appeals to the eye, its primary appeal is to the intellect, as one appreciates the art and individual genius of Palladio through the intellectual theories he subtly explores. The Palladian villa, and particularly the Rotonda, has a worldly quality deliberately avoiding the more spiritual resonances evoked by, for instance, the medieval cathedral. The significance of the Gothic structure represents humanity's devotion and subservience to God, whereas the mathematical perfection of Villa Capra implies that humans are no longer subservient to God. The symbolism of the temple as the residence of the muses, divinities who concerned themselves with the intellectual rather than spiritual life of mortals, further underlines this idea. The Rotonda has immense cultural significance and has set the key guidelines for architectural theory up to the present day. Yet because of its singular appeal to the enlightenment intellect, and its failure to reflect myths of earlier periods, it remains the archetypical 'heavy man-made temple' (Summerson 1963: 9).

If the architecture of the Renaissance quattrocento is expressive of intellectual humanistic concerns, the baroque, which followed on from the Renaissance, is expressive of a revival in spiritual values experienced

Figure 1 *Balthasar Neumann's abbey church at Neresheim.*

sensually. Where the Renaissance was static, the baroque was concerned with movement and tension. To illustrate this distinction, it is worth referring to the late baroque/rococo, since this was a high point in the exploration of the intuitively designed, emotionally charged space, immediately prior to the classical revivals of the nineteenth century.

The late baroque of the eighteenth century was an expression of the renewed faith in Catholicism after the ravages of the Thirty Years War. It also sought to assert the new-found security and independence of the German sovereign states; one of its main exponents was Balthasar Neumann, who worked for the Schönborn Prince Bishops in southern Germany. Neumann was an engineer by training but was gifted with the ability to take disparate ideas and influences and formalize them into new and original forms. His final work, the abbey church at Neresheim, achieves a synthesis of the almost intangible spiritual and worldly qualities which make great sensual space.

The building sits on a hill and has a bluff, well-proportioned exterior (Figure 1). Its interior is informed by a classical order and the overall organization obeys the rules of east–west orientation (Figure 2). Neumann was working with the idea of a highly articulated wall thickness, where the classical order almost fuses with the wall surface. The columns remain free-standing however, and support three interlocking domes over the crossing and transept. Although the design was severely compromised in its execution (only the foundations existed when Neumann died), the overall effect of movement and dynamism remains. The image of the space is of a series of stretched membranes (the roof), tied down by heavily sculpted walls. This creates a perfect fusion of heaviness and lightness, providing a sense of ordered complexity which reflects the state of human beings within their world.

In describing the characteristics of the Bavarian, John Bourke accurately defines the essentially sensuous pictorial nature of the baroque art, as compared to the more intellectual approach of the Renaissance:

The Bavarian, broadly speaking, is what has been called an 'Augenmensch', a 'man of the eye'; one, that is to say, for whom the eye is the primary channel by which he establishes contact with, and draws significance from, the world around him. His attitude is essentially sensuous, perceptive, intuitive. He is a sharp and fascinated observer of nature and of his fellows. Like the Austrian he has much of the Southerner's delight in the variety and fullness of the world of sense in its pageantry of shape, colour, light and shade. Even where his approach is intellectual or reflective his thought tends to be of a strongly pictorial cast in which the 'inner eye' is quite as much at work as the intellect. We think too of his fondness for play and drama which shows itself alike in a love of formal ritual of theatre and opera and in a sense of the dramatic in ordinary human intercourse which often saves him from taking himself and his life too seriously.

(Bourke 1958: 53)

The art of the baroque, particularly the late baroque of Neumann, has more connection to the primitive than the intellectual tradition within architectural theory. Whilst one cannot 'study' the complexities of the piece in the same way as one can the Rotonda, the experience of entering Neresheim as the sun sets through the west window on an autumn afternoon never fails to lift the spirits. It has qualities which enable it to transform and 'dissolve the heavy prose of building into religious poetry' (Summerson 1963: 9).

The Villa Rotonda was completed in about 1580, at about the same time as Wollaton Hall in Nottingham, England (Figure 3). The Renaissance did not have as strong an influence on architecture and life in Britain as it had in mainland Europe. However, Wollaton was one

Figure 2 *The church at Neresheim obeys the rules of east–west orientation.*

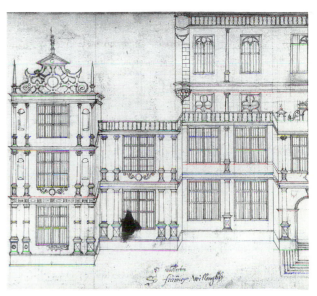

Figure 3 *Wollaton Hall.* (Source: *The Trustees of Sir John Soane's Museum*)

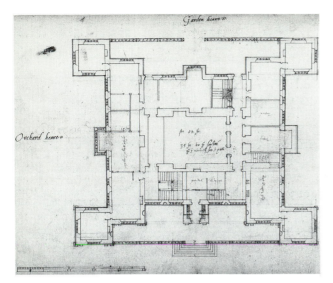

Figure 4 *Serlio's influence can be seen in the plan of Wollaton.* (Source: *The Trustees of Sir John Soane's Museum*)

of the earliest buildings to be strongly influenced by the new spirit of enlightenment in Europe at the time. Like Neresheim, Wollaton is unmentioned by the academic architectural establishment. Yet, also like Neresheim, it is part of an architectural tradition which synthesizes different ideas to express the spirit of the people and the times.

Alice Friedman links the social customs of the family to the unusual layout of Wollaton (Friedman 1989). Whilst recognizing the influence of Serlio and the French castle tradition, Friedman sees the main source of the originality of Wollaton as deriving from the fusion of the social traditions of the clients' family with new Renaissance ideas. The clearest way this can be understood is in the plan (Figure 4). Serlio's influence (derived from Italian villa design) could be seen in its compact character and the omission of an open central courtyard, the tight organization and, most importantly, symmetry. At first glance, all of these characteristics are in evidence at Wollaton. But on closer inspection, the inclusion of the medievally derived central hall and screens passage, side by side with a symmetrically planned upper floor, suggests that Wollaton marks the transition from medieval concepts of social organization to the modern, more compact, organization. The plan and section read together show the deliberate way in which the idea of the past and the future are fused; although the hall entrance is symmetrical about the face of the building, the actual entrance route (as originally planned) sidesteps the hall once within the façade, and since the hall is planned longitudinally, on entry the first encounter with the hall is at the short north end behind the screen. The space then becomes a subsidiary corridor, reversing the central significance it had throughout the medieval period.

Immediately above the hall is the main gathering space. Called the prospect room, it is, as the name suggests, a room with extraordinary views across the countryside. Its light, open structure not only contrasts with the heavy hall space beneath, but also draws analogies with the imagery of the heavy, fortified structures of the medieval period, to which Wollaton makes deliberate reference. It is, then, a building that takes up a reconciliatory position, adopting new ideas but also accommodating traditional themes, and creating a unique and resonant form. It is a building which seems to mediate between the earth and the sky, a quality which is further underlined by the rhythm of the balusters at the rooftop as compared to the ground floor level. Its verticality, visual transparency and overall texture give it a harmonious relationship with its natural setting.

The Villa Savoye (Figure 5), a seminal Modernist building, is by comparison to Wollaton almost wholly at odds with its site. The comparison between the two may not be an obvious one to draw, yet it helps to illustrate this difference between the fundamental nature of the two kinds of architecture: the purist Modernism of Villa Savoye and the composite nature of Wollaton.

This is especially clear in the treatment of the interior of Villa Savoye, where the ramp dominates the plan, producing a sequence of spaces which tends to make the object or the individual within the building more vivid. The use of ribbon windows around the whole building and a predominantly white finish evoke the evenness of a light, almost shadowless, quality often associated with dreams, and accentuates the feeling of horizontality, as compared to Wollaton. Qualities such as the purity of the villa's form, and its elevation above the ground on *piloti*, gives the piece a shocking, almost surreal appearance. Rather than effecting a harmonious relationship with its natural setting, Villa Savoye dominates the surrounding countryside through this deliberately unequivocal imagery. This dichotomy was of course intentional, and the new interest in psychological self-analysis at that time, and increasingly through the twentieth century, further underlines the human-centred nature of the piece.[6]

Figure 5 *The Villa Savoye by Le Corbusier.*

Giorgio de Chirico, a proto-surrealist painter of the early twentieth century, defined a world which predicted the essential nature of modernist architecture.[7] The critic Soffici described de Chirico's technique in 1914:

By means of almost infinite escapes – arcades and façades of bold straight lines, of looming masses of simple colour of almost funereal lights and shadows – he ends by expressing this sense of vastness, solitude, immobility and ecstacy which is sometimes produced in our souls by certain spectacles of memory when we are asleep.

(Soffici, cited in Soby 1955: 48)

The references to horizontality and deep perspective in de Chirico's paintings help to clarify this new spirit. It was fundamentally interested in humanity's domination of urban space, as compared to the soaring verticality of the medieval and Gothic spires or the dynamic containment of space within the baroque which exemplified the myths of those periods in history. The Modern Movement was thus revisiting the classical intellectual obsessions of the Renaissance, albeit employing a completely different language. It was essentially horizontal in its expression, compared to the vertiginous qualities of the forms it replaced.

Two of the examples illustrated, Wollaton and Neresheim, speak of an architecture which is highly ambiguous in its source and references. Yet it can be seen that it is memorable precisely because it adopts the philosophy of the middle ground. It is neither extremely disciplined by classical or mathematical rules, nor does it step profoundly outside the accepted norm to create shocking or extreme effects as is the case with Villa Savoye.

Clearly we should not attempt to reuse the architectural languages of the past. Architecture must mirror society, and it must now seek out a new language which expresses the true nature of our world at the end of the twentieth century. And whilst that world must look forward with optimism to a future where technology and science can service the requirements of all people, the recognition that our past is of equal importance hints at the adoption of a more composite approach to architecture. The assumptions of both classical and modernist architectures are based on purity, lucidity and the domination of space. Modernism added a new ingredient, that of abstraction, which intended to shock or make intellectual statements about the modern world. The search for meaning in modern art and architecture centred on interpreting often abstracted pieces as primitive references, whether they were seen through the eyes of children, graffiti artists, aborigines or peasants (Krauss 1986: 74; Rykwert 1972). The effects of people's misuse of their natural environment is only one of the areas where the notion of the return to a more simple, harmonious relationship between human beings and their world has relevance.

Today certain architects and critics use the analogy of the modern corporate bank and insurance headquarters as the 'cathedral to money' just as in the 1930s the power station was the 'cathedral to electricity'.[8] The analogy is highly problematic, because it is an analogy based on formal issues concerning scale rather than meaning. These buildings are more analogous to the temple than the cathedral, since they are concerned with commerce and tend to exclude the possibility of contemplative experiences. This distinction between the temple and the cathedral, which I believe is fundamental to an understanding of spirituality in the architecture of our towns and cities, is expressed more clearly by Summerson in his comparison between the 'heavy man-made temple' and the light 'heavenly mansions' which provoke 'religious poetry' (Summerson 1963: 9). Western culture is rooted in two thousand years of Christianity, and earlier myths related to natural phenomena. Society is bonded by opposing ideas such as good and evil, earth and sky, old and new, intellectual and intuitive. Historically, architecture was the mediator between these extremes rather than individual expressions of the extremes, as is the case of much contemporary architecture. We should attempt to mirror these values rather than the more superficial values which have generated much of the architecture of the past fifty years.

One of the new generation of buildings which reflect this spirit in architecture is the Mound Cricket Stand in London, designed by Michael Hopkins (see Farrelly 1986). A modern structure built into an existing Victorian arched wall, the new penetrates the existing to form a complex yet clearly definable base and middle. The roof is an articulated and extremely light tent structure which completes the layering of the piece. When viewed from the side, almost in section, the phenomenological reading may be the building that 'stretches from earth to sky. It possesses the verticality of the tower rising from the most earthly, watery depths, to the abode of a soul that believes in heaven' (Bachelard 1969: 25)[9]. We may not believe in heaven, but this building mediates between earth and sky in a way that makes our primitive roots and spiritual beliefs harmonize with the modern world. It is a significant pointer for the future of architecture.

NOTES

1   Logical positivism – philosophy of Compte recognizing only facts and observable phenomena.

2   Gaston Bachelard (1969) writes of the loss of distinction between the words 'soul' and 'mind' in French philosophy and psychology. 'As a result, they are both somewhat deaf to certain themes that are very numerous in German philosophy, in which the distinction between mind and soul (*der Geist und die Seele*) is so clear.' (Bachelard 1969: 25). Bachelard quotes the onomatopoeic

reading of the word 'soul' as deriving from the variations of breathing, a reading common to nearly all peoples.

3   The President of the RIBA, Maxwell Hutchinson, in his inaugural speech to the institute in July 1989 spoke of 'facing up to our responsibility of rationalism' and the revival of Modernist architecture, which he later described as 'Neo-Modernism'.

4   This idea was explored more fully by Doug Clelland in his essay 'In our times' (1987). The idea is illustrated on the one hand by Ludwig Hilberseime's project for a city centre of 1924: 'Its illusion lies in its barbaric simplicity and indifference to plurality which must underpin individual and social life again'; and the plan of the Sanctuary of Apollo, Delphi, 'a vision of stability based on the mythical and the uncertain, the symbolic and the energetic, in individual and social life' (Clelland 1987: 44).

5   Entasis can be defined as the way in which a slight convexity is introduced to column shafts to correct the visual illusion of concavity. See Ackerman 1966.

6   This idea is further explored in Richard Sennett's *The Fall of Public Man*, where he describes this new state as a form of narcissism: 'The myth of Narcissus has a double meaning, his self-absorption prevents knowledge about what he is and what he is not' (Sennett 1977: 324).

7   The iconographic imagery in the series of paintings entitled *The Disquieting Muses* by de Chirico includes an interpretation of the Castello Estense, Ferrara, and is worth comparing to Wollaton in its deliberate lack of transparency and refinement in what is a similarly contrived form.

8   Summerson discusses further this analogy between the cathedral and the power station in Summerson 1963: 203. A similarly erroneous version of this analogy was discussed by Martin Pawley on *The Late Show* (BBC2 TV, 27 March 1990) from his book (1990) *Theory and Design in The Second Machine Age*, where he likened modern financial buildings to the medieval cathedral in their functional need to communicate information. He thus denies the density of ideas within the fabric of a building such as Chartres, which refer to complex numbers theory, primordial and natural phenomena, and mystical symbolism, as well as ecclesiastical references. The buildings then are about layers of ideas rather than functions, often buried so deeply that their understanding becomes subconscious and thus truly spiritual.

9   The phenomenological reading of this idea may seem pretentious, but is worth pointing out because it encapsulates the fundamental difference between the Modernist building programme, which is derived almost exclusively from the plan, and a more poetic approach which refers initially to the section, but also includes literary and primitive elemental references (Bachelard 1969: 25).

REFERENCES

Ackerman, J.S. (1966) *Palladio*, Harmondsworth, Pelican.

Bachelard, G. (1969) *The Poetics of Space*, Boston, Mass.: Beacon.

Bourke, J. (1958) *Baroque Churches of Central Europe*, London: Faber & Faber.

Clelland, D. (1987) 'Berlin: origins to IBA' *Architectural Review* CLXXXI (1082): 43–6.

Constant, C. (1979) 'Mannerist Rome', *Architectural Design* 49 (3–4): 19.

Farrelly, E.M. (1986) 'The new spirit', *Architectural Review* CLXXX (1074): 7–12.

Friedman, A.T. (1989) *House and Household in Elizabethan England, Wollaton Hall and the Willoughby Family*, Chicago: University of Chicago Press.

Krauss, R.E. (1986) *The Originality of the Avant Garde and Other Modernist Myths*, Cambridge, Mass. and London: MIT Press.

Pawley, M. (1990) *Theory and Design in the Second Machine Age*, Oxford: Basil Blackwell.

Rykwert, J. (1972) *On Adam's House in Paradise*, New York: Museum of Modern Art.

Sennett, R. (1977) *The Fall of Public Man*, Cambridge: Cambridge University Press.

Soby, J.T. (1955) *Giorgio De Chirico*, New York: Museum of Modern Art.

Summerson, J. (1963) *Heavenly Mansions*, New York and London: W.W. Norton.

3 Buildings as social objects

Thomas A. Markus

The use of the word 'architecture' raises the fundamental problems addressed by this section. The word bears a resemblance to others which also stand for major classes of entities – concrete objects, phenomena or experiences – transformed by these words into abstractions. In the case of 'architecture' the entities are buildings and all their internal and external components such as rooms, courtyards, stairs, roofs, windows and gardens. Other words of this kind are 'family', standing for visible entities which may include adults, old people, children, domestic animals and servants; 'nature', standing for mountains, lakes, forests, grassland, trees, birds and animals; or 'art', standing for sculptures, paintings or photographs.

These abstractions share some features. First, whilst the entities they stand for are experienced through the senses – they are tangible, visible, audible or whatever – the abstraction is not. Second, the meaning of the words that stand for the entities has a great homogeneity across cultures and over time – change is slow – whereas the meaning of the abstract words changes rapidly with ideological shifts and serves to sever cultures rather than unite them. And third, the abstractions are arguable. In theory it should be possible to have a lively debate about whether something is a work of architecture, or art; whether a group of people comprises a family; or whether an urban park is part of nature. The resolution of such debates depends on examining the pattern of relationships within which the entities exist and then agreeing the rules by which membership of a class of entities is established. But a debate about whether something is rightly called a building, a painting, a child or a tree seems much less interesting.

In practice debates about these abstractions are rare once they shape the way we see things, and the ways we feel, think and speak about them. They have then become accepted as part of reality and their meaning is

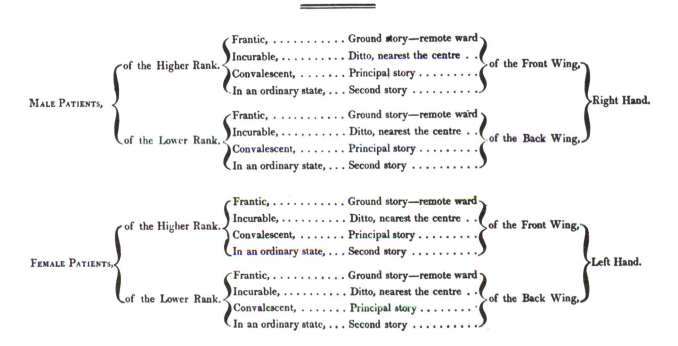

General View of the Plan of Classification, and of the Distribution of the Classes in the GLASGOW LUNATIC ASYLUM.

Figure 1 *Diagrammatic brief for Glasgow Lunatic Asylum, 1807 (architect: Stark). The sixteen classes of patients were classified in a three-layer hierarchical structure by gender, economic status (ability to pay or paupers), and medical condition (effectively, productive disability). These appear on the left of the diagram and map into the sixteen plan locations on the right. (Source: Author's photograph from Stark 1807)*

put beyond debate. When words like 'architecture' become as powerful as this, and so deeply embedded in a culture, it is right to speak of them as myths. Such myths have important functions. This essay examines the myth of architecture and analyses how it functions to obscure the social meaning of buildings.

The most direct way to start revealing architecture's mythical nature is to distance ourselves from the abstraction 'architecture' and to focus on concrete experiences of its objects – buildings. We can recognize at least three very powerful ones.

First is the experience of what we see (feel, hear, smell, etc.), that is, the geometry of the volumes and their enclosing surfaces – their ornament, colour, texture, articulation, transparency, etc. – in short, of forms. When the images formed by these elements form a coherent language we call it a style.

Second, we do things, and we see others doing things. Either we participate as actors, or we observe as audience. If the building is empty we deduce what is done there, what each of its spaces is for, from its location in the total structure of space, its furnishings and equipment, possibly from actual labels. In short we know its function. We describe it by function-related words for whole buildings ('airport', 'health centre', 'museum') or for individual spaces ('corridor', 'atrium', 'gallery', 'living room'). Within a given culture each of these words carries a rich parcel of meanings. 'Museum' or 'atrium' do not define simply a material process, but a space, an activity and a culture whose essence is a set of complex relationships between people, things, places and ideas. Such words serve not only to *de*scribe what exists, but *pre*scribe what is to come into being (Figure 1).

Third, whatever is done is done some*where*: in a space which is related to all the other spaces and the outside. These relationships of 'nextness' are topological, not geometrical, and are matters of continuous experience as we enter or move through a building. A space can be 'deep' within such a structure, that is we have to pass through many others before reaching it, or 'shallow' – we come across it almost at once (typically, an entrance lobby). It may be reachable by a single route only – that is, it lies somewhere on a branching tree – or by one or more alternative routes – that is, it lies on one or more rings. In short there is a spatial structure (Figures 2 and 3).

Form, function and space. They each mean something; they tell us something about ourselves, others, and the world – about relationships which are therefore social in that they involve ourselves and other people. At the deepest level it makes sense to speak of the elemental relationship of self-to-self as social. As we develop our understanding of it we begin to form answers to Gauguin's age-old questions (which he formulated in the first person plural) – 'where do I come from?', 'who am I?', 'where am I going?'. The relation-

ship of self-to-others is the very fabric of our childhood development, of our experience of family, friendship and conflict, and of our work and professional life. That of self-to-Other is the attempt to engage with the cosmos within which, with others around us, we struggle to find a meaning for life in terms of reason, nature, science, society, explicit religious belief or perhaps existential disorder. At any of these three levels of relationships if

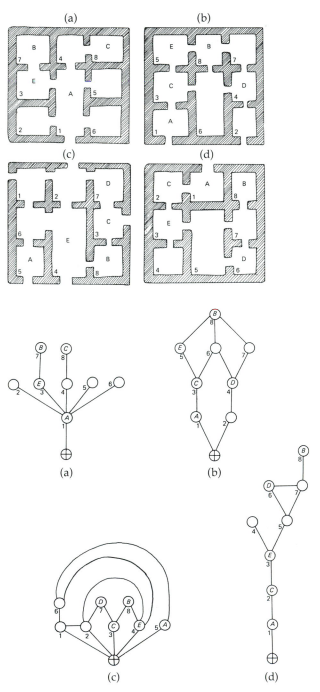

Figure 2 *Four formally equivalent but spatially different plans, with their spatial maps in which all connections between the outside and an interior space, and pairs of interior spaces, are represented by a line as a topological graph.* (Source: *Hillier and Hanson 1984*)

there is no meaning we have what Marx defined as alienation – from self, from others and from nature (the only 'other' to possess the concrete reality to make it admissible within a materialist framework).

We extract a variety of meanings about each of these three levels of relationships through our experience of form, function and space. The forms act as metaphors, signs or symbols. The analysis of meaning involves iconography, art criticism and semiotics. There is an enormous body of scholarly and critical work in this area. Functions speak directly of social relationships at their deepest level. They reveal the status, role and productive or reproductive purpose of every participant.

These purposes are describable in speech or writing – hence the close link between function and language. Analysis of language is needed to get at these meanings. Unlike philosophy, literature and science, where linguistic methods are highly developed, in architecture the methods are totally undeveloped. Spatial relationships, on the other hand, speak indirectly of these relationships; they can be analysed to show how control and power is distributed in social structures (Hillier and Hanson 1984).

There is no internal link, within 'architecture', between form, function and space. A health centre can have any spatial structure or style. A Post-Modernist

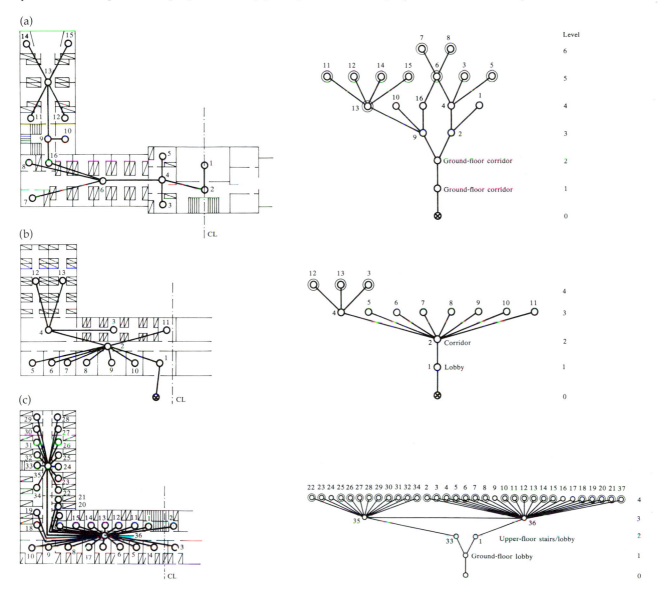

Figure 3 *Three eighteenth-century U-shaped formally similar but spatially different hospital (half) plans, with their spatial maps on which spaces with patient accommodation are ringed. In (a) the patient spaces are in the three deepest layers and some are on the route to others. In (b) they are all in the deepest layer and not on any route. In (c) they are also at the deepest point but, through the use of the corridor for the entire plan, are highly articulated at the tips of the branches of the tree. Here the shallow 'ring' is for staff. (a) Edinburgh Infirmary, 1738, William Adam; (b) The London Hospital, 1752, Boulton Mainwaring; and (c) Manchester Infirmary with extensions, 1754–91, architect unknown. (Source: Markus 1982; Markus 1987)*

building defines nothing about its function or spatial structure. A deep, tree-like spatial structure can be used for a wide variety of purposes, and its spaces can be baroque or High-Tech. So the discourse of 'architecture' has no coherence except in a world outside itself – the world of relationships, of society. Questions can be asked, in turn, about the meaning of each of the three properties of a building. Finding answers involves analysis in a common field, external to the building – society. Once answers are yielded these can be mapped back into the building to give it an overall, unified meaning. This unity is specific and unique to each building and is derived from the common external field (Figure 4).

The impossibility of finding a general relationship between the three discourses, internal to the field, is one of the powerful pieces of evidence which suggest the mythological nature of 'architecture'.

So experiencing buildings is experiencing relationships. The most obvious ones have to do with power arising from the distribution of finite resources – money, energy, time, security, control, information. This is a cake-slicing operation – more here is less there. There is a host of ways in which the relationship of power is evident in buildings. It determines the location of the building, the status of its *quartier* and hence the value of its site. It determines the relative amount of space allocated to individuals and groups; the quality of the finishes, furnishings, and environment of these spaces; the distribution of information about the design and management of the building; and its formal imagery (whose favoured imagery dominates?). Power and control determine the spatial location of individuals and groups – with respect to the outside, to each other, to choice of routes, to major communication routes. Role, authority, hierarchy and resource control are the instrumental means through which the relationships are translated into built form.

The critique of power is justice – resources can be shared out justly or unjustly. But justice is irrelevant to another experience of relationships – friendship, or that which poets and theologians call love, or which in politics is solidarity or community. Here it is not cake-slicing – in fact it is the opposite. The stronger the bonds the more there is to share out. The possibilities are no longer finite; bonds have no bounds. The form, function and spatial structure of buildings can encourage, express, give room for, sustain or deny the formation of bonds. Images can symbolize it; functions can be based on open-ended, easy-to-redefine programmes; spaces can have such links that free communication and choice, and hence solidarity and friendship, are possible between a wide variety of individuals and groups.

It is impossible to produce a building which is entirely just and has no barriers against bonds – such a building would be a 'heavenly mansion'. All buildings make both power and bond relationships concrete. That is, they are both instruments of control about resources and places where bonds are formed or suppressed. Sponsors of buildings (other than small houses, workshops, etc.), are those with access to resources for such major investments – land, labour, money, tools, machines and materials. History teaches that they are also those with political power. Their huge investments have not only overt purposes – to exhibit pictures safely, run a health service, produce microchips or teach children – but the covert one of reinforcing the social relationships on which their power is based. This involves so defining art, health, production or education that certain ideologies dominate, that professional groups' status is strengthened, that control of production is welded to ownership.

This is not a question of politics in general – though clearly that will affect what buildings are produced and how they are designed – but about the fact that the design, production and management of all buildings, and all their bits, inescapably make them into theatres of power, and, with rare exceptions, reinforce the asymmetrical distribution of power. They are, inevitably, also theatres of bonds; but since bonds tend to undermine asymmetrical power, buildings are required to limit the freedom, open-endedness and unpredictability which are necessary for easy formation of bonds. They tend to separate, classify, control and formalize relationships – in other words to make other, to alienate. It was this tragic paradox at the heart of architecture, that a practice committed to creativity should produce a rigid, rule-ridden system of order, that Piranesi grappled with

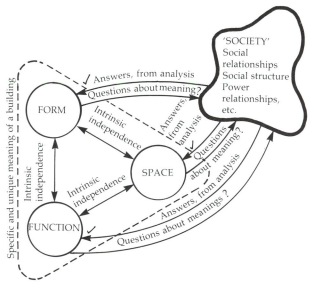

Figure 4 *Diagram of relationships between society and form, function and space, which are assumed to be intrinsically independent of each other. In a specific case their relationship, in terms of the building's meaning, results from the analysis of each property in social relationships.*

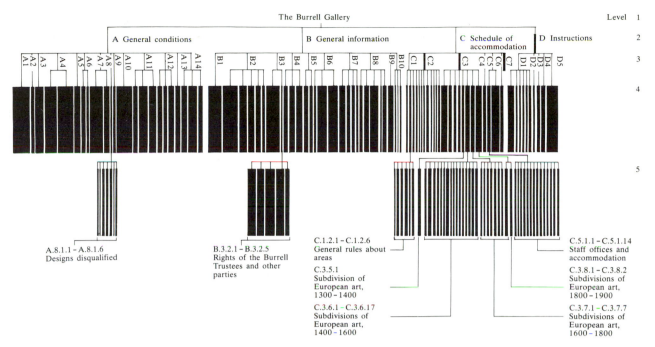

Figure 5 *Text of the Burrell Art Gallery, Glasgow, competition brief, represented as a hierarchical structure in five levels. The length of each bar is uniform and the width is proportional to the length of each part of the text. The area of each volume is therefore proportional to the text length. At levels 2 and 3 there are merely a series of headings, except for those shown in a thicker line, where there is a short piece of text. Volume of text and its depth in the layered structure represent elaboration and emphasis. Only European art is classified down to level 5, other parts of the collection remaining at level 4. The only other matters treated at level 5 are the reasons for disqualification of entries, and the legal rights of the Trustees and other parties. (Source: As for figure 2, based on original produced by Salman Othman as part of an undergraduate dissertation, 1985).*

in his great *Carceri* etchings. Here impossible perspective created mysterious, dark underground space above which, in the light of day, we catch glimpses of the familiar world of classical order. It was that world, not the underground space, which was the true prison at the heart of his work.

Prior to the industrial revolution there was a substantial identity of values between sponsors and their architects. Their shared social and educational backgrounds, through shared class origins, and the well-established traditions of the few building types in existence, ensured that there was little risk of the hidden agendas not being fulfilled. There was little need to spell out programmes (today's 'briefs') in detail.

However, the upheavals of the industrial revolution shook this secure relationship. A host of new and unexplored building types were needed by the state, municipal authority and entrepreneur. Both sponsors and architects came from a much wider social background – identity of class interest could no longer be assumed. Moreover, users of buildings began to develop their own voices. It was now necessary to take steps to safeguard sponsors' interests and, at the same time, to camouflage the link between buildings, and power and bonds, by means of an unwritten pact which was based on the myth.

With regard to form this was easy – by treating it as autonomous, demanding a personal rather than a social

response, by blocking out symbolic meaning and by pushing experience into the stratosphere of other myths, such as history, heritage, nature and the 'spiritual'. Architects were given freedom over the form of specific projects. They were, thenceforward, to absorb all their energies in stylistic debate – if necessary they could kill each other (metaphorically). They were to be artists; their workplaces 'studios', their education in art institutions based on the Ecole des Beaux Arts. They were to exhibit framed drawings in the Academies, today even those drawn by computers. The media, textbooks and professional institutions were committed to architecture-as-art. So successful has this definition of architecture been that it has become classless – it is shared by royalty, scholars, professionals, patrons, most community architecture workers and their clients, the bougeoisie and the working class. It is shared by east and west, First World and Third World. In other words, it has become nearly universal. Control over form – stylistic development – was achieved by other, more subtle and stronger ways. The sponsors, the selfsame elites, took control of the resources for architectural education, the media, publishing and exhibitions. Form could be censored at an institutional level, without destroying the apparent freedom of architects.

With function there was greater difficulty. Sponsors could not afford to be so cavalier. So they explicitly and elaborately *pre*scribed it in a text – the brief – which was presented as 'neutral', 'technical' or 'objective' and thus beyond argument. But language can never be innocent – it is the unique human invention for transmitting values. The speaker or writer chooses the vocabulary, structures the text, selects the silences and inevitably betrays this pretended neutrality. These briefs deal overtly with material processes – 'function' has been redefined to exclude relationships and to include dimensional, work-study, anthropometric, biological and simple environmental issues, as well as detailed technical requirements. By means of specific briefs, general design guides, Codes, Standards and legislation, a battery of written and graphic prescriptions were produced. The covert, social-reproduction aspect of the brief was ever more deeply submerged in this material. But the texts became powerful prescriptions which, in many important ways, designed a building long before a so-called designer appeared on the scene.

Thus in a typical competition brief, for instance for an art gallery, the definition of art and of the relationship between patron and viewer, the classification of art objects and the required spatial organization of the 'schools' of art which the scholars have produced, all occur within the text (Figure 5). No matter what formal variations the competitors produce, the ideology governing the collection and exhibition of art is embedded inescapably and in an apparently objective text.

Space was even more crucial to maintaining power. Who is where, who acts as gatekeeper to whom, surveillance, privacy, groupings and segregations – these are all maps of relationships. Space is controlled implicitly by unquestioning reproduction of customary spatial structures. It is a language, just like speech. Spatial experience is all-pervasive and potent, but as long as sponsors, architects or users lack analytical techniques for discovering the meaning of spatial structures, spatial knowledge does not exist. It remains untaught, unconscious, uncriticised and undebated.

Two other traditions gained legitimacy alongside that of buildings as art objects. The first was formalized, also in France, more or less at the same time as the architecture-as-art tradition was institutionalized in the Ecole des Beaux-Arts, in the Ecole Polytechnique. This was the tradition of buildings as technical, engineering objects. The second matured later – the development of economic criteria for building performance, so that buildings could be analysed as investment objects. This coincided with the final abandonment of use as a value criterion and the acceptance of buildings as commodities, long after other products had suffered this transformation. Throughout these two hundred years silence reigned and continues to reign over buildings as social objects.

This brief critique has explored a few of the historical causes for an astounding silence. It is astounding in the sense that even though buildings are predominantly treated as art-objects, architectural scholarship and criticism has not even advanced to the stage of much modern art scholarship and criticism, especially in literature, film and painting, where both the production of works of art and the production of the experiencing subject are analysed as social and historical processes. The best work in architecture has remained in the groove of nineteenth-century German idealist art scholarship, whilst the worst of it has developed through fads that use ill-understood ideas from major intellectual streams, such as semiotics, structuralism and, most recently, deconstruction. The trivial influence of these only emphasizes the real intellectual isolation of architectural thought from the arts, sciences and social sciences.

There are three core aspects of the mythical architecture discourse that have to be conserved if the social meaning of buildings is to remain unanalysed, untaught and unpractised: first, its autonomy and coherence; second, the dominance of the art, technology and investment discourses; and third, the fable of a neutral building text. The new interest in theoretical issues and growing awareness of the power of analysis is so far limited to narrow, academic circles. When it is allied to the continuing popular crisis of disenchantment with successive waves of stylistic 'isms' and technical acrobatics this well-established core may weaken.

REFERENCES

Hillier, W.R.G. and Hanson, J. (1984) *The Social Logic of Space*, Cambridge: Cambridge University Press.

Markus, T.A. (ed.) (1982) *Order in Space and Society: Architectural Form and its Context in the Scottish Enlightenment*, Edinburgh: Mainstream.

—— (1987) 'Buildings as classifying devices', *Planning and Environment B, Planning and Design* 14 (467–84).

Stark, W. (1807) *Remarks on Public Hospitals for the Cure of Mental Derangement*, Edinburgh.

4 Needs and means

Ben Farmer

Architecture is the art of designing good buildings, buildings that are attractive, well planned and well built, and that are both appropriate and meaningful to society. For centuries it has been known as the 'Mistress of the Arts'.

If one takes a long-term view, it can be seen that no form of architecture takes root unless it relates to the needs and expectations of society – it therefore speaks both to and for society by bringing messages from the past and making statements about the present. It is, at base, building, but rather special building, and perhaps paradoxically the practice of architecture has as its central skill the handling of space.

People build for their needs, and the patterns or codes that evolve directly reflect their priorities, resources and capabilities. Not all aspects of these needs are universal – much building is place-, time- and culture-specific – and, of course, buildings, if they are to be used, have to be accessed. This would suggest that architecture has three fundamental responses to make: response to people, response to place and response to routes.

PEOPLE

Response to people is architecture's *raison d'être*. The needs of people, as individuals or in small groups or whole communities, fairly directly influence built form, from single cells to whole cities.

We cannot survive without shelter, and we need protection from the elements and nature. We are aggressive and possessive and need protection from each other. Beyond the basic needs for survival, however, there are extremely complex societal patterns, which generate needs for facilities of all kinds. The ranges of buildings 'needed' by societies that have developed at different rates, or in different ways, make fascinating study and offer one indication of the influence on architecture of 'culture', in the sense of 'way of life'.

Architecture reflects the culture of society by accommodating or giving witness to a society's ideas of religion, leadership, political structure, institutions, values, art forms, products, family type and so on (see Figure 1). More specifically, good architecture requires a good client and a brief that reflects the client's needs and

Figure 1 *The Pyramids represent some of the world's finest buildings, built by the Egyptians when, as a society, their intentions scarcely changed for 3,000 years. They are massive, hard, durable, precise structures, epitomizing order and durability, which were the dominant characteristics of their society.*

respects the community's interests. In the most general sense, the impact of culture upon what is built can be seen:

1   by comparative analysis of the ranges of buildings built by societies;
2   by considering typological variations of particular kinds of buildings from one culture to another;
3   by examining how what is built within a society varies over time: serious building requires social stability and confidence, while new building types are generated by dynamic societies;
4   by noting what is built within a society by sub-cultures;
5   by comparing the building output of different peoples building in the same place: for example, in cities such as Zaria in Northern Nigeria, one can see large differences in built provision for the indigenous Hausa Northerners, for Nigerians from other parts of the country, for immigrant peoples such as Indians and Lebanese and in areas originally built by and for colonial expatriates;
6   by comparing the use of space between cultures: this can reflect different ideas and values, response to privacy being an obvious example.

On a longer time-scale one can see that archaeologists, having unearthed buildings and artefacts, interpret societies from such evidence.

PLACE

As an art form, architecture cannot detach itself from contextual circumstances, which should therefore be respected.

Places are unique and deserve a unique response. They vary in climate, landscape, plant life, topography, geology and, most importantly, in what might be called the rules of play for building (see Figure 2). Early constraints on such rules of play were almost certainly the need for climatic shelter and the possibilities afforded for meeting such a need by the materials to hand. There is a fortuitously good relationship between climate, territorial condition, materials available, sensible and direct use of such material, built form derived from such use, and the performance of such building as environmental filter or modifier (see Figures 3 to 6).

Over the centuries it has been by investment in structure and fabric that environment has been controlled – indeed, until comparatively recently there was little choice. It is now possible to use energy to modify climatic conditions and produce built forms that disregard local climate, but there is a price to pay – indeed often several different prices.

Building that is traditional to place is concerned not only with the form and fabric of individual buildings, arranged and crafted in ways refined by experience, but also with the deployment and disposition of buildings so

Figure 2 *Clear rules of play are apparent in the Spanish town of Villa Hermosa.*

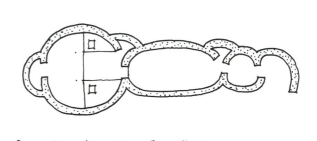

Figure 3 *Typical Inuit igloo. Materials available are snow, ice and animal products. Insulation and protection from wind chill are the main requirements of shelter. Animal skins form an important inner lining.*

Figure 4 *Lead miners' cottages in Northumberland, England, a temperate zone. A wide range of materials was available and a wide range of climatic conditions had to be coped with. This prompted a disciplined material selection (stone, rendering, glass and wood), a pitched roof to accommodate high rainfall, trim verges and eaves because of high winds, and the use of open fires to provide heat in winter.*

Figure 5 *Mud building typical of northern Nigeria, where there is low humidity and extreme diurnal temperature variation. Thermal response of fabric and inter-shading are essential features. Cold air is admitted at night and retained by the baked earth's slow thermal response aided by the domical roof form, small openings in walls, and part protection from insolation.*

that they make sense as part of larger systems. They may perhaps be close together to offer each other and the routes between them a measure of shade (Figure 5), they may be sensibly distanced to ensure minimum inhibition of important air movement, and they may relate to each other as cascading developments on hillsides with the roof of one serving as outside terrace to another, and so on.

To build new buildings in established places is a great challenge. It may be that such building must be new in

type or form or scale or material, it may be that it must complement rather than conform, but if it is different in every respect it is seldom successful. The second half of the twentieth century has, unfortunately, thrown up all too many buildings whose failure is in essence a failure to respond to place.

Figure 6 *Kipsig house, south-west Kenya. This is typical of mud pole and thatch building, and is an extremely effective response to temperature and humidity fluctuations.*

Figure 7 *Road and rail routes oversailing the river route at Newcastle upon Tyne, England. This intersection is sufficiently close to the sea to give ready access to sea routes, but sufficiently inland to be easy to defend – an ideal set of circumstances for the development of a settlement.*

Figure 8 *Diagrammatic plan of part of Venice showing the essentially discrete nature of land and water routes.*

ROUTES

Routes influence settlement patterns, and the disposition and location of buildings; they have always been important in architecture and not simply because buildings must be accessed.

The intersection or conjunction of routes – particularly of different kinds of routes (path, road, rail, river, canal, sea and air) – can be seen to be of major importance to the establishment and development of towns and cities (see Figure 7). Road patterns – grid, radial, linear, contour hugging, etc. – are often the generating or controlling factors of development, influencing if not determining character.

Venice and Amsterdam are obvious examples. In Venice, an island city, the curving Canale Grande forms the main spine of the city and is lined with the city's most renowned palaces – originally the houses of rich merchants and a reflection of the importance of the city as a sea trading centre. Where this canal meets the Canale della Guidecca and the Canale di San Marco, literally where the city offers itself to the sea, we find the major buildings and spaces: Santa Maria della Salute, San Marco, Palace Ducale and Libreria Vecchia and the world-famous Piazza San Marco with the campanile signalling it so dramatically.

Peculiar to Venice is that the minor canals, which subdivide the city into a matrix of small islands (Figure 8), serve as exclusive routes for the transport needed to make the city work (the transport of goods and services) with three- to five-storey buildings built to the edges of the canals (Figure 9), whereas many of the 'land routes' are pedestrian routes periodically passing over the canals and feeding and interconnecting public and private open spaces (Figure 10). Engagement with, or points of exchange between, the two kinds of routes are few, and are attractively arranged. These two, largely discrete systems of movement give Venetians many privileges and privacies enjoyed by few other city dwellers.

Amsterdam, on the other hand, which has so many features in common with Venice, has canals organized concentrically, with roads flanking the canals as well as intersecting them (Figure 11). In this case there is a maximum engagement between the two route systems with buildings offering their faces to both, and with all of life taking place on and along the canals. Private open spaces are behind the tall, deep-plan buildings, and public open spaces can be in the form of swellings to both systems – for example, Dam Rak and Spui Centrum. The composite concentric routes, often attractively tree lined, give the city an individual charm and vitality.

Figure 9 *The minor canals of Venice are discrete service routes for the city which enable many of the land routes to be pedestrianized.*

Figure 10 *Piazza San Marco, Venice. A world-famous public space, offering itself to the water and protected from vehicular traffic by the discrete route patterns of the city.*

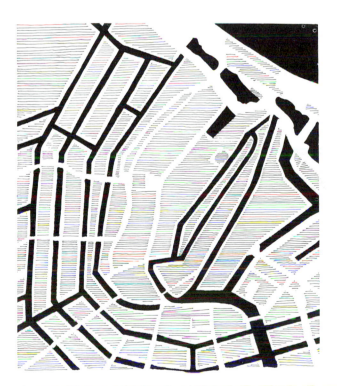

Figure 11 *Diagrammatic plan of part of Amsterdam showing the conjunction of land and water routes.*

Amsterdam's many bridges have an important part to play in the city's character, in that they both connect and separate streets. They make connections for road and path traffic, but often, because of necessary elevation for canal traffic, they offer visual and spatial punctuation (Figure 12).

Routes have their own hierarchies, their own form and order; they must enable people to interact as well as move about (Figures 13 and 14). This is as true for routes internal to buildings as it is for those external to and between buildings. Where routes do not enable people to interact there is no sense of place, and where routes and buildings do not interact there are all sorts of discomforts (Figure 15).

If response to people, place and routes are the three fundamental responses, how are they met and by what means? People build what they need or what they choose to build, but also they build only what they *can* build. More specifically, they build what they can afford to build, whether by investment or effort, skill, time, material, risk or money – the latter, of course, enabling them to buy or harness the resources of others – and they build what they can build by technological command.

Figure 12 *Singel Centrum. Amsterdam's bridges connect roads and paths but offer visual and spatial punctuation.*

WEALTH

Wealth, in some form, is needed, as are authority and expertise. The Welsh Castles built as a series in the thirteenth century were only possible because the Royal Ordinance had the authority to command a workforce and acquire materials, and had the technical and organizational expertise to deal with the constructional and logistical challenges. Wealth is, of course, not an unmitigated blessing, and many European and Scandinavian cities have been preserved in form for our generation because in past times such cities were too poor to change.

TECHNOLOGY

Technological command is a basic requirement if architectural concepts are to be realized. Theoretically, one can now build almost anything. In practice, particular ways of building with particular materials may have to be employed and, traditionally, structural or constructional factors have exercised considerable influence on form and arrangement. Pitched roofs, for example, exercised geometric discipline on plans and made location and strength demands on walls or other support systems.

Figure 13 *A route in Dieppe where people interact as well as move about, creating a vital sense of place.*

Figure 14 *A route in Dubrovnic with similar properties to that in Figure 13.*

Figure 15 *The urban motorway system in Newcastle upon Tyne, which respects neither people nor place. A bleak non-place through which vehicles can speed but by which pre-existing buildings are blighted.*

Typologies such as very tall buildings or Sydney Opera House (Figure 16) were simply not viable before the advent of high-speed lifts and the computerization of structural calculations.

Figure 16 *Sydney Opera House; Jørn Utzon 1959–73. A Gestalt design realized (in somewhat modified form) by computerization of the structural calculations.*

COMMUNICATIONS

The development of the railway system in Britain in the nineteenth century made it possible to live remote from place of work. Such cheap, high-speed, reliable, scheduled transport was essential to the development of suburbia. Electronic communications of all kinds are now being harnessed that in part qualify this trend, by offering the prospect of a reduction in the need to work remote from home with all that might entail. Transport and movement systems of all kinds continue to form an essential means of response – thus routes have a dual role: they both provoke response and facilitate it.

In another sense, ever since the designing function has been split from the building function, communications have been important in conveying advice on what is proposed and instructions as to how it is to be built. Drawing ability is vital to architects if they are to test and communicate ideas, and lack of it can quite fundamentally limit concepts that can be entertained, declared, tested and negotiated.

SOCIETAL FORCES

Societal forces are, of course, the ultimate means of response. There are three types of societal force that are particularly significant. First and foremost there are political systems and systems of government, which determine the deployment of resource. For example, the Pax Romana made possible the development of fenestration as we know it today, and the rebuilding of Warsaw as a reincarnation of its pre-1939 self was a deliberate political act.

Second there is legislation, which can determine what, where and to what standards one may build. Most building legislation springs from interests of health and safety but may reflect a society's priorities for building performance as, for example, with respect to energy use and conservation. It may also relate to taxation systems. Amsterdam's narrow-fronted, deep-plan, crosswall structures, in addition to making good sense given the city's subsoil conditions, reflect the fact that buildings were taxed by frontage rather than volume or other measures.

Third there are ideas. Architecture draws upon ideas of all kinds: ideas from other art forms, architectural precedent, mathematical concepts, relationships, series and progressions; ideas from the world of nature; ideas from the world of business and management, analogy generation and data classification; ideas from religion, whether inspirational, symbolic, prescriptive or proscriptive; ideas about buildings as a series of interrelated systems – space systems, movement systems, structural systems, energy systems, money systems; ideas that society has about itself, and so on. We are surrounded by examples: Corbusian buildings influenced by Cubism (Figure 17); mosques with their domes symbolizing heaven and their walls symbolizing earth; whole developments springing from the idea of the city in the park; buildings as metaphors, and so on.

These inescapable universal and timeless considerations, and the means by which they are met, come together in special and peculiar ways each time to give buildings and settlements such rich variety. They are underlying factors to be noticed and understood; they form a framework for creativity but do not, of course, guarantee success, being necessary but not necessarily sufficient. As ever, they are most obvious in retrospect – success and failure can be readily categorized in their terms but prediction and prescription are less easily determined. If architecture is an art form, whether or not it is the 'Mistress of the Arts', it is certainly the inescapable art – inescapable, but also indirect, as architects build for others with other people's money. Client and community are, therefore, of central importance.

I have isolated considerations in order to examine them here, but in reality they form part of an indivisible whole with, in each case, a unique combination of importances. A designer must look for fit, and while, in one sense, design is always a matter of compromise (efficiency in one respect traded against that in another), one must never compromise the issue of quality or the controlling idea. In such respects, to be able to avoid compromise, from concept to the smallest detail, is to demonstrate mastery of the art and, when achieved, the resultant architecture is the hallmark of civilization.

NOTE

All drawings and photographs by the author.

FURTHER READING

Alexander, C., Ishikawa, S. and Silverstein, M. (1977) *A Pattern Language*, New York: Oxford University Press.
—— (1979) *The Timeless Way of Building*, New York: Oxford University Press.
Bronowski, J. (1976) *The Ascent of Man*, London: BBC.
Clark, K. (1975) *Civilisation*, London: BBC and John Murray.
Oliver, P. (1987) *Dwellings: The House Across the World*, Oxford: Phaidon.
Rapoport, A. (1969) *House Form and Culture*, Englewood Cliffs, NJ: Prentice-Hall.
Rudofsky, B. (1974) *Architecture without Architects*, London: Academy Editions.

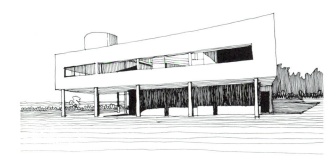

Figure 17 *Villa Savoye, Poissy, 1929, by Le Corbusier, showing obvious Cubist influence. The structure, of ferro-concrete, enables space to penetrate the cubic form from above and below.*

5   In praise of the house that Anon built

Hugh Casson

My favourite architect or designer is, I suspect, the same as most people's . . . 'Anon'. He – (seldom I fear 'she') – is historically the designer/builder of fishing boats and hay-barns, lock-keeper's cottages and farm gates, terrace housing, harbour walls, tiny village churches, warehouses. Welsh village chapels and huts for permanentway inspectors – each one a product of necessity and of contemporary technology and not one is pretentious, wilful or 'witty'. Does it sound dull? Perhaps. But it isn't, for my category includes also the dottiest of follies, the most daring of nineteenth century engineering structures and not a few cathedral-sized churches or cornexchanges. Missing, admittedly, are some of the world's masterpieces – the Pantheon, the Temple of Segesta, the Palace of Westminster – all those buildings that carry designer labels – but the weight of numbers and the average of excellence lies with 'Anon'.

Why were they so good?

First, they sprang from the necessity to fulfil a simple need. Second, they were built often by people on the spot from the few skills and materials locally available – brick, stone and timber. They lasted well and aged gracefully. Third, they obeyed Ruskin's precept – (though few had heard of him) – that art is craft and if you begin your work by seeking 'beauty', in inverted commas, it will almost certainly evade you.

Take one example – our family is lucky enough to be tenants in a piece of 'Anonery'. It is a cottage – one in a row of eight – built in 1853 by un-named Trinity House engineers on the shores of the Solent to house a posse of coastguards. It is protected from sea damage by a low turfed 'bund' and a stretch of salt marsh which almost dries at low water. Each cottage has three bedrooms, a living room, a kitchen and larder. A small separate washhouse was built to serve everybody, in the back gardens where earth privies once stood. The small front gardens fringed by formal wood palings demarcate tiny zones of individual privacy.

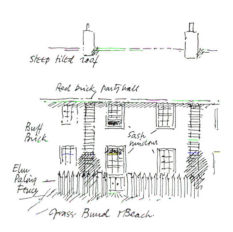

Inside, the kitchen floor is paved, the sitting room timbered, the spiral wood stair leads to and through ledged and braced doors to the bedrooms. All the windows are small-paned sashes sliding vertically or sideways. The sitting room window is constructed ingeniously to be dismantleable and to permit passage into the front garden. The walls are of brick, the steep roof is tiled. The chimneys are robust. The two end cottages are given bow windows to denote the rank of the owners. Although only a few steps from the sea at high tide, each cottage is as weatherproof and snug as a wellfound fishing boat. Today the terrace is listed – rightly. The coastguards have gone. The cottages since the 1960s are holiday homes with electricity, bathrooms and indoor WCs and at night television blinks its blue light through the Beatrix Potter window panes. But to the sailor half a mile out there is no visible change and to the passer-by very little more.

Coastguard Cottages.

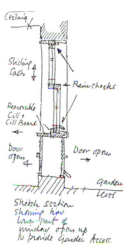

First published in the *Guardian*, 24–5 December 1988.

I discovered the cottages some sixty years ago when sailing inexpertly with two schoolboy friends. We ran ashore opposite them in a fast-falling tide and were clearly stuck for six hours. (A seagull we thought was floating nearby was, in fact, wading.) We placed an anchor out and waded grumpily ashore. The cottages were all dark and empty. Mousedroppings on the floors, salty caking on the windows, cow parsley in the tiny gardens, but smoke curled from the chimney pots and in one window an oil lamp glowed. An elderly Arrol Johnson rusted among the blackberry bushes. Crouched over an oil-clothed table was exactly the sort of occupant we expected. Silent, huge, elderly, bearded, gumbooted. He preferred tea in enamel mugs and showed us silently around. Although all the rooms seemed modestly spacious it seemed as if every personal want was reachable from a single well-positioned chair. The tour over he drove us along a farm track to the nearest village.

It was twenty years before I saw the place again. The bathroom had arrived – but not electricity. The cottages – such was the thoughtful simplicity of their design – continued to stand their ground. But the simplicity was deceptive.

That dismantleable window, for instance, leading into the garden boasted an ingenious system of checks and weatherboards that ensured a watertight fit and looked equally handsome whether open or closed. Timber, weathered and painted, slid or opened without strain or jamming. Fires drew properly in the tiny grates. When the South-West gales blew spray on to the windows and pebbles rattled on the glass the spiders rocked on their webs like experienced sailors. Part of Anon's achievement was always to include the elements and the weather in the creative process.

Is to admire and enjoy all this part of the current English disease? ... to look always to memory for reassurance rather than to reason? The risk is there. The builders of these cottages stretched their skills and to the limits of what was known and what was needed – so do today the designers of oil rigs, suspension bridges, of check-out counters and windscreen wipers, staple-guns and zip fasteners, squeeze torches and tube-doors, aircraft landing gear and sticky tape, 'trainers' and cats-eyes in the road, apple-corers, pillar boxes and Xerox.

Who are these designers? They are Anon of course – they do not wear dark glasses nor are they photographed in fashion mags looking mean. They're too busy. Anon still Rules ... OK?

NOTE

Drawings by the author.

PART 2

RESPONSES

SECTION 2.1

Response to people

Human need is at the base of all building, from single cells to entire cities. We are social animals and our nature and our psychology are as important as our physical needs when it comes to requirement for built provision.

The basic social unit in any society is the family, the structure of which differs from society to society, but the functionalist view of sociology establishes that the four universal characteristics of 'family' are that: all have a socially accepted way of reproduction; all care for and maintain their young; all socialize (educate and condition) their young, introducing them to the culture of their society; all families, to a large degree, determine the social position of their children in a society.

Given these universal essential functions, it is not difficult to perceive the importance of shelter as a psycho-physical and psychological need, albeit expressed in many different physical forms.

Although it cannot be argued that architecture is behaviourally deterministic – certainly not in an absolute or prescriptive way – human behaviour is interactive with the built environment. It is, of course, true that in a negative sense built provision can be inhibiting or unhelpful and that built form, management and behaviour are interdependent. One can see too how building forms that worked well for particular societies at particular times are not timelessly successful if society itself changes.

Designers responding to people therefore must provide environments conducive to human well-being and must cater for people anthropometrically and ergonomically. The dimensions and characteristics of skeletal, muscular, corporal and nervous systems must be understood and systems of perception and interpretation responded to if built environments are to make sense in a detailed way.

At a larger scale, group and mass characteristics must be understood and catered for and here, once again, architects must not only be intelligent and observant, they must take advice from others and be aware of, and sensitive to, cultural climate.

Patronage, vision and confidence are all-important.

Architecture, the inescapable art, is enjoyed or suffered by the majority of people who have no direct access to or use of particular buildings, and in the general sense it becomes a backdrop to our lives, setting the qualitative scene.

Bruce Allsopp's essay deals with the importance of patronage to start this section, the body of which addresses societal concerns, and the essay by Hala Kardash and Nick Wilkinson rounds off the section by illustrating the fact that few environments can defeat people's ability to adapt. Adaptation (transformation as it is currently called) seems to be one of our basic instincts.

B.F.

RECOMMENDED READING

Chermayeff, S. and Alexander, C. (1966) *Community and Privacy: Toward a New Architecture of Humanism*, Harmondsworth: Penguin.

Hall, E. (1969) *The Hidden Dimension: Man's Use of Space in Public and Private*, London: Bodley Head.

Fathy, H. (1969) *Architecture for the Poor*, Cairo: American University Press.

Jukes, P. (1990). *A Shout in the Street: The Modern City*, London: Faber.

Lennard, H. and Crowhurst Lennard, S.H. (1984) *Public Life in Urban Places: Social and Architectural Characteristics Conducive to Public Life in European Cities*, Southampton, NY: Gondolier Press.

Marc, O. (1977) *Psychology of the House*, London: Thames & Hudson.

Moore, C., Allen, C. and Lyndon, D. (1979) *The Place of Houses*, New York: Holt, Rinehart & Winston.

Newman, O. (1973) *Defensible Space*, London: Architectural Press.

Rapoport, A. (1969) *House, Form and Culture*, Englewood Cliffs, NJ: Prentice-Hall.

Raskin, E. (1974) *Architecture and People*, Englewood Cliffs, NJ: Prentice-Hall.

Rudofsky, B. (1964) *Architecture Without Architects*, New York: Doubleday

Sennett, R. (ed.) (1969) *Classic Essays on the Culture of Cities*, New York: Meredith.

—— (1991) *The Conscience of the Eye: The Design and Social Life of Cities*, London: Faber.

Turner, J.F.C. (1976) *Housing by People: Towards Autonomy in Building Environments*, London: Marion Boyars.

Ward, C. (1977) *The Child in the City*, London: Architectural Press.

Wilson, F. (1984) *A Graphic Survey of Perception and Behaviour for the Design Professions*, New York: Van Nostrand Reinhold.

6 Patronage and professionalism

Bruce Allsopp

Vitruvius, whose book *De Architectura* enshrines what he knew about the theory and practice of Greek and Roman architecture up to the first century BC, was proud to describe himself as a 'client' of Augustus. The Emperor was his 'patron'. The modern professional architect reverses these roles and speaks of the employer as the 'client'. Until about the end of the eighteenth century artists of all kinds – musicians, poets, painters, writers, sculptors, architects, as well as scholars, physicians, engineers and astrologists – sought patronage and addressed their patrons in sometimes extravagant terms of flattery. The patrons were drawn mainly from the social, political and religious aristocracy, from the papacy and the monarchy, through the various ranks of church and state down to the minor nobility and gentry, to bankers and, latterly, to the prosperous bourgeoisie. To put it bluntly, architecture was dependent upon those who had money and were prepared to spend it on building. It still is. In the Roman Empire prosperous citizens gave public buildings, partly out of civic pride but mainly to impress their neighbours and commemorate their names, so such buildings were intended to be monumental in the true sense of that word. Emperors gave even larger buildings such as the Thermae (baths) of Caracalla and Diocletian in Rome, and of Constantine in Trier.

With the rise of Christianity, established by Constantine in the fourth century as the official religion of Rome, and the transfer of the capital of the Empire to Constantinople, God rather than the civic community became the focus of prestigious building and architectural patronage. Constantine set the fashion with his church of the Holy Apostles in Constantinople and Justinian consummated it in Hagia Sophia, which was designed by two architects who might be supposed to be 'professional' in the modern sense.

The declining Eastern Empire was curtailed by the rise of a Frankish empire and the Roman Church in the west, and by Islam in the south and east, but it extended its religious and artistic influence into Russia. State and private patronage of religious architecture, for the Orthodox Church, was dominant. The style invented in Byzantium (Constantinople) and properly named by W.R. Lethaby as Hellenesque, because of its basically Greek origins, profoundly influenced the architecture of Islam and extended it as far as Spain in the west and India in the east, as well as influencing Western Christian architecture (possibly via Ripoll in Spain) – witness the horseshoe arches of Fountains Abbey and Winchester Cathedral in England.

In western Europe, after the final collapse of the Roman Empire, the state of patronage is obscure. Barbarians (i.e. foreigners from outside the Roman Empire) were establishing an overlordship which eventually coalesced into the Holy Roman Empire with the coronation of the Frankish Charlemagne by the Pope in AD 800. The simple fact that most of the barbarian rulers could neither read nor write made them practically dependent for administration, communication and accounting upon the clergy who could. Latin became the cultural and administrative language of Europe and, with the commitment of the Franks to Christianity by Clovis I in 506, the bishops, abbots, and, significantly, the abbesses, who in some cases were retired queens, preserved the literary and to some extent the architectural traditions of Rome. The medieval church became the main patron of the art of architecture. It was, in theory, a vicarious patron because churches and monasteries were dedicated, through their patron saints, to God who was, in medieval thinking, the real 'client'. None the less the role of the human patron is indicated by the inscription in the chancel of Saint-Denis in Paris:

> C'est moi, Suger, qui ai en mon temps agrandi cet édifice.
> C'est sous ma direction qu'on l'a fait.

It must also be noted that the money came very largely from secular sources, given out of piety, prudence or penitence.

With the Renaissance, secular patronage, especially in Italy, became much more important, as palaces in towns replaced the austere and redundant castles perched tediously upon promontories. Though this has been called the age of humanism it must be remembered that religion flourished and so-called humanist artists were devout Christians. Alberti, the author of *De Re Aedificatoria*, the most important theoretical book on architecture since Vitruvius, performed a remarkable reconciliation of pagan and Christian theology in the service of aesthetics and it was in the early sixteenth century that the re-building, in classical style, of St Peter's was undertaken with Papal patronage. The master-masons of the previous age became subject to the direction of architects, such as Michelangelo, who were *employed as artists*, many of them practising several arts. Michelangelo himself was primarily a sculptor (like Phideas) but also a painter and a poet. Brunelleschi was a sculptor and had a craft training in the art of watch-making.

From the Renaissance to the beginning of the Second

World War in 1939, architecture was regarded as an art – indeed it was called the mistress art, using that word mistress in its most respectable meaning, and architects themselves became patrons, on behalf of their 'clients', of all the arts which might adorn buildings. The half-century up to 1939 may well be regarded as a golden age of craft-based design, consummated in the composite art of architecture. The Arts and Crafts movement, with its nucleus in the Art Workers' Guild (in London) and profoundly influenced by the teaching of William Morris and W.R. Lethaby, as well as the example of such architects as C.F.A. Voysey, Norman Shaw and Sir Edwin Lutyens, became a world-wide phenomenon with offshoots in Art Nouveau and Art Deco.

During this period architects had the confidence of their clients to such an amazing extent that, whatever style they chose, whether it was in the idiom of the Arts and Crafts movement itself, or Gothic revival, or monumental classical as we see it in the work of McKim, Mead and White in the USA, the client accepted the financial obligation to pay for the ornamentation and embellishment with costly materials which architects told them was necessary for the achievement of beautiful buildings. This immense privilege of continuing an age-old tradition was rapidly destroyed, not by clients but by architects themselves, not so much for aesthetic as for social-moral-political reasons, though it must be noted that the decline of aesthetics as a major branch of philosophy was a contributory factor. Modernism was propagated with puritanical zeal and like other puritan movements it had a component of righteous destructiveness.

Founded in 1919 at Dessau, in the strange climate of post-war Germany, the Bauhaus initially sought to purify art by accepting the discipline of tools and materials, but it also linked architecture to the emerging Modern Movement in painting and sculpture and then to the extraordinary paradox of an abstract painter, known by his sobriquet as Le Corbusier, whose book *Vers une architecture* became a foundation-stone of functionalism, a creed which was to cut architecture away from patronage of the other arts. But in fairness, it must be said that the Modern Movement in the other arts, with emphasis upon self-expression and originality, made collaboration with architects increasingly difficult.

This is not the place to consider the development of the so-called 'Modern Movement'. Its emphasis may now be seen as being upon modernity as such but initially it was puritanical, in a curious alliance with emerging totalitarian concepts of government which led architects to impose architectural fantasies upon the living conditions of 'working class' people. The Modern Movement also extended the role of the architect, from a traditional role as a designer of buildings, amplified by the architect's emergence as a supervisor of their construction, to an arbiter of how people should live and the conditions in which they should work, even to the way they should work.

Meanwhile the very word 'patron' has acquired disreputable overtones. Whereas in earlier times the architect, like other artists, wanted to be patronized, that word has now become pejorative, if not actually abusive. Yet the fact remains that architecture is the most expensive of the arts and cannot be practised unless somebody is prepared to pay the bill. The question which thoughtful and socially concerned architects must ask is: who is the real patron?

In some parts of the world there are still wealthy people who commission grand houses, and architects who cater for this type of client in the old way, but the rising cost of domestic service, even in the most socially backward places, the proliferation of expensive activities outside the home, and the high cost of modern domestic technical equipment, limit even the most luxurious homes to the scale of a villa rather than a palace.

Despite the arrogance of some modern architects there is evidently an instinct for survival in a changing world and it may well be that, underlying the cult of austere design, devoid of decoration, architects were conforming to their age-old affinity with the chameleon, instinctively adapting to a climate of patronage in which investment companies, bureaucracies, both commercial and governmental, banks, insurance companies and other faceless organizations, employed architects in much the same way as they employed lawyers and accountants. Paradoxically this has resulted in architects having to work for clients with immense financial resources and no aesthetic interest in the end product. To deal effectively with giant organizations the architect's office became larger and more comprehensive in the services it could offer. The name of the principals, the partners in the firm, generally persisted as a kind of trade mark, even posthumously, but the real designer of a building was, and still is, obscure, an assistant, or group within the organization which provides what may be called a professional service. The relationship between the designer – the architect – and the client becomes tenuous or disappears altogether. There is much criticism of the ugliness of many modern buildings. No doubt architects deserve to be blamed, but throughout history architects have been servants of their patrons, and when the patron becomes anonymous the architect is deprived of an essential component in the practice of his or her art.

If buildings are ugly, inconvenient, socially demeaning, even structurally unsound, the buck should stop with the patron, the architect's employer, and this is just as true in a communist society as in a capitalist society. Medieval bishops claimed credit for cathedrals, and are even shown in gold and silver reliquaries holding a cathedral in their hands, but their achievement depended upon the artists they employed. The credit for medieval cathedrals must be divided between the clergy and the masons. The discredit for bad modern buildings should go, in large measure, to the patrons who employ bad architects.

So far we have been considering the kind of architecture which appears as an evolving sequence in books on the history of architecture. The standard histories of architecture are extremely selective. They concentrate upon buildings which, at least until the middle of the twentieth century, were based upon arcane principles relating to proportion, geometry, symmetry, and, as is made very clear by Alberti, divine ordering. The English poet Alexander Pope expressed this in the epigram: 'Those rules of old discovered, not devised/Are nature still but nature methodised.'

A key example is Stonehenge in which the problem, which was to intrigue Renaissance architects, of resolving the liturgical axis with the centralized plan (i.e. the plan within the circle which was theoretically the ideal form) was triumphantly solved three thousand years earlier. Stonehenge is an archetype of arcane architecture based upon humanity's relationship to the cosmos, but hardly any traces remain on Salisbury Plain of the people who supported and laboured to erect this architectural medium between human beings and nature, except the mounds which cover the tombs of their aristocracy. Time and decay, as well as the – dare I say – social prejudices of historians, have left us ill-informed about the buildings in which the great majority of people lived and worked. The 'folk' throughout the ages and all around Earth created traditions, sometimes rich in beauty, which were the expression of themselves, their way of life and the adaptations they had made – by long experience, in the light of their perception of divinity in nature, and social pressures – to the climate and the available materials. A leading characteristic of folk architecture is continuity of traditions which embody an intuitive understanding of natural principles. As with folk music, song and dance, folk architecture has sometimes been developed by great artists to a very high level but always within the nature of the traditional style. East of Suez, and especially in South-East Asia and Japan, it has been dominant until modern times.

The patronage of folk architecture has sometimes been communal, sometimes ecclesiastical, but the wealthy patron has had an important role. That of the architect has often been merged in the practical business of building, but in the modern world building is seen as a trade, certainly not a profession. Furthermore, although speculative builders have earned a bad name, some very fine developments have been carried out by them, especially in the eighteenth and early nineteenth centuries. In some cases the architect has been the speculator, adopting the roles of patron *and* client.

The role of patron is distinguishable everywhere and at all times in that the patron pays for the building and, where appropriate, employs the architect. Patronage may become professional – as it was for example in medieval England, where the promotion and administration of building for the King was delegated to a Clerk of the Works who was a high-ranking official – and it

becomes increasingly clear that, throughout Europe, cathedrals were built by a succession of firms (teams or lodges of masons) while supervision and continuity were the responsibility of an official. This was probably a monk specially qualified in architecture but, significantly, the word 'architect', though not unknown, dropped out of use. The word 'architect' is defined in a modern dictionary as 'one who designs and supervises the construction of buildings or other large structures, such as ships'. This is acceptable to modern professional architects but historically, as we have seen, it is not true. Some of the world's finest buildings have not been supervised by their designers. Some influential designs were never actually built. Some patrons gave detailed supervision and indeed inspiration to the designers and, like Abbot Suger, claimed, not unreasonably, a large share of the credit. Furthermore, in modern large-scale practice a relatively small proportion of qualified architects do design buildings, while in both architecture and town planning it is not unknown for firms of architects, or patrons acting independently, to employ design consultants.

The word 'profession', and hence 'professionalism', has so many meanings as to be almost meaningless, but in general it implies the exercise of acquired skill for pay, whether it be in football or medicine. Most of the professional organizations claim to have standards of competence and integrity. Entry is commonly by training and examination. After the final professional examinations competence is rarely tested and integrity is essentially a personal quality. Few if any professional societies are inclined to test resistance to temptation except in cases of actual crime and prosecution. The main claim for professionalism in architecture is that it protects the client. It is an ethical rather than an aesthetic ideal. Significantly, many professional architects have turned against the concept of architecture as an art. One may sympathize with this because many architects are not artists either by inclination or training; but unless we ignore almost the whole of architectural history, architecture has been an art and, whatever the 'professionals' may say, public expectation is that it should remain so.

A heavy responsibility for architects and architecture rests upon teachers of architecture, many of whom are qualified architects, but increasingly the schools need to employ specialists in fields such as engineering, computing, heating and acoustics who are not architects. This reflects the composition of the staff in major architectural practices and the growing demands upon architects for the provision of services as the building design process becomes more and more complex. A certain amount of tension, and even conflict of interests, occurs between teachers and practising architects. Teaching is a profession in its own right and has its own skills. But the relationship between university-level teachers and the profession resembles, in many respects, the relationship which exists between the nursing profession and the medical profession and, indeed, the non-clinical staff of the medical schools. In varying degrees, in different countries, the practising architects want to have control of the education of the people they will employ. Understandably they may exercise this surveillance with more regard to their own interests than to recognition of the fact that the schools are educating the architects who will, sooner or later, displace or succeed them. In considering professionalism in architecture we need to be aware of the overlap of professions, of a profession of teaching and research over a wide field, which may in some cases be supervised, even dominated, by architectural professionals who are amateurs in teaching and unskilled in some of the disciplines which now contribute to an architectural education.

The trend of the profession which the schools of architecture must serve is towards technology and administration. The profession recruits and indeed depends upon getting assistant architects who can take their place in a team amongst engineers, surveyors, accountants, even sociologists, on at least equal terms, and this has resulted in a major change of intake to the architectural profession. Until the 1960s, plus or minus ten years in various places, entrants to the profession were judged, at least to some extent, on their potentiality as designers in the artistic sense. No doubt this proclivity is still valued in some places, but generally academic attainment in school subjects, especially mathematics and physics, but not excluding linguistic, social and technical subjects, is prerequisite to artistic ability. This is what the profession in our time requires, and it reflects what the patrons require from architects – a professional service like that which they expect from lawyers and accountants.

Over the years the architectural profession has shed many opportunities in, and commitments to, town planning, interior design, the stage and cinema, shopfronts, landscape design and conservation. The question which looms is whether the profession can retain the fundamental ability to design beautiful buildings; and here the central interest is neither that of the 'patron' (the organization or individual with money to invest) nor of the population (whose environment is being created), and it is focused not on the interior of the buildings but, as most of our progenitors realized, on their external appearance.

Is professionalism destroying architecture? The answer depends upon the modern patrons; but they need, as they do in other sectors of our economies, a positive contribution from the centres of education, creative thinking and research, not only in training putative architects but in propagating beauty as an essential element in human development of the environ-ment which we bequeath to future generations, as well as practicality and comfort for the people who live and work in buildings. So we come back to Sir Henry Wotton's famous dictum that building well has three conditions: commodity, firmness and delight. Its achievement depends upon a creative relationship between patron and architect. Professionalism in architecture is a means to an end. It is a relatively modern means, based upon an ideal of service, of financial integrity, technical competence and, by implication, a commitment to architecture as an art which contributes beautiful buildings to the human environment. An important, indeed vital, question is whether this commitment to architecture can be fulfilled unless the present professional priorities are reversed. Just as the legal profession is now being challenged as to whether or not it achieves justice, so the architectural profession is being challenged, at many levels of society, as to whether or not it achieves architecture.

Architecture, even more than the other arts, provides a measure of the level achieved by extinct civilizations and an indicator of what they bequeathed, through their arts, to their successors. Until the now-extinct 'Modern Movement', arcane architecture – the architecture in the history books – was an art, and was closely related to philosophy and religion. Folk art in all its forms, including architecture, was congenial, expressive of the taste and character of people, occasionally instructive or monitory, as in fairy tales and the miserere carvings in Christian churches, but generally pleasing. It was by and for people.

Whatever questions there may be about the quality of professionally produced contemporary architecture, it is, for better or for worse, evidence of the quality of our civilization. Whether this is of the slightest interest to patrons whose sole concern is with profitability and cost-effectiveness, either in the public or private sector, is a question which will define and determine our place, *and theirs*, in history.

REFERENCES

Alberti, L.B. (1485) *De Re Aedificatoria*, trans J. Rykwert, N. Leach and R. Tavernor, *On the Art of Building, in Ten Books*, 1988, Cambridge, Mass. and London: MIT Press.

Le Corbusier (Jeanneret-Gris, C.E.) (1923) *Vers une architecture*, Paris: Editions Crès; trans F. Etchells, *Towards a New Architecture*, 1927, London: Architectural Press, reprinted 1970.

Vitruvius, Pollio, M. (before AD 27) *De Architectura*; trans. M.H. Morgan 1914, *The Ten Books on Architecture*, Cambridge, Mass.: Harvard University Press; facsimile edn 1960, New York: Dover Publications.

7 Urban space design and social life

Suzanne H. Crowhurst Lennard
and Henry L. Lennard

We have attempted to summarize – from traditional urban space design theory, and from analysis of successful urban spaces in European cities – the principles involved in designing urban places that promote social life and well-being.

Architecture and urban space design employ a non-verbal 'design language' to create contexts and to make value statements. If these values are not identified, an urban space all too frequently is designed without people in mind and is experienced by the user as inimical.

The accumulated wisdom of centuries of city-making documents the connection between urban space design and forms of public social life; between building use and the presence of persons on streets and squares; between aesthetic qualities of architecture and the attention and interest of city dwellers in their environments; between the form of the city's public places and city dwellers' social and emotional well-being.

The design of a space should define the kinds of behaviour and social contacts most appropriate to that place. The architect's and urban designer's concern must be: how can urban space design foster a sense of well-being, and encourage contact and connection? Donald Appleyard called such settings 'caring environments' (Appleyard 1979: 275).

The experience of well-being in cities comprises the sum total of all encounters, relationships and experiences with other people during the course of the day. Well-being arises from contacts that are satisfying, and enjoyable, that affirm persons as individuals and as members of a community. A liveable city provides occasions and places for such good experiences to occur.

SOCIAL PRINCIPLES

From an examination of Europe's most successful urban spaces we have identified the following social functions and social experiences that they make possible:

1 Provide all members of the community, especially children, the elderly and the handicapped, safe and easy access.
2 Facilitate frequent and regular use by local residents.
3 Make persons feel significant and support their self-esteem.
4 Reinforce a sense of belonging to an identifiable community.
5 Encourage curiosity and exploration.
6 Frame meaningful and memorable experiences.
7 Orient people and facilitate differentiated activities.
8 Make it possible for a variety of persons to feel at home in the space.
9 Amplify channels for interpersonal communication (eye contact, vocal and facial recognition).

DESIGN PRINCIPLES

When we look more closely at the physical context for each of the social functions identified above, we find that specific architectural elements contribute to their achievement.

Provide all members of the community safe and easy access

Young adults have no difficulty in travelling to a public space. Children, the elderly and the handicapped must first be considered if all members of the community are to be allowed to participate equally in public life in safety and comfort (Uhlig 1979: 8). Traffic-clogged streets are too dangerous for these groups to negotiate safely, but by creating pedestrian networks the safety and equal rights of all members of the society can be greatly enhanced.

Providing pedestrian access to urban spaces is a very different concept from creating traffic-free pedestrian islands. Ultimately, what is implied here is the creation of a city-wide pedestrian network separate from traffic routes.

In this respect Venice has always provided the exemplary model: independent of the waterway traffic arteries is a city-wide pedestrian network of narrow alleys, wide main thoroughfares and community open spaces scaled to the walker and hospitable to the variety of social life that takes place in public (Mumford 1961: Plate 21).

Facilitate frequent and regular use by local residents

Urban spaces conducive to public life are centrally located in the community, easily accessible to all, and contain in the surrounding buildings a mixture of commercial, cultural and residential functions. They are places that most inhabitants are likely to use on a weekly basis for shopping or cultural outings, or on a daily basis to and from work.

They are identified as the heart of the city, where the

most historic buildings and monuments are to be found. They dramatize the city and create a strong image of the character of the city. Munich's Marienplatz, Kaufinger-strasse and Viktualienmarkt together embody this heart. Similarly, the interconnected Kaerntnerstrasse, St Stephans Platz and the Graben form the heart of Vienna.

Urban spaces that best serve as centres of neighbour-hood community life reflect many of the same character-istics on a smaller scale. They are located at the heart of their community, and at a crossing point of routes through the neighbourhood, allowing serendipitous meetings and use by varied groups. They are directly accessible from surrounding dwellings, and are thus territories that belong to an identifiable community, and they accommodate many of the facilities required on a daily or regular basis by all in the neighbourhood. The Venetian *campo* is the epitome of this second type of successful urban space (Crowhurst Lennard and Lennard 1987: 133).

Urban spaces conducive to public life are never a single-function space; they are multifunctional, accom-modating as many uses and activities as there are citizens, and thus serve the community's social inte-gration and generate membership in the community.

These spaces owe their great vitality to the fact that recent concepts of zoning have not affected them; as shared spaces between buildings that epitomize every aspect of the city's life, these spaces function as the essential unifying element. If we are to create urban places with this vitality it is clear that Mumford was correct in his rejection of current zoning practices: 'We must scrap the monotonous uniformities of American zoning practice, which turns vast areas, too spread out for pedestrian movement, into single-district zones, for commerce, industry, or residential purposes. (As a result, only the mixed zones are architecturally interest-ing today despite their disorder.)' (Mumford 1953: 244).

Make persons feel significant and support self-esteem

To create a setting that enhances self-esteem and social competence requires the co-ordination of architectural and spatial relationships. The goal is to create a setting appropriately dimensioned to the social needs, a setting that 'breathes and pulsates with a very human feeling and a very human scale' (Kidder Smith 1955: 45).

The optimal size of the urban space is related to the social life that takes place there. The space should barely accommodate the busiest regular daily or weekly events. It should not be too large, for its success depends on its feeling of cheerful bustle and busy concentration of activities.

The architectural scale and proportions of the façade design of surrounding buildings, their overall height, vertical and horizontal dimensions, must be scaled to human proportions and human use.

Small-scale buildings reflecting varied activities, needs and styles convey the variety and diversity of human society. The vertical emphasis of narrow façades, or a façade design that emphasizes the vertical, retains the focus of attention on the foreground and draws the eye to ground level. By comparison, horizontal strip windows draw the eye into the distance (Curran 1983: 82).

The street level is the most critical element of the façade, and deserves special handling, since it is here that the greatest degree of interaction between inside and outside should be possible. The street level must be designed to engage our attention. There should not be blank walls to the street, as William H. Whyte explains (Whyte 1980: 82), but rather windows, window displays, doorways, alcoves and outdoor cafés.

The building façade is the 'face' of the building presented to the public. Like the face of a person this façade can be friendly or hostile, open, expressive, bland or closed. It can facilitate an interchange between people inside the building through windows that open, sills that are at a comfortable height for leaning on, balconies, doors, etc., or it can prevent interaction by sealed windows and blank walls. The character of the façades surrounding a public space thus exerts a strong influ-ence over the atmosphere in the public domain, making people feel either welcome or unwanted.

The knowledge that windows and balconies overlook the space, and that residents may well be looking out, exerts a favourable influence, increasing the sense of community and discouraging antisocial activity. This is the phenomenon that Jane Jacobs termed 'eyes on the street' (Jacobs 1965: 45).

The possibility of interaction between inside and outside is extended also to upper floors by the provision of balconies on the second, third and even fourth floors. But beyond the fifth or sixth floor the distance makes it impossible to conduct a conversation, call to a friend, or even recognize an acquaintance. For this reason five or six storeys is the limit of a human-scale building.

Reinforce a sense of belonging to an identifiable community

The world's most successful urban places – Piazza San Marco in Venice, Il Campo in Siena, Plaza Mayor in Salamanca, Vigévano's Piazza Ducale, or Brussels's Grande Place – foster a sense of belonging by the design of the threshold experience and by a sense of visual enclosure. As Camillo Sitte emphasized, 'The essential thing of both room and square is the quality of enclosed space' (Sitte 1979: 20). A public urban space gains much of its sense of place from its enclosed character. Ideally the space is surrounded by buildings or other barriers forming the walls which seem to support the sky. This quality of visual enclosure focuses attention on the people and events within the space.

The creation of a threshold experience has been identified by many urban theorists as one of the essential elements in creating a sense of place. Entrances are often bridged by an archway. Passing beneath a dark arch heightens the experience of crossing the threshold, and raises one's awareness of the fact that one is entering an open area. Many of the Venetian *campi* are entered through tunnel-like *sottoporteghi* – alleyways with buildings bridging them – and these emphasize the drama of arriving in the *campo*.

In order to maintain this sense of enclosure, streets or passages providing access are small, or angled in such a way that there is no direct view out of the space. The ancient and medieval cities evolved many satisfactory solutions – concealing entrances beneath arcades, curving or angling the access street, closing a vista with an important building, or using dramatic natural phenomena to emphasize the visual enclosure.

If a wide exit is visible even before the square has been entered, the square itself seems to be merely a temporary resting-place, an alcove off the major experience of progressing along the street. If, on the other hand, the entrance seems to lead into a totally enclosed area, with no immediately visible exits, then one seems to have arrived at the end of one's journey.

Visual enclosure is traditionally created in streets, too, by a turn in the street (a mechanism used in almost every medieval city; High Street in Oxford is a celebrated example), by a tower gate (as on Neuhauserstrasse in Munich), by an archway over the street (as at Rouen), or even by natural features (such as at Innsbruck, where the mountains tower above the Goldenes Dachl, closing the view down Maria Theresien Strasse, or the Moenchsberg cliffs that close one end of Getreidegasse in Salzburg).

Encourage curiosity and exploration

Richness of façade details and varied textures and colours of building materials provide sensual stimulation and draw the eye into exploration of the building surfaces. A row of small buildings each designed by a different architect, or built at a slightly different period, is intrinsically more intriguing than a single, large building of uniformly bland details. While all the buildings may respect a basic set of rules governing size and scale, building materials and aperture dimensions, the unpredictable detailing of each next façade invites exploration.

A modelled building façade creates hourly changing patterns of light and shade, increasing awareness of the time of day, the strength of the sun. Natural building materials weather gradually over time and acquire a fine patina that reminds one of the slow passage of time and the beautifying effects of age.

Variety of historic building forms stimulates curiosity in the city's past, changing values and life-styles. Historic buildings stand as a salutary reminder that our present ideas are not infallible, that previous ages may have something to teach us if we pay attention.

A special blend of historic buildings gives a place its unique character, sets it apart from all other places and makes it worthy of our affection. Buildings that have long been cherished instill a sense of pride and engage our interest.

Curiosity is stimulated by views that offer a glimpse of a beautiful building but hide the full façade, or by a narrow, dark vista that hints at a bright, open plaza at its end, or by an unusual spire or tower that rises above the skyline. Narrow apertures between buildings invite exploration. Inexplicable sculptures and signs stimulate imagination.

And one of the best rewards and inducements for further exploration is to stumble accidentally on a well-hidden architectural gem like the Palazzo Contarini del Bovolo, in Venice.

Frame meaningful and memorable experiences

Intimate and personal territories adjacent to significant and historic buildings structure meaningful experience and crystallize memories. Our memories are tied to identifiable locations where meaningful experiences took place. Urban spaces, therefore, must provide locations perfectly suited to our social needs. The old well-head in the middle of the Venetian *campo* is no longer a water source, but is still a gathering place. Children find it the perfect size and height for their home-base. The well's previous significance continues into the present, adding a historic dimension to the children's experience; for they are not only playing in the present moment, they are also echoing the lives of many generations past.

Orient people and facilitate differentiated activities

Architectural 'backdrops', level changes, floor textures and focal-points orient people in the space and facilitate differentiated use of the space. Urban spaces need to be articulated by defining clearly one part of the space as being distinct from other parts of the space, otherwise one loses one's sense of bearing and location.

An outstanding façade locates itself firmly in the mind, and one orients oneself in relation to that building. A particularly dramatic and beautiful façade acts as a theatrical 'backdrop', intensifying the experience of being in the public arena, and emphasizing those qualities expressed in the architecture.

Without Basilica San Marco as a backdrop, Piazza San Marco would lose much of its exuberant joy. The Basilica coveys a profound sense of wonder and delight in the variety and richness of life, and sets the tone for the atmosphere in the Piazza.

Urban spaces need articulation, some expression in the floor surface design, in variations of level, or in placement of objects and monuments, so that the different parts of the space have a clearly defined personality, clustering activity to one part, providing an audience at another, allowing free movement in still another section.

People are naturally gregarious and like to gather where others are present, but they need anchors (Cullen 1961: 104), or focal elements to provide memorable and distinct points around which they can meet and cluster. Focal points may be fountains, works of art, or small, free-standing structures such as bandstands or historic monuments. Typically, they provide places to sit, ledges to lean on, shelter from the sun and rain, and a topic of conversation so that even strangers pausing briefly have a legitimate reason to affirm each others' presence by initiating informal conversation.

For the pedestrian, the floor of the city can convey subtle messages, offer varied sensual experiences, and provide information about the history of the area, as well as articulate routes for walking fast or slow, hazards, and places for pausing. Through the unique patterning and texture of paving materials – flagstones, cobbles, setts, bricks, pebbles and mosaics – the design of the city's floor can give each place a unique identity.

A carefully detailed floorscape conveys specific information about the history of a location, but it also subtly demonstrates the community's sense of pride and investment in its environment.

Freiburg in Germany has treated the floor of the old city as the city's carpet. The main square is surfaced in large, split cobbles with a flat surface comfortable for walking on; streets are finished in squared setts or smaller, smooth cobbles and closely laid split pebbles. Designs unique to each street reflect that street's character, and at the entrance to many public buildings, shops and businesses, are emblems signifying the building's use.

Make it possible for a variety of persons to feel at home in the space

The primary requirement for being able to feel at home is being able to use the space comfortably, or take possession of a corner of it for a while. People take possession in different ways – children climb on to sculptures, young people lean on walls or lounge on steps; elderly people need more comfortable seats with backrests. A good urban space provides the maximum variety in types of seating.

Low walls define boundaries, but if they are appropriately dimensioned they can also be used as a temporary resting place, a support to lean on, or a surface for sitting and reclining on. Well-designed railings can be useful adjuncts to public life. They are often used by young people, in lieu of benches, walls or steps, as a place to perch and watch the passing scene.

Planters can be arranged to divert pedestrian traffic, and to create quiet enclaves, suitable for individuals and groups to sit in or children to play in away from the pedestrian flow. Planters are usually designed in connection with seating; but whether designed for the purpose or not, the edges of the planters themselves are invariably used as seats. If this use is not foreseen in the design, the plants can be badly damaged.

Steps offer opportunities for sitting or lounging, and may be designed in combination with trees, planters or walls to create tables, back- and armrests, alcoves for small groups, or amphitheatres in which large crowds can watch entertainment. From an upper level it is often possible to look down on a crowd and to feel both separate from, yet part of, the social scene.

The popularity of the Spanish Steps in Rome is due in no small part to their theatricality, combining stage sets and balconies for watching and taking part in a variety of scenarios and social situations. The steps rise in four tiers, each platform a stage in itself, a place to rest, to perform or to lean on the balustrade to scan the crowd in the Piazza di Spagna below.

Amplify channels for direct interpersonal communication (eye contact, voice and facial recognition).

Seating is too frequently ill-conceived and not supportive of good social life. Insufficient seating reflects the donors' grudging tolerance of the 'non-productive' activity of social life; benches set in a row demonstrate a lack of understanding of the human need for conversation and sociability; artfully designed fixed seats betray a self-conscious desire to decorate the space rather than to provide hospitable seating. An absence of comfortable seats demonstrates lack of concern for the elderly, while the omission of sit-on-able steps and ledges exhibits intolerance towards the young.

A great deal of subtle social interaction takes place in public, even between strangers, but this interaction is not possible if people are prevented from facing each other and making eye contact. The face is the most interesting human feature, and people-watching would lose much of its attraction if one could not muse on the expression of emotion in a stranger's face, wonder how a person's life formed the character to be read in the face, or catch a glance from a stranger that communicates a shared response to an event in the public realm. These kinds of subtle interaction require seating angled towards, rather than away from, others.

In the most successful public spaces one finds that, as in good stage design, seating has been designed to create settings that enhance a variety of interactions. Individuals and groups can select from several possible choices the territory that will best accommodate their personal agenda, and are able to move through the space from one level of involvement in public life to another, as they desire. Seating offers people who are alone the possibility of remaining in the public domain until they meet a friend.

SUMMARY

History has shown that care and attention in the design of urban spaces, making them appropriate settings for festivities, as well as for everyday social events and functional activities that all can participate in, inspire in all city dwellers a sense of citizenship.

What is needed is a more ecological approach to city design – one that respects the historic function of cities, the systemic connection between urban forms and social processes, and the need to involve all city dwellers, from experts to community members, in decision-making.

It is essential that we do not forget the age-old wisdom of city making: the necessity to place people again in the foreground of attention, and to provide the settings and occasions for sociability and dialogue, for civic and communal participation, for aesthetic experience and, last but not least, for joy and celebration.

NOTE

A more comprehensive discussion of these issues can be found in *Public Life in Urban Places* (1984) Southampton, New York: Gondolier Press, and *Livable Cities: Social and Design Principles for the Future of the City* (1987) Southampton, New York: Gondolier Press, both by Suzanne H. Crowhurst Lennard and Henry L. Lennard.

REFERENCES

Appleyard, D. (1979) 'The Environment as a social symbol', *Ekistics* 278 (September/October): 275.

Crowhurst Lennard, S.H. and Lennard, H.L. (1987) *Livable Cities: Social and Design Principles for the Future of the City*, Southampton, New York: Gondolier Press.

Cullen, G. (1961) *The Concise Townscape* New York: Van Nostrand Reinhold.

Curran, R.J. (1983) *Architecture and the Urban Experience*, New York: Van Nostrand Reinhold.

Jacobs, J. (1965) *The Death and Life of Great American Cities*, Harmondsworth: Penguin.

Kidder Smith, G.E. (1955) *Italy Builds*, New York: Reinhold Publishing Corp.

Mumford, L. (1953) *The Highway and the City*, New York: Harcourt, Brace & World.

—— (1961) *The City in History*, New York: Harcourt, Brace & World.

Sitte, C. (1979) *The Art of Building Cities*, trans. C.T. Stewart, Westport, Conn.: Hyperion Press.

Uhlig, K. (1979) *Die Fussgaengerfreundliche Stadt*, Stuttgart: Verlag Gerd Hatje.

Whyte, W.H. (1980) *The Social Life of Small Urban Spaces*, Washington, DC: The Conservation Foundation.

8 Architecture and people

Steven Tiesdell and Taner Oc

INTRODUCTION

In recent years concern for human needs and welfare within the environment has been overshadowed by debate in architectural circles that is exclusively concerned with the aesthetics of styles and of packaging. The imbalance is neglectful of the totality of architecture. There are at least two fundamental ways of assessing architectural works: as aesthetic objects or displays and as environments (Lang 1989). The first is insidiously seductive since much received architectural appreciation is presented through the two-dimensional medium of photography, rather than through direct, and prolonged, firsthand experience. Whilst not dismissing the importance of the symbolic and aesthetic attributes of architecture, this essay is a discussion of architecture as environment and its interaction with people.

ENVIRONMENT

There is an apparent paradox amongst architects with regard to the influence of the built environment on people. On the one hand there is a necessary, but often unstated, idealism which suggests that a better physical environment will improve people's social behaviour. On the other there is a disclaimer, where it is argued that there are many examples of ostensibly similar buildings, some of which are successful whilst others are not. In addition, there are highly desirable high-rise flats, and, equally, unsuccessful houses and gardens. Clearly the explanation of this pattern of causation is complex, particularly since local and individual differences will inevitably disrupt general or simplistic theories.

Consideration of the behavioural influence of the physical environment must inevitably start with environmental determinism, where the physical environment determines social behaviour. From this essentially Victorian belief sprung the positivist idea that the amelioration of the physical environment would inexorably produce a resultant social reform. Consequently the physical environment was seen as the principal instrument of social reform. Such a concept would have had some currency in the extreme conditions of the nineteenth-century slums, since any physical improvement would probably precipitate a resultant behavioural improvement. Nevertheless, the narrowness of this simple linear causality is nicely illustrated in Mark Twain's epigram: 'If your only tool is a hammer, all your problems are nails.' In reality, the belief was an intuitive normative conviction about what ought to be, rather than being rigorously based on factual knowledge. In effect, it was well-intentioned paternalism. 'Like all good Victorians, they choose to believe that if the masses will only wash and go to sunday school they will be happier' (Anson 1986: 16). Similarly if they were to have better housing: it was this attitude which underpinned Edwin Chadwick's Public Health Acts of the mid-nineteenth century (see Fig. 1).

Nevertheless it remained a potent idea throughout the early twentieth century, perpetuated in differing ways by expansive concepts, such as Le Corbusier's Radiant City and Ebenezer Howard's Garden City. The belief was that if the environment was changed in the ways prescribed by these ideologies, then human behaviour would improve and human happiness increase. Whilst this was a retention of Victorian beliefs, it was also a reflection of the broad humanist social concerns that underpinned the early Modernist ideology, and of its faithful, but in hindsight misguided, adherents who were firmly committed to the idea that architecture would lead to a better world. This deterministic outlook was contained, rather too literally, in Le Corbusier's famous aphorism: 'Architecture or revolution: revolution can be avoided' (Le Corbusier 1946: 269). The literal interpretation was that revolution could be avoided by better housing. Unfortunately this viewpoint held a very fixed notion of humanity, which was that it saw no need to consult people because it already knew what they wanted (Kostof 1989: xiii).

By the mid-1960s, due to the increasing influence of the maturing social sciences, this rather crude belief was disputed and contested by arguments that placed their emphasis on cultural, social and economic factors. Where previously stress had been placed on the nature of the physical environment, such that the friendliness of the street was considered to be a product of the pub, the corner shop and the church hall, social scientists

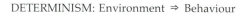

DETERMINISM: Environment ⇒ Behaviour

NON DETERMINISM: Environment ≠ Behaviour

Figure 1 *Static conception of environment-behaviour.*

placed greater emphasis on the deep roots of the inhabitants of working-class streets and on the close family and economic ties of the street system. The reaction by some in the environmental professions, particularly in response to the increasingly manifest failings of the brave new world of modernist architecture, was a welcome to these counter-arguments and a renouncement of determinism, with the emphatic denial that architecture could influence people. Such a ploy was a masterly stroke in reconstructivist self-preservation, absolving them of any blame for any ill effects of their designs, and providing them with an accusative word, determinism, to cast at critics who had the insolence to suggest that their designs were at fault (Coleman 1985). Some observers even put the built environment on trial (Coleman 1985); as it was regarded, by some, as the sole defendant, if convicted it would carry the whole charge. To have the capacity to denounce the built environment was to find a malleable scapegoat for the more manifest urban ills and deleterious behaviour, and thus to marginalize, and deflect attention from, the consideration of other contributory factors, such as poverty, unemployment and other social problems. Equally, if the built environment could be shown to have no effect then the environmental professions were absolved of any responsibility, or blame.

Thus the argument became polarized. The physical environment was either a total determinant of social behaviour or it had no effect. As Lawrence has noted, such a situation tended to reinforce concepts of linearly determined causality, or non-causality, rather than inter-relationships and interconnections (Lawrence 1987). In reality both the original determinist ideology and the reconstructivist non-determinacy theory were over-simplifications. This all-or-nothing view is inherently reductionist: it is not a matter of absolutes, but rather one of relativity. A more realistic approach is to accept that both environment and behaviour are variable factors, possibly, but not necessarily, mutually inter-active, and that physical factors are not the exclusive influence on behaviour (see Figure 2). Gans has developed this aspect:

> Between the physical environment and empirically observable human behaviour, there exists a social system and a set of cultural norms which define and evaluate portions of the physical environment relevant to the lives of the people involved and structures the way people will use (and react to) this environment in their daily lives.
>
> (Gans 1968: 5)

In amplification of this point, where a reliance on purely physical factors would be too simplistic, take the socially deleterious activity of crime (the criminal activity referred to here is that of environmental crime – for example, crimes against the person or against property). Environmental criminology had its roots in the work of

Figure 2 *Dynamic conception of environment-behaviour.*

Oscar Newman (1973), and as such is often vulnerable to charges of a simplistic determinism due to an inadequate discussion of the distinction between motivation and opportunity. Criminal activity is a combination of both sociological motivation and environmental opportunity. For example, some people, for reasons such as social position or economic and social pressures, will rarely be motivated to commit a crime despite the opportunity or temptation, equally, some people are almost habitually motivated or pressured to commit crime whenever the opportunity presents itself. Realistically these are extremes and at any particular moment in time people will form a distribution between these poles, such that a crime may be committed when the particular threshold of motivation in the individual coincides with ease of opportunity. Thus whilst environmental design is unlikely to affect motivation directly, it may possibly affect the ease of opportunity.

Amos Rapoport (1977: 2), amongst others, has offered an expanded view which promulgates a spectrum of determinism, where determinancy is a generic term for the continuum between determinancy and non-determinancy (see Figure 3). On the 'determinism' level, the view is that the physical environment determines human behaviour, whilst on the 'possibilism' level the physical environment provides opportunities and constraints within which people are able to make choices based on other criteria. Between these two positions is a level of determinism called 'probabilism' where the physical environment provides possibilities for choice and is not determining, but in a given physical setting some choices are more probable than others. Rapoport's models reiterate the notion of environmental opportunities. Thus what people are able to do is consistent with, and limited by, the set of environmental or spatial opportunities available to them. Thus behaviour is still

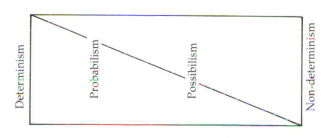

Figure 3 *Spectrum of determinism.*

'situational' or contextual (Lawrence 1987: 205). In part this is because certain activities require particular means of support from an appropriately designed or facilitative environment. Additionally, however, people make rational choices about the opportunities available to them within particular physical settings. These choices are made with respect to personal normative criteria such as individual social values and goals, which are not static but are related to lifestyle and its anticipated development, or what Stokols labels 'subjective life stages' (Stokols 1982: 191). These are defined as 'spatially and temporally bounded phases of a person's life that are associated with particular goals and plans'. Subjective life stages are related to, but distinct from, developmental stage and life cycle, which are usually defined in terms of age-specific variables; hence people of the same age may construe phases of their lives differently owing to dissimilar professional experiences and different residential biographies (Lawrence 1987: 158).

Gans (1968: 5) has made a distinction between potential and effective environments, whereby a physical setting is interpreted as a potential environment providing a range of opportunities for satisfying individual and group needs in diverse ways. At any particular moment in time, what is achieved is the resultant or effective environment (Lawrence 1987: 157). In this context, the inherent potential of an environment relates to the quality and quantity of opportunities available, although the availability of an opportunity does not necessarily equate with an individual's ability to exercise it. As Lawrence observes (ibid.), Gans's concept implies that there is no deterministic relationship between human requirements and physical settings, since both individual and group requirements can be fulfilled in diverse ways. The notion of diverse ways postulates that most needs apparently dependent on the environment may be equally well satisfied in other ways: for example, by the alteration of economic, social or cultural conditions, or of the prevailing managerial regime, or by a combination of these. Hence people are not hopelessly moulded by their environment but are able to modify the immediate conditions of their environment. For example, people are able to moderate feelings of dissatisfaction in residential settings by selecting among neighbours for the purpose of interaction or by spending more or less time in their neighbourhood (Fried 1982). Similarly, the apparent success of former public-sector flats sold off to the private sector may be (politically) attributed solely to the change in the pattern of tenure, but is also related to the installation of controlled access and the social backgrounds of the new inhabitants.

Nevertheless there are pragmatic limits to the physical scope of this modification beyond which the environment is a relatively fixed entity. In a fundamental way it is architects who, in creating the built environment, necessarily put limitations on people's be-

havioural opportunities by establishing the general context for those opportunities. For example, consider the architectural determination of privacy. Whilst acknowledging that people are able to exert a personal or social control on their contact with other people, built-form determinants of privacy take two forms: barriers, which physically establish the general privacy state, and filters, which allow the individual to modify or control that general state. Barriers, in general, concern the permanent physical aspects of the design: for example, audio-privacy between adjacent dwellings is fundamentally a barrier situation. Filters are to an extent beyond the designer's control, but play a vital role in increasing the adaptability of the environment and the ability of the inhabitant to control and to determine his or her own environment. The filter aspects of privacy are best exemplified by the innocuous net curtain, which despite its ostensible simplicity is actually a very sophisticated device for the delimitation of semi-private and semi-public space (Taylor 1973).

In addition there is also a dynamic perspective to environment–people interaction, where the influence of the built environment varies over time. For example, Ellis (1975) has noted that initial friendships on housing estates are strongly based on propinquity, but with time people acquire a more dispersed circle of friends through contacts at, for example, the school, the shops, the pub, etc. Thus with the passage of time, the influence of the physical design is displaced by social factors. This example suggests that there can be differential quality in environments in the sense that some may possess more potential to be effective than others. Hence if the physical environment has a *conducive* effect or, in Gans's terms, more potential to become effective (for example by affording more opportunities for contact) then, paradoxically, the built environment may be a dominant factor for a reduced period, since the individual is projected more quickly into the development of choice-oriented social relationships, rather than those based merely on residential propinquity. Conversely, where the built environment has an *inhibitive* or disabling effect, it remains the principal or dominant influence, in an obstructive manner, on social relationships for a longer period. However, in moderation of this, the concept of diverse ways would suggest that it would still be possible for the individual actively to alter this situation, for example, by membership of local sports teams or local community organizations.

PEOPLE

Having examined their relation with the built environment, the inherent nature of people needs examination. Ellis and Cuff (1989: 8) speculate that architects, in considering people, create an image or model, a homunculus, which offers guidance as to their reactions in given situations, particularly in their spatial comprehension of two-dimensional plans. The development of this conceptual homunculus is based on various influences, including personal social experience and observation, innate sensitivity and insight, and even direct, concious consultation and participation with real people. Inevitably much also depends on the personal sensibilities of the individual architect, whether megalomanic or servile, and his or her view of humanity. To a limited extent the social sciences also offer guidance, although their value as a prescriptive tool without necessary qualification may be unreliable (Jenks 1988). Nevertheless, whilst the concept offers a general truth about relatively abstract populations, the inexorably individual nature of people cannot be discounted. Implicitly the concepts of environmental opportunities and of diverse ways imply criteria of rational individual selectivity. As has been stated, people make choices and decisions based upon past experience of built environments, motivated by shifting criteria in terms of goals and values, relative to both temporal aspirations and available resources. These various motivational factors collectively establish a particular lifestyle which assesses satisfaction with physical settings.

Despite the individualistic and complex nature of human values, goals and aspirations, many authors have proposed a hierarchy of those human needs that are considered to be innate or omnipresent (e.g. Lawrence 1987: 159). These hierarchies tend to be derived from Maslow's original work on human motivations (Maslow 1968). Lang defines them as follows (Lang 1987: 10);

Need	Psycho-physical mechanisms for satisfying needs
Survival	Shelter
Safety	Privacy, territorial control, orientation in place and time
Belonging	Communal settings, symbolic aesthetics of the group
Esteem	Control, personalization, symbolic aesthetics of the self
Self-actualization	Choice, control, symbolic aesthetics of the consideration of others
Cognitive/Aesthetic	Formal aesthetics, art for art's sake

Whilst these needs provide an initial framework, what they mean for people in a specific setting and how they can be achieved is not clear. There are two major criticisms of this approach. First the universal, or absolute, nature of these needs runs the risk of being too simplistic without more expansive qualification, and second, the hierarchy tends to ignore the relativity of these variables, particularly in the differentiation of those that are constant and generalizable and those that are not (Lawrence 1987: 160). Nevertheless the most

pertinent departure point for the examination of the relationship between environmental parameters and human needs would appear to be the related study of territoriality. Most environmental psychologists tend to agree that the provision of territory satisfies people's basic needs for identity (both communally and individually) as opposed to anonymity, security and privacy (and equally socialization or stimulation). Unfortunately, these psychological concepts do not have core definitions that are used consistently within this field. Whilst these needs may also appear simplistic, they are broad concepts that may be resolved in diverse ways, together with the recognition that people's needs vary over time and life situation, particularly with regard to Stokols's subjective life stages.

Identity relates to a need for a sense of identification with a specific territory, or possibly a group of people, often of a defensible nature. Essentially it relates to a need for the individual to create, and also to express, a sense of both belonging to some collective entity or place and of personal or individual identity, although equally there is a concomitant duality with anonymity (Wirth 1938). The collective or corporate sense of identity with a particular place is termed association, for example the feeling of belonging or of possession. This level of identity, beyond that of the individual, is often gained by a degree of physical separation or isolation. Within an urban context, the distinction is less clearly achieved by physical means, even if such expression should be desirable. However, one clear example is the multi-storey housing block in Newcastle known as the Byker Wall, which is, simultaneously, a collective shelter to the low-rise housing on its inner side and an identifying image. Such bold imagery, however, may be incompatible with the aspirations of the inhabitants. Gosling and Maitland (1987) have observed that the powerful imagery bestows a vivid identification with that community, such that it requires extra confidence to be identified as a resident of the Byker Wall. The individual, or ego-identity, relates to a need for 'personalization': the ability to create for oneself or to put a distinctive stamp on one's personal environment. Richard MacCormac (1978) has suggested that this need for individual expression may be inverse to the acceptability of the overall architectural or environmental image: thus satisfaction from associational identity compensates for the relative lack of individual identity. Personalization typically occurs (and makes explicit) the threshold or transition between public and private domains, particularly the judicial boundary of the property or territory of the individual. In this respect, small-scale architectural details contribute to the cultural and social symbolism of such thresholds and delimitations of space. A well-documented example of inhabitants' autonomous personalization is that made by the residents of Le Corbusier's resolutely modernist housing development at Pessac (Boudon 1969). It may be noted that the stone cladding of ostensibly brick dwellings is also an expression of this need for personalization.

Security relates to the perceived necessity for a sanctuary from which to address and deal with the external world. Unsolicited invasion or desecration of this sanctuary may be personally destabilizing, which helps to explain why burglary is one of the most personally distressing of environmental crimes. Whilst security may relate to continuity of tenure or ownership, it also relates to the notion of security as the mutual 'protection' of individual and communal territory, for example the limitation of opportunities for environmental crime. As such it has been most associated with Oscar Newman's ideas of 'defensible space' (Newman 1973), the main thrust of which was increased casual surveillance and the clear demarcation of personal and communal territory.

Privacy appears to be a vital necessity against the threat of overexposure. Thus the home environment is a base for reflection, restoration and for the creation and maintenance of personal relationships. Equally, an excess of privacy can lead to isolation and loneliness. Rapoport defines privacy as 'the ability to control interaction i.e. to avoid unwanted interaction' (Rapoport 1977: 201). This unwanted interaction includes both visual and aural intrusions. Within a residential setting, for example, lack of privacy can create, internally, depression and illness and, externally, conflict and stress which can be alienating and potentially destructive to collective well-being. The physical context of privacy has been discussed earlier. The dialectical companion of privacy is socialization or stimulation. Inherently, it is based on contact and relationships between individuals. The implicit presumption is that people need to form social networks with a corresponding sense of mutual caring and protection. When these networks break down, crime and vandalism may result (Lawrence 1987). Socialization may also act to modify or enhance the other perceived needs, for example by assisting the creation of identity with a specific group of people, or enhancing the feeling of security within a known group of people. Nevertheless the inherent implication that we are instinctively and unreservedly 'social animals' has been questioned. Murdock has suggested that:

> Unlike the ants and birds, man is not biologically a social animal equipped by heredity with prepotent capacities for complex associative life, but in every individual case must be bent and broken to group living through the arduous process of socialisation and be kept in the paths of conformity by the imposition of social controls.
>
> (Murdock 1965, cited in Malmburg 1980: 239)

Nevertheless each viewpoint places stress on the promotion of the social experiences and contacts necessary to educate the individual in group living.

Socialization contacts can be broadly grouped into two interrelated types: 'formal' and 'informal' (Thorns 1976). Formal contacts are those of an institutional, associational and leisure nature and, as such, are inseparably linked with the physical provision of amenities: for example, shops, clubs, sports fields, etc. These contacts are relatively explicit, whilst the informal, unstructured contacts between individuals, such as the casual nod of acquaintance, are inherently less explicit. The provision of informal socialization opportunities has tended to rely on site planning techniques which increase the frequency of external visual contacts between near neighbours, such that through repetitive visual contact, more meaningful oral contact may be provoked. However, motivation for socialization is also required such that contact is merely the beginning. As Gans (1961) has noted, whilst propinquity may initiate many social relationships and maintain less intensive ones, friendships also require homogeneity. Essentially this means 'something in common', for example lifestyle homogeneity, expressed through common norms of behaviour. Gans stressed compatible child-raising methods as being particularly important, the implication being that too great a variety in norms of behaviour can lead to stress and conflict which, whilst stimulating, can be detrimental to collective well-being. Nevertheless, Gans also considered that some conflict was healthy to engender a sense of tolerance, which was only destructive where it was beyond the abilities of the inhabitants to contain that conflict.

A pertinent criticism of many approaches to territoriality, however, is that they are overly concerned with the aggressive defence of territory. But as Sebba and Churchman (1983) note, hospitality is rarely cited as a specifically territorial behaviour. Yet hospitality – for example, an invitation on to one's territory – is subject to one's control, or ownership, of that territory. Thus the important quality is the control, rather than the defence, of the given territory. Equally important may be the perception of control rather than its actuality. Research by Karen Franck (1980) has shown that social factors, such as the intensity of friendship or kinship bonds within a community, have a significant positive effect on the perceived level of safety within its bounds.

ARCHITECTS

Having discussed the interaction between people and the built environment, the architect's role needs to be considered. Following the Industrial Revolution, the supersedence of craft-based trades by industrial rationalization led to the relative estrangement of the sponsor, the designer and the eventual user of the built environment. In self-determined environments such as squatter settlements and the villages of primitive tribes, where the various parties are one, there is no estrangement. Such an estrangement makes the architect's precise role in the process confused. The architect has to deal with the goals and aspirations of both the sponsor, which may increasingly include the ability to negotiate and manage a conflict-ridden, litigious construction process (Montgomery 1989: 276) and the ultimate achievement of profit, and those of the users, who may be simply unknown. In this respect, public participation and consultation may be seen as an attempt to reconcile the various parties by restoring a direct dialogue and giving the users a measure of control over their environment.

Whilst acknowledging that it may be impossible for us all to construct our own houses, and that we are forced therefore to adapt ourselves within the setting with which the architect has furnished us, Candilis has cogently outlined the notion of the architect's role as being to design a physical framework to the point at which an individual can take over and exert real influence over his or her home (Candilis 1968 cited in Team Ten 1972: 384). A reflection of this attitude, in the ordering of the architect's priorities, was illustrated in Vernon Gracie's approach as project architect for Ralph Erskine's Byker Redevelopment:

> Housing gets built over a period of four or five years and these houses stand for an economic life of sixty years; the community will adjust and change during that period of time. The architect's involvement therefore, is not so much in the sticks and stones of the exercise in determining the sort of doorknobs, but in getting the social structuring right.
>
> (Gracie 1980: 42)

Nevertheless, probably correctly, architects yield only the power invested in them, being merely the tool of other forces in society, such as politicians and developers. But whilst architects are becoming increasingly embroiled in their professional and business roles, they are, in their principal role, intrinsically concerned with modifications of the built environment. As Lee states: The architect is a professional manipulator of the environment' (Lee 1971: 257). The sinister and totalitarian overtones of this statement imply a high degree of control over the process, since in reality architects are merely tinkerers. However, architects must have a positive faith in what they do, since their decisions constrain the opportunities of the users over whom, in a practical sense, they have no further control. Nevertheless from Gans's argument (Gans 1968), the 'potential' of an environment can only be made manifest or 'effective' by those users. Hence the necessary stress on their consideration, and even involvement, which the static admiration of architecture as purely aesthetic object effectively negates (see Figure 4).

Thus whilst architects necessarily oscillate between the apparent contradictions of the aesthetic object and the pragmatic requirements of the user, the position is not dichotomous since a spectrum extends between them. Indeed, it is possible to speculate that they are dialectically related, whereby a synthesis is able to subsume the initial contradictions such that the presence of people transforms abstract architectural space into meaningful and experential place. Such a synthesis, which necessarily includes people within its definition, is a total conception of architecture as a conducive and responsive environment. As Lang (1989) has noted, it is this total conception of architecture which has been

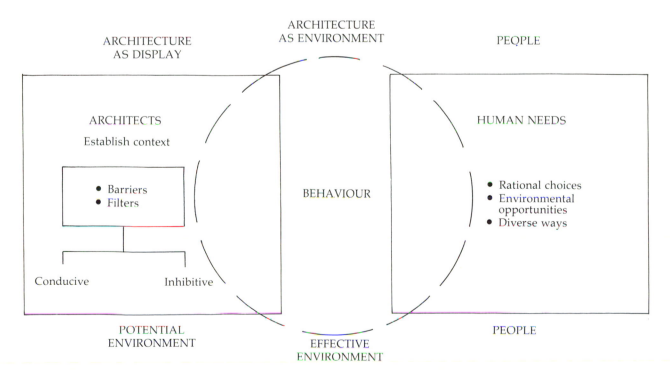

Figure 4 *Dynamic conception of architecture–people interaction.*

neglected as architects have moved on, or away, from Modernism into Post-Modernism and Decontructivism, and to which architecture must return if architects are to maintain their relevance into the twenty-first century.

REFERENCES

Anson, B. (1986) 'Don't shoot the graffiti man', *Architects' Journal* 184 (2 July): 16–17.

Boudon, P. (1969) *Lived-in Architecture: Le Corbusier's 'Pessac' Revisited*, Cambridge, Mass.: MIT Press.

Coleman, A. (1985) *Utopia on Trial: Vision and Reality in Planned Housing*, London: Shipman.

Ellis, P. (1975) 'Letterbox living: making friends on housing estates', *New Society* 33 (2 October): 10–12.

Ellis, R. and Cuff, D. (eds) (1989) *Architects' People*, Oxford: Oxford University Press.

Franck, K.A. (1980) 'The social experience of living in urban and non-urban settings', *Journal of Social Issues* 36 (3): 52–71.

Fried, M. (1982) 'Residential attachment: sources of residential and community satisfaction', *Journal of Social Issues* 38 (3): 107–119.

Gans, H.J. (1961) 'Planning and social life: friendship and neighbour relations in suburban communities' *Journal of the American Institute of Planners* 27 (2): 134–40.

—— (1968) *People and Planning: Essays on Urban Problems and Solutions*, London: Penguin.

Gosling, D. and Maitland, B. (1987) *Concepts of Urban Design*, London: Academy.

Gracie, V. (1980) 'Politics and Participation in Byker', *RIBA Journal* 87 (8): 41–2.

Jenks, M. (1988) 'Housing problems and the dangers of certainty', in N. Teymur, T.A. Markus and T. Woolley (eds) *Rehumanising Housing*, London: Butterworth, pp. 53–60.

Kostof, S. (1989) Foreword to R. Ellis and D. Cuff (eds) *Architects' People*, Oxford: Oxford University Press, pp. ix–xix.

Lang, J. (1987) *Creating Architectural Theory: The Role of the Behavioural Sciences in Environmental Theory* New York: Van Nostrand Reinhold.

—— (1989) 'Psychology and Architecture', *Penn in Ink* Newsletter of Graduate School of Fine Arts, University of Pennsylvania, Fall.: 10–11.

Lawrence, R.J. (1987) *Houses, Dwellings and Homes: Design, Theory, Research and Practice*, New York: Wiley.

Le Corbusier (1946) *Towards a New Architecture*, 1970 edn, London: Architectural Press.

Lee, T. (1971) 'Psychology and Architectural Determinism (Part 1)', *Architects Journal* 154 (4 August): 253–62.

MacCormac, R. (1978) 'Housing and the Dilemma of Style', *Architectural Review* 163 (April): 203–6.

Malmburg, T. (1980) *Human Territoriality*, New York: Mouton Publishers.

Maslow, A. (1968) *Towards a Psychology of Being*, New York: Van Nostrand.

Montgomery, R. (1989) 'Architecture invents new people', in R. Ellis and D. Cuff (eds) *Architects' People*, Oxford: Oxford University Press, pp. 260–81.

Newman, O. (1973) *Defensible Space: People and Design in the Violent City*, London: Architectural Press.

Rapoport, A. (1977) *Human Aspects of Urban Form: Towards a Man-Environment Approach to Urban Form and Design*, Oxford: Pergamon Press.

Sebba, R. and Churchman, A. (1983) 'Territories and territoriality in the home', *Environment and Behaviour* 15 (2): 191–210.

Stokols, D. (1982) 'Environmental psychology: a coming of age', in A. Grant (ed.) *The G. Stanley Hall Lecture Series*, Vol. 2, pp. 155–205, Washington, DC: American Psychological Association.

Taylor, N. (1973) *The Village in the City*, London: Temple Smith.

Team Ten (1972) 'The role of the architect in community building', in G. Bell and J. Tyrwhitt (eds) *Human Identity in the Urban Environment*, London: Penguin, pp. 376–93.

Thorns, D.C. (1976) *The Quest for Community: Social Aspects of Residential Growth*, London: George Allen & Unwin.

Wirth, L. (1938) 'Urbanism as a way of life', *American Journal of Sociology* 44: 1–24.

FURTHER READING

Ellis, P. (1977) 'Social psychological evaluation of Chalvedon housing area, Basildon, Essex', *Architects' Journal* 166 (14 September): 488–94.

Gans, H.J. (1961) 'The balanced community: homogeneity or heterogeneity in residential areas?', *Journal of the American Institute of Planners* 27 (3): 176–84.

—— (1967) *The Levittowners: Ways of Life and Politics in a New Suburban Community*, London: Allen Lane and the Penguin Press.

Norberg-Schulz, C. (1971) *Existence, Space and Architecture*, London: Studio Vista.

Proshansky, H.M., Ittelson, W.H. and Rivlin, L.G. (eds) (1970) *Environmental Psychology: Man and His Physical Setting*, New York: Holt, Rinehart & Winston.

Smithson, A. (ed.) (1968) *Team Ten Primer*, Cambridge, Mass.: MIT Press.

Willis, M. (1963) 'Designing for privacy. Part 1: What is privacy?' *Architects' Journal* 137 (29 May): 113–14.

9 Housing as if people mattered

Stuart Cameron

There is a deliberate ambiguity in the use of the word 'housing' in the title. On the one hand it can refer to houses – physical structures whose quality of design, of accomodation and of the environment which they collectively create, matter to people. On the other hand it can refer to the process of being housed, the economic, social and political opportunities and constraints which people may face in finding their way into these houses. The essay seeks to address both of these issues, but particularly the relationship between them in past and in current housing policy.

HOUSING POLICY BEFORE THE 1980s

The history of housing in Britain since the First World War, and especially since the Second World War, can be viewed as mainly concerned with two great juggernauts. These were the private house-building industry, providing housing for sale with the crucial backing of the powerful financial institutions of the building societies, and the local authorities building housing for rent.

This dual system of housing provision had two great achievements. First, it produced a transformation of housing conditions on a massive scale through housing production and renewal, peaking in the 1960s. This produced average levels of housing quality, of space and amenity, which were undreamed of even in the recent past. Second, it was a system which created improved housing opportunities throughout the social spectrum from top to bottom. It did not rely solely on the creation of housing for the better-off to filter or trickle down to the poor; it directly addressed the housing conditions of the poorer sections of society.

The private housing sector played a major role in the overall improvement of housing conditions through the construction of new housing and the improvement of the existing stock (often with grant aid from the State). It was, though, the public sector which most directly addressed the poorest housing conditions through programmes of slum clearance of the worst older housing, and the needs of the poorest in the population through the construction of council housing within the means of those on low incomes.

Set against those achievements are major problems which are now seen to have emerged from this system of housing provision. On the one hand there are problems of poor quality and insensitivity in the physical form of some housing of the recent past, and in the effect of housing processes on the urban fabric and the environment. On the other hand there are problems

of social polarization and division, reflected in, if not produced by, the past patterns of housing provision.

The symptoms of these problems are seen most clearly in the council housing sector. They come together in the notion of 'hard-to-let' council housing where a combination of unpopular design, poor physical condition and a concentration of the most disadvantaged in the population makes an area so undesirable that – in the midst of housing shortages – housing lies vacant because people are unwilling to live there.

PROBLEMS FROM THE PAST – A DEBATE

The use of the word 'symptom' above raises a highly contentious issue – do problems such as these arise from the nature of council housing itself or from the context within which it operates? Is the cause of the problem to be found within council housing, or merely the symptoms of a problem that has its more fundamental root in the relationship between the public and private sectors of the housing system?

In the mid-1980s the former view was very forcefully represented by Alice Coleman in her influential book *Utopia on Trial* (Coleman 1985). The book is perhaps best known for its attack on Utopian design, on the non-traditional, high-density, high-rise flatted housing built in the public sector in the post-war years. Likewise, the extensive critical commentary on Coleman's work (e.g. Hillier 1986) has tended to concentrate on the apparent architectural determinism of her emphasis on physical design as the primary source of social malaise in housing areas – an emphasis perhaps rather ameliorated in the second edition (Coleman 1990). However, Coleman's attack is clearly as much on a Utopian process of housing provision as on Utopian design. She clearly feels that design problems and resulting social malaise have arisen directly from the intervention by the State – at central and local level – to provide housing on the basis of need. For her the answer lies in a return to market processes of housing provision to produce an evolution of housing design which gives people what they want – which produces housing as if people mattered.

In contrast, Dunleavy (1981) suggested that, within a complex of factors, it was the context within which the public sector operated *vis-à-vis* the private sector which produced the Utopian housing of the post-war years. In effect, in the 1950s and 1960s the public housing sector was burdened by a number of tasks which the burgeoning private, owner-occupied sector escaped. It fell largely to the public sector to address the problem of the renewal of inner city slums and to demolish and rebuild in these areas. It was the public sector that experienced pressure to increase overall residential densities in the interests of urban containment and the preservation of agricultural land. It was in the public sector that ways were sought to find a 'technological fix' for the provision of mass housing as cheaply as possible in terms of costs, land and the use of scarce traditional materials and skilled labour. In contrast, the 'market-led' housing provision of the private sector was left to concentrate on low-density housing built in traditional ways on greenfield sites in suburban locations. This unequal burdening of one of the two elements of the dual system of housing provision set the context within which high-rise and related housing forms emerged.

Dunleavy, too, emphasized that the system of local authority housing of the time gave little power or choice to the tenants of this housing; these were people with low incomes who also had little power in the market.

The Conservative government in power since 1979 has clearly seen council housing itself as the cause of problems in our housing system, and has sought to reduce its role and to strengthen the role of the private sector. This preference for market solutions has formed the context within which attempts have been made to remedy some of the problems created by the housing policies of the recent past. These are examined in relation to two issues – the renovation of difficult-to-let local authority housing, and the creation of new housing in derelict inner city areas.

REHABILITATING COUNCIL HOUSING

In the period since the late 1970s when the problem of difficult-to-let council housing began to gain the attention of policy-makers (DoE 1980), there have been three main strands of action to counter these problems. These are redesign and environmental improvement; management change involving more local and responsive housing management; and tenure change involving the privatization of local authority housing. These approaches are not mutually exclusive. Indeed, local authorities are encouraged to develop packages of measures which include all of these elements by the agency which (in England) is their main source of funding for such measures – Estates Action.[1]

Often the rehabilitation of these housing areas requires major investment in the physical improvement of the housing. In many cases, though, this is not primarily a matter of remedying structural problems in the building, or deficiencies in the internal amenities of the dwelling. More usually it is the organization of space around dwellings and the form of access to dwellings which create problems such as vulnerability to antisocial behaviour, and the issue is one of re-design of these features to provide a more pleasant and secure environment for the individual dwellings. The works of Coleman (1985), and of early writers such as Oscar Newman (1973) have played an important role in providing a vocabulary – analytical and architectural – for addressing these problems.

Making more human the design of some of the most de-humanizing of housing environments can, perhaps, be seen as one of the major examples of 'housing as if people mattered' in recent times. Sometimes these changes are made for the benefit of existing residents, but often they have been associated with tenure change, with the local authority passing the housing over to a housing association or private developer for renovation, usually for sale. The transformation of unpopular council housing into housing for sale provides other important design lessons, one which is very clearly seen in an example from Tyneside. In the early 1980s a row of very run-down, five-storey blocks of flats/maisonettes at Percy Main were handed over by North Tyneside Council to a private developer for improvement for sale (Cameron 1987). The redesign of these blocks, in what became known as St John's Village, was so striking that it was used to illustrate the cover of the brochure which introduced the work of Estates Action (DoE 1985). It is clear that this redesign made little functional change to the dwellings, but was overwhelmingly concerned with changing the visual appearance and image of the blocks to symbolize their change of status. Long-standing research (DoE 1972) has suggested that the appearance of housing and its social and symbolic meaning has much to do with the popularity of areas of council housing, as opposed to purely functional issues relating to the standard of accommodation, and the issue of meaning as well as function is an important one in making housing more human.

The handing over of housing for improvement to other agencies has arisen partly because local authorities have, because of spending cuts, not had the resources to undertake renovation themselves, and because an element of tenure change is often required as part of a funding package from Estates Action. Such an approach can offer new opportunities for low-cost home ownership, and introduce a more mixed population to an estate. It is, though, an approach which may encourage housing policy-makers to move away from a people-centred approach, to see the problem in terms of housing stock rather than in terms of the living conditions of tenants.

This reinforces the point made at the beginning, that housing is a process as well as a product, and it has become clear that the way in which housing is managed can be as important as its design. A major influence on this approach in England has been the Priority Estate Project (PEP) of the Department of the Environment (DoE) (Power 1982). It set out to address the bureaucratic and insensitive traditions of local authority housing management, particularly in a situation where 'local authorities have grown in size from running 1,400 properties each on average after the War, to running 14,000 each by 1975, so relations between landlords and tenants have become more complex and remote' (Power 1984: 2). Through demonstration projects, monitoring and publicizing initiatives and providing best-practice advice, the project has encouraged a trend, now widely adopted, towards more localized and sensitive management. PEP has also addressed the paternalism of traditional management and encouraged new forms of tenant participation and representation. The most recent initiative in this direction is the development of Estate Management Boards (Bell *et al.* 1990) where a local board including tenant representatives takes over the budget and management of the estate. In this respect, though, the English experience has been less wide-ranging and radical than that of Scotland, where in recent years there has been an extensive development of tenants co-operatives actually taking over control of their housing areas. These were pioneered in Glasgow (Clapham *et al.* 1987) – sometimes linked to the renovation of a run-down housing area – and were very much a tenant-led initiative. However, recently there has been extensive promotion of tenant co-operatives by Scottish Homes which appears mainly to reflect their political objective of divesting both local authorities and themselves of their housing stock.[2] A 'top-down' imposition of new management forms seems destined to fail, since it requires a great deal of commitment for tenants to take over full responsibility for the management of their housing, and by no means everyone wants to do this.

HOUSING IN THE INNER CITIES

Inner-city policy has by its nature been people-focused, an attempt to respond to the needs of the most deprived areas of cities. Housing policies of the past which could be seen as part of an inner-city programme – such as the large-scale rehabilitation of older housing through GIA and HAA declarations in the 1970s – directly addressed the needs of inner-city residents.

In the 1980s, though, the character of inner-city policies has been radically changed by the Conservative government with the main emphasis on strengthening the role of the private sector of the economy and limiting the role of the public sector (Cabinet Office 1988, 1989). With this change has come less direct concern with the problems of inner-city residents, to be replaced by an emphasis on private-sector business realizing the commercial potential of unused inner-city land. This is associated with a change in spatial focus of inner-city policies which can most clearly be seen in the 'flagships' of inner city policies in the 1980s – Urban Development Corporations (UDCs). The boundaries of UDCs have typically been drawn to exclude as far as possible inner-city residential areas and to include only areas of derelict inner-city land with potential for commercial develop-

ment. The housing development which has been an important element in the regeneration policies of the UDCs has typically been seperate from existing inner-city housing areas.

While this has done much to bring housing and people back to derelict inner-city areas, questions have been raised over the relationship between the people coming to these areas and the existing communities. The questions have been raised most sharply in the case of the London Docklands (Church 1988) but in the case of the Tyne and Wear Development Corporation (TWDC), too, this is an issue which is well illustrated in two nearby, but very different, housing developments within the TWDC area in the east of Newcastle.

Staines Road is a development of housing for rent by a local housing association. It includes 107 houses, bungalows and flats – about 20 per cent for the elderly – and most of the new residents come from the local area. Rents in 1991 were between £30 and £50 per week, and it is really the only significant example of social housing developed in the TWDC area. One interesting aspect of Staines Road is that it is located some distance from the river frontage, and is the only one of the new housing developments within the TWDC area which is alongside existing housing areas and forms part of the existing community. This is in sharp contrast to the other development in east Newcastle, known as St Peter's Basin, which is on a riverside site on formerly industrial land, still surrounded by industrial uses and forming a walled enclave, cut off from existing areas of social housing in the neighbourhood. This is a 'marina village' development of 285 houses by a major national house-building firm, and includes also a large marina and some shopping and leisure facilities. Within the development is some mixing of housing; there are some housing association flats for rent or shared ownership, and some private renting at the 'luxury' end of the market, but most of the housing is for sale, much of it again at high prices. It aims to create a 'village community', but it is clear that it is likely to remain isolated, socially as well as physically, from the mostly low-income housing areas in the vicinity. In itself, St Peter's Basin has provided an attractive housing environment on what was previously unused derelict land, but in reality it – and developments like it – appear to reinforce the polarization in our housing system, rather than counteract it.

SOCIAL POLARIZATION

There has since the early 1980s been a major debate in housing about the increasing degree of social polarization in our housing system, especially between owner-occupation and council renting (Hamnett 1984).

This has particularly focused on the impact of the sale of local-authority housing to sitting tenants under the 'Right-to-Buy' provisions of the Housing Act, 1980 (Forrest and Murie 1988). This emphasis on the impact of Right-to-Buy is perhaps rather misleading because the increasing tendency for the poorest and most deprived to be concentrated in local authority housing is a more general and long-standing trend. It is, though, a trend which does seem to have accelerated in the 1980s. For example, a comparison between 1981 and 1987 (General Household Survey 1987) showed the mean income of council tenants declining from 81 per cent to 67 per cent of the average. The same concentration of those with low incomes is also seen in the much smaller housing association sector – the other arm of social housing in Britain.

There are conflicting views and interpretations of the significance of this trend. On the one hand, some commentators suggest (Clapham and Maclennan 1983) that it simply reflects social housing doing the job it should do, helping those in most need. On the other hand, some (Malpass 1983) associate polarization with the creation of a residual and stigmatized social housing sector: ghettos in which the poorest people live in the least desirable housing.

One element which is sometimes overlooked in this debate is the spatial dimension. It is an issue which is difficult to quantify – although analysis of the data from the 1991 Census may help – but it seems clear that there is a trend towards an increasing physical, spatial separation of the poorest within the housing system.

Potentially, the effects of Right-to-Buy could have been to reduce this polarization. Indeed, one argument for this policy was that it might break up the 'monolithic' areas of council housing and create a mixture of tenures on estates. However, the evidence suggests that, while this might be true to a small extent, the spatial distribution of Right-to-Buy sales has tended to produce the opposite effects. At a variety of levels, it is the areas with least existing council housing which have had the highest rates of sales. Sales have been highest in the South, lowest in areas such as Tyneside. Sales have been higher in rural than in urban areas – in many rural areas virtually removing the entire council housing stock. Sales have been much higher in suburban than in inner areas of cities. At the very micro-scale, it is often the council housing which is mixed with, and looks similar to, owner-occupied housing which is sold. The Kingston Park Estate on the northern edge of Newcastle, for example, was built by a private developer but some of the housing was subsequently taken over by the local authority and made available as housing for rent. However, since 1980 this estate has seen the highest rate of Right-to-Buy sales in the city, to the extent that virtually all of the housing has now been transferred to owner-occupation. As a result, what was an area of mixed tenure has now reverted to 'monolithic' owner-occupation. Overall the effect of Right-to-Buy has been to remove access to many areas through social rented housing, to in effect deny the possibility of locating in many rural and suburban areas except through owner-

occupation. It has reinforced the polarization fostered by the dual system of housing provision of the post-war years. Returning to the policies previously discussed – the attempts to humanize the environments of council estates and inner cities – it is difficult to see that this can be achieved unless this wider process of polarization can be reversed.

HOUSING AS IF PEOPLE MATTERED

There was in the 1980s a very significant shift away from the approach to meeting people's housing needs which had dominanted the previous decades. This shift is an international phenomenon, and is not peculiar to Britain. In most Western countries the influence of New Right ideas and governments has moved housing policy in similar directions – massive reductions in the output of social housing and increasing reliance on the private, especially the owner-occupied, sector. It has also produced similar results – a decline in the total output of housing, increasing homelessness and problems of access to housing for the poorest, and the marginalization and stigmatization of areas of social housing.

As is often the case, in addressing the problems created in the past new problems have in turn been created, and it cannot really be said that the result is a system which does provide housing as if people matter – if nothing else the existence of the cardboard cities of the homeless attest to that.

It is clearly time for the wheel to turn again. There is a need to recreate some of the achievements of the earlier decades in housing policy while learning the lessons of the problems created. Specifically, there is a need to increase the provision of housing in general, but the provision of affordable social housing in particular, while guarding against the paternalism and polarization of the earlier decades.

What are the requirements for this? First there is a need to recognize that the housing needs of the population as a whole cannot be met purely by reliance on the market, and to allow social housing agencies – local authorities, housing associations and others – to expand their role once more. This does not necessarily mean more subsidy – local authorities in particular now provide housing with almost no external subsidy,[3] and have huge resources locked up in the capital receipts from Right-to-Buy sales which they have not been permitted to use. What they need is more freedom to meet local housing needs.

This does not necessarily mean a return to large-scale council house building. Certainly, given the experience of the past, the creation of more large-scale, single-tenure estates would not seem to be desirable. What may be preferable is a wider development of the 'enabling' role which the present government has suggested for local authorities in housing. One aspect might be the support of housing association development, but a further element could be the purchase of private housing to make available for rent, an approach which would directly address the issue of polarization.

Ideally, a way forward in housing should involve dissolving our hard-and-fast tenure divisions. It needs an emphasis on the mixing of tenures within areas, and also the possibility of making the same housing available in a flexible mix of tenure forms. Ironically, some of the emergency housing situations of the moment provide clues to how this approach might develop – the current use of leasing of private-sector homes to house the homeless, for example, or the 'mortgage rescue' packages being developed by housing associations and others which allow people in mortgage arrears to, in effect, rent their homes for a period. Each suggests the possibility of local authorities and housing associations acting as 'umbrellas' under which people can make flexible choices about housing tenure.

The other major priority is the continued process of democratizing social housing, continuing to make its management more sensitive and responsive, and extending the power of tenants over their housing. There is no single blueprint for this. The tenants' co-operative may be the ideal, but it cannot be imposed, and people may make a variety of choices about the extent to which they want to take on the management of their housing – again it is an argument for a flexible mixture of forms of housing provision and control.

This essay began with the two meanings of the word 'housing'. It has not suggested any prescriptions for the physical forms of 'housing as if people matter', and the reason for that is the belief that such housing cannot be designed in isolation from the process of housing, that is, how people gain access to and control their housing situation.

NOTES

1   Estates Action is a unit of the Department of the Environment, established in 1985 and originally called the Urban Housing Renewal Unit. It controls a significant element of the annual capital spending allocations for housing of local authorities. An annual round of allocations is made to regeneration schemes for specific council housing estates in specific local authorities, on the basis of choices made between schemes submitted by local authorities.

2   Scottish Homes was established in 1989 through the amalgamation of the Housing Corporation for Scotland, which funded housing associations and co-operatives, and the Scottish Special Housing Association, which was a strategic housing agency which had built and managed about 100,000 dwellings. It is an agency which has no direct equivalent in England. It is pursuing an aggressive

policy of encouraging the transfer of housing from the public sector in Scotland, a policy applied to local authority housing and to its own stock.

3   Most local authorities now have no general subsidy to reduce the overall level of rents in council housing. The only remaining form of subsidy in most areas is Housing Benefit, which provides a means-tested rent subsidy to those on low incomes.

REFERENCES

Bell, T., Bevington, P. and Crossley, R. (1990) 'Estate Management Boards – a way forward for council tenants?', *Housing Review* 39: 4: 95–8.
Cabinet Office (1988) *Action for Cities*, London: HMSO.
—— (1989) *Progress on Cities*, London: HMSO.
Cameron, S. (1987) *Recent Approaches to Problem Council Housing in Tyneside*, Department of Town and Country Planning WP No. 3, Newcastle upon Tyne.
Church, A. (1988) 'Demand-led planning, the inner city crisis and the labour market: London Docklands evaluated', in B.S. Hoyle, D.A. Pinder and M.S. Husain (eds) *Revitalising the Waterfront*, London: Belhaven Press.
Clapham, D. and Maclennan, D. (1983) 'Residualisation of public housing; a non-issue', *Housing Review* 32 (1): 9–10.
Clapham, D., Kemp, P. and Kintrea, K. (1987) 'Cooperative ownership of former council housing' *Policy and Politics* 15 (4): 207–20.
Coleman, A. (1885) *Utopia on Trial: Vision and Reality in Planned Housing*, London: Hilary Shipman.
—— (1990) *Utopia on Trial: Vision and Reality in Planned Housing* 2nd edn, London: Hilary Shipman.
DoE (1972) *The Estate Outside the Dwelling*, Design Bulletin 25, London: Department of the Environment.
—— (1980) *An Investigation of Difficult-to-let Council Housing*, Vols 1 and 2, Housing Development Directorate OP 3/80 and 4/80, London: HMSO.
—— (1985) *New Homes for Old*, London: HMSO.
Dunleavy, P. (1981) *The Politics of Mass Housing in Britain 1945–1975*, London: Clarendon Press.
Forrest, R. and Murie, A. (1988) *Selling the Welfare State: The Privatization of Public Housing*, London: Routledge.
Hamnett, C. (1984) 'Housing the two nations: socio-tenurial polarisation in England & Wales 1961–81', *Urban Studies* 21 (4): 389–405.
Hillier, B. (1986) 'City of Alice's dreams', *Architects' Journal* 9 July: 39–41.
Malpass, P. (1983) 'Residualisation and the restructuring of housing tenure', *Housing Review* 32 (2): 44–5.
Newman, O. (1973) *Defensible Space*, London: Architectural Press.
Power, A. (1982) *Priority Estates Project*, London: Department of the Environment.
—— (1984) *Local Housing Management: A Priority Estates Project Survey*, London: Department of the Environment.

10 An architect for the poor

Chris Abel

Global statistics on housing for the poor are daunting. In 1988 it was estimated that 1 billion people lack proper shelter. Most live on the edges of the already swollen cities of the Third World in rudimentary shelters built by themselves, without adequate water, electricity, sewerage, or other essential services. By the end of the century, if current trends hold, those same cities will somehow have to accomodate a further 750 million people (Habitat 1988).

Clearly, there can be little hope of any real change in this growing human tragedy without a massive transfer of economic resources from the developed nations of the North to the developing nations of the South. Equally clearly, the geopolitical difficulties involved in any such transfer, evidenced by the 1992 Earth Summit in Rio and other initiatives (Gillermopriento and Burmmer 1981), imply that developing countries cannot afford to wait for outside help, and must do what they can to alleviate the problem themselves. The growing attention given to 'self-help' housing solutions is an outcome of such hard realities.

In addition, the now widely acknowledged failure of government subsidized mass-housing programmes to keep pace with growing populations or rural–urban migration, or to achieve the necessary social and environmental quality, has led to a rethinking of housing strategies. One result has been a new emphasis on making the most of the willingness of the disadvantaged to help themselves, where government aid is not available. Recognition of the important dual role of even the most basic shelters as both home and workplace is also reshaping attitudes towards self-help housing as an economic factor (Benjamin and McCallum 1985), linked with opportunities for self-employment. The concept of self-help therefore goes beyond solving problems of inadequate housing, which many view as only a symptom of wider economic and social ills, to embrace the social, economic and physical infrastructure needed to create and maintain a viable and healthy community.

The pattern of such housing settlements is similar throughout the developing world. Typically, having found a suitable empty space, usually on undeveloped state-owned land, the urban immigrant would enlist help to construct his or her shelter from a number of *ad hoc* sources. A local builder would provide the materials and semi-skilled labour required, and possibly even a small credit to help finance the project. The builder would probably obtain materials from enterprising merchants who in turn might have salvaged materials from development projects in the city. More materials and labour might be supplied by friends and relatives from the immigrant's own village. A basic shelter would be put up within a few hours, usually overnight to minimize the possibility of police obstruction. Once erected and occupied immediately, the house has a better chance of being allowed to stand. Eventually, if the local authorities remain tolerant (attitudes vary widely between countries) and the immigrant is successful in finding work in the city, he or she would make progressive improvements to the house, creating a durable family home. As the settlement consolidates, the residents might grow bold enough to organize themselves to ask local government authorities for help in providing essential infrastructure and social services. In time, the dwellings themselves contribute to the urban economy by providing rental income from spare rooms or a base for small-scale economic activities, such as shopkeeping or home-based manufacturing and services. In this fashion, the settlement may take on the character of a permanent urban or suburban neighbourhood, always depending that the local authorities remain willing, or at least indifferent.

The self-help housing surrounding Ankara, Turkey, known locally as *gecekondus,* exemplifies the varied kind of support activities involved, and the changing government attitudes toward this form of settlement.

The *gecekondus* account for more than 60 per cent of Ankara's population – the highest proportion of any large city in the world – most of it the result of rural–urban migration since the 1940s. The explosive growth was made possible by a combination of abundant and accessible state-owned land, and relatively tolerant government policies. Recognizing the value to the urban economy of a large pool of cheap labour but unable to initiate or afford suitable housing projects, local government virtually turned a blind eye, requiring only that *gecekondu* owners pay their taxes. The Gecekondu Act, 1966, consolidated the government's tacit acceptance with a series of supportive measures, including credits for house improvements, infrastructure and services, aimed at upgrading the quality of informal settlements (Payne 1982).

The Turkish example is revealing for the extent to which it shows how self-help building may be recognized and even institutionalized as an essential method of housing provision for the poor. At the same time, and despite this acceptance, it also emphasizes the marginal role played by professional architects, even under a relatively benign government. It is the dwellers themselves, the 'barefoot architects', who, out of necessity, create their own environment.

The career of Jorge Anzorena, who writes in these pages of similar case studies elsewhere in the world, is therefore all the more remarkable for going against the professional grain. Born in Buenos Aires, Argentina, Anzorena has followed a path which has been influenced both by his religious beliefs as a Jesuit and by his willingness to look at architecture in a global perspective. The latter factor was already apparent when, as a student architect, he went to complete his studies in Japan. In 1968 he became a professor of architecture at Sophia University in Tokyo. Anzorena's moment of truth came a few years later on a visit to Calcutta, where he observed the wretched living conditions of the homeless there: 'I felt that my architectural studies were useless for them, and I began to look for ways in which I could continue to be an architect and a Christian; an architect for the poor'.[1]

As a result, Anzorena became engaged in a Church in Asia project aimed at encouraging contacts between people involved in low-cost housing projects. They included the dwellers themselves and supporting non-government organizations (NGOs), political activists, and committed professionals, academics and students as well as government officials; anyone, in fact, who was willing to help the poor improve their housing conditions. To facilitate the exchange of information and skills Anzorena produced his own newsletter, documenting the experiences of different self-help groups throughout Asia and passing it on to others, steadily building up an international network of concerned organizations and individuals. He also became the Asian representative of

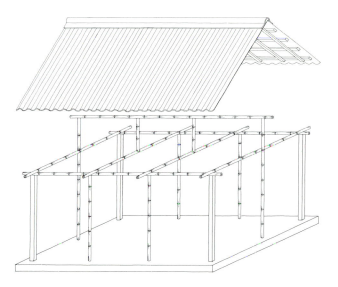

Figure 2 *Grameen-Bank Housing Programme: structural system. Pre-cast building materials are mass-produced off-site and made available to the beneficiaries at low prices. The residents construct their houses themselves, employing family labour, thus keeping the cost per unit low.* (Source: *Aga Khan Award for Architecture*)

Servicio Latino-american Asiatico de Vivienda Popular (SELAVIP), which was formed to help exchange experiences between similar groups in Latin America and Asia. These informal contacts and exchanges eventually led to the formation of the Asian Coalition for Housing Rights, which is related to Habitat International Council, as well as numerous regional and international workshops aimed at sharing relevant skills and techniques.

Spending six months each year teaching in Tokyo and the remaining six months touring Asia on his mission, Anzorena sends his newsletter out from each destination as he finds new projects to report on. Reading the newsletter – usually bashed out on any available typewriter and copying machine – is much like opening a window of hope on to an otherwise depressing global landscape of human deprivation. Especially, it confirms the practical virtues of mutual aid and both the courage and effectiveness of community-based organizations in achieving real improvements in living conditions. It also shows how a growing number of dedicated individuals are ditching professional role stereotypes and adapting themselves to the special needs of these groups. Encouragingly, they include architects, academics and students, like the group in Bali who combined to form the Architectural Clinic to help poor villagers solve their housing problems, or the female architect in Bombay, who worked part-time to train women community leaders in skills and techniques needed to improve their informal settlement to meet government conditions for land tenure; both were reported in Anzorena's newsletter. In the last case study presented here, he gives news of similar moves taken by young architects in South Korea and Argentina.

Figure 1 *Grameen Bank Housing Programme: healthier homes for the poor. 'The small housing loans average US$350 each and include the provision of four concrete columns, a prefabricated sanitary slab and 26 corrugated iron roofing sheets. The rest is left to the borrower to procure on an incremental basis. In the course of five years, hundreds of thousands of landless rural Bangladeshis benefited from the Grameen housing project, resulting in some 44,500 simple, healthier, diverse but equally beautiful houses'* (quoted from the *Aga Khan Architectural Award Jury's citation*). (Photograph: *Anwar Hossein*)

Figure 3 *Kampung Improvement Programme for Jakarta's dense autonomous settlements. The municipal infrastructure programme included building access roads, and sewage, sanitation and medical facilities. Before the programme began, the street shown here was virtually an open sewer, unfit for use. Today sewage is controlled and streets filled with children connect these communities with the rest of the city. The programme won an Aga Khan Award for Architecture in 1981.* (Source: *Aga Khan Award for Architecture*)

Such work represents a marked departure from the usual egocentric and elitist practices of architects tied to surplus economies. Increasing pressures on scarce economic and physical resources, especially urban land, also inevitably place a continuing emphasis on the importance of 'non-architectural' factors, such as problems of land tenure, legal aid, financing, infrastructure and sanitation. It is therefore of especial interest that one of the projects described below by Anzorena, the Grameen Bank Housing Programme in Bangladesh (Figures 1 and 2), received an Aga Khan Award for Architecture. Though not the first such Aga Khan Award for basic shelter schemes – the first series of Awards in 1981 included a Kampung Improvement Programme in Jakarta (Holod 1983) which was mostly concerned with essential infrastructure (Figure 3) – it is notable that a prestigious architectural award should be given to a project which has as much to do with providing credit support for the poor as with physical shelter. Just as food aid agencies now recognize that famines are the outcome not so much of a shortage of food as of a shortage of money with which the poor could buy or grow food, so housing agencies are recognizing that credit programmes aimed at helping the poor to help themselves are not only viable but even contribute to the regional economy. Significantly, the Grameen Bank Housing Programme is aimed, like many recent aid programmes, at improving conditions for the rural poor, thereby helping to alleviate the problem of rural–urban migration at its source.

For architects, however, the sobering conclusion to be drawn from such projects, and from Anzorena's own personal journey from detached academic to the barefoot architects' advocate, is that, for the poorer sections of the world's population struggling to build their own homes and environment, the architectural profession as we know it is mostly an irrelevance. Given that the current professional ethos, especially in the West, encourages architects to reject any moral connotations in their work, this is hardly surprising. Fortunately, as Anzorena and his colleagues around the world have shown, other role models are available, should architects take a different view.

NOTE

1   Quoted from personal correspondence with the author.

REFERENCES

Benjamin, S.N. and McCallum, D. (1985) Abstract from 'Low-income urban housing in the Third World: broadening the economic perspective', in J. Anzorena (ed.) *SELAVIP Newsletter*, Jakarta, March.

Gillermopriento, A. and Burmmer, A. (1981) 'Spirit of Cancun merely a ghost', *Guardian*, 1 November.

Habitat (1988) *Summary, Global Strategy for Shelter to the Year 2000*, Nairobi: United Nations Centre for Human Settlements (Habitat).

Holod, R. (ed.) (1983) *Architecture and Community*, New York: Islamic Publications, pp. 211–21.

Payne, G.K. (1982) 'Self-help housing: a critique of the gecekondus of Ankara', in P.M. Ward (ed.) *Self-help Housing*, London: Mansell Publishing.

FURTHER READING

Abel, C. (1992) 'Ecodevelopment: toward a development paradigm for regional architecture', *Traditional Dwellings and Settlements Working Paper Series*, Vol. 44, Berkeley: University of California Press.

Dwyer, D.J. (1975) *People and Housing in Third World Cities*, New York: Longman.

Fathy, H. (1973) *Architecture for the Poor*, Chicago: University of Chicago Press.

Hamdi, N. (1991) *Housing without Houses*, New York: Nostrand Reinhold.

Swan, P. (ed.) (1980) *The Practice of People's Participation*, Bangkok: Asian Institute of Technology.

Turner, J.F.C. (1976) *Housing by People*, London: Marion Boyars.

Turner, J.F.C. and Fichter, R. (eds) (1972) *Freedom to Build*, New York: Collier Macmillan.

11 Informal housing and the barefoot architect

Jorge Anzorena

For the city slum dweller who lives in a self-built house the architect is an unknown person or luxurious item whose functions are very little known. In the slums most of life is informal; that is to say, outside the formal and legal structure of the city. The acquisition of land for building is informal; the construction of the house is informal. In 1984, 64 per cent of all houses built in Lima, Peru, were informal. In the slums even the way of earning the daily bread is informal. For the slum dweller, the legal alternative is often simply too costly. In order to estimate the cost to slum dwellers of bureaucratic procedures, a research group in Lima followed step by step the procedures an applicant had to go through to register a small workshop with the local authorities. The registration took more than eight months working full-time to complete and cost as much in time lost and unavoidable bribes as most basic salaries.

This case is no exception. Illegality is very much related to the survival of the poor in the slums. Building a house is conditioned by the same considerations; the informal way is the reverse of the formal. First the land is obtained through an invasion or an illegal purchase. In a very short period a temporary house is built and then improved in stages. Finally, if at all possible, the property is legalized. Such invasions of land can be organized or unorganized; in the latter case hundreds or thousands of families may be involved.

The land invasions and unauthorized housing are usually accompanied by a host of social problems, including corruption of government officials, politicians, landowners and real estate entrepreneurs. Despite these hazards, in many countries tens and even hundreds of thousands of poor families have been able to find a shelter which would otherwise have been impossible to obtain through the normal bureaucratic and market systems. With these essential points in mind I should like to refer, by way of example, to the kinds of projects which are helping the poor to do better what they are already doing for themselves.

PREFABRICATED LOW-COST DWELLINGS

The firm of Hogar de Cristo in Chile believes that it is better to have a bad house for the majority of the poor here and now than a good house for a minority. The firm makes prefabricated panel walls for its low-cost house from the most available trees in Chile: pine.

The panels are made in the main factory of Hogar de Christo in Santiago and in two branches at Copiapo and Vina del Mar, and delivered directly to the beneficiary's site. The cost of a house is about US$12 per sq. m. (US$1.10 per sq. ft.). The smallest unit provided is of 10 sq. m., (108 sq. ft.), and can be assembled by three persons in as many hours. Hogar de Cristo has thirty years of experience and has built around 3 million sq. m. of housing, mainly for the most needy.

Also involved in low-cost housing, the firm of Servivienda has built more than 30,000 prefabricated houses – mostly for poor clients – totalling more than 1 million sq. m. The cost of a house is around US$20 per sq. m. (US$1.90 per sq. ft.). The firm has a staff of 200 and produces, transports, assembles and sells the houses, often through its own credit system. Production is carried out at both permanent and mobile factories. Servivienda also promotes community development and various socio-economic activities to ensure the success of its housing settlements. In addition to housing, the firm is involved in urban development projects and emergency (disaster) programmes.

NON-PROFIT-MAKING HOUSING VENTURES

The Marian Housing Foundation in Manila, Philippines, has finished two projects for slum dwellers and low-income groups. A third project, Peace Village, is under development and involves 1,389 housing units. The project is a joint venture between the government, as landowner, and Marian Foundation as developer. The housing packages are formulated to suit low-income wage earners (US$57–128 per month) and poor self-employed individuals. The cost of the land plus site development comes to US$600 for an 80 sq. m. (860 sq. ft.) plot. The cost of a 24 sq. m. (258 sq. ft.) single detached core unit, including septic tank and toilet facilities, is US$2,000. A similar self-help unit of 20 sq. m. (215 sq. ft.) costs US$1,100. The total is payable over 25 years with monthly amortizations.

Freedom to Build is another non-profit making, or utility, company. It began in 1977 as a shop selling second-hand construction materials to resettlers evicted from the squatting areas in Manila. The company has now moved into the development of low-cost housing to prove that it is possible to cost housing at lower prices than those which are currently available on the open market. Several similar companies are at work in South Africa.

In Mangalore, India, St Joseph's Seminar Organization works with local housing co-operatives to help people build their own low-cost houses. For INDR1,000 (US$77) they are able to build simple shelters of bamboo posts and country-style tile roofs, leaving the occupants to finish the walls with whatever materials are available to them. In Semerang, Indonesia, the Sugyapranata Foundation has a similar project in which a bamboo house with tile roofing is offered to destitute people living in the most difficult situations, like street dwellers, ragpickers, etc.

PRIVATE HOUSE FINANCING FOR THE POOR

The main reason for the existence of slums is poverty. Increased incomes make house financing easier. Working on this premise, the Grameen Bank in Bangladesh began giving loans to landless farmers to help generate additional income. A group of farmers takes collective responsibility for each individual loan as a kind of collateral. A combination of hard and fast rules for implementing Grameen Bank-financed projects and the creation of a social and organizational environment which involves the people concerned help this process succeed. By November 1992 the Bank had 1,385,324 members and was growing at a rate of 30 per cent a year.

For the poor the house is not only a place to live but also frequently a place of work. Housing and employment are interactive. Improvements in economic conditions enable improvements in the house, and vice versa. Recognizing this, Grameen Bank provides its members with a housing loan package consisting of: four reinforced concrete columns costing 1,300 takas; two bundles of galvanized iron sheets costing 7,000 takas; one sanitary latrine costing 500 takas, and other materials (bamboo walls etc.) costing 1,200 takas. The total cost for a house measuring 3.5 m. by 5.8 m. (11 ft. 6 in. by 19 ft.) is 10,000 takas (around US$303).

In order to support this process the Bank itself takes responsibility for producing the reinforced concrete columns and the rings and slabs for the sanitary latrines in fifteen construction units in three different zones across the country. To decrease transportation costs, the permanent construction units are supplemented by thirty-four mobile units. By November 1992 the Bank had financed 153,113 houses.

GOVERNMENT-SPONSORED FINANCING SCHEMES

Some governments provide special housing loans for low income groups. In Uruguay, government loans cover 75 per cent of the total cost of co-operative housing projects (including land costs); the remaining costs are shouldered by individual members of the co-operative.

Fideicomiso Fondo de Habitaciones (National Fund for Popular Housing – FONHAPO) is based in Palo Alto, Mexico, and is the first government-sponsored attempt to increase lending to self-help housing co-operatives.

In Sri Lanka the government has introduced new and promising legislation to support the vital interests of organized communities in building their own houses, in collaboration with the local authorities and non-government organizations. There are four categories of housing options:

1   Upgrading package; for repairing or extending an existing house.
2   New house package; for use where only a basic house is required and land is already available.
3   Utilities package; for use where individual services and title clearance are required (i.e., water connection, pit latrine, septic tank, electricity, registration on deeds, etc.).
4   Sites and services package; for group needs.

The guiding principles of fund allocation at FONHAPO consist in: decentralizing decision-making; planning and implementation of urban housing programmes; giving all urban local authorities equitable access to funds based on the population to be served; giving local authorities innovative opportunities to improve the environmental conditions of the poor.

In 1988 the Philippines government launched a new initiative, the Community Mortgage Programme, aimed at increasing land and housing assistance for the poor. The government's intention is to provide land tenure to the more stable squatter communities not only in Metro Manila but in other urban centres. To be eligible, communities must be legally established as a homeowners' association, corporation or co-operative; they must also assume responsibility for a communal mortgage on all of the property involved in the housing project.

The Philippines scheme provides for successive mortgages. The initial mortgage is for land acquisition; second mortgages are allowed two years later to provide funding for infrastructure improvement. Only lastly may the community request home improvement loans.

The Community Mortgage Programme is a whole new concept aimed at cutting through the complexity of bureaucratic requirements related to the acquisition of lands and distribution of individual title rights and demands a responsive community.

TECHNOLOGY TRANSFER

The Orangi Pilot Project (OPP) sanitation programme in Orangi Town, Karachi, Pakistan, offers a number of useful general lessons.

When organized, people are a resource in themselves, even when poor. Based on this premise the Orangi Pilot Project has been able to carry out a massive self-help sanitation programme, financed entirely by the people themselves at a cost less than one quarter of what the local government spent on similar development projects.

The achievement was made possible by a team of experts who were able to communicate their knowledge of low-cost sanitation technologies to community members in steps they could easily assimilate.

Understanding the most effective sociological units around which community resources can be mobilized is crucial to the success of the project. In the OPP sanitation programme this appropriate unit is the group of usually twenty to forty families living in the same lane, who collaborate to install a sewage pipe. The collaboration includes financing and responsibility for management, labour and execution of the project. In 1989 around 86,000 households participated in the project.

Collaboration amongst households was further strengthened by engagement in a number of related community projects and activities. These included: connecting several lines in common secondary drains; the maintenance of the sewage system; garbage disposal and spraying; environmental improvements of various kinds; other projects such as small family enterprises run on co-operative lines, housing research and evaluation.

By organizing themselves poor people have successfully pressured local authorities to implement policies more appropriate to their needs.

LEARNING FROM INFORMAL HOUSING: TWO EXPERIMENTS IN INDIA AND PAKISTAN

A unique experiment in housing for the poor is being undertaken at Huaycan in India: 12,000 families are being settled in ways which resemble illegal invasions of land except that they have been organized and planned by the government. The site infrastructure was planned in advance but is being developed in a progressive way according to the resources of the poor settlers and local authorities.

The Municipality is providing services not to the private household, as is usual for government projects, but to the organized neighbourhood or condominium of sixty families, called the Communal Housing Unit (CHU). Each CHU has connections with the public service network and is responsible for internal distribution. Each family owns 90 sq. m. (970 sq. ft.) of land but public spaces belong to the condominium. The design of each neighbourhood is done by the community together with a team of technical advisers from the Municipality.

The Incremental Development Scheme at Hyderabad was launched in November 1986. After overcoming initial difficulties, 2,500 allottees are occupying their plots and building their houses. The scheme followed government studies into both the reasons for government failure in providing shelter for the poor and the

success of the informal sector. In response, the Hyderabad Development Authority devised an innovative solution aimed at providing shelter at prices and standards of development within the resources of poor people.

Attention was focused on important issues which have previously been ignored in traditional housing schemes: targeting and affordability; land allocation procedure; and the time-lag between allocation and possession of the plot. A basic feature of the new approach is that the land offered is affordable by the poor; a down-payment of only Pak.R1,000 (US$56) is required. Thereafter, as the name suggests, development of the scheme is incremental. Initial services are limited to the absolute minimum; at the start only communal water supply and public transport are provided. Later, house-to-house water supply, sewerage, road paving, electricity and gas are provided as the allottees pay their monthly installments, which range from Pak.R50 to Pak.R100 (US$2.80 to US$5.60). Prescribed standards pertain only to items that cannot be changed later. Thus only the layout of the settlement is fixed, otherwise no standards are imposed on either the plan or the quality of the house. Settlers can start with a *jhuggi*, or basic shelter, if they cannot afford something better; the crucial factor for the people concerned is that they are guaranteed title to the land. Once they have it, then each family pools and invests its resources in the house to make gradual improvements.

THE FORMAL ARCHITECT MEETS THE BAREFOOT ARCHITECT

During 1985 and 1986 young architects in Seoul, South Korea, began to form groups to reflect on the related problems of land speculation, the deterioration of the housing situation of the poor and the responsibilities of architects who normally work only for the rich.

Early discussions were held at two independent levels: one amongst architects in their twenties who entered university in 1976–9, and the other amongst architects in their thirties who had graduated six years before. Eventually the two groups combined, forming the Young Architects' Association in November 1987. By the end of 1988 the Association had around 300 members.

The Association's main aims are to encourage social consciousness amongst professionals and to offer professional advice to poor settlers. In April 1988 a seminar on the housing situation in Korea was held to promote the Association's cause.

A similar movement is under way in Argentina where young professionals argue that gaps in their education do not allow them to lend adequate support to informal housing groups. As a result, a series of Regional Workshops on Popular Housing are being organized, in which grass-roots representatives and professionals come together to debate the problems of informal settlements in specific regions.

The workshops promote communication between the settlers themselves and between architects seeking to enrich their profession through exposure to the hard realities; most importantly, they promote understanding and co-operation between the two different groups, who have different experiences, perceptions and feelings about popular culture and forms of habitat.

In articulating their experiences and values the informal settlers can learn from their own actions and so further their aims. The process works in the opposite direction for the professional architects involved, since their privileged education did not arise from the same needs and therefore separates them from the dis-advantaged. In order to overcome this, the architect has to drop his or her normal professional values and concerns, and learn from the settlers' experiences.

In the workshops the role of the settler was the main focus for the informal housing process and the role of the professional technician was to help catalyse the common task. To succeed, the professional must learn from the people themselves what is valuable in their regional traditions, culture and experiences, digest those values and then, through dialogue, find ways to channel this local energy by helping people improve their own environment.

CONCLUSION

A truly universal architect needs to be an architect for everybody, including the poor. But if the architect wants to work with the poor he or she needs to respect them, to believe that it is possible to improve the situation in the slums, and that the greatest resource lies in poor peoples' own energies. Above all, the architect must believe in mutual aid; that people do things better together and that all willing people can collaborate effectively to improve things for the poor. In doing so, the architect will find many creative and rewarding ways of helping the poor to help themselves.

FURTHER READING

Anzorena, J. and Iyori, N. (1988) *Slum: Records of People's Life* (published in Japanese as *Slum: Minshu Seikatsu shi*), 3rd edn, Tokyo: Akashi Shoten.

Anzorena, J. and Poussard, W. (1985) *A Time to Build: People's Housing in Asia*, Robertsbridge, E. Sussex: Plough Publications.

Anzorena, J., Iyori, N., Uchida, K. and Hosaka, M. (eds) (1987) *The Struggle for Housing: From the Slum Community of Asia* (published in Japanese as *Kyoju he no tatakai: Asia no Slum Community kara*), Tokyo: Akashi Shoten.

Habitat (1987) *Global Report on Human Settlements, 1986*, United Nations Centre for Human Settlements (Habitat), Oxford: Oxford University Press.

Hardoy, J.E. and Sattarthwaite, D. (1989) *Squatter Citizen: Life in the Urban Third World*, London: Earthscan Publications.

Hardoy, J.E., Cairncross, S. and Sattarthwaite, D. (eds) (1990) *The Poor Die Young: Housing and Health in Third World Cities*, London: Earthscan Publications.

MacDonald, J. (1987) *Vivienda Progresiva*, Chile: CPU.

Schütz, E.J. (1987) *Städte in Latinamerika: Barrio – Entwicklung und Wohungsbau*, Misereor.

Soto, H. de (1987) *El Otro Sendero: La Revolución Informal*, Bogota, Colombia: La Oveja Negra.

Turner, B. (ed.) (1988) *Building Community: A Third World Case Book*, London: Building Community Books.

12 Development within development: user extensions of five-storey walk-up housing in Cairo

Hala Kardash and

Nicholas Wilkinson

INTRODUCTION

In studying the spontaneous development of informal settlements, problems of distinguishing between the *raisons d'être* and outcomes are commonly confronted by researchers. Similar difficulties could be expected in following up the development of a process such as extensions of public housing in Cairo.

Reasons of a social, economic or political nature could be singled out as the catalysts which start the process. These, however, on their own do not provide enough evidence as to why different types and qualities of development occur in cases which share similar social, economic and political backgrounds.

This essay sets out to examine why and how different qualities of user extensions develop in different public housing projects in Cairo. Three different projects were chosen as case studies. A series of in-depth interviews were conducted with the different parties involved in the process in each of the three cases. The parties involved were the user, the contractor and the responsible local authority. The three projects chosen were: (1) Helwan Economic Housing, (2) El Tebeen Marazzik Housing and (3) Imbaba Nasser Housing.

PUBLIC HOUSING IN EGYPT

Typical public housing in Egypt has always had the stigma of inflexibility and lack of adaptability for the varying and changeable needs of the users. Production of cheaper housing in short periods and in large quantities has always been the main goal of the mass housing programmes in Egypt. This automatically led to the construction of small identical housing units in five-storey 'walk-up' type blocks of flats. Social and cultural mismatches were often the result of high occupancy rates in public housing projects. In contrast to the tightness and lack of space inside the dwelling, the neighbourhood layout was usually generous in terms of the availability of public open space between the blocks.

Although the planning and construction of all three projects made no allowances for user input, the users took the initiative to resolve their space problems by extending their dwellings into the unused public open spaces outside the dwellings. The form the extensions take is usually affected by the attitude which the local authority takes towards the extension process.

When the attitude of the local authority is relaxed enough all five households living above each other co-operate in building a five-storey extension. On the other hand, when the local authority adopts a stricter attitude a feeling of insecurity develops and a less explicit type of extension develops. The form this type of extension takes would be a cantilevered type projecting out from one of the upper storeys, carried out by one household only. Under these conditions ground-floor extensions are rare.

The communal type of extension is represented in the Helwan and El Tebeen projects, whilst in the Imbaba project only the individual type is found. This essay pays more attention to the communal five-storey type, since it more frequently occurs and is a more consistent type which achieves a better quality of extension.

Three main factors were found to have a strong influence on the organization of the extension process and thus on the resulting quality of the built environment. These were: the user's decision-making process; the financial mechanism; and the government's initial built provision.

The user's decision-making process

The basic social unit involved in the communal type of extension is the group of neighbours who share the same vertical section of the five-storey block of flats. There are several issues on which these five households have to agree; these may be to agree to extend or not, when to build the extension and how. Generally speaking economic logic provides the main motivation but the importance of other social and cultural, as well as political, factors should not be underestimated.

The risk calculation factor

This factor has decisive influence on determining whether the process will be carried out communally or individually. In other words it determines the basic social unit responsible for the building of the extension. Whether the responsible social unit is to be individual or communal is usually the result of households weighing up the benefits against the risks, as well as the costs involved. In order to do this two considerations are taken into account. First the size of the opposition is weighed up, i.e. the local authority's power versus the significance of the user's power. This is influenced by relevant events such as nearby slum-clearance schemes. It is also affected by any previous confrontations which the user(s) have had with the local authority. Security of tenure is also a very important factor. In the early 1980s the majority of households were able to acquire ownership (by then it was decided that households who had completed a fifteen-year period of paying rent would automatically obtain ownership). This does not necessarily mean that renting households do not extend their flats. It simply means that security of tenure is established in a collective manner. Second, an estimation is made of the costs and benefits of the extension. If a household does not want to join in a communal scheme, that household's decision can negatively influence the economic success of the extension project. In this case social pressure will most likely be exerted to influence the decision for a more favourable outcome.

Communication between households

In the individual type of extension the communication required between neighbours is minimal compared to that required in multi-storey extensions. In the latter case, communication amongst the group of neighbours who share the same vertical section of the block is essential. Two distinct stages of communication can be identified: first, regular encounters, and second, planned meetings.

The regular encounter stage starts when the households who are willing to extend begin to declare their intentions, explaining their needs for extra space to each other and discussing the benefits which would result from carrying out the work immediately. This, generally speaking, would take place between the men working in the factories (Helwan and El Tebeen), or in the cafés, or when they meet by chance in the street. A more reliable way of exchanging views on the subject would be the daily visits of women neighbours to each other. The women's role in the extension process is essential and undeniable, not only because they are partly responsible for the affordability of the process but also because they are important participants in contributing towards the 'social pressure factor' (see below).

The planned meeting stage starts after informal approvals have been obtained from the participating households, and it is a stage of agreement about the details of implementation. These meetings might be held in one of the participant's flats or in one of the nearby cafés. In these meetings, suggestions about the appoint-

ment of a contractor and the estimation of costs are made. There are other cases where the contractor is the main motivator of the process; in this case the sequence of events would only differ slightly.

Although the group works in a communal pattern, the element of leadership is not by any means missing from its organization. The leading character could be the person who started the whole thing going in the first place. In other cases the person generally with the most experience of building and construction would be the leader. The leader is not appointed but his or her leadership is gradually established as the project progresses.

Social pressure factor

In the communal type of extension certain levels of pressure are applied to persuade neighbours to join in the process, especially where their reluctance to join would seriously effect the other members. However, some members might experience a degree of freedom of choice in relation to the location of flat they occupy. For example, the top, fifth-floor householder could always pay only his or her share towards the implementation of the foundations, and then later can extend individually according to circumstances. On the other hand, the ground-floor resident enjoys much less freedom of choice, being forced to pay immediately for the extension structure.

There are two kinds of social pressure which are applied to reluctant neighbours. First, direct social pressure can be applied in many forms, for example by accusing those concerned of working against the common good of the group, or of causing financial losses by delaying the construction of the project whilst material and labour costs are continually rising. This could easily provoke the loss of old friendships, and the threat of this has a strong impact, especially on the women. Second, indirect social pressure can be applied; the extensions, like any other material goods, are considered a source of self-realization and social status in Egyptian society, at no matter what level. Investing money in house improvements is one way of expressing economic status; from another angle, a larger house offers a better opportunity for the household to set aside a room for receiving guests, which in itself is a way of confirming social status. Failing to join in the extension project because of economic difficulties could affect the householder's image amongst his or her neighbours.

The financial mechanism

The extension process is carried out through a unique financial mechanism. In order to show the significance of the financial investment of the users, Helwan Economic Housing was chosen as an example. If it is assumed that only three-quarters of the total number of flats have been extended (quite an underestimation, according to the local authority) and assuming that every unit was extended by only one room (also an underestimation), the total investment in the extensions, calculated at LE120 (UK£24) per sq. m. (LE11 (UK£2.25) per sq. ft.), would amount to LE7,344,000 (UK£1,468,800).

Users' affordability

The expenditure pattern of Mahmoud was chosen as an example from the Helwan case study. Mahmoud represents a wide sector among Helwan Economic Housing householders. He is middle-aged at 45 years old, and has been a public sector worker for the last fifteen years. He decided to send all his children to school, and so is the only earner in the family. Comparing his monthly income with his average monthly expenditure on the extension, it is found that the extension cost represented 39 per cent of his total income, and resulted in a monthly deficit of at least LE15 (UK£3). It was established that the difference was made up out of auxilliary resources, which were: first, borrowing from the contractor, i.e. credit; second, selling his wife's jewellery; third, borrowing credit-free from co-workers; and fourth, joining a savings club.

The contribution of each source can be seen from Figure 1, which illustrates the estimated household income, sources of income, and the auxilliary resources, as well as the improvement in internal occupancy rates. Mahmoud is represented in Figure 1 under columns headed 'A'.

Mahmoud's extension consists of two rooms with a

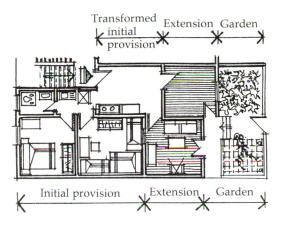

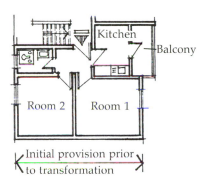

Figure 2 *Mahmoud's extension: ground floor*

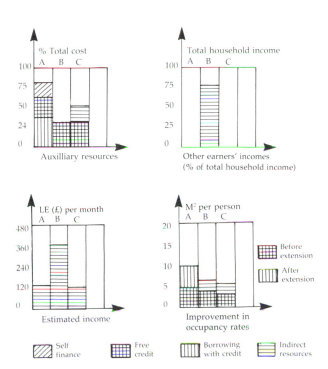

Figure 1 *Resources, income and occupancy rates in Helwan and Imbaba housing projects, Cairo.*

concrete skeleton structure and brick walls; it has quite a reasonable standard of finishing (Figure 2).

Two cases were chosen from Imbaba because of the difficulty in finding one household which would represent a reasonable sector of the Imbaba Nasser Housing households. Abou Abdou was chosen to represent the higher, variable income group and Abou Farag to represent the low, stable income group.

In the case of Abou Abdou the extension was created by the construction of the load-bearing walls of a two-bedroomed flat on the roof. The new flat is supposed to be similar to the original flat on the fifth floor. Only one room has been roofed, with corrugated sheets, and is the only habitable room in the extension. The area of the room is about 12 sq. m. (130 sq. ft.) (see Figure 3). The extension was built four years ago and no further development has taken place since then. A steel ladder had to be constructed at that time to give access to the roof within the initial staircase space. The cost of the extension was LE750 (UK£150); at that time the total family income was about LE280 (UK£56) per month. The cost of the extension represented 22 per cent of the total annual income. Abou Abdou is referred to in Figure 1 under columns headed 'B'.

In the case of Abou Farag, who lives on the ground

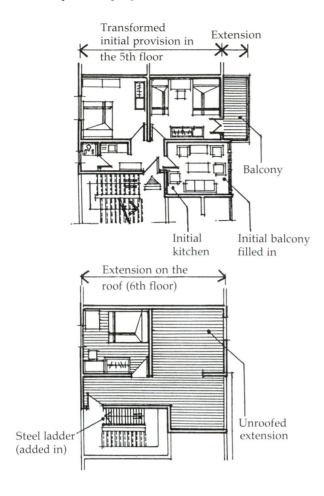

Figure 3 *Abou Abdou's extension: fifth floor and roof.*

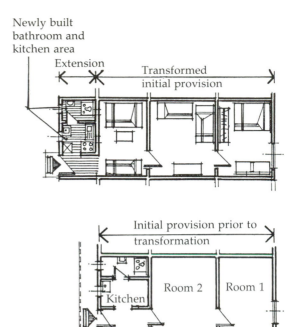

Figure 4 *Abou Farag's extension: ground floor.*

floor, the area gained is only about 6 sq. m. (see Figure 4). The area gained was used as a bathroom and a kitchen, which were moved from elsewhere to allow space for another room inside the flat. Half of the gained area was already roofed by the balcony of the flat above.

Abou Farag is now in early retirement on a pension. Three years ago, when the extension was built, he was working at the Public Weaving and Spinning Factory. His salary then was about LE110 (UK£22) per month. As the total cost of the extension was LE200 (UK£40) it represented only about 15 per cent of the total annual household income. Abou Farag is referred to in Figure 1 under columns headed 'C'.

The variation in income levels in the three case studies previously outlined is due mainly to the existence of more than one earner in the household, most likely an elder son. However, having additional earners does not necessarily mean that more funds are available for the extension costs, as other financial obligations are likely to arise, such as preparing daughters for marriage. But in most cases the additional earners did contribute to the extension costs if required to do so, as well as to the regular household expenditure.

A higher income does not necessarily affect the householder's decision to join a savings club in order to raise the down-payment – he or she would most likely still be willing to join. Higher-income households still prefer to follow the same financial mechanism by dealing on a credit basis with the contractor rather than paying the whole cost in cash.

In some cases, the future rather than the present need for more space determines the householders' decision to extend their flats. In other words, the extension is considered a future investment.

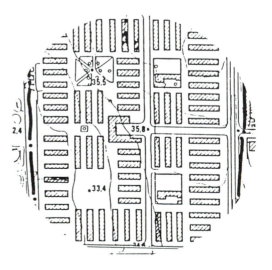

Figure 5 *Block layout of Helwan Economic Housing.*

In Imbaba the decision of the user not to extend is not a financial one, but is mainly because of fear of demolition. However, when some decide to extend in spite of the insecurity involved, they tend to minimize their investment in terms of materials and space. They also seem to be slightly more confident if they build their extensions as cantilevers, or roof extensions, so that the local authority would find it more difficult to demolish it.

The government's initial built provision

The five-storey blocks are laid out in a very regular fashion, with approximately 50 per cent of the blocks facing north–south and the remaining 50 per cent facing east–west (Figure 5).

In the Helwan Economic Housing development, initial provision consists of either two or three rooms, bathroom and kitchen, accessed from a public staircase serving the five floors. A two-roomed flat measures around 35 sq. m. (377 sq. ft.). A small balcony is provided on the side opposite the staircase, where the service pipes and ducts are also located.

The impact of this initial provision on the extensions is rather a two-way process. On the one hand, the access side is never used for extensions because of the space taken up by the proximity of the public staircase. Whilst more space is available on the other side, the service ducts and pipes are always a controlling factor for the ultimate width of the extension. The services are always left uncovered and accessible for maintenance purposes. On the other hand, an extension when built has an unmistakable effect on the initial provision and its environment. Generally speaking daylight to the middle room is cut out except at the end units where a hole can be made in the flank walls to let light in. Although the blocks and flats were designed not to be extended, the extensions have been made quite naturally and easily (see Figure 6).

Location of the flat in the block

The position of the flat affects the freedom of choice of the household whether to extend or not. The fifth- and ground-floor flats have the privilege of separate external access. When an extension is made through the roof to the new sixth floor, the staircase is extended to give separate and private access. The ground floor has the additional advantage of having a private garden, a shop or a workshop. The location of the flat at the end of the block gives the householder the opportunity of gaining additional space to the side of the block.

Access and cultural considerations

In the two-bedroomed flats there are basically two forms of circulation concerning internal access to the extension.

The first form occurs when a central, multi-purpose space such as a hall is created. This hall, besides acting as a circulation area, accommodates various activities such as eating, sitting, cooking and sometimes even washing clothes. The role played by such a space resembles that of the courtyard in Egyptian rural housing. In this case the mixing of different activities in one space does not seem to represent any cultural problems. Allocating a specific room for the kitchen, for example, does not seem to be of much concern to the users.

In the second form, the newly built rooms are individually accessed through one of the existing rooms. The through-room circulation does not cause cultural problems, even if the rooms crossed are utilized as bedrooms. Separation between different activities seems to be more of a priority here, and this is typically urban rather than rural behaviour.

CONCLUSIONS AND PROPOSALS

The user's extension phenomenon will take place whatever attitude the local authority takes. However, the quality of the extension declines when the local authority's attitude is one of prevention and prohibition; this tends to produce a single cantilevered extension of one flat.

When the local authority takes a more relaxed attitude towards the extensions by ignoring them, this encourages a communal and collective type of extension of better quality with a generally better quality environment.

There are large stocks of public housing settlements where unused outside space is widely available. To use this space to increase the internal areas of dwellings seems fair and reasonable, given the overall parameters of housing in Egypt.

The importance of any proposals to improve the extension process must be seen against the following background. First, those users who have already managed to build extensions without any financial help

Figure 6 *Initial provision and extensions.* (Source: *Tipple* et al. *1985*)

from the government have achieved relatively good standards of accommodation, considering their circumstances. The extension process requires a great deal of communal action and organization which residents successfully manage to achieve without the interference of any organizing body. Second, there is still a large stock of five-storey walk-up flat blocks in many of the public housing projects around Egypt. The households in these projects would benefit greatly if they were allowed the opportunity to extend them, and if they were given management, organizational, financial and design advice as outlined below by the setting up of on-site project technical offices. And third, if people's own construction is seen as a healthy social, cultural and economic activity the process should be measured and more support given to those areas which are weakest.

The user extension process is looked upon as a positive approach towards achieving a better quality environment. However, these suggestions are in the form of guidelines which are aimed at achieving a better quality product at a low cost. The main recommendation is that the control of the process of extension-building should remain in the users' hands.

Learning to work together

The involvement of the government is required as a positive participant in the following areas: (a) the organizational and political framework; (b) financial mechanisms; and (c) planning and building guidelines.

The organizational and political framework

The government should act as a legalizing power and provider of services. A change in the classification of unused public spaces in housing projects is essential, so that land currently in the public domain could be obtained by individuals for development purposes.

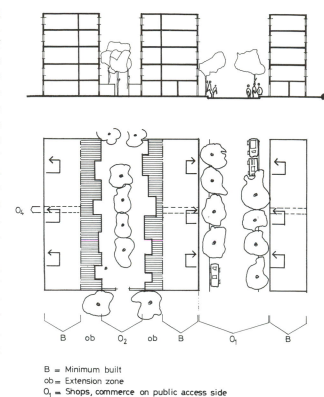

B = Minimum built
ob = Extension zone
O_1 = Shops, commerce on public access side
O_2 = Semi public (extension sides facing eachother)

Figure 8 *The urban tissue for development within development.*

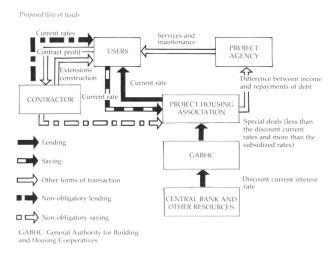

Proposed flow of funds

GABHC: General Authority for Building and Housing Cooperatives

Figure 7 *Financial mechanism: proposed flow of funds.*

The setting up of a local project technical office as an intermediary organization is essential. Such an office could act as an intermediary body between the government and the contractors. If the office held legalizing powers similar to those of a local council, central governmental bureaucracy could be avoided. Generally speaking, the office should act as a type of core housing project agency, a co-ordinator between users and contractors (as the developers of extensions) and the government (as a services, land and utilities supplier).

Such an office would also maintain the cost efficiency of the project as a whole. The money made from the sale of land required for extensions could contribute towards the recovery cost.

A project technical office of this type could offer immediate technical advice in structural design and extension planning to the developers, users and contractors, covering comprehensive planning for the whole project. Such house planning and project information would be disseminated in an accessible and understandable form, and should make residents more aware of mistakes and successes by using visual aids such as slide documentation. Promoting the objectives of the project might include education (for example, related health matters) as well as the aesthetic aspects of the built environment.

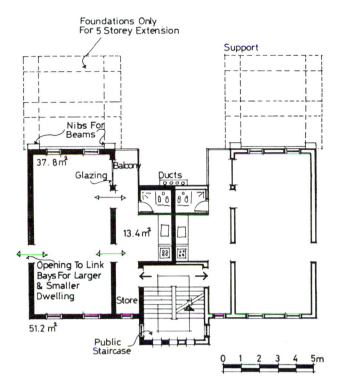

Figure 9 *Proposed initial provision.* (Source: *Tipple* et al. *1985*)

Another essential role of the proposed project office would be in cutting down costs by having access to controlled construction materials (cement, iron and glass) at official prices. Lastly, the office would be able to intervene in the case of problems arising between neighbours, and should try to resolve them.

Financial mechanism

The involvement of the project office as a mobilizer of financial resources would be essential to the success of such a scheme. The project office would encourage both saving and borrowing within market interest rates. In fact, at present, the contractors often lend money at lower interest rates than those of commercial banks.

The project office would therefore have to play the role of both contractor and savings club. A system of package deals might be appropriate whereby the users would have to save up a certain amount of money before they could borrow. This would lead to the setting up of a type of housing association bank, borrowing from the General Authority for Building and Housing Co-operatives (GABHC). The housing association should have the right to do the same, borrowing at discount current rates rather than at subsidized rates (as is the case with housing co-operatives), so no further financial pressure would be put on the government. The project office's contractor role as a financier should be encouraged too, either as a direct financier to the user, or as a saver in the project housing association. Figure 7

explains the flow of funds which is expected in the proposed mechanism.

Planning and building guidelines

A physical survey would be required to produce detailed updated layouts for the project. Land available for extensions should be clearly defined and a classification of land use and land ownership should be provided through detailed layout plans. The area of land which is held under public use title should be reduced to the minimum. Detailed plans of blocks and permissible extension limits should be defined.

The building programmes in the new cities are by no means finished. The cities have been planned in phases, some of which do not reach completion till after the year 2000. The housing which remains to be built should therefore take into account the fact that the people themselves have already made, and will continue to want to make, an important contribution to development within development. The physical planning framework of the urban tissue should take this contribution into account (see Figure 8) by setting limits which encourage and guide the process but which do not stifle or kill the future building of extensions.

The physical properties of the five-storey blocks should likewise respect the fact that the extension-building activity must be guided and not inhibited by the provision of structural walls, openings, public staircases, roofs, floors, façades and services. Judicious positioning and dimensioning of these elements by professionals can lead to positive decision-making by

Figure 10 *Proposed initial provision unextended but planned according to individual requirements.*

3 Rooms 71 m²   4 Rooms 71 m²

0 1 2 3 4 5m

Figure 11 *Fully extended flats.*

households; the result would be many individual different solutions for each household's domestic requirements (see Figures 9, 10 and 11).

Final recommendation

This investigative essay has implications for 'old' projects such as Helwan, El Tebeen and Imbaba which were built *not* to be extended. However, it also has implications for the housing stock in the new cities, such as Fifteenth May, Sadat City, Sixth October, Tenth Ramadan and many others, which has already started to show signs of user extensions, even though these are not yet allowed or fully developed.

The proposals also have implications for the housing which has yet to be built. What has been proposed in this essay should be tried out on a small-scale pilot demonstration project, perhaps for a small, new-build scheme or, more appropriately, for an extension scheme to existing housing stock.

The first step would be to gain the support of the local community and government, and begin to pull together, to advise on and initiate the ideas discussed here. With a planner, an architect, a technician, an engineer, and social workers, only a small sum of money would be required to put such an operation into action. In our view the results would be immediately tangible.

BIBLIOGRAPHY

Abt Associates (1982) *Informal Housing in Egypt*, a report submitted to the US Agency for International Development, Cambridge, Mass.: Dames and Moore; Cairo: General Organization for Housing, Building and Planning Research.

Abu-Lughid, J. (1971) *Cairo: 1001 Years of the City Victorious*, Princeton, NJ: Princeton University Press.

Aref, H. (1989) 'The latent potentialities of the low-income in housing projects', Masters thesis, Cairo University.

Bakr, S. (1981) 'Form and territory: a comparison between four areas in Cairo', Masters thesis, Massachusetts Institute of Technology.

Bass, H. (1979) 'Urban low-cost housing in Egypt', *Building Research Establishment* No. 141/79, Graston Watford.

Blower, A., Brook, C., Dunleavy, P. and McDowell, L. (1986) *Urban Change and Conflict*, London: Harper & Row.

Bouchair, J. (1984) 'The problem of adaptability in mass housing in Algeria', Masters thesis, University of Newcastle upon Tyne.

Dasgupta, A. (1990) 'Negotiating for growth and change: a study of users' initiated transformation of public sector', *Open House International* 15 (4): 34–40.

Davidson, F. and Payne, G. (1970) *Urban Projects Manual*, Liverpool: Liverpool University Press.

El Messiri, S. (1989) 'The squatters' perspective of housing: an Egyptian view', in W. van Vliet, E. Huttman and S. Fava (eds), *Housing Needs and Policy: Trends in Thirteen Countries*, Durham, NC: Duke University Press.

Fathy, A. (1987) 'A report on the living conditions in a Workers' City public housing project', *El Talia Journal* 2: 24–32.

General Organisation for Housing, Building and Planning Research (1989) 'The Shelter', Health and Family Seminar, Cairo.

Habraken, J. (1970) *Three R's for Housing*, Amsterdam: Schelteing & Holkemea.

—— (1983) *Transformation of the Site*, Cambridge, Mass.: Awater Press.

—— (1985) *The Appearance of Form*, Cambridge, Mass.: Awater Press.

Koch, J., Selim, T. and El Gamal, O. (1979) 'Organisation and operation of the construction industry', in *The Housing and Construction Industry in Egypt*, interim report and working papers, Cairo: Cairo University and MIT Technology Planning Program.

Malpazzi, S. (1986) 'Rent control and housing market equilibrium: theory and evidence from Cairo', Ph.D. thesis, George Washington University.

Metwally, M., El-Batran, M., Kardash, H., Serry, A. and Serageldin, H. (1986) 'A seminar on Ismailia Demonstration Project', Cairo: General Organisation for Housing, Building and Planning Research.

Ministry of Housing (1979) National Urban Policy Study, Cairo.

—— (1982) Marketing Reports of the 15th of May New City, Cairo.

Sakr, S. (1983) 'In use modification of existing public housing in Cairo', Masters thesis, Massachusetts Institute of Technology.

Serageldin, M. (1985) 'Planning and Institutional mechanism in the expanding metropolis coping with the growth of Cairo', Aga Khan Award for Architecture, Geneva: Aga Khan Award Series.

Steinberg, F. (1984) 'Ain El Sira in Cairo: the architecture of poverty', *Open House International* 9 (2): 35–42.

—— (1987) 'Cairo informal housing and urbanisation – positive contribution and challenge for the future', paper delivered at the Seminar on Official and Informal Supply for Low-income Housing in Third World Cities, Rotterdam: Institute of Housing and Development Studies.

Tipple, G., Wilkinson, N. and Nour, M. (1985) 'The transformation of the workers, City of Helwan', *Open House International* 10 (3): 25–38.

Turner, J. (1976) *Housing by People*, London: Marion Boyars.

Wikan, U. (1980) *Life among the Poor in Cairo*, New York: Livistock Publications.

Yin, R. (1989) *Case Study Research: Design and Methods*, London: Sage Publications.

Zahlan, A. (1983) *The Arab Construction Industry*, New York: St Martin's Press.

SECTION 2.2

Response to place

Until the advent of powered transport, the architecture of every place tended to be constructed from the materials of that place. If the primary task of architecture is to offer shelter, then the climate of each locality on earth requires its own particular response – for example, excluding or filtering bright light in some climates and taking full advantage of weak light in others. For much of the last two hundred years these special properties of individual places were either played down or ignored. Technological progress, increased communication through exploration, political expansion and global trade, all broke down natural barriers to cultural interchange and influence. Universal ideals for all humankind led to concepts of equally universal architectural ideas. The 'International Style' of the second and third quarters of this century most boldly proclaimed its independence from the unique requirements of place. City centres all over the world bear witness to the naivety of this perception as well as its power to destroy local architectural character. The essays in this section promote the current view that all architecture must respond to the particular characteristics of the place where it is located. They reflect four ways in which place can be regarded.

Jay Appleton and Barrie Greenbie approach it from the perspective of the landscape architect with special concern for the area around the building, landscape being treated in the sense of all open ground, not just the rural countryside. They stress the cultural and emotional content of place in a general exploration of the issue.

In contrast, Ronald Brunskill, in 'The traditional building of Cumbria' considers the vernacular architecture of an isolated part of England. It is, for England, mountainous, wet and remote and a distinct form of building developed steadily over several centuries dominated by the local building stone, the

agricultural lifestyle and the relatively harsh climate. The theme is further elaborated in essays in Part Three which explore the contemporary significance of vernacular traditions in Romania, Greece and Malta.

A.N.

RECOMMENDED READING

Alexander, C. (1979) *The Timeless Way of Building*, New York: Oxford University Press.

Appleton, J. (1990) *The Symbolism of Habitat: An Interpretation of Landscape in the Arts*, Seattle: University of Washington Press.

Beeler, R. (1989) *Architecture and Nature*, London: Architectural Press.

Calvino, I. (1979) *Invisible Cities*, London: Pan Books.

Canter, D. (1977) *The Psychology of Place*, London: Architectural Press.

Correa, C. (1989) *The New Landscape: Urbanization in the Third World*, London: Butterworth.

Day, C. (1990) *Places of the Soul: Architecture and Environmental Design as a Healing Art*, London: Aquarian Press.

Duly, C. (1979) *The Houses of Mankind*, London: Thames & Hudson.

Hudson, E.S. (1976) *A Geography of Settlements*, 2nd edn, Plymouth: Macdonald & Evans.

Lynch, K. (1972) *What Time is This Place?*, Cambridge, Mass.: MIT Press.

Mugerauter, R. (1976) *Dwelling, Place and Environment*, Lancaster: Marthinus Nijhoff.

Norberg-Schulz, C. (1980) *Genius Loci: Towards Phenomenology of Architecture*, London: Academy Editions.

Olgyay, V. (1963) *Design with Climate: Bioclimatic Approach to Architectural Regionalism*, Princeton: Princeton University Press.

Relph, E. (1976) *Place and Placelessness*, London: Dion.

Rossbach, S. (1983) *Feng Shui: The Chinese Art of Placement*, New York: Dutton.

13 Landscape and architecture
Jay Appleton

ARCHITECTURE AND THE HUMAN HABITAT

There are two distinctive but complementary kinds of demand which creatures of all species make on their environment. They require, first, an area which will furnish their requirements in food and other necessities, and, second, a place within or accessible to that area where they can raise a family. The precise demands made in respect of both these needs will be particular to every species, but, except in the very lowliest forms of life, this twin concept of foraging-ground and nesting-place will be found to be the basis of that interaction between a creature and its habitat on which the survival of the species ultimately depends (Appleton 1990).

There is still a widespread scepticism about the validity of comparisons drawn between the behaviour of *Homo sapiens* and that of other creatures, and clearly there are crucial differences; but there are also fundamental similarities (Morris 1967), and these extend to the interaction between the individual and the environment. We may think that architecture is the prerogative of the human race, but the ability to enclose space within an artificial structure, beneficially altering its microclimate, ensuring privacy and excluding unwanted intruders, is well within the competence of innumerable species of birds and other animals which are capable of procuring building materials, transporting them, processing them, assembling them on the building site and using them to construct an edifice which conforms to a standard design (Frisch 1975).

We are, in short, the heirs to not just a few thousand but many millions of years of architectural experience, and the houses in which we live and raise our families are the nesting-places of our own species, the direct linear descendants of a phenomenon of immense antiquity.

What we call 'landscape' is, for us, the equivalent of the primeval foraging-ground, that outer zone of our habitat with which we enjoy an equally important if quite different relationship. Among environmental scientists there is an increasing recognition that we are attached to both of these contrasting elements by deep bonds of association involving attraction, anxiety, repulsion and other feelings, but, above all, curiosity.

For some these emotional links are best understood, in Jungian terms, as 'archetypes'; for others the very concept of atavism as a characteristic of an economically advanced, culturally sophisticated society whose nesting-place is an apartment and whose foraging-ground is the supermarket, is unacceptable; but to everyone the terms 'indoors' and 'outdoors' suggest a pair of complementary concepts whose importance can be easily understood in everyday environmental experience. What I am about to suggest in this essay is that many problems of architectural aesthetics hinge on the interaction between these two conditions, call them what we will.

THE INDOORS–OUTDOORS INTERFACE
The architectural expression

The façade of a building represents the interface between indoors and outdoors in its simplest form. A powerful statement of it, such as may be found in the walls of a castle, can communicate the idea of an effective protective screen which may afford a high degree of privacy and seclusion to those who shelter behind it, but at the same time may strengthen the sense of *ex*clusion for those who perceive it from the outside. For them, as a symbol of a place of refuge (Appleton 1975), it is ineffective; it says 'Keep out!'. By contrast a façade which appears to offer opportunities for passing easily between outdoors and indoors, while it may well be less effective as a protective screen, is likely to be more appealing to the outside observer because its symbolic message is 'Come in!'.

Any device which breaks up the visual impenetrability of a building will add to its capacity symbolically to invite admission and thereby enhance its image as a potential place of refuge from the 'great outdoors'. The feelings of the observer will be correspondingly warmed towards it, and the building, in so far as it is judged by that criterion, is more likely to have a spontaneous appeal. Any unambiguous visible entrances, or any kinds of breaches in a wall which suggest opportunities for admission, can discharge such a symbolic function. Doorways provide the most usual and obvious invitations to admission, since they have manifestly been provided for precisely that purpose, but the effect can also be achieved to some extent by any apertures, such as windows, even if they occur in relatively unattainable situations, since, at this stage, we are talking about symbolic rather than actual means of access. Arcades, porticoes, verandas, balconies, overhanging eaves, exterior staircases and recesses of all kinds render the separation of indoors and outdoors to some degree less absolute. If they do no more than cast shadows they will have begun to suggest a zone of transition between the bright light of the open air, the zone of exposure, and the subdued light of the interior, the zone of conceal-ment.

Many of those large, post-war buildings which have so conspicuously failed to appeal to the public, however staunchly defended by architects, will be found to have façades which are *impenetrable* in this sense. Typically they consist of huge surfaces in a single, unrelieved plane, devoid of both recesses and projections, and therefore untouched by shadow. Although they may present to the observer a very high ratio of glass to other materials, the windows themselves are usually flush with the walls, and in an air-conditioned building it is most unlikely that any of them will be open. In many cities office buildings have been constructed whose façades consist almost entirely of reflecting glass, but to the observer in the street these surfaces appear totally opaque and conspicuously lack the capacity to suggest visual, let alone actual, access. Symbolically they are powerful 'No admittance' signs.

If, however, we look at some of those changes which within the last decade have become widespread in domestic architecture, particularly in areas of urban renewal or infill, we often find a strong emphasis on those devices which soften the severity of the interface, making for symbolic penetrability and strengthening the visual importance of that zone of transition; and undoubtedly buildings of this sort have begun to find a renewed favour among the public even though some of them may invite the use of pejorative terms, such as 'kitsch', from the critics. Recessed surfaces are once more a feature, eaves tend to overhang more generously, balconies, porches and covered passageways proliferate, sometimes also exterior staircases, all embellishing buildings often set at irregular angles; and, in spite of some astonishingly high densities, the general effect is widely considered to be cosy and inviting, the sort of place, in fact, where one could live in a pleasing kind of aesthetic equilibrium. Dare one hope that buildings of this sort are a pointer to the bridging of that gap which, over the last few decades, has so regrettably opened up between the architects and the public?

The land-use expression

So much for the interface as perceived in elevation. What of its perception in plan? In land-use terms the usual device for toning down the immediacy of the interface between indoors and outdoors is the garden. The medieval *hortus conclusus* discharged this role exactly. As *hortus*, 'garden', it belonged to the foraging-ground. Its plant materials, though they might have been artificially positioned, were nevertheless growing organisms, a part of the natural world. Microclimatically it may have been more sheltered than the world outside, but it was still open to the wind and the rain and its ceiling was the sky. As *conclusus* it shared the property of 'enclosure' with the nesting-place. Screened from prying eyes it provided a little theatre of privacy into

which the domesticity of the house could overflow without conceding its protected status. By Tudor times it commonly contained a 'prospect mount' artificially constructed to permit a view of the landscape over the encircling wall.

During the seventeenth and eighteenth centuries the balance of this zone of transition moved towards the 'landscape' side and at the same time its scale became larger as the visual role of the park became more important. The element of enclosure was preserved, not by the garden wall but by the peripheral 'belt' of trees so monotonously favoured by Capability Brown (1715–83), who often eliminated the garden altogether, bringing the grass of the park right up to the house. (The kitchen garden survived as a unit functionally, morphologically and visually quite separate.) Because of their larger scale, however, and the huge expanses of grass only sporadically punctuated by clumps of trees, Brown's parks lacked the intimacy of the old *hortus conclusus*, and Humphry Repton (1752–1818) played a leading part in reintroducing the garden close to the house while retaining the park in something like the style of Brown, dividing the zone of transition, as it were, into an inner, more intimate, and an outer, more expansive, shell.

Over the years the outer limits of the zone of tran-sition have ebbed and flowed like the tide, and numerous devices have been employed to give it expres-sion. The terrace, a perambulating area immediately adjacent to the house and often accessible through French windows, belonged more closely to the foraging-ground over which it frequently commanded a view. The conservatory belonged more closely to the nesting-place but incorporated the symbolic representatives of the foraging-ground.

MUTUAL EXCHANGE

The conservatory provides a good illustration of the mutual interdependence of indoors and outdoors, and shows how objects or concepts which are thought of as properly belonging to the one may be transferred to the other. Many articles of furniture have their counterparts specially adapted for outdoor use. The 'sun-lounger' is a recent example. At the same time garden plants are allowed, not only into the conservatory, but into every room in the house. Nor are these simply small flowers and pot-plants. Rubber plants, vines and shrubs of all sorts have invaded the domestic residence as well as the foyer of the hotel and the circulating area of the shopping complex. The ornamental water of the lake, the 'canal' and the decorative fish-pond have their counterparts in the tropical fish tank and the goldfish bowl. The fountain is not an unusual sight in a hotel, nor are we surprised to find fireplaces and other parts of the interior of the house almost ostentatiously made of rough-hewn, natural rock.

The typical English park at its heyday contained quite

elaborate architectural features; temples, gazebos, summer-houses and numerous lesser structures invaded the domain of grass, trees and water. The arbour, a structure with a medieval pedigree, consisted, as its name implies, of tree-like material fashioned into a small shelter. The pergola was a structure whose function was to support growing plants in such a way as to enclose outdoor space, within which one could enjoy the sensation of being indoors and outdoors at the same time.

Descriptive terms which properly belong to 'indoors' find their way into the description of landscape. The American landscape architect Richard Haag, for example, applies the terms 'Ante-room' and 'Reflection Room' to components of the design for which he was awarded the 1986 President's Award of the American Society of Landscape Architects (Frey 1986). The term 'coulisse', which is in general use among landscape architects to describe screens of opaque material projecting into an open space from the sides, is borrowed from the theatrical stage where it is used to describe pieces of scenery which discharge a similar function.

It is perhaps less usual to find 'landscape' terms used to describe interiors, but in a recent book (Hildebrand 1991) an American architect has taken not only the terminology but the whole conceptual system which I proposed some years ago for the aesthetic analysis of landscape (Appleton 1975), and applied it to the interpretation of the interiors of the domestic buildings of Frank Lloyd Wright.

BLENDING WITH THE LANDSCAPE

The concept of nesting-place and foraging-ground as complementary components of 'habitat' may suggest why we attach importance to the blending of buildings in the landscape. One of the most attractive features of vernacular buildings is the way they reflect the geological character of the district. Many planning authorities in Britain, particularly in National Parks and Environmentally Sensitive Areas, insist on the use of building materials which, even if they are reconstituted, give the appearance of locally quarried stone, in spite of the additional cost. The Spanish architect Antoni Gaudí went to great lengths to imitate natural forms in many of his buildings, visually minimizing the difference between the natural and the artificial.

The covering of façades with plant material is another device for achieving a similar effect. The late Alec Clifton-Taylor had an obsessive dislike of creeper, but the frequency with which he was presented with opportunities for denouncing it illustrates how far, on this point, he was out of line with popular opinion. If people didn't like it they wouldn't plant it, but it is just one of a number of devices for making buildings merge into landscape, devices ranging from the roses round the cottage door to the setting of the new Australian Parlia-

ment House in Canberra into a hill, thereby symbolising the integration of the Australian people with the Australian landscape. The South African Parliamentary seat, the Union Building, also makes a concession to the supremacy of 'landscape' by literally maintaining a 'low profile' in compliance with planning policies which have aimed at maintaining free from development the skylines formed by the prominent ridges which are such a distinctive feature of the built-up area of Pretoria.

AMBIENCE

If the relationship of a building to its surroundings is analogous to that of the nesting-place to the foraging-ground we should expect that visual contact between the two would be one of the more important criteria by which we judge its aesthetic merit. 'A room with a view' is always at a premium. If we are in any doubt about the value which the public attaches to 'ambience' we can find corroboration in financial terms by checking house prices in any estate agent's window. While a private garden, a screen of shrubs and trees, an enclosing garden wall, all suggestive of a reinforcement of the symbolism of 'refuge', are widely esteemed properties of the nesting-place, and will be reflected in the market value, a huge bonus will also accrue from a good view, particularly if it encompasses trees, water, or preferably both, and if it extends into the far distance (Orians 1980).

These values find expression in many common features of architectural design, such as the picture window. The positioning and orientation of a building within the site can often be seen to exploit its potential as a viewpoint, and the deciding factor could well be a mountain, a lake or a glimpse of the sea many miles away. The advantages of a property adjacent to a golf course or public open space, unlikely to be built over, are so self-evident that purchasers will gladly pay substantial premiums without ever stopping to ask why an open view is so important to them.

This whole system of environmental aesthetics is full of ambivalent symbolism (Appleton 1990), and therefore it is not surprising to find anomalies, ambiguities and examples of paradox. Thus the high-rise apartment block, for example, often presents magnificent opportunities for visual contact with the distant prospect, but at the cost of the sensation of being incorporated within the landscape, enveloped by it, swallowed up in it. One of the most cherished images of 'home' in landscape painting is the cottage in the wood, where a man-made symbol of refuge is encompassed within a natural one. The tower block is so out of scale even with the largest natural objects, like forest trees, that it almost inevitably reverses the situation, so that the symbols of nature appear to shelter under its shadow rather than vice versa. If a mountain is high enough, steep enough and close enough it may reassert the domination of nature over a tower block, but such situations are extremely rare.

Many of the theories of architectural aesthetics have become hallowed as if they embodied established truth when, in fact, they are no more than speculations fortified by tradition; and among the ideas which are in urgent need of reappraisal those which concern the relationship between architecture and landscape should be high on the list. The Gestalt psychologists tell us that the meaning we attach to an object cannot be separated from the context in which we perceive it, and why should this apply to buildings less than to anything else? My little model of the nesting-place and the foraging-ground is not intended to be taken too literally, but it may be useful to think of it as a kind of mirror in which we can see familiar issues reflected in a fresh light.

REFERENCES

Appleton, J. (1975) *The Experience of Landscape*, London and New York: Wiley (paperback 1987, Hull University Press).

—— (1990) *The Symbolism of Habitat: An Interpretation of Landscape in the Arts*, Seattle: University of Washington Press.

Frey, S.R. (1986) 'A series of gardens: Bainbridge Island, Washington', *Landscape Architecture*, September/October: 54–61, 128.

Frisch, K. von (1975) *Animal Architecture*, London: Hutchinson.

Hildebrand, G. (1991) *The Wright Space*, Seattle: University of Washington Press.

Morris, D. (1967) *The Naked Ape: A Zoologist's Study of the Human Animal*, London: Cape.

Orians, G. (1980) 'Habitat selection: general theory and applications to human behaviour', in J. Lockard (ed.) *Evolution of Human Social Behaviour*, New York: Elsevier, pp. 49–96.

14 The traditional buildings of Cumbria

Ronald Brunskill

INTRODUCTION

Cumbria is one of the most well-defined regions in Britain. More than half its perimeter consists of water (sea or estuary), while the remainder includes clear topographical boundaries such as the Pennines, or old-established political boundaries such as the Scottish border. Only in the Lune Valley is the regional boundary imprecise. Present-day Cumbria consists of the ancient counties of Cumberland and Westmorland, the detached part of Lancashire 'north of the Sands', and a little of the former West Riding of Yorkshire.

The beauty of lakes and mountains and a largely (though not entirely) unspoilt coastline attract foreign tourists and British residents to Cumbria. But they are attracted also by the buildings of the region; not only by the country houses such as Muncaster Castle and Levens Hall, or the rather fragmentary remains of great churches such as Shap Abbey or Carlisle Cathedral, but also by the humbler buildings for which the term 'vernacular architecture' is coming to be adopted. Works of vernacular architecture comprise cottages and farmhouses, farm buildings and associated structures, watermills and smithies, wayside chapels and some of the smallest and least pretentious of the parish churches. These vernacular buildings, humble though they may be, are monuments to the persistence of traditional designs and traditional building practices in this proud and self-sufficient part of the country.

The design of these traditional buildings was subject to influences of climate, topography and history, and to social and economic factors, some of which were shared with other parts of the country, others peculiar to Cumbria. All combined in a unique fashion to guide and restrain the designers – whoever they may have been.

It goes without saying that most of Cumbria is hilly and some is mountainous, and that, consequently, many buildings occupy hillside positions: few on the hill tops, few in the marshy valley bottoms, but many on sloping sites. Equally, it has to be acknowledged that much of Cumbria is wet and cold at times; buildings had to be substantial, weather-resistant and sited with a wary eye to the cold north-eastern winds which sweep down from the Pennines.

Life in Cumbria has always been hard and rarely has there been much surplus wealth to be spent on extravagant building. For long the region formed one of the most distant parts of the kingdom. Its agriculture was backward and unproductive, its mineral wealth was largely unexploited, manufactures were few, raw materials as likely to be taken elsewhere as converted within the region. Until the early seventeenth century, even until after the Civil War, life was insecure for the poor and warlike for their rulers. However, prosperity came in the late seventeenth century and encouraged a great wave of new building and reconstruction; agriculture and manufacturing flourished, minerals such as coal, lead and iron ore were exploited, mountain streams were harnessed to power factories and furnaces, and the many buildings of the late eighteenth century and the nineteenth century testify to a welcome though not permanent turn in the economic cycle.

The trim farmhouses, extensive farm buildings and substantial cottages of the nineteenth century indicate a prosperous agriculture largely based on family farms. The solidly built but often quite elegant water-powered mills indicate that industry was still on a human scale, and was still more closely tied to the countryside than to the towns. The chapels and schools of a prudent and god-fearing community complete a picture of new but not over-obtrusive buildings.

SITES AND SETTLEMENT

One sometimes thinks of Cumbria as a region of scattered buildings, distributed in an apparently haphazard fashion over the hills and dales, but, in fact, the characteristic settlement of most of the region is the nucleated one of a collection of families and their buildings gathered together for security and mutual aid. Such settlements are not necessarily as large as those in other counties: the township or hamlet rather than the village is the unit of settlement; nor are they always compact: some cluster tightly around a village green while others straggle along a wide trackway. The place names with endings such as 'thwaite', 'ton', 'by', 'burgh' and 'ergh' indicate occupation by successive waves of Celts, Saxons, Danes and Norse.

But isolated farmsteads are, of course, also to be seen. Some are of ancient foundation, tribute to the fortitude of a single family taming the wasteland. Some indicate that a permanent farmstead has been established on the site of a 'scale' or 'shield', a summer homestead occupied as part of the formerly widespread practice of transhumance. Many more, however, represent more recent colonization, the enclosure of the previously undivided fells during the late eighteenth and early nineteenth centuries.

The settlement pattern also demonstrated the ebb

and flow of human endeavour in Cumbria. Farmers pushed upwards into newly enclosed land; miners and quarriers retreated from worked-out mineral deposits; farmers retreated in turn as declining agriculture met expanding demands for water-gathering grounds or afforestation.

The towns, too, had their vicissitudes. Some, such as Newton Arlosh, never developed at all; some, such as Appleby, never fully recovered from some ancient disaster; some, such as Carlisle, flourished, declined and flourished again; some, such as Kendal, maintained a perpetual quiet prosperity, developing one trade or industry as another declined. All the towns contain a wealth of vernacular buildings where design is governed by the special circumstances of siting and occupation which distinguish town from countryside.

TRADITIONAL DOMESTIC BUILDINGS

The traditional houses and cottages do not survive in a uniform fashion in Cumbria any more than in other parts of the country. Many centuries are completely unrepresented by houses, apart from the castles or mansions of the privileged few. Most recent times are represented mainly by the rootless buildings whose design belongs to the nation as a whole rather than to Cumbria as a region. For traditional medieval houses one has to look to the towers and manor houses of the minor gentry. Traditional farmhouses date mainly from the late seventeenth century to the mid-nineteenth century. Traditional cottages are rarely older than the mid-eighteenth century; by the end of the nineteenth century they have virtually lost their traditional characteristics.

In many parts of Cumbria the larger houses of the fifteenth and sixteenth centuries were designed as tower-houses, or incorporated the so-called peel towers in a range of non-defensive structures. For obvious reasons such houses are concentrated near the Scottish border, but examples can be seen in many other parts, especially where raiders could approach by sea or along Pennine tracks. In other parts of the region the conventional manor house design of a hall with one or two cross-wings was adopted. Improvements to such houses during the mid-sixteenth century and early seventeenth century led to the design of taller buildings, almost symmetrical in elevation and often with many gables and chimney stacks. During the seventeenth century the larger houses became more compact, except that boldly projecting staircases and porches were popular. By the eighteenth century the houses recognized as Georgian in all parts of the country were built in Cumbria but were making use of local sandstone, limestone and slate.

Throughout Cumbria there was a great rebuilding of farmhouses beginning in the late seventeenth century; very many houses bear datestones and, especially, dated door lintels of this period. Such houses have two rooms

on the ground floor and a loft space (usually raised in more recent times) up above. In the northern part of the region these basic houses are often extended into subsidiary rooms or have attached farm buildings (see Figure 1); in the southern part the simple house plan generally remained intact, though built to quite generous dimensions.

No sooner was the substantially sized, solidly constructed farmhouse flooding the landscape at the end of the seventeenth century than its transformation into the familiar Victorian farmhouse was about to begin. Both increasing prosperity and improving living standards led to an increase in size, achieved through rearward additions, rearward extension and a general increase in height.

Rearward extension began with the introduction of a fixed stone staircase projecting slightly from the rear wall and replacing the internal ladder or wooden staircase. This projection was covered by an extension of the main roof of the house. Alongside the projecting staircase first a pantry or dairy was added to one side, then a scullery or back kitchen to the other. All were covered by a continuation of the main roof, which in some parts of the country is called a 'catslide' but which in Cumbria is called a 'teufall' roof. Gradually rooms or storage space were added to the back of the first floor until the late Georgian farmhouse plan of four rooms on each floor was produced.

An alternative form of rearward extension had a wing containing the staircase and a dairy and scullery on the ground floor with bedrooms above. This wing was roofed at right angles to the roof of the main house and produced an L-shaped plan. Once the arm of the L had

Figure 1 *Farmhouse at Great Ormside, Westmorland. This house is basically a longhouse of 1687 with farm buildings to the left and domestic accommodation to the right of a cross-passage. The farm buildings were extended outwards and both parts extended upwards in the mid-eighteenth century to create the present eaves level. In the late nineteenth century the new front door was inserted and further farm buildings were added to the right. (Photograph: R.W. Brunskill)*

been filled in, the late Georgian plan had been reached by a different route.

Upward extension began with the draughty undivided loft occupying the roof space over the two main rooms of the seventeenth-century farmhouse. In later years the eaves were raised, windows inserted at the front, and two full storeys of accommodation secured. Later still the garret space above the eaves was brought into use for storage or occasional occupation, lit usually by gable windows rather than the front dormer windows so commonplace in, say, the Cotswolds.

So the solid, square farmhouse of four rooms on each floor, two full storeys in height, stands with its air of stability and permanence in village and countryside throughout Cumbria. Only with the second half of the nineteenth century does this image break down as more and more Gothick touches compromise the spare elevations, and more and more projections to walls and skyline modify the simple silhouette.

Cumbria has never been a region of large agricultural enterprises; the family farm has always been the norm and farm servants, where employed at all, were accommodated in the farmhouse as part of the family. The cottage did not appear as part of the building inventory of rural Cumbria until about the middle of the eighteenth century, and then it was as likely to be occupied by an artisan or a quarrier as a farm labourer. The earliest cottages consisted basically of a single room functioning as a living room and kitchen, and even as a bedroom, though usually there was some slight extension of the accommodation into the roof space or to one side. Improvements followed even more swiftly for the cottager than the farmer, and by the beginning of the nineteenth century the usual cottage plan consisted of a

combined living room and kitchen on the ground floor, and one large and one small bedroom above, the two floors being connected by a fixed staircase of reasonable dimensions. Such cottages were built singly, in pairs, or, in the mining villages, in long rows. This same basic plan remained in use throughout the nineteenth century, the rooms increasing in height and floor area rather than in number.

TRADITIONAL FARM BUILDINGS

Most Cumbrian houses were farmhouses and the traditional farm buildings are as characteristic of the region as the traditional farmhouses. Some of the larger farmsteads, and especially those which were the work of the farming improvers, consist of continuous ranges of buildings around a farmyard with its covered midden; but many others consist of an L-shaped, U-shaped or continuous row of buildings incorporating barn, cowhouses and stable as well as the farmhouse; yet others consist of a scattering of buildings with the tall two-storey bank barn dominating the farmhouse. Most surviving farm buildings appear to date from the period between about 1750 and the end of the nineteenth century but a few, and especially those related to larger houses such as Rydal Hall, are much older, and often, as at Cark Hall, a nineteenth-century stone wall and slated roof conceal the timber structure of a much older farm building.

As in many other parts of Britain the barn is the principal farm building. In spite of the severity of the climate it was customary until about a century ago for Cumbrian farmers to have a fair proportion of their land under the plough – mainly in oats and barley. The capacious barns were used for the conversion of the sheaves of corn into grain and straw through threshing and winnowing, at first by hand but later with the use of the fixed threshing machine, of which a few were powered by steam engines, some by water wheels, but most by horsepower. The graceful polygonal or apsidal horse engine-house may still be seen projecting from barns on many of the larger farms. Following the collapse of farming based on corn growing towards the end of the nineteenth century the barns were used mainly for storage of hay, but now that much grass is converted to silage even that is no longer significant.

There is one type of barn which is so common in Cumbria that it does not have a local name and so the American term 'bank barn' has had to be imported for its description (Figure 2). As the term implies, such a barn is built along a bank or slope but is arranged in such a way that the barn proper is approached from the upper part of the slope, while underneath, and approached from the lower or farmyard level, there are cow-houses, stables and cartsheds. This type of farm building is economical in use in that hay and straw can be dropped down from the barn level to the mangers

Figure 2 *Farm building near Shap, Westmorland. This building is of bank barn arrangement with the barn door reached by way of a ramp at one side, and cow-houses reached from a lower level at the other side (though light penetrates and there is limited access from the upper level). It differs from most bank barns in being placed in the fields away from the farmstead, though the barn doors and threshing floor indicate that it was designed to accommodate grain crops as well as cattle.* (Photograph: R.W. Brunskill)

and feeding troughs below, and economical in construction in that one roof covers what would otherwise be two sets of buildings. In many examples there is a slated canopy to protect the cow-house and stable doors. In some examples the canopy is designed more as a platform – the so-called 'spinning gallery'. Bank barns are found throughout the southern two-thirds of Cumbria and are especially common in the Lake District itself. A variation in which the building is placed *across* the slope is also found, especially in the Lune Valley.

One other type of farm building is worth mention as it is found in many parts of the region. This is the field barn or – locally – the 'field house'. An isolated building occupying a position which could provide a sheltered area either in the middle of a field or along a field wall, the field barn was used to hold hay gathered in upland meadows and fed day by day to young cattle kept in a cowhouse or loose-box entered from the lower part of the slope. Most field barns appear to date from the late eighteenth century or nineteenth century.

Naturally, few of the farm buildings have the subdued ornamentation which so often enriches the houses of Cumbria but they generally make up in simple lines and good proportions whatever they may lack in architectural adornment.

BUILDING MATERIALS

Much of the character of the vernacular buildings of the region comes from the ubiquitous use of stone. There are the olive-greens of the Lake district slates, glistening in the rain, patterned by the sharp thin shadows of unmortared joints. There are the warm sandstones, pink and grey, red and brown, of the Eden Valley and West Cumberland. In Lunesdale, Kentdale, the Furness District and the eastern fringe of the Lake District one finds the water-moulded shapes of carboniferous limestone. In many places the deep colours of split cobbles pattern the walls of buildings. The grey-green slates or red sandstone flags on the low-pitched roofs complete a picture homogeneous in its use of stone.

Yet there is one part of the region where stone is less common, at least among the older houses and farm buildings. On the Solway Plain, the rendered and whitewashed walls of clay buildings give hints of the Devon countryside which the occasional thatched roof helps to fill out. But in the same area the brown bricks which succeeded clay as a walling material remind the visitor more of Staffordshire or Cheshire.

Thatch was once commonplace and the use of clay

walling more widespread than now appears, as old prints and paintings will confirm. It is odd to think of such materials in a land overflowing with stone and bursting with slate. But then, buildings in Carlisle, Kendal and Hawkshead show that, once, timber framing was used even for buildings as important as the Guildhall.

REGIONAL AND SUB-REGIONAL CHARACTER

There is a detectable regional identity in the vernacular architecture of Cumbria comparable to that of East Anglia, Snowdonia or the Peak District. Simple outlines of buildings, rectangular in plan and two storeys in height, with blunt gables, low-pitched roofs and squat chimney stacks portray the traditional forms of Cumbria. Their identity is different from that given by the timber and plaster of Suffolk, the cyclopean masonry of Gwynedd or the sharp, precisely cut gritstone of Derbyshire.

Yet there are variations within the region. In the Lake District one finds the slate walls, sometimes rendered and whitewashed, the crow-stepped gables, the rough window and door openings with rarely a mullion, a label mould, or a carved lintel. In the Eden Valley, the soft sandstone is used for neatly moulded mullions or architraves to windows, while elaborately decorated lintels of the late seventeenth century and carefully copied pattern-book details of the late eighteenth century abound. The Furness District and Kentdale provide light-coloured buildings: gleaming limestone or the staring whitewash which so upset William Wordsworth. Much of the limestone is difficult to work and small pieces were assembled together to create the characteristic chimney stacks of tapered cylinder shape.

FURTHER READING

Brunskill, R.W. (1974) *Vernacular Architecture of the Lake Counties*, London: Faber.
—— (1987) *Illustrated Handbook of Vernacular Architecture*, 3rd edn, London: Faber.
—— *(1987) Traditional Farm Buildings of Britain*, 2nd edn, London: Gollancz.
Denyer, S. (1991) *Traditional Buildings and Life in the Lake District*, London: Gollancz.
Rollinson, W. (ed.) (1989) *The Lake District: Landscape Heritage*, Newton Abbot, Devon: David & Charles.

15 Harmonizing the human habitat

Barrie B. Greenbie

Architecture began when cave dwellers first hung skins in front of their caves to keep out the cold. By so doing they enclosed space, and thus they created space, rather than merely discovering it. But the discovery preceded the creation in their imagination. The cave was already there, along with the hill and the valley or the plain which the hill enclosed, and the fact that it was there to begin with was essential to the creation. Forest dwellers bent trees together and wrapped them with skins or leaves to form a tepee, and in time learned to cut the trunks into poles and tie them together to shape a house. But the trees were there before the house, as was the forest, and they were all part of the habitat which humans shared with other animals. For early humans, the sense of what could be built must have been inseparable from the setting in which the building occurred.

The first humans, as they discovered they could shape space, were impelled to decorate it, and art was inseparable from building, from technology. Since one purpose of art was to evoke or propitiate spirits, the art of building was inseparable from religion, as religion was from life. The grandest efforts at early architecture were reserved for temples and community spaces, for religion was inseparable from politics. In front of the caves, in or near the main buildings, or in otherwise defined sacred spaces, dances were held, songs were sung, and stories told, and so music and theatre were linked to architecture.

The fusion of architecture with its setting in the surrounding landscape and with the other arts continued, despite increasing elaboration, complexity and social stratification, for most of human history. However, with industrialization a number of unprecedented changes occurred in building as in other aspects of life. One of them was the separation of ever larger numbers of human beings from the land and the organic processes of survival. Another was the specialization of human activities and with it the specialization of spaces. A third was the separation of the designer from the builder and the builder from the user. With increased specialization accompanied by increased scale, interconnections became increasingly difficult to perceive.

In our time, architecture has become a largely technical speciality, the construction of buildings as structural objects conceived in isolation from their settings. Art, where it connects with buildings at all, is applied after construction by specialists known as 'artists'. The setting has become the lot, or plot, largely a legal delineation, and specialists in landscape architecture, when they are known or employed at all, provide vegetative cosmetics for the face of architecture as object. Other specialists, called 'interior designers', perform cosmetic operations on the inside of the structure, which often has little relation to the outside.

Specialization obviously has its benefits, but there are costs – often hidden, but heavy, costs. Among them is the lost sense of place, that endangered species of the mind, the *genius loci*. Paradoxically, specialization spawns standardization and obliterates distinctions. The social concomitant of spatial standardization is conceptual bulldozing of cultural territories.

The problem for modern designers, as well as for their clients and other decision-makers, is that of finding a common experience among pluralistic populations. In pre-industrial times, except for the upheavals of war and natural disasters, environmental changes generally occurred slowly. People were born, married, raised children and died in the same essential setting. Under such circumstances, the shaping of architectural and agricultural space involved commonly accepted forms and symbols peculiar to the local culture. To a great extent, geographic space itself was defined by the social customs that took place within it – when in Rome one did as the Romans did, and that is how one knew where Rome was. Several generations of living people could share the same essential view of what was appropriate, significant, or important in their world. In our time, both culture and environment change with bewildering speed, often much faster than the human psyche can cope with them. What Alvin Toffler called 'future shock' (Toffler 1970) takes place not only across national boundaries, but within them. Children emerge into societies and inhabit landscapes their parents have difficulty comprehending, and culture shock can be experienced at home by anyone over the age of 30. These jolting transformations must be assimilated by human beings whose basic neurological equipment has remained essentially unchanged since the old Stone Age.

Enclosing space is not, of course, an activity limited to human beings – nest-building birds, beavers, burrowing animals, bees, and even worms do it – and so in this sense architecture ties us not only to our physical world, but to other living things. A phenomenon related to space creation, which is perhaps even more pervasive in the animal world, is the organization of territories. All architecture, for better or worse, defines territory of one kind or another by enclosing space with walls. But the concept of territory is a perceptual rather than a structural one. Among animals, different *species* may define territories differently within the same geographical area. Among humans, diverse *cultures* may perceive the same space as constituting different kinds and degrees of territory. Often boundaries significant to one culture are unimportant or even invisible to another, a factor that continually complicates international relations. Within modern nations, overlapping, variously stratified sub-cultures in the same geographical space make competing demands on the environment, based on different symbolic systems of what is desirable.

The psychoanalyst and psychohistorian Erik Erikson reasons that because human infants are born into the world so helpless and so dependent on learned exper-ience, our evolution requires that the young be bound firmly to their native group and the place it inhabits in order to assure that they would learn its ways of survival. He calls that 'pseudospecies', the compulsion of human beings to identify themselves not as human beings but as members of a tribe in a tribal territory, and to define being human in terms of the culture of their tribe, to respond to the tribe as other animals do to their species (Erikson 1966, 1974). While human activity is generally thought to be less governed by instinct than that of lower animals, tribal territoriality which spatially focuses learned behavior seems in itself to be a kind of instinct.

However, in all civilized societies there are spaces which are not territories within the ethological meaning of the word as defended spaces, but which are freely accessibly to all who do not interfere with the rights of others. They are closer to the ethological concept of an animal's *home range*. Such spaces can be thought of as a world-wide locale of a community of strangers. While most people do not think of strangers as forming a community, spaces of this sort foster co-operation to the extent that those who use them for civilized purposes, as a centre or forum for social diversity, have a common interest in keeping them usable and safe. Such a community is achieved by relatively arbitrary and abstract laws, as compared with the social pressure that controls behaviour in cultural territories. It is in such spaces that we meet as human beings, not primarily as members of a tribe (Greenbie 1981, 1988).

In design terms, the intricacies, the natural variety, the subtleties and ambiguities of form that are possible in a local neighbourhood are practical because the people who live in them or use them regularly can be expected to know them well. The complex and often cryptic characteristics of cultural territories make them sensually and emotionally interesting to residents and strangers alike. But such places can also be highly confusing to strangers, and the typically small scale, while reassuring, can also be confining. In spaces struc-tured largely for the cosmopolitan community of strangers, clarity and legibility are important, and at best they are achieved without monotony. Landmarks must

convey recognizable and meaningful symbols to strangers, often through abstract form. These forms must call forth universal human responses to the en-vironment. The two kinds of space are not mutually exclusive – on the contrary they are complementary, and the best cosmopolitan places comprise both. But they are different.

It is easy for modern urban people to idealize village life and to overlook the fact that the price of mutual support offered by a close community is a good deal of meddling. In such communities, interpersonal conflicts can be hard to escape. At least for some people of all ages, there is a special kind of delight in roaming freely in a public place, surrounded by human beings with whom one is not personally involved. Under such circumstances, free of threat to one's own ego, where status and achievement are irrelevant, one can really see humanity as part of nature.

Architecture is essentially a public art, one that at its best accommodates basic tribal needs, as it does other animal functions, in order to transcend them. When it does so, it is somehow related to the specific space that surrounds the building, to the context, to the *genius loci*, and thus acknowledges the holistic art of place-making as the pinnacle of all the arts, not as a profession, but as a way of looking at, comprehending, and then tran-scending the limitations of what we call the real world.

There is hierarchical order to all fine works of architecture. Whether it is a Gothic cathedral or a Japanese pagoda, one finds a clear progression from bottom to top, of dominant and subordinant elements, with entrances at ground level and a pinnacle which is both sheltering from and open to the sky, and a supporting structure connecting them. Natural land-scapes also have their hierarchies, from mountain ranges with tributary streams to river basins reaching to coastal plains. The true nature of architecture is to fit nature's pre-existing hierarchies while defining its own. The Houses of Parliament by London's Thames Embank-ment, Notre Dame cathedral on its island in the Seine, or Prague Castle above the Vltava river and its bridge of saints, are all given their full grandeur in hierarchical relation to their settings. Even the kind of undifferen-tiated high-rise buildings that have lately acquired the opprobrium of being 'modern' as they passed out of high style take on interest and beauty and their own *genius loci* when they are grouped against a mountain slope, as in Hong Kong or Vancouver.

Theoreticians of landscape aesthetics who try to explain the spirit of place come up against the fact that the word 'spirit' covers what cannot be defined, described, or explained, but can only be evoked. As Louis Armstrong said of jazz music: 'If I've got to explain it to you, you'll never understand it.' Neverthe-less, in all cultures and all times there are talented individuals who manage to implant or evoke the spirit of designed objects and spaces without being able to describe how they do it. Talent is a mysterious capacity that is no easier to define than spirit and is somehow related to it (the word 'genius' applies to both). Indeed, talent can be defined as *the capacity to evoke the spirit in things*. In many professional schools today, 'talent' has become a dirty word, banned as elitist. The word now commonly used to distinguish the work of professional environmental designers is 'skills', a word almost always attached to specialities. The result is a global landscape with less and less of the *genius loci*.

Architectural theorists talk of mass and void, floor plane, walls and ceiling, figure and ground. But, unless we are consciously theorizing, none of us upon entering a room says to ourselves, 'Aha, there is the floor and those are the walls and above it all is the ceiling. I am now entering a void, having passed through an opening in a mass.' We take it in all at once, as a *room*, perceiving a continuous progression from outside to inside, linked as well as separated by a threshold, the perceived forms filtering through our associations with the whole of it and our motives of the moment. Design schools stress process, usually a linear process: data gathering → analysis → design. But creative designers generally acknowledge that design ideas emerge, as if by themselves, seemingly out of nowhere, usually after a hard struggle to harmonize seemingly random and contradictory factors with infinite connections to everything else. Information and idea are rarely separate in a freely functioning mind; they come together reciprocally and continuously, if not always smoothly, as the brain assimilates continually changing experience.

Rudolf Arnheim, in his book *Visual Thinking*, argues that human intelligence is based on the 'spontaneous grasp of pattern', something which computers cannot do. The 'artificial intelligence' of computers, he notes, is a blind and random running through of possible reactions until a successful one is found, a process which a nineteenth-century psychologist took as proof that animals cannot reason (Arnheim 1969: 72). Spontaneous recognition of pattern is not based on vision alone. We do not 'see' only with our eyes, but with all our senses, including the sense of moving through and acting upon our surroundings, combining immediate sensations with stored memories. Pattern recognition is also selective; the wholeness depends as much on what is left out as what is included, sifting experience for those relationships which provide some sort of meaning. The geometrical standardizations of so many bland modern buildings are mindless because they are so predictable. Meaning is found only in the effort to probe mysteries. The Post-Modernists have returned a measure of variety and surprise to building design, but for the most part their eclectic forms are randomly organized, as if randomness and chaos were in and of themselves meaningful. Meaninglessness is a luxury only people who survive entirely on products of machines can contemplate. Few humans really live by machine alone. Historically, architecture has been the most concrete and enduring consequence of this human desire to find meaning in the physical world.

Despite current trends, there are examples of late-twentieth century architecture the world over which continue to reorder space so as to include both human and non-human nature. Among American examples is the corporate headquarters of Deere and Company at Moline, Illinois (see Figure 1). The company is a venerable manufacturer of farm machinery whose management made a symbolic decision to locate its administrative centre out on the Midwest prairie that had brought it into being, rather than in or near a large city. Thus the building began with its environment. Architect Eero Saarinen chose as his basic material exposed steel 'in big forceful, functional shapes' to express the activities of his client (Saarinen 1962), for the first time using Corten steel – originally developed as a purely industrial material – for aesthetic effect. That effect is truly forceful, but as Saarinen achieved it, also magically delicate, almost a filigree. The dark steel spandrels and sunshades are reminiscent of a Japanese wooden pavilion. The structure was welded to its environment with the collaboration of Hideo Sasaki's firm of landscape architects. The result is not a true prairie but a magical place in which the hard steel is joined to plants, water, landform, and Midwestern sky so meaningfully that this private corporate centre has become virtually a public park, a major tourist attraction. The building and outdoor plazas are filled with artworks, including a historic museum of the company's products which displays farm machines as things of beauty as well as utility.

In Boston's Quincy Market, architect Ben Thompson and his colleagues at the Boston Redevelopment Authority, a city agency, rehabilitated largely abandoned dockside warehouses and a dilapidated historic meeting hall (see Figure 2), transforming them into a symbol of the new social class who became known as 'yuppies'. In this case the setting was highly urban, and the result was a triumph of commercial contemporaneity inte-

Figure 1 *John Deere headquarters building, Moline, Illinois.*

Figure 2 *Quincy Market, Boston.* (Photograph: *B. Greenbie*)

rials, which, however 'natural' in appearance, is wholly contrived in arrangement, from the grain of a floor plank to the moss on a stone bridge. Stepping stones, each formal in its square shape but asymmetrically arranged on the ground, lead by the veranda of the pavilion, as if inviting the passer-by to wander from side to side while looking around (see Figure 3). A clearly articulated railing lies restfully above its cleanly spaced posts. The ends of the rails, turned up at the corners, echo the upturned eaves of the projecting, sheltering roof, which in turn echo the branches of surrounding trees. There are continual surprises in every square foot of space, yet one is left with a profound awareness of the unity of all things and a curious feeling of comprehension and stability. But of course it is all in constant change, as living things are, while its *genius loci* has presumably remained constant for nearly a thousand years. One author has defined soul as 'that which persists through change'. In some mysterious way the spirits of the people who build places like this stay with them. The intelligent human energy required to put together all the elements of a landscape like Byodo-In, evoking the spirit of the place and sustaining it through the centuries, is present but not seen. Even crowds of tourists seem to blend in quietly with the landscape.

grated with one of America's most historic townscapes. The method has been copied all over the world since, but nowhere has the architecture of the present been better fitted to that of the past.

More recently, a Post-Modernist masterpiece has appeared on Boston's waterfront at Rowes Wharf. This hotel and office complex picks up architectural elements from the older city and combines them in striking new ways, not all of which are harmonious. But what is remarkable about this place is the way its walled and domed spaces connect with the harbour place. Completing the transit context, Logan Airport is visible from the esplanade, linked to it by a ferry.

Perhaps in no other modern nation is the *genius loci* so pervasive as in Japan. Traditional Japanese gardens are, of course, famous for their harmonious relationship of buildings, plants, water and stone. An exquisite example is the Byodo-In, south of Kyoto, a villa of a feudal lord converted to a Buddhist temple in the eleventh century. The centre-piece is the Phoenix Hall, shaped to resemble that mythical bird, a most appropriate symbol for Japan. The graceful wooden structure seems literally to be growing in its environment. Inside and outside are part of a single composition, a seemingly infinite constellation of living things and inorganic mate-

Figure 3 *Pavilion veranda, Byodo-In, Kyoto.*

Figure 4 *Shinjuku, Tokyo.*

However, the striking thing about present-day Japan is that so much integration is to be found in its exceedingly advanced, high-tech, industrial and commercial cities (see Figure 4). To talk of harmony and integration regarding a metropolis like Tokyo may seem surprising to the casual visitor, even absurd. But there is much more order there than meets the unperceptive foreign eye. As a city, Tokyo seems to have no boundaries at all, but spreads out into a mosaic of districts and suburbs, contained only on the east by Tokyo Bay and spreading otherwise towards the distant mountains. But out of sight, behind fences, under grey tile roofs, as well as in the side streets off the main centres, are firmly bounded cultural territories in which not only the private life, but also much of the richly ritualized public life of local restaurants, drinking places, street festivals, and other entertainments, thrives. On the other hand, modern, commercial Tokyo welcomes the community of strangers with a dazzling variety of hospitalities (at least to those who can afford them) in cosmopolitan spaces which, despite the congestion, are remarkably legible and easy for the visitor to get around in. Japan's other cities are smaller and therefore more comprehensible than Tokyo,

but all its urban centres are as open and accessible as its local territories are enclosed or obscure. The disparate elements of the Japanese landscape seem to fit together, even those that perhaps should not.

The great difference between Japanese modernism in architecture and most of the genre found elsewhere is in the texture of building facades at street level. This texture is created partly by surface decoration – signs, lanterns, sculptured objects, potted plants – but great attention is given to threshold subspaces (see Figure 5). Public places such as restaurants often have gates, or screens, or narrow entrance corridors like those of private houses, but many others have the ubiquitous strips of hanging cloth called *noren*, which are more easily penetrated than a foyer with doors but which still serve to give one the sense of entering another zone. Bounded spaces are everywhere, including many which do not enclose but merely define, such as the black borders of tatami mats. Often restaurants and places for intimate public gathering still have the traditional raised floors like those in homes. Modular design, the essence of International School Modernism, has long been the essence not only of Japanese design, but also of Japanese thought. At the same time, the sometimes jarring, but nevertheless curiously harmonic, juxtaposition of contrasting elements which is also part Japanese design tradition fits in with the return to decoration which characterizes the best of Western Post-Modernism.

What is needed by all nations now is a new profession which will have as its central mission the construction of regionally diverse but interestingly harmonious habitats for human beings under the conditions of post-modern society, integrating technical activities with nature and human nature as well. Landscape architects aspire to do this, but so far have generally failed to live up to their aspirations. Since professions inevitably become specialities that are defined as much by what they are not as what they are, perhaps we need not another profession as such, but rather a way of looking at the world which can be adopted by all the environmental arts. Architect Philip Thiel has coined the word 'envirotecture' for this purpose but it is clumsy on the tongue. An alternative might be 'habitecture'. Whatever it is called, this outlook should redefine the nature of architecture as the conscious harmonizing of the human habitat in all its organic and inorganic aspects.

Figure 5 *Street scene, Kyoto.*

REFERENCES

Arnheim, R. (1969) *Visual Thinking*, Berkeley: University of California Press.

Erikson, E.H. (1966) 'Ontogeny of ritualization', in R.M. Lowenstein *et al.* (eds) *Psychoanalysis – A General Psychology: Essays in Honor of Heinz Hoffman*, New York: International Universities Press.

——— (1974) *Dimensions of a New Identity: The 1974 Jefferson*

Lectures in Humanities, New York: W.W. Norton.

Greenbie, B.B. (1981) *Spaces: Dimensions of the Human Landscape*, New Haven: Yale University Press.

—— (1988) *Space and Spirit in Modern Japan*, New Haven: Yale University Press.

Saarinen, A.B. (ed.) (1962) *Saarinen on His Work*, New Haven: Yale University Press.

Toffler, A. (1970) *Future Shock*, New York: Random House.

SECTION 2.3

Response to routes

Buildings and routes are interdependent. All journeys start and finish in places of shelter, normally buildings, and, if they are to be used, all buildings must be accessed.

Routes influence settlement patterns and the disposition of buildings. In cities, towns and villages, routes have their own hierarchies and patterns – grid, linear, radial and so on – which give orienting clues and which prompt the location of major buildings and spaces.

As well as allowing people to move about, routes provide opportunities for people to interact and it is often the provisions for social interaction that give routes a sense of place – so important to urban and building design.

The same is true within buildings, where routes can give a sense of order and clues about expected behaviour – in such respects entrances (zones along routes) are particularly important, prompting as they do ritualized behaviour of many kinds in addition to their basic function, the control of admission.

There are, of course, many examples where routes are the exclusive preserve of a particular kind of movement – expressways for high-speed vehicles, railway tracks, foot-bridges to cross such routes, and vertically segregated traffic systems. Such deliberate provisions invariably work against a sense of place.

Architecture, being three-dimensional, is best and most fully enjoyed dynamically, and routes are important to the prospect of being able to approach, pass, sweep round, over, under and into buildings – a marvellous example being the approach to Le Corbusier's chapel, Notre Dame du Haut, at Ronchamp in the Vosges hills. Because of the climb involved, the chapel, which can be glimpsed from afar, has to be approached gradually, obliquely, with several changes of direction, and the periodic, changing and progressively more informative views of the building induce a heightened sense of anticipation in the visitor.

Movement and circulation systems lie at the heart of city plans and circulation is more often than not the controlling idea in the plan of a building, for example, in Courts of Law where, for obvious reasons, judges, jurors, defendants and general public may well have discrete routes to a common space – the courtroom. Without doubt response to routes is a timeless and universal generator of architectural form and space.

The essays in this section address the several importances of routes from the most general (Patsy Healey and Ali Madani Pour's essay) through issues of nature, capacity and quality (Hartmut Topp and Dietrich Garbrecht) to their ordering significance (Tom Ellis) and, finally, to one leading modern master's philosophical approach (Steven Groák).

B.F.

RECOMMENDED READING

Alexander, C., Ishikawa, S. and Silverstein, M. (1977) *A Pattern Language*, New York: Oxford University Press.

Anderson, S. (ed.) (1978) *On Streets*, Cambridge, Mass.: MIT Press.

Bacon, E.N. (1967) *Design of Cities*, London: Thames & Hudson.

Bednar, M.J. (1990) *Interior Pedestrian Spaces*, London: Batsford.

Cullen, G. (1971) *The Concise Townscape*, London: Architectural Press.

Lewis, D. (ed.) (1969) *The Pedestrian in the City*, London: Elek Books.

Lowe, J.C. and Moryadas, S. (1975) *The Geography of Movement*, Boston: Houghton Miffin.

Lynch, K. (1960) *The Image of the City*, Cambridge, Mass.: MIT Press.

Passini, R. (1992) *Wayfinding in Architecture*, New York: Van Nostrand Reinhold.

Richards, B. (1976) *Moving in Cities*, London: Studio Vista.

—— (1990) *Transport in Cities*, London: Architecture Design & Technology Press.

Tregenza, P. (1976) *The Design of Interior Circulation: People and Buildings*, London: Crosby, Lockwood Staples.

16 Routes and settlement patterns

Patsy Healey and Ali Madani Pour

ROUTES AND SETTLEMENTS

Routes are for people and products on the move. Settlements are where people put down roots and build structures to shelter themselves and their goods. People on the move bring wealth, culture and trade to places. But such movement may also disrupt settlements. Tension between people on the move and people in their settlements – neighbourhoods, towns and cities – is as old as settlement itself.

Routes predate permanent settlements. Early human societies moved around the landscape, using natural features for shelter. Many were nomadic, leaving their mark as tracks on the ground, or in the mind, as myths and travellers' tales. Bruce Chatwin in *The Songlines* (1987) vividly describes the role of Australian ancestor myths as route maps. Settled peoples have commonly felt threatened by the arrival and temporary settlement of nomads. Many modern societies, which have built enormously complex settlements for themselves, still share territory with such 'travellers', whether as survivals from local aborigine societies, or as the 'travelling people' of Europe.

The routes and settlement patterns of one society are commonly layered over those of another. This may happen within a society. Commuters from suburbs to the central business districts of modern cities may peer through train windows at the dwellings of families who may rarely leave their neighbourhood. Some people whose pattern of life is spatially confined may be in this position as the result of poverty, disability, lack of access to transport, or ethnic disadvantage. Others prefer the confined lifestyle of the 'village in the city' (Taylor 1973).

Routes are inherent to settlements, made by and for the circulation of people and goods. As settlement has developed, there has been a complex two-way inter-action between the social dynamic of cities, towns and villages and their internal and external relationships, and the routes which express the physical dimension of these relationships. Some routes have had an extra-ordinary persistence through human history, such as many of Europe's Roman roads and prehistoric tracks. The location of settlements and their internal arrange-ment may be patterned by the influence of these routes for centuries.

Others have been generated by economic and techno-logical change. The new transport needs and possi-bilities of the industrial revolution produced canals and railways. The mobile, globally communicating, late twentieth century has spawned airports, motorways and telecommunication cabling. Once built, these generate possibilities for new locations and forms of settlement. Suburbia is a peculiarly twentieth-century built form, linked to the invention of personalized transport in the form of the automobile.

Patterns of routes thus record the past and help to structure the future. A new route can threaten the economic future of a place, which is why bypasses are often viewed with such hostility by local business interests.

The construction of a major piece of transport infra-structure may transform the pattern of economic opportunities in a place. In Newcastle, the building of high-level bridges above the old quayside which had been the established city centre for centuries drove the location of the city centre to the north, leaving the old centre to decline slowly.

Motorway construction around British cities has had the same effect on many older industrial zones, the traffic from which may now have to pass through congested urban roads to reach the new route network. The provision of modern motorway access routes may be seen as essential, in such circumstances, to regenerate the economic potential of these bypassed locations. This is a critical issue in the regeneration strategies of many older industrial cities at the present time.

But while the economic effects of new transport investments have long been recognized, calculating precise effects is an unreliable business. The range of effects may be complex to unravel and the time-scale over which they are realized means that they may be inextricably mixed with effects caused by other factors, such as trends in economic development.

ROUTES AND TECHNOLOGY

The changing impact of routes on settlement patterns has depended critically on transport technology. New transport forms have allowed settlements to expand outwards and have influenced how this happened.

Technology not only affects the competition between routes and hence the qualities of specific locations, it also influences urban design through the structures needed for routes, their interchanges and their vehicles. Until the nineteenth century, travel technology was rudimentary. The main structures required were bridges and gates. Sea and river travel was the most technically sophisticated, and the changing location of port facilities had a major impact on the growth of many cities.

In the last 150 years, transport innovation has proceeded at an accelerating rate, as we have sought through technology to annihilate space with time, as Karl Marx noted. Networks of roads and motorways are paralleled by canal systems, railway networks, light rail connections, air routes, airports and heliports, and tele-communication networks. These routes pass across, over and under land, constantly reorganizing space through the competitive search for efficiencies in travel time and packaging. For example, the advent of containers, and the large lorries and ships needed to carry them, has required the relocation of port facilities, producing new nodal points in the transport network as road and rail traffic converges at container depots. Large articulated lorries have in turn had destructive effects on the urban fabric as they rumble through cities, towns and villages (Figure 1).

In the search for time savings, not only have new forms of transport been invented, there has also been a parallel search for ways of separating fast traffic from local traffic, and to cut down the delay inherent in the dense structures of complex settlements. Railways, canals, motorways, tunnels and overpasses are all examples of the attempt to separate out fast 'through' traffic from local traffic, although all too often the 'through route' of one age has become the local route of another.

With the invention of air travel, another solution has been provided, which brings airspace into use, as well as land and sea. The critical structures are then airports, although 'noise shadows' now have an important effect on the areas around airports as air traffic has grown and citizens have become less tolerant of environmental pollutions. These 'shadows' then affect the pattern of

settlements, as property values change to reflect them and public policy guides noise-sensitive activities away from them.

The transmission of 'knowledge' has similarly sought to 'escape' the need for people and goods to travel over the land surface. Such transmission originally required people to meet, or to carry documents to each other via mail services. Computerized telephone technology has shrunk the physical unit of transmission to minute proportions. It was once thought that this technology would finally liberate society from spatial constraints as it would be universally available. It would, in effect 'deconstruct' spatial patterns. It now appears that it is instead constructing new patterns, focused on tele-communication nodes. Schemes for 'Teleports' are innovations of the 1980s which seek to build on this advantage.

What is interesting about this 'knowledge tech-nology' is that its routes are minimal space consumers and, once installed, are largely invisible. Its major archi-tecture impact is in the design and organization of space within buildings. In this, information technology par-allels another major transport innovation of the modern period, the elevator. This transformed routes from the street into the building and had a massive effect on settlement patterns by allowing increases in the density of activity, in city centres in particular, while increasing space standards. The Chicago shoreline was the first result of the architecture this produced.

ROUTES AND INTERNAL SETTLEMENT PATTERNS

Changing transport technology has thus been a constant challenge to the spatial organization of settlements. The elevator may have allowed increasing densities in urban cores, but road and rail developments have allowed cities to explode outwards. The pattern of the pre-industrial city was built around horse-power. The typical European city was focused around its central markets, business district and administrative offices, with deve-lopment radiating outwards along the main routes into the central zone. Economic activity and property values were strongly concentrated in the central core of the city.

The automobile city, symbolized by the expansion of Los Angeles, broke away from this, producing an environment where economic activity could be much more evenly spread across the city, because people and businesses could move freely around the network. There are, nevertheless, capacity constraints to this pattern, as Los Angeles has now discovered. But the automobile has allowed lower density neighbourhoods to proliferate around cities, and has enabled the development of 'suburbia' or 'commuterland', separating where people live from where they work. It has also enabled people to segregate themselves from each other, with the ghettos of the pre-industrial city subtly reappearing in the class

Figure 1 *Modern traffic navigates a medieval street in the City of London.* (Source: *Lloyd 1984*)

and ethnic differentiations of housing markets. Transport innovation has not of course by itself caused what American urbanologists refer to as 'white flight' to the suburbs. But it has enabled this.

American cities have tended to sprawl progressively outwards from their cores. In Europe, the pressure for decentralization has encouraged expansion over much denser landscapes of existing settlements and routes, enabled by motorway networks. As people have come to value rural environments for their space and landscape, and as infrastructure constraints in rural areas have been overcome, a new sort of settlement structure can now be identified, a sort of 'loose-knit' or dispersed pattern of settlement in an urban region. Individual settlements no longer perform a clear role within a spatial hierarchy of settlements, or of neighbourhoods, within a city. Rather, social, economic and cultural networks within an urban region are dispersed spatially, with a factory in one place obtaining its workers and supplies from many other places, and distributing along yet further networks. This reflects the dissociation between social and spatial networks. Places and routes thus become locales for a range of activities which may have little connection with each other. 'Community' and 'place' are thus more dissociated than ever. In this context, routes within settlements may become critical issues should the various activities come into conflict with each other.

Despite all the transport innovations which reduce the constraint of space, routes can still make or break the value of locations within settlements. Site values for industrial and commercial activities are critically affected by location with respect to access to the transport routes needed for their inputs and outputs. Equally, site values may be blighted by traffic congestion and noise, the physical structure of a flyover, or the impossibility of access due to some gyratory road system impenetrable to pedestrian office workers.

ROUTES AND PLANNING

Faced with these complex relationships, a critical issue in settlement planning has been the connections between land use and transport. Planners initially thought of these primarily in physical terms. This was replaced by a more sensitive appreciation of the nature of the activities which generate ways of using sites, and their respective transport needs. In the immediate post-war period in Britain, the focus was on physical structure. In Abercrombie's pioneering plan for Greater London, a central issue was how to equip the expanding metropolis with a road structure to take the growth in road traffic. Abercrombie's plan in effect sought to maintain the established activity patterns of London and improve economic efficiency and the quality of life by decentralizing high-density development in the centre, limiting further expansion by a 'green belt', and overlaying a series of ring roads to take the pressure off

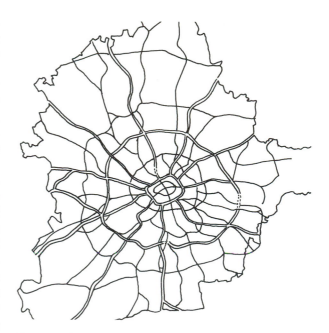

Figure 2 *Abercrombie's Greater London plan.*

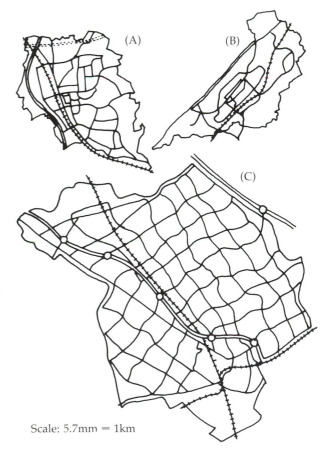

Scale: 5.7mm = 1km

Figure 3 *Three approaches to transport patterns in the post-war British new towns: (a) Stevenage, 1940s; (b) Cumbernauld, 1950s; (c) Milton Keynes, 1960s. (Source: (a) and (b): Osborn and Whittick 1963; (c) Milton Keynes Development Corporation (1970))*

London's main radial arteries (Figure 2).

The post-war British new town programme also initially promoted urban structures which reflected the traditional radial route patterns of British cities.

As it became evident that road traffic could be increasingly dangerous and polluting, solutions which separated cars from people more clearly were developed, as in the linear structure for Cumbernauld new town, with its multi-level central area. Another alternative was to spread activities out in a network of neighbourhoods, linked to an expandable, grid-shaped road network. This pattern underpinned the spatial structure of Milton Keynes new town, and took Los Angeles as its model (Figure 3).

Perhaps more important than this preoccupation with road patterns in the overall urban structure from the 1960s onwards has been the struggle to safeguard the environmental qualities of places as living and working environments which provide a human scale, and which are pollution-free and safe from the threat of the steadily increasing scale of movement in and around settlements, and the increasing size of transport structures and vehicles. This was the prime objective of Colin Buchanan's famous report, *Traffic in Towns*, produced in 1963. At the level of the city, this effort has produced the urban motorway schemes which gouged their way through and around city centres in an attempt to remove road traffic from places where people congregated as pedestrians.

To complement this, city planners and engineers have greatly contributed to environmental quality by slowly piecing together pedestrianization schemes, inserting walkways and bicycle tracks through the urban fabric, and separating cars and lorries from people through careful traffic management.

More ambitiously, planners have also sought to realize Buchanan's ideas of residential neighbourhoods segregated from through traffic. But to achieve this in many existing cities requires substantial resources and careful traffic management. Nevertheless, many cities have managed a great deal through closing 'rat-runs' which had been used as short cuts by through traffic, or by inserting 'traffic calming' devices to slow down vehicles. Such devices are now widespread in towns and cities in many countries.

Within residential areas, early neighbourhood design sought to cope with the car by segregating it from pedestrians and play areas. The classic approach to this was the Radburn layout. Cars were channelled along distributor roads into short culs-de-sac and the family garage. The house then opened on its other side on to an open space dedicated to pedestrians and cyclists. But typically, children have played in the streets. Where security is a problem, the Radburn layout could be threatening as it produced two possible ways of entering someone's property. More recently, urban designers have pioneered a multi-functional approach to residen-

tial street spaces, merging private drives into pavements and streets to create open spaces which, by their design, guide and slow down the access traffic of the neighbourhood.

Quality of life with respect to routes and transport is, however, not only about safety and reducing the pollution of traffic. It is also about having access to transport when needed. Much of the effort of transport planners in the 1960s and 1970s in Britain was devoted to equipping cities to accommodate the needs of car-users and of firms transporting goods by lorry. Yet many people, then and now, have only limited access to cars and are dependent on public transport. This is particularly so for poorer people, the elderly, the disabled, children, and women, who still lose out in the 'one-car' household. Where the emphasis in transport planning is on road transport, as it has been in Britain for a long time, these groups may find themselves increasingly disadvantaged. Where public transport is given more emphasis, their needs may be recognized not only with respect to the availability of routes in relation to where they live, but in the design of vehicles, and the entry and exit points to them.

ROUTES AND TOWNSCAPE

Routes not only contribute to structuring settlement patterns, distributing transport opportunities and creating or destroying the economic value of sites. They also create spaces and produce architecture. They are thus critical elements in the urban fabric. Stations and termini, places for starting and ending journeys, or transferring between forms of transport, are also important commercial zones and social gathering places. Streets have always been places of meeting, used for processions and street parties, as well as daily traffic. In high-density cities, they may provide highly valued open spaces for families with very little personal space in the home.

The battle for control over street or 'station' space may often become a major issue in city planning. Segregating activities may not always be the answer, as the multiple use of street space may contribute to the ambience which everyone values. It may also help to make streets and pathways feel safe to those who use them. It is at this level that the qualities of urban design are of such importance. It is the little things, the alignment of pavements, the positioning of landscaping and of sitting places, and the alignment of buildings to streets, which may enable or destroy the potential role of streets as open space, and the extent to which the street experience conveys a sense of threat or safety to passers-by.

Finally, the architecture of transport can itself become a major feature of the urban environment. Nineteenth-century railway builders understood the importance of grandly designed stations in attracting people to use the railways. Chicago's loop or Hong Kong's carefully nego-tiated walkway systems are certainly dominant features of the urban landscape, if aesthetically jarring. Some places are fortunate in possessing beautiful bridges and viaducts.

Transport innovations, because they often require vast reorganization of the urban fabric, are increasingly seen as a destructive force. Yet they can equally be seen as a creative force. To realize this, however, requires great sensitivity to the detailed impacts of a transport structure on the places through which it passes.

ROUTES IN THE FUTURE

New transport technologies and economic change seem likely to continue reorganizing settlement patterns into the future. As we try to reduce the pollution from motor vehicles and realize that more road building leads to more traffic congestion rather than relieving it, attention is turning more vigorously to new public transport systems, with major technological innovations in high-speed trains and light rail systems. As our urban space becomes increasingly crowded, technological innovation may be expected to speed up and ease congestion in air travel. It is still unclear where the telecommunications revolution will lead.

But technological development and new economic priorities are unlikely to remove some of the major dilemmas embodied in the relationship between routes and settlements patterns.

Should new routes be encouraged to sustain and reproduce existing settlement patterns, or should they be allowed to generate new opportunities? This is a critical issue in all countries whose settlement structure and economic development is such that present patterns are likely to be around for a very long time. In Britain, at the intra-regional scale, it means addressing the contra-diction between green-belt policies designed to contain urban development in established settlements, and a motorway building programme which has created major development opportunities outside existing settlements.

How are the benefits of the new transport technology to be combined with the continuing assertion of a human scale as a context for social and economic activity? This means that people still want the chance to meet, talk, walk around and organize parties and pro-cessions even while they are also travelling. The transit lounge at Dubai Airport, where tired and displaced passengers pause for an hour or so on intercontinental flights, or *en route* to a more buoyant labour market than can be found in their home countries, is a sad contrast to the social world of Chaucer's *Canterbury Tales* or the adventure of a journey on the Trans-Siberian railway.

One solution is to encourage people to travel less. Some have thought that the telecommunications revol-ution would allow more people to work from home and reduce commuting. This may happen on a small scale, but such hopes ignore people's desire for social contact, and enjoyment of travel. Work is not just about producing things, nor is travel just about getting to places. It is also about social relationships and personal enjoyment. For many people, work is a way of escaping or at least taking a break from the demands of family relationships. Another solution is to contain the strong demand for private travel, where individuals and family groups sustain their personal space and carry their goods in the 'car capsule'. Within the car, they can sustain a human scale under their own control. Yet the congestion and pollution costs this creates for all of us are increasingly intolerable. Can a form of public trans-port be recreated which is convenient, well-designed and consumer-friendly? Perhaps the major challenge for the future is to invent and manage forms of public transport which people will enjoy using. How could this relate to the diversity of existing settlement patterns, and what patterns might it tend to produce?

REFERENCES

Abercrombie, P. (1945) *Greater London Plan*, London: HMSO.

Buchanan, C. (1963) *Traffic in Towns*, Ministry of Transport, London: HMSO.

Chatwin, B. (1987) *The Songlines*, London: Picador.

Lloyd, D. (1984) *The Making of English Towns*, London: Victor Gollancz.

Mayer, H. and Wade, R. (1969) *Chicago: Growth of a Metropolis*, Chicago and London: University of Chicago Press.

Milton Keynes Development Corporation (1970) *The Plan for Milton Keynes*, Vol. 1, Milton Keynes.

Osborn, F. and Whittick, A. (1963) *The New Towns, the Answer to Megalopolis*, London: Leonard Hill.

Taylor, N. (1973) *The Village in the City*, London: Temple Smith.

17 Transport in cities

Hartmut H. Topp

Feet, bicycles, buses and rail systems, private cars, delivery vans and trucks are all part of the backbone of urban transport. They differ in speed and range as well as in danger potential, availability and convenience, experience quality, expenditure, space requirement and environmental impact, in the ability to integrate into town – and landscape and in their compatibility with other street uses.

The car determines the pace and scale of a city. Commuter trips of over 30 to 50 km. (20 to 30 ml.) are commonplace with people living in the country and working in the city, made possible because of the car. The price for this is high: roughly 70 per cent of all traffic accidents in what was West Germany occur within towns and villages, with about 300,000 people injured and about 3,000 killed annually. Approximately 30 per cent of the urban population suffers noise pollution beyond any acceptable limits. Dense and fast car traffic restricts the freedom of mobility of pedestrians and cyclists, and the one-sided adjustment of the streetscape to private cars has resulted in a serious loss of the streetscape's character.

In spite of that, we want to live with the car, even in the city. This means that the car must be integrated into the town – and landscape, and that traffic must be made safer and more compatible with urban life. Therefore, the target of municipal traffic planning must be the reduction of car traffic in volume, in speed, and in its dominance in the street. The approach to this lies on three levels:

- Level 1: Freezing the total amount of traffic by developing a land-use structure of short distances.
- Level 2: Shifting traffic to transport modes which preserve the environment and save energy.
- Level 3: Urban compatible layout of the traffic systems themselves.

First, the possibility of freezing or even reducing the total amount of traffic through promotion of a settlement structure of short distances is rather limited. But despite this limitation, approaches to reduced traffic can lie in the co-ordination and mixture of land uses, in securing the existence of central urban residential and mixed areas, and in increasing the provision of schools, shops and services within walking distance.

Second, shift traffic to environment-preserving and energy-saving modes of transportation by following ecological priorities: pedestrians and bicycles, public transport, car pools, and, last of all, individual drivers. This main approach should consist of parking strategies

and promotion of urban public transport and pedestrian and bicycle traffic.

Third, any urban-compatible layout of the traffic systems themselves must involve vehicles which produce less pollution and noise, with environment- and town-compatible arrangements and design of traffic routes, and, moreover, environmentally favourable traffic regulations which may, for example, aim at the stabilization of car traffic with neighbourhood-compatible speeds.

The integration of traffic into the townscape is not solely the task of the cities. The federal and state governments are, in a legal and financial sense, equally responsible. The idea of responsibility also applies to the car industry as far as vehicle anti-pollution equipment and noise reduction are concerned. Responsibility also applies to each one of us, in general in our choice of lifestyle, and in particular in our modal choice of transport, and in our own behaviour as car drivers.

Possibilities of transferring car users to other modes of transport are judged differently. They really differ according to each city's specific situation. The possibilities are probably, to a large extent, already depleted in cities where car trips make up 30 to 35 per cent of all journeys (a relatively small percentage), as in the cities of Groningen, Delft, Uppsala or Göttingen (Apel 1984). In many German cities of comparable size, the car's share of all journeys is considerably higher, with 45 to 50

Table 1 Modal split of inhabitants in medium-sized European cities, without inbound commuters

City Population	Bicycle On foot (%)	Public transit (%)	Car Motorcycle (%)
Groningen 160,000 (1982)	60	8	32
Uppsala 140,000 (1981)	48	17	35
Göttingen 130,000 (1982)	50	13	37
Erlangen 100,000 (1985)	50	12	39
Medium-sized centres in Germany (1982)	42	10	48
Kaiserslautern 106,000 (1985)	36	14	50

Sources: Apel 1984; Brög 1986

per cent; and in American cities much higher still. Also, considering different conditions of settlement structure, catchment area and topography, the range of possible changes becomes obvious (see Table 1).

Let us take the example of Kaiserslautern which today has about 50 per cent car traffic. Kaiserslautern is a town of about 100,000 inhabitants with a large rural catchment area. Motor ownership is about 480 cars per 1,000 inhabitants. A public transport study for Kaiserslautern was based on two scenarios:

1 'Status quo'. This means no changes in the transport policy.
2 'Changes'. This deals with the redistribution of traffic as a result of a new transport policy.

Model calculations show that today's 50 per cent car traffic could be reduced to 44 per cent by pursuing the 'Changes' scenario, through promotion of bicycle traffic and through a considerable increase in the frequency of service of the buslines, in conjunction with park-and-ride services and a restrictive parking policy. In the 'Status quo' scenario, with no change in urban traffic policies, an increase to 53 per cent car traffic could be expected. A comparison of both scenarios results in a 21 per cent difference in the number of car trips and, more important to the stress on a city, a difference of 13 per cent in car kilometres (Retzko & Topp 1986). The different contrasts between numbers of trips and kilometres result from the different trip lengths of bicycle, car and bus traffic (see Table 2).

Table 2 Kaiserslautern, Germany: different development of traffic due to different urban traffic policies (inhabitants' journeys only)

	Scenario 1 'Status-Quo'	Scenario 2 'Changes'	Scenario 2 versus Scenario 1 for 1995
	1995 versus 1985 (%)	(%)	(%)
Public transit	− 8	+ 21	+ 31.5
Car journeys	+ 6	− 16.5	− 21
Car kilometres	c. + 3	c. − 10	c. − 13

What can be learned from this example is that the amount of car traffic in a town is not a given technical figure: it can be shaped through municipal traffic policy over a relatively wide range.

If, for reasons of town and social compatibility, redistribution of traffic from the car to public transport is seriously and increasingly desired, then it is not enough to increase the frequency of public transport, synchronize traffic signals to accommodate public transport, and use special bus lanes; these changes must be accompanied by area-wide parking restrictions. Merely increasing the supply of public transport will not overcome the advantages of the private car, but, certainly, a good supply of public transport is a prerequisite of reducing car traffic.

A greater frequency of service naturally raises the operating costs of public transport; however, a part of these increased costs can be defrayed through the synchronization of traffic lights along bus routes and bus lanes to accommodate public transport by shortening the travel time. The increased operating costs are offset by the greater income from the increased patronage. Even if the increase of public transport is not economic in itself, it is sensible from the viewpoint of social economy by considering the effect of the reduced social costs resulting from reduced car traffic. In most countries the hidden subsidies for private car traffic are higher than the paid subsidies for public transport because of the only partially paid environmental impacts and accident burdens of private car traffic.

The success of transferable monthly tickets for public transport in several towns in Switzerland and Germany has shown, contrary to former beliefs, that tariff policies in connection with the advertisement and 'image' effect lead to distinctly greater demand. These results might also be applied to constructional, layout and operations measures in the direction of the general enhancement of urban public transport. This includes shape and colour, visual understanding of public transport in the street picture, furnishings at the stops, and priority of buses, rail traffic and pedestrians over car traffic at stops – in short, the visual appearance of the importance of public transport in the city.

The second lever to change the competition between private car traffic and urban public transport in favour of public transport requires restrictions of car traffic. Here, parking restrictions are better than restrictions to the flow of car traffic. As parking restrictions do not cause obstructions to traffic flow, they are better ecologically as far as exhaust, petrol consumption, noise, stress and danger are concerned.

In contrast to restrictions of traffic flow, parking restrictions are selectively applied. This means that easy accessibility by car for residents, customers, visitors and business traffic is compatible with, and even results from, restrictions towards employees for whom the change to public transport and park-and-ride causes the least problems.

Area-wide parking concepts with complete parking control aimed at modal-split alterations see parking space as a steering factor of municipal transport policy, in contrast to the nowadays common laissez-faire outside the city centres.

The shift of car traffic to other modes of transport was, for planners, politicians and citizens, overshadowed for a long time by the locational shift of car traffic to efficient main thoroughfares. Since Buchanan's authoritative publication Traffic in Towns (1963), the organiza-

Figure 1 *Perfectionism in a side street: the pavement alteration cannot be derived from buildings and streetscape.*

tion of urban road networks has seen the concentration of car traffic on main roads and the relief and reduction of traffic in the adjacent residential areas (see Figures 1 and 2).

Two coincidentally incompatible demands for reduction of car traffic on the one hand and ease of flow on the other were locationally separated and perfected – this applies to many measures of traffic reduction as well as to the one-sided, car-traffic oriented urban structural devastation of many main thoroughfares.

The concentration concept is based on two fundamental ideas, the first being the objectively slight increase of environmental stress – especially of noise level – by the relatively slight increase in traffic volume, when the basic volume is high anyway. The second basic idea is in many cases a false premise: that a main street should be changed into a main thoroughfare through suggested land-use changes along the street. This means that flats should become offices or should be oriented away from the street to the back of the building. In fact, it is along such streets that we often find the urgently needed cheaper flats (for low-income people in particular).

Figure 2 *Perfectionism in an arterial street: pedestrians are supposed to use the footbridge from where the photograph was taken.*

The concept of concentration of traffic on main thoroughfares is in conflict with two facts:

1   Many main thoroughfares with high volumes of traffic are also main residential or shopping streets.
2   The quality of the surrounding area of many of these streets is already unbearable, even without the additional stress.

Is this the break-down of the concentration concept, since it makes better what was already good, makes quieter what was already quiet and makes worse what was already bad? Would the alternative be equal noise for all, with traffic pushed into the residential areas? Certainly not. But what we urgently need is a further development of the concentration concept in a manner whereby we still try to make the different street functions at least somewhat more compatible, preferably on main roads with dense traffic, where a reduction of traffic volume can hardly be achieved. Even where the traffic volume cannot be changed in the near future, it is possible in many cases to lessen the threat to the residents and passers-by, through compensatory measures such as improving the streetscape by planting trees, and reducing the speeds (see Figure 3). Such measures effect psychological improvement, in the sense of reducing stress, as much as a real, objective improvement. Consequently, slower car traffic with equal or slightly higher density is safer for the use of the street by pedestrians and bicycle riders. Thus a wider pavement allows more non-traffic usage than a narrow pavement; streets become safer for pedestrians and bicycle riders by helping them to cross the street with traffic islands and centre strips; and a street planted with trees appears friendlier, more pleasant, and, at the same time, improves the climate.

Because there is no meaningful alternative in respect of a moderate concentration of car traffic on urban arterial roads, some sort of social justice can only be achieved if the expenditures for traffic calming and streetscaping are not used – as today is most common – for accumulating the advantages in the low-traffic side streets, but are aimed at a partial balance and compensation for the strains caused by car traffic in the arterial streets. Compensatory measures would include:

1   improving the streetscape;
2   planting trees;
3   slowing down car traffic;
4   broadening the pavement;
5   installing traffic islands and centre strips for easier street crossing.

Further concentration and traffic separation in pedestrian zones at one extreme and car-oriented, ring, radial and relief roads with subways for pedestrians at the other should be replaced by an 'integrating' approach of town-compatible car traffic.

Among all compensatory measures, speed reduction

Present state:

Planned:

Figure 3 *Proposals for an arterial street in Berlin with heavy traffic and a large amount of business and residential usage. The photograph and illustration at the top show the present state. After a long dispute the concept of Planwerk's research project (below left) will be realized. The Traffic Authorities' counter-proposal (below right) was finally rejected.* (Source: *Schilcher* et al. *1988*)

has a key function. Car traffic in towns is usually too fast – on feeder streets as well as on arterial streets. High speed ranks first as a cause of accidents. Speed restrains the freedom of pedestrians and the access functions of a street, more than traffic volume.

A reduction of speeds on arterial streets from the presently common 65 to 70 k.p.h. (40 to 45 m.p.h.) to the legal speed of 50 k.p.h. (30 m.p.h.) would already cause a noticeable steadying of the traffic flow, leading to a noise-level reduction of approximately 3 dB(A) – roughly the noise-level reduction that would be achieved by halving the traffic volume. Apart from this a considerable reduction in injuries and fatalities (especially of pedestrians and cyclists) could be achieved since about 80 per cent of these accidents within built-up areas occur in arterial streets.

Beyond the arterial street network, speeds should not exceed 30 k.p.h. (20 m.p.h.), as can be easily deduced from the typical conflict between a child entering the carriageway from behind a parked car and the car driver who needs about 16m. (53ft.) to stop from 30 k.p.h. –

even under favourable conditions. (The stopping distance from 50 k.p.h. is about 33m. (108ft.).) In some cases – near schools, kindergartens and playgrounds – even 30 k.p.h. is too fast.

During the last five years 'tempo 30-zones' have been applied very successfully in German cities, with injury reductions varying between 27 per cent in Hamburg and 44 per cent in Heidelberg, though the speed limits of 30 k.p.h. were only partially observed. It is typical for most measures aimed at traffic taming that the total amount of accidents is not, or is only slightly, decreased, but the accidents are usually less severe.

The second most remarkable benefit of 'tempo 30' compared with 'tempo 50' is a noise reduction between 3 and 5 dB(A). And even the controversy over the effect of a speed limit of 30 k.p.h. on the exhaust of cars could be clarified by tests in Buxtehude – a medium-sized town in northern Germany: compared to 50 k.p.h., a speed limit of 30 k.p.h. results in distinctly lower pollution levels (see Figure 4). The explanation for this finding lies in the reduced amount of acceleration and the altogether

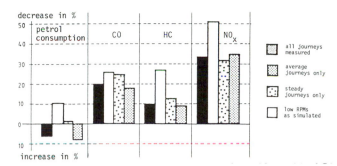

Figure 4 *Reduction of pollution with a speed limit of 30 k.p.h. (20 m.p.h.) compared to 50 k.p.h. (30 m.p.h.). (Source: Holzmann 1988)*

smoother flow of traffic with a reduced target speed.

From these results, the conclusion for the organization of the urban street network is the necessity of a general speed limit of 30 k.p.h. combined with a right-before-left priority (left-before-right in countries which drive on the left), with the exception of arterial streets, which should have a speed limit of 50 k.p.h. (or 40 k.p.h. (25 m.p.h.) within the inner city) combined with priority or traffic lights at junctions.

The choice of driving speed is influenced by many factors: the characteristics of the road; the surroundings of the road; the conditions of the traffic, the driver and the vehicles; the traffic regulations and their degree of enforcement; and many other things.

At present, the main starting point for reducing speed is the street: through speed bumps, narrower areas (chicanes), gates, and alterations of the carriageway within the street, and by right-before-left priority regulations. All will make car drivers drive more slowly. All function to some extent. However, it is totally impossible from an economic and urban design point of view to cover completely our towns with these constructional measures for speed reduction. Some of the increasingly popular and generally universally applied constructional measures (such as barriers and alterations) are often totally unacceptable in a historic street scene, and also questionable, from a town planning viewpoint, for less sensitive street areas (see Figure 1).

Therefore, the question arises whether it would make sense to redesign the streets in those areas where some car drivers behave to social detriment in such a way that fast drivers must drive more slowly. Or, would it not be more correct to begin with the car driver as cause instead of the street, and try to achieve driving compatible with a given situation through education and publicity, and better regulations and enforcement?

'The freedom with which a person can walk about and look around is a very useful guide to the civilised quality of an urban area' (Buchanan *et al.* 1963: 40). This basic issue is to be applied not only to residential areas, pedestrian zones or environmental zones between arterial streets, but to the city as a whole, to the continuum of the urban network of streets, places, paths, and to the continuum of open spaces.

Lower driving speeds – as discussed – are an indispensable prerequisite to achieving the freedom of walking and looking around. But lower speeds alone do not suffice. A second basic principle suggests that pedestrians and cyclists belong to the normal level, to the natural ground of the city. This sounds like a self-evident claim, but the reality of our towns is far away from this.

In most European cities – especially in western Germany, the Netherlands and the Scandinavian countries, but in other countries as well – we find ambitious, well-designed pedestrian zones in city centres. In many cases former arterial roads with high loads of car traffic were converted into pedestrian zones. Today, strolling around in the Zeil of Frankfurt am Main, one can hardly imagine that this main shopping street carried about 35,000 cars per day. And interestingly enough – contrary to traffic forecasts – only about one half of this traffic was shifted to neighbouring streets; the other half could not be detected in other parts of the road network. This is a common experience also found in other cities.

Without any doubt pedestrian zones in city centres are a convincing success on the way to liveable cities, and they remarkably ushered in a new thinking about priorities in traffic management. But one should not forget that most pedestrian zones, roofed malls and passages are all too often isolated islands surrounded by ugly inner-city rings with heavy car traffic which form barriers for pedestrians and cyclists (see Figure 2).

In many such cases pedestrians are encouraged to use subways or – more often in American cities – skyways. Even if subways are well equipped with elevators, they run contrary to the natural behaviour of people (see Figure 5). Only in special cases – with 'natural' grade separation which avoids 'steps down/steps up', with shops and kiosks accompanied by high pedestrian density – might subways be acceptable or even comfortable. Most subways are far away from such ideal

Figure 5 *Subways are usually alien to the natural behaviour of people.*

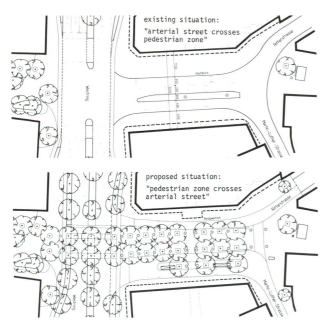

existing situation:
"arterial street crosses
pedestrian zone"

proposed situation:
"pedestrian zone crosses
arterial street"

Figure 6 *'Pedestrian zone crosses arterial street (combined with bus station)' instead of 'arterial street crosses pedestrian zone', Hamm, Germany.* (Source: *Retzko & Top 1987*)

standards; usually they are chilly and uninviting, with marks of vandalism inducing a feeling of danger. Subways of this type are against the nature of people and against the tradition of cities.

Having the right priorities in mind – pedestrians produce urbanity – in most cases amenable at-grade solutions for pedestrian crossings (i.e. crossings at the same level) are obtainable. In Hamm, for example, a medium-sized city in Germany, the pedestrian zone was divided into two parts by an arterial street and a central bus station (Figure 6). Without changing the traffic functions – neither that of car traffic in the arterial street nor that of the central bus station – a new quality of streetscape and environmental amenity for pedestrians was achieved while the trees hide the bad architecture that dominates the situation.

Ideas and examples could be continued endlessly. Transport in cities is such a broad subject, with very different situations from city to city in developed and developing countries, that a comprehensive discussion of all its aspects needs a book of its own, therefore this essay is limited to basic issues concerning medium-sized and big cities in highly motorized countries. The central plea focuses on urban compatibility of car traffic; that means less car traffic at lower speeds, resulting in less dominance of car traffic over other urban values.

REFERENCES

Apel, D. (1984) *Umverteilung des städtischen Personenverkehrs – Aus- und inländische Erfahrungen mit einer stadtverträglicheren Verkehrsplanung*, Berlin: Deutsches Institut für Urbanistik.

Brög, W. (1985) *Changes in Transport. Users' Motivation for Modal Choice: Passenger Transport – The Situation of the Federal Republic of Germany*, Paris: ECMT Publication: 68.

Buchanan, C. *et al.* (1963) *Traffic in Towns – A Study of the Long Term Problems of Traffic in Urban Areas* (The Buchanan Report), London: HMSO.

Holzmann, E. (1988) 'Flächenhafte Verkehrsberuhigung in Buxtehude: Auswirkungen der Maßhahmen zu Tempo 30 auf die Umweltsituation', in BfLR (ed.) *4. Kolloquium zum Forschungsvorhaben 'Flächenhafte Verkehrsberuhigung' – Ergebnisse aus drei Modellstädten*, Buxtehude/Bonn: Bundesforschungsanstalt für Landeskunde und Raumordnung, pp. 128–42.

Retzko & Topp (1986) *Neuordnung des Busverkehrs in Kaiserslautern*, Darmstadt/Düsseldorf: Planungsbüro Retzko & Topp.

———— (1987) *Verkehrskonzept und Platzgestaltung Westentor in Hamm*, Darmstadt/Düsseldorf: Planungsbüro Retzko & Topp.

Schilcher, J., Guggenthaler, H. and Tibbe, H. (1988) 'Flächenhafte Verkehrsberuhigung – Ergebnisse aus Berlin-Moabit/ Darstellung der Maßnahmen', in BfLR (ed.) *4. Kolloquium zum Forschungsvorhaben 'Flächenhafte Verkehrsberuhigung' – Ergebnsse aus drei Modellstädten*, Buxtehude/Bonn: Bundesforschungsanstalt für Landeskunde und Raumordnung, pp. 251–70.

Topp, H.H. (1987) *Ways to More Comptatible Urban Transportation*, Proceedings of the Seminar 'Transport Policy' at the PTRC Transport and Planning Summer Annual Meeting in Bath, UK.

FURTHER READING

BfLR (1988) *4. Kolloquium zum Forschungsvorhaben 'Flächenhafte Verkehrsberuhigung' – Ergebnisse aus drei Modellstädten*, Buxtehude/Bonn: Bundesforschungsanstalt für Landeskunde und Raumordnung.

Hass-Klau, C. (ed.) (1986) New Ways of Managing Traffic, special issue of *Built Environment* 12 (1/2).

Müller, P. and Topp, H.H. (1986) 'Verkehrsberuhigung durch Straßenumbau: Eine neueu Art der Stadtzerstörung? – Über den Versuch, sozial- und umweltschädliches Verkehrsverhalten mit baulichen Maßhahmen zu kurieren'. *Der Städtetag* 5: 327–30.

Organization for Economic Cooperation and Development (1975) *Better Towns with Less Traffic*, Proceedings of an OECD Conference in Paris.

Topp, H.H. (1987) *Ways to More Comptatible Urban Transportation*, Proceedings of the Seminar 'Transport Policy' at the PTRC Transport and Planning Summer Annual Meeting in Bath, UK.

18 Walkability: a prerequisite for liveable cities

Dietrich Garbrecht

WHAT IS LIVEABILITY?

When we talk about the liveability of a city we mean housing and jobs, retail, educational and leisure facilities, to mention just a few criteria. In the context of this essay, I am concerned with individual and social development, with the autonomy of getting around, with the accessibility and permeability of the urban environment, and with the safety and comfort of movement. I am concerned with transport, with streets and piazzas, with their spatial and architectural quality, and, not least, with beauty.

When we say of a city that it is beautiful, what do we mean, and how do we experience this quality? I suggest we mean the beauty perceived from streets and piazzas, that is, from public space. It is this space I am going to deal with.

LIVEABILITY FOR WHOM?

Liveability for all groups! For children, teenagers, adults, and the elderly. For men and women, for people with a job, for housewives or husbands, for the unemployed, for the healthy and the sick or the disabled, for people who have access to a car and for those who have not.

However, cities and metropolitan areas in industrialized countries today are much more liveable for the motorized middle- and upper-class professionals than for any other group of the population. Involved, then, are issues of equality, and of power.

But, are we not all car drivers? No! About half the population does not have access to a car, which means it depends on walking, or cycling or on public transport. We all walk a lot; even car drivers walk.

LIVEABILITY AND WALKABILITY

There are different types of pedestrian journeys, for example from the home to the bus stop, or from the parking garage to the office. Then there are 'pure' walks – the child leaves the apartment and walks to the kindergarten (and later walks back), the housewife walks from house to store (and then walks back). In Europe 30 to 40 per cent of all movement in settlements is on foot. If we add all those other walks to this figure (those between home and bus or subway, between school or work and streetcar), the pedestrian share in urban traffic becomes even more impressive. Incidentally, the amount of walking is greater in big cities than in small towns. And in areas with a mix of housing and offices or other work-places, significantly more work trips are entirely by foot than in cases where place of residence and job are separated.

But then walking is not only a means of transport, walking is also fun! In Europe one of the main outdoor leisure time activities, if not the most important, is going for a walk. This is especially true for the elderly. In fact, for many, going for a walk is the only outdoor leisure activity they can still enjoy.

There are extremely few statistics which show how the amount of walking has developed over the years. The little data there are exhibit a decrease over the last thirty years, a decrease of walking of all kinds.

Two points can be made about children and the elderly. We know from developmental psychology that children need to stroll, need to explore and to appropriate the environment in an autonomous way. Also, when children have the opportunity to move safely they will make the environment, be it country, suburb, urban fringe or inner city, their own – playing, and this means walking, within it. Children need to move. Witness any urban space that has been given back to them, be it a street in a residential neighbourhood or a plaza in Barcelona – immediately, they take over, ball playing, skateboarding, bike riding, etc.

The elderly need to walk for other reasons. The older we get, the more dependent we become on walking, and the more our life-space shrinks, not only because of the limitations of walking, but because this limited life-space is even more limited by motorized traffic. Main arterial routes, for instance, turn into real boundaries. Ironically, the more time we have to take advantage of our immediate environment, and to do so on foot, the less safely and securely we can do so.

There are many more reasons why walkability is a prerequisite for liveability. A street and piazza environment that is pleasant to walk in is an environment that makes many other individual and social activities possible. Pedestrian movement is a 'soft' mode of transportation (it has also been called 'autonomous' since it needs so little infrastructure and so few instruments), and has all the ecological arguments going for it – not forgetting that walking is the oldest and most elementary way of getting from one place to another.

We must remember too that in the walkable city we can enjoy architecture. In the walkable city Mary McCarthy is being taken seriously: years ago the writer complained that many of Florence's famous monuments had become literally invisible since there was no spot from which to look at them in safety (McCarthy 1973:

14). In the walkable city her comments must be taken seriously.

The walkable city can be a place truly urbane in character. The rudeness and frequent brutality that go with today's traffic are not inherent in the concept of 'urbanity'. On the contrary, urbane interaction is one characterized by tolerance, politeness and cosmopolitan conviviality.

The walkable city is liveable, the liveable city is walkable. Liveable City and Walkable City – two names for the same place!

Liveable City is not a city without cars. The private automobile is not only comfortable and fun, it is useful and very often indispensable. With respect to liveability, the question is not: cars – yes or no? The question is: how can we use the car in a reasonable way? The issue is the number of cars, and the amount of car driving, and the rules of the game (for instance, speed and priorities whenever other modes of transport are being crossed). The issue is one of a balanced, that is equitable, approach to accessibility.

CRITERIA AND WALKABILITY

Walkable City – isn't it everywhere? Does not almost every town or city have a 'pedestrianized area'? (Pedestrianized, a monster of a word!) What we have are a few streets and piazzas reserved for the pedestrian, islands in a network of public space hostile to the walker. Even Munich's famous downtown streets where the pedestrian reigns supreme are no more than an island within a street network between 3,000 and 4,000 km. in length. (A few years ago in a small town in Italian Liguria I saw a sign which called things by their proper name: *Isola pedonale*, it read – pedestrian island.) Conversely one could even argue that whenever a few streets in a town are being turned over to the walker, this is being done so that at least some streets are friendly to the pedestrian, streets which indicate that, by contrast, the overwhelming majority of streets and piazzas do not treat the walker nicely. But these are not walkable cities.

In Walkable City the network of sidewalks, paths and streets adapted to the needs of the pedestrian is:

1   continuous,
2   ubiquitous,
3   of shortest possible connections,
4   a provider of variety and choice.

Why? Because continuity of movement is one of the pleasures of walking. There are many reasons why Venice is so humane, the ability to walk without being forced to stop not being the least, and remember the continuity we enjoy in cross-country hiking, an experience totally different from the stop/go we suffer in today's cities! Continuity is also a prerequisite for high average walking speeds, and so are short connections.

Ubiquity means networks that span a whole city. Ubiquity and continuity are needed because subjective life-spaces, those parts of the environment that we use regularly, overlap. To this basic fact, area concepts do not correspond; rather, they disadvantage those living near the borders of a residential neighbourhood when it is limited by main arterial routes. For those living near such streets the potential walking life-space is drastically reduced. What of variety and choice? We expect and enjoy them in everyday life. Variety and choice correspond to fundamental psychological needs – we must make them performance criteria of a truly humane network of pedestrian ways. (Again, remember Venice?) All dimensions of the footway network must meet these criteria, not least the surfaces on which we walk. The possibilities for hard surfaces are endless, but there must be soft ones as well.

How can we realize continuous and ubiquitous networks for walking? The basic elements will be existing pavements, adequately adapted – or readapted – to pedestrian use wherever necessary, sidewalks that are carried across carriageways (giving priority to the pedestrian when he or she crosses a street), and streets that are punctuated. Incorporated in the network are malls, mixed-use or space-sharing streets, piazzas and open spaces.

The footway network of Walkable City is both safe and comfortable. Safety applies to the crossing of carriageways as well as to the protection of pavements against the intrusion of car drivers. Montpellier in the south of France is a case in point: in the centre of this old university town virtually all sidewalks are protected by physical means; fines for cars parked on walkways are high.

A comfortable footway network requires adaptation to the needs of the pedestrian. Walking has characteristics that no other transportation mode has. Stop when you feel like it, meet somebody and start a conversation, react spontaneously to stimuli of the environment, daydream, react to thoughts, change speed or direction, sit down, play – all such behaviour is integral to walking, with spontaneity being the most prominent. Furthermore, we do not always walk alone and with empty hands, we often carry bags or an umbrella, push a pram, walk with a friend or in a group – and we need adequate space!

NODES

In Liveable City – just another name for Walkable City – entrances to buildings, or spaces which have high pedestrian frequencies or which are important for the citizens' identity and the city's image, or both, are connected to the network of pedestrian ways. Examples would include entrances of department stores, post offices, schools, sports facilities, concert halls, theatres and museums.

Included in the network are assets such as lines of junction and edges of interest (for example, those which provide views) as well as buildings of remarkable architecture. Also included are the stops and termini of public transportation. In Liveable City an attractive public transit system (to which taxis belong) complements the walkway system: for short distances people walk, for long distances they are driven. Both systems are perfectly integrated ('walk-and ride'). Whenever possible, the nodes where entrances to important activity centres connect with the footway system are made to coincide with the nodes where the footway system connects with public transportation. People living close to a museum can easily walk there; people living further away can conveniently get there by public transportation.

The land use of nodes or interfaces is influenced by public policy. When interface areas are given adequate space, a piazza, tiny as it may be, comes into existence. Interface areas have high priority in terms of comfort and amenity, and design. They are the jewels of Walkable City.

THE OPEN CITY

Pedestrian space in Walkable City is stimulating and complex, reflecting the complexity of the city itself. It is a learning environment for children. However, when walking in this city everyone 'learns' about what the city *is*, about the manifold activities people pursue, and about changes the city undergoes.

Harbours in a sense are such open cities. In Liveable City, regulations and codes are such that many more parts of the city are opened up to the footway system. Harvard University's Carpenter Center for the Visual Arts, designed by Le Corbusier, exemplifies how, by a ramp leading through the building, the passer-by can watch students engaged in visual arts experiments.

In Walkable City not only the present but also the past are made as visible and touchable as possible. And conservation is no issue: many architects, having learnt from collage and mixed-media art, incorporate in a very natural way the remains of buildings into excellent avant-garde designs. All this contributes to a rich walking environment, to a liveable city.

Architecture along the footways is a matter of public concern; so is the footway system itself and so too is city development. Intended changes are exposed, explained and discussed in walkable public space which has become a space of public debate.

Walking in Walkable City is a sensuous pleasure and an intellectual adventure, and the mysteries and miracles of the city can be experienced.

THE NON-WALKING PART OF WALKING

Intrinsic to walking is that it is frequently interrupted,

that it is structured by episodes of associated activities. We stop to stand, to sit down, to lean against something, to lie down. We do so to relax, to take a nap, to put something down (be it to rest, be it to have hands free for something else); we pause from walking to sunbathe, to talk to somebody, to show something to somebody, to watch and to be watched, to read or to eat, and children 'interrupt' a walk to play (in fact, with children walking and playing are interwoven; they are almost identical). Hence, to make Walkable City liveable, standability, sitability, leanability, and playability along the footway network must be ensured.

The myriad secondary activities need not be supported by street furniture added to or put into public space. In Walkable City the supports take the form of small walls, projections, ledges, niches, balustrades, stairs, and ramps. And these are integrated. Integration is achieved by plastic modelling of the ground, of the ground-floor zone of the buildings running along the footway system, and of the edge where building and pavement meet. Two criteria are relevant here, first, integration, and second, polyvalence; this means plastic elements of the walking network being designed in such a way that they may be used for different activities. In this way choice is enhanced, children can play anywhere along the footway system and most special equipment can be dispensed with. To summarize: the open city welcomes people in its open space.

BEAUTY AND BEAUTY

In Walkable City the beauty of the footway system is considered a prime prerequisite of liveability. Take the sequence of spaces: wherever it is without contrast or suspense, the shape of buildings forming the lateral walls of a walking space is changed. Often walking from a street into a piazza lacks excitement because the width of the street was similar to that of the piazza. Usually in such a case, either the whole street was narrowed, or a narrow space was created between street and piazza by enlarging the respective buildings.

Sections of high and low design control alternate. Even in streets, alleys or piazzas of high design control, citizens are being consulted. In sections of low or zero design control, popular taste (which really is also a definition of beauty by other than expert or elitist standards) may manifest itself.

In Walkable City there is space to look at buildings. And pedestrians, as a consequence of walking speed, do look. That is why architectural quality is regarded as being very relevant to liveability.

INVENTING LIVEABILITY

The city as we know it is hardly more than 150 years old. The transportation problem is even younger, dating back merely four decades. We feel that a certain liveability has been lost. Some look back to the nineteenth century, the eighteenth century, nay to the Middle Ages, to find a concept of liveability. This search cannot be successful. Looking back can, however, help us by locating ourselves in time, by making us aware how variable the social and physical fabric of a city is. And we can learn from history that developments may be influenced by imagination and will. If we truly want a more liveable city we can realize it. Walkability will be one indispensable prerequisite.

NOTE

This essay is dedicated to my parents.

REFERENCE

McCarthy, M. (1973) *Florenz Venedig*, Munich and Zurich: Droemer Knaur (German translation of *The Stones of Florence*, 1959, New York: Harcourt Brace).

19 The discipline of the route

Tom Ellis

One of the essential elements of good architecture is the route – the way in, the way through and the way out of a building.

At one time or another we must all have had the experience of losing ourselves in some building. We must have missed the ground floor on the way out and ended up in the basement; have failed to reverse the directions – 'third right and second on your left, you can't miss it' – and been baffled and irritated. Yet very often these same buildings, which seem like rabbit warrens or tins of worms, have been planned with the greatest care after a detailed analysis of circulation diagrams, and the results are these ill-defined routes which lose themselves or peter out in a cupboard.... Confusion and frustration!

This whole question – of the way in and the way out – has exercised my mind for many years. Some time ago when I was refreshing myself with a study of Letarouilly's *Rennaissance Palaces in Italy* and brooding on the possible significance of certain planning features common to all these plans, I began to feel my way towards a solution. Certain principles became apparent; they seemed both clear and consistent.

The theories I gradually arrived at I have since tested out and, most rewardingly of all, on the work of Le Corbusier. In all his finest work he submits to these disciplines of the route. I find the same ideas rigorously adhered to by Alvar Aalto and I have seen it in the work of Mies van der Rohe.

In fact I feel that these 'disciplines of the route' have been rediscovered by our great contemporaries and given new meaning. The conditions in themselves do not make great architecture, but great architecture always contains them.

I propose first to describe to you what I believe to be the key points in this context of the typical Rennaissance plan, illustrating the idea of the way in, the way around and the way out.

Then I shall go on to analyse various plans of Le Corbusier and illustrate how in each case the rule of the route has been adhered to, the ideas developed and transformed and how new ideas have been generated – all within the framework of this theory.

RENNAISSANCE PALACES

In the typical palace the entry is made through the building into the courtyard which is the 'dominant

First published 1960 in *Architectural Design* 30 (November): 481–2.

element' immediately recognized. The number of floors of the palace can be seen at one glance, the importance of the varying floors recognized and the destination noted. The staircases are invariably in the corners of the courtyard and are dog-leg, so that on arrival at the first floor you are immediately above the point where you started and recognize the courtyard – therefore the position is known (see Figure 1). In these pre-Versailles plans there were no corridors and the principal rooms looked on to the courtyard which had been previously identified, so that the views were always related to the dominant element.

The doubling back of the dog-leg staircase is the key to the way in and the way out in that the same thing is seen in both directions. Where single flights of stairs are used, they are open and usually stand within halls of double height or more, so that their destination is easily recognized.

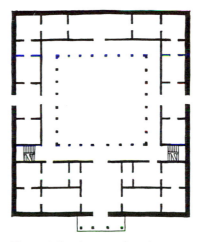

Figure 1 *Renaissance palace plan*

MAISON LA ROCHE

Here the courtyard has become the hall which rises through three floors. On the first and obviously more important floor the gallery extends from the left-hand side over the entrance round the right-hand side. On the second floor the right- and left-hand galleries are not connected. The back wall facing the entrance rises blank and unbroken through the three floors. In the left- and right-hand corners are dog-leg staircases, but the right-hand staircase is so inconspicuous that the route to the first-floor studio is clearly shown to be by the left (see Figure 2).

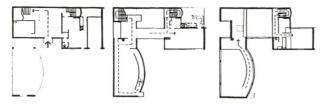

Figure 2 *Maison La Roche by Le Corbusier*

At the top of the stairs you look down into the hall and pass along the gallery to the double doors leading to the studio which is of double height, and on the left of which is a curved ramp rising back to the library gallery which looks down on to the hall. Thus the route doubles back up the ramp over that previously traversed at a lower level to a destination previously identified. To have taken the dog-leg staircase up to the library would have been banal. It would have robbed the studio of its importance, and the privacy and surprise of the library would have been lost. The dining-room is on the first floor also and is reached by the gallery over the entrance. It is directly on the right of the entrance hall. This means that to pass from one room to any other in the house you must pass through the hall, the dominant element, which is sustained for all routes. The route swings back and forth over the limits of the house, the position of the windows indicates the peripheral condition and a rooflight in the library indicates the upward limits.

By taking you to the external limits of the building and then bringing you back as you rise to a point above the place where you started, Le Corbusier not only makes you see the same things on the way out as on the way in, but he makes you see the whole of the building. It is all part of the 'Unity of Intention'. There is no alternative route on the way out in the form of a short cut, which if once known makes the so-called route of entry purely paper architecture. There is not a single portion of this building which can be considered as arbitrary in its planning. It is fugal.

MAISON À GARCHES

On entering Garches one is made aware of the importance of the first floor by the opening in the ceiling at the left of the entrance and also by the free-standing dog-leg staircase on the right, used in this way for the first time by Le Corbusier. Here too the staircase leads back to the point of importance previously identified (see Figure 3). The shape of the staff staircase is negative on the ground floor, but the sculptural form is more positive at the first floor as its use changes from a staff staircase to the staircase to the owners' bedrooms.

One can see the development of Le Corbusier's idea from La Roche to the Savoye house, in that in Maison à Garches there is the curved opening in the ceiling which

may be compared with the courtyard or the hall in La Roche and which identifies the importance of the first floor, and also there is the sculptural use of the free-standing staircase as a point of identity which replaces the court in some of his later work.

Here within the now rigid geometrical form of the exterior we have a further development of the identity of the peripheral walls and the limits of the house, for now all internal partitions are curved and modelled shapes so that they read as sculpture.

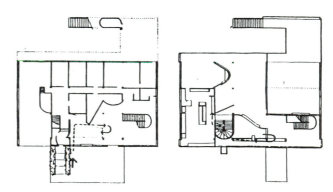

Figure 3 *Maison à Garches by Le Corbusier*

VILLA SAVOYE AT POISSY

The identification of the first floor as being the most important one is made externally. It is interesting to note that on entering the Savoye house the identifying element is now the sculptural dog-leg staircase on the left which passes through all the floors of the house. The front entrance doors at the bottom of the ramp are immediately below the focal point of the first floor. The dog-leg staircase faces outwards towards the window on the ground floor, and at the first and second floors there are windows in exactly the same position. From the ramp, position is known by the identity of the sculptural staircase; and from the staircase, by the views from the windows (see Figure 4).

You will see that to enter the house, the external route takes you around all the façades before coming to the front door. Le Corbusier so often either takes you all round the building first or he takes you through it so that you know the external limits before entering. It is another version of the double-back.

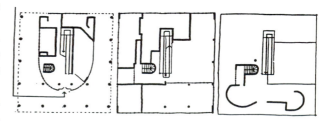

Figure 4 *Villa Savoy at Poissy*

ARMÉE DU SALUT, PARIS

Whilst the external appearance of the route to the main block of the Salvation Army building may appear to be complex, the discipline of the way in and the way out are as clearly defined as ever. It is now changed from the dog-leg, the doubling back and seeing the same views on the way in and the way out, to two L-shaped barriers, a turn right at the entrance and a turn left to the staircases of the main block.

It is the way out that is particularly interesting. On arrival at the bottom of the main staircases the daylight through the glazed screens to right and left indicates that one has left the multi-storey block. Then one comes to the toplit, L-shaped walls, so that the turn is instinctively right, and through the circular glazed foyer (external position known), and through the glazed doors and across the bridge to the second L-shaped screen and the street (see Figure 5).

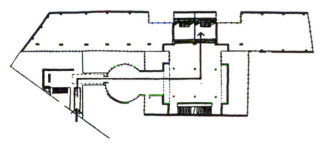

Figure 5 *Armée du Salut, Paris, by Le Corbusier*

On the way out the use of glazed screens and toplights show when one has left the multi-storey part of the building; the limits of the entrance hall are known and there is no doubt as to the direction the visitor must take. For the staff their circulation routes are clearly separated. Here is an example of a simple route made into great architecture by the changes in volume and shape and daylighting.

By rising on to the small podium at the entry the building is immediately divorced from the surrounding property; and what is more important, on the way out the plane of this podium makes the building extend in its route to the street – and not to the building opposite.

HIGH COURT, CHANDIGARH

The entrance to the High Court can be described as a covered court rising through the full height of the building but open on one side (see Figure 6). The route takes one through the limits of the main building to the dog-leg ramp which rises through all the floors and which has, as the staircase in the Savoye house, the window at the landing in the same position on each floor, and the dog-leg staircase in one corner. There is the lift shaft, also an identifying element throughout the building and the external condition is always known.

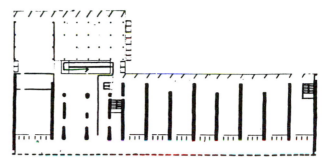

Figure 6 *High Court, Chandigarh, by Le Corbusier*

The destination is seen from the covered court. All the staircases double back. The court is seen from the external corridors. Views on the way out as on the way in are identical.

THE SECRETARIAT, CHANDIGARH

All the previous examples deal with buildings without central corridors which may be likened to pre-Versailles planning, but the Secretariat is a large administrative slab block with a central corridor (see Figure 7).

Externally it is seen that the important rooms are not confined to one or two floors but rise through all floors of the building in an off-centre element within the block. The entrances are through *piloti*, using the same principles as in the Savoye house. The route rises to an open platform within the *piloti* and here Le Corbusier has brought down from the floors above the elements he will use on all the upper floors, staircase, curved screen to the toilets and the lift shaft. As in La Roche, the first staircase up to the platform does not continue through

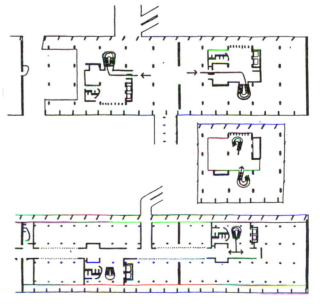

Figure 7 *The Secretariat, Chandigarh, by Le Corbusier*

the building although it is the same sculptural shape as the one which continues from the platform. It is this bringing down from an upper floor an element which you identify and then see in the same position on the way through the building which is the key here.

The staircases are placed alternately along the spine of the building and the large landings reach from the corridor to the face of the building, so that as you walk along these corridor 'streets' the daylight pours through the piazzas containing the sculptural shapes of the staircase, the lifts and the toilet screens.

The position of the external ramps which rise at an acute angle to the front and back façades of the building seems ambiguous in their relation to the corridor, although their position externally is a very happy one. As one studies *L'Architecture Vivante*, the early designs of the Pavillon Suisse, the first scheme for Maison Savoye in Volume 1, and the alterations already shown in the Secretariat designs in Volume 5, one recognizes that changes in design show adherence to Le Corbusier's order of identifying elements which is consistent throughout his work.

THE PALACE, CHANDIGARH

From the drawings of the proposed Palace it appears that this building will be an example of closely interwoven 'fugal' planning which will be as perfect in its way as La Roche.

Le Corbusier has planned all the roads to the group of government buildings and the Palace to be run in deep cuttings through the plateau on which all the buildings stand. The road cutting to the Palace opens out to a large area which is about 7.5 m. (25ft.) below the plateau level.

Entry is made through *piloti* with the familiar route under a gallery to a hall of double height (court) to pass in the usual way to the back of the court before doubling back up the staircase and over the point of entry at the mezzanine floor level and complete the dog-leg route through the cutting in the ceiling of this court to the plateau 'ground floor' level. The lift shaft has been identified, daylight has entered this lower court only from the entrance façade, there are blank walls on the other three sides (as in Armée du Salut). This ground floor is the *piano nobile* and light now penetrates from all sides of the square plan. Again one is in a hall of double height and the various destinations are seen. The shape of the lift shaft is still clearly defined, and, as in the Secretariat, shapes are brought down from upper floors for identification as the route passes to these floors. A small dog-leg sculptural staircase leads to the apartments of the guests of the governor. This private staircase opens up into another court at the next floor level, again of double height, but there is that masterly twist that we now see a reversed route – a staircase that falls from the governor's apartments to a bridge across this

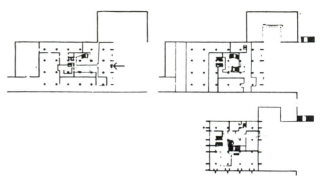

Figure 8 *The Palace, Chandigarh, by Le Corbusier*

court to link him to his guests' apartments.

The shape and treatment of the various parts of this building have changed with each different function. The private staircase rising finally into the governor's apartments consisting of flowing sculptural shapes within the square perimeter (see Figure 8).

Looking at Alvar Aalto's plans one knows that he has solved the analysis of his problem before attempting to make physical plans, and from this arises the conceptual idea which is sustained throughout. The route and destination within his buildings, the way in and the way out, the changes in volume and daylighting, the awareness of the external conditions from within, the identity of your position anywhere within the building, the clarity of the segregation of the parts of his building, and the dramatic use of changes in level – all these illustrate once again the discipline of the route in great architecture.

In the office block the Rautatalo, you climb through the building to a covered court, and that court is the dominant element. It is surrounded by continuous stepped galleries at each floor and the ceiling is pierced by dome lights. In the corners of the court are two dog-leg staircases, so that as you arrive at each floor you are exactly over the position where you started.

THE TOWN CENTRE AT SAYNATSALO

The Town Centre, Saynatsalo, marks the unfolding of a new phase, the phase of flowing growth.

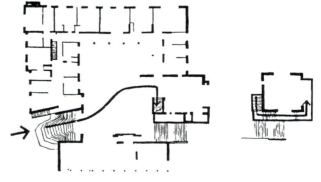

Figure 9 *The Town Centre, Saynatsalo, by Alvar Aalto*

You see this virile climbing composition. The route is as clearly defined as ever; you see the dominant element of the council chamber rising behind the pine trees. A staircase at the side of the council chamber rises to an open courtyard surrounded by the council offices, the caretaker's house and the library. You turn right to enter and see through the foyer windows the courtyard on your left. You double back up the brittle brick staircase which is wrapped around the council chamber. The stairs are lit by a continuous window at ceiling level. The transition from the open courtyard up the completely enclosed staircase into the council chamber is most impressive (Figure 9).

In Saynatsalo and the MIT Building, Aalto has shown that the idea of his order is not one of apparent clarity. It is not geometrical and final as a Rennaissance idea, but it is an order which emerges as the building is used. His buildings do not all speak at once. The dominant elements externally are the important parts within; they are all given their true significance.

20 Aalto's approach to movement and circulation

Steven Groák

In modern architecture, where the rationality of the structural frame and the building masses threaten to dominate, there is often an architectural vacuum in the left-over portions of the site. It would be good if, instead of filling this vacuum with decorative gardens, the organic movement of people could be incorporated in the shaping of the site in order to create an intimate relationship between Man and Architecture.

(Alvar Aalto)

INTRODUCTION

The work of Alvar Aalto's office is the most encyclopaedic of any major Western architect this century. Recent research has revealed that over 5,000 projects were undertaken in his office during his professional working lifetime of some 55 years, of which probably more than 800 were for buildings – of which in turn perhaps 600 were built.[1] In examining these records, we discover the astonishing amount of residential and industrial architecture he proposed – often in symbiotic relationships. Some important designs have been completed since Aalto's death in 1978, such as the very successful Theatre at Seinäjoki, which completes his most complex 'citizen's square'. The range – of site conditions, clients, scales, functions, principal building materials, etc. – is extraordinary, as is the inventiveness of the solutions.

In many ways, Aalto's work defies interpretation. This is partly because he simultaneously displays a wide array of precedential reference and unique forms; yet these have not induced a stylistic 'school'. And, of course, he often eschewed any critical purpose or theoretical programme: 'I build.'

At one time, it was thought that Aalto's 'styles' conformed to 'periods' in his work associated with his supposed changing relationship to Modernism. Today, there is a greater tendency to recognize an underlying coherence and consistency of approach in all the work despite superficial visual differences. This is also part of the more public acknowledgement that Aalto was a highly cultivated and educated man, with wide sympathies in European culture: he was not – as has sometimes been implied – an unselfconscious naïf.

An important aspect of this underlying coherence is what might be termed a 'humanistic functionalism', not to mention 'humane functionalism', in which Aalto considered not only what task the person is seeking *to do* in and around a building, but also what it is like for one person *to experience* that position, that environment, on that site. To use current formulations, that person partakes of 'Being' and 'Becoming', of both aspects of Modernist sensibility (Berman 1982).

It is significant that Aalto travelled to Italy and Greece early in his career (1924) and was permanently affected by the architecture he saw. He was entranced by the way in which the Mediterranean sun was used to model classical buildings – indeed, a sub-programme of his work might be seen as the systematic pursuit of these qualities under a Nordic sun. This perhaps helped to consolidate in his mind a constantly refreshed approach, a modern reformulation of the classic concept of architecture as mediating between 'Man' and 'Nature'.

This approach must be understood as dynamic – both Man and Nature are moving and changing. The particular formulation which concerns us here is Aalto's approach to movement and circulation. However, it is worth first rehearsing the extraordinary array of architectural conditions which are explored in Aalto's building designs, leaving aside his office's work in art, glassware, ceramics, door fittings, and furniture design (which itself assures his position as a major designer of the twentieth century).

A FUNCTIONALIST'S PROGRAMME

This section identifies critical parameters and scales of Aalto's work, which stem from his perceptions of the Finnish condition. They mark out a broader framework for the interpretative points made in relation to routes, movement and circulation. I emphasize that these are one way of examining the built and drawn work; the evidence comes from these sources, rather than from explicit research programmes set down by Aalto. The critical features I would draw to the reader's attention include:

- the industrial economy
- urban design
- civic complexes
- the synthesis of tradition
- the continuous experiment
- materials and 'dematerialization'

- site, route and memory
- light, standing for Nature
- the natural order and the rational order.

Aalto's functional analysis of the Finnish economy was based on its timber industries, and the changes therein following the Finno-Russian War – such as major demographic movements to the South. Although some of these developed only in the post-War period, the basic propositions were there from the late 1920s onwards. They informed his whole approach to the development of Finnish settlements.

Aalto's ideas of urban design, such as his industrial-residential plans, his town centres, etc., grew from a conception of modern life. (It is notable that many of his most famous buildings and groups of buildings were placed in towns for which previously he had put forward planning ideas.) In the late 1980s, several analysts have rediscovered the power and fertility of these proposals, few of which were properly realized at the time (Rautsi 1986).

Aalto developed many civic complexes – his 'citizen's squares' – which were combinations of building types. These formed the practical architecture which united his analysis of the changing industrial society with his 'humanistic functionalism', often related to a particular concept of public space which inhabits all his buildings – even the most private.

Aalto is notable for his synthesis of many European building traditions, his encyclopedic coverage of architectural problems and typical conditions of the twentieth century. This relates to his interest in 'types' of buildings.

Aalto used virtually all building materials (except exposed steel), and in a Constructivist tradition, in part exploring a 'layering' of the architectural volume, to convey an ambiguity and dynamic of the solid materials of walls and planes. The frequent striated or 'reverse fluting' effects which he displays in so many surface finishes to his buildings are a clear reference to the play of sunlight on the fluted classical column.

We can see Aalto's approach to his work as a continuous experiment, in which no one project is complete. In physical terms, many of the buildings appear to be broken fragments of a typological whole. There are various interpretations of this characteristic. Baird suggests that this is because Aalto was appalled at the rapid decay of modern materials and details in his buildings, and sought to pre-empt the effects of time by deliberate 'ruination' (Baird and Futogawa 1970). Porphyrios (1982) has attempted to use Foucault's concept of 'heterotopia' to help analyse the plans and forms of Aalto's designs, so that they may be seen as the unification of fragments from different sources. Porphyrios sees each design as a complete statement in that sense. I disagree, and believe that the designs are both indicative and incomplete, in some sense, and

demonstrate the sacrifice of the type to the demands of the site.

Aalto demonstrates a preoccupation with the site and with routes, with what I suggest is the 'memory' of their physical attributes as part of the architectural experience, and with conjuring the experience of movement across the previously unbuilt site.

Pearson (1979) has documented Aalto's interest in environmental comfort. Many, such as Mosso (1960), have noted his special interest in light. I suggest that Aalto treated light as almost metonymic of Nature, arising from his concern with a humanistic – often Nature-oriented – functionalism. The famous optical geometry diagrams for acoustic analyses of concert halls, etc., demonstrate how comprehensively the description and manipulation of light rays and waves is used in his work to represent the more complex behaviour of Nature at large. Light rarely enters his buildings without being modified, baffled, screened, reflected.

Wilson (1979) has noted that many features of Aalto's work can be expressed in the ideogram of a straight line set against a free-form or wavy line. I would also link this to the 'fan' motif which appears so often in Aalto's designs, evoking both the point source of a radiating light 'cone' and the scanning view of an observer from a point on the route. Together, then, these graphic symbols, both static and dynamic, almost independent of scale, can stand for Aalto's concern to design communities and buildings which mediate between the natural order and the rational order, between the natural and the synthetic environment. At a detailed level of construction, as Tatarian (1982–3) has observed, we can see examples in the combinations of 'the raw and the cooked', the mixture of sawn and unsawn timber – for example, the columns of the Finnish Pavilion at the 1935 Paris Exhibition.

These preoccupations of Aalto's work can be seen to presage those of the 1970s and 1980s, especially when contrasted with Louis Kahn, who has similar but opposite interests in site, structure, light and materials. This points to why Robert Venturi – a pupil of Kahn's – is such a perceptive commentator on Aalto's work, taking as he does the confrontation of the canonic architectural tradition with an anonymous and ordinary vernacular as the critical condition of post-war suburban architecture in Europe and North America.

We can characterize the difference in their approaches as a 'Theory of Sites' (Aalto) versus a 'Theory of Types' (Kahn).[2] Aalto starts with 'the Type', but then dismantles it in the unravelling of 'the Site' through the dynamics of the route.

THE IDEA OF ROUTE

Commentators have always recognized Aalto's profound understanding of the basic organization and properties of a site. There have been attempts to link his use of the route to other masters of the Modern Movement, such as Le Corbusier (Ellis 1960, 1966). This virtuosity should be placed in terms of the concepts elucidated above.

Aalto evokes the idea of a person wandering over the site, of succumbing to the spectacle, of experiencing the site morphology, as is plain in his explanation of the approach to the design of the Viipuri (Vyborg) Library, one of his first buildings to attract international acclaim:

> Whilst designing the library for the town of Viipuri (and I had plenty of time at my disposal – five whole years), I spent a long time making child-like drawings representing an imaginary mountain, with different shapes on its sides and, over it, a celestial super-structure crowded with suns which lit the sides with an even light. Visually these drawings had nothing to do with architecture but from their apparent childish-ness there arose a combination of plans and sections whose interweaving it is difficult to know how to describe, and which became the basic concept for the library. . . .
>
> The concept grouped the reading-rooms, meeting-rooms and the lending library on different levels around the central control – just as the sides of a mountain build up around the ridge. And overhead, a system of suns: the round conical rooflights of the glazing system.

(Aalto 1957: 138)

From this, we are given three crucial elements – the moving person, the arrangement of the ground, and the light from the sun. These define the underlying site morphology and the concerns most clearly subject to the mediation of the building. From this base, Aalto elicits a functional route structure for each building which defines movement and circulation in and around that building.

There is the route of the sun, as it moves over the site, which produces a modelling – through light – of the exterior and interior spaces and surfaces. There is the route of people circulating outside the building. There is the route of people within the building, which is related to the central functions of that building – in the sense of 'humanistic functionalism' – and the sequences of actions associated with those functions. Each building is the intersection of these different routes; and they are mutually animated by the functional movement of people, the effect of the moving sun, and the site morphology – for instance, by the closing and revealing views of openings in the built volume as light or observer change position, or both.

One of the functions of natural light brought into the buildings is to identify critical junctures along the functional routes. A particular version occurs with one of Aalto's trademarks – the conical rooflights. These are used sometimes to illuminate vertical circulation and sometimes to mark major 'atrium' spaces (as we now call them) where people gather and swirl between different routes. The original version of the Viipuri Library is an obvious example, as is the Rautatalo in Helsinki with its bringing of the public realm into the building – and, as it were, writing a record of the previous site on the architecture of the internal space.

Another straightforward example of route lighting is over the stair to the Main Building at Jÿväskylä University, around whose campus several other minor examples are to be found. A more elaborated version is the main public space of the academic Bookshop, which adjoins the Rautatalo in Helsinki. As has been convinc-ingly demonstrated by Arias, the very complex array of rooflights can be deciphered according to the precise use of space below (Arias 1983–4).

The bookshop lighting condition is not the same as that of the libraries, which follow the archetype of Viipuri, because in the former the books are for display and sale, whilst in the latter they are to be read – requiring directional light without shadows for the functioning reader. These can be contrasted again with the role of sunlight in the Paimio Sanatorium – orig-inally designed for tuberculosis patients, for whom sunlight and forest air were the principal healing methods: that is, sunlight is central to the 'humane functional' purpose of the building.

The functional route can be most immediately demonstrated in the Finlandiatalo, the complex of concert halls and conference facilities. (What could be more contemporary than that combination?) Following a clear entry from any one of several approaches to the site, the pedestrian is shown the cloakrooms – large and spacious to allow for the exchange of outdoor clothing in the severe Finnish winters. The staircases drop into these spaces, showing the next stage, which leads to a set of antechambers, for gathering, waiting, coffee, etc. From there, we can see the doors to the stalls, the stairs to the gallery, and so on. Despite their strange forms, Aalto's buildings are not mysterious. This organizational form occurs in many of his public buildings.

The most elegant version of functional route linked to building use is in the Helsinki Atelier, which is distinct from the concert halls because we do not find the same clear separation between functional groups (performers, administrators, audience, etc.).

THE AALTO ATELIER

A more detailed analysis can be proposed for the 1956 Atelier (see Figure 1), which is one of the Aalto master-works, a building in which we can find almost all of Aalto's architectural preoccupations developed with clarity and rigour – but with the lightest of touches. The plan repays detailed analysis.

The flow of space from the forest fragment (A) divides either side of the 'prow' of the building (B), one part to the main door (C), the other through the South-

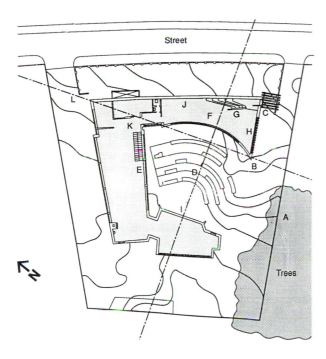

Street

L

J

F G C

K H

E D B

A

Trees

Figure 1 *Plan (main level) of Alvar Aalto's 1956 Atelier.*

facing amphitheatre (a formalization (D) of the contours, which also encapsulates the ideas in Aalto's various grass-stepped courtyards – such as those at Säynätsalo, Seinäjoki Town Hall and Paris Centre – memories of the sites before the buildings came). The spatial flow here also represents the potential movement of people around the site. It is balked at the wall to the main drawing office (E); this has its counterpoint in the flow of space through the master studio (F), which divides to the interior of the main door (C), around the freestanding wall (G) and which is also balked at the high end wall (H). In both cases the high-level clerestory windows reinforce the termination of space and the blocking of the pedestrian routes. These two flows sweep either side of the great curved wall.

From the blank wall (I), which with the curved wall formally identifies the axis of the amphitheatre (D), the space also steps up the contours and 'through' the low window in the curved wall to balk at the blank back wall (J): this appears to be one of the few – if not the sole – windows in Aalto's buildings to demonstrate a Modern Movement precept about the continuity of internal and external space and to give deliberate views to the exterior. (Usually, we find in Aalto's designs that windows exist to bring light into the buildings, not to give views outwards.)

Within the master studio (F), this flow of space also bifurcates around wall (G) upwards to the small roof-light.

The plan pivots around a 'knuckle' (K) – where the

doors make the transition between interior and exterior and where the stair joins upper and lower levels on the north-west element of the building. That is, it is the crossing-point of the various routes around and through the building. The amphitheatre makes plain the memory of the site, which in this instance illustrates the preconditions of a garden city. And the building as a whole demonstrates in almost programmatic terms Aalto's concern to use architecture as the mediation between the natural and the fabricated world: we can draw a 'gradient line' from the (almost) right-angle of the street pattern (L), through the knuckle (K) to the forest (A).

This gradient is virtually perpendicular to the amphitheatre axis and together these form the matrix of spatial complexity in the whole building: the mediating function can be read along the gradients either way. One gradient is (North) from the natural to the rational world; the other takes us from the most impenetrable (enclosing) wall through a series of screens to the street. The two axes also acknowledge the movement of the sun during the day.

The only free-form element, the great curving wall rising to its 'prow', is also the only wall which is permeable to space: this ambivalence is reinforced by the treatment of the wall beneath the long window, which (as noted by Wang)[3] has a clear reference to the fluting of classical columns, a motif which I have argued elsewhere (Groák 1978) is at the root of Aalto's conception of the dematerialized wall. The classical reference is of course also explicit in the reference to the Greek theatre embedded in the hillside.

At an everyday level, the building is light and airy, quiet because it turns its back on the street, calm, and organized. Whether full of people or virtually empty, the scale is always appropriate because of the articulation of the plan into smaller semi-volumes. Moreover, whilst in and around the building, one is not conscious of the highly abstract ordering of the space in any formalistic way; rather, one feels the quiet dynamic as an animation of site, light, space and structure which supports work and repose.

This specific analysis indicates the complexity and abstraction of Aalto's conception of space as a particular set of flows – notably of light (Nature) and people. It touches on their implications for the treatment of materials and building elements. The examination of the functional route shows it to be the operator which breaks down traditional types into specific solutions for specific sites.

ACKNOWLEDGEMENT

This essay has drawn on many discussions and joint work with my friend Jussi Rautsi, the benefit of which I gratefully acknowledge. He is not responsible for the views expressed here.

NOTES

1 Private communication from the Archivist of the Alvar Aalto Trust Archive.
2 I am indebted to David Dunster for this formulation.
3 Personal communication from Wilfried Wang.

REFERENCES

Aalto, A. (1957) 'The egg of the fish and the salmon', *Architects' Year Book* 8, London: Elek Books.

Arias, R. (1983–4) Essay for B.Sc. course in Construction Analysis, Bartlett School, University College London.

Baird, G. and Futogawa, Y. (1970) *Alvar Aalto*, London: Thames & Hudson.

Berman, M. (1982) *All That is Solid Melts Into Air*, New York: Simon & Schuster.

Ellis, T. (1960) 'The discipline of the route', *Architectural Design*, November.

—— (1966) 'The discipline of the route – 2', *Architectural Design*, August.

Groák, S. (1978) 'Notes on responding to Aalto's buildings', in *Architectural Monographs No. 4: Alvar Aalto*, London: Academy Editions.

Mosso, L. (1960) 'La luce nell'architettura di Alvar Aalto', *Zodiac 7*.

Pearson, P.D. (1978) *Alvar Aalto and the International Style*, New York: Whitney Library of Design.

—— (1979) 'The legacy of Viipuri', *Architectural Design* 49(12).

Porphyrios, D. (1982) *Sources of Modern Eclecticism*, London: Academy Editions.

Rautsi, J. (1986) 'Alvar Aalto's urban plans, 1940–70', *RIBA Transactions 9* 5(1).

Tatarian, G. (1982–3) Essay for B.Sc. course in Construction Analysis, Bartlett School, University College London.

Wilson, C. St J. (1979) 'Alvar Aalto and the state of Modernism', *International Architect* 2(1) Issue 2.

PART 3

INFLUENCES

SECTION 3.1

Influence of society

Every society has its own culture, its own way of life comprising the ideas, values, beliefs and knowledge it has about itself, that are passed on from one generation to another. Culture, in all its various forms, is a major determinant of built form. Institutions within cultures – that is, formal and regular ways of doing things, established procedures and structures – are important in that respect (for example, the family, the economy, the law, political systems, education, religion and social stratification). Many building types are generated by these institutions – varying again in form from culture to culture – but are common within all cultures.

The ranges of building types generated by institutions are easily envisaged but, because they are common to most if not all societies, the impact of societal influence is most readily seen by comparing particular forms of building types between societies. Domestic building is the most fundamental of all provision and here one can readily see variations on the theme, the nature of families and communities, attitudes to privacy, wealth, religion, ideology and culture (in the sense of artistic ideas and traditions of behaviour) being the underpinning considerations.

The very act of building is a social activity and architecture forms a comparatively permanent record of society, reflecting as it does a society's values.

Architects design for others and need other people's money to realize buildings. They also design within obvious legislative and technological contexts. However, in the most fundamental way, it is the commissioning process that essentially determines what is built (or what is not built). Architects therefore are not free agents, nor should they seek to be so; their task is rather to harness ideas, space-making and form-resolving ability, technological command and building expression in the service of society.

The essays in this section collectively address these issues.

B.F.

RECOMMENDED READING

Agnew, J., Mercer, J. and Sopher, D. (eds) (1984) *The City in Cultural Context*, Boston: Allen & Unwin.

Castells, M. (1976) *The Urban Question: A Marxist Approach*, London: Edward Arnold.

Harvey, D. (1973) *Social Justice and the City*, London: Edward Arnold.

—— (1989) *The Urban Experience*, Oxford: Blackwell.

Jacobs, J. (1984) *The Death and Life of Great American Cities*, Harmondsworth: Penguin.

King, A.D. (ed.) (1980) *Buildings and Society: Essays on the Social Development of the Built Environment*, London: Routledge & Kegan Paul.

Lerup, L. *Building the Unfinished: Architecture and Human Action*, London: Sage.

Pahl, R. (1970) *Whose City?: And Other Essays on Sociology and Planning*, London: Longman.

Rapoport, A. (1977) *Human Aspects of Urban Form – Towards a Man–Environment Approach to Urban Form and Design*, Oxford: Pergamon.

Smith, M.P. (1980) *The City and Social Theory*, Oxford: Blackwell.

21 Buildings and Society

Anthony D. King

The conceptual understanding of the relationship between 'buildings' and 'society' has, in recent years, become increasingly problematic. This is not because buildings, their social uses and meanings, have become less real or tangible but rather that the notion of society, and especially its spatial and temporal boundaries, has become increasingly controversial. This essay will focus on some of the recent ways in which the relationship has been understood.

Buildings are articulated with society in many different ways: economically, socially, politically and culturally. Economically, they house activities, occupy land, create work and, in modern market societies, they provide for investment and store capital. Socially, buildings house institutions, provide shelter, support relationships, express social divisions, permit hierarchies, embody property relations and enable the expression of status, identity and authority. Culturally, they store sentiment, symbolize meaning, embody history and express identity. Politically, buildings represent authority, symbolize power, become an arena for conflict and are a political resource (King 1990a: 11). Perhaps the first point to note, therefore, is that buildings, consisting of a variety of building types distinguished by, among other criteria, their age, size, form, design, function, location, and degree of permanence, are socially produced. Buildings, and the larger built environment of which they are a part, represent a given social order and the way that economic, political, cultural and social power is distributed within this.

In some peasant or pre-industrial, pre-capitalist societies, a relatively undifferentiated range of building types and forms may exist; dwelling functions, as well as functions associated with religion, and the political and economic organization of the social unit, may be accommodated in broadly similar structures, though the actual forms in which these exist will clearly vary according to location, climate, culture and materials (Oliver 1987). In other cases, as in the most 'advanced' industrial and post-industrial market economies, a vast range of socially and functionally differentiated building types exist, each classified according to a socially and culturally significant terminology. Thus, the catalogues of contemporary architectural libraries will list over 1,000 terms (in English) describing identifiably different building types, and this could certainly be expanded by referring to other languages.

In these examples, it is being assumed that building types may be explained primarily by reference to the prevailing mode of production (or system of socio-economic organization and political control), whether this is peasant agriculture, early industrial capitalism or state socialism, but also by taking note of historical and cultural variation at different times and places. This probably provides the most effective starting point for understanding the social contexts in which buildings are produced.

Historically, buildings have performed enduring social functions, most obviously those of the accommodation and representation of religious and political authority (the temple and the palace), of sheltering a household and, where it exists, the storing of the surplus product (the granary or bank). Based on a social theory which analyses society according to its principal institutions (understood as the established ways of doing things), for example, kinship and the family, the economy, polity, religion and social control, socially specialized building forms have been explained, within a cross-cultural, comparative and historical context, by reference to the institutions with which they are associated (King 1980). Such an approach, while having an initial appeal, also has its problems. It may suggest, for example, that there are in all societies unchanging 'social needs' which specific buildings are designed to fulfil.

'Social needs', on the contrary, are constantly created and vary according to changes in historical modes of production. Multi-storey accommodation for labour in European or American industrial cities, provided either by the state or private capital, or the self-built squatter settlements of Rio de Janeiro or Calcutta are each different ways of satisfying the 'need' for shelter which is determined by the social relations of production and state policies, rather than some social law that exists in an organic society.

Moreover, building types do not relate only to one social institution, such as the dwelling to the family, the temple to religion, the school to the polity, but to many: in contemporary market societies, all buildings are forms of property and are, therefore, linked to economic institutions. Indeed, as has been argued by Harvey (1985), one of the prime functions of building in contemporary market societies is the accumulation and circulation of capital.

The historical development of many modern public institutional buildings – the school, hospital, prison, police station, asylum, town hall – is a direct outcome of the rise of the modern nation-state and its intervention into the realm of social life (Scull 1984). These developments may be interpreted in a variety of ways, whether from a Marxist perspective (that they were the specific instruments by which the institutions of capitalism were established) or from a Foucaultian one (that they were simply a means of disciplinary control; Foucault 1979). It is, however, the difference in political and economic organization of modern nation-states that governs which buildings (from museums to monuments, factories to farms) are produced by the state and which by the private sector, or whether, indeed, they are produced at all.

It should, nevertheless, be recognized that specific forms of buildings and the institutions and activities they both represent and contain have, for centuries, been transplanted geographically from societies with one mode of production to those with another (e.g. Holston 1989). The radial prison, first developed in the United States, was later adopted in Britain, then elsewhere in Europe (Evans 1982) and in overseas colonies. The global diffusion of specific building types is the outcome of various processes: colonialism, the spread of world religions, international migration, and the growth of the idea of the nation-state. This last has been particularly important since the early nineteenth century, with the number of nation-states increasing from some 25 in 1815 to almost 200 in the last decade of the twentieth century.

The effect of this multiplication has been to introduce the apparatus of the modern state – national archives, museums, government complexes, universities and prisons – on an unprecedented scale around the world. The globalization of communications and technologies and the internationalization of professional practices since the nineteenth century has enabled these developments to take place.

Buildings are also 'classifying devices' (Markus 1987). An increasing number of studies have demonstrated that buildings embody the social ideas of those in power which, translated into language, become represented in space (e.g. Goodsell 1988, King 1980, Markus 1982). The process of classification operates on at least two levels: first, in the appropriation of a given realm of social life to particular social institutions (such as the task of educating the young by the church, the state or the market); and, second, through the classification of both space and the social subjects within a building according to particular ideologies and systems of social rules.

In this way, buildings, as well as the larger urban space in which they frequently exist, reproduce to varying degrees the different criteria – gender, class, ethnicity, religion, age, race, nation or culture – by which social life is organized. Likewise, the realm of culture, understood as the forms and social organization of knowledge, the constructions of cultural value, all find their place in the constructed spaces of society, whether these are the 'biochemistry laboratory', the 'jazz club' or the 'history library'.

Yet neither in the past nor especially today does 'society', understood simply as the nation-state, provide an adequate economic, social, political or spatial context in which to consider the social production of building form (King 1990b). Religious movements, giving rise to similar building forms, albeit varied according to local cultures, have been transcontinental in their scope. Empires, as political, economic and cultural systems, have redistributed resources and people around the world, in the process creating cultural and spatial forms (of buildings and cities) which embody both the power of politically dominant cultures and the subordinated cultural forms of societies they have set out to oppress. Especially from the eighteenth century, though also earlier, many building forms and the architecture in which they are expressed, as well, generally, as the urban settings where they exist, are best understood in relation to the old and, from the late twentieth century, the new international division of labour. This can be illustrated by two examples.

The extensive development in the late nineteenth century in parts of northern England of cotton weaving and spinning mills simultaneously with the extension of agricultural cotton production in Egypt and the colonial 'modernization' of Cairo (King 1990a: 36) or, in the USA of the late twentieth century, the massive development of high-rise office towers housing the headquarters of global corporations (of which New York, with fifty-nine in 1987, has the highest number of any city in the world) whose production facilities and low-cost labour factories are to be found in Taiwan, Mexico or elsewhere, are both examples of the extensive economic and social foundations from which buildings arise. Such a broad political-economic framework also provides at least part of the relevant context for understanding the disappearance, rehabilitation and conservation of buildings; though here it would be necessary to add that buildings, and the built environment in general, also obviously have symbolic, historical and cultural values over and above the economic.

If buildings are socially produced, they are also socially consumed. Buildings, and the larger built environment in which they exist, do not simply 'reflect' or 'represent' a particular societal and social order, they actively engage in the constitution of social and cultural existence: society is to a very large extent constituted through the buildings and spaces that it creates (Prior 1988). It has been said that how people think affects how people build, and how people build affects how people think (Rapoport 1980). This is not to argue for any kind of architectural determinism; rather, it implies that the symbols and images that buildings provide form the basis for the lexical concepts by which people make sense of their material world. In so far as it is those groups in power in any particular society who exercise hegemonic control over what is produced, providing most of the models, the symbols and the images of a certain mass culture, the way in which these are indigenized, subverted and consumed depends on people in their positions as social subjects. This concern with the meaning of the built environment turns our attention from considering the social production of buildings to thinking about the production of people as social, cultural and political subjects.

A major contribution of feminist and also psycho-analytic theory for understanding the 'buildings and society' problem has been to make visible, and articulate, the fact that people, as social subjects, do not have one identity, but, rather, multiple identities: in different contexts, they operate as gendered subjects, class subjects or national subjects, belong to different ethnicities, races, professions and occupations, or possess different political and sexual orientations. These theoretical developments, and the practical consequences which flow from them, have injected a new understanding into the way buildings, as socially produced objects, are understood. We may take as an illustration the growing number of feminist analyses in architectural and urban studies (e.g. Hayden 1981, Spain 1992) which demonstrate the extent to which the production, design and form of buildings (as well as cities in general) has been the outcome of a society where patriarchal decision-making has been the rule.

In other spheres, in some ways exhibiting contradictory tendencies, the consciousness of specific religious, social, ethnic or racial identities has led to social movements at the level of the neighbourhood, region or even state, to contest notions of 'modernization' and redevelopment in the name of the community or a larger religious or social group. Other examples might be cited. In the United States, adjusting to new waves of immigration and abandoning the old 'melting pot' idea, ethnicity is increasingly celebrated through the identification of 'ethnic buildings' and architecture (Upton 1986). In the coming decades, it will be of particular interest to see how the institutional buildings and housing forms of the former centrally planned, socialist states of Eastern Europe and one-time Soviet Union are appropriated, and modified, to meet the needs of emergent social, ethnic and national categories. The buildings, and larger social and spatial divisions of a society, are constantly subject to change, reconstruction and subjective redefinition.

Such concepts can be of value in understanding the present urban and architectural transformation of those societies in Asia, Africa and Latin America whose major cities are expanding at a phenomenal pace. Superficial opinion would suggest that many of these cities, influenced by the transnationalization of economies, the internationalization of capital and of labour, and increasingly influenced by 'Westernization', are moving to some form of 'homogenization of culture' on a global scale: increasingly, global solutions are sought to building and urban development, whether in the universalization of technology and materials (steel and concrete), professionalized knowledge, or planning and land policies, or in, for example, the practices of international organizations such as the World Bank promoting site-and-services schemes and low-cost housing.

The extent to which nationally organized societies either ignore these developments or respond to them by identifying and objectifying unique cultures for themselves – maintaining culture-specific buildings and the institutions and cultural practices they contain – will in itself demonstrate the degree to which nation-states have themselves resisted or succumbed to an increasingly pervasive modern global culture (Featherstone 1990, McGrew 1992). Ironically, therefore, the degree to which the buildings and architectures of nationally organized societies will be maintained and reproduced as 'different' will be evidence of the degree to which they are increasingly the same. In the twenty-first century, there will be no capital city in the world where representations of the national culture are not embalmed in a museum.

REFERENCES

Evans, R. (1982) *The Fabrication of Virtue: English Prison Architecture, 1750–1840,* Cambridge: Cambridge University Press.

Featherstone, M. (1990) *Global Culture: Nationalism, Globalization and Modernity,* London and Newbury Park: Sage.

Foucault, M. (1979) *Discipline and Punish. The Birth of the Prison,* New York: Vintage Books.

Goodsell, C.T. (1988) *The Social Meaning of Civic Space: Studying Political Authority through Architecture,* Lawrence: University Press of Kansas.

Harvey, D. (1985) *The Urbanization of Capital,* Oxford: Blackwells.

Hayden, D. (1981) *The Grand Domestic Revolution: A History of Feminist Designs for American Homes, Neighbourhoods and Cities,* Boston, Mass.: MIT Press.

Holston, J. (1989) *The Modernist City: An Anthropological Critique of Brazil,* Chicago: University of Chicago Press.

King, A.D. (ed.) (1980) *Buildings and Society: Essays on the Social Development of the Built Environment.* London: Routledge.

King, A.D. (1990a) *Global Cities: Post-Imperialism and the Internationalisation of London.* London: Routledge.

King, A.D. (1990b) 'The global production of building form', in *Urbanism, Colonialism and the World-Economy: Cultural and Spatial Foundations of the World Urban System,* London: Routledge, pp. 100–29.

Lawrence, D.L. and Lowe, S. (1990) 'The built environment and spatial form', *Annual Review of Anthropology,* Palo Alto, Calif.: Annual Reviews Inc.

Markus, T.A. (1982) *Order in Space and Society: Architectural Form and Its Context in the Scottish Enlightenment,* Edinburgh: Mainstream Publishing.

Markus, T.A. (1987) 'Buildings as classifying devices', *Environment and Planning D: Planning and Design* 14: 467–84.

McGrew, A. (1992) 'A global society?', in S. Hall and A. McGrew (eds) *Modernity and its Futures,* Cambridge: Polity Press.

Oliver, P. (1987) *Dwellings: The House Around the World*, London: Phaidon.

Prior, L. (1988) 'The architecture of the hospital: a study of spatial organisation and medical knowledge', *British Journal of Sociology*, 39 (1): 86–113.

Rapoport, A. (1980) 'Vernacular architecture and the cultural determinants of form', in A.D.King (ed.) *Buildings and Society*, London: Routledge, pp. 283–305, esp. p. 292.

Scull, A. (1984) *Decarceration, Community Treatment of the Deviant*, Cambridge: Polity Press.

Spain, D. (1992) *Gendered Spaces*, Chapel Hill and London: University of North Carolina Press.

Upton, D. (1986) *America's Architectural Roots: Ethnic Groups that Built America*, Washington: Preservation Press.

FURTHER READING

Foucault, M. (1975) *The Birth of the Clinic*, New York: Vintage Books.

Gad, G. and Holdsworth, D. (1987) 'Corporate capitalism and the emergence of the high-rise office building', *Urban Geography* 8: 212–31.

Giddens, A. (1990) *The Consequences of Modernity*, Cambridge: Polity Press.

King, A.D. (1984) *The Bungalow: The Production of a Global Culture*, London: Routledge.

Lawrence, D.L. and Lowe, S. (1990) 'The built environment and spatial form', *Annual Review of Anthropology*, Palo Alto, Calif.: Annual Reviews Inc.

Markus, T. (1993) *Buildings and Power*, London: Routledge.

Matrix (1984) *Making Space, Women and the Man-made Environment*, London: Pluto.

Roberts, M. (1991) *Living in a Man-Made World: Gender Assumptions in Modern Housing Design*, London: Routledge.

Schorske, C. (1987) *Fin-de-Siècle Vienna: Politics and Culture*, Cambridge: Cambridge University Press.

Wallerstein, I. (1987) 'World-systems analysis', in A.H. Giddens and J. Turner (eds) *Social Theory Today*, Cambridge: Polity Press.

Wilson, E. (1991) *The Sphinx in the City: Urban Life, the Control of Disorder and Women*, London: Virago.

22 Temples in China

Evelyn Lip

INTRODUCTION

Temple architecture in China is deeply rooted in the country's history. An understanding of the basic architectural principles and character of these temples thus involves the study of the historical background of temple buildings (Lip 1984: 207–10).

The first major Buddhist temple, built in the western part of Luoyang, Henan, was called Bai Ma Si, dated AD 67. It was fashioned after the Chinese palace and official residence.[1] The architecture of Chinese temples has not changed considerably since the seventh century. The planning was, and still is, based on symmetry and, very often, the *si-he-yuan* principle (Chi Ying Tao 1965: 17–18). However, the structural and supporting systems had evolved gradually since the Tang dynasty of AD 618–907.

In geographical terms, China is large. The natural resources, climate and customs vary from area to area. For these reasons, the temples in the Northern part vary in detail from those in the South.[2] These variations, however, were modified by the long period of the Chinese feudal systems which tended to predetermine building requirements and styles. Building size, planning, construction, materials and the themes of decorations were determined and executed according to the edicts of the feudal system of the various dynasties

Figure 1 *Map of China showing the provinces and autonomous regions. The northern region consists of Heilongjiang, Jilin, Liaoning, Hebei, Shandong, Shanxi, Shaanxi, Gansu and Qinghai. The central region comprises Jiangsu, Anhui, Henan, Hubei, Sichuan, Yunnan, Guizhou, Hunan, Jiangxi and Zhejiang. The southern region includes Guangxi, Guangdong and Fujian.*

(Wang Yun Wu 1926: 34–8). In short, the architecture of China was generally developed and to some extent constrained by thousands of years of Chinese traditions and practices under its feudal system. Consequently, constructional systems, usage of materials and building techniques did not change very much. Even though feudal lords and rulers changed from one dynasty to the next, the basic concepts of planning and structural system continued. A stereotyped courtyard plan and unique beam-frame structure prevailed in China and exerted influences elsewhere, such as in Japan, Taiwan, Korea, Vietnam, Malaysia and Singapore.

The aim of this essay is first to identify the principal architectural characteristics of temples and the dynastic changes that were related to this study. Second, it is to compare the architectural features of temples in northern, central and southern China and to distinguish the differences between them, if any, so that the origin of the Chinese temples in Singapore can be traced more precisely (see Figure 1).

BASIC ARCHITECTURAL CHARACTERISTICS AND DYNASTIC CHANGES

Introduction

Chinese architecture was already well developed during the Han dynasty (206 BC). During the Northern Wei dynasty (AD 386–534), 12,700 temples were built (Gin Djih Su 1964: 49). The greatest of monasteries, the Yun Ning Si, was constructed by Empress Dowager Hu. Since then, the craft of temple building has been transferred from generation to generation of master builders, who made reference to the *Treatise of Architectural Method* (Ying Zuo Fa Shi), which was written by Li Jie in AD 1097.[3] During the Qing dynasty (AD 1616–1911), the Ministry of Works produced a publication on the subject of Chinese construction methods. This publication became the standard manual for builders and, as a result, the style of traditional temple architecture was standardized.

Planning

The plan of the large temple can be identified easily with that of the imperial palace, while the plan of the community worship hall or ancestor worship (Ci) is similar to that of a residential house (Wang Yun Wu 1926: 43–6; see Figure 2). For example, the palaces of the Forbidden City, Beijing, are similar in planning to the Kong Fu Zi Miao, Shandong, with similar symmetrical

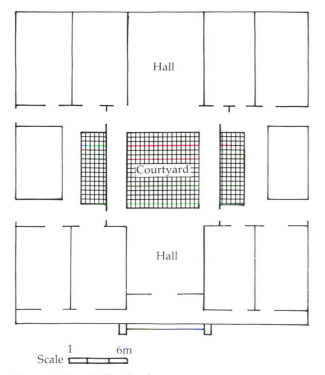

Figure 2 *Plan of a Chaozhou house.*

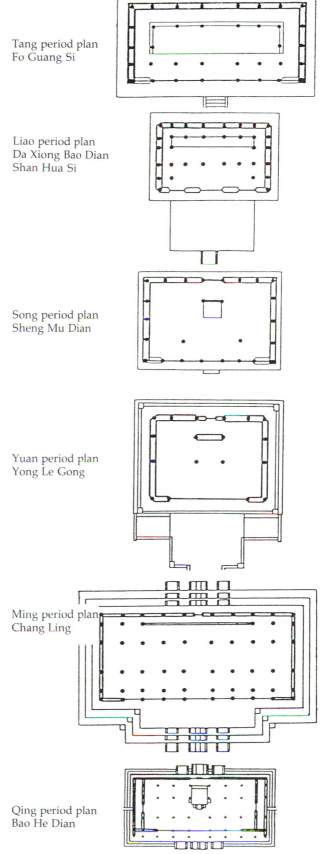

Tang period plan
Fo Guang Si

Liao period plan
Da Xiong Bao Dian
Shan Hua Si

Song period plan
Sheng Mu Dian

Yuan period plan
Yong Le Gong

Ming period plan
Chang Ling

Qing period plan
Bao He Dian

Figure 3 *Plans of temples from the Tang to the Qing dynasties.*
(Source: *Watson 1981*)

layout, axial planning, walled enclosure and north–south orientation.

The palace enclosure, *tai he dian*, is a rectangular enclosure with colonnades and built-up, beam-framed trusses, as is the prayer hall of Kong Fu Zi Miao.

Many of the Taoist and Buddhist monasteries were renovated or converted from private residences (Gin Djih Su 1964: 68). In fact, the design of palaces, temples and residences was in general similar and indeed, in use, they were quite interchangeable.[4] Palaces, official buildings, residences and temples were basically of the *si-he-yuan*, or courtyard plan, with strict adherence to symmetry, axiality, north–south orientation and walled enclosure (Chi Ying Tao 1965: 17–18).[5] Large temples consisted of successive courts and porticoes with halls on the sides. Usually there were three blocks of buildings grouped around a central court. The first was *shan men*, or entrance hall, beyond which was the court. On the right and left of the court were the bell and drum-towers. Across the court was the *tian wang dian*, or internal courtyard, beyond which was the *da xiong bao dian* or main hall (Lip 1981: 41; see Figure 3). For small temples which consisted of one block there was only one forecourt.

For larger temple complexes there were at least two internal courtyards. The first building block was called the *shan men*, the second the *tian wang dian*, the third the *dai ziong bao dian*, and the fourth the *hou dian* or *ting*. As an example, the Pu Lo Si Changde, Hebei, is drawn to scale and shown in Figure 4 to indicate the relationship and the hierarchy of space and height of the building blocks.

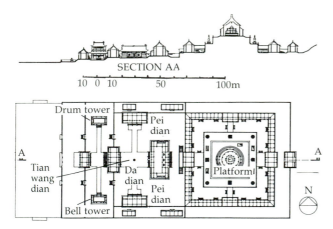

SECTION AA

Figure 4 *Plan of Pu Lo Si, Changde, Hebei (northern China).* (Source: *Boerschmann 1925: 220, pl. 125*)

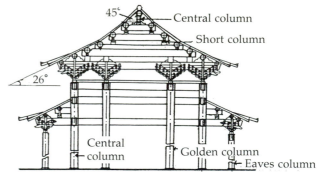

Figure 5 *Section of a temple.* (Source: *Li Jie 1103*)

The planning of temples during the dynasties of Tang (AD 618–907), Liao (907–1125), Song (960–1279), Yuan (1206–1368), Ming (1368–1644) and Qing (1616–1911) is exemplified in Figure 3. From the drawings it can be concluded that the concept of planning of temples had not changed very much through the dynasties as it was based on symmetry and rectangular layout.

Structural system

Though the structural system had undergone gradual changes, the basic elements of the Chinese structural system remained substantially the same. Chinese temples were built on the beam-frame system developed by the Chinese during the Han dynasty. The roof support took the form of a built-up triangle, consisting of a system of beams of diminishing length placed precisely one over the other between columns, and separated from each other by struts. Above the beams and purlins, rafters were placed to support the tiling boards and battens which in turn supported roof tiles. The roof finish consisted of one insulating layer of clay on which segmental roof tiles were laid in two interlocking layers (Wang Yun Wu 1926: 282). These roof tiles were either unglazed terracotta or glazed in various colours. The whole superstructure was supported by timber columns resting on stone bases. The columns and the entire framework were tied by longitudinal beams and transverse beams. Many temples had five types of columns, namely the eaves, 'golden', centre, intermediate and short columns. There were two or more rows of columns that divided the hall into the central and side spaces. There was often an additional exterior colonnade forming a portico in the front of the temple (see Figure 5).

The structural system gave considerable freedom in the design of the roof curvature because the relative positions of the struts and purlins could be changed so as to form a straight or a curved roof profile.

Eaves posts were built around the temple underneath the eaves. The 'golden' posts were built on the outer

perimeter, but inside the eaves posts; the intermediate posts were those in between the 'golden' posts. The structural elements were joined by tenons and mortices (Wang Yun Wu 1926: 215 and Li Jie 1097: 109–10). To build substantial overhanging eaves, the Chinese invented the *dou-gong* as early as the Zhou dynasty (Chinese Academy of Architecture 1979: 110). Since then the *dou-gong* was used in temples throughout China. The inner end of the *dou-gong* first abutted a transverse tie-beam over which various blocks and struts conveyed the support of the roof. By the Song period the forces from the inner end of the *dou-gong* or bracket were transmitted through the construction system of the bracket to

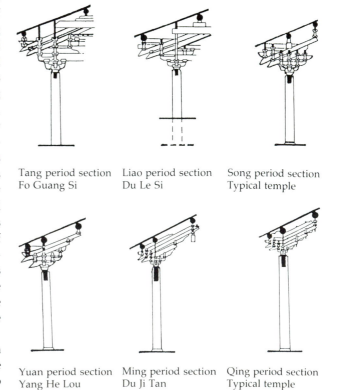

Tang period section
Fo Guang Si

Liao period section
Du Le Si

Song period section
Typical temple

Yuan period section
Yang He Lou

Ming period section
Du Ji Tan

Qing period section
Typical temple

Figure 6 *Sections of temples from the Tang to the Qing dynasties.* (Source: *Watson 1981*)

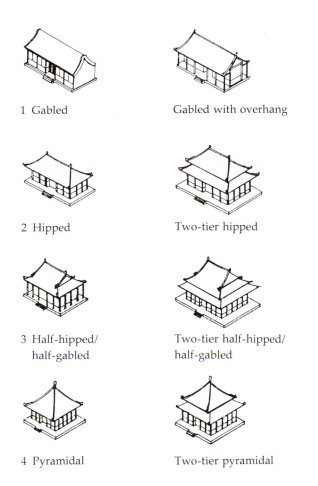

1 Gabled

Gabled with overhang

2 Hipped

Two-tier hipped

3 Half-hipped/
half-gabled

Two-tier half-hipped/
half-gabled

4 Pyramidal

Two-tier pyramidal

Figure 7 *Roof forms showing the four basic types (left), with variations (right).*

the purlin in the same way as that under the eaves of the roof (Watson 1981: 502–4). From the Yuan dynasty onward the ends of some of the transverse bracket arms were carved to an oblique point. By the Qing period the module (formation of the bracket) was as broad or thick as the bracket arm.[6] From Figure 6 it can be seen that the Tang brackets took up 40 per cent of the total height of the roof support, while the Qing brackets took up only 12 per cent (Wang Yun Wu 1926: 188).

Roof forms and ridges

Since the Han dynasty, Chinese roof forms were developed to give emphasis to the overall form and shape of the building and to protect it from rain and other elements. The beam-framed system made it possible to form the roof in many ways. Basically there were four types of roof: the gabled, the hipped, the half-hipped or half-gabled, and the pyramidal (see Figure 7).

The rank of a temple was reflected by its roof form since this was considered the most important part of a building. Generally, the most important block of a temple complex had a double-hipped roof, while the

least important had a gabled roof. The beam-frame and bracketing system also made it possible to curve the roof eaves and verge. The curved roof was developed as early as the Han dynasty (Boyd 1962: 38). Symbolically, the most important part of the roof was the main ridge; on it were placed symbols and sculptured animals, birds, plants or figurines to 'repel' evil influence and 'capture' good fortune (Lip 1979: 90–5).

Walls and finishes

The walls and partitions of temples were screens, and were non-structural with the exception of small temples in southern China (Wang Yun Wu 1926 and Gin Djih Su 1964: 203). External walls were used to exclude rain, sun or snow. The use of wall infills between columns originated over three thousand years ago (ibid.). The internal partitions were not always carried to the ceiling and were often made of wood. The materials used for external walls were brick, stone and timber. Important temple walls were faced with glazed tiles, or granite or marble panels (Fletcher 1956: 919).

Openings in walls and windows ranged from square to oval in shape. The types and shapes of openings did not appear to be consistently identified with stylistic origin. Substantiating this, Wang Yun Wu wrote, 'All forms and shapes of windows are used throughout China. I have collected as many as three hundred types by travelling for one to two months (Wang Yun Wu 1926: 52–3).

Colour and decoration

The colour schemes of Chinese temples were designed both with reference to symbolism and for practical purposes. Since the main structural members were of timber, oil paint was applied for two purposes: to protect the timber from insect attack and decay, and to give colour and symbolic value to the temples. Selection of colours was based on the principle of harmony of *yin* and *yang* (cool and warm), and each part of the temple had its designated colour.

The colours applied were believed to exert influence on the destiny of the occupants (Gin Djih Su 1964: 224). The main colour scheme for imperial temples was yellow, for mandarin temples it was red, and for others green.

Colours are expressed through the 'yin-yang polarity' of the universe, and the five elements, as shown below (see Wang Yun Wu 1926: 63; also Lip 1978b: 17–21):

Element	Colour	Direction	Symbolism
wood	green	east	posterity, peace
fire	red	south	happiness, blessings
earth	yellow	centre	power, wealth
metal	white	west	peace, purity
water	black	north	mourning, bad fortune

Chinese decorative motifs applied to temple roofs, ceilings, beams, walls, columns and floors could be divided into five main categories, based on the themes of animals, plants, natural phenomena, geometry and legend (see Lip 1978: 33; Wang Yun Wu 1926: 57). Dragons were popularly used as decorative motifs and sculptures on roofs and columns because they represented power and royalty. *Hu-lu*,[7] pagodas, pearls, phoenixes, unicorns and figurines were also popular symbols of virtue, power and benevolence (Lip 1978a: 39–42 and Wang Yun Wu 1926: 56–7). The themes for decorative motifs and their significance can be summarized in the following table (see Morgan 1942: 110–21):

Themes	Symbolic representation
willow	meekness
plum	endurance
bamboo	longevity
orchid	superiority
peony	affection
jasmine	fairness
lotus	uprightness
chrysanthemum	joviality
dragon	royalty
phoenix	virtue
tortoise	longevity
unicorn	felicity
chimera	virtue
elephant	wisdom
eagle	boldness
duck	felicity
Eight Immortals	longevity

COMPARISON OF ARCHITECTURAL STYLES OF TEMPLES IN NORTHERN, CENTRAL AND SOUTHERN CHINA

Introduction

Generally, in all regions of China, temples were based on courtyard, axial and symmetrical forms. In large temples, the plan consisted of the front hall, the main hall and the rear hall. The left and right wings and the corridors were symmetrically placed on the sides of the halls so that the plan was axial. In smaller temples, residential courtyard-house plans were adopted. The structural system and constructional details had gone through several stages of development and changes; however, the principle of construction remained basically the same throughout China. The extent of elaboration depended on the location and importance of the temples.

China is a large country. The northern part consists of provinces such as Shandong, Jilin, Shanxi and Hebei.

The central part includes Jiangsu, Zhejiang, Anhui, Jiangxi, Henan, Hubei, Hunan and Sichuan. The southern part includes Fujian, Guangdong and Guangxi (see Figure 1). The purpose of the following section is to distinguish the architectural characteristics of the temples in the northern, central and southern parts of China.

General characteristics

The northern part of China is barren and timber is generally scarce. Mud bricks, stone and clay are used for building. The architecture, consequently, is unpretentious and robust. The central region has forests as well as fertile rice fields. Timber is used as the main building material. The architecture is less robust and richer in decoration than that of the North. The southern part has the mildest climate of the three regions and timber is found in abundance. There are numerous rivers and lakes. Boat or water navigation is common and the people are outgoing and adventurous. The architecture of this region is finer and more attention is given to details.

Planning

The *si-he-yuan* (four-in-one unit), a form of courtyard planning, was typical of temples in the northern region (see Figure 8). The courtyard was surrounded by a main prayer hall facing south, an entrance hall facing north or south, and the east and west halls. In the south, where the climate is milder and more humid than that of the north, the courtyard was also usual, but it was narrower and smaller (see Figure 9).[8] Windows of the northern

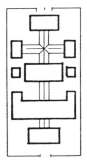

Figure 8 *Shuang Lin Si, Ping Yau, Shanxi (northern China).*

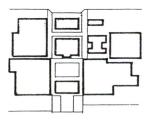

Figure 9 *Yong Quan Si, Ku Shan, Fujian (southern China).*

temples and houses opened on to the internal court-yards, while those of the southern temples opened on to the courtyards as well as the streets. Windows of the temples in the southern region are smaller, to exclude the strong sunlight (Gin Djih Su 1964: 232).

Structural system

The structural system for northern, central and southern China was based on the typical beam-frame construction (see Figure 10). Details of the built-up beam frames and cantilevered brackets varied not so much from region to region, but rather with the size and importance of the temples.

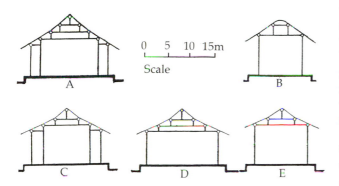

Figure 10 *Typical beam-frame constructional system.* (Source: *Wang Yun Wu 1926*)

Roof forms and ridges

Although the basic roof forms of temples in all three regions of China were the hipped, gabled, half-hipped or half-gabled, and pyramidal, those in the southern region were not as large in scale as those in the central and northern regions because, generally, temples in the south had smaller span.

The most significant difference between temples in the three regions is in the main ridge and corner rib design of the roofs:

> The great halls of the Imperial palace ... important temples, and similar buildings, have roofs which curve considerably ... but the ends of the corner ribs do not point upward. ... The roofs on the temples in Suchou and Hangchou are not only exceedingly large ... their corner ribs ... point upwards at the end like raised snouts or trunk. ... at Chuanchou, a further development of the roof lines are not only at the sides and corner-ribs but also at the main ridge.[9]
> (Siren 1970: 42)

In short, the roof ridges of the northern and central temples were straight while those of the southern temples were curved. The corner ribs of the northern temples were slightly curved, but those of the central and southern temples curved and tilted upward.

The curved and tilted southern Chinese roof not only provided shelter from the heat of the midday sun, admitted more light, and led the rain-water further away from the foot of the wall, but also looked more graceful. The southern tendency to an exaggerated upturn of the corners of the eaves, according to scholars such as Wang Yun Wu, Andrew Boyd and William Willets, was due to the aesthetic refinement of the elevation of the building.[10]

Walls and finishes

In terms of construction, the main difference between the northern and southern temples was in the use of materials for walls. The gable-end walls of the northern temples were built of thick mud or bricks to keep out the severe cold in the winter, and to keep the heat in during the summer. The southern region was warmer, and building construction was simpler and used a lighter framework. Walls were quite often made of bamboo mesh plastered with lime and mud. Bamboo lattice walls were also common. For important buildings bricks and masonry were used.

Colour and decoration

The colour schemes applied to the southern temples were generally brighter than those on the temples in the other regions. But large and important temples in northern and central China were just as colourful and bright – for example, Guan Di Miao at Shanxi, Ling Ku Si at Jiangsu, and Tai Miao at Shandong. The type and arrangement of ornaments and symbols on the roofs of the temples in the south were impressive, and a few distinctive examples with extremely ornamental roof and ridge decorations were found on the coastal regions of the south. Temples in the southern region were generally more ornate and had more variety in their decorative motifs compared to those in northern China (Wang Yun Wu 1926: 24).

The variety in the design of roof beams, brackets and wood carving of the southern temples was impressive. Frequently, at the ends of the corner-ribs of the roofs were dragon tails, while on top of the main ridge a pearl and two sculptures of dragons were placed. Other ornaments such as pagodas, phoenixes and flowers were also used.[11] At the entrance areas of the southern temples, the columns usually had dragons entwined (ibid.).

SUMMARY

The northern style was more robust than the central and southern styles, and comparatively, in elevation was less decorative. The significant difference in planning between the three regions of China was in the size of the interior courtyards. The south, having the mildest climate, had narrower and smaller courtyards. The roof forms of the temples in the southern region were not as

Guan Yin Ge, Tu Lo Si
Datong, Shanxi
N. China

Shan Ku Miao
Anping, Hebei
N. China

Huo Hsing Shan Ku Miao
He Xian, Hebei
N. China

Long Shan Si
Zhengding Xian, Hebei
N. China

Jiu Li Miao
Jiu Li lake, Fujian
S. China

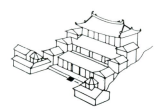

Qing Shui Si
Penglai, Fujian
S. China

Figure 11 *Freehand sketches of temples in China.*

large as those of the centre and north.

In terms of wall construction, the main difference between the northern and southern temple was in the use of materials. For example, walls of the small Northern temples were built of mud bricks, whereas those of the Southern temples were built of a lighter material such as bamboo mesh.

In terms of colour and decoration, temples in the southern region were more ornate and decorative than those in the other regions. However, the most significant difference in the architectural characteristics of the temples of these two regions was in the main ridge and the corner rib design of the roof. Generally, the roof ridge and corner ribs of temples in the southern region curved and tilted up, whereas the ridges of temples in the central region were straight, although the corner ribs also tilted and curved up. But in the northern region both the ridges and the corner ribs of temples were usually straight (see Figure 11).

NOTES

1   Many scholars have testified that Chinese temples were modelled on palaces or residential buildings. See Chi Ying Tao 1965: 17–18, Wang Yun Wu 1926: 43 and Gin Djih Su 1964: 70–1.

2   See Wang Yun Wu 1926: 20–5 and 26–34. Wang explained the natural resources and weather conditions of northern, central and southern China which affected the architectural characteristics of these regions.

3   The *Ying Zuo Fa Shi*, written by Li Jie, is a detailed and methodical illustrated summary of the Song practice of building and decoration. The first edition was printed in 1103 at Kaifeng, and was reprinted in 1145.

4   It is evident that plans of temples in China are similar in many ways. As an example of the way a temple was used for residence, or vice versa, Yong He Gong was originally the residence of Emperor Yong Zhen when he was a prince. It was turned into a temple after he became Emperor. The layout was, and still is, entirely in traditional style, complete with *pai-lou* (entrance arch), gatehouse, pavilion, and a hall for the Buddha.

5   Other scholars who confirmed these architectural characteristics were Andrew Boyd, Alexander Soper, Hugo Munsterberg, Joseph Needham and William Willetts.

6   Beams and columns of the structure were joined to simplify the construction and free the interior framework from restrictions imposed by the brackets.

7   A *hu-lu* is a magical gourd-shaped object for repelling evil influence.

8   Because the main and side halls are usually adjacent to each other, the courtyard is narrow and small. See Gin Djih Su 1964: 323.

9   Suchou, Hangchou and Chuanchou are old spellings of Suzhou, Hangzhou and Quanzhou, the latter being in southern China. The Imperial palace and important temples mentioned were in northern and central China. See Siren 1970: 42 and Hamlyn 1963: 229.

10   The reasons for the development of the curved roof were subjective. Some historians maintain the curved roof was designed for aesthetic reasons. See Willets 1958: 716–17.

11   The practice of placing a pearl and two dragons on the ridge was popular in the provinces around the southern coastal areas such as Fujian and Guangdong. According to Buddhist texts, the pearl was a miraculous object and a relic of Buddha.

REFERENCES

Boerschmann, E. (1925) *Chinesische Architektur*, 2 vols, Berlin: Waomuth.

Boyd, A. (1962) *Chinese Architecture and Town Planning 1500 BC–AD 1911*, London: Alec Tiranti.

Chinese Academy of Architecture (1979) *Ancient Chinese Architecture*, Beijing: Chinese Building Industry Press.

Chi Ying Tao (1965) 'Zong guo gu jan zhu shi qi de jian ding' ('The examination of the dates of ancient Chinese architecture', *Wen Wu* 4: 17–18.

Fletcher, B. (1956) *A History of Architecture on the Comparative Method*, London: Batsford.

Gin Djih Su (1964) *Chinese Architecture – Past and Contemporary*, Hong Kong: Sin Poh.

Hamlyn, P. (1963) *World Architecture*, London: Hamlyn.

Li Jie (1103) *Ying Zuo Fa Shi*, reprinted 1981, Beijing: Wen Wu Chu Ban She.

Lip, E. (1978a) 'Symbols, colours and decorations on Chinese temples in Malaysia', *Journal of the Malaysian Institute of Architects*, March: 39–42.

—— (1978b) 'Feng shui, Chinese colours and symbolism', *Journal of the Singapore Institute of Architects* 89: 17–21.

—— (1979) *Chinese Geomancy*, Singapore: Times Book International.

—— (1981) *Chinese Temples and Deities*, Singapore: Time Books International.

—— (1984) 'Chinese temple architecture in Singapore', Ph.D. thesis, National University of Singapore.

Morgan, T. (1942) *Chinese Symbols and Superstitions*, California: South Pasadena.

Munsterberg, H. (1954) *A Short History of Chinese Art*, London: P. Owen.

Needham, J. (1954) *Science and Civilization in China*, Vol. 2, Cambridge: Cambridge University Press.

Siren, O. (1929) *A History of Early Chinese Art*, London: E. Benn.

Soper, A.C. (1942) *The Evolution of Buddhist Architecture in Japan*, Princeton: Princeton University Press.

Wang Yun Wu (1926) *Zong Guo Jan Zhu Shi*, Beijing: Zong Guo Jan, Zhu Gong Yi, Chu Ban She.

Watson, W. (1981) *Art of Dynastic China*, London: Thames & Hudson.

Willetts, W. (1958) *Chinese Art*, London: Penguin.

FURTHER READING

Chow Kang Chang and Werner, B. (1987) *China, Tao in Architecture*, Boston: Birkhauser Verlag.

Silcock, A. (1935) *An Introduction to Chinese Art*, Oxford: Oxford University Press.

23   Client, community and climate:
Byker – a case study
Ben Farmer

Ralph Erskine's redevelopment of Byker for the city of Newcastle upon Tyne is without doubt the most comprehensive and convincing example of community participation and community response in England. It has attracted international interest and acclaim and has been widely reported in the architectural journals.[1] It has a major presence on the northern bank of the Tyne to the east of the city centre (see Figure 1) and is famous for its 'wall' and the fact that its architects set up their office on site and listened to the people.

During the latter half of the nineteenth century rows of terraced housing had been built at Byker to house the workers of the rapidly expanding shipbuilding and heavy engineering industries. To gain maximum use of space the streets were laid out in a gridiron pattern, with steeply sloping streets running east to west, bisected by the main thoroughfare of Raby Street – within this area a very close-knit, homogeneous, working-class community grew up.

By the 1950s, with overcrowding at 120 per acre (49 per hectare) and many of the houses declared unfit for habitation, this still close-knit community was scheduled to be cleared as part of an overall slum-clearance plan by the City Council. The programme began in the mid-1960s and by 1979 was complete. What made Byker

Figure 1 *View of Byker forming the skyline to the northern bank of the Tyne.*

special was that in 1968 the City Council decided to respond to local demands, acknowledging that there was a cohesive community which should be preserved. The local people declared a preference for new houses and argued for the preservation of community spirit (Arkitektokoutor AB and Department of Housing 1981).

The brief was formulated in the late 1960s. What may now be described as the council areas were built in the 1970s and the 'build for sale' areas in the early years of the 1980s.

It might be helpful if, at the outset, I show my hand. I believe Byker to be a great success. If one walks around now, some two decades after its inception, and more than a decade after most of it was built, one cannot help but be struck by two things: first, its size – it is a very large-scale redevelopment,[2] and second, its overall quality, which is head and shoulders higher than most, if not all, developments of a similar nature in Britain. It has to be regarded as a success, too, if measured against the views of the city's Housing Department,[3] the expressed attitudes of Byker's population (Cameron and Thornton 1986: 54), and claims that its seminal significance rivals that of Stuttgart's Weisenhof Housing Exhibition of 1927 (Egelius 1980: [2]).

It is, however, not an unmitigated success. Peter Malpass argued that the two key questions – have the people been able to remain in their home neighbourhood, and have the people of Byker been closely involved in the formulation of policies and their subsequent execution? – properly deserved the answer 'no' (Malpass 1979). More recently, when Ralph Erskine was in the news again, as a result of being nominated for the RIBA Gold Medal, the following extracts featured in the editorial news page of the *Architects' Journal*:

> Police plan a 'designer-crime' scheme on RIBA Gold Medalist Ralph Erskine's award winning Byker Estate in Newcastle upon Tyne to stem what they claim is a rising crime wave. . . . Erskine has become a soft target for complaints about maintenance and is being blamed for a whole range of problems from the height of garden trees to poorly filled potholes. 'Half the people here would hang Erskine if they could get their hands on him', said Sid Jones, Chairman of Grace Street Tenants' Association. 'Parts of the estate are just falling to bits.'
>
> 'Things have changed a lot, mind, since Byker was first planned,' said Jones. 'Now we are paying £48.00

for rents, rates and heating, although 8 out of 10 people here get subsidy.'[4]

Problems change as they are worked on, and perception of problems and the ability to respond to them change with changes in 'climate'. With respect to client, community and climate, there have in Byker's case been many significant changes.

AIMS

The stated aims of the redevelopment set out by Ralph Erskine in a memorandum in November 1968 were as follows:

> At the lowest possible cost for the residents, and in intimate contact and collaboration with them particularly, and with relevant authorities generally, to prepare a project for planning and building a complete and integrated environment for living in its widest possible sense. This would involve us in endeavouring to create positive conditions for dwelling, shopping, recreation, studying and – as far as possible – working in new contact with the home. It would involve us in considering the wishes of the people of all ages and many tastes.
>
> We would endeavour to maintain as far as possible, valued traditions and characteristics of the neighbourhood itself and its relationships with the surrounding areas and the centre of Newcastle.
>
> The main concern will be with those who are already resident in Byker, and the need to re-house them without breaking family ties and other valued associations or patterns of life.
>
> We would endeavour to exploit the physical character of the site, more especially the slope towards the south, its views and sunny aspect.
>
> (Erskine 1977: 839)

'The political aim for the redevelopment was "Byker for the Byker people" and an overriding problem was to preserve social unity.' (Egelius 1980: [2])

CLIENT

Specifically to address the theme of this essay, with respect to client, Ralph Erskine is on record as having said:

> A clear distinction needed to be made between the sponsor clients and 'the real clients – the users themselves'. He had been lucky with Byker he said, 'because the clients were already living there when we started'.
>
> (*Architects' Journal* 1987: 11)

But he is also on record as having said that he is conscious of the influence of money, and conscious too that its source can be as important as its amount, as

Figure 2 *Fast-growth plants helped to create character and a sense of place.*

funding agencies may well have priorities for cost allocation, for example, high priority on internal equipment rather than on planting and landscaping (Edwards 1982: 21). As ever, the real client is the person who will pay for the venture.

Byker's client in the sense of commissioning agency has been the City Council but that Council has changed its political persuasion over time and has been in and out of sympathy with national government. During the formation of the brief and the early phases of the Byker development there were national and local commitments to social housing and high levels of funding for the public sector. There was also the avowed interest of wishing to make the development look good as quickly as possible. To that end, for example, landscaping was realized by fast-growth plants (Figure 2).

Towards the end of the 1970s and into the 1980s, not only was there a Conservative government in power nationally but a Conservative government geared to monetarism, to an enterprise culture and to the general belief that market forces should carry the day. Public spending was to be reduced severely in order to be able to reduce the apparent level of taxation – that is to say, to bring down the standard rate of income tax. As a result of such declared policies, the government exercised 'rate-capping' on local councils – a form of financial penalty for overspending. Additionally, council houses were to be available for sale throughout the land. Newcastle City Council was not able to complete the redevelopment as proposed by Ralph Erskine, and entered into 'build for sale' partnerships with two developers, with licensing agreements which allowed the Council to place a variety of conditions on those developers.

COMMUNITY

The community has changed; first, in respect of a dramatic reduction in population;[5] second, it is growing older; third, it is a community 'of the north', i.e. subject to comparative deprivation *vis-à-vis* those of the south, with high unemployment and with some 80 per cent of the householders in receipt of 'benefit'; and fourth, it is no longer exclusively a community renting property. There is now a low-cost owner-occupied development, the population of which, although not markedly different in terms of social class, is different in being younger and having more young children, and with having 12 per cent out of work, as against 62 per cent out of work (Cameron and Thornton 1986: 54). It is no longer a community united by common employment in nearby heavy industry and with extended family patterns.

CLIMATE

The north-east of England has perhaps the world's worst natural climate for building materials in having long, quite cold (often below freezing), very damp or wet winters. For much of the year the outside spaces are not places in which to linger. Culture and climate are always close neighbours but even in summer the outside benches and tables are now used less than was initially the case.[6] In particular, such a climate is lethal for low-quality softwoods,[7] and the prevailing weather conditions, with much drizzle and dribble, are notorious for causing pattern stains on buildings. Reference has already been made to the economic climate which currently obtains, and, unhelpfully, Byker is more expensive to maintain than are most local authority developments in Britain. 'Environmental maintenance' is high – there is a special team on Byker, geared to maintaining the spaces between the buildings, and to maintain the buildings themselves. Because of the extensive use of softwoods, the maintenance programme for that material is particularly onerous and not at all helped by the fact that much of the timber is difficult to access.

To place these considerations in context, it must be acknowledged that there is real interest in maintaining the development to a high level, both on the part of the local authority and of the residents. A contemporaneous development in Newcastle at Rye Hill – a development for some 300 houses – is now deemed completely out of date, is extremely unpopular, and is to be remodelled at a unit cost of some £10,000 – altogether a cost to the local exchequer, therefore, of some £3 million.[8]

With respect to social climate, since the inception of the redevelopment, society in Britain has more violence, less prosperity on comparative if not absolute terms, more unemployment and reduced educational opportunities. Vandalism, crime (particularly housebreaking) and graffiti seem to be natural by-products of these changes. At Byker graffiti are marked by their absence, and damages to buildings and external features are surprisingly few, but many of the local residents are concerned about the profuse vegetation which, in combination with the levels and the locations of external space-lighting, they believe gives too many opportunities for evil-doers to avoid detection. Whether this is a real rather than a perceived problem is difficult to measure.[9]

Nationwide, the philosophical climate has changed out of all recognition in the past few years with the Conservative government's commitment to, and recommendation of, 'the enterprise culture', leading to a major shift in the percentage of the population who now own their own homes. However, in common with most inner areas of Newcastle, council house sales in Byker have been very low. At the time of a survey carried out by the Department of Town and Country Planning at Newcastle University in 1984, only eleven of the 2,000 dwellings had been sold. The explanation in the case of Byker, which is generally well regarded by residents, is that their income is low, many of them being unemployed or elderly, and that the design of the redevelopment is not thought to be appropriate to owner-occupation on the open market. In other words, people are concerned about resaleability. Sales are also prejudiced by a government control called a 'cost floor', with tenants being allowed large discounts on the market value of the dwelling, provided that the price they pay is no lower than the construction cost. House prices have risen slowly in the north-east of England, which in effect reduces the discount which can be given.

GENERAL CONSIDERATIONS

If we now address issues which are timeless and universal in presenting architecture with challenges to which it must respond – response to people, response to place and response to routes – one can see that, with

Figure 3 *Kendal Street, Byker, pre-redevelopment.* (Source: *Konttinen 1983. Copyright: Amber Associates, Newcastle upon Tyne*)

Figure 4 *The containing north wall follows the site's contours and forms a shield to traffic noise.*

respect to response to people, the community could not be retained in its entirety simply as a function of the reduction of density on site and because of external systems beyond the control of the architect. As Malpass has argued, 'participation has become merely an aspect of urban management, rather than the means of giving people a decisive voice in their area' (Malpass 1979b: 1013). With respect to community involvement, in the initial pilot scheme for forty-six dwellings, there were detailed consultations with the prospective tenants for each dwelling. In the event, only thirty-three such tenants occupied the forty-six dwellings in the pilot scheme and this exercise was not repeated, in part because it had set up tensions and jealousies between those chosen to participate and those not chosen. Consultation thereafter became very much more generalized:

Figure 5 *Building forms and public spaces in complete contrast to what went before.*

Specifically, the idea of an on site architect's office should not mislead us into thinking that priority really was given to the residents as clients. The value of the office is in drawing attention to the contradiction of aiming to work for one set of clients while the key resources are controlled by another. From the attempt to involve tenants in design we should learn that what was more important was the overall distribution of decision-making power. The real question remains who gets what, when and how and who decides?

(Malpass 1979a: 969)

With respect to place, Byker breaks the rules of play for buildings in that area. Traditionally, Byker had what in England are called terraced houses – in many other countries known as 'row houses' – stepping down the contours, with gradients of up to 1 in 7 giving dramatic

Figure 6 *Within the site the containing wall offers itself to the sun.*

form. Even this typology was misleading as the 'houses' were in fact 'Tyneside flats' – a rather special configuration which causes flat (apartment) development to read like house development. The townscape was hard with no trees and no gardens (Figure 3). The redevelopment did, however, preserve some key buildings and facilities – swimming pool, churches, pubs and some shops – but the form of redeveloped Byker with its containing northern wall, following the contours, and its low-rise buildings defining and containing open spaces which are public and semi-private, was a totally 'foreign' solution and, being quite outside the experience of Byker residents, would not have been a solution which they would have proposed (see Figures 4, 5 and 6).

With respect to routes, the existing route patterns were severed. New routes were to be accommodated, principally the urban motorway and the 'Metro' railway development. The philosophy of traffic segregation carried the day. Byker, then, represents a major implant on the pattern of the city and, in particular, having severed many of the existing routes, has caused interference with some aspects of broader community life. Priory Green United Reformed Church on Gordon Road has closed partly because many of its congregation had been dispersed as a result of Byker's reduced population, and others of its congregation found the 'wall' between their homes and their Church. Additionally, public transport services were re-routed.

Byker can, therefore, be seen as being foreign in form, foreign in scale and foreign in typology. It disregards local rules of play for building and the genetic codes of building, responding not at all to existing routes but to a proposed route in a self-protective way, and introduces new segregated routes which, arguably, have as many disadvantages as they have advantages (orientation is a problem). It used building form and building materials and colours never before seen in the north-east of England (Figure 5).

THE ARCHITECT AS A COMPONENT OF THE PROBLEM

Erskine was the problem-solver and if we examine his approach to such problems we find the following.

1   Wherever possible he tries to get the users involved at the design stage (Edwards 1982: 6) – at Byker, such participation was necessarily limited by the sheer size of the project.

2   He is concerned with people's needs (Erskine 1977b: 37), particularly their needs for privacy and their need for some private outdoor space. Most Erskine houses have gardens or balconies – balconies giving territorial but not visual privacy and therefore offering self-policing prospects (Edwards 1982: 12).

3   He regards traffic danger, traffic noise and traffic fumes as invasive forces. He is committed therefore to partial or total vehicular segregation. He argues that identity with schemes and with individual dwellings is vitally important, and he uses colour as a key to identity of location (ibid.).

4   The concept of a 'boundary wall' of flats or houses is a strong and recurrent theme in his work.[10]

5   He enjoys exploiting sloping sites which face south in order to take advantage of solar radiation, often with the open spaces oriented to the south-east to take advantage of the early morning sun, and with living rooms oriented to the south-west so that balconies or immediately accessible private outside spaces can be enjoyed in the late afternoons and evenings. He is committed to the use of forms which protect and embrace (Erskine 1976: 96), and as a deliberate policy he tries to get interest and variety of forms of building with richly planted external spaces (Buchanan 1981: 339) by using low-cost materials (Edwards 1982: 24). He has used timber a great deal in Scandinavia, claiming that 'timber is a friendly material that is pleasant to touch'. (Erskine 1976: 32)

All of the above form a complete prescription for the redevelopment of Byker as carried out by Ralph Erskine, and with his interest in protective perimeter walls coinciding with the policy which the planners had produced to protect the redevelopment from traffic noise, the concept of the wall and its form were a precondition and not open to negotiation or consultation.

What is, however, also very obviously true is that there is an unusual degree of pride of possession and sense of involvement with the redevelopment on the part of its residents, and that the presence of the architect's office on site in major part led to that, first, because it was accessible, second, because it worked hard to listen to people's interests and their declared needs, and third, and perhaps most importantly of all, it really did try to communicate with the 'folk' of Byker in terms that they could understand.[11]

That investment of energy has proved to be well placed. The lesson seems to be that, inevitably, public participation will have very severe limits, but that its existence is so much more important than any of its specifics; that if a venture is big enough and bold enough and carried out with courage and flair, both its active and its passive users will enjoy it, come to take pride in it and sustain it.

Much mention is made of community response and community architecture in Britain today. In part it is due to the crisis we have in our inner cities and by the fact that one of its leading exponents, Dr Rod Hackney, recently served as President of the Royal Institute of British Architects. Much of this, certainly as practised by Rod Hackney himself, can be seen as community building rather than community architecture, and (although obviously good for the morale of the people who have built their own homes) Hackney invites us to suspend judgement in certain respects, claiming that if such people on such occasions are able to build things which serve them well and of which they are proud, then that is sufficient in itself. There is, too, a test to be

Figure 7 *The banal architecture of the build-for-sale development.*

made in future with respect to the resaleability of such property.

The lesson which is apparently eternally true of Britain is that 'he who pays the piper, *does* call the tune'. The latest phases of Byker, with the 'build for sale' partnership between the City and developers, has led to architecture which is banal in the extreme, and to a miserable approach to external space-making and, indeed, to general overall character. Private money seems to be able to respond only to the interests of the market-place (see Figure 7).

CONCLUSION

The generalizable lessons to emerge from Byker would seem to be:

1   Consultation and communication are invaluable in leading to understanding and a sense of involvement which can have long-term benefits.

2   Improved living conditions initially generate much goodwill towards the architect whereas estate deterioration generates ill-will, with neither being absolutely deserved.

3   Good management and good behaviour are all-important and interdependent.

4   There should be maximum possible investment in build quality.

5   The nature and the source of funding are of critical importance – inescapably, the real client is the funding agency.

6   There is a clear relationship between quality of realization and the quality and amount of invested thought.

7   Designers are prone to the 'Sinatra Syndrome' – they do it their way.

Byker is the implantation of an entirely different approach to residential development in Newcastle – replacing a most characterful earlier approach which had

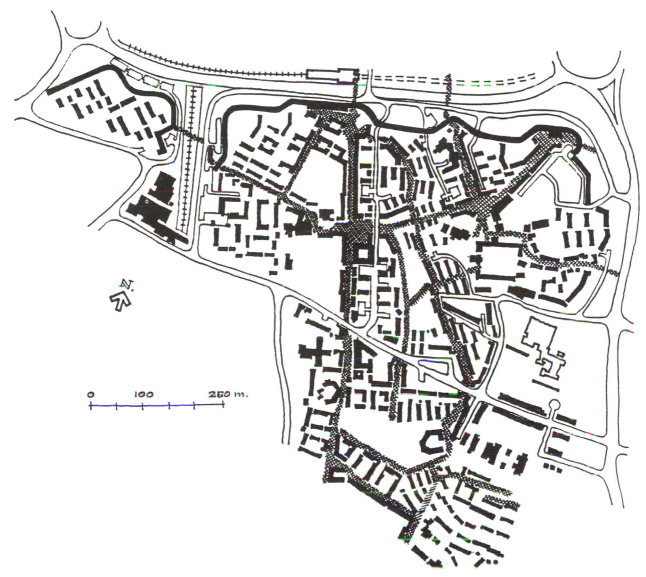

Figure 8 *Diagrammatic plan showing wall to the north (acting as a barrier to road and rail noise) and the pedestrianized through routes.*

been completely overtaken by changing standards and expectations and which was in extreme disrepair. It is big enough to be a new system – a new game – rather than the breaking of existing rules of play (Figure 8).

The medical analogy of surgical transplantation seems apt. Newcastle has had a 'pacemaker' fitted, the body is alive and has recovered from the operation, there is no sign of rejection, health care is good but medication (in the form of financial subsidy) will be a lifelong requirement. The budget for medication is subject to pressure.

NOTES

1   See list of *Further Reading*.
2   The site is approximately 81 hectares (200 acres) with 2,000 council-owned dwellings and some 300 privately owned dwellings. The perimeter block is in some places eight storeys high – within this 'wall' is an area of two-storey housing, in small terraces and around courtyards. The low-rise development is of timber-framed construction faced in brickwork. There is a district heating scheme.
3   Interview with John Cornhill, Assistant Director of Renewal Housing Department, Civic Centre, Barras Bridge, Newcastle upon Tyne, 21 January 1988.
4   In Britain there are two major forms of Social Security benefit:

- *contributory benefits*: those paid in return for National Insurance contributions, e.g. unemployment benefit, sickness benefit and retirement pensions;
- *income support*: a 'top-up' for people not in full-time employment whose income falls below a certain level. Generally, people on income support will have their rent and local government tax paid.

See Lakhani and Read 1987.

5   Byker population estimates quoted by Malpass (1979a: 964) are as follows:

1960	17,450
1968	12,000
1975	6,200
1979	4,400

So, since the start of the demolition the population has declined by 75 per cent and since the decision to retain the community it has fallen by 64 per cent.
6   Interviews with John Cornhill and residents, January 1988 (see n. 3).
7   'The generous use of wood has caused some problems in Byker, as it is a rarely used building material in that area of Britain. The craftsmanship in the endless details is often of low quality and the wooden houses are often associated with pre-fabricated, emergency shelters' (Erskine 1977a: 841).
8   Interview with John Cornhill, January 1988 (see n. 3).
9   'Northumbria Constabulary are to implement an Alice Coleman style overhaul of the estate which it is said is prey to burglars and muggers because of the poor lighting and landscaping which provides cover' (*Architects' Journal* 1987: 11).
10   For example, Brittgården, in Tibro, and also Erskine's 1958

studies for an ideal arctic town (Edwards 1982: 14–16).
11   The office was led by Vernon Gracie and Roger Tillotson, and their thinking, although fundamentally aligned to Erskine's, is reflected throughout the realization of Byker. Their availability, compassion, intelligence and energy were critically important to the genuine feeling the Byker folk had of 'being listened to'. Roger Tillotson is now Director of Studies to the BArch Course at the School of Architecture, University of Newcastle upon Tyne.

REFERENCES

Architects' Journal (1987) 'News', *Architects' Journal* 185 (13) 1 April: 11.

Arkitektokonter AB and Director of Housing, City of Newcastle upon Tyne (1981) *The Byker Redevelopment*, City of Newcastle upon Tyne.

Buchanan, P. (1981) 'Byker: the spaces between', *Architectural Review* 170 (1018): 339.

Cameron, S. and Thornton, G. (1986) 'Build for sale partnerships in Byker', *Housing Review* 35(2): 53–4.

Edwards, S. (1982) 'A very nice place to live – Ralph Erskine's approach to housing', dissertation for BA in Architectural Studies, School of Architecture, University of Newcastle upon Tyne.

Egelius, M. (1980) 'Byker', *Global Architecture* 55.

Erskine, R. (1976) 'Construire dans le nord', *L'Architecture d'Aujourd'hui* 134: 96.

—— (1977a) 'The Byker Wall', *Architectural Design* 47 (11–12): 837–41.

—— (1977b) 'Wie bewohnbare Umgebung entsteht', *Bauen und Wohnen* 32: 37.

Kontinnen, S.-L. (1983) *Byker*, London: Jonathan Cape.

Lakhani, B. and Read, J. (1987) *National Welfare Benefits Handbook*, 17th edn, London: Child Poverty Action Group.

Malpass, P. (1979a) 'The other side of the wall: a reappraisal of Byker, Part I', *Architects' Journal* 169 (19) 9 May: 963–9.

—— (1979b) 'A reappraisal of Byker, Part II', *Architects' Journal* 169 (20) 16 May: 1011–21.

FURTHER READING

Byker has won many architectural awards and attracted international interest from architects, landscape architects, sociologists, planners and housing managers. It continues to be studied and written about but the following short list of published material serves as an introduction:

Arkitektokontor AB (1974) 'Urban redevelopment – the Byker experience', *Housing Review* 23 (6) November/December: 149–56.

Avery, C. (1974) 'Byker by Erskine', *Architectural Review* CLVI (934): 356–62.

Les Architects (1976) 'Pragmatisme romantique et continuité lyrique', *L'Architecture d'aujourd'hui*, no. 187: 51–5.

Cameron, S. and Thornton, G. (1986) 'Build for sale partnerships in Byker', *Housing Review* 35 (2) March–April: 53–5.

Egelius, M. (1977) 'Profile No. 9 – Ralph Erskine', *Architectural Design* 47 (11–12) December: 751–2.

Malpass, P. (1979) 'A reappraisal of Byker', *The Architects' Journal* 169 (19) 9 May: 961–9; 169 (20) 16 May: 1011–21.

Saint, A. (1977) 'The Byker Street Irregulars', *New Statesman* 93 (20 May): 897.

24 Privacy as a culturally related factor in built form

Miles Danby

The way our homes are designed and our settlements arranged reflects the relationship between individual, family and community. How the individual relates to family and community, of course, varies from one culture to another. Consequently, the organization of space in the home, the layout of residential areas, and access to the home and places of socialization are influenced by the way of life of the community. Nowhere is this more clearly demonstrated than in the world of Islam, where religious principles govern the way of life and affect the resultant built form.

Islam is a world religion and its community of faith is shared by approximately 400 million Muslims, distributed from Mauretania to Indonesia in one direction and from Mongolia to Malagasy in the other. The principles of Islam are established by the revelation of the Holy Qur'ān, the wisdom of the Prophet Muhammad and the inherited commentaries of the spiritually learned of the Islamic community. Islam is both monotheistic and patriarchal, sharing the religious traditions of Abraham with Judaism and Christianity. According to the Qur'ān, the Kaaba, the liturgical centre of the Islamic world, was built by Abraham and his son, Ishmael, and it was Abraham who initiated the yearly pilgrimage to Mecca. Muslims pray five times a day facing the direction of the Kaaba, and it is this axis that fixes the siting of the mosque and is given physical expression by the niche (*mihrab*) in the wall facing Mecca.

In an Islamic settlement the mosque is the most important building and access to it is the prime factor in the layout. In traditional towns and cities, the residential quarters are arranged in clusters of houses in culs-de-sac leading to minor through-streets which in turn lead to a main street, where the mosque, shops and markets are sited but clearly distinguishable from each other. In the Islamic way of life, the respective roles of man and woman are strictly defined in relation to the physical environment. The public areas are the domain of men while the private and family areas are the domain of women. The privacy of the family and the home are paramount and shape the plan form of all traditional Muslim houses. Male visitors who are not close relatives do not enter the family zone or meet the women of the household. In this way, Islamic culture requires physical space to be clearly public, semi-public and private.

Because Islam was founded in Arabia, Arab culture and language have influenced all Islamic countries. Not least of these influences is the tradition of hospitality, which results in all householders being hospitable in a way that is unknown in the Western world. The traditional greeting to a guest is, 'Welcome, my house is yours.' All visitors are welcome to stay as long as they wish, and the obligations of kinship combined with the tradition of hospitality require the keeping of an open house. In rural areas each settlement is regarded as a large family and houses are open to all members of the village, and especially to relatives from other villages. Formality hardly exists and individuality within the family is at a minimum. Consequently, there is little variation in the house form, furnishings and equipment. Because of the obligations of kinship, relatives from rural areas who may be visiting urban centres to find employment, or for business or medical treatment, can expect board and lodging for the duration of their stay.

The often conflicting needs for privacy of the family and traditional hospitality for visitors and relatives can only be resolved by the division of domestic space into two zones relating to the separation of the sexes. The male zone is also used for the reception and accommodation of male guests. The women have access to this zone when there are no males present who are outside the immediate family, but are otherwise excluded. The family zone is dominated by the women, and the men of the family use this zone as 'beloved guests'. The form of the home may reflect this duality in the simplest way. For example, the tent of the Bedouin, the desert nomads of Arabia, is divided into two zones (Figure 1) by a central curtain with a separate entrance to each division.

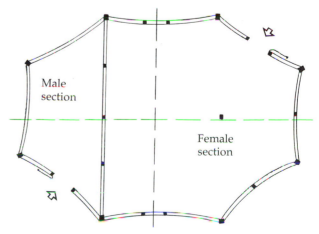

Figure 1 *The Bedouin's tent is divided into two zones.*

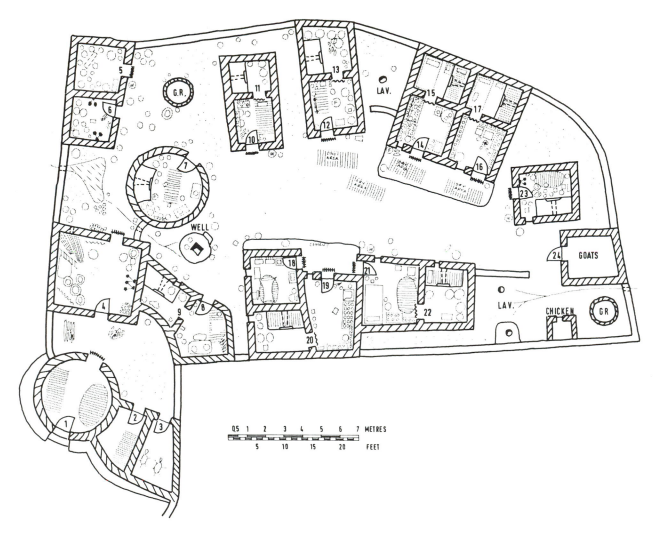

Figure 2 *Northern Nigerian compound accommodating one household head in three separate domestic units.* (Source: *Schwerdtfeger 1971*)

Permanent houses, on the other hand, are more complicated and contain a series of rooms and spaces which is planned in accordance with the same duality. The house may be large because of the need to accommodate guests as well as relatives who may reside permanently, forming an extended family. In urban situations, the male zone is sometimes extended because of the need to conduct the business of the householder, requiring space for business visitors and the storage of goods.

Another aspect of Islam that affects house form and layout is the permission given in the Holy Qur'ān for the practice of polygamy. Muslims are allowed to take up to four wives, but economic development and urbanization mean that polygamy is now relatively rare. However, in some areas quite extensive house plans are found that provide separate accommodation for each wife and respective children within the dual system. Such examples have been described by Schwerdtfeger (1971) in Zaria, northern Nigeria (Figure 2), where a single-walled compound with one household head may contain many different units, each unit consisting of as many as six rooms in some cases.

The cultural and religious emphasis on visual privacy in Islamic communities has tended to produce an inward-looking plan with external containing walls that have no openings that permit strangers outside to look inside. The entrance doorways, of which there are two where possible, allow an indirect approach to the interior, obtained by two right-angled turns in the vestibule, which avoids direct visual access even when the door is opened. The entrance is the main external feature at ground-floor level, and is frequently decorated in an attractive way that indicates its function, although ostentation is discouraged because of the egalitarian basis of Islam.

The courtyard plan is the most common arrangement used to achieve the degree of privacy needed. It has existed since 1900 BC at least, adopted from the Graeco-Roman tradition; with the advent of Islam, it was found that the courtyard concept suited its religious and social demands as well as providing a satisfactory response to the environmental problems of the hot and dry climate of Arabia and other parts of the Middle East. It also permitted the development of a housing layout that provided a high density and, at the same time, reduced the area of external surfaces exposed to solar radiation. The public circulation spaces are shaded during most of the day because the streets and alleyways are kept to the minimum width needed for pedestrians, horses and donkeys with average loads. In some urban areas where the development is two to three storeys high, some parts of the street are bridged at first-floor level, often linking neighbouring family apartments. This leaves repetitive rectangular areas open to the sky above, providing sufficient light and ventilation to the street as well as a beautiful pattern of light and shade.

The size of the courtyard varies as does the number of them provided in each household. It is common, where space and resources permit, to create two courtyards, one for male residents and visitors, and another for family use. The number of storeys varies from one to three; the flat roofs are used for sleeping out when the season permits. Development therefore was to be carefully controlled so that neighbours cannot observe the roof next door or another householder's courtyard. Screen walls at least two metres (six-and-a-half feet) high are built to maintain visual privacy of roof terraces.

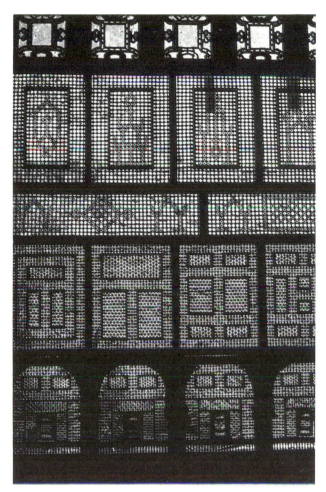

Figure 4 Mashrabiyya.

Figure 3 *Room on ground floor of three-storey courtyard house, Cairo, with one side open to the courtyard, viewed from loggia at first-floor level.*

A number of large courtyard houses, three storeys high, survive in the older districts of Cairo, and one has been described and analysed in some detail by Nour (1979). The rooms on the ground floor were used by men and were seldom entered by women. Casual meetings with male visitors of no great social standing would take place in a room with a side open to the courtyard (*taktabosh*) (Figure 3) and a central column supporting the family reception hall above (*ka'a*). Male vistors of importance, however, would enter indirectly from the courtyard to a large reception hall (*mandarah*), divided symmetrically about a lofty central space with a fountain and two subsidiary lower spaces at a slightly higher level on either side. These side spaces were simply furnished with carpets and cushions and were used for discussion and, sometimes, meals. In this example, there are two other reception halls of lesser proportions at ground-floor level, as well as various store-rooms. In the summer season, important male guests would be received in an open loggia (*maq'ad*) (Figure 3) facing into the courtyard at first-floor level, accessible by stairs from the courtyard close to the main entrance. The remaining spaces at first- and upper-floor levels were devoted to the family and no male stranger was allowed to enter. To ensure this, the stairs giving access to the family section are sited in a remote position as far as possible from the main entrance.

The main spaces used by the family at first-floor level are lit by large projecting windows of elaborate timber latticework which exclude the direct rays of the sun but provide a fair amount of reflected light and ventilation. The latticework was made from turned hardwood by skilled artisans working in a long-established tradition using very beautiful, complicated designs based on abstract geometrical patterns. The higher panels of these windows (*mashrabiyya*) are often decorated with coloured glass. There are some small opening panels provided to allow observation of the courtyard below but, in any case, it is possible to look out through the narrow gaps in the latticework without being seen. Screens of similar latticework are placed in the walls of the higher section of the *mandarah*, making it possible for the women to observe without being observed. *Mashrabiyya* are also placed in the street elevation at upper levels only (Figure 4). The ground floor of the street elevation has no windows, but there are some grilles at a level higher than the eye-level of a mounted passer-by.

So far the visual aspects of privacy have been emphasized, as these have most influenced built form, but acoustic privacy was also considered desirable, and was achieved. Many visitors have described the remarkable transformation from the noisy, bustling street, no doubt accentuated by the narrow width and hard stone surfaces, to the tranquil effect of the quiet reception rooms within. Nour measured the noise level in two reception halls of the described house (Beit El Siheimi) as well as in the street outside. The reception halls averaged 36 dB compared with 68 dB recorded in the street (Nour 1979: 327). This considerable reduction is probably due to the heavyweight construction of the thick stone walls at ground-floor level, the close-packed courtyard plan resulting in minimum external walls with a few small openings at high level, and the 'sound lock' formed by the indirect arrangement of the sets of doors of the entrance. The heavyweight construction also contributes to the good environmental conditions of the interior, which were also measured by Nour. In this way, the design of the built form has achieved visual and acoustic privacy as well as thermal comfort.

A smaller and more compact two-storey version of the traditional courtyard house (Figure 5) in the Mzab district of Algeria has been described by Etherton (1971). In this case, the courtyard has been reduced at ground-floor level to the minimum, becoming a central living space with a horizontal, rectangular grille above, allowing the ingress of reflected light and the escape of hot air, which is replaced by cooler air drawn in from the shaded streets. Alternatively, the courtyard has been raised to first-floor level where the opening to the sky has an area larger than the grille below, but smaller in proportion to the site coverage of the house than the Cairo example. This is probably due to the greater severity of the hot, dry and dusty climate of the Mzab.

Climate is thus seen to be a moderating factor that acts in a complementary way to the cultural and religious need for privacy. That this does not necessarily mean the adoption of the courtyard plan is shown by the example of the traditional 'Red Sea' house-type so beautifully observed by Greenlaw (Figure 6) in his survey of the coral houses of Suakin (Greenlaw 1976). Unfortunately, Suakin is now abandoned and in ruins, but there are some houses of this type surviving in Jedda, Saudi Arabia. The climate is hot and humid, and so requires as much through ventilation as possible to create reasonable internal conditions of thermal comfort. Both dual zoning for privacy and high density are, nevertheless, maintained. The houses are built three storeys high in the case of Suakin and sometimes up to six storeys in Jedda, usually in blocks so that each house has two sides open to the street for light and ventilation, the other sides being party walls shared with neighbours. There is no courtyard and they are sometimes referred to as 'tower houses'. The dual zoning is achieved in the vertical dimension with the male zone at ground-floor level, including reception hall, shops and storage areas, while the family zone, including kitchen, is at the upper levels. There are two separate entrances, one for the family and the other for the men and their visitors. The stairs are used as ventilating air shafts for the remote parts of the house.

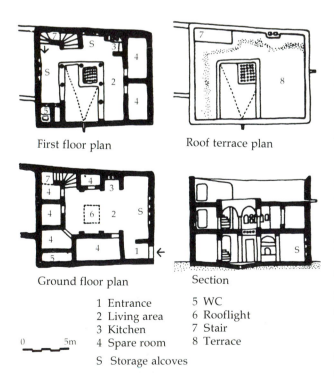

First floor plan

Roof terrace plan

Ground floor plan

Section

1 Entrance
2 Living area
3 Kitchen
4 Spare room
S Storage alcoves

5 WC
6 Rooflight
7 Stair
8 Terrace

0   5m

Figure 5 *Plan and section of a typical traditional two-storey courtyard house, Mzab, Algeria.* (Source: *Etherton 1971*)

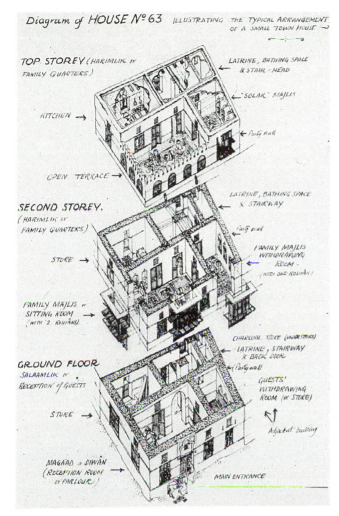

Diagram of HOUSE No 63   *ILLUSTRATING THE TYPICAL ARRANGEMENT OF A SMALL TOWN HOUSE →*

TOP STOREY (HARIMLIK or FAMILY QUARTERS)

← LATRINE, BATHING SPACE & STAIR-HEAD

KITCHEN →

'SOLAR' MAJLIS

← Party Wall

OPEN TERRACE →

SECOND STOREY. (HARIMLIK or FAMILY QUARTERS)

LATRINE, BATHING SPACE & STAIRWAY

Party Wall

FAMILY MAJLIS WITHDRAWING ROOM - (WITH ONE ROSHAN)

STORE →

FAMILY MAJLIS or SITTING ROOM (WITH 2 ROSHANS)

CHARCOAL STORE (UNDER STAIRS)
LATRINE, STAIRWAY & BACK DOOR (Party Wall)

GROUND FLOOR. SALAAMLIK or RECEPTION of GUESTS

GUESTS' WITHDRAWING ROOM (or STORE)

STORE →

Adjacent building

MAGAAD or DIWAN (RECEPTION ROOM or PARLOUR)

MAIN ENTRANCE

Figure 6 *Traditional 'Red Sea' house, Suakin.* (Source: *Greenlaw 1976*)

As in Cairo, projecting lattice windows (called *roshan* in Suakin and Jedda) are used to bring light and ventilation to the larger rooms and, where possible, are placed on two outside walls to allow maximum through ventilation. The top storey and roof have terraces used for sleeping out at night, often with an adjacent shaded or enclosed area. The householder and his wife would normally have a space separate from the rest of the family. Unlike Cairo, the *roshan* was often used in the male reception and guest rooms at ground-floor level to give through ventilation, but sufficient privacy was considered to have been obtained because only men were permitted to use these rooms. As a result of a recent series of interviews with former occupants of such houses in Jedda, Al Lyaly has prepared a space and activity chart (Figure 7) for a typical day in the summer season (Al Lyaly 1990: 186). It can be seen that the uppermost floors are only used at night for sleeping and socializing, whereas the family midday meal and siesta take place in rooms on the first floor. Field measure-

ments of air temperature and relative humidity demonstrate that the purpose of this diurnal movement through the house is to obtain the most comfortable environment at the appropriate time.

A very different house form is to be found in the urban areas of Omdurman in Sudan. In a study of the relationship between privacy and built form in four districts there, Adam (1990) observed that the majority of houses were single storey with a courtyard used by the family, whereas 40 per cent had two courtyards, the second for use by men. From an analysis of interviews, it seems that privacy is particularly important to the women, who named the bath, WC and kitchen as sensitive spaces. Children, however, are generally allowed to sleep anywhere except on special social occasions when they are confined to the women's zone. Visual and acoustic privacy are considered to be of prime importance, and this view was reinforced by the fact that it was considered wrong to be able to observe passers-by from inside the house by 72.9 per cent of those interviewed. On the other hand, 65.7 per cent approved of the possibility to view the street from the house. This appears to create some doubt concerning the acceptance of one-way observation of the public realm. The difficulty may be related to the use of space in front of the house as semi-private for socialization with male visitors, especially where there is no second courtyard reserved for men.

A typical house plan reveals fairly dense, single-storey development on a relatively large plot, with common walls shared with neighbours on three sides. There are no openings in the single outside wall except for the doors of the men's entrance direct into the men's courtyard and the doors of the family entrance opening into a passage which leads indirectly via another passage to the family courtyard. There is a long bench (*mastaba*) in front of the outside wall to define the semi-private space for male friends and neighbours. In some cases, this space was reserved for group usage and blocked off from vehicular access by trees or bollards. This group space is used for weddings and funerals, which are important social occasions, with the participation of many relatives and neighbours. These districts of Omdurman are relatively modern and the layout of plots and roads is on a rectangular grid accommodating through passage of motor traffic. This is a fundamental departure from the older, traditional Islamic residential quarter, as in Cairo, where groups of neighbouring houses are clustered in a cul-de-sac accessed by a narrow alley, sometimes provided with its own gate.

The traditional layout is informal, apparently haphazard, and anything but rectangular. Nevertheless, it clearly defines a semi-private space for use by inhabitants of the quarter. The present dominance of the motor car, the introduction of modern building techniques and, perhaps most far-reaching, the application of alien planning laws, has led in many Islamic countries to the majority of new residential buildings assuming an

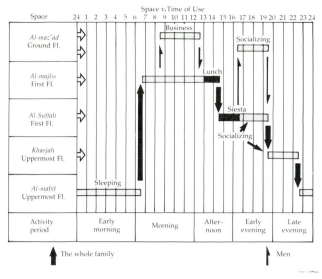

Figure 7 *Space and time use chart for the summer season.* (Source: *Al Lyaly 1990*)

outward-looking character that follows the modern international model. Setback rules are applied in many places to all four boundaries of a rectangular house plot, forcing the owner to place the house in the centre, making it virtually impossible to create a courtyard. This means that all windows are on outside walls, often overlooking the neighbour's house and garden. Inevitably, the plot is surrounded by a two-metre (six-and-a-half foot) high wall, but upper floors are frequently provided with Western-style balconies and large, glazed windows. The balconies can never be used because of the impossibility of maintaining privacy and all external openings must be visually screened. The internal planning is based on Western models, causing difficulties with the definition of dual zones when visitors are entertained. The lack of party walls means that larger external surfaces are exposed to solar radiation giving increased heat transmission to the interior, requiring almost continuous use of mechanical air-conditioning and expensive energy consumption. The use of the external space between the house and the boundary walls is inhibited by the fear of observation from the

upper floors of the neighbouring houses, creating yet another disadvantage.

The requirements of the need for both privacy and pleasant internal comfort are again seen to be complementary, but in so many modern examples they are almost completely denied. However, with the recent Islamic revival in political, social and religious terms, there is a growing realization that the physical environment is a demonstration of the values of the society that creates it. There is now a trend among Muslim architects to try to create a contemporary house form that adequately responds to the cultural and religious need for visual and acoustic privacy. That is not to say that the need for privacy is not present in other cultures. The need to be able to observe and not be observed is felt even in the most industrialized Western nations, but in Islamic communities it is normally more clearly expressed in terms of building and urban design.

REFERENCES

Adam, El Tayeb (1990) 'Culture, architecture and the urban form', Ph.D. thesis, University of York.

Al Lyaly, S. (1990) 'The traditional house of Jeddah', Ph.D. thesis, University of Edinburgh.

Etherton, D. (1971) 'Algerian oases', ch. 11 in P. Oliver (ed.) *Shelter in Africa*, London: Barrie & Jenkins.

Greenlaw, J.P. (1976) *The Coral Buildings of Suakin*, Stocksfield: Oriel Press.

Nour, M.M.A. (1979) 'An analytical study of traditional and domestic architecture', Ph.D. thesis, University of Newcastle upon Tyne.

Schwerdtfeger, F. (1971) 'Housing in Zaria', ch. 4 in P. Oliver (ed.) *Shelter in Africa*, London: Barrie & Jenkins.

FURTHER READING

Al Shahi, A. (1986) 'Welcome, my house is yours', in A.D.C. Hyland and A. Al Shahi (eds) *The Arab House*, Newcastle upon Tyne: CARDO/University of Newcastle upon Tyne.

Burckhardt, T. (1976) *Art of Islam*, London: World of Islam Festival Publishing.

Lane, E.W. (1836) *Manners and Customs of the Modern Egyptians*, reprinted 1978, London: East–West Publications.

25 The Scottishness of Scottish architecture

Charles McKean

INTRODUCTION

This essay offers elements for the retrieval of Scottish architecture from its inappropriate position as an appendix to British architectural history, and provides an opportunity to redress myth and scotch well-meaning but fundamentally ignorant paternalism, which has relegated Scottish architecture to a picturesque but provincial vernacular. As will become clear, Scots architecture may be a footnote but, if so, it is to European and not to English architectural history; and much that has been misunderstood as vernacular was the product of deliberate design.

INFLUENCES

Sir Banister Fletcher's belief that the architecture of a country derived from the fundamentals of its geography, geology, climate, politics, religion and wealth provides a suitable point of departure. Scotland is the remote northern half of an island falling off the north-west corner of Europe where – as Tacitus put it – the world and all things come to an end. It is only rarely a fertile country, and its climate is adverse. Wind-driven rain comes horizontally in Scotland, and not infrequently upwards. Of necessity therefore, Scots architecture is defensive and frequently hunched against the prevailing wind, but rarely ground-hugging as, say, in Finland.

Scotland has a short growing season, which results in limited crops. It was therefore often low in ready cash. One consequence was a dearth of specie with which to pay for imported skill such as foreign artisans like stonemasons. It was, however, rich in people and materials, as Etienne Perlin reported to the French government in 1553: 'nothing is short here save money' (cited in Brown 1973: 72). One can infer that the expense of foreign artisans, who had to be imported over the North Sea after the opening of the English wars (*c.*1290), was the cause of the development of an architecture sparing in high craft, concentrating instead upon massing.

Scotland had many burghs, but few major towns or cities until called into being by mid-nineteenth century agricultural and industrial expansion. The vast principality of modern Buchan contained virtually no community of size in the seventeenth century. Turriff, the oldest, was a single street of houses with an old church, and the new fishing burghs of Peterhead, Fraserburgh, and Rosehearty were of limited size. The ancient Royal Burgh of Woodhead of Fyvie (now virtually vanished) had fewer than thirty houses. As may

be inferred from its *chateaux*, seventeenth-century Buchan was prosperous; but the population inhabited dispersed settlements, fermtouns and kirktouns, with communication generally by water until the arrival of turnpike roads and railways in the nineteenth century.

The particular influence of Scots Law may best be understood by reference to the development of London's Regent's Park. When John Nash presented his proposals for the construction of Regent's Park to the Crown, he justified the landscaping, the lake and the tree-planting on the grounds that the houses were built on a ninety-nine-year lease. The landscape would survive beyond that to enhance the value of subsequent rebuilding. No comparable attitude existed in Scotland. Ownership in feu tenure gave the land proprietor perpetual rights to set building conditions; and yet the building's owner still owned. Both therefore had an interest in good quality construction. Those with money to spend spent more upon initial capital cost.

Scotland is a country of stone: many various stones, but stone none the less. What long-span timber existed had mostly been burnt by the Middle Ages. The absence of long-span timber before seventeenth-century Baltic imports led to Scottish buildings almost invariably the width of a stone vault, for that comprised their structure. It also proved wonderfully indestructible in times of turmoil.

THE MIDDLE AGES

Culdee, Celtic, Pictish and Norse buildings – such as they are known – seem to have taken the form of circular stone enclosures, some thatched, some underground like soutterrains, and some soaring upwards hugging rocky outcrops, such as the brochs and duns. Little, save the door in the round tower of Brechin Cathedral, survives of a self-consciously architectonic nature.

The Normans invited north by Queen Margaret to join the Scottish thanes were followed by their craftspeople – particularly masons. Norman plan forms and Norman masonry were adapted for Scots traditions, climate and materials, resulting in buildings plainer, taller, more compressed, and deeper in mass and profile than the norm. That mutation of European influence to Scots conditions persisted for centuries. Glasgow Cathedral, for example, is notably spare of decoration in nave and transept; as Sir Walter Scott put it: 'plain, weel-jointed mason work: none of your curly wurlies, open steeked hems.' (Scott 1829a: 29) The massing successfully conceals its diminutive scale: two Glasgow Cathedrals would fit inside that of Amiens.

Norman influence in Scotland was partial and tended to follow the great families of de Moravia, Comyn and de Vaux. The native Scots architecture of plain, undecorated enclosure inherited from the brochs persisted in the non-hierarchical, curtain-walled castles that enclose rocky defensive outcrops throughout the Highlands and Islands, not infrequently amended by the addition of later tower houses and palace blocks – as in Dunstaffnage, Tioram, Kilchurn, Duntrune, Dunvegan, and Mingarry.

THE DEVELOPMENT OF A NATIONAL ARCHITECTURE

From 1296 onwards, Scotland was unwillingly embroiled in a 300-year war against English colonization, and Scots trade, culture and political alliances switched eastwards. Trading colonies were established throughout the Baltic coastline, with churches and colleges in Antwerp, Gothenburg, Amsterdam, Paris and Danzig, and a Scottish street in Riga. The Scottish Staple was at Middleburg, later Campveere, in Holland and many Scots attended the universities of Leyden, Paris, Utrecht and Louvain.

Save for the masons accompanying the invaders (James of St George is known to have worked at Linlithgow), Scotland shipped its masons expensively across the North Sea. Beyond the wealthier religious buildings or the greatest palaces, carved or dressed stone was deployed sparingly on Scots architecture. It is to France, particularly, that the religious (Melrose) and the kings (James V) look for that special refinement. Instead, a new architectural identity was called into being: solid, plain and vertical, still to the width of a stone vault, now composed of plain, harled walls increasingly highlighted by dressed stone details and brilliantly gilt carvings.

An indication of masonic rarity can be found in the *Calendar of State Papers* for 1595. It is reported that, restored to favour after the Glenlivet rebellion of 1594, the Earl of Huntly wished to restore his House of Strathbogie (Huntly) 'were masons to be had' (*Calendar of State Papers* 1595). Masons of the calibre Huntly sought were not to be had until 1600 – although to judge by the magnificent results, the English mason Ralph Rawlinson who executed them was well worth waiting seven years for.

Sixteenth-century Scotland was a fully fledged participant in the northern European Renaissance. Consorts for its kings were sought in Hungary, Spain, Corsica, France and Denmark; its historians Buchanan, Boethius and Bellenden enjoyed a European reputation – as did its poets Dunbar, Montgomerie and Sir David Lindsay. The Stuart monarchs – pre-eminently James V – were notable patrons of architecture. Lindsay of

Pitscottie witnessed the celebrations of King James V near Pitlochry in 1531. From his description of the entire timber palace erected by the Earl of Athol, round tower in each corner, the plan closely resembles that of the Loire Château de Bury (now vanished), and the Palace of Boyne in Buchan (ruined).

> The Ambassador of the Pope, seeing this great banquet and triumph, which was made in a wilderness, where there was no town nearby 20 miles, thought it a great marvel, that such a thing could be in Scotland considering that it was named *the arse of the world* by other countries.
>
> (Pitscottie 1778: 228).

James V was the greatest of Scottish building monarchs, and his expenditure was extraordinarily lavish. He appointed Sir James Hamilton of Finnart (arguably Scotland's first architect to deserve that title in the modern terminology) to refit Linlithgow, and to build a stunning Royal Pavilion of the finest stonework and Louis XII detail within Stirling Castle. His favourite hunting palace of Falkland was extended in François I manner. He had begun in 1529 by adding the tall, round-towered palace-lodging to his father's glittering palace of Holyrood in Edinburgh, intending to balance it by another to the south. It was perhaps the first inkling of a preoccupation with symmetry which began to manifest itself strongly by the end of the century.

Possibly in emulation, the vertically stacked tower houses of Scotland became extended by one or more 'palace' wings containing horizontally planned apartments of processional rooms *en suite*, ending in a projecting bedroom tower with its own private mural staircase. Construction remained the width of the ground-floor stone-vaulted kitchens and cellars (now widened to include a service corridor). In smaller buildings and châteaux (or 'castle-wise houses of country gentlemen' as the English visitor Sir William Brereton put it) (cited in Brown 1973: 148), laird and lady's apartments of usually three rooms would be above each other. 'Castle-wise' can be translated into French as 'château'; and it is châteaux like Terpersie and Carnousie – not castles nor tower houses – that one can see almost every league. Carved detail from France, Italy, Germany and from Spain adorned their superstructures, their windows, doors, turrets and dormer windows: so carefully disposed (as both Robert Billings and C.R. Mackintosh spotted in the nineteenth century) as to indicate the hand of deliberately creative and picturesque design. They were not vernacular buildings, but the work of designers. The roundels at Thirlestane may be traced directly to the royal château of Loches (south of the Loire), the first-floor arcade of now vanished Castle Gordon to Blois, and Palatial Lodgings at Balvenie and Huntly to the château of Amboise.

That is the pattern that may yet be discerned today in the châteaux of Kilcoy, Ballone, Redcastle, Edzell and

Muness. Ruins of buildings like the sadly vanished palace of the Earl Marischals of Scotland at Inverugie are not those of Z-plan tower houses; as revealed by their *corps de logis* with a round bedroom tower at one end and a projecting staircase at the other, they are mock military country mansions comparable to many a Loire château. The best local artist would generally have been commissioned to paint the plaster walls within.

Influence from Denmark and Holland was most noticeable in the burghs – particularly those seafaring ones founded by James V – but peculiarly so in Glasgow, whose 1636 university had remarkable visual similarities to the Frederiksborg palace.

Edinburgh, with its king in Parliament, was a European rock-girt capital city more like Bohemia than Britain, which struck visitors with its similarity to Prague, or to Salzburg with its dense High Street crammed with arcaded merchants' lodgings. Edinburgh's brief spurt of immense mercantile wealth between 1600 and 1637 is naturally reflected in stately mansions and gracious arcaded merchants' tenements faced in expensive dressed stone, such as Gladstone's Land, Acheson House, and the noble monuments of the time – the Tron Kirk, the 1633 Parliament House, work within Holyrood Palace, the Palace buildings within the castle, nobles' lodgings and ambassadors' hotels in suburbs such as the Cowgate and Canongate. It was a period when central Scotland enjoyed a distinctive 'court style' under the hand of Sir James Murray of Kilbaberton.

Arcaded tenements are also recorded in Elgin, Aberdeen, St Andrews, Dumfries and Dundee, but nowhere was arcading so thorough or so significant as in the boom town of later seventeenth-century Scotland, Glasgow. Glasgow rebuilt its centre four streets with regular stone arcades after a dreadful fire in 1652, and the resulting regularity of its streets attracted the admiration of all visitors. To appreciate what the city must have been like you would now need to visit towns in southern Germany, Austria and northern Italy.

The nobility and greater merchants lived in U-plan courtyard *hotels* like Argyll's Lodging in Stirling, or in suburban villas of similar form like Baberton, Pitreavie and Dean (now demolished). Essential characteristics persist – still the width of a stone vault, principal apartments upon the first floor. This 'most national of Scottish architectural periods' (Hurd 1938: 120), evolved a recognizable architecture of plain form and contrasting geometries in light: 'the masterly, correct and magnificent play of masses brought together in light', as Le Corbusier was to put it 300 years later. The horizontal plan is deliberately contrasted with a vertical proportion, often focused upon projecting round, square, hexagonal or octagonal stairtowers, not infrequently with a study, special room, or balustraded flat at the top.

Light harling or limewash for the walls had as much to do with design as with weather protection. Dressed stone, being rare and expensive, required a smooth background to set it off, particularly where Francophile lairds were aware of the glowing châteaux of the Loire, and of the architectural need for light in this weakly lit country. It was also an easy means whereby poor construction and loosely pinned rubble could be concealed. Thus evolved an aesthetic of two-tone Renaissance architecture in Scotland – part-harl and part dressed stone – of which the Palace of Huntly was possibly the most stunning exemplar. Huntly implies the probability that much of the superstructure above the corbel course in houses like Fyvie, Craigston and Castle Fraser might also prove to be dressed stone beneath the harl.

After 1660, direct contact between Scotland and northern Europe began to wither, and after 1707 it largely ceased. Instead, particularly after its occupation by the Commonwealth army, Scotland became more susceptible to ideas emanating from the south, and the nobility took to a Scottish version of baroque. Those who travelled abroad sought to recreate in Scotland an equivalent grandeur. To meet the demand appeared an altogether more sophisticated personage than the 'architector' who advised Glasgow on its arcades; even more sophisticated, indeed, than James VI's architect, Sir James Murray. The first such (indeed, one of the architects of the Restoration – in every sense of the word) was Sir William Bruce. And others soon emerged: James Smith, James Gibbs, Alexander McGill and William Adam. Scots indigenous building traditions and plan forms were either adapted to the new baroque or became relegated to houses for lairds.

The sophisticated U-plan noblemen's lodgings of the Jacobean renaissance developed into a closed U-plan at Prestonfield House, Edinburgh, Panmure and Gallery. William Adam's Duff House has a plan like a compressed Heriot's Hospital or Drumlanrig, and corner or closet towers persisted in Floors, Hamilton Palace and Black Barony. Adam's mansions of lavishly dressed stone (he had his own masons' workshop) protrude four-square from the landscape in a manner not dissimilar to their predecessors; their room sequence perpetuates that already apparent in the châteaux, their ground floor often stone-vaulted. Their roofs remain a prominent feature long after they vanished behind a balustrade in England.

Second-rank houses remained light harled with carefully placed dressed stone, retaining the architecture of geometry: four-square lairds' houses, staircases contained in projecting drum towers (a motif to appear later in all three of Mackintosh's masterly houses – the Art Lover's House, Windyhill and the Hill House). In several, the entrance is through a depressed ground floor of subsidiary rooms, and up a magnificent staircase into a *piano nobile* of statuesque proportions: very much in the French manner. The aesthetic of combined harl and dressed stone gradually assumed similarities to central

European baroque (e.g. that at Salzburg), in which poor stone was concealed beneath a smooth, coloured finish, dressed stone being used sparingly as highlight. A Scots variant is John Adam's Gaelic Church in Inveraray; and it proved to be surprisingly persistent in remote areas, appearing in William Robertson's buildings – notably in Cullen, Portsoy and Buchan. The dominant characteristic of quality rural architecture remained one of plain volume with limited surface decoration of which the small 1804 church at Scalasaig on Colonsay, a composition of white geometric mass, is the purest example.

Money resided in the towns, as it always had done, and it was in Edinburgh and Glasgow that substantial quantities of buildings faced with dressed stone began to appear. There was little urban development before 1770 save in Glasgow, whose Tobacco Lords adopted a curious and aberrational pattern of detached, steep-roofed, urned and pedimented classical villas with flanking pavilions, reminiscent of those in Virginia and Maryland, laid out in a fundamentally suburban pattern. Free-standing houses of this type in such formal proximity were scarcely emulated by even the highest in London, who went uncomplainingly into terraces. The even more curious Glasgow Square, which enfolds a major public building (as compared to the central garden that was the norm elsewhere), may well derive from the American custom of thus enfolding their courthouses.

Edinburgh favoured a denser, almost baroque urbanism of formal streets and squares in its New Town, which was originally intended to provide houses like those in London to attract Scottish aristocrats back to Scotland's capital. In that purpose, it failed. What it did do was to suck the wealthy and the intelligentsia away from the Old Town, leaving it to fester. Grand things were done in St Andrew's and Charlotte Squares (individual houses by Robert Adam and Sir William Chambers in St Andrew's Square, and palace fronts à la Spalatro in Charlotte Square), the plain dignity of the rest of the New Town (and of the succeeding four New Towns) unified by magnificent blocks of dressed Craigleith ashlar, mostly the result of individual building according to strict feu conditions which governed height, scale and materials. They were generally houses in the principal streets and superior tenements disguised as houses (with bow fronts or superimposed pediments) down the cross streets.

Edinburgh's seventy years of classical development, emulated in Glasgow, Dundee, Aberdeen and most county towns with aspirations to one degree or another, initiated what became called the 'stone period' of Scots architecture. The legacy of Robert Adam was that houses became collectively much more important in their massing and layout than in their individuality. Streets became polished stone walls with holes punched through, not dissimilar to the smooth, harled but punctured walls of the previous century.

The glory of early nineteenth-century Scotland was the collection of splendid neo-classical temples erected from one end of the country to the other, fulfilling the functions of grammar schools, town halls, libraries, churches, hospitals and country houses. Many were in the functionally useless (because theoretically windowless) form of a Greek temple, their details deepened to take account of the weak Scots sunlight. These buildings are of a scale and grandeur far in excess of the requirements of their ordinary sublunary purpose. The creators of the 'Athens of the North' had aspirations to eternity.

Yet certain native characteristics persist even in this 'international style'. The siting and detailing of these buildings was governed by the antithesis of Grecian reason: picturesqueness – a picturesqueness inspired by artists such as Hugh 'Grecian' Williams, whom architects like Thomas Hamilton were pleased to follow. Within the walls of these sturdy, thick-set and immensely powerful buildings in their picturesque settings burgeoned the wildest of romantic revivals as the influence of the novels of Sir Walter Scott began to take hold of the country.

The picturesque movement had mid-eighteenth-century romantic origins. The Ossian controversy had transformed Scotland from a land of inaccessible savages, ill-disposed to civilization, to a nation of Dark Age poetic heroes, with a primitive culture haunting heather-clad fastnesses. Travellers ventured north to emote at frightful waterfalls and suitable ghastly grottoes; moss houses, hermitages, ancient springs, vista-fillers and doocots were constructed to satisfy the yearning. Original towers were inadequate: Sir John Dalrymple, client of Robert Adam at Oxenfoord Castle in Midlothian, wrote to a friend: 'I have repaired a noble, old castle, and with the help of Bob Adams, *have really made it much older than it was*' (cited in Rowan 1974: 94 (my italics)). The preferred architecture of the romantic movement was the Adam brothers' sturdy, geometric castles, such as Culzean. Nothing flimsy here. Not a Gothick window among them. Monzie, built by Adam's chief draughtsman, John Paterson, in derivative style, was described in 1798 – and these are the important words: 'a pile of building highly suitable to the surrounding scenery. Mr Paterson has very judiciously introduced this style of house into those parts of Scotland which are on a grand and wild scale' (Fittler 1804: Plate XV).

The inspiration was to find an architecture of a scale and presence to complement the grandeur of the scenery. In the absence of a genuinely Scottish voice, the fashion grew for things English, and the Smirkes and the Atkinsons surged north in their smartly crocketed and buttressed neo-Elizabethan or neo-Tudor garb. Schools and academies, which at the beginning of the century were housed in magnificent Doric temples to impart the most heavy instruction, fell prey to the scenic imperative – modified first by baroque, and then by Jacobean. Its apotheosis was William Playfair's

Donaldson's Hospital, of which he said, 'I try hard to produce a building which, in the correctness of its parts shall be worthy of comparison with the remains of Old English architecture' (cited in Walker 1980: 84). A picturesque mock window dressing began to appear, and when Abbotsford, Sir Walter Scott's house, seemed to have been built in this idiom everybody wanted a bit of it.

Although nothing was exempt from Scott's romanticism, Scott himself regarded revivalism as something serious. In *The Pirate* he speculated that the Earl's Palace in Kirkwall might

> be selected … as the model of a Gothic mansion, provided architects would be contented rather to imitate what is really beautiful in that species of building, than to make a medley of the caprices of the order, confounding the military, ecclesiastical and domestic styles of all ages at random with additional fantasies and combinations of their own device.
>
> (Scott 1829b: 175)

Having been directly involved with the design of Abbotsford (more his than anybody else's), he would have rejected that charge against his own house, and was pleased that William Burn approved of it. The odd thing was that English architects were happy to ape old Scots features in the illiterate manner thus condemned by Scott, but Scottish grandees demurred. Even though Scots architects also practised the art – Playfair at Bonaly, Burn (reluctantly) at Laurieston and Bryce at Castle Menzies – lairds were generally terrified of being thought provincial. What was needed was an authoritative document to restore to Scots architecture its sense of *amour propre*.

The radical mid-century change to what the *Building Chronicle* christened 'modern old things' can best be understood by comparing Old English Donaldson's Hospital to the maturely Scots Baronial Fettes College: two major charitable schools split by the first Scottish revival.

The Scottish revival took off with the tragic drowning of George Meikle Kemp in 1844, half-way through constructing his masterly medieval monument to Sir Walter Scott in Princes Street. The Scott monument was the first notable breach in the neo-classical consensus that had held Edinburgh and most of Scotland in thrall for almost fifty years. Kemp had been engaged in drawing old Scots buildings for a tome intended to reveal ancient Scottish architecture, whilst preparing designs for the restoration of Glasgow Cathedral, Melrose Abbey and Rosslyn Chapel, and for several churches. The following year, inspired to replace Kemp's now lost knowledge of old Scots architecture, William Burn and David Bryce brought to Scotland Robert William Billings, an English antiquarian, to carry out that task. By 1852 his four volumes of *The Baronial and Ecclesiastical Antiquities of Scotland* had achieved their

purpose. Lairds had seized them as pattern books. Amongst the well over 1,000 subscribers, many from England, were those who ran or owned Scotland, and some 200 architects (150 from England including Cockerell, and almost every member of the Architectural Institute of Scotland). A legitimate Scottish voice had been rediscovered.

Billings's term 'Baronial' has as much meaning in Scotland as the phrase 'English Manor House architecture' would have in England, for what he had thus christened was simply the grander architecture of the aristocracy and lairds of Scotland over 200 years. His thus inappropriate term 'Baronial' stuck – and soon devalued everything it touched. The *Building Chronicle* was troubled by the resultant controversy: 'We would fain discover, in the present mania of fashions and conflict of styles, some symptoms of a principal which may hereafter be worked out in the ultimate production of a distinct national architecture.' (*Building Chronicle* 1858: 69).

Mid-nineteenth century architects tended to produce architecture appropriate to function. Baronial was inappropriate for city offices despite the furious attempt in Glasgow's Trongate by J.T. Rochead, because Baronial fantasist imagery was unsuitable for mercantile purposes. Its power, rather, lay in its application to country houses, schools, monuments and those symbols of ancient authority – town halls and sheriff courts. There was nothing incongruous in the manager of the sternest of classical banks retreating each night to a romantically turreted tower house in the country where he became transformed into a laird. Few would trust a romantic bank, but what people did in their own time was their own affair. The *Building Chronicle* was peculiarly diverted by Balmoral:

> now, in north Britain, we have old Scottish, thanks to Burn and Billings 'Baronial Antiquities', taking its place, as par excellence, the style for nine tenths of our domestic buildings. And oh! What oddities are being perpetrated in its name. The grim bastion towers of Caerlaverock and Craigmillar are being revived in the retreats of peaceable country gentlemen. Heavy battlements surround their doorways and loopholes command it; to sweep off marauders should they prefer that means of access to lifting the sash of the larder window.
>
> (*Building Chronicle* 1855: 143)

The symbol of the first Scottish revival is J.T. Rochead's Wallace Monument on the Abbey Craig, Stirling, an embarrassingly Scottish monument that received adulation from the Hungarian patriot Kossuth, from Garibaldi, and from nationalist patriots throughout Europe. Generally, however, the revival was restricted to the application of derivative detail and massing (which Billings astutely perceived as being the product of deliberate design) assembled with an appropriate picturesqueness upon standard mid-century plans.

In 1854, however, Scotland gained its first cast-iron building in Glasgow's Jamaica Street and, as the workshop of the world, the city became distinguished for innovation in the architectural application of technology – particularly cast iron. Alexander Thomson sought to construct in stone buildings of the transparency and explicit structure offered by cast iron, thereby forging a unique architectural language. Thus came the origins of the architecture debate that has dominated Scotland ever since: is structure the servant of architecture, or is architecture decorated structure? Eclectic mercantile Scotland preferred the former, in cosmopolitan European models, creating an Italian hill-town at Park Circus, Glasgow, Venice's Golden House in cast iron in Union Street, Glasgow, and Venice's Doge's Palace in polychromatic brickwork as a built advertisement for the international aspirations of Templeton's carpets.

A renewed interest in a specifically Scots architecture became apparent by the 1870s, possibly under the influence of Sir Robert Rowand Anderson, and the product of his School of Applied Art. From 1856, Anderson had shown a specific interest in the drawing and measurement of Scottish architecture. Those student drawings were, he said, analogous to anatomy in the study of medicine. 'They brought the student into actual contact with work of all kinds. He was taught to dissect, to analyse, to work out for himself all the reasons that gave rise to various features he saw in buildings' (cited in Gow 1984: 545). Whilst it had become *de rigueur* for those who could afford it to travel abroad for sketching and drawing (publishing volumes of the results on their return as a way of publicizing their services – in exactly the manner adopted by Robert Adam and his Spalatro volume a century earlier), Anderson's energies were focused upon the need to study native Scots buildings as well; and thus created the impetus for the second Scots revival.

It was fundamentally different from the first, Billings-inspired revival in that it was not based upon pictures and a picturesqueness (however authentic) imposed upon an otherwise rational plan, so much as upon an accurate recording and measuring of buildings. There is a stunningly tactile if not sensual dimension to this second revival. Moreover, the buildings studied were largely different from those drawn by Billings. His were Baronial antiquities, whereas the focus of this new revival may be gauged from the title of the series of books that accompanied it – the 'Castellated and Domestic Architecture of Scotland' by David MacGibbon and Dr Thomas Ross. These mock-military country mansions of the Renaissance were neither Baronial nor vernacular.

In 1889 Anderson, as President of the Architecture Section of the National Association for the Advancement of Arts, advanced a very Scots base to design:

It is still too much the fashion to rely on the clever imitation of old work, without its reality and functional truth. I am told that many of the picturesque modern timber-framed houses in England have very little framing in them: it is all on the surface – a mere external show.... How can any good come out of such work?

(Anderson 1889: 39)

Into that context fell James MacLaren, Robert Lorimer, Charles Rennie Mackintosh and their followers.

MacLaren's native genius is apparent in the 1879 white Kirkton Cottages and farmhouses in Glenlyon, amongst the first buildings of the new generation of Scottishness to display the rational planning and simple massing from seventeenth-century Scotland. MacLaren died in 1890, and although indeed an 'architect for connoisseurs' (McAra 1970: 28), taking the long-span view of Scottish architecture his hand was only given the opportunity to make a slight nudge at the tiller. That the time was propitious, however, was signalled by the appointment of a Chair of Celtic Studies at Edinburgh University. Two strands emerged. The first was a desire to reintegrate art and craft, promoted by Sir Patrick Geddes in his short-lived journal *Evergreen*; and the second a retreat from the evils of industrialization and urbanism into a suburban or rural haven of distant Celtic or mythological past.

Rowand Anderson's mantle was picked up by Robert Lorimer (whom Mackintosh regarded as the best house designer in Scotland). Lorimer, like Henry Kerr, Henbest Capper, A.N. Paterson, and many others, returned to seventeenth-century Scotland for inspiration – and largely stayed there. He referred to Formakin as the best seventeenth century he had ever done. Whilst city centres were built up with iron-framed elevator buildings faced with machine-cut sandstone, out there in the suburbs or along the river valleys, pretty, seventeenth-century-influenced white cottages were being occupied by wealthy bourgeois who contented themselves with stiff-leaf Art Nouveau book jackets and the plaintive strands of Marjorie Kennedy-Fraser's Gaelic laments. English architects were stimulated by the challenge to design in a manner appropriate to Scotland, and there was no longer any client resistence. Apart from the somewhat eccentric attempt by Sir George Gilbert Scott to create a new Scots architecture of his own devising for Dundee's Albert Institute and Glasgow's University (a blend of Low Countries medieval adorned with crow-steps), the legacy of the second English tilt at Scottishness is five outstanding pieces of architecture by *aficionados* of the Arts and Crafts revival: Macharioch by George Devey, Arisaig House by Philip Webb, Melsetter (Orkney) by W.R. Lethaby, Greywalls (Gullane) by Edwin Lutyens, and Cour (by Carradale) by Oliver Hill.

Glasgow shared the nationalist sentiment but produced radically different results. The continuing preoccupation with technology led to James Salmon's deployment of Hennebique concrete in 1904 in his aspiration to be Scottish in a contemporary way, in Lion Chambers, Hope Street. His friend Charles Rennie Mackintosh, who maintained that 'we should be rather less cosmopolitan and rather more national in our architecture' (Mackintosh, ed. Robertson 1990: 196) also returned to the seventeenth century for inspiration. He understood, as had Billings, that the châteaux of the seventeenth century were the product of as yet unknown designers' but, unlike Lorimer, he did not remain in the seventeenth century. Ancient inspiration provided the synthesis for a new architecture, most magnificently exemplified in the Hill House (1904) and the Glasgow School of Art (1910). Mackintosh's Hill House can be read as the transformation of a standard north-corridor Edwardian house, with a family wing to one side, into a seventeenth-century Z-plan tower extended with an eighteenth-century wing: very like a handed version of Crathes. The exterior of his buildings reveal his tendency toward greater abstraction which culminated in that totem for inter-war architects – the Willow Tea Rooms, with its white façade, oversailing flat roof, long strip window, and smaller windows deep set into a white façade. The interiors, following a different programme of different aesthetic origins, comprise a series of light and frequently colourful magical spaces in contrast to the solidity of the exterior.

The inter-war period was dominated by housing. In 1918 the tenement was banned as anti-social, and all future houses were to be redeveloped to the density of 12 houses to the acre (5 to the hectare) with back drying greens to an imported Art and Crafts aesthetic. Similar restrictions applied to the private sector, which led to the growth of the bungalow. For the first time, Scotland was faced with a suburban aesthetic on a large scale which – with the rare examples of continentally inspired tenements of the late 1930s – failed to develop an appropriate form.

During the 1920s, the architectural profession concentrated upon refining its identity and its education through the medium of the newly established Royal Incorporation of Architects in Scotland. In the 1930s, there arose a momentum for a new contemporary architecture that was truly Scottish – a Celtic response to the stirrings upon the Continent. They looked to Holland for efficiency, to Sweden for pragmatism, to Czechoslovakia for style, and to Finland for poetry; but most of all Robert Hurd, Ian Lindsay, Sir John Stirling Maxwell, Sir Frank Mears, Basil Spence and others looked for inspiration to Scotland of the period around 1600.

Sir Frank Mears wrote in the *RIBA Journal*: 'buildings from the earliest to the latest, especially when they were faced with rough stone, harled and white-washed, have a certain monolithic character; they are definitely Cubic if not Cubist.' (Mears 1938: 310) Charles Rennie Mackintosh (and the façade of the Willow Tea Rooms) was regarded as the master to be studied. Indeed, in 1937,

John Summerson reviewed the new fire station in Dunfermline by James Shearer as being peculiarly Mackintosh in influence, whilst in 1938 Robert Hurd thought likewise of T.P. Marwick's National Bank in Edinburgh's George Street.

Those favouring architecture as embellished structure were led by James Miller to some twenty grandiose steel-framed American classical banks and offices, particularly in Glasgow, from which the classical stone façade was gradually peeled back; and eventually to the prefabricated Empire Exhibition. Despite experimentation with prefabricated steel and timber, and poured concrete houses, it had made only marginal impact upon Scottish construction by the Second World War. Instead, the proto-nationalists, who had sought to adapt Rowand Anderson's second Scottish revival to contemporary idioms and materials, had began to turn the tide in favour of a spare white geometry based equally on Nordic models, Mackintosh and Scots Renaissance châteaux.

Nationalism was not an attractive concept after the war, and the priority was the rehousing of half-a-million people. That preoccupation with technology which had been germinating in the Scottish psyche for the previous hundred years now dominated, and the programmatic and structural aspects of speedy construction took priority over the architectonic. It was the period of comprehensive redevelopment, high-rise (usually system-built) flats, Hutchesontown, motorways and New Towns: fundamentally an aesthetic of prefabrication and lightweight construction. Yet beneath that, two trends persisted against the odds. First, the creation of highly crafted poetic spaces integrating the arts – notably in the churches of Gillespie Kidd and Coia; and second, the solid, spare, white, Cubist-inspired geometry inherited from the 1930s, particularly in churches, houses, factories, distilleries and schools, examples of which are Mary Erskine's School, Edinburgh, and Stirling University. Yet it is very curious that one of Scotland's leading Modernists, Peter Womersley, deliberately chose in 1968 to favour white, geometric Scottishness for his Doctor's Surgery in Kelso.

Prefabrication has now taken a lesser role: and in the new solid construction, a continuation of Scottish characteristics may be inferred from heavy modelling such as the vertical expression of stair and service towers in the National Library extension, and in Distillers Company headquarters; the patterning of heavy masses in Tollcross fire station; and from the return of walls of buildings as urban areas are knitted together once more – in Ingram Square, Glassford Street, Craigen Court, Maryhill and much other housing in inner Glasgow, Edinburgh and Aberdeen. The white geometric tradition shone in the Glasgow Garden Festival, and is much preferred for non-urban housing, although the advent of facing brick seems set to change that.

The future of Scottish architecture lies in the hands of its architects, who are subject to international inspiration and an international palette of materials. The quality of the resulting architecture will depend entirely upon their understanding of how Scottish architecture developed, their sensitivity to their culture and to the particular climatic needs of location; and to the creativity with which they marry international opportunity to the task of building in and for Scotland.

REFERENCES

Anderson, R.R. (1889) *Place of Architecture in the Domain of Art*, Edinburgh.

Brown, P.H. (1973) *Early Travellers in Scotland*, Edinburgh: Mercat Press.

Building Chronicle (1855) 'Modern Old Scottish', *Building Chronicle* 11 (1 February).

—— (1858) *Building Chronicle* 8 (9 November).

Calendar of State Papers (1595) London.

Fittler, J. (1804) *Scotia Depicta*, London.

Gow, I. (1984) *Sir Rowand Anderson's National Art Survey*, Architectural History, Vol. 27, London.

Hurd, R. (1938) in J.R. Allan (ed.) *Scotland 1938*, Edinburgh.

McAra, D. (1970) 'James MacLaren', *Scottish Art Review* 12 (4): 28–33.

MacGibbon, D. and Ross, T. (1897) *The Castellated and Domestic Architecture of Scotland*, Edinburgh: David Douglas.

Mackintosh, C.R. (1990) *The Architectural Papers*, ed. P. Robertson, Bicester, Oxon: White Cockade.

Mears, F. (1938) *RIBA Journal* (January).

Pitscottie, R.L. of (1778) *History of Scotland*, Edinburgh.

Rowan, A. (1974) 'Oxenfoord Castle', *Country Life* 156 (15 August): 94–8.

Scott, W. (1829a) *Rob Roy*, Edinburgh.

—— (1829b) *The Pirate*, Edinburgh.

Walker, D. (1980) *Studies presented to Howard Colvin, Donaldson's Hospital Competition and the Palace of Westminster*, Architectural History Vol. 27, London.

26 Russian Revolution: politics or art?

Bill Risebero

At the end of *Vers Une Architecture*, Le Corbusier gives his views on the contradictions and opportunities of a changing world:

> the man of today is conscious, on the one hand, of a new world which is forming itself regularly, logically and clearly ... and on the other hand he finds himself ... living in an old and hostile environment.... Society is filled with a violent desire for something which it may obtain or may not.
>
> (Le Corbusier 1927: 268)

His answer to this problem is both bourgeois and technocratic:

> It is a question of *building* which is at the root of the social unrest of today.... Architecture or Revolution. Revolution can be avoided.
>
> (ibid.: 269)

It is hardly surprising that he should have made such a conservative response; what is much more remarkable is that in the bourgeois-democratic society of which Le Corbusier was part, architecture and revolution should be mentioned in the same breath at all. That they were is due to the Bolshevik Revolution of 1917 and the short-lived but immensely influential cultural episode it gave rise to – what John Berger later called:

> a movement in the Russian visual arts which, for its creativity, confidence, engagement in the life and synthesising power, has so far remained unique in the history of modern art.
>
> (Berger 1979: 29)

Committed though it was to the dynamism of modern life, the Russian avant-garde presented a paradox too. What was the relevance of a Constructivist manifesto to a Siberian peasant? What was the point of the extravagant architectural fantasies of Tatlin or Leonidov when there was not enough steel even for nails, never mind a construction 400 metres (1,300 feet) high? The relevance of Constructivism must be that, like the revolution itself, its fulfilment lay in the future.

The theory of permanent revolution, advanced by Marx and developed by Trotsky, recognized that:

> Society keeps on changing its skin ... economy, technique, science, the family, morals, and everyday life develop in complex reciprocal action ... there is established between the democratic revolution and the socialist reconstruction of society a permanent state of revolutionary development.
>
> (Trotsky 1962: 6–10)

More than anyone, Lenin knew that the revolution which had been started was far from completion. 'As though one can set about a great revolution', he said on one occasion, 'and know beforehand how it is to be completed.' The revolution had to be worked for, through housing, through the construction of railways, through the electrification programme, industrialization and agricultural reform. A great new political system and new social relationships were to be created, and this might take 'a whole historical epoch.'

It was necessary to use all the resources of information, education and propaganda. The Constructivist designers, through the Agit-Prop programme, through their propositions for new ways of living or the harnessing of modern technology, suddenly found themselves carrying out a real and urgent examination of the future. Lenin himself did not totally reject the culture of the bourgeois past, but was also tolerant of what he called 'the chaotic ferment, the feverish search for new solutions' (quoted in Hill 1971: 163) among the young designers as they attempted, in Lissitzky's words, 'the destruction of the traditional' (El Lissitzky 1970: 68).

All architecture, whether bourgeois or revolutionary, has to be seen in the context both of the productive process and of the prevailing ideology of the time. Under capitalism, architecture displays the effects of alienation, among them a marked disunity of theory and practice; practice obeys the logic of capitalist production while theory seeks not to express this fact but to obscure it through mystification. Le Corbusier's proposition that the new society can be achieved through architecture, without the need for social revolution, is one example.

Constructivism, however, sought to destroy alienation, to stitch society together, to unite theory and practice in a way impossible under capitalism. Lissitzky spoke, in Marxist terms, of an ideological superstructure which informs the designer's work and which is based in turn on a substructure of 'social economic reconstruction' (El Lissitzky 1970: 68). He recognized the subtlety of the relationships between base and superstructure and the changing, dialectical process through which they develop. Like Le Corbusier, the Constructivists set great store by technology as a liberator; the difference is that for them technology – like all else – was subordinate to the aims of socialist reconstruction and not, as it was for bourgeois reformers, an alternative.

Bourgeois history tends to emphasize the destructive aspects of Bolshevik politics and to present pre-Revolutionary society as liberal and reformist, as if in 1917 something wholly admirable was wantonly destroyed.[1]

By the same token, emphasis is placed on the vitality of modern art before 1917 and its destruction by the Soviet State during the 1920s. Both propositions have some truth in them, but they fail to give due weight to the excessively crude, exploitative and repressive nature of the tsarist regime which, for all Stolypin's reforms, was incapable of responding to the growing demands for freedom and equality. They also fail to recognize that the very vitality of pre-revolutionary art was due not to an expansive, liberal capitalist system but to the undercurrents of revolution which sought to overthrow it.

Revolution had been on the agenda ever since the Decembrist uprising of 1825, and became increasingly possible as the nineteenth century progressed. Then with the events of 1905, revolutionary activity intensified rapidly. A workers' *soviet* (council) was set up in St Petersburg; Lenin's pamphlets, the publication of *Iskra*, and the wide circulation of *Pravda* established a culture of revolution.

And in parallel with this, modern art developed rapidly. In 1905 art had been dominated by the traditionalist Narodism of painters like Goncharova and by the Post-Impressionism of Larionov and Malevich. But by 1911 all three had developed into Rayonism and Cubo-Futurism, the latter having become the fundamental style of Russian modernism, distinct in character from the Cubist and Futurist experiments in the West – with which there was little contact. It soon became the basic vocabulary of Tatlin, Popova, Rodchenko and Exter, but meanwhile Malevich had progressed still further, into the 'supreme' restraint of Suprematism, with paintings like *Black Square* (1913). This relentless drive towards abstraction was the ultimate expression of alienated art under the capitalist system; it is difficult to see how much further it could have gone under the circumstances in its rejection of the bourgeois tradition.

However, the year 1917 provided the opportunity to extend this struggle in a number of ways. The pivotal month was October of the old-style Julian Calendar, then still used in Russia, when the Bolsheviks adopted Lenin's proposal for an armed uprising against the Provisional Government and set up the Petrograd Revolutionary Military Committee to see the task through. The revolution of 25 October established Soviet power in Petrograd (formerly St Petersburg) and in Moscow soon after. The first Soviet government was set up, and an All-Russian Congress of Soviets made Declarations on Land and Peace. Almost immediately, NARKOMPROS – the People's Commissariat of Education – was set up. Its director was Anatoly Lunacharsky, a returned exile who had worked with the avant-garde in Europe; a revolutionary role was about to be established for modern art.

The circumstances could hardly have been more different from the stability of the old bourgeois world. Russia was plunged straight into a civil war, as Kolchak's White forces fought back against the revolution. The Peace of Brest-Litovsk brought the war against Germany to an end, but as early as February 1918 foreign capitalist governments were landing counter-revolutionary troops on the northern and eastern coasts of Russia. A complete collapse of the economy brought homelessness and famine, which the Soviet government was forced to counter by its programme of 'War Communism', and the mass appropriation of dwellings and food.

Despite these desperate events, plans for socialist reconstruction went rapidly ahead. Planning studios were set up in 1918 in both Moscow and Petrograd to prepare city plans on 'garden city' principles. A national planning agency was also set up; this was the Office for Town Planning, Regulation and Building, whose first programme included a set of priorities:

> The first goal shall be the elimination of the housing shortage.... The second shall be the creation of the city and the development of its parts as an organic whole.... The city master plan is a programme for organising urban life and a vehicle for social creativity.

> (Ikonnikov 1988: 79)

The relationship between town planning theory and practice, particularly the argument between 'urbanists' and 'disurbanists' was debated fervently through the 1920s, as the search for 'social creativity' went on. At first, radical social aims were not always expressed in radically new architectural forms. The concept of a workers' palace was wholly new, but the designs devised for Petrograd by Ivan Fomin and Andrei Belogrud in 1919 were neo-classical in inspiration.

The idea of commune-houses was also a new one, but the highly expressionist designs produced late in 1918 by Krinski and Ladovsky belonged to the Cubo-Futurism of pre-revolutionary times and were not dissimilar in mood to the early work of the Weimar Bauhaus.

As yet, these were unrealized designs. The first practical contribution to social reconstruction made by the avant-garde designers, and one in which modern abstract art played its full part, was that of communication and propaganda. 'Propaganda by Monuments' was launched in Moscow in May 1918, and Agit-Prop trains were inaugurated in December the same year: the Revolution had been started, but to win against the counter-revolution, want and famine, and to spread the revolutionary message across the country, required an enormous effort of persuasion. Altman's anniversary celebrations of the Revolution helped keep the idea alive: Tatlin's gigantic tower, designed in 1919 and constructed in effigy to be dragged through the streets on demonstrations, celebrated the newly-established Third International; Aleksander Vesnin, Liubov Popova and Anton Lavinsky began to design Constructivist sets for the avant-garde productions of Mayakovsky, Meyerhold and others; Agit-Prop trains and steamers took entertainment, slogans and films to all parts of the country; revolutionary verse was declaimed through megaphones at street corners; abstract constructions appeared in the cities, representing the triumph of the Revolution and the death of capitalism; and the revolutionary message was proclaimed from billboards through posters of unsurpassed modernity and vigour, like El Lissitzky's *Beat the Whites with the Red Wedge* (1920).

All this time, the Red Army was engaged in a desperate struggle, expelling the German armies from the Baltic states, engaging foreign forces in the north at Archangel and in the east at Vladivostok, and fighting the Whites on the Volga and the Don. As a result of the war and the famine, Moscow lost some 40 per cent of its population, and Petrograd 70 per cent. But gradually the tide turned; during 1919 and 1920 sections of the country were being liberated, and states added to the newly formed Union.

At the beginning of 1921, reconstruction began in earnest, under circumstances that were still desperate, with the implementation of the GOELRO plan for electrification, and the adoption by the 10th Party Congress of the New Economic Policy, a stop-gap measure to restore incentives and create economic growth. Trade agreements with Britain, Germany and other European countries paved the way for cultural exchange.

By now, the relationship between the artistic avant-garde and the Revolution was a close one, reinforced by the setting up of numerous art societies which formed and re-formed following the tendencies of the moment. Malevich formed UNOVIS at Vitebsk in 1919 'to affirm the New Art', and simultaneously a group of artists and architects including Ladovsky and Rodchenko founded JIVSKULPTARCH in Moscow, dedicated to the overthrow of classicism and to a kind of Cubo-Futurist modernism. The shifts that took place within the architectural avant-garde are shown by the successive dominance of three major groupings. In 1923 ASNOVA was founded by Ladovsky, Krinski and others; they called themselves 'rationalists' but it would be more accurate to say their approach was formalist and intuitive. In response, the Constructivists founded OSA, the Organization of Contemporary Architects, in 1925, dedicated to productivism and a strong sense of social purpose. By the end of the 1920s, the situation was to change sufficiently to bring VOPRA to the fore, an organization of 'proletarian' architects who worked for a return to a more traditional form of architecture and rejected the 'left-wing' tendencies of the Constructivists.

Dominating design education, from 1920 onwards, was VKhUTEMAS in Moscow, organized mainly by the ASNOVA group. VKhUTEMAS offered a wide variety both of approaches – ranging from classical to modern – and of courses, including architecture. The school was made as accessible as possible and its education began with a common 'basic course' run by Rodchenko.

From 1921 onwards, Constructivism began to influence the avant-garde. Its chief theorist was Moisei Ginsburg, and its chief practitioner Aleksander Vesnin, but it drew many other progressive designers into its orbit. In 1921 it developed the concept of productivism, of designing artefacts – furniture, clothes, utensils and, ultimately, buildings – for the purposes of factory production. Much of the experimental work – by Rodchenko, Popova, Stepanova and even Tatlin – was developed later by the Bauhaus. A productive exchange of ideas between eastern and western Europe took place in 1922, when an international conference of the avant-garde took place in Düsseldorf, at which Lissitzky and Theo Van Doesburg came together and established a 'Constructivist International', and when a major exhibition of Soviet art was mounted by Lunacharsky in Berlin. Gropius was prompted to reappraise his social aims and to overhaul Bauhaus policy and design, replacing the mystical expressionist Johannes Itten as head of the *Vorkurs* by the Hungarian Constructivist László Moholy-Nagy. Western designers had suddenly been confronted with the idea of progressive art for a progressive social purpose, a concept of the most profound influence in the development of modern architecture.

This concept was reinforced in the Soviet Union itself during the early 1920s. In 1922, a meeting between Lenin and Lunacharsky established a new role for film-makers and resulted in the social masterpieces of Eisenstein, Pudovkin and Dziga-Vertov. Architectural competitions, for new workers' quarters or great public buildings, brought avant-garde architecture considerable success; the Vesnin brothers' design for the Moscow Palace of Labour was highly influential. El Lissitzky began to experiment with designs for 'horizontal skyscrapers'. In 1923, Mayakovsky became editor of LEF, the newest, most progressive and most seminal art magazine of the period. The same year, an all-Russian Agricultural Exhibition in Moscow, though dominated by traditional and classical architecture, also included dynamic modern pavilions by Exter, Boris Gladkov and Vera Mukhina, and by the up-and-coming Konstantin Melnikov.

Early in 1924, Lenin died; he had played relatively little part in politics for the last year of his illness, and leadership of the Communist Party had been assumed by a triumvirate which included Stalin; in 1923 the censorship organization Glavrepertkom had been set up, a taste of what was to come. Lenin had not been opposed to coercion, even to terror, in political life if it would save the Soviet State; on the other hand he had been resolutely opposed to repression in civil life. His 'testament' of 1923 makes it clear that he saw the way ahead as one of gradual reconstruction, avoiding narrow nationalism, breaking the power of the bureaucracy, enlarging the Central Committee to bring into it specialists and professionals to enrich Soviet cultural life, and extending democracy to all Soviet institutions. It cannot be doubted that the seeds planted by the avant-garde designers could have flourished in such a climate.

Lenin also recognized Stalin as a barrier to such progress. It is common among bourgeois historians to represent Stalinism as the inevitable result of the Bolshevik Revolution, as if socialism, by its very nature, could achieve political stability and economic growth only through bloodshed and oppression. Roy Medvedev's view is more convincing:

> It was not Stalin who inspired the people with the ideas of Socialism ... the door to education and culture was opened by the October Revolution.... Prisoners in Stalin's concentration camps accomplished a great deal, building almost all the canals and hydro-electric stations, many railways, industrial plants, oil pipelines, even tall buildings in Moscow. But industry would have developed faster if these millions of innocent people had worked as free men.... Stalin did not choose the shortest path; he did not speed up, he slowed down the movement towards socialism and communism.
>
> (Medvedev 1971: 560)

Here then is an explanation of how and why the great experiment in art and architecture was cut short. The second half of the 1920s is full of ironies: the irony that gradual economic growth now made it possible to put the productivist theories of the Constructivists into practice, but that Constructivism itself was under threat; that the new Soviet State was attracting avant-garde architects from all over Europe, anxious to participate in reconstruction, at a time when modernism was beginning to meet with official disapproval.

After Lenin's death it took about two years for Stalin to achieve absolute power. Paradoxically, during that time, the Constructivists began to build, and achieved some of their most notable successes.

During 1924, a competition was held for the Leningradskaya Pravda building, which produced the Vesnin brothers' famous design. The following year, work was begun on Grigoriy Barkhin's Moscow Izvestiya building, and 1925 was also the year of the Paris Exposition des Arts Decoratifs, at which two seminal modern building designs appeared: Le Corbusier's Pavillon de L'Esprit nouveau, and Melnikov's Soviet Pavilion, an instructive contrast between cool Purism and dynamic Constructivism.

In 1926, for the first time, the post-war economy climbed back to its pre-war level of productivity. There seemed to be greater potential now for using industrial processes to manufacture housing, and OSA did numerous studies. The next year, Moscow's first purpose-built workers' clubs were constructed, among them Ilya Golosov's Zuyev Club, with its characteristic glass corner turret, and Melnikov's Russakov Club, which established a standard architectural treatment for an auditorium for many years to come. Melnikov was constructing his own house, too, in which the dynamic interlocking shapes and big windows expressed new ways of living.

But all this lively experiment belied the political changes taking place. In 1927 Trotsky, Bukharin and Zinoviev were excluded from office, with Trotsky being exiled the following year. There was a political purge of the Dramatic Studios in Leningrad, and the freedom of VKhUTEMAS was curtailed through its merger with the Moscow Engineering faculty, when it became VKhUTEIN. Most significant of all, pressure was being put on the peasants, in anticipation of the first Five-Year Plan and the horrors of repression which were to accompany it.

1928 was a year of further ironies. Ginsburg's superb DOMNARKOMFIN was built for Moscow government workers, a prototype apartment block with communal facilities, which represented the peak of Constructivist logic, imagination and social commitment; the collective social philosophy it represented had a particular influence on Western housing design where, of course, the different social system made its progressive forms much less appropriate. A competition for the Lenin Library brought Ivan Leonidov, most brilliant of all the young Constructivists, into prominence; his stunning design seemed to refer directly to the future, but politically it was already out of date. And the international competition for the Moscow Centrosoyuz building was won by Le Corbusier, who had adopted Constructivism at a time when official Soviet design was turning elsewhere.

1929 saw the creation of VOPRA, to act as Stalin's watchdog on architectural design; increasingly, *Pravda* attacked modern literature, art and architecture as 'formalist' – the exact opposite of what Constructivism had always sought to be. It also saw the adoption of the first Five-Year Plan, with its drive towards enforced collectivization and industrialization. Some modern architects were drawn into the design programme for the auto and tractor plants, hydro-electric schemes and new cities; the Vesnins collaborated on the design of the Dnepr barrier, and Miliutin on the planning of Stalingrad and Magnitogorsk. Many others lapsed into theorizing or inactivity; others escaped the country, or met imprisonment and death, along with peasants, intellectuals and old Bolshevik revolutionaries. In 1930 VKhUTEIN was closed down and the poet Mayakovsky, 'drummer of the Revolution', following prolonged attacks in *Pravda*, killed himself.

From this point on, control of the arts was taken over by the state and its puppet Unions into which all the smaller groups were subsumed. 'Social realism' was officially defined and striven for, and a new artistic chapter was opened. A final irony, perhaps, came in 1933 when the Nazis took over in Germany. Almost at once, they denounced modern design, that of the Bauhaus and the Weissenhof, as *Kulturbolschewismus*, even though by then both Bolshevism and the dynamic culture it had given rise to had been destroyed.

NOTES

1   See, for example, Fitzlyon and Browning 1977.

REFERENCES

Berger, J. (1979) *Art and Revolution: Ernst Neivestry and the Role of the Artist in the USSR*, London and New York: Readers and Writers.

Fitzlyon, J. and Browning, T. (1977) *Before the Revolution*, London: Allen Lane.

Hill, C. (1971) *Lenin and the Russian Revolution*, Harmondsworth: Penguin.

Ikonnikov, A. (1988) *Arkitektura Sovyetskoi Rossii*, Moscow: Raduga.

Le Corbusier, (1927) *Towards a New Architecture*, trans. F. Etchells, London: Architectural Press.

Lissitzky, El (1970) 'The ideological superstructure', in *Russia: An Architecture for World Revolution*, London: Lund Humphries.

Medvedev, R. (1971) *Let History Judge: The Origins and Consequences of Stalinism*, New York: Alfred A. Knopf.

Trotsky, L. (1962) *The Permanent Revolution*, New York: Pioneer Publishers.

SECTION 3.2

Influence of function

As a general rule architects much prefer images to words, and reading is a time-consuming distraction from drawing. In this context slogans have had a long and honourable role in the theory of architecture.

Vitruvius via Wotton gave us 'Commoditie, Firmness and Delight', which is still apposite after a couple of millennia.

Over the last century 'Form follows Function' has been one of the more popular aphorisms amongst those who aligned themselves with Modernist doctrine. Coined by Louis Sullivan, it was used to justify the tripartite form of an office block by reference to natural phenomena. Such justifications were felt necessary in order to move architecture forward into the twentieth century.

At the end of the nineteenth century, architecture seemed out of step with contemporary ideas. Since the scientific revolution of the eighteenth century, the industrial revolution of the nineteenth century and the evolutionary revolution of Darwin, rational explanations of the nature of the world dominated contemporary thought. Debates about whether Gothic or classical was the 'correct' style for the buildings of the material world seemed increasingly irrelevant. Factories, railway stations or office buildings should look like themselves, not like some religious temple of the past. Symbolic gestures to a higher spiritual power seemed unnecessary when wealth and power were being so successfully produced by human endeavours.

For much of the twentieth century architects and designers sought a rational design process that would legitimize their creative decisions.

Engineers and scientists, both social and technical, were called upon to explain and organize the needs of people, the morphology of materials, the psychology of aesthetics, so that the architects, having fully understood the programme, could, by the application of their creativity, produce an artefact that was the correct solution. Up to now little has emerged from their efforts. The influential figure of the second half of the century, Robert Venturi, challenged these arguments with his reference to 'The Duck and the Decorated

Shed'. This somewhat enigmatic notion divided buildings into two types. The 'ducks' were those where the form was a direct expression of the programme of the building, such as the restaurant which specialized in selling duck and was, therefore, shaped like a 'duck'. All other buildings were 'decorated sheds' where the programme was accommodated in an anonymous space and the architecture came from arbitrary external decoration. This argument has yet to be resolved but the successful adaption of many old buildings has demonstrated that the same form can accept widely different functions.

Ben Farmer's essay considers a range of 'ducks' and discusses how very specific functions have generated specific forms.

One of the major difficulties about recognizing functional effectiveness is that very few buildings are tested objectively. Indeed, few engineering artefacts are rigorously tested against objective criteria and this nullifies the support given to the functionalist cause by reference to aeroplanes and silos. One of the very few machines to conform ruthlessly to a functional requirement is the Grand Prix racing car. The absolute test is to cover the set distance in the minimum time, and they are continually modified to ensure this. Yet still it requires designers who have talent to make the successful cars.

Roger Day and James Powell recall early optimism and expectations but bring the story up to date, indicating that the simulation of virtual reality is now the ultimate goal of the computer, and functional considerations are still in the care of the architect or designer.

A.N.

RECOMMENDED READING

Alexander, C. (1964) *Notes on the Synthesis of Form*, Cambridge, Mass.: Harvard University Press.

Beckett, H.E. and Godfrey, J.A. (1974) *Windows: Performance, Design and Installation*, London: Crosby, Lockwood, Staples.

Ford, E.R. (1990) *The Details of Modern Architecture*, Cambridge, Mass.: MIT Press.

Granath, J.A. (1991) *Architecture, Technology and Human Factors: Design in a Socio-Technical Context*, Goteborg: Chalmers University of Technology Press.

Greenough, H. (1962) *Form and Function: Remarks on Art, Design and Architecture*, Berkeley: University of California Press.

Kennedy, R.W. (1953) *The House and the Art of its Design*, New York: Robert E. Krieger.

Kent, S. (ed.) (1990) *Domestic Architecture and the Use of Space*, London: Cambridge University Press.

Lawson, B. (1990) *How Designers Think: The Design Process Demystified*, 2nd edn, London: Butterworth.

Mills, E.D. (ed.) (1985) *Planning: The Architect's Handbook*, 10th edn, London: Architectural Press.

Pye, D. (1982) *The Nature and Aesthetics of Design*, New York: Van Nostrand Reinhold.

Richards, J.M. (1958) *The Functional Tradition in Early Industrial Buildings*, London: Architectural Press.

Zurko, E.R. de (1957) *Origins of Functionalist Theory*, New York: Columbia University Press.

27 'Commoditie'

Ben Farmer

Architecture is a collaborative art practised within a complex framework of societal, technological, climatic and economic factors. It is at base building, but rather special building – special because of significance or excellence, scale or form. Serious building is generally produced only by societies that are stable or dynamic, because the large investments that have to be made require confidence.

It is obvious, therefore, that no building is built without cause, but what that cause might be is often less than obvious. Certainly if one considers the purpose of buildings, as distinct from their cause, one is on unfirm, if interesting, ground, because purpose is seldom precisely definable, may well be complex and may change over time.

Sir Henry Wotton's 1624 definition of architecture as offering 'commoditie, firmness and delight'[1] (which, of course, sprang directly from Vitruvius' 'durability, convenience and beauty')[2] puts 'commoditie' as the first condition to be met. It is 'commoditie' in the sense of purpose, utilitarian need, or simple *raison d'être* that this essay will address.

The function of buildings is the function required of them by people (individuals, groups or whole societies). Function is seldom absolute even at the time of commission and certainly never absolute over time because standards, expectations and needs for buildings are continually changing; and subjective as well as objective criteria obtain.

Furthermore, the influence of function on what is built has become bedevilled by the many uses of the words 'functionalist' and 'Functionalism' with their implications of philosophical, moralistic, attitudinal or even merely fashionable or stylistic stances. In the mid-1930s it had become common to use the word Functionalism to stand for the progressive Western architecture of the 1920s.

Peter Rayner Banham (1972: 320) rehearses the belief that Le Corbusier is held responsible for the introduction of the term, having offered 'Functional' as a term to oppose 'Academic' (rather than, more logically, 'Rational' to oppose 'Academic'). He then goes on to dismiss Louis Sullivan's expression 'Form follows Function'[3] as 'an empty jingle'. Be that as it may, there is to be no engagement with Functionalism as a creed in this essay and no wish to associate the influences of function with a particular style.

Function may be seen to influence building in three main ways – by required performance, by the requirements of what is to be housed, and by symbolic need.

REQUIRED PERFORMANCE

Required performance may influence location, orientation, size, shape, disposition of parts, environment, cost, maintenance, quality of materials and finishes, and what might be termed character. Within this category function may be seen to exert very strong, if not determining, influences.

Some obvious examples of buildings or structures where this is the case are: cooling towers, fortresses, gasholders, glasshouses, grain silos, grandstands, lighthouses, observatories, planetaria and windmills. Let us examine a few using three of David Pye's four requirements of a design, that is to say, from the points of view of embodying an essential principle of arrangement, of geometric relationship and of required component strength (three of his four requirements of use, the fourth being the requirement of access (Pye 1982).)

Lighthouses are built where lighthouses are needed; they are located at the ends of piers or breakwaters, on rocky promontories, on cliff tops or in the sea itself.

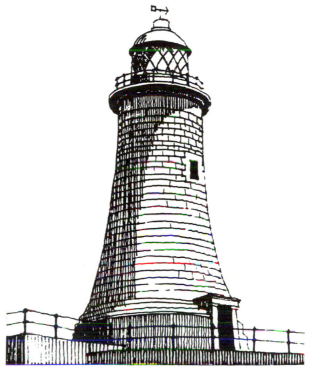

Figure 1 *Granite north pier light at Tynemouth, England, 1909. The focal plane of the light is 26 m. (85 ft.) above the high spring tide water level. The doorway faces south-west, towards the river mouth and away from the open sea.*

Their essential feature, the light itself, is always given the maximum possible elevation. Their navigational need is greatest in conditions of fog or storm and their form, therefore, has to withstand high wind and wave action. Strength, durability and resistance to the deleterious effects of seawater are essential characteristics. The light may need to sweep and have an identifying pattern of signals which dictates the plan geometry, at least at the level of the light itself.

Lighthouses are, therefore, tower structures, invariably wider at base than top. Automatic lights may well have open structures with ladder access to a working platform at the level of the light, and the lantern itself may be circular or multi-faceted on plan. Traditional lighthouses that are operated and inhabited by lightkeepers are perforce solid, tapering and/or curving towers, invariably circular in plan at all levels. Proportions, materials, patterns of applied colour and particular features may vary to advantage (so that the structures may be recognized as 'daymarks') but the generic form is clear (see Figure 1).

Windmills, by tradition, all over the world, have common features. Although there are many examples of vertical axis windmills designed to harness windpower, for example, to generate electricity, in buildings that are designed to use windpower for motor purposes, the axes are normally horizontal, and the windmills multi-bladed. The material and shape of the blades, or sails, vary as do the means by which the wind may be harnessed or slipped, but what can be seen in common are exposed

Figure 3 *Bamburgh Castle. One of many castles in Northumberland, England, with its towers and projecting turrets signalling offensive potential. The ramparts and central tower afford visual command of the coastline.*

sites, tower structures (in part to elevate the sails above ground and/or obstructions, and in part to accommodate the milling process), sails and transmission devices which are sensibly strong, and slip or release mechanisms to prevent overload or to disengage force. Some designs (post mills) enable the entire mill to be turned into or out of the wind. There are differences in size and shape and material but commonality with respect to principles underlies the range of solutions (see Figure 2).

Gasholders, although not buildings as such, are structures which can make dramatic contributions to British townscapes. They are essentially engineering solutions to the containment of variable (but always large) amounts of gas under a more or less constant pressure, and the classic form for such structures is a steel framework containing telescopic, vertical cylinders. The precise mechanisms for effecting seals and for controlling volumetric expansion or reduction vary (some actually can measure contained volume and so properly deserve the term gasometer) but the logic of geometry and strength of material relative to form is inescapable.

Fortresses offer a much richer range of expression but here again the requirements of their nature can be clearly seen to influence location, control of access, durability, strength and arrangements of building elements. They all offer protection (most offer means of engaging an enemy while under attack) and the ability to withstand seige – with all that that implies logistically and in particular with respect to water supply. Such influences are clearly reflected in simple fortified houses through castles of increasing size and complexity to veritable citadels, and, of course, other than simple fortified houses, which are defensive in nature, military architecture is the most power-charged symbol there can be (see Figure 3).

While people in fortresses may throw stones, the

Figure 2 *Chillendon Mill, Kent, England – a late example of an open trestle post mill. Post mills are the earliest form of European windmill; the body revolves on a stout upright post.*

folk-saying has it that people in glasshouses should not. The whole purpose of a glasshouse, or greenhouse, has been to create a privileged environment for plants (it is, of course, true that the necessary attention currently being paid to energy has led to a dramatic increase in the erection of conservatories as integral elements of domestic buildings in cold countries so that humans too may benefit from their environmental control capability). But glasshouses as independent or composite structures have been built for centuries, and the concept of artificial climates can be traced to the fifth century BC. This recently has been proposed even at city scale – Buckminster Fuller's 2 mile (3 km.) diameter Tensegrity dome over Manhattan, for example, and there are many examples of glasshouses within which are 'living packages' for people (see Figure 4).

Greenhouses proper work on the eponymous 'greenhouse effect'. Glass allows certain wavelengths of energy to pass through it, which are then absorbed by plants and internal materials. Although some of the absorbed heat is lost (by convection and conduction), the remaining re-emitted heat radiates at a different wavelength, which glass will not transmit, and so heat builds up within the glasshouse (Figure 5).

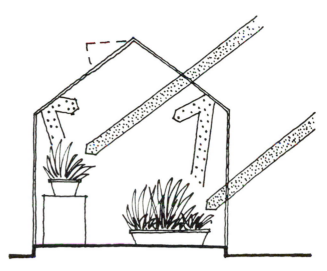

Figure 5 *Typical greenhouse section. The energy that passes through the glass is short-wave, while the reflected long-wave energy is trapped and so heat builds up. The angle of glass to sun is critical to efficiency.*

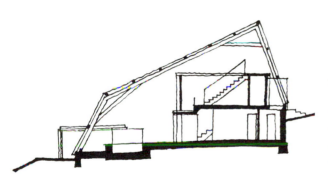

Figure 4 *Part section through Frei Otto's south-facing hillside house in Stuttgart, Germany, showing the flat-roofed domestic accommodation inserted at two levels within the vast glass space. Radiant heaters are used in winter, and in summer the roof slides open to provide ventilation.*

Critical to the efficiency of such structures are orientation and angle of glass relative to sun. There may well be supplementary sources of heat and there certainly will be ventilation systems to limit heat build-up as well as to introduce fresh air, but glasshouses are highly disciplined structures.

As we have seen, not all the structures within the 'required performance' category properly deserve to be described as buildings and even those that do are mostly mono-functional.

Most buildings are, of course, far from being mono-functional. Building design does not exemplify simple cause and effect but rather the interdependence of parts within a system, but even here there are many examples of function being a primary and obvious consideration.

HOUSED REQUIREMENTS

Buildings which house activities which are special by nature, agreement, tradition, legal requirement or performance specification fall into this category. Buildings which store things and buildings which accommodate production processes; religious buildings the world over which may have to be special with respect to location, orientation, form and layout; sports facilities which may have to comply with internationally agreed dimensions or environmental standards; concert halls and auditoria of all kinds where visual and aural criteria are critical; operating theatres in hospitals where state-of-the-art hygiene must be practised; laboratories and assembly spaces for spacecraft which must be absolutely dust-free; and so on. The list is virtually endless.

The provisions which have to be made for such buildings influence the performance of structure, fabric and services, as well as plan form, access and means of movement in and around the buildings.

Invariably there is legislation to ensure certain minimum standards for structural stability, health and safety, fire protection and fire-fighting, or which influences form and fabric because of property taxation. There may well be legislation that influences fenestration as, for example, the requirement to provide a minimum of 2 per cent daylight factor on children's desks in British schools in the 1960s, which led to the rash of glass boxes which performed so badly from the points of view of glare and heat loss. Now, with changed priorities and the need to conserve energy, legislation in Britain limits the percentage of fenestration in walls, on a sliding scale depending on the nature of the glazing (single, double or triple).

Figure 6 *High-rise pots, Sudan.*

Let us consider a few building types that fall into this category. Storage buildings, whose basic functions are to contain, preserve or protect, have a noble history. The big pot granaries of Greater Africa (Figure 6) are splendid in themselves and highly regarded within communities that owe their very existence to them. Granaries often form the dominant features of villages and have significances beyond that of merely storing food and seedcorn. Location gives possible clues about village society (such as confidence or insecurity – are the granaries central and well protected or peripheral to domestic areas?), size signals social hierarchy.

If warehouses can be taken as the generic term for storage buildings, bonded warehouses are good examples of such buildings where the basic provision of safety and security is enhanced in the interests of the Department of Customs and Excise. Located at points of entry to a country, they are traditionally large and four-square buildings with small openings (sensible in any store to limit the entry of potentially harmful light) heavily protected against forced entry. Since the advent of air-conditioning, they may of course have no openings other than for delivery and dispatch of goods.

Warehouses are invariably large in volume and scale, epitomizing the strength and security they must offer, and their structure and fabric are often redundantly strong, so the buildings lend themselves to adaptation. The British dockland scene is currently undergoing much change, as surplus storage buildings are converted to apartments, shops, galleries, offices and restaurants – many good buildings outlive their original purpose (see Figure 7).

Supermarkets and out-of-town stores are large buildings of an entirely different nature. To these the public at large is welcomed. They presuppose (and have generated) access by car for bulk purchases. They are located away from city centres, they are large sheds surrounded by very large car parks. The buildings themselves may be expressed in many ways – as simple

containers or with clip-on architectural features or, less frequently, as buildings that celebrate their structure and fabric.

In the United States of America, we have the consumer society with the fastest metabolic rate where not only are buildings built for a short life, to be torn down and replaced as commercial drive dictates, but where some buildings are designed to look as though they are about to fall, or have already fallen, down. Best Products' famous Notch, Peeling, Intermediate Façade, Tilt, etc., projects are real eye-catchers and have tremendous advertising impact (see Figure 8).

While recent developments suggest that future attention might well focus on the car parks themselves rather than the buildings, supermarkets as a building type are by now well researched and developed, and have had great attention paid to layout – the anthropometric and ergonomic considerations of galley widths, shelf design, cabinet arrangements, lighting levels, and so on – and to sales psychology. Entry and exit arrangements, graphics,

Figure 7 *Albert Dock, Liverpool, England. Robust, characterful dockside warehouse, now part of a conversion scheme for leisure, commerce, art and business. The great strength required in such buildings for their original purposes and their directness of character makes them a valuable resource.*

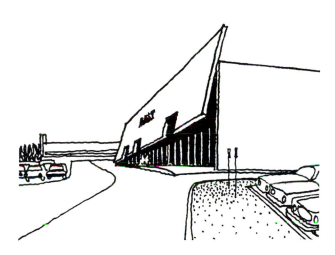

Figure 8 *The Endowood Mall Best Products showroom, Maryland, USA, 1978. It is argued that the function is not expressed, but simply revealed by lifting one corner. However, from the passing highway the façade appears to have collapsed dramatically and constitutes an arresting feature.* (Source: *SITE 1980*)

colour usage, materials and, most importantly, what is on sale where, have all been very carefully considered. In many cases the customer first encounters fruit and vegetables, and at the far end of the store will find protein foods and/or (in Western societies) alcoholic drinks. The ploy is to draw the customer through the entire store.

Theatre design makes a particularly rewarding study from the point of view of function. Large Western theatres are extremely complex buildings with challenging front-of-house and backstage needs. In so many ways the challenge is symbolic or atmospheric, or, indeed, simply theatrical.

For the theatre-goer the sense of theatre should begin with the first glimpse of the building – approach, entry, reception, orientation, sense of occasion, self-awareness and awareness of others are all important, with lighting and circulation being of paramount importance.

The auditoria may, indeed do, take many shapes and are of many different sizes, but actor–audience engagements are the fundamental provision. Sight lines, distance from seat to stage, nature of stage (proscenium, in the round, thrust, etc.), form and disposition of the seating, reverberation times or general acoustical tuning must all be critically considered.

Backstage considerations or the problems of front-of-house control or direction are equally demanding. Workshops, wardrobes, green rooms, changing rooms, rehearsal rooms, paint frames, fly galleries, control rooms, fly towers, and so on, form the engine of the theatre, and they have conflicting needs within themselves and with the front-of-house in general. Access, circulation, lighting provision, sound systems, sound separation and visual control must all be dealt with.

Additionally, because theatres attract large numbers of people who arrive and leave virtually simultaneously, and because backstage areas are potentially dangerous as sources of fire, there is invariably the need to be able to compartmentalize the theatre. This is critical where stage meets audience, and great attention has to be paid to fire protection of the building fabric and fire escape routes for both actors and audience. Whether one then expresses the theatre as a jewel box or black box seems almost incidental (Figure 9).

As a final example within this section and to make connection with the next, let us consider religious buildings. At first sight it might seem that different religions need such different kinds of buildings, which may be or are perforce expressed in such different ways that it is difficult to find common functional threads – indeed, the symbolism of such buildings, which differs so dramatically from one religion to the other, may be seen to be the overriding priority.

If, however, one examines the incredibly rich stock of such buildings that exists, one can see that importance is given to religious buildings by their siting; that particular orientation may be important or an absolute requirement; that approach and entry is carefully considered or controlled, often with ritual observance at the point of entry; that the spaces within the buildings have liturgical or worshipping significance that makes them essential as provisions if not to a particular pattern; that worshippers and those leading the worship use zones in the buildings in different ways; and that form and layout may be of fundamental importance, as may be 'furniture' or its absence. It may be too that men and women may worship together or must do so separately, but all such things are functional requirements, often non-negotiable requirements (see Figures 10, 11 and 12).

Arrangements of people, layout and form of the buildings are, of course, symbolic, as are the ways in which such buildings may be expressed, but designers of

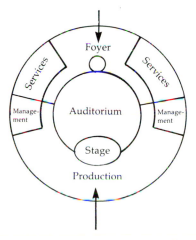

Figure 9 *Diagram showing functional relationships of Western theatre.*

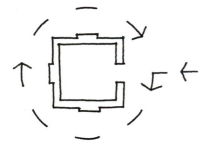

Figure 10 *Diagrammatic plan of a Hindu temple, which is approached and circumambulated in a clockwise direction. The temple is conceived as a place of transit. Passage through the doorway symbolizes the transition from the temporal to the eternal, usually on an east–west axis. The plan functions as a sacred geometric diagram, usually a square subdivded into a number of smaller squares. In association with horizontal penetration over the central, most sacred part of the sanctuary, a vertical axis links the temple's summit to the sacred centre. There are symbolic images of cave, mountain and cosmic axis in the temple's section.*

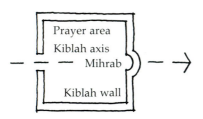

Figure 11 *Diagrammatic plan of an Islamic mosque reduced to the bare essentials of prayer area, a kiblah wall at right angles to the kiblah axis of prayer in the direction of Mecca, and a mihrab (a niche in the centre of the kiblah wall). A mosque may therefore be understood as a building erected over an invisible axis which is the principle determinant of its design. Ancillary structures are the minaret, from which the muezzin gives the call to prayer, and a fountain for ablution. Shoes are removed before entering the mosque.*

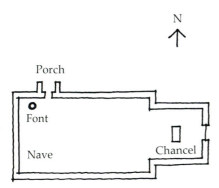

Figure 12 *Diagrammatic plan of an early Christian church in England. East–west orientation was probably influenced by pre-Christian pagan values and the advantages of an eastern window in the comparatively poor light. The porch acknowledges the climate and offers a transitional zone for arrival and departure. The position of the font symbolizes admission to the Faith.*

religious buildings are in many ways interpreters rather than creators and may indeed feel that their inspiration is divine – that they are conduits of creative energy, serving their god or gods by application of their talent.

SYMBOLIC NEED

The final form of functional influence is that of symbolism. Symbolism can either be direct, as in the design of monuments, or in the form and expression of religious buildings, or those to give witness to leaders of society, or it can be less than direct, as a by-product of buildings, which gives clues to the nature of society. Vernacular domestic building in villages and mass housing by totalitarian regimes not only provide different living conditions, they symbolize and signal different cultures.

Governments and political leaders often make serious investment to their own greater glory with formal planning, ceremonial avenues, triumphal arches and grandiose buildings which form stages on which they perform. The spirit in which this is done and the time-scale over which it is done would seem to be critical to one's appreciation, but, of course, symbolic appreciation is learned and is peculiar to a society rather than being universal, and so a measure of humility is appropriate to us all.

Arguably the world's most famous monuments are the Egyptian pyramids, which truly are monuments rather than buildings, since they contain almost no space. They represent enormous investment to signal the immortality of the Pharaohs, and are powerful abstract symbols of a long-lasting, dominating, culturally enriching society on the world's stage. Their function is clear and is brilliantly met.

Function as a factor in the design of buildings has been identified and isolated, in order that it may be examined. In practice, of course, design factors are not separable, nor can any one of them be solved precisely; there is always a range of solutions that will serve, and a designer's job is complicated by the fact that problems change as they are worked on, caused by the designer's or the design team's developing understanding.

There is no single correct solution to any problem. There are no easy design problems, but few are critical in the sense of endangering life, or defeating our ability to adapt; all too easily designers start operating crudely, designing semi-automatically, in soft-focus.

Design is always a matter of compromise, with efficiency in one respect balanced against that in another – what designers must do is to be alive to compatibilities, to look for, and see, fit. What must not be a matter of compromise is the essential nature of, the essence of, a design, and designers must ruthlessly avoid an arrangement, an idea, a form or a quality that subtracts from or masks, rather than adds to and confirms, that essence.

To follow through from concept to the smallest detail

with absolute consistency is to demonstrate mastery. To develop an idea to its limit stretches the mind and uplifts the spirit – the best of architecture does that and 'commoditie' is surpassed.

NOTES

1 'Well-building hath three conditions, Commoditie, Firmness and Delight' (Wotton 1624: [14]).
2 Vitruvius regarded architecture from the point of view of 'durability, convenience and beauty' (Vitruvius 1914: 17).
3 The expression 'that form ever follow function' was first used by Louis Sullivan (Sullivan 1896, quoted in Benton and Benton 1975: 13).

All drawings and photographs by the author.

REFERENCES

Banham, P. Reyner (1972) *Theory and Design in the First Machine Age*, London: Architectural Press.
Benton, T. and Benton, C. with Sharp, D. (eds) (1975) *Form and Function: A Source Book for the History of Architecture and Design 1890–1939*, London: Crosby Lockwood Staples/ Open University Press.
Pye, D. (1982) *The Nature and Aesthetics of Design*, New York: Van Nostrand Reinhold.
SITE (1980) *Architecture as Art*, London: Academy Editions.
Sullivan, L. (1896) 'The tall office building artistically considered', *Lippincotte's Magazine* 57 (March), Philadelphia; revised version in L. Sullivan (1947) 'Kindergarten chats', New York: Schultz Inc., p. 208.
Vitruvius Pollio, M. (1914) *The Ten Books on Architecture*, trans. Morris Hickey Morgan, Cambridge, Mass.: Harvard University Press, Book 1, ch. 3, p. 2.
Wotton, H. (1624) *The Elements of Architecture*, a paraphrase of Vitruvius, printed London: John Bull.

FURTHER READING

De Zurko, E.R. (1957) *Origins of Functionalist Theory*, New York: Columbia University Press.
Hix, J. (1981) *The Glass House*, Cambridge, Mass.: MIT Press.
Reynolds, J. (1970) *Windmills and Watermills*, London: Hugh Evelyn.

28 The vision, the potential and the virtual reality: technologies to inform architectural design

Roger Day and James Powell

THE INDUSTRY AND THE TECHNOLOGY: A CONTEXT FOR CHANGE?

Information is now, more than ever before, fundamental to all activity in the construction industry. The complex task of designing and constructing improved environments for human habitation and use depends critically on the transfer of information between the participant roles (client, designer, consultant engineer, contractor) and the processing of information by participants to increase its value. For example, the production of an architect's drawing combines and converts numerous items of information into a coherent design proposal, represented in a form that communicates with other participants, such as those from whom planning permission must be sought, or those who will eventually construct the building. These items of information range widely, to include the client's perception of need, the architect's design conceptions, technical information about the performance of building components and the necessary expert knowledge about construction technologies and building regulations. To a very large extent, the quality of the built product is determined by the success with which information is represented, interpreted, processed, stored and exchanged.

The simplicity with which this is stated conceals the difficulty with which it can be achieved. Two aspects of the industry have contributed much to compound this difficulty. First, the systematic study, interpretation and reporting of the variety of design responses to the vast range of building types now required to support civilized communities have combined with an accelerating development of alternative construction materials and technologies to create an *information explosion*. Second, the trend which has seen most industries progressively dominated by a reducing number of multi-national companies has *not* been shared by the construction industry. In 1986, in the UK alone, there were over 8,000 component manufacturers, 170,000 private contractors who employed fewer than seven people and 3,000 design practices employing fewer than four architects (DTI 1987). The industry remains fragmented and this is not only true of the employment and distribution of its workforce but also of the information structures which serve and co-ordinate them.

Thirty years ago, the growth and persistence of these problems were not foreseen. In the early 1960s, amidst the glare of 'the white heat of technology', it appeared that computer science would anticipate every information need. Even tasks as complex as architectural design seemed certain to benefit from the improved co-ordination that would follow from their computerization, just as soon as the speed and the capacity of the hardware increased sufficiently. In this climate of unguarded optimism the Science Research Council funded large computer installations, such as the ATLAS, at selected research establishments, and eager researchers queued to add the one remaining ingredient: the rational thought and reasoning necessary to access and harness the computer's undoubted power.

These early efforts to establish Computer Aided Architectural Design (CAAD) were contemporary with those of another group of researchers whose interests were not centred on the role of the computer in design practice but who nevertheless sought to analyse and represent the activity of design in terms of systematic *design methods*. Typical of their search for an all-encompassing design process was the 'Plan of Work' published in the RIBA Handbook of Architectural Practice and Management (1965). The Plan set out the contributions of all the participants in design and construction in a sequence of stages from 'Inception' to 'Completion and Feedback'. However, some of the difficulties encountered by design teams attempting to adopt such systematic approaches were soon apparent to design methods researchers.

One study, based at the Tavistock Institute of Human Relations, included case studies during which the actual 'process' of design was observed. Under the title *Interdependence and Uncertainty*, the report stated:

> each time a decision was taken it set in train a chain of circumstances which could and did cause the initial decision to be changed.... Since the full implications of any decision or action can seldom if ever be forecast with absolute accuracy, a communications system which assumes that they can will simply not work.
>
> (Tavistock 1966)

By the beginning of the 1970s, design methods research had revealed the variety and complexity of strategies used in architectural design. An early, some would say prophetic, expression of the corresponding complexity necessary in any machine environment that might inform and assist designers appropriately emerged from the Massachusetts Institute of Technology, where Negroponte proposed the 'Architecture Machine'. His challenge to those developing CAAD systems was issued in the following words:

> Imagine a machine that could follow your design methodology and at the same time discern and assimilate your conversational idiosyncrasies. This same machine, after observing your behaviour, could build a predictive model of your conversational performance. Such a machine could then reinforce the dialogue by using the predictive model to respond to you in a manner that is in rhythm with your personal behaviour. This dialogue would be so intimate (even exclusive) that only mutual persuasion and compromise would bring about perceptions and ideas – ideas, in fact, unrealizable by either converser alone. In such a symbiosis, it would not be solely the designer who would decide when the machine is relevant.
>
> (Negroponte 1970: 11)

Negroponte's vision of the future is yet to be achieved, but has much in common with the intelligent, knowledge-based systems now under development and the machine environments proposed as a unifying framework for their application to design. With the benefit of hindsight it is possible to recognize that many of the basic hardware technologies necessary to support such an environment were already available when the 'Architecture Machine' was first envisaged.

UNCHANGING CULTURAL DIVIDES: THE SUCCESSES AND FAILURES OF SYSTEMS ANALYSIS

Why then has design practice yet to be transformed, as predicted by the confident assumptions of the 1960s and the prophetic visions of the 1970s? In many other fields, especially in science and engineering, very significant advances have followed the rapid development of information technology, to meet, and in some cases outstrip, the predictions of the enthusiasts. Some might protest that, to a substantial degree, architectural practice has embraced the benefits of office automation. Word-processors have replaced typewriters. Fax machines are used almost as frequently as telephones. More and more practices are installing computer drafting systems. However, the fact remains that the extent to which computer *modelling*, as opposed to computer *drafting*, contributes to *design* procedures falls far short of the dreams of the proponents of the 'Architecture Machine', nor does it yet approach more modest ambitions widely held for CAAD.

Many now believe that the answer to the question

that this poses is rooted in what has been called 'the two cultures'. Psychology explains their existence in terms of the functions of the two halves of the brain and the dominance of either the left side or the right. Recent research has identified a number of sub-cultures, membership of which, or temporary alignment with which, influences the ways in which individual designers interact with the world and construct models of it (Powell 1987 and Newland *et al.* 1987). In everyday terms we might label the two dominant cultures 'science' and 'art', but this can be an oversimplification and a more useful characterization distinguishes between *analysis* and *synthesis* as the bases of alternative problem-solving strategies.

The tasks to which computers were first successfully applied required a type of process support that could be identified, specified and programmed using a purely analytical approach. This kind of programming seeks to model complex systems – for example, a nuclear reactor or transport to the moon – by observing and representing the behaviour of component parts before assembling them as a logical sequence of mechanisms and operations to produce a complete model. Given the sequence

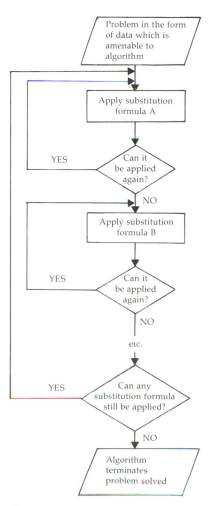

Figure 1 *Flow chart for an algorithmic procedure.*

and the definition of its stages, the output of the model is fixed and completely predictable. Theoretically, all such representations could be modelled and used without computers. However, when problems submit to this approach, it is indeed the speed of computer hardware and the size of machine memories that can make so much more achievable within practical, human timescales.

The critically important stage in analytical problem-solving and process-modelling is the *systems analysis* required to identify a linear sequence of steps from the definition of the problem to its solution. The success of this approach in many fields of science and engineering was well established long before the arrival of computer technology. When it did arrive, its potential to underpin and extend such rigorously analytic techniques was immediately apparent. As a result, the early high-level languages, for example FORTRAN and ALGOL, were structured to suit this basic methodology and to support a style of programming now distinguished from other styles by the generic term 'procedural programming'. The flow diagrams routinely used to represent the sequential logic of procedural programming (see Figure 1) provide a simple representation of these inherent structures.

In seeking the right kind of machine environment to support architectural design, the inappropriateness of software structured only in this way now seems clear. For example, the validation of its sequential logic normally requires results to be precisely repeatable. The same data as input should always produce identical solutions as output. This test is clearly unsuited to any model representing architectural design, which draws much of its interest from the variety of responses that can legitimately be made to the same design brief. Indeed, the celebration of the richness of this variety is an essential aspect of all great and appropriate architecture.

In this fundamental way, the first interpretations of the potential of computers and the applications for which they were first developed largely determined the view taken of all other possible applications. It is impossible to believe that the inadequacy of this view can have escaped the notice of many of those who worked closely with the profession to model and support design activity. Indeed, the importance of 'resolving a conflict that exists between logical analysis and creative thought' had been central to the aims of the first Conference on Design Methods in 1962, as interpreted by Jones (1963). He went on to say:

> The difficulty is that the imagination does not work well unless it is free to alternate between all aspects of the problem, in any order, and at any time, whereas logical analysis breaks down if there is the least departure from a step by step sequence. It follows that any design method must permit both

kinds of thought to proceed together if any progress is to be made.

(Jones 1963: 54)

However, belief in systems analysis and sequential models remained strong, particularly within the science-based culture that adopted and raised the new technology. The mismatch between the models that procedural languages were structured to construct and the ways in which architects actually tackled design was for some time ignored.

In spite of this mismatch, some progress was made. Components of design processes were identified and modelled as algorithms suitable for procedural programming. *Task-oriented* software was written to make these models accessible to potential users, particularly in two kinds of applications. The first was in areas relating to building science such as structural analysis, energy and environmental performance predictions and the specification of building services. The second kind of application was in computer graphics, particularly for the rapid drafting and revision of working drawings and the visualization of buildings in perspective projection.

TERMS OF ENGAGEMENT:
ENABLING AND DISABLING THE USER

During the late 1970s and early 1980s, pioneering attempts were made to overcome the limitations of procedural programming. Most notable were those which linked computer drafting systems to performance modelling software, so that one could inform the other (Lawson 1982). However, while capable of supporting many design tasks when treated in isolation, it became increasingly apparent that existing software structures were not sufficiently flexible to support the pluralism of working strategies adopted by creative designers and design teams. As a consequence, use of the software was conditional on the acceptance of prescribed terms of engagement, which can be summarized as 'do things my way and I can help'. It is the implied terms of engagement that distinguish truly informing and enabling technologies from those that are too prescriptive to be used without imposing unacceptable change on established working patterns and practices.

It is our view that, even now, few of the computer-based systems developed as aids to architectural design offer appropriate terms of engagement at the user interface. Rather, many of these systems, in effect, disable their users because they do not respect and reflect the preferred strategies of building designers. However, the necessary reinterpretation of the potential of computer technology has begun. There are now clear signs of convergence between an improved understanding of the real needs of designers, resulting from more open-minded observation of the strategies that they adopt, and emerging information technologies, such as artificial intelligence (AI) and knowledge engineering (McCorduck 1979). They promise more appreciative and enabling design information systems.

The search is on for a new type of CAAD with a user interface as familiar and responsive as a soft pencil drawn over paper and which offers the freedom to explore design space in ways that are, from the designer's viewpoint, mind-opening and creative rather than mind-closing and prescriptive. The developers of these new systems now realize that it is not only speed and capacity that are critical to the uptake of informing technologies. The important issue is to create a machine environment which appropriately represents data *and* knowledge of many types, from a wide range of sources. These representations must be so structured as to respond to the information needs of all participant roles in architectural design, and so presented at the user-interface as to appear appreciative of the alternative information-processing strategies adopted by different participants at different design stages.

A PARADIGM CHANGE: FROM COMPUTING TO INFORMATION TECHNOLOGY

Concurrent with this reappraisal of CAAD is an initiative, recently taken by the Science and Engineering Research Council, to stimulate new research into the applications of information technology (IT) to the built environment. The Council has expressed particular interest in design assistance, calling for 'more intelligent systems which could offer advice and active assistance, rather than just passive modelling and evaluation' (SERC 1990). In drawing attention to the new opportunities presented by potential applications of emerging information technologies, the initiative echoes Negroponte, recalling that:

> systems have been envisaged which could interface more intelligently by sustaining models of the user and of the product under design, in order to fashion and support an appropriate dialogue between the user and the advisory system; to provide assistance for the designer rather than a designer for an assistant.
>
> (SERC 1990: 1)

Attempts to structure such an integrating environment and to facilitate information flows between the user and various assisting knowledge resources have proposed systems with the components illustrated in Figure 2. The role of these components and the nature of the environment which they combine to create can be compared to a meeting of design professionals: the architect and various expert consultants. A designer (the user) might arrange such a meeting to offer project proposals for review by those from whom advice and stimulation is sought. We must picture this team gathered around a blackboard, the shared display/workspace on which

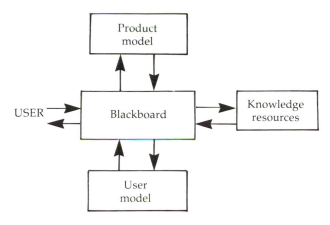

Figure 2 *The components of an intelligent design assistant.*

they record and exchange views about the project. The blackboard acts as a central communication and temporary storage device. It is ideally flexible, being equally suited to the variety of representations that different team members might use, such as sketches, diagrams, graphs, formulae or text.

All members of the team have particular contributions to make, based on their experience and expertise. They are the *knowledge resources*, possessing information which they interpret and process expertly to the mutual benefit of the team. Each expert interpretation of the current status of the project and the corresponding views of the alternative ways forward are written on to the blackboard and so offered to the other team members for their evaluation, development and advice. Through the blackboard, all members of the team have a constantly updated view of the developing ideas of all other team members.

Together, they work on a *product model*, the building(s) under design, which will be represented in various ways, perhaps including site plans, photographs or video footage, conceptual sketches or models, and progressing through many development stages to a final set of formal drawings. At any one time, the product model is the accumulation of all existing representations that can inform the design team about the proposal under consideration.

The overall aim of meetings of this kind is to facilitate a dynamic, free-ranging exchange of interacting views, in order that fully informed choices can be made from as wide a range of design alternatives as the team can generate. It has much in common with *brainstorming* (Osborn 1957). There is no prescribed formal agenda, corresponding to any fixed view of a sequential design procedure. No attempt is made to anticipate the order in which contributions from individual team members will be made or to place immediate value on them, once expressed. Ideas which appear untimely when first proposed will nevertheless remain on the blackboard, to be picked up and revived if they are subsequently recognized to be constructive. Such a process cannot be automated, but the advisory environment which supports and assists it can be simulated.

INTELLIGENT SYSTEMS: NEW SOFTWARE STRUCTURES TO INFORM DESIGN

CAAD research, currently in progress, aims to develop prototype decision support that would place the user at the control centre of an information system simulating the meeting of minds described above (Carter and McCullum 1991). It would offer continuous access to the knowledge and expertise of those from whom advice might be sought, captured and represented in the various knowledge resources that share access to the machine equivalent of the blackboard (Corby 1986). Some aspects of this knowledge, particularly those which are supported by numerical calculation, are already represented by software modules structured in the conventional style of procedural programming, but most will require the implementation of newly maturing technologies and software structures characteristic of artificial intelligence, knowledge engineering and expert systems.

These technologies can simulate the information processing strategies of human experts, by representing and implementing the rules on which they are based. Used in conjunction with laws of logical inference they can construct reasoned arguments to simulate deduction and judgment. For example, artificial intelligence structured in this way might be used to select design strategies, which, taking account of all the information to hand, are 'judged' to have good chances of success. Prompted by these expert propositions, the user would be free to accept or ignore advice, adopting those strategies which he or she judges to be progressive, but only for as long as they remain so. When the current strategy is no longer working, the user will look for an alternative, perhaps prompted by further advice from another of the knowledge resources writing to the blackboard.

The potential of advisory modules of this kind to cope with uncertain and incomplete data, using probability and inference to select promising design strategies, seems certain to offer a more appropriate interpretation of the fragmented information that characterizes construction design processes. However, to ensure that the advice offered at the user interface is presented in a manner that is truly informing, important research and development is also in progress to establish suitable technologies with which to construct knowledge bases of another kind. Rather than knowledge of alternative design strategies, these would possess knowledge of the alternative conceptual frameworks employed by different types of users.

These *user models* would act as interpreters, choosing between alternative representations of the information written on the blackboard, in order to present it at the user interface in a form that is *known* to be familiar and enabling to the user engaging the system. Successful user models would bridge the cultural divides that currently separate disparate professions within the construction industry. They might also recognize and respond to the temporary cultural alignments between which individual users alternate in their search for design solutions (Powell 1987 and Newland *et al.* 1987).

The intelligent design assistant described above is one example of a knowledge-based system. Intelligent knowledge-based systems (IKBS) are programmed using the new rule-based structures characteristic of *declarative* languages, such as PROLOG and LISP. The rules that they apply are normally formulated at the stage of systems development that roughly corresponds to the systems analysis stage required to program using procedural languages. This stage is called 'knowledge acquisition'. The knowledge is normally acquired from human experts (those whose presence the knowledge resources discussed above are intended to simulate), often by structured interviews or formal observation of the expert at work.

Knowledge-bases, like databases, can be updated as the software is used. When this is a function of the user, we can say that the system is being 'taught' new knowledge. The need to make assumptions about the cultural differences and alignments to which user models must respond could be avoided by the use of systems capable of simulated *learning*. Such highly intelligent systems might record and interpret the manner in which each individual user engages the system to identify patterns in the choices made so that they may be incorporated into a continuously updated user model capable of anticipating user needs more accurately. A particularly exciting technology that may eventually provide an alternative to the rule-based systems now being implemented in user modelling is the neural network.

Neural networks offer a new kind of hardware structure in which many small information processors are connected in networks characteristic of the human brain. Their most interesting property allows patterns to be extracted from data and representations of these patterns to be constructed without the system having been programmed to anticipate patterns of any particular type. In effect they 'learn' from experience. Their implementation in applications of the type discussed here remains a distant but enticing prospect.

So, after several sections of this essay dealing with the fundamental reinterpretation of software structures necessary to build appropriate models of design activity, it is in considering this most important component, the user model, that new hardware structures begin to be suggested. Could it be that a similar reinterpretation of hardware structures will be just as fundamental? The recent research interest in transputers and parallel processing provides further evidence to suggest that from now on software and hardware development cannot be treated separately. Indeed the following sections, which describe some recent successes in the application of information technology to design, re-inforce this view.

NEW TECHNOLOGIES AT THE USER INTERFACE

A recent survey of the use of information technology in general British industry (Aris *et al.* 1990) identified inflexibility at the user interface as the most important deterrent against the uptake of new information systems. Arguably the most successful user interface so far introduced is the WIMP (window-icon-mouse-pointer) environment pioneered by Apple Macintosh and now rapidly becoming a *de facto* standard for design-based industries. The *mouse* replaces the keyboard as the main tool at the user interface. It is used to move and locate a screen *pointer* (cursor) and thus to access facili-ties which are represented on the screen by *icons* (graphic symbols) and, when selected and activated by clicking a button on the mouse, are opened as *windows* to display their contents.

In its original form, the icons used to represent the environment's standard facilities were chosen to estab-lish an analogy with basic office equipment, such as the filing cabinet (for permanent storage), a clipboard (for temporary storage) and the waste-paper bin (for disposal of unwanted items). Inside the filing cabinet (i.e. on disc) *files* contained *documents* grouped in *folders*, all identified by appropriate icons to reinforce the analogy. The general office simulation concept was extended further by calling the whole screen area displaying the icons the *desktop*. Using the mouse, docu-ments could be removed from the filing cabinet, opened on to the desktop and edited with various pieces of mutually compatible applications software for word-processing, drawing, etc. Text and graphics could be transferred between applications using the clipboard. Updated documents were refiled and unwanted drafts assigned to the waste-paper bin.

This desktop metaphor and the WIMP environment has proved enabling to the inexperienced user while not hindering the expert. It has enjoyed wide acceptance because it is a truly appreciative system which makes use of familiar strategies to increase the value of skills and knowledge already possessed by most of its poten-tial users. The distribution and communication centre that the desktop represents is perhaps the nearest thing to a machine blackboard in general use today. The choice of icons and the names given to them amount to a simple user model. However, these are passive devices, as yet with no ability to structure advice in response to the input from particular users.

Further very important changes in human–computer interaction (HCI) can be anticipated when the voice-recognition technologies now under development become standard at the user interface. One of the most successful information technology tools in the practice office is the telephone. Indeed, voice communication is the mainstay of the construction industry. Those respon-sible for the telephone network are endeavouring to add value to their systems in terms of local area networks and wide area networks (see next section). Intelligent applications of voice-processing technologies, especially voice recognition in combination with advanced data and knowledge processing, will significantly affect the use of all information technology and thence construc-tion information handling and communication.

NEW TECHNOLOGIES FOR NETWORKING AND DATA EXCHANGE

Some architects are intimidated by networking, partly because of the jargon that surrounds it – bandwidths and bridges, twisted pairs and topologies – and partly because it provides so many sharing options. The best way to conquer this fear is to start small and add new capacities as they are needed. At the lowest level, simply networking to a laser printer adds economic value to an expensive peripheral. Linking to others in the office enables you to share ideas and information. Adding *file server software* allows you to store, in one place, files everyone needs to access: for example, client databases, downloadable laser printer fonts for special presen-tations, or templates for frequently produced docu-ments. Using *electronic mail software*, you can send messages and files to colleagues. With *multi-user software*, everyone can access the same files without the need to store separate copies on each machine and without fretting over whose version is the latest.

The fax communications board added to an informa-tion system is perhaps the most important development to date. This can simply be plugged into a computer so that workstations can send and receive digitized images and data communications over conventional telephone lines at facsimile rates. The logical extension of networking is the development of a global network, acting as a world-wide conduit for all types of informa-tion.

Organization of and access to massive databases are perhaps the most fundamental concerns faced by the construction industry. Unlike a physical library where every book has a spatio-temporal location and com-petent individuals can easily build and retain a mental map of where required items are, the 'black box' syndrome of intangible mega-storage can become an offensive Pandora's box. However, many of the new interfaces access massive databases in a manner similar to the way professionals think about, design and make construction itself. Point and click on a roof component of a drawing and this 3-D object, held in the CAAD system, becomes the search string which retrieves struc-tural characteristics, manufactures' specifications and optional products. In advanced systems such objects are automatically recorded and any updates (for example, by dynamic links to manufacturers' source databases) are communicated to the designer by colour changes in the relevant components.

To make such system databases accessible to all requires standardization. The NEDO Working Party on CAD data and other information exchange in the building industry recognized this and recommended the DXF format as a standard, but only for graphics. This, originally pragmatic, intermediate solution has now evolved towards the much more widely embracing European STEP standard for the exchange of all types of building and construction data. One of the unifying ideas to emerge from STEP is the concept of *life-cycle* within an information model and standard system. This will lead to as-planned, as-designed, as-built and as-used models in all data sets. The ISO STEP (1988) standard seems likely to be adopted, at least within Europe, so that translators can be written which will transform data from a given application into the standard, and from the standard into a new application. In this way the standard will act as a vehicle for passing of information between databases.

NEW TECHNOLOGIES FOR INFORMATION STORAGE AND RETRIEVAL

While floppy discs, hard discs and tape backup are familiar, proven technologies that will remain important to IT and continue to be widely used, optical discs have been called the 'new papyrus' of the information handling industries. Optical storage media allow fast, easy and reliable computer access to a large range of information types including moving video, still images, graphics, sound or pages of text. Different systems allow cost-effective storage of different types of information. What follows can only hint at their enormous potential. For a fuller treatment of optical media see Powell (1991).

Imagine combining 15 hours of audio with over 55,000 still images or 37 minutes of moving video, all in vivid colour. This is the extraordinary capacity of a single 30cm. (12 in.) video disc. All such information is available with random access within seconds or split seconds of demand, comparing favourably with the rate of retrieval from a purely computer-based archive, or material stored on conventional videotape. Team the rapid reflexes of the videodisc player with the organizing, calculating, textual and graphic powers of the computer and you have interactive videodisc. A typical system is shown in Figure 3.

GLIMPSES OF THE FUTURE: REALITY AND VIRTUAL REALITY

A turning point has been reached in the history of the computer's involvement in architectural design and construction. New interpretations of its potential have produced technologies which can be truly informing. Some progressive practices are already providing us with glimpses of the future by using these technologies in experimental, designerly ways. A principal designer (Catalano 1990) describes the use of state-of-the-art IT at his New York office in the following words.

> Our 12-person firm represents an example of a totally electronic, computerised design practice increasing its value as a small business through commitment to state-of-the-art information technology, from network computing linking us with clients, consultants and manufacturers, to voice controlled CAAD and related technologies, to in-house developed software for solid modelling and animation, to expert and decision support systems, to multi-media. Our computerised design firm is a structurally flexible, knowledge-based organisation where the emphasis is placed on information creation. Here, work is performed by computer experts, brought together electronically in spontaneous work groups that reach well beyond the boundaries of the firm.
>
> (Catalano 1990: 60)

Finally, Figure 4 is a graphic by Castle (1990) depicting the technology that has been called *virtual reality*. It promises to allow architects of the future to take a surrogate wander through buildings still under design, without leaving the office.

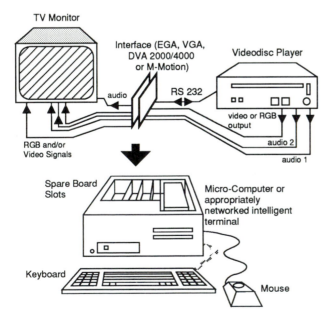

Figure 3 *Typical interactive video system configuration.*

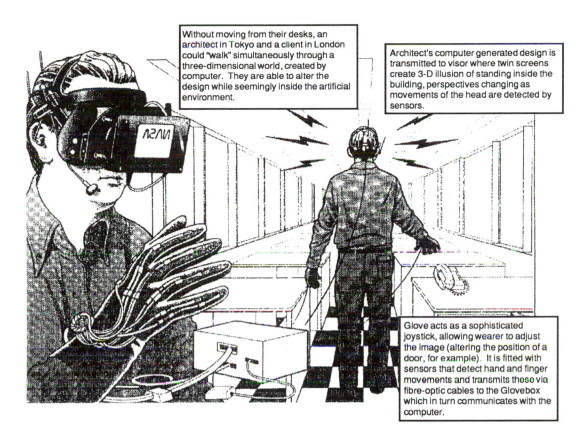

Figure 4 *A graphic by Roy Castle showing an architect's surrogate wander through his designed environment.*

REFERENCES

Aris, J. *et al.* (1990) 'Survey of IT user needs', Pub. DTI (private communication)

Broadbent, G.H. (1973) *Design in Architecture*, London: Wiley.

Carter, I.M. and MacCallum, K.J. (1991) 'A software architecture for design coordination', in J.S. Gero (ed.) *Artificial Intelligence in Design*, Butterworth-Heinemann, pp. 859–82.

Castle, R. (1990) 'Step this way into a world of illusion', *Daily Telegraph*, 26 March: 27.

Catalano, F. (1990) 'More than meets our ears – voice technology in CAD', *Architects' Journal*, 14 November: 59–62.

Corby, O. (1986) 'Blackboard architectures in computer aided engineering', *Artificial Intelligence in Engineering* 1(2): 95–8.

DTI (1987) *Housing and Construction Statistics*, London: HMSO.

International Standards Organization (1988) *Draft STEP Proposal*, ISO TC184 SC4/WG1.

Jones, J.C. (1963) 'A method of systematic design', in J.C. Jones and D.G. Thornley (eds) *Conference on Design Methods* Oxford: Pergamon.

Lawson, B. (1982) 'Know your building', *Architects' Journal* 175(25): 81–4.

McCorduck, P. (1979) *Machines Who Think*, San Francisco: W.H. Freeman.

Negroponte, N. (1970) *The Architecture Machine*, Cambridge, Mass.: MIT Press.

Newland, P.M., Powell, J.A. and Creed, C. (1987) 'Understanding architectural designers' selective information handling', *Design Studies* 8(1): 2–16.

Osborn, A.F. (1957) *Applied Imagination: Principles and Practices of Creative Thinking*, New York: Scribners.

Powell, J.A. (1987) 'Is architectural design a trivial pursuit?', *Design Studies* 8(4): 187–206.

—— (1991) *Proceedings of the First National RICS Conference*, Barbican Centre.

RIBA (1965) *Handbook of Architectural Practice and Management*, London: RIBA.

SERC (1990) 'Intelligent design assistance', IT Applications Research Theme.

Tavistock Institute (1966) *Interdependence and Uncertainty: A Study of the Building Industry*, London: Tavistock Publications.

29 The building skin: scientific principle versus conventional wisdom

Michael Wigginton

In human societies the intention to build is driven by two fundamental aims: the wish to create platforms (and thus make better use of land), and the need, in the varying climates of our planet, to provide shelter.

The concept of 'architecture' carries with it the spiritual and cultural overtones of building, but it is these two generative forces behind the act of building which constitute the basis for the form-making process, and the essential requirements for performance.

Shelter, and environmental control, may seem utilitarian and prosaic aspects of the potentially poetic creation of architecture. However, they set the most important agenda in the building process, and the one most related to the climatic and socio-historic characteristics of a place and the people who inhabit it. In the twentieth century, the century of functionalism and science, they can also provide the basis for the aesthetic.

In considering the earliest buildings, subjects of anthropological rather than architectural attention, we see the earliest attempts people made to provide stable shelter, from the cave to the elementary stone shelters still visible in all parts of the world.

Primitive, but simple and elegant, forms of sheltered platforms can still be seen in the village huts of countries such as Thailand (Figure 1).

Figure 1 *A Thai village house. A timeless and perfectly integrated combination of shelter and platform.*

An elevated platform provides the floor for the living accommodation, and the base for the sheltered enclosure in which the family sleeps and obtains privacy. The raised floor gives shade and shelter from the burning sun and torrential rain experienced in the monsoon climate. The family's animals share this shelter with their human owners. The raised enclosure lifts the living accommodation above flood and mud, and gives limited but important protection against vermin and insects. The enclosure itself provides privacy, protection against the weather and a certain elementary security.

The building is a holistic and simple response to the needs of its owners. In its fusion of structure (platform, walls and roof) and envelope it provides identity as well as protection. It is designed in response to the exigencies of climate and socio-economic structure. It is elementary, but perfect architecture.

In such a building, the envelope incorporates exemplary physical attributes in the climate it inhabits. Using easily obtained materials and simple construction techniques, it provides a lightweight (thus easily supported), low thermal capacity, well-ventilated enclosure. A modern analysis of the physical requirements of such an envelope would lead to a solution of exactly such a type.

Building in northern Europe presents a completely different agenda. The ancient black houses of the Highlands of Scotland demonstrate how enclosures in northern European climates are formed to respond to a different set of criteria (Figure 2). The building provides a wind-proof enclosure, arranged around the central position of the fire. The wall is massive, and its thermal capacity provides an effective heat store, soaking up the heat from the fire, and giving it back, slowly, when the fire is out.

In both of these buildings, the provision of envelope is an intrinsic reason, if not the principal reason, for the very existence of the building. It is also, of course, its external manifestation; it is what the building looks like.

To all intents and purposes, and for most of the

Figure 2 *A Scottish black house.*

people who experience it, the envelope of a building *is* the building. It is the place where interior space meets the exterior. It constitutes the boundary between the internal environment and the climate outside. It defines ownership, and provides privacy, security and view. It is the energy filter, and in its material quality lies the effectiveness of the building in mitigating or welcoming the vagaries of weather. In its design is embodied the expression of those who built it, whose inner world is concealed from or open to the world outside, only to the extent provided by the envelope itself.

At the same time, it assists in the formation of exterior space, as it defines the streets, squares and courts of our urban environment.

Le Corbusier, the great Swiss/French architect said, at the beginning of his canonical book *Vers une Architecture* (1927), 'The plan is the generator'. In this statement lies a great truth of architecture, that the form of a building is the result of its internal organization. However true this may be, we know that books on architecture are actually filled with photographs of the exteriors of buildings, images of envelopes. These correspond with our experience of the buildings themselves, as architecture.

In considering the building envelope *per se*, historically and as a matter of cultural, aesthetic and technical study, we are dealing with two essential types: those in which it is withdrawn within the confines of structure, and those in which the envelope is wrapped around the structure, as a skin. The Greek temple (Figure 3) and the Gothic cathedral exemplify these two types. In the temple, conceived in a culture and at a latitude in which climate control was almost unnecessary, the envelope is set well back in the structure. It provides an enclosure in response to requirement set by religious criteria.

In the Gothic cathedral, an essentially northern European phenomenon, the exterior of the building is a membrane, stretched between the structure elements (Figure 4). The form is closed.

In the buildings of the Renaissance we see the fusion

Figure 4 *King's College Chapel, Cambridge, England. At the zenith of European Gothic architecture, the envelope is a membrane of decorated glass stretched between stone structure.*

of the dichotomy in European architecture: the combination in infinite permutation between the membrane and the colonnade. In their wish to recreate the order of classical architecture in a climate which demanded enclosure, architects created the forms which gave us centuries of building to a pattern, in which the column (or pilaster), the wall, and the window became the prime means of individual external expression (Figure 5).

The 1,000 years of European architectural development between the early medieval period and the industrial revolution saw modes of architectural expression derived essentially from stylistic criteria. The building skin certainly existed as climate modifier and structural support, but the window/wall assembly, the envelope, existed primarily as a means of expression: the surface on which the 'architecture' was drawn. This is not to say that Renaissance exteriors were usually comprised of walls. The great colonnades of St Peter's,

Figure 3 *Greek temple, Paestum. In the warm Mediterranean climate the outward expression of architecture could be purely structural. The colonnade, not the wall, was the envelope.*

Figure 5 *Palazzo Rucellai, Florence, by Alberti. In their wish to recreate the forms of classical antiquity, Renaissance architects applied the orders of Greece and Rome to otherwise flat window-walls.*

Figure 6 *King's Cross Station, London. The industrial revolution brought the long span and the glazed roof, early hints of the mega-enclosure and artificial climate.*

the cloister of the Ospedale degli Innocenti in Florence by Brunelleschi, and the rich perimeters of Borromini deny this. However, in most buildings we see limitless permutations of holes in walls.

In only a few building types (such as conservatories, where the growing of plants demanded an understand-

Figure 7 *Glass skyscraper project, Berlin, by Mies van der Rohe. One of the first great architectural proposals for a glass 'skin', seen here in the form of the original 1922 model.*

ing of microclimate) was the *performance* of the envelope much considered.

The industrial revolution created new demands. Railway terminals required wide and lofty halls, daylit and capable of accommodating the smoke of the new railway engines (Figure 6). The development of commerce created a requirement for large spaces in which goods could be exhibited and marketed. Most important, a new engineering aesthetic developed out of the inevitable, increasing use of the machine. In Britain, Europe and America, the awakening of the industrial aesthetic led to the birth of modern architecture.

In Germany in particular, the Deutsche Werkbund and the subsequent founding of the Bauhaus produced a fresh awareness of the potential of new (and in some cases, such as glass, very old) materials. Concrete, steel and glass provided new means of expression which the architects of the twentieth century were quick to exploit.

What has become known as the International Style provided a new language for architecture. The Villa Savoye by Le Corbusier, of 1929–31, follows the formal organization of the Thai house, but its construction and appearance exemplify the new architecture of our century.

Le Corbusier went on to develop richer and more complex forms of envelope in buildings such as the Salvation Army Hostel, also of 1930, in which air-conditioning and a glazed envelope were designed to combine to produce an artificially controlled environment. The glazed wall provided view, light and climatic protection, and the wall itself carried air as part of the breathing system of the building.

Ludwig Mies van der Rohe, another great Modernist, produced his 'Glass Tower' project in 1922 (Figure 7), and here we see demonstrated even more clearly the new attitude towards the building envelope. Made entirely of glass, the wall is designed to exploit the material with its ambiguous properties of light transmission and reflection. Here we see the paradigm of the twentieth-century idea of the architectural skin. It is a paradigm in terms of image only, however, and was, significantly, only made as an architectural model. Mies van der Rohe's Seagram Building of 1959 (Figure 8), nearly forty years later, represents a simplified and more overtly classical version: it was left to Foster Associates in their Willis Faber Dumas office building to realize the earlier vision, with its undulating wall, albeit only three storeys high (Figure 9).

These buildings manifest a uniquely twentieth-century attitude to technique and metaphor. Without overt reference to historical models in terms of appearance, avant-garde architects between 1920 and 1940 used machine-age imagery to develop a new architecture.

In the Seagram Building, and many other buildings of undoubted quality built since 1945, we see the climax of one phase of the Modern Movement in architecture, accompanied by the creation of an architectural model

Figure 8 *Seagram Building, New York, by Mies van der Rohe. A great and classic curtain wall building, with the envelope as a celebration of metal and glass technology – in this case bronze, and a specially made brownish-pink, selenium-based glass.*

Figure 9 *Willis Faber Dumas offices, Ipswich, England, by Foster Associates. Truer in some ways to the Berlin Tower than Mies's own Seagram Building, this building embodies the idea of architecture as 'skin', in frameless bodytinted glass.*

which was to be the cause of a major reappraisal of the Movement itself.

We saw a proliferation of commercial buildings using so-called curtain walls, in which a thin frame of metal (usually aluminium) supported membranes of metal and glass to form the building envelope.

This new 'architecture of commerce' exploited the metaphorical building skin on the constructional sense: they were continuous membranes apparently stretched around the structure behind. In terms of performance and appearance however, they were extremely inadequate.

Moreover, the curtain wall has only proved itself at all appropriate for certain types of commercial building and, at the end of the twentieth century, we have seen

an entirely understandable reaction against this form of architecture (Figure 10). We are currently seeing a reworking of much of the architecture of the previous 300 or more years. Many architects, to the apparent relief of a public frightened by the machine-age aesthetic, have turned to the historical model for the cladding of their steel and concrete frames.

Such an architecture is only 'skin-deep' however, and we must consider more carefully the essential relationship between the building 'skin' and architecture itself.

It is an irony of history that we have grown to use the word 'skin', a word borrowed from the world of biology, to describe the envelope construction in the buildings of our industrial and (so far) highly mechanistic age. The irony is compounded into embarrassment when we consider how poorly we have manipulated the metaphor. In an age characterized by technology transfer, we have shown that we can produce skins for ships, aircraft and space vehicles which are efficient, correctly designed interfaces between the inner and outer worlds.

In buildings we have, of course, produced envelopes which approach the quality of such skins in certain respects, provided we spend the price of an automobile for about 10 sq. m. (100 sq. ft.). In general, however, we have hovered uneasily between the banality of the curtain wall of the office building, and the inadequacy and super-redundancy of traditional methods. When we mix the two, we all too often produce failure: the panellized, prefabricated, brick-clad masonry wall, prey to condensation, leakage, and (ultimately) collapse.

Much of this is due, of course, to the fact that the envelope of a building *is* its physiognomy, and we have set up rules for physiognomy which defy the laws of Darwin: they do not relate to an evolutionary response to performance criteria, but are superimposed styling. We have decided as a society that the faces of our buildings must satisfy the preconceptions of the public at large. Whilst evolution proceeds in the inner organism, we are held by the process of Planning Approval to familiar and conventional forms.

Figure 10 *Offices, Richmond, London, by Quinlan Terry. As a reaction to the banality of 1960s curtain walls, many developers and their architects sought refuge in new 'Renaissance' envelopes.*

This reactionary tendency in the public view of architectural physiognomy is understandable in some ways in an age characterized by what many would say is urban and rural vandalism. It is nevertheless unparalleled in the history of Western architecture – and artistic culture in general – which is itself characterized by the regular overturning of form and appearance, as technology and social priorities have developed and changed.

However, if the interior of the organism is changing, we must expect the skin to change too. Our century has seen the burgeoning of a scientific culture, and the building envelope, the essential protective screen between us and the external environment, must eventually respond to the evolutionary process.

We are now acutely aware of a (comparatively recent) set of objectives written around the needs of performance. We realize, perhaps almost too late, the importance of energy, of the economical use of materials, of environmental care. In this new culture, the design of the envelope has become a matter of performance.

Increasingly hemmed around by regulations concerning water and energy leakage, and by the demands of clients who are more educated about what is possible, the necessary physical characteristics of the envelope are becoming more defined. It is worth asking, in this situation, whether conventional wisdom about the building skin is in accordance with the scientific principles which we increasingly find we must follow. The answer to the question is 'sometimes, but very often not.'

Let us consider a simple example, separated from the contentious matter of the curtain wall (generally only a concern for commercial buildings), or the arguments revolving around the use of brick, stone, metal and glass: the example of the house in a temperate climate, at a latitude of about 52°, in the British Isles.

The climate is characterized by diurnal and seasonal temperature ranges which are unpredictable and overlapping: a summer's day can be colder than a winter's night. The only contrasts are the annually cyclical

pattern of the sun's movement, and the statistical norms of temperature, wind, rainfall, relative humidity and other climatic variables.

Now consider one of the historically most favoured building types originating in such a climate, the Georgian terrace house (Figure 11).

The constraints of materials availability and constructional techniques lead to a prototypical solution for the envelope. A brick skin is built solid for stability. Holes are made in it, and building details conceived, which permit the incorporation of timber-framed, sliding sash windows. The width of the holes is constrained by the limits of shallow arched brickwork or short lintels. The fronts of these building are rendered and painted to imitate the stone which cannot be afforded; the backs are left unrendered and dark. Security, privacy and extra protection are provided behind the window by shutters which fold into boxes: these shutters are angled to mitigate glare and increase the effective width of the window. The window itself is rather leaky, since two sliding elements are difficult to seal. The sliding solution is considered better than side-hung casements, however: it gives better control of ventilation and rain.

The pattern of openings up the façade is derived from the social hierarchy of the floors. The largest windows are at first-floor level (the major reception rooms). The smallest are at the top where the servants live.

The pattern is repeated regardless of orientation. In considering the building skin the 'presentation' of the physiognomy of the building is considered more important than the function of the wall/window arrangement for the occupants. It is considered that the arrangement is quite good enough, no matter which way the building faces, and in any case that the symmetry of the street is of overriding importance.

Much of the rationale behind this designed result is difficult to fault. In our age of science however, we must ask whether it is the best we can do.

In many respects it is. The high proportion of masonry wall gives the building a thermal performance which smooths out diurnal temperature ranges. Given the technical and historical limitations of the hole-in-wall solution to the window, it performs quite well. Draughts abound, and the insulative qualities of the wall are not very good, but such buildings are still valued, and for good reason.

If, however, we were to adopt the same approach to the envelope of the terrace house as we do to a modern kitchen, what would we aim for? What criteria would apply, what techniques would we study, research and implement, and what materials would we use?

We would of course, look at the climate and the sun. We would know that we wished to welcome the sun at certain times, and exclude it at others. We would consider the amount, and the location, of thermal capacity, to ensure that we stored heat when we wanted to. We would conceive solutions to the problems of the

Figure 11 *A Georgian street, Pimlico, London. Simple and elegant skins of brick and windows, embellished with mock stone on the street façades, plain and functional in the rear, and oblivious of orientation.*

sudden rainstorm on the summer day, and the warmth of a sunny day in winter.

In some parts of the world this more careful and considered view of envelope design already leads to a richer architecture, with more amenity and better performance. This is particularly true in places where the climate is harsher, such as Scandinavia or California. In these cultures designers have had to create envelopes which respond to climate, and have happily produced architectures to suit the sun and snow.

When we in the temperate zone decide to respond to climate, and use our technology, we will design differently. We will require the envelope to behave like the petals of a bell flower; to open in the sun and close in the rain and at night. We are talking 'anatomy' here, however, and we should not be afraid to extend the metaphor, because it is entirely appropriate.

As we seek to set out the agenda for the design of the building skin for the twenty-first century, it is to anatomy we should look for our conceptual models. Since humanity is at the centre of our particular stage, it is the human skin we may consider.

The human eye and epidermis represent the biological interface between the body and the environment. The eye opens and shuts, and the pupil contracts and dilates, in response to the conditions of light and air encountered. The transparent protection to the lens is kept tirelessly clean throughout the life of the organism by a continuous supply of appropriate fluid. A shutter protects, and cuts off stimuli during the hours of rest.

The skin provides a waterproof, self-repairing and

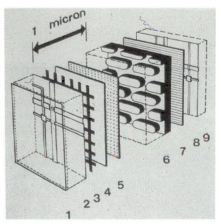

Figure 13 *Multi-layer membranes. Future building skins may comprise multiple layers of glasses and plastics, coated with invisible films a few nanometres thick, capable of variable performance. (Diagram by Michael Davies)*

elastic membrane, at the same time porous to the internally created moisture essential to its cooling apparatus (Figure 12). Built-in sensors carry messages in micro-seconds to the brain, which activate heating and cooling. The combined performance of the active epidermis and the insulative fat layer below enable sensitive internal organs to be kept at $\pm$ 1°C of their required constant temperature with external ambient temperature variations of 30°C or more. Such a skin does not enable us to do without clothes or buildings in our 52° latitude environment, but it provides an exemplary model for our future designing.

The building skin is the essential expression of most architecture, whether wrapped tightly around the structural form, or inflated to produce a bubble container, or deeply modelled as it contrives to provide an envelope for complex interior organization.

Materials are now available which enable many of the desirable attributes of an epidermis to be achieved (Figure 13). Suitable coatings on glass, liquid crystal technology, and automatic control systems already make it possible to design buildings with elementary 'intelligence', which open and close automatically in response to exterior conditions or pre-programmed intention. We can lie in bed and watch the stars, knowing that when we fall asleep the roof/wall/skin will close itself to keep us warm. If we want the sun to wake us up at 7.00 a.m., the wall can transform itself gently from opaque to translucent to transparent, at just the right time. The window can be designed to incorporate fibre-optics, to transmit light to the building interior: we can switch off the lights during the days when there is plenty of light in the sky.

The comparison between such building skins and the wall/window of the eighteenth century, is similar to that between the Georgian skin and the medieval wall: it represents a quantum leap. Such, however, is the history of the physiognomy of building, and of architecture.

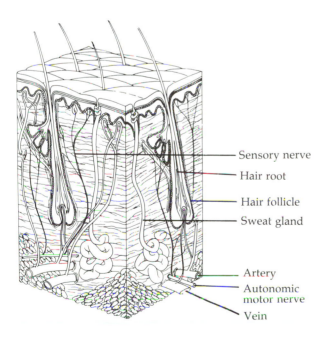

Figure 12 *Human skin. A section through human skin shows the complexity of performance to which architects may aspire, in its complex of tissue, nerves and blood vessels, all typically within a thickness of 2 mm.*

Sensory nerve
Hair root
Hair follicle
Sweat gland

Artery
Autonomic motor nerve
Vein

SECTION 3.3

Architectural precedent

Architects are not the only group in society to have been challenged about their attitude towards the past over the last few decades, but the impact of this experience on the profession has been unusually traumatic, causing a widespread collapse of confidence.

The root cause of this crisis concerning the relationship between contemporary architectural practice and history lies, it is frequently stated, in the combined effect of the entrenched historicist and relativist doctrines which deny any fixed norms for human action. Whether or not this view is accepted, few would dispute the need to find a way out of the impasse reached when Modernism failed in its revolutionary objectives. The question is how to proceed. It is clear that it is no longer a serious option to attempt a return to the kind of tradition prevalent amongst cultures of the pre-industrial era which demands a blind adherence to the ways of the immediately preceding generation, however idyllic that condition might appear to some. A more positive (and realistic) approach would seem to be to search for a new critical awareness that could guide our interaction with history – one that would invigorate and not debilitate.

In an essay called 'Tradition and the individual talent', written before the 'anti-historical' stance of the modern avant-gardes had become a destructive force, the poet and critic T.S. Eliot gave some clues as to what this might involve. He argued for a more democratic concept of tradition which would allow scope for individual creativity whilst constantly reaffirming our links with the past. This, he thought, could be achieved through what he called a 'historical sense', i.e. a perception 'not only of the pastness of the past, but of its presence'.

This desire for past and future to be united in a confident present is gaining ground as a cultural objective over a broad front. As David Lowenthal points out in a recent book, *The Past is a Foreign Country* (1985), it is the most sensible way forward:

> We can use the past fruitfully only when we realize that to inherit is also to transform. What our predecessors have left us deserves respect, but a patrimony simply preserved becomes an intolerable burden; the past is best used by being domesticated – and by our accepting and rejoicing that we do so.
>
> (Lowenthal 1985: 412)

However, for the reference to historical precedent (in a utilitarian as well as symbolic sense) to become once again a force for good in modern practice, it is essential that both its nature and limitations be understood.

The twelve essays in this chapter, even though they draw on human experience over a wide geographical spectrum and time span, can only identify some of the aspects worth studying. That need not concern us. The reasons for our interest in historical buildings (including those from the recent past) are many, and the ways we engage with them both complex and varied. What is important is that we approach this task in the right spirit. The past can be an infinite source of inspiration for an architect, but it does not divulge its secrets lightly. Only when we have learned to ask the right questions will it provide us with the appropriate answers.

H.L.

RECOMMENDED READING

Alexander, C., Ishikawa, S. and Silverstein, M. (1977) *A Pattern Language*, London: Oxford University Press.

Bourdier, J.P. and Alsayyad, N. (eds) (1985) *Dwellings, Settlements and Tradition: Cross-Cultural Perspectives*, London: University Press of America.

Colquhoun, A. (1989) *Modernity and the Classical Tradition: Architectural Essays 1980–7*, Cambridge, Mass.: MIT Press.

Lowenthal, D. (1985) *The Past is a Foreign Country*, Cambridge: Cambridge University Press.

Pelt, R.J. van and Westfall, C.W. (1991) *Architectural Principles in the Age of Historicism*, New Haven: Yale University Press.

Rapoport, A. (1990) *History and Precedent in Environmental Design*, New York: Plenum Press.

Summerson, J. (1980) *The Classical Language of Architecture*, London: Thames & Hudson.

Tafuri, M. (1980) *Theories and History of Architecture*, London: Granada.

Thiss-Evenson, T. (1987) *Archetypes in Architecture*, Oxford: Oxford University Press.

30   What makes the past matter?

David Lowenthal

We live in the present, and all we see around us are things that currently exist. What is yet to come is of obvious concern, for we are bound to care about the future we are going to inhabit. But for what reasons do we concern ourselves with the past – a past presumably over and done with? Modern times appear to have cost the past two of its most hallowed values: pedagogy and empowerment. Yet the past still commands our attention and our affections as strongly as ever.

Before our own epoch, the past was generally valued as an indispensable guide to the present and the future. Only by studying the lives of past people and by learning what had happened in history could people understand their present selves and circumstances and hope to foresee what life would be like in times to come. These twin beliefs were predicated on three widespread assumptions: that the past was knowable and the future ordained; that change was gradual, cyclical, or inconsequential; and that human nature was more or less the same in all times and places. Hence the past was a fount of useful lessons, lessons that could serve as precepts for the present and the future.

These certitudes and assumptions are no more; the past has lost most of its pedagogic functions. Popular fears that we may repeat past errors are still widespread, but not even the best understood past is any longer felt to enable us to forecast the future. And faith in a knowable past is itself in tatters. Though historical research continually throws light on myriad realms previously unexplored, the lineaments of the past in general have become increasingly murky, its consequences ever less certain. The actual past forever eludes us: all we have is partial accounts of it, based on our own or other people's memories, and fragments of much-altered material residues from former times. And the past we reconstruct as a substitute for that lost realm is anything but fixed and solid: it shifts from viewer to viewer and from decade to decade, as recent events crowd on to our chronological canvas and as later perspectives supersede earlier ones. Perhaps the only valid lesson that is left for the past to teach is that there *are* no lessons the past can teach.

The past used to be of especial interest to those able to benefit from the privileges antiquity and precedence conferred. An attested and ancient lineage and time-honoured traditions gave their fortunate possessors privilege and power, property and prestige. The aggrandisement validated by this frequently fabricated past 'seeped through the interstices of society, staining all thought, creating veneration for customs, traditions and inherited wisdom', and acted as a 'bulwark against innovation and change' (Plumb 1969: 66). But in democratic and egalitarian societies these past-based privileges had ceased to be credible. The authoritarian past was being replaced by a truly objective chronicle of what had actually happened, creating 'a new past as true, as exact, as we can make it' (ibid.: 115). Modern historical insights and industrial democracy have largely extinguished the prerogatives formerly conferred by antiquity and genealogy. The past as a source of profit and power, no less than the pedagogic past, is becoming *passé*.

Yet loss of faith in the past both as an exemplary guide and as a fount of privilege has not diminished our profound attachment to it. Ordinary people as well as elites everywhere seem more than ever devoted to the past, or at least to *some* past. These attachments manifest themselves at every level from individual and family annals through chronicles of communities, ethnic groups, and nations, and even the history of the earth and of the whole universe.

These interests touch on every imaginable aspect of existence. People manifest a concern with the past of natural objects and of living beings, with relic artefacts and archives, and with the origins and careers of traditional ideas and practices.

Such interest increasingly takes the form of zealous campaigns to protect and preserve outstanding, rare, or representative specimens of past forms or features against the apparent threats of accelerating change and loss. Such attachments are especially manifest in concerns with the built environment, notably with the architecture of the past.

Why should this be? What benefits can we now hope the past will yield, since for the most part those who treasure the past no longer believe that it will guide or enrich them?

Attachment to the past is in any case inescapable. Although the strength and character of our concerns vary with time and place, with culture and mentality, and although we may focus now on certain residues and now on others, no humans are exempt from myriad forms of dependence on the past. It is an essential component of the human condition; we have no choice but to concern ourselves with what has been, for it is built into our bones and embedded in our genes.

The survival of our very existence is based on the facility of habit and the faculty of memory; without them we could neither learn nor long endure in any environment. Habit enables us to perform actions previously learned without having to think about them or to make new decisions each time we repeat them; memory enables us to recognize familiar features, to negotiate familiar routes, and to cast back to previous experience in order to assess the likely outcomes of actions undertaken by ourselves and others, now and in the future.

The pervasive influence of recollection and repetition in everyday life stresses our need for environmental continuities. Habit and memory can be effective and efficient only if the world around us is stable enough so that we can readily recognize and act on our environs in a way that will yield expectable results. Hence we utterly rely on the familiarity of our surroundings.

The natural world generally causes few problems in this regard; except when interfered with by human agencies, most landscape components long endure essentially unaltered, changing at a pace seldom noticeable in a human lifetime. And living beings with life-spans briefer than ours are succeeded by beings so similar that they appear wholly familiar.

Change becomes a major problem only for the things we ourselves do and make, especially where natural things are subordinated to the realm of artefacts – notably in cities. But even urban environments include routes and spaces, buildings and façades, many of which – save for large-scale wars and other major upheavals – persist much longer than we ourselves do.

Nowadays, however, buildings as well as other commodities are increasingly designed to be replaced ever more rapidly by things that look and function quite differently. Planned obsolescence pervades the built environment along with most objects of everyday use. We are not equipped by nature to cope with continually new arrays of unfamiliar things. Swift and massive environmental replacement hence induces stress from which people seek surcease, anchoring themselves to familiar worlds by clinging to whatever survives from or reminds them of the past. We indulge habit and memory not simply out of nostalgic yearning for times gone by, but out of a rational need for security in a world become perilously unstable.

In short, attachment to the past is innate and natural. Amnesiacs deprived of the ability to recognize, recall, and retrieve memories of the past, long-time residents whose neighbourhoods have been transformed beyond recognition, and refugees ejected from life-long locales, are alike dispossessed of cherished linkages – cherished because they are familiar, and familiar because they are cherished. And when we are dispossessed we turn to other pasts for support.

Alongside these more or less involuntary attachments, we cultivate and celebrate the past in myriad acts of appreciation, emulation and preservation. Beyond the need to ensure survival in a not too unfamiliar present, what motivates us deliberately to seek out the past?

Manifold individual and communal benefits – identity, enrichment, diversity, escape – come readily to mind. There is not space here to discuss them all; this essay simply highlights a few that seem significant for a wide range of cultural milieux. Familiarity with the past enables us to achieve a keener sense of our own individual and collective selves. It enlarges us by linking ourselves with a community embracing ancestors and descendants, with those who came before and those who will come after us. It enriches our present lives with an awareness of folk of earlier times, and it counters modern monolithic forces of global sameness with the greater diversity of the past's many alternative places, products, peoples, and ways of life.

To know who we were and where we came from is a prerequisite for a stable and fulfilling present. As history and psychoanalysis variously demonstrate, knowledge of one's past need not – and in many ways cannot – be wholly accurate, but it must be substantial and self-confident. Those who lack knowledge of their previous selves tend to conflate past with present and fail to project themselves realistically towards the future; they are compelled to relive the past they do not remember. A mature sense of present identity is possible only through an awareness of life as a continuing career. To become familiar with our own ancestry, to retrace in recollection the steps and scenes of childhood and youth – these are not mere antiquarian pastimes, they are vital ingredients of our personalities. Concerned interest in the past grounds us in time and space and connects our lives with historical contexts.

Cultural and social identity require an analogous awareness of the collective past. To be a member of a group one must at least empathetically share that group's origins and history. Rites of initiation, including induction into citizenship, emphasize familiarity and identification with the collective past. Whatever traits are held to be most germane to group identity have, especially since the rise of nationalism in the early nineteenth century, been apotheosized and protected under the general rubric of 'heritage'. The past celebrated within the concept of heritage is typically quintessential – it highlights traits felt most characteristic of, or unique to, the group, notably language, folklore and founding myths, outstanding artistic creations, and monumental and traditional architecture.

Indeed, architecture plays a triple role in the collective past. Three distinct types of structural remnants enter the valued heritage: the finest achievements of past epochs, felt to embody the immortal aspirations of its people; representative buildings of former times, felt to embody the collective genius of their makers and possessors; and 'monuments' created to celebrate particular individuals and collective entities, historic events, tragedies, triumphs and achievements.

The role of past architecture in forging cultural identity goes beyond its material survival; buildings of previous epochs also provide models for architects and builders of later days, including our own, to emulate.

Much of the built environment consists of conscious or unconscious revivals, echoing manifold attachments to forms and features of the past.

This heritage links us not only with our precursors but with our descendants. We enjoy our inheritance in substantial measure as a trust to be handed down to future generations. Our investment in that future is closely interwoven with our interest in the past.

The past we thus recognize and remould to secure our identities need not, indeed cannot, simply mirror the past as it was; we are inevitably selective, inaccurate, anachronistic and creative in what we know about the past and how we apply that knowledge. But there is nothing wrong with such manipulations: difficulties arise only if antiquarian reverence compels us to claim that we are reviving a wholly authentic past, the true version of bygone times that brooks no alternatives. Quite to the contrary, the utility of the past inheres in its manysidedness, in being all things to all people. It is the flexibility, not the fixity, of the past that makes it so useful in enhancing our sense of ourselves: our interpretations of it alter according to the perspectives and needs of present and future moments.

The past we deploy to forge our sense of identity is, however, not the whole of the past but only *our* past. To serve other purposes we have to transcend the heritage that is particular to ourselves and make imaginative use of other pasts as well.

Our need for these other pasts is less apparent than our need for our own legacies, but it is none the less essential. Awareness of pasts that lie beyond the confines of our own kinfolk, our own community, our own country, enhances our understanding and whets our appetite for more. Through these exotic pasts we view our own past – indeed, our own being – in comparative context. They show us that how we were, and how we have come to be what we are, are not the foreordained consequence of some divine or other grand plan, but are contingent realities explicable as much by chance as by design. A catholic concern with the memories and relics and heritage of others safeguards us against narrowly partisan chauvinism, a self-aggrandizing and exclusively celebratory (or tragic) view of our own heritage.

To ask that we attend to pasts that extend beyond our own purlieus may seem quixotically selfless. But the growing popularity of museum-going and historic-house visiting, of biography and autobiography, of historical romance and of fictional accounts of former lives, demonstrates that the interest in pasts beyond our immediate ken is already enormous. And relics and ruins – the characteristic features of the built environment along with the architectural masterpieces of former times – fascinate millions of tourists the world over. Public curiosity about the collective pasts of remote cultures is already pervasive. The zest for exploring exotic lives and landscapes attests the expansion of many horizons beyond the here and now, and the power of a far-flung past to illumine and transform awareness of our own.

Viewing what he termed the rising cult of historical monuments, Alois Riegl in 1903 categorized three broad strands of past-linked concern – their visible marks of physical deterioration, their role as historical witnesses, and their deliberate use as memorials. Almost a century on, we have only begun to chronicle the shifting tides of sympathy for and among these and other sentiments. Different kinds of past – collective or personal, classical or Gothic, national or local, remote or recent – suit different purposes. So do the myriad particular benefits we seek to derive: the past now enhances pride and pleasure in present life, now compensates for present deprivations and disappointments.

The benefits the past is felt to confer vary with epoch and culture, individual and stage of life. Heightened awareness of more and more kinds of past leaves us dazzled by their differences, uncertain how best to construe them. But all concern with the past has two common elements: it enables us to function in the present and to plan for the future; and it links our individual and corporate identities with the comprehensive community of the dead, the living, and the still unborn.

REFERENCES

Plumb, J.H. (1969) *The Death of the Past*, paperback edn 1973, Harmondsworth: Penguin.

Riegl, A. (1903) 'The modern cult of monuments: its character and its origin', trans. K.W. Foster and D. Ghirardo, *Oppositions* 25 (Fall 1982): 21–51.

FURTHER READING

Connerton, P. (1989) *How Societies Remember*, Cambridge: Cambridge University Press.

Koselleck, R. (1979) *Futures Past: On the Semantics of Historical Time*, trans. K. Tribe (1985), London: MIT Press.

Lowenthal, D. (1985) *The Past is a Foreign Country*, Cambridge: Cambridge University Press.

Munz, P. (1985) *Our Knowledge of the Growth of Knowledge: Popper or Wittgenstein?*, London: Routledge & Kegan Paul.

31 Tradition and innovation

Jakub Wujek

Tradition and innovation together make architectural history. They correlate. They are interdependent. Without tradition, which imposes standards of behaviour on generations of followers, it would be impossible to talk about the 'new', the 'different' or the 'better'. An innovation which has been generally accepted becomes, in time, a tradition.

Fathers to sons, teachers to pupils, elders to youngers, all passed on their knowledge and experience acquired year after year in harmony with people and environment. Local standards, in communities separated from one another by natural geographical barriers, existed unchanged for a very long time.

The need for a new kind of innovation appeared when the most influential centres of civilization began the process of subordination of highly individualized regional forms according to strictly defined principles.

Ancient Greece had played the most significant role. Philosophers and artists, utilizing the experiences of developed cultures situated around the Mediterranean Sea, created the classical base for the aesthetics of the whole of Europe. For Plato the most important concept was the 'idea'.[1] The real world, as perceived by human senses, was merely an imperfect and ever-changing reflection of the existing truth. Intellectual solutions, through their connection with the absolute, could occupy the time and thoughts of a philosopher in accordance with Socrates' dictum that knowledge is a virtue, and had very important consequences in practice. If an artist succeeded in approaching the ideal through his or her work, another artist, in imitating the first, was equally successful in reaching toward perfection. This perception of artistic activity made imitation inevitable, sanctioned it and gave it theoretical justification. Giorgias, sophist and the pioneer of aesthetics, defined sculpture, painting and architecture as imitative arts, because the need to follow the work of their predecessors was an intrinsic part of their nature. Once created, the image of the ideas of people – a temple, or a city, in fact all the ideas of *real* work – were waiting for future artists to copy and continue the standards. Plato's division of the world into perfect ideas and their imperfect representation was taken up and developed by his great pupil, Aristotle.[2] To the latter, form was what the idea had been for Plato. Aristotle considered it as the real counterpart of every concept. An artist's task was to extend the life of the form into the future.

Ancient vision of the world of art was based upon the hierarchy of values: a graded order defining with mathematical precision the different levels of meaning, interactions and mutual relations, easily understood by all, the public as well as the creators. The absolute form presenting the eternal idea had to be defined, that is, the work as a whole and each of its constituents had to remain within their confines as prescribed in the terms of art. All architects, masters, builders or artisans, irrespective of education, knew that when they were building a house they should define all contours of the mass and single out, by means of ornament, the main doorway and the windows according to their importance. Each knew how to design the base, that is, the area of contact with the ground; to develop the relation of roof with the sky; to work out all corners and angles. There could be no doubt that a given structure was made with references to the tradition of building and as such could be compared to others.

These standards, popularized by Vitruvius' book *De Architectura*, captured the imagination of later generations, with full acceptance by the Christian Church, which adopted the complete philosophy of Aristotle.

During the many centuries of flourishing Mediterranean civilization, empires rose and fell and political borders continuously changed until the ancient civilizations were destroyed by Barbarian raids. But the timeless quality of the aesthetic language created on the Greek peninsula retained its relevance.

Architects who inherited the alphabet had to rely on talents to create from this a work that would either become a symbol of their times or be relegated as an insignificant and undistinguished scribble.

These aesthetic principles, which persisted throughout the Romanesque, Gothic, the Renaissance and baroque periods until the beginning of the twentieth century, are sometimes referred to as 'The Great Aesthetic Theory of the Past'. The Theory's language could easily describe all new developments of civilization which led to the creation of the well-known architectural monuments. The most resilient and vital political structures received the appropriate form to depict the power of a new state system. Thus the demands of royal prestige inspired French classicism.

Previously unknown technological possibilities presented true challenges to the restless creative mind searching for innovation in the field of building technique. For example, the constructional experiments of Isidore and Artemios of Tralles at the Hagia Sophia in Constantinopole, or Joseph Paxton's new method of building, based upon the use of standardized, factory-produced elements which were assembled on the building site, respectively won immediate public approval.

Different economic orders created new social groupings, which tried to establish their identity in the most conspicious way, such conditions prompted the Chicago architects to build the first skyscrapers.

Mutable trends in philosophy and religion inspired innovators to search for new solutions adequate to the changed condition. Villard de Honnecourt provided instructions on how to raise the vast Gothic cathedrals connecting the earth with heaven;[3] Filippo Brunelleschi's dome of Santa Maria del Fiore in Florence demonstrates a new understanding by humanity, as did Michelangelo's Basilica of St Peter's, Rome.

All this innovation fitted within the framework of the 'Great Aesthetic Theory'. It was the twentieth-century avant-garde which rejected this tradition and adopted innovation at all cost as the only goal. In order to understand what happened it is necessary to outline the origins of those changes which go back to the Age of Enlightment.

Apart from the impact of industrial development and the rise of new social strata, the most important factor was the appearance of new philosophical doctrine. Empiricism, which gave priority to experience over dogma, encouraged the denial of existing order in the world and proclaimed the freedom of people from the role they had until then been playing on the stage of history. No longer were they actors repeating the words that others had written a long time ago. Instead they were offered the opportunity of becoming simultaneously playwrights, stage managers and directors.

At the beginning of the nineteenth century, the rationalism of the encyclopedists was replaced by a number of successive idealistic doctrines. The Enlightenment, with its desire to change the poorly organized world, found an ally in the new ideas based on faith in intuition, which held that if theory was incompatible with the facts it was the facts that were to be disregarded, not the theory.

The first of many romantic idealists was Johann G. Fichte, who was fascinated by 'action' and believed that it was the most important thing in the development of society. His ideas were continued by Georg W. Hegel, who proposed a dialectic interpretation of the world, where the mechanism defined by the principles of thesis, antithesis and synthesis was successful in interpreting the past but useless in regard to the future. Karl Marx found in the dialectic the inspiration for his revolutionary ideas; Saint Simon deeply believed that industry would bring about a greater happiness of the people in the name of Humanity, Progress and Order. Thomas Carlyle preached the hero cult. Henry Bergson, towards the end of the nineteenth century, ranked intuition amongst the supreme laws. Edmund Husserl and Max Scheler propagated Phenomenology as the new philosophical foundation for all intellectual movements to come.

The general tendency of thinkers to turn towards the future had a crucial influence upon creative activities.

The artists of romanticism were the first to challenge the Great Aesthetic Theory. They preached individualism and the cult of emotion. Through their own example they imposed standards and attitudes which are binding to the present day. At first, there was only an avid pursuit of primitive innovation which was still being drawn from tradition. This accounted for the pervasive historicism of the second half of the nineteenth century, until an attempt was made to establish a new visual world.

This new movement was Art Nouveau. Its other names – Secession, Jugendstil, New Style, Liberty – all express the yearning for a totally new art, free from tradition, which encompassed all spheres of human activity. It was an extremely important precedent. If it was possible yesterday to create by artificial means a new, contemporary art, then there should be no reason why the same could not be accomplished – only better – today, and again tomorrow, and yet again the day after. The achievements of Art Nouveau, however, soon lost their disturbing revolutionary significance and became simply a continuation of Great Aesthetic Theory.

Then came the Futurists. Their artistic manifestos assumed not only the ultimate destruction of all the buildings erected in the past but, worst of all, the annihilation of all ideas which drew their inspiration from the past. In their manifestos, drawn up early in the twentieth century, they demarcated the limits of artistic individualism for the future generations of the avant-garde.[4] One cannot overestimate the significance of Futurism as a turning point in the history of art of our century.

The influence of Marinetti's group differed according to political, economic and social conditions. In stable countries Futurism was a short-lived novelty; in those parts of the world where radical changes were taking place, it merged with the existing artistic ideology with astonishing results as, for example, in pre-revolutionary Russia.

Cubo-Futurism, which next arrived on the scene, was an extra-ordinary mixture of Futurist manners and behaviour and Cubist experiments in self-expression.

During the October Revolution, the whole artistic avant-garde, bursting with the desire to act, joined in the building of the new state with great enthusiasm. The rise of a new and different social structure created unique opportunities. The borders between the possible and the impossible blurred and became gradually obliterated. Through their art artists wanted to participate in the building of the new; through active participation in various organizations they helped to destroy the old.

Having joined the current of the country's political life, and by becoming the leaders of new schools and institutions, the Cubo-Futurists turned into teachers who tried to innovate not art but their own society against the will of their own citizens. They became Constructivists.

Figure 1 *The English designer from* The Architect and Building News *knew perfectly well in 1930 that the experiences of Modernism soon became part of our common tradition.*

The birth of the new movement in Eastern Europe took place in unique socio-political conditions, the scene of remarkable passion and desire. Russia was erecting the first utopian state in a sea of blood. Poland, Czechoslovakia and Hungary were trying to rebuild their fragmented state structures. Germany and Austria shuddered under the collapse of their empires.

The first stage of Constructivism – mystical Suprematism led by Kasimir Malevich – was quickly replaced by extremely orthodox Productivism. Its leader, Vladimir Tatlin, saw art as the production of functional objects. Beauty meant novelty – standardized and manufactured on a large scale. It also meant a complete break with all tradition.

Irrespective of formal experiments, which were observed with great attention by the avant-garde throughout Europe, one of the most significant Constructivist experiments was the identification of the artist with the state. Totalitarian attitudes resulted in multi-million population cities with a single type of urban housing, the commune-house, where new architectural forms were used to organize the lives of their future tenants according to the principle of social equality.

In the West, egalitarian ideas were also a source of local experiments based on utopian socialism and primitive rationalism. In 1928, Le Corbusier consolidated all of these groups and founded the Congrès Internationaux d'Architecture Moderne – an international organization which united the hitherto dispersed activities of various centres.

Only architects who were sure to have similar views were ever invited to the congresses of the 'Modernist International', replete with slogans about 'the housing for working people'. Undoubtedly influenced by the utopian ideas of Constructivism, dreaming of totally free and unrestricted use of space, they made declarations which negated the existing aesthetic order and advocated a new one – their own.

The signing of the Charter of Athens in 1933 was the turning-point for the movement. The revival of conservative tendencies and the Second World War closed this common chapter of architectural history. In the East European countries, because of political reasons, architects were forced to continue the ideology of Constructivism in its extreme form – 'Productivism'. In the West, where democracy and private property imposed restrictions upon the totalitarian inclination of the designer, the process took a decidedly different course.

From the heritage of Modernism and, partly, Constructivism, only certain aesthetic proposals were selected and applied, because the time had obviously come to say a final farewell to the utopian dream of high-tech, mass-produced human happiness. Creators no longer spoke about changing the world in a revolutionary way; they tried to improve it, not as mentors or instructors, but merely as advisers.[5] Familiar and easily understood signs and symbols from old alphabets reappeared on drawing boards, beyond the reach of the heritage of Modernism, as a part of our tradition (Figure 1). The failure of the political and economic systems of Eastern Europe has taught us that the innovations which enter social and sociological spheres are doomed to fail.[6]

Instead of one all-embracing 'international style' there is now a multitude of distinctive artistic attitudes, resulting from individual conditions and possibilities of execution, respecting tradition, and trying to find new ways of handing over our natural environment to future generations as little changed as possible.

NOTES

1   Plato's theories on imitation in art are mostly expounded in his book *State,* in the dialogue between Socrates and Glaukon.

2   In *Poetica and Rhetorica,* Aristotle explains that the image of a thing can be created in three ways: what it is, what it pretends to be, and what it ought to be.

3   The thirteenth-century French architect Villard de Honnecourt wrote a book, *Livre de Pourtraiture,* on the standards of details in churches.

4   The Futurists intended to change everything. It is very characteristic that the proposition of new orthography was done in stylish Italian language.

5   The social revolt of 1968 was the turning-point in the history of Western Modernism: society demonstrated against the theories of industrialization which originated in the nineteenth century.

6   Eastern Europe has greater problems with saying farewell to utopian dreams of Modernism because a whole economic infrastructure was created for a productivistic model of activities. This is the reason why, for instance, Polish Post-Modernism is mainly political rather than aesthetic.

32 The history of a rupture: Latin American architecture seen from Latin America

Ramon Gutierrez

This essay may perhaps depart from traditional historical exegesis, which has explained Latin American architecture from a Eurocentric viewpoint, projecting us as dependents whose experience has been determined by decisions of the central power.

It does not ignore the persistent process of political, economic, and cultural colonization, which has left deep impressions on us, evident to this day in numerous characteristics of dependence. The intention is simply to identify one of the most typical forms of pedagogic colonialism as the denial of our right to explain ourselves in our own terms. This already constitutes a new point of departure from which to highlight the vast apparatus reinforcing our inferiority complex.

To tie ourselves to an inferior role in a foreign history fixes us into a closely linked, cumulative and inescapable system on which our hold will always be partial and fragmentary because of our peripheral position. But if we can shake off some of this predictable inertia and analyse our achievements – both successful and unsuccessful – in terms of their own time and place, we will learn that, far from being linear, history is complex and open-ended, and capable of inspiring in us a sense of our own worth and a quite different perspective on ourselves.

Architecture is a basic element in the formation of our historic memory, and hence in the definition of our identity. As a historical document a building can explain not only the complex of ideas and circumstances which gave rise to it, but also the usages and ways of life which, by a process of sedimentation, our society built into it over time (see Figure 1). To these we may add the functions and charges of its symbolism, which enable us to understand its meaning over history and to give form to its accumulated inheritance, the vitality of which continues today and conditions our future.

To understand the context in which a building was produced is, in short, to incorporate into our own culture a fragment that can be brought to life – if the work is extant – or else documented with parallels from similar systems. So without binding ourselves too strictly to chronologies or categories of style, we shall try to grasp this broad scene with ideas that may overlap one another and even conflict: so disparate a reality can

be reduced to a consistent linear vision only by the facile conception of dependence.

THE TRANSFER OF CULTURE

The American peoples 'discovered' by the Europeans at the close of the fifteenth century had a variety of levels of organization and forms of settlement. The *Conquista* would melt down the whole territory, flux-like, into a single unit, transplanting to it its political authority, its system of administering justice, its unifying language, and its new creeds.

Figure 1 *Formal continuity and concealed rupture. The concept of the covered street is lost in this neighbourhood in the city centre. Each property has fragmented the continuous run of the arcade. Pedestrians can no longer use this perfectly adequate architectural solution.*

First published in Spanish in *A & V* (*Monographias de Arquitectura y Vivienda*) 13 (1988) as 'Historia de una ruptura'.

The Iberian 'donor'-culture would undergo its own transformation. Not everything in its territory was transferred to the new continent, but only those elements retained through a process of selection and synthesis: physically, only what a ship could carry; culturally, out of the many languages spoken on Spanish territory, only the dominant Castilian (to give two examples).

Architecture was subject to a similar process. The Catalan farm house, the Valencian cottage, even the rural manor house of Castile, would give way to a synthesis. Its dominant types, forms and functions stemmed from Andalucia and the Extremadura, but many regions contributed elements from their own traditions.

We should also mention the solutions devised to problems that were novel in their circumstances or scale, where European experience was stimulated to creative response. Such was the case with the problem of founding thousands of towns, for which a standard pattern was worked out incorporating both European and American theories and experiences. Or again, the need to evangelize millions of natives involved the creation of architectural structures bringing religious ceremony into the open (open chapels, enclosed atria, 'wayside' chapels, etc.).

The 'colony' was a ferment of creative and well-worked-out solutions to concrete problems. Increasing participation by native Americans led to hybridization and cultural syncretism.

IMPLANTATION

The transferral of Spanish architecture to Latin America, even to areas where the native culture had no substantial tradition, involved a process of integration and a specific synthesis.

There is a clear example in the cathedral of Santo Domingo in the Dominican Republic, the first significant work completed in America, where the architects – brought from Spain for the purpose – constructed within thirty years a building with the ground plan of a Gothic hall-church, ribbed vaulting, pillars with Isabelline decoration, and a presbytery with a neo-Mudéjar window and Renaissance façade. That is to say, a process that took centuries in European architecture was here brought together in concrete form within decades.

The same can be said in another paradigmatic case, the church of San Francisco in Quito, Ecuador, where the discovery of a treatise by Serlio (in the Spanish edition published by Villalpando) shows that it was the same Spanish master of works who had a command of the Mannerist language of the treatise who set up the guidelines for the rough carpentry hoardings.

The tasks of supporting imperial rule required the European masters of works to set aside their specializations and take on work of all kinds. At San Francisco in

Quito, furthermore, we find that Bramante's design for a concave–convex staircase, which as far as I know, was never carried out in Europe but which Serlio recorded, was actually built in the courtyard of the church.

What the Europeans brought was modified by the materials available, the work-force, and the limitations of the situation. The Europeans had to blaze their own trail, to bring into full play their talents and special skills.

SUPERIMPOSITION

For pragmatic reasons, as well as to assert formal and symbolic dominance, the Spaniards often decided to re-use the old American buildings as the foundations for their own.

The standard examples are those of Cuzco, capital of the Inca Empire of Peru, and Mexico City, imposed on old Aztec Tenochtitlan, but one should add the many medium-sized and small urban centres, which to various degrees were treated in the same way.

Superimposition involved accepting the continued presence of sizeable physical components of the old city, both in its plan and in the organization of public spaces and the location of symbolic buildings (temples, palaces, etc.).

It also meant the adaptation of the old structures to new uses. For example, the *canchas* of Inca dwellings which grouped a nucleus of four units round a central yard, gave way to a single Spanish house, transforming the density of occupation of the ground in the town centre and causing the city to expand over areas previously devoted to agriculture.

Sometimes superimposition deliberately altered the public spaces. The command of great spaces which the native had enjoyed gave way to the much more confined urban experience of the European, who was accustomed to intensive land-tenure and small public spaces. So the big Inca square at Cuzco was broken up by the construc-

Figure 2 *The appropriation of symbolic values and the ratification of power. The cathedral, Mexico City, built on the site of the major Aztec temple.*

tion of streets of housing, clearly marking off the Spanish Parade Ground, the civic amusement ground, the native market (or *tianguez*), and the Plaza de San Francisco, with its spacious residential quarters.

This superimposition of spaces also led to the destruction, above all, of those buildings which expressed the political and religious power of the native empires. On the site of the main temple of Mexico City was built the cathedral (see Figure 2), on the Inca Coricancha of Cuzco rose the church and convent of Santo Domingo; while the campaign to eradicate idolatry razed to the ground the native shrines, in many cases thereby reconstituting the sacred platforms of temples that had been destroyed earlier (Colula, Haquira, San Geronimo, etc.).

Superimposition on Inca or Aztec foundations testifies to dominion: presence is the primary form of the assertion of power. But it also recognizes that 'other' which the Spanish vision aspired to integrate, whereas in the Puritan ethic of the north it was marginalized and finally destroyed.

ADAPTATION

The encounter of the two worlds had lessons for both cultures. The asymmetric relationship of the *Conquista* shaped new patterns of behaviour and organization to which the American native communities had to submit. Their icons, language, ways of life and scale of values underwent deep changes which, combined with the movement of the population, involved deep traumas. This was expressed in the loss of appetite for life and an alarming death-rate, arising mainly from the epidemics which they did not have the biological resources to resist.

The Spaniards who reached the forests of Paraguay and eastern Bolivia in search of El Dorado soon had to accept that this chimera did not exist, and to resign themselves to a process of settlement and a rapid mingling of races. Where stone was scarce, they had to learn from the experience of the natives the right time to cut timber in the woodlands (the latter part of the year when the sap is low). They failed in their efforts at great cost to build stone fortresses, since these were obsolete by the time they were finished – left behind by the mobility of the fronts in the wars against rebellious natives. They learnt that this fast-moving war called for flexibility, and began to develop field-fortifications in wood, whose materials could be gathered up as the lines advanced, allowing the fort to be moved quickly.

In technology the Spaniards also learnt. When their method of laying foundations was unsuccessful at Mexico cathedral, they returned to the traditional *tablero tocado* (ground raft) which suited the difficult soil-conditions in a city built on a partly-dried-up lake.

Adaptation is the process which, in the culture of conquest, generates a new reality exhibiting what some call 'Indian culture' and which others recognize as a constituent of our 'American culture'. The natives adjusted themselves to the use of large covered spaces. To come to terms with them they covered them with mural paintings, polychrome plasterwork, or sculptures in wood, paper, glued fabric or plaster. The natives adapted themselves to them, but they also transformed them decisively.

The Europeans learned to handle the monumental proportions of the open spaces. They also transformed them, so as to dominate them; alternatively, they launched out on the conquest of immense distances in search of their dreams. In both cases they relocated Utopias for which there was no room or possibility in pragmatic Europe. America was a testing-ground, where the prophetic visions of the monk Eiximemis or the communities of Thomas More were tried out in hundreds of regular town plans, or in the hospital-villages which the indefatigable bishop Vasco de Quiroga built in the Mexican region of Michoacan.

CULTURAL HYBRIDIZATION

Adaptation was bound to lead to collaboration. From the middle of the seventeenth century, the rapid rise in the American population and the reorganization of craft-activities in the main towns made possible the greater involvement of the natives, creoles and different breeds in the creation of architecture.

This collaboration did not imply the dismantling of native social and cultural relationships, which were still effective. Thus the craft-guild (a labour organization) was matched with a system of *cofradias* or lodges (an organization involving religion and social security). In many cases there was a link with the ancient Inca *ayllu* (a social organization), which was the native family unit. The last of the Inca architects of the fortress of Sacsahuaman at Cuzco lived in the late fifteenth century and was called Hualpa-Rimac (the Man who Commands with a Shout), and in the eighteenth century we find stone-cutters in the San Cristobal district, at the foot of the fortress, who called themselves Valgarimache in Castilian.

The Inca habit of grouping together artisans of similar skills merged with the medieval system of streets devoted to particular crafts. The streets of silversmiths, sword-makers, tanners and carpenters, or the age-old names of the arcades around the squares attest to the process of assimilation of like with like. The ideology of the Conquistador was, and still is, affected by daily contact with the conquered.

If the ground plans of the key buildings (churches, palaces, mansions) reflect forms that were well-tried in Europe, the spatial results were quite different, with a world of colour and profuse ornament spreading all around and allowing the artisan control of vast surfaces. This gave rise to the analysis that was very much in vogue with art historians over many decades: European architecture – American decoration.

This equation was mistakenly applied to analysing decorative elements in terms of their original and their derivatives – for example, the sirens playing American musical instruments, or the distinguishing marks of a universal abstract lion as against a European puma. This, together with attempts to see in American decoration similarities with forms of Asiatic origin kept us entertained – and entangled in sophistry.

The deductions were correct, the premise was false. Architecture is a unity, not to be dismembered for formal analysis.

To sum up, we were forgetting that conquerors and conquered learnt together from a common starting point. Durer's *rhinoceros*, of which a copy was painted in the sixteenth century at the house of the notary Juan de Vargas at Tunja (Colombia), was as new-fangled for the native who painted it as for the notary who commissioned the painting.

Of course there were architectural forms subject to a higher degree of European control, which come close to the best work of the old world. American fortifications of the sixteenth to the eighteenth century are among the finest expressions of Iberian military architecture, and there was no lack of writers of treatises like Felix Prosperi, who in 1744 published from Mexico his book *La Gran Defensa* (The Large Fortification) setting out ideas at the forefront of contemporary thought.

LATIN-AMERICAN BAROQUE

We cannot be accused of chauvinist reductivism if we analyse Spanish and American baroque comparatively. Quantitatively the movement is represented in Spain by only a handful of buildings; in many more cases there were modifications – many of them doubtless noteworthy – of existing buildings. But in Mexico alone thousands of completely new buildings brought alive this fusion of Spanish and native. This work is of astonishing quality, and goes far beyond any interpretation derived from a traditional reading of European baroque.

The presence of the 'the other' was an imposition on the ideas of historians, whose closed minds were not prepared for readings outside the accepted axioms of the central universe. No critic would think of calling the baroque of Bavaria provincial with respect to that of Rome, but they do not blanch at applying this kind of analysis to Latin-American baroque. Only from a highly ethnocentric point of view would the products of distinct cultures be considered anachronistic, or those cultures persistently be explained, without taking their own products as the starting point for analysis.

To explain ourselves through others is the surest way never to get to know ourselves, and to remain dependent on the central model assumed to be our source of inspiration. There were outstanding experiments in

Figure 3 *The Mexican baroque. The intentional exuberance of the syncretism between the persuasive Counter-Reformation and the participation of the indigenous sensitivity. Thousands of temples sanctified the territory, leaving an imprint of American* mestización. *Santa Prisca, Taxco, Mexico, eighteenth century.*

Latin American social and cultural integration – for example, the Jesuit missions to the Guarani Indians, which in a century-and-a-half evolved forms of high social solidarity, and produced art and architecture of a high order, clearly demonstrating the potential of the Americans once the Europeans took the risk of giving scope to their cultural potential.

Cultural hybridization (*mestizaje*) found expression in syncretism in religion, and in enriching life-styles, and in architecture in the eloquent testimony of a multitude of works of the Mexican, Guatemalan or Andean baroque (see Figure 3). This is not to discount contradictions and class-distinctions, the continuing injustices and the conflicts. It was not a question of a paradise on earth, but of a new society in gestation, with the Americans gaining significance. In about the middle of the eighteenth century the archbishop, the governor, and the judges of the powerful court of Charcas had to resort to a native and a mulatto (neither of whom could read or sign their names) to determine how to repair the lavish cathedral church of Chuquisaca, thus recognizing the authority acquired through their craft by fringe elements in colonial society.

When in the presbytery of a church – a sacred place of importance alongside the main altar – there are angels playing instruments like the organ or the violin, and suddenly we identify a figure clutching the native *maraca* (a dry gourd containing pebbles), we realize there is a new reality going far beyond the imperial dialectic of the Conquest.

Think of the façades covered with tiles, the use of local stones (the pink *tezontle* and yellow *chiluca* in Mexico, the white coral-stone in Cartagena and Havana, the volcanic ashlar in Arequipa), the Cuban timber that crossed the ocean to be used in the Royal Palace at Madrid, the plasterwork in the American *pueblos*, the indigo of Guatemala, and the cochineal covering walls and gilt reredoses with red. Latin American baroque exceeds in its expressiveness the limits of European tactile experience: it appeals to the senses and to a 'cosmovision' which welds together age-old rifts, and socializes daily activity in a continual ritual of the kind found in the thought and life of the old American cultures: a syncretism in liturgy and ritual which transcends the inconsistent meanings that have been superimposed.

A CENTURY OF ONE-HUNDRED-AND-FIFTY YEARS

For us the nineteenth century begins in 1780 and ends with the crisis of 1930. This reading does not tally with the usual calendars or with stylistic periods, but it stands out clearly as significant in the formation of the new reality, which determines architectural thinking.

With the foundation of the academies of fine arts in the mid-eighteenth century, the Bourbon court set in motion the radical transformation of the conception of architecture (see Figure 4). It gradually withdrew from mathematics and sciences of construction to enter the field of the 'three noble arts', in which it was to play a leading role. But at the same time there appeared two essential requirements – theory and drawing – which increased the content of the discipline and shattered the old craft-base of the master-masons, who dominated architecture often without being able to read or write.

Without any deliberate plan of dominance, the standards in architecture set by the Academy, with royal backing, began to be applied in the Peninsula and the Canaries in the last decades of eighteenth century.

The Enlightenment devalued the expressions of popular baroque and welcomed neo-classicism openly, barbarously destroying altarpieces and façades in Spain and Latin America. But above all, the main effect of the dialectic was to establish that there was only one valid way of doing architecture, and that no one in Latin America was competent to do it. So all projects had to be sent to Spain, where royal academies, with no knowledge of the continent, had to lay down rules for how the job should be done.

Some projects took a decade of correspondence – and were already complete by the time the design finally arrived from Madrid; others were never executed; and over some there were notable arguments. Such was the case with the Cathedral of Santiago in Cuba. The bishop refused the design from Madrid, telling the academicians that there was wood but no stone in Cuba; that the estimate for their scheme far exceeded the diocese's revenues for decades; and that there were experienced master-masons there, but the highest scaffolding they had erected was 12 metres (40 feet) high, while the dome designed in Madrid was more than 64 metres (210 feet high).

The dialectic between plan and reality had started to operate. The American cultural project, the fruit of hybridization, was called into question by the Court, whose enlightened despotism gradually led it to the destruction of the guilds, entailing loss of the social bases, and launching Latin Americans (for the most part

Figure 4 *The 'Small Temple', Havana. The beginning of the neo-classical century in Cuba, and one of the first neo-Greek temples of the South American continent. The abstract modernity and universality of the 'classic' distorted the process of cultural integration that had been gestating in Latin America. It marks the beginning of the didactics between 'civilization' and 'barbarism'.*

natives and creoles) on a supposed liberalization of the exercise of their art; but it also moved them to the side-lines in the social and cultural role which they had acquired in colonial society.

The few academic architects who reached America (basically Mexico, Guatemala, and Chile) left important works resembling metropolitan models (the Mint at Santiago, the Palace of Mining at Mexico, etc.) but which, while manifesting the spirit of the time, fail to express the spirit of the place.

THE RUPTURE

The principal new feature of the academic Enlighten-ment was the Rupture, marking the collapse of the process of cultural integration and the beginning of Latin American moves towards independence, with their varied consequences.

In reality, our independence meant a change of model. Spain was replaced by the new dominant Euro-pean powers – principally England and France – while a fiction of political and economic autonomy was main-tained.

The Rupture called for loss of memory. Morelos, at the Congress of Chipalcingo on 13 September 1813, said: 'After the 12th of August 1521 comes the 14th of September 1813' (Sarmieuto 1845). This was a fanciful blotting out of selected passages of history that were distasteful.

This anti-historical attitude of the Enlightenment exhibits one constant feature of the Rupture: the nega-tion of reality and the substitution of the arbitrary and of foreign models. Denying one's own history led to denying one's own people. So Sarmiento coined the antithesis: 'civilization (Europe) or barbarism (America)', and as a deduction advised 'no sparing of gaucho blood'.

Exterminating 'in Saxon style' the native and the creole was the new model for these civilizers, who at the

Figure 5 *The Church of the Conception, on the beach at Bahia, Brazil, was designed and fabricated in Portugal and erected in the Lusitanian colony. A notable case of linear transplantation.*

Figure 6 *European neo-classicism arrived in Brazil through the 'French Maison' of Grandjean de Montigny. However, buildings like the Chamber of Commerce in Salvador, Bahia, illustrate the extent of this trend.*

same time promoted the mass migration of the im-poverished European peasantry to 'improve the stock'.

Contempt for our reality led to an inferiority complex and efforts by the elites to mimic European culture in its eclectic and cosmopolitan version. There was nothing innocent about this operation: it was a clear policy of displacing the Hispanic presence in our culture.

In 1817, even before much of South America had achieved independence, the French engineer Jacob Boudier, under contract to the 'Enlightened' Rivadavia, stated in a report on the Market of the Plaza Mayor in Buenos Aires that:

> When the institutions of the country are moving to eliminate the last traces of Spanish subjection, the public buildings should be in a style other than that of *los godos* (sci. 'the Dagoes'), because as monuments they have to reflect the public attitude at the time of their erection. This is not at the dictate simply of good taste, which may err, but of what is appropriate, which is perhaps more certain.
>
> (Boudier, cited in Pillado 1910: 106)

In Brazil, the Napoleonic invasion of Portugal trans-formed the colony into a centre to which the Lusitanian court moved (see Figure 5). Here too the French artistic mission, contracted to set up the School of Fine Arts under the direction of Grandjean de Montigny, imposed classical academic assumptions (see Figure 6). The excel-lent baroque was set aside in favour of a doctrine based on Graeco-Roman models.

In the rest of America, the wars of independence were followed by internal struggles, stubborn regional conflicts stimulated by assiduous businessmen offering loans, and ideologists from Britain who were in a position to create states and 'Balkanize' the continent as a basis for their domination. Here they continued to hold a mirror to European architecture. Thus the professionals imported by our Enlightened governments adopted the historic 'revivals' of the history of others. There were vogues for neo-Gothic and neo-Greek, while the academicism of the Ecole des Beaux Arts in Paris reinforced its position as the most respected model.

A popular neo-classicism, the work of the Italian *cucharas* (literally 'trowels') recreated the townscapes of the cities that were progressively consolidating themselves in the second half of the century. A regular vocabulary of plinths, columns, friezes, cornices, rectangular openings, and a variety of balustrades, was now *de rigueur* for prestige façades on houses that otherwise were not much different from the colonial house with its patio.

BUENOS AIRES, EUROPEAN CITY

The steps taken to transform our capital cities into little third-world Parises were based on the notions of 'prefectural aesthetics' made fashionable by Baron Haussmann, on the hygienist premises of the German functionalist and positivist school, on studies of traffic flows and, more than anything, on the whims of changing governments.

Economic liberalism, hand in hand with political authoritarianism, made possible the dizzy enrichment of social sectors linked with British interests or investments from elsewhere, while on the fringe the workers on the land, imported from Europe (preferably Spain or Italy), were grouped in new types of 'slums', communal houses with shared facilities, or settlements.

At the same time industrial workers' housing schemes appeared (see Figure 7) – exhibiting another form of dependence, since these had been conceived to solve a problem we lacked, not having industries but only cheap labour amassed through the failure to deliver the land that had been promised.

Alienation from their own reality showed up in the training of the first Latin-American architects. Those

Figure 8 *'The historicist rediscovery' and the archaeology of Latin America. Mayan houses by the French architect Viollet-le-Duc and the Mexican pavilion at the Paris Exhibition of 1889 – between exoticism and anachronism. The form has been stripped of content in favour of sheer eclecticism.*

who did not go to Europe received instruction here from imported teachers. Even in 1934 the School of Architecture entrusted the Argentine ambassador with securing a winner of the Grand Prix de Rome to take charge of the studio in Buenos Aires. In 1919 the final-year architecture students at Montevideo designed a 'tourist centre for a battlefield' for a victorious country.

The outcome of the crisis of the Academy at the end of the nineteenth century was eclecticism: the incompatibility between the routine of the standard and particularist individualism was resolved in an escape into the past, including the picturesque. In 1890 Barberot, writer of academic treatises, included some exotic 'Peruvian and Mexican' styles, rescuing pre-Columbian decoration from oblivion, while a year earlier Viollet-le-Duc had roused us with his Aztec and Mayan houses at the Paris Universal Exhibition (see Figure 8).

At the beginning of this century we got on our feet and began producing a 'modernist' architecture simultaneously with that being created in Europe. It was of no concern that our Catalan Modernism or our Secession style did not answer to any specific cultural context that would justify it, and was no more than an uncritical copy lacking logical basis. When Clemenceau in 1911 spoke of 'Buenos Aires, this great European city', fiction had been made fact.

But underneath this brilliant stage-set lay the real America, ignored, decimated, withdrawn into impotence, attached to its traditions and ways of life, and with the conviction of a historic sense of age-old wisdom which did not bank on the ephemeral fireworks of those who looked only abroad.

THE TURNING POINT

The foundations began to move in the first decades of the twentieth century with the Mexican agrarian revolu-

Figure 7 *Barrio Rues, Montevideo, Uruguay, early nineteenth century. One of the first collective housing estates done through private initiative.*

tion, the rise of the native movements in Peru, social tensions in the south, and university reform throughout the continent.

In the field of literature, Marti, Ruben Dario, and Ricardo Rojas, with their 'National Restoration' (1909) raised the question of the neglect of Latin American issues by the elites then in power.

The First World War signalled a crisis for Europe as a model of civilization, and opened the way to reflection on what was one's own. This happened in a confused and casual way, without clarity of ideas but with a bursting impulse to shake off the heavy yoke of spiritual dependency.

The revindication of the Hispanic heritage went hand in hand with that of its native alternative. Spanish culture had been vilified as mainly responsible for 'barbarism', and so had appeared only occasionally among the picturesque exoticisms (principally in the form of 'neo-Mudéjar') or among the 'modernisms'.

Now for the first time there was talk of Hispano-American architecture as having its own values, and as worth study. Architects mused about 'the Nation and national architecture' (like Mariscal in Mexico in 1915), or on 'the Hispano-native fusion' (like Angel Guido in Argentina in 1925). Alongside them some Europeans succumbed to the 'seduction of barbarism' and carried out important studies of our colonial architecture. This marked the turning-point in attitude and consciousness, but could not destroy the conceptual assumptions of the rupture.

Figure 10 *The historicism of someone else's history, the creation of a world of fiction. Latin America seen as a laboratory for experiment with theories, or as a depository of all the forms – universal, national and regional styles. Everything goes . . . except the American. The Post Office Building, Mexico City, twentieth century.*

Being caught in their own academic and social contradictions, the architects of the 'neo-colonial' only managed to propose a change in the repertory of forms and architectural language so as to incorporate the decorative and compositional elements of the old colonial architecture (see Figure 9).

Some opted for Americanist tendencies, others – openly Hispanophile – made an intellectual return to the Peninsula in quest of their models, while yet others (many fewer) quarried the Pre-Hispanic. All were adopting an academic historicism, if under a different skin (see Figure 10). In 1920 a prize was won at an architectural competition in Buenos Aires by a 'neo-Aztec' house. The designers explained that they had arrived at it by tilting the outside face of the walls of a French *petit hotel* inwards. Inability to take on board at the same time the co-ordinates of their own space and their own time meant that this movement would be side-tracked into the picturesque of another kind, without contributing any new direction.

There was a positive legacy in the shape of the discussion of theory – the first to take root in Latin America – and in the documentation and revaluation of its architecture. This gave rise to systematic studies and a concern with protecting the architectural and urban heritage.

The 'worried introspection', which Arnold Toynbee detected during the 1860s, recognized this turning point which, in spite of failure in the short term, showed up unmistakably what was unreal.

But the unreal continued. In 1926 we were doing Art Deco imposed on us by the previous year's Exhibition of Decorative Arts in Paris. From then on, close on each other's heels, came the International Style, the *barco* (ship) style, and the first rationalism.

The nineteenth century blotted out the eighteenth, and we are now engaged in blotting out the nineteenth

Figure 9 *The new symbols of power. The displacement of Euro-centrism, with the Capitol at Havana based on that in Washington – the fatal reality of neo-academicism which led to the inception of the Modern Movement.*

in the drive for historic loss of memory, and in hot pursuit of change, which we take for the inexorable engine of that elusive 'progress'.

The Modern Movement was introduced into the city by property speculation and by planning based on models, and consequently contributed further to the Rupture. It bore witness to its time and was determined to ignore its space, being seen in due course as just one further style in the series presented by feverish foreign modernity.

It was all the more destructive because it altered irreversibly the scale of the city, swamping the old colonial town-plans which had stood up to the impact of the academies right up to the first decades of this century.

The crisis of 1930 and the switch of tutelage to the north presently brought in those new models of the Rupture which seem themselves now to be in a state of crisis. It is a crisis which, if we can learn from history, shows us that there does exist a space for our space, and a task for those who want to be equal to the situation facing us: to mend the Rupture; to recognize our history as a whole, with its successes and mistakes; and to realize an architecture that can find its identity in the equation of time and place – in short, to marry the popular wisdom of our Latin America with the science we command as 'modern' human beings.

That is, modernity made our own.

BIBLIOGRAPHY

Angulo, I.D.-M., Dorta, E. amd Buschiazzo, M.J. (1945–56) *Historia del Arte Hispanoamericano*, Barcelona: Salvat, 3 vols.

Buschiazzo, M.J. (1961) *Historia de la arquitectura colonial en Iberoamérica*, Buenos Aires: Emecé.

Clemenceau, G. (1911) *Notes de voyage dans l'Amerique de Sud: Argentine-Uruguay-Bresil*, Paris: Hachette et Cie.

Gutiérrez R. (1983) *Arquitectura y urbanismo en Iberoamérica*, Madrid: Ed. Cátedra.

Gutiérrez R. *et al.* (1981) *La casa cusqueña*, Resistencia: UNNE.

Pillado, J.A. (1910) *Buenos Aires colonial: edificios y costumbres*, Buenos Aires: Compañía Sud Americana de Billetes de Banco.

Sarmiento (1845) *Facundo o civilización y barbaria*.

Zavala, S. (1950) *La utopía de Tomás Moro en la Nueva España*, Mexico City: Colegio Nacional Mexico.

33 Is there a modern vernacular?

Michael Manser

Over thirty years ago J.M. Richards identified in the following passage a situation which is still a challenge to the modern architect:

> The modern architect has reached a crucial point in the development of his art, which has been utterly changed by new technical resources, new planning responsibilities and new aesthetic ideals. Its impetus has, up till now, been a revolutionary one, but no art can remain for ever in a state of revolution. Innovation gives it its vitality and its capacity to develop, but after the revolution comes consolidation, depending on the creation of a vernacular language in which the most worth while ideas of all the innovators gradually become merged. Architecture's special need now is to perfect such a vernacular, even in the face of the difficulty that it means achieving the unselfconscious virtues in an age peculiar for its self-consciousness. How can this better be done than by striving to carry on the functional tradition which inspired the anonymous vernacular of these early industrial buildings? In them we see a preoccupation with functionalism similar to our own, with the disciplines that functionalism imposes transformed into a flexible architectural language.
>
> (Richards 1958: 18)

This essay sets out to examine the same issues from a current perspective and to answer the question: is there a modern vernacular? But before the question can be answered the question must be defined. What does vernacular mean?

The term is derived from the Latin *vernaculus* meaning domestic, indigenous, a home-born slave, a native. It was in use in England by 1601 to describe the nature or indigenous language of a country or district. Not until 1857 was it used referring to buildings, viz. 'The vernacular cottage building of the day' (Shorter Oxford English Dictionary 1964).

In the late nineteenth century the term vernacular was adopted by the Arts and Crafts Movement, which romanticized the rural idyll and the simple life. This movement, however, was celebrating the social history of architecture – the human demand which inspired the building types rather than the available materials which influenced their form and structure. And the post-Second World War revival of interest in vernacular architecture, which spawned the Vernacular Architecture Groups, referred to the Arts and Crafts Movement of the preceding century and, like it, was again concerned with the human need for particular buildings rather than the structural variations imposed upon them due to geographical location.

The meaning of vernacular referring to buildings must therefore be assumed to describe buildings which are indigenous (for which vernacular is a synonym) to a particular geographical area.

The modern use of the word vernacular for buildings still implies a structure made of locally found or crafted materials. In 1962 Alec Clifton-Taylor drew a scholarly and interesting relationship between the geology of various areas of England and buildings produced as a result of the geological strata on which they were built. He showed how, area by area, there were distinct physical and aesthetic qualities generated by the geology. He also made clear that these were mainly manifest in domestic buildings since extraordinary efforts were made to transport enduring materials over considerable distances for the great structures like Stonehenge or the Gothic cathedrals, because of their exceptional importance to the community. He demonstrated that the availability of timber spawned different types of construction in different areas. There were regionally derived characteristic house forms from crux or box frame construction to claddings of shiplap boarding, shingle roofs, pargeting, brick nogging and the traditional black and white buildings.

However, as Clifton-Taylor points out, sixteenth- and seventeenth-century wood-framed buildings are now generally only to be found in England south and east of the limestone belt, as far north as a line from Huntingdon to Yarmouth, and west of the limestone belt from the Severn Estuary, to Leicester, and west of the Pennine chain as far north as central Lancashire. Where there were deposits of stone or granite, houses were built of these materials, and where clay subsoil was found, houses were made of bricks. In valleys and lowlands where water was plentiful there was extensive reed thatching, and on the uplands roofs were clad with stone or slate depending upon which was available.

The architectural qualities of houses built from local materials are well known. Cotswold stone cottages, East Anglian thatched plastered cottages (see Figure 1) and Cumbrian, Welsh and Cornish granite cottages (see Figure 2). The Home Counties and the Midlands were areas where brick was used widely and with great diversity.

Clifton-Taylor showed that although in earliest times in England probably all domestic buildings were made of easily available timber, few of those which survive date further back than the sixteenth century. By this time the

Figure 1 *Thatched cottages in Suffolk.* (Photograph: *courtesy of British Tourist Authority*)

Figure 2 Cornish granite cottage.

supply of felled timber was becoming limited. In Norfolk and Suffolk during 1604 there was a royal proclamation which decreed that new houses must have walls and window frames of brick or stone, and that cutting timber for firewood must cease altogether. Even so, the builders of the time were hard-pressed to satisfy their timber needs despite the great Scots pine forests. High fire risks then increasingly became a deterrent to constructing timber houses in towns.

Such factors leave us today with timber-framed buildings mainly surviving in rural areas and small country towns (with the exception of Chester and Shrewsbury), or in those parts where the supply of oaks remained plentiful throughout the sixteenth and seventeenth centuries.

Thus, although in pre-medieval times timber was almost the universal vernacular material in England, shortages due to over-use then forced builders to find alternative materials close to hand and thereby made more pronounced regional and geological differences.

There were of course local influences, apart from materials, which impinged visibly on architectural design, such as climatic conditions, a particular society's way of life, economic conditions, or restraints caused by terrain. But these were not usually as dramatic as the differences imposed by construction materials. A log hut in northern Canada and an igloo in the Canadian Arctic have much the same purpose, but the spectacular visual difference between the two is due to the material from which they are made. A medieval Cotswolds stone house has the same purpose in design as a black and white timber house in Shropshire, but their materials make them instantly recognizable for what they are. Likewise, when the Georgian pattern books spread through Britain and then to its colonies there was a sharp difference, despite following the same models, between those designs built in Massachusetts of timber (see Figure 3), in Hertfordshire of brick (see Figure 4) or in Cornwall of stone. Moreover, those built in Kent sometimes have more in common with those in Massachusetts because of their timber construction, and those built in Maine with those in Cornwall, because they are made of stone. So it can be said with reasonable certainty that the true vernacular building is the result of building from readily available materials, locally found. The influences of style or use – cottage, stable or water mill – do not determine whether or not a building is vernacular.

By the early eighteenth century all but the most significant buildings were still made from whatever

Figure 3 *Massachusetts timber house.*

Figure 4 *Hertfordshire brick house.*

materials were readily to hand. Each village had a brick-yard or a quarry or timber merchant. It had a blacksmith and a tileyard or slate quarry, or water meadows, reed beds and osiers. This was local building, and was truly vernacular.

But this pre-industrial world was about to change, presaged by the development of canals to provide cheap bulk transport, by the establishment in Britain of the first (and, in design, the best) and most universally adopted standardized building system since Roman times: Georgian Palladian architecture. The effect of canal transport on architecture was that alternative building materials could be transported far from where they occurred naturally; this was the beginning of the end of genuine 'out of the ground' building. The spread of Palladian classicism then further diminished regional design variations. Pattern books were available to lay down design criteria, including standard details for doors, windows, fanlights, staircases, panelling and decorative plasterwork. It was, in retrospect, a remark-ably pervasive voluntary adoption of an exceedingly comprehensive, centralized design standard. This was, in my view, the point at which true vernacular archi-tecture began to disappear. From then on construction from local materials became less and less prevalent.

The next significant step in improved distribution of building materials and components came during the second quarter of the nineteenth century with the advent of the railways. The railways in turn helped to establish regional centres of manufacture and supply of building materials, such as pottery from Staffordshire, bricks from Bedfordshire and roofing slates from Wales. What had been exceptional in earlier years, when Caen stone from Normandy was exported to Chichester for its cathedral, or large Scandinavian roof timbers were shipped for Wren's new palace extension at Hampton Court, now became routine for ordinary building projects.

The development of efficient and reliable bulk trans-port finally terminated vernacular building. Local brick-works were no longer economic. The local joiner could

not compete with a joinery factory, and when transport distributed cheap tiles and slates throughout the land, the risks and hazards of vermin and fire made even local thatch unattractive.

Vernacular is about local materials and the effect they have upon appearance, and has nothing to do with function. Function concerns design – the efficient resolution of an architectural problem in the simplest and most direct way. J.M. Richards was not talking about the vernacular, but rather was commenting upon how, over the ages, buildings erected to house industrial functions have invariably had a strong, simple formality and minimalist, engineered elegance (see Figure 5). He calls for a modern equivalent of this, not a modern vernacular. But the modern equivalent of industrial architecture can only be found in high technology. Brunel was struggling at the sharp edge of the tech-nology of his time designing bridges and warehouses. Nowadays the span of his bridges and sizes of his ware-houses are simple structural problems. We have to look to the greatest skyscrapers, the vast, modern indoor stadia, or the space programme, to find the true successor of the functional tradition of industrial archi-tecture. And this is where the tradition of extracting the maximum benefit from the simplest and most econ-omical advances of available technology lives on.

Returning to the original question of whether or not there is a modern vernacular, the answer leads us by an intriguing circular route to an unexpected conclusion. Vernacular architecture was built 'out of the ground'. It was made of materials found on or near its site. Its demise, as for so many local traditions and culture, folkfore and dress, was brought about by ever more efficient and fast transport and communications. By the end of the nineteenth century, roughly the same building materials were available at similar costs throughout the length and breadth of Britain. Those made or found locally made up but a small percentage. Now, at the end of the twentieth century, materials and components similar or the same are available throughout

Figure 5 *Buildings erected to house industrial functions usually have a strong, simple formality and minimalist engineered elegance.*

the developed world at comparable prices. It was recently assessed that about 40 per cent of the components of a sophisticated London building like the Hilton Hotel, Heathrow (1990), came from abroad – some from as far away as Japan.

There are now very few areas in the world where current conditions still command a genuine vernacular. One is the Mediterranean island of Malta, where every building commodity except the local limestone has to be imported. The limestone is machine cut and marketed in various standard sizes and shapes, and is still the most economical material for most types of building. Thus there is to this day truly vernacular building in Malta.

In the Middle Ages and earlier, vernacular architecture varied at a local scale. The appearance of buildings changed district by district. There was a distinctly locational 'look' due to the use of 'out of the ground' components. As new ideas about construction spread over generations, and as techniques and materials changed and were then exported to other areas and countries, this 'look' became first regional, then national, and finally international. A major modern building today in Paris, New York, Sydney or Hong Kong is made of the same materials and employs the same construction techniques. Components and cladding are standardized.

The buildings look the same because, ironically, their materials are designed and produced internationally and are transported all over the globe. Just as in the past local materials created a local took, we now have the ultimate, a global look.

If there is a modern vernacular, it must surely be that which has come to be known as international Modernism. QED.

REFERENCES

Clifton-Taylor, A. (1962) *The Pattern of English Building,* London: Batsford.

Richards, J.M. (1958) *The Functional Tradition in Early Industrial Building,* London: Architectural Press.

Shorter Oxford English Dictionary (1964), Oxford: Oxford University Press.

A living tradition?

34 Romanian vernacular architecture

Jennifer Scarce

Romania's varied and lively cultural traditions are as yet all too little known and appreciated beyond its boundaries. Awareness of Romania among the general public is usually confined to the 'hype' of the Dracula legend as exploited by the tourist industry, and package holidays to the beach resorts of the Black Sea coast and to the ski slopes of the Carpathian mountains. Specialist Western interest in Romania has been equally selective, concentrating on the political and economic situation of this strategic and at times volatile region, on the opening up of business relations, and in the context of culture on language and literature. Romanian architecture, which has been little studied in the West, does however function as a point of contact between both general and specialist audiences. Tourists are routinely taken on short trips to the Bukovina region of north-east Romania to see the five monasteries of Arbore, Humor, Moldovita, Sucevita and Voronet, which range in date from the late fifteenth to the early seventeenth centuries. Their churches are remarkable for the vitality and quality of their external wall paintings, which depict the saints and narrative cycles of Orthodox religious iconography, and the scenic beauty of their natural environment. The churches are equally known to art historians both for their role in the survival and transmission of the Byzantine heritage and as comparative material to the mainstream traditions of Constantinople.

The five Bukovina monasteries, Romania's most famous monuments, are, apart from their own interest and merit, also representatives of a deep-rooted and prolific architecture which is admirably suited to its physical and social environment. Here the churches, houses and farm buildings of Romania's many villages, built and decorated according to distinct regional styles, still testify to the survival and continuing development of a living architectural tradition. This is dependent on local artisans in wood, stone and plaster who rely on experience gained through transmitted skills rather than formal training. Village architecture is indeed so distinctive and attractive that features such as open porches and deeply overhanging roof eaves have been integrated into town buildings to their structural and decorative enrichment, thus contributing to the creation of modern vernacular forms.

Paradoxically, the political and economic conditions of post-Second World War Romania have collectively ensured the survival of a living tradition. The bureaucratic principles of an orthodox state socialism required control of the movements of both town and village populations and supervision of their contacts. This policy effectively sealed off Romanian villages, many of which were already isolated by poor communications, from the stimulus of external influences. In terms of architecture, villages continued to be built according to tried and proven traditional forms and techniques. Economically this conservatism contributed towards their survival as functioning social units.

A ruthless programme aimed at developing heavy industry in Romania had disastrous results, burdening towns with the pollution of old-fashioned factory plant, sacrificing people's need for food and services to a currency-earning export drive, and neglecting the development of an efficient agriculture for which Romania's land is so well-suited. In this deprived environment only the villages following a basic self-sufficient life managed to both survive and support neighbouring towns through the produce of their smallholdings. Eventually this precarious symbiosis was threatened by the late President Nicolae Ceauşescu's plans for 'agricultural rationalization', which aimed to uproot most of Romania's villages and forcibly resettle their inhabitants in the concrete apartment blocks of new agro-industrial complexes. The process was abruptly stopped by the 1989 revolution.

The architecture which has now survived has to be understood in the contect of Romania's unique cultural and historical position in relation to central and south-east Europe. This position is perhaps most obvious in language. A traveller in Romania with a knowledge of French or Italian is soon able to recognize basic phrases and read street signs as the dominant Romanian language has reputedly evolved from the Latin dialect spoken during the Imperial Roman occupation of AD 106–275. As such it survives encircled by Slav, Magyar and Turkic-speaking neighbours.

The boundaries of modern Romania, as elsewhere in the Balkans, give a deceptive appearance of unity, as they are the result of a series of political and military decisions. The two historical provinces of Moldavia and Wallachia had functioned as independent medieval principalities within a broadly based Byzantine Orthodox cultural tradition. They then passed during the fifteenth and sixteenth centuries to a singular form of Ottoman Turkish control as autonomous tributary Christian provinces, whereby they retained their own native princes as rulers in return for supplying funds and military levies. These two provinces were united in 1856 and finally emerged as the independent kingdom of Romania in 1878 after the Congress of Berlin. The third province, Transylvania, ceded to Romania in 1918, had an equally eventful history. Progressively linked to Hungary, briefly to Ottoman Turkey, and to Austria, its cultural traditions had a strong Western bias influenced by Roman Catholicism, classical humanism, and Protestantism.

In view of this history it is not surprising that Romania has inherited a remarkable ethnic and religious diversity through boundary changes, immigration, trade, and invasion. Romanians, Hungarians, German Saxons, Bulgarians, Armenians, Greeks, Serbs, Jews, Turks, Tartars and Russians have all contributed their influences in various ways. This is reflected visually in the exuberant architecture which features Byzantine forms mingled with Gothic steeples, roof shingles, and stone tracery in the monasteries of Moldavia, and buildings of neo-classical and French Second Empire inspiration in Bucharest; the influence of the Islamic world is seen in the mosques of the Turco-Tartars of the Black Sea coast and the fluent, interlaced motifs carved in the stonework of city church and palace.

Romania's greatly varied terrain and plentiful natural resources have been dominating factors in shaping a rural building tradition which is both practical and aesthetically pleasing. Conveniently, the three provinces also have distinct geographical features. The Carpathian mountains sweep around the Transylvanian plateau in a bold loop from north to south to west; Moldavia is characterized by wooded hills and high, isolated grazing pastures; Wallachia has broad, open plains. Despite harsh winters, climatic conditions are generally favourable; there is sufficient rainfall and the land is fertile, resulting in abundant forest and arable land. There is no shortage of suitable building material, notably wood, which is much used in Moldavia, Wallachia and north-west Transylvania, reeds and thatch, which are supplemented by locally available stone and masonry as required. Here Romania is one of the main centres where the techniques and styles of the timber construction – especially that of horizontal blockwork – of central and eastern Europe have survived. Remains of wooden houses have been excavated from the early Iron Age village site of Lake Biskupin in Poland and dated to 700–500 BC, and from the medieval city of Novgorod, ranging from the tenth to fifteenth centuries. They demonstrate the use of a simple plan, based on a living room and entrance lobby, and the technique of intersecting notched corner joints, which are still found in Romanian villages.

The Romanian communities where this architecture is found are still complex social units, defined by one eminent Romanian authority on peasant societies as 'a mode of economic exploitation of collective territory by pastoral and very rudimentary agricultural techniques' (Stahl 1980:37). Here a network of mutual obligations and rights underlies a rural economy which uses clearings and enclosures in both forests and plains as common lands for animal husbandry, haymaking and

Figure 1 *Wooden church, Răpciuni village, Neamţ district, Moldavia, eighteenth or nineteenth century.*

planting, and harvesting of grain crops. This type of organization favours a relatively open and spacious village plan of self-contained units of farmhouse and attendant outbuildings such as barns, stables and haylofts. This social structure is reflected in the architecture.

One type of building which was always a focal point in a village was the church, although its location is not always central. Churches can be found in comparatively isolated positions at the end of a village or, as in the rural monastic tradition, within an enclosure set amid pastoral lands. Church building, unlike farmstead construction, required the services of specialist carpenters, who also functioned as architects, drawing up a ground plan after discussion with the villagers. This plan was usually simple in the case of Orthodox churches, requiring three sections – the narthex, the nave, and the sanctuary located in the apse. Columned porches could be added at the west end for aesthetic and social gathering reasons, and also belfries and steeples. The choice of wood varied according to area – pine and fir in the upper Carpathian mountain village, oak at lower levels. The example here (Figures 1 and 2) is a

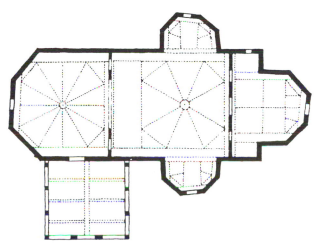

Figure 2 *Plan of the wooden church at Răpciuni.*

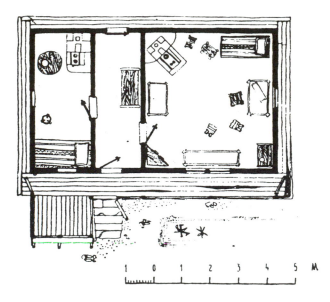

Figure 3 *Plan of a balconied house at Trăisteni, Prahova district.*

wooden church of eighteenth to nineteenth century date from the village of Răpciuni in the Neamţ district of Moldavia, distinctive for its steep roof, kiosk-like belfry set over a deep porch, and a broad trilobed apse. The church is built on a shallow stone foundation in the traditional blockwork technique, in which wall timbers ascend horizontally, leaving spaces for doors and windows. The roof is also constructed in this manner and covered with overlapping wooden shingles. The problems of angles and corners have been elegantly solved by the use of intersecting notched joints which fit smoothly into place.

These construction techniques are also found in village houses, whose stylistic and decorative range is one of the most appealing features of Romanian architecture. Traditionally house plans are simple, based on a living and guest room separated by a central vestibule which can also function as a kitchen extension (see Figures 3 and 4). A household still continues to be built as a self-contained unit usually within a retaining fence but with some concessions to modern building methods.

Two houses from the village of Gara Humorului in Moldavia illustrate compromise solutions. One (Figure 5) retains such features as a deep encircling veranda

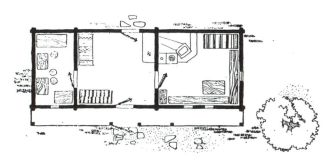

Figure 4 *Plan of a house at Prundul Birgăului.*

Figure 5 *House at Gara Humorului village, Moldavia, twentieth century.*

with wooden eaves and supporting columns, but the steep roof has overlapping red earthenware tiles instead of wooden shingles. Walls are constructed of white-washed brick, while doors and windows are no longer hand-crafted but standard units from a builder's stock. Another house in the same village is more faithful to tradition in its use of wood timbers and roof shingles. Appearances are, however, deceptive as these wooden constructions are applied over a plastered foundation.

The use of painted plaster provides a colourful version of the village house near Rădăuţi, an important market town in Moldavia (Figures 6 and 7). Here the construction is bland, with smoothly finished masonry walls and a neatly tiled roof. This provides a base for rich decoration, worked in plaster, carved and moulded in relief of foliate scrolls and panels, and painted in boldly contrasting colours. Many elaborate variations can be seen indicating the owner's personal taste and technical skills.

A modest treatment of house building which makes use of local materials is seen in the islands of the delta of the river Danube. This area is one of the most extensive flat regions of Romania where a seemingly endless network of waterways mingles with reeds and rushes.

Figure 6 *House with painted plaster decoration in a village near Rădăuţi, Moldavia, twentieth century.*

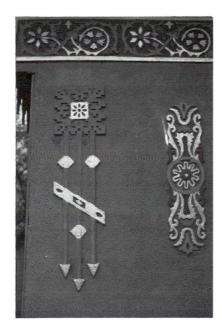

Figure 7 *House with painted plaster decoration in a village near Rădăuţi, Moldavia, twentieth century. Detail.*

Figure 8 *House built for Dr Nicolae Minovici, Bucharest, 1905.*

Here in a house from the island of Maliuc reeds are arranged in vertical bands on a light wood frame to construct both the walls and the shallow sloping roof.

The forms of traditional village architecture greatly influenced urban buildings of the late nineteenth and early twentieth centuries, resulting in the construction of many picturesque and comfortable villas and houses, all within spacious gardens, located in the more affluent suburbs of cities such as Bucharest, Iasi and Craiova. These buildings were nostalgic in concept and adapted features such as the columned porch and steep shingled roof, typical of village farmsteads, to a middle-class environment. One of the most successful and attractive of such homes is the villa (Figure 8) designed and built for Dr Nicolae Minovici (1868–1941) – who founded the Casualty Hospital and Ambulance Society of Bucharest – by the architect Cristofi Cerchez (1872–1955) in 1905. Here the village porch and roof is blended with panels and friezes of stonework, carved in relief with the interlaced foliage motifs of eighteenth-century Romanian court architecture, in an agreeable eclecticism. The interior decoration of the villa, based on the wooden furniture, household utensils, colourful woven textiles and painted pottery of village origin, complements the external appearance. While this may seem a self-indulgent pastiche it is more sympathetically understood in the context of Romanian nationalism. The stages of Romania's progress towards independence were naturally accompanied by a revival of ethnic literature, music and visual arts. It is to the credit of Romanian intellectuals, such as Dr Minovici and his circle, that they recognized the value of village societies and pioneered and developed the disciplines of ethnography and material culture.

REFERENCE

Stahl, H.H. (1980) *Traditional Romanian Village Communities*, Cambridge: Cambridge University Press.

FURTHER READING

Buxton, D. (1981) *The Wooden Churches of Eastern Europe – An Introductory Survey*, Cambridge: Cambridge University Press.

Ionesco, G. (1972) *Histoire de l'Architecture en Roumanie*, Bucharest: Editions de l'Académie de la République Socialiste de Roumanie.

A living tradition?
35 Greek vernacular architecture
Dimitri Philippides

To measure the tenacity of traditional architecture in Greece, one has to proceed along two seemingly unrelated paths. The first is direct: it follows its evolution during the past 150 years; the second is indirect: it concerns its impact on contemporary architectural theory and practice.[1] In order to do so, though, a working definition is absolutely essential, but we discovered that there is a surprisingly wide choice of conflicting interpretations of what actually constitutes tradition. Once again there is a choice of two schools of thought: one that regards traditional architecture solely in terms of a certain historical period;[2] and another that perceives it in a time continuum where it never ceased to undergo protean transformations. We will face the issue by attempting to pinpoint the two most crucial definitions of traditional architecture at hand; from there we will move to the relevant theoretical background in use by Greek architects; and finally we will sum the argument and examine traditional architecture on its own terms.

The first definition considers traditional architecture as a distinct historical phenomenon, hence something which started at some point in time and ended at another, owing to a radical change of social and economic conditions. The shift from a pre-industrial era to the present constitutes exactly such a shift. The historical essence of this architecture is coupled with a unique formal and structural syntax, uniform and unchanging throughout the period (Figure 1). Remnants or derivations from that architecture may have survived afterwards but they are insignificant replicas devoid of any meaning. The sheer imitation or even simplification of such an architecture by today's practitioners is pointless because it cannot be recreated. It is only fit to be preserved and studied as part of the national heritage.

The second definition takes a more lenient position. Whereas traditional architecture in Greece is undoubtedly identified with the period of Turkish occupation, there still exists another architecture which defies easy categorization. It cannot be grouped either with official architecture or with any late survivals of the traditional. This architecture is not necessarily illegal and does not correspond to a subsistence level of economy, although it usually relates to low-income housing. It is certainly not built by authorized architects or engineers, simply because its users cannot afford them. In short it lacks a common formal language, its main characteristic being its frugality – an economy of expression and materials which transcends the mere fullfilment of needs. This is essentially the central argument of Aris Konstantinides,

the most respected living architect in Greece (awarded the Herder Prize, Vienna 1990). He has propagated his ideas both in writing and in designing for the last forty years.

Yet historically speaking such clear-cut distinctions were not always recognizable. During most of the history of modern Greece, the study of vernacular architecture has not been a respected field of study.[3] This was partially due to an overemphasis placed on the study of oral tradition, where it was hoped to establish a direct link with ancient Greece, thus proving the ethnic continuity of modern Greeks with their glorious antecedents.

A systematic research on traditional architecture started as late as the 1930s. Up to that point the field was monopolized by folklorists whose priorities have always differed from those of architects: their task was to prove that this architecture was purely Greek with no other significant admixtures. The absence of geographers being an additional factor, it is no surprise that there still exists a marked residue of ethnocentric romanticism embedded in the issue, even if it is now studied by 'impartial' architects. This has helped perpetuate a confusion of the terminology in use which emphasizes the traditional rather than the historical aspect, the emotional rather than the scientific, and the

Figure 1 *The 'true' tradition: a house of Platanos, a village in Arcadia in the interior of the Peloponnese.*

ideological rather than the pragmatic dimensions of this type of architecture. For example, there is no clear distinction between 'vernacular' and 'traditional', and the terms invariably in use, such as 'folk' (*laiki*), are totally misleading.[4]

To trace the shifts in ideology concerning traditional architecture, one has to start with the second half of the nineteenth century. A number of socio-political crises that climaxed around the turn of the century and up to the 1920s always involved the turbulent relations of Greece with neighbouring Turkey. Since Turkey was the acknowledged source of Greek traditional architecture, this helped perpetuate its neglect and consequent destruction throughout the past century. It was a European style, i.e. neo-classicism, which was accepted as the appropriate model fit for the major drive towards Westernization at the time. All local architecture – practically speaking, anything built in the late eighteenth and early nineteenth century – was considered backward, unhealthy and a painful reminder of past hardships under Ottoman rule.

In the wake of an exchange of populations between the two countries in 1922,[5] the influx of Greek refugees from Asia Minor to the Greek mainland consolidated a shift toward a period of national introspection, which helped further emphasize a latent 'return to the roots' movement among intellectuals. One of the side-effects was an open acceptance of the long-despised local architectural idiom as a viable alternative to imported styles of the past. It was widely felt at the time that contemporary Greek architecture should be based solely on this particular model if it were ever to amount to anything worthwhile.

To put this axiom into practice, architects began to study such prototypes and openly copied them, while arguing that this was in line with the climatic and social needs of the country. A prominent figure among these was Aristotelis Zachos (1871–1939); his mixture of Byzantine and traditional forms was then considered a legitimate answer to the search for a national architecture. A similar approach was followed by Dimitris Pikionis (1887–1968), whose instinct led him further out, towards various stylistic borrowings from Greek insular architecture down to reconstructed Hellenistic houses (Figure 2).

The courageous emergence of such a 'back to the roots' trend in the 1920s and later was none the less only one of several competing alternatives open to Greek architects, who frequently travelled to Europe to study or work. Therefore it was only natural that at least some of them would attempt to 'modernize' (update) the local idiom by experimenting with various mixtures of traditional and eclectic or modernistic forms. A representative example in this category was Nicholas Mitsakis (1899–1941), who attempted the fusion of former Greek styles, including the vernacular, with modern architecture in the 1930s.

Figure 2 *The 'learned' tradition: a suburban house in the Athens area, designed by D. Pikionis, 1954.*

The ensuing impact on Greek architecture is obviously outside our scope; yet it should be pointed out that this mixed 'official' architecture has been the subject of a raging debate since then. On the one hand, D. Pikionis and his followers in practice supported the direct application of vernacular forms to contemporary architecture; on the other, immediately after the war Aris Konstantinides fervently preached the unconditional avoidance of imitation of vernacular forms.[6] In his work instead he tried to incorporate the abstract principles of vernacular architecture, which, as he insisted, distinguished 'true' architecture from false. He was actually fighting a losing battle: popular taste eventually remained unconvinced. People just loved those picturesque touches and freely spent their money in costly villas dressed like traditional mansions. Even low-income home builders tried hard to apply as much 'vernacular decoration' as possible to structures raised in their place of origin – sometimes next to genuine vernacular specimens. Neo-vernacular style, however vulgar and at odds with traditional architecture, has become the uncontested dominant 'Greek' architecture at present.

Although some leading architects at first say this as a healthy reaction against the vagaries of Modernism and eagerly followed the trends, it took them more than a couple of decades to realize how damaging such a direction was. It was too late. In the meantime virtually every tourist development or official building constructed in a traditional locale after the 1960s routinely sported elaborate arcades and other fake traditional elements on

Figure 3 *The 'fake' tradition: a neo-vernacular cultural complex built in Yiannina, Epirus, in the early 1980s.*

a colossal scale (Figure 3). In addition, strict formal regulations had been imposed on new construction in traditional settlements. The legal protection of traditional settlements in Greece hastened the creation of a series of custom-made building codes for new construction in such cases. These codes explicitly tried to regulate even the formal aspects of new buildings, thus giving rise to a neo-vernacular style.

If that was in general terms the picture in the area controlled by architects, traditional architecture itself was presenting a real challenge which was difficult to ignore. The newly acquired sensitivity of architects in the 1920s and 1930s had led them towards the makeshift shelters of refugees, which dotted the urban 'landscape' of major Greek cities. Whatever was found there co-incided with their need for a low-key, self-sufficient architecture, picturesque and totally 'Greek'. But it was not yet clear to what purpose the appreciation of such material would be put.

The connection was made in the post-war period, when a fresh wave of refugees flocked to the cities as a result of a bitter civil war (1947–9) and afterwards, when urbanization forced rural immigrants into large cities, where they created vast areas of illegal housing (Figure 4). Architects again 'stooped' to study this unique built environment and some started to question whether the forms of such low-income structures represented the immediate descendents of the glorified traditional architecture, transposed from the rural to the urban milieu. It was argued that the restricted scale of such buildings, the importance given to the use of open space and the intense socializing among residents in such areas was the equivalent of rural Arcadia, long lost among city dwellers. Such opinions were quite fashionable during the 1960s, at which time a number of studies on Greek illegal housing were first published.[7]

Again, it took some time for these ideas to affect the architectural practice. Encouraged by new trends

towards 'ad-hocism' – a movement which reached Greece in the late 1970s – the models of illegal housing began to appear on drafting boards, if only slightly adapted to gain respectability. A number of recent competitions were won as projects which vaguely followed such principles, and before long a number of such buildings will have risen around the country. Thus a second-generation connection will be established between the living tradition, i.e. the architecture of the underprivileged, and official architecture.

So far we have not discussed the ways in which traditional architecture itself succeeded – or failed – to adapt to changing conditions during the past century-and-a-half in Greece. On the contrary, we seemed to presume it defunct – a total fallacy. Although not yet commonly acceptable, there is enough evidence to indicate that traditional architecture continued to thrive. According to reliable estimates, most of what is presently considered as 'genuine' traditional architecture, especially in the dense urban tissue of older towns, belongs firmly to the late nineteenth century. Besides, traditional architecture has evolved, forming admixtures which are sometimes heavily indebted to a neo-classical vernacular. Even more important is the fact that it retained its vitality practically up to the 1920s – in some cases, it can be traced up to the 1940s. Beyond that one finds the traces of yet another 'tradition', still not respectable but at least recognizable.

In conclusion, we side firmly with the second definition of traditional architecture given above (p. 206), namely a minimalist architecture characterized by frugality regardless of the formal aspects used, and can testify to its longevity despite the long shadow cast by

Figure 4 *The urban tradition: a 1966 photograph of refugee housing in the centre of Athens, first settled by refugees from Asia Minor in the 1920s, now demolished.*

official architecture. It may not be the dominant 'style' it was some centuries ago; it may have no relation to the absurdities of the neo-vernacular architecture which is the current rage; still, it resists all efforts at blatant uniformity and holds a promise for the future of a living Greek architecture.

NOTES

1   The emphasis placed on vernacular architecture is directly related to a search for identity in the face of cultural annihilation (cf. Sherrard 1978: 1–16).

2   The Turkish occupation of the Greek peninsula lasted from the fifteenth century to the first quarter of the nineteenth century; some regions of northern Greece though were liberated as late as the 1910s (see Campbell and Sherrard 1968: 83 ff.).

3   For a more thorough discussion of such currents, cf. Philippides 1983: 33–50.

4   See Bouras 1983: 21–32.

5   The Greek army defeat in Asia Minor in 1922 signalled the sudden end of a number of bustling Greek communities there. Survivors, approximately 1.5 million strong, subsequently settled on the Greek mainland (see Campbell and Sherrard 1968: 138 ff.).

6   See Konstantinides 1950.

7   See for example Romanos 1969: 137–55.

REFERENCES

Bouras, C. (1983) 'The approach to vernacular architecture. General introduction', in D. Philippides (ed.) *Greek Traditional Architecture*, Vol. I, Athens: Melissa.

Campbell, J. and Sherrard, P. (1968) *Modern Greece*, London: E. Benn.

Konstantinides, A. (1950) *Ta Palaia Athinaïka Spitia* (*Old Athenean Houses*), Athens.

Philippides, D. (1983) 'Historical retrospect', in D. Philippides (ed.) *Greek Traditional Architecture*, Vol. I, Athens: Melissa.

Romanos, A. (1969) 'Illegal settlements in Athens', in P. Oliver (ed.) *Shelter And Society*, London: Barrie & Jenkins.

Sherrard, P. (1978) *The Wound of Greece*, London: Rex Collins.

FURTHER READING

Konstantinides, A. (1964) *Architectural Design* 5 (special issue): 212–35.

—— (1972) 'Life vessels or the problem of a "genuine" Greek architecture' (with English summary), *Architecture in Greece* 6: 27–48.

Lavas, G. (1972) 'Anonymous and modern architecture' (with English summary), *Architecture in Greece* 6: 49–59.

Philippides, D. (1972) 'In search of anonymous architecture' (with English summary), *Architecture in Greece* 6: 63–72.

—— (1986) 'The inheritors' (with English summary), *Architecture in Greece* 20: 70–4.

Philippides, D. and Kizis, Y. (1989) 'Neo-vernacular masquerade in the traditional context', *Design and Art in Greece* 20: 68–70.

Pikionis, D. (1989) *A Sentimental Topography*, London: Architectural Association.

Porphyrios, D. (1982) 'Classicism is not a style', in D. Porphyrios (ed.) *Classicism Is Not A Style*, London: Academy Editions/St Martin's Press, pp. 51–7.

Zannos, A. (1989) 'Caricatures of traditional fashion' (with English summary), *Design and Art in Greece* 20: 66–7.

A living tradition?
36 Maltese vernacular architecture

Denis De Lucca

Throughout history, the Maltese islands have been particularly susceptible to east–west and north–south currents of influence because of their geographical location. Their built environment consequently reflects the input of a wide variety of cultural traditions. This phenomenon, particularly pronounced in the aftermath of the many armed invasions to which the islands have been subjected in the past, and often reinforced through widespread trading, has resulted in a tremendously rich architectural heritage as the strong evolutionary process due to insular isolation was repeatedly strengthened or, indeed, interrupted by alien forces of change at different points in time.

Within this ever-changing pattern of development it is nevertheless possible to identify a number of interesting historical constants which governed the development of a vernacular architecture in Malta. Amongst these one can identify a marked preoccupation with security; the presence of a small population of subsistence farmers whose poverty determined clear priorities; the use of an indigenous building limestone coupled with the tendency to adopt primitive, labour-intensive types of building technique; and, finally, the predominant influence of a typical Mediterranean island climate benevolent to building activity. The successive building phases of the Maltese islands, namely Prehistoric, Punic, Roman, Islamic, Medieval-Christian and Renaissance-baroque, must necessarily be viewed within the context of these basic parameters.

PRIMITIVE STONE SHELTERS

The limestone vernacular architecture of Malta presents us with two intriguing examples of a living tradition. The first can be traced back to at least the fifth millenium BC when Neolithic farmers from Sicily introduced a hut-building tradition of Asiatic origins. Around 3800 BC this evolved into a monumental architecture which used megalithic construction and had a sacred, medical or cosmic significance (Bonanno 1986: 10).

The most primitive contemporary expression of this limestone architecture consists of isolated specimens or groups of rural buildings locally known as *giren* (singular: *girna*) (Figure 1). In terms of typology and construction the *giren* are considered by many to be the direct descendants of the megalithic architecture of the fourth and third millenium BC for which the islands are renowned. These primitive stone shelters have several interesting features. First, although it would be difficult to establish conclusively the link with prehistoric

building traditions, the *giren* constitute a vernacular building type which has widespread formal and constructional parallels in neighbouring Mediterranean countries. Especially close in this respect are primitive structures in the Jabal and Ujlah areas in Libya (Libyan General Committee for Participation in the World of Islam Festival 1976: 48–9); stone huts in the Palermo area of Sicily; the Sardinian *nuraghi* (Piggott 1965: 156–7); the *bunje* of Yugoslavia (Fabor 1970: 237–46); and the remarkable *trulli* of the Apulia region in Italy (Allen 1969: 77–131) (an area where a number of still uninvestigated cultural cross-currents with Malta can be identified in prehistoric and post-prehistoric times, two important examples occurring in the form of free-standing Bronze Age dolmens (Evans 1959: 179)) and baroque palace architecture.

The second interesting aspect of the Maltese *giren* is their geographic distribution (Fsadni 1990: 13), camouflaged as they often are amid dry stone walls and other manifestations of the manufactured landscape which characterizes what is still considered to be rural Malta. It is important to note that the territory where these remarkable clusters of stone shelters are situated was historically the most inhospitable and dangerous area of the islands, well away from the earliest hamlet and village concentrations in the southern part of Malta. Does this clear contrast to the later closed settlement patterns of the post-medieval period suggest the survival of a prehistoric settlement pattern of isolated stone dwellings? Whatever the reason for this may be, it is clear that the Maltese *giren* represent a class of vernacular building in its own right – a primitive form of shelter which until recent years did not require skilled labour, architects or professional builders, so that it was

Figure 1 *Typical Maltese rural structure or* girna.

historically totally impervious to the external forces of change which made such a powerful impact on the plans, sections and elevational treatment of the more refined cubic architecture associated with the villages and fortified towns on the islands.

A third distinguishing feature of the limestone *giren* of the Maltese countryside concerns their visual form. This normally results from a direct translation of the inside spatial form in that unsubtle manner that one expects from farmer-builders more concerned with security, shelter and other functional qualities than with aesthetic considerations. The plans of the buildings are mostly based on the circle, this giving rise to the shape of a truncated cone. The double-skin wall of the *girna* curves inwards as successive courses of stone are made to corbel slightly until a point is reached where the enclosed space can be sealed by means of a single limestone slab in a manner reminiscent of the second-millennium BC prototype beehive tombs associated with the Mycenaean culture. In some cases the base of the Maltese *girna* is strengthened on the outside by a low skirting wall of undressed limestone, or, alternatively, by a ramp that encircles the *girna* from its base to the roof, representing a technique well known in other Mediterranean areas.

Occurring next in frequency to the circular plan is the square plan *girna*, followed by the rectangular, the oval and numerous intermediate stages which demonstrate the ingenuity and fertile imagination of generations of farmers who were responsible for their construction and maintenance at different points in history. The use of different sized stones, variations in the entrance theme, with horizontal, arched or triangular lintels, and a total lack of standardization in internal and external measurements all bear testimony to what can best be described as a fascinating architecture without architects, having very primitive roots indeed.

THE CUBIC EXPRESSION

In sharp contrast stands the second type of limestone-based vernacular architecture associated with the Maltese islands. The cubic buildings of Malta also form part of an age-old tradition. Their origins can be traced back to a period spanning from approximately 800 BC to AD 1200 when the islands appear to have been firmly within the North African rather than the European sphere of influence. This was due to the presence of a deeply rooted Punic culture which survived through the Roman occupation until it was reinforced in the ninth century by the presence of the Aghlabid Muslims of Tunisia. The latter remained in Malta well into the twelfth century, and documents dated 1175 still refer to Malta as 'a Saracenis abitata' (Luttrell 1975: 28).

The tradition of cubic limestone architecture in the Maltese islands is therefore decidedly North African in inspiration. A present-day Maltese village profile seen in

silhouette at sunset, and without the typically domed Roman baroque church, still has very strong formalistic associations with many an African settlement, which points towards common roots prior to the main period of Christianization (1530–1796) when Malta was ruled by the crusader knights of St John of Jerusalem.

Irrespective of whether they occur in isolated forms scattered in the countryside, as traditional farmsteads or contemporary pleasure villas, or whether they occur within the higher density context of hamlets, villages, fortified settlements or contemporary sprawling suburbs, the unique character of the cubic architecture of Malta stems from the innumerable permutations and combinations of a few basic shapes. These are modelled in a seemingly endless series of visually interesting spaces: internal courtyards, narrow winding streets, wide, straight thoroughfares associated with baroque gridiron patterns and, more significantly, typically Mediterranean piazzas. The piazzas can range from mere left-over clearings tightly enclosed by buildings to more sophisticated and spacious forms that hinge on the presence of some dominant baroque palace or church, or both.

In terms of scale, mass, architectural language and the exuberant decoration of the European baroque academies, these major monuments collectively bear testimony to the absolute political power of the Grand Master of the Knights, the terror of the Inquisition, the counter-influence of the Bishop of Malta, or the haughtiness of a local nobility – with strong ancestral affiliations to the royalty of medieval Spain. It is undoubtedly these forces and their European connections which, after 1600, were responsible for transforming a humble cubic architecture of North African origins into a more sophisticated European version dressed in the garb of the Renaissance and baroque styles. The primitive Maltese rural farmhouse or *razzett*, based on cubic forms, traditionally consisted of a number of rooms informally planned around two or three sides of a central courtyard which contained a well and an open staircase providing access to the *ghorfa*, or sleeping quarters, at first-floor level (see Figure 2). The building was essentially the

Figure 2 *Typical Maltese razzett.*

basic dwelling unit of an agriculturally based economy. It was very closely attached to the fields that were cultivated and, among other things, contained ample space for an extended family as well as for the storage of field produce and animals. The principal space, in accordance with the common Mediterranean practice of outdoor living, was the courtyard. Here such activities as cooking, playing, resting and dining took place.

In this vernacular type of architecture, the cubic forms furnished their own decoration through simple composition, clear lines and sunlit masses. The only overt attempts at decoration consist of masonry projections, especially around small windows, woodwork painted in pale colours, pointed roof corner decorations clearly of North African origin (Libyan General Committee 1976: 50, 54–5), simple rain-water gargoyles and, perhaps the most interesting feature of all, limestone blocks decorated with so-called 'roundels' (Buhagiar 1984: 15–18). The latter echo the exciting geometric forms associated with Islamic culture, but also incorporate well-known Christian symbols.

These cubic dwellings were simple in form and camouflaged in the landscape, the natural bedrock providing their building material and the soft stone the opportunity for an infinite variety of sculpted symbols portraying old Mediterranean pagan traditions overlaid on a primitive view of the new Christian world with strong Islamic overtones, all very reminiscent of the situation in Spanish Andalus after 1492.

In about 1600, the introduction of the practice of living in closed settlements for security reasons in medieval Malta led to a reinterpretation of the basic cubic farmhouse layout. Community living, as opposed to extended family living, linked with the typically medieval Mediterranean tradition of walking to one's fields in the early morning and returning to the security of the village at sunset, led to the establishment of a typical village pattern of two distinct types. The earlier type consisted of a closely knit web of winding streets and alleys radiating from a central square, echoing the introverted central courtyard of the farmhouse building; the later type, most popular on Malta's sister island of Gozo, consisted of a sprawling pattern based on open-ended streets and alleys leading into the countryside, offering less security and introversion but infinitely more visual rapport with the terraced fields around the settlement.

Within the context of these two types of village fabric, cubic architecture evolved rapidly in the period 1530–1798. A particular model and spur for development was the sudden appearance after 1600 of a large, baroque parish church strategically dominating the village square, its exterior and interior exclusively designed to impress humble farmers, who were largely illiterate and certainly not accustomed to such an expression of large-scale, baroque decorum and artistic sophistication.

The result of this development was that, after about 1650, the simple façades of the village cubes – then still honestly portraying the exciting combinations of solids and voids, and underlining the introverted character of the roots of this architecture – were suddenly transformed as a direct result of the introduction of the classical orders of architecture, skyline mouldings, a new emphasis on scale and symmetrical composition, Renaissance door and window ornament, and wooden balconies. The latter feature can be interpreted as one of the many signs of the Spanish influence which seems to have been dominant in Malta in the first half of the seventeenth century.

The outcome of all this was that the simple village street developed, as in Islamic settlements, exclusively for communication purposes (Figure 3), soon became a pseudo-baroque vista where the new ornament of the cube reflected the purpose of the building and the occupier's position in society. The three-dimensional traditional architecture of cubic mass and shadow play was now transformed into a two-dimensional exercise in Façadism designed to boost the ego of both client and architect, to enrich the urban scene and to crown the repeated efforts of the Knights to introduce an urban lifestyle into a land where it had been hitherto unknown (see Figure 4). The sixteenth-century foundation and the seventeenth-century baroque redevelopment of the bastioned city of Valletta, scientifically laid out on a gridiron pattern as the embodiment of what was meant to be one of the finest urban military machines in Europe (Mangion 1989: 21–31), completes the picture of the transformation of the cubic expression in Maltese architecture in the historic period.

This process of change continues and its underlying spirit still largely dominates the architecture of contemporary cubic dwellings designed by Maltese architects for Maltese clients. There are, of course, exceptions to the rule who draw inspiration from the simple cubes of primitive Malta, and some enterprising Maltese and foreign architects have created some interesting buildings in the idiom which are either applauded, criticized

Figure 3 *Simple village street indicating Islamic origins.*

Figure 4 *Seventeenth-century transformations of the street in Malta.*

or rejected, depending on one's standpoint.

At the present time one can see two distinct tendencies at work: either a return to the traditional simplicity of cubic forms, noticeable in some recent touristic developments, or a stylistic change from the formal baroque or neo-classical idiom to informal International Modern or Post-Modern. The latter trend is clearly visible in mass housing schemes meant to accommodate an ever-increasing population.

One is therefore faced with a situation where a very old vernacular tradition persists. It does so because of a seemingly unlimited supply of limestone building blocks, and because of the introduction in this century of a new 'superstone' called concrete, which has enabled architects to dispense with unfashionable labour-intensive and space-limiting techniques of flooring and roofing using limestone slabs, limestone arches and limestone-based waterproofing materials.

The recent transformation process of the cubic architectural expression in Malta deserves further comment. Observing the traditional methods of construction involved in the cubic farmhouses in the Maltese countryside that have managed to escape adulteration through centuries of foreign influence, Harrison and Hubbard wrote:

> Yet if the architects of Malta were destined to make an original contribution to the architecture of the new world, they would be inspired by the forms not of the massive Auberges, nor of the splendid Parish churches, but of these humbler creations of the master-masons. The opulent masses and turgid ornament of the baroque monuments, their twisted columns and broken pediments, admirable as the

expression of other times and other people, are, in relation to the future, and to the Maltese, sterile and moribund. On the other hand, the clear-cut three dimensional forms of the rural houses are, like those of comparable buildings in the High Atlas, in the Palestinian Hills and in the Cyclades, pregnant with suggestion, and strangely in accord with the spirit of the age.

> (Harrison and Hubbard 1945: 103–5)

WHAT CONSTITUTES A LIVING TRADITION?

The question of whether vernacular architecture in Malta represents a living tradition or not would seem to hinge on the evolutionary process concerning the constructional methods used to create the characteristic built forms of the islands. It is perhaps significant in this respect to point out that in Malta the limestone block, itself of cubic shape and typically measuring 58 cm. (23 in.) in length, 15–23 cm. (6–9 in.) in width and 28 cm. (11 in.) in height, is very much a reflection of the completed building, and vice versa. There is therefore, in the very best sense of the word, 'vernacular' – an overt relationship between form, material and the land from which the material is extracted. This accounts for the overall homogeneity of the built environment of a Maltese village (Spiteri 1984: 10–11) before the introduction of modern imported materials, such as aluminium, façade paints and concrete, and their respective fashionable applications.

Prior to the introduction of concrete in prefabricated or *in situ* form, there were only three materials available for building purposes on the islands of Malta: limestone, clay and lime. The cubic vernacular expression therefore relied on a heavy load-bearing system of construction (Agius 1977: 26) using thick external walls with an outer and an inner skin of coursed dressed stonework and a filling of rubble and soil, the minimum section thickness being approximately 80 cm. (32 in.). The ceilings of rooms were normally constructed of 10 cm. (4 in.) thick limestone slabs known locally as *xorok*. These rested on arches, projecting stone corbels or wooden beams, the latter imported from nearby Sicily and mainly used in upper floors where it was desireable to avoid the heavy thick walls which the thrust of arches would necessitate. Staircases were built either in straight flights of a size and scale depending on the degree of baroque effect required or, alternatively, in a spiral form without newels, with cantilevered steps and carried up to roof level, thus forming the characteristic tower feature of the Maltese village. The roof slabs of the buildings were normally covered with a layer of clay and chippings laid to falls. This in turn was covered with a rendering made of lime and finely ground pottery which had the merits of being resistant to extremes of temperature and being easy to patch. Sometimes a thin layer of dried seaweed was also introduced to provide insulation.

If one were to compare the cubic vernacular architecture in Malta with the primitive *giren* forms or even with such remarkable Mediterranean manifestations as the Apulian *trulli*, one immediately becomes aware of the significance of a living, as opposed to a moribund, tradition. Whereas the latter two vernacular built forms largely ceased to be built in the post-war period due to a variety of factors – the most important being the obvious inadequacy of their curved interiors in terms of contemporary standards of living – the cubic architecture of Malta seems to have flourished considerably in recent times. This is mainly due to its unique capacity to receive, within its traditional limestone fabric, new constructional materials and techniques which furnish it with the flexibility that is essential for survival in the late twentieth century.

The way in which the Maltese builders have, for better or for worse, been able to play games of addition and subtraction within the time-honoured context of their built environment is, in itself, a tribute to the marked capability of the basic form of expression to change – both on the basis of the individual building unit and on the scale of the village, suburb or city – without losing that holistic quality associated with the Maltese built environment. The very fact that the architects of these modern limestone buildings are very much concerned with the search for new ways of expression using traditional cubic limestone blocks, coupled with an emphasis on historical and conservation studies in the curriculum of the architecture course at the University of Malta, indicates that the will and determination still exist on an individual and corporate level to keep alive a tradition of architectural expression and building with

ancient roots – a vernacular tradition in its truest sense which, together with a unique language, gives identity and charm to the Maltese islands.

REFERENCES

Agius, R. (1977) 'Human settlements in Gozo', B.E. and A. (Hons) dissertation, University of Malta.

Allen, E. (1969) *Stone Shelters*, Cambridge, Mass.: MIT Press.

Bonanno, A. (1986) *An Illustrated Guide to Prehistoric Gozo*, Gozo, Malta: Gozo Press.

Buhagiar, M. (1984) 'Some random reflections on Maltese vernacular architecture: the razzett and the roundel carvings on town and village houses', *Atrium* 3: 15–18.

Evans, J.D. (1959) *Malta*, London: Thames & Hudson.

Faber, A. (1970) 'Le Bunje sul littorale nord-est dell'Adriatico e il problema delle loro origini', in *L'Architettura a Malta*, unedited proceedings of the XVth Congress on the History of Architecture, Malta 1967, Rome.

Fsadni, M. (1990) *Il-Girna – Wirt Arkittetoniku u Etniku Malti*, Malta: Interprint.

Harrison, A.St B. and Hubbard, R.P.S. (1945) *Valletta and the Three Cities*, Malta: Government of Malta.

Libyan General Committee for Participation in the World of Islam Festival (1976) *Islamic Art and Architecture in Libya* (1976) catalogue for the World of Islam Festival prepared in co-operation with the Architectural Association, London: Ernest G. Bond.

Luttrell, A. (ed.) (1975) *Medieval Malta - Studies on Malta Before the Knights*, London: British School at Rome.

Mangion, G. (ed.) (1989) *Maltese Baroque*, Malta: Union Print.

Piggott, S. (1965) *Ancient Europe*, Edinburgh: Aberdeen University Press.

Spiteri, J.M. (1984) 'Towards an understanding of the character of the Maltese town and village', *Atrium* 3: 10–11.

37 The temple of Solomon and its influence on Jewish, Christian and Islamic architectural thought

Joseph Gutmann

Probably no ancient work of architecture has elicited so many attempts at archaeological reconstruction as the Temple of Solomon. Moreover, this ancient temple has been the object of constant imitation by architects erecting houses of worship in Jewish, Christian and Muslim cultures. In addition, it has also excited interest and inspired profound symbolic theological interpretation in the three major religions of the Western world.

The Temple reportedly took seven years to build. It was commissioned by King Solomon around the middle of the tenth century BC, although there is no scholarly agreement on its exact date or location. All reconstructions are largely based on two chapters of the Hebrew Bible (I Kings 6–7), as few archaeological remains are at hand. These biblical chapters are brief, ambiguous, contradictory, and confusing; the Hebrew terms used are frequently unintelligible. Whereas the furnishings and utensils of the Temple are described in great detail, only sparse information has been preserved about the building itself. Later editorial additions and contradictory evidence presented in the books of II Chronicles (2–4) and Ezekiel (40–3) make any architectural renderings difficult. Leroy Waterman has justifiably seen in the biblical description 'the damaged "blueprints" of the Temple of Solomon' (Waterman 1943: 284–94). The temple was 60 cubits long (31 m. or 103 ft.), 20 cubits wide (10.5 m. or 34 ft.) and 30 cubits high (15.5 m. or 51 ft.).[1] It was a 'long-house' type building with a tripartite division: an open vestibule or entrance hall called the *ulam*, a main hall or nave known as the *hekhal*, and an inner sanctuary or adytum called the *devir*. The orientation of the building was east–west. The best parallel, the building with the most striking similarities, is the excavated ninth-to-eighth-century BC Temple of Tell-Tainat in northern Syria. No similar Phoenician temple has yet been found. A craftsman, Hiram of Tyre (I Kings 7: 13, 40), was in charge only of the bronze works at Solomon's Temple; he was not, as has been frequently claimed, the architect supervising the entire temple project.

There is no scholarly agreement on many details of Solomon's Temple. We are not certain whether it was an independent temple or simply a royal chapel, an adjunct to the palace structure. The purpose and appearance of its side wings with three storeys (I Kings 6: 5–10), which may have surrounded the Temple like a horseshoe up to the portico, remain unclear. Some scholars even maintain that these side structures may deserve a later dating. Whether the inner sanctuary (the *devir*) was a separate room or whether it was partitioned off by a screen and functioned as an interior chapel within the temple is not determinable from the available evidence. Whether a stairway led from the main hall to the inner sanctuary is also disputed. What the hybrid, winged creatures called *keruvim* (I Kings 6: 23–8), which stood in the inner sanctuary, looked like is open to question. As in other Western Asian cultures, they served as a throne for the Israelite divinity. After all, the entire temple was God's residence and he dwelled in darkness in the innermost shrine. Whether the biblical desert ark had a place under the wings of the *keruvim* and served as a sort of footstool for the deity in the Temple of Solomon, an assumption made by most scholars, is far from certain. The reputed Solomonic ark may simply be a later retrojection into the biblical narrative of the Temple in order to authenticate later biblical ark traditions.

The two bronze pillars (I Kings 7: 15–22) have elicited much scholarly controversy. Usually thought of as free-standing and having a purely decorative and symbolic function, these pillars have been interpreted as sun and moon symbols, indicators of the equinox, dynastic markers, sacred pillars, incense burners and phallic symbols. Actually, they may not have been free-standing, but may have had a structural function. Perhaps they were an intricate part of a pillared portico, patterned on the familiar Western Asian *bit-ḫilani*. As in some *bit-ḫilani*, the Solomonic bronze columns may have supported a roof or canopy that projected in front of the vestibule. The height of the portico is not given in the Bible and thus further complicates a reconstruction of its possible architectural appearance. Any attempt at reconstruction of Solomon's Temple is doomed to failure, as too many vitally needed details are missing in the biblical narrative (see Figure 1).[2]

The Temple of Solomon was destroyed by the Babylonians in 587/6 BC. On the site of the Solomonic Temple another sanctuary was built, the so-called 'Second Temple', when the exiles returned from Babylonia under the aegis of the Persian dynasty of Cyrus-Darius around 515 BC. Enlarged and rebuilt probably between 23 and 15 BC by King Herod the Great, this temple stood until its destruction at Roman hands in AD 70. Traces of either Herod's Temple or the Temple of Solomon cannot be

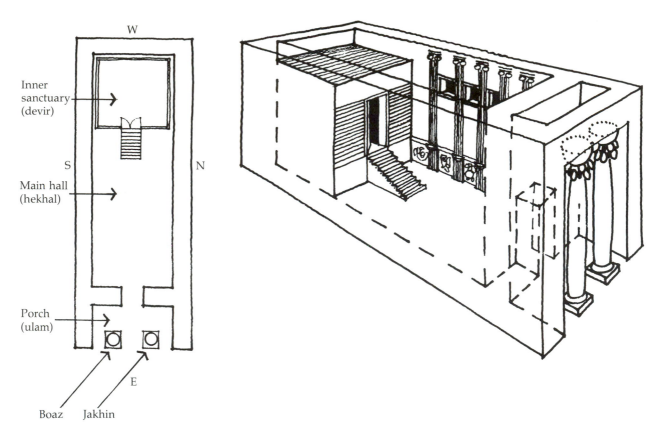

Inner sanctuary (devir)

Main hall (hekhal)

Porch (ulam)

Boaz   Jakhin

W

S   N

E

Figure 1 *Solomon's Temple: hypothetical reconstruction.*

searched out because the Muslim Dome of the Rock, a building of great holiness and beauty, now occupies the site of the former temples.

The significance of Solomon's Temple a.id the later Herodian Temple of Jerusalem was largely eclipsed with the rise of Christianity under the emperor Constantine. By the fifth century, Calvary and the Holy Sepulchre had replaced Mount Moriah and the erstwhile temples of Jerusalem. The Holy Sepulchre became the new Temple, the Sanctuary of Christ. Calvary and the Holy Sepulchre were now the true locations of traditions formerly linked with the Jewish Temple and its site. The Temple Mount upon which Solomon's Temple once stood was referred to by St Jerome 'as the dung heap of new Jerusalem' (Ferber 1976: 22–3; see also Gutmann 1985). It visibly expressed the fulfilment of Christ's curse: 'Verily I say unto you, there shall not be left here one stone upon another [in the Temple], that shall not be thrown down' (Matthew 24:2 and Mark 13:2).

Yet symbolically both Solomon and his Temple continued to live on in Christianity. Theodorus of Cyrus stated that the Temple of Solomon should be the model or prototype for all churches, Eusebius of Caesarea compared those who built churches to Solomon while Prudentius felt that 'wisdom builds a temple by Solomon's hands' (Ferber 1976: 22–3). To these early Christian Fathers, the Temple of Solomon was seen as a prefiguration of the Temple of God, the church of the

New Law established by Christ. Identifying the church with the Temple of Solomon, Christians sought symbolically to incorporate it – the mystic church was the spiritual Temple of Solomon. 'It is our most peaceful Solomon who built this Temple', cried an orator at the site of one of Constantine's vast rotundas, and 'the latter glory of this House is greater than the former' (ibid.). In a poem inscribed in the church of St Polyeuktos, one of the largest and most sumptuous churches in early sixth-century AD Constantinople, we read that the patron Anicia Juliana 'alone had conquered time and surpassed the wisdom of the celebrated Solomon, raising a temple to receive God' (Harrison 1983: 277; Scheja 1962). It is further suggested that the great Justinian, standing under the huge dome of Constantinople's Hagia Sophia in AD 537, raised his hands and exclaimed:'Glory to God who has found me worthy to complete such a work. Solomon I have outdone you!' (ibid.). These dynastic statements refer, of course, to an imaginary rival who has been vanquished. They place the church above the 'Old Testament' temple. They may also equate the church with the Solomonic Temple. Like Solomon's Temple, these churches were probably conceived as royal chapels appended to larger palaces. Especially in Anicia Juliana's church, such carved decorations as the palm trees, pomegranates, capitals overlaid with network, may have been conscious references to Solomon's Temple.

During the Carolingian period in the ninth century Alcuin and Notger likened Charlemagne and Charles the Bald to Solomon and their church buildings to his Temple. Later kings, too, were glorified in similar terms – Philip II of Spain was called a second Solomon; he built El Escorial in imitation of Solomon's whole building complex. In the eighteenth century Frederick I of Prussia wrote to his architect Jean de Bodt: 'Before I die, I desire to build a temple, like Solomon, to the glory of the Eternal' (Blunt 1972: 258).

In the Romanesque and Gothic periods, the church came more and more to be understood as a new Solomonic Temple. As such it was outfitted with the seven-branched biblical lampstand. In St Veits Cathedral in Prague, a twelfth-century candelabrum is actually inscribed as hailing 'de templo Salomonis in Jherusalem'. The candelabrum was deemed symbolic of the seven gifts of the Holy Spirit; its central stem represented Christ, who illumined and united the three lights on the right, the New Testament, and the three lights on the left, the Old Testament. The early twelfth-century baptismal font fashioned by Renier de Huy for Notre-Dame-aux-Fonts in Liège was carried on the backs of twelve oxen. This baptismal font, according to medieval Christian interpretation, had been prefigured by Solomon's large bronze sea resting on twelve oxen (I Kings 7: 23–6). The waters collected in Solomon's bronze basin or tank, which stood in front of the Temple, were equated with the baptismal waters and the twelve oxen symbolized the twelve apostles (Bloch 1961). Additional Solomonic features are also found. For instance in the thirteenth century the Würzburg Cathedral featured two knotted columns identified with the spoils of Solomon's Temple. They therefore had inscriptions, *Iachim-Booz*, on their capitals, consciously alluding to Solomon's bronze columns, *Jakhin* and *Boaz*, which had stood in the Temple portico (I Kings 7: 21). From the twelfth century on, four bronze columns in San Giovanni in Laterno in Rome were said to have come from the Temple of Solomon, while by the fourteenth century, twelve columns in St Peter's in Rome had become linked with the Temple of Solomon (Cahn 1976; Nilgen 1977; Kalavrezou-Maxeiner 1985). In addition to the placement of Solomonic elements in churches, cosmological and mystical speculations led some medieval builders to consider Solomon's Temple a sort of ideal prototype for their own church projects. In particular, the dimensional units of Solomon's Temple were considered divinely inspired and therefore at times were employed as ideal proportions for churches (Bannister 1968; von Simson 1956; Renna 1990).

Early Christian depictions of the Temple of Solomon pictured a simple, oblong, antique-derived classical temple. At times Solomon's Temple was rendered as a ciborium. Most frequently, it was represented as a contemporary Romanesque or Gothic church (Krinsky 1970). This image of the Temple changed dramatically when the Crusaders conquered Jerusalem in 1099. Hoping to eradicate all vestiges of Muslim rule and religion, they appropriated the splendid Muslim buildings that stood on the Temple mount. The beautiful octagonal Dome of the Rock was converted in 1104 into a church in honour of Christ's Presentation in the Temple and the Virgin Mary. It was administered by the Augustine Canons, and was called Templum Domini ('Church of the Temple of the Lord'). Some Christian writers even claimed it had been built by Solomon. The al-Aqsa mosque was identified as the Templum Salomonis and became at first a royal palace for the Crusader kings. It was later given to the Order of the Templars and used as a church. No doubt the Christian rulers, hoping to link themselves with a sacred tradition and place, looked to the kings of Israel as their ancestors. By the fifteenth century, long after the demise of the Latin kingdom in Palestine, some travel books began to label the Crusader Templum Domini the Templum Salomonis (Schein 1984).

King Solomon, known as Sulayman in Islamic tradition, plays a significant and glorified role; many 'Old Testament' stories about him are embroidered in Islamic lore. During Umayyad sway over seventh- and eighth-century AD Jerusalem, the Temple area was chosen as the site of the earliest Islamic buildings. In the 691/2 AD Dome of the Rock (Qubbat as-Sakhrah), the mosaic decorations with unusual trees, vines and jewelled ornaments may have been intended to evoke the splendours of Solomon's Temple. Thus the Dome of the Rock was perhaps conceived as a continuation of Solomonic traditions – a propaganda effort on the part of the Umayyad caliphs to affirm their kingship by linking themselves with a sacred, ancient, and royal tradition, thereby evincing superiority and victory over Judaism. No doubt the anti-Christological themes discernible in the Qur'ānic quotations that embellish the building were intended to demonstrate Muslim triumph and power over Christian Jerusalem and to diminish the significance and magnificence of such important Christian buildings as the domed Church of the Holy Sepulchre. In addition, both Caliph Mu'awiyah and his successor 'Abd al-Malik may have wanted to de-emphasize the importance of the Arabian peninsula as the religious centre of the newly established Empire and temporarily to divert the *hajj* (pilgrimage) from Mecca, which was then under the control of 'Abdullah ibn al-Zubayr, to Jerusalem. The Dome, a shrine with an inner ambulatory for a liturgical *tawaf* (or circling) of the Rock, may have been intended as a rival for the Kaaba in Mecca. In both venues, the rocks were linked with Abrahamic traditions; a later belief had Muhammad make his miraculous Ascension (*Mi'raj*) to Heaven from the Rock in the Jerusalem Dome (Soucek 1976; Grabar 1988).

Within Judaism, two distinct Temple of Solomon traditions developed in medieval Spain and Central Europe. The synagogue was considered only a *mikdash meʿat*, a temporary substitute, for the hoped-for rebuilt Solomonic Temple of the messianic future. It therefore became customary to illustrate Spanish Hebrew bibles, dating from the thirteenth to the fifteenth centuries, with cult implements such as the seven-branched lampstand, altars, tongs, snuffers, the ark, and the table of Showbread, that had once stood in the Temple of Solomon. God, according to Jewish tradition, had hidden or caused to be hidden for his faithful the precious vessels of Solomon's Temple. Sincere moral reconstitution would bring about restoration not only of the appurtenances but the Temple itself in the time of the Messiah. Furthermore, the Hebrew bible came to be called in Spain *mikdashyah* or *mikdashiyah* ('Lord's Sanctuary') and its threefold division – into Pentateuch, Prophets and Hagiographa – was likened to the partitions of the ancient Solomonic Jerusalem Temple. Placement of the hidden Solomonic Temple appurtenances on the opening pages in Spanish Hebrew bibles – rather than accompanying the descriptive passages of these cult objects in the books of Exodus, Leviticus and Numbers, as is the usual practice in many Christian and Hebrew manuscripts – visually expressed the Spanish Jews' belief in resurrection and kept alive their hope that they might be priviliged to view and serve in the Third Temple in messianic times. When they daily prayed for the speedy rebuilding of the Solomonic Temple and studied from their *mikdashyah* (Bibles), they were sheltering themselves, as it were, in a surrogate temporary Sanctuary while awaiting the permanent Sanctuary (the restored Temple of Solomon) with the coming of the Messiah.

In medieval Central Europe, it became standard practice to have synagogal appurtenances resemble those associated with the ancient Solomonic Temple and thereby ensure its rebuilding in the messianic future. The Torah ark was given the same designation as the biblical Temple ark, *ʾaron ha-kodesh*. A curtain, called the *parokhet*, was hung in front of the ark, since the biblical ark had also been placed behind the *parokhet*. An eternal light (*ner tamid*) was introduced in remembrance of the Temple. Finally, a large candelabrum was placed in the synagogue on the south side of the ark. This was also done in memory of the Temple *menorah* that had stood on the south side. These practices in Central European synagogues attest to the fact that the synagogue was considered a surrogate Temple in the Exile. Praying in their *mikdash meʿat*, surrounded by Temple objects, all Jews dreamed that they might behold the magnificent objects of the messianic Solomonic Temple at a time when all Jewish exiles would be gathered to the Holy Land (Gutmann 1986).

It was only from the sixteenth century on that attempts were actually made to reconstruct the Temple of Solomon – both in large printed volumes and in actual scale models. These efforts rendered the biblical descriptions of Solomon's Temple in contemporary baroque and rococo architectural styles since biblical archaeology had not yet come to the fore. In the Middle Ages, the Temple of Solomon and its objects were understood symbolically; no efforts were made to comprehend it or render it architecturally. Early attempts at reconstruction were made in the sixteenth century by Benedictus Arias Montanus. The most elaborate and famous reconstruction was that of the Jesuit fathers Geronimo Prado and Juan Baptista Villalpando. Their reconstruction, however, had little to do with the actual appearance of Solomon's Temple, but conformed to classical Vitruvian principles. In the seventeenth century Jacob Jehudah Leon built a model of what he conceived to be Solomon's Temple – it is now lost – which had a direct architectural influence on its contemporary Portuguese synagogue in Amsterdam. Similarly, such timber models of Solomon's Temple as that of Gerhard Schott, still to be found in the Hamburg Historical Museum, influenced contemporary church architecture (Rosenau 1972, 1979; Hermann 1967; Reuther 1980).

In the nineteenth and twentieth centuries, now considerably aided by archaeological excavations, many books have been devoted to the subject of the Temple of Solomon. They have influenced constructions of contemporary synagogues and led to the introduction of Solomonic elements, thereby evoking the ancient Solomonic Temple tradition.

The Temple of Solomon thus continues to live on in the imagination, art and thought of Judaism, Christianity and Islam. Solomon was the first biblical king to construct a major sacred shrine – the Temple in Jerusalem – for his divinity. He became the model for later Christian and Muslim rulers, the spiritual heirs to the Jewish traditions so minutely described in the biblical books of Kings. These rulers considered themselves descendents of King Solomon and consciously strove to emulate the example of this divinely appointed monarch. Solomon, who was the biblical paradigm of holy wisdom, inspired Christian and Muslim sovereigns who felt that his mantle of sapience also rested on them. Thus they conceived it to be their consecrated and prescribed mandate not only to equal Solomon's glory and sagacity, but to surpass this ideal figure.

The longing to behold the sanctified rebuilt Solomonic Temple in the messianic future is firmly embedded in traditional Jewish theology and liturgy. In Christianity, the fulfilment of the Jewish longing for the rebuilt Solomonic Temple was construed to be the cathedral, which was regarded as the legitimate holy inheritor and the rightful successor to the Jerusalem Temple.

ACKNOWLEDGEMENT

My thanks to my good friend Professor Stanley F. Chyet for reading this essay and for making suggestions for its improvement.

NOTES

1   A royal cubit equals 52.5 cm. (20.7 in.).
2   Cf. Ouellette 1976 and Fritz 1987.

REFERENCES

Bannister, T.C. (1968) 'The Constantinian Basilica of Saint Peter in Rome', *Journal of the Society of Architectural Historians* 27: 16, 24–5.

Bloch, P. (1961) 'Siebenarmige Leuchter in Christlichen Kirchen', *Wallraf-Richartz-Jahrbuch* 23: 55–190.

Blunt, A. (1972) 'The Temple of Solomon with special reference to South Italian baroque art', in A. Rosenauer and G. Weber (eds) *Kunsthistorische Forschungen. Otto Pächt zu seinem 70. Geburtstag*, Salzburg: Residenz Verlag, pp. 258–62.

Cahn, W. (1976) 'Solomonic elements in Romanesque art', in J. Gutmann (ed.) *The Temple of Solomon: Archaeological Fact and Mediaeval Tradition in Christian, Islamic and Jewish Art*, Missoula, Mont.: Scholars Press, pp. 45–72.

Ferber, S. (1976) 'The Temple of Solomon in early Christian and Byzantine art' in J. Gutmann (ed.) *The Temple of Solomon: Archaeological Fact and Mediaeval Tradition in Christian, Islamic and Jewish Art*, Missoula, Mont.: Scholars Press, pp. 21–44.

Fritz, V. (1987) 'What can archaeology tell us about Solomon's Temple?', *Biblical Archaeology Review* 13: 38–49.

Grabar, O. (1988) 'The meaning of the Dome of the Rock', in M.J. Chiat and K.L. Reyerson (eds) *The Medieval Mediterranean: Cross-Cultural Contacts*, St Cloud, Minn.: North Star Press, pp. 1–10.

Gutmann, J. (1985) 'Josephus' Jewish antiquities in twelfth-century art: renovatio or creatio?', *Zeitschrift für Kunstgeschichte* 48: 440.

—— (1986) 'Return in mercy to Zion: a messianic dream in Jewish art', in L. Hoffman (ed.) *The Land of Israel: Jewish Perspectives*, Notre Dame, University of Notre Dame Press, pp. 234–40.

Harrison, R.M. (1983) 'The church of St Polyeuktos in Istanbul and the Temple of Solomon', *Harvard Ukrainian Studies* 7: 277–9.

—— (1989) *A Temple for Byzantium*, London: Harvey Miller.

Hermann, W. (1967) 'Unknown designs for the "Temple of Jerusalem" by Claude Perrault', in D. Fraser *et al.* (eds) *Essays in the History of Architecture Presented to Rudolf Wittkower on his Sixty-fifth Birthday*, London: Phaidon Press, pp. 143–58.

Kalavrezou-Maxeiner, I. (1985) 'The Byzantine knotted column', in S. Vryonis, Jun. (ed.) *Byzantine Studies in Honor of Milton V. Anastos*, Malibu, Calif.: Undena Publications, pp. 95–103.

Krinsky, C.H. (1970) 'Representations of the Temple of Jerusalem', *Journal of the Warburg and Courtauld Institutes* 33: 1–19.

Nilgen, U. (1977) 'Das Fastigium der Basilika Constantiniana die Vier Bronzesäulen des Lateran', *Römische Quartalschrift* 72: 20–3.

Ouellette, J. (1976) 'The basic structure of Solomon's Temple and archaeological research,' in J. Gutmann, (ed.) *The Temple of Solomon: Archaeological Fact and Mediaeval Tradition in Christian, Islamic and Jewish Art*, Missoula, Mont.: Scholars Press, pp. 1–20.

Rabbat, N. (1989) 'The meaning of the Ummayad Dome of the Rock', *Muqarnas* 6: 12–21.

Renna, T. (1990) 'Bernard of Clairvaux and the Temple of Solomon', in B.S. Bachrach and D. Nicholas (eds) *Law, Custom and the Social Fabric in Medieval Europe, Essays in Honor of Bruce Lyon*, Kalamazoo: Medieval Institute Publications.

Reuther, H. (1980) 'Das Modell des Salomonischen Tempels im Museum für Hamburgische Geschichte', *Niederdeutsche Beiträge zur Kunstgeschichte* 19: 161–93.

Rosenau, H. (1972) 'Jacob Judah Leon Templo's contribution to architectural imagery', *Journal of Jewish Studies* 23: 72–81.

—— (1979) *Vision of the Temple. The Image of the Temple of Jerusalem in Judaism and Christianity*, London: Oresko Books.

Schein, S. (1984) 'Between Mount Moriah and the Holy Sepulchre: the changing traditions of the Temple Mount in the Central Middle Ages', *Traditio* 40: 175–95.

Scheja, G. (1962) 'Hagia Sophia und Templum Salomonis', *Istanbuler Mitteilungen* 12: 44–58.

Soucek, P. (1976) 'The Temple of Solomon in Islamic legend and art', in J. Gutmann (ed.) *The Temple of Solomon: Archaeological Fact and Mediaeval Tradition in Christian, Islamic and Jewish Art*, Missoula, Mont.: Scholars Press, pp. 73–124.

von Simson, O.G. (1956) *The Gothic Cathedral: The Origins of Gothic Architecture and the Medieval Concept of Order*, London: Routledge & Kegan Paul.

Waterman, L. (1943) 'The damaged "blueprints" of the Temple of Solomon', *Journal of Near Eastern Studies* 2: 284–94.

38 A horn of plenty

James Stevens Curl

Architects and architectural students rarely read: on the other hand they respond to images, and illustrations are the means by which architectural themes and motifs are disseminated. This was just as true in the last century, for William Burges (1827–81) himself was to write that he and his contemporaries all imbibed from the works of E.-E. Viollet-le-Duc (1814–79), 'although not one ... in ten ever (read) the text' (*Building News* 1865: 115, 225). Most Victorian architects absorbed 'Ruskinian' and other ideas by looking at appropriate pictures: Ruskin's notions about social and economic theory, and Viollet-le-Duc's 'Rationalism' were never truly grasped by architects (see Brooks 1989).

Eclecticism implies borrowing and, especially, borrowing from diverse sources, unencumbered by the niceties of one style or another; so it suggests a broad approach in matters of taste, although there might be pretensions to the choosing of the best points from a multitude of forms. Eclecticism is a virtual cornucopia, or horn of plenty, fabled to be the horn of the goat Amalthea by which the infant Zeus was suckled.

Professor J. Mordaunt Crook has noted that during the eighteenth century, considerations of the Picturesque multiplied the 'range of stylistic options' available to architects of the time (see Figure 1). He continues:

During the late nineteenth and early twentieth century, the problems created by the need to choose a style ... accelerated two complementary trends: the cult of eclecticism and the concept of modernity. The Modern Movement tried – and failed – to abolish style by abolishing choice. Post-Modernism – or rather Post-Functionalism – has recreated the

Figure 1 *A group of buildings in Devonport all designed by John Foulston (1772–1842) in order to produce a 'picturesque effect'. It shows a typical series of styles available to Regency architects, and includes a terrace of houses with a Roman Corinthian order, a town hall with a prostyle tetrastyle portico of the Greek Doric order, a commemorative Greek Doric column, a chapel in the 'Indian' style with vaguely Gothic overtones, and a library in the Egyptian revival style.* (Source: *author's collection*)

dilemma by resuscitating choice. Today the wheel of taste has turned full circle. The twentieth century has had to rediscover what the nineteenth century learned so painfully: eclecticism is the vernacular of sophisticated societies; architecture begins where function ends.

(Crook 1987: 11)

An Edwardian architect, faced with a multiplicity of stylistic choices, be they baroque, Surrey vernacular, northern Renaissance, or even neo-classical, at least had a solid grounding in draughting, history, and the orders which provided the tools, the dictionary, and the language with which to fashion architectural designs. The position today is rather different, for, although there is once more a free choice (after the tyranny of Modernism, when there was none), understanding of the languages and complexities of style needs to be painfully acquired. To judge from some current work, that acquisition is halting, slow, and only fractionally evident. Architectural illiteracy, encouraged by the free-for-all when non-architecture was *de rigueur*, promoted in the educational establishments, and applauded by the critics, cannot be reversed overnight.

No discussion of architecture, and of eclecticism in architecture, can avoid taking seriously the question of style: Pevsner (1961) noted that if a historian of architecture does not take style seriously he stops being a historian at all. During the Roman Empire architects drew on a wide variety of motifs for their designs (although the student would hardly think so from a study of the relevant chapters on Roman architecture in Banister Fletcher's *A History of Architecture*, even though that work has recently been revised (Musgrove and Farron 1987).[1] The syncretic processes by which Egyptian deities and mystery cults were absorbed into the fabric of the Empire also ensured that not only were Egyptian objects imported in great numbers into Italy, but that artefacts were made in Italy in the Egyptian style.[2] Couchant lions, sphinxes, canopic vases, obelisks, and cult statues were manufactured in huge quantities during the first four centuries of our era, and testify to the great importance of the Egyptian religion in the Roman Empire as well as to the popularity of Egyptianizing furnishings and ornaments among the members of polite society (see Curl 1982 and Roullet 1972).

One of the greatest of temples in Imperial Rome was the Isaeum Campense, part of which lies under the church of Santa Maria sopra Minerva, and we know from excavated fragments that its aedicules had segmental pediments with winged globes and *uraei*, as well as Egyptianizing capitals and *uraeus* friezes. The shape of the segmental pediment is suggested by the bow of Diana/Artemis (with whom the goddess Isis is identified) and by the crescent moon. Now the segmental pediment, which is such a common feature of classical architecture, does not occur before the first

century of our era, and is essentially associated with Isiac cults and with buildings used for the worship of Isis and her consort Osiris/Serapis. Processes of eclecticism simply absorbed the segmental pediment into the vocabulary of classical architecture (see Figure 2), and it became used over aedicules alternating with triangular pediments, losing its Egyptian connotations in the process (Gilbert 1942).[3]

Among the most remarkable architectural ensembles in which eclecticism played a major role was the Villa Adriana at Tivoli, with its deliberate allusions to parts of the Empire by means of architectural and landscape devices. The *Canopus*, for example, conjured Egypt, an association emphasized by the Egyptianizing Nemes-head-dressed statue of the Emperor's 'favourite' (as he is primly described), Antinoüs. This Antinoüs figure recurs not only in neo-classical statuary like the Coade Stone figures at Buscot Park near Faringdon, Oxfordshire, or the statue by Beauvallet at the fountain in the rue de Sèvres in Paris, but in the project by E.-L. Boullée (1728–99) for a cenotaph in the form of a gigantic sarcophagus, where a whole frieze of repetitive Antinoüs figures occurs under the 'lid' (Figure 3).[4]

Throughout the following centuries, eclecticism played an enormous part in architecture. One only has to consider Romanesque and Gothic buildings to see how widespread it is, and it was nothing to do with 'functionalism'. Publications during the Renaissance period gave the orders a status of immutability almost like holy writ, but many other aspects of decorative design were disseminated by means of the printed page. The colossal impact of 'Palladianism' can be ascribed to illustrations, notably in Colen Campbell's *Vitruvius Britannicus* (1715–71).

Richard Payne Knight (1750–1824) noted that in the landscapes of Claude and Poussin, Greek and Gothic co-

Figure 2 *Segmental pediment with winged globe and* uraei, *probably the crowning feature of an aedicule or niche. This is Roman work in the Egyptianizing style from the Isaeum Campense in Rome. Segmental pediments are Egyptianizing features that appear in classical architecture for the first time from the second half of the first century* AD *or the beginning of the second century* AD, *and are associated with the crescent moon (Isis/Artemis/Diana) and the bow of Artemis/Diana.* (Source: *Ägyptisches Museum, Staatliche Museen zu Berlin, No. 16785*)

Figure 3 *Project by E.-L. Boullée for a cenotaph for a national military hero. The building is in the shape of a huge classical sarcophagus from Antiquity, but the frieze is a repeated figure based on the Antinoüs figure from the Villa Adriana, which itself was a Roman work in the Egyptian Taste.* (Source: *Bibliothèque Nationale, Paris, H.A. 57 No. 27*)

existed happily, with no sense of incongruity, and he proceeded to create a Gothic house with a Grecian interior for himself at Downton Castle, Herefordshire, in the 1770s. He recognized that there was no such thing as 'pure' Gothic, and that Gothic, to him, was a corrupted Roman architecture anyway. The mixing of columnar-trabeated and arcuated forms had been pioneered by the Romans in their triumphal arches, the Theatre of Marcellus, and the Colosseum, and these precedents had influenced generations of Renaissance designers, including the lushly opulent creations of Sansovino in Venice.

Payne Knight's eclecticism was deliberate synthesis, and he anticipated the work of Thomas Hope (1769–1831), who mixed Gothic, Greek, Lombardic, Pompeiian and Tuscan elements at The Deepdene (see Watkin 1968), and created an astonishing essay in the Egyptian Taste at his house in Duchess Street, London. The real popularizer of eclecticism in the nineteenth century, however, was John Claudius Loudon (1783–1843), whose *Gardener's Magazine, Encyclopaedia of Cottage, Farm, and Villa Architecture,* and many other publications had a profound effect on Taste. Loudon was influenced by the theories of 'Architectural Associationism' as propounded by Archibald Alison (1757–1839), and proposed that style would die away because the multiplicity of styles he illustrated would create a *modern,* synthetic, almost unclassifiable, and style-less architecture. Although also influenced by Humphry Repton

(1752–1818), who was an eclectic, but who never proposed a synthesis of styles, Loudon associated a multiplicity of styles with different purposes. For example, he was to commend several works by John Dobson (1787–1865) – Schinkelesque chapels, entrance-gate, and lodge for the General Cemetery, Jesmond Road, Newcastle upon Tyne, for their severe neo-classical appearance, seeing the ensemble as expressive of its purpose (see Loudon 1843: 25, 115). Payne Knight, on the other hand, saw a mixing of styles as essentially modern, and went so far as to see his eclecticism as expressive of his own age and nation. Thus the notion of building 'for our own time', that mischievous phrase trotted out by the flabby of mind, derives from a period of eclecticism, in which modernity was seen as a synthesis of two or more styles. There is another aspect to all this, and that is that the eighteenth-century reverence for antiquity was not only a rediscovery of ancient Rome, then Greece, then Egypt, but of the past generally. One has only to think of Chinoiserie, or rococo Gothick, as shorthand evocations of ancient Cathay, Exoticism, or the Middle Ages, to make the connections and observe that there was indeed a wide choice of style in the various antiquities available.

Eclecticism had come a long way from Tivoli, but in the eighteenth century it was essentially part of the cult of the Picturesque, when pictorial values superseded ideas of absolutes, and when formal elements of the classical tradition were subordinated to the sensational, to associations, to composition, to the creation of interesting silhouettes, and to the illusion of utility. The Abbé Marc-Antoine Laugier (1713–69), in his *Essai sur L'Architecture* of 1753, proposed a rational view of a classical architecture derived from the 'primitive hut', in which elements such as columns would be expressed as such, rather than engaged with walls, but he also referred to apparent functions in the revised edition of the book (Laugier 1755), indicating that he knew full well the functional argument was shaky.

Eclecticism was evident in the architectural development of Munich under Crown Prince (later King) Ludwig (1786–1868) (see Watkin and Mellinghoff 1987). With his architect Leo von Klenze (1784–1864), he embellished the Bavarian capital with buildings such as the Propylaeum (Greek Doric with Graeco-Egyptian pylons at the top of which are square mullions derived from the Choragic Monument of Thrasyllus), the Glyptothek (Greek Ionic with Renaissance aedicules and vaulted polychrome interiors), the Pinakothek (Palazzo Cancellaria and Vatican Belvedere Courtyard), the Königsbau (Palazzo Pitti with pilaster system derived from the Palazzo Rucellai), and the Allerheiligenhofkirche (North Italian Romanesque, with an interior of Neo-Byzantine sumptuousness), all intended to create a museum of styles reminiscent of the plates in Jean-Nicolas-Louis Durand's *Recueil* (1800). Eclecticism had cultural and educational overtones already apparent in many examples of eighteenth-century garden design. At Wörlitz in Saxony, for example, Prince Franz of Anhalt-Dessau (1740–1817) and his architect, Friedrich Wilhelm Freiherr von Erdmannsdorff (1736–1800), created a park and *Schloss* between 1766 and 1799 which included an Anglo-Palladian house, an island with Rousseau cenotaph based on the Île des Peupliers at Ermenonville, a Villa Hamilton and rockwork[5] Vesuvius, a rockwork Labyrinth inscribed with the Masonic/Enlightenment exhortation to the wanderer 'to Choose His Path with Reason', a synagogue (to demonstrate lack of bigotry and adherence to liberal ideals), a Pantheon, a Temple of Flora, a Gothic house, an iron bridge based on the original in Shropshire, and much else (see Alex and Kühn 1988; see also Alex 1986 and Hempel 1987). Thus ideals of the Enlightenment, suggested in a wide eclecticism, are explicitly enshrined in this extraordinary and beautiful garden of allusions.[6]

Perhaps as interesting is Klenze's remarkable Walhalla, high above the Danube, a Greek Doric temple with tympana featuring Germania and her restored provinces after the War of Liberation of 1813–15, and the victory of Arminius over the Romans. Inside, where King Ludwig I presides in Roman toga over the marble portrait-busts of eminent Germans, the polychrome Ionic scheme is derived from Cockerell's restoration of the Temple of Apollo Epicurius at Bassae, but there are Caryatides too in bearskins representing the Valkyries who carry dead heroes to Valhalla. The programme here

is to create a place of secular pilgrimage to German achievement and nationhood, the victory over the Romans being associated with that of the Greeks over the Persians; and so Germany was compared with Greece, therefore the Greek style was appropriate for the monument (Watkin and Mellinghoff 1987).

In Berlin, too, Karl Friedrich Schinkel (1781–1841) used his own version of Greek Architecture to help to identify the Spartan qualities of Prussia with those of Ancient Greece in such buildings as the Neue Wache and the Museum in the Lustgarten. In the former he combined a modified Greek Doric with a square, fortress-like guard-house (planned asymmetrically inside), and in the latter he introduced a long Ionic colonnade *in antis*, and a circular, Pantheon-like hall set within a cubic block. At the Schauspielhaus (Figure 4) he merged a motif from the Choragic Monument of Thrasyllus with the square-columned temples of Ancient Egypt, but he also mixed exedrae, the *Rundbogenstil*, Greek themes, Neo-Gothic, and even a warehouse architecture derived from exemplars he had seen in England in 1826 in his massive *œuvre* for the Prussian monarchy and state. He experimented with Picturesque asymmetry at Schloss Babelsberg, but handled stereometrically pure forms of cube, drum, dome and apse with tremendous elan at the Nikolaikirche in Potsdam (Schinkel 1866; see also Curl 1991b,c). There can be no doubt that Schinkel was a master of eclecticism, and one of the greatest of architectural synthesizers.

Many experiments in eclecticism combined not only styles but also historic forms, with new materials. The University Museum in Oxford of 1854–60 (Figure 5), by Benjamin Woodward (1815–61) and the Deanes father and son, has Venetian Gothic windows, Veronese mouldings, Byzantinesque carving, a North European roof reminiscent of buildings in Ieper, Italianate polychromy, a laboratory based on the kitchens at Glastonbury Abbey, and an iron-and-glass structure within the central arcaded court. The design was considered

Figure 4 *Schauspielhaus in Berlin by Karl Friedrich Schinkel, showing the Greek Ionic portico and the square mullions derived from the Choragic Monument of Thrasyllus and from Egyptian square columns.* (Source: *author's collection*)

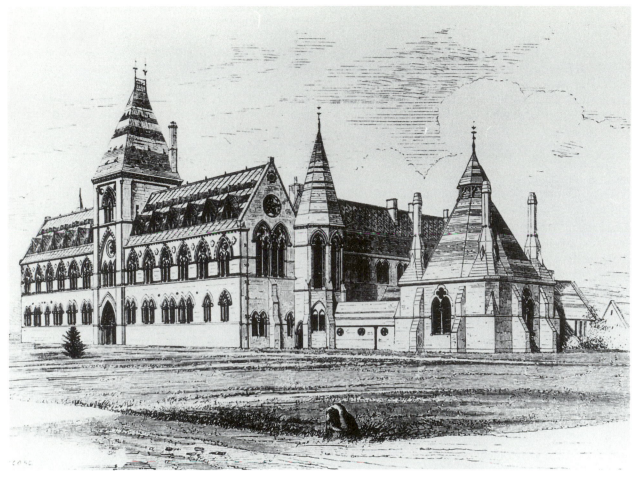

Figure 5 *University Museum, Oxford, 1854–60, by Deane and Woodward. It mixes elements from Italy, Flanders and England. On the right is the laboratory based on the Abbott's Kitchen at Glastonbury.* (Source: *author's collection*)

progressive, modern and educational, in that the building itself, with its different colonnettes and carvings, was a museum (Curl 1990a).

Alfred Waterhouse (1830–1905), too, with his Manchester Assize Courts of 1859 and his Town Hall of 1868–76, created buildings that were essentially of the nineteenth century (*Builder* 1868), synthesizing many elements in his free eclecticism, and adapting the Gothic elements to new conditions. With materials such as iron, glass, terracotta, and encaustic tiles, he produced buildings that are not copies of, and which cannot be confused with, medieval structures. So it is with William Butterfield (1814–1900), who mixed English Middle Pointed, German *Backsteingotik*, Tudor brick diaper patterns, and Italian polychromy in his masterly church of All Saints', Margaret Street (Curl 1990c). The design he evolved was startlingly new, for Butterfield created a perception of the past, and invented a new synthesis of styles, mixing them with great originality. He designed an urban minster, a citadel of faith, built of materials intended to withstand the ravages of the urban atmosphere and usage. Here is no feeble pot-pourri, garnered from medieval rural churches, but a powerful and vital

design, assured and tough, and brilliantly conceived for its site.

The fact that Italian Gothic was rather more of a hybrid, stylistically, than Northern European Gothic made it a model for many nineteenth-century architects to follow, but it did have the added attraction of built-in colour. In particular, its structural polychromy appealed to Victorian innovators, and, when Gothic freed architects from the tyranny of symmetry, it was perceived as the ideal style for the complex secular buildings required at the time. George Edmund Street (1824–81) saw in Continental Gothic, and especially in Italian Gothic, a prime element in a new eclectic synthesis that would mix the verticality of Pointed with the serenity of classical architecture (Street 1852). Street's Law Courts complex in the Strand combines elements from England, France, Italy, Spain, and Flanders with a strong dose of Burgundian toughness and Sienese layered structural colour. George Gilbert Scott (1811–78) mixed in Caledonian features in his buildings north of the border, while he gave a convincing performance in the German Gothic style at the Nikolaikirche in Hamburg.

High Victorian eclecticism, then, was an intelligent

and modern solution to different design and massing problems using materials such as brick, stone, iron, glass, terracotta, and faience, but it also responded to local conditions. Its quotations are rarely verbatim, and in fact it was free from the shackles of historical precision in its use of elements.

Yet from the records of lectures, from the copious printed sources, and from memoirs pours a constant stream of agonized doubt. Eclecticism had been seen as a way of arriving at a sound, consistent and original style, worthy of the nineteenth century (Crook 1987: 101), but it seemed to some that this was not happening. Victorian architects had to struggle daily with problems of function, form and style as the mechanical requirements of buildings increased in complexity in a way the eighteenth century never knew.

When Butterfield reduced his Gothic forms to their basics, and introduced the sash-window into ostensibly 'Gothic' buildings at Margaret Street and Milton Ernest Hall, Bedfordshire, he was heralding that freedom of mix which we so admire in the work of Philip Speakman Webb (1831–1915) and Richard Norman Shaw (1831–1912). The Gothic Revival had progressed from the accumulation of elements to a synthesis of eclectic forms, and wedded progressive concerns and historical precedents. Alexander James Beresford-Hope (1820–87) put his faith in progressive eclecticism, which he saw as combining Egyptian massiveness, Saracenic lightness, and Greek proportions, with Gothic as the main ingredient because Gothic was the universal style of Christian Europe. He also visualized a universal eclecticism suitable for the British Empire, in which the sources would be ever more broad and comprehensive. Eclecticism, however, to just about everyone, was a means to an end, a transitional phase that would lead to some sort of new style. Webb and Shaw, taking their cue from Butterfield, experimented with a 'Queen Anne' style, which within a few years brought English architectural expression back to classicism. In fact the last quarter of the nineteenth century is distinguished for its vast range of eclectic styles, leading firmly back to a revival of baroque forms, then to a reaction and neo-classicism (Curl 1990b).

And what of the situation today? It is quite clear that the architecture of the future merges themes from the present and the past after the failure of the Modern Movement to establish a 'functionalist' and international vernacular for architecture. The Modernist consensus fell apart in the 1970s, and in its place rose a diversity that recalls the end of the Gothic Revival and the rise of the free styles a century earlier. Architects are having to learn how to use languages they only dimly comprehend, for the Modernists destroyed not only the grammar and language of architecture, but the vocabulary as well.

Stirling's Staatsgalerie in Stuttgart is an example of modern eclecticism, but it is very odd and very different compared with the eclecticism of a century before. It has an Egyptian cavetto cornice, striped polychromy that recalls the Gothic Revivalist concerns with Sienese 'structural' colour, nods to the *Rundbogenstil* and to Giulio Romano, and parodies the primitive Doric of James Playfair (1755–94) at Cairness House, Aberdeenshire, or possibly the 1785 dockyard gate at Karlskrona by C.A. Ehrensvård (1745–1800).[7] Yet the eclecticism is somewhat jokey, and even the 'masonry' walls are only skins, applied to the structure.

The richly eclectic diversity of the latter half of the eighteenth century, exemplified at Wörlitz, has its parallels in the free, or progressive, eclecticism of the last twenty-odd years of the nineteenth century, and in what is haltingly happening today. Eclecticism is associated with freedom of choice, and with an open-minded view of society. Adherence to one approved style, or to the fiction of functionalism, indicates totalitarian tendencies. New Objectivity was a myth, but it was a dangerous myth, as unworthy of serious consideration as the parrot-cry of a 'building for our own time', used to justify crass insensitivity to context. Eclecticism is alive today, just as it was in Imperial Rome and during all the other creative phases of our civilization. It is a sign of health, not a cause to bewail. There is not that much originality around: it is what you do with the parts that count (see Figure 6).

Figure 6 *Mortuary Chapel at Arbroath, begun in 1875, by Patrick Allan-Frazer. A free eclectic mixture of Scottish and Continental medieval and Renaissance motifs, freely treated.* (Source: *author's collection*)

NOTES

1   In the revised version the chapters on the architecture of Antiquity virtually ignore the enormous number of publications that have shed new light on syntheticism in architecture, especially the Egyptian influences.
2   Discussed in detail in Curl 1982: 5–42.
3   Gilbert favoured the second century AD as the time when the segmental pediment came into its own. Evidence from Pompeii, however, suggests that it was used for Isiac buildings in the first century.
4   See Curl 1982, plates 5, 69 and 111.
5   Rockwork is grotto-work, or rough stone-work arranged to resemble natural outcrops of rocks, commonly found in eighteenth-century garden design. (It can also be a type of rusticated masonry, very rudely or roughly dressed as though it had been taken in partly natural state from the quarry, but it is, of course, contrived, and is often found on the plinths of classical façades or in garden-buildings. In this article, the term is used in the first sense.)
6   For developments of this theme see Curl 1991a.
7   Illustrated in the Catalogue of the Fourteenth Exhibition of the Council of Europe (Arts Council 1972: plate 103a).

REFERENCES

Alex, R. (ed.) (1986) *Friedrich Wilhelm von Erdmannsdorff 1736– 1800*, Wörlitz: Staatliche Schlösser und Gärten.

Alex, R. and Kühn, P. (1988) *Schlösser und Gärten um Wörlitz*, Leipzig: VEB E.A. Seeman Buch-und Kunstverlag.

Arts Council (1972) *The Age of Neo-Classicism*, Catalogue of the Fourteenth Exhibition of the Council of Europe, London: Arts Council of Great Britain.

Brooks, M.W. (1989) *John Ruskin and Victorian Architecture*, London: Thames & Hudson.

Builder (1868) 'The designs of Manchester Town Hall', *The Builder* XXVI: 259–62.

Building News (1865) *Building News* 12.

Campbell, C. (1715–71) *Vitruvius Britannicus; or, The British Architect, containing the plans, elevations, and sections of the regular buildings, both publick and private in Great Britain, with variety of new Designs ... by Colen Campbell*, London: The Author.

Crook, J.M. (1987) *The Dilemma of Style: Architectural Ideas from the Picturesque to the Post Modern*, London: John Murray.

Curl, J.S. (1982) *The Egyptian Revival: An Introductory Study of a Recurring Theme in the History of Taste*, London: George Allen & Unwin.

—— (1990a) *Victorian Architecture*, Newton Abbot: David & Charles.

—— (1990b) 'All Saints', Margaret Street', *Architects' Journal* 191 (25) 36–55.

—— (1991a) *The Art and Architecture of Freemasonry: An Introductory Study*, London: Batsford.

—— (1991b) 'Altes Museum Berlin' *Architects' Journal* 193 (25): 30–49.

—— (1991c) 'Charlottenhof, Potsdam', *Architects' Journal* 194 (4–5): 22–39.

Durand, J.-N.-L. (1800) *Recueil et parallèle des édifices de tout genre anciens et modernes, remarquables par leur beauté, par leur grandeur, ou par leur singularité, et dessinés sur une même échelle*, Paris: Impr. Gillé, an IX.

Gilbert, P. (1942) 'Le Fronton Arrondi en Égypte et dans l'art Gréco-Romain', *Chronique d'Égypte: Bulletin Périodique de la Fondation Égyptologique Reine Élisabeth*, Brussels: Musées Royaux du Cinquantenaire, Year 17, pp. 83–90.

Hempel, D. (ed.) (1987) *Friedrich Wilhelm von Erdmansdorff: Leben, Werk, Wirkung*, Wörlitz: Staatliche Schlösser und Gärten.

Laugier, M.-A. (1755) *Essai sur l'architecture*, Paris: Duchesne.

Loudon, J.C. (1843) *On the Laying Out, Planting, and Managing of Cemeteries, and on the Improvement of Churchyards*; reprinted 1981, with an introduction by J.S. Curl, Redhill: Ivelet Books.

Musgrove, J. and Farron, J. (eds) (1987) *Sir Banister Fletcher's A History of Architecture*, London: Butterworth.

Pevsner, N. (1961) 'The return of historicism in architecture', *The Listener* LXV (16 February): 299–301.

Roullet, A. (1972) *The Egyptian and Egyptianizing Monuments of Imperial Rome*, Leiden: E.J. Brill.

Schinkel, K.F. (1866) *Sammlung Architektonischer Entwürfe*, Berlin: Ernst und Korn.

Street, G.E. (1852) 'The true principle of architecture, and the possibility of development', in *The Ecclesiologist*, Vol. XIII (new series X), London: Joseph Masters, pp. 246–62, esp. p. 253.

Watkin, D. (1968) *Thomas Hope and the Neo-Classical Idea*, London: John Murray.

Watkin, D. and Mellinghoff, T. (1987) *German Architecture and the Classical Ideal 1740–1840*, London: Thames & Hudson.

39 The uses of architectural history today

Derek Linstrum

Once upon a time there was only Banister Fletcher, the big blue bible first published in 1896, in which we were told that architecture is:

> essentially a human art as well as an affair of material.... It ... provides a key to the habits, thoughts and aspirations of the people, and without a knowledge of this art the history of any period lacks that human interest with which it should be invested.... The study of Architecture opens up the enjoyment of buildings with an appreciation of their purpose, meaning and charm
>
> (Fletcher 1938: 18)

The last sentence is as true today as when it was written, although 'charm' has a curiously period ring, and the objective of the study seems a little limited. However, human interest, enjoyment, purpose and meaning are still relevant goals. Banister Fletcher is still with us, now in its nineteenth edition, although the lovely blue and gold Art Nouveau design of the binding is no longer used, and we do not have the wonderfully simplified but decorative 'Tree of Architecture' to welcome us under its spreading branches on the first page; but we do still have the familiar line drawings which are an essential part of the book's image and which once represented architectural history to the majority of architects in the English-speaking world.

How different the situation is today when we look at what is available in print. Few major figures have not been accorded the distinction of a monograph, and many minor figures have been handsomely treated too. Such subjects as the English country house have reached saturation point. Many regions and major cities have been thoroughly researched and documented: Sir Nikolaus Pevsner's *The Buildings of England* series (1951 onwards) is being supplemented by those of Scotland, Ireland and Wales. Building types and materials have received their share of attention and influential movements and organizations have been studied. Some of this has been the result of scholarship for its own sake – an entirely praiseworthy activity; but that accounts for only a part of this upsurge of research and publication.

A significant change has been a move away from architectural history as one of styles, and instead there has been a relating to the society that produced it and

for which it was produced. There has been a greater interest in understanding an architect's thought process in designing, and in his or her working methods. Another change has been the greater tendency to place individual buildings within their physical environment, and to examine the lesser and more common buildings within that environment. Hence the enormous increase in studies of vernacular and industrial buildings.

But all this activity, this increase in knowledge, this widening and deepening of the scope of architectural history, must be seen as complementing two other tendencies. One is the growth of conservation, first as a process of pressure and a popular movement, and then as a respectable professional activity enshrined in our legislation and so imposing certain duties and obligations. Architects, planners and conservation officers need to know what they are dealing with. So do the craftspeople whose traditional skills were rapidly being lost in the long interval between the 1930s and the 1970s before conservation became firmly established as an element in professional practice. The second tendency has been the widespread rejection of the belief that 'Modern Architecture', or what passed for it, can provide an automatic design solution, although sometimes this rejection has been as unthinking and without understanding as an earlier generation's rejection and destruction of Victorian architecture.

And so in the field of new design there has been a backward look at precedents and principles, as well as at pediments and pillars. There has been a remembrance of things past which in its realized form has required a better understanding of history – even if we might think this is sometimes a superficial assemblage of elements rather than either a scholarly exercise or a creative reinterpretation.

There has also been a growing tendency once again to claim links with the past, as if to establish a respectable and legitimate pedigree. The 1986 Royal Academy show devoted to the work of Foster, Rogers and Stirling made far from obvious references to similarities between new designs and historical precedents (Royal Acadamy of Art Catalogue 1986). 'In order to progress we need to seek a greater understanding of the past,' confirming Richard Rogers in his television programme, *A Modernist View* (November 1988), while Quinlan Terry, two weeks previously, had chosen in *The Rejected Alternative* a return to order rather than progress as his interpretation of the lessons of history; both agreed those lessons could not be ignored.

It seems that each generation wishes to claim

This essay is a revised and shortened version of the David Saunders Memorial Lecture read to the Society of Architectural Historians of Australia and New Zealand at the University of Adelaide in May 1987.

dependence on the past. Le Corbusier confessed 'to having had only one master – the past; and only one discipline – the study of the past' (Le Corbusier 1930: 34). Sir Joshua Reynolds recommended his students to study 'the great masters . . . for . . . it is by being conversant with the inventions of others that we learn to invent' (Reynolds 1975: 98). Sir Christopher Wren liked to think that when working on an old building he was doing so in agreement with 'the original Scheme of the old Architect, without any modern Mixtures to shew my own Inventions (Wren 1750: 302). Such advice implies a perceptive knowledge of history, as does Viollet-le-Duc's recommendation that in such cases the best plan 'is to suppose one's self in the position of the original architect, and to imagine what he would do' (Viollet-le-Duc 1896: 32).

It was in 'The Lamp of Memory' that Ruskin laid down two duties on an architect 'whose importance it is impossible to overrate; the first, to render the architecture of the day, historical', and the second 'to preserve, as the most precious of inheritances, the architecture of past ages' (Ruskin 1849: 164). At no time since 1849 has the latter been so widely proclaimed as it is today as a desirable, indeed obligatory, professional duty; and yet it cannot be divorced from the first duty, and in both it might be thought that illumination can come not only from the 'lamp of memory' but even more brilliantly from the 'lamp of truth'. It is a platitude to say that history is about truth; but that is what must be an ideal. Yet truth has many facets, and depending on who we are and why we are examining this precious stone we shall see different facets.

In suggesting the uses of architectural history today, we can begin at the level of investigation, at the basic need to understand our building whether we are historians, archaeologists, architects, skilled artisans or teachers. In the work of the professional investigator, the compiler of inventories, we ought to be nearer than in any other work to an objective assessment, in which we shall be using all the documentary sources that are available to help us to discover the truth about the building, its dating, the genesis of the design, the changes that have occurred to it. But then we use the plain, unvarnished tale in order to interpret its significance and what it represents. We begin to consider its artistic value, its relative rarity, its associations, its symbolic quality. And in doing this we need to have a wider knowledge and understanding of other buildings of the same date, by the same architect, of the same type. To the archival investigation we are adding the historical investigation, and the relatively simple truth begins to be more complicated as layers of interpretation are added to it. We can still have objectivity as our goal. We must have. But why are we engaged on the exercise? This is where we open the windows of our ivory tower to the real world, to the architects and planners in the courtyard, to the private clients and commerical developers at the gate, to the building contractors and craftspeople in their workshops, and to the public at large. What do they all make of architectural history? How do they use it? How is it used to benefit them?

Now if we consider the world of architectural practice we find two distinct activities. There are those that come within the general definition of conservation, that is, work to an existing building of architectural or historical quality, or the design of a new building in an existing historical context, or the design of a new context around a historical building. And here we find a wide range, from a careful restoration of a building to its original appearance at some time in its history, through the relatively straightforward repairs which do not change its appearance, to an adaptation to a new use. But whichever activity it is – even the last, which might involve dramatic changes – a detailed knowledge of the building is an essential prerequisite. Obviously a historical assessment prepared objectively on the basis of available documentation can be a great advantage, which becomes a tool to be used in conjunction with an architect's investigation; but that architect's research of the building itself, of its structure, of its construction, of its materials, is of equal importance. The architect's professional knowledge and experience of the behaviour of structures and materials will add other facets of that truth we are looking for. But his or her research and detailed inspection will be a complementary extension of the documentary history. In an ideal world each will confirm the other.

It has sometimes been suggested that an intimate knowledge of a building's history and its condition will more or less automatically suggest potential solutions to defects that have been identified; and up to a point this may be true. It is like the relationship between someone and his or her personal physician, who has the patient's history plainly in view. But it would be misleading to think that, as on a computer screen, a specification will be instantaneously revealed by pressing the button marked 'Truth'. But we might imagine another button marked 'History', which acts as a caution. Once destroyed, historic fabric has gone for ever, and so has all the evidence contained within it; that is obvious, and the simplest rule is to accept that the latest state of the building is the truth. That is the best documented truth, as revealed by the fabric itself. But that present state will not necessarily suit the present requirements or the possibilities of the building's economically sound future. Or it might be an unacceptable falsification of the original concept because of later alterations; or it might be an impractical building. There might be various reasons why that nice simple idea of minimal repair cannot be the answer, and that is when architectural history ought to be a principal witness in decision-making, because the scale of permissible latitude ought to be based on knowledge of the building's quality and historical significance, and on a recognition of authenticity in the fabric itself.

There is a long tradition of the architect as historian – Sir Christopher Wren was curious enough about the origins of Gothic architecture to attempt to elucidate it even though he was not especially sympathetic to it; and until relatively recently all architectural history was written by architects – and very well they did it. An architect can bring a special knowledge to his or her investigation as well as an understanding of how architectural predecessors thought about their design problems, taking into account current limitations, and how they organized the preparation of drawings and the control of the building work. But it must also be recognized that by the very nature of their vocation and training they are primarily creators rather than conservators. So are craftspeople, who would rather recarve than consolidate and repair decaying stonework, rather replace old timber than treat it for beetle or rot, rather regild than accept worn gold leaf.

Nevertheless, those aspects of architectural history which relate to building materials, the applied arts and furnishings are now perceived to be of great importance both as history and for their use in conservation. Pattern books and technical manuals have been thoroughly researched, so that today's craftspeople can follow exactly the same information and instructions as their predecessors. Historical research has given us details about textiles, furnishings generally, the way to drape a window or arrange the chairs, the manner in which a room was lit and heated. And if we go outside the building we are now much better informed about the plants and trees that were available at a given date, the sort of edging a path might have had, and all the other details of garden design. Architectural history, and its sisters furniture and garden history, have in theory made the present generation better informed and better prepared to undertake work on existing buildings – Ruskin's first duty to preserve.

But what about the second duty to 'the architecture of the day'? What can architectural history offer the creative architect? Looking at some recent designs we might remember Ruskin and how he upbraided one of his audiences by accusing them of sending for him 'that I may tell you the leading fashion; and what is, in our shops, for the moment, the newest and sweetest thing in pinnacles' (Ruskin 1866: 53). We have only to change the word 'pinnacles' with its Gothic connotations to one more suitably classical to feel the same comment could be made today. But the trend in favour of traditional architecture as a reaction to the Modern Movement was noted more than thirty years ago by Henry Russell Hitchcock. He wrote how the broadening of 'the canons of the permissible and the desirable' was leading 'by current theory and practice towards various aspects of what may still be called the traditional'. He recognized in 1958 how 'to some critics certain earlier urban conditions, against whose vices the ideals of the 20s were first invoked as correctives, have come to seem, by nostalgia, preferable in various human ways to the "brave new world" of the 1920s which has, to such a surprising extent, become the real world of the 1960s' (Hitchcock 1963: 442–3).

Hitchcock was foreseeing the widespread reaction to 'Modern Architecture' which was to come. But already one work of architectural history, Rudolf Wittkower's *Architectural Principles in the Age of Humanism* (1949), had exerted a surprisingly profound influence in some architectural circles. The harmonic proportions, geometrical perfection and intellectual discipline of Alberti and Palladio seemed to offer a possible direction in which the tired cliché of form and function might be placed, according to Peter Reyner Banham, in a 'significant relationship to objective and eternal laws governing the Cosmos', offering architects 'a way out of the doldrum of routine functionalist abdication' (Banham 1955: 358). Even if this influence was greater on student projects than on executed designs, it reintroduced some important principles. So did Sir John Summerson's influential little book, *The Classical Language of Architecture*, which first appeared in 1963 to accompany six broadcast talks. The 1980 revised edition ends on a new note by questioning if the Modern Movement is dead, but then observing that this is the first really inspiring idea since the Movement was born. 'It is, anyway, liberating. It means that there may be, once again, some point in discussing architectural language, in trying to define the nature and value of ornament and entering into the whole question of architecture as a vehicle of social meaning. . . . The understanding of [classical architecture] will surely remain one of the most potent elements in architectural thought' (Summerson 1980: 114). Arthur Drexler, who edited the publication resulting from the 1975–6 exhibition mounted by the Museum of Modern Art in New York on *The Architecture of the Ecole des Beaux-Arts*, made a similar point. 'Some Beaux-Arts problems, among them the question of how to use the past, may perhaps be seen now as possibilities that are liberating rather than constraining' (Drexler 1977: 8)

'Liberating' is, coincidentally or not, the word used by both historians; and architectural design over the last decade has revealed without any doubt that, as always after a liberation, there has been a reaction. Neo-Rational, Neo-Realist, Neo-Vernacular, Neo-almost anything seems to be in order within a wide-spreading Post-Modernist umbrella, provided that it can find a literary advocate. Then there is the new classical revival, which its zealous adherents claim is a complete programme for all architecture, rather than just another style.

What is the role of the architectural historian in all this? He or she can observe, note, stand aloof and wait until it is time to write about the architectural scene in the 1980s. But if we can foresee a future for the present genuine interest in reviving traditional architectural values, then there must be an important role in architectural education. In an ideal programme history should be all-pervasive, the primary basic element, with a positive contribution right across the curriculum. It is not an isolated subject to be confined to a weekly lecture period and then dropped once an examination has been passed. But are architectural historians equipped and ready to accept such an implied role? There is a need for historians who will provide the objective facts, the truth so far as can be ascertained, as discussed earlier. But there is also a need for architect/historians who can communicate with students on the drawing board, who know how designs evolve, how structures and materials behave, as well as being conversant with the grammar of classical composition and the well-tried theories of proportion and harmony. Indeed, the art of communication is a necessity in the wider world to which architectural history has been introduced. The opening of historic buildings to visitors and the growth of interested participation in questions of conservation have, in their different ways, brought a variety of people within the orbit of architectural history and stimulated a desire for knowledge that needs to be satisfied with accuracy, but painlessly and enjoyably. The opportunities for stimulating presentation and popular education are unlimited.

It is all a far cry from the big blue bible and Banister Fletcher's line drawings which, as Bruce Allsopp said, made 'all buildings, of all ages and sizes . . . look more or less alike' (Allsopp 1979: 67). And it is equally a far cry from the dark days of the 1950s when many schools of architecture dismissed history as irrelevant and removed it from their curricula. Now the situation is reversed to some extent; history has become a part of general professional practice, and to some people 'real architecture' means columns and pediments (Catalogue of the Building Centre 1987). A historian should never be surprised, but it seems as if history once again has been recognized as having a profound influence in the realization of Ruskin's definition of an architect's two duties.

REFERENCES

Allsopp, B. (1979) *The Study of Architectural History,* London: Studio Vista.

Banham, P. Reyner (1955) 'The new brutalism', *Architectural Review* 118: 355–61.

Building Centre (1987) *Real Architecture,* catalogue, London: Building Centre.

Drexler, A. (ed.) (1977) *The Architecture of the Ecole des Beaux-Arts,* London: Secker & Warburg.

Fletcher, B. (1938) *A History of Architecture on the Comparative Method,* 10th edn, London: Batsford.

Hitchcock, H.-R. (1963) *Architecture: Nineteenth and Twentieth Centuries,* Harmondsworth: Penguin.

Le Corbusier (1930) *Précisions sur un Etat Présent de l'Architecture et de l'Urbanisme,* 1960 edn, Paris: Vincent Freal & Cie.

Pevsner, N. (1951 onwards) *the Buildings of England,* Harmondsworth: Penguin.

Reynolds J. (1975) *Discourses on Art,* ed. R.R. Wark, London: Yale University Press.

Rogers, R. (1988) 'A Modernist View', in *Visions of Britain* series, TV, 20 November.

Royal Academy of Arts (1986) *New Architecture: Foster Rogers Stirling,* catalogue, London: Royal Academy of Arts.

Ruskin, J.(1849) *The Seven Lamps of Architecture,* London: Smith, Elder.

—— (1866) *The Crown of Wild Olive,* London: Smith, Elder.

Summerson, J. (1980) *The Classical Language of Architecture,* London: Thames & Hudson.

Terry, Q. (1988) 'The Rejected Alternative', in *Visions of Britain* series, TV, 6 November.

Viollet-le-Duc, E. (1896) *Dictionnaire Raisonné de l'Architecture Française,* Vol. VIII, Paris: Morel.

Wittkower, R. (1949) *Architectural Principles in the Age of Humanism,* London: Tiranti.

Wren, S. (ed.) (1750) *Parentalia,* London; reprinted 1965, Farnborough: Gregg Press.

40 Architectural history and archaeology: an understanding relationship?

Peter Fowler

INTRODUCTION

Architectural history is a significant but small part of the academic discipline of archaeology. The considerable potential of the two subjects together in furthering the study of the past must be based on this assertion, especially if it is accepted that one of the purposes of such study is to help understand not only the past but also the present, now and in future.

It is significant in itself that a professor of archaeology, rather than of architecture, should be invited to contribute this chapter. The invitation, well meant and gladly accepted, nevertheless continues the conventional academic tradition that the two subjects are indeed different and unequal (archaeologists should know about architectural history but architectural historians do not need to know about archaeology). That tradition is set in tablets for all to see in, for example, the volumes of Pevsner's *Buildings of England* series.

There, an 'Introduction' characteristically contains a nod towards pre-Saxon times, almost like clearing the road of minor obstacles before the real procession parades its pomp. Sometimes the 'Archaeology' of the county under review is fuller. Pevsner's *Wiltshire* (1963), for example, was published 'With Notes on the Prehistoric and Roman Antiquities' announced on the title page. By p. 57, as if with some uncertainty as to what this strange bedfellow was, they had become an 'Introduction to the Prehistoric and Roman Remains'. All is explained, however, on p. 14: 'for many visitors Wiltshire means Stonehenge and Avebury rather than even Salisbury. So a special introduction to Wiltshire prehistory and Roman Wiltshire was called for'. That Stonehenge and Avebury might conceivably be 'architecture' clearly never occurred to the author or editors. Indeed, the county's architecture gets off to a slow start altogether for, furthermore, 'Wiltshire is poor in Anglo-Saxon remains' (Pevsner 1963: 15).

To be fair, in *Wiltshire*'s case and elsewhere, such summaries were, and in some cases still are, useful syntheses of a sort of archaeology up to a date somewhere between Romans and Normans. Their implicit parameter, however, is not just that 'archaeology' is something with a definite upper date-limit but also, and more fundamentally, that it happens before, and is something exclusive of, the study of buildings including the history of architecture. Such a view is of course misinformed and quite unacceptable.

THE DISCIPLINES AS TAUGHT

Assumptions about the relationship between architectural history and archaeology also persist in another, perhaps even more influential, field: that is, in the way in which teaching and research in the two subjects are organized in separate departments in universities. By and large, there is no place for archaeology in schools of architecture, largely, one suspects, because of the anachronistic perception of the former as concerned only with digging and with early, 'pre-architectural' times and material. Thus, for example, standing Classical structures are architecture, not archaeology, while a Neolithic chambered tomb is archaeology and not architecture. Such a false dichotomy is not a problem from the archaeological point of view in which *all* fabricated structures are evidence.

Not only was there, obviously, architecture in Roman Britain as elsewhere in the Empire but major structures designed and built to visual and aesthetic effect were a characteristic of prehistoric societies in Britain and elsewhere in the world over some three thousand years and more before that (Fowler and Sharp 1990; Sherratt 1980).

One of my more stimulating teaching experiences was as guest lecturer over several years at the Architectural Association, London. At that time, in the mid-1970s, the experience was particularly interesting. On the one hand, students were being encouraged to disregard historical precedent intellectually and the rigours of graphic discipline technically. On the other, the discipline of archaeology was simultaneously expanding almost exponentially in its theoretical range while at the same time imposing a more and more demanding technical competence on its increasingly professional practitioners. A little later, when I was Secretary to the Royal Commission on Historical Monuments (England) (RCHME), the results of this divergence were all too apparent (Fowler 1981).

COMMON GROUND AND DIFFERENCES

Despite this traditional separatism, in practice the two fields of study have in some respects already moved closer together. A basis for a common future probably lies in this development. A brief exploration of the theory and objectives of the two disciplines is, however, first desirable. Since the whole of this book is about the nature of architecture, including its own history, little need be added here except from an archaeological point of view. If architectural history is concerned to study buildings in terms both of their individual histories and of their place in the evolution of style, two of its particular characteristics are presumably to relate such history to named individuals and to make aesthetic judgements, both in isolation and comparatively. While the first two objectives are common to an archaeological approach, the latter two are not fundamental in archaeology. Both are of course elements to be taken into account and used interpretatively where present, but neither is of primary concern in assessing evidence. A building is a mass of archaeological evidence, about which a lot can be said and inferred, whether or not its owner is known or its form is pleasing. So there is a difference in emphasis here, reflecting the contemporary theoretical bases of the two disciplines.

Yet, of course, historically both share common origins in the same antiquarian strain of post-Renaissance European scholarship. They developed from that all-embracing 'curiositie' which wrestled with 'Remains' on the ground and the concepts of a pre-classical and, especially in Britain, of a pre-Roman antiquity in the mind (Piggott 1989). Scholars in this mould before the mid-nineteenth century coped also with the practical demands of catholic enquiry in fields which we would now regard, but they did not, as diverse, wide-ranging and specialist. It is we, not they, who label as separate such as genealogy, armorials, (noble) family history, forklore, geology, natural history, classics, antiquities (archaeology), and architectural history.

Before the intellectual upheavals that worked through the second half of the nineteenth century, all such were conceptually one to the scholar. He would, perhaps inspired by a 'Grand Tour', work out and record for posterity the details of the descent and armorials of a family, of the buildings of its ancestral home, and of the natural history and antiquities of the surrounding countryside. 'I think I might collect matter enough,' wrote Gilbert White while preparing his *Natural History of Selborne* for publication (1789), 'especially as to the ornithological part. . . . To these might be added some circumstances of the Country, its most curious plants, its few antiquities, all of which might soon be moulded into a work.' His friend, The Revd John Mulso, urged him not to 'take too much time in ascertaining the Size, the Marketts, the Tolls, the Souls, the Priories, & religious Houses of Selbourne', adding later, 'I fear the sweet & elegant Simplicity of your Observations will be overwhelmed by the Rubbish of the Antiquities'. When published complete with 'the Rusts & Crusts & Frusts of Time', the work was, however, immediately praised by Mulso who wrote, 'As to the Antiquities, you have given to them such a Grace in your manner of treating the subject' (White 1950: 14–15).

Such holistic achievement by one person is something lost in the last four generations. Yet surely a capacity to reclaim the intellectual integration that lay behind it must be an objective of joint endeavour in the still-too-separate academic disciplines of architectural history and archaeology.

LANDSCAPE ARCHAEOLOGY

In fact, such is already happening. The development may be pragmatically led, but doubtless theory is not far behind. One particularly useful concept is 'landscape archaeology', in essence what Gilbert White was attempting as the, to him, natural way of investigating a particular area. Hoskins (1955) reinvented the approach, paving the way for what is now over a generation's extremely active and productive work. The resultant widely relevant concepts and changed appreciation of the English landscape are synthesized in Taylor's introduction to, and commentary on, Hoskins (1988). (It is essential that any newcomer to the field starts with this version since, great work though the original was, inevitably the research it inspired has shown it to be conceptually flawed and factually wrong in numerous respects.)

Basic to the approach is that as much evidence as possible be taken into account in trying to elucidate how the present landscape has come about (e.g. Taylor 1983). Buildings of all sorts are therefore included with everything else and, while this approach may not initially elucidate the detail of a change in the moulding on a baluster of the country house's back stairs in the eighteenth century, it has the great virtue of providing a whole series of contexts in which the origins, evolution, relationships and present state of any one building can be viewed and indeed questioned. And by the phrase 'any one building' is not meant only the major edifice in a landscape: *any* building, indeed any structure whether or not it be regarded as 'architecture', is initially as relevant evidentially as any other. To begin by looking only for the 'biggest' or the 'best', or to start by labelling some buildings 'important' or 'pleasing' is to beg questions and even risk wrong assessments from the start.

To do exactly that has of course been a tendency in archaeology as well as in architectural history; witness the concentration of work and publications on particular, 'obviously important' monuments such as Stonehenge (Chippindale 1983) and King's College Chapel (RCHME 1959: 105–31). If the practice of landscape archaeology has taught us anything it is that while, as the result of a *scientific* mode of enquiry, we may hope to identify and interpret sites important in their time, nothing is obvious. Indeed, on the one hand, the 'obvious' is often misleadingly so; on the other, investigation of the context of what appears to be the 'obvious' monument can significantly change perception of it. Again, Stonehenge is a classic example (RCHME 1979; Chippindale *et al.* 1990; Richards 1990).

CONTEXT

The landscape approach is but one manifestation of a wider syndrome of which the key element is context. The value as a piece of evidence of an individual potsherd is enhanced by the exact recording not only of its position in a particular excavated context but also of all its relationships to everything else in that and associated contexts. So too, for example, is the interest of an individual item of furniture enhanced if its original place at one moment of time in a particular room in a specific house is known. Archaeology and architectural history are methodologically at one here.

Similarly, a class of artefact, and indeed of something a little less tangible such as 'style', in, for example, La Tène art (Megaw and Megaw 1989) and English Palladianism (RCHME 1988), can also be studied in context, though of course the contexts themselves can vary. In those examples, that of the former is in cultural and technological as much as in artistic terms, and that of the latter is 'The National Context' and 'Some Wiltshire Houses'. Wilton House and its *comparanda* could clearly be considered and presented differently if studied in another – but equally legitimate – context, and that such has been and is being done *in addition to* (not instead of) mainstream architectural history is surely to be encouraged.

CHURCHES

Parish churches lie in the heartlands of architectural history and voluminous is their literature. They lend themselves to individual consideration; the parish is their obvious context. RCHME (1987) tried, not entirely successfully, to break out of this model in south Wiltshire; its relative failure lay in starting with the monuments rather than in asking questions other than 'what have we physically-surviving here?' Quite a good question is 'Why is it here?', for a whole approach and a consequent investigative methodology follow.

Morris (1989: 2) writes 'Archaeology ... has recently emerged as a generous provider of new knowledge about churches'. He could have been referring to the results from the now numerous excavations in and around ecclesiastical buildings, ranging from York Minster (RCHME 1985a) to chapels (generally Rodwell 1989). The application of this particular archaeological method of enquiry to churches has not just modified but has drastically altered perceptions, especially of early structural phases and of their non-ecclesiastical predecessors. Or Morris could have been referring to intensive, above-ground structural investigations of churches, for example those by RCHME in Northamptonshire (1984 and *forthcoming*). They too are adding to knowledge in a way different from that of conventional architectural recording hitherto.

In fact, however, Morris's book is about something else. 'There is', he correctly observes, 'one aspect of the parish church which up to now has been largely overlooked. This is ... the parish church as a place, a component of the pattern of settlement, and churches together as a pattern of places.' As but one example of the results of this approach, the fifty-two isolated churches in western Suffolk may serve:

> at least 35 stand beside existing halls or moated sites.... To claim all of these as the successors to pre-Conquest halls would be unjustified. But most of the churches in this area were in position by 1086, and the possibility that many of them adjoined the homes of local power-holders is an hypothesis that goes further than any other to explain the positions of most medieval churches in [this] landscape'
>
> (Morris 1989: 274).

This would seem to suggest lines of approach different from those of conventional architectural history, yet surely the reasons for a building, church or otherwise, being where it is ought to be at least as interesting as details of its decoration.

To say as much is not to criticize the studies of architectural historians as such for, consistently and properly, they have addressed major questions by their own terms of reference; but it does mean that materials of architectural history can be questioned as legitimately in other ways and about other themes. It would be a pity if such were done entirely by non-architectural historians.

VERNACULAR ARCHITECTURE

The example of churches is but one type of building considered nationally in space as a contrast to all types of evidence in one small area. The approach need not of course be confined to 'obvious' architecture of the sort represented by ecclesiastical buildings and great houses. The relatively new field of vernacular architecture, developing largely outside the traditional confines of an art historical approach, has from the start been much more open to the influences of historical research, archaeology and the social sciences. Wood's intention with *The English Medieval House* 'to reflect the social history of England' (Wood 1965: xxv) was echoed a decade later in the stated purpose of the pioneer, heavyweight academic study in the field: 'to relate changes in the nature of small rural dwellings to changing social relationships in the countryside in such a way that each may be made to say something about the other' (RCHME 1975: xvii). The Welsh counterpart opens expansively with a high-powered rationale on the subject of vernacular architecture in general, ending 'Thus while the architectural historian cannot often supply a precise chronicle, the themes he deals with are vital, and can have a greater bearing on the life of the people than the *minutiae* of historical narration' (RCAMW 1975: 5).

Building on such social and economic aspirations

from the start rather than only recording for recording's sake or making judgements of an aesthetic nature, this approach had already developed strongly in the work of Fox and Raglan (1951–4) and Barley (1967). Research in this field has moved rapidly from *merely* data-collecting (though that is essential and continues) to addressing major historical themes or at least to seeking to illuminate them regionally (e.g. Gailey 1984, Beaton *et al.* 1989).

Models in this respect are RCHME 1985b and 1986a. The former aims to consider the rural houses of the Lancashire Pennines between 1560 and 1760 'as historical documents which contribute to our understanding of the economic and social history of the area in the pre-industrial period' (RCHME 1985b: 1); the latter 'employs the house primarily as evidence for the evolution of rural society in the late and post-medieval periods, that is, as a valid historical source which can throw new light on old problems and suggest conclusions which more conventional documentary sources fail to illumine' (RCHME 1986a: xviii) The latter is in fact a good definition of the archaeological approach to anything, whether or not documentary sources are available. Barley (1961) in particular showed, nevertheless, in a way long-recognized by architectural historians, the crucial importance of documentary evidence to an understanding of how, in this case post-medieval, buildings were used. His influence remains strong in archaeologically based studies.

There is no archaeological antipathy to documentary evidence as such; problems of interpretation apart, its limitation is merely that it is unavailable for most of time and inappropriate to answering, indeed unable even to pose, certain questions about human behaviour in historic times. So it is extremely helpful that buildings have locked within themselves, individually and collectively, an evidential value in historical terms, just like any other material evidence considered as such, regardless of documents. Indeed, one school of archaeological thought argues, with a logic seeking objectivity, that such evidence should be recorded and assessed on its own terms without reference to written evidence.

The archaeology of the nineteenth- and twentieth-century English terraced house, still standing in its thousands, may seem an unlikely topic, but it is one in effect explored, in a sense within the vernacular architecture tradition exemplified above, by Muthesius (1982). He asked, stressing the need to use documentary sources, 'What happened before the house was built, who were the developers and builders, what was the financial situation?' and, of the occupants, 'What were their incomes? how many servants did they have?' (Muthesius 1982: viii), questions not readily answered by the buildings themselves whether 'read' by archaeologist or architectural historian. This list of questions is very similar to that asked in a rather different social and functional context of a whole range of buildings sharing

but one common factor, a royal origin in medieval times (Colvin 1963).

Another RCHME (1986b) study, this time of workers' housing (note: '*housing*', not 'houses'), posed similar specific questions for itself: 'who provided the housing? why was it provided? and why did it take the particular forms that it did?' (1986b: [xvii]). The approach has also been exported: Meirion-Jones's survey in Brittany 'attempts to combine techniques from several disciplines in an interdisciplinary approach' (Meirion-Jones 1982: 6) concerned 'to extend existing knowledge of certain west European house-plans and constructional techniques, making possible new definitions and hypothesis' (ibid.: 4) on the premise that 'Buildings are historical documents in their own right' (ibid.: 3). The archaeologist thinks exactly that of his or her material, which comes in all shapes, sizes and forms from the beginning of human history to the present day – and includes buildings just like any other artefact.

SOME APPLIED TECHNIQUES

Another way forward is in the further application of archaeological techniques to the study of these 'historical documents' which physically exist in the landscape. Excavation has already been mentioned; however complete and analytical a survey of standing structure may be, excavation can often add not just detail but whole chapters to structural and functional history of both individual buildings and of types in different periods. Knowledge, for example, of prehistoric and Anglo-Saxon buildings, especially houses, is largely the creation of excavation. That a discussion of 'social structure' can be undertaken of Romano-British villas, for example, is possible only because of the results of excavation (Smith 1978). Knowledge of medieval buildings such as town houses and rural dwellings has similarly benefited, in some cases fundamentally (Carver 1987; Beresford and Hurst 1971). Excavation in and around complex standing buildings, architecturally important as such, can add significantly to their interest: the huge excavations around and in the Louvre provide an outstanding contemporary example. In England, currently Calke Abbey, Derbyshire, and Sutton House in east London, both National Trust properties being prepared for public access, are more modest examples. A detailed survey of the former's surrounds emphasizes the point about context in bringing to the fore the significance on the estate of its industrial function, lime-making.

More generally, so-called 'industrial archaeology' is another field where, at its best, an archaeological approach to buildings, and a whole range of other structures, communications systems and plant, can be related to major themes in economic and social history (Buchanan 1980). Complementarily, such work at its best can play effectively to the concept of landscape archaeology (Trinder 1982) and the illumination of a particular theme through the archaeology of its buildings in various places (RCHME 1989).

Among other techniques developed by archaeology to study the past and particularly applicable to the history of architecture are radio-carbon and dendrochronological dating. Their potential is already being realized, for example in dating barns in Essex and in RCHME's current work. Denrochronological research has now provided us with the capacity to date precisely, i.e. to the exact year of its felling (Hillam *et al.* 1990), not just individual timbers but a whole series of them from, most obviously for architectural history, the same and different roofs and framing. This is clearly a breakthrough which could in the immediate future revolutionize the study of buildings. It will have a particular place in 'buildings archaeology', a jargon term attempting to express the application to upstanding structures of routine archaeological techniques and standards developed in excavation and field surveys.

Photogrammetric and air photographic survey techniques, often backed up by computer data-storage and interpretative modelling, for example, are becoming norms of best practice rather than luxuries. Such detailed recording and structural analysis is now widespread, much of it not initiated as research but as contract work in advance of or during development of various kinds, including conservation (as at Sutton House, p. 234).

DEVELOPING UNDERSTANDING

Archaeologists can learn much from the traditional high standards of scholarship, acute observation and fine judgement of architectural history. Now that structures above ground are as much part of archaeology's evidential base as anything below, it is important that they do. It is as important that the custodians of that architectural high ground recognize two developments: one, they are no longer alone on their chosen territory, and two, rather more importantly than sharing the same building with another group of investigators, there is now available a complementary discipline to further and indeed widen understanding in their own field of enquiry. Architectural history has already been enhanced by the contributions of mainstream archaeology to knowledge of the range of structures, standing and no longer so, in type, distribution and significance, and all over a much longer time-span than that to which the subject is conventionally accustomed.

Furthermore, it is essential to mutual understanding to grasp that archaeology does not *precede* history, and especially architectural history. Rather is it a different approach, applicable to all time and with its own intrinsic validity. Its relevance to the study of buildings and their architecture, 'fine' or 'polite', 'vernacular' or 'industrial', documented or not, would seem to invite a

widespread reinvigoration of that intellectual integration practised by the common forebears of today's specialist practitioners in both disciplines. The opportunity is certainly there, and the taking of it, whether or not it helps those respective academic disciplines, would undoubtedly improve understanding of their subject matter, the built environment, then and now.

REFERENCES

Barley, M.W. (1961) *The English Farmhouse and Cottage*, London: Routledge & Kegan Paul.
—— (1967) 'Rural housing in England', in J. Thirsk (ed.), *The Agrarian History of England and Wales, IV, 1500–1640*, Cambridge: Cambridge University Press.
Beaton, E. *et al.* (1989) *Highland Vernacular Building*, Edinburgh: Scottish Vernacular Buildings Working Group.
Beresford, M. and Hurst, J. (eds) (1971) *Deserted Medieval Villages*, London: Lutterworth Press.
Brunskill, R.W. (1982) *Traditional Buildings in Britain. An Introduction to Vernacular Architecture*, London: Gollancz.
Buchanan, R.A. (1980) *Industrial Archaeology in Britain*, Harmondsworth: Penguin.
Carver, M. (1987) *Underneath English Towns: Interpreting Urban Archaeology*, London: Batsford.
Chippindale, C. (1983) *Stonehenge Complete*, London: Thames & Hudson.
Chippindale, C. *et al.* (1990) *Who Owns Stonehenge?*, London: Batsford.
Colvin, H.M. (ed.) (1963) *The History of the King's Works*, London: HMSO.
Fowler, P.J. (1981) 'The Royal Commission on Historical Monuments (England)', *Antiquity* 55: 106–14.
Fowler, P.J. and Sharp, M. (1990) *Images of Prehistory*, Cambridge: Cambridge University Press.
Fox, C. and Raglan, Lord (1951–4) *Monmouthshire Houses, Parts I–III*, Cardiff: National Museum of Wales.
Gailey, A. (1984) *Rural Houses of the North of Ireland*, Edinburgh: John Donald.
Hillam, J. *et al.* (1990) 'Dendrochronology of the English Neolithic', *Antiquity* 64: 210–20.
Hoskins, W.G. (1955) *The Making of the English Landscape*, London: Hodder & Stoughton.
—— (1988) *The Making of the English Landscape*, London: Guild Publishing
Megaw, R. and Megaw, V. (1989) *Celtic Art, From its Beginnings to the Book of Kells*, London: Thames & Hudson.
Meirion-Jones, G.I. (1982) *The Vernacular Architecture of Brittany. An essay in Historical Geography*, Edinburgh: John Donald.
Morris, R. (1989) *Churches in the Landscape*, London: Dent.
Muthesius, S. (1982) *The English Terraced House*, New Haven and London: Yale University Press.
Pevsner, N. (1963) *The Buildings of England, Wiltshire*, Harmondsworth: Penguin.
Piggott, S. (1989) *Ancient Britons and the Antiquarian Imagination*, London: Thames & Hudson.
RCAHMW: Royal Commission on Ancient and Historical Monuments in Wales (1975) *Houses of the Welsh Countryside, A Study in Historical Geography*, London: HMSO.

RCHME: Royal Commission on the Historical Monuments of England (London: HMSO unless otherwise stated):

(1959) *An Inventory of the Historical Monuments in the City of Cambridge, Part I.*

(1975) *English Vernacular Houses: A Study of Traditional Farmhouses and Cottages.*

(1979) *Stonehenge and its Environs: Monuments and Land Use,* Edinburgh: Edinburgh University Press.

(1984) *An Inventory of Architectural Monuments in North Northamptonshire.*

(1985a) *Excavations at York Minster, Vol. II: The Cathedral of Archbishop Thomas of Bayeux.*

(1985b) *Rural Houses of the Lancashire Pennines 1560–1760.*

(1986a) *Rural Houses of West Yorkshire 1400–1830.*

(1986b) *Workers' Housing in West Yorkshire 1750–1920.*

(1987) *Churches of South-East Wiltshire.*

(1988) *Wilton House and English Palladianism.*

(1989) *The Royal Dockyards 1690–1850: Architecture and Engineering Works of the Sailing Navy,* Aldershot: Scolar Press.

Richards, J. (1990) *The Stonehenge Environs Project,* London: English Heritage.

Rodwell, W. (1989) *Church Archaeology,* London: Batsford.

Royal Commissions *see* RCAHMW and RCHME.

Sherratt, A. (ed.) (1980) *The Cambridge Encyclopedia of Archaeology,* Cambridge: Cambridge University Press.

Smith, J.T. (1978) 'Villas as a key to social structure', in M. Todd (ed.), *Studies in the Romano-British Villa,* Leicester: Leicester University Press.

Taylor, C. (1983) *Village and Farmstead. A History of Rural Settlement in England,* London: George Philip.

Trinder, B. (1982) *The Making of the Industrial Landscape,* London: Dent.

White, G. (1950) *The Antiquities of Selborne in the County of Southampton* (ed. by W.S. Scott), London: the Falcon Press.

Wood, M. (1965) *The English Mediaeval House,* London: Dent.

41   Revivals as phenomena in history

James S. Ackerman

Revivals incorporate into current architectural design aspects of a past style which had run its course and been abandoned. Usually they focus on the formal and symbolic characteristics of a style and rarely the building techniques, craft or accommodation of utilitarian functions. As a rule they are not generated simply by a shift in architectural taste, but reflect new aspirations – often decisively opposed to prevailing ones – in the culture from which they emerge. Though they turn to the past for inspiration, they are not always conservative, but often serve progressive social aims.

In stable and conservative societies such as those of ancient Egypt and most tribal communities, which revere the achievement of ancestors, marked innovation is discouraged: there one finds a pattern of survival rather than of revival. Vernacular architecture also manifests such conservative traits, though in industrialized societies the vernacular is disturbed by the intervention of escalating standards of living and taste, pressures that also have led to the destruction of the bulk of pre-modern vernacular.

All Western architecture of the past two millennia – with the exception of the pre-Conquest architecture of meso-America – derives in some sense from the classical tradition of Greece and Rome, but the distinct culture of Christianity, as it emerged within the Roman setting, progressively differentiated its buildings in the course of the Middle Ages from the first Early Christian forms to the point at which it had developed more radically different structures and expressions in the Byzantine, and subsequently in the Carolingian/Ottonian,

Romanesque and Gothic styles. Even within that sequence, however, there were revivals, notably in the return to Early Christian models of Rome and Jerusalem in the Carolingian period, around AD 800, recognized by Richard Krautheimer (1969) (Rome, Sta Prassede (Figure 1); Abbey Church at Fulda; Palatine Chapel at Aachen), and in Romanesque architecture of the eleventh century, which emulated both Roman architecture (St Gilles du Garde, portal) and Byzantine (Venice, St Mark (Figure 2), and the domed churches of the Perigord). In the post-Renaissance centuries, ancient and medieval Christian styles offered an alternative to Greek and Roman models, and from that time architectural revivals have oscillated between classical and medieval inspiration.

Egyptian architecture remained on the periphery of Western vision, occasionally emerging to exert its influence, more in decoration than in building. The Romans imitated the pyramids in smaller scale for memorials, and imported obelisks which, in turn, Renaissance urban planners adopted as centrepieces for major squares, primarily in Rome. In the late eighteenth century, Piranesi produced a series of etchings that stimulated a taste for Egyptian furnishings and architectural decorations. This was soon amplified by Napoleon's Egyptian campaign and the incorporation of Egyptian motifs by his architects Percier and Fontaine and others into the *Style Empire*. Occasional public buildings and, particularly in America, innumerable cemetery gatehouses were built in the Egyptian style throughout the mid-nineteenth century.

In the early eighteenth century, a proto-romantic

Figure 1 *Sta Prassede, Rome. Interior.* (Source: *Art Resource 2720: 4*)

Figure 2 *Basilica of St Mark, Venice.* (Source: *Art Resource 2720: 1*)

taste for the exotic prompted deviations into Islamic or Chinese and, much later, Indian and Japanese design. These differ in spirit from classical and medieval revivals, which represent an effort to reaffirm roots within Western culture.

The first and most far-reaching architectural revival was that of the Renaissance, originating in Italy in the fifteenth century and extending in the course of the following century to the rest of Europe. The term 'Renaissance' originated in the nineteenth century, but the concept of a rebirth of 'good' (Roman) architecture after centuries of irrational, barbaric medieval building was already articulated by writers of the period. The ancient inspiration was specifically Roman because Greek architecture was virtually unknown; Greece itself was in the control of the Ottoman Turks, with whom Westerners were at war, and Greek sites in Italy and Sicily remained unexplored. Renaissance architects found inspiration in two different approaches to Roman building: the remains of monuments; and the text of the first-century BC architectural theorist Vitruvius, whose manuscripts had survived through the Middle Ages and were rediscovered in the early 1400s.

Florence, which already had fostered an indigenous renascence of ancient forms in the eleventh and twelfth century (Baptistery, San Miniato), was the locus of the first Renaissance style as formulated principally by Filippo Brunelleschi (Foundling Hospital, Pazzi Chapel), and the humanist Leon Battista Alberti (Florence, Palazzo Rucellai; Mantua, Sant'Andrea (Figure 3)), who also wrote the first modern architectural treatise, based on Vitruvius (*De Re Aedificatoria*, completed by 1450). The fifteenth-century revival of ancient architecture was more allusive than precise; designers took liberties with their sources, and easily accommodated late medieval elements into non-antique contexts. But sixteenth-century architects became proto-archaeologists in their eagerness to learn and to use the full range of the Roman

Figure 3 *S. Andrea, Mantua. Begun by L. Fancelli, 1494, after a design by Alberti. The dome is by Jurarra.* (Source: *Art Resource 2720: 5*)

vocabulary and planning principles. Every architect sketched in the ruins, and innumerable drawings of ancient monuments were passed around, copied and used as illustrations for treatises. The work of Donato Bramante and of his pupil Raphael in Rome first reflected the mass and volume of ancient Roman monuments (Tempietto of S. Pietro in Montorio; St Peter's in the Vatican; Villa Madama). In the next generation, Andrea Palladio, a still more passionate scholar of Roman architecture, formulated in his writing (especially *I quattro libri dell'architettura*, 1570) and in his designs (Vicenza, Villa Rotonda; Venice, il Redentore) a synthesis of ancient and modern principles that became in later centuries the paradigmatic statement of the classical tradition. Michelangelo, on the other hand, took such liberties with Roman models (most extravagantly in the Porta Pia, Rome) that his biographer Vasari feared he would lead younger architects astray.

Theorists of the sixteenth century, particularly Sebastiano Serlio, Andrea Palladio and Giacomo Barozzi da Vignola, were responsible for establishing a canon for the five ancient orders (one not clearly articulated by Vitruvius) that was adhered to in classical architecture of the following centuries.

Roman models continued to provide inspiration in baroque designs throughout the seventeenth and early eighteenth centuries. Some baroque architects, particularly in the France of Louis XIV, were more orthodox and archaeological (Perrault, Mansart), and some more fantastic and independent (Borromini, Fischer von Erlach, Vanbrugh) in interpreting the ancient past. The most precise of all published drawings of Roman monuments, made for Louis XIV by Antoine Desgodets (*Les Édifices antiques de Rome*, 1682), provided models for generations of classicists.

By this time the Renaissance offered alternative models to ancient Rome, and in England the architecture of Palladio was revived on two occasions, first by Inigo Jones in the early 1600s (Queen's House, Greenwich) and again a century later – as a reaction against baroque monumentality – in the domestic architecture of the Whig circle of Lord Burlington (Villa at Chiswick; Holkham Hall). British Palladianism was brought to America by Peter Harrison (Newport, Market) and Thomas Jefferson (Monticello).

Occasional outcroppings of the Gothic style throughout the Renaissance and baroque periods can be attributed either to the survival – as distinct from revival – of a local tradition, or to an effort to make new construction conform to an existing medieval structure or environment, as in designs for San Petronio in Bologna, the Cathedral of Milan, or Christopher Wren's Tom Tower and Nicholas Hawksmoor's All Soul's in Oxford. Exceptions can be found in the appropriation of Gothic elements by baroque and rococo designers like Borromini in Italy and Santini Aichl in Bohemia.

In ancient China, especially following the establishment of Confucianism as the state religion in the first century AD, respect for tradition and precedent encouraged imperial patrons to demonstrate their legitimacy by building capital cities, palaces and ritual structures in the style of early dynasties – especially the Chou. By that time the original buildings had disappeared and the 'revivals' had to be based on classical texts, especially the chapter of the ritual canon *Chou Li* (Rites of the Chou Dynasty) that documented the dimensions and shapes of cities and building types. In later dynasties the effort to build structures that should appear 'new' usually implied a desire to reinterpret the ancient texts.

Twice in Japanese history, in the train of devastating civil wars, attempts were made to rebuild ancient monuments in past styles. First in the eleventh century, after the thirty-year Gempei War, destroyed temples were reconstituted in their past, partly Chinese, form with the advice of Chinese craftspeople. The rejection at this point of the preceding Heian style characterized the direction of all the arts. A second renaissance of around 1600, centred in Kyoto, emerged paradoxically as the manifestation of the cultural clout of those who had lost political power to the military regime of the Edo (Tokyo)-based Tokugara family. They sponsored a revival of Heian arts and literature, expressed in architecture through an innovative element of rusticity, simplicity and a harmony with nature that related to the re-establishment of the Tea Ceremony.

In India, the increasing influence of the West from the eighteenth century on brought the potentiality of revivals to the foreground. The styles of the Mogul period (sixteenth to eighteenth century) were especially favoured in the formation of an 'Indo-Saracenic' revival, particularly in Gwalior, Jaipur and the cities under British rule. The basic forms tended to be European with Indian decorative surfaces. Vigorous advocacy of an Indian revival at the time of the British decision to rebuild New Delhi in the classical style stimulated an effort on the part of Indians to revive pre-Islamic Hindu forms (Benares Hindu University; Alwar Railway Station (Figure 4)). The temple architecture of recent decades

has revived the form's ancient prototypes with exceptional accuracy.

Revivals in the pre-modern Islamic world are found rather in individual monuments than in widespread styles, as in the Mamluk mausoleum of Qalaun in Cairo (1283–5), which refers to the Dome of the Rock in Jerusalem, or in the mosque of Mehmet II (1766), modelled on the classical Ottoman mosque of Sehzade Mehmet (1548). In the nineteenth century, contact with Europe stimulated participation in the revival styles of Western architecture, as in the classical-revival Dolmabahce palace in Istanbul (1856) and Abdin palace in Cairo (1874); neo-Gothic features appear in mosques later in the century. European architects even brought an Islamic revival to Islam (Cairo, Jazirah Palace, 1863). More recently, Islamic architects have sought to re-establish contact with their tradition (mosques by Abdel Wahed El-Wakil, and later architects).

By the late eighteenth century in the West, much of the continental baroque style had given way to the rococo, in which the ties to the classical tradition were increasingly tenuous. And because rococo design was associated in Enlightenment culture with a declining old regime, a neo-classical taste – promoted by the most original theorists of the period (Lodoli, Laugier, Winckelmann) – developed for the simplicity and severity of early antiquity. This was fortuitously fuelled by the rediscovery of the Greek architecture of the Peloponnese (first published by Stuart and Revett, *The Antiquities of Athens*, 5 vols, from 1762), and by the excavations of Herculaneum (from 1738) and Pompeii (from 1748). Although some neo-classical architecture remained authentically ancient (Jefferson's Capitol at Richmond; the Madeleine, Paris (Figure 5)), the finest architects (Soane, Ledoux, Schinkel) worked in a classical-geometrical spirit permitting unlimited invention. The term 'romantic classicism' has been coined for this tendency.

A second proto-romantic development was initiated in England, stimulated, paradoxically, by new ideas about landscape design, which produced not only the informal garden, but the artificial ruin or grotto, and other architectural follies in diverse styles, the Gothic and the Chinese being most favoured (Temple of Liberty, Stowe; Pagoda, Kew Gardens). The appearance of exotic elements in architecture most often took the form of overlays on basically classical buildings and tended to remain decorative and superficial (Betty Langley's pattern books; Strawberry Hill – both Gothic, or Gothick as this phase has been called). At the end of the century, Picturesque theory (which recommended designing gardens and buildings to resemble the pictures of admired landscape painters, especially Claude Lorraine and Salvador Rosa) gave impetus to the diverse historical revivals of the nineteenth century by emphasizing the values of association (reminding the viewer of a painting or of a work of literature or historical

Figure 4 *Railway Station at Alwar, India, built by a master builder for the Maharajah of Alwar, c. 1910–12. (Photograph: E.B. Howell)*

Figure 5 *The Madeleine, Paris, 1804–49, by Pierre Vignon.* (Source: *Art Resource 2720: 6*)

event) and character (reflecting in a design the nature of the owner or the setting). Architectural values, which in classical theory had been based on immutable laws and were immanent, thereby became personal and subjective, doing away with firm rules. This was one of the routes to nineteenth-century romanticism.

The aesthetic of the Picturesque helped to make the nineteenth century the great era of non-classical revivals, and architects and institutions worked in as wide a variety of historic styles as experience and knowledge would permit. Books were essential to the revivals of the nineteenth century; model books suggested designs in hitherto unfamiliar styles and precise surveys of historical monuments permitted architects at their drawing tables to call up images of past buildings in their totality and often in minute detail. As neo-classical taste waned in the early years of the century, a great outpouring of British (and later, American) model books for country gardens and villas educated the expanding middle class in styles such as Gothic, Tudor, English Cottage, Italian Villa, Castellated, Swiss Chalet, and many others, adapted to increasingly irregular plans The classical tradition was not forgotten, but took its place as one among many options.

The equivalent to the medieval options of the Picturesque in Germany and to some extent elsewhere on the European continent was given the name *Rundbogenstil*, which stood on the one hand for Romanesque (particularly Lombard) or Byzantine, and on the other for Italian Renaissance, particularly of the Florentine quattrocento. It was motivated partly by the desire of German patrons and designers to reaffirm a style associated – more than the Gothic – with German medieval architecture, and partly by the theory, anticipated already by Schinkel in 1811 (Berlin, Petrikirche), that a round-arched style combined the rationality of classical architecture with the spirituality of the Middle Ages. The style was adopted in England, particularly by Nonconformist congregations, where it was often called 'Norman', and

was brought to America by emigrant German architects; it later inspired H.H. Richardson to design some of the most original and powerful nineteenth-century buildings (Cambridge, Mass., Austin Hall (Figure 6)).

The Gothic revival became more than merely one Picturesque option because of its importance for ecclesiastical design. In this sphere it was seen not merely as a style but as an affirmation of faith and of the values of tradition. In England it was vigorously and effectively promoted for Catholic churches and institutions by James A.W. Pugin, who deplored the superficial Gothicism of his predecessors as represented in the Houses of Parliament, and devoted his life to publishing articles and books affirming the ethical and liturgical superiority of correct late Gothic ('Perpendicular') architecture. Pugin designed exceptionally fine and authentic churches (St Giles, Cheadle, Staffordshire). The Anglican revival, led by the Camden Society, initially formed by Cambridge undergraduates, was equally vigorous and exhorted the public through a journal, *The Ecclesiologist*. Their major American disciple was Richard Upjohn (Trinity Church, New York, 1839–). G.E. Street's Royal Courts of Justice, Strand, London (1874–82) (Figure 7), a serious essay in thirteenth-century Gothic, is one of the few secular buildings of the period that stand comparison with the churches.

John Ruskin, the most influential architectural critic of the century, adhered to Pugin's moral imperative, but directed his readers rather to Italian medieval architecture, focusing on Venice. Like Pugin, he called for a return to fine crafting which should respect the nature of materials. Ruskin, and the Arts and Crafts movement that he inspired, wanted to hold at bay the capacity of the industrial revolution to replace the individually crafted object with the mass-produced. In this he differed from his French counterpart, Viollet-le-Duc, a pioneer of cast-iron construction who was at the same time the chief exponent of Gothic in France. Viollet's

Figure 6 *Austin Hall, Harvard University, Cambridge, Mass., 1881, by H.H. Richardson.* (Source: *Harvard University*)

Figure 7 *The Royal Courts of Justice, London, 1874–82, by G.E. Street.*

involvement in Gothic architecture (he restored – with a heavy hand – Notre-Dame in Paris and many other Gothic ecclesiastical and domestic monuments) was motivated not by religious considerations, but by the conviction that the style represented the most structurally rational of all historic models. Indeed, Viollet was more interested in the rationalism than in the style itself.

The palaces of sixteenth-century Italy inspired many of the large commercial and institutional buildings and dwelling blocks of the mid-nineteenth century in major Western cities; Rome particularly, which had contributed a major share of the original models, experienced a *Neocinquecento* vogue in the decades 1830–80.

The Second Empire style of the public buildings of Napoleon II, reinforced in architectural education by the École des Beaux-Arts, influenced official architecture throughout the West during the third quarter of the century, and Beaux-Arts principles, grounded in the Renaissance and baroque practice of Italy and France (Paris, Opéra), continued to exert their influence well into the twentieth century. In Soviet Russia, after a brief flirtation with Modernism in the 1920s, a diluted version of Beaux-Arts classicism became the official style. In the late Victorian period in England, the style known there

as 'Queen Anne', which had little to do with that monarch, represented a return to indigenous seventeenth- and eighteenth-century sources, primarily in domestic architecture. Gilbert Scott, its most effective British formulator, contributed to the genesis of the Shingle Style in America. But the term 'Queen Anne' in America denotes the colonial revival of the 1880s and 1890s.

The mainstream of architectural design forked in the late nineteenth and early twentieth century. The major Modernist architects abandoned overt historical allusion and ornament, though Mies van der Rohe, Walter Gropius, Le Corbusier, Oud and others adhered in their principles of form to the classical tradition. Others, particularly in domestic architecture, sought inspiration in their traditional regional vernaculars – for example, Webb, Voysey and Lutyens in England. In Scandinavia, architects like Asplund, Eliel Saarinen and Aalto created a Modernist–regional fusion. Frank Lloyd Wright is more difficult to categorize, because his borrowings from past vernacular, Japanese and pre-Colombian architecture were so assimilated into his personal idiom that the reference is not overt.

The Post-Modern taste of the later 1970s and 1980s, a reaction against the purism of Modernist architecture, stimulated the use of superficial elements of classical, and occasionally Gothic, architecture with the intention of reintroducing greater variety and allusion into architecture. Post-Modernism was not strictly a revival style, though it was accompanied in Britain and America by occasional instances of literal reproduction of historical – particularly Georgian – styles.

The architecture of the nineteenth century, being almost exclusively committed to revivals of various sorts, does not at this time appear likely to be itself seriously revived. The various versions of Modernism seem the most likely candidates to take a place alongside the classical and medieval as the stimulus for revivals in the twenty-first century.

BIBLIOGRAPHY

AARP (various authors) (1977) 'European influence in nineteenth- and twentieth-century oriental architecture', *A.A.R.P.* 11 (June).

Burns, H. (1971) 'Quattrocento architecture and the antique: some problems', in R.R. Bolgar (ed.) *Classical Influences on European Culture, AD 500–1500*, Cambridge: Cambridge University Press.

Clark, K. (1962) *The Gothic Revival*, 3rd edn, London: Murray.

Crook, J.M. (1972) *The Greek Revival: Neo-Classical Attitudes in British Architecture, 1760–1870*, London: Murray.

—— (1987) *The Dilemma of Style: Architectural Ideas from the Picturesque to the Post-Modern*, London: Murray.

Curran, K. (1988) 'German *Rundbogenstil* and reflections on the American round-arched style', *Journal of the Society of Architectural Historians*, XLVII: 351 ff.

Eastlake, C.L. (1872) *A History of the Gothic Revival*, London: Longmans Green.

Forssman, E. (1973) *Dorico, Ionico, Corinzio nell'Architettura del Rinascimento*, Bari: Laterza.

Frankl, P. (1960) *The Gothic: Literary Sources and Interpretations through Eight Centuries*, Princeton; NJ: Princeton University Press.

Girouard, M. (1977) *Sweetness and Light: The 'Queen Anne' Movement, 1860–1900*, Oxford: Oxford University Press.

Günther, H. and Thoenes, C. (1985) 'Gli ordini architettonici: rinascità o invenzione?', in *Roma e l'antico nell'arte e nella cultura del Cinquecento*, Rome: Istituto della Enciclopedia Italiana.

Hautecoeur, L. (1912) *Rome et la Renaissance de l'antiquité à la fin du XVIIIe siècle*, Paris: Fontemoing.

—— (1943–57) *Histoire de l'architecture classique en France*, 7 vols, reprinted 1963–7, Paris: Picard.

Krautheimer, R. (1963) 'Alberti and Vitruvius', in *Actos of the XXth International Congress of the History of Art*, II, Princeton, NJ: Princeton University Press.

—— (1969) 'The Carolingian revival of early Christian architecture', in *Studies in Early Christian, Medieval and Renaissance Art*, New York: New York University Press.

Leeds, H. (1839) *The Travellers Club House . . . and the Revival of the Italian Style*, London.

Lotus International 26, (1980/1) Issue on colonial architecture in Asia and the third world.

McCarthy, M. (1987) *The Origins of the Gothic Revival*, New Haven and London: Yale University Press.

Onians, J. (1988) *Bearers of Meaning: The Classical Orders in Antiquity, the Middle Ages, and the Renaissance*, Princeton, NJ: Princeton University Press.

Panofsky, E. (1960) *Renaissance and Renascences in Western Art*, Stockholm: Almqvist & Wiksell; reprinted 1972, New York: Harper & Row.

Pevsner, N. (1969) *Ruskin and Viollet-le-Duc*, London: Thames & Hudson.

Pugin, A.W.N. (1843) *An Apology for the Revival of Christian Architecture*, London.

Stanton, P. (1968) *The Gothic Revival and American Church Architecture 1840–56*, Baltimore: Johns Hopkins University Press.

Stillman, D. (1988) *English Neoclassical Architecture*, London: Zwemmer.

Weiss, R. (1969) *The Renaissance Discovery of Classical Antiquity*, 2nd edn 1988, New York: Blackwell.

Wiebenson, D. (1969) *Sources of Greek Revival Architecture*, London: Zwemmer.

SECTION 3.4

Influence of technology

Building technology is a huge subject and this section only offers a number of discussions on how in general terms the specific requirements of technology influence architecture. In general terms, technology is concerned with what is possible or practically feasible, and for many centuries a major impulse for designers and builders was simply to push back these frontiers. Later, new methods and materials began to offer ever-increasing choices for architects. Today, a technological condition has been reached in architecture whereby any conceivable technical advance could be achieved if sufficient political will and finances existed. In reality, the challenge for the contemporary architect is how to harmonize the technological opportunities with every-thing else, since most building technology is not confined by what is possible but by what is conven-tionally believed to be appropriate. However, many architects are still inspired by the prospect of using their design skill and courage to create something that has not been done before.

Seen from another perspective, technology does not move forward continuously. In the twentieth century we would be hard pressed to emulate the expertise of the master masons whose work is discussed by Robert Mark in his essay 'Gothic structural engineering'. Similarly, while the technology of timber engineering has developed enormously over recent years, the skills of the craftspeople of previous centuries, discussed by David Yeomans in his article 'The changing pattern of the use of timber', cannot be reproduced. As befits the engineer who designed the structure of the tallest building in the world, Fazlur Khan describes with enthusiasm new developments in the structural engin-eering of reinforced concrete and structural steel.

Environmental engineering has been a particular development of the nineteenth and twentieth centuries, and higher and higher standards of comfort are expected by the users of buildings. But both John Martin in 'Building the total system' and Ian Murphy in 'The impact of the environment' emphasize that contemporary reliance on machines and energy to modify climate has its limitations. Everywhere we must be on our guard against the attraction of mere innova-tion. The value of technological progress must be assessed in the wider context of architecture.

A.N.

RECOMMENDED READING

Banham, P. Reyner (1985) *The Architecture of the Well-Tempered Environment*, 2nd edn, London: Architectural Press.

Fitch, J.M. (1975) *American Building: The Environmental Forces that Shape It*, 2nd edn, New York: Schocken Books.

Gordon, J.E. (1978) *Structures or Why Things Don't Fall Down*, Harmondsworth: Penguin.

Guise, D. (1991) *Design and Technology in Architecture*, New York: Van Nostrand Reinhold.

Mainstone, R. (1983) *Developments in Structural Form*, Harmondsworth: Penguin.

Markus, T.A. and Morris, E.N. (1980) *Buildings, Climate and Energy*, London: Pitman.

Martienssen, H. (1976) *The Shape of Structure*, Oxford: Oxford University Press.

Perez-Gomez, A. (1983) *Architecture and the Crisis of Modern Science*, Cambridge, Mass.: MIT Press.

Salvadori, M. (1980) *Why Buildings Stand Up*, New York: W. Norton.

42 Gothic structural engineering

Robert Mark

Reflecting the resurgent prosperity of western Europe in the middle of the twelfth century, a cadre of professional builders began to push the construction of Gothic churches to unprecedented heights. And in this quest, the builders encountered a new environmental realm. Lofty clerestory walls, in addition to having to resist the outward thrust of vaulting, were now subject to great wind forces, as were the high wooden roofs resting upon them. As the buildings grew larger, too, the design problems were exacerbated by what must have appeared to be the almost insuperable costs of obtaining and transporting stone, often from distant quarries, and of shaping and setting it into place.[1] Still another design restraint was imposed by the need to reduce the weight of the superstructure to relieve foundation loadings and hence reduce building settlements. It was the combination of all of these factors that led to the invention of the flying buttress and the consequent redefining of the *style* of Gothic churches.

Surviving records tell us almost nothing of the design techniques that were employed for so marked a technological achievement. We stand on firm ground, however, in ruling out the use of any kind of scientific methodology; more than four centuries would pass before the appearance of Galileo's seminal work in mechanics. The absence of structural theory eliminates also the possibility of quantitative modelling at small scale. Hence, the builders could not have predicted with any certainty whether or not structural elements perfectly valid in smaller buildings would perform reliably at the large scale of new construction. An important exception which is independent of scale, however, is gross stability against overturning under dead weight loadings. Indeed, a bench-top-size model could have served to indicate the gross stability of a full-scale building. And although the principles of this fact of structural behaviour would not have been known, its existence helped to offset some of the problems of new, large-scale design.

In view of the builders' inability to predict structural behaviour scientifically, the elegance of many Gothic structural solutions demanded some explanation. We suggested, on the basis of our structural studies, that the details of design could have been worked out with a crude type of experimental stress analysis performed during construction: tensile cracking observed in the weak lime mortar between building stones during the relatively long periods of construction could have led to refinements in design (Mark 1982: 56). Building programmes in fact often called for the erection of one high bay at a time. In these instances, the first bays could have acted as experimental, full-scale models to fix the form of new building elements.

NOTRE-DAME DE PARIS AND THE INFLUENCE OF WIND

A case in point is the cathedral of Notre-Dame de Paris. The 33 m. (108 ft.) interior height of Notre-Dame's nave (*c.* 1180) exceeded that of all earlier Gothic churches by some 8 m. (26 ft.). No doubt it was this singular increment in height that led its designers to employ flying buttresses for the first time to support the high clerestory walls. Unfortunately, we have only indirect evidence for the original configuration of this seminal structural device. Massive rebuilding of the cathedral, which altered the entire buttressing system, was begun in 1225, and extensive rebuilding was carried out again in the fourteenth and nineteenth centuries.

An archaeological reconstruction of the original, twelfth-century configuration of the Notre-Dame nave which included also structural modelling was recently developed by W.W. Clark and myself (Figure 1). The

Figure 1 *Analytical drawing of the reconstructed twelfth-century nave of Notre-Dame de Paris.* (Source: *after Clark and Mark 1984*)

modelling indicated that the reconstructed nave was structurally sound except for probable cracking occurring during major storms in the mortar near the ends of the windward flying buttresses. Because the cracking would have been highly localized, it is doubtful that serious damage occurred – provided that the custodial staff repaired the joints promptly enough after a storm to prevent more general deterioration. But bear in mind that there would have been many such affected regions along the full length of the nave, making this type of maintenance costly.

It has been generally assumed that the thirteenth-century campaign of rebuilding was undertaken to modernize the cathedral and to bring in considerably more light than had been permitted by the earlier wall structure (see, for example, Frankl 1962: 16). According to this line of reasoning, changes to the structural system were only a by-product of the need to change the window design. Inherent structural problems within the original design had never been considered, despite the fact that anyone visiting the cathedral today will see that the benefit of the larger clerestory windows has been overrated; Notre-Dame remains a dark building. After completing the model study, however, we speculated that the problems of maintenance led the cathedral chapter to consider reconstruction. And while this observation is noteworthy, a more important observation for gaining an understanding of the technology of the era concerns the effect that this experience seems to have had on the two giant buildings whose construction closely followed that of Notre-Dame, the cathedrals of Chartres and Bourges.

In addition to lateral spur walls and two tiers of stout flying buttresses, Chartres exhibits a tier of largely ineffective, light upper flyers that were hastily erected during the last stages of its construction (Mark 1972) (see Figure 2b). Archaeological evidence also reveals that the efficient, lightweight buttressing of Bourges (see Figure 2c) resulted from alterations made during a later phase of construction (Branner 1962). (Although the Bourges vaults at 36 m. (118 ft.) are slightly taller than those of Chartres, the Bourges buttressing weighs but 40 per cent as much as that of Chartres; cf. Figures 2b and 2c.) In the light of the Notre-Dame analysis, both structures indicate a technological response to an increased awareness of wind effects on tall buildings – which must have come first from Paris.

The new evidence suggests that information about on-site modifications to eliminate structural problems at a particular building site was passed on rather quickly, influencing the design of other buildings. The steep flying buttresses of Bourges then represent a spectacular level of structural refinement in apparent response to the problems of Notre-Dame de Paris. And if the upper flyers of Chartres are not fully effective in themselves, they none the less appear to have pointed the way to the mature High Gothic buttressing systems of the ca-

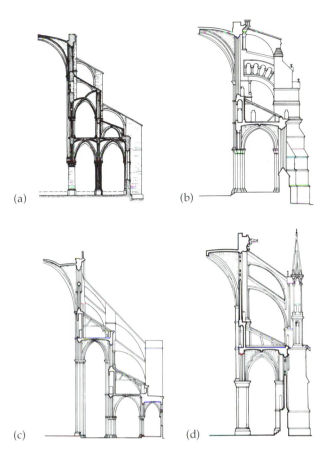

(a)   (b)   (c)   (d)

Figure 2 *Comparative cross-sections: (a) Paris, Notre-Dame Cathedral, nave reconstruction (c. 1180); (b) Chartres Cathedral, nave (begun 1194); (c) Bourges Cathedral, choir (begun 1195); (d) Reims Cathedral, nave (begun 1210).*

thedrals of Reims (Figure 2d) and Amiens, where upper flying buttresses are strategically placed to receive the thrust of the high wind loadings on their tall superstructures (Mark and Clark 1984).

Such a 'learning cycle' has a parallel in our own time. The 854 m. (2,800 ft.) main span of the Tacoma Narrows suspension bridge which opened in July 1940 was the third longest in the world and its weight per metre of roadway was by far the lightest of any long span. Four months after the bridge opened, a fairly steady 65 k.p.h. (40 m.p.h.) morning wind produced severe twisting oscillations in the span, which collapsed by midday. Soon afterwards, many long-span suspension bridges built during the period between the two world wars were stiffened by the addition of trusses to their roadway decks. And when the second Tacoma Narrows Bridge was opened a decade later, it too incorporated deep trusses (see Leonhard 1984: 287–9).

THE TRANSITION FROM SEXPARTITE TO QUADRIPARTITE VAULTING

Gothic vaulting provides another important instance where technological imperatives altered earlier convention.

With few exceptions, prior to the year 1200, square-planned, six-part (sexpartite) vaults were used in the high bays of all the larger Gothic churches (including the cathedrals of Paris and Bourges). After 1200, and evidently following the example of Chartres Cathedral, only rectangular-plan, four-part (quadripartite) vaults, sprung from a point well above the clerestory base, covered the soaring interior spaces. A causal relationship between the development of the raised High Gothic clerestory supported by flying buttresses and the shift in vault configuration seems obvious, yet the literature on Gothic architecture has been somewhat vague on this point.

Stylistic explanations predominate discussions of the sudden shift in vaulting – the implication being that the use of sexpartite vaults arose from the introduction of alternating nave piers. Since the number of vault ribs springing from the piers is alternately one and three, this system is claimed to be a logical visual complement to alternating piers.[2] By the same reasoning, the stylistic theories attribute the adoption of quadripartite vaulting to the introduction of uniform, non-alternating piers (but note that Notre-Dame de Paris and Chartres and many other churches are exceptions to this schema).

Nor have constructional theories provided adequate explanation. These are generally based on the premise that quadripartite vaults were easier to build than sexpartite vaults. Some scholars, however, have concluded that the centring was more difficult to erect for quadripartite than for sexpartite vaulting. It has also been suggested that the Gothic builders adopted quadripartite vaults because they were lighter than sexpartite vaults (Fitchen 1961: 75). But a series of model studies of ribbed vaulting (of the type illustrated in Figure 3) performed at Princeton in order to determine the structural role of the vault rib (these indicated the rib to be a useful constructional device, but unimportant structurally) also revealed that the weight of sexpartite vaults,

having fewer ribs than quadripartite, was significantly *less* than the weight of equivalent quadripartite vaults covering the same area (Mark 1982: 114–15). The finding that the thirteenth-century builders, who generally favoured light construction, chose to construct heavier vaults over increasingly slender piers and walls in the tallest churches did nothing to clarify the enigma surrounding the abrupt change in vaulting form.

This question was resolved, though, by examining the forces necessary to support the vaults during a previously unconsidered phase of vault erection. Consider first the salient structural feature of Gothic vaulting: the 'focusing' of the distributed forces within the vaults at the points of vault support along the clerestory wall. There are three components of this focused force resultant at the springing: (1) a downward, vertical component equal to the weight of the ribbed vaulting supported by the clerestory wall, which in turn is carried by the piers of the main arcade; (2) a lateral outward, horizontal component tending to overturn the clerestory wall, but resisted in the mature Gothic church by flying buttresses; and (3) a longitudinal, horizontal component against the adjacent bay along the axis of the church. This last force is ordinarily stabilized by the adjacent bay of vaulting whose longitudinal component acts in the opposite direction to that of its neighbour (and eventually by the rounded apse with radial flying buttresses at one end of the church, and by a pair of massive towers at the other end). In effect, the completed bays of vaulting all 'lean' against one another.

From this brief description of the mechanics of vault support, it is evident that mature Gothic buttressing could handily support any reasonable form of vaulting, sexpartite or quadripartite. A different condition is present, however, during the *construction* of the vaulting, which was generally carried out, one bay at a time, on movable centring. Since the erection of the vaulting was necessarily preceded by the erection of the piers, the walls, and the flying buttresses, the vertical weight and the outward horizontal thrusts of the vault bay after its centring was removed were resisted by the same structural elements as in the finished church. On the other hand, the longitudinal thrust along the axis of the church at this stage of construction must have been supported by the clerestory wall, and likely by timber props, since an adjacent vaulting bay to provide stabilization was not yet in place. As the springing of the vaults was carried upward from the base of the clerestory in later buildings, coping with this thrust at higher elevations became a far more serious problem of construction. The sexpartite-vaulting model corresponding to Bourges indicated a longitudinal thrust of 19,000 kg. (42,000 lb.). For the equivalent quadripartite vaulting of Chartres (from modelling based on vaulting from the choir of Cologne Cathedral), the longitudinal thrust is indicated to be only 9,000 kg. (19,900 lb.), or more than a 50 per

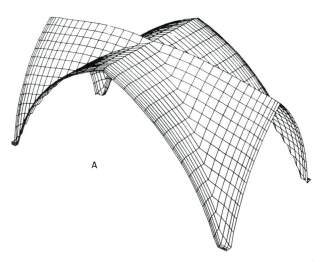

Figure 3 *Computer-drawn numerical; (finite element) model of quadripartite vaulting.*

cent force reduction compared with sexpartite vaulting (Taylor and Mark 1982).

The constructional problems presented by the intensity of these longitudinal thrusts do not appear to have been crucial in the early Gothic churches where the vault springing could be anchored in the typically massive walls below the clerestory. The countering of this force became an acute problem only with the demand for greater clerestory height and the accompanying fenestration which brought an end to the practice of having the vault spring from a solid wall. Slender segments of the clerestory wall could have displayed cracking, even if braced with temporary timber falsework, and this might well have brought the conviction to the Gothic builders that the walls were unable to resist forces of such magnitude. As with the flying buttresses, quadripartite vaulting was probably adopted in High Gothic churches for structural reasons; the flying buttresses provided support for the outward thrusts of the high vaults, while the quadripartite vaulting reduced longitudinal thrusts to manageable levels during construction. As a result, stone structures become more truly skeletal and Gothic tastes for greater clerestory height and increased light were satisfied.

WELLS CATHEDRAL AND VERTICAL BUTTRESSING

The extremely high Gothic churches of France, later emulated in Germany, Italy and Spain, were never adopted in England. Even the high vaults of Westminster Abbey, the tallest and most French of any English church in structure, are 2 m. (6.5 ft.) lower than those of Notre-Dame de Paris. In discussing Wells Cathedral, whose construction began in the decade following the establishment of the nave design of Notre-Dame, architectural historian Peter Kidson observed:

> The tendency at Wells to stress the horizontal divisions of the building at the expense of the vertical was to become very characteristic of English Gothic in the thirteenth century; and it is one of the things which distinguishes English Gothic of this period from all Continental versions of the style.
>
> (Kidson *et al.* 1965: 77)

This 'horizontality' contributed also to another distinguishing characteristic of English churches: only rarely were flying buttresses required for lateral stability. Indeed, in many of these buildings, flying buttresses were added only later on to prevent the spreading of clerestory walls (usually caused by foundation problems), or, often in the nineteenth century, to create a more romantic aspect.

Wells Cathedral suffered the fate of many English churches when, around the beginning of the fourteenth century, it became the fashion to crown them with great towers and spires. Because these buildings, and parti-

cularly the monastic establishments, were often sited near water and on marshy soil, damaging settlements ensued. At Wells, the problem manifested itself as differential settlement of the two western crossing piers following the erection after 1315 of a new central tower and spire. To forestall further settlement, the cathedral chapter authorized the repairs that were undertaken in 1338 (Bony 1979: 84). Three sets of great inverted arches were placed between the piers of the crossing on the north, south and west, and the clerestory windows adjacent to the crossing were partially filled with stone and what appears to be a steeply sloped 'flying' buttress (see Figure 4). These relatively slight wall buttresses, whose form places their constituent stones in compression, are most effective in transferring much of the tower weight to adjoining footings. The great masonry arches, on the other hand, were found to be wanting in transferring loads, which would have to be done by shearing action across their centre section (see Figure 4).

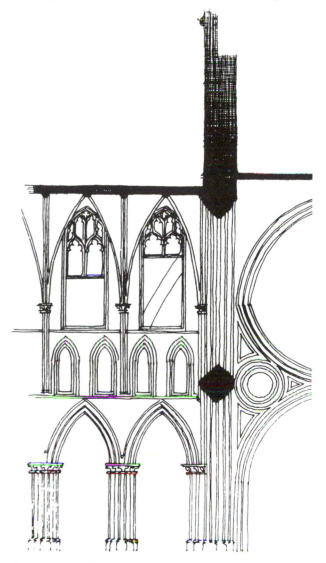

Figure 4 *Wells Cathedral, England: section drawing showing disposition of wall buttress and inverted arch. The darkened section at gallery level is that of the inverted arches at the centre of the nave.*

In fact, the wall buttresses were found to be more than four times as effective as the arches (Mark 1982: 83–6).

The failure of the inverted arches alone to provide significant relief to the piers leads to speculation about their other possible functions. The other role that they might play is to brace the piers laterally below the arches of the crossing in a manner similar to that achieved at Salisbury Cathedral with comparable, but lighter, inverted arches. However, the relatively low height of Wells – the springing of the crossing arches begins only 15 m. (50 ft.) above the floor – should preclude a need for such additional bracing.

In any event, the effectiveness of steeply sloped buttresses of the type used at Wells was not lost on the English masons of the fourteenth and fifteenth centuries who had to cope with placing towers over similarly poor foundations. Indeed, the use of actual flying buttresses to transmit *vertical* loadings to adjacent structures seems to have been an English, late Gothic innovation. Flying buttresses of this type are widespread; they may be seen, for example, at the cathedrals of Salisbury and Gloucester (see Figure 5).

Figure 5 *Gloucester Cathedral, England: crossing tower. The flying buttress helps to transfer some of the crossing tower weight to an adjacent footing.*

Even though the French fascination with tall structure and its subsequent refinement is missing from the original design of Wells, modifications made to the building's structure over the years presented opportunities to test new ideas. As the present state of the building fabric attests, a scientific theory of structure was not necessary to achieve success; yet our observations on the inverted arches illuminate the pitfalls of employing novel technological designs and, for that matter, historical speculation without recourse to analytical techniques.

HISTORIOGRAPHY

Modern understanding of medieval building technology derives largely from the observing and recording of details of construction carried out during restorations made in the nineteenth century. The two giants in this field of that era are Robert Willis (1800–75) – whose major contributions include an early publication on the construction of medieval vaults and a series of papers on the architectural history of English cathedrals (Willis 1842)[3] – and Eugène-Emmanuel Viollet-le-Duc (1814–79), author of the monumental ten-volume encyclopedia *Dictionnaire raisonné de l'architecture française du XIe au XVIe siècle*, published between 1854 and 1868.

Although Willis was also a prominent engineer and a fellow of the Royal Society, he did not (perhaps prudently, in his time) attempt to deal with the major questions of Gothic structure (see Mark 1977: 52–64). On the other hand, Viollet-le-Duc, who directed the restoration of many French buildings, became convinced that important architectural elements (such as the ribs of Gothic vaults) were originally derived from the demands of the construction process or of the physical laws governing structural forces. And to prove this, he attempted to discern their structural function. But Viollet-le-Duc was not trained as an engineer, and despite the considerable influence of his writings on 'structural rationalism', his necessarily simplistic analyses provoked, in 1934, a full reassessment of Gothic structure by the French architect Pol Abraham. In the light of Abraham's more systematic studies, some inconsistencies in Viollet-le-Duc's reasoning did indeed become apparent; but Abraham also encountered difficulty in attempting (with inadequate mathematical theory) to explain the workings of such complex structures. So rather than resolving the issues, the main outcome of Abraham's study was a continuing lively debate.

Modern engineering studies of Gothic structure date from the 1960s. By extending to masonry the so-called limit theorems then being used for the design of modern steel-framed buildings, structural engineer Jacques Heyman was able to reliably assess the overall stability of medieval construction and to estimate factors of safety against catastrophic failure (see Heyman 1966,

1968). At that time too, the writer began to apply two- and three-dimensional photo-elastic modelling (a technique of experimental stress analysis developed for the design of aircraft and nuclear reactor components) to determine the internal force distributions within Gothic structures (described in Mark 1982). By the mid-1970s, numerical (finite-element) models generated in a computer (as illustrated in Figure 3) become a practical tool for quantitative analysis of complex structures. And, in what can be viewed as the closing of the circle back to the building site, by the mid-1980s the application of finite element, computer modelling has become almost routine in helping guide major projects of medieval building restoration.

NOTES

1   For background on early commercial transportation, see Landels 1978: 133–85.

2   This view was almost universal. See: Focillon 1965: 35; Frankl 1962: 18–19, 80, 118; Jantzen 1962: 13; Pevsner 1963: 100–9; Seymour 1939: 69–71, 134–5; Simson 1962: 205–6; and Stoddard 1966: 130, 140, 181.

3   This article and all of Willis's known studies of individual cathedrals have been reproduced in Willis 1972–3.

REFERENCES

Abraham, P. (1934) *Viollet-le-Duc et le Rationalisme Médiéval*, Paris: Vincent, Fréal & Cie.

Bony, J. (1979) *The English Decorated Style*, Ithaca: Cornell University Press.

Branner, R. (1962) *La Cathédrale de Bourges et sa Place dans l'Architecture Gothique*, Paris/Bourges: Editions Tardy.

Clark, W.M. and Mark, R. (1984) 'The first flying buttresses: a new reconstruction of the nave of Notre-Dame de Paris', *The Art Bulletin* 66 (1): 47–65.

Fitchen, J. (1961) *The Construction of Gothic Cathedrals*, Oxford: Clarendon Press.

Focillon, H. (1969) *The Art of the West in the Middle Ages*, ed. J. Bony, Vol. II, 2nd edn, London: Phaidon.

Frankl, P. (1962) *Gothic Architecture*, Baltimore: Penguin.

Heyman, J. (1966) 'The stone skeleton', *International Journal of Solids and Structures*, 2: 249–79.

—— (1968) 'On the rubber vaults of the Middle Ages and other matters', *Gazette des Beaux-Arts* 6(LXXI): 177–88.

Jantzen, H. (1962) *High Gothic: The Classic Cathedrals of Chartres, Reims and Amiens*, London: Constable.

Kidson, P., Murray, P. and Thompson, P. (1965) *A History of English Architecture*, Harmondsworth: Penguin.

Landels, J.G. (1978) *Engineering in the Ancient World*, Berkeley: University of California Press.

Lemaire, R.M. and Van Balan, K. (eds) (1988) *Stable-Unstable? Structural Consolidation of Ancient Buildings*, Leuven: Leuven University Press.

Leonhard, F. (1984) *Brücken/Bridges: Aesthetics and Design*, Cambridge, Mass.: MIT Press.

Mark, R. (1972) 'The structural analysis of Gothic cathedrals: Chartres vs. Bourges', *Scientific American* 227(5): 90–9.

—— (1977) 'Robert Willis, Viollet-le-Duc and the structural approach to Gothic architecture', *Architectura* 7(2): 52–64.

—— (1982) *Experiments in Gothic Structure*, Cambridge, Mass.: MIT Press.

Mark, R. and Clark, W.W. (1984) 'Gothic structural experimentation', *Scientific American* 251(5): 179–85.

Pevsner, N. (1963) *An Outline of European Architecture*, 7th edn, Harmondsworth: Penguin.

Seymour, C. (1939) *Notre-Dame of Noyon in the Twelfth Century*, New Haven: Yale.

Simson, O. von (1962) *The Gothic Cathedral*, 2nd edn, New York: Harper & Row.

Stoddard, W.S. (1966) *Monastery and Cathedral in France*, Middletown: Wesleyan University Press.

Taylor, W. and Mark, R. (1982) 'The technology of transition: sexpartite to quadripartite vaulting in High Gothic architecture', *Art Bulletin* 64(4): 579–87.

Viollet-le-Duc, E.E. (1854–68) *Dictionnaire raisonné de l'architecture française du XI⁰ au XVI⁰ siècle*, 10 vols, Paris: Morel.

Willis, R. (1842) 'On the construction of the vaults of the Middle Ages', in *Trans. Royal Institute of British Architects*, Vol. I, Part II.

—— (1972–3) *Architectural History of Some English Cathedrals*, 2 vols, Chiceley: Minet.

43   Changing challenges: the changing pattern of the use of timber

David Yeomans

The task of the carpenter is sometimes to provide a purely utilitarian structure for either roof or floor but at other times to express this structure in a decorative way. At the same time designers in wood have had to work within the limitations of this natural material: the limited sizes available, and therefore the relatively high cost of large sections, and the difficulty of forming effective joints between members. Limited by the sizes of members that could be obtained, early structures were confined to simple frames, or to arch-like structures, while the modern timber designer can achieve similar structures with relative ease with glued laminated timber or by using timber connectors, both of which enable large structures to be built with small sizes of timber.

Early roof structures either used light sections of timber to form common rafter roofs or heavy frames to carry purlins which in turn supported the rafters, and while the former could be given some modest decorative treatment in the form of carved crown posts, there were much greater opportunities for decoration of the large frames. Although regional traditions differed, most roof structures depended upon a beam spanning between masonry or timber walls, from which an arrangement of struts took load from the principal rafters. The same basic structures were used for both utilitarian buildings and the larger houses, but in the latter the structural members were often decoratively carved. In churches the use of lead enabled flat roofs to be used where the beams carried the purlins directly, with these main members decoratively moulded.

The alternative to structures based on beams was to use arch-like arrangements to brace the principal rafters. This required long, deep timbers and produced what we might regard today as a dramatic structure of simple elegance, but this would not have suited a taste for richly decorated structures. The hammer-beam roof, which reduced the maximum size of timbers needed for the structure, provided a greater opportunity for decorative work. In the simplest form of this roof the arch brace was divided by a hammer beam into two shorter pieces; once this had been done, the line of the arch no longer needed to be continuous and the upper part could be brought forward along the hammer beam, giving a more dramatic effect. In church roofs, hammer beams were sometimes carved in the form of angels who thus appeared to carry the roof, because the arches sprang from their backs. When a hammer post was stood on the beam the space behind it could also be filled with decoration. This suggests that the development of this type of roof was for its decorative rather than structural possibilities, but whether this was the principal motivation is not certain.

The origin of the hammer beam is still a matter for debate, but its visual form must have been a powerful influence on its adoption because variations on this structure were used in many parts of the country where the carpenters adapted the form to quite different carpentry traditions to produce distinctive hammer beam types.

The best-known and one of the earliest surviving examples of this kind of structure is the roof of Westminster Hall which, with its arch braces, has come to be the archetype for the hammer beam roof, still illustrated in books today (see Figure 1). However, it was not the most frequently used, probably because of the complexities of construction involved in the use of the arch brace. Since these early structures the form has continued to fascinate designers. In the eighteenth century James Smith published his *Specimens of Ancient Carpentry*, which was simply a collection of drawings of hammer beam roofs, and in the nineteenth century it became popular with the architects of the Gothic Revival. Although much of the church roof building during that period was in simple imitation of Gothic forms, there were a few architects who seem to have used the inspiration of these forms as the basis for designs which were not simply imitations but rather adaptations of the spirit of the Gothic structure, like Brunel's Temple Meads Station, Bristol, or Lamb's church at Addiscombe.

The floor naturally offered fewer opportunities for decorative arrangements, but in the sixteenth century Serlio published a drawing of a structure which, although not new, he claimed as his own invention. It was a floor constructed of pieces of timber each of which was shorter than the total span but which intersected in such a way that they mutually supported each other. Whatever structural advantages this arrangement had, the beams of the floor produced an intriguing pattern if exposed in the ceiling below, and in England during the seventeenth century there was some interest in the use of this type of structure for its decorative possibilities. The basic arrangement was adapted to form a floor in

ROOFS.
ROOF OF WESTMINSTER HALL

Figure 1 *Westminster Hall roof.* (Source: *Newlands 1865*)

the Schools Tower, Oxford, but regrettably this and other examples have not survived. The type of layout attracted sufficient attention at the time for John Wallis to attempt its structural analysis and to design variations on the same theme. But because they depended upon the soundness of a large number of joints they were hardly a practical proposition and were not much used. The largest span known for which the structure was used is in the floor of Independence Hall, Philadelphia, but this was for its ability to produce a long span rather than to give an interesting ceiling below.

During the seventeenth century the trussed roof was being developed in England, and although this was a purely utilitarian structure, hidden above a ceiling rather than exposed for decorative effect, its development was essential to the architecture of the day. Architectural ideas which had been imported from Italy were scarcely possible using the traditional structural forms used in England. Long spans, beyond the capacity of simple beam structures, were needed for such buildings as the Banqueting House, Whitehall, by Inigo Jones, and Wren's Sheldonian Theatre, Oxford, and the only way to construct these efficiently was to use roof structures based on the trussed roofs that were already being used in Italy. However, this type of structure was developed by architects and carpenters in England. Wren designed

a unique structure for the Sheldonian Theatre based upon the trussed roof and later designed dramatic, long-spanning queen post trusses for roofs in the hospitals at Chelsea and Greenwich.

In part these roofs depended upon imported softwoods from Baltic countries which produced longer timbers than the native oak, which by that time was in short supply. Eighteenth-century architects continued to develop and exploit this type of structure, adapting it to cope with wider spans and different architectural forms. It was adopted for the church roofs of the eighteenth century, in which it supported vaulted plaster ceilings, for the replacement of steep-pitched and wide-spanning Gothic cathedral roofs and for the building of domes like that of the Radcliffe Camera, Oxford. It was to be some time before spans as large as the Sheldonian Theatre were again needed – not until the riding schools and the theatres of the later eighteenth century – but by then the roof truss was better understood and simpler forms had developed.

The great advance in the means of constructing trussed roofs came with the introduction of iron fasteners and the use of iron members in combination with timber. Although this did not lead directly to the timber structures of today, it was a foretaste of the truss forms that might be possible. The main structural problem in building a timber truss was that pieces of timber had to be joined together to form the tie beam in such a way that they could transmit tensile forces and so contain the outward thrust of the principal rafters. This was possible but not easy to do in timber. At the same time a joint had to be formed so that the principal rafters were properly restrained by the ends of the tie. More-over, the tie itself had to be suspended from the principals if it was not to sag, either under its own weight or from the loads of the struts that were brought to bear on it. From the very beginning, iron connectors of some form were used to construct such trusses and help form these critical joints. Tie beams were suspended from the king and queen posts of the trusses with metal straps, principal rafters were strapped to the ends of the tie beams and iron bolts were used to connect parts of the tie beam together. With these simple devices, long-spanning trusses could be built to serve a variety of purposes.

It was the more extensive use of iron in the late eighteenth and nineteenth centuries that enabled the timber truss to develop beyond the simple early forms. At first, cast-iron connectors were used between the members, eliminating complex carpentry and simplifying the problem of transmitting forces from one member to another. Wrought-iron rods, which could be fixed to the castings, were then used in place of timber tension members and this gave designers much greater freedom in arranging the members of the truss because the tie beam no longer need be straight, and joints could be made at any angle.

Early trussed roofs were all hidden structures. They served their purpose in facilitating an architecture which required large roof spans, and where elaborate plastered ceilings were hung from the tie beams, but although this was an architecture made possible by such timber structures it was not an architecture of timber like that produced by the decorative medieval roofs. In the nineteenth century the structure was exposed once more but although the structures were often dramatic in scale they were seldom designed for architectural effect. Combinations of timber and iron were used for the roofs of sheds, workshops and railway stations. Brunel designed a number for his buildings on the Great Western Railway, and many later stations on the same line had roofs on this principle. More recently, structures like this have been used with effect because in an interior there may be an advantage in exposing the roof, the timber compression members providing an acceptable finish while thin steel tension members give a lightness to the structure that would not be possible with timber alone. The roof of the Maltings concert hall at Snape is a good modern example of this combination.

The nineteenth century inclusion of iron was the prelude to the development of iron-trussed roofs, as rolled sections became available that could be used instead of timber. Although timber continued to be used in conjunction with iron throughout the nineteenth century, it was a period when iron and steel structures were more important; the revival of timber structures needed the development of the modern mechanical fastener, which enables the more direct connection of smaller sections of timber and the transmission of larger forces than is possible with bolts or nails. A fastener was patented in America before the First World War but there was little interest in it and the real development of this type of device began in Germany after the war, stimulated by timber shortages. This enabled long-span timber structures to be built by simply assembling small pieces, and the timber truss enjoyed a period of revival and development throughout Europe. Major industrial structures were built in France by the company of Antoine Mole, although the greater availability of timber in America naturally resulted in its more extensive use there.

Even with modern timber connectors it may still not be a simple matter to design effective joints in timber, but the great advantage of the material is its high strength-to-weight ratio when compared with other materials. This makes it suitable for long-spanning structures and, in spite of the comparatively small sizes of members that can be used, timber has been the material chosen for some of our largest structures. A number of airship hangars have been built of timber, and during the Second World War two such hangars were built at Tillamook, on the Oregon Coast, which at the time had the largest roofs in the world. By combining metal connectors with timber ties and struts

it has also been possible to construct three-dimensional trussed timber structures. Aalto used exposed, three-dimensional trusses as both the structure and a decorative feature of the council chamber of Saynatsalo Town Hall.

The recognition of the possibilities of joining quite small pieces of timber to form large structures, in what today we call laminated timber, dates from de l'Orme's invention in the sixteenth century. This relied upon some form of mechanical fastener to join the pieces together. This form of construction could not be used for beams where timber was in bending, but it was a useful means of building timber arches. Although it did not receive much attention in this country it enabled forms to be built in timber that were not otherwise possible. Wren used it in some of his church roofs, in particular for the dome of St Stephen's, Walbrook. This arrangement of parallel planks set vertically, known today as vertical laminations, seems to have been little used in Britain during the eighteenth century but enjoyed a revival in the nineteenth century with the need for larger spans. Its advantage was that the large cross-sections which these required could easily be framed from small planks cut to shape, and by staggering joints in each layer long, continuous arch members could be formed. This was the structure used for the vaulted roof of the transept of Crystal Palace and the domes of the later exhibition buildings at South Kensington. It was also used in Britain for a number of more utilitarian structures. For example, a large roof which was built for a roller-skating rink in the nineteenth century survives in the centre of Norwich. In America, when Thomas Jefferson built Monticello he used this form of construction, and it was later used by a number of other American architects for framing domes.

Horizontally laminated timber, which has effectively superseded vertical laminations, developed in the early nineteenth century (see Figure 2). Bridges of curved boards of timber fastened together had been used in Switzerland for bridges, but the development of this

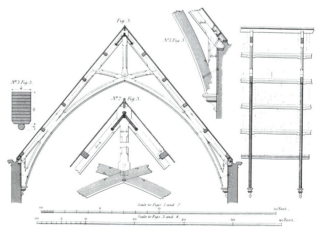

Figure 2 *Roof truss with laminated members, nineteenth century.*

type of structure for buildings came largely through an interest in it by French military engineers who used it for roofing riding schools, a building type that required a large span. Known in Britain at the time as 'bent timber', a number of planks were fastened together mechanically, either by nailing or bolting. This method attracted the attention of railway engineers who used it for bridges, but it was also used for railway stations at Newcastle and King's Cross, London, neither of which survive. It was used for drill halls and for at least one church roof in Liverpool. But this last example looks little different from any other Gothic Revival structure, and where 'bent timber' was used in utilitarian structures they have largely perished unrecorded. Today the best surviving example in Britain is the German Gymnasium, quite close to King's Cross station. Because both types of laminated timber were used for simple utilitarian buildings that are unremarked by history, it is difficult to know how extensively they were used.

Glued laminated timber (Glulam), which is used extensively today, was developed by Hertzer in Germany before the First World War, but was little used there afterwards because of a shortage of glue-making materials. Instead it was extensively used elsewhere in Europe. During the inter-war period this method of construction attracted the attention of American engineers, who carried out a number of experiments on laminated timber arches and visited Europe to examine structures that had been in use for several years to assess their durability. The effect of this was that America became the centre of interest in this technology and, following the Second World War, it was essentially reimported into Europe from there. Laminated timber is now used for simple beams as an alternative to steel structures, where it enjoys the advantage of lightness, and in very long-spanning structures because laminating overcomes the limitation of the natural sizes of timbers. It seems to have found particular application in sports buildings where spans of 70 m. (230 ft.) are not uncommon. The combination of a good finished appearance and the ability to curve structural members using this method has also led to its use in dramatic works of architecture, especially in churches and market halls. Some of the largest structures recently built which take advantage of the high strength-to-weight ratio of timber have combined the use of laminated members with steel connectors to form large-spanning goedesic domes.

In contrast, some more recent developments in timber structures have used the idea of joining small pieces together in ways which have no precedents in the past. There are two developments of this kind. The first involves connecting small pieces of timber in a shape which is capable of long spans rather like a shell roof. There have been two systems for doing this which are structurally unrelated. The earlier is the lamella roof, which was largely developed in America between the wars. Short pieces of timber, all in the same plane, are

fastened together with bolts, or other metal fasteners, to form a kind of net that can be constructed as a vaulted roof. A more recent version for the Federal Garden Show at Mannheim shows how a net of timbers can be used to roof an amorphous area.

The other recent development is the glueing together of boards to form a surface structure of some kind. Hyperbolic paraboloid roofs constructed like this have enjoyed some popularity, but other surfaces are equally possible. The roof of Oxford Road Railway Station, Manchester, is a combination of three conoids constructed in this way, and the shell roofs of the Thames Barrage are prefabricated components of boarded timber shells on laminated timber ribs. In this way timber has adopted forms which are perhaps more commonly associated with concrete shells, but which can be constructed with much simpler temporary supports (see Figure 3).

Figure 3 *Canterbury Teachers Training College, engineers Harris and Sutherland.*

REFERENCES

Newlands, J. (1865) *The Carpenter's and Joiner's Assistant*, Glasgow: Blackie; reprinted 1990, London: Studio Editions.
Smith, J. (1733) *Specimens of Ancient Carpentry*, 2nd edn 1787, London.

44 Structural theories and their architectural expression: a review of possibilities

Fazlur R. Khan

The fundamental function of architecture, which is to provide protection and shelter from the elements of nature, was indeed the origin of all artificial shelters of the first settlements of *Homo sapiens*. From primitive mud and straw huts to elegant stone and masonry forms in later civilizations, architecture remained deeply rooted in humanity's basic needs and the level of structural technology. Architecture without structure can exist only as art. Yet, art applied to basic structure can bring in an aesthetic and spiritual quality which structure itself cannot always achieve. Even in the most primitive settlements of people, structural theories were used in an intuitive and empirical, if not mathematical, way. Construction techniques and the capability of handling materials also affected the final architectural forms and proportions. The spacing of the massive columns of Karnak in Egypt, the proportions of the stone beams and columns of the Acropolis, the stable shapes of the pyramids and Mayan temples, the grand spaces created by Brunelleschi, the elegance of the Taj Mahal, and even the elegant form of the pagoda were based on structural principles of the day.

Only around the eighteenth century did a structural theory based on mathematical formulations begin to emerge. The simple formulations $\Sigma M = 0$, $\Sigma V = 0$ and $S = Mc/I + P/A$ established relationships which are the basis for understanding and designing both the simplest and the most complicated structures. The development and understanding of new materials has gone hand in hand with the refinement of mathematical theories. The capacity of building materials to carry precisely determined axial loads, moments and shear stresses is primarily responsible for the innovation of new structural systems more sophisticated than classical masonry construction.

In the late nineteenth century the invention of steel for construction was a significant step in the development of many new structural systems. Steel trusses and frames were developed and concordant structural theories were established. The early suspension bridge by Brunel, the Crystal Palace by Paxton, and the first skyscrapers in the United States all resulted from the invention of structural steel and structural theories which predict and interpret the behaviour of trusses and frames. Although concrete developed in the early twentieth century as a significant alternative to masonry

First published in the *Chicago Architectural Journal*.

construction, it soon was combined with steel reinforcing rods to emerge as the totally new reinforced concrete construction material. Structural theories quickly followed to understand and predict the behaviour of such a composite material. Through all these developments, the original basic structural theory of bending, axial and tortional forces was adapted to special conditions.

THE FRAME

Just as the forms of arches and domes developed out of the structural possibilities of masonry construction based on empirical and intuitive structural theories, newer architectural forms began to emerge to represent and heighten the structural possibilities of steel and reinforced concrete in frame-type construction. The industrial urban centres facing increasing population needed multi-storey buildings. New structural materials and their concordant theories rose to the challenge of developing tall buildings. The massive stone wall construction of earlier times was replaced by frame construction for taller buildings. These frames consisted of a series of columns connected to each other at each floor level by girders and beams in a rigid way so that the resulting structure, while carrying the vertical floor loads down to the foundation, can also withstand the horizontal forces caused by wind and earthquake. Frame construction found its clear and distinctive expression in the elegant proportions of buildings by famous Chicago architects like Jenney, Burnam and Root, *et al.* The Chicago window was the outcome of the frame's regular column spacings expressed through the practical detailing of large plate-glass windows which fit between those columns. From the late nineteenth century to the early twentieth century the 'Chicago school of architecture' influenced the expression of the structural frame for tall buildings, which become taller and taller under socio-economic pressures and came to be known as skyscrapers. The first Leiter building built in 1893 was already a grand departure from the traditional masonry bearing-wall construction, and created a new architectural form. The structure was simply expressed in the architectural façade of the building. For an extreme expression of such structure one has to look at a building done in the 1960s, the BMA Building in Kansas City. Here the structural frame is expressed without any hindrance by moving the glass line inside the exterior frame. The structural frame, symbolizing the inherent structural theory, becomes the clear architectural expression of the building. If the early twentieth century was the 'modern era' perhaps this building should have been called 'post-modern' in its freedom from the earlier tradition.

The structural theory of the beam-column frame system for tall buildings pointed out that the required stiffness of such a frame was the controlling factor for design rather than simple strength. The bending of columns and girders accounts for about 90 per cent of the total sway. The remaining 10 per cent is due to the cantilever action of the entire frame, causing tension and compression in the columns. This is generally known as the column-shortening effect. The horizontal racking of the frame at each floor due to lateral shear can be approximated by the simple assumption that points of counterflexure exist at mid-height in a storey and at the midspan of a beam. This approximation is reasonably valid for most of the building except the top and bottom floors, and leads to the following equation for calculating the sway factor at any intermediate floor:

$$E\phi_n = V_n h_n / 12\Sigma K_{cn} + V_n h_n / 12\Sigma K_{gn}$$

where:

E	=	modulus of elasticity
ϕ_n	=	shear sway factor at n^{th} floor, i.e. the ratio of sway to the storey height
V_n	=	total horizontal shear at n^{th} floor
h_n	=	height of nth floor
ΣK_{cn}	=	sum of column stiffnesses (I/h) at n^{th} floor
ΣK_{gn}	=	sum of girder stiffnesses (I/L) at n^{th} floor

An examination of the above equation will immediately show that the shear sway is caused partly by the flexibility of the columns and partly by the flexibility of the beams. Therefore, when a building is taller than about ten stories the designer is often faced with the need to increase the size both of columns and beams in order to keep the shear sway within an acceptable limit. To establish economic control of the overall cost of a high-rise building, the design can be divided into two phases. The first phase involves designing the building for gravity loads alone, without considering the effects of the lateral loads. The columns, the beams and the slabs are sized to carry only the dead and live loads. Because gravity loads cannot be reduced or dissipated by any structural manipulation, the first phase sets the lower boundary of the proportions and total quantity of material and labour cost. After this the designer has to consider all the sway and the lateral strength of the structural design, as outlined earlier. To provide adequate resistance to lateral sway and to control the perception of lateral motion, the designer may have to increase the sizes of columns or beams or both. The second phase, therefore, constitutes the final design of the structure and represents the upper bound of the

proportions and total quantity of material and labour cost. A steel structure's economy can be fairly well defined by the average weight of steel per square foot of floor area. Therefore, for a typical building frame one can show how an increase in the number of storeys increases the gap between the lower bound (phase I) and the upper bound (phase II) in design quantities. The gap between the upper bound and the lower bound represents the premium paid for height, as discussed earlier. The structural engineer's challenge has to refine a known system or to find and develop newer structural systems to reduce or eliminate the premium for height in any given building.

THE TUBE

In the search for new structural systems which would allow the construction of buildings without any premium for height, structural theories played a very strong role. It was easily proved that for a given series of columns in a building the most efficient behaviour in strength and in stiffness can be obtained by tying all the columns so that they act together like a rigid 'box' or 'tube' cantilevering out of the ground. However, from the practical point of view, it is easier and more efficient to tie the exterior columns rigidly, rather than interior ones. In the ideal case, therefore, under lateral loads the entire building will act like a hollow cantilever projecting out of the ground and the deflections and stresses in the perimeter columns can then be computed on the assumption of an equivalent hollow tube. Such an ideal case would require almost infinitely rigid diaphragms connecting these exterior columns. Although in an actual building this is never possible, in recent years, a number of new systems have been proposed and used which aim at achieving the ideal tube-like action.

These rigid box or tube-type structural systems generally consist of an exterior tube, simulated by the exterior columns, and a central core of rigid or simply connected columns and beams confined within a central service area for lifts, stairs, toilets, service ducts, etc. The floor beams can then span from the exterior wall to the central core and thereby provide column-free open space for the tenants. Because in a tube-type structure most of the necessary stiffness and strength for lateral loads is provided by the exterior columns acting together, the floor construction does not have to participate in resisting lateral load. It can therefore be simply supported and relatively shallow, and any interior columns can be located as needed for the best floor plan. For this same reason, longer spans can be used between the exterior walls and the interior core.

COMPOSITE SYSTEMS

In 'tube-in-tube' structures, shear-walls in the central core can drastically reduce flexibility in the planning and utilization of that area. For instance, when elevators drop off at different height levels it is difficult to use the freed space as rental area because the shear-walls cannot suddenly be eliminated. In steel buildings, however, the central cores are much more flexible than in the concrete building, and any area freed due to dropping off of the elevators can be immediately utilized as rentable area. Further, tall steel structures can be built relatively quickly, generally one floor every three days, whereas in concrete construction even one floor every five days is an optimistic projection. Why not combine the advantages and eliminate the disadvantages of concrete and steel systems? This is what led the author to develop the 'composite system', consisting of structural steel columns, beams and floor construction inside the building, whereas the exterior framed-tube is formed by closely spaced columns and spandrels which act as the window wall as well. In order to keep the rate of construction equal to the normal rate for a steel building, and also to keep the structural steel trade separate from the reinforced concrete trade, the entire inside structure in steel is built ahead of the exterior concrete tube structure *cum* cladding. Three major buildings recently constructed with this system are the 45-storey Union Station building in Chicago, the 50-storey One Shell Square building in New Orleans and the recent 55-storey Three First National Plaza building in Chicago. The quantity of structural steel used in this system is approximately half of what is needed for a normal steel building, making it one of the most efficient systems for tall buildings.

The 100-storey John Hancock Center in Chicago, on the other hand, achieves its architectural expression – the visual recognition of its strength and stability – through the interplay of horizontal, vertical and diagonal members. For the structural design of the John Hancock Center, the truss-tube concept is based on the interaction of exterior columns, spandrels and the large diagonal members, which simulate a hollow tube consisting of the entire exterior perimeter of the building. The diagonals in this building were not designed as wind bracing in the classical sense, but as inclined columns which also distribute the gravity loads uniformly to all vertical columns. This integral structural composition of the building's exterior was thus responsible for both its unusual economy, and its aesthetic quality. The decision to express the structure by cladding the main structural members with black anodized aluminium, and filling in the remaining surface with a slightly recessed glass curtain wall, was a deliberate act to highlight its visual strength. The clear expression of the structure helped to give the building a character and architectural quality that a preconceived façade could have never achieved. The very possibility of expression makes the engineer more conscious of the need to design the structure as efficiently, elegantly and articulately as possible. The John Hancock Center in Chicago is a structural expression of strength and vitality that gives it a distinct architectural presence in its urban setting.

Structural aesthetics goes beyond the visual expression of the structure on the outside of the building. The visual and physical environment it creates for the occupants within the building is of great importance. The John Hancock Center's diagonal truss tube also contributes to the sculptural elegance of the spaces within. The juxtaposition of vertical and diagonal members in its fenestration gives a special visual effect. The two intersecting diagonals inside the second floor lobby as well as the lobby of the apartment on the forty-sixth floor are particularly good examples of the structural expression of this frame as perceived from within.

The steel built truss concept for intermediate height buildings of forty to sixty stories was developed to reduce the building sway under wind load. Steel trusses have their own natural proportions, and when set at intermediate levels on the exterior of a building they create a structural form worthy of full expression. The First Wisconsin Bank Building in Milwaukee is an excellent example of such a structural expression.

In tall reinforced-concrete buildings, the visual expression of structure has only recently been integrated in the overall architectural façade. In the framed-tube concept the exterior walls of the building are indeed classical bearing walls in contemporary materials with punched-through openings to create windows. Once this is understood it is easy to look at the larger openings that can be necessary at the ground floor as an integral part of the bearing wall, rather than as an independent opening created by a very rigid transfer girder. In the early 38-storey Brunswick Building in Chicago the large opening at the ground floor was created by a solid 7.3 m. (24 ft.) deep and 2.4 m. (8 ft.) thick reinforced concrete girder all around the perimeter to support the framed bearing wall above that level. This was a monumental solution and its clear expression of structure had a strong architectural impact. But in a later building a more transitional transfer was achieved through the understanding of load flow around an opening in a classical bearing wall. In the Marine-Midland Bank Building in Rochester, New York, the large opening on the ground floor was achieved through a gradual transition of load paths from the upper floors to the far spaced ground floor columns. The intermediate floor columns and spandrel beams were shaped and sized according to the actual load flow. The result, a visual impression of the classical arch in traditional masonry bearing-wall construction, was the result of honest structural expression.

BUNDLED TUBES

The original concept of bundled tubes, first used in the Sears Tower, is now being explored as a more 'organic' shape in a number of new, tall concrete buildings. Each of these buildings is being studied for proportion and form through a totally integrated structural and architectural expression.

Bundling square framed-tubes established the concept in the Sears Tower. What soon became apparent was that it was not so important to give the single tubes any particular plan shape, but that adjacent tubes can be attached to each other in such a way that the bundled shape develops into a closed mega-tube, with single tubes forming cells within it. The framed-tubes, whether single or bundled, could be rectangular, square, hexagonal, octagonal or parallelograms in plan. The columns and the spandrels of the tube must be sized so that their flexural contribution to the lateral sway of the building must be relatively small, perhaps on the order of H/1500, while the major portion of the deflection will be caused by the cantilever behaviour of the entire building.

The multi-rise One Magnificent Mile Building at Oak and Michigan in Chicago is an example of the three hexagonal framed-tubes bundled together to respond to the site on one hand and the need for more views of Lake Michigan on the other. The manifestation of this structural theory is a truly architectonic massing-vocabulary for future buildings.

THE THEORY OF CABLE STRUCTURES APPLIED TO LONG-SPAN ROOFS

Steel cable suspension bridges have been in use for around a hundred years. These bridges all derive their aesthetic value from the natural form created by the structure. In enclosed buildings, however, the use of cables has not yet been fully explored and experimented. The possibility exists of creating large clear spans by hanging the roof structure from cables spanning between masts. A recent example of this is the Baxter Lab Cafeteria Building near Chicago, which has a 90 m. by 45 m. (295 ft. by 148 ft.) roof. The need for an enclosed, column-free space was social as well as functional; social in the sense that it was desirable to create an inner environment with a spirit of celebration and relaxation which would be enhanced by a clean structural grid on the roof and a feeling of unobstructed extension of inner space into the outer landscaped area; and functional in the sense that the large gatherings of people throughout the day could be facilitated by the elimination of as many supporting columns as possible. The structural concept of the roof offered the possibility of expressing the roof's unusual slenderness and floating characteristics and to honestly create the visual impression that the entire roof is supported by the radiating cables from the two central masts. From inside, stabilizing cables radiating from the mast up to the roof beams give the inner space a convincing and distinct structural aesthetic character. The structural concept of

the stayed cable suspension bridge has opened up superb possibilities in architecture.

TENSION STRUCTURES WITH FABRICS

Cable network tension structures have been used successfully for a number of years, and structural simplicity and elegance have always been the essence of the architectural expression of these buildings. The pioneering work done for the German Pavilion in the Montreal Expo, 1967, and the Munich Stadium for the Olympics in 1976 are two excellent examples of this kind of structure. A logical extension of this structural system was developed for the Haj Airline Terminal in Jeddah, which required a roof surface of almost 500,000 sq. m. (5 million sq. ft.). The pilgrims coming through Jeddah for their final destination of Mecca needed an open-air environment rather than an enclosed building. In a search for the most appropriate kind of roof for the desert environment of Saudi Arabia, the fabric tent appeared to be the most attractive and natural, and it also evoked the cultural heritage of the land. Using fabric as a permanent structure required the development of a special structural theory, which in turn dictated the optimum shapes for the tents. The structural tent thus derived uses teflon-coated fibreglass fabric 1 mm. (0.039 in.) thick, interacting with radiating cables. These tent units are hung from piers spaced 45 m. (150 ft.) apart and they soar from 20 m. (65 ft.) above the ground to a height of 36 m. (118 ft.). They are arranged in modules of twenty-one such units (3 × 7 units). All told, ten such modules (210 units) provide the pilgrims with an environment of transition from the air-conditioned aircraft to the generally open environment of the Haj process. Repeating the tent itself 210 times helped make the structure more economical compared to possible alternative steel or concrete roof systems. The expression of the simplicity and naturalness of the structure provides an aesthetic ambience and a cultural identification which will undoubtedly evoke the spirit of Haj to the millions of Hajiis who pass through it.

In describing these examples of steel, concrete, bearing-wall, cable and fabric-tension structures, I have attempted to focus upon the essence of structural aesthetics in buildings. Structure is based on a kind of reason (expressed in mathematical theories) which has its own inherent aesthetics. Well-detailed and efficient structures possess the natural elegance of slenderness and reason, and have possibly a higher value than the whims and a-priori aesthetics imposed by architects who do not know how to work closely with engineers, and who do not have an inner feeling for natural structural forms. Most preconceived architectural expressions and forms are the result of a dichotomy created in the last century with the splitting of the classical master-builder's task into architecture and engineering, each separate from the other. Simple and honest structure, with its implicit strength and stiffness and its elegantly optimal slenderness, can provide an architectural expression that has its very own vitality and aesthetics. A clear understanding of structural behaviour and the resulting inherent forms will help future teams of archi-tects and engineers to design buildings in which the aesthetic qualities of structure and technology can give form to social and architectural values, to create build-ings that will eloquently speak of our time even though we are not sure whether we are Modern or Post-Modern.

45 The impact of the environment: the shock of the new

Ian Murphy

This essay addresses salient contemporary issues which have resulted in the current pluralist approach to architectural design. It is argued that the interest in revivalist architecture is largely attributable to social disunification and attendant uncertainties which have been sustained by the technologies of decentralization.

Neophobia, the fear of new objects, is a common response mechanism in the animal kingdom (in which the human race features as a relative newcomer). The 'phobia' becomes apparent when a new object is placed in, or near, the selected habitat of the animal in question. At first the alien object is treated with great suspicion and normally avoided. After a time, when the object is discovered to be benign, it will be accepted as a constituent part of the habitat, albeit that it may cause some discomfort and embarrassment initially. In due course the animal may establish a rapport with the object and eventually this may cause the animal to change the general habitat in order better to accommodate the object.

Naturally, the same response syndrome can be identified in humans. In this instance 'habitat' can be interpreted as village, town or city, and 'object' as a building or other manufactured structure. The conscious decision to reside for some time in a particular location generally infers that people accept, and probably feel at ease with, the environmental fabric of that location. Familiarity with the surroundings engenders a sense of relative security and, perhaps, an affinity is eventually established. When a building is erected within the 'habitat' which impinges upon, and challenges, this experiential pattern then a negative response to the instrusive element is often apparent. This is particularly true if the building is perceived to contrast vigorously with the existing environmental grain of the surroundings in terms of function, scale and visual treatment. The discord is frequently borne out of insecurity caused initially by the 'shock of the new'. The shock, in time, may manifest itself as a fear or dread if the discomfort continues (either physically or psychologically, or both), and ultimately as a 'phobia'.

However, in times when cataclysms and traumas of every description are being treated with increasing complacency it is justifiably difficult to believe that architecture can any longer make a significant impact on, let alone shock, society. That it continues to do so is simply because architecture is difficult to ignore. It is unavoidable. Society is compelled to experience it on a more or less daily basis, as it has done throughout history. Architecture is potentially one of the most readily accessible and digestible of all art-forms. It will only shock when it becomes indigestible, when it is 'force-fed' to an unsuspecting and unwilling society.

Contemporary society, rightly or wrongly, is seen as multivalent and amorphous, and it is relatively easy, therefore, to understand why architectural pluralism exists and is accepted *sine dubio*. If the word 'society' is taken to mean the customs and organization of an *ordered* community then it is tempting to think that architecture can only shock if it causes *disorder*, either directly or indirectly. A dichotomy instantly arises, however, since it is frequently argued that the *creation* of order is axiomatic to architectural design and practice. If this argument is translated literally then the intentional, even unintentional, disarrangement of the built environment cannot be considered to be of value to society, or to be of architectural merit. Clearly, this is not the case since the long-term results of disorder need not be entirely negative if they lead, at a later date perhaps, to reappraisal, reform and improvement. Historical perspective is a powerful panacea. The post-rationalization of society's ills and preoccupations is cold comfort to those actually exposed to them at any one time and who experience the 'shock'.

History is littered with examples of buildings and other structures which have 'shocked'. It would be a fruitless task to attempt to list them all, whether they be early examples such as the Egyptian pyramids or of more recent origin such as the Beaubourg Centre in Paris or the Lloyd's headquarters in London. In most instances, however, the initial surprise and distrust of the public has been displaced by tacit acceptance, and occasionally fondness. More often than not, each example represented advances in design, technology, management and production which have left an indelible mark on history and which still confound to this day.

More convincing arguments about the puissance of architecture in this context can be developed if the impact of the work of one architect upon a particular city is explored. In this instance, the work of Antoni Gaudí (1852–1926) can be considered in relation to the city of Barcelona. Contrary to popular theory, Gaudí was a pragmatist, despite the complex sculptural and decorative qualities of many of his buildings. He would often make 'upside-down' models using string and small bags of sand to determine the structural performance of his buildings. Apparently the public was taken aback by his Casa Batlló (1904–6), and the Casa Milá (1906–10) caused an uproar in a city used to inventiveness and arrogance. Gaudí was interested in architectural and structural 'brinkmanship' (as witness the parabolic arches at Colegio Teresiano which quiver when touched) and surreal interventions (ventilation towers masquerading as church spires at the Güell pavilions) which still arouse strong passions even today. There is no doubt that Gaudí's architecture and enabling technology shocked when the buildings were first revealed, and their power remains unabated.

Some cities have been reluctant to change and have been cocooned by over-enthusiastic conservation policies. The urban centres of Bruges, Prague and Krakow spring to mind. Despite their undoubted qualities, the centres of such cities resemble architectural mausoleums. Other cities, however, have remained faithful to progress and have absorbed new 'layers' of architecture and technology with panache. The character of the city in these instances has been considered as a permanent reflection of history and has been transformed accordingly with wit and enthusiasm. Vienna is such a city.

New interventions in Vienna have always been seen as positive and assertive, rather like surgical incisions within the urban fabric which have been skilfully executed according to a carefully devised strategy. Such examples have spanned several centuries, from the work of J.B. Fischer von Erlach in the early eighteenth century to Coop Himmelblau in the late twentieth century. The recent work of Hans Hollein may also be cited, principally the New Haas building of 1989 which confronts St Stephan's Cathedral without equivocation and without apology. In the intervening period the immensely innovative work of Otto Wagner shines like a beacon. His Postal Saving Bank (1904–6) incorporated the most modern materials (glass blocks, aluminium) used in conjunction with advanced methods of construction (marble veneer secured with bolts) and pioneering environmental control systems. The engineering expertise of Wagner can aso be seen at the Nussdorft Weir and Floodgate scheme (1894–8) and at the Schutzenhaus project, which contains a moveable crane and a 'cockpit' of corrugated copper. Vienna had, and still maintains, an insatiable appetite for the new and an ability to absorb the resultant 'shockwaves' with ease. It is a fascinating city because of this.

In the current context the disadvantages of a consumer-orientated society which is heavily dependent on 'manufactured' energy are readily apparent. There are those who prophesy the ultimate demise of civilization because of global warming, which results directly from the abuse of current technologies. With biblical fervour it is claimed by others that this abuse will lead to various global combinations of famine, flooding and nuclear irradiation. This may prove to be the case. It is not, however, the 'fault' of technology. In contradistinction, it is the misapplication of technology that causes this distrust. Technology does not invent itself. Given the will and the right incentives (and this would require enormous moral and ethical circumspection) society could ensure that the development of future technologies would be used constructively to ameliorate the distasteful and, in the long term, hazardous by-products of current technologies.

It is difficult to know whether architecture is the recipient and user of new technologies or the generator of them. In truth, architecture has probably acted throughout history as a kind of propagator where technological seeds, which have been germinated elsewhere, are nurtured and reared, eventually to be transplanted in, and consumed by, society in diverse ways. A classical example of this is the interdependency of the elevator and the high-rise building. Whatever the social, aesthetic or constructional pressures, the height of the multi-storey building was limited as long as it depended on stairs for vertical circulation. Once Otis developed a safe elevator the way was open for the transformation of the urban environment. Subsequently the technology that was developed for high-rise buildings could be applied to all forms of lifting apparatus. The technology of mechanical ventilation followed a similar pattern.

When an architectural 'product' proves to be 'inedible' or 'indigestible', society should not criticize it in isolation. Instead, society should look within itself to discover how and why it was created in the first instance. Thus the symbiotic relationship between architecture and technology is as unique and particular now, with a new millennium in sight, as it has been throughout history. We are living in a society whose uncertainty causes it, and hence architecture, to fragment. Yet each faction is certain that the narrow, selective stance which it has adopted from within the pluralist *milieu* is entirely appropriate and correct. It is often a case of maladroit architecture emanating from a rhetoric of malapropisms.

The legacy of the Modern Movement is clearly seen in the faction which believes that technology can always provide suitable compensatory mechanisms to deal with all eventualities. Thus the International Style of 'anti-climatic' architecture demands sophisticated and extensive artificial endo-climatic control. Another faction, the Alternative Society, is concerned to protect what remains of our much-abused social and ecological systems and is once again gaining political momentum after first flourishing a quarter of a century ago. Yet another, the Neo Vernacular, adopts picturesque styles based on Arts and Crafts values chosen on a seemingly arbitrary basis. Post-Modernism uses crude symbolism loosely based on often inappropriate historical precepts. There is a resurgence of interest in classicism. Many other factions prevail. Contemporary architecture is confused. It appears to the lay person that self-indulgent, egotistical games are being played by so-called professionals at the expense of society at large.

Like the majority of art-forms, the creation of architecture depends principally on the conscious, or unconscious, intentions of its creators, which, in turn, are moulded by a wide spectrum of social, cultural and political influences and allied determinants. Architecture readily mirrors the preoccupations and values of the society in which it is spawned, and it is consequently an excellent indicator of coeval morals, tastes and expectations. As with architecture in general, technology in particular cannot be isolated from society because it too is dependent on such factors for its evolution and development.

Since a principal feature of contemporary society is disaggregation, it follows that resultant technologies are essentially concerned with decentralization. We live in a society with a rapidly diminishing heavy industrial base and an increasing service economy. Physical decentralization is made attractive by the sheer burden of urban congestion and the advent of relatively cheap telecommunication facilities, such as facsimile transmission and access, via remote secure terminals, to centralized computer banks. Communication networks, on a global and national basis, are the key to future developments both in terms of urban planning strategies and also at a detailed, technological level. Enormous emphasis is placed on speed of communication and transaction, which, in turn, means that buildings and associated technologies need to be adaptable and responsive (see Figure 1).

The symbolism of architecture will remain as strong as ever, whether it be conscious or inadvertent. Yet the iconographics of indeterminate buildings required by an ever-changing society will be particularly difficult to reconcile. Buildings which are specifically designed to accept change, perhaps many times within their allotted life span, will result in chameleon-like, metamorphic architecture. This concept is not new, but the technologies which permit the environmental control systems within buildings – and also their external fabric – to respond rapidly to fluctuating demands are the result of recent advances in the integration of artificial intelligence and precisely engineered control mechanisms.

An electronic 'brain' which operates the various environmental monitoring and control systems and layering devices of the building's fabric can be designed and installed with ease. The 'brain' can relay infinitely complex messages to remote controls to orchestrate a building's response to variable functional and climatic demands. A computer can even be programmed to anticipate changes and independently instigate the necessary control strategies, although these can always be overridden manually. The creation and use of such technology, based on heuristic principles, is a matter of fact. It should also be a matter of concern.

The principal concern of architecture in the twenty-first century should be the attempt to unite the technologies of decentralization and the concept of *genius loci* – that presiding, welcoming sense, or spirit, of belonging. To achieve this, both society and architecture have to be at peace with technology. These aspects are often absent in modern buildings and urban centres in general. The superimposition of revivalist styles of architecture on a matrix of contemporary, enabling technology simply leads to confusion and discord. The resultant buildings lack integrity and represent the unfortunate offspring of stylistic mayhem and social uncertainty. They represent the fruit of the Age of Unreason.

The spectre of the Modern Movement still looms large but is suffering from the backlash of failed social and cultural reforms and a legacy of architectural prosaicism. The doyens of the Modern Movement produced prototypes which broke down the barriers of architectural stereotypes. The preconceptions and aspirations of those architects have been seen retrospectively to be generally alien to those of the people who inhabited their buildings. Worse still is the fact that the building clones which followed were often thoughtless, sometimes cynical, misrepresentations of the incipient values of the Modern Movement. The architects of that age endeavoured to be both physical *and* social engineers in the broadest sense. They failed on both counts. The often egalitarian and worthwhile principles of the Modern Movement have now been eschewed, to be replaced by speculatory avarice and the 'objectivity' of diffident clients concerned more with quantity than quality.

The technology of decentralization can be the saviour or assassin of contemporary and future society. The role of architects may be uncertain, but the role of architecture is not. In order to look forward society may sometimes have to look back. This it should do in order to learn from previous mistakes and oversights and to preclude similar eventualities in the future. This does not imply historical dependency, as some would assert. The symbiosis of architecture and technology should prevail, engendered by honesty and integrity. The task will not be easy.

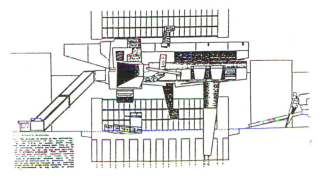

Figure 1 'Gobot' intervention, Brno. Andrew Budd, 3rd year BA (Hons) Architecture, University of Westminster; Tutor: Dr Ian Murphy.

46 Building the total system: the integration of the competing demands of modern technology

John Martin

The title I was set for this essay troubled me considerably as I will explain, but I decided that since it makes my first point for me very nicely I would leave it as it stands.

The fact is, of course, that technology should be serving us, not making demands of us, let alone competing demands. If it gets to the point where we think of technology as anything other than our servant, then building design – any design – is off to a bad start.

The consequences of letting technology in, without having it under control, are dire. Unfortunately that is exactly what happens more often than not. The engineering 'systems' which are installed in a building are, like the cars parked beneath it, quite beyond the user to look after. But, unlike the cars, they cannot be 'taken in' for expert service, they cannot easily have pieces exchanged and, worse, the owner rarely understands what they are really capable of doing, and increasingly finds that he or she cannot even run them properly.

At this point, I must make a distinction between the technology which is an integral part of the building and that which is clearly an 'extra', like the radio in the car, designed to suit the needs of the occupant but not necessary for the proper functioning of the car. These latter systems, like those for security, for communication and for computing – all of which are likely to be outmoded long before the building is worn out – vital though they may be to today's user, will certainly be replaced by tomorrow's. The trouble about this distinction is that modern building-management systems blur it. The air-conditioning will be monitored and controlled by the same computer which looks after building security and, no doubt in due course, everything else.

I suggest that the primary function of modern buildings, like ancient ones, is to provide shelter. This means that they are there to provide an appropriate environment for whatever is to take place inside. Let us not forget that this implies many things. We seek shelter not only from wind and rain, heat and cold, but also from the intrusion of discomfort – whether it assails by sight, sound or smell, or as polluted air. Not an easy matter to do all that in a city centre without resorting to a lot of modern technology, which may be well-understood by its designer, half-understood by its installer and understood barely at all by its user, particularly by the one who inherits it five years later. Ten years later it probably needs a major overhaul anyway, but it won't get it.

So a modern building, in order to serve its primary purpose of providing shelter, works only through a combination of the static parts, the fabric, and the active parts, the machinery, which every year become more complex. This raises the difficult question of the relative life-span of these two parts of the building. Things which are not expected to move or which don't consume energy can be expected to last far longer than those which do. It is not generally desirable to solve the problem of the incompatibility of life-span of building fabric and of building 'systems' by downgrading the quality of the fabric and the structure. The very creation of the materials used for the fabric of our buildings has, generally, involved the expenditure of large quantities of energy, and little of this material is recyclable. We cannot attempt to design our buildings for a short life. The alternative, of designing the moving parts to last longer, is not a practical proposition either. First, the client could not afford it but, second, even if they could, ten years hence they would want to change the mechanical and electrical systems in the building for something more modern.

What then is the answer?

One hears less often than before the once-popular slogan 'long life and loose fit'. It had a lot to commend it, though in practice far too little notice was taken. It implied a clear separation between the passive 'shell' of a building, made to last and capable of adaptation, and the other parts of the building which must change to suit changing times, changing needs and because active 'systems' wear out quite quickly.

But I think this never quite answered the question. 'Architecture', surely, implies something more than a two-part answer to the problem, where the two parts – the permanent and the temporary – are not perceived as one whole. If the fabric of a building evidently fails by itself to provide the shelter which is the *raison d'être* of the whole edifice, but has to be driven by machinery which is a temporary addition, how then can the whole aspire to be architecture? Of course, it is easy to take this argument too far. The issue is not so simple. What of the need for artificial light? Light is certainly related to architecture, and if lamps have to be added why not air-conditioning?

Perhaps it is all to do with the extent to which we find it necessary to fight against the adverse circumstances we have created for ourselves. If we could choose where to live, then we could build a perfectly comfortable home of natural materials which would last virtually for ever, be pleasant to live with, and need nothing more than a fire in winter and, if we insist on staying awake after dark, a light in the evening. But we have now contrived a way of life which results in a need to build high, and hence lifts which wear out before the building does, to build deep, and hence mechanical ventilation which wears out too, to build in an unhealthy – polluted and noisy – environment, and hence air-conditioning, which is even more complex and vulnerable. It is small wonder that in the most sophisticated cities of the world the scope of architecture has, with a few notable and expensive exceptions, been confined to the choice of cladding. It is not easy to produce real architecture where there is no space.

It is pleasant to dream of a time, far in the future, when we have learned how to live in this world without spoiling it for ourselves, and in which our skills will enable us to live at peace within it instead of making yet more hazards from which our buildings must shelter us. It is not in sight, and, till then, architecture for the many is a difficult challenge to meet.

The privileged few – the rich – remain, on the whole, unaware of their good fortune. I recall discussing the brief for a new building to house a group of highly paid scientists working in ancient ex-army huts in deep and lovely country. On analysing what they said they wanted, it became clear – more beautiful huts in deep and lovely country. They did *not* want one big building or air-conditioning or any of the trappings of 'high technology' building. But they could do without them, and until we all can – and have learned to want to – we have a difficult problem to solve: to make good architecture in a bad environment.

Earlier, I made a distinction between the technology which is essential to the primary function of the building as a place of shelter and that which serves the changing needs of its inhabitants, like communications systems and computers. These latter facilities, the 'add-ons', often tend to dominate in the client's briefing to the designers. Their impact on design is mainly to do with the space they may need rather than on the form or substance of the building. Certainly the screens at the terminals of communications systems call for a special environment – which they rarely get – but the need for this will surely disappear as the technology improves.

Much the more interesting problem is to do with the building itself. As things are, we are forced to design buildings in a hostile environment. The fabric of it is made from a wide range of mainly synthetic building materials, generally of rather poor quality and of which the long-term performance is not fully understood, assembled by a very mixed assortment of skilled, semi-skilled and unskilled people working in frequently unpleasant conditions. This building shell is then rendered habitable by the introduction of increasingly complex mechanical and electrical systems, each of a shorter life than the shell it services and each needing expert attention from time to time, which it probably doesn't get.

So what can be done now, and what can we hope for in the future?

Given that the complete building is, after all, a 'total system', then one can choose, to some extent, how much of the 'sheltering' function shall be provided by the passive shell and how much by the active mechanical and electrical systems. They do, after all, complement each other. A tent does little except keep the rain out. Anything more must be added. A massively constructed house can be designed to be comfortable as it is for most of the time. As the 'physics' of building becomes better understood, so does it become more feasible to rely on the fabric to provide the comfortable environment needed, which seems to me to be a good thing. Is it right that a building, like an aeroplane, should depend upon machinery and an input of energy to keep it useable?

It is still rare, but for some time now modern buildings have been made which require relatively little energy to keep them comfortable. Such buildings might not be thought of as examples of 'high technology'. They tend not to look as if they are, anyway. But high technology is there, certainly in the design, if not in the ultimate complexity of the construction: it takes the form of applied physics. It entails designing the fabric of the building to admit or exclude light, heat and sound, perhaps to store heat or cooling, in fact all that can be done naturally, within the constraints of the external environment. The more hostile, the more polluted the environment, the more difficult does this become. Surely this is a step in the right direction, towards an architecture which could properly be described as 'total' – when the building, as perceived, really works, not when what is seen represents only a façade behind which the real guts of the building hum and grind out the necessities for life within it.

Much more could be done in this direction, but there is a question of education involved. 'Professional' building clients, like most of us, are motivated mainly by profit, and generally this means short-term profit. Until circumstances change so that users, then building developers, find that it is better value to invest more in the permanent and less in the temporary parts of the building, progress in this direction will be very slow, and the total system – more, total architecture – will be very imperfect. At present there is little chance unless the building is paid for by those who will use it, and even then the case is hard to make on financial grounds alone.

What of future possibilities – the 'intelligent building', for example? If the external fabric of the building is seen as a complex filter, designed to cope with heat, light and sound, and given that the total natural energy falling upon the building over a day and a night could, were it not wasted, provide most, if not all, of the comfort conditions needed inside, then the challenge is evidently to design a fabric to act in just such a way. As external and internal conditions change, so the performance of the fabric as a filter must alter, and probably so must the function of the system within the building which is needed to redistribute the air, the light, the heat or the 'coolth'. Still too complicated? Probably. But materials already exist which can by themselves change their filtering characteristics to suit the need, for example, to allow more or less light and heat through. Whether or not such materials can be made to perform reliably for a worthwhile life-span remains to be seen.

But there is another element in all this, the most important of all – the people themselves, inside the building. In speaking of architecture, or of comfort or convenience, we are referring as much to the perception of the person as to the characteristics of what is perceived. If the expectation, the aim, is to have 'air-conditioning' or, more specifically, controlled conditions of temperature and humidity within a narrow range, then that will very directly determine the nature of what is designed and built, but very likely may not at all determine whether the user remains healthy and happy. There is, as yet, very little appreciation of what it is that really produces the feeling of well-being and joy which surely is the objective.

People and their buildings, together, make the 'total system'. Without understanding people, the building cannot be designed which will work in harmony with them.

It is gradually beginning to be known – as a theory – that our own in-built system needs the stimulus of changing conditions to function well. But you try convincing a letting agent or a developer of that! Steady 'perfect' conditions have been found to lead to a breakdown of the nervous system. On the other hand, a day out in rough weather – in the hills or on the sea – does a lot for one's health and happiness. Of course it is not that simple. The answer is not to ignore comfort. But some things are surely clear. We need fresh air, we like natural light, we like to exercise our individuality and open or shut the window or the heating or the blinds; we don't thrive in 'battery' conditions. Less obviously, we benefit from change – the dawn, full daylight and dusk, from pullover weather to shirt-sleeve order. We do not thrive on pollution, whether it be visual, aural, olfactory or chemical, and I am sure we vastly underestimate the positive effect of a good environment, let alone a beautiful one.

Surely architecture is about stimulus, and technology must support it, not get in the way. But, increasingly, the technology is understood by technologists and not by architects. The next few decades will give us the opportunity of getting technology to serve us, and that will entail a much better integration of understanding between those engaged in the design and the construction and with the use of the building.

In the meantime, I am happier and more effective amid uncomfortable beauty than comfortable dreariness, and I would be classed, I suppose, as a technologist!

PART 4

ELEMENTS AND ATTRIBUTES

SECTION 4.1

Architectural form

Debates about the relative importance of the form and content of objects, including buildings, go back to the ancient world, but we do seem to have reached an extraordinarily confused situation at the moment with respect to this central theme of architectural theory. Between the two extreme schools of thought – those who approach content almost exclusively via form, who prize extrinsic qualities over intrinsic ones, and their arch-opponents, those who place the emphasis on the single-minded pursuit of universal, atemporal values as perceived through the intellect rather than the senses – there are many shades of opinion.

This reflects the simple fact that in architectural form and content, extrinsic and intrinsic aspects are inextricably linked, and gives credence to the arguments of those who call for a middle way – a new kind of realism which would relate to, as Michael Benedikt puts it, 'a reality neither potential nor ideal, but actual . . . a world of things in themselves seen clearly' (Benedikt: 1987: 8).

Whatever the outcome of this war of words, ultimately our concern must be with the establishment of a framework or set of conditions that would encourage (or, at least, permit) the development of lasting and meaningful architectural forms – forms that could enhance the quality of human existence. It is to this end that our energies should be directed irrespective of the specialisms or ideological standpoints we hold.

The collection of essays in Parts 4 and 5 of the book were put together with this objective in mind. The nine contributions to the first section, 'Architectural form', deal with some of the principles behind architectural form-making as well as its physical properties in general terms: the interaction between forces and forms; the fundamental disciplines upon which architectural design procedures are founded; the nature of architectural creativity; the limits of associative thinking in the field; the connection between the development of architectural components and the wider socio-technological milieu from which they emerge;

and, finally, the way in which form is (and has been over time) qualified or articulated, or both, through the manipulation of physical factors such as colour, texture and light according to culturally determined decorative traditions.

H.L.

REFERENCES

Benedikt, M. (1987) *For an Architecture of Reality*, New York: Lumen Books.

RECOMMENDED READING

Alexander, C. (1964) *Notes on the Synthesis of Form*, Cambridge, Mass.: Harvard University Press.

Arnheim, R. (1977) *The Dynamics of Architectural Form*, Berkeley: University of California Press.

Bacon, E.N. (1970) *Design of Cities*, 3rd edn, London: Thames & Hudson.

Baker, G.H. (1989) *Design Strategies in Architecture: An Approach to the Analysis of Form*, New York: Van Nostrand Reinhold.

Benton, T. and Benton, C. (eds) (1975) *Form and Function: A Source Book for the History of Architecture and Design 1890–1939*, London: Open University Press.

Birren, F. (1988) *Light, Color and Environment*, 2nd edn, West Chester, Penn.: Schiffer.

Brolin, B. (1985) *Flight of Fancy: The Banishment and Return of Ornament*, London: Academy Editions.

Brown, G.Z. (1985) *Sun, Wind and Light: Architectural Design Strategies*, New York: John Wiley.

Ching, F.K. (1979) *Architecture: Form, Space and Order*, New York: Van Nostrand Reinhold.

Habraken, N.I. (1985) *The Appearance of the Form*, Cambridge, Mass.: Awater Press.

Saarinen, E. (1985) *The Search for Form in Art and Architecture*, New York: Dover.

Scholfield, P.H. (1958) *The Theory of Proportion in Architecture*, Cambridge: Cambridge University Press.

Steadman, P. (1979) *The Evolution of Designs: Biological Analogy in Architecture and the Applied Arts*, Cambridge: Cambridge University Press.

47 Forms versus forces

Sabine Chardonnet and Marcel Maarek

What is the expression of a face? Is it the surface? Is it the underside of the skin? Is it the skin itself? Is it the flesh under the skin? The bones? Or is it all that, which is the fulcrum of all the spaces in between?

Space/time/body are enigmatic and inexplicable, like the architecture that is based upon them.

(Abraham 1988: 140)

'The urge to form' is stronger than the urge to 'impose conformity'.

(Gombrich 1992)

The present state of Nature's system is obviously a sequel to what it was immediately before, and if we conceive of an intelligence which, at any given moment, embraces all the interrelations between creatures and this Universe, then such an intelligence will be able to determine the relative positions, the movements, and the affections in general of all these creatures at any time whatever in the past or the future.

(Laplace 1774 (explaining determinism))

It would indeed be curious that all nature, all the planets, were subject to eternal laws, and that one small animal 1.65 metres tall could behave as he thinks proper and according to his whim, despite those laws.

(Voltaire, quoted in Stewart 1989: 181)

'Does free-will really exist? Everything persuades us to act as though it did.' This means that if all the atoms in my body, by virtue of the immutable laws of nature, led me to attack an old lady, then by virtue of those same immutable laws the magistrate would send me to prison for five years.

(Stewart 1989: 181)

New forms create new contents.

(Victor Chklowski, quoted in *Encyclopedia Universalis* 1980)

New forms, functions and species raise questions for us. Can it be thought that an object, an attractile to be discovered, resolves the new into something already there?

– The new is not a product (in the strong sense of an artefact) of what exists already.

– The new is recognized, understood, captured.

(Milgram 1985)

INTRODUCTION

'Give me a list of your needs and I will give you the corresponding form!' This injunction, like a modern counterpoint to Archimedes' 'Give me somewhere a fulcrum and I will lift the world', is often quoted as the foundation to the architectural act. Certainly its promoters, who over a long period of time have been exploring the issue in a number of ways, were well aware of the trap that lay there: they knew they had to replace the subjective and imprecise notion of needs with the richer and more general one of forces (see in particular, Alexander 1966: 96–107; 1964). Beside the actual needs, in the notion of forces appear the constraints of an architectural project – those which depend on the intended use as well as those that arise from the environment. Unfortunately, a paradox is always lurking around the corner: the fulcrum, as Archimedes suspected, is also an intrinsic part of the world. So is the potential form; any form is always already present in embryo within the expression of the forces and the architect cannot afford to ignore it.

We must therefore analyse the *forces* → *form* connection with care, not simply as implied but as an interplay of reciprocal references, in order to gauge its pertinence, its problems and its effects.

The forces → form schema is similar to the classical concept of cause and effect, which enjoyed its hour of glory, particularly in the physical sciences. Unfortunately, this formula only works effectively if a single cause can be isolated, or at most a very small number of intimately related causes. That was Descartes's old scheme: the separation of complex events into simple elements, and then the reconstitution of the complex. Certain sciences, especially the sciences of life such as biology, have demonstrated that such a process can have no sense. When a large number of causes exist side by side, things often happen in a way that may at first seem chaotic and irrational. But on closer inspection we perceive that, right from the start, reality engenders a summary form that emerges from the complexity of causes. This is the phenomenon we call 'self-organization',[1] the effects of which have been demonstrated in biological structures as well as in human society. This auto-organization sometimes expresses itself in terms of adaptation (the form gives the impression of adapting naturally to the modifications of the forces acting there), and is easily discernible in the usage of an architectural form or in the equilibria of urban life. Architects and town planners have often failed to foresee that things would turn out in the way they have, and that the users would unconsciously impose an organization that would prove very difficult to modify *post factum*. Everything happens as though this organization were responding to a very powerful logic; the situation might also be described in terms of the 'pregnance' or 'resistance' of the form.[2] The 'habits' of a place are not easily changed.

The complexity of an organization, therefore, cannot always be recomposed from its simple elements and described on this basis. Not only is this difficulty additional to the multitude of forces, but it actually represents in itself a phenomenon that overturns our attempts to grasp reality. So the form is engendered at the same time as the forces emerge, not afterwards. Likewise, in a great number of fields ranging from biology to the learning of language and artificial intelligence, it has been noticed that problems involving a tangle of causes cannot be treated, even marginally, by splitting them up into simple traditional elements. A substantial science of complexity is being evolved at present, at the basis of which we find the concept of self-organization. The architect who wishes to analyse his or her own procedure must take advantage of these new approaches.

When trying to identify all the forces that seem to concern the origin of the form to be determined, either for individual users or for institutions, one cannot avoid the presence, real or imaginary, of a form that haunts all expression of needs or forces, like a ghost. Whether this form is inherent in reality or in the inevitable framework of our discernment, the very fact of perceiving a form is in itself a force. This perception forms part of the forces described, for example, by the end-user. In architecture there never is a clean slate! Except perhaps in matters of strictly technical requirements, users always have a form engraved on their memories which they use as a reference, positive or negative. This pre-existing form (which they will probably not mention) is essential to them for expressing the forces in question. Moreover, it is often the same for the designer, either architect or town planner. The difficulty lies in the very fact that this form is not explicit and manifests its presence in an indirect way. A form is always present, probably arising from the past or simply from habituation, but this 'ghost' is nevertheless the framework or the detector of the play of forces, their point of take-off. Its action is indirect and is revealed often in the form of a resistance to change or, conversely, as a great capacity for adaptation.

The minimal nucleus of the forces → forms relationship is therefore, in fact, the chain *form → forces → form*. It remains for us to find ways to apprehend it, highlight it, to make it workable and use it effectively.

SELF-ORGANIZATION

Let us start with a metaphor. Imagine a forest in spring. The grass has grown, and the first passer-by will begin

Figure 1 *Finding a way through space: the formation of a footpath in a forest.*

to leave footprints on it. Perhaps this person has a pressing reason for walking there rather than elsewhere. Nobody knows, but subsequent walkers, though knowing nothing about the originator of the footprints, will take account of them and little by little form a track that will be imposed on everybody. Everyone will adapt the goal of their walk to the existence of this track. A multitude of objectives, certainly different and perhaps even contradictory, will be moulded into this form. To give the process a more theoretical setting, a model has been constructed that illustrates it very well: Blackwell and Kendall's ballot-box (Blackwell and Kendall 1964). The box contains one white ball and one black. The method consists in drawing one out, then replacing it in the box together with another of the same colour. When this operation is repeated a great number of times, its peculiar result is that the proportion of black balls to white will tend towards an arbitrary but stable figure. To put it another way, the probability of modifying the proportion becomes ever fainter, regardless of the fact that it is in no way predictable. Like the forest track, the ballot-box experiment creates a situation that stabilizes itself every time with no one being able to foresee its value (Figures 1 and 2).

Figure 2 *Finding a way through space: the formation of a route in an ordered and yet occupied space.*

These metaphors demonstrate that the form generated by a complex interplay of forces does not correspond to this or that precise need, but a reciprocal adaptation does take place. When a confusing number of causes are superimposed, it is in the interplay of balance between forces and forms that the practical solution may perhaps be found. It is therefore useless to try to rationalize the process and invent for it a hierarchy of causes that has no meaning for any of its users taken in isolation. What will in fact take place is that everyone will adapt their demand or their objectives to the form that is already there, at least in embryo. This is the way biology explains the ability that living organisms have to reconcile a considerable number of objectives. That is probably the way our brains work: each cause finds its place in a form already there, although taking shape only gradually.

As far as architecture is concerned, we ought probably to start thinking along these lines. Instead of hoping to have a complete and rational inventory of the forces before producing the form, the dialogue between forces and forms must be allowed to work itself out. Each factor will take its meaning from the others. It is certain that this dialogue explains, over the course of time, the shaping of ancient cities that have resisted many vain attempts at imitation.

It may not be easy to revise attitudes and adapt the act of creation to this process, but it is nothing else than the anticipation of what will effectively take place in practice. This reciprocal adaptation is often revealed, as shown by the 'catastrophe theory', when an impossible circumstance arises and a profound modification of form is imperative. Only then is it perceived that the earlier form was perfectly appropriate. These 'catastrophes' can be well simulated within the framework of research, as work carried out in the field of ecology has demonstrated. It would be curious if the forces ↔ forms equilibrium, so well organized in practice, were to be inaccessible to the act of creation.

THE GROWTH OF THE FORM

The growth of the form is one of the points at which the form → forces → form chain comes into effect. Various examples of growth situations of complex forms are provided by the conception and realization of large, aggregated facilities such as airports. The development of a large airport depends on a variety of complex considerations. Its capacity depends essentially on the number and lay-out of its runways. For the last twenty years, however, it is the concept of airport terminals that has evolved most.

The Charles de Gaulle airport at Roissy (Paris North) was intended from the start to be constructed in successive phases, so that its growth could keep pace with the increase of air traffic and with technical evolution. Whereas the first terminal was conceived as a complete, finite object, the second, a modular form, was conceived as a growth form in a reproduction system. The airport's territory of 3,000 hectares (7,400 acres) can afford the opportunity to set up a third terminal, the form of which has yet to be determined. The car–aircraft relationship having been given priority, a central unit situated between the two terminals groups together the ground transport services (buses and regional express network) and the hotels. This unit, the objective of which was to avoid the multiplication and dispersal of facilities linked to user requirements, constitutes the first point of connection. Passengers have to use some on-site local transport to reach their final destination.

Roissy I: the impossible growth

The concept of an airport terminal as 'a machine for catching a plane' has been guided by one central preoccupation: the essential function of Roissy I is that of an interface between car and aircraft with an annual handling capacity of 10 million passengers. Starting from there, the architects have attempted to achieve maximum concentration of the terminal, both horizontally and vertically, so as to miminize walking distances. This explains the cylindrical form, as horizontal moves are developed over the shortest distance, or the radius, while fast elevators deal with vertical links. Vehicles move on longer, helicoidal paths, while passengers move on shorter, more direct ones. The latter extend to the satellites which can handle a maximum number of aircraft at boarding points. Travolators have mitigated the problem of these increased distances. This formal concept has allowed two parameters to be united: the life of the central body is inward-looking, while the satellites are open to the outside space, appearing as islands in the traffic area. The form of this terminal is at once concentrated and open, reductionist and expansionist, but it does not allow for further growth. It could perhaps be called a total or a finite form. Any externally imposed demand for growth can lead only to breakdown or to the creation of a new and totally independent unit. This complex and complete form bears its end within itself.

This is the reason why, facing up to the saturation of terminal I, the Paris Airport Authority and the national company Air France have put their efforts together to study the concept of Terminal 2.

Roissy II: the self-reproduction

Terminal 2, with its linear form, is composed of reproducible traffic units or modules, with an annual passenger-handling capacity of 5 million. Originally, the general form at which the development was to aim was a string of eight terminals or modules (arcs of circles) arranged, as in a plant growth, in two rows on either side of the access route.

Unlike Terminal I, where arrivals and departures are separated horizontally, Terminal 2 opts for vertical

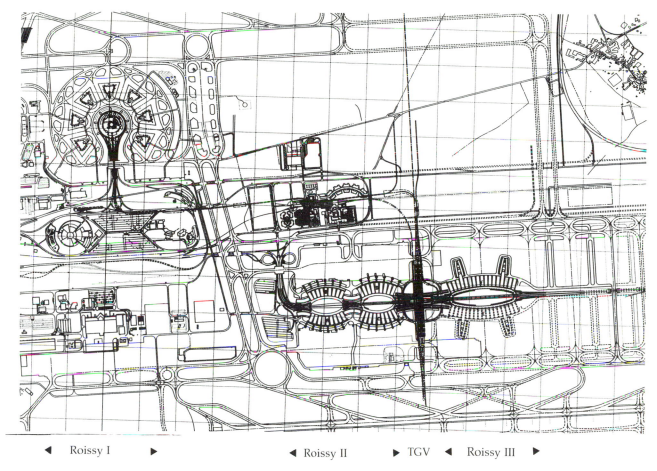

◄   Roissy I   ►   ◄ Roissy II   ► TGV   ◄   Roissy III   ►

Figure 3 *General Plan after 1990 of Roissy I, II and III, with TGV station.* Source: *Salat and Labbé 1990*)

separation. According to the current plan of 1978, this terminal will eventually grow to a length of about 1.5 kilometres (1 mile), which does not avoid creating circulation problems for walking trips. This will make internal communications and interconnections very difficult. Walking from one module to the opposite one necessitates taking a shuttle or changing level, which makes it a difficult trip. Already in the present situation, with four modules in service, a passenger who goes the wrong way or becomes disorientated is up against a problem of internal circulation and baggage-handling. The lengthening of access runways and on-ground movements, made necessary in order to follow the linear development of terminals, has also considerably increased the fuel consumption of aircraft.

The module can, of course, be reproduced to accompany the growth in traffic, in satisfactory economic and technical conditions. This was one of the determining factors in its formal conception. But it is this very growth that is going to render it inefficient. Beyond a certain threshold (apparently lower than that initially envisaged with eight modules) discontinuity starts to prevail over the consistency of the form. It is becoming evident that the planners will have to terminate this form and consider a new, independent implantation or its restructuring around a central point.

A closed form was abandoned in order to create an open form, but in due course this was leading to a discontinued open form, or, in the mathematical sense, a 'catastrophic' one. The new concept of Roissy III is developed now with a larger module, a condensation and deformation of the linear structure. Terminals 2 and 3 will then be settled on both sides of the future railway station of the TGV, acting as a new centre (see Figure 3).

THE NEUTRALITY OR ADAPTABILITY OF A FORM

The form adapts itself. It works like a melting-pot, its action consisting either of a resistance to change or else of a great capacity for adaption or extension.

The Louvre or the awaited void: the metamorphosis of the place

In 1993 the Louvre Museum in Paris appeared in its full glory, open to the city and the outside world. Of course the Pyramid has monopolized attention in its role as a new interpretation of an ancient form sited at the heart of a complex of visual perspective (Figure 4). But something more important is to be found in the underground spaces of the Cour Napoléon and the transformations still being effected in the Richelieu Wing and the Cour

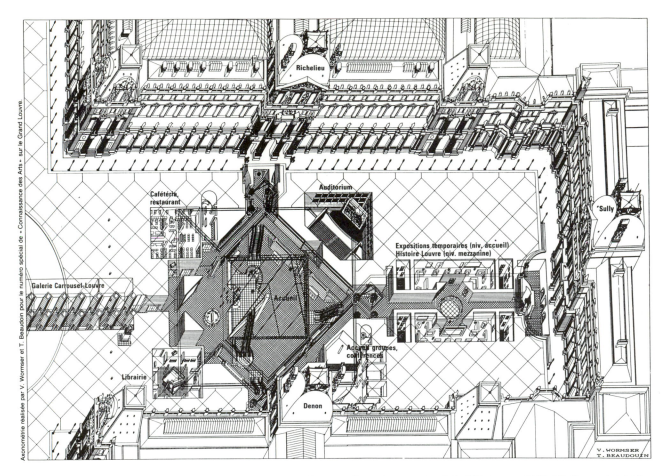

Axonométrie réalisée par V. Wormser et T. Beaudoin pour le numéro spécial de « Connaissance des Arts » sur le Grand Louvre.

Figure 4 *Original axonometric projection of the Grand Louvre.* (Source: Connaissance des Arts *307, January 1990: 71. Reserved rights*)

Carrée. The project is in the hollow, the void, of which the pyramid is only the transparent signal announcing the event. In fact, the centre of a new life for the Louvre lies hidden within this funerary symbol (unless it is simply a pure geometric form).

The works undertaken now, at the end of the twentieth century, affect the organization and the very substance of the Louvre. Two centuries after it was first set up, the Palace is actually being successfully transformed into a Museum. Standing right in the heart of Paris, the Louvre suffered from being enclaved, parcelled out, broken up. Access was difficult and fragmentary, internal circuits were illegible, and horizontal linearity was developed interminably through the sequence of different blocks. The creation of under-

ground spaces has achieved not a growth but an organization, a fulfilment of the already existing form. An organizational principle has taken over from one of circulation. With the emergence of the vertical, of natural light from above, and the organizing void, the space has become three-dimensional. We have passed from a collection of different circulations to an organization legible in the round, where it is simple to find our way, thanks to the cross-roads of orthogonal axis corresponding to those of the surrounding city (see Figure 5).

It is by this added simplification, this adaptation of the form, that we now accede to the complexity of the whole. This new neutrality permits the set of combined forces to interact freely through the dialogue of forms.

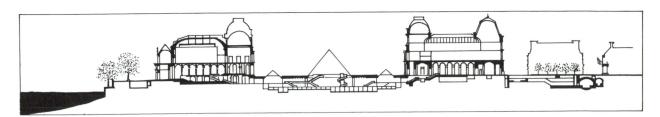

Figure 5 *The Cour Napoléon, the Louvre and their liaison with the city.*

The formation of the organizational principle, the hollow space, has managed to conclude and reorganize the earlier form long after its initial creation, and the Louvre is regenerated. Suddenly the form becomes immediately perceptible and its pregnance evident. We then wonder how we have managed to wait so long for this crucible, this organizational hollow that was missing.

After this first phase of metamorphosis, concerning liaison with the city, visitors' reception and public circuits, the great project of the museum's conception was divided between three architects' offices. One feared that the end result would be fragmentation. But that would be to reckon without the pregnance of the form so far completed, the strong presence of the Palace's previous form into which the museum has to fit and, finally, the spirit of the project (which can be defined according to terms of austerity, quality of lighting material, geometric elegance and restrained solemnity).

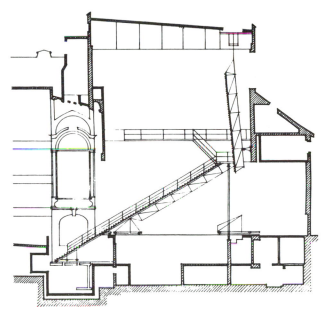

Figure 6 *Sketches for a production of the* Beggar's Opera *at the Theater des Westens, Berlin, 1987.*

A production in a Berlin theatre – the amplification of form

In 1987 the Theater des Westens in Berlin staged a remarkable production of Bertolt Brecht's *Beggar's Opera* directed by Günther Krämer with décor by Andreas Reinhardt. This production and its spatial organization, both revised, interest us because they evince certain interaction effects of the form → forces → form chain.

The production broke with the Brechtian tradition of austerity. It was decided to mark the dichotomy between auditorium and stage, public space and acting space, by leaving the auditorium in its traditional state and totally transforming the stage by a contemporary spatial operation. The entire width of the acting area was occupied by an enormous flight of steps descending towards the stalls and disappearing into the depths below stage (inevitably reminiscent of the famous steps in *Battleship Potemkin*; see Figure 6).

The audience therefore found themselves looking at a space possessing a precise and active formal structure, although the form in its entirety was perceived as unfinished at both ends, that is, a form previous to the

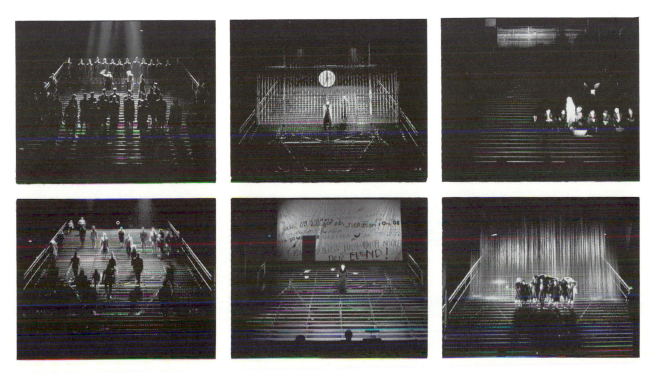

Figure 7 *Interplay of spaces on the staircase,* Beggar's Opera, *Berlin, 1987.* (Photograph: *Lothar Dahlmann, lighting director*)

action and the actors performance; and at the same time a structure capable of neutralization, the strong orientation of this initial form not detracting from its neutrality which permitted the free play of forces and multiple readings (neutrality being neither absence nor polyvalence, let us remember).

The monumental steps constituted the basic form of the stage space, but placing this space on an inclined plane had several consequences. First, it annulled the traditional effect of perspective in the visual perception of the scene from the auditorium. There was no horizon, only two extremes top and bottom, but undefined and unfinished. This had the additional effect of bringing the actors closer to the audience, flattening the stage picture and compressing it in place and time. Second, although perspective was eliminated, there was none the less a constant evocation of inside and outside, either by the occupation of the space on the steps (from the centre out to the sides, towards an imaginary world, and from the centre upwards and downwards, towards the real world) or by the new dimensions of space. The simple production of a vertical plane, even evanescent, out of paper, water or light instantly creates an interior and an exterior. And the marking out of certain surfaces in the inclined plane by the interplay of lit and unlit areas produces a sense of remoteness, or confinement, or a new perspective (see Figure 7).

Not so much neutral as rich in reality, the flight of steps amplified the action in all its forms because it was the place of movement. It could be divided into a series of small horizontal and stable spaces, one on each step, or else become the focus of total movement and fluidity. The static state, emphasized both by the actors' immobility and the shadows of their motionless bodies, expressed itself as a particular moment (or form) of movement.

Emphasis must also be put on the particular role of sound (other than music) allied to movement, which gave a supplementary dimension to the scenic space. Here the play developed three sound registers, three languages: words or songs, music, and the sounds of movement (metallic vibrations or stamping of boots as the actors poured down or climbed up the steps). Move-

ment through space was thus expressed by the change of place, and through time by the sounds.

Such an example demonstrates that, in a complex reality, the opposition developed, for example, by René Huyghe between 'form-stability' and 'force-mobility' remains purely conceptual (Huyghe 1971: 144 ff.).

THE SUPERIMPOSITION OF FORMS

What happens to the resistance or the transformation of forms over the course of time and when their environment changes? It is not rare to encounter places, particularly in towns, where several forms have a face-to-face dialogue.

The Place des Prêcheurs in Aix en Provence

The Place des Prêcheurs is one of the high spots of public life in Aix, from daily life in the market to civic life in the Palais de Justice (law-courts), which symbolizes the city's dominant tertiary function. Several forms

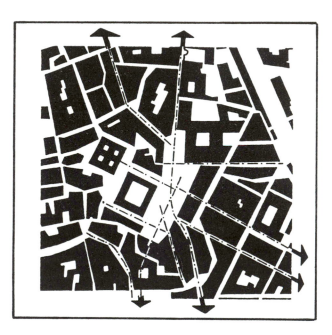

Figure 8 *The relation of the Palais de Justice and the Prison to the urban form.*

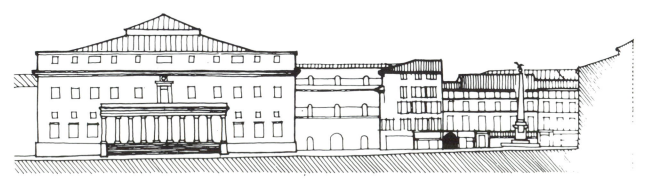

Figure 9 *Elevation of the Palais de Justice and the Prison.*

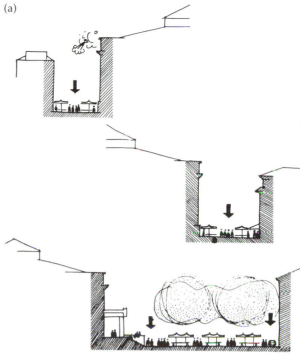

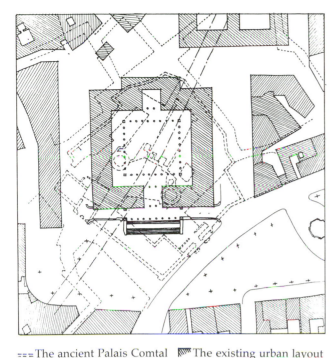

===The ancient Palais Comtal ▧▧The existing urban layout and the Palais de Justice

Figure 10 *The formal evolution of the Place des Prêcheurs.*

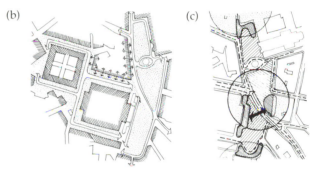

Figure 11 *Schemes of space-occupation in the Place: (a) and (b) on a market day; (c) on a normal day.*

are imprinted on this urban space, not one of them having totally eliminated the others (see Chardonnet 1980).

The first contrasts appear in the morphology of the built environment: in this city, the important buildings and monuments stand among others in the cohesive built mass, surrounded by their neighbours and not displaying precise boundaries. The emergence of the Palais de Justice above the general mass, its monumental flight of steps and its independent position are an exception in the Aix townscape.

The Palais de Justice and the Prison behind it bring a strong orientation into the urban space, thus emphasizing the functions represented (Figures 8 and 9). The ensemble has a symbolic amplitude. It was realized in 1822 on the strength of a vast project of architectural arrangement by Claude-Nicolas Ledoux, for which it was decided to demolish the Palais Comtal which stood on the site (see Figure 10). The end of the environmental project was lost sight of after a time.

It is imperative to see both aspects of the Place, with and without the market. When there is no market, traffic carves the space up into three zones commonly occupied by a sea of parked cars. There remain two zones of adaptable space for the use of pedestrians: the shady transition areas with pedestrian footpaths and sunny Café-terraces in the centre. The Palais de Justice dominates and orders the surrounding space (Figure 11).

On market days, vital space for cars, compressed and slowed down, becomes hazardous, while pedestrians appear in greater numbers moving more actively. They

spread out and saturate a widened space beyond the Place, absorbing the Prison. The canopy of trees assumes a new scale and significance, forming a second layer above that of the sunshades which brings about a concentration of the already crowded and animated space. There then occurs a reversal of the frontal space of the Palais de Justice and a change of scale. The effects of human scale and monumental scale are inverted. Alone or in a group, passer-by or tramp, tourist or student, people sit down in the sun and watch the scene of urban life. They 'rest their backsides' on the steps of the law-courts to while away the time, playing some music or nibbling some food bought in the market.

This flight of steps, which indicated the authority of the institution, the setting at a distance and the non-accessibility to each and all, becomes the site of a daily collective ritual. People are far from caring about formal symbols, for a temporarily stronger form has super-imposed itself on the previous one. The new form is an intermittent one, but always there, simultaneously fluid and concentrated, assembling rather than selecting, a form that has resisted the other one despite its breadth.

Here we find a perfect example of an urban public space where social use alters the form for a while and transforms the identity of the place. This place is a complex space, but a total space where all forms of urban life can cohabit against a background of anonymity: an open space *par excellence*.

If form is, as conceived by René Thom, a zone of stability in a system of forces (the moment when they achieve balance and minimize each other), the Place des Prêcheurs presents two distinct stabilities with the major changes in its use. The use of space therefore reveals forces and is itself a force. Stability does not signify immobility, and in the competition between forms, the pregnance level may be determined by usage.

Fortifications

There exist cases, such as that of the military fortress, where form and forces are linked in a close relationship of cause and effect. One may wonder, however, about the role and the meaning of such monumental forms today. Should these buildings be looked at as objects bearing witness of the past?

The Fort Carré of Antibes was built in the seventeenth century at the time when France was developing its southern fortifications under the driving force of the Marquis de Vauban. It was sited and designed to respond to a field of determining constraints or forces. The project consisted of four bastions around a Genoese tower already standing on a promontory situated at the harbour entrance. The overall form was raised on a regular geometric plan slightly distorted to ensure good firing coverage in four precise directions landward and seaward (Figure 12).

For ages the fortress fulfilled its role solidly, thanks to the adequacy of its form and its function. But with evolving methods of military attack, particularly in the vertical dimension with the advent of aviation, its defensive form and function have collapsed. The obsolescence of the defensive form has left us with a form for its own sake. The Antibes landscape today would be inconceivable without its fortress. The form has remained while its whole environment has changed. It has a permanent place in the city and the forces that apply to it are not concerned with usage but with symbolism. The Fort Carré is now a pure form acting as a force.

Paris after Haussmann

We should not attempt to believe, however, that a previous form will always resist an upset or a disorder. A famous counter-example is provided by the brutal transformation of Paris between 1853 and 1882. This was the work of one of the first modern administrators, Baron Haussmann. It is staggering to realize that the Paris we know today was planned and carried out in just thirty years and with relatively rudimentary means. Leaving aside the attempts at political and historical explanation of the emergence of a city constituted as an institutional centre, it can only be said that it is impossible for us to read in present-day Paris what the city was like before 1853. The vestiges of the former town,

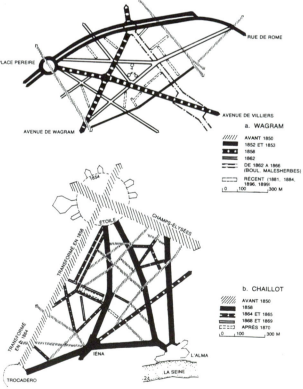

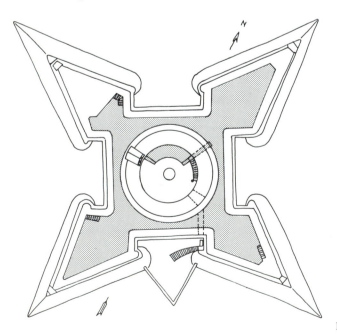

Figure 12 *The Fort Carré of Antibes.*

Figure 13 *The layout out of the new arterial routes in Paris: the structuring of the city by means of arteries and borders.*

which are numerous, have been almost naturally integrated into the modern structure and are now inseparable. Nobody can convincingly explain this extraordinary success: the old city being absorbed by the newborn city (see Figure 13).

CONCLUSION

It has often been admitted that the architectural process was scientifically formulated when using the method of starting from the demands expressed in terms of forces and deducing a form from that. Unfortunately this approach proves impossible, which is probably not really a bad thing.

This failure is due to several factors. In practice, an exhaustive inventory of forces – in the sense understood by, for example, Christopher Alexander (1966), namely all that an architectural project can take into previous consideration in the way of requirements or constraints – is quite simply unrealizable. We have tried to demonstrate two reasons for this: first, that forces express themselves in terms of forms, and come to life in the context of previous or imaginary forms; and second, that it is impossible to isolate them rationally, and measure their weight and relative importance. Inspired by current research, particularly in the sciences of living organisms, we have tried to indicate some useful lines for a new methodology in the architectural act.

These sciences are precisely characterized by their complexity and by forms that are generally a well-adapted expression of this complexity. Such a process is obviously only at its beginnings and postulates a profound modification of habits and traditions, but there is no reason why the revolutions that are taking place today in the life sciences should not be feasible within a practice that has always attempted to ally the expression of an individual art with the consideration of collective requirements, however explicit they may or may not be. The starting point of this methodology will probably be a language that allows the elements concerned to be more closely combined. It is possible that these methodological revolutions will bring back into focus approaches where architects will have the surprise of rediscovering their daily practice. It nevertheless holds true that what we are looking for is an epistemological revolution, since the quest for the cause → effect mechanism is firmly anchored in our cultural habits. The language that enables us to tell about complexity in simple terms has yet to be invented!

NOTES

1   Self-organization: a biological term.
2   Pregnance: a term used in psychology, in Gestalt theory, to denote temporal solidity, permanence and stability despite apparent changes. The French mathematician René Thom (1989) adopted it after having used 'structural stability' to describe the concept in 'catastrophe theory'.

REFERENCES

Abraham, R. (1988) 'The anticipation of architecture', in J. Hejduk, E. Diller, D. Lewis and K. Shkapich (The Cooper Union) (eds) *Education of an Architect*, New York: Rizzoli.

Alexander, C. (1964) *Notes on the Synthesis of Form*, Cambridge, Mass.: Harvard University Press.

—— (1966) 'From a set of forces to a form', in G. Kepes (ed.) *The Man-made Object*, London: Studio Vista.

Blackwell, D. and Kendall, D. (1964) 'The Martin Boundary for Polya's Urn: scheme and application to stochastic population growth', *Journal of Applied Probability* 1: 284.

Encyclopedia Universalis (1980) 'Formalisme Russe', in *Encyclopedia Universalis*, Vol. VII, Paris: Encyclopedia Universalis France.

Gombrich, E.H. (1992) *Réflexions sur l'histoire de l'art*, trans. J. Morizot and A. Capet, Nîmes: J. Chambon.

Huygue, R. (1971) *Formes et forces: de l'atome à Rembrandt*, Paris: Flammarion.

Laplace, P.S. (1774) 'Mémoires de mathématiques et de physique présentées par divers savants 1773–1776', in *Oeuvres de Laplace*, Vol. VIII, pp. 5–27, Gauthier-Villard.

Milgram, M. (1985) in J.-P. Dupuy (ed.) *L'Auto-organisation*, Colloque de Cerisy 1983, Paris: Seuil.

Salat, S. and Labbé, F. (1990) *Paul Andreu: Métamorphose du cercle*, Paris: Electa Moniteur.

Stewart, I. (1989) *Les Mathématiques*, Paris: Pour la science, Belin; trans. of *The problems of mathematics*, Oxford: Oxford University Press, 1987.

Thom, R. (1980) *Modèles mathématiques de la morphogenèse*, Paris: Bourgois.

—— (1989) *Structural Stability and Morphogenesis*, trans. D.H. Fowler, Reading, Mass.: Addison Wesley.

FURTHER READING

Atlan, H. (1982) *Entre le cristal et la fumée*, Paris: Seuil.

Chardonnet, S. (1980) *Sentier urbain à Aix en Provence*, Paris: Centre de Recherche d'Urbanisme/Ministère de l'Environnement et du Cadre de Vie.

Gleick, J. (1987) *Chaos*, New York: Viking.

Science et pratique de la complexité (1986) Actes du colloque de Montpellier Mai 1984, Paris: La Documentation Française.

48   The invisible foundations

Robert Lawlor

European Architecture is founded on the astonishing geometric and mathematical mental development peculiar to the ancient civilizations, which flourished around the eastern Mediterranean: ancient Egyptian, Semitic, Babylonian and Arab peoples, and more prominently, the ancient Greeks (Ghyka 1938).[1] Each of these source cultures utilized a mathematization of musical harmony, along with sets of irrational relationships, found in pure geometric figures and volumes. The varied schema based upon music and geometry in every case served as metaphors that intellectually affirm the underlying unity and order of creation.

The same primary musical tones have been discovered in all musical scales throughout history. The aural response to consonants and harmony seems universally associated with a common group of sound qualities. Visually, there is also a universal utilization and response to the perfect symmetry and balance of simple geometric figures such as squares, circles, triangles and rectangles. Early Greek contemplatives such as Pythagoras, Plato and Archetys formalized a philosophy based on the universal, invariable aspects of music and geometry, which had a profound effect upon the development of Western aesthetic and proto-scientific thought. This philosophy, the origin of which is attributed to Pythagoras, begins with the invisible world of sound. It proposes that the 'inaudible music of the spheres' resonates in musical sounds which physically result from ratios of concurrent wave frequencies vibrating proportionally one to the other. These sounds, or tonal intervals, can be measured or defined by whole number ratios such as: 4:2, the octave; 4:3, the fourth; 3:2, the fifth. Once the invisible tonal world is symbolized by number it can then be represented graphically or structured visually. Thus the inner, 'felt', musical consonants and harmony are transported from subjective, auditory perception to a visual, formal realm through the intermediate agency of number. Pythagorean philosophy views these numbers as symbols, representing active, metaphysical agents, which mediate between the invisible, preformative realms of pure energy and the formed, material world (Smyrna 1979).

Pythagoreans observed that number, like the energetic world, exhibits several important primary polarities such as odd/even and commensurable/incommensurable. Each opposition indicates an important division in the physical and metaphysical world and also provides different possibilities for contemplation and aesthetic or architectural application. The significant, commensurable numbers were the first four whole numbers: 2, 3, 4,

and 5. There is no musical sound which does not result from frequencies defined by these four numbers, or by their multiples, or powers. These numbers were viewed as 'states of being' or archetypal qualities emerging from the continuum of infinite, successive self-replication of the ever-mysterious monad. The monad was considered the creative source, which was paradoxically both the absolute unity, as well as the infinity of individual units, and referred to, in Eastern thought, as the All/One. This philosophy was encapsulated in the famous diagram named the Pythagorean tetractys (Franz 1974: 114–35).

Table 1 The Pythagorean tetractys

No	Monad continuum	Musical ratio	Metaphysical principle	Geometric form
1	1		unity	point
2	1 1	1/2 (octave)	polarity	line
3	1 1 1	2/3 (fifth)	trinity (form)	triangle
4	1 1 1 1	3/4 (fourth)	quadrature (substance and meaning)	square

From this simple diagram, the Pythagoreans visualized the co-origination of the organizational foundations of the universe: vibration, number and form.

> One can understand that this staggering discovery made the Greeks believe that they had seized upon the mysterious harmony which pervades the Universe and, on this, was built much of the number symbolism and mysticism, which had an immeasurable impact on human thought for the next 2,000 years.
>
> (Wittkower 1973: 104)

The books of the Roman Vitruvius expounded Pythagorean number philosophy and embedded it deeply in the European imagination. Without exception, the great artists and architects of the Renaissance (Alberti, Giorgio, Leonardo, della Francesca, Michelangelo and others) adapted the Pythagorean principles of music and geometric proportion originating from the works of Vitruvius. For example, we read from the notes of Renaissance architect Palladio: 'Suppose a room measures 6 × 12 feet; its height will be 9 feet. Second example: a room is 4 × 9 feet; its height will be 6 feet. Third example: a room is again 6 × 12 feet; its height will be 8 feet.' (Palladio, cited in Wittkower 1973: 135–6). Without mentioning the source, Palladio has named the arithmetical, geometric, and harmonic proportions which define the fundamental tones in the Pythagorean diatonic musical scale.

The incommensurable numbers provided another standard or guide for both philosophical contemplation and architectural design. An incommensurable number is the type of non-recurring, 'irrational' decimal which can never be reduced to an exact quantity. For example: the square root of 2 is 1.4142135.... Each of the primary geometric figures contains a characteristic incommensurable ratio: the square (side/diagonal, $1:\sqrt{2}$); the equilateral triangle (half base/height, $1:\sqrt{3}$); the pentagon (side/diagonal, $1:\Phi$) the 1:2 rectangle (side/diagonal, $1:\sqrt{5}$).

Embedded in these primary geometric forms are the root functions ($\sqrt{2}$, $\sqrt{3}$, $\sqrt{4}$, $\sqrt{5}$) of the same whole numbers (2, 3, 4 and 5) which define the vibratory frequencies of the musical scale. In Pythagorean number cosmology, these incommensurable ratios symbolize the immeasurable (disembodied) archetypal principles that are immanent in the visible world of form. The incommensurable ratios pose a problem for architectural application because their values can never be rationalized for structural purposes. The second-century Pythagorean mathematician Theon de Smyrna revealed a means of generating sequences of whole-number ratios which progressively approximate, with increasing accuracy, the desired incommensurable relationship (Lawlor 1982).

Incommensurable ratios such as $1:\sqrt{2}$ or $1:\Phi$ (known as the Golden Ratio) act as controlling ratios in two-number progressions, which are important mathematically, and also as models of natural growth. They are the geometric: $1:\sqrt{2}$, with its progression 2, 4, 8, 16, etc.; and the additive $1:\Phi$, with its progressions such as 1/2, 3/2, 5/3, 8/5, 13/8, 21/13, 34/21, etc. These sorts of numerical progressions provided architects with a variety of numerical relationships in which the proportions remained the same but the sizes varied. With such a system, for example, a door could be formed from an 8:5 proportion for a room with the dimension of 34:21. This process of selecting ratios from a progression, in which each element oscillates close to an archetypal, controlling, incommensurable relationship (in this case $1:\Phi$), fulfils the goal of symmetry and harmony as defined by Vitruvius: 'Symmetry consists of an accord of measure between the diverse elements of the work as between the elements separate and together, as well as each element or part to the whole' (Ghyka 1938: 14). As Schwaller de Lubicz (1957) demonstrated, these additive and geometric progressions can be graphically arranged to form logarithmic spirals. Thus, the proportions selected from these progressions, for an architectural work, are integrated by an underlying flowing and rhythmical spiral pattern quality, also prevalent in natural growth. Vitruvius and his followers maintained that designs which follow these laws of proportion create a rhythm between diverse and reoccurring architectural elements, which is visually and psychically pleasing, in that they convey a sense of a unity prevailing amidst the diversity of growth and evolution (see Figure 1).

There are numerous works which verify that the forms and growths of nature abundantly exhibit proportions, patterns, shapes and scalar relationships which conform to these same geometric, mathematical and musical principles (see Figure 2).

Vitruvius and his followers believed that the ideal human body uniquely contained *all* the proportional principles upon which music, geometry and the forms of nature are based. The human body was considered a living representation of the Creative Archetype; the part that reflects the whole. Following Vitruvius' famous

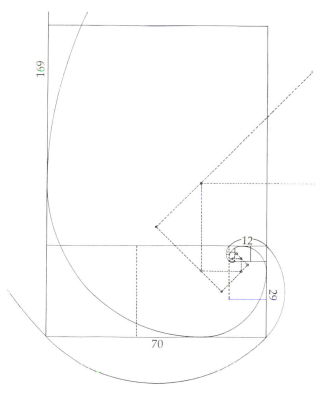

Figure 1 *The $\sqrt{2}$ spiral, starting from ratios 1:2 and 1:3, but with the successive addition of two squares. For the $\sqrt{2}$ spiral we begin with the two creative relationships 1:2 and 1:3 to initiate progressions which will form the numerators and denominators of a series of fractions: (origin 1:3)/(origin 1:2) 1/1 3/2 7/5 17/12 41/29 99/70 diagonal numbers/lateral numbers.*

The growth is made by the addition of two similar squares having the larger side of the preceding rectangle for sides. Thus to the original 1:2 rectangle add two squares having 2 for their sides, to give a side of $1 + 2 + 2 = 5$; then, to the 2:5 rectangle, add two squares of side 5, which makes $2 + 5 + 5 = 12$, etc.

To the original 1:3 rectangle we add two squares of side 3, making $1 + 3 + 3 = 7$, and to this 7 we add two squares of side 7, that is, $3 + 7 + 7 = 17$, etc. The series 1, 2, 5, 12, 29 ... etc. represents the sides of the squares in which the diagonals are respectively 1, 3, 7, 17, 41 ... etc. (Source: *Lawlor 1982*)

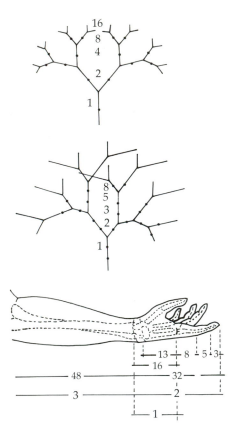

Figure 2 *(a) The two major branching patterns, one demonstrating the geometric progression by 2(√2), and the other the Fibonacci Series (ø). (b) The appearance of the Fibonacci Series in the relationships between the bone lengths of the human finger, hand and arm is another instance of the numerous ø relationships in the human body.*

description of the 'man in the square-and-circle', Renaissance architects such as Leonardo, Giorgio and Cesariano created striking images of the human body as a generator of geometric planes and spacial modules.

Lying beneath the invisible geometries (the *linée occulte*) of architectural renderings was an even deeper image of the naked perfection of the human body. The mystical humanism of Renaissance architecture was not simply a poetic metaphor, but a deeply held belief: a building, designed with respect to the proportional laws of creation, as summarily revealed in the fascinating beauty of the ideal human body, would structurally resonate with the psychic and vital energies that pervade and sustain the visible world. A building so conceived was considered to be, in essence, a living being. Cornelius Agrippa, a generation later, re-expressed this attitude:

> Man is the most finished and beautiful work and image of God, and a smaller version of the world. Therefore in his most perfect form and sweeter harmony, and in his more sublime dignity he has all the numbers, measures, weights, motions, and elements, etc. All component things stand within and are sustained in him, all things are in him as in the

supreme artificer, and he has a supreme destiny beyond the common range of other creatures. As a result all ancient peoples first counted their fingers and then established (abstract) numbers from them. And all the articulations of the human body itself, and all numbers, measures, proportions and harmonies that they found were measured against it. Whence, from this commensuration, temples, shrines, houses, theatres, and beyond them boats and machines and all sorts of technical devices and craft objects, and buildings in all their parts and members e.g. columns, friezes, bases, antae, stylobates and so on and so forth, were born and brought forth from the human body.... And there is no member of the human body that does not respond to some point or sign, some star, some being, some divine name within the archetype of it all, God.

(in Hersey 1976: 92–3)

The image of Ideal or Cosmic Man as the generator of creative symmetries and patterns again links the rebirth of Western art and humanism to the anthropocosmic myths of ancient India and Egypt. The Purusha in Indian cosmology is both the cosmic plan and perfected human form, and was used as the basis for all Hindu temples. Likewise, the Egyptian coffin texts tell of the 'first born' of creation, King Pepi, whose body held the geometric essence (seed) for the entire manifestation. These philosophies are, in some ways, the reverse of the later Platonic derivations, in that pre-Greek antiquity conceived the ideal geometric forms (the ideas of God) to be generated by the embodied form. This implies that the abstract intelligible or mental world, so revered by Plato, is secondary to, or derived from, an innate beauty and organization of the physical body (Wind 1980).

The rich depth of antiquity from which Renaissance architecture grew made the architect not only an engineer and artisan, but a mystical symbolist in whose designs every element breathed with layers of spiritual meaning and psychological associations. The philosophers who inspired architectural humanism (della Mirandola and Ficino) extended the exaltation of the beauty of the physical body to a spiritual philosophy based on abandoned ecstacy and heightened pleasure. They adopted the 'blind cupid' as their symbol, and their teachings so closely paralleled, in many respects, the sexual philosophy of Indian Tantric that it is difficult to dismiss the possibility of a cultural transmission (Wind 1980; Danielou 1984).

Prior to the Renaissance, the inspiration for the other surge of Western architecture – the Gothic cathedrals – can also be traced to geometric and musical cosmology, along with Gnostic mysticism associated with sexual imagery (cloaked in alchemical images to preserve Christian propriety) (Michell 1988). At the threshold to the Gothic period, ancient thought entered Europe primarily through Hebrew and Sufi mystics, who had

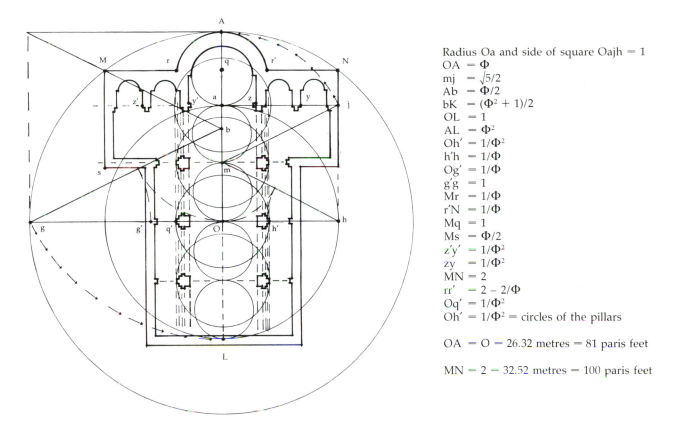

Radius Oa and side of square Oajh = 1
$$OA = \Phi$$
$$mj = \sqrt{5}/2$$
$$Ab = \Phi/2$$
$$bK = (\Phi^2 + 1)/2$$
$$OL = 1$$
$$AL = \Phi^2$$
$$Oh' = 1/\Phi^2$$
$$h'h = 1/\Phi$$
$$Og' = 1/\Phi$$
$$g'g = 1$$
$$Mr = 1/\Phi$$
$$r'N = 1/\Phi$$
$$Mq = 1$$
$$Ms = \Phi/2$$
$$z'y' = 1/\Phi^2$$
$$zy = 1/\Phi^2$$
$$MN = 2$$
$$rr' = 2 - 2/\Phi$$
$$Oq' = 1/\Phi^2$$
$$Oh' = 1/\Phi^2 = \text{circles of the pillars}$$

$$OA = O = 26.32 \text{ metres} = 81 \text{ paris feet}$$

$$MN = 2 = 32.52 \text{ metres} = 100 \text{ paris feet}$$

Figure 3: *Floor plan of the Abbey of Thoronet.*

established themselves in the universities of Spain during the tenth and eleventh centuries. The great European exponent of these teachings was St Bernard de Clairvaux, who established the Cistercian monastic order in 1134. With his close associate Ashad, a Persian cabbalistic geometer, Bernard developed the plans which resulted in nearly 500 vaulted abbeys which for centuries have been celebrated for their wonderful architectural and acoustic properties. These abbeys are relatively small, but provide an acoustic volume which perfectly enhances the human voice.

Cistercian abbeys became the prototype for the great Gothic cathedrals which followed. All evidence points to the probability that the almost uncannily beautiful acoustic properties of these abbeys are due to the fact that every element of the architecture adheres to the proportions of sacred geometry and music. In France and Germany a number of these twelfth-century abbeys still stand at Fonteney, Citeaux, Silvacane and Senaque. The abbey in Provence, near the tiny village of Thoronet, is considered the purest example of Cistercian architecture and exemplifies the interweaving of proportions, derived from geometry, music and human form (Audibert 1978) (see Figures 3, 4 and 5).

The Cistercians challenged the authority of Rome and, through their power of discipline and the unparalleled expansion of their monastic order, temporarily turned the face of Christianity toward a deeper symbolic and mystical direction. Bernard's famous architectural dictum, 'no decoration, only proportion', resulted in a purity of church design which was never excelled, even in the great cathedrals (Jean-Nesmy 1979). The Church of Rome finally suppressed the Cistercian movement, labelling it heretical, and, with the removal of the Cistercian brotherhood from Chartres, the cosmology of mystical geometry went 'underground' to emerge for the last time as an inspiration for the Italian Renaissance. The conceptual impetus of the Renaissance ended when the Church of Rome once again slammed down its totalitarian fist upon the Academy of Rome. Leon Alberti, Nicholas Cusano, Prospero Colonna, and others who formed this Academy (according to historian Emmanuela Kretzulesco-Quaranta) were, one by one, poisoned by the Borgia Popes. Leonardo da Vinci, who as a youth attended meetings of the Academy, escaped with his life, but from then on the occult mystical tradition began to decline (Kretzulesco-Quaranta 1976). The last work of the mystical architects was a mysterious book published under the pseudonym Francesco Colonna in Venice in 1496, entitled *The Dream of Poliphilo* or *The Hypnerotomachie* (a coined word from the Greek meaning 'The Dream of the War Against Love'). The work contains long poetic passages of architectural descriptions, in which buildings have the psychic characteristics of the living. *The Dream of Poliphilo* is the final expression of the symbolist architects, who explored the mystical identity

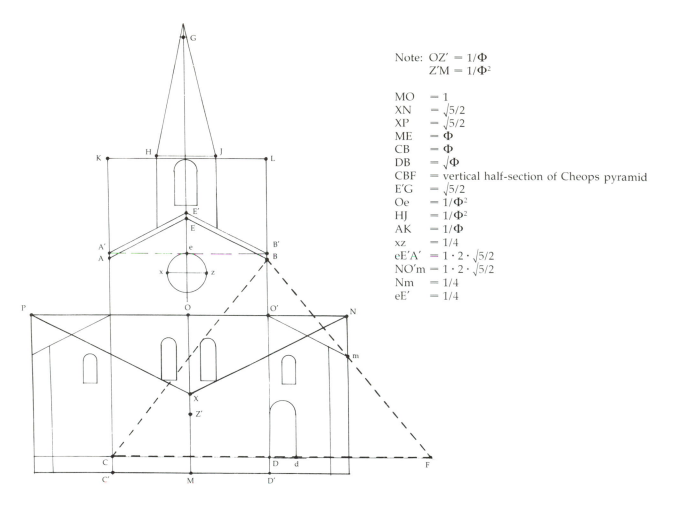

Note: $OZ' = 1/\Phi$
$Z'M = 1/\Phi^2$

MO	$= 1$
XN	$= \sqrt{5}/2$
XP	$= \sqrt{5}/2$
ME	$= \Phi$
CB	$= \Phi$
DB	$= \sqrt{\Phi}$
CBF	$=$ vertical half-section of Cheops pyramid
E'G	$= \sqrt{5}/2$
Oe	$= 1/\Phi^2$
HJ	$= 1/\Phi^2$
AK	$= 1/\Phi$
xz	$= 1/4$
eE'A'	$= 1 \cdot 2 \cdot \sqrt{5}/2$
NO'm	$= 1 \cdot 2 \cdot \sqrt{5}/2$
Nm	$= 1/4$
eE'	$= 1/4$

Figure 4: *Exterior elevation of the Abbey of Thoronet.*

between the two most profound experiences of our existence; that of the physical body and that of the 'supra-body' of the surrounding environment of earth and sky.

The knowledge and use of musical and geometric proportions declined in Europe from a mystical to an aesthetic tradition and, from there, to an academic dogma. It was finally dismissed in the seventeenth century, first by Claude Perrault, who denied that beauty in art depended upon universal ratios and proportions. In the nineteenth century Burke and Hume, following Perrault, overthrew classical aesthetics and completed the rupture between mathematics and art, between science and spirit, and encouraged science and art to go on their divergent paths: the one toward rational empiricism and the other towards subjective expressionism.

European architecture, having lost its invisible foundation has, in the intervening centuries, oscillated between periods of excessive decorativeness to the other extreme of engineering and economic expediency based on utilitarianism. Since the industrial revolution, aesthetic design has been applied to an increasingly

small proportion of Western architecture, and for the most part has become a language of shifting styles and personal taste. The bulk of standardized domestic and commercial architecture has followed the path and the language of scientific materialism. In contrast to the age of humanism, architectural design has, for the most part, become stifling in its reductionism, utterly empty of any sense of metaphor, imaginally impoverished and almost devoid of any meaningful analogy. Taking into account the history of repression, it remains astonishing that European civilization, having once conceptually achieved an architecture of symbolic imagery, an architecture with the beauty of 'frozen music' and the 'poetry of number-form', could willingly deny itself that source of inspiration and knowledge in its structured environment, and academically banish the invisible foundations of its own culture.

NOTE

1   Many historians trace inspiration for these developments to contacts with ancient India through the Persian empire. See Sedler 1980.

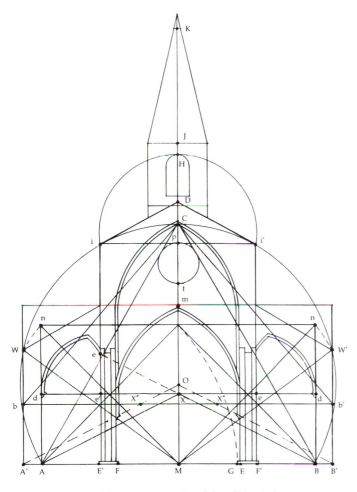

$$MA = 1 \atop MB = 1 \Big\} = \text{unity}$$

$$xB = \sqrt{5}/2$$
$$MB' = \sqrt{5}/2$$

$$XA = \sqrt{5}/2$$
$$mA' = \sqrt{5}/2$$

$$Mn = \sqrt{2}$$
$$MW = \sqrt{2}$$
$$AC = 2$$
$$AB = 2$$
$$MC = \sqrt{3}$$
$$cb' = \sqrt{3}$$
$$cb = \sqrt{3}$$
$$ii' = \sqrt{5}/2$$
$$tJ = 1$$
$$tR = 2$$
$$mH = \sqrt{\tfrac{5}{2}}$$
$$MG = 1/\Phi^2$$
$$GB = 1/\Phi$$

$$\left.\begin{array}{l} ME \\ MF \\ AE' \\ mp \\ DJ \end{array}\right\} = 1/\Phi - (1/-\Phi^2)/2$$

Figure 5 *Section of the interior elevation of the Abbey of Thoronet.*

REFERENCES

Audibert, P. (1978) *La Geométrie au service de la prière*, Le Thoronet: L'Eglise, Abbatiale du Thoronet.

Colonna, F. (1496) *The Dream of Poliphilo*, English trans. 1592, facsimile edn (Vol. 1) 1986, London: Magnum Opus.

Danielou, A. (1984) *Shiva and Dionysius*, New York: Inner Traditions International.

Franz, M.-L. von (1974) *Number and Time*, Evanston, Ill.: Northwestern University Press.

Ghyka, M.C. (1938) *Essai sur le rhythme*, Paris: Gallimard.

Hersey, G.L. (1976) *Pythagorean Palaces*, Ithaca and London: Cornell University Press.

Jean-Nesmy, Dom C. (1979) *Les Sœurs provençales*, Saint Leger (Vauban): Zodiac.

Kretzulesco-Quaranta, E. (1976) *Les Jardins du songe*, Paris: Magma.

Lawlor, R.T. (1982) *Sacred Geometry, Philosophy and Practice*, London: Thames & Hudson.

Michell, J. (1988) *The Dimensions of Paradise*, San Francisco: Harper & Row.

Schwaller de Lubicz (1957) *Le Temple de l'homme*, Paris: Caractères.

Sedler, J.W. (1980) *India and the Greek World*, Totowa, NJ: Rowman & Littlefield.

Smyrna, T. de (1979) *Mathematics Useful for Understanding Plato*, San Diego: Wizards Bookshelf.

Wind, E. (1980) *Pagan Mysteries in the Renaissance*, Oxford: Oxford University Press.

Wittkower, R. (1973) *Architectural Principles in the Age of Humanism*, London: Academy Editions.

FURTHER READING

Danielou, A. (1959) *Traité de musicologie comparée*, Paris: Hermann.

Duby, G. (1978) *Saint Bernard l'Art Cistercien*, Paris: Flammarion.

Fabre d'Olivet, A. (1972) *La Musique expliquée comme science et comme art*, Collection Delphica, Lausanne: Age d'Homme.

Ghyka, M.C. (1931) *Le Nombre d'or*, 3 vols, Paris: Gallimard.

Jenny, H. (1974) *Cymatics I and II*, Basel: Basilius Press.

Michel, P.H. (1950) *De Pythagore à Euclide: contribution à l'histoire des mathématiques preeuclidiennes*, Paris: Belles Lettres.

Vitruvius (1960) *Ten Books on Architecture*, New York: Dover.

49 Instruments of order

Hans van der Laan

With the passing of centuries, architecture has lost touch with its origins. During the thirty years following the Second World War a group of Dutch architects attempted a renewal of architecture by rediscovering its primitive foundations. I set down the results of this attempt in the book *De Architectonische Ruimte* (*Architectonic Space*), which first appeared in 1977.

That study comprises the complete architectonic process, from the establishment of a first space between walls, up to the whole town. In the first chapter, this process is described as the withdrawal of a limited, horizontally oriented space from the space of nature, which is limitless and vertical, being oriented entirely towards the earth's surface. This is achieved by means of solid elements which in their turn must be drawn from the unlimited mass of the earth. And because a continuous enclosure of space cannot be drawn from the earth in one piece, these elements must be multiple. So it is always a matter of a composition of solid elements – of a *construction*.

If the house is to fit harmoniously into the space of nature, its making must be guided by the intellect. For nature includes a being who, in order to adapt it to his or her existence, must employ his or her intellect to complete it. Therefore our human, intellectual products necessarily belong to nature.

Thus between the two extreme terms of the housing process – the human intellect and the natural spatial given – two intermediate terms appear: the material drawn from the earth, and the interior space withdrawn from the space of nature. The essence of architecture consists in the bringing together of limited solid elements so that limited living-spaces can arise between them.

The first question in architecture is not, therefore, what we make the house of, or what kind of house we make, but the making as such. In our book, this making process is explored in depth, but the two extreme terms of the process – the first contact of the human intellect with the extension of the natural spatial given, and the place in nature of the artefact as end-product – receive less attention. They will be enlarged on here.

Human making is of great significance for creation as a whole, because it gives an image, within nature, of nature's own origin. A limited, created intelligence here does in a limited way what in nature an unlimited, creating intelligence has brought about in an unlimited

way. This analogy is more important than the house as a material object.

Like every analogy, it contains not only a similarity but also a difference. For our making is not, like nature, an independent phenomenon, but dependent on natural creation. We do not make a space, but extract it from the space of nature, and moreover this extraction is brought about by solid elements which are themselves drawn from the mass of the earth.

As soon as a part is removed from the earth's mass, it acquires something that mass lacks: a form. Of course we know that the earth is round, but as long as we live upon it we can only experience it as a surface, without any corresponding opposite surface to define it as a form. But every mass drawn from the earth has two opposite surfaces that correspond to each other.

Once, in the depths of a granite quarry, I saw the satisfaction on the face of the quarry-master as a huge block of stone, already prepared by drilling, was brought crashing down by an explosive charge. The single face of the rock that had till then been visible was now matched by the sheared face, and together these corresponding surfaces sufficed to define the form of the block. And because it was now possible to determine its volume, the block took on not only a form, but also a size.

So from the start the building process involves a limited space, a limited form and a limited size. We experience space by being and moving about within it; we see forms; but the appraisal of size is an intellectual matter.

However, in estimating size, which is a *continuous quantity*, the intellect has need of an instrument. This is because it only has direct access to *discrete quantity*, the 'how-manyness' of the things we count on the basis of their unity. Each number then expresses the quantity by its relation to this unit, and we can give this relation a name: two, three, four.... We can hold only a limited number of these relations in our mind, but by means of an established number-system we can extend them to infinity. So the unit of discrete quantity, being the unity of the things that we count, is completely fixed; but the system, in our case the decimal system, is established by convention.

We can translate this grasp of number into a certain grasp of size, that is, of continuous quantity or 'how-muchness'. To do this we need only consider a part of the size as a unit, in other words as an indivisible whole, and relate the whole size arithmetically to this unit. In this case both system and unit must be established by convention.

Translated from the Dutch by Richard Padovan

The advantage of this completely artificial way of measuring, which is universally applied in practice, is that it allows 'measuring-up' and 'measuring-out' to be harmonized with each other. In measuring-up we convert a concrete length into an abstract number, which can then be converted back into a concrete length by measuring-out. The only prerequisite is that the same unit and system be used in the second operation as in the first.

But in the case of an initial measuring-out, no previous measuring-out has taken place; that is, when we first determine the size of something we are going to make, no number is given. No intellectual basis seems to exist for this initial contact with spatial extension. And in fact Western civilization has been content with determining the size of its artefacts on a purely sensory or instinctive basis. To this we have given the name *inspiration*, and associated it with the image of the artist; but this must be seen as a sort of Western idolatry. The image of the inspired artist leads us to see art, not just as analogous to natural creation, but as identical with it, just as other civilizations identified the graven images of gods with the gods themselves.

The ancient civilizations applied themselves far more deeply than has ours to this problem of the intellectual determination of size. Perhaps the decline of architecture and of the whole manufactured environment during the last century or two can be put down to this intellectual ignorance.

We experience space, we see form and we appraise size with our intellect: these three levels at which human existence encounters the spatial given are all reflected in architecture. The problem of how to deal intellectually with size – with continuous quantity – must be approached in the same way as space and form. In order to make natural space habitable for ourselves, we cut off limited pieces of it with solid walls. In order to get a visual grasp of the earth's mass, of which we only perceive the upper surface, we split off pieces from it. So too with size. In order to make accessible to the intellect the continuous series of possibilities, from infinitely small to infinitely large, we must make a sort of separation within it.

When I was a small boy, before the First World War, my father built an estate of workers' dwellings, and I enjoyed visiting the site. There I watched the workmen using two sieves to sift the gravel to be used for concrete foundations. One sieve was large-meshed, the other small. Only the gravel that passed through the first sieve but was caught by the second would be used. I still recall vividly the question that sprang up in my mind, a childish question but one which it has taken me a lifetime to answer: stones that are smaller than the mesh pass through, those that are larger are trapped; but where is the stone that is exactly the same size?

My first reaction was that no such stone exists, because the size of the meshes is determined by human beings, the size of the stones by nature. The lack of stones equal in size to the meshes could be attributed to the essential difference between measures determined by a limited, created intelligence and by an unlimited, creating one. Later I was to learn more about our own way of determining measures.

Just as the interior space comes into existence only when it is delimited by its opposite, that is by solid walls, and the forms of these walls are defined only by surfaces which themselves have no volume, so too we can know the sizes of concrete things only by containing them within certain limits – limits which do not themselves belong to the concrete sizes. When gravel is sieved, it is not a matter of the size of a stone, but of stones *of a certain size*, a size that we hold in our mind by determining its limits. At this point we really make contact with continuous quantity.

In the 1930s, where the garden now lies behind our monastery, there used to be a gravel pit. A few metres below ground level lies a thick stratum of gravel, which geologists say is a former bed of the river Meuse which now flows past Maastricht. This is why in the paths of our garden one finds beautifully coloured, smooth shaped pebbles, varying in size from 2 to 8 centimetres (1 to 3 inches). I cannot resist picking up these unusual stones, and little by little I have built up quite a collection of them, which lies on the window-sill of my workroom. Unconsciously I began to sort these out by size, obeying a lifelong fascination with the sizes of things, equivalent to the interest painters have in their colour.

By rejecting those pebbles whose difference in size was too small to be perceptible, I reduced my collection to a series of 36 whose size-difference just began to be noticeable; according to psychologists this difference amounts to about 4 per cent of the size of the stones.

It at once became apparent, however, that if the pebbles were spread out at random, they could be seen to belong to clearly different groups. One could start by picking out the largest ones, until a point came when none were left that belonged to that size. A smaller group, again of a same type of size, then revealed itself.

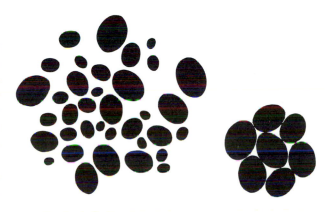

Figure 1 *Pebbles spread at random can be seen to belong to clearly different size groups.*

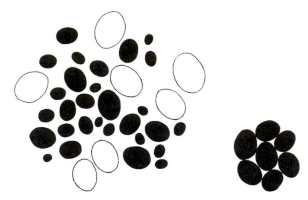

Figure 2 *The remaining pebbles can again be grouped by size.*

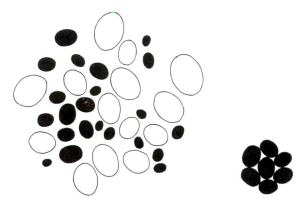

Figure 3 *Once more, a clearly discernible gradation takes shape.*

Figure 4 *The pebbles that are left can still be easily divided by their size.*

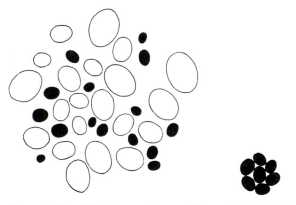

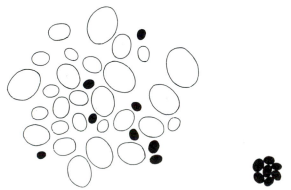

Figure 5 *The last batch of pebbles all belong to the same size group.*

In this way the pebbles sorted themselves out into five groups, each of six or seven stones which one assessed to be of the same size (see Figures 1–5).

In saying that the stones in each group were of the same size, I declared that the difference between the largest and smallest in each group just failed to count in relation to the size of the stones. And since the smallest stone of the smallest group roughly corresponded to the difference between the largest and smallest stones of the largest group, I also had to acknowledge that the five groups thus differentiated represented the complete range of sizes that could be related to each other (see Figure 6).

Figure 6 *The five groups of pebbles represent the complete range of sizes that could be related to each other.*

The seventh chapter of *Architectonic Space* is devoted to a mathematical confirmation and further development of this method of sorting, by which we pay attention not to the concrete size of each stone but to the size to which each stone belongs. Although this size is derived from the size of the available stones, it is none the less clearly of an intellectual nature. This shows that there exists an objectively establishable scale of measures, equivalent to the musical scale which Plato explains in detail in the *Timaeus*, and from which all great music derives its firm foundation.

In music, however, nothing is fixed but the intervals, and every piece of music can be played at different pitches; the actual pitch of the notes must be established *from outside*. Everyone knows how the instruments have to be tuned before the performance of a piece. As soon as one tone is fixed, so too are all the others, and all intermediate tones are false. Likewise the measure scale is determined only by the mutual proportions of the measures, and is independent of the concrete size of the measures as such.

Here we encounter a very important phenomenon. The unit of discrete quantity, or 'how-manyness', is an absolute given, while the system by which it is counted, like our decimal system, is based on convention. But with continuous quantity, or 'how-muchness', it now appears that the system can be determined objectively, while the unit must be established from outside. In architecture it can be derived from the smallest habitable space or 'cella', or more readily on the thickness of the walls that bring this cella into being.

All human determination of measure, and above all that of a first measuring-out without any preceding measuring-up, is therefore the result of combining discrete quantity with its fixed unit and continuous quantity with its fixed scale. This scale is, as it were, impregnated by the unit, and it is this impregnation that makes possible the dimensional ordinance of all our artefacts – in this case, of our houses.

By limiting ourselves, in making, to measures or relations of measures that arise from this impregnation, and avoiding all others as false, we make accessible to the intellect not only the measures but also, by way of these measures, the forms and spaces that they determine. This gives architecture that eloquence which the people who must live in our houses have a right to.

As we noted at the beginning of this essay, the house is essentially a whole made up of parts, because the delimiting boundary of the interior space cannot be extracted from the earth's mass in one piece. Houses or towns are assemblages of parts into wholes which in their turn are parts of still greater wholes.

In the beginning of his *Histoire de l'architecture* (1899), Auguste Choisy describes such a primary whole composed of parts when he observes: *Une pierre à plat sur deux pierres debout, voilà le premier type d'une construction monumentale que l'homme ait réalisée.* (A stone laid flat on two upright stones; there is the first type of monumental construction realized by man.) What he has in mind is surely the trilithons of Stonehenge, where three stones together make up an elementary wall-section, which with four others encloses the cella (see Figure 7).

At this beginning of all architecture, where a few stones act as parts to form a whole, we must make a clear distinction between two ways of measuring. The Greeks had separate names for these, *eurhythmy* and *symmetry*, the meaning of which has been preserved for us by Vitruvius in the second chapter of the first of his ten books on architecture. Eurhythmy defines the parts of the building, as well as the building as a whole, by relating height to breadth and breadth to length. Symmetry, on the other hand, concerns the mutual relations between the parts, and between the parts and the whole.

In the case of the trilithons of Stonehenge, as primary wholes composed of parts, both these ways of

composing measures are clearly distinguishable. Each of the three stones has a height, breadth and length, whose mutual proportions determine the form of the stone. But besides this, the heights of the lintel and of the two uprights have a proportion to the total height of the trilithon, and the breadth of each upright has a proportion to the total breadth. In the first case we are dealing with eurhythmy, which is a matter of form, while in the second case it is a question of symmetry, which concerns the relations between the parts and the whole, and is a matter of size.

Thus eurhythmy indicates proportions between the different measures of a single thing, and symmetry, proportions between corresponding measures of different things.

Moreover, the trilithon as a whole has its own eurhythmy, and becomes in turn a part in the symmetry of a greater whole – the demarcation of the cella – which is, once again, a part of the whole monument.

The ultimate form of the whole is thus born of a progression of alternating eurhythmies and symmetries which begin with the eurhythmy of the smallest part and ends with that of the largest whole. This ultimate form directly confronts the spatial given of nature.

We must see this great confrontation of architecture and nature as the counterpart of our intellect's initial encounter with the infinite extent of that spatial given. And since this same spatial given itself gave rise to the measure-scale that enabled the form of the smallest part to grow out into that of the largest whole, the confrontation with it of the ultimate building-form completes a sort of cycle.

From my youth, I have always been fascinated by the fact that while for animals a single insemination is enough to maintain the species, plants and trees need a double one. First, a fruit is set in the flower, producing a seed with which the earth itself must be inseminated to bring forth a new plant. It is much the same when we make things. First, the measure-scale develops in our mind from the confrontation between the unit of discrete quantity and the sorting of sizes. It is this measure-scale with its unit and system that lies at the root of all our artefacts with their wholes and parts. The form of the ultimate whole that we envisage, together with those of other artefacts, must then be absorbed into the created natural continuum in order to transform it into a human environment. Now it is no longer a matter of the relation between the different measures of one form, but of the relation between different forms.

In nature, forms become more distinct the more they raise themselves above the earth's surface, to which they are bound by gravity. To mark the place where he had his dream, Jacob raised up the flat stone which had served as his pillow (Genesis 28: 10–22). Between the lying of a flat form and the standing of an upright one there exists a continuous series of possibilities, which, recalling our own bodies, we classify as lying, sitting

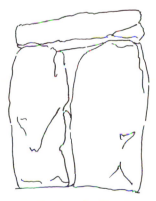

Figure 7 *A primary whole composed of parts: the trilithons of Stonehenge make up an elementary wall-section.*

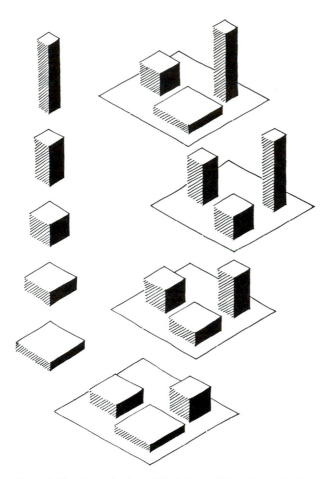

Figure 8 *Varying eurhythmy of block forms with unchanged volume but different dimensions.*

and standing. Which category the form belongs to depends on its eurhythmy, which itself is based on the measure-scale.

Now, however, it is no longer a matter of changing the form by lengthening or shortening one of its dimensions, but of *transforming* it while maintaining its volume constant.

Starting from a cubic block with equal dimensions,

and therefore without eurhythmy, the lying form comes into being by decreasing its height and simultaneously increasing its length and breadth, and the standing form by the contrary process. To keep the volume unchanged, the height must change by twice as many intervals of the measure-scale as the two horizontal dimensions (see Figure 8).

The measure-scale allows five distinct forms to be built up, rising successively from a lying slab to a standing bar, with midway, expressing the sitting position, the square block. When these forms are placed in each other's neighbourhood, a new relationship arises between them, a sort of super-eurhythmy, for which the Greeks used the word *thematismos*: the ordered arrangement of different forms.

It is therefore no longer just a matter of defining the forms of things by their height, length and breadth – that is, by imposing upon them the three dimensions of our bodies. We now impose our standing, sitting or lying posture upon the things themselves, in this case upon buildings, which rise up, as towers, houses and galleries, within the space of nature. By this means we give the primary given – the exclusively vertical orientation of natural space above the earth – a threefold intensity. This is the ultimate achievement of architecture, for, through the coming together of these building-forms around squares and courts, the whole natural space above the earth's surface is mastered, just as the immediate space around us is mastered by the form of the walls.

A few natural pebbles and a few squared pieces of stone have helped us arrive at these insights; we might well call them 'instruments of order'.

REFERENCES

Choisy, A. (1899) *Histoire de l'architecture*, Vol. 1, Paris: Gauthier-Villars.

Laan, H. van der (1977) *De Architektonische Ruimte*, Leiden: E.J. Brill; English trans. 1983; French trans. 1989; German trans. in preparation.

50 Creativity in architecture

Tom Heath

MYTHS OF CREATIVITY

Like the existence of the world, the existence of human technology requires explanation. In strongly traditional, pre-literate societies both were explained in the same way. They were the work of gods. Creation was a prerogative of divinity. Mortals who took on the role of creative innovator either became gods, like Aesculapius, or suffered the penalty of hubris, as in the story of Daedalus and Icarus. With the growth of civilization, originality was recognized to have a part in productive work, but it remained a subordinate part. Thus Vitruvius, whose *Ten Books* are the oldest surviving document of European architecture, acknowledges the contributions of historic innovators. His main concern is nevertheless to represent architectural design as conforming to tradition and rule. Genius and inspiration he mentions as being required only in certain exceptional circumstances. This view of the matter did not change substantially until the Renaissance, and older views persisted even up to the beginning of the modern period, around two hundred years ago.

Today creativity is highly valued. Nevertheless its status is still ambiguous and it remains the subject of an elaborate mythology. The dominant ideology of modernism includes a distinctive view of individual psychology and of social organization which was from the first and correctly described as 'mechanical',[1] though it is also instrumental and commercial. Psychology and society were thought of in terms of a quite literal analogy with clockwork like Babbage's calculating engines. Rationality has become identified with this mechanical view of mental processes. Unfortunately the mechanical view is incompatible with even the superficially observable facts of productive thinking. Therefore an alternative, supposedly 'irrational' way of thinking had to be invented. At first this was confined to artists, but it was later extended to other original people; in popular fictions, creative scientists are often 'mad', or at least eccentric. The social role of 'artist' was itself invented, at the beginning of the nineteenth century, for persons who thought in this 'non-rational' way. They were distinguished from artisans and 'mere mechanics' by virtue of their creative powers, and were admitted to bourgeois society while remaining apart from it in significant respects. Convention permits them a high degree of personal autonomy and a considerable or even complete indifference to ordinary social obligations. The artist thus occupies an ambiguous status, respected but socially irresponsible, which exactly matches the status of creative thinking, which, in a future-oriented society, is held to be 'irrational' but beneficial. From the first, architects were admitted to the 'creative' status of 'artist'.

The myth of the romantic, bohemian artist and of the division of mental powers into two fundamentally distinct elements, one rational and mechanical, the other irrational and creative, has been enormously successful. Indeed it has been so successful that it is popularly accepted as fact. Nevertheless, it is today a considerable obstacle to our understanding of the psychology of creativity, of creativity as a social process, and of the place of creativity in architectural practice. Its effects on architectural practice and the well-being of individual architects are particularly damaging. Applicants to architecture schools commonly give as a reason for aspiring to the profession that it is 'creative'. What this means to them must be understood in terms of the myth. They desire freedom and autonomy. In reality, the freedom they hope for cannot be attained. The architect is not less but more than other professionals bound by the web of social obligation. As a result many architects in mid-career are deeply frustrated and unhappy.[2]

CREATIVITY AND THE INDIVIDUAL

Modern psychology may be said to begin with Locke, who in the late seventeenth century rejected the Platonic doctrine of innate ideas and proposed instead that all we know, we learn. Since that time psychology has made great progress. There are, however, obvious difficulties in accounting for creativity and innovation in terms of learning. These difficulties have been increased by the prevalent conviction that only mechanical and reductionist views of the world qualify as 'scientific'. There have been repeated and necessarily unsuccessful attempts to explain productive thinking in terms of a restricted selection from the known range of mental processes.

The two processes which have, mistakenly, been treated as accounting for all describable thought processes are logical inference, or deduction, and the association of ideas. Deduction has a very ancient and respectable history, having been first formalized by Aristotle. It does in fact play a role in productive thinking, but that role is strictly limited. The conclusions of a correct logical inference can say nothing that the premises do not already say. To overcome this limitation, the new category of 'inductive' logic was invented in the nineteenth century. Here observation of instances was by itself supposed to lead to new generalizations. Induction was never technically satisfactory, and in this century the sustained criticism of Karl Popper (1963, 1972) seems to have destroyed its remaining credibility. However, there are some signs that it is making a comeback, along with association, in the field of artificial intelligence and expert systems.

The association of ideas depends on the frequent occurrence of two or more different things or events simultaneously or in close association. Once such an association is established, an encounter with one member of the set will bring the others to mind. Also first discussed by Aristotle and developed into an elaborate system in the eighteenth century by Hartley, the association of ideas was rigorously investigated by Pavlov and others of the behaviourist school during the first half of our present century. Thanks to its apparently purely mechanical character, 'conditioning', as the behaviourists called it, became for a time the *only* respectable psychological process. Opposition nevertheless persisted, even among experimentally inclined psychologists, particularly the Gestalt school.

The reductionist efforts of behaviourism were all the more deplorable in that a sound and comprehensive theory already existed. At the beginning of the nineteenth century Samual Taylor Coleridge, working on the basis of his own experience as a poet, proposed a tripartite theory of the imagination.[3] First of all he saw that *all* mental activity has an imaginative or constructive aspect. Even the categories of 'thing' into which we divide the world are not simply given; we have to construct them. Further, the boundaries between categories are not fixed, but plastic. This general insight has recently been clarified by the work of Rosch and others (Rosch *et al.* 1976). Once constructed, our categories can then be mechanically connected and rearranged by the processes of inference and association, which Coleridge lumps together under one heading: 'The Fancy'. However, Coleridge also perceived the need for another *kind* of imagination, operating at a higher level and depending on ordering principles. Finally, he realized that the ability to do this kind of structuring and restructuring depended on the plasticity of our most basic concepts.

Coleridge's theory lacked empirical support. The experimental exploration of the constructive basis of mind was begun independently by the Gestalt school early in this century. When Wertheimer came to summarize the implications of this work for 'productive thinking' in the late 1930s, he reached conclusions similar to Coleridge's (Wertheimer 1945, 1978). His subdivision of mental processes has been adopted here. Like Coleridge he saw that basic concepts could not be rigid if the observed processes of structuring and restructuring were to be possible, but he did not assign a separate category to the construction of basic concepts.

The influence of Wertheimer's work was limited while behaviourism was dominant. In the late 1950s, however, a certain weakening of mechanical conceptions of the mind happened to coincide with a significant incident of the cold war: the launching of the first Sputnik. Concern that the non-communist countries were falling behind technically stimulated research into creativity. The 1960s saw the publication of a number of important books on the theory of creativity and on management techniques for encouraging innovatory thinking (see, for example, Schon 1963, Gordon 1961, Koestler 1964, Osborn 1963). Most reached fundamentally similar conclusions. Perhaps the most penetrating analysis was that of Schon in his *Invention and the Evolution of Ideas*. Schon extended Wertheimer's approach to include all kinds of metaphorical thinking and the transfer of concepts from one context to another in general. Such transfer depends essentially on the recognition of structural similarity, based on analogy of internal relationships rather than of superficial features.

By recognizing and creating structure, the mind can do more than inference and association would permit. This 'more' is what is usually meant by the term 'intuition'.[4] Without intuition, in this sense, architectural design would be impossible. However, as in psychology itself, some theories of architecture have rejected this formative role of the individual mind. Functionalism, exemplified by the teaching of Hannes Meyer at the Bauhaus and the operations research-based approaches of the 1960s, proposed that architecture could be produced by calculation. For example, the sizes and shapes of rooms were to be determined by the dimensions of the furniture and people they must contain, and their relative placing by counting the number of trips which must be made between them. There are two related mistakes here. The first is to suppose that any set of abstract relationships, such as the anticipated number of trips between rooms, can in itself be sufficient to determine the form of something. There must also be forms to be related. The second is to think that, even if this were possible, the result would be either intelligible or aesthetically acceptable. The selection of an organizing principle on the basis of an intuitively perceived 'match' with the pattern of constraints imposed by the physical and social conditions is an essential part of architectural design. Such intuitions are essentially individual, and deserve the title of 'creative'.

On the other hand, logical inference and associative thinking play a much larger part in the day-to-day practice of design than formative intuition. All three are involved in any productive work, as Coleridge perceived, but the balance varies with the number and severity of the social demands imposed. Further, the order which the architect imposes or discovers need not be in any broad or deep sense original. In most cases it will have a strong family resemblance to the organizing principles found in other buildings of the same type. In this respect architectural design often falls short of the demands of the myth. To be 'truly' creative implies conspicuous originality, innovation which achieves social recognition. Creativity is thus not only an individual, but also a social process.

CREATIVITY AS A SOCIAL PROCESS

The general forms of mental activity identified by psychology are, reassuringly, apparent in socio-cultural studies of innovation. There are four basic kinds of social innovation: variation; cultural borrowing; invention; and trial-and-error (see Murdock 1956). Of these, variation and cultural borrowing depend mainly on the logical and associative processes, while invention depends mainly on processes which grasp the structure of a situation and result in the reorganization of the field and the transfer of concepts.

Variation in this special sense is a slight modification of an established way of doing things. Variation generates the well-known historical sequences of artefacts: in architecture, the development of the Doric temple towards the classic form of the Parthenon, or that of the Gothic cathedral from its Romanesque origins.[5] In the latter case, though, the changes initiated by variation posed problems which had to be solved by other processes. The development of the Gothic vault and the flying buttress cannot be explained in terms of variation alone. This sequence, in which directed or purposeful variation creates conflicts which cannot be resolved within the existing paradigm, is historically common.[6]

Cultural borrowing is the most commonplace mechanism of change. The ordinary process of imitation, by which social practices are transmitted within a culture, is extended to include material from long ago or far away, or both. (Long ago and far away are highly relative terms in this context.) Architectural forms have always been subject to diffusion from one culture to another. Amongst the most striking of the many examples are the architecture of the Renaissance, and English Palladianism. In modern times systematic historical research and international distribution of architectural books and journals have greatly increased the speed and scope of cultural borrowing. The ideology of the Modern Movement sought to restrict the range of permissible borrowing. Within the last few years, however, this restriction has been questioned if not entirely removed.

Invention demands structural understanding. Ideas or forms are transferred from one context to another superficially quite different one, on the basis of this perception of underlying community of organization. Again, a set of ideas or forms may be radically reinterpreted, so that the 'same' elements are given quite new tasks in the new structure. Well-known architectural inventions include Palladio's translation into classical forms of the medieval organization of the façade of the church with nave and aisles; the similar reworking of the English church spire by Wren and the English baroque school; and Frank Lloyd Wright's synthesis of the 'Prairie House' out of a diversity of architectural traditions.

Trial and error is a tactic of desperation, and desperate social groups seldom engage in architecture. Errors do of course occur in the history of architecture, but seldom as a result of mere random experiment. The repeated collapses and reconstructions of the dome of Sancta Sophia, Istanbul, during the Byzantine era, for instance, were certainly not the result of random activity.[7] The architects concerned had developed a correct qualitative theory of the causes of collapse and took intelligent measures to overcome them. They simply had no notion of the magnitude of the forces involved, and no means of calculating them. In general, design as an activity is the antithesis of trial and error.

These four social processes of innovation are uniform throughout history. So, it may be assumed, is the distribution of the corresponding psychological abilities. The distribution of innovation is not uniform. In architectural history, there are periods of exceptional 'creativity' and others of placid competence. This is not a paradox. Culture is essentially conservative. Even in modern societies which have incorporated change and progress into their value systems, cultural drag is strong. Variation, spiced with a little cultural borrowing, is the normal form of change. However, societies and cultures are never homogeneous. Different elements and systems within a culture move at different rates and in different directions. Tensions accumulate, and eventually surface as perceived problems which become increasingly urgent and well publicized. Such problems attract the attention of able and ambitious people. In science and technology where such problems are relatively autonomous and well structured, a solution is often reached by several people simultaneously, or almost so.[8] In architecture and the arts similar processes create the conditions for the emergence of new schools or styles. To be a genius requires not only exceptional ability, but a great problem, and problems are defined by the state of the art.

CREATIVITY IN ARCHITECTURAL PRACTICE

The opportunity to contribute to a 'paradigm change' in architecture may not occur in a working lifetime. Other kinds of change give rise to lesser opportunities. New settlements and the symbolic self-definition of newly wealthy groups produce regional or local 'schools'. Human-made or natural disasters, such as the great fires of London and Chicago, or the destructive bombing of the Second World War, lead to large-scale rebuilding. New patterns of work and recreation call for new or radically modified building types. Technical change may render old forms obsolete or suggest new ones. Fluctuations in demand for established building types drive the 'design cycle': an upsurge in demand after a pause in production is often accompanied by substantial modification of the type. Finally, there is always a certain amount of superficial, fashionable change. Even the chance to introduce fashionable or decorative variations in building types, however, comes, if at all, only at quite long intervals in the life of the average architect. Much of the work of an architect is administrative. Most of the remainder is concerned with details rather than overall arrangement and form. There are, after all, many more details to be settled. Architects who cling to the myth of the creative artist with god-like powers are bound to be frustrated. What productive work they do seems menial and insignificant in relation to the myth.

Nevertheless, people from other professions who work with architects, such as engineers, are often quite convinced that architectural work is 'creative' by comparison with their own. And so it is. The range of objectives in an engineering design task is usually limited, and the objectives themselves are well defined and structured. Buildings, on the contrary, usually serve a wide range of purposes, and the detailed nature and relative importance of these purposes may be far from clear. People's knowledge of their needs is often surprisingly vague and inexplicit. Their descriptions of what they want and do are correspondingly inaccurate. They quite commonly want contradictory things. The physical constraints on a design will in most cases be much less significant than the beliefs, values and habits of the people concerned. Architectural design is thus much concerned with defining objectives.

In order to define objectives, to bring the inexplicit knowledge of clients and users out into the open, and to secure agreement on contentious issues, architects must make proposals. These proposals cannot be mechanically derived from 'the facts of the case'. Their purpose is, in part, to elicit the facts through a dialectic process. The proposal will contain more, and more precise, information than has been given. It will also, as argued previously, necessarily embody some organizing principle which is connected to the function or 'content' of the building by analogy, and mainly by analogy in the realm of visual thinking. In generating it the architect must act creatively and use imagination. However, the process is a tiresome and frustrating one. Some of the additional information which the architect has introduced will in all probability prove to be wrong. Proposals elicit new information which invalidates them. Design 'homes in' on an acceptable solution, but often at a high emotional cost to the designer.

In practice, then, architects are highly creative, but their creativity is stressful because it is largely employed in the definition of acceptable solutions to practical problems. Much of their effort is devoted to matters of detail, in the context of variations to established patterns. The inherent difficulties and frustrations of this work are made worse by a widely accepted mythology which pictures the architect as free, innovatory on the historic scale, and concerned with broad concept rather than detail. In order to break out of this vicious circle it is first of all essential to recognize that the mental processes by which new ideas are produced are commonplace rather than mysterious or exceptional. They are no more, but no less, mysterious than many other human performances, such as managing to find and put on one's shoes in the morning. They can be learned and practised like other skills. Opportunity in architecture on the other hand is rather scarce. Great architects have, almost without exception, had to work hard at making their opportunities. They have also been fortunate in their timing. Creativity in architecture must be seen as both individual and social, and the social aspect should be given its proper weight.

NOTES

1 On this point, see the chapter on the use of 'Creative' in Williams 1958.

2 See, especially, Blau 1984, ch. 3, for the results of a sociological survey. Other writers on the profession have reached similar conclusions, for example Saint 1983.

3 Coleridge's theory of imagination is to be found in *Biographia Literaria* (1817).

4 See Arnheim's essay 'The double-edged mind' in Arnheim 1986.

5 The relationship between historical sequences of artefacts and creativity are explained in a most illuminating and accessible way in Kubler 1962.

6 The notions of a paradigm and paradigm changes or 'revolutions' in ideas were first developed by Kuhn (1962).

7 The curious and instructive history of St. Sophia, Istanbul, is outlined in ch. 16 of Mainstone 1975.

8 The classic paper of William F. Ogburn and Dorothy Thomas (1922) 'Are inventions inevitable: a note on social evolution', *Political Science Quarterly* 37: 83–98 lists 148 cases of multiple discovery, some involving as many as six co-discoverers. Reprinted in Brady and Isaac 1975.

REFERENCES

Arnheim, R. (1986) *New Essays on the Psychology of Art*, Berkeley: University of California Press.

Blau, J.R. (1984) *Architects and Firms*, Cambridge, Mass.: MIT Press.

Brady, I. and Isaac, B. (1975) *A Reader in Cultural Change*, New York: John Wiley and Sons.

Coleridge, S.T. (1817, 1847) *Biographia Literaria*, London: J.M. Dent & Son.

Gordon, W.J. (1961) *Synectics*, New York: Harper & Row.

Koestler, A. (1964) *The Act of Creation*, London: Hutchinson.

Kubler, G. (1962) *The Shape of Time*, New Haven: Yale University Press.

Kuhn, T. (1962) *The Structure of Scientific Revolution*, Chicago: University of Chicago Press.

Mainstone, R. (1975) *Developments in Structural Form*, Harmondsworth: Allen Lane/Penguin Books.

Miller, G. (1956) 'The magical number seven, plus or minus

two: some hints on our capability for processing information', *Psychological Review* 63 (2): 81–96; reprinted in G. Miller (1967) *The Psychology of Communication*, London: Allen Lane/Penguin Press.

Murdock, G.P. (1956) 'How culture changes', in H.L. Shapiro (ed.) *Man, Culture and Society*, New York: Oxford University Press.

Osborn, A. (1963) *Applied Imagination*, New York: Scribner.

Popper, K. (1963) *Conjectures and Refutations*, London: Routledge & Kegan Paul.

—— (1972) *Objective Knowledge*, Oxford: Clarendon Press.

Rosch, E., Mervis, C., Gray, W., Johnson, P. and Boyes-Braem, P. (1976) 'Basic objects in natural categories', *Cognitive Psychology* 8 (3): 382–439.

Saint, A. (1983) *The Image of the Architect*, New Haven: Yale University Press.

Schon, D. (1963, 1967) 'Invention and the Evolution of Ideas', London: Social Science Paperbacks.

Wertheimer, M. (1945, 1978) *Product Thinking*, Westport: Greenwood Press.

Williams, R. (1958) *Culture and Society 1780–1850*, London: Chatto & Windus.

51   A face in the cloud: anthropomorphism in architecture

Andrew Ballantyne

PARANOIAC SPACE

'I must not', said the poet Paul Eluard, 'look on reality as being like myself' (Bachelard 1938: 1). He failed of course. Even the most prosaic of us has heard the wind sigh and reacted to a symptom of melancholy. Engines routinely roar, brakes squeal. In the artificially constructed world of poetry and novels emotional crises link with thunderstorms, and melancholy seems actually to cause the condensation of delicate mists and gentle rain, so closely does one follow on the other. The world is becoming human when the sea utters a melancholy, long, withdrawing roar, no less than when the earth is made to scream in pain.[1]

Anthropomorphism – the finding of human form – has its roots deep in our psyche: we begin by finding human form in ourselves. It is one of our most powerful and adaptable tools for making sense of things. We compare the familiar with the unfamiliar, and if we find a similarity then we feel that we have learned something, that we understand. One side of the comparison, whatever the object of scrutiny, is often the body (Foucault 1966: 22). We project ourselves into other things, finding 'faces in the moon, armies in the clouds' (Hume 1757: 29), ascribing:

> malice or good-will to every thing, that hurts or pleases us … trees, mountains and streams are personified, and the inanimate parts of nature acquire sentiment and passion.
>
> (Hume 1757: 29)

For each act of projecting ourselves into inanimate things there is a corresponding possible *becoming* of those objects in ourselves. If we are like a thing then it follows that the thing is like us: the face becoming a moon, the army turning into a cloud. Trees are animated as Dryads, Daphne rooted as a laurel tree. A dangerous mountain is an ogre, the Eiger, a craggy rock the Old Man of Hoy, Medusa's gaze petrifies; Pygmalion's story tells of a statue becoming flesh while, moving in the opposite direction, Lot's tells of his wife becoming salt. We project human characteristics into a skyscraper, and then reciprocate by becoming skyscrapers ourselves (see Figure 1). Becoming human or becoming mineral is one process moving in different directions. Even empty space takes a human imprint when there is a sense of up and down: the directions are charged with meaning by reference to the body.

Without anthropological association such words as 'on', 'under' and 'beside' become indistinguishable (Merleau-Ponty 1962: 101). The head is higher than the abdomen: rationality and spirituality dwell in the first, sensuality and the gut-reaction in the second. A relation of up and down cuts across culture: it is buried in language and projected across the universe. We look 'up' to those we respect, look 'down' on those we despise (and call them by names drawn from our 'nether' regions). We applaud 'high' ideals, condemn 'low' morals. Before we have buildings we have anthropomorphic space. We have words which send us out into things, projecting our own shape into nebulous space, giving it a direction and purpose of which it is itself unaware. And on the other hand we are invaded by those same things: we suspend the sense of our own shape in order to empathize with them. One extreme of this thinking stretches into anthropomorphic space, where human form is understood even though there is nothing but indifferent void. The other reaches the schizophrenic's aconceptualized body: human, but without a sense of its form and limits. In between is the range of equilibrium which can find expression in buildings:

> by remembering 'houses' and 'rooms', we learn to 'abide' within ourselves. Now everything becomes clear, the house images move in both directions: they are in us as much as we are in them.
>
> (Bachelard 1958: xxxiii)

Figure 1 *New York architects dressed as their buildings at the Fête Moderne, a Fantasy in Flame and Silver, 23 January 1931.* (Source: *Koolhaas 1978*)

FERTILITY AND INTELLIGENCE

As in the body, so in the house, the forest, the universe: we see, because of the fact that plants grow, that earth is the source of fecundity, and we deduce that the first of our species was born of earth. Prometheus, we learn, modelled the first man from clay and water, but (the earth having been recently formed) the clay had in it traces of sky. It is because of these traces of sky that man walks upright: the sky is charged with intellect as the earth is charged with fertility. Yahweh Elohim formed Adam from the dust of the ground and breathed life-giving air into him. Lucretius tells us that the first of each species was born from a womb with roots, from the earth (Lucretius 1947, Vol. 1: 474–5). Burial confirms kinship with earth, cremation kinship with sun and sky: the body is returned to the fire from which (according to Heraclitus) everything was made. Animated during life by an invisible sun within, the body consumed by fire is *interred by angels*: buried in sky (Browne 1658: 169).

As individuals our earliest dwelling place is the womb; collectively, as a species, it was a cave, imitated in the earliest known buildings: the temple-tombs on Malta. Here, constructed buildings are buried under earth mounds with cave-like, womb-like chambers which use a vocabulary of form related to that used in the contemporary modelling of the female figure (Figures 2 and 3).

A related arrangement is found at Newgrange in Ireland where a tunnel leads to a chamber which is penetrated by a shaft of sunlight for a few minutes only on the shortest day of the year, when the sun is reborn to perform its next cycle. As the earth is fertile, so it is the sun who fertilizes. As the earth is instinctual and substantial, so is the sky intellectual and spiritual. The logic works so long as we understand the unstated term in the syllogism: the human body. There is fertility below *therefore* there is reason above. A mound of earth and irregular stones, a dead place, is transformed into a site for the annual dramatization of an act charged with vitality. The building which seems casually hewn is transformed into a miracle of precision. This precision is

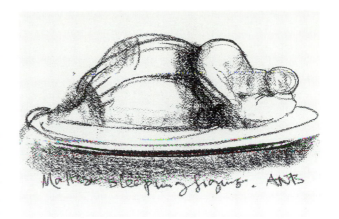

Figure 3 *Maltese sleeping figure drawn by the author.*

not in the *shaping* of the stones but in their *positioning* in the universe. The wonder comes not from the stones but from the assemblage of stones *and* ideas, earth *and* sky, instinct *and* intellect. The anthropomorphism is not in the substances but in the connections.

The same thinking is found in a tower of learning, Filarete's *House of Virtue and Vice*, described by Antonio Averlino (1461–3, Vol. 1: 245–9; Vol. 2: 142v–151v), who enthusiastically anthropomorphized the whole process of design and construction: the architect and client are lovers, the architect gives birth to the building. His tower has brothels and drinking saloons on the ground floor, with above them dormitories for prostitutes and headquarters for police. Moving higher the occupants become more sedate, pursuing liberal studies in an ascent to the heights of sophistication: an observation platform where 'the art of astronomy is used to explore all of Creation, Heaven as well as Earth' (Leeuwen 1988: 68).

This is a vision of a building which is a whole world in itself (a precursor of Le Corbusier's Unités), consciously anthropomorphic and consciously mediating between earth and sky, between the sensual and the intellectual. The Gothic cathedral had, perhaps unconsciously, made the same transition from cave-like crypt to a closely implicated involvement in sky. The interior, disembodied into light, was a zone on earth which mediated with heaven: 'dwelling, as it were, in some strange region of the universe which neither exists entirely in the slime of the earth nor entirely in the purity of Heaven' (Suger, in Panofsky 1979: 65). This mediation is dramatized for example in the west façade of the abbey at Bath, where angels climb up and down ladders which reach from earth to heaven.

SYMPATHETIC ACTION

A person standing upright crosses the horizon at a right-angle – human and ocean: each feels gravity's pull and responds, one adopts the vertical, the other the horizontal.

Figure 2 *Maltese temple-tombs drawn by Birgit Cold.*

The human feels kinship with others who have chosen the same response. Ledoux's primitive man projects himself into the clouds, fills his sky with gods, but is alone between earth and sky. His tree has more to offer as a companion than as a shelter (Figure 4).

If we turn large stones upright then they stand, and in the act of standing they become giants: Nine Maidens (Cornwall), Whispering Knights (Oxfordshire). The carved standing-stone column becomes a sentinel: caryatids in ancient Greece, apostles in the chevet and prophets in the ambulatory at Saint-Denis in medieval France (Panofsky 1979: 21). We project human characteristics into things which stand, from standing stones and trees to skyscrapers, not because of what they are but because they stand: by virtue of their stance they become interchangeable.

Thus the Greek temple becomes a cella, housing the god, attended by a disciplined phalanx of sentinels. Sometimes the column-sentinels are explicitly anthropomorphic, like the Erechtheion caryatids; but even when the conventionally abstract orders are used they are continually described in anthropomorphic terms, following Vitruvius who explained the proportions of the Doric, Ionic and Corinthian columns with reference to the proportions of the man, the woman and the young girl. Indeed the fact that columns had *capitals* and *pedestals* (which is to say *heads* and *feet*) invites some such understanding. Vitruvius tells us, no doubt correctly, that symmetry derives from the body (Vitruvius 1914, ch. 1: 72–5), but what he meant by 'symmetry' was not the bilateral uniformity of a mirror image but the regulation of one part with respect to the others: *proportion*. A larger building, like a larger person, needs larger parts, not a greater number of them. Axial symmetry goes unremarked, perhaps because it seemed self-evidently necessary: it is certainly favoured in natural organisms.[2] In ceremonial and monumental buildings the principle of axiality was established very early: in a relaxed way in the Maltese temples, with unrelenting rigour in ancient Egypt.

Figure 4 L'Abri du Pauvre (The Poor Man's Shelter) *by Claude-Nicholas Ledoux (1736–1806).* (Source: *Ledoux 1847*)

The projection of the human form into architecture via the abstracting systems of mathematics has had long currency. Vitruvius explains how to centre a circle on the navel to make it touch the outstretched fingertips and toes, and how the distance from head to toe is equal to that from one outstretched fingertip to the other, meaning that a man with outstretched arms can be inscribed in a square as well as the circle. Leonardo da Vinci's drawing of this formula is one of the most celebrated images of Renaissance thinking. Drawings trying to reconcile geometric and human forms from the Middle Ages, the Renaissance and after are legion, from Villard de Honnecourt to Le Corbusier's *Modulor*. If we compare the symmetry and the proportioning ratios in a human and in a church plan then we can find the same number, which might be thought to show that they have something in common, that they share some abstract essence, that the building can shadow the divine, since systems of proportion are the spiritualized essence of the person, made in the god's image. Even the purest of geometries can become human. In Vitruvius a square implies a man. In the Renaissance we find the idea extended into three dimensions:

> The cube is formed from the square, and the square in turn is formed from the man of perfect proportions.
>
> (Giovanni Paolo Lomazzo, quoted in Hersey 1976: 88)

More recently, Frank Gehry in California designed himself a kitchen window, a tilted cube, imagining it as the ghost of Cubism escaping from the old house which was being extended (Friedman 1986: 42–3). His dining room has a window turning a corner, and here the shape was influenced by Duchamp's attempt to catch an image of movement in his *Nude Descending a Staircase* (Friedman 1986: 39). The human image here is evoked at a remove: the first association is with a painting, the second with the human form. Yet a comparable process could have shaped the ancient Maltese temples. Art does not merely depict, it gives us ways of seeing.

The stance of a stone turns it into a whispering knight. The twist of a cube turns it into a Cubist ghost. The action of the body turns into the action, the function, of the building:

> as in the human body there are some noble and beautiful parts, and some rather ignoble and disagreeable, and yet we see that we stand in very great need of these, and without them cou'd not subsist; so in fabricks, there ought to be some parts considerable and honoured, and some less elegant; without which the other cou'd not remain free, and so consequently wou'd lose part of their dignity and beauty. But as our Blessed Creator has ordered these our members in such a manner, that the most beautiful are in places most exposed to view, and the less comely more hidden; so in building also, we

ought to put the principal and considerable parts, in places the most seen, and the less beautiful, in places as much hidden from the eye as possible; that in them may be lodged all the foulness of the house, and all those things that may give any obstruction, and in any measure render the more beautiful parts disagreeable.

(Palladio 1570: 38)

The increasing sophistication of building services makes a parallel with metabolism increasingly clear. The body's temperature is maintained at a comfortable level, like the building's, by a system of interacting sensors and mechanisms which in the building might include its inhabitants (as sensors) feeling too warm and therefore (as mechanisms) opening a window. When the regulating machines are activated by a computer which has its own sensors then we have an 'intelligent building'. When it gives its inhabitants dry throats, influenza epidemics or legionnaires' disease it becomes a 'sick building'. However, it is not necessary to have a computer and air-conditioning in order to have a sick building. It can be achieved using traditional methods, even using technology available in the mid-fifteenth century:

I will show you that the building is truly a living man. You will see that it must eat in order to live, exactly as it is with man. It sickens or dies or sometimes is cured of its sickness by a good doctor. I will show you that the building is truly a living man. You will see that it must eat in order to live, exactly as it is with man. It sickens and dies or sometimes is cured of its sickness by a good doctor. Sometimes, like man, it becomes ill again because it neglected its health. Many times, through the cares of a good doctor, it returns to health and lives a long while and finally dies in its own time. There are some that are never ill and then at the end die suddenly; others are killed by other people for one reason or another.

(Averlino 1461–3, Vol. 1: 15)

MASKS AND SOULS

A façade (as the word says) is a face, and we respond to it as such, finding expressions of mood and character in arrangements of windows and doors as easily as we see a face in the moon, or in a cloud. Sometimes a façade is treated literally and heavy-handedly as a face and given anatomical detail, as in the cave in the gardens at Bomarzo (Figure 5). The anthropomorphism here is direct and absolutely unmistakeable. The orotund entrance is a black hole which exerts a gravitational pull on everything else in this essay. Sometimes there is no direct correspondence of features, but there lingers a sense of physiognomy and expression, for example in Lequeu's work, where disturbing studies of human form

Figure 5 *Cave in the gardens at Bomarzo, Italy, drawn by the author.*

relate to equally disturbing ideas for buildings (Vidler 1987: 120–2).[3] There need be no direct correspondence, feature by feature, for us to respond as if to a face: a reflective surface, a white wall, with light-absorbing black holes, has a way of becoming a face whether or not it is arranged like one (Deleuze and Guattari 1980a). A façade is immediately scrutinized as a face and if it does not submit to the interpretation then it looks *blank*. Architects' conventional elevations emphasize a building's façades and allow their scrutiny. They can be a trap, bringing about the neglect of other things:

What is the beauty of a building to us today? The same thing as the beautiful face of a mindless woman: something mask-like.

(Nietzsche 1878: 218)

Avoiding the superficial façade-mask can lead to another level of anthropomorphism where the psyche rather than the body is modelled. Gehry's Winton Guest House fragments a single house into a cluster of separate-seeming room-buildings. Here, in an appropriately unconscious modelling of *role-diffusion*, each aspect of the individual's domestic life takes on separate identity. The individual house becomes a society of rooms just as an individual person can be a social structure composed of many souls: a society of mind with micropolitical interactions between the parts (Thiele 1990; Minsky 1987; Deleuze and Guattari 1980b).

We might expect to find a portrayal of the psyche in the work of Peter Eisenman, who draws ideas from a wide range of sources including psychoanalysis. He has declared an intent to make architecture of complete abstraction. Nevertheless his design for a house in Spain can be radically 'misread' in anthropomorphic terms (Eisenman 1987: 172). Not only does its geometry derive from the cube (which, as we have seen, has been anthropomorphic since the Renaissance) it is also a thorough realization of Duchamp's nude – a portrayal of rationalism's etiolated ghost descending a hillside, nervously edging its way towards the brink of the Gulf of Cadiz (see Figure 6).

The further limit of anthropomorphism is reached at such a building as London's National Theatre. The dominant image in the mind of Sir Denys Lasdun, the designer, was not an idea of the body but of geology: continuous concrete decks run across terraces and foyers stratifying the space. People move in flows from theatres to bars, from terraces to car parks, the strata causing them to be arranged as spectacles for one another. This is a mainstream ambition for a modernist architect: the blurring of boundaries between inside and outside should make the building mesh inseparably with its surroundings. The foyers are much used, it would seem very happily, but yet the building's unpopularity is notorious.

If we are inclined to try to understand unfamiliar buildings in anthropomorphic terms, then when we approach the National Theatre we face a challenge. The human state in which there is a blurring of boundaries, in which the mind loses its conceptual grasp of the body and loses its ability to separate self from surroundings, confusing inside and outside is *schizophrenia*. A schizophrenic body which has lost its self-image can feel itself being invaded by foreign bodies: 'the surface of the uncreated body swarms with them, as a lion's mane swarms with fleas' (Deleuze and Guattari 1972: 16). The

theatre's foyers – which extend beyond the building into riverside terraces, blur boundaries, merge with surroundings, mix inside and outside – accommodate people who lend animation, but (as has been said with reference to this building) 'the visible commotion of its inhabitants no more gives life to a building than the wriggle of worms gives vitality to a corpse' (Scruton 1981: 17).

Bernard Tschumi has drawn on this image of the schizophrenic body in describing his *cinegramme folie* for the Parc de la Villette in Paris. This surprises because his architecture of arbitrarily colliding points, lines and planes seems so far removed from an anthropomorphic outlook. However, his punning use of the term '*folie*' – evoking not only the *follies* of the English landscape tradition but also *insanity* – seems the more apt once this connection has been made (Tschumi 1987: 17; Vidler 1992).

HALF A UNIVERSAL ATLAS

Thus anthropomorphism has two limits. One corresponds to the schizophrenic deterioration of the personality: if we are to find human form in the building then we must resort to a specialized body which cannot securely imagine itself. The other limit is correspondingly paranoid: with no building at all, only a predisposition to find human form, motivation, meaning and purpose – even in indifference, in empty space. A line is traced from one limit to the other, and anthropomorphic architecture positioned along it: in one direction the architecture fades from view, in the other the human form dissolves.

From the cave-becoming-womb in ancient times, buildings have been conceived and conceptualized with reference to the body. Other ideas have been available, and they have been used. But if confronted with the unfamiliar, then an idea of human form is with remarkable persistency understood. Alternatives may be more reasonable, or more ingenious, but inevitably they are more demanding. They entail imagining things other than ourselves as being different from ourselves. This is something that, to some degree, can be learned. But we cannot understand without reference to something we already know; and the thing that lies at the root of our understanding of space and form is the body. It tends to be an idea of first resort.

The persistence of anthropomorphic thinking is a testimony to our failure to understand things as they are, as different from ourselves. The failure is, however, so regular as to be counted upon, and when it is experienced it does not feel like failure. It feels like understanding. How majestically Orion strides across the sky! Who would sacrifice him? To abolish anthropomorphism would be to divest the world of meaning. On the other hand, an uncritical anthropomorphism would bring with it too much meaning. Teeming swarms of faces, bodies,

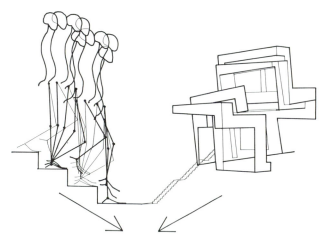

Figure 6 *Guardiola House, Santa Maria del Mar, Spain, by Peter Eisenman.*

bodily actions and passions would overwhelm the most commonplace occurrence. One would be unable to see the wood for the Dryads.

A multiplicity of levels of involvement of the person in the world is necessary for the most practical understanding, for survival. Anthropomorphism infiltrates even scientific thinking; it need come as no surprise to find it in architecture (Bachelard 1938). Our buildings are as artificially constructed as the world in our novels. Form in buildings is connected with our sense of our own form as surely as the weather in novels is connected with fluctuating states of mind.

NOTES

1   For example, Matthew Arnold's poem *Dover Beach*, and Sir Arthur Conan Doyle's short story *When the Earth Screamed*.

2   (William) Bateson's Rule: 'When an asymmetrical lateral appendage (e.g. a right hand) is reduplicated, the resulting reduplicated limb will be bilaterally symmetrical, consisting of two parts each a mirror image of the other and so placed that a plane of symmetry could be imagined between them' (Bateson 1972: 350).

3   Lequeu's work is sometimes taken to be a hoax perpetrated by Marcel Duchamp, but attribution does not affect the observation made here.

REFERENCES

Averlino, A. (1461–3) 'Il filarete', *Treatise on Architecture*, trans. J.R. Spencer 1965, 2 vols, New Haven: Yale University Press.

Bachelard, G. (1938) *La Psychanalyse de Feu*, Paris; trans. A.C.M. Ross, *The Psychoanalysis of Fire*, 1987, London: Quartet.

—— (1958) *La Poétique de l'espace*, Paris: Presses Universitaires de France; trans. M. Jolas, *The Poetics of Space*, 1969, Boston: Beacon Press.

Bateson, G. (1972) 'A re-examination of Bateson's Rule', in *Steps to an Ecology of Mind: Collected Essays in Anthropology, Psychiatry, Evolution and Epistemology*, New York: Chandler.

Browne, T. (1658) 'Hydriotaphia: Urne-Buriall or, A Brief Discourse of the Sepulchrall Urnes Lately Found in Norfolk' (originally printed in a volume with 'The Garden of Cyrus'); reprinted in *The Works of Sir Thomas Browne*, Vol. 1 of 4 vols, ed. G. Keynes, London: Faber.

Deleuze, G. and Guattari, f. (1972) *L'Anti-Œdipe: Capitalisme et Schizophrénie I*, Paris: Editions de Minuit; trans. R. Hurley, M. Seem and H.R. Lane, *Anti-Oedipus*, 1977, New York: Viking.

—— (1980a) 'Visagéité', in *Mille Plateaux: Capitalisme et Schizophrénie II*, Paris: Editions de Minuit; trans. B.

Massumi, *A Thousand Plateaus: Capitalism and Schizophrenia*, 1987, London: The Athlone Press.

—— (1980b) 'Micropolitique et segmentarité', in *Mille Plateaux: Capitalisme et Schizophrénie II*, Paris: Editions de Minuit; trans. B. Massumi, *A Thousand Plateaus: Capitalism and Schizophrenia*, 1987, London: The Athlone Press.

Eisenman, P. (1987) 'Misreading', in *Houses of Cards*, London: Oxford University Press.

Foucault, M. (1966) *Les Mots et les choses*, Paris: Editions Gallimard; trans. A. Sheridan, *The Order of Things: An Archaeology of the Human Sciences*, 1970, London: Tavistock.

Friedman, M. (ed.) (1986) *The Architecture of Frank Gehry*, New York: Rizzoli.

Hersey, G.L. (1976) *Pythagorean Palaces: Magic and Architecture in the Italian Renaissance*, Ithaca, NY: Cornell University Press.

Hume, D. (1757) *The Natural History of Religion* (originally in *Four Dissertations*), Edinburgh: Andrew Millar; published separately in 1956, ed. H.E. Root, London: Adam & Charles Black.

Koolhaas, R. (1978) *Delirious New York*, London: Thames & Hudson.

Ledoux, C.N. (1847) *Works*, Ramée edn, Paris; reprinted 1983, Princeton, NJ: Princeton Architectural Press.

Leeuwen, T.A.P. (1988) *The Skyward Trend of Thought: The Metaphysics of the American Skyscraper*, Cambridge, Mass.: MIT Press.

Lucretius (Titi Lucreti Cari) (1947) *De Rerum Natura: Libri Sex*, 3 vols, ed. C. Bailey, Oxford: Oxford University Press.

Merleau-Ponty, M. (1962) 'The spatiality of one's own body and motility', in *The Phenomenology of Perception*, trans. C. Smith 1962, London: Routledge & Kegan Paul.

Minsky, M. (1987) *The Society of Mind*, London: Heinemann.

Nietzsche, F. (1878) *Menschliches Allzumenschliches*; trans. R.J. Hollingdale, *Human, All Too Human*, 1986, Cambridge: Cambridge University Press.

Palladio, A. (1570) *I Quattro Libri dell'Architettura*, Venice; trans. 1738, *The Four Books of Architecture*, London: Isaac Ware, Book II.

Panofsky, E. (ed.) (1979) *Abbot Suger on the Abbey Church of St-Denis and its Art Treasures*, 2nd edn, Princeton, NJ: Princeton University Press.

Scruton, R. (1981) 'Architecture on the horizontal', *PN Review* 25: 15–170.

Thiele, L.P. (1990) *Friedrich Nietzsche and the Politics of the Soul*, Princeton, NJ: Princeton University Press.

Tschumi, B. (1987) *Cinégramme Folie: Le Parc de la Villette*, Princeton, NJ: Princeton Architectural Press.

Vidler, A. (1987) 'Asylums of libertinage: de Sade, Fourier, Lequeu', in *The Writing of the Walls*, Princeton, NJ: Princeton Architectural Press.

—— 'Architecture dismembered', in *The Architectural Uncanny*, Cambridge, Mass.: MIT Press.

Vitruvius (1914) *The Twelve Books on Architecture*, trans. M.H. Morgan, Cambridge, Mass.: Harvard University Press, Book III.

52 'The advantage of a clearer light': the sash-window as a harbinger of an age of progress and enlightenment

Hentie Louw

The sash-window is well enough known not to have to explain what it is and how it works. Suffice it to say that the counterbalanced, vertically sliding wooden window received the format it retained until this century during the 1670s–80s in England. How that came about is in itself a fascinating story, but not one which can be related here. The aim of this essay is to demonstrate the extent to which even such a mundane object as a window can reflect the nature of the socio-technological milieu which gave birth to the buildings of which it forms a part.

Despite the fact that the revolutionary nature of the sash-window was understood from the beginning, surprisingly little seems to have been written about the topic at the time. The first detailed appraisal of the novel window type came from the poet and translator Charles Cotton (1630–87). In a poem of his called 'Chatsworth', and first published in 1681 as part of a volume of poems on the Peak District, England, Cotton describes amongst other things the new sash-windows installed in the house only a few years earlier by the Third Earl of Devonshire. While hardly inspiring as poetry, Cotton's description nevertheless gives a good enough impression of the impact the sash-window's appearance made on contemporaries to serve as the basis for our analysis:

> And all these Glories glitter to the sight
> By the advantage of a clearer Light
> The *Glaziers* work before substantial was
> I must confess, thrice as much Lead as Glass,
> Which in the Suns *Meridian* cast a light
> As it had been within an Hour of night.
> The Windows now look like so many Suns,
> Illustrating the noble Room at once
> The primitive *Casements* modell's were no doubt
> By that through which the Pigeon was thrust out,
> Where now whole shashes are but one great *Eye*
> T'examine, and admire thy beauties by
> And, if we hence look out, we shall see there
> The *Gardens* too i'th *Reformation* share.
> (Cotton 1683: 81–2)

From this account it would appear as if the following five properties of the sash-window hold the key to an understanding of its immediate appeal:

1   It allowed more light into buildings than other window-types available at the time.
2   It was seen as progressive.
3   It enhanced display.
4   It strengthened the visual link between inside and outside.
5   It fulfilled a particular aesthetic ideal.

The superiority of the sash-window in terms of daylight penetration over other window types even at the early stages of its development is relatively easy to demonstrate, and this difference became even more pronounced as its technology was refined in the course of the next century.

It owes this to a novel method of operation and to its rigid constructional framework which not only allowed larger panes of window glass to be employed safely, and with minimum interruption of the view, but also permitted substantially larger window openings than traditional methods. For example, some of the sash-windows installed in the William and Mary wing at Hampton Court Palace in the early 1690s measure no less than 14 ft. × 6 ft. (4.3 m. × 1.8 m.), while 10 ft. × 5 ft. (3.1 m. × 1.5 m.) was considered big for its main rival the cross window (see Figure 1). It is therefore not surprising that it became customary for contemporaries to refer to sash-windows as 'large' or 'big' windows.

Figure 1 *Fountain Court, Hampton Court Palace, with sash-windows dating from the last decade of the seventeenth century. (Photograph: author)*

What made this particular advantage of the sash-window so crucially important, however, is the special significance which had come to be attached to light.

The immense fascination in which the whole concept of light (in both a physical and metaphysical sense) was held in virtually every important sphere of intellectual life is one of the distinguishing features of an age which we now refer to as the baroque. Painters from Caravaggio to Rembrandt and Vermeer, from Poussin to Claude, all in their different ways found the symbolism of light a constant source of inspiration, and relied heavily on light effects to animate their subject matter, be it of secular or religious origin.

Bernini's mastery of theatrical illusion generated by light in both his sculptural compositions and his architecture never fails to amaze the modern observer. And in the churches of the Italian, Spanish and German/Austrian baroque, the use of light as the 'visible manifestation of the supernatural' often rivalled even that of the great cathedrals of the Middle Ages. In the Protestant north the imagination was fired by the clear white light of truth rather than the magical chiaroscuro effects of the Catholic south, but the fervour with which these ideals were pursued was no less acute.

In literature the blind poet Milton's quest for a celestial light to compensate for his disability stood as a beacon for later generations of English poets, who drew further inspiration from the discoveries of scientists like Newton in the field of optics (Nicholson 1946).

In politics the imagery of the sun as the primary source of light on earth was adapted to fit the doctrine of Divine Hereditary Right, culminating with Louis XIV's appropriation of the title 'Sun King'. His palace at Versailles, which was the envy of rulers throughout Europe for generations, contains a fine series of allegorical paintings supporting this concept. Of these, La Fosse's *The Rising Sun* (c.1680), in the Room of Apollo, is the best.

Light remained a favourite theme for seventeenth-century religious writers and philosophers alike, and from that unique blend of spiritual and material enquiry of the era was born the new science of optics, i.e. the systematic study of the physical properties of light, in which most of the leading scientists of the day participated.

Cause-and-effect relationships are never easy to establish in matters as complex as this, but it is inconceivable that such a level of attention to a particular aspect of the environment would have been maintained for so long a period of time, and by so many different people of high intellect active in so many different walks of life, if there was not some unifying ideal, however ill-defined, sustaining it. The most plausible explanation seems to be that during the course of the seventeenth century there was a growing conception amongst the peoples of northern Europe, especially in England, France, Germany and the Netherlands, of the birth of a new, progressive age of light and reason.

Frances Yates has traced the origins of his world view to the Rosicrucian movement's prophecy, early in the seventeenth century, of a coming Enlightenment (Yates 1972). Rosalie Colie found similar ideas prevalent amongst the Cambridge Platonists and Dutch Arminians of that period (Colie 1957).

In this scheme of things, natural philosophy was to become the key with which to unlock the new era, and the scientists, according to Comenius in his book *The Way of Light* (1668), became the 'Torchbearers of this Enlightened Age'.[1] A number of these so-called 'Torchbearers' in both France and England had strong connections with architecture, notably Charles Perrault, Robert Hooke and Christopher Wren. It is therefore not surprising to find these concepts well ingrained in architectural thinking by the end of the seventeenth century.

The progressive amount of daylight available inside buildings as a consequence of a sustained period of advancement of the flat glass-making and woodworking technology related to fenestration had revolutionized people's attitudes towards interior design. The development was largely confined to secular building where lofty, well-lit, well-ventilated halls and staircases, lavishly decorated with mirrors, stucco painted and with wood ornamentation now became the aesthetic norm. And the sharp contrast this formed with the architecture of preceding ages came to symbolize for the people of the time the superiority of their own age – an era of light and knowledge – over previous centuries which were considered to have been times of darkness and ignorance.

The Dutch architectural writer, Willem Goeree, wrote in 1681:

> Formerly, painted glass was used stupidly and unnecessarily, and most glass windows of churches and houses were so stained that one couldn't see daylight. . . . our estimation which loves light will never desire to live in the dark, or on a clear day by candlelight, as one must do in many houses.
> (Goeree, cited in Meischke and Zantkuijl 1969: 433, my translation)

I have not yet come across an equally emphatic call for the banishment of all coloured window glass from a contemporary Englishman, but the sentiments were undoubtedly shared. Christopher Wren, when he surveyed Salisbury Cathedral in 1669, especially admired the ancient builders' sensitive handling of the light effects. He wrote:

> The windows are not made too great, nor yet the light obstructed with many mullions and transomes of Tracery-work, which was the ill-fashion of the next following Age: Our Artist knew better, that nothing could add Beauty to Light.
> (Wren, cited in S. Wren 1750: 304)

Richard Neve, in his *City and Country Purchaser and Builders' Dictionary*, called light 'God's eldest daughter [and] the principal beauty in building' (Neve 1703: 68). It is from Neve too that we get the clearest statement as to how contemporaries viewed the results of the architectural revolution:

> When I compare the modern English Way of Building with the old Way, I cannot but wonder at the Genius of our Times. Nothing is, nor can be, more delightful and convenient than Height, and nothing more agreeable to Health than free Air. And yet, of old, they used to dwell in Houses, most of them with a blind Staircase, Low Ceilings, and dark Windows; the Rooms built at random (without anything of Contrivance) and often with steps from one another. So that one would think the People of former Ages were afraid of Light, and good Air; or loved to play hide and seek. Whereas the Genius of our Times is altogether for light staircases, fine sash-windows, and lofty Ceilings.
>
> (Neve 1703: 68)

These standards were not only applied to past cultures. Other European nations who either could not afford the amenities, or did not share the same attitudes towards light in buildings, now came to be seen as inferior as well. Bishop Gilbert E. Burnet of Salisbury, for example, when he visited Italy in 1685–6, was evidently much influenced in his views of Italian architecture (and, in a sense, of Italian society as a whole) by the fact that they rarely used glass in their windows. To the Bishop this was a sure sign of the Italians' general backwardness as compared to his own culture, and he expressed himself in no uncertain terms to this effect in a letter from Milan, written in 1686:

> There is one inconvenience in Milan, which throws down all the pleasure that one can find in it; they have no glass windows, so one is either exposed to the Air, or shut up in a Dungeon: and this is so Universal that there is not a House in ten that hath Glass in their Windows: the same defect in Florence, besides all the small towns of Italy, which is an effect of their poverty.[2]
>
> (Burnet 1687: 115)

Better quality clear window glass was obviously the critical factor in the development of widespread glazed windows, but the role that the sash-window played in England as the principal vehicle for utilizing the superior lighting potential of the improved glazing product should not be under-estimated. Both Cotton and Neve testified to its importance in this respect and the prestige that was attached to the big sash-window as the sign of a new age soon led to its widespread adoption.

The high cost involved as a result of the expensive glass used in, and the complicated joinery required for, sash-windows may initially have deterred some from employing them, but since it was still considerably cheaper to have your house sashed than to build a new one according to the latest style emanating from London, the sash-window became increasingly popular as a status symbol towards the end of the seventeenth century. Celia Fiennes' *Diaries* of her travels through England (1685–1703) gives a good account of the progress of the new window across the country (Morris 1947).

Needless to say, common sense did not always prevail as fashion-conscious owners came to compete with each other for the size and number of windows they had put into their buildings. Not only was the environmental control of buildings affected by this desire for more and larger windows, but structural damage to the buildings was often done in the process. The great number of sagging lintels that one still observes in old buildings which had their mullioned windows ripped out indiscriminately for sashes in the late seventeenth and eighteenth centuries testifies to the scale of the problem.

There were some, like the amateur architect Roger North (*c*.1653–1734), who warned against this tendency towards, as he puts it, 'punching the wall full of windoes like pidgeon holes' (North 1981: 54), but the general inclination of the period (on the part of laity and professionals alike) was to allow the maximum amount of light to enter the building. Those who did not conform to this notion were censured, as North himself discovered when making alterations to a relative's house in Oxfordshire (1680–5). He wrote some years later:

> I advised that Most of the windoes should be covered which in great part was approved [by the client] and I should still have stopt up more, but there being sometimes accidentally bad lights folck think they are never secure of enough, and are tender of it, as of the foundation of their houses, Not considering how small Apertures with a fair sky lights a room.... Aperture is onely for use, and if there be more than the Nature of the Building declares needful, it is a foolish superfetation.[3]
>
> (North 1981: 57n.)

It took a complete aesthetic sea-change and the strict regime of the Palladian movement to create a climate of opinion where warnings like these were heeded.

Another factor which may have contributed to the sash-window's image as a progressive element is that contemporaries seem to have regarded it as the product of the new science, or 'Mechanic Knowledge', propagated by the natural philosophers. By the 1670s, when the sash-window made its appearance, the marriage between science and technology, so passionately advocated by people like Bacon, Galileo and Descartes earlier in the century, had begun to show material benefits, and it was quite common for some of the greatest scientific minds of the day to be actively engaged in attempts to solve a wide range of everyday technical problems. Utility was also one of the principal concerns of the first really important scientific societies, the Royal Society of London (founded in 1660) and its French counterpart, the Académie des Sciences (founded in 1666 in Paris).

The building industry received much attention and both the crafts which underpinned the sash-window's development, glass-making and joinery, benefited from these efforts to find practical outlets for scientific knowledge.

What places the sash-window firmly in the category of new inventions of the era is that it did not come about as the logical outcome of the progressive refinement of an earlier craft product, but as a consequence of the specific application of a mechanical principle, the counterbalance, to a known window-type, thus transforming it from a purely manually operated object into a mechanical device or machine.

It is not known who was responsible for this 'act of insight' – to borrow a phrase from Gestalt psychology. It is tempting to attribute it to either Christopher Wren or Robert Hooke, both of whom we know were involved with the development of the sash-window during its early stages, but the issue has not yet been resolved. The counterbalance was quite widely used in mechanical devices at the time, for example, the ribbon loom and pendulum clock, so the inventor could have been any of a number of people, including artisans (Louw 1983).

The important point, however, is that the sash-window was immediately recognized as something special. A French visitor to London in 1685 observed:

In the newly built houses I noticed one very convenient thing. That is the big glass windows with sliding sashes which one lifts without needing a notch to hold them in place. There is a counterweight which one cannot see at all, as heavy as the sash, which holds it back in any position in which one leaves it, and without fear that it will fall on the head of those who look out of the window, which I thought very convenient and agreeable. The English are very skilful.[4]

(quoted in Hollister-Short 1976: 159)

When the sash-window was introduced into Holland at about this time, it met with a similar response, but of the two nations – France and Holland – who share with England the honour of perfecting the new window type, it was only the Dutch who took the sash-window to their hearts in a way comparable to the English, for whom it became the very epitome of modernity and convenience.

Across the Atlantic, where the burgeoning communities of English colonists sought to keep abreast of architectural progress in the mother country, the sash-window was adopted with enthusiasm in the early eighteenth century. Here, too, the symbolic implications of the development did not escape notice. In his first

address to the grand jury sitting in the New Courthouse, Boston (1711–13), Chief Justice Samuel Sewall held the building's new sash-windows up as an inspiration for justice – a symbol of enlightenment and truth.[5]

By then, the initial experimentation with the sash-window had already turned into a national craze in England, and opposition against it was mounting in several sections of society.

Criticism was raised on moral, aesthetic and practical grounds. To moralists such as Defoe and Richardson, the sash-window was a sign of decadence, because it encouraged imprudent display. Typical of this attitude is the remark in the *Spectator*, No. 175 (1711), to 'a Jezebel [who] appears constantly dressed at her sash' (*Notes and Queries* 1895: 257)

Traditionalists, amongst whom members of the aristocracy and clergy figured prominently, saw the sash-window as a threat to an older order.[6] But even architects like Nicholas Hawksmoor and Robert Morris, who themselves regularly employed the sash-window, found it necessary to warn against its indiscriminate use (Hawksmoor 1960; Morris 1728: 90–2).[7]

One particular incident encapsulates the spirit of the controversy which developed over the use of the sash-window in traditional settings. It concerns the alterations to the Master's Lodge, Trinity College, Cambridge, in 1701, and the story goes like this: Dr Bentley, who became Master of the college in February 1700, immediately upon his appointment set in motion a comprehensive renovation programme for the Master's Lodge at a final cost of about £2,000. These so-called 'convenient improvements' included the installation of no fewer than thirty-four new sash-windows – an extravagance which brought Dr Bentley a severe reprimand from his paymaster, the Bishop of Ely. In his 'Articles against Dr Bentley' (11 July 1710), the Bishop specifically singles out the sash-windows as an unwarranted waste. He wrote:

When only convenient Improvements ought to be made in your said Lodge, why did you, according to your own extravagant Fancy, cause between 30 and 40, or some other great number of sash-windows to be made in the same [lodge], which was not only an excessive Charge to the said College, and a wasting of their Money and Goods, but besides broke the Uniformity of the rest of the Quadrangle, contrary to a former order or Conclusion?

(Willis and Clark 1886: 614)

In his reply to this accusation, Dr Bentley defended himself by saying that as the Quadrangle was not uniform to start with the sash-windows made little difference and that, moreover, sash-windows were desirable because they give more light to rooms in excess of 25 ft. (7.6 m.) in depth. On an earlier occasion he had, however, stated that the intention of the project was to entertain and impress important guests, which it certainly did! A German aristocrat who visited Dr Bentley in 1710 thought him 'lodged as the Queen at St James or better'; the visitor also admired the 'very large and high' windows with the glass panes of 'extraordinary size' (Willis and Clark 1886: 616).

There seems to be no contemporary view of Trinity College showing the sash-windows in question, but James Beeverell's engraving of the courtyard of Clare College in 1707 illustrates the points made (Figure 2). A few years later, Nicholas Hawksmoor also singled out Dr Bentley's sash-windows as a particularly good example of how *not* to introduce the new window type into historic buildings (Hawksmoor 1960).

Objections such as these could, however, do little to stem the tide of popularity upon which the sash-window was riding by now. Everywhere it had become the byword for 'seeing and being seen'. 'She ventures now to lift the sash; the Window is her proper sphere', wrote Swift in 1716 (Swift 1755, quoted in the *Oxford English Dictionary* under 'sash'). Remarks of the kind abound in English literature of the first quarter of the eighteenth century, suggesting that 'shining out of the sash', as Thomas Browne put it in 1704, may have become an important part of the fashion-conscious young town girl's daily routine (Browne 1709, ibid.)

Shopkeepers too were not slow to recognize the opportunity for public display of their wares and the tradition of the glazed shopfront was born, as the poet John Gay observed: 'Shops breathe Perfumes, thro' Sashes Ribbons glow' (Gay 1716: 141).

Even the Palladians, who went out of their way to wean the public from the baroque love of many and large windows, showed an uncharacteristic lack of restraint when it came to that most ostentatious of classical window forms, the Serlian or Palladian window.

In fact, so important had this particular characteristic of the new mode of fenestration become by Dr Johnson's

Figure 2 *Clare College, Cambridge, courtyard.* (Source: *Beeverell 1707 (Bodleian)*)

Figure 3 *Izaak Ouwater,* The Bookshop and Lottery Office of Jan de Groot in Kalverstraat, Amsterdam, *1779.* (Source: *Rijksmuseum, Amsterdam*)

time that he attempted to connect it with the origin of the sash-window's name. 'Of the word' [i.e. *sash*], he wrote in his *Dictionary*, 'etymologists give no account: I suppose it comes from *scache* or *scavoir*, to know, a sash worn being a mark of distinction: and the Sash window being made for the sake of seeing and being seen' (Johnson 1755).

For exactly the same reason, bow windows became immensely popular later in the century – much to the disgust of someone like William Cauty, who campaigned for better fire-proofing of buildings. He complained:

> If a maggoty landlord or tennant takes it in his head that he is not sufficiently seen from the window, especially when his head is just finished by a French hair-dresser, the best carpenter and bricklayer that he knows are directly sent for; down comes the front of his house in a mighty hurry, and bow-windows are erected in prodigious haste without paying the least regard either to the complaints or damage of his neighbours, though he often affronts them all.
>
> (Cauty 1772: 36)

Judging from Izaak Ouwaters' painting *The Lottery Office* (1779) (Figure 3), the Dutch too had come to share in this sash-window-induced mania for more light and display.

Charles Cotton identified another benefit brought about by the improvement in fenestration, namely that prospects of gardens and natural scenery could now be enjoyed in comfort from within buildings. This development is of more than purely aesthetic and practical importance. The enhanced link thus established between the inside and outside of buildings, with the implied dominance of humanity over nature, parallels the conclusions drawn by the natural philosophers of the period about the relationship between the synthetic and natural worlds. It is the architectural equivalent of the naturalism of the baroque painter, the nature-orientated empiricism of contemporary science and the political establishment's insistence on a natural order in society. The picture which seems to embody all the converging ideologies of this confident age is the famous engraving by Sebastion Le Clerc of Louis XIV's visit to the Académie des Sciences in 1671 for Denys Dodart's *Recueil de Plantes* (1676).

The development of flat panes of clear glass was again of central importance, with the French, who led the field in window glass manufacture at the beginning of the seventeenth century, being the first to respond to the challenge. By the 1630s, as can be seen from the engravings of Abraham Bosse, the picture window figures prominently in some fashionable Parisian houses (see Figure 4).[8] Many of these were sliding windows of the kind that the sash-window developed from, but the window type that really caught the imagination of the French was the tall casement window which opened like a door, and which in England became known as the 'French window'.

The advantages of the French window were described as follows by the antiquarian H. Sauval, *c.*1670:

Figure 4 *Abraham Bosse,* Les Vierges Folles, *1630s. (Source: British Museum)*

These windows without sills, which extend from top to bottom, from ceiling to the ground, make a room extremely cheerful and permits one to enjoy without hindrance the air, the view and the pleasures of the garden.

(Sauval, cited in Thornton 1978: 81)

Within a few years the tall French window was established as an inseparable part of the 'grand manner' of Louis XIV's court, and it has remained a prominent feature of French architecture ever since (see Figure 5).

Figure 5 *Design for a room elevation with French windows from Blondel (1737), Vol. II, Paris.*

In England, on the other hand, although gardens and prospects of them had also come to play an increasingly important role in architectural thinking from the early seventeenth century onwards, the very much poorer quality of early English window glass and the persistent use of iron casements, with small quarries set in lead, placed severe restrictions on the 'viewing potential' of windows. It is only after the Restoration of Charles II, when timber windows with square glass panes after the French manner became popular, and the English glass-making industry was transformed, that a more direct relationship between inside and outside was established in English architecture.

Then, suddenly, everyone seems to have become aware of the importance of views, or 'vistas' as they were called in contemporary parlance. The antiquary John Aubrey (1626–97), for instance, appreciated the views from the dining room of Danvers House, Chelsea, so much when entertained there (probably in the late 1670s) that he made a special note in his diary:

> As you sitt at Dinner in the Hall, you are entertained with two delightfull Vistas: one southward over the Thames and to Surrey: the other northward into the Garden.
>
> (Aubrey, cited in Charles 1977: 62)

For Celia Fiennes a fine vista was a definite factor in judging the quality of the habitation of the nobility and gentry she visited on her journeys through England (Morris 1947).

Horticulturists like John Worlidge (d. 1698) extolled the virtues of a close connection between the garden and the house. Richard Neve quotes him as saying:

> Let the garden joyn to one, if not more sides of the house, for what can be more pleasant and Beautiful for the most part of the Year, than to look out of the Parlour and Chamber windows into the Gardens.
>
> (Worlidge, cited in Neve 1703: 69)

No doubt the introduction of the French window into England (it was already employed by Inigo Jones and the Smythsons during the second decade of the century) encouraged this interaction between house and garden, as did the use of greenhouses, gazebos and banqueting halls, such as the one described by John Worlidge, in *The Art of Gardening* with 'Windows and Doors, the one or other respecting every Coast ... glazed with the best and most transparent Glass to represent every Object through it the more splendid' (Worlidge 1677: 40–1). But the single most important element (and this is confirmed by contemporary building accounts as well as other records) was without question the new type of window which made its appearance at this time: the big sash-window with large square panes of clear glass.

This association of the sash-window with views became increasingly stronger in England as the sash bars got thinner and the panes of glass larger during the

course of the eighteenth century. It was not simply the technical advances in window design progressively improving visibility which secured for the sash-window the role of picture window *par excellence* in English architecture. Nor can its triumph over the French window, which incidentally had undergone similar improvements, be attributed purely to the fact that the English weather is less conducive than that of France to the kind of activity which the French window encourages, however compelling that argument may seem.

There is, I believe, another fundamental reason why the sash-window appealed to the English, namely that it conformed closely with their conception of the landscape and the place of buildings and people within it.

John Dixon Hunt has demonstrated how, parallel to the rise of the French school of geometrically ordered landscape design, in seventeenth-century England a counter movement grew which propagated a contemplative rather than an overtly interventionalist approach to the landscape, and which eventually culminated in the English landscape garden and the Picturesque Movement of the eighteenth century (Hunt 1976).

Unlike the French window, which is in effect a door and thus facilitated the direct and immediate appropriation of the outdoors which suited the baroque spirit, the sash-window remained – despite efforts to make it function in ways similar to the French window – essentially a window which presented excellent views to the outside but which limited direct participation with it.

Figure 6 *Francis Cotes,* Portrait of Paul Sandby, *1761.* (Source: *Tate Gallery*)

Figure 7 *S. Fokke*, In de Herberg de Zon na de Kolfbaan te zien, *1761.* (Source: *Amsterdam Gemeentelijke Archief*)

By enforcing an abstract relationship between the inside and outside of the building, the sash-window constantly places the user in the position of observer, whether approached from inside or outside – hence its attraction, I would argue, for the 'grave and contemplative Genius' (John Lawrence 1714, quoted in Hunt 1976: 34) so much admired by English writers and painters of the period (see Figure 6). From a mid-eighteenth century Dutch inn scene by S. Fokke, it would appear as if the sash-window might have played a similar role in that country, too (see Figure 7).

The final clue which Charles Cotton gives us is contained in the phrase 'whole sashes are but one great Eye' (Cotton 1683: 81–2). The obvious reference here is to Plotinus' equation of the eye and the sun, which made the sash-window too a symbol of light and rational understanding. Put in its architectural context, however, the emphasis falls on the outward form of the sash-window – the fact that it was not fragmented by an over-elaborate internal framework like earlier window types, and which militated against the window being seen as an autonomous, rationally designed object.

For Cotton the sash-window was clearly part of a modern classical idiom and his analogy of the 'one great eye' reminds one of the practice of purists of the Italian-ate school of designers who, for the sake of simplicity and in order to stress the abstract nature of their compositions, left the window openings in their designs blank. The casement window, on the other hand, is definitely seen as a relic of England's medieval past, and by comparing it with the window in Noah's Ark, through which the 'Pigeon was thrust out' (Cotton 1683: 82), Cotton branded it as primitive.

It took another generation for the sash-window to become exclusively associated with the English classical tradition, but once that link was forged and it became accepted as part of the rational system of design which sustained Palladianism, the sash-window found a lasting place in English architectural history.

NOTES

1   *The Way of Light*, which Comenius wrote in England in 1641, was published in 1668 with a preface dedicating the book to the members of the newly founded Royal Society of London, as the 'Torch bearers of this Enlightened Age' (see Yates 1972: 190).

2   Comments like these were fairly common during the eighteenth century, and the attitude persisted into the nineteenth century.

3   The wording used is that of the unpublished manuscript in the British Library.

4   From a letter written by C.A. de Sainte-Marie to the Marquis d'Auvers, from London and dated 8 May 1685.

5   Samuel Sewall's diary entry for 5 May 1713 states: 'May the Judges always discern the right, and dispense Justice with a most stable, permanent Impartiality; let this large, transparent, costly Glass serve to oblige the Attornys always to set Things in a True light (Halsey Thomas 1973: 713–14). Information from Professor Abbott Cummings.

6   For a discussion on this trend, see Allen 1958, Vol. 1: 43–6; Vol. 2: 71–3. See also William Cowper, 'Winter Evening', lines 762–3, in Milford 1950: 198.

7   For Hawksmoor's views on the subject see Hawksmoor 1960.

8   A series of Bosse's engravings has been published; see Blum 1924.

REFERENCES

Allen, B.S. (1958) *Tides in English Taste 1619–1800: A Background for the Study of Literature*, New York: Pageant Books.
Beeverell, J. (1707) *Les Delices de la Grande Bretagne*, Leyden.
Blondel, J.F. (1737) *De la Distribution des Maisons de Plaisance et da la Décoration*, Vol. II, Paris.
Blum, A.S. (1924) *L'Oeuvre grave d'Abraham Bosse*, Paris: Blum.
Burnet, G. (1687) *Some Letters Containing an Account of What Seemed Most Remarkable in Travelling Through Switzerland, Italy and Some Parts of Germany . . . in the Years 1685 and 1686*, 2nd edn, Rotterdam: Abraham Archer.
Cauty, W. (1772) *Natura, Philosophia and Ars in Concordia*, or *Nature, Philosophy and Art in Friendship*, London.
Charles, A.M. (ed.) (1977) *A Life of George Herbert*, Ithaca, NY: Cornell University Press.
Colie, R.L. (1957) *Light and Enlightenment: A Study of the Cambridge Platonists and the Dutch Armenians*, Cambridge: Cambridge University Press.
Comenius (Komensky, J.A.) (1668) *The Way of Light*, Amsterdam.

Cotton, C. (1683) *The Wonders of the Peake*, 2nd edn, London: J. Wallis.

Dodart, D. (1676) *Recueil des Plantes*, Paris.

Gay, J. (1716) *Trivia, or the Art of Walking the Streets of London*, Vol. II, London.

Goeree, W. (1681) *D'Algemeene Bouwkunst, Volgens d'Antyke en de Heden daagse manier*, Amsterdam.

Halsey Thomas, W.H. (ed.) (1973) *The Diary of Samuel Sewall, 1674–1729*, New York: Farrar, Strauss & Giroux.

Hawksmoor, N. (1960) *Explanation of Designs for All Soul's, 17 February 1715*, pamphlet, Oxford: Oxford University Press.

Hollister-Short, G. (1976) 'Leads and lags in late seventeenth century English technology', *History of Technology* 1.

Hunt, J.D. (1976) *The Figure in the Landscape: Poetry, Painting, and Gardening during the Eighteenth Century*, Baltimore: Johns Hopkins University Press.

Johnson, S. (1755) 'Sash', in *A Dictionary of the English Language...*, Vol. II, London.

Lawrence, J. (1714) *The Clergy-Man's Recreation Showing the Pleasure and Profit of the Art of Gardening*, London.

Louw, H.J. (1983) 'The origin of the sash-window', *Architectural History* 26: 49–72.

Meischke, R. and Zantkuijl, H. (1969) *Het Nederlandse Woonhuis van 1300 tot 1800*, Haarlem: H.D. Tjeenk Willink & Zoon.

Milford, H.S. (ed.) (1950) *The Poetical Works of William Cowper*, 4th edn, London: London University Press.

Morris, C. (ed.) (1947) *The Journeys of Celia Fiennes*, London: Cresset Press.

Morris, R. (1728) *Essay in Defence of Ancient Architecture or a Parallel of the Ancient Buildings with the Modern*, London.

Neve, R. (1703) 'Building', Chapter III in *The City and Country Purchaser and Builders' Dictionary*, London.

Nicholson, M.H. (1946) *Newton Demands the Muse: Newton's 'Opticks' and the Eighteenth Century Poets*, Princeton, NJ: Princeton University Press.

North, R. (1981) *Of Building: Roger North's Writings on Architecture*, eds H.M. Colvin and J. Newman, Oxford: Clarendon Press.

Notes and Queries (1895) Series VIII.

Swift, J. (1755) 'Progressive beauty', *Works*.

Thornton, P. (1978) *Seventeenth Century Interior Decoration in England, France and Holland*, London: Yale University Press.

Willis, R.J. and Clark, J.W. (1886) *The Architectural History of the University of Cambridge*, Cambridge: Cambridge University Press.

Worlidge, J. (1677) *The Art of Gardening*, London.

Wren, S. (ed.) (1750) *Parentalia*, London; reprinted 1965, Farnborough: Gregg Press.

Yates, F.A. (1972) *The Rosicrucian Enlightenment*, London: Routledge & Kegan Paul.

53 Architectural form and colour

Tom Porter

The relationship between colour and architectural form is a tenuous one because, due to a series of historical phenomena, they have progressively been conceived as quite separate entities. For the most part architectural colour has been approached as a dispensable facet of the creation of the built environment, that is, one which is either ignored or employed as an afterthought. By contrast, our visual perception of the world represents a holistic process; it is an integrated faculty in which each aspect of a spatial sensation is experienced by us in context with all the others. Therefore, our evolved ability to perceive colour is constantly and simultaneously modified by a supplementary experience of surface condition, quality of illumination and nature of form. Consequently, we experience each spatial component as an integrated factor of all others.

Several writers, such as the architect Waldron Faulkner (1972) and the artist Victor Vasarely, have described the separation of colour and architectural form (see Porter and Mikellides 1976: 26). Vasarely cites the beginning of the process as coinciding with the birth of archaeology in the 1440s, when Flavio Biondi systematically catalogued the surviving relics of imperial Rome. Subsequent excavations in the city transformed Rome into a vast museum, and a fashion was started for the collecting of relics as *objets d'art*. Wealthy Italian patrons not only collected the archaeological finds but also commissioned paintings and sculpture by contemporary artists. This, for the first time, isolated the artists' creations as entities or 'works of art' to be viewed out of context from their original setting.

Hitherto, the experience of architecture had been extended visually through a deliberate and symbolic use of applied colour. For example, the astrologically motivated Assyrians stratified their great ziggurats using metal plate and vitrification to assign their stages to the solar system, while the ancient Egyptians assigned hues to the manifestations of a deity system. Perhaps the most spectacular example of an architectural polychromy which is still discernible is found on the ruins of the fabulous temple of Karnak at Thebes. Here, red, yellow, green and blue pigment not only brought a brilliant decoration to the massiveness of its architectural members but also imbued the temple with a complex and divine significance (see Figure 1). This tradition of a painted architecture spread north via the Minoans to ancient Greece where, it is thought, even the earliest wooden structures were decorated in colour. However, what is known is that the Greeks almost entirely covered their marble temples and statuaries with pigment in the belief that the natural colouration of stone was no substitute for the artistic creation of the city as a work of art.

On one level the role of colour in the Greek experience of architecture was not simply a capricious decoration; it appeared to respond to an established code of practice. This assigned a palette comprising chalky red, dark brown, pale yellow, bright blue, black and white to specific architectural components (see Figure 2). Modern evidence shows striking similarities between the painted treatments of different structures, which display a use of colour contrast, that is, hues being juxtaposed and counterchanged to control visual emphasis and clarification. However, a second look at the colours reveals more deep-rooted functions, for the pediments and friezes also acted as information systems. For example, those on

Figure 1 *The use of colour in ancient Egyptian temples at Karnak, Edfu and Philae.* (Source: *Uhde 1909*)

Figure 2 *The decorative scheme for the Greek Doric order.*
(Source: *Durm 1910*)

combining brilliant hues with a developing geometry of oblique projection, the Romans attacked the interior wall plane with remarkable vitality. For example, apart from rural scenes and ornamental landscapes, the painted walls of Pompeii and Herculaneum dissolve under *trompe l'oeil* illusions of an idealized and architectural form and space (see Figure 3). Wall painting is also associated with a Christian colour tradition that began in the catacombs of Rome and later flowered in the rich blues and golds of a Byzantine iconography. This was expressed in mosaic, variegated marble and fresco, and followed a precise geometrical hierarchy of form designed to draw the eye upward, through the mystical circle, and into the ethereal chamber represented by the dome (see Figure 4).

Rich colour was an intrinsic element of glass-making because, until the Renaissance, clear glass was very difficult to achieve. Therefore, a multicoloured sunlight poured into medieval cathedrals, but it also illuminated the bright painted surfaces of their interiors (see Figure 5) – a colour experience that was often matched and, according to James Ward (1913: 74–5), often over-shadowed by a corresponding application of pigment and gilding to external surfaces (see Figure 6). Traces of medieval colours are still distinguishable on the exteriors of many French cathedrals, such as the flecks of red,

the Parthenon functioned as gigantic hoardings that narrated the mythology of a golden age, a legendary and social state of perfection toward which (aided by a clearly defined colour and precious metal symbolism) the Greeks strove. Here, hues played a highly significant role, much as they do in their psychological use in modern advertising and package design. Blue, for instance, was associated with truth and integrity – colour attributes (ascribed earlier by the Egyptians to Isis as the hue of divinity) that were to re-emerge later in the cloaked Madonna of Christian symbolism. White was the basic colour of the Parthenon and of Athena's statue. The meaning of the word 'parthenon' in Greek is syn-onymous with 'purity', and this association still colours our idealized conception of a classically pure form. Red is ascribed to love, sacrifice and fertility, and this is reflected in depictions of the red face of Dionysus during the period of the annual wine festival. Like the Egyptian gods before them, other Greek gods were also vested in their appropriate hues, some being painted different colours to reflect the changing cycles of seasons.

The symbolic painting of architecture was eagerly adopted by the Romans, and advances in the tech-nologies of fresco painting, pottery, glazing and glass-making combined to extend the architectural colour range. Using sophisticated fresco techniques and

Figure 3 *Portions of a painted wall, House of the Second Fountain, Street of Mercury, Pompeii.* (Source: *Gruner 1850*)

Figure 4 *Longitudinal section, Hagia Sophia, Constantinople.* (Source: *Salzenberg 1854*)

blue and green pigments at Angers and the red stain on Notre-Dame.

As the 'pagan' colours of the medieval period faded under the cleansing action of a puritanical zeal, one aspect of the use of architectural colour should be kept in mind: namely, that the desire to decorate with colour

Figure 5 *Painted pillar and vault, church of S. Francisco at Assisi, thirteenth century.* (Source: *Gruner 1850*)

and the potency of colour symbolism was much stronger than the pigments at people's disposal. It can only be surmised that the ancient architectural polychromies held deep-seated meanings because the experience of a city, temple or cathedral was not merely that of an architecture, but of a structure that perhaps communicated tribal concepts about survival, as did the totemic cave paintings at Ariège and Altamira.

During the Renaissance, colour became the tool of an individualistic and artistic endeavour. Armed with a highly advanced pigment technology, artists created two-dimensional illusions of their insights and inner compulsions in oil, tempera and fresco. The conception of architecture as an art-form was gradually exchanged for one that considered built form as a 'container' of art – a palace or cathedral being designed as a receptacle to house an extroverted art and decoration (see Figure 7).

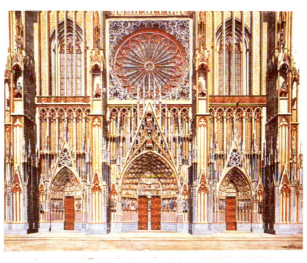

Figure 6 *Colour reconstruction by Hermann Phelps of the west façade of Strasbourg Cathedral.* (Source: *Phelps 1930*)

Figure 7 *Ceiling at the Palazzo Vecchio, Mantua, sixteenth century.* (Source: *Gruner 1850*)

Indeed, as the late Faber Birren put it: 'If the Greeks had a Golden Age in the philosophical sense, the Italian Renaissance had one in the materialistic sense' (Birren 1982: 113).

However, if the experience of a brightly polychromed architecture became tempered by the shift in the Renaissance/Reformation paradigm, then the bifurcation of colour and architectural form was to be later compounded by new and rational design attitudes in the second half of the eighteenth century. For instance, the architecture of the so-called French Revolutionary period between 1750 and 1800 is characterized by exaggeratedly simple forms. Two of the most spectacularly inventive architects of this time were Etienne-Louis Boullée and Claude-Nicholas Ledoux. Both produced projects which flouted architectural convention and derived their forms from almost purely mathematical concepts. Typical of this revolutionary style is Boullée's spherical cenotaph designed in 1784 and dedicated to one of the heroes of the enlightenment, Sir Isaac Newton. Here, a concern for the extreme signification of form denies colour and provides an achromatic foretaste of the severe geometry characteristic of the early twentieth century and the ensuing International Style.

Even Johann Wolfgang von Goethe – famed for his theoretical experimentation with colour and his attempt to rescue its understanding from the abstract mathematics of Newtonian optics – designed an achromatic altar in 1777, consisting of a pure sphere mounted on a stone cube. According to Professor Werner Spillmann of Winterthur Polytechnic, this represents a further milestone in the detachment of colour and form (Spillmann 1981). In order to realize the essential purity of form, designers were now no longer dependent upon polychromy. It is as if colour would hinder their abstract perception of a pure plastic form.

Spillmann suggests that the root of our modern disregard of colour can be traced back to those philosophical preconditions that formed the basis of the development of modern science. In this context the influence of the philosopher John Locke is important, because in the second half of the seventeenth century he distinguished between the primary and secondary features of an object. On the one hand, according to Locke, there are the quantitative and mathematically calculable characteristics of a body, such as its position in space, its size and shape. On the other, there are its qualitative and external properties, such as sound and colour. In excluding the qualitative features from the scientific cognitive process, this philosophical influence not only formed the basis of modern science but also further compounded the artificial detachment of colour from form. Moreover, suggests Spillmann (1981: 46), if colour is known to affect our emotions, then an intellectual approach will simply underestimate its experience. Indeed, in a 'rational' context colour will either be viewed with suspicion or be dismissed as merely trivial.

However, during the latter half of the seventeenth century in England, and in the wake of Inigo Jones's emphasis on a colour palette reflecting structural materials, the classical style consolidated and confined itself to a few 'common' colours. Hentie Louw's survey of house painting (or 'vulgar painting' as it was known) of the period finds a sober external palette comprising 'red oaker, umber, red and white lead', with richer colours used in interiors (Louw 1990). This tradition persisted until the late eighteenth century, when a move towards a greater variety of colours, drawn simultaneously from nature and antiquity, resulted from the rise of neoclassicism and the Picturesque. Furthermore, this shift in emphasis was accompanied by the romantic movement's insistence that the whitewashing of façades defied the laws of nature.

According to Louw, the first decades of the nineteenth century were 'characterised by the free exploration of colour combinations with the only discernible constraints being the cost and availability of materials' (Louw 1990: 50). By the 1830s this upsurge in interest saw the revival in the colouring of built form using the 'primitive' hues found on Greek temples. Led by the French artist Jacob-Ignaz Hittorff and the German architect Gottfried Semper, this movement was not only reminiscent of the early Renaissance passion for the past, but it also came to intensify the debate between those who practised an applied polychromy and those who considered that architectural incidence of colour should derive from the intrinsic colours of building materials.

Perhaps the bravest attempt at a restoration of colour and form came with Joseph Paxton's appointment of Owen Jones to decorate his Crystal Palace. This was a commission that gave Jones the opportunity of applying a theory of architectural colour based on his initial studies of the colours of the Islamic palace of the Alhambra, which he published in 1845. Jones's restoration illustrated its columns painted in red, blue and gold.

However, not only did Jones's colours for the Crystal Palace borrow from antiquity, they were also tempered by a growing interest in the science of colour vision; his colour system followed Michel-Eugène Chevreul's rules for colour clarity and George Field's laws of proportion. For instance, the slim iron columns were painted with narrow stripes of red, blue and yellow, each separated by a field of white. This also responded to a proportional harmonic that related three parts yellow to five parts red to eight parts blue. Nearby, these hues were perceived as distinct but over increasing distance an optical mixing of atmospheric perspective caused Jones's hues to fuse progressively and visually into a vibrant, blue-grey haze (see Figure 8). This phenomenon of a formal diffusion was first noted by Leonardo da Vinci and was later to be exploited in the Neo-Impressionism of Seurat's pointillism and, again, in the colour interaction experiments of Joseph Albers.

Figure 8 *Owen Jones's colour scheme for the Crystal Palace.* (Source: *Nash, J.* Comprehensive Pictures of the Great Exhibition (1851–3), *courtesy Henry Southern*)

Prior to its installation, Jones's scheme was not without stern criticism. For instance, the *Illustrated London News* ran a competition among its readership to find a less 'offensive' alternative. The competition drew over thirty proposals and several of these have been researched and restored by Professor Giovanni Brino at Turin Polytechnic. However, as the majority of these proposals demonstrate, the colour schemes created by laypeople were just as anxious to celebrate Paxton's forms and, in many respects, were more colourful than the one that they were intended to replace (see Figure 9). Furthermore, a report written later in the same newspaper turns criticism into high praise, for the journalist who visited the Crystal Palace on its opening day in 1851 reported:

> To appreciate the genius of Owen Jones, one must take his stand at the extremity of the building.... Looking up the nave, with its endless rows of pillars, the scene vanishes from extreme brightness to the hazy indistinctness which Turner alone can paint.
> (*Illustrated London News* 1851: 424)

Strong criticism had also come from John Ruskin. Indeed, he despised the Crystal Palace but his criteria provide an insight into the values that were instinctively cherished by the bourgeois nineteenth century. In 1849 Ruskin had published his *Seven Lamps of Architecture* and in the chapter 'The Lamp of Beauty' discussed at length the relationship between architectural form and colour.

Figure 9 *Inspired by Newton's spectrum, this speculative colour scheme for the Crystal Palace was submitted in 1850 to the* Illustrated London News *competition by reader C.B. Allen.* (Source: *courtesy Giovanni Brino, Turin Polytechnic*)

He envisaged form as a concept to be coloured by the mind of the beholder. In reality he prescribed that architectural colour 'should be as fixed as its form' (Ruskin 1889: 137). Ruskin conceded that he could not, therefore, consider architecture as in anywise perfect without colour' (ibid.). However, he proposed that it was better to rely on the colours of stone for its polychromy, as to paint stone required the hand of a 'true painter'. Furthermore, rudeness in painted colouration was far more offensive than rudeness in the cutting of stone.

When Ruskin considered applied colour, he turned to nature for guidance. Based on his observations that nature colours individual organisms rather than orchestrates the entire landscape, he proposed that a building be approached as a single object and be subject to a basic rule, that is, that colour should be arranged as an entirely separate system and exist without reference to any underlying formal anatomy. In citing the colouring of animals but, seemingly, ignoring the function of camouflage, Ruskin observed: 'The stripes of a zebra do not follow the lines of its body or limbs, still less the spots of the leopard' (Ruskin 1889: 138). However, he admitted that these two independent systems of colour and form will occasionally coincide, but briefly like a musical harmony and 'never discordant but essentially different' (ibid.). From this he drew his 'First Great Principle of Architectural Colour' – that is, that colour should always be visibly independent from form. Therefore, it follows that a column should never be painted with vertical lines, but always crossed. Furthermore, in connection with the painting of ornament, the figure and ground should not be distinguished by different hues but should be varied by the same harmony. Moreover, formal points of interest should not be further highlighted by colour contrast as 'it is a safe rule to simplify colour when form is rich and vice-versa' (ibid.: 139).

It is, therefore, no surprise that Ruskin condemned the form-following polychromy that was promoted two years later by Jones. Indeed, the Ruskinian stricture of 'coloured stones' found strong echoes in the British sense of architectural good taste and was to be exploited by, among others, William Butterfield and George Edmund Street. Meanwhile, in 1856, Jones published his thirty-seven axioms of colour and form for an architecture worthy of the machine age in his *Grammar of Ornament*. But, being confined in application to agricultural and industrial machinery, his colour concepts became architecturally dormant.

Although Ruskin's central colour thesis is still in widespread currency today, further attempts were made to 'liberate' colour for application in the architectural setting. The most significant of these coincided with advances in the study of the psychophysiological impact of colour at the beginning of the twentieth century. The experience of colour was now known to be not just a property of the object or merely a sensation in the eye, but a complex and integrated process involving the modifying effect of the brain. Also, having been confined to the painter's easel, colour expertise had been traditionally explored as a two-dimensional phenomenon, and a new generation of artist-designers became anxious to exercise its three- and four-dimensional effects.

Early experiments began in Russia in 1913 and developed the simultaneous contrast theories of Post-Impressionism and Fauvism into a new and kinetic colour language. As part of a Suprematist rejection of the natural appearance of objects, colour kinetics were seen as inherent in complementary hues – the resultant energy or 'dynamism' resulting from the fact that different wavelengths travel perceptually at different speeds and are, therefore, in motion. However, the pioneer of a Suprematist dynamism, Kasimir Malevich, insisted that this phenomenon was influenced by conditions other than hue. Indeed, Malevich came to believe that, in his work, colour and form had no direct relationship.

Experiments conducted at around the same time by the Dutchman Piet Mondrian extended the dissected structures of Cubist painting to their logical and abstract conclusion in the form of Neo-Plasticism. Unlike Malevich, Mondrian confined his colour experiments exclusively to painting and attempted to tame the primitive hues of red, blue and yellow (now stripped of their historical associations) in grid-plan abstractions. However, Mondrian's works in themselves constitute a sort of architecture, but in a functionless, ideal form which came to influence De Stijl designers, such as Bart van der Leck, Theo van Doesburg and Gerrit Rietveld.

For example, Rietveld's Schröder House, built in 1917, enlists the three primary hues of red, blue and yellow against the non-colours of black, white and grey to reposition perceptually the modulations of its internal and external elevations. When necessary, Rietveld engaged the pushing and pulling qualities of hue to adjust the building's planes as coloured screens. Although no published texts exist documenting his architectural use of colour, a lecture presented by Rietveld in 1962 in Amsterdam describes two colour approaches. The first sees colour as a secondary element, that is, as a feature introduced to form in order to rectify any imbalance in the composition; the second approach, described by Rietveld as the 'best application of colour in architecture' (Overy et al. 1988: 71), is the use of colour to translate the constituent greys of an achromatic formal composition into corresponding degrees of light reflection using complementary hues.

Despite their philosophical differences, Theo van Doesburg and Le Corbusier both conceived an architecture rich in applied colour. Theo van Doesburg wrote: 'The new architecture is against decoration. Colour (and whoever distrusts colour must realise it!) is not ornament or decoration, but an organic element of architectural expression' (Doesburg 1924: 78). In contrast to a popular misconception proliferated by a monochrome publication of his work, Le Corbusier loved the 'powerful hum of colour' (Doesburg 1924: 83), especially as stabs of bright paintwork against the white concrete of his facades.

On his large projects Le Corbusier loved to emphasize the indented rhythms of the envelope, employing bright colours to separate inside from outside and also to 'tint' deflected sunlight in the transitional spaces of balconies, such as his Unité d'Habitation in Marseilles and in the deep recesses of roof- and wall-lights in La Tourette monastery (see Figure 10). The relationship between Le Corbusier's interior and exterior colour use is of interest because, in contrast to the sheer white and primary hues of his façades, his schemes for interiors are borrowed directly from his Purist paintings – created in collaboration with the artist and colour theorist Henri Ozenfant – and deployed earthy, muted colours with umbers, siennas and green-greys.

Like Rietveld, Le Corbusier approached colour as a means of modifying the experience of architectural form and space. Colour could be imported at the end of the design process to cause 'a lightening of the volume and enlarging [of] surfaces'. In 1927 he wrote: 'This polychromy is absolutely new, it is essentially rational. To the architectural composition, it adds elements of extreme physiological power. By harmoniously arranging the physiological sensations of volume, surfaces, surroundings and colours, it is possible to achieve an intense lyricism' (Le Corbusier 1927: 30).

A lyrical colour sense was also thematic in the work of the German designer Bruno Taut. In 1919 he, together with several militant architects of the time, such as Peter Behrens and Hans Poelzing, had endorsed the text of 'A Call for Colour in Building', which sought to reinstate a liberated, colourful townscape after the horrors of the First World War (Taut 1919). While a councillor for Magdeburg in the 1920s, Taut continued to battle for

Figure 10 *Interior of the church at La Tourette, near Lyon, 1956–60, by Le Corbusier, showing the effect of colour in the recessed wall and rooflights.* (Photograph: *H.J. Louw*)

applied colour in the belief that an architectural polychromy was the only natural means of defining space. Basing his colour combinations on a complex musical harmony, he would either disrupt the verticality of façades in his low-cost housing projects with horizontal bands of colour, or simply diagram them clearly in steps of Pompeii red, yellows and lilacs, such as those of the now-restored Onkel Tom Hutte estate in Berlin (1926–31) (see Figure 11).

By contrast to the more psychologically uplifting and scientifically controlled use of modernist colour, remnants of a more revivalist and decorative colour began to appear on London factories and cinemas during the 1920s and 1930s. Inspired by the colour decoration of ancient Egypt, Greece and China, these modern 'temples' to industry and entertainment were each invested with an antiquarian character that, albeit superficially, appeared to rediscover briefly the Victorian revivalist and form-following prescriptions of Owen Jones.

However, apart from its function to dissolve form with the protective hues and disruptive patterns of camouflage, architectural colour was to fade into the drabness of the Second World War. A revitalized colour display had to await the late 1960s, where it performed acts of aggression against a lingering post-war austerity. The colour-coding of an architecture of high technology which occurred in the 1970s saw designers returning to a basic and formal colouration in the diagramming of building components using raw primary and secondary hues. Paradoxically, this was preceded by the renewed experiments of artists who used colour to attack the walls of inner cities; urban wall painting not only revived a tradition as old as building itself but heralded the decomposition of the wall plane. In treating city walls merely as a support on which to hang an illusory narrative or abstract paintwork, environmental artists began to reintroduce the concept of formal erosion through the application of a totally independent and supergraphic colour system. The widespread popularity of this type of public art – especially in America – was to have a profound influence on an ensuing generation of architects.

The 1970s also witnessed the emergence of a new breed of environmental designer, the colourist, who specialized in identifying traditional patterns of colour in the built landscape. In Italy, Giovanni Brino had begun his restoration of historic 'colour maps' based on surviving city archives, such as those in Giulianova and Turin. Meanwhile, Jean Philippe Lenclos had turned to nature and begun to classify systematically the traditional and naturally occurring palettes across the regional diversity of his native France. This was a vast project that, even before its publication in the mid-1980s, was to have a major impact on the site-related colouration of new towns in both France and Japan.

While wall painting and a high-tech colour-coding used a language of reference to events beyond the form, Lenclos's work – in linking the colour of form to its setting – represented chromatic attachment (see Figure 12). This back-to-nature methodology of colour mapping finds echoes in the earlier and organic philosophy of Frank Lloyd Wright. For example, in an article

Figure 11 *Riemeisterstrasse, Onkel Tom's Hutte housing estate, Berlin, 1926–31, by Bruno Taut.* (Photograph: *G. Higgs*)

Figure 12 *Jean Philippe Lenclos's methodology for site-related coloration of architectural schemes.* (Photograph: *courtesy J.P. Lenclos*)

written in 1908 Wright reiterates his six 'Propositions' first formulated in 1894. His fourth Proposition states:

> Colours require the same conventionalising process to make them fit to live with that natural forms do; so go to the woods and fields for colour schemes. Use the soft, warm, optimistic tones of earths and autumn leaves in preference to the pessimistic blues, purples or cold greens and greys of the ribbon counter; they are more wholesome and better adapted in most cases to good decoration.
>
> (Wright 1908: 55)

By the 1980s, however, a Post-Modernist movement has established a literal colour use that could either transform material by nudging our memories of an architecture of the past or make polychrome statements that attempt to integrate built form with its setting. This diversity can often be found in the work of individual designers; compare, for example, the humorous references to antiquity in John Outram's Isle of Dogs Pumping Station with his essay in polychrome concrete on his New House, used to harmonize with a strongly coloured Sussex landscape.

The 1980s also witnessed a whole series of miniature colour revivals, such as Zaha Hadid and Terry Farrell's respective debts to Suprematist and Art Deco palettes. Possibly, this more catholic attitude to colour and form relationships is best exemplified in the work and words of Michael Graves (see Figure 13).

Graves suggests that the thematic basis of colour is not quite the same as that of form. On the one hand, the traditional, classical basis of form has been derived from two sources: nature and humanity. For example, the orders are drawn from the partitions, symmetry and geometry from the human body, while 'floor' represents 'ground', 'ceiling' represents 'sky', and 'column' represents 'tree'. On the other hand, the classical language of colour is derived not from humanity but from nature and nature's materials. In this sense, colour can either refer to nature or to another event. For instance, if a surface is coloured terracotta in order to allude to brick, then our first reaction is to brick, in its full measure. Therefore, no matter that one knows colour to be an application *to* a form, we see colour first as representational. To some degree, Graves writes, 'colour possesses the quality of an object, an artifact'. Consequently, it is the polychromed wall as artefact that allows the full gamut of thematic significance. He concludes: 'It is because the wall has lost its neutrality, has taken on figural qualities through the elaboration of form and colour that we are able to make the connection between ourselves, the architecture, and nature' (Graves 1978: 58).

This current and seemingly magical use of colour to transmute our perceived first impression of form takes us full circle back to the very earliest function of applied pigment. For example, this approach to colour is reminiscent of the daubing of corpses with red ochre by primitive societies so that life was symbolically given in death; it also reminds us of ancient Greek statuaries where marble faces were painted pink in order to bring them to life.

REFERENCES

Birren, F. (1982) *Light, Color and Environment*, revised edn, New York: Van Nostrand Reinhold.

Doesburg, T. van (1924) 'Verso un'architecture plastica', *De Stijl* 6/7: 78–83.

Durm, J. (1910) *Handbuch der Architektur*, Vol. 1, Leipzig: Alfred Kröner Verlag.

Faulkner, W. (1972) *Architecture and Color*, New York: Wiley-Interscience.

Graves, M. (1978) section of N. Miller 'The re-emergence of color as a design tool', *AIA Journal* 67 (12): 41–71.

Gruner, L. (1850) *Specimens of Ornamental Art*, London: Thomas M'Lean.

Illustrated London News (1851) 17 May: 424–5.

Jones, O. (1845) *Plans, Sections, Elevations and Details of the Alhambra*, London.

—— (1856) *Grammar of Ornament*, reprinted 1910, London: Bernard Quaritch.

Le Corbusier (1927) 'Pessac', *L'Architecture Vivante* 30 (Autumn/Winter): 29–32.

Louw, H. (1990) 'Colour combinations', *Architects' Journal* 192 (1): 44–53.

Overy, P., Büller, L., den Oudsten, F. and Mulder, B. (1988) *The Rietveld Schröder House*, The Hague: De Haan/Unieboek.

Phelps, H. (1930) *Die Farbige Architektur bei den Römern und im Mittelalter*, Berlin.

Porter, T. and Mikellides, B. (1976) *Colour for Architecture*, London: Studio Vista.

Ruskin, J. (1889) *Seven Lamps of Architecture*, 6th edn, Orpington: George Allen.

Salzenberg, W. (1854) *Altchristliche Baudentmale von Konstantinopel*, Berlin: Verlag von Ernest & Korn.

Figure 13 *Rear façade of the Dolphin Hotel seen from the Swan Hotel, Walt Disney World, Lake Buena Vista, Florida, 1990, by Michael Graves.* (Photograph: *courtesy Michael Graves*)

Spillmann, W. (1981) 'Architektur Zwischen Grau und Super-bunt', *Achitektur und Farbe* 4: 43–52.

Taut, B. (1919) 'A call for colour in building', *Die Bauwelt,* 18 September.

Uhde, C. (1909) *The Architectural Forms of the Classic Ages,* 2nd edn, London: Batsford.

Ward, J. (1913) *Colour Decoration of Architecture,* London: Chapman & Hall.

Wright, F.L. (1908) 'In the cause of architecture', *Architectural Record* 23 (3): 53–63.

FURTHER READING

Lenclos, J.P. and Lenclos, D. (1982) *Les Couleurs de la France,* Paris: Moniteur.

Porter, T. (1982) *Colour Outside,* London: Architectural Press.

——— (1988) 'Colour in architecture', in J.A. Wilkes and R.T. Packard (eds) *Encyclopedia of Architecture: Design and Construction,* New York: John Wiley & Sons.

Van Zanten, D. (1977) *The Architectural Polychromy of the 1830s,* New York: Garland.

54 Architectural form and light

Pieter de Bruyne

Licht und Finsternis führen einen bestandingen Streit miteinander.

(J.W. Goethe)

Light is so fundamental that it has come to symbolize life itself just as its opposite, darkness, symbolizes death.

We are influenced by the gradations in light which, almost unperceived, alter our moods. The sharpest contrasts in light and shade are associated with joy and sorrow: we associate bright, glittering light with festivities and freedom, but in times of sorrowful happenings we seek darkness. Between these extreme situations infinite gradations occur, sometimes brutally, sometimes imperceptibly altering our inner tranquility.

Despite its immaterial and intangible nature, light is inseparable from the notion of architecture. For, beside structural and functional properties, architecture can call forth an aesthetic response, create an atmosphere and generate emotions through the use of light as one of its fundamental elements.

Metaphysical and philosophical as well as symbolic and scientific interpretations of light regularly appear in architecture and frequently have a great impact. From the very beginning of architecture, temples, churches, palaces and other important buildings have, in their massive strength, demonstrated at least one and often a combination of these interpretations. In our domestic dwellings too, light provides vigorous and inspiring architectural forces. There too light acts upon the state of mind in such a way that it transcends its merely functional role.

The intensity of light can be accurately measured nowadays, and light coefficient tables already have a history behind them. The subtle properties of light we wish to deal with here are, however, far more difficult to measure, yet we cannot do without them in living architecture.

We may tend to think that modern technology has succeeded in superseding darkness. Large glass windows provide the interior with almost unlimited floods of light and, at night, artificial light can simulate a midday atmosphere. Yet, this range of technical aids seems unable to satisfy a number of specific human needs. Builders often revert to small windows and sparse light. Restaurants frequently have candlelight. Does this not point to the fact that the architect cannot

First published in Schofield, M. (ed.) (1980) *Decorative Art and Modern Interiors*, Vol. 69, 'Environments for people', London: Studio Vista.

supply all requirements with mathematical indices alone? Yet, what is the origin of these forces of attraction and repulsion between light and darkness, both within and without the architectural space?

Paradoxically, the history of architecture begins with defining darkness. The first human beings ventured, torch in hand, into the naturally formed 'interior': the cave. They were surrounded by mysterious darkness; only the glow of their torches allowed them to perceive forms. The enclosing space contrasted with the infinite 'outer' space, where light alternated naturally with darkness. The discovered space became the first people's shelter and the place where they expressed their fearsome experiences.

In the first buildings, people *intentionally* created dark spaces where they could express these experiences, as is proven by archaeological discoveries. In the neolithic settlement of Catal Hujuk (Anatolia) for example, the paintings in the houses were very much like those in the caves. In these dwellings, the infiltration of light was kept to a minimum; it penetrated the space through a small opening in the ceiling which, at the same time, served as an entrance. The same technique was used in ceremonial spaces. In megalithic buildings (for example, in Malta) and in the first temples, the interior was totally dark. The contrast between natural light and artificial darkness was the actual base on which a plurality of interpretations grew. Eventually the tendency prevailed to use dark spaces as a medium for expressing psychological, symbolic, metaphysical and philosophical interpretations.

It goes without saying that there is no conclusive evidence that these interpretations of light could be found as archetypes, separately or in combination, at the very origin of history. Nor can we easily draw the line between these interpretations and the builder's merely functional intentions.

In religious buildings the association between the architectural solutions of light and the metaphysical aspirations can be more clearly determined than in secular dwellings. Yet it may be assumed, despite a few exceptions in modern architecture, that our appreciation of any light situation is not influenced by the purely functional properties of light alone. The triumph of the 'luminous wall' over the solid stone wall meant not just the provision of more light, but a psychological victory over reticence and darkness. Thus, the intensity of light achieved in secular buildings may be said to have psychological value in so far as it is in direct ratio to an 'open' as opposed to a 'closed' way of life.

A particular light atmosphere dominates a whole environment in which forms, people and objects are interrelated, while each obtains an independent reality. Therefore, the light atmosphere that has been created inside a building is related to the natural light atmosphere in a village, a town, or a region where it is determined in turn by the condition of the soil (vegetation or desert), natural materials (wood or stone), coloured or monochrome buildings, and the people (naked or clad). But the light atmosphere inside a building also depends on other determining factors such as the light system, the materials used, and ultimately on the style of living. The light atmosphere is a clear indication of the attitude to life of the people who created the building. Painters aptly synthesize this all-embracing and enveloping light in their work. We find examples of natural light atmosphere in the landscapes of van Ruysdael, van Gogh or Cezanne. The interiors of van Eyck, Vermeer or van Gogh provide us with examples of contrived light atmosphere. In paintings the sensory light becomes transcendental light. For example, in van Eyck's work *Het Echtpaar Arnolfini* (1434) (National Gallery, London), the blissful intimacy between man and woman harmonizes perfectly with the sunwarmed, sunlit interior. This painting is an example of the 'Gothic light' in the middle-class house and is very much like the 'Gothic' light we can still admire in the cathedrals built in that time.

In his work *The Philosophy of Interior Decoration* (1964), Mario Praz analyses the Western way of life in a series of illustrations of paintings. Image after image demonstrates the multiple significance of light limited by time and function. Here the value of painted illustrations is twofold, giving us a personal, emotional interpretation of light atmospheres and providing us with a survey of the various light systems.

The determining elements utilized in creating a light atmosphere in building cannot be fully analysed here. By way of illustration, however, we may give a few of the many striking achievements in this field.

A clear distinction should be made between the determining factors that deal respectively with the outside or inside of a building, bearing in mind that outside and inside are always related, whether they are in sympathy with or contrast to each other. We find an example of the latter in the pyramids: the outside catches the light and reflects it over an immense surface, thus identifying the building as an indestructible 'light beacon' and an undeniable witness to humanity's energetic presence on the surface of the earth; the inner corridor and tomb are wrapped in total darkness and, enclosed as they are within a solid mass of stone, become integrated into the earth itself. The whole demonstrates the utmost contrast, both formally and symbolically, between light and darkness.

The play of light and darkness is not restricted to the internal–external relation. The use of the contrasting

Figure 1 *Detail of the colonnade of the second terrace, Temple of Queen Hatshepsut, Dair-el-Bahri, Thebes, Egypt, 1520 BC. Light creates a rhythm of longitudinal planes on the polygonal columns, and these delicately shade light around their form, from brightness to darkness.*

properties of light (surface) or dark (relief or aperture) parts on the outside of the building becomes fundamental and inspiring after the rhythmical quality of the walls of King Zoser at Sakkara and the terraced temple of Queen Hatshepsut (see Figure 1). The contrast between light and dark parts creates positive and negative forms, while the rhythmically constructed parts of the building (columns) use to a maximum one property of natural light: the effect of shadows.

Shadow-entities optically divert planes and volumes and divide space in ever-moving parts, while maintaining a harmonious relationship with the architectural elements. Open or covered planes or elements may be placed in sharp contrast and as a result they are neatly, graphically outlined. Alternatively, they may blend together to achieve a plastic whole. In the entrance hall of Queen Hatshepsut's terraced temple there is an ever-varied intensity of natural light, created by the polygonal structure of its columns.

Figure 2 *Residence of the Middelheimpark, Antwerp, Belguim. Light falling across the simple white façade produces a delicately modulated effect.*

Figure 3 *Detail of the Basilica, Vicenza, Italy, 1549, by Andrea Palladio. The use of one material, a fine white stone, and the simplicity of the architectural decoration create a contrast of extremes of light and darkness, revealing the fine proportions of the façade.*

The delicate composition of the architectural elements in the Residence of the Middelheimpark, in Antwerp (Figure 2), creates an intensely poetical effect: a single tone, white, brings about a wide range of greys and creates optically intriguing effects.

The negative forms on the façade of the Basilica at Vicenza, by Andrea Palladio (Figure 3), seem to be drilled clear through – an effect which is particularly striking in the lunettes. Details become subordinate to the whole and openings and arched forms are accentuated.

Figure 4 *Pavilion in the garden of the Musée de l'Ecole de Nancy, France, by Eugène Vallin. The glass roof shades a terrace on the top of the building, mediating between the solid form below and the open sky above.*

In the Greek temple, where the architectural accent is mainly on the outside, every nuance of contrast and rhythm is accentuated. There is extreme contrast between the overwhelmingly lit exterior, the colonnade, and the shadowy interior, hermetically sealed for the uninitiated, the cella. Rhythm and contrast exist too between the columns themselves and in their chiselled fluting. An intermediate zone between the interior and the exterior is formed by a transitional space, the peristasis, where the shadows of the columns are projected on to the walls of the cella. This passage between the interior and the exterior acquires an independent atmosphere which is characteristic also of later buildings, for example religious houses and galleries.

The intermediate zone 'catches' the light in an exceptionally intimate way, divorced as it is from direct exposure to natural or reflected light. The shadows act, in perspective, like the steps of a staircase inviting the spectator to explore the temple or gallery.

Other elements too are used to link natural light and space. The *torii* of the Inari shrine in Kyoto, placed as they are at regular intervals, allow the light to penetrate playfully from above and from both sides. In combination with the colour shades a 'light tunnel' is formed, similar to that which one might see in a pergola.

In the pavilion in the garden of the Musée de l'Ecole de Nancy, a sand-blasted glass roof mediates between light and the building (see Figure 4). The glass entity relates to the wide sky, but the matt material gives it independence, thus creating in the space beneath an atmosphere adaptable to climatic changes. The shadows of plants and trees become part of the massive, organic substructure, thus integrating form and light. A similar visual link between building and nature can be seen on the façade of Antoni Gaudí's Casa Milá, in Barcelona. The ideal interrelation of building and surroundings and the effect of penetrating light touch our aesthetic senses when we enter the Campo Monumentale in Pisa, walk in the Piazza San Marco in Venice or stroll around a parish church which is flanked by trees.

The surface of a building itself may reveal the architect's intent, both by its texture and by any elements added to it. In the Casa de las Conchas in Salamanca (sixteenth century) shells occupy the surface (Figure 5). Floodlight, however, seems to cut them off the wall, an illusion strengthened by their cast shadows.

The interplay of light and darkness, of volume and shadow, is also to be found between several buildings. A narrow gap, such as narrow streets, staircases or arches, accentuates the illuminated area which thus appears to be a surface cut out of the infinite light source (see Figure 6). The distance between the tower and the church of San Biagio at Montepulciano, by Antonio de Sangallo il Vecchio, allows a blade of natural light to penetrate. The 'freeing' of the tower creates an 'imprisoned' light zone between both constructions,

Figure 5 *Detail, Casa de las Conchas, Salamanca, Spain, 1512–13. The architect has enriched an otherwise fortress-like building, with small windows, by decorating the wall with shells, which at certain times of the day appear to be independent of the structure. The elaborate decoration around the windows makes them appear larger, stressing their importance and providing a transition between the brightly lit wall and the dark opening.*

composing a fascinating whole. The very concentration of light raises the tension between both massive volumes.

Roman architects applied this technique with maximum expressive force. In the Pantheon, for example, the space is integrated with the cosmos while the interior is given a pronounced independence from the outside solid mass. Here, the various interpretations of light mentioned earlier are concentrated in one place. The very interaction of space-mass and the natural effects of light enhance symbolic values.

The Roman 'Domus' enclosed in its atrium and peristyle a cut-out piece of heaven from where the zenithal light came in. The enclosed 'living cocoon' is

Figure 6 *Detail of cortile, Palazzo Vecchio, Florence, Italy, 1470, by Michelozzo Michelozzi. The upper edge of the courtyard frames a section of the sky, which thus appears to be cut out. The opening illuminates the walls with varying intensity of light.*

enlarged internally by perspective interplay, while the light streams unimpeded through the opening, destined for the inhabitants alone. Later examples of this pronounced accentuation of symbolic values are to be found in Guarino Guarini's architectural work.

In architecture, both natural properties and interpretations of light are linked to the expressions that are characteristic of people or time. The architectural style is in a way complemented by a light style.

The Egyptians preferred a sparingly lit space. The tombs within the pyramids were dark and the ceremonial buildings were dimly lit through light grooves near the ceiling, as in the temple in the valley of Chephren or the celebration hall of Thoutmosis III at Karnak. From a well-chosen angle the light was often projected onto the image of a god. The same method of illumination was followed in the inner-space of secular buildings, as in the working-class houses of Dair-el-Bahri.

It was not until the Gothic period that the aspiration of drawing up transparent walls was realized. The 'lateral' light facilitates a direct contact between the interior and exterior of a building, and the architect has more possibility to create the optimum light atmosphere. In the Gothic cathedral, the walls radiate an autonomous colour. Light is tied to intense, vivid hues and helps the architectural space to take shape. Natural light is exalted to 'supernatural' light. It penetrates the space in an endless series of directed beams and facets.

As opposed to the Gothic cathedral, the Renaissance temple is full of 'natural' light. The light sources are spread out regularly, with precise speculative intention. All the architectural elements are illuminated with equal intensity. The space as a whole prevails, not the separate accentuation.

The Islamic mosque shows a remarkable resemblance to this Renaissance conception of light, as we may observe in Sinan's Suleymaniye Canii in Istanbul. Here the even intensity and the nature of the light are enhanced by the delicate use of colours which has the effect of turning the inner space into a homogeneous colour entity.

In the baroque church, the passage of light is woven into the architectural concept to become an illusive and symbolic element. In the Church of San Lorenzo in Turin, by Guarino Guarini, the play of light emphasizes the bold construction of the dome and creates illusionary effects. The upper part of the building becomes a 'vision of light', the perforation and the concealed light spaces seem to detach the lantern from the dome.

In the parish church at Villa Pasquali, by Antonio Bibbiena, both the double dome and its perforation create a theatrical effect. The massive structure acquires the fragility of lace, and, as in a vision, light pours through its meshes. The colour of the outer wall, a light blue, intensifies the illusion and enhances the reflections.

In addition to these historical examples there are realizations of more recent origin which indicate how light can determine the character of the building and realize special intentions. In the chapel at Ronchamps (Figure 7), Le Corbusier obtains an archaic character by placing irregular niches in the massive walls; a massiveness that is openly exposed, for the wall is fenestrated on the outside. Light beams are literally guided and directed by the oblique niches.

In the church of Borgomaggiore at San Marino (Figure 8), by Giovanni Michelucci, form and light create a dramatic effect in the irregular structure of the interior. The sources of light are indirect and create sharp contrasts in the perforated structure. The violent opposition of bright planes and dark openings results in an overwhelming atmosphere. Here light saves us from the appalling darkness. The struggle between light and darkness has been elaborated into an architectural poem about life and death.

Coloured glass reduces the intensity of light and creates a specific light atmosphere in accordance with the colour pattern, as in coloured windows. Its effect influences our psychological attitude towards the space and it may lead to symbolic associations. In the San Francisco Cathedral, by McSweeney, Ryan and Lee assisted by Pier Luigi Nervi, the architectural volume is split up in the symbolic form of the cross and light penetrates through narrow apertures filled with coloured glass. In this building, the most advanced technical, mathematical and geometric realizations are in perfect harmony with light and colour. In Paolo Soleri's studio in Phoenix, the light atmosphere is determined by

Figure 8 *Church of Borgomaggiore, San Marino, 1961, by Giovanni Michelucci. The perpetual struggle between light and darkness is here dramatically realized in three dimensions.*

the coloured dome. Natural and coloured lights are in sharp contrast to each other. Red colour tones create an illusion of unreality, for 'red' has been used instead of the more familiar 'blue', the symbol of the heavenly colour.

Coloured light may create an autonomous element inside a space filled with natural light. In one of my furniture designs that consists of a frame filled with blue glass I enclosed, as it were, an amount of blue light within the volume of the structure. I did the same in a room: natural light penetrates the space through blue windows and becomes an autonomous and intense blue mass. Listening to music in this space is a deeper and more intense experience: beside the psychological factors of calm and reflection, the unreal atmosphere is associated with the infinite. In a bathroom I realized the opposite (Figure 9). There the delicate colour-tones, the reflections of light provided by glossy materials such as mirrors and ceramic walls, create a surrounding suggestive of water and nature. The materials, united by light, acquire not only a symbolic character, they also enhance the natural atmosphere. As a consequence, the bathroom is used more intensively. Our homes could become spaces where a succession of light and colour-tones surprise us agreeably and dispel the monotonous light. The interior would radiate calm, intimacy and poetry.

By contrast, light entering through a window which is considered as a plane cut out of the light source can dramatically intensify the character of an interior space. One of Paolo Soleri's windows in Arcosanti looks like the frame of a majestic landscape. Beyond the large window is a second screen of precise geometric dimensions: an unusually large circle. Horizontal and vertical lines divide the window into small frames, each of which cuts a large plane out of the landscape beyond, where atmospheric conditions keep evoking new visions. The beholder is deeply impressed by the varying facets of

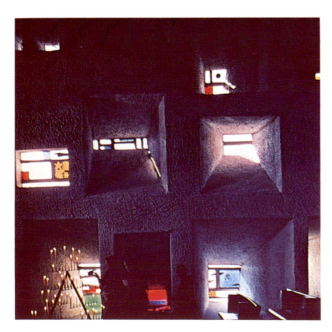

Figure 7 *Notre Dame du Haut, Ronchamp, France, 1950–3, by Le Corbusier. Deep-set, splay-jambed windows send shafts of coloured light into the gloomy interior, producing an archaic effect to express the religious symbolism of the building.*

Figure 9 *Bathroom, Aalst, Belgium, 1975, by Pieter de Bruyne. The highly reflective materials suggest the presence of water and nature.*

natural light, from the diffused light at sunrise till the red afterglow at sunset. He or she is inevitably influenced by light and colour and the atmosphere determines the beholder's attitude towards nature.

A glass roof illuminates the corridors within the Lewis Medical Building in San Diego, by Simpson and Gerber, and at the same time splits up the architectural volume. The result is a neat ensemble of coloured structures, natural light and some white planes. Subdued light and the specific choice of the fragile streak of light enhances the suspense. The view has been diverted from the heavy traffic alongside the building to the serene heaven. The atmospheric conditions are more intensely experienced and working inside the building becomes more agreeable.

In the Villa Savoye in Poissy, by Le Corbusier, the inner wall receives along its entire length a lateral illumination. Horizontal light enhances the concept of 'free plan' on which the building is based, and pervades the whole space according to its gradation which, in turn, depends on the high or low position of the sun. The wall in architect Neutra's own house in Los Angeles is as transparent as possible. The inside almost forms one whole with the outside, also in terms of light. In both solutions (Le Corbusier's and Neutra's) the choice of the light scheme corresponds to the 'open' character of the space. Atmospheres of light and colour are in close harmony with nature.

The opposite of these 'open' light solutions are those solutions which create an intimate atmosphere by their 'close' construction. In the corridor of the town-hall of Säynätsalo, by Alvar Aalto, the windows are built near the ceiling, between the rafters. The space is a closed, warm one, because of the reflection of the light onto the wooden ceiling. Alvar Aalto often used such window constructions: they offer the spectator a view on to surrounding tree tops and catch the reflections of the leaves.

It is obvious that between those extremes, 'open' and 'closed', lies a wide range of possibilities. All of them have a distinct influence on the inhabitant, both through form and psychological intent. There is no doubt whatever that we should attempt to reach a better understanding of the possibilities and significance of light in architectural composition. Properties such as intensity, atmosphere and character of light should be studied and evaluated in every architectural structure. As a result, purely formal construction of windows, such as we see in prefabricated houses for example, would prove to be unjustified when we consider the impact of adequate light diffusion and the significance of light. Any architectural structure that has been built at a given place can become an autonomous entity through the skilful deployment of light.

The examples mentioned earlier illustrate many of the possibilities in the use of light. The poetic, calm and intimate character of the house requires particular consideration and should be subject to closer study. Good architecture is only possible when we are willing to experience all the properties of light. It requires a feeling for subtle light-gradations which is probably not consciously present yet, although it might be stimulated by successful architectural realizations. In this process, psychological as well as purely technical requirements should be taken into account.

In the search for an harmonious surrounding, light and its modulating properties in architecture may become a contributing factor to the creation of a more complete and agreeable atmosphere in life.

REFERENCE

Praz, M. (1964) *The Philosphy of Interior Decoration*, Milan: Longanesi.

55 Architectural form and ornament

Stuart Durant

Ornament enhances the status of a building by indicating that labour and wealth have been lavished upon it. The relationship between ornament and architectural form is, ideally, one of successful symbiosis. Traditionally, the ornamenting of buildings has formed a sophisticated part of architectural culture. Ornament is invariably associated with the concatenation of the familiar components of architecture – columns, capitals, entablatures, pediments, arches and domes.

An important function of ornament has always been to explicate as well as to emphasize form. For the present discussion 'form' is understood as 'shape' or 'mass'. It is the conjunction of the vertical and the horizontal that the eye naturally first lights upon in a building. And it is here that the most elaborately ornamented component of a classical building – the capital – is placed (see Figure 1).

Architectural ornament can take the form of representations, both stylized and naturalistic, of human, animal and plant forms. It may also be purely geometrical and abstract in character. Frequently, combinations of these varieties of ornament are employed at the same time. Contrasting bands of material or arrangements of bricks are often employed for ornamental purposes. The deployment of ornament in all architectural modes, or systems, is regulated by practice, subsequently codified as rules, which appear analogous to those governing the ordering of language, or music.

Complex, or agglutinative, structures may themselves possess ornamental qualities. The Hindu temple is the prime example of this. The architectural fantasies of Antonio Filarete and Leonardo da Vinci fall into the same category.

The temple architecture of medieval India is worthy of special attention in the context of the relationship of ornament and form. Totalities composed of a multiplicity of subsidiary forms – themselves sometimes miniature versions of the temple structure itself – are of considerable complexity. In such an architecture, ornament does not seem entirely subservient to form. In addition to being highly ornamented, the external surfaces of Hindu temples are often devoted to hierarchically organized figure sculpture employed for iconographical purposes. Canonical examples include: the tenth-century Kandarya Mahadeva Temple at Kujaraho; the tenth-century Lingaraja Temple at Bhuvanesvara; and the twelfth- to thirteenth-century Hoysala dynasty temple at Hullebid (Figure 2). The Victorian architect and historian James Fergusson (1808–86) described Hullebid as the very antithesis of the Parthenon – 'the best example we know of pure refined intellectual power applied to the production of architectural design'. Hullebid was 'the opposite . . . every part exhibits a joyous exuberance of fancy scorning every mechanical restraint' (Fergusson 1891: 403–4).

Islamic architecture, while frequently highly ornamented, relies principally upon monumentality for its effect. This is the case with the late seventh-century Dome of the Rock (al Aqsā Mosque), Jerusalem, which is the earliest major Islamic building.[1] Its form is a drum – surmounted by a pointed dome which is enclosed by an octagonal ambulatory. This form is of great visual power and external ornament is applied, rather than integral, to the structure. In Islamic buildings decorative use is often made of the squinch – a system of subsidiary arches placed at the internal angles of structures to support a dome. Complex geometrical window tracery – as at the Great Mosque, Damascus, probably completed in 714–15 CE – is also sometimes used. Other early examples of geometrical decoration are to be seen in the soffits of the arches of the late ninth-century Mosque of Ibn Tūlūn, Cairo. Polychromatic faience tiles are sometimes applied to the exteriors as well as the interiors of buildings.

Figure 1 *Corinthian capital, Temple of Jupiter Stator, Rome, 146 BCE.* (Source: *Cresy and Taylor 1822*)

Figure 3 *Castle of Himeji, Japan, 1580–1610. Drawn by the author.*

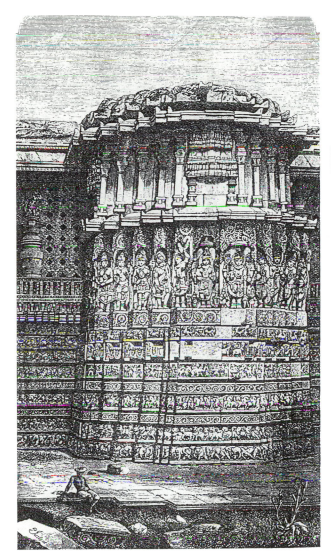

Figure 2 *Hoysala dynasty temple at Hullebid, Kamataka, Southern India, twelfth to thirteenth century.* (Source: *Fergusson 1891*)

associated in all architectural cultures. In Chinese and Japanese architecture it is the bracket, not the capital – as in the classical tradition – which is the main point of decorative focus (see Figure 4). Elaborate compound brackets demonstrate the skills of joiners. Virtuoso construction, as in other architectural systems, is here exploited to considerable decorative effect. The pagoda – a tower form composed of square, hexagonal or octagonal segments which progressively diminish in size at each storey – owes its origin to India whence it was exported by Buddhist missionaries. The more highly ornamented *gopura* or *vimana* of southern India have a somewhat similar form.

In the West ornament and form were traditionally considered together. This is the case in the only surviving classical text devoted to architecture – *De Architectura*, of Marcus Vitruvius Pollio, the Roman architect and military engineer, who was probably writing during the early part of the reign of Augustus (*c*.22 BCE). The ten books of *De Architectura*, in part, reflect the received wisdom of subsequently lost Greek texts.

These often carry designs of considerable geometrical sophistication – Iranian (Isfahan) and Central Asian (Samarkand) examples are particularly noteworthy. The multi-faceted niche (*mihrab*), which is found in many mosques, seems to manifest the same joy in complexity – seemingly for its own sake – which is found in the Hindu temple.

Traditional Chinese and Japanese architectural practice was based upon wooden constructional principles. The elegantly curved roofs of Chinese and Japanese buildings – at Beijing in China and Nara in Japan, for example – are vigorous expressions of form which display the prowess of their carpenter-builders. The five-storied fortified stone castle of Himeji, Japan, built between 1580 and 1610 (Figure 3), employs the elaborate traditional wooden roof form at each level. A complex hierarchy of gables and projecting roofs produces an outline which is both monumental and ornamental – the monumental and the ornamental are invariably closely

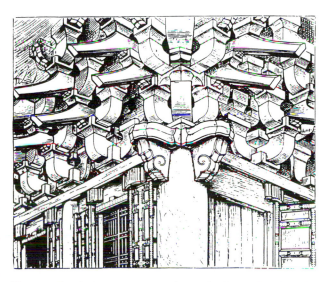

Figure 4 *Bracketing supporting the roof of the temple gate, Chionijin, Kyoto, Japan.* (Source: *Dresser 1882*)

A particular order, which would predicate the proportions and, to an extent, the form of a building, could be selected for iconographical reasons. Vitruvius recorded the well-known stories connected with the origins – and hence the iconography – of the orders. The Doric, the most primitive of the orders, was essentially masculine in its character and its proportions were those of a man. It was appropriate for the temples of Mars and Hercules, as well as those of Minerva, the goddess of handicrafts. The Ionic order, with its volutes representing the flowing hair of women, had the proportions of a woman. It was appropriate to temples dedicated to Diana – a goddess principally worshipped by women. During the Renaissance, the Ionic order was to be associated with female saints. Later architectural theorists reproduce the salient ideas of Vitrivius. One of the most enduring of these is: that the stone architecture of the orders was derived from, and indeed imitated, wooden construction. Vitruvius deals with this in his Fourth Book. The triglyph in the Doric order, for example, represented an attempt on the part of 'ancient carpenters' to conceal the unsightly ends of large timber

Figure 6 *Section and plan of the Pantheon, Rome.* (Source: *Cresy and Taylor 1822*)

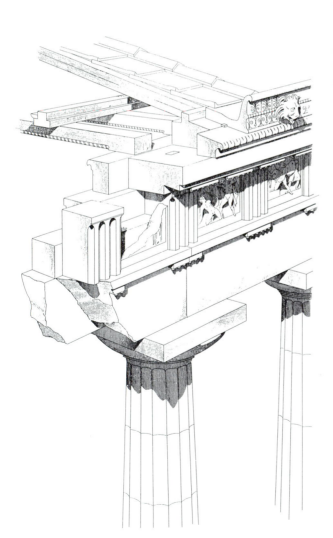

Figure 5 *The Greek Doric order.* (Source: *Viollet-le-Duc 1864*)

tie-beams with wooden planks, which were then embellished with the simple incised grooves which characterize the Doric entablature in its final and perfected manifestation (Figure 5).

Roman architectural form is of greater complexity and diversity than Greek. Its ornamentation is generally richer and often coarser. The dome was widely used by the Romans; the coffering of the dome of the Pantheon, built in CE 120–4, during the reign of Hadrian, is evidence of a highly developed understanding of the principles of structure (see Figure 6). Coffering, which reduces the weight of a roof, may function structurally as well as ornamentally. Indeed, all repeated architectural elements, irrespective of function, may be turned to decorative use. The introduction of the arch, which was probably first used in ancient Assyria, added an important new element to the Roman architectural vocabulary. Widespread decorative as well as structural use was made of the arch.

East Roman, or Byzantine, civilization produced an architecture of great inventiveness, particularly in terms of form. However, Byzantine churches – frequently an agglomeration of discrete tectonic elements, which were themselves simple – were not generally highly decorated externally. The façade of the ruined monastery of Saint Simeon Stylites, at Qal'at Siman, near Aleppo, Syria, probably built at the end of the fifth century, is a bold symmetrical composition consisting of a major and two minor arches surmounted by pediments – the model being the Roman triumphal arch. Mouldings and capitals lack the refinement of their earlier classical equivalents. Hagia Sophia, Constantinople (now Istanbul), built in the sixth century – 'the most interesting building on the world's surface', according to W.R. Lethaby (1894) – is formally complex. Externally it is decorated sparingly with bands of variegated marble and simple mouldings at the eaves. In Byzantine buildings ornament – often of mosaic depicting saints – is generously applied to interiors, particularly in apses and the underside of domes.

The architecture of the Gothic Middle Ages is of great importance in any examination of the relationship between ornament and form. The pointed arch, the rib vault, the traceried window, the vertiginous spire and the flying buttress, were the elements of architecture with which medieval builders demonstrated their skill. In Gothic architecture ornament and form seem to co-exist in perfect symbiosis.

The ruined Benedictine Abbey of Saint Jumièges, Seine-Inférieure, built in the latter part of the eleventh century, was externally without ornament – apart from the cursorily carved capitals of columns. The two square-plan towers on either side of the porch adopt an octagonal plan above the level of the pediment – prefiguring the constructional and formal virtuosity of later medieval builders. The Benedictine – Cluniac – Priory of La-Charité-sur-Loire, Nièvre, consecrated in 1107, which is also largely un-ornamented externally, has a conical and faceted roof above the transept – an assertive formal device denoting ecclesiastical power. However, it is in the cathedral of Chartres, begun in 1194 and finished in 1260, or the cathedral of Amiens, the façade of which dates from c.1245, that the Gothic style is manifest in its mature form. Other examples include Salisbury, begun in 1220, and Exeter, begun in c.1257, which were both built over a comparatively short span of time and show a stylistic homogeneity which is untypical of British cathedrals. Drawings in the one surviving architectural manuscript of this period – the famous 'lodge book' of Villard d'Honnecourt, a Norman master mason – exemplify contemporary interest in structure, tracery and formalized floriated ornament. At Rouen Cathedral, Normandy, begun in 1063, one can trace the full scope of the development from the austere forms of the Romanesque to the elaborate ornamentation of the later phases of the Gothic merging with the equally ornamental early Renaissance (see Figure 7).

During the Renaissance, the architect and humanist Leon Battista Alberti (1404–72) in *De Re Aedificatoria*, written in about 1450, which first appeared in a printed from in 1485, accepted, like Vitruvius, that the Orders were based upon timber constructional practice. Alberti's views on ornament are set out in four of his Ten Books.[2]

Alberti believed that a building should be appropriate for its usage, durable, and pleasing to the eye. Of these qualities, the last was 'the noblest and most necessary of all' (Alberti 1485, Sixth Book: 155). The ornamentation of a building was thus of primary importance. Ornament

Figure 7 *Rouen Cathedral, west end.* (Source: *Cotman 1822*)

was to be placed on a building according to the proper division and subdivision of the parts of the structure – Alberti spoke of 'compartition' (*partitio*). This conception subsumes an inextricable association between ornament and form.

Ornament, according to Alberti, must contribute to the total harmony of a building. At the same time, it must itself be governed by the rules of order and propriety:

> The faults of ornament which must be avoided most of all are the same as those in the works of Nature, anything that is distorted, stunted, excessive, or deformed in any way. For if in Nature they are condemned and thought monstrous, what would be said of the architect who composes the parts in an unseemly manner?
>
> (Alberti 1485, Ninth Book: 311)

In his buildings, Alberti made innovative and scholarly use of the orders. S. Francesco at Rimini, also known as Temple Malatestiano, begun c.1450 (see Figure 8), is particularly noteworthy in this respect, but the somewhat later Santa Maria Novella is perhaps the most remarkable. Here, upon a medieval structure, Alberti imposed Renaissance order, by means of an ingenious system of applied classicizing elements. His marble marquetry, with its clearly defined linear divisions, demonstrates the power of simple geometry in the articulation of a façade.

Figure 8 *S. Francesco at Rimini, c.1450, by L.B. Alberti.* (Source: *Knight 1842–4*)

Leonardo da Vinci (1452–1519), whose architecture remained, for the most part, on the manuscript page, occasionally conceived buildings which depend for their effect upon an aggregation of elements. Leonardo's fantasies sometimes possess a considerable complexity; they confirm the assertion that form may yet function as ornament. The chapel of S. Satiro, Milan, which was remodelled by Donato Bramante (1444–1514) from its original Romano-Lombardic form, has something of the formal and geometrical complexity found in Leonardo's architectural sketches.

In the wake of Alberti's *De Re Aedificatoria*, many illustrated treatises describe the contingent relationship of form and ornament – mediated through the orders. In this context, the works of Sebastiano Serlio (1475–1554) and Andrea Palladio (1508–80) were of immense importance in codifying the orders and their usage. Palladio's influence was the greater and the more lasting. His use of ornament was restrained and invariably clarified his structural propositions. His precisely rendered drawings – of the most elegant simplicity – are manifestly the work of one who had himself worked as a stone-carver.

Mannerists like Michelangelo Buonarotti (1475–1564) or Giulio Romano (1499?–1546) created an architecture in which the classical orders were used in unconventional ways to achieve dramatic effects. Romano in his Cortile della Cavallerizza, Palazzo Ducale, Mantua, of 1538–9, with its twisted and contorted Roman Doric columns and its exaggerated Serlian rustication, achieved an effect which is barbarous and exciting (see Figure 9).

This decorative tradition was further developed by Giovanni Battista Rosso (1494–1540) and Francesco Primaticcio (1504–70), who had worked in Giulio Romano's studio at the palace of François I at Fontainebleau during the 1530s. This influence was, via the Netherlands, to become widespread throughout northern Europe.

In France, Philibert de L'Orme (*c.*1515–70), the first French Renaissance master, in his *Le Premier Tome de l'architecture* (1568), also demonstrated how the elements of the Serlian structural and ornamental vocabulary could be used in a highly original and, on occasions, idiosyncratic manner. Other French architects, particularly the members of the Du Cerceau family – of whom the best known is Jacques Androuet Du Cerceau (*c.*1510–*c.*1585) – exhibited a similarly vigorous and inventive approach to form and ornament.

The enduring legacy of the Middle Ages is often apparent in the work of these earlier French Renaissance architects. The famous screen in St Etienne-du-Mont, Paris, of *c.*1585, often attributed to Philibert de l'Orme, with its delicate fretted staircase rails and fulsome Renaissance mouldings, reveals a decorative sensibility and attitude to form which is still in part Gothic.

The baroque style of the seventeenth and early eighteenth centuries produced an architecture in which complex form and the manipulation of space were all-important. In Italy, the work of Francesco Borromini (1599–1667) and Guarino Guarini (1624–83) represented baroque virtuosity at its most brilliant. Here, without question, form takes precedence over ornament. The remarkable undulating façade of Borromini's S. Carlo alle Quattro Fontane, Rome, seems almost to prefigure

Figure 9 *Mannerist architecture: side elevation, Cortile della Cavallerizza, Palazzo Ducale, Mantua, 1538–9, by Giulio Romano.* (Source: *Haupt 1931*)

the late nineteenth- and early twentieth-century architecture of Antoni Gaudí in its plasticity.

By contrast, in France, during the reign of Louis XIV, another baroque characteristic – namely that of formal *gravitas* – is manifest in the Versailles of Louis Le Vau (1612–70) and Jules Hardouin Mansart (1646–1708). Here, ornamentation is essentially temperate.

Rococo architects did not, in general, venture beyond the already rich vocabulary of baroque forms. In terms of ornament, however, they were inclined to abandon all restraint. The work of the brothers Asam – Cosmas Damian (1686–1739) and Egid Quirin (1692–1750) – is particularly worthy of consideration. The decoration of their Abbey Church at Weltenburg, Bavaria, is so highly wrought that it achieves a visual saturation. As, indeed, a Bach fugue can induce aural saturation. Both can only be comprehended with sustained concentration. Visual 'unravelling' may well contribute to the enjoyment of rococo ornament.

The reappraising of Renaissance architectural practice began in France during the Enlightenment. Jean Louis De Cordemoy (1651–1722) and the Abbé Marc-Antoine Laugier (1713–69) were the most important figures in advocating a rationalism which may be taken as a reaction against baroque, and particularly rococo, excess.

Jacques-Gabriel Soufflot (1713–80) the first major neo-classical architect, was much admired by Laugier. Soufflot's Panthéon, originally the Church of Ste Geneviève, begun in 1757, marks the starting point of a purist and reductionist neo-classical tradition – which culminated in the buildings of Charles-Nicolas Ledoux (1736–1806), the visionary projects of Etienne-Louis Boullée (1728–99), and the work of Charles Percier (1764–1838) and Pierre Léonard Fontaine (1762–1853). Under the patronage of Napoleon, Percier and Fontaine were largely responsible for creating the so-called Empire decorative style. The Regency style in England has obvious affinities. In all neo-classical architecture, ornament is subservient to form.

In the history of ornament the case of Sir John Soane (1753–1837) is a particularly interesting one. While his house in Lincoln's Inn Fields also served as a museum of ornament, Soane's own ornament was of the simplest kind. The block-like, symbolized columns on the façade of his house, for example, were decorated merely with incised lines, while entablatures were represented by panels of incised Greek key pattern.

At an empirical, or intuitive, level, Soane appears to have understood the aspect of perceiving pattern which was later designated as 'Gestalt perception'. In consequence, his minimal representations of classical elements function quite adequately as ornament.

From the succeeding generation of architects, Pierre-François-Henri Labrouste (1801–75) is noted for the innovation he brought to the neo-classical tradition. His Bibliothèque Ste Geneviève, Paris, 1844–50, was the earliest work of academic architecture in which internal

Figure 10 *Neo-classicism – combined with the new iron technology: Bibliothèque Ste Geneviève, Paris, 1844–50, by H. Labrouste. Decorative ironwork in the roof of the main Reading Room.*

structural ironwork was exploited decoratively (see Figure 10). This ironwork possesses a neo-classical refinement and discreetness. Externally, Labrouste's austere decoration – of festooned garlands, which was a common neo-classical decorative motif – is reminiscent of Soufflot's decoration of the Pantheon, which is in close physical proximity.

The Ecole des Beaux Arts, the premier nineteenth-century architectural teaching institution, enthusiastically received Labrouste's ideas. Subsequently, the Ecole did much to further the advance of the understanding of the potentialities of structural ironwork.

The Palais des Machines, completed in 1889 and designed principally by Charles Louis Ferdinand Dutert (1845–1906) was conceived according to Beaux Arts principles. It was by far the largest and most spectacular of all the great nineteenth-century glass and iron buildings (see Figure 11). It was – though sometimes misrepresented in Modernist histories – a highly decorated building. The elegant deportment of the Palais des Machines derives from an architectural culture which was steeped in rational classicism. Structural elements – principal and subsidiary trusses as well as lattice braces to restrain the immense curtain wall façades at either end – are deployed in a manner which accords entirely with Alberti's principle of 'compartition'.

A rebellion against the prevailing view of a noble pagan past, from which architectural culture should be drawn, began towards the end of the eighteenth century. During this period, that of the ascendancy of the romantic movement, an increasing interest came to be taken in the Gothic Middle Ages. This was to set in

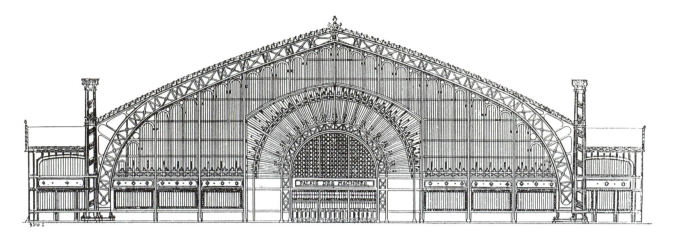

Figure 11 *Echoes of neo-classicism – advanced construction: Palais des Machines, Universal Exhibition, Paris, 1889, by C.L.F. Dutert.* (Source: *(1889)* Engineering *XLVII*)

motion an intensive study of medieval archaeology and religion. Increasingly, a superior spirituality was to be attributed to an era which, during the Enlightenment, had been described as redolent of superstition. Inevitably, Gothicism was destined to become preoccupied with moral issues.

A.W.N. Pugin (1812–52) was the first of the great Gothic moralists. He was also a stirring propagandist and had a good deal to say about ornament. Pugin's 'two great rules' are of importance in the present context:

> 1st, that there should be no features about a building which are not necessary for convenience, construction, or propriety;

> 2nd, that all ornament should consist of enrichment of the essential construction of the building.

> The neglect of these two rules is the cause of all the bad architecture of the present time.
>
> (Pugin 1843: 1)

Paradoxically, it was Owen Jones (1809–74) the champion of modernity and 'intelligent eclecticism', who echoed Pugin, the medievalizer. Jones asserted that:

> Construction should be decorated. Decoration should never be purposely constructed. That which is beautiful is true; that which is true must be beautiful.
>
> (Jones 1856: 5)

Jones was enthusiastic about the use of iron in building and championed its use in a lecture of 1835. In about 1860 he prepared designs for a glass and iron exhibition building at St Cloud, Paris – which appear to have been based upon his competition designs for the building to house the Manchester Art Treasures Exhibition of 1857. Had the St Cloud building been executed it would have established that rational form and ornament could happily coexist in the new iron and glass architecture of the nineteenth century – almost thirty years before the

triumph of the Palais des Machines.

John Ruskin (1819–1900) in his two most influential books on architecture – *The Seven Lamps of Architecture* (1849) and *The Stones of Venice* (1851–3) – is mainly concerned, besides issues of morality, with details and ornament. Hardly ever did Ruskin illustrate complete buildings. This concern for the intimate aspects of architecture – the micro-scale, rather than the macro-scale – was to become embedded in the attitudes of the generation of Arts and Crafts architects who were to be nurtured on Ruskin's teachings. The form of Arts and Crafts buildings is, in consequence, all too often indeterminate.

Nevertheless, William Richard Lethaby (1857–1931) was a master of form. His startling and innovative competition design, of 1902, for Liverpool Cathedral, with its barrel-vaulted roof and Byzantine massing, possesses a strength which few contemporaries could have matched in their work (see Rubens 1986: 160–6). Here ornamental details are employed with particular skill to emphasize form.

The same can also be said of the work of Sir Edwin Lutyens (1869–1944). This is as true of his early Arts and Crafts, as it is of his later, classicizing work.

In continental Europe Eugène-Emmanuel Viollet-le-Duc (1814–79) exerted a considerable influence. His precise drawings for a new architecture, which would make full use of cast and wrought iron, appear in the Atlas which accompanied his *Entretiens sur l'Architecture* (1863–72). In this Viollet-le-Duc endeavoured to apply the lessons learned from his rationalist, or scientific, interpretation of medieval structure.

Viollet-le-Duc saw no inconsistency in ornamenting iron structural components. While none of Viollet's iron projects was actually built, Hector Guimard (1867–1942) paraphrased Viollet's suggestion of angled cast-iron columns in his Ecole du Sacré Coeur (now Les Colonnes de Guimard), Paris, 16ᵉ arrondissement, of 1895. Guimard invariably ignored, in a way that was reminiscent of the master masons of the Middle Ages, the frontier between form and ornament.

Another architect who manipulated form and ornament with virtuosity was Baron Victor Horta (1861–1947). His Maison du Peuple, Brussels, of 1896–9 – now unfortunately demolished – with its elegant concave façade, and its undulating iron trusses, was among the most inventive of late nineteenth-century buildings.

Antoni y Cornet Gaudí (1852–1926) was probably the greatest exponent of modern medievalizing architecture. The forms of his buildings, while obviously related to medieval models, were never merely exercises in archaeology. The Church of the Sagrada Familia, Barcelona, begun in 1884 and not yet completed, is the best-known example of his work. But the crypt of his church at the Colonia Guell (1914) is, probably, Gaudí's most adventurous essay in form (see Figure 12). Ornament is here sparingly used. Some, though not all, columns are built of ingeniously arranged brick, while ceilings in the porch are composed of patterned tiling. Nevertheless, the entire form of the building, which is irregular and complex, can be seen as ornamental – in precisely the same sense in which Leonardo's or Filarete's fantasies can. The familiar enigma of 'what is form?' and 'what is ornament?' is utterly insoluble in the case of the Colonia Guell church.

Louis Henry Sullivan (1856–1924) has long been recognized as one of the great architect-designers of ornament. His method of designing ornament is set out in *A System of Architectural Ornament According with a Philosophy of Man's Powers* (1924). The materials from which Sullivan created his ornament are essentially those of the nineteenth century. His ornament is not, in actuality, very far removed from that of Pugin and the British floriated tradition (particularly the work of J.K. Colling (1816–1905) and Christopher Dresser (1834–1904)). Frank Lloyd Wright (1869–1959) – who worked

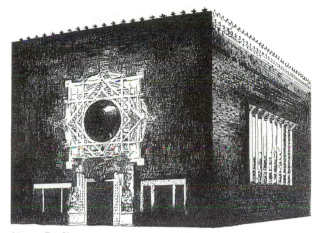

Figure 13 *Merchants' National Bank, Grinnell, Iowa, 1914, by Louis Sullivan. Drawn by the author.*

for a time in Sullivan's office – eulogized Sullivan's ornament in *Genius and the Mobocracy* (1949). It is interesting to observe how many Modernists had an almost morbid interest in Sullivan's ornament.

Sullivan's ornament was always consistently complex – no matter what the size of the object, or building, decorated. His design for a doorplate has the same visual consistency as an ornamental panel high on an office building. With one of those shafts of common sense which often illuminate his pages, Ruskin wrote that there were no ways in which ornament was 'more painfully lost' than by excessive delicacy, or too great a distance from the eye (see Ruskin (1851–3: 237 ff) for a detailed discussion of this phenomenon). This criticism can certainly be applied to Sullivan's ornament, while it can not be levelled against that of his fellow-Americans Frank Furness (1839–1912) and Henry Hobson Richardson (1838–86).

Sullivan possessed a brooding, Richardsonian, sense of form which was most successfully realized in his Walker Warehouse, Chicago (1888–9) – a distinctly Richardsonian structure, which he designed with his partner Dankmar Adler (1844–1900) – and his Merchants' National Bank, Grinnell, Iowa (1914) (Figure 13). In both these buildings ornament is comparatively restrained – although only in the Walker Warehouse are any adjustments made in the scale of the ornament in relation to the distance of the onlooker.

Adolf Loos (1870–1933) despite his famous article 'Ornament und Verbrechen' ('Ornament and crime') (1908), which was to enter into the folklore of the Modern Movement, was not fundamentally opposed to ornament – certainly not to classical ornament. This assertion is confirmed by his store for Goldman and Salatsch in the Michaelerplatz, Vienna (1910), with its correct Roman Doric columns and entablature. There was also his well-known Chicago Tribune project of 1922 – a skyscraper in the form of a colossal Greek Doric column. Here, in a distinctly humorous, if not ironic, manner, Loos conflates form and ornament.

Figure 12 *Medievalism – innovation. Crypt of the incomplete church at the Colonia Guell, Barcelona, 1914, by Antoni Gaudí. Drawn by the author.*

True Modernists, however, vehemently despised architectural ornament. Le Corbusier ridiculed it. With brilliant polemic and tendentiously selected illustrations he successfully undermined its status (Le Corbusier 1923; 1925). One should remember that ornament had once been thought able to transform a mere building into a work of art.

Post-Modernism and revived classicism have prompted us to question again the issues of form and ornament. Form is again being viewed as not necessarily wholly determined by function. Architectural forms might once again be devised for purely aesthetic reasons. While Viollet-le-Duc's assertion, that only with the solution of the 'problem' of ornament would the architecture of the future be born (Viollet-le-Duc 1863–72), Vol. 2), might seem untenable, we are now again at least contemplating the serious study of ornament.

NOTES

1　See Cresswell (1969, Vol. 1, chaps 4 and 5) for a detailed discussion of the Dome of the Rock. The issue of whether this was the first 'major' Islamic building is a somewhat vexed one. The Great Mosque at Kufa, rebuilt 670 CE, is known only by description, as is the Mosque of ˻Amr, 673 CE. However, Creswell has written of the Dome of the Rock as 'the earliest existing monument of Muslim architecture' (Cresswell 1958: 18).

2　In Alberti (1485), see the Sixth Book: *On Ornament*; the Seventh Book: *Ornament to Sacred Buildings*; the Eight Book: *Ornament to Public Secular Buildings*; the Ninth Book: *Ornament to Private Buildings*.

REFERENCES

Alberti, L.B. (1485) *De Re Aedificatoria*, trans. J. Rykwert, N. Leach and R. Tavernor, *On the Art of Building, in Ten Books*, 1988, Cambridge, Mass. and London: MIT Press.

Cotman, J.S. (1822) *Architectural Antiquities of Normandy*, London.

Cresswell, K.A.C. (1958) *A Short Account of Early Muslim Architecture*, Harmondsworth: Penguin.

—— (1969) *Early Muslim Architecture: Umayyads* AD *622–759, With a Contribution on the Mosaics of the Dome of the Rock in Jerusalem and of the Great Mosque in Damascus by Marguerite Gautier van Berchem*, 2nd edn, Oxford: Clarendon Press.

Cresy, E. and Taylor, G.L. (1822) *The Architectural Antiquities of Rome*, London.

Dresser, C. (1882) *Japan, its Architecture, Art and Art Manufacture*, London.

Fergusson, J. (1891) *History of Indian and Eastern Architecture . . . Forming the Third Volume of the New Edition of The History of Architecture*, London: John Murray.

Haupt, A. (1931) *Renaissance Palaces of Northern Italy and Tuscany*, London: Batsford.

Jones, O. (1856) *The Grammar of Ornament*, reprinted 1910, London: Bernard Quaritch.

Knight, H.G. (1842–4) *The Ecclesiastical Architecture of Italy from the Time of Constantine to the Fifteenth Century*, London.

Le Corbusier (1923) *Vers une architecture*, Paris: Editions Crès; trans F. Etchells, *Towards a New Architecture*, 1927, London: Architectural Press.

—— (1925) *L'Art Décoratif d'aujourd'hui*, Paris: Editions Crès; trans. and introd. J.I. Dunnett, *The Decorative Art of Today*, 1987, London: Architectural Press.

Lethaby, W.R. (with H. Swainson) (1894) *The Church of Sancta Sophia, Constantinople: A Study of Byzantine Building*, London and New York: Macmillan.

Loos, A. (1908) 'Ornament und Verbrechen', in *Trotzdem (Sämtliche Schriften)* 1: 282–3; trans. (into French) G. Besson, 1913, in *Les Cahiers d'aujourd'hui*, Paris.

L'Orme, P. de (1568) *Le Premier Tome de l'architecture*, Paris: Frédéric Morel.

Pugin, A.W.N. (1843) *The True Principles of Pointed or Christian Architecture: Set Forth in Two Lectures Delivered at St Mary's, Oscott*, London: H.G. Bohn.

Rubens, G. (1986) *William Richard Lethaby: His Life and Work, 1857–1931*, London: Architectural Press.

Ruskin, J. (1849) *The Seven Lamps of Architecture*, London: Smith Elder.

—— (1851–3) *The Stones of Venice . . .*, 3 vols, London: Smith Elder; 5th edn 1893, Orpington: George Allen.

Sullivan, L. (1924) *A System of Architectural Ornament, According with a Philosophy of Man's Powers*, New York: Press of the American Institute of Architects.

Viollet-le-Duc, E.E. (1863–72) *Entretiens sur l'architecture*, and accompanying Atlas (1864), Paris: A. Morel; trans. B. Bucknall, *Lectures on Architecture* [1877], London: Sampson Low, Marston, Searle & Rivington; facsimile edn 1959, London: George Allen & Unwin; New York: Grove.

Vitruvius *De Architectura*, trans. M.H. Morgan 1914, *The Ten Books on Architecture*; facsimile edn 1960, New York: Dover Publications.

Wright, F.L. (1949) *Genius and the Mobocracy*, New York: Duell, Sloan & Pearce; enlarged edn 1971, New York: Horizon Press.

FURTHER READING

Blunt, A. (1953) *Art and Architecture in France 1500 to 1700*, Harmondsworth: Penguin.

Bony, J. (1979) *The English Decorated Style: Gothic Architecture Transformed 1250–1350*, the Wrightsman Lectures delivered under the auspices of the New York University Institute for Fine Arts, London: Phaidon.

Durant, S. (1986) *Ornament: A Survey of Decoration Since 1830*, London: Macdonald.

Evans. J. (1948) *Art in Mediaeval France, 978–1498*, Oxford: Clarendon Press.

—— (1931) *Pattern: A Study of Ornament in Western Europe from 1180 to 1900*, Oxford: Clarendon Press.

Gombrich, E.H. (1979) *The Sense of Order: A Study in the Psychology of Decorative Art*, the Wrightsman Lectures delivered under the auspices of the New York University Institute for Fine Arts, London: Phaidon.

Hitchcock, H.-R. (1958) *Architecture: Nineteenth and Twentieth Centuries*, Harmondsworth: Penguin.

Lewis, P. and Darley, G. (1986) *Dictionary of Ornament*, London: Macmillan.

Physick, J. and Darby, M. (1973) *Drawings and Models for Victorian Secular Buildings* (catalogue of an exhibition at the Victoria and Albert Museum), London: HMSO.

Summerson, J. (1980) *The Classical Language of Architecture*, London: Thames & Hudson.

SECTION 4.2

Architectural space

In realized architecture there is a form/space paradox. In built form, having been defined and expressed, at least in part, by structure and fabric, all architecture has physical presence; and yet space is understood to be the raw material of architecture.

This form/space paradox is resolved if space-handling is seen as the art of architecture and building as its craft.

Architectural space, created to meet the needs of people, ranges from single cells to whole cities, and is as fascinating and as complex as human need itself. Our responses to space, territory, atmosphere, thermal comfort, sound, smell and touch are properly the study of philosophers, anthropologists, physiologists and behavioural psychologists, but architects must have a real appreciation of human need and response if they are to design spaces that satisfy more than the needs of utility. Architects have to imagine or anticipate reaction to space and spatial connection and interaction at the point of concept.

Conceptual space (the space we see or visualize), physical space (geometrically describable and measurable space), behavioural space (the space available for use after structural, circulation or other obstructive influences are accounted for) and the interconnections between such spatial categories must be understood.

Of the four essays in this section, Peter Aspinall's sets the scene in the most general way, ranging as it does over the fundamental issues and their importance to designers.

Paul Rabinow's interview with Michel Foucault offers historical and sociological perspectives seen from a twentieth-century viewpoint, while David Gosling addresses urban space, the major spatial preoccupation of the second half of the century – certainly in Western societies. Cornelis van de Ven's essay, 'The theory of space in architecture', stands as a positional statement of current understanding.

Conceptual space is governed by perception, and by our mental make-up, some of which is universal whilst some is learned and culture-specific. It is therefore vital that architects understand the cultural stage upon which they work so that the general issues addressed within these essays can be responded to with discrimination and sensitivity.

B.F.

RECOMMENDED READING

Alexander, C., Ishikawa, S. and Silverstein, M. (1977) *A Pattern Language*, New York: Oxford University Press.

Bachelard, G. (1969) *The Poetics of Space*, Boston: Beacon Press.

Giedion, S. (1971) *Architecture and the Phenomena of Transition: The Three Space Conceptions in Architecture*, Cambridge, Mass.: Harvard University Press.

Hillier, B. and Hanson, J. (1984) *The Social Logic of Space*, Cambridge: Cambridge University Press.

Krier, R. (1979) *Urban Space*, London: Academy Editions.

Laan, H. van der (1983) *Architectonic Space*, Leiden: E. Brill.

Norberg-Schulz, C. (1971) *Existence, Space and Architecture*, London: Studio Vista.

Tuan, Y.-F. (1977) *Space and Place: The Perspective of Experience*, London: Edward Arnold.

Van de Ven, C. (1980) *Space in Architecture*, Assen: Van Gorcum.

Zevi, B. (1957) *Architecture as Space*, New York: Horizon.

56 Aspects of spatial experience and structure
Peter Aspinall

INTRODUCTION

An awareness and a facility in ordering space is central to an architect's skill. In general, plans of buildings are described in terms of spaces and there is a rich professional vocabulary for describing the appropriateness of a space. Much of this centres on the potential of a space to accommodate the required activities and functions which are destined to be carried out within it. In addition, however, there are anticipations of the effect of the space on people (for example, whether enclosing or inviting, or both) and how, in moving through space, the perception of architectural forms can be revealed by the nature of the spatial viewing route. It is common experience that moving from a small enclosed space into a larger space seems by its contrast to make the latter more impressive. Figure 1 illustrates how the experience of space B can be altered by approaching it from A or from C. Combining such a transition with a change in level of observer seems to enhance the effect. Part of the experience and fascination of Italian hill towns relate to similar spatial variety.

Various effects have been studied in relation to spatial experience or spatial use. The following are typical findings.

1 Apparent spatial size – lighting and the lightness or darkness of the colour reflected from walls can influence the spaciousness of a room (Lam 1977). Furthermore any clues for apparent distance can affect perceived spatial size. Particularly interesting is the way in which a familiar object when created out of scale shifts the reference point for apparent distance – an effect known as size constancy (Canter 1974).[1]

2 Spatial use – in public areas or in restaurants preferred locations are at the edges of a space, suggesting a desire to see without being too obvious to others (Gehl 1980). Personal space has been studied as a function of gender, culture and situation (e.g. Hall 1966, Sommer 1969). Argyle (1973) and Morris (1977) describe the role of eye contact and body language on interpersonal distance and the consequences for the arrangement of seating or furniture. At an urban level, housing layouts have been shown to influence the patterns of friendships, people centrally placed being more likely to have more friends (Aiello 1987).

3 Wayfinding – many studies suggest it is the mental or cognitive map we form of a spatial layout which directs our wayfinding or orientation behaviour. This mental map may be a distorted or partial version of the physical map (see Figure 2) and will be easier to form in some environments than others (Lynch 1960; Appleyard 1976; Smyth *et al.* 1987).[2] Large buildings, such as hospitals or government buildings, often present users with significant problems of wayfinding with associated feelings of stress and incompetence (Evans *et al.* 1982) – problems which become crucial in emergency situations. Weiseman (1981) produced guidelines for the institutionalized elderly for 'legible' housing which emphasized architectural features such as visual landmarks at key choice points. More recently Peponis *et al.* (1990) have shown that an objective measure of the floor plan configuration is significantly related to the relative use of the space in search tasks in the building. Reference to this will be made in the last section.

Finally, a general point is worth emphasis. It is common to imagine space as a neutral backcloth which contains people and other objects and which may be described by its surfaces and volumes, etc. Even terms

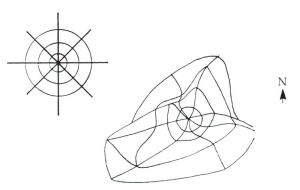

Figure 2 *Mental maps: students were asked to name places falling at the intersection of radial lines and concentric circles. If mental maps coincided with the physical map the drawings would be circular, as on the left. (Source: studies by Annetta Pedretti at the Architectural Association, London)*

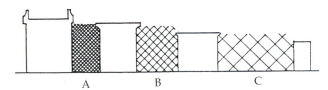

Figure 1 *The experience of space B is influenced by whether space A or space C precedes it.*

like 'built' or 'physical' environment encourage a view of humanity as a living, experiencing being encapsulated in a material container – a being behaving within an environmental shell. It is more difficult to think of space as something positive such that it can be 'charged with energy which varies according to the nature and proximity of the façades, of buildings which surround it' (Arnheim 1977: 35). What is at issue, therefore, is the common tendency to study the nature of environments as if this can be separated from people's experience and images of that environment. In attempting to group the significant transactions which take place between persons and the environment, Alexander writes: 'True feelings arise only when you thoroughly and deeply recognise the structure of a situation that exists and you do exactly the right thing at the right moment to respond to that situation' (Alexander and Davis 1981: 20). The corollary of feeling right and acting right is an environment which possesses 'quality without name'. There appears in such an environment to be compatibility between the activities the environment suggests and supports and the plans and activities people need or wish to carry out within it. There is a long history of phenomenological research into such places – on home, on what it means to dwell or belong, on 'existential insideness', i.e. unselfconscious immersion in a place (Relph 1976: 55; Norberg Schulz 1980).

Two recent approaches – one on spatial experience, one on spatial structure – will now be presented. Each challenges the assumed Cartesian split between the human or subjective world and the objective, physical world. The first links our perception of space and architecture with the emerging awareness of our bodies we have as children – an unconscious feeling level at which space is experienced. The second suggests that space itself has a social logic. Through an analysis of spatial structure, the way in which architects organize space for social purpose, and the consequences of this organization for human interaction can be revealed. As the crucial role of the human participant is emphasized, both views differ from sculptural conceptions of space or of architecture as an abstract art.

EXPERIENCING SPACE

The world of a child seems very different from the world of adults. For the infant there may be no distinction between self and not self (Donaldson 1978) and no clear differentiated body boundary, so that body and environment fuse (Wapner and Werner 1965).[3] In this early phase, the self, rather than being thought of as an isolated individual, may be seen as constituted by the relationship of other persons (MacMurray 1961) with early interpersonal responsiveness, the source out of which human intelligence springs (Trevarthen 1977).

All our subsequent knowledge (including scientific) is for MacMurray anthropomorphic, in that characteristics attributed to the 'other' must first be included within the full characterization of ourselves. It is certainly true that in childhood we seem to inhabit a world filled with animate beings. Trees might cry, animals might have conversations and tank engines might be proud of themselves. We draw houses with doors like a mouth and windows like eyes. As we struggle with gravity we distinguish up from down, we learn left from right and back from front. All these spatial relationships may begin from an awareness of ourselves in which our early dialogues set a pattern for our later relationships with the world. This point has been made by Merleau-Ponty (1962) who made the body the primary reference point of perception from which all spatial co-ordinates are derived. This body-centred sense of space and things used to be extended into architecture. Bloomer and Moore (1977: 49) give an account of the significance of the body in early built form to its 'virtual elimination from architectural thought in this century'.[4]

Recent views of perception appear in keeping with a body-centred view. Furthermore, touch, in which we act and directly engage with objects, has for some authors a primacy in perception. For example Gibson (1966), in seeing all five senses working together in actively seeking information, postulated a basic orientating and haptic system particularly relevant for our understanding of three-dimensionality. Basic orientating is the postural sense of up and down establishing our knowledge of the ground plane. The haptic sense is the sense of touch which Gibson reconsiders to include the entire body. No other sense deals as directly with the 3D world; no other sense engages feeling and doing simultaneously.

Beginning from an awareness of our own bodies, Peled (1976, 1978, 1990) has developed new techniques to assist architects in their spatial location of activities and events.[5] For Peled we are always in dialogue with the environment, we always find ourselves inside a place which we cohabit with other entities – people, objects, walls, trees – surrounded by outside places. Experiencing means being in a situation. Rather than experiencing *space* as a distinct entity we experience *place*, which is the spatial givenness of the situation in which we find ourselves. All entities in a place present themselves to us in their spatiality. For Peled all of these are partners in a dialogue; all are experienced in the holistic context of being in the place. Spatial experience is understood therefore as a whole. Because all entities are partners in a dialogue we project properties on to them seeing even objects as purposeful entities – responding partners in an encounter.[6] Peled uses Erikson's model of psycho-social development (Erikson 1965) as a basis of the interaction between person and place. This emphasizes key dimensions in our interactions with place as direction (reception to production), intensity (involvement to detachment) and control (dominance to submission).[7] In brief place experience is characterized by balance or conflict along these existential dimensions.

Ecoanalysis

How are these ideas applied to everyday practical design decisions on spatial organization? 'Ecoanalysis' is the method Peled (1990) uses to provide designers with relevant information for initial design decisions. It is in two parts. First, for each individual or group the analysis begins with an exploration of the experience of a place as a whole. Peled uses a Personal Construct approach to do this (Kelly 1955), in which the whole place is compared and contrasted with other similar and dissimilar places. From these comparisons 'constructs' are generated which represent the ways of seeing the places as a whole. An example of this approach was used by Aspinall and Sefre (1986) in the way elderly residents perceived their sheltered housing. Figure 3 shows the way in which perceptions of the present house were compared with perceptions of other houses and with the idea of the 'ideal' house. For this resident the main difference between the present house and the ideal is experienced as feelings of security or threat. The greatest contribution to resident satisfaction would be made therefore by addressing this issue.

In the second phase of ecoanalysis a location task is carried out in which the spatial organization of design is explored. As individuals carry out this task the meanings and feelings which are invested in places are made much more explicit, giving insight and understanding to spatial layouts. The task is designed to be free from actual design constraints but not detached in the manner of a bubble diagram. Individuals think about a place as they would like it to be, and list the component spaces they would wish to include. These component spaces often emerge from the holistic exploration of the personal construct approach. Counters representing spaces are manipulated on a board indicating their inter-relation. An important aspect of the resulting arrangement is the way in which inside and outside, back and front, core and periphery, and left and right are experienced. These key terms are based on the notion that at a direct 'feeling level' we experience and interact with the space that surrounds us as we experience the regions of our own bodies. In subsequent analysis of the direct expression of feelings embodied in the counter arrangement we assume an 'expressive analogue', that is, central spaces placed near the core rather than the periphery are an expression of a wish for integration; the front spaces are public while the back spaces are turned away from society and more inward looking; the left location is seen as the rebellious side while the right is more accepting and a region allocated to looking after the functioning and operation of the system.

A simple example of the technique has been used in an educational context where primary school children designed a garden for local use (Aspinall and Ujam 1990). Figure 4 shows the location board for the arrangement of objects and activities. An architectural application using the location task as input to the project brief was given by Moran (1978) for the design of a day centre. The composite location task and architect's plans are shown in Figure 5. Moran observed that the location task was 'very powerful'. Not only did it produce a projective arrangement of space at a 'feeling' level but it went 'beyond given experience with any existing buildings to the exploration of future places in both physical and conceptual terms' (Moran 1978: 294). Other uses by

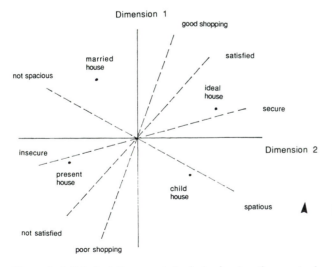

Figure 3 *A Principal Component Analysis showing the perceived similarities and differences between the houses. The closer in space, the more similar the houses are seen to be. Lines represent dimensions of perceived differences. In order to bring the present house closer to the ideal, a move is necessary along the line which corresponds to perceived security.*

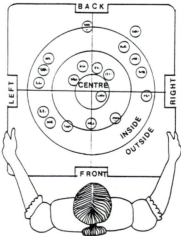

Figure 4 *Ecoanalysis: objects and activities are located on the board and distributed as the person or group wishes. This arrangement is then translated into an actual design.*

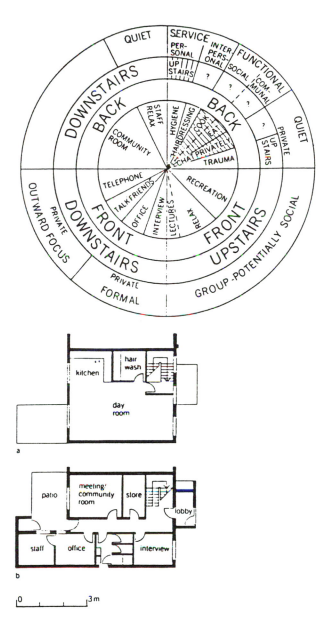

Figure 5 *Ecoanalysis: the topology of the diagram at the top, reflecting user needs and wishes, was presented as a brief to the architect who produced the design underneath.* (Source: *Peled 1990*)

Peled have been towards the design of houses, schools, hospital wards and an airport terminal.

SPATIAL STRUCTURE

So far we have considered aspects of spatial experience and the fundamental dimensions upon which that experience might be grounded. In this section aspects of spatial structure will be considered. Once again the idea of buildings or spaces as having merely physical properties is challenged, but now from a different point of view. It is apparent that buildings and urban spaces are themselves the products of human intentions. Therefore in asking how an aspect of architecture (i.e. space)

might influence behaviour we have to recognize that human behaviour is already part of the built environment. Moreover, one of the most important ways in which the built environment carries the imprint of society is in the way space is organized for human purposes. Perhaps the writer who has most fully developed these views is Bill Hillier with his colleagues at the Bartlett School of Architecture in University College, London. Space syntax is the name given to this new approach for the representation, quantification and interpretation of spatial configurations in settlements and buildings.

Urban level

It is widely believed that 'good' urban design involves the design of spaces which will be used and in which there is always the likelihood of encountering others. Simply being aware of others can reduce anxiety, and can be the springboard for the developments of friendships or neighbourhoods (Gehl 1980). In addition, one function of the spatial structure of a town is to facilitate encounters between inhabitants, and between inhabitants and strangers (Hillier and Hanson 1984).

In attempting to achieve these goals, and improve the liveliness of street life, most design intervention is at a local level (for example by pedestrianizing zones, introducing benches and local facilities, removing fumes and noise, etc.). While all these are important in context, Hillier has shown that a key factor in understanding urban form and its use is how a space relates to other spaces in a system. It is this global pattern which seems to affect how a town works and where people are likely to be encountered within it. Furthermore, as will be shown, this information can be used as a predictive design tool for creating new urban developments or building complexes.

There is, moreover, a general awareness that something has gone wrong with urban space. Architects can no longer create the informal liveliness which seems to characterize some of our best-loved towns. Hillier shows that these older towns, which appear to be lacking order and to be fairly random in their evolution of space, actually possess subtle properties which are vital to aspects of use and movement. Sadly and paradoxically these properties are absent from many of our recent 'planned' developments, which often exhibit the 'urban desert' problems. The plans of older towns (see Figure 6) suggest an irregular continuity or deformed spatial grid. This contrasts with a pattern regularity (which looks intelligible from above but which may not be intelligible to a user at ground level, as parts are too similar) or with a fragmentation of space apparent in many recent developments.

Spatial descriptors

There are several alternative ways to describe space. At a one-dimensional level streets on a map may be

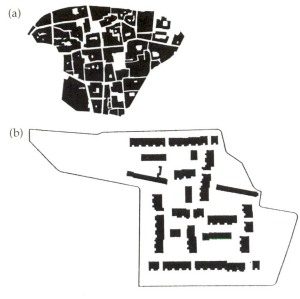

Figure 6 *(a) The irregular continuity of the traditional zone (Apt in France) contrasted with (b) fragmented space (Marquess Road Estate in London) or (c) patterned, bird's-eye regularity (Bofills village in Algeria).* Source: *Hillier 1983: 50 (a and c), 53(b))*

Figure 7 *(a) The fewest and longest straight lines to cover the entire street system of a town; (b) The same area divided into the fewest and fattest convex spaces.* (Source: *Hillier (1983): 50*)

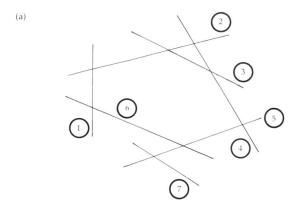

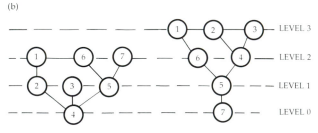

Figure 8 *Measuring integration: each line in the spatial system of (a) can be given a number. Starting at any line, the connections to all other lines can be made. The number of levels needed to do this reflects the integration value of the starting line – fewer levels means higher integration, hence in (b) line 4 is more integrated than line 7.*

covered by the longest and fewest straight lines – like sight lines. At a two-dimensional level a convex space can be defined as a space within which all points are directly visible from all other points (Figure 7). Before concentrating on one-dimensional analysis of urban spatial structure, one special property of convex spaces in traditional settlements should be noted. Most convex spaces have building entrances opening on to them. This means that as a pedestrian you are nearly always adjacent to someone's door. Should the convex space you are in not contain an entrance, then the adjacent one surely will. This simple spatial property (which can be easily checked by observation) is not present in many modern developments.

The global measure of integration

If the fewest and longest straight lines covering a spatial system are connected, it is possible, starting at any line and by placing each direct connection on a separate level, to see how many levels are required to join up all other lines. Figure 8 shows this for two starting lines in a simple spatial system. The figure shows that for line 7,

four levels are needed to join up all the lines in the system. On the other hand, for line 4 only three levels are needed to connect up all lines. By multiplying the number of lines on a level by the level number, summing across levels and dividing by the number of levels in the system, the average mean depth of the system from the chosen starting line can be calculated. The mean depth reflects the integration value for the line – the actual integration value is inversely related to mean depth and corrected to enable comparisons between spatial systems of different size. It is therefore possible that for every line in a spatial system, an integration value can be calculated. These integration values can be sorted and placed in order from the highest to the lowest. The location of the top 10 per cent or 20 per cent of integration lines can then be identified on the map of the system.

Properties of 'good' towns

Hillier has discovered two important properties of 'good' urban areas. First, there is a high correlation between the integration values of spaces and likely encounter with others as assessed from counts of people on the streets. This means spatial layout predicts usage. This is not the case in 'bad' urban areas where, in addition, encounter rates are much lower. Second, if we examine the top (say 25 per cent) integration lines we find in a good town that these tend to form a pattern which relates to all other areas. In other words, wherever you are in a town, you are never far (around two or three lines) from a high integration line. The patterns vary but the principle holds. On the other hand, many modern estates exhibit a quite different pattern. The top integration lines often border an estate without penetrating its centre. The centre is therefore several steps deep from the outside, and there is no high integration network available to all parts of the spatial system.[8] Finally, in addition to integration there is the important property of intelligibility. This is the relation between the number of immediate connections a line has and its integration value. If locally well-connected lines are also high-integrating lines then the system will possess intelligibility – the whole can be read from the parts.[9]

This brief sketch gives some properties which have been used in design contexts to gain understanding and to redevelop urban areas. By analysing an existing structure, redesigning an area within it, then reanalysing the whole, the new design can be assessed for the degree to which it works with, or against, the existing spatial structure. In addition, the possibility of predicting spatial use has been a major contribution against the 'urban desert' phenomenon.

Buildings

From a space syntax perspective, the relevant set of questions in understanding buildings relates to how different groups of people (such as different kinds of inhabitants, and strangers) inhabit, interact, and carry out their activities in buildings. The central question is therefore how these social events are mapped into the spatial structure of buildings, and how this spatial structure affects these social events.

A useful way of looking at the spatial relationships in buildings is by means of a depth diagram. In this type of diagram, each room can be represented by a dot, and connections between rooms by a line. Simple properties of a building become immediately apparent, for example, which and what type of spaces are deep in a building and which are shallow, which spaces lie on rings (and thereby have more than one point of access) and which do not.

Such a diagram can be drawn from any room or space as a starting point. Calculations for each space can then be made (as for the lines in Figure 8) to find how integrated that space is with all others in the building. Certain patterns may then become apparent. For example in a study of several different house types and geometries, Hillier and Hanson (1984) found a stable rank order of integration values, with the living room having highest integration, kitchen next highest, and the parlour least integrated – different functions consistently mapped into spatial structure at a level not evident from an inspection of the different house plans. Again, in a study of factories, people occupying more integrated spaces were found to know more people and to talk to them more frequently (Peponis and Stansall 1987).

Mention has already been made of inhabitants and strangers. It can be instructive to see how these different groups are distributed in a building. Inhabitants are people with special access who have control of space and whose existence (status or activity) is mapped into space. From the set of strangers there is the subgroup of visitors – people who temporarily enter buildings but who do not control them (such as pupils in a school, patients in a hospital). Buildings exercise control in terms of how these different groups interact or are brought together. The layout of a building can therefore reinforce the differentiation of status, influence the potential for supervision or control, and affect the potential for encountering others. These are the social functions of space which may be compatible or at variance with the organizational structure of the office or the factory.

Finally, it is possible to cover all the available connections between convex spaces in a building with the fewest and longest straight lines, as was done at the urban level in Figure 7. Here lines are chosen because previous research has shown them to be closely related to patterns of spatial use. The integration value of each line can be found, and the top (say 10 per cent) of lines plotted to form the integration core of the building. This is a summary of the spatial system which allows comparisons with other layouts. Recently Peponis *et al.* (1990) have shown that wayfinding and search behaviour in a building is determined by the integration value of spaces and choice points in the circulation system, high-integration spaces being crossed most frequently during search. This brief account has scarcely touched the complex sociological thesis developed by Hillier and Hansen (1984) and has only made use of a few of the many measures developed in connection with the space syntax programme. None the less the practical implications of this work are clear and are increasingly being recognized.

In this essay two areas of current research into spatial experience and structure have been selected. Each has been characterized as a break from the Cartesian view, deeply embedded in our minds and still underpinning much debate on how environments influence people, which separates mind from body, reason from emotion, and people from their environments. In developing personal construct psychology, Kelly (1955) refused to make these distinctions and saw individuals construing the world and validating their construals in action. This closer link between action and place is in keeping with the general trend of research development in the field. The spatial location techniques of ecoanalysis begin from the personal construct perspective but extend it further into environmental dialogues at a feeling level. In developments of space syntax, the spaces surrounding us are not treated as neutral physical entities but are seen as social products already possessing a built-in social logic. We ignore this to our cost in the creation of a built environment. This research and that on ecoanalysis are ongoing. Both are attempting to provide us with greater understanding and encourage better practice in the design of urban and built space.

NOTES

1　The relevance of more general environmental constancies originally suggested by Ittelson (1973) has received more recent support. For example, a church may still be seen as a 'church' even when converted to a disco. This categorization process will in part determine the affective responses and evaluations. These appear related to properties of the category into which an object has been placed (Purcell 1986).

2　Similar errors resulting from simplifying heuristics and framing effects are not confined to mental maps but regularly occur in many perceptual and decision-making situations (Tversky and Kahneman 1974).

3　Psychologically, body image relates to the unconscious awareness individuals have of their body boundary. The boundary is unstable, changing with mood and physiological state. Fisher (1970) has suggested that the strength of the primary boundary in 'penetration' or 'barrier' characteristics relates to capacities for environmental experience – strong barrier persons being more individuated and capable of greater strength and range of experience.

4　For example, the hearth was seen as the heart of a building, Christian churches had plans resembling the body of Christ, while columns, walls and roofs were talismans with invested qualities to give meaning to the building.

5　These emerged as a result of attempts to deal therapeutically with people's experience of place, aligning the goals of design with those of psychotherapy.

6　For Peled we construe all other entities as the bodies of actual or metaphorical beings.

7　People, objects and places are located along these existential dimensions. We receive food and ideas. We also produce and communicate ideas and manipulate objects or people. Similarly, a room receives us; so does a chair, which can also be manipulated. Places rich in sound or colour tend to be experienced as intense and involving. Interplay between participant and place can give rise to complementary or conflicting combinations in which each can be either dominating or submissive.

8　Note it is not that high-integration streets are 'good' while low-integration streets are 'bad'. What matters is the relative patterning which gives access to high-integration streets and gradation of use across all streets.

9　Note that this definition of intelligibility is on the basis of how one local property (connections) helps predict one global property (integration). The relationship between this term and ease of mental mapping has still to be established.

REFERENCES

Aiello, J. (1987) 'Human spatial behaviour', in D. Stokols and I. Altman (eds) *Handbook of Environmental Psychology*, New York: Wiley.

Alexander, C. and Davis, H. (1981) 'Beyond humanism', *Journal of Architectural Education* (Fall): 20.

Appleyard, D. (1976) *Planning a Pluralist City*, Cambridge, Mass.: MIT Press.

Argyle, M. (1973) *Social Encounters*, Harmondsworth: Penguin.

Arnheim, R. (1977) *The Dynamics of Architectural Form*, Berkeley: University of California Press.

Aspinall, P. and Sefre, F. (1986) 'An investigation of "place" with reference to old peoples' housing', 5th year study, Heriot Watt Architecture Department.

Aspinall, P. and Ujam, F. (1992) 'A projective approach to designing with children', *Journal of Landscape Research* (in press).

Bloomer, K. and Moore, C. (1977) *Body, Memory and Architecture*, New Haven and London: Yale University Press.

Canter, D. (1974) *Psychology for Architects*, London: Applied Science.

Donaldson, M. (1978) *Children's Minds*, London: Fontana.

Erikson, H. (1965) *Childhood and Society*, Harmondsworth: Penguin.

Evans, G., Smith, C. and Pezdek, K. (1982) 'Cognitive maps and urban form', *Journal of the American Planning Association* 48: 232–44.

Fisher, S. (1970) *Body Experience in Fantasy and Behaviour*, New York: Appleton-Century-Crofts.

Gehl, J. (1980) 'The residential steel environment', *Built Environment* 6 (1): 51–61.

Gibson, J. (1966) *The Senses Considered as Perceptual Systems*, Boston: Houghton Mifflin.

Hall, E. (1966) *The Hidden Dimension*, New York: Doubleday.

Hillier, B. (1983) 'Space Syntax – a different urban perspective', *Architects' Journal*, 30 November.

Hillier, B. and Hanson, J. (1984) *The Social Logic of Space*, London: Cambridge University Press.

Ittelson, W. (1973) *Environment and Cognition Seminar*, New York: Press Network.

Kelly, G. (1955) *The Psychology of Personal Constructs*, London: Routledge.

Lam, W. (1977) *Perception and Lighting as Form-Givers for Architecture*, New York: McGraw Hill.

Lynch, K. (1960) *Image of the City*, Cambridge, Mass.: MIT Press.

MacMurray, J. (1961) *Persons in Relation*, London: Faber & Faber.

Merleau-Ponty, M. (1962) *Phenomenology of Perception*, London: Routledge & Kegan Paul.

Moran, R. (1978) 'The spatial brief of a day centre', in D. Canter, M. Krampton and D. Stea (eds) *Environmental Policy Assessment and Communication*, Vol. 2, pp. 233–59, Aldershot: Avebury.

Morris, D. (1977) *The Naked Ape*, London: Grafton.

Norberg-Schulz, C. (1980) *Genius Loci: Towards Phenomenology of Architecture*, New York: Rizzoli.

Peled, A. (1976) 'The place as a metaphoric body', report from Faculty of Architecture and Town Planning, Technion, Israel Institute of Technology.

—— (1978) 'Explorations in ecoanalysis', in D. Canter, M. Krampton and D. Stea (eds) *Environmental Policy Assessment and Communication*, Vol. 2, Aldershot: Avebury.

—— (1990) 'The ecoanalysis of places', *Architects' Journal* 192 (7): 49–55.

Peponis, J. and Stansall, P. (1987) 'Spatial culture', *Design Journal* 27 (June): 52–6.

Peponis, J., Zimring, C. and Yoon Kyung Choi (1990) 'Finding the building in wayfinding', *Environment and Behaviour* 22 (5): 555–90.

Purcell, A. (1986) 'Environmental perception and affect: a schema discrepancy model', *Environment and Behaviour* 18 (1): 3–30.

Relph, E. (1976) *Place and Placelessness*, London: Pion.

Smyth, M., Morris, P., Levy, L. and Ellis, A. (1987) *Cognition in Action*, London: Lawrence Erlbaum Associates.

Sommer, R. (1969) *Personal Space: The Behavioural Basis of Design*, Englewood Cliffs, NJ: Prentice Hall.

Trevarthen, C. (1977) 'Descriptive analyses of infant communication behaviour', in H.R. Schaffer (ed.) *Studies in Mother-Infant Interaction*, London: Academic Press.

Tversky, A. and Kahneman, D. (1974) 'Judgements under uncertainty: heuristics and biases, *Science* 185: 1124–31.

Wapner, S. and Werner, H. (eds) (1965) *The Body Percept*, New York: Random House.

Weisman, J. (1981) 'Evaluating architectural legibility: wayfinding in the built environment', *Environment and Behaviour* 13 (2): 189–204.

57 Space, knowledge and power

Michel Foucault and Paul Rabinow

P.R. *In your interview with geographers at* Herodote, *you said that architecture becomes political at the end of the eighteenth century.*[1] *Obviously, it was political in earlier periods, too, such as during the Roman Empire. What is particular about the eighteenth century?*

M.F. My statement was awkward in that form. Of course I did not mean to say that architecture was not political before, becoming so only at that time. I only meant to say that in the eighteenth century one sees the development of reflection upon architecture as a function of the aims and techniques of the government of societies. One begins to see a form of political literature that addresses what the order of a society should be, what a city should be, given the requirements of the maintenance of order; given that one should avoid epidemics, avoid revolts, permit a decent and moral family life, and so on. In terms of these objectives, how is one to conceive of both the organization of a city and the construction of a collective infrastructure? And how should houses be built? I am not saying that this sort of reflection appears only in the eighteenth century, but only that in the eighteenth century a very broad and general reflection on these questions takes place. If one opens a police report of the times – the treatises that are devoted to the techniques of government – one finds that architecture and urbanism occupy a place of considerable importance. That is what I meant to say.

P.R. *Among the ancients, in Rome or Greece, what was the difference?*

M.F. In discussing Rome, one sees that the problem revolves around Vitruvius. Vitruvius was reinterpreted from the sixteenth century on, but one can find in the sixteenth century – and no doubt in the Middle Ages as well – many considerations of the same order as Vitruvius; if you consider them as *reflections upon.* The treatises on politics, on the art of government, on the manner of good government, did not generally include chapters or analyses devoted to the organization of cities or to architecture. The *Republic* of Jean Bodin does not contain extended discussions of the role of architecture, whereas the police treatises of the eighteenth century are full of them.

P.R. *Do you mean there were techniques and practices, but the discourse did not exist?*

M.F. I did not say that discourses upon architecture did not exist before the eighteenth century. Nor do I mean to say that the discussions of architecture before the eighteenth century lacked any political dimension or significance. What I wish to point out is that, from the eighteenth century on, every discussion of politics as the art of the government of men necessarily includes a chapter or a series of chapters on urbanism, on collective facilities, on hygiene, and on private architecture. Such chapters are not found in the discussions of the art of government of the sixteenth century. This change is perhaps not in the reflections of architects upon architecture, but it is quite clearly seen in the reflections of political men.

P.R. *So it was not necessarily a change within the theory of architecture itself?*

M.F. That's right. It was not necessarily a change in the minds of architects, or in their techniques – although that remains to be seen – but in the minds of political men in the choice and the form of attention that they bring to bear upon the objects that are of concern to them. Architecture became one of these during the seventeenth and eighteenth centuries.

P.R. *Could you tell us why?*

M.F. Well, I think that it was linked to a number of phenomena, such as the question of the city and the idea that was clearly formulated at the beginning of the seventeenth century that the government of a large state like France should ultimately think of its territory on the model of the city. The city was no longer perceived as a place of privilege, as an exception in a territory of fields, forests and roads. The cities were no longer islands beyond the common law. Instead, the cities, with the problems that they raised, and the particular forms that they took, served as the models for the governmental rationality that was to apply to the whole of the territory.

There is an entire series of utopias or projects for governing territory that developed on the premise that a state is like a large city; the capital is like its main square; the roads are like its streets. A state will be well organized when a system of policing as tight and efficient as that of the cities extends over the entire territory. At the outset, the notion of police applied only to the set of regulations that were to assure the tranquillity of a city, but at that moment the police become the very *type* of rationality for the government of the whole territory. The model of the city became the matrix

First published in *Skyline*, March 1982, Rizzoli Communications. This interview with Michel Foucault was conducted by Paul Rabinow and translated by Christian Hubert.

for the regulations that apply to a whole state.

The notion of police, even in France today, is frequently misunderstood. When one speaks to a Frenchman about police, he can only think of people in uniform or in the secret service. In the seventeenth and eighteenth centuries, 'police' signified a programme of government rationality. This can be characterized as a project to create a system of regulation of the general conduct of individuals whereby everything would be controlled to the point of self-sustenance, without the need for intervention. This is the rather typically French effort of policing. The English, for a number of reasons, did not develop a comparable system, mainly because of the parliamentary tradition on the one hand, and the tradition of local, communal autonomy on the other, not to mention the religious system.

One can place Napoleon almost exactly at the break between the old organization of the eighteenth-century police state (understood, of course, in the sense we have been discussing, not in the sense of the 'police state' as we have come to know it) and the forms of the modern state, which he invented. At any rate, it seems that, during the eighteenth and nineteenth centuries, there appeared – rather quickly in the case of commerce and more slowly in all the other domains – this idea of a police that would manage to penetrate, to stimulate, to regulate, and to render almost automatic all the mechanisms of society.

This idea has since been abandoned. The question has been turned around. No longer do we ask: What is the form of governmental rationality that will be able to penetrate the body politic to its most fundamental elements? but rather: How is government possible? That is, what is the principle of limitation that applies to governmental actions such that things will occur for the best, in conformity with the rationality of government, and without intervention?

It is here that the question of liberalism comes up. It seems to me that at that very moment it became apparent that if one governed too much, one did not govern at all – that one provoked results contrary to those one desired. What was discovered at that time – and this was one of the great discoveries of political thought at the end of the eighteenth century – was the idea of *society*. That is to say, that government not only has to deal with a territory, with a domain, and with its subjects, but that it also has to deal with a complex and independent reality that has its own laws and mechanisms of reaction, its regulations as well as its possibilities of disturbance. This new reality is society. From the moment that one is to manipulate a society, one cannot consider it completely penetrable by police. One must take into account what it is. It becomes necessary to reflect upon it, upon its specific characteristics, its constants and its variables. . . .

P.R. *So there is a change in the importance of space. In the eighteenth century there was a territory and the problem of governing people in this territory: one can choose as an example* La Métropolite *of Alexandre LeMaitre – a utopian treatise on how to build a capital city – or one can understand a city as a metaphor or symbol for the territory and how to govern it. All of this is quite spatial, whereas after Napoleon, society is not necessarily so spatialized. . . .*

M.F. That's right. On one hand, it is not so spatialized, yet at the same time a certain number of problems that are properly seen as spatial emerged. Urban space has its own dangers: disease, such as the epidemics of cholera in Europe from 1830 to about 1880; and revolution, such as the series of urban revolts that shook all of Europe during the same period. These spatial problems, which were perhaps not new, took on a new importance.

Second, a new aspect of the relations of space and power was the railroads. These were to establish a network of communication no longer corresponding necessarily to the traditional network of roads, but they none the less had to take into account the nature of society and its history. In addition, there are all the social phenomena that railroads gave rise to, be they the resistances they provoked, the transformations of population, or changes in the behaviour of people. Europe was immediately sensitive to the changes in behaviour that the railroads entailed. What was going to happen, for example, if it was possible to get married between Bordeaux and Nantes? Something that was not possible before. What was going to happen when people in Germany and France might get to know one another? Would war still be possible once there were railroads? In France a theory developed that the railroads would increase familiarity among people and that the new forms of human universality made possible would render war impossible. But what the people did not foresee – although the German military command was fully aware of it, since they were much cleverer than their French counterpart – was that, on the contrary, the railroads rendered war far easier to wage. The third development, which came later, was electricity.

So there were problems in the links between the exercise of political power and the space of a territory, or the space of cities – links that were completely new.

P.R. *So it was less a matter of architecture than before. These are sorts of technics of space. . . .*

M.F. The major problems of space, from the nineteenth century on, were indeed of a different type. Which is not to say that problems of an architectural nature were forgotten. In terms of the first ones I referred to – disease and the political problems – architecture has a very important role to play. The reflections on urbanism and on the design of workers' housing – all of these questions – are an area of reflection upon architecture.

P.R. *But architecture itself, the Ecole des Beaux-Arts, belongs to a completely different set of spatial issues.*

M.F.   That's right. With the birth of these new technologies and these new economic processes, one sees the birth of a sort of thinking about space that is no longer modelled on the police state of the urbanization of the territory, but that extends far beyond the limits of urbanism and architecture.

P.R.   *Consequently, the Ecole des Ponts et Chaussées. . . .*

M.F.   That's right. The Ecole des Ponts et Chaussées and its capital importance in political rationality in France are part of this. It was not architects, but engineers and builders of bridges, roads, viaducts, railways, as well as the polytechnicians (who practically controlled the French railroads) – those are the people who thought out space.

P.R.   *Has this situation continued up to the present, or are we witnessing a change in relations between the technicians of space?*

M.F.   We may well witness some changes, but I think that we have until now remained with the developers of the territory, the people of the Ponts et Chaussées, etc.

P.R.   *So architects are not necessarily the masters of space that they once were, or believe themselves to be.*

M.F.   That's right. They are not the technicians or engineers of the three great variables – territory, communication, and speed. These escape the domain of architects.

P.R.   *Do you see any particular architectural projects, either in the past or the present, as forces of liberation or resistance?*

M.F.   I do not think that it is possible to say that one thing is of the order of 'liberation' and another is of the order of 'oppression'. There are a certain number of things that one can say with some certainty about a concentration camp to the effect that it is not an instrument of liberation, but one should still take into account – and this is not generally acknowledged – that, aside from torture and execution, which preclude any resistance, no matter how terrifying a given system may be, there always remain the possibilities of resistance, disobedience, and oppositional groupings.

On the other hand, I do not think that there is anything that is functionally – by its very nature – absolutely liberating. Liberty is a *practice*. So there may, in fact, always be a certain number of projects whose aim is to modify some constraints, to loosen, or even break them, but none of these projects can, simply by its nature, assure that people will have liberty automatically, that it will be established by the project itself. The liberty of men is never assured by the institutions and laws that are intended to guarantee them. This is why almost all of these laws and institutions are quite capable of being turned around. Not because they are ambiguous, but simply because 'liberty' is what must be exercised.

P.R.   *Are there urban examples of this? Or examples where architects succeeded?*

M.F.   Well, up to a point there is Le Corbusier, who is described today – with a sort of cruelty that I find perfectly useless – as a sort of crypto-Stalinist. He was, I am sure, someone full of good intentions, and what he did was in fact dedicated to liberating effects. Perhaps the means that he proposed were in the end less liberating than he thought, but, once again, I think that it can never be inherent in the structure of things to guarantee the exercise of freedom. The guarantee of freedom is freedom.

P.R.   *So you do not think of Le Corbusier as an example of success. You are simply saying that his intention was liberating. Can you give us a successful example?*

M.F.   No. It *cannot* succeed. If one were to find a place, and perhaps there are some, where liberty is effectively exercised, one would find that this is not owing to the order of objects, but, once again, owing to the practice of liberty. Which is not to say that, after all, one may as well leave people in slums, thinking that they can simply exercise their rights there.

P.R.   *Meaning that architecture in itself cannot resolve social problems?*

M.F.   I think it can and does produce positive effects when the liberating intentions of the architect coincide with the real practice of people in the exercise of their freedom.

P.R.   *But the same architecture can serve other ends?*

M.F.   Absolutely. Let me bring up another example: the *Familistère* of Jean-Baptiste Godin at Guise (1859). The architecture of Godin was clearly intended for the freedom of people. Here was something that manifested the power of ordinary workers to participate in the exercise of their trade. It was a rather important sign and instrument of autonomy for a group of workers. Yet no one could enter or leave the place without being seen by everyone – an aspect of the architecture that could be totally oppressive. But it could only be oppressive if people were prepared to use their own presence in order to watch over others. Let's imagine a community of unlimited sexual practices that might be established there. It would once again become a place of freedom. I think it is somewhat arbitrary to try to dissociate the effective practice of freedom by people, the practice of social relations, and the spatial distributions in which they find themselves. If they are separated, they become impossible to understand. Each can only be understood through the other.

P.R.   *Yet people have often attempted to find utopian schemes to liberate people, or to oppress them.*

M.F.   Men have dreamed of liberating machines. But there are no machines of freedom, by definition. This is not to say that the exercise of freedom is completely indifferent to spatial distribution, but it can only function when there is a certain convergence; in the case of divergence or distortion, it immediately becomes the opposite of that which had been intended. The panoptic qualities of Guise could perfectly well have allowed it to be used as a prison. Nothing could be simpler. It is clear that, in fact, the *Familistère* may well have served as an instrument for discipline and a rather unbearable group pressure.

P.R.   *So, once again, the intention of the architect is not the fundamental determining factor.*

M.F.   Nothing is fundamental. That is what is interesting in the analysis of society. That is why nothing irritates me as much as these inquiries – which are by definition metaphysical – on the foundations of power in a society or the self-institution of a society, etc. These are not fundamental phenomena. There are only reciprocal relations, and the perpetual gaps between intentions in relation to one another.

P.R.   *You have singled out doctors, prison wardens, priests, judges and psychiatrists as key figures in the political configurations that involve domination. Would you put architects on this list?*

M.F.   You know, I was not really attempting to describe figures of domination when I referred to doctors and people like that, but rather to describe people through whom power passed or who are important in the fields of power relations. A patient in a mental institution is placed within a field of fairly complicated power relations, which Erving Goffman analysed very well. The pastor in a Christian or Catholic church (in Protestant churches it is somewhat different) is an important link in a set of power relations. The architect is not an individual of that sort.

After all, the architect has no power over me. If I want to tear down or change a house he built for me, put up new partitions, add a chimney, the architect has no control. So the architect should be placed in another category – which is not to say that he is not totally foreign to the organization, the implementation, and all the techniques of power that are exercised in a society. I would say that one must take *him* – his mentality, his attitude – into account as well as his projects, in order to understand a certain number of the techniques of power that are invested in architecture, but he is not comparable to a doctor, a priest, a psychiatrist or a prison warden.

P.R.   *'Post-Modernism' has received a great deal of attention recently in architectural circles. It is also being talked about in philosophy, notably by Jean-François Lyotard and Jurgen Habermas. Clearly, historical reference and language play an important role in the modern episteme. How do you see Post-Modernism, both as architecture and in terms of the historical and philosophical questions that are posed by it?*

M.F.   I think that there is a widespread and facile tendency, which one should combat, to designate that which has just occurred as the primary enemy, as if this were always the principal form of oppression from which one had to liberate oneself. Now this simple attitude entails a number of dangerous consequences: first, an inclination to seek out some cheap form of archaism or some imaginary past forms of happiness that people did not, in fact, have at all. For instance, in the areas that interest me, it is very amusing to see how contemporary sexuality is described as something absolutely terrible. To think that it is only possible now to make love after turning off the television! and in mass-produced beds! 'Not like that wonderful time when . . .' Well, what about those wonderful times when people worked eighteen hours a day and there were six people in a bed, if one was lucky enough to have a bed! There is in this hatred of the present or the immediate past a dangerous tendency to invoke a completely mythical past. Second, there is the problem raised by Habermas: if one abandons the work of Kant or Weber, for example, one runs the risk of lapsing into irrationality.

I am completely in agreement with this, but at the same time, our question is quite different: I think that the central issue of philosophy and critical thought since the eighteenth century has always been, still is, and will, I hope, remain the question: *What* is this Reason that we use? What are its historical effects? What are its limits, and what are its dangers? How can we exist as rational beings, fortunately committed to practising a rationality that is unfortunately criss-crossed by intrinsic dangers? One should remain as close to this question as possible, keeping in mind that it is both central and extremely difficult to resolve. In addition, if it is extremely dangerous to say that Reason is the enemy that should be eliminated, it is just as dangerous to say that any critical questioning of this rationality risks sending us into irrationality. One should not forget – and I'm not saying this in order to criticize rationality, but in order to show how ambiguous things are – it was on the basis of the flamboyant rationality of social Darwinism that racism was formulated, becoming one of the most enduring and powerful ingredients of Nazism. This was, of course, an irrationality, but an irrationality that was at the same time, after all, a certain form of rationality. . . .

This is the situation that we are in and that we must combat. If intellectuals in general are to have a function, if critical thought itself has a function, and, even more specifically, if philosophy has a function within critical thought, it is precisely to accept this sort of spiral, this sort of revolving door of rationality that refers us to its necessity, to its indispensability, and, at the same time, to its intrinsic dangers.

P.R.   *All that being said, it would be fair to say that you are much less afraid of historicism and the play of historical references than someone like Habermas is; also, that this issue* *has been posed in architecture as almost a crisis of civilization by the defenders of Modernism, who contend that if we abandon modern architecture for a frivolous return to decoration and motifs, we are somehow abandoning civilization. On the other hand, some Post-Modernists have claimed that historical references per se are somehow meaningful and are going to protect us from the dangers of an overly rationalized world.*

M.F.   Although it may not answer your question, I would say this: one should totally and absolutely suspect anything that claims to be a return. One reason is a logical one; there is in fact no such thing as a return. History, and the meticulous interest applied to history, is certainly one of the best defences against this theme of the return. For me, the history of madness or the studies of the prison ... were done in that precise manner because I knew full well – this is in fact what aggravated many people – that I was carrying out a historical analysis in such a manner that people *could* criticize the present, but it was impossible for them to say, 'Let's go back to the good old days when madmen in the eighteenth century ...' or, 'Let's go back to the days when the prison was not one of the principal instruments....' No; I think that history preserves us from that sort of ideology of the return.

P.R.   *Hence, the simple opposition between reason and history is rather silly ... choosing sides between the two....*

M.F.   Yes, well the problem for Habermas is, after all, to make a transcendental mode of thought spring forth against any historicism. I am, indeed, far more historicist and Nietzschean. I do not think that there is a proper usage of history or a proper usage of intrahistorical analysis – which is fairly lucid, by the way – that works precisely against this ideology of the return. A good study of peasant architecture in Europe, for example, would show the utter vanity of wanting to return to the little individual house with its thatched roof. History protects us from historicism – from a historicism that calls on the past to resolve the questions of the present.

P.R.   *It also reminds us that there is always a history; that those Modernists who wanted to suppress any reference to the past were making a mistake.*

M.F.   Of course.

P.R.   *Your next two books deal with sexuality among the Greeks and the early Christians. Are there any particular architectural dimensions to the issues you discuss?*

M.F.   I didn't find any; absolutely none. But what is interesting is that in imperial Rome there were, in fact, brothels, pleasure quarters, criminal areas, etc., and there was also one sort of quasi-public place of pleasure: the baths, the *thermes*. The baths were a very important place of pleasure and encounter, which slowly disappeared in Europe. In the Middle Ages, the baths were still a place of encounter between men and women as well as of men with men and women with women, although that is rarely talked about. What were referred to and condemned, as well as practised, were the encounters between men and women, which disappeared over the course of the sixteenth and seventeenth centuries.

P.R.   *In the Arab world it continues.*

M.F.   Yes; but in France it has largely ceased. It still existed in the nineteenth century. One sees it in *Les Enfants du Paradis*, and it is historically exact. One of the characters, Lacenaire, was – no one mentions it – a swine and a pimp who used young boys to attract older men and then blackmailed them; there is a scene that refers to this. It required all the naiveté and anti-homosexuality of the Surrealists to overlook the fact. So the baths continued to exist, as a place of sexual encounters. The bath was a sort of cathedral of pleasure at the heart of the city, where people could go as often as they want, where they walked about, picked each other up, met each other, took their pleasure, ate, drank, discussed....

P.R.   *So sex was not separated from the other pleasures. It was inscribed in the centre of the cities. It was public; it served a purpose....*

M.F.   That's right. Sexuality was obviously considered a social pleasure for the Greeks and the Romans. What is interesting about male homosexuality today – this has apparently been the case of female homosexuals for some time – is that their sexual relations are immediately translated into social relations and the social relations are understood as sexual relations. For the Greeks and the Romans, in a different fashion, sexual relations were located within social relations in the widest sense of the term. The baths were a place of sociality that included sexual relations.

One can directly compare the bath and the brothel. The brothel is in fact a place, and an architecture, of pleasure. There is, in fact, a very interesting form of sociality that was studied by Alain Corbin in *Les Filles de Noces*. The men of the city met at the brothel; they were tied to one another by the fact that the same women passed through their hands, that the same diseases and infections were communicated to them. There was a sociality of the brothel, but the sociality of the baths as it existed among the ancients – a new version of which could perhaps exist again – was completely different from the sociality of the brothel.

P.R.   *We now know a great deal about disciplinary architecture. What about confessional architecture – the kind of architecture that would be associated with a confessional technology?*

M.F.   You mean religious architecture? I think that it has been studied. There is the whole problem of a

monastery as xenophobic. There one finds precise regulations concerning life in common; affecting sleeping, eating, prayer, the place of each individual in all of that, the cells. All of this was programmed from very early on.

P.R.   *In a technology of power, of confession as opposed to discipline, space seems to play a central role as well.*

M.F.   Yes. Space is fundamental in any form of communal life; space is fundamental in any exercise of power. To make a parenthetical remark, I recall having been invited, in 1966, by a group of architects to do a study of space, of something that I called at the time 'heterotopias', those singular spaces to be found in some given social spaces whose functions are different or even the opposite of others. The architects worked on this, and at the end of the study someone spoke up – a Sartrean psychologist – who firebombed me, saying that *space* is reactionary and capitalist, but *history* and *becoming* are revolutionary. This absurd discourse was not at all unusual at the time. Today everyone would be convulsed with laughter at such a pronouncement, but not then.

P.R.   *Architects in particular, if they do choose to analyse an institutional building such as a hospital or a school in terms of its disciplinary function, would tend to focus primarily on the walls. After all, that is what they design. Your approach is perhaps more concerned with space, rather than architecture, in that the physical walls are only one aspect of the institution. How would you characterize the difference between these two approaches, between the building itself and space?*

M.F.   I think there is a difference in method and approach. It is true that, for me, architecture, in the very vague analyses of it that I have been able to conduct, is only taken as an element of support, to ensure a certain allocation of people in space, a *canalization* of their circulation, as well as the coding of their reciprocal relations. So it is not only considered as an element in space, but is especially thought of as a plunge into a field of social relations in which it brings about some specific effects.

For example, I know that there is a historian who is carrying out some interesting studies of the archaeology of the Middle Ages, in which he takes up the problem of architecture, of houses in the Middle Ages, in terms of the problem of the chimney. I think that he is in the process of showing that beginning at a certain moment it was possible to build a chimney inside the house – a chimney with a hearth, not simply an open room or a chimney outside the house; that at that moment all sorts of things changed and relations between individuals became possible. All of this seems very interesting to me, but the conclusion that he presented in an article was that the history of ideas and thoughts is useless.

What is, in fact, interesting is that the two are rigorously indivisible. Why did people struggle to find the way to put a chimney inside a house? Or why did they put their techniques to this use? So often in the history of techniques it takes years or even centuries to implement them. It is certain, and of capital importance, that this technique was a formative influence on new human relations, but it is impossible to think that it would have been developed and adapted had there not been in the play and strategy of human relations something that tended in that direction. What is interesting is always interconnection, not the primacy of this over that, which never has any meaning.

P.R.   *In your book* The Order of Things *you constructed certain vivid spatial metaphors to describe structures of thought. Why do you think spatial images are so evocative for these references? What is the relationship between these spatial metaphors describing disciplines and more concrete descriptions of institutional spaces?*

M.F.   It is quite possible that since I was interested in the problems of space, I used quite a number of spatial metaphors in *The Order of Things*, but usually these metaphors were not ones that I advanced, but ones that I was studying as objects. What is striking in the epistemological mutations and transformations of the seventeenth century is to see how the spatialization of knowledge was one of the factors in the constitution of this knowledge as a science. If the natural history and the classifications of Linneas were possible, it is for a certain number of reasons: on the one hand, there was literally a spatialization of the very object of their analyses, since they gave themselves the rule of studying and classifying a plant only on the basis of that which was visible. They didn't even want to use a microscope. All the traditional elements of knowledge, such as the medical functions of the plant, fell away. The object was spatialized. Subsequently, it was spatialized in so far as the principles of classification had to be found in the very structure of the plant: the number of elements, how they were arranged, their size, etc., and certain other elements, like the height of the plant. Then there was the spatialization into illustrations within books, which was only possible with certain printing techniques. Then the spatialization of the reproduction of the plants themselves, which was represented in books. All of these are spatial techniques, not metaphors.

P.R.   *Is the actual plan for a building – the precise drawing that becomes walls and windows – the same form of discourse as, say, a hierarchical pyramid that describes rather precisely relations between people, not only in space, but also in social life?*

M.F.   Well, I think there are a few simple and exceptional examples in which the architectural means reproduce, with more or less emphasis, the social hierarchies. There is the model of the military camp, where the military hierarchy is to be read in the ground itself, by the place occupied by the tents and the buildings reserved for each rank. It reproduces precisely through architecture a pyramid of power; but this is an exceptional example, as is everything military – privileged in society and of an extreme simplicity.

P.R.   *But the plan itself is not always an account of relations or power.*

M.F.   No. Fortunately for human imagination, things are a little more complicated than that.

P.R.   *Architecture is not, of course, a constant: it has a long tradition of changing preoccupations, changing systems, different rules. The* savoir *of architecture is partly the history of the profession, partly the evolution of a science of construction, and partly a rewriting of aesthetic theories. What do you think is particular about this form of* savoir *? Is it more like a natural science, or what you have called a 'dubious science'?*

M.F.   I can't exactly say that this distinction between sciences that are certain and those that are uncertain is of no interest – that would be avoiding the question – but I must say that what interests me more is to focus on what the Greeks called the *techne*, that is to say, a practical rationality governed by a conscious goal. I am not even sure if it is worth constantly asking the question of whether government can be the object of an exact science. On the other hand, if architecture, like the practice of government and the practice of other forms of social organization, is considered as a *techne*, possibly using elements of sciences like physics, for example, or statistics, etc. . . . , that is what is interesting. But if one wanted to do a history of architecture, I think that it

should be much more along the lines of that general history of the *techne*, rather than the histories of either the exact sciences or the inexact ones. The disadvantage of this word *techne*, I realize, is its relation to the word 'technology', which has a very specific meaning. A very narrow meaning is given to 'technology': one thinks of hard technology, the technology of wood, of fire, of electricity. Whereas government is also a function of technology: the government of individuals, the government of souls, the government of the self by the self, the government of families, the government of children, and so on. I believe that if one placed the history of architecture back in this general history of *techne*, in this wide sense of the word, one would have a more interesting guiding concept than by considering opposition between the exact sciences and the inexact ones.

NOTE

1   See the article on Foucault in *Skyline* (March 1982), p. 14.

REFERENCES

Bodin, J. (1576) *Six Livres de la république*, Paris.
Corbin, A. (1978) *Les Filles de Noces*, Aubier; trans. S. Alan, 1990, as *Women for Hire: Prostitution and Sexuality in France after 1850*, Cambridge, Mass.: Harvard University Press.
Foucault, M. (1966) *Les Mots et les choses: une archéologie des sciences humaines*, Paris: Gallimard; trans. 1970 as *The Order of Things: An Archaeology of the Human Sciences*, London: Tavistock.
LeMaitre, A. (1682) *La Métropolite*, Paris.

58   The spaces in between

David Gosling

It is widely accepted that planning methods over the last four decades have failed to produce a satisfactory environment. The proliferation of land-use plans, traffic studies and economic and demographic surveys has little to do with the way in which the city dweller perceives, uses and enjoys the urban environment (Gosling and Maitland 1984: 7). Physical urban planning has tended to be disregarded and replaced by long-term strategic planning. Four new planning acts became law in May 1990 and they are intended to replace the Planning Act, 1971. It is doubtful, however, that this new legislation will actually improve visual aspects of the environment or halt the degradation of cities which has occurred throughout the twentieth century. Yet, if the planning process is seen by most people to have become increasingly bureaucratized, recent experience in London Docklands suggests that the total abandonment of that process, with the creation of Enterprise Zones, does not work either, with spiralling land costs and speculation, wildly fluctuating property values, followed by market collapse and the resulting visual and environmental anarchy.

It has become apparent that the physical development of world cities has been going wrong and that the gulf between architects and planners must be bridged. Urban design is a rapidly emerging discipline which specifically attempts to build a bridge between the two vital areas of built form and land use within a three-dimensional framework. The recent projects of James Stirling and Michael Wilford in Germany have shown an understanding of these links. Possibly the most notable built example of an urban design project in Europe is the Stattsgallerie in Stuttgart by James Stirling and Michael Wilford, completed in 1984, in which the new art gallery was skilfully designed as a major urban link and pedestrian route between upper and lower city.

Wilford suggests that it is

> difficult to distinguish between urbanism, urban design and architecture save perhaps consideration of scale ... urban design *is* architecture and not a separate activity. It involves areas of concern which do not recognise boundaries between public and private domains. Urban design should integrate physical design with the power of policy making to shape the larger scale public realm and manage its growth and change.
>
> (Wilford 1990)

Wilford further noted that Aldo Rossi defined the city as an icon signifying attitudes to historical process and social change (Rossi 1981). William Safire suggests that the idea of 'icon' has its roots 'in semiotics, the theory of the relationships of signs in language ... an icon is a sign chosen to stand for its object because it looks like, or triggers an association with, the thing it represents' (Safire 1990: 12). Safire points out that a gas (petrol) station may have a star as its sign but that unless you are a Texan you are unlikely to associate the symbol with the name Texas. However, the symbol used by the Shell Oil Company is familiar to all and is an icon in semiotics.

The city as a cultural investment tends to be imbued with meaning for its inhabitants and is similar to a language in terms of syntactic structure or through the study of the meaning of signs, as in semiotics. Gordon Cullen suggests that 'communication between people and the towns they live in is primarily effected by signalization' (Cullen 1980).

URBAN DESIGN ANALYSIS

Urban design analytical systems were developed some three decades ago, particularly in the United States, by such authorities as Kevin Lynch and Gyorgy Kepes at the Massachusetts Institute of Technology, and Donald Appleyard at the University of California (Berkeley). The pioneering work of Kevin Lynch (1960) was the first attempt to test user response at a city scale. In urban design practice, there are two quite different schools of thought. One approach, relating to Lynch, is characterized by user response, advocacy planning and consumer surveys. The other grows out of an objective analysis of the three-dimensional fabric of the city including morphological and typological studies. Ideally, for urban design to be truly effective, both these forms of analysis need to be combined into a single approach.

The results of Lynch's work were in the form of maps showing the existence of perceived images such as nodes, landmarks, barriers, districts and monuments (see Figures 1 and 2). An extension of this idea was the more subjective analysis developed originally in the 1920s at the Bauhaus as part of Gestalt psychology, and later by László Moholy-Nagy (1956) and Gyorgy Kepes (1956) in the United States. In this, areas of tranquillity, repose, confusion, permeability and imageability can be defined either by the urban designers themselves or from surveys of various groups of respondents such as residents, inhabitants and visitors, or different age groups.

The urban designer working in such a manner needs

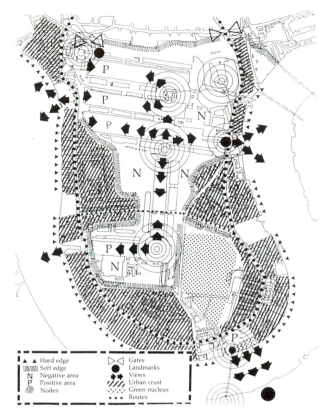

Figure 1 Urban visual analysis based upon Kevin Lynch's studies, Isle of Dogs, London, 1982, by David Gosling.

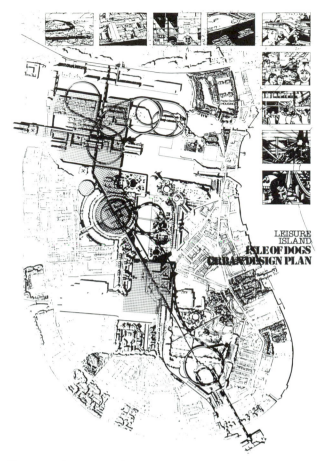

Figure 2 Alternative urban design study for a Royal Academy exhibition, 1984, based upon Nicholas Hawksmoor's 'Greenwich Axis' (1714), Isle of Dogs, London, by David Gosling and John Ferguson.

to be able to appreciate both subjective and objective data in their spatial context, and to make connections between the many different factors under consideration. In essence, what is required is a way of representing this information in a manner which integrates it with the three-dimensional physical fabric. Such a tool should allow for easy progression from analysis to synthesis without interrupting the flow of thought or imposing artificially discrete steps in the design process. In terms of information technology, such a facility might be created by linking relational data-base systems (RDB) and geographical information systems (GIS) to ground surface models and computer-aided design (CAD), though such a cumbersome combination is unlikely to prove to be a satisfactory design tool for analysis and eventual synthesis.

Had Lynch or Appleyard had access to the advanced computer techniques available today, an urban design process might easily have been incorporated into British and American planning legislation. There is clearly a need for an urban design planning system which can identify problems of the existing city fabric, analyse the needs, aspirations and opinions of the inhabitants as well as committees, and put forward proposals which are easily understood by those inhabitants and committees. Present planning tools are negative in the way in which they are used for development control purposes, and are not easily understood from either a graphical or literary point of view.

Lynch, in trying to analyse the city images of the inhabitants, had to rely upon relatively small sample surveys and manual data processing. Appleyard, in his attempts to investigate the visual problems and significance of movement systems (particularly urban highway design) relied upon expensive scale models, 16 mm. film cameras, gantries and modelscopes. Video technology and computer-based animation techniques would have played an important role in this research had they been available at the time. In fact, such techniques could create what Gordon Cullen described in his writing, also three decades ago, as 'serial vision' in the form of sequential, computer-generated three-dimensional images. Research by psychologists, such as David Canter (1977) at the University of Surrey, into such areas as cognitive mapping would also have been greatly enhanced by computer-generated systems.

THE URBAN DESIGN PLAN

An urban design plan can be seen as the amalgam of two sectors – the public realm and the private realm. The public realm is concerned with the public spaces formed by: new and existing buildings; public movement systems (including pedestrian routes, access roads and rapid transit systems); and the squares, streets, arcades, parks and open spaces of the *quartier* (district). All of these elements make up the urban morphology, or physical shape of the city. They are the 'Spaces in Between' which, as Wilford says, bring about the indivisibility of building from place. The visual harmony and social success of the city is possible only if urban development or redevelopment is within a public framework which has sufficient coherence and identity. This is the purpose of an urban design plan as opposed to an urban design guide (such as the Essex design guide) which sets down rules about detailed architectural design and the use of materials. The urban design plan is *not* a master plan in the sense that it is finite and fixed. Instead it should be flexible, variable and capable of inumerable permutations and change.

The public realm, then, is the skeletal structure of the city; it does not necessarily imply that it is based entirely upon public-sector investment. Given a public realm plan, as part of the urban design process, which is sufficiently strong and functional as well as visually memorable, and a system which is easy to navigate and enjoy, then the private realm of buildings created within this framework can be created with greater freedom of architectural expression, whether they are public buildings, such as schools, or private buildings, such as offices and apartments.

Without a strong public realm, visual anarchy prevails and the very fabric of the city is destroyed. A public realm plan must have flexibility for incremental growth as well as change. In British planning legislation, land-use control, zoning, building densities, plot ratios and traffic systems are catered for at one end of the spectrum. Development control, including aesthetic guidance, at the other end, does not include statutory provision for the urban design plan. This should occupy the present void in the centre of the planning process.

GRAPHIC TECHNIQUES AND THE PLANNING PROCESS

Most urban design proposals are in the form of 'interventions' in the existing city fabric. It is important that the historical layering process of the city and its morphological form are fully understood, and that later additions are seen as accretions to the fabric rather than autonomous insertions. 'Figure-ground' studies are popularly used to analyse the disposition of built form and void which create the texture of the urban fabric and identify the density and direction of the urban grain. Such techniques are, of course, not new. It has been noted that they relate to the Gestalt theories of the 1920s and the phenomenon of figure-ground goes even further back, to Giambattista Nolli's plan of Rome in 1748. The concept of urban design relies on a classic figure-ground reversal, in which what is normally regarded as figure (buildings) must be read as ground, and what is normally seen as ground (the surrounding spaces) becomes figure. Nolli's plan extended this technique to include the ground-level plans of the major churches, temples and basilicas, since he regarded them as extensions of the public realm carved out of building blocks which were represented by black tones. The production of figure-ground studies by computer, rather than burdensome hand-drawn techniques, would make them a normal part of analysis.

Aerial photographs, or perspectives traced from photographs, provide a base illustration for analytical overlays. Thus, if computer-generated images of air views of cities could be overlaid by cognitive maps produced from opinion surveys taken from inhabitants of or visitors to that city, a major step forward could be taken along the lines of citizen participation in the planning process and advocacy planning. This would replace the somewhat primitive analytical maps of Lynch's nodes, barriers and landmarks, which are still used by planners today.

Such experiences and responses could be expressed in an animated form (as in Cullen's idea of 'serial vision'), with computer-generated helicopter rides over the city, the pedestrian's walk through the city at ground level, the car driver's view of the city, or the rapid transit passenger's view of the city. These might be used in the form of analytical presentations to public meetings or official committees. Computer-generated images are already widely used in various ways and are the key to an understanding of the spatial sequences of the urban environment, and whether the spatial structure of the city is coherent or otherwise.

URBAN DESIGN GUIDELINES

Urban design guidelines are a commonly used tool in American city planning. They differ substantially from design guides in Great Britain, which tend to address detailed architectural design issues mainly associated with domestic architecture and residential estates. American urban design guidelines are far more prescriptive in nature, but necessarily so in the case of complex and massive city-centre redevelopment schemes. The Canary Wharf Urban Design Guidelines prepared by Skidmore, Owings and Merrill of Chicago are intended to set rules for the design of major buildings on individual plots within the urban complex. That they produce an architectural imagery which has been widely criticized is probably due to a misunderstanding on the part of the American architects concerning the precedent and nature of historical London. It was suggested that Georgian London was, in part, an inspiration for the design of Canary Wharf. However, the carefully conceived proportions of terrace housing and their relationship to the space of tree-lined squares and gardens of Bloomsbury have little to do with the enormous spatial relationships between fifty-storey skyscrapers and massive boulevards. Other urban design guidelines have been employed with greater success in cities such as Boston, Baltimore and San Francisco.

THE PUBLIC REALM PLAN

In an issue of the American periodical *Progressive Architecture* (January 1989: 110–12), a design award in urban design and planning was given to Johnson Fain, Pereira Associates for Design Guidelines for Highway III in Indian Wells, California. This was the result of the City Council's decision to limit future commercial development of highway frontage through an urban design plan that determines land uses, circulation improvements and landscape, and would be enforced through urban design guidelines and development controls. It was praised by the assessors for its sensitivity and its explicit nature in controlling strip development on a 3½ mile (6 km.) stretch of highway. Instead of using traditional zonal techniques, it manipulates formal elements designed as a series of events and nodes. It is perhaps the first implementation of a sequential urban design guideline document.

The Heron Quay Urban Design Guidelines, completed in September 1988 and subsequently commented upon by Peter Buchanan (1989: 40), were based upon the the Skidmore, Owings and Merrill precedent. The Canary Wharf Guidelines are two-dimensional control systems, but Heron Quay is three-dimensional and capable of adaptation through CAD systems. The sequential fly-round perspectives, for example, were incorporated in the document.

The importance of this study is that it can be seen as a major development in urban design methodology capable of eventual incorporation into planning legislation on a statutory basis. The present non-statutory status creates current difficulties in the realization of urban design plans, whereas building regulations affecting architecture and planning regulations affecting land use are an accepted part of legislation.

If the Heron Quay Design Guidelines may be considered, in retrospect, as too prescriptive and too restrictive for individual architectural designs, the positive factors include the definition and description of public spaces, boulevards, waterspace relationships and building relationships. The guidelines address aspects of the public realm, such as the connection and interface between buildings and streets and other public spaces. These are the relationships between horizontal and vertical elements of the city. An applied system of colonnades, arcades, promenades, canopies, street walls, water walls and gateways supplements the more usual regulations concerning floor areas and permitted uses. In viewing the urban context, it is the pedestrian's reaction to the spatial sequence and its relationship to the first

three or four storeys of the adjacent buildings which is of primary importance. Colonnade systems, for example, have provided an ordering element throughout the history of architecture, whether it is Brunelleschi's Founding Hospital in Florence or the Federal Office district in late twentieth-century Washington.

The containment volume regulations are probably the most controversial elements of the guide, in that they define building envelopes, including set-back planes and horizontal expression lines. Nevertheless, the attempt to bring urban articulation into the system, combined with site easements, might provide a satisfactory planning evaluation method for the first time. Present tools, including the laborious assessment of individual proposals, item by item, could be replaced by more objective and infinitely quicker appraisal which would respond to the accelerating process of urban change in all major cities.

This kind of system would require a responsive information technology language which is applicable to urban design in the same way that a responsive language already exists in computer-aided architectural design. A typical list of urban elements might be allocated in the following categories:

1   **Site**: outlines and boundaries; plot ratios; building densities; daylighting; sunlighting; overshadowing; set-backs; car parking; building envelopes; sloped massing planes; site footprints; building floor plates; vertical access; horizontal access.

2   **Streets**: length; width; gradient; curve; sequence; connections; continuity; discontinuity; traffic generation; traffic flows; traffic noise; underground infrastructure (sewerage, water, electricity, telecommunications, gas, cable television, fibre-optic systems); boulevards; tree avenues; landscaping; traffic–pedestrian interface; alleys; service streets; footstreets; pedestrian ways/networks; traffic feeders; dual carriageways; urban motorways; street transit systems.

3   **Public spaces**: parks; built forms; squares; piazzas; plazas; greens; gardens; arcades; *quartiers*; nodes; landmarks; monuments; atria; foyers; *loggias*; gateways; vistas.

4   **Building envelopes**: streetwalls; waterwalls; colonnades; cornices; building lines; building heights; building surfaces; peristyles; real walls; false walls; screens; free-standing walls.

APPLICATIONS

It has already been noted that the pioneering work of Lynch and others could be developed into testing use response to the urban environment at a city scale, with sampling methods allowing surveys on a scale unimaginable in the days of data-card processing. CAD images could provide a vivid alternative allowing overlays of user response images. In addition, analytical methods could be used for a vivid mapping system of urban planning control such as land use, land and rental values, and traffic flows, as well as environmental issues such as sunlighting, aerodynamics and traffic noise evaluation. Guidelines should avoid instructing architects at detailed design level but should be more concerned with the compatibility of adjacent building massing, building envelopes, sloped massing planes, and so on. There should be some built-in flexibility in terms of maximum height, minimum height, maximum and minimum floor areas, alternative uses, and horizontal and vertical projections such as balconies. The guidelines could also test agreed plot ratios, densities, site footprints, and building floorplates, as well as environmental considerations such as car parking, overshadowing, daylighting, wind vortices and traffic-generated noise-levels.

The most positive attributes of these techniques would concern the public realm itself: the interface between the private realm of built form and the public realm of city spaces and networks, such as colonnades, arcades, water walls and street walls. What is proposed is the application of CAD techniques to public realm planning. It is an attempt to discard and replace the cumbersome and unworkable development control system with a positive, creative planning framework.

Accompanying illustrations testing these ideas include the 1988 Heron Quay Urban Design Guidelines, which were seen as a first step towards changing the planning process (see Figures 3 and 4). The precedent studies upon which these were based were in the form of a group of Sheffield architectural theses written in

Figure 4 *Heron Quay, London Docklands: computer-generated sequential perspective, 1988, by David Gosling and Stephen Proctor in association with Scott, Brownrigg and Turner.*

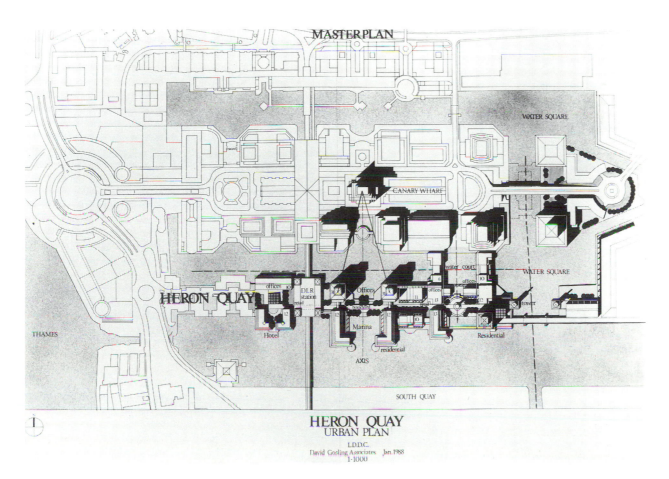

Figure 3 *Heron Quay Urban Design Plan, by David Gosling and Stephen Proctor.*

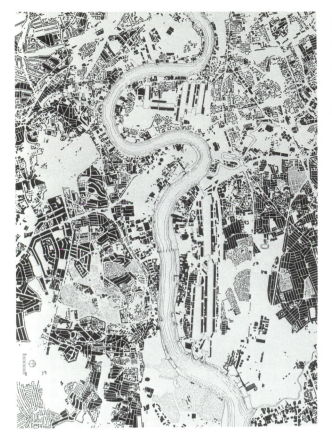

Figure 5

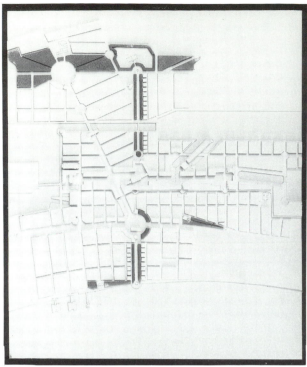

Figure 7

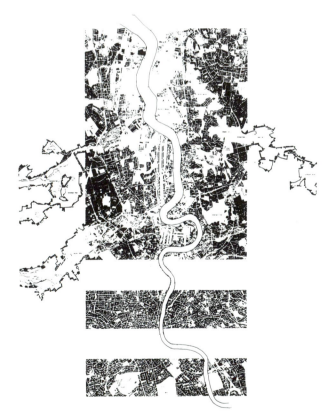

Figure 6

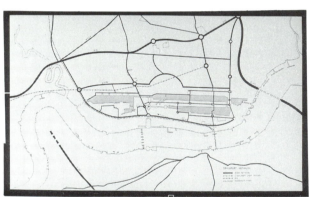

Figure 5 *Existing figure-ground, Royal Docks Study, 1985, Sheffield University thesis by Proctor, Soper, MacDonald and Simons (tutors: Michael Wilford and David Gosling).*

Figure 6 *Figure-ground in the context of the city, Royal Docks Study, 1985, Sheffield University thesis by Proctor, Soper, MacDonald and Simons (tutors: Michael Wilford and David Gosling).*

Figure 7 *Massing study, Royal Docks Study, 1985, Sheffield University thesis by Proctor, Soper, MacDonald and Simons (tutors: Michael Wilford and David Gosling).*

1984–5. Seen as an antidote to the perceived need to build high to achieve sufficient densities to recoup land costs and land values, the authors of the Heron Quay Guidelines devised an alternative urban design strategy. It indicates a different design approach which might achieve a better balance between community aspirations and commercial necessity.

Dock City was a project based on the derelict Royal Docks of London and offered an urban revitalization strategy for an abandoned industrial area within the metropolis (see Figures 5–8). Its intention was to repair the urban structure, a phenomenon of post-industrial Europe and the product of economic decline and the reorganization of operational procedures within the industrial and commercial sectors. The 'figure-ground' studies were used by the authors to analyse the disposition of built form and void, creating the texture of the urban fabric and identifying the density and direction of the urban grain. In this way, boundaries and districts were established. Similar studies were made of both physical characteristics (patterns of open landscape, topography, vistas, urban landmarks, etc.) and functional data (road networks and transportation systems). The extensive analysis enabled the designers to identify existing morphological patterns and provide a guide for the future development of the old docks, whilst maintaining coherence within the fabric rather than the sudden obliteration of themes and structures embedded within the historical matrix. It is an interlacing of themes and systems.

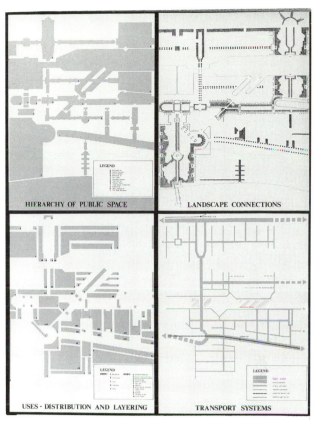

Figure 8 *Royal Docks Study, 1985, Sheffield University thesis by Proctor, Soper, MacDonald and Simons (tutors: Michael Wilford and David Gosling).*

REFERENCES

Buchanan, P. (1989) 'Quays to design', *Architectural Review* 185 (1106): 39–44.

Canter, D. (1977) *The Psychology of Place*, New York: St Martin's Press.

Cullen, G. (1971) *The Concise Townscape*, London: Architectural Press; first published as *Townscape*, 1961.

——— (1980) 'Language of gestures', in G. Broadbent, R. Bunt and C. Jencks (eds) *Signs, Symbols and Architecture*, New York: J. Wiley.

Gosling, D. and Maitland, B. (1984) *Concepts of Urban Design*, London and New York: Academy Editions, St Martin's Press.

Kepes, G. (1956) *The New Landscape*, Chicago: Paul Theobald.

Lynch, K. (1960) *The Image of the City*, Cambridge, Mass.: MIT Press.

Moholy-Nagy, L. (1956) *Vision in Motion*, Chicago: Paul Theobald.

Rossi, A. (1979) *Projects and Drawings*, London: Academy Editions.

Safire, W. (1990) 'On language', *New York Times*, 4 February: 12–14.

FURTHER READING

Alexander, C. (1979) *The Timeless Way of Building*, Vol. I, New York: Oxford University Press.

——— (1987) *A New Theory of Urban Design*, New York: Oxford University Press.

Alexander, C., Ishikawa, S. and Silverstein, M. (1977) *A Pattern Language*, Vol. III, New York: Oxford University Press.

Appleyard, D., Lynch, K. and Myer, J.R. (1964) *The View From the Road*, Cambridge, Mass.: MIT Press.

Architectural Design (1988) Special Issue, Deconstruction I and II.

Arnell, P. and Bickford, T. (1984) *James Stirling: Buildings and Projects*, New York: Rizzoli.

Banham, P. Reyner (1976) *Megastructure: Urban Futures of the Recent Past*, London: Thames & Hudson.

Benevolo, L. (1967) *The Origins of Modern Town Planning*, Cambridge, Mass.: MIT Press.

Bloomer, K.C. and Moore, C.W. (1977) *Body, Memory and Architecture*, New Haven: Yale University Press.

Calhoun, J.B. (1971) 'Space and the strategy of life' in A.H. Esser, (ed.) *Behaviour and Enviroment*, New York: Plenum Press.

Coleman, A. (1985) *Utopia on Trial*, London: Shipman.

Davis, B. (ed.) (1989) *Remaking Cities*, Pittsburgh: Pittsburgh University Press.

Downs, R.M. and Stea, D. (1977) *Maps in Minds: Reflections on Cognitive Mapping*, New York: Harper & Row.

Duany, A. and Plater-Zyberk, E. (1986) 'The form of the American city', *Lotus International* 50: 2.

Eco, U. (1976) *A Theory of Semiotics*, Bloomington: Indiana University Press.

Eisenstein, S. (1957) *The Film Sense*, New York: Meridien Books.

Fishman, R. (1982) *Urban Utopias in the 20th Century: Ebenezer Howard, Frank Lloyd Wright and Le Corbusier*, Cambridge, Mass.: MIT Press.

Gibson, J. (1950) *The Perception of the Visual World*, Boston: Houghton, Mifflin.

Giedion, S. (1959) *Space, Time and Architecture*, Cambridge, Mass.: Harvard University Press.

Greenbie, B. (1981) *Spaces: Dimensions of the Human Landscape*, New Haven: Yale University Press.

Howard, E. (1898, 1902) *Garden Cities of Tomorow: A Peaceful Path to Reform*, Eastbourne: Attic Books, 1985.

Katz, D. (1951) *Gestalt Psychology*, trans. R. Tyson, London: Methuen.

Koolhaas, R. (1978) *Delirious New York*, New York: Oxford University Press.

Krier, R. (1979) *Urban Space*, London: Academy Editions.

—— (1982) *On Architecture*, New York: St Martin's Press.

—— (1988) *Architectural Composition*, London: Academy Editions.

Lawson, B. (1980) *How Designers Think*, 2nd edn 1990, Butterworth.

Le Corbusier (1924) *The City of Tomorrow*, trans. F. Etchells, 1971, London: Architectural Press.

Lynch, K. (1976a) *What Time is this Place?*, Cambridge, Mass.: MIT Press.

—— (1976b) *Managing the Sense of a Region*, Cambridge, Mass.: MIT Press.

Miliutin, N.A. (1974) *Sotsgorod: The Problem of Building Socialist Cities*, Cambridge, Mass.: MIT Press.

Mumford, L. (1955) *The Human Prospect*, Boston: Beacon Press.

Newman, O. (1972) *Defensible Space; People and Design in the Violent City*, London: Architectural Press.

Norberg-Schulz, C. (1963) *Intentions in Architecture*, Universitetsforlaget and Allen & Unwin.

—— (1971) *Existence, Space and Architecture*, London: Studio Vista.

Rabbit, P. (1971) *Drop City*, New York: Olympia Press.

—— (1981) *Architecture of the City*, Cambridge, Mass.: Opposition Books, MIT Press.

Seelig, M.Y. (1978) *The Architecture of Self-Help Communities*, New York: Architectural Record Books.

Tafuri, M. (1976) *Architecture and Utopia*, Cambridge, Mass.: MIT Press.

—— (1980) *Theories and History of Architecture*, New York: Harper & Row.

Venturi, R., Brown, D.S., and Izenow, S. (1972) *Learning from Las Vegas*, Cambridge, Mass.: MIT Press.

Wilford, M. (1990) Wolfson Memorial Lecture, University of Cincinatti, Ohio, 17 May.

Wulf, F. (1922) 'Über die Veränderung von Verstellungen' (Gedächtnis und Gestalt), in W.D. Ellis (ed.) (1938) *A Source Book of Gestalt Psychology*, London: Routledge & Kegan Paul.

59 The theory of space in architecture

Cornelis Van de Ven

Architecture is the art of space, and all architectural innovations arise from new concepts of space – intuitive concepts of space preceeding the intellectual recognition of spatial ideas. Simultaneously, the development of ideas of space in the theory of architecture finds its origin in new visions of space in the architecture of that day.

The development of the spatial concepts therefore can only be investigated by the often limited existence of original intellectual ideas. Architecture is art, not science, therefore the intellectual ideas in architecture are impossible without the emotion of the artistic experience. There is one thing that architecture and science have in common: both follow 'inner logic'; however, the experience of architecture and its theory are not always a logical unity.

The history of space in architecture is an account of often contradictory statements by leading architects and theorists. There are always different opinions on the value of spatial concepts in architecture, and it is the investigation of the development of ideas concerning space which brings a number of conclusions to the fore.

The first and most important of all conclusions concerns the general relationship between the idea of space and modern architecture. Space as an architectural idea appeared for the first time in the aesthetic theories of the late nineteenth century, or, more precisely, in the early 1890s. This coincided with the visible emergence of modern architecture, in particular with the Art Nouveau movement. It can be argued that the Art Nouveau represents the first real modern movement in architecture, because it broke definitely with the eclectic tendencies of the nineteenth century. In Art Nouveau both ornament and construction were fused into a new unity; but above all, Art Nouveau was the first movement that visualized the new consciousness of spatial abstraction. The new awareness of the idea of space, as an architectural principle, in the theories of the early 1890s is not a pure coincidence; the fact that the first ideas of space emerged together with the first movement of modern architecture, Art Nouveau, demonstrates that the idea of space is inherent to modern architecture.

The second conclusion concerns the effect the new idea had upon the position of architecture in relation to other visual arts. From the Hegelian aesthetic system, which shaped the stream of aesthetic thinking in the nineteenth century, two major aspects can be derived: beauty in art is attained by the perfect expression of an idea; and, consequently, the hierarchy of the arts will be defined by the degree of immateriality in the means of expression.

The identification of architecture with space in the early 1890s promoted architecture, unquestionably, as the *ars magna*, because space is, by definition, the most immaterial of all means of artistic expression. This conclusion is supported on the one hand by the unprecedented interest in architecture of art historians, and, on the other, by the remarkable movement of painters and sculptors into the field of architecture.

Examples of such art historians are Schmarsow, Hildebrand, Lipps, Riegl, Wölfflin, Worringer, Brinckmann, Scott, Sörgel, Frankl and Giedion. Typical of the artists are van de Velde, Endell, Behrens, Olbrich, Lauweriks, Le Corbusier, van Doesburg, Tatlin, Lissitzky, Malevich, Finsterlin, Moholy-Nagy, Wijdeveld and Kiesler, all of whom were occupied with the synthesis of painting, sculpture and architectural design, with, however, an architectural prevalence in their work. True, not all of these artists carried the new idea of space in their 'aesthetic manifestos'; some had romantic-industrialist views, and others, socio-cultural traditions that called for a synthesis of the arts (*Gesamtkunstwerk*); but the idea of space proved to be the only 'logic' or inherent principle, that was, and still is, capable of crossing the arbitrary boundaries dividing the arts. The use of the concept of space as a catalyst leading to the *Gesamtkunstwerk* culminated in the work of van Doesburg, Lissitzky and, in the Bauhaus school, of Gropius and Moholy-Nagy.

In short it can be concluded that the idea of space contributed to the belief in the early twentieth century that architecture fulfilled a principal role in the establishment of the total work of art.

Third, the aesthetics of space, produced by the majority of the 'third generation' theorists in the 1920s, seem quite antithetical to the ideal of *Gesamtkunstwerk* among contemporary avant-garde architects. Due to the academic tradition in aesthetics since the time of Kant, art historians got entangled in defining the boundaries between the fine arts, especially since the new concepts of space and time were dissolving these boundaries. This created an unbridgeable gap between the artists and the art scholars, with unfortunate side-effects on art education in general. It was to the great credit of Giedion that co-operation was restored between the two diverging creative disciplines.

As a result of these events, it can be concluded that

hierarchical systems of art were proven to be inadequate, in particular, after the development of new concepts of space and time which involved the total environment and blurred the formal distinctions between the fine arts.

The fourth important conclusion deals with the relationship between the idea of space and the problem of 'style'.

Throughout the nineteenth century, most architectural theorists struggled with the significant question 'What is style?'. The manifold eclectic tendencies of the nineteenth and early twentieth century were symptomatic of the architectural confusion that gave rise to this question.

Many attempted to provide guidelines to a way out of this aesthetic maze: Ruskin discussed the concept of 'style' in 1848; Semper developed his '*Stillehere*' in 1860; Berlage dealt thoroughly with the problem in 1904; van de Velde examined the question of 'new style' in 1907; Scott defined 'style' as 'coherence' in 1914; Steiner searched for ways to a new Style in 1914; and, to close the ranks, van Doesburg's magazine was called *De Stijl* (1917–31).

The dispute around the concept of 'style' was aggravated by the seemingly endless conflict between the appearance and reality of material form in architecture or, as van de Velde put it, between '*Schein und Sein*'. Ruskin attached greatest value to ornament, whereas van de Velde strove for the amalgamation of ornament and structure into a new unity.

The idea of space, once it had been introduced and generally accepted, allowed architects and theorists to escape from nineteenth-century hybrid aspects in the material treatment of Style. The unambiguous doctrine of Berlage, equating style with space, caused a breakthrough in the formation of the modern movements in architecture.

The idea of space established a new prospect that finally abolished eclecticism, because it gave rise to an immaterial meaning to the concept of Style.

The conclusions which have been drawn so far are limited to the rise of the idea of space in general. As to the evolution of its content, two major trends seem to have prevailed. From the introduction of the idea of space in about 1890, the aesthetic interpretation confronted the functional one. Schmarsow defended the functionalist tradition of Semper and disputed the view of Riegl, Hildebrand and Wölfflin, where the aesthetic idea of space ('*Raumaesthetik*') prevailed.

Both trends, aesthetic and functional, emerged from the nineteenth-century arguments about the nature of beauty. On the one hand, Durand, Semper, Schmarsow and, later, Berlage considered beauty to be an expression of function, an attitude called *Sachlichkeit* since the beginning of the twentieth century. It is not at all surprising that the proto-modernists equated beauty with space. Space embodied, logically, our functional

activities in three dimensions. On the other hand, opposition came from the Rieglian school of thinking, which considered space to be a result of cultural artistic volition ('*Kunstwollen*'). This attitude to space as an artistic perception came to full fruition in the *l'art pour l'art* movements of Cubism, De Stijl and El Lissitzky's Suprematism.

It was the great skill of Gropius that prevented the segregation of art and function, initially in the German Werkbund, and later in the Bauhaus school; perhaps Gropius foresaw that Functionalism might take over completely. Nevertheless, after 1930, Neue Sachlichkeit (New Objectivity) became the face of international architecture, when it became evident that functionalist-materialist theories of space overruled the weaker, artistic ones.

Yet Functionalism as a true architectural movement transformed into 'functionalism' in its narrowest sense. The tragedy was that the process of formal abstraction, resulting from the idea of space, reduced Functionalist aesthetics to mere repetition and *Minimum-Existenz*. The functional beauty of Neue Sachlichkeit, coinciding with economic building techniques, has gradually deteriorated into poor 'profit-making' practices for building the environment.

The idea of space, initially both an aesthetic and a functional concept, evolved into a prevailing functional principle in the first half of our century.

The physical content of the idea of space caused architectural ideas to move in a direction parallel to ideas on space in philosophy and natural sciences. In the first part of this essay, these lines were treated as concisely as possible. One of the most stunning finds was a lucid essay by Albert Einstein in 1953 on the various meanings of space in physics, which are directly applicable to the variety of physical interpretations in architecture. Einstein's distinctions were threefold: (1) the concept of space as a place indentifiable by a name; (2) the concept of absolute space; and (3) the four-dimensional concept of relative space.

One may reason, *a posteriori*, that architecture has simply borrowed from innovations in the sciences, and the whole idea of space–time within architecture is an afterthought; however, cultural overlappings within the *Zeitgeist* refute such facile deductions. The concept of space–time was already explicit in Hildebrand's kinetic vision, as early as 1893; the fourth dimension was used by the Cubists in 1912. Van Doesburg suggested his aesthetics of space–time in 1916, the same year in which Einstein formalized his (general) theory of relativity. Such cultural intertwining justifies the standpoint that architecture created an aesthetic interpretation of space, whereas physics, in its own right, developed a scientific one.

Thanks to the clarity of vision of the physicists, we are now able to disentangle the often hybrid statements of the artists. Einstein's three conceptions of space in physics also apply to architecture, for the simple reason that all three exist simultaneously in any work of humanity. Yet the concept of space–time has been gradually replaced, since the early 1960s, by the more existential concept of 'place'. Despite such shifts in emphasis, regardless of the course architecture may take, any work of architecture follows three premises of physical space: that of space as place; that of the absolute concept of three-dimensional space; and that of the relative concept of space–time.

The positive attitude to space is generally considered the main theme; however, the negative attitude appears to be just as important. Theorists, such as Riegl and Wölfflin, dwelled upon the phenomenon of *horror vacui*, or 'Raumscheu', because it is our natural reaction to the bewildering chaos of space around us.

The gist of the argument is that space is a *sine qua non* in architecture, but corporeal mass in all its aspects is equally meaningful. How meaningful corporeal mass is can be judged from the general theory of empathy. The process of empathy encompasses personal involvement with the internal dynamics of structural mass, as well as the message that radiates from external surface treatment. For example, the work of the contemporary architect Robert Venturi shows that commercial propaganda is recognized as the most important method of directly establishing empathic communication with the consumer of today. It continues – in modern terms – the function of the cathedral's west front: a powerful religious propaganda to draw in the medieval crowds.

Theories to explain the dread of space in architecture emerged soon after the positive aspects of space had been established. At first, the discovery of claustrophobia in psychology influenced Sitte's attitude to the perception of urban space. Later, in the beginning of this century, Riegl and Worringer propounded that the love for corporeal mass was an essential aesthetic urge of humanity – a notion that came to a climax in the Expressionist movement soon afterwards.

Since the 1970s, Post-Modern architecture shows a revival of interest in corporeal mass and its symbolic meaning and message, rather than in space. The reasons are twofold; first, the recognition that getting the user involved depends on the external typology of the architectural mass and, second, the recognition that using the envelope of the building as the message itself is quite effective, especially in modern, commercial situations. These two recognitions gained aesthetic interest in the 1960s and 1970s, thanks to the work of Louis Kahn, and the architectural research of Venturi in Las Vegas. In general we may conclude that positivist ideas of space have evoked the recognition that its negation, mass, is just as important, due to the perceptional and behavioural influence of empathy.

The negation of space, and its antagonism, the negation of mass, have led architectural theorists to recognize that perhaps the only correct answer to the dilemma will be found in a balance of the two aspects. This attitude has been developed in the materialist theory of spatio-plastic unity. This notion can be traced as the leitmotiv of the theories of Sitte, Schmarsow, Brinckmann, Frankl, Sörgel and Giedion, from 1888 until 1941. In this respect, the materialist interpenetration of interior and exterior space (*Raumdurchdringung*) culminated in the De Stijl models and the work of Frank Lloyd Wright. Here too, the aesthetic system of Hegel was the starting-point, since spatio-plastic relationships were indicative of the particularities of the various style-periods in architecture.

In this century, modern movements have either intensified the expression of space (e.g. De Stijl) or intensified the expression of mass (e.g. Expressionism), or they have intensified the interpenetration of both (Giedion's 'Universal Architecture'). Modern material renewal in architecture will modify, in one way or another, these seemingly exhausted possibilities; however, the innate contradiction between interior and exterior space, as propounded by Sitte before 1890, is still a vital inspiration to design. We can draw the conclusion that from a material standpoint, the idea of space leads to the thesis of spatio-plastic unity, finding expression in three ways: exterior space (mass); interior space; and culminating in the interpenetration of both interior and exterior space. All renewal in spatial expression will start from one of these universal premises.

The definition of an aesthetic perception of space was initiated in 1893 with the theory of form by Hildebrand. His knowledge of the psychology of perception allowed him to develop the startling thesis of kinetic vision that became, later, the notion of space–time, or Moholy-Nagy's vision in motion. Other theorists, such as Lipps, Riegl and Wölfflin, attached great value to Hildebrand's amazing relief-concept, a thesis that was paralleled in the two-dimensional perception of space by the pre-Cubist philosopher Bergson. Two-dimensional space perception advanced further with synthetic Cubism, Suprematism and its extreme form, Mondrian's Neo-Plastic conceptions.

Four-dimensionality of space perception was developed by the Futurists (the succession of movement) and in Moholy-Nagy and van Doesburg's concept of space–time (the simultaneity of movement). These artistic perceptions exerted a great influence on the perceptional systems of theorists such as Paul Frankl and Dagobert Frey. The aesthetics of space-perception were brilliantly defined by El Lissitzky in 1925, when he derived four ways of seeing space from the various ways that the image or illusion of space can be evoked. From his thesis, we may conclude the general theory that all possible aspects of the perception of space can be reduced to four: (1) planimetric or two-dimensional space; (2) one-point perspective or three-dimensional space; (3) 'irrational' space–time, or four-dimensional space; and (4) imaginary space as produced by motion pictures. Our perception of architectural space is, in one way or another, the synthesis of these four phenomena.

FURTHER READING

Van de Ven, C. (1977) *Space in Architecture. The Evolution of a New Idea in the Theory and History of the Modern Movements,* 3rd revised edn 1987, Assen/Maastricht: Van Gorcum.

SECTION 4.3

Elements of architecture

The elements that might be thought to constitute a basic 'grammar' of architectural form are many and have been variously defined. The most comprehensive attempt yet made at codifying these and integrating them into a coherent design language was the French Beaux-Arts system developed in the nineteenth century. The Beaux-Arts method, which had strict rules for progression from the study of the individual components of a building (doors, windows, stairs, etc.) to their arrangement in the plan and elevation, rested on the rich formal vocabulary of the classical tradition. This ensured that the increasingly abstract compositions of Beaux-Arts designers never entirely lost their comprehensibility, nor the constituent parts their autonomy within the broader scheme.

When the Modern Movement rejected this carefully crafted system for articulating built form and embraced modern technology and the abstract formal/spatial language of the fine artists, it gained much freedom of expression. Since architectural form was now conceived as part of a space–time continuum, the objective was to destroy the boundaries between the different structural elements of a building. The price for this liberation from the formal conventions and material constraints of traditional ways of building was an ever-present risk of visual anarchy and the breakdown of communication between designers and their public.

So far none of the efforts to restore the balance by establishing an alternative grammar based on the forms and spatial arrangements developed by the Modernists and their progeny has met with much success. This gave rise to renewed calls for a return to the classical tradition with its emphasis on typological enquiry and elemental composition.

On the face of it, the latter may appear the simplest option but, as the twelve essays in this section demonstrate, the matter is still far from being resolved. The papers have been divided into two groups. The first consists of those dealing with the nature and role of specific components within the framework of the architectural setting, and the factors conditioning the formation of an effective design discipline for architecture. The second part – as the subtitle 'Architecture in the making'

suggests – concentrates on the working methods and personal design philosophies of six leading modern architects. Three of these were written by critics, three by practising architects.

In view of the attention usually paid in theoretical discussions on architecture to formal issues like style, one is struck by how little such aspects figure in the accounts these practitioners give of their respective approaches to particular design problems. It would seem to bear out the axiom that with highly skilled artisans technique is invisible – it is merely the means to an end, not an end in itself. As Pierre von Meiss observes in his book *Elements of Architecture: From Form to Place* (1990), 'an *a posteriori* debate on architecture is never as rich as architecture itself, which has less need to "speak" than to "exist with man". The built works of great architects are therefore always finer than their writings'. Perhaps therein lies the hope for the future.

H.L.

RECOMMENDED READING

Alexander, C., Ishikasua, S. and Silverstein, M. (1977) *A Pattern Language* London: Oxford University Press.

Curtis, N.C. (1935) *Architectural Composition*, 3rd edn, Cleveland: Jansen.

Heath, T. (1984) *Method in Architecture*, Chichester: John Wiley.

Herzberger, H. (1991) *Lessons for Students in Architecture*, Rotterdam: OIO Publishers.

Krier, R. (1988) *Architectural Composition*, London: Academy Editions.

Lawson, B. (1990) *How Designers Think: The Design Process Demystified*, 2nd edn, London: Butterworth.

Meiss, P. von (1990) *Elements of Architecture: From Form to Place*, New York: Van Nostrand Reinhold.

Mitchell, W.J. (1990) *The Logic of Architecture: Design, Computation and Cognition*, Cambridge, Mass.: MIT Press.

Steadman, P. (1979) *The Evolution of Designs: Biological Analogy in Architecture and the Applied Arts*, Cambridge: Cambridge University Press.

Thiss-Evenson, T. (1987) *Archetypes in Architecture*, Oxford: Oxford University Press.

Tzonis, A. and Lefaivre, L. (1987) *Classical Architecture: the Poetics of Order*, Cambridge, Mass.: MIT Press.

60 A 'thick' description of windows

Herman Neuckermans

Architecture as a part of the real world cannot be reduced to a realm that is exclusively rational. Consequently a scientific discourse on architecture, like any design project, will necessarily rely upon value judgements. Values always play a role in architecture, explicitly or implicitly, due to that inextricable connection with the real world.

Built architecture as well as projects reveal the underlying system of thought and the value system upon which they are based. Sometimes it is obvious, as for example in institutional buildings of totalitarian regimes; sometimes it can only be discovered through careful reading. For instance, the location of the mortuary in a hospital can teach us how a society thinks about life and death, about illness and health.

Value systems give rise to currents and tendencies in architecture. They are the object of study or architectural theory. A quick *tour d'horizon* shows a great variety of theories coexisting or competing with each other: conservative versus progressive attitudes towards monuments, traditionalism and historicism versus real modernism, and so on. However, similar to the shift that has occurred in philosophy, from a modern conception of science (Descartes, Popper) to *la condition postmoderne* (Lyotard 1979) – mainly under the influence of Kuhn, Feyerabend, Lakatos and Habermas – a parallel evolution can be observed in architectural theory from Modernism to Post-Modernism, denying the existence of universal values and truths (Heynen 1983: 15–16). At the same time this tendency is somehow contradicted by Neo-Modernists trying to bring a new order into our fragmented space using the formal vocabulary of the avant-garde and pure Modernism. There is also a growing belief in the autonomy of architecture, i.e. that the shaping of architecture follows its own logic without being subjugated to mere functional needs. This shift in attitude towards architecture also challenges design methodology, which emerged from the problem-solving paradigm, and which is now seriously questioned by the semantic approach to design. As Aldo Rossi's project for the Modena cemetery demonstrates, the latter approach proves the predominance of metaphorical thinking.

It becomes clear that architectural theory cannot formulate normative rules. There is no longer a single truth, one single *grand récit* as legitimation, but a collection of several (minor) stories. Architectural theory, like many humanities, is still in a state of *paralogie*, to quote Lyotard (1979: 63). However, variety in tendencies is a sign neither of weakness nor of inferiority of architectural thinking. On the contrary, this pluralism just reflects the pluralism of contemporary society, where tendencies enrich each other through dialectic interaction, and proves once more that architecture is well and alive.

Given this pluralism in thought, we advocate an approach to architectural design which transcends the mere discussion of style and pure architectural morphology. We argue for an architecture which offers something to the user; an architecture which leaves traces in the mind, which positively contributes to our experience; an architecture dense with sensory stimuli, rich in capabilities for plural use in line with Kenneth Frampton's argument for plurifunctional structures (Frampton 1975: 112).

Too often a design is treated as a mere addition of monofunctionally solved parts. Decompositional methods – our natural strategy when facing complexity – stimulate this kind of attitude. We have all experienced the results of dividing the city into zones for housing, working, recreation and circulation by now – a world taken apart, non-efficient and uneconomic use of space, cities like trees (Alexander 1966).

Even today many architects approach their design problems with the same meagre mentality – one element serving one function only. Likewise in education we see a lot of fragmentation and frequently also a predominance of 'hard', factual topics. A course in technology, for example, deals with building elements as if they exist without shape, meaning and history. 'Soft' aspects are not taught or left to the design studio.

The glasses we are looking through condition our behaviour and actions as designers. The way we synthesize reflects the way we analyse; or, to paraphrase De Saussure: analysis and synthesis, the recto and verso of design. On the one hand the multiplicity of tendencies reduces somewhat the importance of shape in architecture, on the other it forces the architect to produce a design which has deeper or structural qualities capable of taking many shapes.

Design decisions are always based upon many criteria. The more arguments that support a decision the better it will resist criticism. Design decisions have to reinforce each other, they have to add evidence to the story told by the other decisions. The stronger the arguments the more chance that the building will become timeless. Multiplicity and coherence of argument guarantee the consistency of the building within its own logic. Multiplicity of argument presupposes a multiplicity of knowledge, that means a rich picture of architecture. According to Mackinnon, creativity – and that is the core of design – is 'putting the elements of one's experiences into new combinations' (MacKinnon 1970: 29). This definition is very close to what happens in metaphorical thinking, namely the bringing together and mixing of the semantic content of concepts which did not have such a relationship, or any relationship, before. Both definitions strengthen the importance of cumulative knowledge in architecture, or, in more general terms, culture in architecture. They also presuppose an openness of mind, a fundamental characteristic of creative individuals.

'Seeing' architecture (Zevi 1948), or consciously experiencing it, has to be learned and taught, not only to architects, but from the primary school on, because all people will inevitably be confronted with buildings. You don't know what you miss when you ignore what is. Those who never look under the water in the Mediterranean are missing half of the scene. Whoever is a complete layperson in non-figurative painting probably will not enjoy it. The problem is that in architecture it matters to be acquainted with the whole picture, not only for architects, but for everybody involved in decision-making about the built environment.

The richer the experience the more it is worth experiencing. A design will stimulate arousal when it shows characteristics which provoke this psychophysical activation. Novelty, incongruity, surprise, ambiguity, diversity and structural complexity introduced as collative factors by Berlyne (1960) and Wohlwill (1976) are such characteristics which make objects catch our attention. Complexity and ambiguity are well known in architecture (Rapoport and Cantor 1967). Umberto Eco, too, highlights the importance of ambiguity and auto-reflexivity as stimuli for sensory activation in texts. And also architecture as a means of communication can be read as a text carrying a message that can provoke aesthetic response: 'the message assumes an aesthetic function when it is structured in an ambiguous and auto-reflexive manner, that is to say when it wants to draw the attention of its recipient to its own shape in particular' (Eco 1972: 124).

Multiplicity of meaning is strongly linked with multiplicity of use and interpretations. Barthes writes: 'Interpréter un texte, ce n'est pas lui donner un sens (plus ou moins fondé, plus ou moins libre); c'est au contraire apprécier de quel pluriel il est fait' (Barthes 1970: 11).

As an illustration of such a multiple approach to architecture, we take the window (especially the domestic window) as an example, because it lends itself admirably to the purpose. Plenty of books exist about the technological and quantitative aspects of windows; other books show pictures only, but very little has been written about its 'soft' aspects, about those aspects which make the window become architecture. It is therefore our intention to paint a 'rich' picture of windows in the following pages. In other words, to give a multifaceted image or 'thick description' of windows, to paraphrase Geertz (1975: 3–30).

THE WINDOW AS A TRANSITION

As a part of the outer wall the window regulates the transition from inside to outside in a very subtle way. The window-pane is both separation and link; its meaning vibrates between these two poles, depending on the observer's intention, depending also on the differing light conditions between inside and outside. The window has a *dunamis* (power), according to Claes (1970).

Like all objects windows also determine the space around them: a space in front and a space behind, a zone inside and a zone outside, different in nature by more than by climatic factors only (Heidegger 1968: 183).

The window settles visual privacy: seeing and not being seen. It is able to regulate in a very sensitive and versatile manner the inward and outward views. This can be achieved by an appropriate location, and by the dimensions and shape of the window itself, as well as by way of the purposeful organization of space and attributes in front of and behind the window-pane.

It is remarkable how inventive and subtle people have been in the past in structuring the transition between inside and outside, using all kinds of devices conditioned by culture and religion (see Figure 1). We think of, for example, lattices, meshing, folding blinds, shutters, sliding panes, Venetian blinds, louvres, Persiennes, awnings, curtains, draperies, overhangs, window bays, and so on (Ching 1987: 218). We also think of the manifold forms derived from windows, as for example in balconies, loggias, alcoves, greenhouses and the like; each of which exist in numerous shapes and decorative patterns (Alexander (1977).[1] It would be interesting to make a cross-cultural and historical study of these.

Figure 1 *Window shutters outside, Albergo Italia, Urbino, Italy.*

On the other hand it is amazing to see how poor some solutions are, windows nothing more than translucent holes in walls, solutions also which are exported all over the world, failing to reinforce the cultural specificity of each region.

The articulation of the transition between the inside and outside through all kinds of patterns of voids and solids, through the interposition of screens, in-between spaces, barriers, and points of control, reflects the mental transition between the private and the public domain. This appears to be very fundamental to human behaviour. When this transition neglects the cosmology of the inhabitant, conflicts arise. These are expressed in various ways: vandalism; the barricading of windows; hostility towards ignorant visitors seen as unwanted intruders in a domain that is public by status, but considered to be private or semi-private by the inhabitants. Only a careful analysis of human behaviour by means of suitable anthropological categories can bring insight in such a complex phenomenon. This complexity, however, must be the basis for design (Loeckx 1982).

A window is not only a link regulating the mental transition between inside and outside. It is also the separation between the inner and the outer climate. Often the window is the weakest link in this climatological transition. Thermal and acoustic insulation have become particularly important as a consequence of the growing demand for comfort, the energy crisis and increasing noise pollution.

All these aspects can be solved within a plurifunctional approach: in a situation of heavy noise pollution, for example, the widow can be doubled with a wide, absorbing space in between, which can be converted into a small botanic garden, a greenhouse or wintergarden, or an alcove for sitting; the inner window can be left open or can be closed according to choice.

THE WINDOW AS AN ELEMENT IN THE INTERIOR SPACE

The space on the inside, near to the window, is a very particular place: the natural light, the contact with the outside, with nature, with life, with people and moving objects, all these make this place a favourite spot for many. The window is regarded as a place for sitting, especially by children and elderly people.

The window is often a place for plants: plants growing with light, a changing light which, close to the window, and only there, follows the natural movement of sun and clouds, the diurnal and seasonal rhythm (Figure 2). Plants inside buildings make human presence visible. For some, screens of plants between the inside and the outside are somehow a substitute for nature. Frequently too, objects are displayed in the window; objects symbolizing (pseudo-)social and cultural status, objects put there for the sake of decoration which benefit from contrasting light conditions.

Windows also frame the environment. They enable, hide or mask views (it is no coincidence that in computer graphics 'windowing' is used to frame a picture on the cathode ray tube) (Ching 1987: 206–7).

Sufficient daylight can be expected when the glazed area measures at least one sixth of the floor area, although the real figures will depend on the translucency of the glazing, and on the height, the shape and the position of the window (Van Santen and Hansen 1989: 11–26). Daylight, however, is more important for architecture because of its quality rather than its quantity. Sunshine illuminates directly and generates shade and shadow patterns. Daylight produces more diffuse lighting when bouncing from walls, floors or ceiling (Moore, Allen and Lyndon 1974: 96–9) (see Figure 3). Skilful architects master the art of lighting through sensitive fenestration (Ching 1979: 181–91). Horizontal and vertical windows provide substantially different visual information as well as experiential value. Horizontal windows result in a horizontal stratification of the view; vertical windows induce a movement parallax, a kind of 'motion in between the pictures', as in cinematography. In the case of a horizontal window the picture is more static, at least with regard to the observer's motion. The vertical window shows a part of the sky, as well as the remote and the immediate environment (Markus 1967). Vertical windows, associated with high interiors, have a connotation of wealth, and are pleasantly surprising with high incoming light reaching deep into the interior (see Figure 4).

Glare and hard contrasts between glass and windowframes, or between the window and the adjoining wall parts, can be avoided by bevelling the inside corners or by providing windows in at least two walls of the same space (see Figure 5). Large-size glass-panes often emphasize bareness or emptiness; partitioning contri-

Figure 2 *A place for plants, private house, Heverlee, Belgium.*

Figure 3 *Light reflecting on the floor, private house, Heverlee, Belgium.*

Figure 4 *High incoming light, Castle of Arenberg, Heverlee, Belgium.*

Figure 5 *Light balanced by windows in different walls, Villa Savoye, Poissy, France, by Le Corbusier.*

butes to scale reduction. Windows also give an orientation to the interior. A bay window, for example, opens new possibilities for sunshine, views and screening (see Figure 6).

Skylights provide an abundance of light, which fascinates when washing the walls, and which surprises when daylighting inner spaces (see Figures 7 and 8). Interior windows create an ambiguous and flexible relationship between interior spaces, keeping them apart and linking them; they allow spatial continuity and visual contact, although they separate physically and even acoustically, when properly designed (Neuckermans *et al.* 1988: 107).

Deep windows gather many of the qualities mentioned so far.

Figure 6 *Bay window, private house, Heverlee, Belgium.*

Figure 7 *Light washing the wall, Chapel of Notre Dame du Haut, Ronchamp, France, by Le Corbusier.*

Figure 8 *Skylight washing the wall, Maison Tassel, Brussels, Belgium, by Victor Horta.*

THE WINDOW AS PART OF THE FAÇADE

The extent to which buildings and their inhabitants relate to the environment can be read from the openings of the outer wall: their number, shape, size, detailing, material, framing, division, articulation, scale, proportion, rhythm, and colour. In particular, the way they open or have to remain closed tells us a lot about this relationship: participation, indifference, or hostility?

Equally, the way in which the inhabitants personalize their windows influences the character of the façade (see Figure 9). On the one hand, façades live their own life; they exist as autonomous objects and can be experienced as such. On the other, they belong and contribute to the architecture of the building and, on a larger scale, to the architecture of the city.

Thoughtless repetition of elements, in our case

widows, can result in monotony or, on the contrary, can become fascinating when the whole becomes more than the sum of the parts – when the whole gets a new identity, an added value in comparison to the individual elements. Take as an example the Royal Crescent in Bath, where identical windows and façades are repeated over and over again, and in doing so constitute a strong urban shape on the larger scale. Or consider the Arche de la Défense in Paris, where identical fenestration is subjugated to the Platonic shape of a strong architectural object dominating the scene by its scale and position.

Windows stand here as *pars pro toto*; they are somehow paradigmatic for the structural complexity of architecture. And indeed the same exercise could be made for other building elements like the entrance, stairs, façades, building tops and so on.

Designers should be knowledgeable about all these facets and have all these strings to their bow. They should design with this complexity in mind and carefully learn the lessons the built environment teaches us, because it still is the container of generations of design efforts. The key issue is, first, to discover these structural qualities and, second, to translate or, better, to actualize them into the architecture of today. Analysis and synthesis, the recto and verso of design.

NOTES

1   In Alexander 1977, see patterns 127, 128, 135, 159, 161, 163–8, 179, 180, 192, 194, 197, 202, 221, 231, 238–40.

All photographs are by the author.

REFERENCES

Alexander, C. (1966) 'A city is not a tree', *Design* 206 (February): 46–55.

Alexander, C., Ishikawa, S. and Silverstein, M. (1977) *A Pattern Language*, New York: Oxford University Press.

Barthes, R. (1970) *S/Z*, Paris: Seuil.

Berlyne, D. (1960) *Conflict, Arousal and Curiosity*, New York: McGraw-Hill.

Ching, F. (1979) *Architecture – Form, Space and Order*, London: Van Nostrand Reinhold.

—— (1987) *Interior Design Illustrated*, New York: Van Nostrand Reinhold.

Claes, J. (1970) *De Dingen en hum Ruimte*, Antwerpen: Nederlandse Boekhandel.

Eco, U. (1968) *La struttura assente*, Milan: V. Bompiani; French trans. 1972, *La Structure absente: introduction à la recherche sémiotique*, Paris: Mercure de France.

Frampton, K. (1975) 'Reflection on the opposition of architecture and building', in J. Gowan (ed.) *A Continuing Experiment*, London: Architectural Association.

Geertz, C. (1975) *The Interpretation of Cultures: Selected Essays*, London: Hutchinson.

Heidegger, M. (1958) *Essais et conférences*, Paris: Gallimard.

Heynen, H. (1983) 'Postmodernisme: een neoconservatieve mode', *Plan* 7–8 (14): 15–16.

Figure 9 *Personalizing windows, Grimentz, Switzerland.*

Loeckx, A. (1982) 'Model en metafoor – bijdragen tot een semantisch – praxeologische benadering van bouwen en wonen', Ph.D. thesis, Afdeling Architectuur, KU Leuven (B).

Lyotard, J.F. (1979) *La Condition postmoderne*, Paris: Minuit.

Mackinnon, D. (1970) 'Creativity: a multi-faceted phenomenon', in J.D. Roslansky (ed) *Creativity: A Discussion at the Nobel Conference, 1970*, Amsterdam: North-Holland.

Markus, T. (1967) 'The function of windows – a reappraisal', *Building Science* 2 (2): 97–121.

Moore, C., Allen, G. and Lyndon, D. (1974) *The Place of Houses*, New York: Holt, Rinehart & Winston.

Neuckermans, H., De Lathouwer, R. and De Petter, H. (1988) *Bouwen om te Wonen*, Brussels:Belgische Radio en Televisie.

Rapoport, A. and Cantor, R. (1967) 'Complexity and ambiguity', *Journal of American Institute of Planners* 33 (4) 210–21.

Van Santen, C. and Hansen, A.J. (1989) *Daglicht, Kunstlicht, een Leidraad*, Delft: Delftse Universitaire Pers.

Wohlwill, J. (1976) 'Environmental aesthetics: the environment as a source of conflict', in I. Altman and J. Wohlwill (eds) *Human Behaviour and Environment*, New York: Plenum Press.

Zevi, B. (1948) *Saper vedere l'architettura*, Turin: Einaudi; trans. 1957, *Architecture as Space*, New York: Horizon Press.

61 Meeting ground

Henry Plummer

Relation is reciprocity

(Martin Buber 1970: 58)

For architecture to become a dwelling place and real home in the world, rather than an alienated object – a prospect increasingly called for in existentialist literature even if peripheral to the current architectural scene – its configurations must become engaged in two-sided dialogues rather than one-sided containments. Instead of merely enclosing and shaping the space within, as an outer shell or envelope, walls and roofs must be formed to exploit their capacity as interfaces shared by, and therefore defining, the interaction between adjoining spaces. Seen as a dualistic membrane, the building enclosure thus becomes paradoxical, alternately acting as a limit that separates and indicates the distance between two spaces – between here and there, my world and your world, private and public – and also acting as the very mechanism by which those same worlds communicate and passage occurs between them. This dialectical capacity to integrate, as well as divide our inhabited spaces, thus enables architectural meaning to transcend any volumetric aesthetics or utility, for the interface actually creates, concretizes, and makes experiential the relationships between our two archetypal worlds of being and belonging – inside and outside. It is by the dialectical exchanges of architectural edges that we are able to dwell within and come into harmonious relationship with our world at large.

Dialectical edges imply conditions both open and closed and particularly a deliberate physical opening where relationships between spaces are to be manifested and concretized. Certainly a variety of architectural elements are needed to form a dialectical fabric capable of overcoming any overall polarization and mutual alienation of inside and outside space. But among these various modes of interchange, the entrance is of paramount importance due to its setting for human passage – dialogues that are literal, bodily, recurring and often momentous. I would like to examine here a dialectical entrance phenomenon that is perhaps least obvious, because it is under our feet – occurring where a portion of the ground surface preceding a threshold projects into, over or below the ground surface outside to form an intermediary landing. Architectural landings of this sort are found in the traditional stoop, porch and veranda, and are directly related to doorless and buildingless landings, such as the pier and dock, that link sea

and earth. All such landings are moments in a dividing boundary where adjacent worlds become bound together and passage between them is encouraged.

RECIPROCITY

The most obvious aspect of reciprocal integration in a landing is overlap. Its under-over action produces an *amphibious zone* occupied inside and outside without exclusive predominance by either side. Think of a sandy beach washed with the sea and inundated by spray, where you can stand on firm ground and yet have your feet bathed in the surf. When we stand on an architectural landing, we are supported by a piece of interior flooring projecting into interior space. Even when a wall prevents our seeing the source of this outward projection, we tend to assume that a similar level lies on the other side of the door and that the landing is an extension of the building's base. The landing is at the same time infused with exteriority by its alfresco qualities of sunlight, atmosphere, wind, sound and precipitation. Differences become softened in this common *meeting-ground* between worlds. The resulting *interspace* contains a synthetic quality unlike either side, although it is composed of their elements, for here antithetical values can be simultaneously experienced. Polar qualities are intermingled to produce unpredictable combinations and juxtapositions. Admixtures are spun together from the extremes of sensory dualities, such as light/shadow, loud/quiet, windy/still, active/passive, natural/artificial, wet/dry, and hot/cold, as well as territorial dualities, such as public/private, collective/individual, native/alien, and inhabitant/visitor.

A second means of integration is spatial. The narrow borderline of a building shell is stretched at the landing into a *borderland* that people can occupy. It is no longer a simple dividing seam. It forms an interspace lying within the inner and outer faces of the split boundary tissue. In a stoop, the outer face is the 'fault line' of the level change and the inner face is the building wall at the rear. The exploded edge is diffused, fuzzy and physically ambiguous. It is not clear where outside ends and inside begins. This double reference turns the landing into an *intermediary zone* – a place of exchange between territorial extremes. The simultaneity of belonging to both individual/collective and private/public domains underlies the timeless attraction of the stoop – for here one sits securely in a still somewhat intimate place that is also out-of-doors, part of the public street, at the edge of he action, and conducive to neighbourly congregation.

First published 1984, as 'Realm of the landing', in *Reflections* 2 (1): 48–61.

Only in such a zone, where an interface is expanded into an interspace, can a person lead the double life of belonging concurrently to thoroughly different worlds and can an ongoing dialogue between those worlds be actually experienced.

Integration is also produced in the landing by transition. It can be experienced during cross-boundary passage, as well as intraboundary dwelling. The stoop, after all, is an entrance as well as a sitting place. Any passage from outside to inside, and vice versa, involves drastic changes of environmental conditions – a complete loss of one set of familiar qualities and sudden assimilation of a new, unaccustomed set. Such values are dovetailed in the landing. The contemporaneous presence of both worlds grants those undergoing passage the space and time for complementary processes of both withdrawal and familiarization to evolve side by side. There is no trauma, for a person belongs to the building before he or she is entirely separated from the outside environs. And since the threshold is the site at which people arrive and depart, the landing becomes a place forged for important ritual functions and occasions. A spatial setting is provided at the junction of two worlds to accommodate greetings and parting words, introductions and valedictories, returns and farewells, homecomings and send-offs.

BASIC FORM AND STRUCTURE

Within the elemental landing constructions of Edwin Lutyens, we can see especially clearly the otherwise unclear anatomy and prototypical composition of an interspace. For instance, Lutyens calls our attention to the reality of a landing as a spatially inflated boundary line and, thus also, to the reality of inner and outer faces of a landing as being split linings of a wall. In a number of outdoor gardens, circular landings between larger levels become kernels within the bisected tissue of retaining walls (see Figure 1). The circle within a line is itself deeply symbolic as the germ of a landing, since its

centric symmetry reflects back directly and entirely to the central line it has dilated. Its geometry simultaneously grows out from and is focused back upon its centre line, emphasizing that the inner and outer faces of the original wall can be transposed and also that its contained space is a cavity in the wall. Rings of steps suggest both an outward expansion of concentric ripples and a pointing back toward their common place of emanation. Even more primordial, concrete circles lie within concrete boundary lines along the edges of entrance porticoes to van Eyck's Children's Home (Figure 2). These irreducible landings seem to be nodes within edge lines, places where the narrow dividing border is deliberately enlarged into a place that people can step into and through as they arrive and depart.

Lutyens also exploits visual tensions to cohere inner and outer boundary faces of a landing. These perceptual forces are not as incidental as they might first appear, for their mending action contributes to the integrative ability of the landing. They pull inside and outside together within the interspace. A subtle connective tension between boundary faces occurs in the twin semicircular stairs at either end of a garden terrace at Ammerdown House (Figure 3). The pair of incomplete forms produce tension towards both closure and unity. They are twin halves of a split circle. They are also mirror-imaged convexity and concavity – reciprocal solid

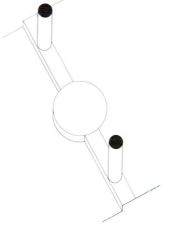

Figure 2 *Children's Home, Amsterdam, by van Eyck.*

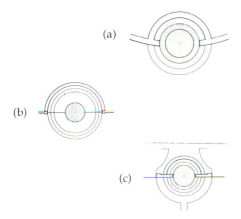

Figure 1 *(a) Great Dixter, Sussex; (b) Marshcourt, Kings Somborne, Hampshire; (c) Heathcote, Ilkley, Yorkshire. All by Lutyens.*

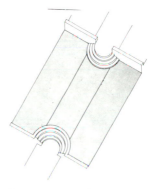

Figure 3 *Ammerdown House, Somerset, by Lutyens.*

and void whose union would complete itself like a form returned to its mould. The *retaining* walls above and below are thus linked as inner and outer faces of the interspace, and the dialogue between stairs draws and binds the lower and higher garden levels closer together.

A far more complex pattern of perceptual tensions is encountered in the entrance to Tigbourne Court (Figure 4). The circular landing is split by the colonnaded edge of the portico. The split circle immediately relates inside and outside as twin halves of a perceptually cohesive geometry. The outer half of the circle, however, has been further interrupted by the narrow strand of a larger landing in the courtyard. Incompleteness results here from superimposition rather than the divergence of twin shapes as at Ammerdown House. Perceptual forces of closure have been brought into play to induce the divided portions of a circle to visually complete themselves in place. While arriving or departing, one steps upon a circular segment of the landing that is perceptually related to another circular segment on the far side of the line of columns. The viewer becomes involved as a visual participant and catalyst in the landing's integrative action.

Primary features of the landing are also seen in the traditional *doorstep*. A small concrete slab or wood deck provides a place for a person to perch at the front door. Here one can step out of the water and mud of a rainy day or kiss a loved one goodbye. Wonderful developments of the doorstep are seen in the traditional Japanese house. A chain of stepping stones carries us to the entrance as if along a series of doorsteps elevated above the more natural and exteriorized ground of grass, moss and water. The broad veranda is itself a kind of collective doorstep for many sliding doors. This transitional experience of stone and veranda is often enhanced by additional intermediate conditions. Stones near the building, for instance, may become progressively elevated and small wood platforms may step down to meet the final *shoe-stone* (see Figure 5). Veranda and stones converge, so that the outer frontier of the dwelling extends to graze the final frontier of ascending

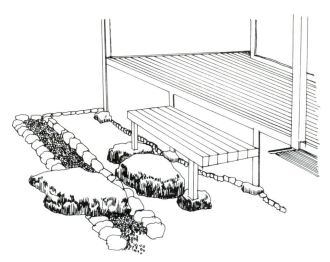

Figure 5 *Garden entrance, Katsura Palace, Kyoto.*

stones. There is a magical moment when stepping from last stone to first platform, for we are made conscious of the heightened, yet gently softened leap between worlds.

The underlying splitting of boundaries in an interspace can be multiplied to produce rich stratifications of *in-between space*. A single continuous landing, as at the entrance to Hertzberger's Montessori School (Figure 6), contains an undivided interspace. More complex aggregations of landings, however, as in the successive *terraces* of Smith's house at Groton (Figure 7), endow the interspace with a complex of layers. A gradation of

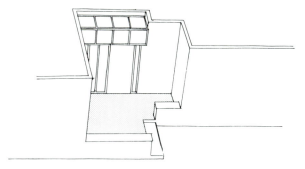

Figure 6 *Montessori School, Delft, by Hertzberger.*

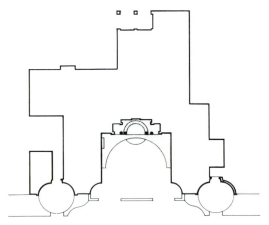

Figure 4 *Tigbourne Court, Surrey, by Lutyens.*

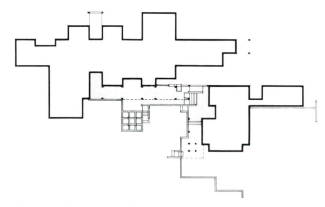

Figure 7 *House, Groton, by Smith.*

interior values unfolds here, so that the entrant is gently withdrawn from exterior surroundings and steps into a faintly interiorized piece of ground long before the front door. Successive spatial strata contain contrasting mixtures of inside and outside qualities, such as farther or nearer the building and less enclosed or more enclosed. Each level thus assumes different ratios of attachment to inside and outside. There are phases of transition outlined by each level change. And since the landing does not produce an even gradation of values, each sublevel of the interspace is rich in sensory and territorial juxtapositions. We see this in the way a person at the outskirts of the landing is in certain locations securely enclosed by building forms, whereas at the end of the landing he or she can step several feet away and be immersed in the garden and sunshine. Polar qualities are reconciled without blurring through endless gradation what we value and enjoy most about them – their distinctions.

Bunches of landings produce a world of terraces outdoors. At the Cheney House (see Figure 8), three platforms extend from the building shell – a higher open terrace leading straight out from the living room and two lower garden courts intermediate in height and accessible from the street. Each landing is walled in – a veritable outdoor room open to the sky. The one level used for entrance is further subdivided to permit passage through the garden court and across a short elevated stretch before reaching the small, intimate landing at the doorway.

Meandering successions of terraced levels at the Villa d'Este (see Figure 9) produce such large, shielded,

episodic and directionally varied landings that the culminating spaces are endowed with those innermost qualities of penetralia and seclusion normally encountered only in a building's deepest recesses. The entrant has become well oriented and acclimated to the interior world by the time he or she arrives at the front door. Each outdoor terrace is a paved room for communing with nature. Moreover, each segment of the diversified interspace has a unique character imprinted with an individuality of shape, height, planting, and water play of its fountains. Continuously flowing water covers, borders, centres and permeates various landings – now streaming down a chute overhead, now spilling along channels in tune with cascading stairs, now rippling in a pool, now calm and still, now floating as a mist. This weaving of an element of nature around and through an interspace, thus revealing so many of its different facets, makes nature more assimilable and part of life without ever losing its dynamic and wild quality through domestication. Nature is only temporarily diverted, untamed, into and through the interspace.

The pluralistic landings of the Pembroke Dormitories (see Figure 10) are an urban counterpart to what the Villa d'Este accomplishes by integrating humanity and nature. Rich topographical sequences in the entrance

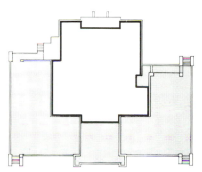
Figure 8 *Cheney House, Oak Park, by Wright.*

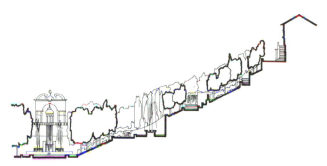
Figure 9 *Villa d'Este, Tivoli, by Ligorio.*

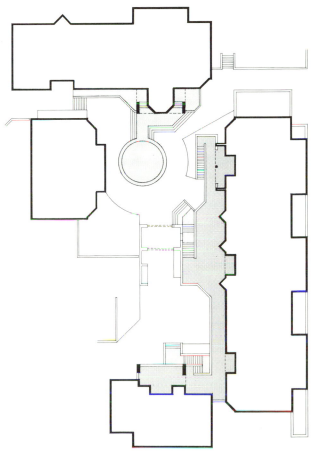
Figure 10 *Pembroke Dormitories, Brown University, Providence, by Lyndon.*

courtyard stretch and diversify the inside–outside boundary into an enormously complex interspace of clustered levels. Landings are not only subdivided into manifold phases along the ground but are spatially interspersed with the elevated landings of bridges and roof-terraces so that boundary elements are scattered, superimposed and intertwined. The courtyard is accessible from the street outside and tends to draw this public world into, through and past the encrusted landings. Stairs, stoops and terraces at varied levels and degrees of exposure offer myriad locations for people to either perch along the edge of the action or nestle back into a quieter alcove, to be surrounded by the passing parade or be left alone, and to bask in the sun or cool off in the shade.

BELONGING AND ADHESION

While it is generally true that the overlapping action of a landing permits a person to stand outside on inside ground, this impression of being within the shelter of a building depends upon the sureness with which the flooring of a landing appears to extend beyond the door. Without visual evidence of continuity, the landing presents itself as an extraneous platform rubbing against the shell rather than a projecting limb. To truly experience reciprocity, as opposed to merely assuming or imagining it, we must see with our own eyes that the landing belongs physically – at a perceptual level – to the building. Since a building's walls usually prevent us from seeing outgrowth literally (as we can in the open-air pier or beach), an impression of configurational interpenetration is needed to visibly fuse landing to building. Without such a bond of adhesion, the landing remains disengaged from interior associations. As a person steps up out of the exterior landscape and upon a surface that is not convincingly integral with the building, he or she lies between worlds – thoroughly suspended and alienated – rather than belonging to both simultaneously.

Let us see how the potential integrative action of a landing is diminished by tenuous attachment to the building shell. The entrance landing of the Tribune Review Building (see Figure 11) touches the envelope along a single plane. The continuity of concrete certainly tends to unite landing and building through identical colour and material; however, there is no physical bond. The landing form merely abuts the wall and appears as

an appendage extrinsic to the shell. We might even say that it seems perceptually unattached, since it only grazes the building and is, therefore, free to 'slide or drift'. If we stand on this landing, we are on a platform backed up against the wall – an independent island rather than a proprietary extension of the building – and so we remain outside the building's grasp. The lower platform to the Farnsworth House (see Figure 12) is even more estranged – literally hovering in mid-air and spatially disjoined from the building. In both examples, the liberated character of the landing separates, rather than integrates, outside and inside. The formerly adjacent territories become further stretched apart, since they are separated by a neutral foreign body. The landing becomes a wedge rather than a connector. A long series of non-involved landings touching along single planes occur at the Amon Carter Museum (see Figure 13). Assembled like radiating strings of ice floes, the stepped landings between planters pass the entrant through five stages of belonging 'nowhere' until he or she finally reaches a landing bound to the building and belonging 'somewhere'.

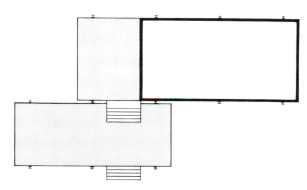

Figure 12 *Farnsworth House, Plano, by Mies van der Rohe.*

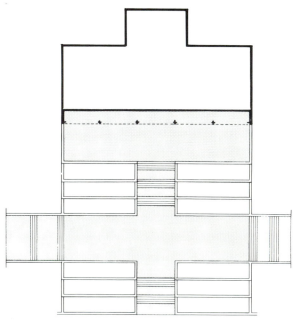

Figure 13 *Amon Carter Museum, Fort Worth, by Johnson.*

Figure 11 *Tribune Review Publishing Company Building, Greensburg, by Kahn.*

The configurational disengagement of no-bond between landing and building can be overcome by adhesive substitutes. At the entrance landing to the Blacker House (see Figure 14), which touches the building shell along a single plane, the broken connection is compensated for by the collective action of weaker methods of adhesion. We find an identification with the building shell in the way canopies and columns reach over to stake the landing in place, in the way the kinship of brick between landing and foundation produces a material continuity of substructure, and by the way 'reinforcing' corners and folds of brick structure stabilize the form and anchor it to the ground. The lack of a direct bond is offset here by a net of entanglement and rooting in place.

A configurational journey of the landing and building shell along two or more sides immediately locks the landing in place by preventing 'detachment' in two directions, by suggesting adhesive tenacity through interpenetration and by asserting physical ownership through a grip. Physical interpenetration, after all, is the very essence of cementation and of secure joints between adjoining elements. A simple, two-sided bonding occurs at the Ward Willits House – the small landing fitting neatly into a recess at the building's corner. In plans for the McAfee House, a similar docking of the landing into a corner is further stabilized by the joggle joint of a vestibular protrusion. The entry level breaks out of a corner and interlocks with both landscape and building at Wright's Oak Park House (Figure 15) and the Greenes' Gamble House, yet the outward projection is counterbalanced by the tenacious bond exerted by so many facets of physical connection. The doubly interpenetrative landing also increases reciprocity by expanding the diversity of innerness and outerness. One can sit in a shaded nook warmly

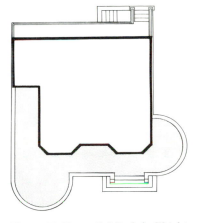

Figure 15 *House, Oak Park, by Wright.*

embraced by the building and shielded from outside winds, or several feet away can sit in a spot thrust into the outside gardens that is enveloped by sunlight and cool breezes and offers panoramic views.

As a landing extends far from the building and is subdivided into different levels, an interpenetration of the various levels maintains interior affiliations through the cohesion of continuous linkage and the territorial outreach of a chain of grips. Association over distance occurs in the series of interlocked landings at Taliesen West (see Figure 16) and Smith House, the levels fitting together like a chain of puzzle pieces and joined into a subdivided but still united interspace, rather than fractured into an archipelagic sequence of independent steps.

Adhesion is also produced when a landing is encompassed by the building mass. We see a slight retention in the way the embedded landing of Unity Church is enwrapped by extremities of the shell. At the entrance of Centraal Beheer (Figure 17), a long and narrow landing stretches out from an implanted nucleus, like tendrils from a root bulb, to pick up entrants at the distant street. The elevated entrance courtyard of Säynätsalo Town Hall (Figure 18) is not only clutched by the main building mass – the extremities pinching the landing at its waist, but the library mass positioned opposite the recess securely boxes in the landing and gives it the core-like quality of an atrium.

Integration is compounded when the landing flows out of a porus field of walls and columns rather than a dividing wall. We not only see the landing physically emerge as inner flooring but also see spatial interpenetration between building and landing. The incomplete shell is stagnant with 'interiority' trickling out to merge with the more fully exposed portions of the landing. Simple examples are found in the traditional portico. Substantial build-ups and outward filtrations of inner territory occur at Centraal Beheer, both in the vestibular cocoon of the street entrance and in the densely sown forest of columns and bridges of the parking entrance. At the Barcelona Pavilion (Figure 19) and van Eyck's

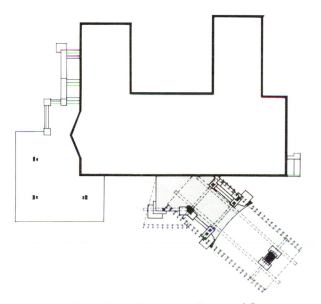

Figure 14 *Blacker House, Pasadena, by Greene and Greene.*

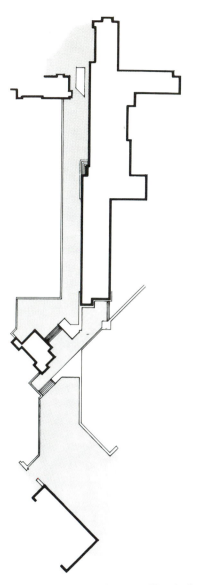

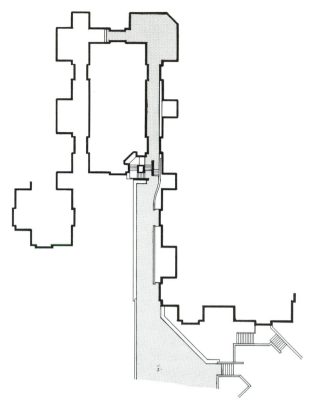

Figure 17 *Centraal Beheer, Apeldoorn, by Hertzberger.*

Figure 16 *Taliesin West, near Phoenix, by Wright.*

sculpture pavilion at Arnheim, barely restrained interior space flows directly out through a field of wall fragments to impregnate and warm up the landing with innerness.

Our perception of interiority also depends upon spatial tangibility. If the space of the landing is not in some way contained at its periphery, as upon the windswept aprons of Niemeyer's Presidential Chapel (see Figure 20) or the Farnsworth House, it appears abandoned by the building. There is no sense of place, and the zone is fully pervaded by outdoor space. Once the landing is slightly defined along its perimeter, however, as by a railing, low wall, or columns, and thus granted a spatial substance different from that outside its periphery, it forms a spatial nest. People are able to dwell in the friendly lap of a building. This hollowed shape also displays adhesion as it is perceptually held, like a cupped hand, by the building from below. Examples of attached basins are found within the parapet walls

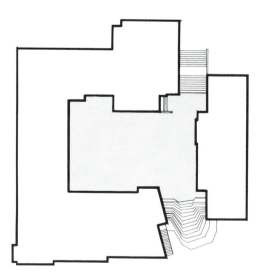

Figure 18 *Town Hall, Säynätsalo, by Aalto.*

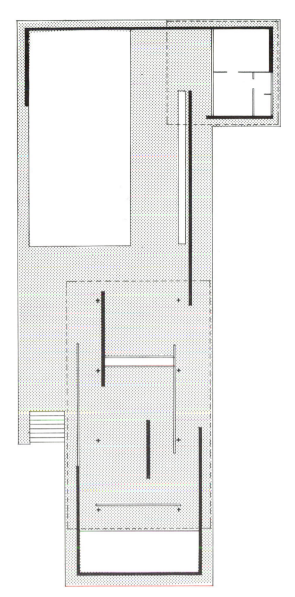

Figure 19 *German Pavilion, Barcelona, by Mies van der Rohe.*

adjoining entry landings to most of Wright's houses, within the retaining walls of Smith House, and in the hollow of the Montessori School landing. A cupping of the interspace, and the dilation of each wall in Wright's buildings at its terminus so as to anchor the landing's extremities in place and assert possession of the level by a corporeal outpost, creates the unmistakable impression of an in-between spatial entity cemented to the building shell.

While a sense of belonging to a building is elicited by stepping on a landing that is itself adhered to that building, the attachment remains vicarious and tenuous if a person does not, at the same time, belong in a territorial sense to the landing upon which he or she stands. While fully developed territorial bonds of in-habitation are not possible in the comings and goings of transitional passage, particularly for a visitor, the embryonic germ of territorial dwelling occurs with every act of sitting. To sit is to temporarily claim territory and appropriate space for oneself, and thus to concretely belong here and now. It is no accident that we use the expression 'to take a seat'. Landings containing built-in benches, as in the traditional stoop and the Amsterdam Student Hostel (see Figure 21), or low walls that serve as seats, as at Hertzberger's Montessori School and Smith's House, invite such existential attachment to the inter-space. Intermediate landings of the Guell Park contain an assortment of ceramic faced benches – both inwardly cave-shaped and outwardly fan-shaped. Concrete parapet walls at Centraal Beheer are formed as benches with railing back, and occur along lengthy stretches of overhang, as well as brief depressions and folds of wall. These lodging points provide existential footholds. Only

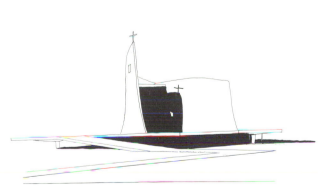

Figure 20 *Presidential Chapel, Brasilia, by Niemeyer.*

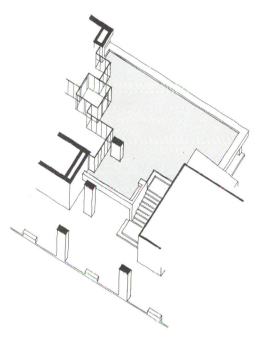

Figure 21 *Student hostel, Amsterdam, by Hertzberger.*

by coming to a stop can a person become fixed and rooted to a place, and the seat offers a deliberate physical invitation to pause and briefly settle. By contrast, the empty aprons of the Presidential Chapel and Amon Carter Museum fully alienate people by preventing any bond with landings they traverse and by reducing the landings to paths of pure circulation. They propel movement and forbid settlement.

WELCOME MAT

The phenomenon of reciprocity underlies the universal meaning of the *welcome mat* and *red carpet* as greeting elements. These two-dimensional landings are friendly and gregarious gestures to the outside world, affirmations of human fellowship, and soften the isolating effects of architectural walls. Floor material inside is symbolized by these outside patches of fabric, just as the stoop symbolizes floor structure inside. By stepping on their surface, the entrant is similarly included territorially within while still bodily without.

A more permanent welcome mat is found in the zone of pavement before a doorway that contrasts in texture and colour with surrounding surfaces. The edge between different surface qualities creates a purely graphic boundary line and defines the outer fringe of the interior. At Zonnestraal Sanatorium, a square patch of dark interior pavement lies outside the glass doors. A similar example occurs in the enclosed veranda of the New Palace at Katsura (Figure 22), where an interspace is created deep within the building by a band of tatami mats that have been drawn across a threshold of shoji screen tracks from the reception area to form an inter-

iorized landing surrounded by the exteriorized wood terrain of a corridor.

The 'inness' of an outflowing pavement is enhanced if its composition recalls the building. At Wright's Vigo Sundt House (Figure 23), an interior pavement of hexagonal elements spreads under glazed doors to become the outdoor pavement of a carport-entry landing, thus producing additional interiority through the alignment of its granular indices with the angular planes of the building structure. The composition of flat paving pattern manifests the three-dimensional building pattern, creating an organic unity in their synonymous structures. A similar geometrical linkage of pavement to building is found in the way circular paving elements around the Guggenheim Museum echo, like unit cells of a crystal, the rounded segments and cylindrical shapes repeated through the entire building composition.

A particularly beautiful and evocative landing 'mat' is found at the Inner Gate to the Katsura Palace (Figure 24). The wood threshold of the gate is preceded by a

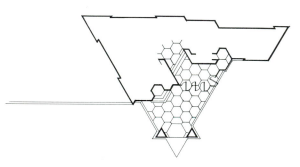

Figure 23 *Vigo Sundt House, Madison, by Wright.*

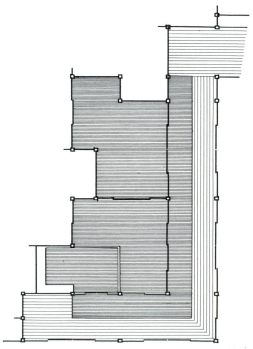

Figure 22 *Enclosed veranda, Katsura Palace, Kyoto.*

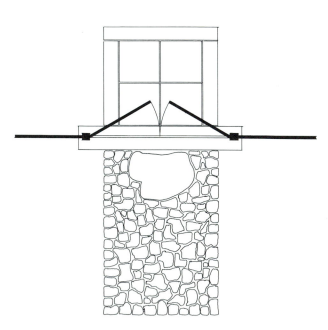

Figure 24 *Inner gate, Katsura Palace, Kyoto.*

rectangular pavement of cobble stones covered by moss, at the rear of which projects the upper surface of a single large, untrimmed stone and beyond the threshold several carefully cut rectangular stones. An effective landing of two stages is formed, with increasing fixity and 'inland' character from beginning to end, passing symbolically from water to pebbly beach, to a solid outcrop of rock, and finally to the dressed stone representing constructed dwelling. This coastal symbolism reminds us of the archetypical meaning of every landing for the act of entrance – it is an instrument for removing the guest from the rootless 'sea' outside and placing him or her upon a prominence of rooted 'land'. As soon as a person steps on to the landing, he or she has come 'ashore' and set foot upon the outermost 'headland' of the territorial world to be entered. Or, to use another voyaging metaphor, the landing provides a territorial 'mooring' upon which the guest can 'dock, drop anchor, and disembark' upon arrival at journey's end.

The foregoing discussion has sought to shed some light on one small piece of the architectural puzzle. The landing may often be a prosaic, homely and inglorious element of architecture; and certainly its design occupies a rather brief moment in the evolution of a whole building. The value of the landing to those who use and inhabit buildings, however, tends to grant it an extraordinary level of importance. Its form alone integrates us inside with our universe outside – at ground level – the realm where most activity occurs in a gravity-bound world such as ours. And since the landing is doubly accessible and connective along the ground, alienation is reduced and mutual belonging enhanced for those outside as well as those inside. If we take the fundamental questions of architecture to be those concerned with human beings – with determining what environmental qualities are fit for and nourishing to people both individually and collectively – then our search cannot help but acknowledge and explore the developmental possibilities of this symbiotic phenomenon.

REFERENCES

Buber, M. (1970) *I and Thou*, trans. W. Kaufman, New York: Scribner.

62 The case for a return to classical composition
Robert Adam

ARCHITECTURAL COMPOSITION

All architects compose buildings. All architects deliberately manipulate elements and parts of buildings to create a design and so engage in the process of architectural composition. The act of composition does not mean that the outcome will be successful or constitute a work of art, but the choice of one arrangement of details as against another will always be the process of composition.

Architectural composition is the final act in the design of the building which gives it both its special character and the individual stamp of the designer. It is the final act because it must bring the situation, function and construction of the building together with the ideology and artistry of the architect and, until all these factors are finally reconciled, the act of composition – and hence the design of the building – cannot be complete.

The distinction between one type of composition and another is created by the differing ideology of the architect. This ideology will affect the way that situation, function and construction are brought together but will not, in any viable architectural design, significantly diminish their significance.

Classical composition, in common with all types of architectural composition, is the practical consequence of a particular architectural ideology. Classical composition will, therefore, be the outcome of an ideology specifically identified as classical and distinguishable from other ideologies.

CLASSICAL ARCHITECTURE

Distinctions between different types of architecture are usually first made on a stylistic and, therefore, visual basis and there are generally acknowledged to be three principal Western stylistic categories: Classical, Gothic and Modernist. (While Modernist architects have disclaimed any stylistic identity, their buildings can be clearly distinguished on a solely visual basis and must, consequently, be counted as an identifiable style.)

Classical architecture is usually distinguished by the use of the classical orders but, as the orders can be so modified or suppressed in a classical design as to make them invisible to all but the trained eye, it is more useful to define all classical buildings as those which owe their inspiration and ancestry to the architectural traditions which originated in classical antiquity.

Relating either of these broad definitions of classical architecture to a single ideology is difficult. Classical architecture has been the dominant style from ancient Greece until the end of the Roman Empire, from the Renaissance until the early nineteenth century, shared prominence with the Gothic Revival in the nineteenth century, and became the principal style for the first half of this century. Altogether this represents some fifteen hundred years – excluding periods such as the Carolingian and Romanesque which can readily, according to the second definition above, be counted as classical. In this fifteen hundred years many ideologies have been represented by buildings which owe their inspiration or ancestry to classical antiquity.

Among the ideologies that inspired classical architects have been: the desire to recreate a imaginary golden age seen in the Renaissance and periods of antiquity; the desire for novelty and originality seen in mannerism and the baroque revival; the desire for a revolutionary reinterpretation of architecture and society seen in neo-classicism; the desire to express grandeur and power seen in the baroque; and the desire to express the democratic nature of government or society seen in the United States in the nineteenth century and Scandinavia in this century. It would be hard to bring together the fine detail of these different, and at times opposing, ideologies in such a way that they could produce a unified attitude to architectural composition.

None the less, it is not only possible to provide a definition of classical architecture that encompasses all of these different strains of classicism, as given above, but it is also possible to distinguish all varieties of classicism on ideological grounds at least from the Modern Movement, if not consistently – as we shall see – from Gothic.

CLASSICAL, GOTHIC AND MODERNIST

If classicism can be defined as drawing its inspiration or ancestry from the traditions handed down from classical antiquity, the distinguishing characteristic in this definition is a particular attitude to the past. In all forms of classical architecture, new design, however original or however dictated by modern needs, respects and makes of use the architecture of the past. History is not only a matter for academic study but also a valuable source of information for the present.

This attitude is the basis of the contrast between the philosophy of all varieties of classical architecture and the philosophy of Modernism and corresponds to the obvious visual contrast between the two broad stylistic groups.

The Modern Movement is notable for its rejection of history as a source for new architecture. Indeed, so confident were Modernist theorists that they had discovered the eternal truth of architecture that they saw no future possibility of the sort of stylistic change that had created the differences between historic periods – in short they believed that they had eliminated style altogether. Design would no longer owe anything to its past but would be created by a process of revolution that would destroy all links with history.

Out of this fundamental difference of attitude to the past comes the essential difference in ideology that distinguishes classical composition from Modernist composition.

The past is the key to comprehension. This applies in architecture as much as in language. Our comprehension of language is based on its historic use, it is passed down and diffused from generation to generation with an unbroken continuity. This natural continuity enables complete strangers to speak to one another and allows great figures of literature to communicate to the ordinary public. This historic consistency, while subject to evolution and change, gives language its richness and complexity. So it is with all the arts. It is impossible to recreate an architecture free from its own past without abandoning the possibility of communication with those not involved in this revolution – the ordinary public. The Modern Movement not only abandoned this possibility but created a theory to support it. According to the theory of the avant-garde, the comprehension of the public is not only unnecessary but even undesirable, the revolution is seen to be so self-evidently correct that the public are obliged to learn to understand rather than the artist to communicate.

The Modernist work of art, and so the Modernist attitude to composition, places little significance on public understanding. The guiding principle is the will of the artist and composition is as subject to revolutionary restructuring as it is to a desire to confuse and so shock the observer. Classical art, and so classical composition, by contrast, seeks to make the work comprehensible. It does so through the medium of history and tradition – the keys to comprehension.

So far these attitudes reveal no distinction between classical and Gothic architecture. Gothic architecture, as distinct from Gothic Revival architecture, evolved out of its own history within the continuity of its own traditions. There is no evidence for a revolutionary departure from classical architecture in its late, Romanesque, forms in the twelfth century. If anything, there is evidence for a revival of interest in antiquity during this period which can most readily be seen in the revival of classical Latin, the revival of Roman decoration and the reliance on classical authors in education.

The revolution in attitudes to history, the reawakening of a perception of anachronism, that occurred in the Renaissance did, however, revive certain specific compositional themes from antiquity which had become subdued and transformed, if not actually lost, in the Gothic period. As a consequence, compositional devices which have become common to all periods of classical architecture are not necessarily found in Gothic architecture. The distinction is, however, often slight and there is a case to be made for including medieval Gothic architecture within the classical tradition.

CLASSICAL COMPOSITION

Different periods of classical architecture have each had their own compositional character. Early Greek buildings employed a simple and uniform assembly of elements, while Hellenistic architecture expanded this repertoire to accommodate more complex building types. In the early Renaissance form was broken down into distinct component parts, whereas in the baroque period form was unified and fluid. Mannerist architecture manipulated and distorted familiar classical themes while neo-classicism relied on a relatively rigid application of ancient precedent. Throughout these and other developments of the classical tradition, however, ran certain compositional themes which acted as the common points of reference necessary to identify each subtle difference of interpretation as different. These acted as the essential grammatical structure of classical buildings which would be understood by the user and observer.

The consistent themes of classical composition can be summarized under five headings: proportion; symmetry; axial planning; spatial definition; and vertical and horizontal hierarchy. Seen in the context of the long history of classical architecture, none of these has been turned into a rigid formula; they are guiding themes that can include different interpretations and in combination make up some of the essential characteristics of classical buildings.

PROPORTION

The classical orders (see Figure 1), the use of which provides the common definition of classical architecture, are formal systems which relate a certain specific range of post (column) and lintel (entablature) details to one another and establish a range of proportions traditionally associated with each range of details or order. Classical buildings, and in particular temples in antiquity, have also had proportional systems calculated to suit their size, order and use. Equally, ranges of interior proportions have been developed by architectural theorists such as Alberti and Palladio with sophisticated methods of adapting these proportions to different circumstances.

These facts led to a great deal of doubtful speculation in the nineteenth century as historians and theorists sought – in typical nineteenth-century fashion – scienti-

Figure 1 *The five orders of architecture: (from left to right) Tuscan, Doric, Ionic, Corinthian, Composite.* (Source: *Richardson 1787*)

fic rules that could be used to govern proportion in architectural composition. These researches have become today's myths and the idea of absolute classical proportion persists to this day amongst both critics and supporters of classical architecture. Principal among these myths is the 'golden section', which is attributed to classical designs in antiquity and the Renaissance and is thus sanctioned by precedent. There is no more than the flimsiest circumstantial evidence and no documentary evidence for these claims.

There are similar misunderstandings about the proportional principles of the orders themselves. While there is no doubt that the orders have, since their earliest development, been based on proportional systems that relate principal overall sizes to details in a way that differentiates one order from another, the application of these proportions has been a great deal less rigid than many authors would have us believe. Factual evidence from both antiquity and the Renaissance demonstrates that, within a generally understood proportional foundation, architects have modified the proportions of the orders for both practical and aesthetic reasons.

Classical proportioning is not a rigid application of rules but a flexible response to an open-ended accumula-

tion of historical experience. Precision is not the determining factor, rather it is a knowledge, understanding and commitment to the classical tradition. This is an intellectual counterpart of commonplace visual familiarity and this correlation between the intellectual and the everyday gives classical proportioning both its cerebral and popular appeal.

SYMMETRY

The arrangement of building plans and façades so that they are identical about a central line or axis – symmetry – is not unique to classical architecture. Prehistoric civilizations and Egyptian and oriental cultures also constructed symmetrical architecture, particularly for important buildings. This seems to be a natural disposition of elements which reflects the symmetry of human and animal forms and is related to simple rational geometric shapes.

The persistence of this basic compositional device over two or more millennia has given cultural reinforcement to its perceptual significance. The location of an entrance centrally on a façade is an accepted convention which facilitates the comprehension and use of a building. The expectancy of a roughly symmetrical arrangement of rooms permits orientation in a strange interior.

While symmetry is generally desirable in classical design, it is not always possible. Narrow buildings, such as terraced houses (Figure 2), cannot have central entrances and make proper use of the space available; complex plans cannot always have symmetrically arranged rooms, and awkward sites often will not contain symmetrical buildings. Indeed, classical planning often arises out of a tension between function, site and symmetry which, if successful, will structure the function in a comprehensible form without any loss of efficiency. This design process is, however, often very testing and requires the assistance of other classical compositional themes such as the use of the axis.

AXIAL PLANNING

The central line of a symmetrical plan is its axis. Early Greek temples had only one central axis which concentrated attention on the entrance and the image of the deity (see Figure 3). From this simple beginning axial planning has become one of the most useful classical compositional devices.

Axes give structure and direction to plans and spaces. The traditional church plan (Figure 4) adds to the central axis from the door to the altar one or more secondary and tertiary axes. Each axis gives emphasis to a door, altar, chapel or other feature according to its relative importance and this is readily comprehensible in the plan. When the use and size of rooms makes a symmetrical arrangement impossible, axes can give the plan

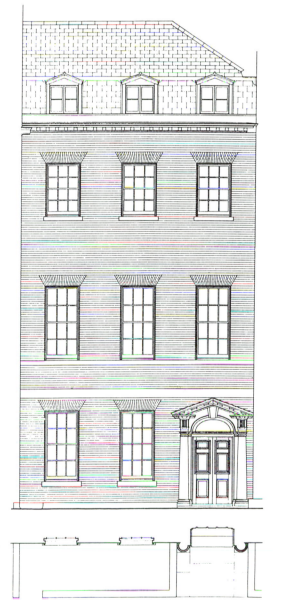

Figure 2 *English terraced house, after a drawing by Peter Wyld.*

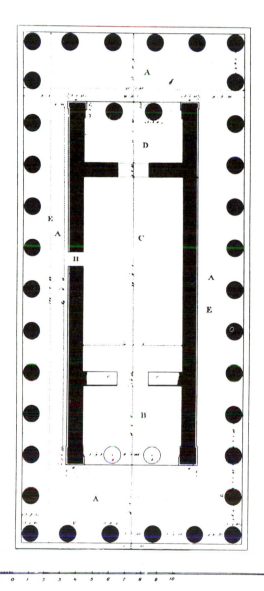

Figure 3 *A Greek temple plan: Temple of Hephaestus, Athens.* (Source: *Stuart and Revett 1787*)

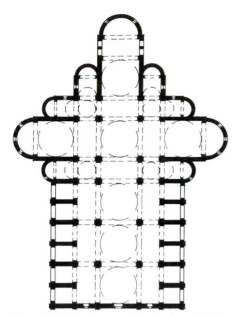

Figure 4 *A Renaissance church plan: Sta Giustina, Padua. The main axis is supplemented by axes to the additional altars in the semicircular apsed spaces, after Jacob Burckhardt.*

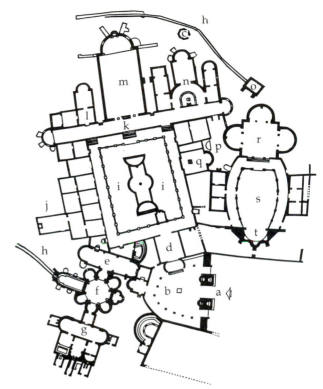

a	Entrance archway	j	North wing
b	Entrance court	k	Grand corridor
c	Latrines	l	Northeast suite
d	Vestibule	m	Basilica
e	Baths, hall	n	Southeast suite
f	Baths, octagon with cold plunges	o	Water tank
g	Baths, heated rooms, and plunges	p	Open connective space
h	Aqueducts	q	Orpheus room (shrine?)
i	Main peristyle and fountain court	r	Triconch
		s	Curved peristyle
		t	Nymphaeum

Figure 5 *Plan of a late Roman villa, Piazza Armerina, Sicily, c.315–25. A series of loosely planned spaces, each with its own axial symmetry and linked together by axial movement through the building.* (Source: *MacDonald 1986*)

a structure which describes how movement from space to space is organized. Irregular plans, such as those of Roman buildings (see Figure 5), can have complicated interrelationships between axes where the axial structures of individual spaces mix with axes connecting one space to another, giving a rationale to the experience of an apparently confusing collection of volumes. Beaux-Arts planning in the nineteenth and early twentieth century used carefully categorized and simple axial systems to bind together large and complex buildings.

The axis is so fundamental to the organization of architectural space that no intelligently considered composition in any style can avoid, at the very least, confronting the issue of axial movement and organization of space. The classical use of the axis, however, through its historical development, is fully integrated with all other aspects of classical design. While the application of the orders may be the surface hallmark of classical design, a regulated axial structure will always lie beneath and reveal itself throughout the design from the plan to details of the interior decoration.

SPATIAL DEFINITION

Axial planning is only the first and most significant element in the classical definition of space. All types of volume and space – rooms, internal courts and external spaces – can be given a geometric structure which explains their form. This compositional principle can be applied to rooms designed according to geometric proportions (Figure 6) as well as to irregular spaces which can be brought together with focal elements and surface patterns creating a regularity and legibility otherwise absent (see Figure 7).

Figure 6 *Salt store by Claude Nicholas Ledoux: design for the entrance vestibule. An example of the use of simple geometry in the organization of space.* (Source: *Ledoux 1847*)

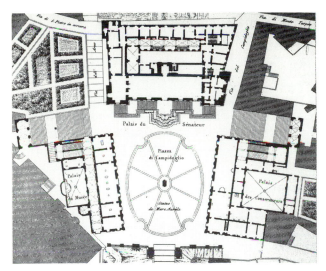

Figure 7 *Piazza di Campidoglio, Rome, by Michelangelo: irregular space made regular.* (Source: *Letarouilly 1840–57*)

The geometry of space is defined either by the use of readily perceivable proportions or by the treatment of the surfaces that surround the volume, or – more commonly – both. To the observer there is a more or less obvious series of clues which will lead to an understanding of the geometry or geometric rationale that has been applied to the space.

There is no single technique and the result can range from bare volumes lucid by their simplicity to the complex decoration of interiors which breaks down the space into multiple geometric components (see Figure 8).

Figure 8 *Staircase from the Palazzo Braschi, Rome: decorative organization of space.* (Source: *Letarouilly 1840–57*)

Figure 9 *A Greek temple: front elevation of the Parthenon, Athens.* (Source: *Stuart and Revett 1787*)

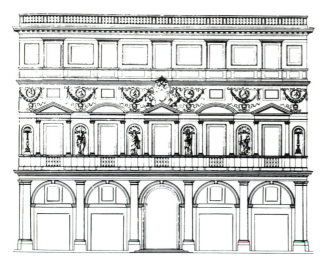

Figure 10 *A Renaissance house in Rome: minor variations only denote the entrance.* (Source: *Letarouilly 1840–57*)

Figure 11 *Palladian villa for Girolamo Ragona at Le Glizze: the entrance as a major feature by the addition of a portico.* (Source: *Scamozzi 1778*)

The classical orders themselves often, but by no means universally, provide the means of describing this framework.

The classical definition of space is a method of allowing the individual to feel secure in the knowledge of the space he or she inhabits. At the same time the visible geometric structure gives the designer a framework within which the emphasis of features and details can be varied to make their relative significance intelligible.

VERTICAL AND HORIZONTAL HIERARCHY

The application of vertical and horizontal hierarchy to a design progressively differentiates elements by changing the visual emphasis of different parts of a building. This device can be used to express the different functions of elements and to organize a rhythmical relationship between component parts.

While simple buildings, such as Greek and Roman temples (see Figure 9), are sufficiently self-contained to require little or no diversity between the parts, large or complex structures can become monotonous and individual elements tend to lose their identity.

The enhancement of the entrance is the most elementary hierarchical exercise. This can be done by little more than increasing the quality of detail in the relevant area (Figure 10) or by introducing a distinctive feature such as a portico (Figure 11). A long façade can include a series of similar modulations often terminated with pavilions of an almost independent design (Figure 12). Vertical variations in emphasis and detail, such as the *piano nobile* (Figure 13) can describe on the exterior the particular importance of different levels in the interior or, in tall buildings, can reinforce the practical and visual significance of the street level and upper floors (Figure 14).

Figure 12 *Electoral Palace at Mannheim, 1670, by Jean Marot: horizontal hierarchy.* (Source: *Courtauld Institute, Conway Library*)

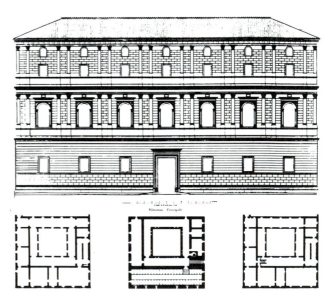

Figure 13 *Palazzo Giraud-Torliona, Rome, fifteenth century. The piano nobile is expressed with decoration: vertical hierarchy.* (Source: *Letarouilly 1840–57*)

The classical orders themselves are both the source and instrument of these hierarchical variations in detail. The details of the orders can be increased or decreased, decoration can be applied or removed and parts can be removed or added back selectively. The long-established use of classical details makes this possible, the orders are so familiar that they can be alluded to by no more than selected elements. This principle can be applied at all scales in a classical composition and so provide the opportunity to communicate the relative significance of buildings and their parts with economy and subtlety.

Classical composition is neither a series of rules nor a method of restricting creativity. It is not specific to any historical period and does not prevent the introduction of new architecture. It will not make bad design good any more than good design bad. It is a traditional framework developed through centuries of practice which not only gives the designer a medium for self-expression but also gives a structure that enables that self-expression to be communicated to the user and observer.

Each element of classical composition is a systematic method of providing a common level of experience between the designer and the user which permits a series of levels of mutual understanding. If these systems are abandoned, so are the possibilities of creating an architecture that speaks to its public. Without a common framework, self-expression and creativity can be squandered in incomprehension and obscurity.

REFERENCES AND FURTHER READING

Alberti, L.B. (1485) *De Re Aedificatoria*, trans. J. Rykwert, N. Leach and R. Tavernor, *On the Art of Building, in Ten Books*, 1988, Cambridge Mass. and London: MIT Press.

Chitham, R. (1985) *The Classical Orders of Architecture*, Sevenoaks: Butterworth.

Ledoux, C.N. (1847) *Works*, Ramée edn, Paris; reprinted 1983, Princeton, NJ: Princeton Architectural Press.

Letarouilly, P. (1840–57) *Edifices de Rome Moderne*, Paris.

Lewis, P. and Darley, G. (1986) *Dictionary of Ornament* London: Macmillan.

MacDonald, W. (1986) *The Architecture of the Roman Empire*, Vol. II: *An Urban Appraisal*, London and New Haven: Yale University Press.

McKim, Mead and White (1925) *A Monograph of the Work of McKim, Mead and White 1879–1915*, New York: Architectural Book Publishing; reprinted 1985, New York: Da Capo Press.

Meyer, F.H. (1974) *Handbook of Ornament*, revised edn, ed. T. Birks, London: Duckworth.

Normand, C. (1819) *Parallel of Orders of Architecture*, London: Alec Tiranti, 1987.

Palladio, A. (1570) *The Four Books of Architecture*, trans G. Leoni (1715); facsimile edn 1965, New York: Dover.

Richardson, G. (1787) *A Treatise on the Five Orders of Architecture*, London.

Scamozzi, V. (1778) *Les Batiments et les Dessins de Andrea Palladio*, Vol. II, Vicenza.

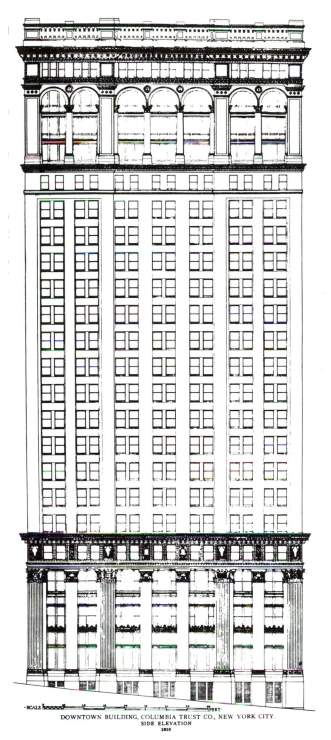

DOWNTOWN BUILDING, COLUMBIA TRUST CO., NEW YORK CITY.
SIDE ELEVATION
1910

Figure 14 *Columbia Trust Company Building, New York, 1910, by McKim, Mead and White: vertical hierarchy in a tall building.* (Source: *McKim, Mead and White 1925*)

The combination of symmetry and hierarchical planning leads to a predominance of uneven numbers of divisions in the plan and façade of a building. A uneven number horizontally will provide a central entrance, and vertically will give a façade a base, middle and top, so duplicating at a large scale the division of the classical column into base, shaft and capital.

Scholfield, P.H. (1958) *The Theory of Proportion in Architecture,* Cambridge: Cambridge University Press.

Serlio (1537–51) *The Five Books of Architecture,* trans. van Aelst (1606), facsimile edn 1982, New York: Dover.

Stratton, A. (1986) *The Orders of Architecture,* London: Studio Editions.

—— (1987) *Elements of Form and Design in Classic Architecture,* London: Studio Editions.

Stuart, J. and Revett, N. (1787) *Antiquities of Athens,* Vol. II, London.

Vitruvius (before AD 27) *De Architectura,* trans M.H. Morgan 1914, *The Ten Books on Architecture;* facsimile edn 1960, New York: Dover.

Wittkower, R. (1988) *Architecture Principles in the Age of Humanism,* London: Academy Editions.

63 Typological theories in architectural design
Micha Bandini

The word typology means the study of types. Typology is concerned with those aspects of human production which can be grouped because of some inherent characteristics which make them similar. The theory of typology is thus that of conceptualizing those categories.

The issue of types and typology becomes of fundamental importance in artistic production whenever the artist is confronted with, on the one hand, the weight of historical precedent and, on the other, artistic invention. If an artist is interested in contributing to the culture of human artefacts he or she will have to confront the problem of type, whether choosing the avant-gardist position of rejecting history, or accepting the continuation of tradition.

It becomes obvious, then, why typology is of central interest to architecture, since architecture cannot exist in a vacuum but will always be found in a context which is often pregnant with historical references. These are precedents which designers might want either to follow or to distance themselves from, but which, nevertheless, because of their nature, condition the act of creative invention itself.

It is of cultural significance that typology becomes relevant in architecture every time the following two issues are simultaneously present: when similar, but different, architectural objects are needed to house similar functions (for example, banks, schools); when the validity of a dominant stylistic convention is being challenged. Thus typology assumed primary significance at the end of the eighteenth century, when the classical tradition of architectural composition was confronted by the emerging needs of an industrializing society; it was again in the forefront of the architectural debate during the 1920s and the 1930s, when the so-called Modern Movement was expected to provide an alternative aesthetic for an ever-increasing number of building requirements. And typology once again became important in the late 1960s and the early 1970s, when a number of architects began to question both the validity of the Modernist aesthetic and its solutions.

In other words, typology appears to become of prime relevance to architectural debates when the cultural parameters which have lent authority to a certain manner of formal expression lose their credibility and thus become less prescriptive. An example of this is when it starts to be acceptable to claim that, say, a bank, which needs to be recognized as such (by belonging to a 'family of banks' and by representing 'bankness' in its design), could convey respectability, security and solidity in ways different from that of the traditionally composed façade with a classical order.

The moment of stylistic doubt, the moment of recognizing the need to form part of a seriality, and yet be different from it, brings typology to the forefront of architectural theory. However, other fundamental questions arise. Is type something easily recognizable and reproducible? Does following a type mean designing something equal to what has already been proposed as a precedent?

To this, two different answers have been traditionally given. The first assigns to type an ideal role, that of a mental construct which is not embodied in any specific form but which is adapted and elaborated by the designer, so that invention can coexist with tradition and the authority of precedents. The second sees type as a tool for the composition of schematic objects which might become real architecture if the needs of social and economic production require their particular conformation.

The first answer is usually attributed to Quatremère de Quincy who, following the Neo-Platonic tradition of neo-classicism, defined 'type' as an a priori which can be further transformed by the designer to fit his imagination and the requirements of the brief (Quatremère de Quincy 1788–1825). The second answer comes from J.N.L. Durand who, following contemporary theories of taxonomy in the natural sciences, believed that the nature of a type is that of a classifiable form, composed from primary architectural elements which, combined with the laws of descriptive geometry, can produce a model to be copied (Durand 1802).

But while the conventions of a tradition characterize these two positions as opposites, a closer reading of Quatremère and Durand shows an absence of that rigid schematization which had been the main feature of their posthumous interpretation.[1] Thus when Quatremère makes the distinction between type and model he is not only reaffirming the predominance of the ideal over the contingent, he is also indicating the need to provide, through an inspiring mental construct, a workable indicator for practising architects. Likewise, J.N.L. Durand, who declares the importance of a 'model' rooted in history in both the *Précis des Leçons* (1802), where he indicates a geometrical compositional procedure, and in the *Recueil et parallèle des tous les édifices anciens et modernes* (1800) where he traces their historical lineage. Thus Durand's conceptual justification of the 'model' is reached through analysing the tradition of the formation of certain types and through successively elaborating on them with the belief, common to the culture of his time,

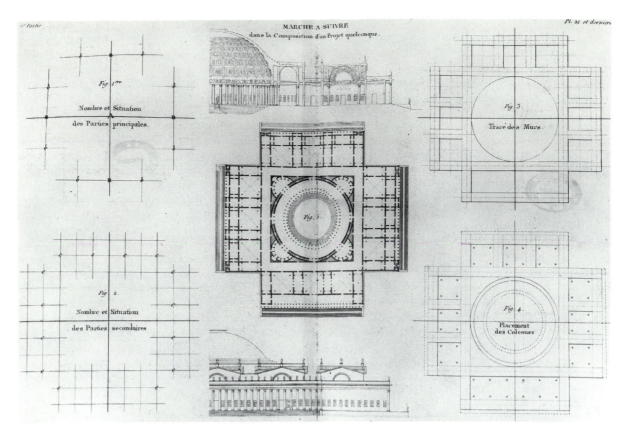

Figure 1 *'Steps to follow in the composition of any project.'* (Source: *Durand 1813, copyright: RIBA*)

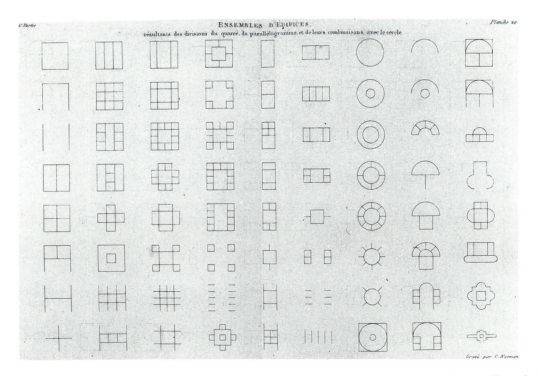

Figure 2 *An ensemble of architectural forms derived from the division of simple geometrical configurations.* (Source: *Durand 1802–5, copyright: Courtauld Institute, Conway Library*)

that if the classical language had been able to sustain architecture over the previous centuries then it would be within that tradition of composition that the requirements of the nineteenth century were likely to be met (see Figures 1 and 2).

It is from this mixed heritage that the theory of typology came to represent within the polemic of the Modern Movement both the perfectibility of the industrially produced mass object and the ideal timeless perfection of certain forms. Muthesius in his advocacy for a better industry, Le Corbusier in his conception of a minimum unit in the composition of a larger 'Unité', and Ernst May, Alexander Klein and the second CIAM congress (1929) in their search for a minimum housing standard, all shared that tradition which chose to keep open the ambiguity between type and model because of the workability of the latter and the formal authority of the former.

Most contemporary evidence now shows that these architects, while taking part, theoretically, in the avantgardist polemic against history, in their practical work often elected to invent on the basis of a tradition which allowed the linking of contemporary creativity with an awareness of the formal richness of the past. But the way in which this manner of working was received, codified and transmitted by critics and historians to others, in order to make it more palatable and useful, is rather different. The flexibility, one could almost say the ambiguity, which was built into early Modernist theorizations was not incorporated in those narrower recordings of architecture which saw type only as a non-specific concept, and model only as a very convenient way for appropriating precedents.

Thus type, in the reductive exception it acquired through its post-Second World War vulgarization, came to be almost synonymous with two trends of thought: either with functionalism, which was negatively equated with the *Existenzminimum* research, or with the classification, and possible further production, of previous architectural examples.

Within the European architectural culture in general the typological issue was quickly recognized and analysed in all of its complexity because of concern that the problem of history was left unresolved by the Modern Movement. By contrast, within the Anglo-Saxon world, up to the late 1960s, only Alan Colquhoun and Nikolaus Pevsner seem to have considered the topic important enough to warrant some serious consideration.

Alan Colquhoun's article (Colquhoun 1967) is intellectually positioned within the Anglo-Saxon debate on design methods, and attacks the underlying design-scientism by demonstrating that social and iconic values are as essential as technological and organizational ones for the development of the physical tools needed for shaping our environment. His belief that 'after all the known operational needs have been satisfied, there is still a wide area of choice in the final configuration' (Colquhoun 1967: 45) is offered as an alternative to the Modern Movement's ideology which had been reduced into 'biotechnical determinism on the one hand and free expression on the other'. The latter he claims could more appropriately be fulfilled if creation is seen as 'a process of adapting forms derived either from past needs or from past aesthetic ideologies to the needs of the present' (Colquhoun 1967: 47). This does not mean the acceptance of all forms from the past as immutable; instead there is a need to work with the possibility for transformation already built into conventionally based typological approaches. These Colquhoun considers as the only appropriate antidotes to the then prevalent mechanisms of empiricist functionalism.

But while Colquhoun's contribution enriched the architectural debate, Nikolaus Pevsner's book on building types (Pevsner 1976) seems to have contributed retrospectively to its impoverishment. Perhaps because of the adoption of a close-to-the-sources perspective, as required by the scholarly apparatus of his later research (for example, the project for documenting all historic buildings in the United Kingdom), Pevsner seems to have abandoned that larger breadth of vision which informed his earlier, seminal work for a narrower view of architecture and its components. Whilst it is to be applauded that Pevsner attempted this work at all – because, as he informs the reader, 'There is, to the best of my knowledge, no history of building type in existence' (Pevsner 1976: foreword) – it is quite lamentable that he would not acknowledge the by then quite conspicuous number of new European contributions on the topic, even if his aim was that of merely documenting the nineteenth-century emergence of new types. Not only does Pevsner not give us the benefit of contributing to the theoretical debate between type and model, but also the descriptive nature of his book suggests an interpretation merely by default. Thus it deprives its readers, most of whom have no access to primary source material in foreign languages, of the richness of the theoretical hypotheses behind the projects as well as failing to alert them to the precariousness of the status of the built examples. Pevsner thus lent his by then considerable authority to the anti-speculative Anglo-Saxon view of theory.

It is mainly because of this anti-intellectual bias that typological debates did not take place during the 1960s and 1970s within an Anglo-Saxon cultural context while they flourished in the Continental one. To be furthered they needed not only a strong tradition in Modernism (and a familiarity with its polemical currents) but also an intellectual curiosity which believes in the unity of theory and practice for architectural design. These conditions being largely absent in Britain and only partially present in the USA, it is easy to see with hindsight how and why the Anglo-Saxon acquaintance with typology has been acquired later through the reception of formally dominated researches and thus why, in a cultural context where legitimization in design still comes largely from following the brief correctly, typological interests have been pursued with diffidence outside a small circle of acolytes.

On the Continent the post-war cultural situation was rather different. Not only was Europe the birthplace of those different trends which historical reductivism labelled the 'Modern Movement', but most architects there regarded as central to the architectural debate the problem of history, which the historical avant-gardes had denied, but which post-war reconstruction had made so important.

So it here suggested that typological interests started to develop again because of two issues merging: history, and the need to operate in urban contexts which had been formed, in most European towns, by morpho-logical aggregates based on traditional housing typo-logies.

Typological debates became very important in Italy, perhaps because immediately after the Second World War history became central to architectural debate. The reason for this was not just that the country needed to obliterate the representational ambiguities of its im-mediate Fascist past by linking itself to the rationality of Modernism and to its Enlightenment roots, but also because younger designers, searching again to ground architecture within specific cultural and geographic settings, questioned the 'internationality' of the Modern Movement and its legitimacy as a 'model' valid for all times and in all contexts.

For a while the debate between model and type seemed to lean on the Neo-Platonic interpretation of type, especially because this was the thesis of an authoritative article by G.C. Argan which has appeared in different versions since 1965 and which achieved its ultimate status when it became the entry on 'type' in the *Enciclopedia Universale dell' Arte*.[2]

Argan's argument, in equating the role that typology serves in architecture with that of iconology in art, not only followed the art-criticism hypothesis current at the time, but also made hypothetical suggestions to those Italian architects who were searching for a rationale from which to operate.

His three-tiered argument, used frequently by those who support the idealist interpretation on type, starts by stating:

> Type is characterized as a set of rules deduced through a procedure of reduction of a series of formal variants from a base-form or from a communal scheme. If type is the product of this regressive procedure, the found base-form cannot be under-stood as a mere structural framework, but either as the internal framework of form in its autonomous artistic value or as the principle which includes in itself not only all the formal configurations from

which it has been deduced but also the possibility of further variations and even the complete modification of the structure of the given type.

(Argan 1958: 3)

Argan then proceeds to demonstrate that type is an integral part of any artistic creation first by stating that 'typological series are not formed in history because of the practical function of buildings but because of their configuration', and second by making the hierarchy of architectural scale the conceptual means by which such formal configurations may be subdivided into categories. In order to do this he chose three all-encompassing categories: 'the first which includes entire configurations of buildings, the second [which comprehends] large building elements, and the third [which is concerned with] decorative elements' (Argan 1958: 4).

The attractiveness of Argan's article is due not only to its intrinsic appeal but also to the way the argument builds up towards a process which closely resembles, in its internal logic, the one which gives rise to rationally based design. It could be reasonably hypothesized, then, that what came to be understood by those European architects who were inclined towards this design approach, and they were the majority, as a basis for a typological debate was:

1   that type is an idea and not a precise form, which means that it can be elaborated upon;
2   that this modifiable concept is similar, in the internal logic of its historical deployment, to the internal logic which the architect employs when creating the forms of his or her projects;
3   that through the analogical combination of the two (the type-ideal-form and the architect-ideal-form) the designer could approach the pressing problem of history; and finally
4   that the procedure through which all of this could be achieved would be to follow a design process which would be careful to identify the appropriate-ness of different hierarchical scales of composition both in appraising and in designing buildings.

These ideas seemed especially relevant, during the 1960s and the 1970s, for the Venice School of Architecture where a number of influential teachers came to regard the investigation of the typological structure of a city as a prerequisite for a morphological intervention into it. Within this tradition of enquiry, begun by Giuseppe Samoná,[3] and furthered by Saverio Muratori, with a detailed survey of the Venetian urban context (Muratori 1960), Aldo Rossi chose typology as the main topic of discussion for the academic year of 1963–4 (Rossi 1963–4). In this way a long series of contributions began through which his approach to typology developed and changed.

While it is clear that Rossi, in this early phase, saw building typology as the repository of the permanent morphological features of the city, the role he attributes to type in respect to the boundaries of architecture is more ambiguous. Does type possess socio-anthropological connotations, which the designer can access through its analysis and elaboration, or is such a method doomed to failure and can architecture only be pursued within an autonomous position? Rossi's contemporaneous 'architecture of silence' seems to further the second hypothesis, especially because it is pursued in conjunction with his concept of the city formed of parts formally concluded where, in the urban structure, building typologies provide the networking tissue and monuments the exceptions (see Figure 3). Rossi writes (almost paraphrasing Argan):

> Type is thus a constant and manifests itself with a character of necessity; but even though it is predetermined, it reacts dialectically with technique, function and style as well as with both the collective character and the individual moment of the architectural artifact.
>
> (Rossi 1976: 41)

If Rossi's initial concept seems to draw on the ideal aspect of type, particularly emphasizing the ethical

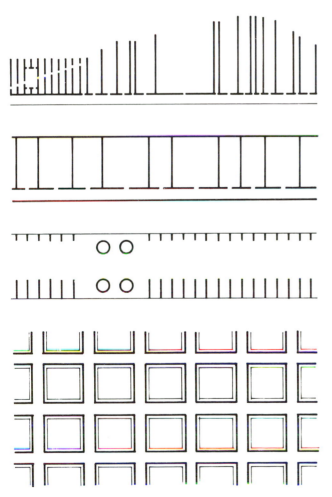

Figure 3 *Typological diagram, 1979, by Aldo Rossi.*

correctness of typology as the appropriate 'political' compositional device,[4] he would, later on, relax into a more all-embracing attitude which would focus on those aspects of the relationship between urban morphology and building typology (as, for example, with 'memory') which the designer could use in order to transform the urban context through his or her own creative sensibility.

But in those years of confusion, when general political issues became mixed up with the intellectual difficulties which architects were encountering in understanding their role in society, liberating themselves from the Modern Movement straitjacket while simultaneously seeking to give 'form' to their projects, these kind of compositional approaches provided security. Thus a 'political' working document, drawn up during the academic year 1967–8 by a group of students tutored by Massimo Scolari, characterized type as a principle of architecture based on formal analysis; twenty years later Scolari would write in appraising this phenomenon:

> Even the definition of 'type as a principle of architecture' was only apparently a theoretical statement. In Rossi's architecture this was, immediately and from the very start, a not reducible model; and it was so close to the idea that it remained ambiguously poised between simplicity and oversimplifcation. To the latter belong all the replicas and the variations produced by the imitators.
>
> (Scolari 1985: 45)

While Rossi pursued, through the ideal type, his own idea of architecture, in the same years Carlo Aymonio saw typology more as part of that current of thought which drew on the rationality of both the Enlightenment and the Modern Movement. To him, building types are architectural hypotheses, 'useful to all just because necessary'. Thus 'type becomes the reference point of the emerging urban structure'; however, 'the boundary between "type" and "model" would often be weak and the prototype will later become the type to be confirmed in the subsequent built examples' (Aymonino 1976: 76–7)

If this represents the reality of the historical process responsible for the construction of the Western bourgeois city during the last three centuries, then it is possible to identify those characteristics which define building types. For Aymonino these are: first, a one-to-one relationship between function and form; second, an indifference to context; and third, a certain independence from building regulations. This stringent logic is followed through to its natural conclusion so that it becomes inevitable that, because of this kind of historical analysis, Aymonino would refute both Argan's negative aesthetic judgment on nineteenth-century functional typologies and Rossi's hypothesis of a city of parts, attributing for himself the possibility of an urban architecture where the relationship of monument to context would not be given, as in Rossi, but would remain dynamic and always in the process of becoming.

The initial emphasis placed within the Italian neo-rational mode of architectural composition on the relationship between urban morphology and building typology might well be due to its initial didactical impetus. To this might also be attributed a certain initial rigidity and schematism of the concept, which in its application to the teaching of students risked degenerating into the belief that the project would follow, *ipso facto*, from the analysis. While it must be recognized that both Aldo Rossi and Carlo Aymonino wrote against such reductive vulgarizations, it must also be pointed out that much of the international fame of this compositional method was due to the fact that its ambiguity lent itself to such reductive experiments. This seems to be the path pursued by the European and American typological experiments which after a wealth of analysis for a time froze into the mechanical reproduction of the investigated models.[5]

Particularly interesting in this respect is the *excursus* of the French followers of the typological school. Notwithstanding their allegiance to J.N.L. Durand, Wittkower and Aymonino, who had become the legitimizing authority for their writings,[6] to them the distinction drawn between analysis and project, so important for the political and cultural correctness of previous elaborations, became of secondary importance. Instead they seek to derive the project from the analysis of its urban components (Panerei 1979: 14).

Such attitude is very evident in the work of P. Panerai, as, for example, when he writes:

> But it is not only up to the project to enlarge the knowledge of the city, which would not be negligible, we must interrogate ourselves on the usage of typology, and ask ourselves if such work could, at a certain point, be of any utility in the process of designing. First of all typology is useless if one does not have any intention of making use of it. Why waste time observing part of a city, understanding the constitutive mechanisms of its tissue, if the hypothesis from which the design process springs is that of a *tabula rasa* operation or a bulldozer operation. If one continues to believe that there is a time for analysis and another for the project which will simply put logical forms to the 'objective' data given by the analysis, then one understands that analysis and project are but two moments, two faces of the same theoretical reflection, of the same responsible attitude towards the city. Urban analysis, and this is the thesis here defended, goes hand in hand with the criticism of those interventions which tend to demolish the city, to violate it, to annihilate it. Without such criticism urban analysis would be nothing but an alibi.
>
> (Panerai 1979: 14)

Bernard Huet's belief in an architecture which sees itself mainly as contributing to the structure of the city is at the centre of most research pursued at the Institut d'Etudes de Recherches Architecturales in Paris. There, a series of studies was spawned on the typo-morphological relationship underlying the structure of French cities. 'L'architecture urbaine' (as this approach is labelled) is seen as a political tool to contrast speculative developments, and a teaching method is proposed as a way to anchor design to a cultural and ideological dimension. It is interesting to note that Huet's response to the problem of mass teaching is conditioned by his belief in the supremacy of typology over other theoretical tools. This extends itself to the point that typology becomes the source of all architectural education, as when he writes:

> All the practical problems given to the students to solve should be considered in terms of urban quantity and repetition of type rather than in terms of the development of subjectivity based on the new and original. Compulsory typology must be a necessary beginning and not an end in itself for architecture consists in going beyond it.
>
> (Huet 1978)

The methodology of the French approach to typological questions seems to me particularly well exemplified by Castex and Panerai's study of the city of Versailles, where four analytical levels of investigation became the basis for reading the city. This prescriptive framework, which in its hierarchy strongly resembles Argan's interpretative categories, constitutes both the strength and weakness of these researches.[7] Castex, Depaule and Panerai seem to acknowledge the inherent ambiguity of their approach, for example when they write with respect to one of their later research projects:

> Among different possible ways of reading the city, we do consider the city as an architectural artefact which can be divided in distinct elements in order to emphasise differences. Such differences, which refer to different levels of meanings, have to be interpreted in the light of evidence external to architecture. In particular we are referring to the relationship between spatial organization and social practices, this being for us of primary importance. In order to do so we will be using the notion of model both from an architectural point of view ... and from a cultural one.... From this stems the apparent ambiguity of our work: it is a morphological study, but referred to examples belonging to a specific historical context, it is an architectural study, but at the urban scale, it is spatial too, but concerned with social aspects.
>
> (Panerai *et al.* 1980: 8–10)

The reputation of the typo-morphological approach is contemporaneous and linked with the emergence of the 'Tendenza' after the thirteenth Biennale of Milan, because those who recognized the necessity of a 'rational' and 'theoretical' framework for design approached the relationship between architecture and the city as a priority, and resorted to typology as being representative of a system of analytical investigation in which the project could be anchored. I think it is interesting to note here that the more widespread this attitude the looser the boundaries of its system of reference became, so that, by the end of the 1970s – either under the banner of 'rational' or of 'typology' – one could find a series of very different designs. These ranged from the purely morphological ones (see Figure 4) to those who saw 'the relationship between building typology and urban morphology' as still belonging to the alternative political climate of urban renewal of the late 1960s. Particularly representative of the formal approach to typology is Rob Krier's *Stadtraum in Theorie und Praxis* (1975), where the notion of urban space seems embodied by that of spatial type, the vessel of all functional, symbolic, social and historical contents. Krier's geometric characterization of spatial types through history clearly aligns itself within the tradition established by J.N.L. Durand (see Figure 5).[8]

In the early stages typology found its followers amongst architects of the Ticino region, perhaps stimulated by the teaching of Aldo Rossi at the Eidgenossische Technische Hochschule in Zurich, while others in France, Spain, Luxembourg and Portugal loosely saw typology and morphology as the rationale behind their crisp, geometric, well-balanced forms. The magazines *Lotus International*, *L'Architecture d'Aujourd'hui* and *Controspazio* used their influence to support these projects and articles within a polemical climate still largely dominated, at the top publishing level, by magazines which either supported an anodyne professionalism or furthered, as did *Domus* and *Architectural Design*, a more expressionist, individual, empirical and technologically based architecture.

A series of questions, now recognized as fundamental for all urban studies, was perhaps overlooked in the 1970s under the combined pressure of two major factors: first, that town planning was being influenced by pressure groups that were different from, and perhaps less concerned about these issues than, those originally envisaged by architects; and second, that architects themselves widely disagreed on the correct approach and expended vast amounts of energy in the polemical pursuit of one or other point of view. Was the relationship between building typology and urban morphology the most fruitful way in which urban form could be read? How does one account, within this approach, for the fact that different socio-political configurations are historically expressed with similar forms (or, even more puzzling, the reverse)? Is a prescriptive framework the

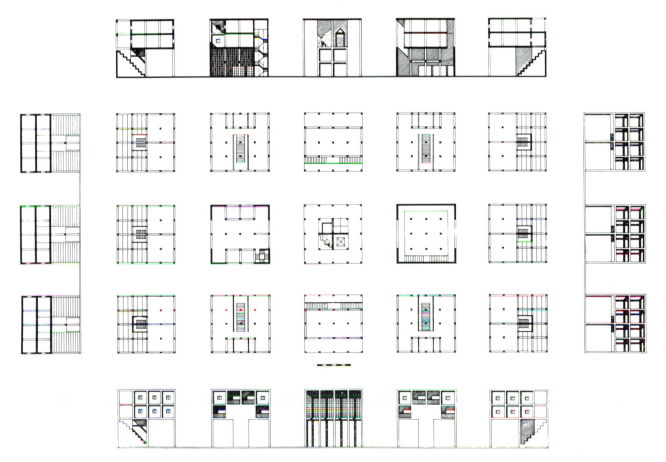

Figure 4 *Luogo e progetto, 1976, Franco Purini.*

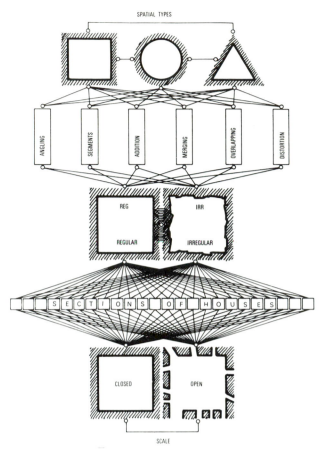

SPATIAL TYPES

ANGLING · SEGMENTS · ADDITION · MERGING · OVERLAPPING · DISTORTION

REG / REGULAR · IRR / IRREGULAR

S E C T I O N S O F H O U S E S

CLOSED · OPEN

SCALE

Figure 5 *Types of urban space by Rob Krier.* (Source: *Krier 1979*)

best way to further the kind of morphological imagination on which the formation of cities has been based in the past? Raphael Moneo aptly summarized the state of the art of typology at the end of this period when he wrote:

> typology has come to be understood simply as a mechanism of composition. The so called 'typological research' today merely results in the production of images, or in the reconstruction of traditional typologies. In the end it can be said that it is the nostalgia for types that gives formal consistency to these works.
>
> (Moneo 1978)

But such research efforts have left cultural traces which cannot easily be forgotten, either at the formal or at the intellectual level of architectural design. Typology was probably only a major issue for architectural theory during the 1960s and 1970s, but many current approaches to the city owe an implicit debt to those who furthered this debate. In a way typology has become another architectural convention and, as such, its usefulness is directly proportional to the looseness of its unverified boundaries, that is, until the cultural assumptions which underwrite it remain stable. After that we may well see another resurgence of the typo-morphological debate.[9]

NOTES

1 See Oechslin 1986 for a most illuminating analysis of both conceptions.

2 It is interesting to note that the English version of the *Enciclopedia* omits this specific entry.

3 Samoná's lifelong interest in the typological question is best represented in the long introduction to the collection of his essays (see Samoná 1978: 11–52).

4 For example, Rossi writes:

> The structural value of typology – and thus its prominence in architecture – is a compositional factor; it concerns first of all a choice, a tendency.... In order to make a typological choice it is necessary to make some references, these references are part of the choice or tendency.... in architecture, typological indifference means disorder. I do not refer to expressionistic disorder but to the disorder of not-architecture of non-choice.
>
> (Rossi 1979)

and also: 'The problem is to design new parts of the city choosing typologies able to challenge the status quo. This could be a perspective for the socialist city' (Rossi 1979).

5 Significantly, the longer Italian way of expressing this approach, i.e. 'the relationship between building typology and urban morphology', was dropped for a *tout court* 'typology'.

6 In this respect it is illuminating to read Panerai 1979.

7 Castex and Panerai's analysis, notwithstanding its historical dimension, is largely based on four categories: the overall form of the city in relation to the territory and with the stages of its growth; the big, monumental, atypical insertions within the urban tissue; the relationship of housing to work-place; and, finally, the single residential configuration.

8 The variety of design positions represented within the so-called 'rationalist' camp is simplified well in *Rational architecture rationelle* (Archive d'Architecture Moderne (AMM) 1978), a book presenting a series of projects which take on board the relationship between architecture and the traditional city. It includes a paper by A. Vidler (1976) which underpins the approach theoretically. He introduces the thesis, an interesting one notwithstanding the circularity of its argument, that a third typology (the one just presented by the rationalist approach) is equipollent to the previous two – the one that 'returned architecture to its natural origins' and the one that 'assimilated architecture to the world of machine production' (Vidler 1976: 28). Of the AAM activities and intellectual overtones, I think the article by Santelli (1981) is representative; in this article a correct urban rehabilitation is seen as being possible only if architects follow traditional typologies in their reconstructions.

9 It is interesting to note that in 1985 a double issue of *Casabella* (1985: 509–10) was dedicated to typology, which needed by then to be appraised both as a cultural phenomenon and as a disciplinary tool. This was provided by the magazine by extending the typological domain to encompass the landscape, and by asking some of the protagonists of the earlier debate to assess it. Today, that issue of the magazine reads more as an obituary than as the account of a lively debate.

REFERENCES

Argan, G.C. (1958) 'Typology', *Enciclopedia Universale dell'Arte* 1, Vol. XIV, Venice: Fondazione Cini.

Aymonino, C. (1976) *Il Significato delle citta*, Laterza.

Casabella (1985) 'The grounds of typology', *Casabella* 509/510 (January/February), special issue.

Colquhoun, A. (1967) 'Typology and design method', *Arena* 83 (June); reprinted in *Essays in Architectural Criticism*, Cambridge, Mass.: MIT Press, pp. 43–50.

Durand, J.N.L. (1800) *Recueil et parallèle des tous les édifices anciens et modernes*, Paris.

—— (1802–5) *Précis des leçons d'architecture données à l'Ecole Polytechnique*, Paris.

—— (1813) *Nouveau précis des leçons d'architecture données à l'Ecole Polytechnique*, Paris: L'Auteur.

Huet, B. (1978) 'The teaching of architecture in France, 1968–1978: from one reform to the next', *Lotus International* 21.

Krier, R. (1975) *Stadtraum in Theorie und Praxis*, Stuttgart: Karl Kramer; trans. *Urban Space: Theory and Practice*, Brussels: Archive d'Architecture Moderne.

Moneo, R. (1978) 'On typology', *Oppositions* 13 (Summer).

Muratori, S. (1960) *Studi per una operante storia urbana di Venezia*, Rome: Instituto Poligrafico dell Stato.

Oechslin, W. (1986) 'Premises for the resumption of the discussion of typology', *Assemblage* 1 (October): 37–56.

Panerai, P. (1979) 'Typologies', *Les Cahiers de la Recherche Architecturale* 4 (December): 3–21.

Panerai, P., Castex, J. and Depaule, J.C. (1980) *Formes urbaines: de l'îlotà la barre*, Paris; Italian edn 1981, *Isolato urbano e città contemporanea*, Milan: Clup.

Pevsner, N. (1976) *A History of Building Type*, London: Thames & Hudson.

Quatremère de Quincy, A.C. (1788–1825) 'Type', in *Dictionnaire d'architecture: encyclopédie méthodique*, Vol. III, part 2, Paris.

Rossi, A. (1963–4) 'Considerazioni sulla morphologia urbana e la tipologia edilizia', in *Aspetti e problemi della tipologia edilizia*, Venice: Venice University.

—— (1976) *L'architettura della città*, Bari: Laterza; trans. 1982 *The Architecture of the City*, Cambridge, Mass.: MIT Press.

—— (1979) 'Due progetti', *Lotus International* 7 (June).

Samoná, G. (1978) *L'unita architettura urbanistica: Scritti e progetti 1929–1973*, ed. P. Lovero, Milan: Franco Angeli.

Santelli, S. (1981) 'Réhabilitation et règles typologiques', *Archive d'Architecture Moderne* 21.

Scolari, M. (1985) 'The typological commitment', *Casabella* 509/510 (January/February).

Vidler, A. (1976) 'The third typology', *Oppositions* 7; reprinted 1978 in *Rational Architecture/Architecture Rationelle*, Brussels Archive d'Architecture Moderne.

64   An anthropology of building

Kenneth Frampton

In the sense in which they are used in the Italian debate, 'projection' and 'composition' are almost entirely absent from Anglo-Saxon architectural discourse. There are no professors of composition in Anglo-Saxon architectural schools. The intent behind exporting this distinction beyond the confines of the Mediterranean is presumably to interrupt the demagogic somnambulism which characterizes so much of the current Post-Modern polemic in the Anglo-Saxon architectural press.

The *Oxford English Dictionary* is of little assistance in elaborating this topic from an architectural standpoint save to indicate that both words have their modern origin in the mid-sixteenth century. During this period, when 'composition' first emerges with the sense of composing and hence of constructing the language itself (and then, by extension, of combining elements, be they architectural or musical), the idea of 'projection' is divided between the epistemology of mapping and the act of alchemical transmutation. England will have to wait until the beginning of the eighteenth century for orthographic projection to come into general usage, and yet another century for the term 'project' to acquire the connotations of a long-term proposal.

Within Western architecture, the intrinsically empirical bias of 'projection' has always been opposed to the formal logic of the academy. This dialogue is made more complex by the qualification of the rules of composition through the processes of projection and realization. In architectonic terms 'projection' seems to have its origins in laying out the arches and vaults, full size, on the floor of the cathedral before cutting the stones to their appropriate contours and raising the final construction.

In shifting from the organic continuity of the medieval period to the projective utopianism of the Enlightenment, the idea of progress transformed this processal aspect of projection by giving it a much more extended and programmatic frame of reference.

From the beginning of the eighteenth century the architectural project becomes increasingly implicated in socio-ideological, instrumental undertakings of a much more ambitious nature. Within the academic tradition, this more programmatic aspect of projection is to be finally facilitated by composition, above all in the work of J.N.L. Durand. In the succeeding century when the projective, instrumental thrust of the Enlightenment was to pass from the application of normative codes to an interrogation of its own constitutive elements, the

'other' of structural projection was to emerge to challenge the *mise en scène* of rational composition. The mid-nineteenth-century critique of Gottfried Semper and Eugène Viollet-le-Duc returns the architectural discourse to a reconsideration of the ontological determinants of projection and construction; the academic line reconsiders the constructional and symbolic nature of its basic elements. One critical line of the Modern Movement surely has its origins in this interaction between the tectonic body of revealed construction and the Neo-Platonic order of rationally composed space and form.

Projection as building first asserts itself as being unequivocally 'other' with the Gothic Revival – with the categorically anti-academic critique of the Enlightenment launched by A.W.N. Pugin. The empirical domesticity of the English Free Style – the irregular additive middle-class country houses – will be totally reconstituted after the First World War in the absolutely abstract, paradoxically *atectonic* pinwheeling compositions of the Constructivist avant-garde. It is significant that the main protagonists are renegade artists rather than architects. Their organic, centralized vortices prove incapable of generating continuous residential fabric or accommodating large-scale collective institutions. The formally discontinuous linear city of the Constructivists seems to be as much a consequence of formal preferences as it is an outcome of revolutionary ideology or an anticipation of the Megalopolis. Both the regressive nostalgia of the Arts and Crafts and the progressive assay of the avant-garde are successively compelled to limit the scope of their application to the private realm.

As Bruno Reichlin has argued, it is to Le Corbusier's lasting credit that he invented and elaborated a method (*le plan libre*) by which to integrate the literative space-form of the avant-garde with the normative academic paradigms of the Enlightenment. The fact that the free plan no longer commands our general attention in no way invalidates its potential for future development. The most monumental demonstration of this synthesis comes with Le Corbusier's project for the Palais des Nations (1927) and the Palais des Soviets (1931) both of which are elemental compositions in terms of method and result. As Le Corbusier was to put it in the caption which accompanied the alternative site plan for his Palais des Nations proposal, 'alternative proposition employing the same elements of composition' (Le Corbusier 1928). That Le Corbusier's method consisted of a combinatory design procedure *à la* Durand is borne out by the caption which accompanied the publication of eight alternative site plans for his Palais des Soviets; 'the

First published in 1986, in Italian and English, *Casabella* 520/1: 26–30.

various stages of the project, whereby the organs which are already established independently of each other, assume, little by little, their reciprocal positions in order to arrive at a synthetic solution'. Elsewhere he writes of the internal circulation in topographic-biological terms:

The vestibule and the entrance hall are truly 'classification machines'; all the numerous categories of users, while mutually seeing each other, follow precise itineraries which lead them automatically to their destination. These 'routes' (comprising inclined planes) are in a certain sense like 'mountain passes'.

Le Corbusier's Palais des Soviets synthesizes the three parallel paradigms of Western architecture first formulated by Vitruvius: the monumental symmetry of rational combination; the intimate asymmetry of empirical convenience; and the formal constitution of primary tectonic elements through the revelation of structural and constructional devices. At this particular juncture, Le Corbusier admits composition while Hannes Meyer *theoretically* rejects it on the grounds of its irrelevance with regard to modern instrumental, productive and ergonomic criteria. The demise of the avant garde after the early 1930s is reflected in Le Corbusier's renunciation of the *plan libre*; he returns to the authentic immediacy of the projective process and to that 'otherness' of fundamental construction which cuts backwards across time to combine the modern with the primordial, in such works as the Maison Errazuriz (1930) and the Maison de Week-End (1935).

Half a century has elapsed since this cellular, structural assembly was projected and realized as a topographically inflected collage of different tectonic elements. Thirty years later, Le Corbusier applied an equally fragmented, albeit systematized, mode of assembly to what was virtually a piece of urban infill: his unrealized hospital for Venice, projected in 1965.

Nothing could be further from Le Corbusier's Venice Hospital proposal than Aldo Rossi and Giorgi Grassi's San Rocco housing, projected for Monza in the following year. What these works share and differ in epitomize two radically different approaches to both architecture and urban form. While both works are rationally arranged in terms of module and grids, they differ markedly, first in the way the typological unit is inflected with regard to the topographic context, and second, where the former is a tectonically layered tactile fabric which is virtually indifferent to the issues of composition and representation, the latter aggrandizes the perimeter block model to bestow upon the residential stock a certain monumental and symbolic significance. Between these two works one may situate the Zen housing quarter projected for Palermo in 1969 by Vittorio Gregotti, which mediates between the projection of the Venice hospital and the composition of the San Rocco housing.

San Rocco not only initiates the Neo-Rationalist *Tendenza* in Italy but also inadvertently inaugurates a highly ambiguous revisionist line in Western architecture today. The *Tendenza* opposed the degenerative empriricism of welfare-state architecture with a *rappel à l'ordre* based on type and on the formal rules of classical composition. It was also unavoidably conditioned by the *retardataire* urban implications of its preferred models, the block, the arcade, the square and the street, which embodied an impossible nostalgia. This *rappel à l'ordre* assumes its most reactionary form today in the Krier-Culot proposals for reconstruction of the European city and in the demagogic prefabricated concrete neo-classical housing recently realized by Ricardo Bofill in France. The fragmentary works of the avant garde were, in 'intent at least', liberative and we would be hard pressed today to equal the delicately detailed, emancipatory spatial planning incorporated in some early works; but where they have been realized they owe their being more to projection than to the rules of composition. And yet while the open plans of the Modern Movement have evident advantage over the traditionally subdivided interior and vice versa, we have not and indeed cannot choose today *in absolute terms*, between the free or open plan of the avant garde and the cellular internal planning of the Western tradition.

As traditional environmental culture finds itself progressively outstripped by the seductiveness of the media and the rapacity of contemporary development, the scope for an architecture apparently predicated on the received rules of composition becomes increasingly limited. This dilemma was already apparent in Louis Sullivan's heroic attempts to adduce a convincing format for the 'tall office building artistically considered'. As with the skyscrapers so with the railway terminus and so with the recent mega-developmental types: the airport, the factory, the mega-hospital, the regional university, etc.

Within the ubiquitous Megalopolis nothing remains for our marginal discipline other than to interpret each fragmentary building task as an occasion for a 'liberative oasis' or place-form, rather than for one more idealized compensatory object which, while bereft, both internally and externally, of any traditional context, can none the less be made to appear as a *posed* or *composed* unity within the photographic frame. The best strategy for doing so may well lie with an 'anthropology of building' rather than with the legacy of academic composition, which tends often today to degenerate into scenography. It is in the light of such reasoning that Semper's (anti-Vitruvian) formulation of the Four Elements of Building comes into its own, since each element constitutes an instrument with which to define the limits of architecture in both specific and general terms. Of these four elements the earthwork is perhaps the most decisive since it proffers a primary component with which both to inflect the adduced type and to define the protective perimeter of its unfolding. This undercroft mediating between the *typological* and the *topographical* is at the same time the matrix within which the inner 'figure' or hearth emerges, and it is this last which establishes that paradigm known in academic terms as the *parti*. There remains, then, for Semper, the frame and its skin; that is to say the fundamental tectonic substance of the work itself and its representative enclosure. Do we not have here a valid theory of pro-jection, one which, while saving the work from empiricism through the primacy of the tectonic, does not, at the same time, degenerate into a regressive unbounded-ness?

REFERENCE

Le Corbusier (1928) *Une Maison, Un Palais*, Paris: Editions Grès.

65 The concept of design and its application to architecture

Mark Gelernter

THE CONFUSION IN WESTERN DESIGN THEORY

Faced with the daunting task of conceiving a building form and then directing its construction, most architects in the history of the West have sought help in a theory of design. In effect, they have looked for a set of principles which would explain how a good building form is created, and which would thereby give them direct instructions about how to organize and direct their work.

Unfortunately, most of the theories about design so far proposed have not explained this activity satisfactorily. In particular, most of them vacillate between two equally unsatisfactory and diametrically opposed conceptions of the designer and of the designing activity (Gelernter 1981). According to a set of theories at one extreme, design ideas are passively discovered by the designer in something external to himself or herself, either in the material constraints of the design brief, or in the prevailing 'spirit of the times', or in the prevailing social and economic conditions; but according to a set of theories at the opposite extreme, design ideas are actively created within the designer's own personal artistic resources, independent of – and even in advance of – outside influences.

For evidence of these contradictions, consider first of all the concept of architectural Functionalism (Zurko 1957). According to this idea, the form of a good building is shaped by the various physical, social, psychological and symbolic functions it is expected to perform. Proponents of this view often speak as if the ideal architectural form is already latently contained in the various functions, and the role of the designer is simply to discover it. Those who espoused this view in the design methodology movement of the 1960s insisted that the designer must be like a scientist, because both are concerned with dispassionately finding some form in an objective body of 'facts'. In both science and design, personal values or dispositions are intentionally kept out of what is considered to be a rational process of discovering that which already exists. Preconceptions about possible ideas are to be avoided in this view because they blind the designer to the objective reality of the problem to be 'solved' (Alexander 1964).

In contrast, the romantic conception of the designer as a creative genius insists that an idea for an architectural form originates within the personal and sub-jective resources of the designer. The designer draws upon some special insights or some special feeling for form such that an original form never seen before magically blossoms in the brain and emerges out of a pencil. In direct contrast to the Functionalist view, this theory expresses concern that a consideration of too many outside constraints will distort or even crush the creative process. Furthermore, preconceptions are encouraged and celebrated in this view, because they reveal the inner creative spirit.

Most other Western theories of design similarly tend to stress either outside constraints or inner resources, and as a result none of them gives a complete and convincing account of the source of design ideas. If a theory can explain the role of the creative individual in the generation of form, then it cannot also explain how individuals seem to fall under the coercive influence of a prevailing style or a predominant ideology; if a theory can explain these coercive influences, then it cannot explain the idiosyncratic characteristics of individual buildings or the procedures by which these coercive influences are overthrown and changed; if a theory can explain how particular and unprecedented requirements of function, site and climate give unique characteristics to forms, it cannot also explain why architects attending strictly to these idiosyncratic requirements alone often generate versions of familiar form types – like courtyard plans – used through all of history for many different functions and climates; and if a theory can explain how certain universal building types are used by architects everywhere, it cannot explain how these types are transformed into particular, idiosyncratic forms with quite different appearances.

THE SUBJECT–OBJECT PROBLEM AND ITS RESOLUTION

This curious dichotomy between objective constraints and subjective resources in Western theories of design results from a philosophical problem well known to professional philosophers but relatively unfamiliar to the architectural practitioners, theorists, historians and educators who have struggled with its consequences. Built deep into the foundations of Western philosophy is a dualistic conception of the individual which allows for two simultaneous but mutually exclusive interpretations: at one moment, an individual can easily be thought of as an integral component of a larger physical and cultural system, in which his or her ideas and actions are largely created and determined by external forces; but at the next moment, the individual can just as easily be thought of as a free agent whose actions are determined by, and whose ideas are created within, his or her own autonomous resources. To resolve the dichotomies in design theory mentioned above requires a resolution of this subject–object problem.

The serious philosophical efforts to resolve this problem originate in the eighteenth-century philosopher Immanuel Kant, and have been refined in the twentieth century by Karl Popper (1959, 1963) and Jean Piaget. Essentially they offer a conceptual model of the individual in the environment which shows how each side influences, and yet at the same time is influenced by, the other. The ideas most directly applicable to design theory come from Jean Piaget and his colleagues, based on their extensive studies of cognitive development in children (Piaget 1971a, 1971b, 1972). Piaget conceives of the individual as a problem-solving mechanism which attempts to negotiate successfully the various problems and challenges faced in life. These include physical problems, like walking or building a table; problems of comprehension, like understanding Hegel's philosophy or finding the front door of a building; and intellectual problems, like solving a quadratic mathematical equation or inventing a new scientific theory. According to Piaget, young children possess few successful solutions to any of their immediate problems like, for example, how to pick up a ball. At first they randomly thrash about, hitting or squeezing the ball with their arms and hands. Occasionally these efforts may meet with some success, and the young child tries the successful efforts again. Eventually the child learns that grasping the ball between thumb and fingers always achieves the desired object of lifting it up. According to Piaget, these actions are remembered by the child as a kind of programme – what Piaget calls a mental *schema* – which can be used whenever the problem of grasping a ball is faced again.

From these simple beginnings develops more sophisticated and eventually innovative behaviour. Faced with any new problem, Paiget discovered, a child will first attempt to solve it with a mental schema it already possesses. When first attempting to pick up a fork the child will grasp it like a ball, for example. If the action is successful, Piaget says the problem has been *assimilated* by the existing schema. On the other hand, if the schema fails to achieve the desired end, then the child randomly experiments with the schema until a new and successful plan of action emerges out of the old. A schema which has been evolved to cope with a new problem is said by Piaget to be *accommodated* to the problem. Once the new schema has been developed, it is retained with all the others as a *repertoire* of possible solutions to problems. These mental repertoires include solutions not only to physical problems but to problems of comprehension as well.

It is this repertoire of solutions that provides the individual with competence to act in the world. Faced with a problem, the individual first tries to resolve it with an existing schema in his or her repertoire. If none of these works, then the individual selects one which comes closest to succeeding and modifies it until a new, successful schema emerges. New ideas and patterns naturally evolve out of old ones as the individual confronts new problems, and in this way the individual's personal repertoire becomes ever more extensive. Innovation of new ideas grows organically out of the old.

Culture plays a fundamental role in the elaboration and use of mental schemata. Many problems faced by individuals in life have, of course, been faced by many other people before. Through much trial and error, and drawing upon the successes of previous individuals and even generations, cultures as a whole discover which solutions work for their particular circumstances. A young child in the West attempting to move food from its plate to its mouth does not have to work through many different possible solutions, but is guided by its parents to try the standard solution of a fork. In almost every conceivable human activity including playing a violin, learning a language, solving a mathematical problem, building a piece of furniture, and dressing appropriately for one's climate, the individual's culture gives explicit guidance about which solutions work and which solutions other members of the culture will understand. Standard cultural solutions provide individuals with competence more quickly than if the individuals attempted always to discover successful solutions for themselves. At the same time, though, accepting these standard solutions has never prevented innovation. When new problems emerge which traditional cultural solutions cannot resolve, individuals experiment with new possibilities grown out of their old ideas. If someone discovers a new solution and others see its worth, it may well enter the culture's general repertoire and then provide competence for others facing a similar problem. Cultural traditions provide rapid competence when recurring and familiar problems are faced, and when new problems emerge cultural traditions provide the essential base of knowledge from which new ideas are derived.

THE CONJECTURE–TEST MODEL OF DESIGN

These philosophical ideas have fruitfully been applied to design theory by Bill Hillier and his colleagues Adrian Leaman, Professor John Musgrove and Professor Pat O'Sullivan. They offer a model of designing activity which tries to explain how an architectural idea is generated *both* by outside conditions and constraints *and* by the inner creative resources of the designer (Hillier *et al.* 1972; Hillier and Leaman 1973, 1974).

The designer faced with a blank sheet of paper and a

design problem, according to their model, necessarily starts with preconceptions about a possible design form, despite the exhortations of Modernist theorists to the contrary. As Kant, Popper and Piaget have pointed out, without some concept of what to look for in the first place, one simply cannot organize or direct subsequent searches either for knowledge in general or for design ideas in particular. The preconceptions are drawn from the designer's personal repertoire of *solution types*, those forms and details which the designer has employed successfully in the past, and which are kept as possible solutions for future problems. This repertoire of solution types includes not only deep syntactical rules about geometry, but also various sets of genotypical building forms like courtyard plans and high-rise blocks, as well as detailed images of ornament and materials.

As soon as the preconception is proposed, the designer tests it against the constraints and requirements of the problem at hand. At this stage a good designer considers the consequences of the form for a variety of factors including orientation, heat loss and gain, construction, behaviour of future inhabitants, and the symbolic meaning of the image within the community. Since the first conjecture almost never satisfies all of these requirements, the designer then adjusts the form, tests it again, adjusts the form, and so on until either it is exactly right or the project runs out of time or money. Because design in this view consists of two stages – making a conjecture about a possible solution and then testing that conjecture against the constraints of the problem – Bill Hillier and his colleagues have termed this the *conjecture–test* model of design.

If the evolved design successfully solves the problem, the designer then adds it to his or her personal repertoire as a possible first conjecture for future problems. In this way the designer's personal repertoire of solutions expands and the designer effectively becomes more capable of solving a wider range of future problems. If other designers facing a similar problem consider this new form to be successful as well, they may well make it their own starting conjecture and thereby avoid the time-consuming task of reinventing a successful solution. In this case the new idea is assimilated into the entire culture's repertoire and becomes a useful tradition. Examples of new ideas becoming design traditions include the basilica form, the Venetian window, and the multi-storey internal atrium, each one creatively evolved from earlier forms in response to a particular problem, and then applied by many subsequent designers to quite different problems. Through inspired adaptations by individual designers of generic building ideas to new building problems, the pool of ideas within the culture continually evolves and adapts to changing conditions in the world.

In the conjecture–test model of design, then, the architectural form is not simply discovered in the outside constraints, nor is it cooked up entirely within a super-heated creative brain. Rather, it originates in cultural traditions which exist independently of individual designers, it evolves as the designer attempts creatively to adapt it to the particular and perhaps unprecedented conditions in which it must operate, and then in its revised form it possibly returns to the shared cultural pool. This model of design arguably bridges the gulf between subject and object, explains what the evidence of architectural history tells us about evolving traditions and styles, and explains more satisfactorily than the standard analysis–synthesis model what actually happens at the designer's drawing board.

This model of design, incidentally, argues against some of the central notions of current Deconstructivist architectural theory. Inspired by the writings of Jacques Derrida in literary criticism (Derrida 1978), a number of architectural theorists led by Peter Eisenman have reasserted the late eighteenth-century discovery that there are no absolute truths, no objective standards upon which an architectural design can be based. These theorists note that design traditions like Modernism or the classical language of form are not objectively based in principles of nature or in principles of logic. Rather, they are merely arbitrary human inventions which, over time, have became uncritically accepted conventions.

This assertion in itself is consistent with the conjecture–test model of design offered earlier. But the Deconstructivist theorists wish to draw more extreme conclusions. Because these design conventions are subjective human inventions and not absolute truths based in an objective reality, the Deconstructivists wish to discount their value altogether. In their view, these conventions are artifical props which prevent individuals from facing bravely the chaotic reality of our subjective world. Eisenman and others even regard cultural traditions as politically and emotionally repressive, because they impose an artificial and arbitrary order on human affairs. These theorists ask for a continuous revolution, in which no conventions are established and each individual privately and creatively constructs his or her reality without cultural props.

Although the language has changed, these Deconstructivist arguments are essentially the same as those of the nineteenth-century romantic artists and philosophers who first struggled with these problems of cultural relativity; and they suffer from the same shortcomings. Just because cultural conventions are arbitrary inventions it does not mean that they are not useful or even essential. Pragmatist philosophers like John Dewey have noted that the true test of a theory, or a convention, or any other human invention, lies not in its adherence to some absolute truths, but rather in its ability to achieve some desirable end (Dewey 1929). The fact that the word 'table' is an arbitrary sound with no objective basis does not prevent an English speaker from using it effectively to communicate to others who accept the same convention. The Deconstructivists are so frightened by the *arbitrary* nature of human inventions that they would rather have us retreat into private worlds where no public communication is possible. Nor, as this essay has argued above (p. 400), are cultural conventions necessarily repressive dogmas which prevent individual insights or inventions. They can be if they are used uncritically, but they are – for better or worse – the essential foundation from which future creative ideas necessarily spring. The Deconstructivists have thrown out the baby with the bathwater.

IMPLICATIONS FOR THE DESIGNING ACTIVITY

Theories of design are invented to give specific directions to architects about how to create good architectural forms. This model suggests several changes to the way in which most architects currently operate.

First of all, the conjecture–test model of design suggests that architects must become more self-consciously aware of the repertoire of forms they use, and of the repertoire of forms successfully used in their culture. Before the Modernist prohibition of preconceptions came to dominate architectural thinking in the middle of the twentieth century, architects throughout history had developed many successful techniques for assimilating solution types. In the apprenticeship system, novice designers learned explicitly how the master solved particular problems, and the master's solutions became the starting point for the novices' own repertoire of possible solutions. In the eighteenth century many architects toured the Continent, sketching and measuring exemplary buildings. Until recently, most architecture students prepared elaborate sketchbooks of historical buildings, and were expected to draw an accurate measured drawing of some exemplary building. All of these helped architects understand how particular problems were successfully solved in the past, and provided them with a basic repertoire of forms upon which they could subsequently build their own evolved solutions in the future.

However, the traditional methods for transmitting successful solution types to designers did not always fully explain to them *why* certain solutions worked for particular problems. Because architects often did not fully understand the inherent consequences of their forms for human behaviour, cultural meaning, technical realization, environmental controls, and so on, they often took a solution type which worked successfully in one set of circumstances and reproduced it unchanged in circumstances quite different. Le Corbusier's high-rise point block solution type might have worked well for commercial developments and privately owned condominiums in America, but it did not answer satisfactorily the problems of state-subsidized housing in Britain.

The conjecture–test model of design suggests that architects need to become more aware of the various consequences of their solution types, so that they can make reasoned judgements about which forms to employ, and so they can make intelligent decisions about how to evolve and adapt their existing ideas to new and unprecedented problems. This requires a serious research programme into the various consequences of the forms we employ. This research programme would be different from much of the current architectural research in one fundamental way. Where the typical research in environmental psychology, for example, starts with concepts of human behaviour and then attempts to determine the consequences of this for architectural form, the research required in the conjecture–test model of design suggests we start with a study of our existing architectural forms and then determine the consequences for behaviour. Research of the former kind has proven notoriously difficult to implement at the drawing board, while the few efforts at research of the latter kind more successfully influence designers' decisions. Examples of the latter kind of research include Christopher Alexander's pattern language (1977), Bill Hillier's space syntax, and the land-use studies in the University of Cambridge (Hillier and Hanson 1984).

So the more architects become aware of the range of generic building ideas available to them, the more likely they are to find the ones most suitable for development in any given situation. Without this broad comprehension, designers are inclined to use one or two solution types over and over again, even if these types are not entirely appropriate to the problem at hand. And the more designers understand the consequences of these forms for behaviour, environmental controls, symbolic meaning, and so on, the more likely they are to adapt their forms sensitively to the actual conditions, rather than to impose an arbitrary form on the problem. More knowledge on these two fronts will provide designers with the cultural traditions which are essential to subsequent creative design, while at the same time it will discourage designers from using these traditions dogmatically.

REFERENCES

Alexander, C. (1964) *Notes on the Synthesis of Form*, Cambridge, Mass.: Harvard University Press.

Alexander, C., Ishikawa, S. and Silverstein, M. (1977) *A Pattern Language*, New York: Oxford University Press.

Derrida, J. (1978) *Writing and Difference*, Chicago: University of Chicago Press.

Dewey, J. (1929) *The Quest for Certainty*, New York: Minton, Balch.

Gelernter, M. (1981) 'The subject–object problem in design theory and education', Ph.D. thesis, University of London.

Hillier, B. and Hanson, J. (1984) *The Social Logic of Space*, Cambridge: Cambridge University Press.

Hillier, B. and Leaman, A. (1973) 'The man–environment paradigm and its paradoxes', *Architectural Design*, August: 507–11.

—— (1974) 'How is design possible?', *Journal of Architectural Research* 3: 4–11.

Hillier, B., Musgrove, J. and O'Sullivan, P. (1972) 'Knowledge and design', *EDRA* 3: 29/3/1–14.

Piaget, J. (1971a) *Structuralism*, trans. C. Maschler, London: Routledge & Kegan Paul.

—— (1971b) *Biology and Knowledge*, trans. B. Walsh, Edinburgh: Edinburgh University Press.

—— (1972) *The Principles of Genetic Epistemology*, trans. W. Mays, London: Routledge & Kegan Paul.

Popper, K. (1959) *The Logic of Scientific Discovery*, New York: Harper & Row.

—— (1963) *Conjectures and Refutations*, London: Routledge & Kegan Paul.

Zurko, E.R. de (1957) *Origins of Functionalist Theory*, New York: Columbia University Press.

66 Le Corbusier: the creative search

Geoffrey Baker

Of the leading figures involved in the development of a modern architecture, none owes more to architecture's historic past than Le Corbusier.[1] Although he brought into being an architectural language which used modern materials and techniques and which always sought to express the values and represent the lifestyle of the twentieth century, he saw architecture as a continuing tradition and believed that key principles discovered from the architecture of previous periods could be reinterpreted in ways which would be appropriate to the present.

Born in 1887, Le Corbusier's formative years were experienced during the first decade of the present century, when it was common practice to select from past styles, using versions of classical, Gothic, Romanesque or Byzantine architecture, dependent on the purpose a building had to serve. Le Corbusier, however, rejected this sterile form of reproduction and instead carefully analysed those aspects of past styles which he felt transcended their period and which he believed remained relevant to the twentieth century.

On two important study tours (to Italy in 1907, and to the countries surrounding the eastern Mediterranean in 1911) he embarked on a thorough survey of architecture, sculpture and painting, which he documented in a series of sketchbooks. In this survey he was selective, paying most attention to the Greek, Byzantine and Romanesque architectural styles, from which he reached important conclusions about form, structure, the use of light, planning and siting. Greek temples and Byzantine mosques convinced him that architecture is the 'masterly correct and magnificent arrangement of forms seen in light'. Le Corbusier became convinced that forms affect our senses directly and that architects can play upon our emotions by their arrangements of form. Such arrangements respond to structural and organizational needs and to the way we move through buildings, so that the *promenade architecturale* may consist of a series of memorable visual experiences.[2]

Conclusions reached on the study tours, together with studies of nature in his youth, convinced Le Corbusier that certain architectural forms evolve in the same way as do natural organisms and ordinary objects. These ideas were further developed in the movement known as Purism, which Le Corbusier established in collaboration with Amédée Ozenfant between 1918 and 1920.

Undoubtedly, Purism formed the theoretical vehicle from which Le Corbusier compounded his mature architectural philosophy. Ozenfant and Le Corbusier sought to rationalize the relationship between art, science and the machine in terms of twentieth-century developments in engineering technology. Basic to this was a belief that machines and other manufactured artefacts respond to the same laws of economy and selection through fitness of purpose that are apparent in nature. Le Corbusier became convinced that this was a universal principle, one consequence of which was a tendency towards harmony, order and balance in all things. Ozenfant and Le Corbusier put forward the idea that art could enable us to establish contact with what they believed to be the universal force that governed existence.

It followed from this argument that art should observe the same laws that applied in nature and science. As Le Corbusier wrote: 'A work of art should provide a sensation of mathematical order ... and the means by which the order is achieved should be sought in universal means.' These ideals were exemplified in a series of paintings in which equilibrium was achieved by a careful balancing of selected objects. These *objet types* – guitars, pipes, books, bottles and glasses – were considered 'pure' because they had evolved by an evolutionary process, and were therefore impeccable extensions of humanity.

In applying Purist principles to his design approach, Le Corbusier assumed certain links between the laws of nature and the design of artefacts. For example, clear visual perception and the use of colour are both part of nature's scheme of things, so primary forms should be used, with colour applied as an enhancement of form; in nature geometry is a necessary ordering discipline for structural reasons, this again having an architectural correlation; the use of light to illuminate forms and space is important in the way we respond to visual stimuli; as in nature, function dictates form, therefore architectural functions should be similarly expressed. From this it followed that ramps, elevators, and spiral or 'dog-leg' stairs would become standard 'organs' of circulation, and a window would evolve in such a way that it optimized viewing conditions whilst giving the best possible internal light; amenities such as roof terraces and the raising of buildings above the ground would enable everyone to enjoy maximum exposure to sunlight.

The theory was intended to be comprehensive and Le Corbusier applied these axioms to the urban fabric. By raising buildings from the ground on *piloti*, entire cities could be placed in a parkland setting. Road networks would be established that separated fast and slow traffic, with complete separation of vehicles and pedestrians. This immaculate, utopian vision was meticulously worked out by Le Corbusier. His ideas were exhibited in Paris, published in several books and were sufficiently persuasive to encourage two generations of architects world-wide to follow his lead.

If these considerations addressed the rational and functional aspects of architecture, Le Corbusier dealt with aesthetic concerns by underscoring one of the key factors in the Purist philosophy – the role of art as a means by which we might have contact with the universal force that governs the cosmos. A new art was needed, one based on rational considerations, yet capable of compositional lyricism.

In his paintings, liberated from the restrictions of architectural problems and the act of building, Le Corbusier merged planes and solids, explored contrasts between opacity and transparency, and suggested ambiguous readings in which shadows sometimes seemed to be objects. These experiments, intended to represent nature's diversity, fuelled his imagination, and the inventiveness of his architectural forms and arrangements is directly traceable to his painting, which he practised each morning before working on architectural projects.

If painting supported Le Corbusier's architecture compositionally, the vast inventory of knowledge of technique acquired by sketching on the study tours informed his intuitive design sensibility. When the comprehensive Purist theory is added to these important design requisites, Le Corbusier was formidably equipped to undertake his self-appointed task of creating a new architectural language for the twentieth century.

In his buildings of the 1920s, Le Corbusier followed the main architectural preoccupation of the period, which was to dematerialize the mass of buildings and reduce them to a series of slender planes. This reaction against the solidity and heaviness of traditional masonry construction had been influenced by Modern painting, with abstraction replacing traditional decoration. In a symbolic sense, this breaking down of the mass alluded to the structural freedom given by modern materials such as steel, concrete and glass. Le Corbusier's architectural language was strongly influenced by painters such as Fernand Léger, whose work celebrated the machine, and sculptors such as Naum Gabo, whose work also captured the precision of modern technology.

During the 1920s, Le Corbusier produced a series of villas that clearly demonstrates his ideology. These villas reach a culmination towards the end of the decade with the Villas Stein and Savoye, each of which may be regarded as exemplary in that they may be read as sculptural objects in which volumes and spaces co-exist as aesthetic and functional entities.

The Villa Savoye (1929–31) (Figures 1–5) follows the Purist ideology and brings together the various strands of Le Corbusier's philosophy at this point in his development. Situated at Poissy on the outskirts of Paris, the villa demonstrates the deployment of forms that exemplify Le Corbusier's personal style, displaying the clarity and rigour which characterize his functional aesthetic.

As part of his grand design for the parkland city, the villa was intended as a standard solution to the problem of the dwelling. The relationship with nature is formalized by raising the living zone above the landscape on *piloti*, allowing the best possible views and maximizing the admission of sunlight. Forms are used that are in essence both simple and clear (a rectangular box hovering over a curved, glazed entry vestibule). Recognizing the importance of the machine, the villa embraces the motor vehicle by having its approach drive turning-circle determine the lower form. The three levels of the house occur in logical sequence: ground for access, garage and servants' rooms; middle for living, sleeping and relaxation; and upper as a secluded sun terrace.

Functional items such as the ramp which threads through the stratified layers, spiral stair, ribbon windows, *piloti*, roof screen and large sliding glass windows act as *objet types* which express the idea of evolutionary perfection. They are also placed together in an arrangement of planes and solids inspired by the Purist aesthetic. The hovering box is eroded at mid-level by the terrace, and the ramp meanders through the centre so that it is inside at ground level, part in/part out at mid-level and entirely outside as it reaches the roof terrace. The gentle, oblique flow of the ramp contrasts with the swirling corkscrew of the spiral stair, and these complementary expressions of movement occur alongside a series of solid and transparent planes in a box which appears complete on the outside whilst its inside is partly cut away.

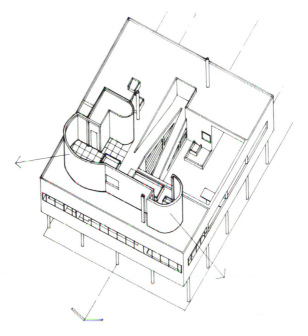

Figure 1 *Villa Savoye, Poissy, 1929–31, by Le Corbusier.*

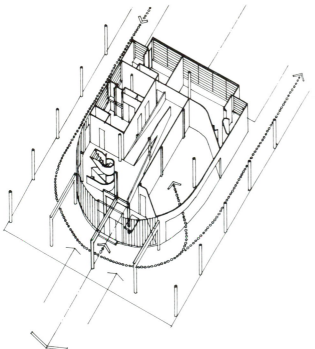

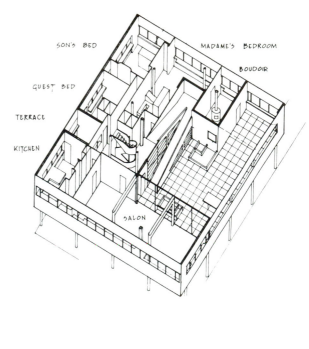

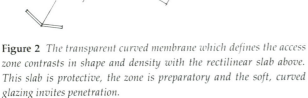

Figure 2 *The transparent curved membrane which defines the access zone contrasts in shape and density with the rectilinear slab above. This slab is protective, the zone is preparatory and the soft, curved glazing invites penetration.*

The enclosing membrane threads its way through the orthogonal framework of columns and is pierced by a beam linking an outer column with an 'arch' formed by twin columns and a beam within. This T-shaped structure is placed on the dominant axis where it marks the point of entry. The entry direction is reaffirmed by beams which link piloti on either side of the centre.

Entry therefore becomes ceremonial, and, directly ahead, on the axis, a ramp extends this theme by providing a gradual ascent, which suggests that the promenade architecturale will gently unfold.

To the left is the spiral stair which, baldachin-like, provides swirling vertical punctuation within the space, extending the curvilinear movement of the perimeter membrane. (Source: *Baker 1989*)

Figure 3 *The living zone, expressed as a piano nobile, has an orthogonal deployment within the rectilinear slab, while being divided on a diagonal into public and private areas separated by the ramp. In the public area the part-glazed box of the salon merges into the open and yet part-closed terrace.*

Le Corbusier controls this spatial interpenetration by his handling of solids and opaque and transparent planes, permitting views through in different ways. The ribbon windows are left out of the long side of the terrace giving a narrow frame for the vista, and horizontal glazing to the ramp gives views within and without. (Source: *Baker 1989*)

The roof terrace concludes the composition with a screen that appears solid from one side but is seen as a plane from the other. This screen picks up the nautical imagery of the villa in its framed support members, and the ramp railings are also ship-like, further evidence of Le Corbusier's infatuation with the ocean liner, whose precise and efficient functional expression he so admired.

Yet the villa has another dimension in its discernible references to classical architecture. The use of columns or *piloti* may be regarded as a modern interpretation of the classical column, symbolizing the freedom afforded by twentieth-century technology. This idea of liberation is also apparent in the roof screen; this has a similar role as the classical pediment in proclaiming the message of the building, but is quite different in being able to flow freely, unconstrained by the limitations of traditional

construction. The mid-level *piano nobile*, compaction of elements and axial control of the design strike chords of comparison with the Renaissance villa, itself derived from a classical temple prototype.[3] In all these ways Le Corbusier states architecture's role as belonging to both past and present, in the process demonstrating his concern to reconcile these inevitable constituents of the architectural phenomenon.

If the Villa Savoye was a culmination of the white Purist architecture of the 1920s, it also marked the end of the first mature phase of Le Corbusier's *oeuvre*. The machine aesthetic, with its abstract, planar language, was gradually replaced by a return to a more primitive style in which natural materials such as stone and timber were used, with concrete now in its raw state. Instead of an architecture of smooth and sometimes fragile-looking planes, the massive strength of concrete was expressed, with the boardmarks of the shuttering forming a rich surface texture. Instead of elegant boxes and glass towers hovering above the landscape on

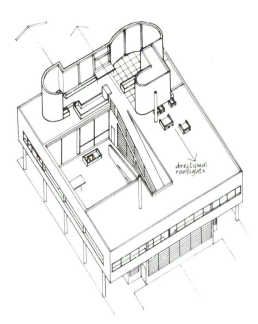

Figure 4 *The promenade architecturale concludes at roof level where Le Corbusier creates a further terrace. This is enclosed by a screen which acts as the final flourish of the design, a flamboyant gesture proclaiming the sense of freedom and idea of liberation made manifest in the villa. As a statement about the nature of the villa, this screen resembles the Greek temple pediment in which a sculptural composition conveys the message of the building.*

The concave/convex planes of the screen both enclose and also proclaim the villa to distant horizons. This is a variation on the theme of contact with the surroundings established on each of the lower levels.

The screen is controlled by the orthogonal discipline of the design and has a solid component which encloses the spiral stair. Depending on the viewpoint the entire screen may be read as solid or planar, an ambiguity similar to that of the piano nobile box, read as a solid container except where a glimpse of the terrace is provided. The screen is stabilized by the solid stair container. (Source: *Baker 1989*)

Figure 5 *Each end of the roof terrace screen has a definite termination and edges to this level are protected by plant containers. Structural ribs supporting the screen are expressed, suggesting that the screen is a thin, wrap-around membrane. This rib and railings to the ramp add to the nautical metaphor.*

The membrane is pierced by an opening which reveals the thickness of the screen and terminates the promenade architecturale. This event is marked by a concrete table which projects out from the base of the opening, a similar device being used at the perimeter of the living zone terrace. The opening frames a distant view and, close by, the edge of the largest plant containers projects out and is raised, helping to define the route.

At piano nobile level the continuous strip of glazing is echoed by the horizontal plane of the window ledge. The opening in the roof screen with its adjacent table confirms this idea. From a practical viewpoint the screen gives shelter from the north and east while admitting the afternoon sun. (Source: *Baker 1989*)

slender columns, the apartment blocks of the post-war era became the *unités d'habitation*, massive concrete megastructures raised on huge *piloti*.

In most respects the architectural language of Purism was abandoned, yet Le Corbusier extended his functional credo in pursuit of greater integrity. During the 1920s the slender planes in his buildings in fact consisted largely of concrete blocks. The apparently thin skin was seldom what it purported to be. After the Second World War, Le Corbusier sought a greater honesty of functional expression in the way materials were now revealed in their natural state. In addition, his interpretation of function became broader, embracing a wider range of symbolism and dealing with environmental concerns in a manner that proved to be conceptually regenerative.

In his Purist buildings, serious solar overheating problems had been caused by large areas of glass. As a remedy to this the *brise soleil* was used as an external skin to shelter buildings from the sun; concrete vaults covered by grass improved both insulation and roof drainage, each of which had proved unsatisfactory in Le Corbusier's earlier language. The 'ribbon' window was abandoned in favour of distributed windows varying in shape and size. These new devices increased the sculptural virtuosity of his work, and in the Jaoul Houses (1954–6) Le Corbusier replaced the hard machine image of the 1920s villas with soft, rhythmic vaults and a concern for the subtle nuances involved in family relationships.

The Jaoul Houses have cave-like interiors which provide a feeling of shelter and security. They were intended for older parents and their son and his family; the parents' house is placed so that it has a protective role and is interlocked with its neighbour in a typical Corbusian geometry. The use of age-old materials such as brick and timber (in other buildings he used natural stone) seems part of a return to nature that first became evident in his paintings in 1928, when bones, animals and the human figure replaced the *objet types* which had previously formed his subject matter.

During this phase of his output, Le Corbusier's greater concern for environmental factors caused him to use site forces in a more significant way. This fresh perception of the interaction between site and building is clearly demonstrated in his two great religious buildings, the Chapel at Ronchamp, and the Monastery of La Tourette.[4] In these buildings and in the Government Buildings at Chandigarh, Le Corbusier engages in fresh explorations of form, geometry and meaning, the latter being informed by a more expressive sculpting of the mass and by a deeper understanding of the way light can be manipulated to play on our emotions.

In this final flowering of his genius Le Corbusier draws on all his previous experience and achieves a fusion between the various strands of his ideology, retaining the inspirational vitality of his painting and drawing increasingly on his inventory of historical knowledge. Always aware of twentieth-century people's dependence on machine technology, he nevertheless infuses his work with that understanding of nature's principles that first guided him as a student in his native Switzerland. The somewhat limited, and in some ways naive, Purist philosophy is extended to take on board the complex diversity and 'imponderables' of life, so that the 'certainties' of the 1920s are replaced by an even greater reference to ambiguities and contradictions. It is in this final phase that we become fully aware of the grandeur of Le Corbusier's vision, the later buildings being characterized by an open-ended approach that absorbs myriad references, controlled majestically by an assured compositional technique. These works are particularly fluent, their message is elusive, yet they resonate with an effusive energy generated by an apparently limitless creative search.

NOTES

1 Le Corbusier's real name was Charles-Edouard Jeanneret. He adopted the pseudonym Le Corbusier in 1920 in order to distinguish his work as an architect from his work as an artist (he continued to sign his paintings 'Jeanneret').

2 The term *promenade architecturale* was coined by Le Corbusier to describe the movement route through a building. In his work he arranges this route to provide a series of memorable experiences that will impress themselves on the mind of the observer.

3 We can directly compare Le Corbusier's Villa Savoye with Andrea Palladio's Villa Capra near Vicenza (1552–). Like the Villa Savoye, Palladio's villa consists of a centralized cubic form with the living area raised to signify its importance (*piano nobile*). In each house the columns have a symbolic purpose. In the Villa Capra, the classical columns suggest a knowledge of Greece and Rome that was considered obligatory for the 'man of taste' in the sixteenth century. In consequence, both villas may be regarded as ideal dwellings for the informed and enlightened patrons of their day.

4 For a full analysis of these works see Baker 1989: 240–97.

REFERENCES

Baker, G.H. (1989) *Le Corbusier: An Analysis of Form*, 2nd edn, London: Van Nostrand Reinhold.

Le Corbusier-Saugnier (Ozenfant) *L'Esprit nouveau* 4.

67 An architecture of imagery: conception and experience in Alvar Aalto's architecture

Juhani Pallasmaa

Contemporary architecture has been criticized for its sensory poverty and lack of meaning by the public and critics alike. When almost any old building, a ruin or an abandoned house evokes our imagination and invites our emotions, standard buildings of our own time often leave us unmoved. The imagery evoked by contemporary architecture seems to be too shallow and uninviting.

Alvar Aalto's architecture, however, is particularly stimulating because of the masterly play on emotions by his architectural imagery. Beyond evoking imagery in the mind of the observer, Aalto utilized the power and complexity of visual imagery in his own creative process.

In his time Alvar Aalto was generally regarded as a charming dissident within the Modern Movement, but marginal as far as the problems of the industrial mass society were concerned. The current re-evaluation of the architectural development of this century has, however, enhanced the importance of Aalto's critical humanism. Although his individualism seemed to have prevented a wider school of followers forming in his lifetime, Aalto's works as well as his working methods promise to open up new possibilities for architecture today.

A PAINTERLY ARCHITECTURE

Alvar Aalto's buildings, sketches and writings provide ample evidence that he worked in a painterly manner using suggestive and unconscious images and associations rather than employing the rationally structured working method typical of his contemporaries.

Aalto began his artistic career in his youth as a painter and he painted to the very end of his life. It is significant, however, that he never exhibited his paintings or sculptures independently.

> The paintings and the sculptures are a part of my method of working, which is why I unwillingly see them as separated from my architecture, as if they could express something beyond it . . . they are for me branches of the same tree whose trunk is architecture.
>
> (Aalto, quoted in Schildt 1978: 172)

But beyond mere visual exercises in painting, Aalto had a profound interest in the manner in which a painter composes and collages images. In an early text of his, written around 1926, Aalto analyses Andrea Mantegna's fresco in Padua, *Christ in the Vineyard*. He praises the

painting as a splendid analysis of terrain and calls it 'an architectonic landscape' and a 'synthetic landscape'. 'For me, the "raising town" has turned into a religion, an illness, a madness, as you wish', Aalto confessed (quoted in Schildt 1986: 12).

It is evident that in his own work Aalto was constantly preoccupied by the notion of a miniaturized architectonic or synthetic landscape. Many of his architectural compositions (e.g. Villa Mairea (1938–9), Seinäjoki Administrative and Cultural Centre (1958–69), Maison Louis Carré (1956–8) (Figure 1)) combine building volumes and terraced earth to create an image of a complete, fabricated landscape in miniature.

A painterly architectural image is particularly evident in the *Gestalt* of Säynätsalo Town Hall, 1950–2, which is a condensation of miniaturized images of an Italian hill-town reminiscent of the representations of towns in medieval or early Renaissance paintings (see Figure 2).

The ruin allusion is another painterly device of Aalto's, which subliminally conjures up an experience of time and longing much in the same way as in nineteenth-century romantic paintings. His own summer house at Muuratsalo, built in 1953, suggests a building put together of the remains of some previous edifice (see Figure 3). The image of a Roman atrium court adds to the surreal effect of historical urban image in the middle of an uninhabited Finnish lake landscape.

Aalto used white marble accents on red brick buildings as a painter would use patches of colour to make a

Figure 1 *Maison Louis Carré, Bazoches, France, 1956–8, by Alvar Aalto.* (Photograph: *H. Havas, Archives of the Museum of Finnish Architecture*)

Figure 2 *Town Hall, Säynätsalo, 1950–2, by Alvar Aalto.* (Photograph: *K. Hakli, Archives of the Museum of Finnish Architecture*)

Figure 3 *Experimental house, Muuratsalo, 1953, by Alvar Aalto.* (Photograph: *E. Mäkinen, Archives of the Museum of Finnish Architecture*)

distant, unconsciously perceived allusion to antique ruins. The amphitheatre motif, almost an obsession in Aalto's work, is, of course, an explicit reference to antiquity.

In his town centre projects (e.g. Seinäjoki town centre, Helsinki centre plan (1961), and Rovaniemi Administrative and Cultural Centre (1963)) Aalto frequently applied diverging shapes and materials in different building units to create a painterly urban collage, which appears more as a product of timeless urban history than of deliberate contemporary design.

THE CREATIVE MIND

Synthesis of the arts was not a matter of physical fusion for Aalto, but a unification at the creative level – *in statu*

nascendi – where artistic ideas and images are born from their common sensual and plastic origins. In his working method he evidently allowed a free interplay and inter-action of the conscious and subconscious mind. In a remarkable article, written in 1947, and called 'The trout and the stream' (reproduced in Schildt 1978: 96–8), Aalto described his working methods and cast light on the still only vaguely understood creative process in an architect's work. Aalto's poetic description of his working method is surprisingly similar to statements by many writers and artists. Aalto believed that the complexity of architectural problems cannot at all be grasped and solved through rational or mechanical means – the subconscious faculties have to be effectively utilized: 'Always there will be more of instinct and art in architectural research' (quoted in Schildt 1978: 77), and, further, 'Salvation can come only or primarily through an expanded rationality' (ibid.: 50).

Aalto describes how his creative attention shifts from an analytical, conscious focusing to a synthesizing subconscious level, and becomes automatic and self-regulating:

> The large number of different demands and sub-problems form an obstacle that is difficult for the architectural concept to break through. In such cases I work – sometimes totally on instinct – in the following manner. For a moment I forget all the maze of problems. After I have developed a feel for the program and its innumerable demands have been engraved in my subconscious, I begin to draw in a manner rather like that of abstract art. Led only by my instincts I draw, not architectural syntheses, but sometimes even childish compositions, and via this route I eventually arrive at an abstract basis to the main concept, a kind of universal substance with whose help the numerous quarreling subproblems can be brought into harmony.
>
> (Aalto, quoted in Schildt 1978: 97)

Abstract visual images are patterns free of reference and scale and they can be applied to any context. Aalto gives clear indication of the use of metaphoric images, which has been found to be a powerful means of expanding the scope of creative search:

> When I designed the city library at Viipuri (I had plenty of time at my disposal, five whole years) for long periods of time I pursued the solution with the help of primitive sketches [See Figure 4]. From some kind of fantastic mountain landscapes with cliffs lit up by suns in different positions I gradually arrived at the concept for the library building.... The childish sketches have only an indirect connection with the architectural conception, but they tied together the section and the plan with each other and created a kind of unity of horizontal and vertical structures.
>
> (Aalto, quoted in Schildt 1978: 97)

Aalto also points to the common sensory origin of the arts:

> my own instinctive belief has led me to the fact that architecture and art have a common source, which in a certain sense is abstract, but which despite this is based on the knowledge and the data that we have stored in our subconscious.
>
> (Aalto, quoted in Schildt 1978: 97)

Figure 5 *Aalto's sketches for the winning competition entry of the Vogelweidplatz, Vienna, Austria, 1953.* (Source: *Archives of the Museum of Finnish Architecture*)

Figure 4 *A preliminary sketch by Aalto for the Viipuri municipal library, c. 1930.* (Source: *Archives of the Museum of Finnish Architecture*)

OBSERVATION AND MEMORY: VISUAL THINKING

In Aalto's sketches and designs the role of memories seems essential. Already in one of his earliest articles of 1921 Aalto emphasizes the importance of tradition and memory in the development of architecture: 'Nothing old is ever re-born. But it never completely disappears either. And anything that has ever been always re-emerges in a new form' (Aalto, quoted in Ruusuvuori and Pallasmaa 1978: 69). His sketches suggest that certain visual patterns or motives came first – emerging almost like unconscious memories in his architectural work. For instance, there are strong visual similarities between aspects of Aalto's travel sketches and his later architectural solutions.

Aalto also seemed to be extremely sensitive and skilful in adapting, assimilating and fusing already existing techniques or formal inventions into his personal synthesis. Many of his later personal idioms, for example, the freely undulating shape, the use of vernacular motifs and apparently accidental configurations, or the practical invention of the bent furniture leg all evidently have historical predecents.

Aalto's sketches are a kind of a creative visual shorthand, which has an inherent graphic quality without conscious artistic intention. His lines are soft and vague and they retain a high degree of ambiguity and obscurity in order to further stimulate creative interpretation (see Figure 5). In his sketches Aalto kept shifting his atten-

tion from the whole to details, from compositional ideas to technical and practical solutions. Subtle interaction between the artist's intentions and the emerging work is an essential element of artistic maturity and Aalto seems to have mastered this interaction and his work remained open to alterations and improvisations to the very end of the actual execution.

A study of his sketches and works reveals the gradual maturation process of an artistic idea: a theme or a structural idea often emerges as an almost unnoticed theme in a secondary context, often merely as a graphic rhythm; it becomes elaborated later in various contexts, becomes a major design theme and, finally, declines into mannerist application in his routine design vocabulary.

PLAY AND EXPERIMENT

Aalto stressed the role of experimentation and play in architectural design. The gradual evolution of his furniture series from experiments in bending and lamination methods of wood (see Figure 6) is particularly illustrative of the role of non-utilitarian experiments in design and the gradual maturation and application of an idea: 'Something that seemed like a game with form but after a long time unexpectedly resulted in a practical architectural form' (Aalto, quoted in Schildt 1978: 98).

Figure 6 *An exercise by Aalto in wood bending, 1930.* (Source: *Archives of the Museum of Finnish Architecture*)

Exercises in painting, sketching and relief sculpture seemed to be for Aalto a playful means of drawing subconscious sensual patterns into conscious design vocabulary. The fact that Aalto did not see intrinsic artistic value in these exercises emphasizes their mediating role in his working method.

Aalto wrote of the 'mentality of play' or the 'art of play' (in Ruusuvuori and Pallasmaa 1978: 40), which should be connected with empirical knowledge and logical deduction. He also stated that even technology and economy should be connected with a playful approach which brings an essential 'life enriching charm' (in Ruusuvuori and Pallasmaa 1978: 40):

> I acquired the idea and instinctive feeling that though we are in the middle of an experimenting, calculating and utilitarian age, we still have to believe that play has a vital role in building a society for man, the eternal child.
>
> (Aalto, quoted in Ruusuvuori and Pallasmaa 1978: 39)

ARCHETYPAL IMAGES

Aalto's architecture often has sensuous associations that seem to derive from the archetypal image of the Primordial Female or Mother Earth, which Erich Neumann has thoroughly analysed in Henry Moore's sculpture (Neumann: 1959). Or, perhaps, one could say that the exterior appearance of Aalto's buildings generally tends toward rugged maleness, while his interior atmosphere has frequently soft and sensuous female associations.

A particularly interesting aspect of Alvar Aalto's work is the repeated appearance of certain patterns of images, such as the dislocated or twisted grid, the wave-like flowing line, or the radiating fan-shape (see Figure 7). The fan pattern, particularly, characterizes his later work and appears in numerous contexts, in details of fittings, floor plan shapes of buildings, as well as in urban lay-outs, to the degree of an obsession. The frequency of this shape invites psychoanalytic interpretations.

Figure 7 *Sketch of fan-shaped terraces, Helsinki centre plan, 1961, Alvar Aalto.* (Source: *Archives of the Museum of Finnish Architecture*)

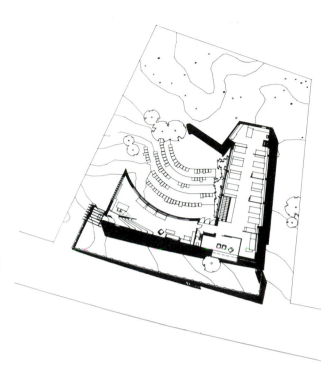

Figure 8 *Amphitheatre motif in Aalto's design: the architect's studio, Helsinki, 1955.* (Source: *Archives of the Museum of Finnish Architecture*)

The fan pattern and the frequent appearance of the related amphitheatre motif in Aalto's work suggest connection with his apparent pleasure in performing or addressing people and being the focus of attention. Even Aalto's own studio is based on the motif of the amphitheatre (see Figure 8) and the somewhat pretentious image of the academician teaching his pupils in the open air. Göran Schildt points out Aalto's strong interest in the institution of theatre, although not as a passive spectator but as the performer who is the focus of attention. Aalto disliked sitting passively in an auditorium, and therefore unwillingly attended theatre or concerts (Schildt 1984: 257).

The radiating pattern is also quite evidently a biomorphism and associated with organic growth and the tree archetype. The radiating lines express the dynamism of growth, but they also have their hidden vanishing point. It is significant, however, that the lines of Aalto's fan patterns do not converge in a single focal point. This illustrates his passionate avoidance of mechanistic constructions.

POLYPHONIC COMPOSITIONAL STRUCTURE

Alvar Aalto himself did not want to analyse the effect of form; he sensed it intuitively: 'The form is a mystery that defies definition but gives people a feeling of pleasure' (quoted in Schildt 1978: 133).

In his architectural compositions Aalto avoided excessive repetition or regularity and he emphasized three-dimensionality and plasticity of forms by deviation from rectangular co-ordinates and utilization of diagonal approaches. In order to stimulate continuous movement of the eye from one aspect of the building to the other he avoided symmetry and used a polyphonic compositional structure with several simultaneously evolving themes. He also created sensorial diversity and richness by the use of rich textures, polyrhythms and variations in materials.

Aalto's compositions are rich, interwoven patterns of overlapping themes, discoveries, whims and improvisations. His compositions have a strong coherence due to interlocking motifs and lines. It seems that his designs were not based on a dominating total idea, but rather on an embracing atmosphere or feeling, which held the complex structure together. His compositions are not predetermined; rather, they seem to grow from below, one invention after the other.

An architectural approach based on a dominant idea and its logical elaboration seems to eliminate improvisation and becomes a gradually narrowing path with less and less choice towards the end of the design process; the internal logic of thinking itself becomes a restriction to freedom for further thematic elaboration. Aalto's design process, on the contrary, kept branching out and suggesting new possibilities.

Aalto interrupted the regular continuity of structural systems and supressed structure and mechanical systems to the sequence of spaces and shapes. He consciously created deliberate discontinuities instead of a penetrating continuity of the main idea. Instead of relying on a single dominant architectural idea and its articulation, Aalto broke the whole into sequences, individual localities and sub-wholes, and contrasted several motifs, or even opposites, in the way that a symphony consists of parts, or a play is made of different acts.

ARCHITECTURE OF COLLAGE

The design of Villa Mairea (Figure 9) is a deliberate collage which amalgamates imageries of modernity and of anonymous vernacular tradition. The assemblage technique ties the architecture of Villa Mairea to the artistic tradition of collage. The masterly application of unrelated architectural motifs, images and recollections is closely associated in technique and spirit with the Cubist work of Picasso and Braque (Pallasmaa 1987a: 42–7).

The collage principle of Aalto allows a shameless fusion of contradictory elements, images of modernity and peasant past, Continental avant-garde and primordial construction, primitive simplicity and extreme sophistication.

In his own description of the Villa, Aalto makes an explicit comment on the relation of painting and his architectural approach:

Figure 9 *Villa Mairea, Noormarkku, 1938–9, by Alvar Aalto.* (Photograph: *Welin, Archives of the Museum of Finnish Architecture*)

The special form concept associated with the architecture of this building is included in the deliberate connection attempted here to modern painting.... Perhaps modern painting is propagating a form world connected to architecture which evokes personal experiences, instead of the former historic and prestige serving ornament.

(Aalto 1939: 135)

PLAYING WITH OPPOSITES

Demetri Porphyrios has introduced the concepts of *heterotopia, discriminatio* and *convenientia* in reference to Aalto's thinking (Porphyrios 1982: 2–3). *Heterotopia* refers to the destruction of continuity of syntax; *discriminatio* to the activity of mind which does not attempt to draw things together under predefined categories but rather investigates and establishes differences; and *convenientia* to the adjacency of dissimilar things.

Göran Schildt has attributed Aalto's negligence of orthodox categories in thinking and design to his fundamentally anarchistic attitudes (Schildt 1984: 242–59). According to Schildt, one of Aalto's most worn-out 'perpetual companions' on his night table was the 1901 edition of Prince Peter Kropotkin's *Memoirs of a Revolutionist* (Schildt 1984: 242).

While the Modern Movement generally was obsessed by defining boundaries, both visually and conceptually, Aalto fused together elements of different categories similarly to the dreaming mind.

Aalto pointed out that a creative mind should achieve the unification of opposites: 'In every case one must achieve a simultaneous solution of opposites' (quoted in Schildt 1972: 87). The notion of unifying opposites should not only be taken literally – it also refers to the psychic dimensions of artistic experience: the simultaneous experience of separate self and its fusion with the world. Logical deduction is evidently unable to reach this goal – it can only be achieved through the synthesizing metaphoric mind.

Aalto played skilfully with opposites and, for example, frequently gave indoor spaces a feeling of outdoors, and vice versa. In an article of 1926 Aalto explicitly expressed his appreciation of the paradoxical nature of indoor and outdoor spaces (see Figure 10). He refers to the hall in an English house as a 'symbol of the open air under the home roof'. Aalto considers this idea as 'the philosopher's stone' for the architect and continues: 'For the same reason as I previously wished to turn your garden into an interior, I now wish to make your hall into an "open air space"' (quoted in Schildt 1984: 216).

MULTISENSORIAL EXPERIENCE

The calm organic or biological sensation in Aalto's architecture seems to result from a simultaneous stimulation of all the senses. There is an abundance of sensorial experiences – kinesthetic experiences of motion, tactile and skin sensations caused by textural variations and an acoustic softness, as well as softness and diversity of illumination.

The organic quality of Aalto's architecture is closely related to the sensory richness of the traditional Japanese house and garden, but the experience of Aalto's architecture also reminds one of walking in a forest. The characteristic 'Finnishness' of Aalto's work, which is very hard to analyse verbally, seems to be related to a distinct 'forest geometry' in Aalto's work (Pallasmaa 1987b).

Figure 10 *Staircase hall, Jyväskylä University, 1952–7, Alvar Aalto.* (Photograph: *H. Havas, Archives of the Museum of Finnish Architecture*)

There are indications that Alvar Aalto emphasized tactile and kinesthetic experiences. His designs are carefully detailed for touch (roundness of edges, softness and warmth of materials) and, characteristically, he disliked metal furniture because of its visual glare, tactile coldness and acoustic hardness (Schildt 1978: 48).

The experience of Aalto's architecture seems to contain unconscious body reactions and rhythmic memories – his visual space is also motor-space. The free, plastic forms of Aalto's designs have usually been associated with the character of Finnish landscape but they can, with equal justification, be associated with his tactile orientation. Free-form architecture also has its evident parallels in the history of contemporary art.

Aalto's twisting of building volumes, and violation of linear or grid-like order gives an impression of movement and force inherent in the mass. Deviations from rectangular order enhance the independence of various parts and approach an experience of chaos. This seeming lack of underlying structure and coherence creates a relaxed and unpretentious impact. The entrance arrangement to Aalto's buildings is always humble, often almost hidden, completely lacking a monumental or symmetrical emphasis, thereby contributing to an experience of secrecy and discovery.

Aalto frequently used exaggerated or reversed perspective in his layouts, either to emphasize distance or to embrace an outdoor space into the building.

Aalto's topological arrangements, deviating from rectangular grids, arouse associations with historical environments, suggesting gradual growth and change. Violation of rectangular order is slight, sometimes hardly noticeable, and gives an accidental, spontaneous effect. These irregularities also contain a seed for further modification by the user and introduce a kind of aesthetic tolerance.

Sometimes his solutions are downright illogical, as, for example, the irregular column arrangement at Villa Mairea, where columns appear single, double or tripled, made of steel or concrete, wrapped in cane or pine slats in apparent arbitrariness in relation to structural situations. The violation of apparent order, however, provokes a mystical sense of question and expectation.

IDEALISM VERSUS REALISM

Aalto did not value a theoretical approach to architecture. He did not aim at theoretically purist goals in his designs, but rather at experiences in the real physical environment. As a consequence, Aalto's buildings reveal their full complexity and charm only when encountered in reality.

The main stream of Modernism represents an intellectualized approach to architecture through abstraction and idealization. Alvar Aalto was a critical realist and his architecture engaged directly with the senses and emotions, not with ideas or idealized abstraction.

As a consequence, Aalto's work belongs to the few popular successes of contemporary aesthetics. His furniture and glass designs are being manufactured today unaltered more than fifty years after their conception. Alvar Aalto's architecture and design possess the rare capacity of satisfying both the critical individual and the public at large.

Aalto's tolerant and flexible approach to architectural problems provides an important lesson. His manner of fusing together contradictory elements, memories, references and allusions, his combination of history, the present and an optimism for the future, as well as his utilization of traditional craft and industrial production methods side by side, are highly valid design strategies today.

An important spiritual heritage of Aalto in today's world is his combination of cultural critique and artistic optimism. He believed in the power of humanist planning, architecture, design and art to improve our living conditions, to soften the encounter of individual and mass, human and technology. He believed in small improvements, and he was concerned with the 'little man', the individual at his or her weakest, rather than the great mass: 'Each solution is in some way a compromise that is most easily discovered when one considers man in his weakest condition' (quoted in Schildt 1978: 49). He saw that the future of society lies in the individual.

REFERENCES

Aalto, Aino and Aalto, Alvar (1939) 'Mairea', *Arkkitehti* 1939(9): 134–5.

Neumann, E. (1959) *The Archetypal World of Henry Moore*, New York: Pantheon Bollingen.

Pallasmaa, J. (1987a) 'Alvar Aalto: image and form – the Villa Mairea as a Cubist collage', *Studio International* 200 (1018): 42–7.

——— (1987b) 'Architecture of the forest', in J. Pallasmaa (ed.) *Language of Wood*, Helsinki: Museum of Finnish Architecture.

Porphyrios, D. (1982) *Sources of Modern Eclecticism*, London: Academy Editions.

Ruusuvuori, A. and Pallasmaa, J. (eds) (1978) *Alvar Aalto 1898–1976*, Helsinki: Museum of Finnish Architecture.

Schildt, G. (1972) *Alvar Aalto: Luonnoksia*, Helsinki: Otava.

——— (ed.) (1978) *Sketches: Alvar Aalto*, trans. Stuart Wrede, Cambridge, Mass.: MIT Press.

——— (1984) *Alvar Aalto: The Early Years*, New York: Rizzoli International.

——— (1986) *Alvar Aalto: The Decisive Years*, Helsinki: Otava.

68 Gottfried Böhm: the quest for synthesis

Svetlozar Raev

Gottfried Böhm is an outspoken individualist, who has often gone against the stream. He was strongly opposed to the devastation and brutalization of the environment by Modernism and Brutalism during the 1950s and 1960s. Instead Böhm stressed the spiritual dimension of architecture. When these values began to be accepted by the new architectural movements in the 1970s and 1980s, he warned of historicist excesses that would only result in the pointless imitation of past epochs. He also warned against short-lived, fashionable stylistic exercises that in the long run would have a negative impact on the built environment.

Like the Bauhaus school, Gottfried Böhm adheres to the principle of relating architecture to the present time, and yet he does not consider innovations and new ideas a breach with tradition; he rather thinks of them as a development which is strongly tied to current events. Like the Bauhaus school, he occasionally makes use of the strength and clarity inherent in simple forms in order to reach his formal objectives. However, typical of him is the will to give complex forms rigour and purity. Referring to these complex forms and alluding to one of Mies van der Rohe's axioms, 'Less is More', Böhm says: 'Less is ... not in itself equal to "More"'. First of all, there has to be a force which, provided it is presented with modesty, turns into this 'More'.

It is also typical of Böhm to overcome real or imaginary contradictions and to create a unity where he finds opposites. In the course of time, he has developed an architecture which could be described as the architecture of synthesis. He himself is not very fond of such designations and simply speaks of an architecture of 'Zusammenhänge' (literally, 'hanging together'), a quality which he considers well worth striving for in his own work.

Zusammenhänge, in the sense that Böhm uses the word, means the complex interaction of material and immaterial components of a building in its actual natural and cultural situation. He thinks that towns and villages in particular should be put in order again by creating links between their functions, structures and (building) materials. The creation of such links does, however, exclude the passive adjustment to the environment. A creation of this kind demands flexibility and variability when integrating the old and the new, spiritual and material values. This explains why Gottfried Böhm has built in so many different styles in the course of time: simple and complex, modest and monumental buildings using concrete, brick, glass, metal, etc. Regardless of how his buildings look – whether sculptural, expressive,

original or related to historical prototypes – they are all marked by a special *Zeichenhaftigkeit* (significance), as in the case of the town hall at Bensberg and the pilgrimage church of Neviges, which acquires a symbolic power to link the unique and ordinary in a joint display of a unified urban aspect.

With regard to the expressive power of architecture and urban development, Böhm nowadays argues for an appropriate emphasis on the connections between small and large, elementary and complex building components. His call for the re-establishment of the *Zusammenhänge* of structures unambiguously opposes the 'free planning' of the previous decades. He himself has never followed that line and has always ensured clear directional relationships through the application of symmetrical and asymmetrical order. Like Mies van der Rohe, Gottfried Böhm hardly ever theorizes. He builds and he builds constantly. His creative reflections stem from the conclusion that human behaviour is determined simultaneously by reason and sentiment. According to him, houses, villages and towns should, therefore, always have a rational as well as an emotional effect.

Seen from this perspective, the chronological development of Böhm's buildings and projects can be divided into three phases: in the first phase, the 1950s, the rational elements dominated the emotional ones. In the second phase, the 1960s, it is the other way round. And, finally, from the 1970s to the present, a more or less balanced mixture of the elements has been evident.

The chapel of St Columbia in Cologne (1949–50), Böhm's first building, already shows the basic, rational forms distinctive of the first phase of his career. Several

Figure 1 *The parish church at Schildgen, 1957–60, by Gottfried Böhm.*

buildings and projects of that time, such as the 'Herz-Jesu' parish church in Schildgen (1957–60) (Figure 1), the church project at Bernkastel-Kues (1969), the parish churches at Oldenburg (1958), Kassel-Willhelmshöhe (1958–9) and Porz-Urbach (1959–60), show compositions of exact shapes such as cubes, cones and pyramids, made slightly more appealing by asymmerical accentuation in elevation and ground plan. Some influence of his father, Dominikus Böhm, is noticeable, and also of Mies van der Rohe, whom Böhm had met during his stay in the USA, and whose buildings inspired him. Unlike Mies van der Rohe, Gottfried Böhm clearly separates the diverse functions within a building; this is especially true for his earlier buildings. The degree of significance that he bestows on his architectural forms corresponds with the particular use of the space they encompass.

The move into the second development phase first became evident in a competition design for the theatre in Bonn (1959) and was fully accomplished in St Gertrud's church in Cologne (1960–1). Reflections on the technical and constructive, as well as formal considerations, may have triggered this, and there are precedents for it in Böhm's family history. Both Böhms, father and son, found the problem of how to span the demarcated areas the most exciting aspect of architectural space-making. Dominikus Böhm developed a system of suspended roughcast shell structures in the 1920s to roof over his buildings. Subsequently he replaced that system with bigger and more massively vaulted concrete constructions. In his turn, Gottfried Böhm developed the so-called 'webbed roof' with the structural engineer Fritz Leonhardt towards the end of his studies, which aimed at suspending the shells upside down in order to utilize the tensile forces.

Such a roof was first executed at St Columba. The shell construction generated here continued in the faceted manner of Gottfried Böhm's buildings of the 1950s. In the case of the parish church in Kassel-Willhelmshöhe, the shell turned into a folded, supporting pillar; at the Cologne university church, it

turned into a folded system which forms the entire roof and, at St Gertrud's church, roof and walls were conceived as a unity. Thus originated the prototypical crystal-like buildings which far exceeded the visionary drawings of German Expressionists of the 1920s and which made Böhm world famous. Gottfried Böhm reached the climax of this development when he built the pilgrimage church in Neviges (1962–4) (Figure 2). In this building, one can literally feel the spiritual source of such forms; a sense of living (*Lebensgefühl*) which connects the present and the hereafter has found its most powerful architectural expression. A broad pilgrims' way leads from the point of arrival to the church and its mysterious interior. This place is, however, shaped like an urban square, so the inside and outside spaces merge. During large festivals the pilgrims' way thus forms a unity with the interior of the church.

Another climax is the town hall of Bensberg (1962–4). Here the new building takes on the original form of a destroyed medieval castle in such a way that the silhouette of the castle with its towers, which is symbolic for the town, crowns the town anew. The altered function of the building, as town hall and central point of focus, is emphasized by the new stair tower which is higher than the building itself. The former courtyard of the castle now serves as the town square.

Other significant buildings of Gottfried Böhm's expressive formal phase include the following.

1 The orphans' village in Bensberg-Refrath (1963–5), a circular village in a forest. At the centre of this village is a square with a small chapel in it, surrounded by community buildings, shops, the administration building, the library, etc. The central area is encircled by a green meadow with a brook. The meadow is bordered by the houses in which the children are accommodated, and a small monastery.

2 A community centre with an old people's home, a nursery school, dwellings, a church and shops in Düsseldorf-Gorath (1962–4). The way the old people's home was built allowed room for little alleys and squares to be created which lead to the centre of the site. Individual rooms are provided with windows overlooking the alleys so that every dweller has the feeling of entering his or her own little house. The alleys on the ground and first floors are connected through a large square with ramps.

3 The *Auferstehungskirche* (Resurrection) in Cologne-Melate (1968–70). A long canal with high trees on either side leads to the churchyard. Inside there are supporting pillars of concrete which branch like trees at the top, becoming progressively denser until a ceiling is finally formed. The spaces between these 'branches' are filled in with masonry. Multi-coloured plastic sheets cast with inset nail patterns serve as windows. The thick plates thus formed shed a most peculiar light.

Figure 2 *The pilgrimage church at Neviges, 1962–4, by Gottfried Böhm.*

Towards the end of the 1960s, changing external conditions began to impact on Böhm's activities. Partly because of technical developments, other materials and construction methods came to the fore in his work. The scope and complexity of his commissions increased. This may have been the cause for new, formal conceptions which became apparent in the 1970s, the third phase of Böhm's development. Strict rational basic shapes and rigorously constructed order appeared once again; however, now the relationship with the emotionally expressive building elements and room sequence is changeable. The town hall and cultural centre in Bocholt (1973–7) may be regarded as a conclusive example. A severe steel and glass structure containing the administrative spaces overlaps a rich sculptural base of brick which, as a public hall and theatre, opens its doors to the social and cultural life of the town. The functional differences between the two domains are expressed through the use of form, materials, colour, etc. None the less, they are unified by the way in which they are combined. An even closer connection between rational and emotional elements is made by Böhm in the Bürgerhaus at Bergisch-Gladbach (1977–80). The strict basic shape of the building is obscured by numerous alcoves. Public ways, external stairs and small squares on all levels, as well as links to the old building, overlay and penetrate the structure in such a manner that it is integrated into the urban picture like a 'living organism'. At the centre of the building complex is an old theatre which had been modified and extended.

In the field of social housing, Böhm's housing scheme at Köln-Chorweiler (1965–75) is worth mentioning. It comprises a small urban square with shops, a restaurant and a playing area for infants as well as a pedestrian route on a higher level connecting with the flats. From the pedestrian way stairs lead to the parking garage on the lower ground floor. Each flat has a balcony, a yard or a garden. Daylight enters from two opposite directions.

Gottfried Böhm's contribution to office building lies in the humanization of the office atmosphere, especially through an appropriate subdivision of the building mass, which facilitated the development of overlooked work areas with adjoining courtyards for employers and employees to relax in (e.g. projects for the technical town hall in Cologne (1975), the Viktoria insurance company in Düsseldorf (1976), and the Mercedes-Benz headquarters in Stuttgart (1982)).

The Züblin building in Stuttgart (1984) (Figure 3) brought Böhm wide recognition. This administrative building is situated in suburban Stuttgart and there was no way of integrating it with the urban fabric. It was therefore designed as an 'independent' structure with the outline of a hipped-roof house. The space between the two office wings has glazed front and rear façades because there are fine views over relatively unspoilt scenery. The setting was exploited by creating an optical link with the scenery through the hall with a row of

Figure 3 *The Züblin building, Stuttgart, 1984, by Gottfried Böhm.*

trees. The hall has a glass roof and the side walls were designed so that the character of an urban square was established.

During the 1970s and 1980s Böhm became increasingly interested in urban planning and development. The focus of this attention now shifted to the problems related to the coherence of private, public and semi-public spaces as well as the revitalization of dead urban zones which he sought to redress by introducing new uses and functions. His observations centred especially on the creation of street and square elevations, considering the interplay between the ground plans and façades. Representative examples of this category are his projects for the Friedrichsplatz in Kassel (1978), the Prager Platz in Berlin (1977–80), the Lingotto district in Torino (1983), the area around the cathedral in Cologne (1984) and the Heumarktplatz in Cologne (1987), where Böhm, in the meantime, had built the Maritim Hotel in co-operation with the architectural firm K.S.P. Only one of his proposals for the redevelopment of the Sanierung area in Saarbrücken (1978) was put into practice. The new building of the central part of Saarbrücken castle was completed in 1988 with staircases, reception halls and a conference hall, as well as a plenary hall and a festival hall with a ceiling decorated with abstract *trompe l'oeuil* paintwork.

Böhm's competition project in co-operation with his

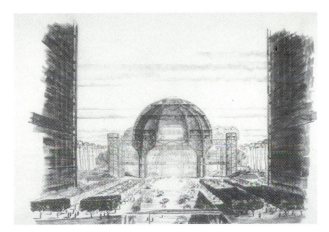

Figure 4 *Competition project for the Walt Disney Concert Hall, Los Angeles, 1988, by Gottfried and Stefan Böhm.*

son, Stefan, for the Walt Disney Concert Hall in Los Angeles (1988) (Figure 4) is also of interest in terms of urban planning. A cupola form was chosen for the music centre because of its prominence amid the variety of high- and low-rise buildings in the city. Since the site opposite the concert hall is also scheduled for redevelopment, the necessary volume was distributed over three linked point blocks which mark the position of the centrum in the urban panorama. Within the cupola building, the required halls and forum spaces were placed in such a way that the concert hall, even with all its stairs, galleries and emporia, would be suitable for various social events such as organ concerts, oratories, theatrical plays and jazz concerts. The theatre foyers are partially located in the space between the halls. A landscaped promenade encircles the cupola building and slopes up from the level of the square to the foyers. This would have made it possible to spend the intervals out in the open. The cupola building was conceived as a steel and concrete construction, partially glazed with coloured glass, etc.

All these plans for urban areas, like the building projects undertaken earlier, illustrate the foundations of Böhm's creative thinking discussed at the beginning of this essay. We may conclude as follows: just as Böhm understands people as existing in the energy field between feeling and reason, so he believes that the built environment created for humans should reflect these tensions, whilst offering people places that satisfy a variety of needs.

Böhm's vision of the city should be understood within this framework. It is a city characterized by the real and the unreal, the intimate and the public, simplicity and magnificence; a city of grand structures and lovingly contrived detail.

FURTHER READING

Böhm, G. (1949) 'Die Gewebedecke', in H. Hoffman (ed.) *Neue Baumethoden 1*, Stuttgart.

—— (1988) Acceptance address for the Pritzker Architecture Prize 1986, The Hyatt Foundation.

Drexler, A. (ed.) (1979) *Transformations in Modern Architecture*, New York: The Museum of Modern Art, New York.

Klotz, H. (1984) *Die Revision der Moderne*: Das Deutsches Architekturmuseum, Frankfurt am Main.

—— (1984–5) 'Der Architekt Gottfried Böhm', *Ausstellungskatalog Kunsthalle Bielefeld*, Bielefeld.

Klump, H. (1980) 'Der Architekte Gottfried Böhm', *Werk, Bauen & Wohnen* 11.

Nestler, P. and Bode, P.M. (1976) 'Deutsche Kunst seit 1960 Architektur', Munich.

Otto, F. (1955) 'Rheinische Kirchenbauten und Hängendes, Dach, *Bauwelt* 51: 1147–50.

—— (1968) 'Der Baumeister Gottfried Böhm', Schrift aus Anlaß der Verleihung des Eduard-von-der-Heydt-Preises 1968 der Stadt Wuppertal, Wuppertal.

—— (1973) 'Works of Gottfried Böhm', *a+u, World Architecture and Urbanism* 7.

Pehnt, W. (1973) *Die Architektur des Expressionismus*, Stuttgart.

Raev, S. (1979) 'Architecture of synthesis', *a+u, World Architecture and Urbanism* 89.

—— (ed.) (1980) *Gottfried Böhm, Bauten und Projekte 1950–80*, Cologne: Konig.

—— (ed.) (1988) 'Gottried Böhm, Vorträge, Bauten, Projekte, Stuttgart: Krämer.

Schirmbeck, E. (1977) 'Gottfried Böhm, Anmerkungen zum Architektonischen Werk', *Bauen+Wohnen* 9.

Architecture in the making
69 Technology in context
Norman Foster

I had just boarded a DC10 at Kai Tak airport, bound for London, after being interviewed in the departure lounge by a journalist who was writing an article on the new Hongkong Bank building. Because he had requested the meeting at very short notice and time was limited, I asked him what he would most like to talk about. He explained that he had studied architecture in England and had become friends with a number of architects in our office who had worked on the Bank. As a result of these insights he suggested that we could forget about the technology behind the building as he was now thoroughly familiar with it and in any case it had been well documented elsewhere. What he was interested to hear from me was how Chinese mysticism and the philosophies of Buckminster Fuller related to the building. Important as these and other issues were, I was immediately suspicious of an approach in which the technology of a building could be isolated out from the wider context. I therefore asked him what his views were on the subject and he gave the opinion that the Bank project had stretched the boundaries of technology far beyond that of any other building to date. If, I ventured, that was the case, then why did he think we had chosen to exploit technology to that degree. Quite unintentionally we had reversed roles; I was now interviewing him, but it was the nature of the question that seemed to disturb him more than the reversal of roles. He could not come up with an answer and it occurred to me that he might believe that we had an obsession with technology to the extent that we could indulge in it simply for its own sake. That idea, imagined or real, was so outrageous that I felt compelled to debate it – and so dispel any such notions.

I tried to explain that the building was the outcome both of its context and the technology that made it realizable. The context would embrace all the functional, social and cultural considerations, and the technology would be another way of saying the making of something or the means of production. How then could the very nature of a thing be separated from the way that it had been made – surely each one informed the other? Which comes first, the chicken or the egg?

Was the design concept of the Bank a response to the specific needs of a financial institution moving upward in the international big league? Or was it a symbol of the colony, with its commanding position at the head of Statue Square facing the mainland beyond – a bastion of

the established order? Or was it a social response to the pressures of Hong Kong – the creation of a better workplace and new public plaza? Or was it a regional response steeped in the spirit of the place? Of course it was all of these and many more. At any stage of its evolution it was also quite literally shaped by its buildability – the technology of its production. The appearance of the Bank both inside and out (see Figures 1 and 2), its internal organization (Figures 3 and 4) and the spatial experience that it offered were all defined, ordered and modulated by the structure which supported it and the walls which enclosed it.

The pressures of time also played a part in shaping the building. Given the looming presence of 1997 in a place already noted for its commercial drive and impatience, at least one signal was unambiguously clear – the new building was to be designed and built in the shortest possible time. This pressure had already influenced the choice of materials away from the concrete

First published in *Process Architecture* (Tokyo), September 1986, as 'A prologue'.

Figure 1 *The Hongkong Bank, Hong Kong: view of the exterior.*

Figure 2 *The Hongkong Bank, Hong Kong: interior of the banking hall atrium.*

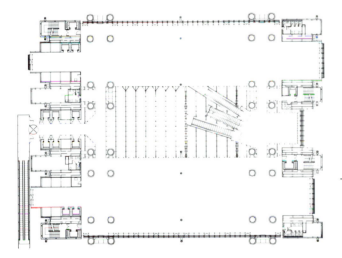

Figure 3 *The Hongkong Bank, Hong Kong: Level 3 floor plan.*

Figure 4 *The Hongkong Bank, Hong Kong: north–south section.*

masts which formed both vertical structure and service cores in the original competition scheme.

To reduce time on site these became separate elements of vertical steel structure and independant service cores (see Figure 5). The means of production were already an integral part of the set of presentation drawings which were approved by the Board of the Bank in 1981, otherwise it would have been impossible to translate them into more than 90,000 sq. m. (1 million sq. ft.) of built space by 1985.

To explain how an undertaking of such magnitude could be achieved within so short a time-span is clearly outside the scope of this article, but four principles can be identified as fundamental to that achievement. First, the site would be more an assembly point than a building site in the traditional sense. Second, the building would be conceived and produced as prefabricated elements, manufactured around the world and then shipped or air-freighted to the assembly point. Third, if industries outside the traditional sphere of the construction industry could offer a better performance then we would attempt to harness their skills and ener-

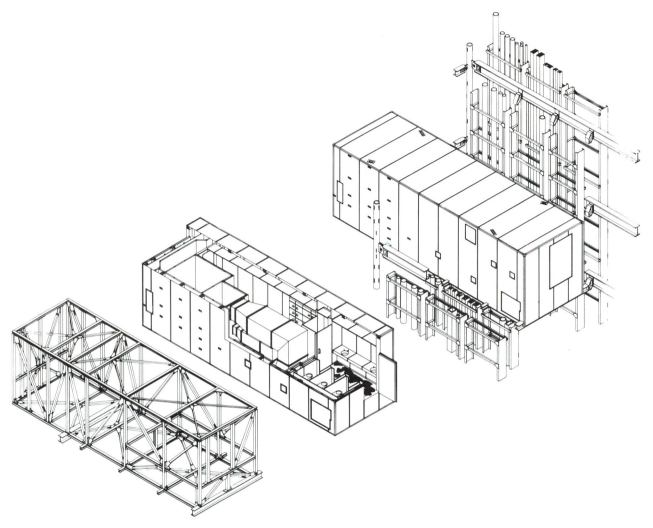

Figure 5 *The Hongkong Bank, Hong Kong: cutaway diagram showing riser connections to service modules.*

gies. Fourth, we would actively collaborate with industry, using mock-ups and testing prototypes to anticipate, as far as possible, the eventual realities on site.

These principles are typical of our approach on other projects; the main difference in this case is a matter of degree. The demanding performance requirements of the Bank as well as the special circumstances of Hong Kong, with its dependence on imports, took these principles to a greater extreme than might have been the case elsewhere – or if more time had been available.

A brief history of the development of one element, the service cores, would serve to illustrate the application of this approach. In a traditional building these cores would contain mechanical equipment, toilets, vertical risers and circulation. They would be located in the middle of layered floors with office space on their periphery – all supported by a compression structure. Such cores would be the subject of extensive fitting-out by a vast on-site labour force of construction workers and this work would occur at the time of maximum congestion towards the end of the building process.

Enough time would have to be allowed for each trade to complete its work before the next one could take over. This would be a lengthy process in which quality control would be subject to all the vagaries of site conditions – typhoons included.

By comparison the new Bank building was conceived as clusters of layered space suspended bridge-like from vertical masts with cores on the outboard edges. These cores were built off site in a factory by a remote labour force who were not normally associated with the construction industry. They were then shipped to the site and clipped on to the building as sealed modules, already fitted out down to the last detail of soap dispensers and taps (see Figure 5). Quality would have been controlled in factory conditions and by being able to work simultaneously on and off site, the overall time-scale for the project would be dramatically reduced.

The manufacturers of the service cores were a Japanese consortium of Hitachi, Mitsubishi and Toshiba, names associated with electricity generation, electronics, shipbuilding and engineering rather than construction. Development work proceeded from drawings to large-scale architects' models, full-size timber mock-ups in Tokyo, and eventually to working prototypes in a remote province of Japan. After extensive testing and detail redesign, the final versions were agreed; meanwhile in Hong Kong the building structure had barely risen to a height of nine storeys.

A factory production line was set up on a waterfront site in Japan and the completed modules rolled off at the rate of four per week on to barges for shipment to Kobe and onward by container ship to Hong Kong. A total of 139 modules were fabricated to contain the air-handling plants and toilets for each floor as well as 'specials' fitted out to house water storage tanks and gas turbine generators. Each module was constructed as a metal box encased in stainless steel, weighing up to 40 tonnes and the size of a small, two-storey dwelling. In the final stages of construction these were driven to the site on low-loaders and craned into position at the rate of two per night. Vertical risers of pipework were similarly prefabricated in frames up to three storeys high and hoisted up alongside the modules. There is an important relationship between design, production, weight and choice of materials. To that extent the module design was also influenced by the capacity of the cranes, which in turn had been designed as an integral part of the building to which they were physically attached.

The edge location for the core modules was ideal in terms of construction management, as the erection process bypassed the main floors, which were saturated with up to 2,000 workers at any one time. It also allowed for later replacement of the shorter-life mechanical equipment from outside, without disrupting banking operations within the building. In real-estate terms this concept also offered a greater proportion of useable area for every square metre built than the traditional solution of one central core. So much for some of the hard-edged, quantifiable benefits of the technological equation – what of the poetry, the spirit of the building? This takes us back again to that analogy of the chicken and the egg.

The most logical way to protect the modules and their related pipework was to sheath them in precision metal cladding and express them as slim vertical towers. By working within the legislation of light angles it was possible to sculpt or articulate the form of the building and create a distinctive stepped profile of these towers on the skyline (see Figures 3 and 4). This was part of a conscious attempt to question the dumb-box of a typical high-rise monolith – visually as well as socially. From inside the building the decision to push the cores to the outer edges liberated all floors to become double-aspect spaces – a generous response to views more dramatic than almost any other city in the world. The quality of a double-aspect space is surely so much superior to that of a single-sided aspect. The French have even coined an expression for it when describing those kinds of spaces – *en lantern*. At the base of the building this arrangement enabled the creation of a soaring cathedral-like space for the banking hall, visually tied by shafts of light from an external 'sunscoop' to the public plaza at ground level. The traditional central core is in effect replaced by the most significant space in the building – a vertical, fourteen-storey-high void.

In one sense the design was a quest for quality at the most strategic level – a quality of space and experience – something that might elevate and transform the otherwise mundane experience of cashing a cheque or working out the humdrum of a nine-to-five routine. That quest for quality also extended to the tactical level of detail – the handling of materials. It is a personal belief that quality is an attitude of mind and quite independent of the actual materials in question – whether brick, concrete, wood, paper, steel, aluminium, stone or precious metal. It is more a matter of respect and loving care, whether on site or on the factory floor. If that sounds a trifle coy, consider our inspections of the prototype core units at the assembly plant in Japan. The threshold at the entrance door was marked by a line of shoes dutifully removed before entry. Everyone, workmen, executives and consultants alike, went through the ritual as if the module had the same status as a hallowed place – home or temple – which in reality it did have. The ritual was not symbolic. Rather it was a symptom of that respect and concern for quality which did not need to be spoken. At that time and place there were certainly no language barriers!

It will by now, I hope, be apparent that I am sceptical of all architecture in which the very nature, the spirit of a building can be tidily isolated out from its technology. How can a Gothic cathedral, classical temple or medieval manor house be perceived except by their spaces and the then state-of-art technology which made them possible?

I hope that by focusing on one small part of the building in some detail I have not only given some insights into the design process but have also communicated why I was uneasy about that reporter's arbitrary separation of technology in my conversations at Kai Tak earlier this year. Maybe this may also explain why I feel similarly uneasy about so much that I see happening at the moment. The phenomenon, for example, of architecture being trivialized to window dressing – this season's new overcoat masking yet another tired old model. The spectacle, as Ada Louise Huxtable put it, of the deck chairs being rearranged on board the *Titanic*. To each his or her own. Earlier on that same day in Hong Kong, the architect Tao Ho asked me how I would sum up the Bank project in one sentence. I said that it was an attempt to try to re-evaluate the nature of a high-rise building in the context of Hong Kong. In retrospect that could now be the beginning of another article . . .

70 For ecology against the odds

Lucien Kroll

In our office we have found ourselves struggling again and again through our architecture towards the same goals: to overturn the dogmas which produce a militaristic architecture, to demonstrate that a congenial place can only arise independently of authoritarian systems, and to show that modern tools, such as methodical organization, industrialized construction and computerization, can also be used to produce a diversified environment.

Two experiences in particular prepared me for this role: the most formative was working for the great Belgian educationalist Claire Vandercam on her Maison Familiale (1965–6, 1968). On questions such as how groups of children can develop their own intuitive planning strategies, or how adults can relate to children in a non-authoritarian way – or, for that matter, designers to inhabitants – she taught me far more than I could possibly have gleaned from specialist literature, academic programmes or practical studies.

The other crucial experience was planning and building the Medical Faculties at Woluwé St Lambert in Brussels (1970–1) (see Figures 1–3). Here for the first time I was able to test at a significant scale the methods that I had already floated experimentally. It was no accident that I was proposed as architect by the medical students on their own initiative, and then only accepted by the authorities with reluctance. I had come to understand how a large number of indistinct and half-defined intentions can construct a much richer programme than is normally imposed through clumsier means. I had also slowly learned how to translate these intentions into complex organizations of built space without distorting them too much in the process. I well understand that this kind of architecture followed quite different rules in its birth and formation than other architectures hitherto, and I knew this would produce a new and intriguing image. I expected it to remain incomprehensible to the unsympathetic.

Over the years we have pursued this yearning for complexity through several further projects, some

Figure 1 *Medical faculty for the Université Catholique de Louvain, Woluwé St Lambert, Brussels: proposed development of the site. Drawing by the author.*

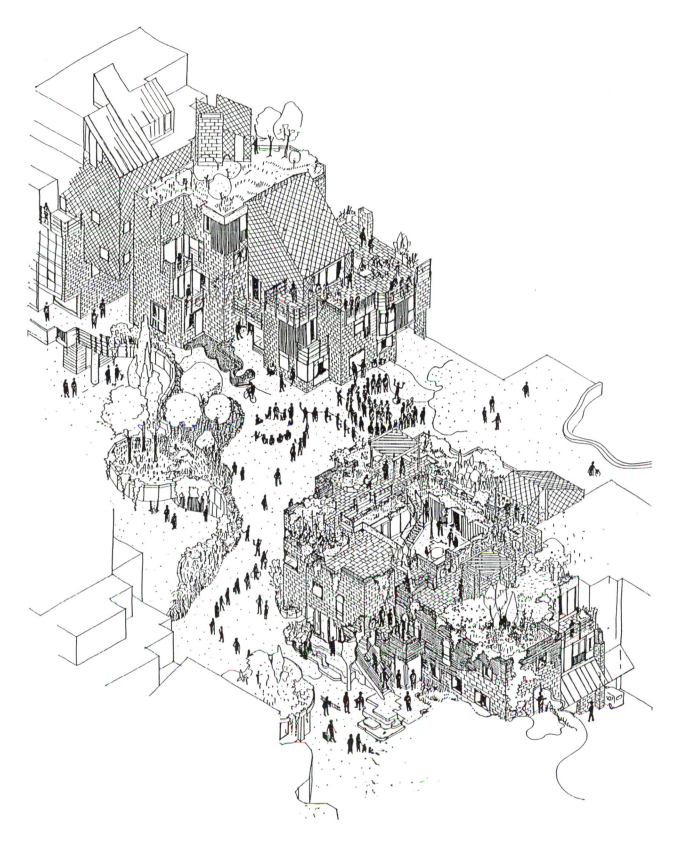

Figure 2 *Detail of Figure 1.*

Figure 3 *View along the glass skirting of the Metro station at Alma, 1979–82, towards the school.*

Figure 4 *ZUP Perseigne, Alençon, Normandy, 1978: converted apartment block on the rue Flaubert.*

similar to the earlier work and others very different. We conceived a new quarter at Cergy-Pontoise in point-by-point collaboration with the inhabitants-to-be, and we worked on the rehabilitation of a large prefabricated housing scheme at Alençon. We pursued both a constructional system and computerized control at Marne-la-Vallée. We grafted new tissue onto a village at Laroche-Clermault, designed some small schools for the Loire area, built an opened-out technical college at Belfort, and replanned an informal suburb at Clichy-sous-Bois. At Utrecht in Holland we transformed some educational buildings, and close to this city lies the site of our first essay in ecological town planning, Ecolonia, which is nearing completion.

At Cergy-Pontoise (1977–9) we went about as far as our physical and cultural strength would allow. There were no fewer than fifty-three evening meetings with potential inhabitants, a constantly changing group who came to design their projects with us, always with different intentions for each house and for the general plan. Later, we had all the problems of the building site, struggles with poor quality of work from contractors, etc. I doubt whether we shall ever again have the time or the energy to pursue such a thing so intensively: it was an ethnological experiment, with unique architecture as the result.

The buildings are banal, and arranged with a studied haphazardness: this was a way of allowing the inhabitants to act naturally, yet encouraging them all the while to be more themselves. As soon as they took possession of their houses, they added and changed things endlessly, so the 'new town' atmosphere evaporated almost immediately. Through allowing the inhabitants to get together without regimenting them, we had achieved by chance an 'animal' planning method which naturally proposes diverse situations to equally diverse participants. At later stages, we found we could extrapolate from what we had learned in the earlier phase, and eliminate the warmth of participation.

At Alençon, Normandy (1978), the initiative also

came from the inhabitants who, rebelling against the prefabricated world they had inherited, invited us to work with them on a rehabilitation, which we attempted to translate into an *ad hoc* architecture (see Figures 4 and 5). We let the inhabitants have their say, then tried to do their bidding. In the event, the political and institutional stakes proved so high that we could realize only a few small prototypes before being ejected, together with the Deputy Mayor, who was the driving force behind the operation.

We had plotted, along with the Deputy, to dislocate this surrealist prefabricated world. New gestures would break it up, bringing an intentional disorder, and it was to be reconquered by organic life, by the familiar, by the liveable and loveable. This needed to be done at a scale to compete with the original crushing order, but we had to be quick, before the guardians of order could reassert themselves. We broke their ranks, but we could not maintain the advantage, and they soon recovered.

Les Chênes at Marne-la-Vallée (1980) also began like a fairy tale: a prefabrication system somewhat more

Figure 5 *School complex, ZUP Perseigne, Alençon, Normandy.*

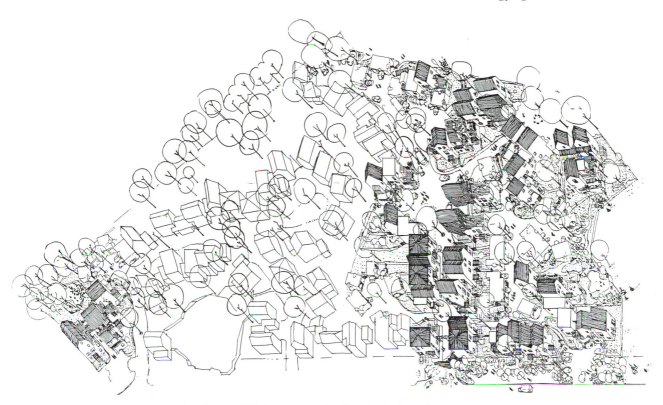

Figure 6 *Emerainville, Marne-la-Vallée, France, 1980: layout of the site. Drawing by the author.*

open-ended than the rest, 110 dwellings to lay out in a cosy, commonplace fashion, variations of type, inhabitant participation, a computer design system under development, a ministry interested in the built result, in fact everything one could ask of a new-town project (see Figures 6 and 7). Then after having constructed the eighty low-rise shared dwellings, the unscrupulous developer lost patience with the procedure, throwing out the results of participation and even the inhabitants. But all the same, there was some success, for despite the houses being built on an industrial system, no two places are alike, and the general atmosphere is almost as friendly as we had wished.

Figure 7 *Houses grouped around a public square at Marne-la-Vallée, France.*

The grafting on of new buildings at Laroche-Clermault (1982) took place in the blissful countryside of the Loire. Questioning a whole village briefly in the course of three meetings is not too difficult. The people quickly made clear their ideas of style and proportion: mix the newcomers with the existing population and get to know them, don't create a closed group of strangers in a ghetto of their own, to become the enemy. Then get on with construction: seen from a distance the new houses are indistinguishable from the old.

Two little schools at Saint-Germain and Cinais on the Loire are designed with everything a bit on the skew; this is not immediately perceptible, but it helps generate an atmosphere appropriate to teaching.

In the case of the Academy of Speech and Drama at Utrecht (1979), we preserved the gesture of the workers smashing holes in the walls. This is evidence of an episode in the building's history, and we did not want to anaesthetize the students by 'making good' these wounds as architects are wont to do in their tidy drawings. Instead we made them all the more obvious (see Figures 8–11).

At Haarlem we were obliged to work within strict Dutch construction procedures which normally tolerate no deviation, producing the kind of repetitive new towns with which we are all too familiar. With the co-operation of the client, however, we sought every possible means to introduce variety, hoping that the inhabitants would follow our lead and transform this excessively sterile environment to their image. This they did, and promptly.

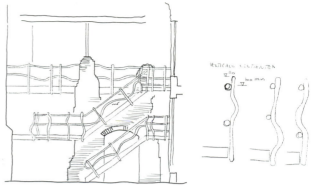

Figure 10 *The Academy of Speech and Drama, Utrecht, Netherlands, 1979: architect's preliminary sketch of interior elevation, showing staircases and balconies.*

Figure 8 *The Academy of Speech and Drama, Utrecht, Netherlands, 1979: architect's preliminary sketch of the interior.*

The Technical College at Belfort (1983) was commissioned by a politician much concerned both with the experience of the user and the relation of the institution to its locality. He distrusted literary declarations which he felt nobody would follow. We proposed to break up the college into its constituent departments and arrange them like a small town, with streets, central square, and urban blocks, pursuing every possible diversity of volume, material and technique (see Figures 12 and 13). We also sought to attach the new institution to the adjacent housing blocks, forging connections to produce continuity, adding new dwellings which were to

surround and even to climb up them. This would have restored to this area the kind of continuity which prevents enclaves and permits a truly urban fabric, but the proposal has yet to be carried out, and the intended continuity seems, for the time being, to have been forgotten.

We placed the outside at the centre, and we managed to treat each block as an independent piece, juxtaposing it with others, accepting both the contradictions and complicities. Each building possesses its own technology and its own materials, and frequently was built by different contractors from those operating in neighbouring blocks. The streets and square at the centre of the institution are public property, with no gates to cut them off from the rest of the area.

At Alphen aan-den-Rijn, the building trust (Bouwfonds) decided to construct a hundred or so 'environment-friendly' houses funded by the state, and asked us to conceive an ecological planning method. What could 'ecological planning' mean? Clearly something more than a purely *biological* solution, such as the lining up of a series of energy-efficient houses, or the bringing together of environmentally conscious inhabitants. It

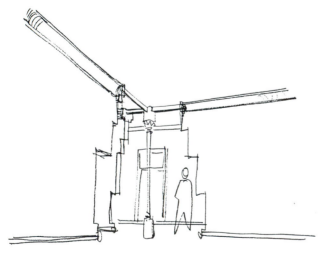

Figure 9 *The Academy of Speech and Drama, Utrecht, Netherlands, 1979: architect's preliminary sketch of the ceiling supports and symbolic holes smashed in the interiors.*

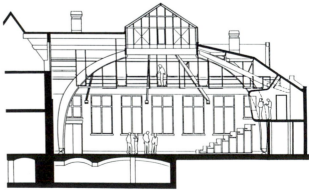

Figure 11 *The Academy of Speech and Drama, Utrecht, Netherlands, 1979: views of the interior as built.*

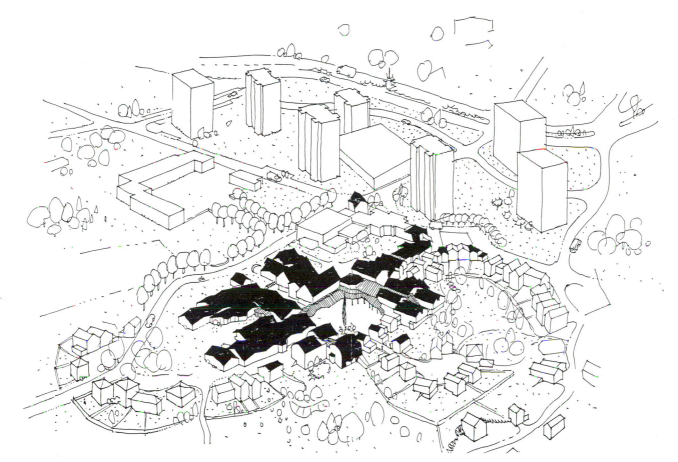

Figure 12 *The Technical College, Belfort, 1983: architect's drawing. The black roofs show those buildings that belong to the college.*

must rather lie in the treatment of the spaces between, the design of public spaces organized in a *relational* way. Is this the first time that the concepts of *ecology* and *planning* are combined? Perhaps all old towns were unconsciously ecological, but now that we have become too conscious, where could one find a real contemporary example?

Evidently, there should be no geometry to dictate the configuration, nor should there be stupid repetition of dumb elements, but rather an uncertain and sensitive

Figure 13 *The Technical College, Belfort, 1983: view of the exterior.*

tissue, and without visible centre, for points of density erupt on their own, slowly. The general form should be carefully dislocated to allow a continuity of urban events to develop. What are the urban elements which might help us form this living and contemporary Dutch landscape? Clearly not those of the old landscape, which one is tempted to imitate, and certainly not the hard and artificial abstractions of the Modernists. Could it be simply a question of following, as literally as possible, those things which weave an everyday complexity? Let us list and draw them to gain an understanding of their characteristics and possibilities of evolution: they thus become components, each with its own personality, its own life, its own freedom.

This is clearly not a question of inventing a new and intelligent arrangement, then repeating it with a little variation, which would just lead to a new kind of autism. It would correspond to nothing existing, remaining just as alienating as any new town. We should not be searching for solutions, but concentrating instead on processes.

We wish to add piece by piece, without subservience to a general scheme, taking a series of autonomous fragments, then making sure of the connections. In this way there will be no reference to a centralized geometry. We could thus put together a huge number of fragments, without limit, and without fear of monotony. It would operate at an increasing scale: each group of fragments represents a larger fragment, which in turn responds to the edges of the largest fragment bordering it.

Bouwfonds invited nine architects to build the scheme: not the militaristic architects who are best known, but others further down the pyramid of fame. Of course the diversity of 'urban motifs' has been multiplied by the varied architectures on offer. The invited architects began by working in isolation, but they gradually became aware of their neighbours and began to negotiate with them. This is something not seen since the birth of the Modern Movement, for it is usually the role of planners to regulate abstractly and thus efface all problems of neighbourly relations, while architects confine themselves within the limits of their allotted sites. This negotiation has returned discreetly, like the butterflies which slipped back into the formal gardens of Louis Le Roy. We also had some discussions about the nature of the *rational*. Fortunately the architecture of repetition is recent in the history of Dutch architecture, hardly half a century old: they can be cured of it.

We are up against an institutional fatality; we struggle to break out of an entrenched state of architectural sterility, a germ-free zone. Those charged with conceiving our environment, in the image of the authorities they work for, cannot imagine operating with the living and changing. The unforeseeable destablizes them, while negotiation with the haphazard processes of a social life which they cannot control makes them anxious. Necessarily, their work turns out just as they have predicted: a utopian, abstract, dream-like world; theoretical and mechanized. It is born and constructed autistically, then the inhabitants set out on the task of habitation. By degrees they take it over and make it loveable, but it takes a long time.

Nothing can give an adequate complexity to this perfectly glossy and artificial image which arises time after time. Nothing is left to chance, to the initiative of urban actions which only reveal themselves slowly, and which only construct themselves in a living logic, that is to say bit by bit through the unfolding of activities, rather than theoretically, and in the abstract. We have deaf planners and dumb inhabitants.

It is with a certain amount of pain that we leave the twentieth century to enter the twenty-first. We already know quite well both factually and intuitively how it cannot be, but we do not know how it *will* be, and above all, we do not know how to take ourselves there and adapt our behaviour accordingly. We are still so conditioned by the deadly and sterile habits of the last few years of the twentieth century, that only with the greatest difficulty can we imagine new ways of acting, of conceiving, of connecting, which could get us away from our old habits.

We could do with some prophets.

Architecture in the making
71 The anatomy of building

Charles Moore

For many years now it has seemed to me that buildings need to be designed by more than just their architects. The notion starts from a perception of a former partner of mine, Donlyn Lyndon, that buildings are repositories of human energy and that if they get enough energy they will pay it back in satisfaction, but if they don't get enough energy they remain incapable of paying back anything. What follows from that is that a building which has the energies of all the people interested in it is more likely to succeed than the masterpiece of a skilled designer operating alone. We had a chance to push this notion even further than we might have otherwise in the Episcopal parish of St Matthew's in the Los Angeles suburb of Pacific Palisades, where land is very expensive, but where a far-seeing bishop had bought long ago a large and very beautiful site which served church and school. The parish had been having a long and difficult time agreeing on a new rector to replace their rector of many years, who had retired when a forest fire burned down their popular A-frame church, which was very small and very pretty. The vestry, anticipating further disagreement about the building (though they had by this time agreed on a new rector) decided to require that a two-thirds majority be cast in favour of the scheme they selected. Our friends in the parish were not confident that even a majority could be found in favour of anything. We were selected to do the job and believed that the only way to get such a majority for any scheme would be to have that scheme designed by the interested members of the parish, hoping that we could get enough interested to carry the day voting for work for which they felt responsible. The process worked surprisingly well. It resulted, after four Sundays of workshops spaced a month apart, in a scheme on which 87 per cent of the voting members of the parish approved.

We have repeated this process now with continuing modifications often enough so that I'm convinced that it works: that people in a creative mode, whatever their differences, are much more positive and co-operative and ready to accomplish something than the same people in the kind of critical mode that a committee structure implies.

A key player was, and has been since, Jim Burns, who with Lawrence Halprin developed the 'Take Part Process'. He choreographed our four meetings with the interested parishioners (see Figure 1). The first Sunday after church we met and had an awareness walk (as these things are called in California) around the extensive site with a notebook for everyone to fill in with verbal descriptions, questions to answer, sketches and diagrams to help figure out where the new church might be placed. Nothing was taken for granted. After the walk we came back, had some lunch on the very pretty lawn of the parish house, and worked together, often on butcher paper on the floor, to draw ideas for the church. Afterward we went into the temporary church/basketball court and were confronted with a set of model-making equipment which Jim Burns had assembled: Froot Loops (breakfast cereal), cellophane, coloured paper, scissors, tape and parsley (parsley is wonderful model-making material since it wilts in a few hours and doesn't let people fall too far in love with their creations). Then people either singly or in groups made models of their ideal church. Froot Loops usually represent people. The designers of all these models then presented them to the group assembled. The group was, as in subsequent sessions, about 150 strong out of a 350-person parish. By that time it was the end of the afternoon and everyone went home.

A month later we architects came back on a Sunday after church with three-dimensional models (quite abstract) of groups of seats, including choir, baldachin, organ, altar, etc., and I learned a lot: I'd been swept away with an architect's fervour and had made what I thought was a wonderful model, for instance, of a four-posted baldachin in bright colours. It was rejected out of hand by everybody. That day there were seven tables set

Figure 1 *Participants in the 'Take Part Process' during the creation of St Matthew's Episcopal Church, Pacific Palisades, California, 1979.*

up in the church with maybe fifteen to twenty people each, and the wonder of it was that the plan of the church that each of the seven tables made was basically the same, of seven rows of pews in a semicircle or half-ellipse around the altar. We were astonished at the fact that all the answers were the same. I guess we needn't have been since the group had already said they wanted to sit as close to their altar as they could but not surround it; they didn't want to look at each other, but to focus on the altar and what lay beyond. No other configuration allowed so many people (288 were asked for) to be so close to the altar. Of course there were discrepancies, mostly in the location of the choir, and our role as architects was to make clear the areas of agreement and minimize the differences, which could get ironed out later. The important thing, we believe, is to seek and find consensus.

Another action that we tried for the first time at St Matthew's, which has since become a standard part of our design process, was to show a carousel of eighty slides of various kinds of buildings that had something to do with the problem at hand. We handed out sheets that gave each viewer the chance with each slide to say 'I like it' or 'I don't', and then separately to say 'this is appropriate for St Matthew's'. We tallied the results and presented them at the third meeting on another Sunday a month thence. They told us interesting things: the most popular pictures (three of them) interspersed among many others were all of Alvar Aalto's Vuok-senniska church in Imatra in Finland, which is white, although almost everyone had said they preferred dark wood; but the church at Imatra does have windows that look out at fine trees. The least popular church was St Peter's in Rome, whether for reasons of doctrine or of cost it seemed unfair to ask. One thing that we first noticed here that we are getting used to is that concrete surfaces, even masterful ones by the likes of Louis Kahn, score very low and that plants casting dappled shadows in a forest or on a wall always score very high. This slide quiz gave us extra information for the third session, a month later after church on a Sunday, to which we brought four models, big dollhouse-like roof models at the scale, as I remember, of one-half inch to the foot (1:24). We knew that the parish wanted a massing of the church that would seem modest and fit well with the wooded site, and we gave each table (there were six that day) the task of deciding which volume or combination of volumes seemed most appropriate. When five out of six tables came up with basically the same volume, we were able to take that as fixed and then concentrate on particular interests of the parishioners: one of the hottest was the desire of many, especially the older members who remembered with fondness their earlier church, to look out at the same prayer garden in a grove of syca-mores that the earlier church had viewed. But the rector was unenthusiastic about the problems of celebrating, for instance, Good Friday on a sunny spring morning,

especially if the sunshine threw him and the other celebrants into silhouette. That was dealt with by having generous windows to the prayer garden, but putting them to one side, not behind the altar.

Behind the altar I was to draw in the next few weeks a series of little houses like an advent calendar occupied by saints, which unfortunately reminded the rector of a *Laugh-In* programme he had recently seen with comics in such a set of niches. The next iteration kept the wall behind the altar simple and blank, which everyone found boring. In the subsequent weeks, after meetings with the liturgical consultant, a wonderful man with whom I swapped C.S. Lewis stories, we were to come up with the four evangelists including St Matthew as they are found in the *Book of Kells* in Dublin. The parishioners said those were weird; finally a tree of life was suggested. It was designed in detail by John Ruble and finally hit the desired note.

There were many issues brought up at this stage, and discussed four weeks later, in which it was important to please both high church and low church parishioners. The floor, for instance: in southern California the most economical and appropriate surface for a floor is Mexican tile, usually large terracotta squares, but that had some of the wrong messages – 'Mexican' meant 'Roman Catholic'. We proposed and they accepted that the corners of the square tile should be sliced away and a small square of blue slate should be inserted at every intersection, carrying the mind across the Bay of Biscay to Devon and home. Somehow it seemed all right that the blue slate for reasons of durability had been replaced by blue-green tile.

Yet another issue was a large cross hanging above the altar, at the specific request of the rector, brooding, as he put it, like a hen broods over her chicks. There was no objection to the cross, but there was considerable discussion about whether the body of Jesus should be on it. I made what I thought was an ingenious solution that involved a giant board with the silhouette of the corpus visible from the side and just an abstract thick line visible from the front. I thought that gave the viewers their choice of corpus or non-corpus depending on their point of view. As it turned out, though, the cross was a gift of a low church lady who banished even the two-dimensional corpus.

A more complex issue, and one that brought on considerable discussion, was the material of the walls of the church. The previous A-frame had been wood and many members of the parish wanted natural wood again. The group that was looking for a fine organ wanted superior acoustics which required, according to the acoustician, dense walls of heavy plaster. We ended up proposing deep wood battens on a plaster wall so that the wall seems mostly of wood if you view it from a raking angle and mostly plaster if you (or the sound waves) address it head on. One of the tenser moments came during a discussion of the plaster-walled nave

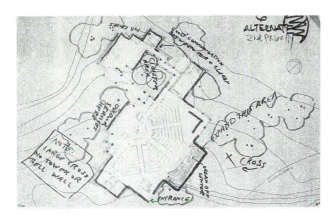

Figure 2 *Sketch plan of St Matthew's, 1979.* (Source: *Moore 1986*)

Figure 4 *Exterior view of St Matthew's Episcopal Church, Pacific Palisades, California, 1979–83, by Moore, Ruble and Yudell.* (Source: *Timothy Hursley*)

which we were drawing with a high ceiling during the fourth meeting. I was vigorously attacked when this was being presented by a woman who cited Jesus' belief in energy conservation with the attendant supposition that the ceiling needed to be low lest heat be wasted warming up the organ in too big a room. Fortunately for me, parishioners interested in the organ responded vociferously, reciting how the organ needed to be cool with a high ceiling. I therefore didn't have to put forward any defence of the high ceiling, which I probably would have on flimsy architectural grounds. Afterward the rector, who had been fairly dubious about the participatory process at first, said he was becoming convinced of its worth and that an important part of the reason why it was working was that we, the architects, never had become defensive. He noted that for us even once to become defensive about the scheme would have killed the mood of involvement of almost all the people taking part. I agreed but laid it to slow metabolism on my part and my partners': we don't get defensive until much later, when the crisis is over.

There were a few other opportunities to steer a course between high church and low church responses. The transept in the scheme, the outlines of which were

Figure 3 *Interior view of St Matthew's church.* (Source: *Timothy Hursley*)

approved in that third meeting, was given round windows (which cheered traditionalists remembering rose windows) with rectangular mullions more like an industrial building and satisfying to the low church parishioners. In the years since, Jane Marquis, who has been doing stained glass for the church, has made softly coloured and non-representational sheets of glass in the panes. The effect is softer than it once was, I think to everybody's pleasure.

I have mixed together in these last paragraphs events of the third and fourth meetings of the parish partly because I don't remember precisely when they occurred, but by the end of the fourth meeting we had a scheme which had been programmed with much greater detail than usual by the parishioners and had on every count their discussion and involvement. The architects' role may seem diminished, but I don't think any of us architects felt that our involvement was less critical or less satisfying. The basic architectural act was to put a Latin cross roof on a half-elliptical floor plan, which seems a suitably pointed challenge to the ability of an architect anytime. We left the fourth session with a detailed set of worked out requirements and produced schematic drawings (see Figure 2) which went up in the parish house a month later, where we had left ballots for the required vote (which came out at 87 per cent in our favour). Not very many people were going to vote against a scheme in which they had had so large a hand, and I for one felt far more comfortable with this effort than I would have with peddling a design that we liked, but about which they were unsure.

Almost a year after that triumphal moment was spent trying to be responsive to the various committees which, no longer unified in that creative thrill of making something, elapsed frequently into long and sometimes bitter disagreements, but the impetus was there from the act of creation which this time included not just the architects but a great many of the people who would inhabit this church. The impetus did, in fact, carry the design (see Figures 3 and 4).

PART 5

APPROACHES AND APPRECIATION

SECTION 5.1

Approaches to architecture

Architecture is not created in a vacuum. It is fundamentally part of our make-up, or, as the Renaissance scholar and architect L.B. Alberti put it, 'firmly rooted in the Mind of Man'.

Therefore, while every building task is about ordering the environment for our benefit, it does so in answer to both our physical and emotional needs, and our cultural aspirations. The extent to which either of these factors influences particular design decisions depends on the situation, but one would be hard-pressed to find built form of any significance anywhere without a cultural dimension to it. The nineteenth-century American sculptor and theorist, Horatio Greenough (1805–52) – who is credited with first enunciating the principles upon which the influential functionalist doctrine was founded – observed that all great developments in the history of architecture had one thing in common: they were the 'fruits of a dominating creed'. He regarded religion as the only human construct pervasive enough to unite the 'motives and means for grand and consistent systems of structure' (Greenough 1962: 115).

A similar claim could possibly these days be made for science, but the objective of this section is not to search for an overriding paradigm governing all architectural activity. Rather, the variety of approaches to the subject identified in the essays included here would seem to emphasize its inclusive nature – the breadth of its scope.

The authors explore recurrent themes linking architecture to other fields in the history of ideas. They consider its place within the age-old arts versus science debate, the concept of style, and the contrasting manifestations of different religious perspectives. They examine the nature of artistic movements, highlight controversies which mark the turning point for particular schools of thought and demonstrate the fascination which apocalyptic visions hold for artists and architects. Finally, our attitudes towards the past and future of the discipline and its end-products are reviewed: how well do we look after the physical remains of our architectural heritage, and how do we ensure that the next generation responsible for the formation of the built environment is properly equipped to do so?

These are only some of the many issues which could be considered relevant to a field of human endeavour that used to be called the 'Mother of Arts'. As architecture continues to draw on such a wealth of sources, perhaps we ought to ask ourselves the question: why is this term no longer in currency?

H.L.

REFERENCE

Greenough, H. (1962) 'Structure and organization', in *Form and Function: Remarks on Art, Design and Architecture by Horatio Greenough*, ed. H.A. Small, Berkeley: University of California Press; first published in *Memorial of Horatio Greenough*, ed. H.T. Tuckerman, New York.

RECOMMENDED READING

Banham, P. Reyner (1960) *Theory and Design in the First Machine Age*, London: Architectural Press.

Benedikt, M. (1987) *For an Architecture of Reality*, New York: Lumen Books.

Brolin, B.C. (1985) *Flight of Fancy: The Banishment and Return of Ornament*, London: Academy Editions.

Collins, P. (1965) *Changing Ideals in Modern Architecture 1750–1950*, London: Faber.

Crook, J.M. (1987) *The Dilemma of Style: Architectural Ideas from the Picturesque to the Post-Modern*, London: John Murray.

Grabow, S. (1983) *Christopher Alexander: The Search for a New Paradigm in Architecture*, Stocksfield: Oriel Press.

Gropius, W. (1955) *Scope of Total Architecture*, New York: Harper.

Laugier, M.A. (1977) *An Essay on Architecture*, Los Angeles: Hennesey & Ingalls.

Le Corbusier (1970) *Towards a New Architecture*, London: Architectural Press.

Lethaby, W.R. (1956) *Architecture, Nature and Magic* London: Gerald Duckworth.

Ruskin, J. (1989) *The Seven Lamps of Architecture*, New York: Dover.

Tafuri, M. (1976) *Architecture and Utopia: Design and Capitalist Development*, Cambridge, Mass.: MIT Press.

Venturi, R. (1977) *Complexity and Contradiction in Architecture*, 2nd edn, London: Architectural press.

Wittkower, R. (1988) *Architectural Principles in the Age of Humanism*, London: Academy Editions.

Wolfe, T. (1983) *From Bauhaus to Our House*, London: Abacus.

Wright, F. Lloyd (1943) *An Autobiography*, New York: Duell, Sloan & Pearce.

72 Frozen music: the bridge between art and science[1]

Stephen Grabow

When Goethe, in 1829, compares architecture to 'frozen music', he says that it is the *tone of mind* produced by architecture that approaches the effect of music.[2] This connection to mind – to the cognitive function of the human brain – is the vital historical link that ties architecture to both art and science. Today, the concept of similar structural relationships occurring in different media is known as 'isomorphic correspondence' – a term from Gestalt psychology to describe the relationship between our experience of order in space and the distribution of underlying dynamic processes in the brain. Goethe's allusion to 'frozen music' – to the simultaneous perception (in buildings) of all of the relationships that (in music) normally develop over time – is a reference to an ancient body of thought and intellectual tradition in which a scientific understanding of the laws of nature could be harnessed to create beauty in art through the principle of isomorphic correspondence.

Figure 1 *Pythagoras at his musical experiments.* (Source: *F. Gafuri (1492)* Theorica Musice *(set of cards)*)

In the sixth century BC, Pythagoras observed that the musical tones produced by vibrating strings create harmonic resonances if their lengths are ratios of whole numbers (see Figure 1). This fascinating discovery turned out to have a profound impact on human thought for the next two thousand years. Following Pythagoras, Plato explained how cosmic order and harmony are contained in certain numbers corresponding to musical proportions (such as 1:2, 2:3, and 3:4 for example, which correspond to an octave, a fifth, and a fourth respectively). According to the historian Rudolf Wittkower (1967), the Pythagorean-Platonic conception of a mathematical and harmonic structure to the universe was guided and supported by a long chain of thought, through the Middle Ages to the fifteenth century where, in the hands of Renaissance architects, it gained wide currency.

Vitruvius' system of proportions based on the human figure, for example, expresses the sizes of the parts in terms of the whole as a *harmonic* progression of ratios (Scholfield 1958: 21). When his work was rediscovered in the fifteenth century, it became the main source of the Renaissance theory of proportion and the inspiration for Alberti's 'musical' analogy: namely, that harmonic ratios inherent in nature are revealed in music and therefore the key to correct proportion in design is Pythagoras' system of musical harmony,

Four centuries before Gestalt psychology, Alberti anticipated the principle of isomorphic correspondence of structure in different media. For him, an inborn sense makes us aware of harmony. Therefore, if a building has been made in accordance with the laws of harmonic proportions, then we react instinctively and feel the resonance of form 'which lies behind all matter and binds the universe together' (Wittkower 1967: 27). With reference to Pythagoras, he said that 'the numbers by means of which the agreement of sounds affects our ears with delight, are the very same which please our eyes and minds' (Wittkower 1967: 110).

Thus, the proportions of room sizes in Alberti's buildings do correspond to the ratios of musical consonances : 1:1, 2:3 and 3:4 for small plans; 2:1, 4:9 and 9:16 for medium plans; and 3:1, 3:8 and 4:1 for large plans, along with similar ratios for their heights (Scholfield 1958: 55). A century later, Palladio applied these so-called harmonic ratios to the internal layout of the whole building (see Figure 2); in other words, to the distribution of the rooms themselves, so as to form a

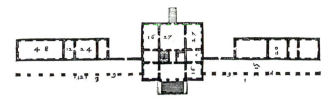

Figure 2 *Villa Emo at Fanzola.* (Source: *Palladio 1570*)

proportional sequence or rhythmic progression, what Wittkower calls a 'fugal' system of proportion (Wittkower 1967: 130).

Although these ideas were extended into the sixteenth century by Vignola in Italy, and the seventeenth century by Francois Blondel in France and Inigo Jones in England, they achieved the widest following and practice during the Renaissance in Italy (Scholfield 1958: 70–1). As Wittkower shows, the theory of musical relationships was widespread throughout the fifteenth century and an important part of one's artistic education (Wittkower 1967: 117). Through music, the visual arts – and especially architecture – were given a *mathematical* foundation. And, as Wittkower notes, the musical analogy was not just theoretical speculation; it testified to 'the solemn belief in the harmonic mathematical structure of all creation' (Wittkower 1967: 117). Along with Alberti and Palladio, many Renaissance architects subscribed to this belief, including Brunelleschi, Leonardo and Michelangelo; and before it eventually lost currency among architects, it was reasserted in scientific circles by Galileo and Kepler.

Stimulated by the Pythagorean quest for a basic harmony in arithmetic, geometry and music, Kepler believed it was possible to represent the motion of the planets in terms of musical notation. His eventual discovery of the laws of planetary motion in the seventeenth century, along with the observations of Newton, Bernoulli and Fourier, laid the foundations for harmonic analysis in contemporary mathematics, physics and engineering. In *Science and the Modern World*, Alfred North Whitehead wrote that 'we have in the end come back to a version of the doctrine of old Pythagoras, from whom mathematics and mathematical physics took their rise' (1967: 36). For architects however, as P.H. Scholfield shows, the Renaissance theory of harmonic proportions had unfortunately 'degenerated' into a 'narrow and inflexible' body of thought focused on a handful of simple arithmetic ratios (1958: 84).

The idea of 'harmonic' proportions belonged to Pythagoras; but he linked musical structure only to mathematics. It was Plato who generalized the notion to all form: that is to say, all form that is 'in tune' with the structure of the universe. Vitruvius, based on studies of human proportions, transferred this general notion into specific visual ratios. But it was Alberti who connected the visual realm of form back to music by

saying that the same Pythagorean ratios by which music creates harmonic resonances to the ear also create visual harmony to the eye. This last point is the one that was eventually refuted, particularly if one is comparing the processes of sight and sound.

The apparently decisive argument was made in the nineteenth century by Helmholtz when he explained how the ear is unable to pass on to the mind any information about mathematical ratios (Helmholtz, cited in Scholfield 1958: 74). When two notes harmonize, he argued, the information that they are coming from two chords of commensurable ratios is incidental to the harmonic vibration of the ear membrane. It simply vibrates as a single consonance, automatically. It doesn't care if the chord came from a violin string, a flute, or a human voice. It responds only to the effect, not the cause. Helmholtz's observations only confirmed a growing suspicion among eighteenth-century critics and philosophers that visual proportion was not something that could be determined by such precise numbers as those contained in the harmonic ratios.[3] After all, one's perceptions of the proportions of a room, for example, are affected by moving around in it as well as by the laws of perspective. Under such conditions it would seem impossible for the eye to detect the exact ratios that the architect had used as precisely and as easily as the ear can detect an out-of-tune chord. And yet no one denied that there was such a thing as harmonic proportions; the argument was simply directed against the belief that they were the same as those on the musical scale.

Although the classical analysis of music shows that there is a relatively simple mathematical underlayer to harmonic structure based on the proportions of tones, contemporary music theorists no longer believe that the recognized units of analysis – like tones, intervals and chords – are also the units of our perception. Rather, the focus is on larger scale events such as patterns, phrases, variations and hierarchic structures (see Serafine 1988: 72–3). The crux of the musical analogy in architecture therefore is not whether the numbers are the same, but that there is a *similar* structure: namely, a system of proportional relationships that repeat with variation, etc. And in fact, as Scholfield has shown, that is the one surviving idea of the Pythagorean-Platonic theory of proportion – repeating ratios (Scholfield 1958: 80).

And here we come closer to the general principles of form that connect music to architecture. Like repeating intervals and rhythm, repeating ratios and harmony help to establish an 'isomorphic correspondence' between the two media. In the case of proportion, repeating ratios means that the divisions between parts and wholes are consistent at different levels of scale. For example, consider the familiar branching pattern of a tree: the spacing of the main branches in proportion to the trunk is actually repeated at a smaller scale in proportion to each branch and again at an even smaller scale in the veins of the leaf membranes (see Figure 3). Repeating ratios generate proportionally similar shapes which, like repeating intervals, unify the pattern of relationships by emphasizing the wholes to which the parts are in proportion.

Christian Norberg-Schulz, using Gestalt theory, explains how the perception of repeating proportional ratios in a building is not dependent upon the ratios being exactly 1:1 or 1:2, for example, but upon our recognition of the *similar* shapes that they generate:

> When this has happened, we may analytically investigate the organization and discover the underlying ratios. But these ratios are never perceived as such; rather, we recognize the dimensions as 'similar,' 'almost similiar,' or 'completely different' . . . This does not mean that we want to abolish the number completely. When we experience *similarities*, the repetition of equal elements implies a numerical order. But the number enters as a purely secondary element of the description. The experienced order thus has to be understood as a characteristic Gestalt.
> (Norberg-Schulz 1963: 94)

In other words, the key to the correspondence between musical and visual form is not in the numbers, as Alberti thought; nor is it in the processes of sight and sound, as Helmholtz and other critics thought. Rather, it is in the cognitive similarity of structure between the two media, in the principles of formation and transformation by which holistic structures in each are created. Like rhythm, harmonic proportion is a unifying force in the differentiation of form. As Alessandro Barca, an eighteenth-century proponent of Renaissance theory said: 'There cannot be beauty or proportion in the whole without unity, which cannot be obtained otherwise than with uniformity of ratios or divisions in all the separate parts' (Scholfield 1958: 80). To the modern reader,

however, it may seem surprising that the repetition of proportional ratios, which is now such an accepted practice in contemporary architectural design (although without any conscious reference to music), originates in the ancient attempt to create forms that were resonant with the harmonic structure of the universe. Yet the intellectual history of architecture is essentially characterized by the attempt to see architectural form as part of a larger realm of form, one that includes both art and science.

For centuries, architects have shown an intellectual passion for the subject of form. Our earliest interpretations of the archaeological past indicate that ancient builders were not only fascinated by geometrical form, they attributed great cosmological significance and purpose to its meaning (see Figure 4). As William Lethaby demonstrates, many ancient buildings, especially temples, were actually scaled models of the proportional structure of the world and of the heavens as perceived by the science of the time, and not merely symbolic representations (Lethaby 1974: 6). And the earliest specifically *architectural* writings address building form as if it were a specific case of a more general realm of natural form.

From Vitruvius, whose *Ten Books* link us to the ancient Greeks, comes the idea of form having reason and laws. His observations on proportion also acknowledge a distinction between the 'parts' and the 'whole' as a general property of all forms. Brunelleschi, who designed some of the most beautiful buildings of the Italian Renaissance, was the first to work out the general laws of perspective. Alberti, whose treatises on architecture link 'fitness' to beauty, said that form arises 'from a secret argument and discourse implanted in the mind itself' (quoted in de Zurko 1957: 48). Leonardo da Vinci attached spiritual significance to the idea of 'force' as the motivating power behind all form. He saw this

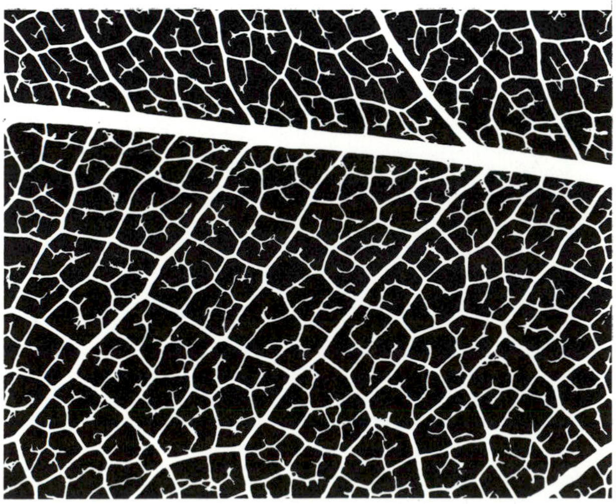

Figure 3 *Venation of a leaf membrane.* (Source: *Feininger 1975*)

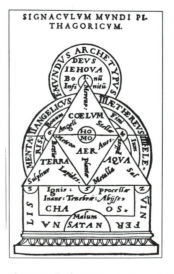

Figure 4 *Pythagorean emblem of the universe.* (Source *Roslinus 1597*)

phenomenon at work whether he looked at nature or at fabricated forms – the existence of which he regarded as a visible embodiment of nature's mechanical principles governing all forms. And Palladio, whose elegant villas continue to influence generations of builders, was also of the opinion that architecture was an expression of the principles of natural form: 'Architecture,' he says, 'as all the other arts, being grounded upon rules taken from the abstraction of nature, admits of nothing that is contrary or foreign to that order which nature prescribes to all things' (quoted in de Zurko 1957: 54–5).

Goethe, whose 'frozen music' analogy echoed many other early nineteenth-century writers and thinkers, connected beauty with fitness in organic forms as well as in buildings, and he conceived of the universe as both an organism *and* a work of art. To him, organic form was present 'not only in the crystal and the bone, in the leaf and the cloud, but also in the painting and the poem' (quoted in Read 1950: 13). For Goethe there was only a single creative process consisting of formation and transformation. Karl Friedrich Shinkel, whose buildings and ideas were influential in shaping nineteenth-century architecture, especially in Berlin, says 'the beauty of form is in the visual structure of nature' (quoted in de Zurko 1957: 197). And Ruskin, who was important in the evolution of twentieth-century architectural thought, says 'all beauty is founded on the laws of natural form' (quoted in de Zurko 1957: 135).

Most architects who have been historically significant in the development of the field have speculated upon form in such general terms, including figures from the more recent past, like Louis Sullivan, Frank Lloyd Wright, Walter Gropius and Eliel Saarinen who, in *The Search for Form*, wrote that 'the structural and organic composition of the universe is *architectureal* by nature' (Saarinen 1948: 44).

These speculations have in common the idea that architectural form belongs to a more general realm of form – even although it is obviously human-made. As an idea, it is astonishing because it is not intended as a metaphor but rather as a matter of both scientific *and* artistic fact. It is based on a parallelism between the search in science for models that illuminate nature and certain crucial processes in art at the level of form. For example, in *Chaos*, the 1987 best-selling story of the discovery of fractal geometry in mathematical physics, James Gleick pays a rare scientific tribute to this tradition of thought. He says that architects no longer care to build blockish skyscrapers because 'such shapes fail to resonate with the way nature organizes itself or with the way human perception sees the world' (Gleick 1987: 116–17).

When the ancients looked at nature, they were attracted to certain states more than others – to the rising and the setting of the sun, the eclipse of the moon, the diurnal rotations of the seasons, the blooming of the flower, or the spiral of the Nautilus shell – and these states represented for them the perfection of the universe, worthy of reverance and respect, and of study and abstraction into fundamental properties like harmony, rhythm, proportion and balance. The isomorphic expression of these same properties – in music, in dance, in athletic contest, or even in politics – was seen as a striving towards perfection and constituted the highest value in life.

In the twentieth century, scientists now look at a wider and deeper range of natural states, including the erratic side of nature; and yet they find the same persistence of formal order. The new science of 'chaos', as physicists and mathematicians call it, studies fluctuations, discontinuities, oscillations, and other irregularities that the ancients avoided. Using the conceptual tools of mathematical topology, physical dynamics, and high-speed computers, they have discovered a fantastic and delicate structure of forms underlying complexity. These forms enable one to visualize the holistic behaviour of an otherwise chaotic system, like a violent thunderstorm, a flag snapping back and forth in the wind, or the way a rising column of cigarette smoke breaks into wild swirls. 'No matter what the medium,' says Gleick, 'the behavior obeys the same newly discovered laws' (1987: 5).

This same concern for form also permeates scientific enquiry at a more subtle level, not just in revealing the beauty of natural forms but in the *process* of doing science. Although rarely mentioned in the body of scientific and mathematical literature, aesthetic sensibility, as the great physicist Henri Poincaré observed, plays the part of a 'delicate sieve' in the formulation of concepts, theories, models and formulae. Aesthetics in science is very much a mode of discrimination and response associated with visualization, structure, metaphor, image, analogy and the recognition of form (see Wechsler 1978: 3). Seymour Papert (1978), commenting on Poincaré's famous essay on mathematical form, acknowledges that there are *resonances* between mathematics and human perception 'which are responsible for mathematical pleasure and beauty' (Papert 1978: 104). And Geoffrey Vickers (1978), demonstrating how Darwin's intuitive sense of the general principles of biological form was the driving force behind the theory of evolution, says 'I regard the creation and appreciation of form by the human mind as an act of artistry, whether the artifact be a scientific theory, a machine, a sonata, a city plan, or a new design in human relations' (Vickers 1978: 147).

We have here the meeting of two perspectives, of both art and science, at the level of form. It is not surprising then that architects should be fascinated by form, or that there should be a tradition of speculation in which architectural form is seen as a special case of a more general realm or continuum of form. Such speculation not only ties architectural thought to a wide and diverse body of knowledge in other, more artistic, scientific or philosophical fields; it provides both an insight to the laws of form and a deeper appreciation of the feelings form evokes in us – its *aesthetic* properties. In 1951, Herbert Read summarized the convergence of these perspectives:

> The increasing significance given to *form* or *pattern* in various branches of science has suggested the possibility of a certain parallelism, if not identity, in the structures of natural phenomena and of authentic works of art.... The revelation that perception itself is essentially a pattern-selecting and pattern-making function (a Gestalt formation); that pattern is inherent in the physical structure or in the functioning of the nervous system; that matter itself analyses into coherent patterns or arrangements of molecules; and the gradual realization that all these patterns are effective and ontologically significant by virtue of an organization of their parts which can only be characterized as *aesthetic* – all this development has brought works of art and natural phenomena onto an identical plane of inquiry.
>
> (Read 1951: v–vi)

What Read is saying is that, at the level of form, human creativity and natural evolution occupy a single plane of enquiry. And it is on that plane that Saarinen could say, with more than poetic confidence, that 'the structural and organic composition of the universe is *architectural* by nature' (Saarinen 1948: 44). It is also the plane on which Vitruvius acknowledged the distinction between the 'whole' and its 'parts', and became fascinated with the relationship between them; where Alberti speaks of a 'secret discourse implanted in the mind itself'; Leonardo, of 'a force behind all form'; Palladio, of 'order which nature prescribes to all things'; Goethe, of the processes of 'formation and transformation'; Shinkel, of 'the visual structure of nature'; and Ruskin, of 'the laws of natural form'. It is also to be found underneath Wright's 'organic architecture', Le Corbusier's 'ineffable space' (see Figure 5), and, in more contemporary theories, Christian Norberg-Schulz's 'existential space' and Christopher Alexander's 'pattern languages'.[4]

The concept of 'isomorphic correspondence' that underlies the 'frozen music' metaphor is seen here as an almost suprahistorical paradigm that ties architecture and its conceptions to both art and science. Architectural principles such as the unity of the whole and its parts, proportion, hierarchy, symmetry, differentiation, equilibrium, adaptation, repetition, alternation, contrast, rhythm and balance – all have their isomorphic counterparts in music, painting, poetry, language and literature, philosophy, mathematics, biology, physics and psychology. The invocation of these principles in the making of buildings is seen like beads on a thread running through almost the entire intellectual history of the field – an allusion to Herman Hesse's 'Bead Game' in which all structures in different fields of both art and

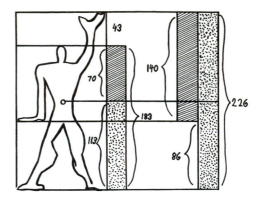

Figure 5 *Architectural proportions based on the human figure.* (Source: *Le Corbusier 1948b*)

science could be seen from a single point of view (suggested by Alexander 1968: 151). Hesse (1945) compared the 'tone of mind' necessary to play this game to a seven-gated cathedral. In this single view, architecture is a highly structured temple of the mind mediating between the earthly beauty of the natural world and the abstract mysteries of the universe. Like 'frozen music', it provides a realm in which the forms of humans achieve their most differentiated articulation, expressing simultaneously the precision of natural law and the dynamic creativity of the human mind.

NOTES

1   The essay is a revised version of an invited talk presented at the fiftieth anniversary of the Icelandic Architects' Association, Reykjavik, July 1989. Research for this project was generously supported by a grant from the Faculty Senate Research Committee of the University of Kansas.

2   J.W. von Goethe, in a letter to his secretary, Peter Eckermann, 23 March 1829, cited in Smith 1969: 49.

3   In France, the leading critic was Claude Perrault. In England, the attack was joined by William Hogarth, David Hume, Edmund Burke and Henry Home (Lord Kames). In the pro-Pythagorean camp were François Blondel, Christopher Wren, Francis Hutcheson and Henry Wotton. See Scholfield 1958: 72–9.

4   See Wright 1943; Le Corbusier 1948a: 7–9; Norberg-Smith 1971; and Alexander 1979; cf. Grabow 1983: 51.

REFERENCES

Alexander, C. (1968) 'The Bead Game conjecture', *Lotus* 5: 151–4.

——— (1979) *The Timeless Way of Building*, New York: Oxford University Press.

de Zurko, E.R. (1957) *Origins of Functionalist Theory*, New York: Columbia University Press.

Feininger, A. (1975) *Roots of Art*, New York: Viking.

Gleick, J. (1987) *Chaos: Making a New Science*, New York: Viking.

Grabow, S. (1983) *Christopher Alexander: The Search for a New*

Paradigm in Architecture, Boston: Routledge.

Hesse, H. (1945) *Das Glasperlenspiel*; trans. as *Magister Ludi*, 1969, New York: H. Holt; trans. as *The Glass Bead Game*, 1987, London: Pan.

Le Corbusier (1948a) *New World of Space*, New York: Reynal & Hitchcock.

—— (1948b) *Le Modulor*, Paris; trans. as *The Modulor*, 1980, Cambridge, Mass.: Harvard University Press.

Lethaby, W. (1974) *Architecture, Mysticism and Myth*, London: Architectural Press.

Norberg-Schulz, C. (1963) *Intentions in Architecture*, Oslo: Scandinavian University Press.

—— (1971) *Existence, Space and Architecture*, New York: Praeger.

Palladio, A. (1570) *I Quattro Libri dell'Architettura*, Venice; trans. 1738, *The Four Books of Architecture*, London: Isaac Ware.

Papert, S. (1978) 'The mathematical unconscious', in J. Wechsler (ed.) *On Aesthetics in Science*, Cambridge, Mass.: MIT Press.

Read, H. (1950) 'Goethe and art', *The Listener* 43: 13.

—— (1951) Preface to L.L. White (ed.) *Aspects of Form*, New York: Pellegrini & Cudahy.

Roslinus, H. (1597) *De opere dei creationis, Frankfurt*.

Saarinen, E. (1948) *The Search for Form*, New York: Reinhold.

Scholfield, P.H. (1958) *The Theory of Proportion in Architecture*, Cambridge: Cambridge University Press.

Serafine, M.L. (1988) *Music as Cognition*, New York: Columbia University Press.

Smith, N.K. (1969) *Frank Lloyd Wright*, Englewood Cliffs, NJ: Prentice-Hall.

Vickers, G. (1978) 'Rationality and intuition', in J. Wechsler (ed.) *On Aesthetics in Science*, Cambridge, Mass.: MIT Press.

Wechsler, J. (ed.) (1978) *On Aesthetics in Science*, Cambridge, Mass.: MIT Press.

Whitehead, A.N. (1967) *Science and the Modern World*, New York: Free Press.

Wittkower, R. (1967) *Architectural Principles in the Age of Humanism*, London: Alec Tiranti.

Wright, F.L. (1943) *An Autobiography*, New York: Duell, Sloan & Pearce.

FURTHER READING

Arnheim, R. (1951) 'Gestalt psychology and artistic form', in L.L. Whyte (ed.) *Aspects of Form*, New York: Pellegrini & Cudahy.

(1970) *Visual Thinking*, London: Faber & Faber.

Cole, Y. (1989) 'Frozen music: the origin and development of the synesthetic concept in art', *Precis* 6: 171–81.

Kepes, G. (ed.) (1965) *Structure in Art and in Science*, New York: George Braziller.

Koestler, A. (1975) *The Art of Creation*, London: Picador.

Maslow, A. (1961) 'Isomorphic interrelations between knower and known', in G. Kepes (ed.) *Sign, Image and Symbol*, New York: George Braziller.

Read, H. (1966) 'The origins of form in art', in G. Kepes (ed.) *The Man-made Object*, New York: George Braziller.

Snow, C.P. (1959) *The Two Cultures and the Scientific Revolution*, Cambridge: Cambridge University Press.

Stechow, W. (1953) 'Problems of structure in some relations between the visual arts and music', *Journal of Aesthetics and Art Criticism* 11: 324–33.

Vergani, G. (1989) 'The question of unification and the musicalization of art', *Precis* 6: 164–9.

73 The meaning of style

Werner Szambien

CONFUSED WORDS AND CONFUSED IDEAS

The age-old debate on the relationship between art and design is as topical today as it has ever been. In the cultural field the race to find something new accelerates with the increase in audiences, mirroring the growth in the economic impact of culture, which may be welcomed or merely tolerated.

Although it remains very difficult to appreciate the necessary association between the democratization of culture and its consumption in its various forms, a number of 'inflationary' phenomena are deplored by the majority of 'professionals' in the cultural field, such as the increase in the number of exhibitions and, indeed, exhibition catalogues, which are tending more and more to replace works of substance, and the growing importance of the media for the economic success of an event (the 'objective' interest of which is of minor importance if it exists at all).

There can be no doubt whatsoever that one of the most irritating of these phenomena is misuse of language, for which the press is largely responsible and which can only prejudice the quality of criticism. Since the 'fashion arts' came into existence (the expression first appeared in the early 1980s), it is impossible to say whether the designer is an artist or vice versa; neo-classicism is no longer an artistic movement dating from 1800, but a 'post-modernist' outlook. 'Post-Modernism' itself – which Charles Jencks is perhaps the only person to have understood – is promoted as an international style which captures elements of the 'language' of classical architecture (so well defined by Sir John Summerson). But has the 'International Style' (Hitchcock and Johnson 1932) ever actually been a style?

Unfortunately, this term is now becoming rooted in the speech of both creators and decision-makers, and is making it impossible to establish a relationship between the physical form of an object and its name, with no precise definition currently available. Leaving aside ephemeral manifestations, an architecture reference can always be made to Pierre Chaussard: 'Architecture demands a more stringent examination than the other arts because of all follies, the folly in stone is the one that costs the most and lasts the longest' (Chaussard 1801: 7).

THE NATURE OF STYLE

The word 'style' only came into use in architecture fairly recently. It comes, of course, from the Latin *stilus*, the point used for writing, and until the end of the eighteenth century it remained a rhetorical or poetic form adopted when composing a text, poem or speech. What we now call style was then called taste, manner or form. Jacques-François Blondel's definition was:

> By *style* in architecture we mean the actual form to be used, relative to the reason for the construction of the building. Style in the design of the façades and the decoration of the rooms is actually the poetry of architecture which helps to make all an architect's compositions genuinely interesting. It is the individual style of each type of building which gives such infinite variety to buildings of the same type and different types; 'style' may also define a sacred, heroic or pastoral type and express a regular or irregular, simple or complex, symmetrical or asymmetrical form; and finally the sublime can be achieved through style.
>
> (Blondel 1771: 401)

When the word was first introduced into architecture, it was simply a metaphor expressing the idea that architecture too can speak.[1]

The word appears to have entered modern usage first in England. Christopher Wren used it for the Saracen Style (Gothic) in 1713. The term was in current use by around 1773 – Germann quotes the example of James Essex (Germann 1972: 24–7). This may be explained by the fact that the Gothic tradition was more alive in England than on the Continent. It is fair to say, however, that the term became universally accepted, particularly in German- and Spanish-speaking countries, via the medium of French theory which enjoyed a position of hegemony until the beginning of the nineteenth century.

A mini-revolution had in fact occurred in France during the second half of the eighteenth century with the emergence of the idea of 'Nature', to which all contemporary writers subscribed (Boullée, Goethe, Le Camus de Mézières, Ledoux, Quatremère de Quincy and many others). The basic tenet of this theory was a return to the virtually exclusive primacy of proportion in architecture and the claim that each form of building had an individual, immediately recognizable nature. This claim was, of course, associated with the fact that many public architectural projects such as museums, libraries, hospitals, prisons and courthouses were being initiated at that time. At heart, however, architects were trying to achieve what their fellow artists (painters and sculptors)

Figure 1 *Prison de la Petite Force, Paris, 1786–91, by Pierre Desmaisons.* (Source: *Vitou*)

had succeeded in doing during the Renaissance period, at least in Italy – the elevation of the status of their profession to a genuine art-form and, by likening it to painting and poetry, its liberation from corporatist constraints (which were later suppressed by the French Revolution in any case).

Architecture then became eloquent and 'speaking'. The porch at the Hospital for Venereal Diseases in the boulevard du Port-Royal (architect Saint-Far, 1785) was intended to frighten and thus satisfy the educational objective of prevention. A prison gate (such as the Petite Force) in the same style had to have chained elements or columns (see Figure 1). The peace and pleasures of the countryside were expressed in irregular forms (the Queen's hamlet at Versailles by Mique and Hubert

Figure 2 *Pavillon des Biches in the Jardin des Plantes, Paris, c.1810, by Jacques Molinos. The 'noble' forms are supposed to illustrate the character of the occupants.* (Photograph: *Vitou*)

Robert, the zoo in the Jardin des Plantes by Molinos, etc.) (see Figure 2). The noblest public buildings demanded the use of distinguished orders (Corinthian for the National Assembly by Poyet, 1806), while convents used simple orders (for example, the Doric order for the Capucines convent, now the Lycée Condorcet, by Brongniart, 1779).

This theory was applied successfully for some time, but its limitations in relation to the canon of classical forms were obvious. In order to escape from the circle of Doric–Ionic–Corinthian orders, it was necessary to return to the wealth of architectural history which had only been a subject for censure up to that time. Until the end of the eighteenth century, Gothic was synonymous with barbaric, itself a synonym for Arabian. Gradually, however, these styles came to be accepted in gardens featuring the picturesque, and despite academic attitudes, popular doctrines and the predominant antipathy, tastes changed and the Gothic, Byzantine, Islamic, Chinese, Persian and Egyptian arts gained equal acceptance with Greek and Roman art (see Figure 3).

The word style then became indispensable, because as far as contemporary architects were concerned history was not 'historical' and did not belong to the past, but constituted a sort of reservoir of forms from which examples could be taken and imitated and which was kept alive in the designs of the present day. One of the most characteristic examples of this view is the building

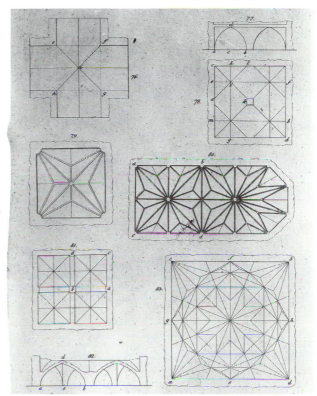

Figure 3 *One of the first comparative plates of Gothic vaulting published on the Continent.* (Source: *Costenoble 1812.* Photograph: *Jean Musy*)

at the entrance to the Passage du Caire (by Prétrel, 1799
– the date when the term was used for the first time in
the Fine Arts class at the Institute) – which combines
Oriental detail with Western ornamentation (see Figure
4).[2] The word 'style' was a means of defining something
which could previously only have been described in
pejorative terms (Chateaubriand was one of the first
writers to use this new meaning).[3]

It remained part of the vocabulary of architecture, but
with a number of different interpretations. To follow the
precise evolution of the word up to the present day
would require too much space. We can, however, see
one basic development up to 1850 – the distinction
between 'style' and 'styles'. Just like the idea of 'Nature',
the theory of 'styles' quickly ran out of steam, mainly
because it could only be applied in the field of decoration. A new caste came into being, that of the art and
architectural historians, who were gradually to transform the analysis of style (but not of form or, really, of
space), holding as they did the trump card of a so-called
scientific approach to the history of architecture.[4]

This was the precise point reached by Kugler in 1842.[5]
For him, style was synonymous with the absolute
beauty of an object resulting from the internal cohesion
of its components. This was also the sense in which

Figure 4 *Houses above the entrance to the Passage du Caire, Paris,
1799, by Prétrel.* (Source: *Vitou*)

Viollet-le-Duc and Semper used the word around 1860,
in the period of eclecticism. Viollet-le-Duc says in his
Entretiens sur l'architecture:

> I am not speaking here of style as a means of classify-
> ing the arts by period but of the style inherent in all
> the arts in every period, and to make this easier to
> understand I would say that apart from the style of
> the writer in every language, there is a style which is
> part of every language because it is part of the human
> genius.
>
> (Viollet-le-Duc 1863–72: 179).

To say that a building had 'style' meant that it had all
the formal characteristics of beauty irrespective of its
allusions to the history of architecture. This idea was
based, particularly on the part of Semper, on a complex
theory of techniques, forms and types which enabled the
presence of 'style' in a work to be measurable to a
certain degree.

What Semper called the stylistic conception of beauty
in art was certainly a rather formalistic equation:

> It does not approach the object in its collective
> nature, but considers it as a unit, as a homogeneous
> result and as a function of several variables which are
> congruent in certain combinations. They constitute
> the variable coefficients of a general value equation
> which provides a solution for a given problem when a
> concrete, predefined value appropriate to the individ-
> ual case is substituted for each variable.
>
> $$U = C\,(x, y, z, t, v, w \ldots)$$
>
> Whenever one or more of the coefficients varies, the
> answer U has to be different.[6]
>
> (Semper, cited in Szambien 1987: 153)

Clearly, the rhetorical aspect through which the introduction of the word 'style' into the vocabulary originated was gradually eliminated. The claim to style was
an expression of the confusion of the eclectic period
when confronted with the inability to achieve an individual nineteenth-century style which would be as
recognizable – or indeed as significant or eloquent – as
Gothic or Renaissance. Its room for manoeuvre, which
was considerable in the structural field (metal structures)
but restricted by historical example with regard to form,
was sanctioned by the emphasis placed on following the
technical path.

This situation did not change fundamentally during
the first half of the twentieth century, with one exception – the functionalist and formalist foundations of the
so-called International Style sought the radical removal
of any element which had meaning, and aimed at self-
sufficiency. Use of the word 'style' then became absurd,
because this 'style' reflected only itself. A similar development can, of course, be observed in the history of art
and architecture, where formalization of the analysis of

style was a conspicuous feature and any search for meaning was suspected of being unscientific.

STYLE AND MANNER

The word 'style' in architecture has thus been the subject of various interpretations between two extremes: first, rhetoric, the message and the expression of architecture; and second, the formal components making up a complex pattern which lends itself to analysis. This explains the contradictory ways in which the word can be used. In order to obtain a less equivocal use of the word, both interpretations would have to be taken into account. Whether an attempt is made to define style in terms of a period, a place or an artist, and whether it is historical, national, regional, local or individual, it only merits the classification if a minimum number of conditions is met. Otherwise the result is the perplexity felt towards most eclectic work – the picturesque, not to say ridiculous, sight of a Bavarian house in China, the unsuitability of a mansard roof on a block of council flats, the crudeness of an imitation of a great architect and the uneasiness felt towards so-called identical replicas.[7] The appropriate words for examples such as these are manner (the theorist Philippe Boudon brought the term 'in the manner of' back into fashion some years ago), design and form. Style is distinct from its imitations or models because of its unique density. Surely this muddled use of words again demonstrates the crisis in a profession whose practitioners are still uncertain whether to call themselves artists or technicians and thus opt consciously or unconsciously for manner? Has there really been any progress since the debates of the nineteenth century and since the dubious restoration of Pierrefonds by Viollet-le-Duc? (see Figure 5).

Figure 5 *Chateau Pierrefonds, restored by Viollet-le-Duc, 1857–68.* (Source: *From an old postcard*)

The meaning of style has yet to be re-established on a firm basis. To quote Quatremère de Quincy:

> In the language of the design arts, style is often synonymous with manner; in order to distinguish between the two words, it may be said that manner

incorporates an idea specifically applicable either to execution of the work or to the practical talent of the artist, while the word style describes the use of moral qualities which determine the manner or general qualities which influence the taste of each century, each country, each school and each form.

> (Quatremère de Quincy 1832: 502).

NOTES

1   See further Szambien 1986 and 1988.

2   In 1798 the Institute invited competitors in the Grand Prix of Architecture 'to abandon entirely the ridiculous affectation of Egyptian, Arabian and Gothic styles'. Cf. Bonnaire 1937: 153.

3   He used the word in 1802 in *Génie du Christianisme*. Like Victor Hugo, he played an important part in the revival of Gothic architecture. See Germann 1972.

4   See Schapiro 1982: 35–38 (first published in Kroeber, A. (ed.) (1953) *Anthropology Today*, Chicago: Chicago University Press). The article contains a bibliography of the major theorists of style in the history of art. See also Crook 1987.

5   Franz Kugler is considered to be one of the 'fathers' of the history of art following the publication of his *Handbuch der Kunstgeschichte*, Stuttgart, 1842. Semper considered that the true value of style had been appreciated for the first time by Rumohr about ten years before the publication of Kugler's work.

6   The theoretical work by the German architect Gottfried Semper (1803–79) remains largely unknown (Semper 1860, 1863). See also Herrmann 1981.

7   For recent misuses in Paris, see Szambien 1990.

REFERENCES

Blondel, J.-F. (1771) *Cours d'architecture contenant les leçons données en 1750 et les années suivantes*, Vol. I, Paris: Desaint.

Bonnaire, M. (1937) *Procès-verbaux de l'Académie des Beaux-Arts*, Vol. I, Paris: Armand Colin.

Chaussard, P. (1801) 'Architecture', *Journal des Bâtiments* 7 (22).

Costenoble, J.C. (1812) *Über Altdeutsche Architektur und deren Ursprung*, Halle: Hemmerde.

Crook, J.M. (1987) *The Question of Style*, London: J. Murray.

Germann, G. (1972) *Gothic Revival in Europe and Britain, Sources, Influences and Ideas*, London: Lund Humphries.

Herrmann, W. (1981) *Gottfried Semper, Theoretischer Nachlass an der ETH Zürich, Katalog und Kommentare*, Basle: Birkhauser.

Hitchcock, H.R. and Johnson, P. (1932) *The International Style: Architecture Since 1922*, New York: W.W. Norton.

Jencks, C.A. (1977) *The Language of Post-Modern Architecture*, London: Academy Editions.

Quatremère de Quincy, A.-C. (1832) *Dictionnaire historique d'architecture comprenant dans son plan les notions historiques, descriptives, archéologiques . . . de cet art*, Vol. II, Paris: A. Le Clére.

Schapiro, M. (1982) 'La notion de style', in *Style, Artiste et Société*, Paris: Gallimard, pp. 35–85.

Semper, G. (1860) *Der Stil in den technischen und tektonischen Künsten oder Praktische Asthetik. Ein Handbuch für Techniker, Künstler und Kunstfreunde*, Vol. I, Frankfurt am Main: Verlag für Kunst und Wissenschaft, Vol. II 1863, Munich: Friedrich Bruckmanns Verlag.

Szambien, W. (1986) *Symétrie, goût, caractère, théorie et terminologie de l'architecture à l'âge classique*, Paris: Picard.

—— (1987) 'Les variables du style dans une conférence de Gottfried Semper', *Amphion* 1: 153–9.

—— (1988) 'Architecture parlante, architecture à caractère, architecture écrite', in *Interférences*, University of Rennes.

—— (1990) 'Aux portes du néoclassicisme', *L'Architecture d'Aujourd'hui* 269: 30–2.

Viollet-le-Duc, E.E. (1863–72). *Entretiens sur l'architecture*, Vol. I, reprinted 1983, Brussels, Liège: Pierre Mardaga.

Architecture and faith

74 The Qur'ān and the Sunna as the basis for interpreting arabic house and mosque architecture

Abdul Aziz Aba Al-Khail

Praise Be to God, the Lord of all Worlds, and peace and blessing of Allah be upon the Seal of Prophets, Muhammad.

THE MOSQUE

God says in *Al-Noor Sura*, verses 36–7: 'In houses, which God hath permitted to be raised to honour, for the celebration, in them, of His Name: in them is He glorified in the mornings and in the evenings (again and again), by men whom neither traffic nor merchandise can divert from the remembrance of God, nor from regular prayer, nor from the practice of regular charity: their (only) fear is for the Day when hearts and eyes will be transformed (in a world wholly new).'

Of course, 'houses', here, means the houses of God (the mosques) and the initial meaning of the verses is that the believer is not distracted by secular things from praying at specific times in the mosque; but there is another inference that the mosque should not contain anything which might disturb the concentration of people at prayer in mosques. Therefore, the first Islamic mosques that followed the pattern of the Mosque of the Prophet (peace be upon Him) at Al-Madinah had hardly any openings: there were none at all in the kiblah wall in front of the people, and just a few at the back of the mosque for lighting; the worshipper should, when entering the mosque, leave behind all secular matters and concentrate on reckoning in the hereafter, fear of hell and interest in paradise. The entrances of the mosque are at the back of the worshippers, and people are supposed to walk between the rows of worshippers. In addition the completion of rows occurs at the back and not at the sides. Muslim bin Jaber bin Samurah narrated that the Prophet (peace be upon Him) said: 'Why do you raise your hands as if they are the tails of stubborn horses? Keep tranquil during prayer.' He said that the Prophet then saw us in circles and said, 'Why you are so circled? Why do you not keep in rows such as angels in the presence of the Lord?' We said 'O, Prophet of Allah, how do angels keep rows in the presence of their Lord?' He said, 'They complete the first line and close in.'

The basic principle of the design of the mosque of the Prophet (peace be upon Him) is the adoption of a rectangular shape, where the kiblah wall forms the length, and the side walls the width. There is evidence in the Sunna that demonstrates the reasons for selecting this shape and helps with an interpretation of the architecture of the Mosque of the Prophet (peace be upon Him), as well as the interpretation of the mosque in general, consistent with the rules laid down by the Qur'ān and Sunna.

Muslim narrated that Abu Saeed Al-Khudri (may God bless him) said that the Prophet (peace be upon Him) saw some of his companions praying in the back lines of the congregation and said, 'Advance and let me lead you, and others come to be led by you. Those who keep to the back, God will make them always stay behind.'

These sayings show that the prayers should follow the leader (Imam) and that this will not be achieved unless they come close to him, which is best achieved by keeping in the first line. The evidence showing the privilege of the first line is clearly indicated in the Qur'ān and the Sunna. God says in *Al-Omran Sura*, verse 133: 'Haste to the forgiveness of thy Lord and a paradise as wide as the heavens and earth prepared for the pious.' God also says in *Al-Hadeed Sura*, verse 21: 'Race to a forgiveness from your Lord and a paradise as wide as the heaven and earth prepared for those who believe in God and His Apostles; that is the favour that God gives to whom He will; God is verily of great benevolence.'

Let us now consider the interpretation of the architecture of the Holy Prophet's Mosque, and the reason behind the adoption of a rectangular shape, where the kiblah wall forms the length of the rectangle. The reason is that the Prophet wanted the first line to become the longest, because of its importance. There is another inference, namely that the length of the lines is of more importance than their number, so that people at the back may be able to hear the leader. Let us look at the first of the two kiblahs, Al-Aqsa Mosque, and study its design in relation to the above citations from the Qur'ān and the Sunna.

Al-Aqsa Mosque is originally the Mosque of Omar Ibn Al Khattab (may God bless him). Omar's Mosque took a rectangular shape parallel to the kiblah wall identical to the Prophet's Mosque. The Omayyads rebuilt Al-Aqsa parallel to it in a rectangular shape like the first Mosque. However, the extensions of the Abbasids, Fatimids and Ayyubids made the Mosque deeper since the extensions were added in sequence to the back, and not to the right or left sides.

The first Islamic mosques, east and west, were the same shape as the Prophet's Mosque; for example the Mosque of Amrou bin Al-As in Cairo originally had the same shape as the Prophet's Mosque prior to expansions. The Omayyad Mosque in Damascus (see Figure 1) is also rectangular in relation to the kiblah wall. And in Maghreb, North Africa, there are the Al-Qairowan and Al-Zaitouna Mosques.

The mosques following the architecture of the Prophet's Mosque were those built by the Abbasids in Sammarah, the Ibn Touloun Mosque in Cairo, the Al-Koufa Mosque and those built in Harran, Aleppo, Hama, Basra, Gordove, Al-Qarawiyeen, Al-Kotobiya, Taza, etc. How does this similarity come about despite such a lapse of time, with so many changes of government and people? The main reason is that the basis of design for the first Islamic mosques drew on inspiration from the Qur'ān and the Sunna. The difference in shape which evolved during the Ottoman Empire came because the Ottomans wanted to surpass Ayasofia; they preferred numerous domes, and did not take the shape of the Prophet's Mosque as a prototype.

The columns in a mosque are architecturally distributed in accordance with the Prophet's Sunna; they follow a rectangular shape so as to form and organize prayer lines, because the Prophet's companion ordered that prayer between the columns should be avoided. Instead he decreed that lines be formed in front or behind these columns. Abdul Hameed bin Mahmoud said: 'We prayed behind one of our leaders and we were forced to form lines between the pillars', but Anas (may

Figure 1 *The Omayyad Mosque in Damascus.*

God bless him) said: 'We avoided this at the time of the Prophet' (narrated by Termedhi and Nisaei). Abu Dawood wrote that Abdul Hameed bin Mahmoud said: 'I prayed with Arab bin Malek on Friday and we were forced between the pillars and front and back.' Unfortunately the mosques which took the Prophet's Mosque as an example have all been altered over time and no longer reflect the system and design of the original.

The provision of water near the mosque can also be attributed to the Word of God and Prophet's Sunna; God says in the *Tauba Sura*, verse 108: 'Do not pray in it; a Mosque founded on piety since the First Day is more entitled to be a place of prayer, where men purge themselves, and God favours those who wish to purge their sins.' It is believed that this verse relates to the Qibah Mosque. The Prophet asked the people there about the words 'They like to be purged', and they said they were cleansing themselves with water, and the Prophet said, 'Keep to it'. From then on water was always made available at the mosque.

We move now to another element of the mosque, the yard. The origin of the word 'yard' can be ascribed to the broad area in front of a house. The yard is also the extension of the house to the sides, hence the surrounding area of the Kaaba is called a yard. The yard is therefore the area that surrounds and extends in front of the house and not inside the building, because the open area inside the house is called the 'enclosure', as it is designated for tethering camels and other animals. The enclosure can also enclose things, meaning it can contain them inside. The enclosure of the house is, therefore, a private area which nobody should look into.

The yard of the mosque should be free from any construction element other than the ablution areas already mentioned. Some people build fountains in the mosque yard claiming that they are for ablutions, but this is very far from the intended function as they are mostly constructed for decoration. The yard should also be free from trees, which would lessen the dignity of the mosque, which is the House of God and different from human houses.

To prove that the yard is one of the mosque elements in general, and not particular to the Kaaba, we can cite more of the Prophet's sayings. Ahmed wrote in his *Musnad* that Muhammad bin Abdullah bin Jahsh said: 'We were sitting at the mosque yard where coffins are put and the prophet was sitting behind us. He raised his eyes toward the sky then turned them down and put his hand on his forehead and said: "Our Lord is great, our Lord is great; what rigidity!" When the Prophet said these words Muhammad bin Abdullah bin Jahsh asked him: "Prophet, what rigidity has God revealed to you?" The Prophet replied: "In religion: by God Who has my soul in His hands, if a man is killed in the way of God, resurrected, and killed again in the way of God, then is resurrected once more and becomes indebted, he will never enter Paradise until he settles his indebtedness."'

This example illustrates that the yard of the Prophet's Mosque also served as a place where the Prophet sat to preach to his companions. Therefore, this is the purpose for which mosque yards could be used.

The mosque yard should also be open to those wishing to pray, and should be a place to sit in the seasons when the climate is moderate. At those times, the yard should be prepared for the purpose of lecturing on religious subjects. The idea behind allocating the yard for lecturing and preaching is that such actions are characterized by loud speech, which should not take place inside the mosque itself because it will upset those praying. Omar (may God bless him) heard some people raising their voices in the mosque, therefore he dedicated a place in the yard and said, 'Whoever wants to speak loud should sit there'.

THE HOUSE

God says in *Al-Noor Sura*, verses 27–8: 'O Ye believers, do not enter houses other than yours unless you ask for permission and say the word of peace to the occupants. This is better for you so that you may remember. If you did not find any inside, do not enter until you are permitted to, and if you are told "Go back", go back; it is better for you for God knows what you do.'

The above verses show the significance of the privacy of the house in Islamic architecture. This means that to enter a house one should seek permission, and keep away from the private areas inside the house. This should be realized by providing a right-angled corridor so that the guest may pass through before entering the sitting room, which gives notice to those inside, especially women, to be able to leave without being seen by such a guest. When he is told to go back or wait, he should do so, so as not to breach the privacy of the occupants. Moreover, the visitor should hear the reply of the occupants when he is still at the door. At Najd, in the central region of Saudi Arabia, an architectural element called *Al-Tarma* was introduced. This is an opening through which the occupants can look to identify the visitor; next to it is a corridor which leads to the interior of the house and which is angled at 90 degrees so that entrance will not be direct in a way that may surprise the occupants.

God says in *Al-Baqara Sura*, verse 189: 'They ask about moon stages, say; they are timings for people and Hajj. It is not good to enter houses from the back, rather, it is good to be pious; enter houses through their front doors and be heeded so that you may win.' The verse shows that the timings of Hajj should be respected, but the basic idea is that houses should be approached from designated doors. The verse also suggests that the private entrance be located at the back of the house while visitors should be received at the front of the house. It follows that in Islamic architecture, houses have two entrances, one at the back and the other at the front. It is regarded as good to enter the house from the front entrance because doing so from the back entrance will breach the privacy of the occupants, since the private elements are always located near the private back entrance. Some houses dedicate this back entrance to women, while visitors are received at the front one, where the sitting room for men is located. The concept of 'back' is an important addition to the privacy of the house; it is something about which pre-Islamic people did not know, nor Arabs before Islam. It is the main factor which secures privacy for some places inside the house, the places about which strangers should not know.

In brief, the Word of God explains to us the characteristics of the Islamic house: privacy and simplicity.

The Sunna complemented and confirmed the principle of the Qur'ān in interpreting Islamic architecture and defining its elements. Al-Bukhari tells us in the Al-Shufa volume that Amer bin Al-Shareed said: 'I was standing with Saad bin Abi Wakkas when Musawer bin Mahrama came and put his hand on my shoulder, and in the meanwhile Abu Rafea, the servant of the Prophet, came. He said: Saad, buy my house in your habitation. Saad said: No, by God, I will not. Al-Musawer said: By God, you will buy it. Saad said: I will not give you more than four thousand pieces. Abu Rafea said: I have been offered 500 dinars. Had I not heard the Prophet say the neighbour has the right in his neighbour's property over others, I would not have sold it to you at 4,000 while I have been offered 500 dinars.' He then sold it to him.

What we are interested in here is the difference between the concept of the house and the habitation. We have already defined the house and the habitation and explained that the habitation is inherited by successive families. God says: 'The Hereafter is the habitation of eternity' (*Ghafer Sura*, verse 39).

After reviewing the explanations of the saying in Fateh Al-Bari by Al-Asqalani, Omdat Al-Kari by Al-Aini, Al-Karamani and Al-Kastalani, it becomes clear that the habitation is a plot of which the house is part.

Al-Termidhi narrated (Ethics) that Jaben bin Abdullah Al-Ansari said: 'The Prophet came to us and said: I dreamt that Angel Gabriel was standing at my head and Angel Michael at my feet and the one saying to the other, give him an example, and the other said, hear, may you hear and understand, may you understand. You and your nation are the same as a king who had a plot where he built a house and organized a feast and sent a messenger to invite people to his feast; some came and some did not. God is the King and you Muhammad the Messenger and the plot is Islam and the house is Paradise. He who responds to you embraces Islam and who embraces Islam enters the Paradise and who enters Paradise eats from its fruits.'

This saying shows that the house is one of the basic necessities of life, and that socially it means settlement.

This is also confirmed by Al-Termedhi when he writes about Okba bin Amer Said: 'I said, O Prophet of Allah, how to win in the Hereafter; he said; "beheed your tongue and keep to your house and cry for your sin."' This may mean that it is enough for you to have a house, and you should not look for more. This confirms what we have already shown about the interpretation of the Qur'ān in relation to the house, i.e. simplicity is regarded as the optimum in Islamic architecture.

Some may say that the house should be large enough; we would accept this as true. The house should not be like those apartments which have nothing to do with Islamic architecture because they are meant to use the plot for commercial purposes; this type of arrangement inside an apartment does not comply with the Qur'ān and the Sunna. The Sunna confirms the privacy of the house in Islamic architecture as already stated in the Qur'ān. Rather, the Sunna clarifies this principle and enhances respect thereof. Al-Termedhi, in the Morals part, quotes Abu Zar as saying that the Prophet had said, 'Whoever uncovers the Privacy of others by looking over the house before taking permission, he has committed a penalizable sin, and if he is stoned to the extent his eyes are extracted, he has been treated well, but if he looks through an open door, he has committed no sin, it is the sin of the household's occupants.' This saying is also narrated by Termedhi under the title 'Permission taken in front of the door'. According to Termedhi, Anas said that the Prophet was in his house and a man looked inside the house; the Prophet threw an arrow head at him, and the man went away. This is a correct saying narrated by both Al-Bukhari and Muslim in the Ethics part.

Al-Bukhari (Al Mathalem volume – the overlooking and non-overlooking of rooms) interprets the verse, 'if you repent, your hearts have thus obeyed', that when Ibn Abbas asked Omar: 'whom does this include among the wives of the prophet?' Omar replied that they were Aisha and Safiya. But the saying also goes 'I prayed the "dawn prayer" with the prophet and then he entered a raised room and isolated himself for he was angry with his wives.'

In the same part, Al-Bukhari claims that Anas said: 'the prophet isolated himself from his wives for one month, so he sat in a raised room. Omar said, Have you divorced your wives? He said, No, but I isolate myself for one month. He stayed for twenty-nine days. In this saying the room and the raised room are mentioned.

The reader may wonder why I have not written about the house yard in the same way as that of the mosque. Does the house not have a yard? Yes, the house has a yard. Al-Bukhari explains in Al-Mathalem. He quotes Aisha as saying: 'My father Abubakr (the first Caliph of the Prophet) built a mosque in the yard of his house for prayer and reciting the Qur'ān, and the pagan children and women were overlooking him to see what he was doing.' Thus, the yard is in front of the house, covered by shades for the head of the household and his guests. It is among the elements of the house built at the yard.

CONCLUSION

To end this essay on the influence of the Holy Qur'ān and the Sunna on Islamic architectural design we confirm that architectural design in Islam is based on two principles, the first being hospitality, the second, privacy. Hospitality is defined by the availability of a space specially designed for reception in the Islamic house (Al-Majliss) or sitting room for male visitors. The Majliss is different from the living room because receiving guests in the living room is awkward and embarrassing for privacy in Islamic tradition. When the guests are gathered in the reception space they sit, which is not a tradition in other cultures.

The public spaces in Islam also offer hospitality: the mosque is open day and night; any Muslim can enter, even outside the time of prayer, and can sit or sleep ad libitum. The space of a mosque is designed for hospitality. Travellers first go to the mosque of a town to take rest and sleep and spend the night; it is like a free-of-charge hotel. Water is always available in every mosque, which is another sign of hospitality since it is always free.

The idea of privacy is not to keep the women in a cloistered space; privacy in the design of the Muslim house means the provision of a space where the inhabitants can relax away from the eyes of intruders or gatecrashers.

To achieve the above-mentioned character in the architecture of Islam, the method is the adaptation of the design to the environment, which is generally desert-like in Dar Al Islam. The umwelt is the immediate environment with which architectural design deals in Islam, because the method that rests on subjugating the environment is not the traditional method in Islam. The Muslim is keen to provide a shelter for his wife and children.

Figure 2 *Architecture in Cairo of the Mameluk period, showing the Moucharabiyas.*

The German term *umwelt* is the right word to define the built space in Islamic architecture, which provides an *umschag* against the aggressive environment. The result must bring about an envelope or cover against the sun's zenith for nine months of the year at least, and against the blowing of the *simoon* hot winds. For that reason, and for privacy, the house in Islam originally did not have a street façade. Finally, we can say that Islamic architecture developed essentially independently from the influence of ancient Rome and Persia only because it issued from two pure Islamic authorities: the Holy Qur'ān and the Sunna. As a result the Islamic approach to design can be defined by the French expression '*sans détour*'; it is uncompromising, it tolerates no deviation.

We can conclude that Islamic architecture was built and designed from within and not without; it forms a *modus vivendi* with the environment, flawlessly. The achievements of architectural design in Islam were therefore more oriented towards the inhabitants' behaviour than formal excellency. The shape of the Muslim city was accomplished with civility in search of respect, of social equality, and mutual regard between the members of the Muslim society (see Figure 2). There is no dividing line between civilian and public or governmental domains in the urban grid. Islamic design deals with urbanity in order to fulfil the urbanism of Dar Al Islam.

The Prophet Muhammad (peace and blessings of God be upon Him) said: 'I had been sent by God for the completion of the most distinguished morals.'

FURTHER READING

Bell, G. (1914) *Palace and Mosque at Ukhaidir*, Coel/Hesperis.

Briggs, M. (1924) *Mohammadan Architecture in Egypt and Palestine*, Oxford: Clarendon Press.

Cresswell, K.A.C. (1932) *Early Muslim Architecture*, Vol. 1: *Umayyad*, Oxford: Clarendon Press.

—— (1940) *Early Muslim Architecture*, Vol. 2: *Umayyad Spain, Abbasid and Tulunid*, Oxford: Clarendon Press.

—— (1951) *The Muslim Architecture*, Vol. 1: *Fatimid*, Oxford: Clarendon Press.

—— (1960) *The Muslim Architecture*, Vol. 2: *Ayyubid and Early Mamluk*, Oxford: Clarendon Press.

Devonshire, E.L. (1935) *Quelques influences islamiques sur les arts de l'Europe*, Paris: A. Picard.

Diez, E. (1917) *Die Kunst der Islamischen Völker*, Encyclopedie de l'Islam.

Dimand, M. (1937) 'Some aspects of Umayyad and early Abbasid ornament', *Ars Islamica* 4: 293–337.

Ettinghausen, R. (1952) 'The bevelled style in the post Samarra period', *Archaeologia Orientalia in Memorium Ernest Herzfeld*.

Herzfeld, E. (1923) *Der Wandschmuck der Bauten von Samarra und seine Ornamentik*, Encyclopedie de l'islam.

Hoag, J. (1962) *L'Architecture Islamique*, Paris: Flammarion.

Marcais, G. (1926–7) *Manue d'art musulman*, Paris: A. Picard.

Richmond, E.T. (1926) *Moslem Architecture*, Harmondsworth: Penguin.

75 Taoism and architecture

Amos Ih-Tiao Chang

Nature eliminates surplus and
Compensates for deficiency

(Laotzu, *Tao-te-ching*)

Dealing with a physical–metaphysical continuum, the above quotation from the bible of Taoism, Laotzu's *Tao-te-ching*, is symbolized by the changing form of a bow in action. This describes the interaction between the diminution in one way and the expansion in the other of any conceivable relativism, including the somehow inter-related time–space relativity and spiritual–physical relativity, that treats our religious concern as one part of the ultra-naturalism of Taoism, or, as Laotzu puts it: 'Longevity belongs to those who die without losing their lives' (Laotzu, cited in Chang 1980: 11).

Being the spatial expression of human life and experience in time, architecture is expressive in terms of the interplay between what is tangible and what is intangible, mainly mass versus void in space and perception versus conception in our temporal reality.

Void is the most perceivable amid intangibles because of its indispensability and its perennial co-existence with mass. By virtue of its intangibility, it is nevertheless inhered with the potentiality to associate itself with the most intangible content of human life, the yearning for freedom from physical inhibition and spiritual frustration.

This association was intentionally used in my own design of the void-filled Bangkok Christian College, Bangkok, Thailand, built during 1965–6. My design of the College's chapel, built in 1967–8, expresses the universally cherished human recourse of looking upward to signify human aspiration and the spiritual inspiration that goes with it.

As for architecture itself, what follows are the main arguments contained in my book *The Tao of Architecture*, first published in 1956. These are augmented by the wisdom gained from twenty years' experience of teaching architectural students at an American university. Highlights or new insights, in either case intangibility is seen as the means and not the end lest Taoism be mistaken for nihilism and lose its positive significance.

INTELLIGIBILITY AND READINESS

The introduction of the book thematically clarifies the intelligibility brought forth by the dual presence of the notions of actuality and potentiality in our thinking. It identifies the realism of 'readiness' in the functional set-up, such as is formed in a fire station, which is unused most of the time but is considered as being constantly occupied and therefore deserves a central position in most, if not all, city planning practice. The inclusion of intangibles such as 'readiness' as legitimate counterparts to the tangible elements in a functional situation is probably what will ultimately make social studies an exact science, in the same way as the inclusion of latent heat for thermal quantification in natural science.

Particularly significant is the ready-made service rendered by an empty core space, which is symbolized by the hub of a wheel.[1]

Architecturally, it represents the concourse of a complex functional entity which co-ordinates all its surrounding functional spaces in a 'currency' field (see Figure 1a) so that all exchanges of traffic to and from all specific functional spaces have to go through the inter-mediacy of the concourse, such as that of a modern shopping mall. This is both diagrammatically comprehensible in our design concept and physically feasible in construction. In contrast to this is a 'barter' matrix (see Figure 1b) that requires unmanageable crisscrossing of direct relationships to confuse both the designer and the users of the facility, if, indeed it can be built at all.

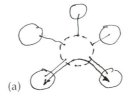 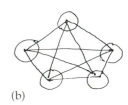

(a) (b)

Figure 1 *(a) Empty core space, symbolized by the hub of a wheel; surrounding spaces are co-ordinated in a 'currency' field; (b) A 'barter' matrix requires unmanageable crisscrossing of direct relationships.*

NATURAL AND ARCHITECTURAL LIVELINESS

The concept of 'natural life movement in architectural vision' concerns the physical context of an architectural environment. Light, for instance, is considered the 'life blood' of architectonic form with darkness being its 'soul'. Addressing the condition of completeness without completion, together they subtly define and enrich the visual variety of our creation.

'Variability and complement' deals with the visual

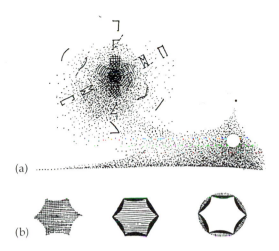

(a)

(b)

Figure 2 *(a) Opposite pairs of shapes create the polarities of a 'form attribute cone'; (b) Concavity enriches architectonic form with opposite, intangible shapes.*

interaction between opposite shapes such as repeated tangible verticality in continuous space that leads to the creation of intangible horizontality. This and other pairs of opposite shapes, i.e. angularity versus rectilinearity and curvature versus straightness, are the polarities of a 'form attribute cone' (see Figure 2a). Concavity is emphasized because it enriches architectonic form inherently with intangible shapes that are the opposite of tangible ones (observe the enriching process of the fluted section of a column in Figure 2b).

The most important implication of this concept is the significant role played by the attribute of size within the 'form attribute cone'. In parallel to this stands a colour cone. I have described their relationship elsewhere as follows: 'The most obvious phenomenon of analogy between them is: when value in color is increasing or decreasing, hues become less manifested; when apparent size is increasing or decreasing, shapes shall also lose their identity (Chang 1980: 38). Size is regarded as the 'value' of form, shape its 'hue', and the degree of concavity its 'chroma'.

In a well-organized system (such as in symphonic music, where pitch variation is more prominent than timbre variety), and in our experience of what I refer to as 'symformic architecture', size variation and proportions – being quantitative and therefore substantive – tend to become negligible in an expansive perspective for the good course of overall unity solely in terms of size variation.

The disparity between the physical and that which is merely visual in architectonic form is a very important design technique. It gives us the opportunity to refine a physical form which derives from functional necessity but of visually inappropriate size by means of colour, texture or merely shades and shadow decomposition. Similarly, by using a reflective material, one can also

create a virtual void and fuse it elegantly with envelopmental space in order to bring about a feeling of relief in a congested urban environment.

BALANCE AND EQUILIBRIUM

The essence of our daily experience is a matter of responding to the perceived balance of physical forms designed on the basis of symmetry, without axiality or asymmetry, without being off-balance. I might add here that the same is expected of continuous equilibrium between action and repose when a person travels in and out of an environment.

Interculturally, for a society of Western heritage, a 'gabled' façade and deep space behind it may express more action than repose, while a 'hipped' façade with wide space behind it may express more repose than action for a society of Far-Eastern heritage (see Figures 3a and 3b). The latter, particularly, is expected to remain balanced when seen from an oblique angle. Alternation of action-prone and repose-prone designs in our environmental experience may well be the basic technique of securing the rhythm of environmental continuity.

In dealing with balance of form and equilibrium of space, Frank Lloyd Wright went one step further by filling architectural space with a lot of extending horizontal elements and free-standing and suspended ornaments whose mission was to fulfil the harmonic balance of an overall design. By adding what are seemingly unnecessary to an otherwise bare and prosaic construction, Wright accomplished dynamic balance and equilibrium and hence brought about tranquility or the feeling of 'lack of irritation' in architectural space. At this juncture, abstraction should be considered a major form of Laotzu's notion of non-being. Accordingly, Wright did not employ Louis Sullivan's more or less realistic floral ornament to achieve the desired effect because the floral ornament would not have been as compatible with the abstract construction as Wright's own abstract ornaments were.

I thought this complex situation could be rightly described as being 'more or less' in contrast to Mies van Der Rohe's approach of 'less is more'. Together, these

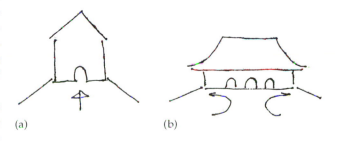

(a)   (b)

Figure 3 *(a) In Western society a 'gabled' façade, with deep space behind it, may express action rather than repose. (b) For Oriental societies, a 'hipped' façade, with wide space behind it, may express repose rather than action.*

two reciprocatively reversible approaches complete the Taoist cycle of complementary transformation in architecture.

A position somewhere between the 'more is less' and 'less is more' type of design approach would produce a variety of formal expression that brings about unlimited pluralism of character expression as well. The following passage may help clarify this important issue of character uniqueness:

> As is always the case for man's recognition of visual form, it is the intangible existence in man's mind or the tangible non-existence in his optical vision of other forms which determines what a specific form could be. Looking back to the past, one would realize that actually an artist's stone lion has no definite being and that it becomes and remains as one of his own only because, by distinction, it is obviously neither a tiger nor a bear.
>
> Knowing that the being of any form is created on the basis of non-being, an architect acquires his maximum freedom of expression.
>
> (Chang 1980: 61).

Thus, the creative design of a church becomes a church because it is neither a warehouse nor an auditorium.

The result of creation on this basis is neither an irresponsible symbol of radicalism nor an obvious repetition of a prototype, but a commensurate abstraction of specific realism of certain functional forms of space. Evolving towards pluralistic abstraction, the styles of architectural designs thus would be highly differentiated and each of them is bound to be honest to itself. The harmony among them then is accomplished on the basis of 'normlessnesses', or common dissimilarity.

THE HIDDEN NUMERICAL LANGUAGE OF ARCHITECTURE

While normless in appearance, creative architectural forms are inhered with the potential of sentient expression in terms of size variation at varied scale.

To demonstrate the possibility of the orderly performance of such a variable scale, I have taken the American football game as my guinea pig on paper to do a playful mathematical modelling of the game, with the hope that it will reveal the secret of a variable modular scale in architecture as well.

The model has a base number 6 to simulate the six full divisions (five full divisions and two half-tones) of pitch variation within the range of each octave in music, which should be considered the father of all arts, in my mind.

The set-up of the model is $6^n = D$, with D being the variable dimension of space involved and n the exponential power of the base number 6. The unit is set to be one inch.

Thus:

$6^0 = 1$ inch	which is supposedly the diameter of a flipping coin at the beginning of the game.
$6^1 = 6$ inches	which is the holding diameter of a ball.
$6^2 = 36$ inches $= 1$ yard	the yardage measurement of the game.
$6^3 = 6 \times 36$ inches $= 6$ yards	which is the extension of a good first down.
$6^4 = 36 \times 36$ inches $= 36$ yards	which is the extension of a good field position for the offence and breathing room for the defense.
$6^5 = 216$ yards	which approximately doubles the length between two goals to complete a cycle of one turn of fortune in a game.

I might add that minute dimensions given by 6^{-1}, 6^{-2}, 6^{-3}, etc., would bring meaningful addition of quality items (of detailing) to the quantity items (of proportion) of the series shown above. Sandwiched between this additional quality series and the quantity series is the basic unit (1 inch) whose smallness and intermediacy together are telling us the reason why the working module of classical architecture, Occidental or Oriental notwithstanding, has to be small in order to relate itself with both qualitative and quantitative expressions.

If we use one metre to replace one yard and extensively employ the technique of half-tone measurement, we may find our search for a variable modular scale in architecture a real possibility. For the time being, incrementally if not exponentially, the variable module in terms of a metre works rather constructively if not as systematically as expected:

(a) 1 metre = 3 ft. 4 in., the width of a window.
(b) 1.5 metres = 5 ft. 0 in., the popular module of a skyscraper.
(c) 2 metres = 6 ft. 8 in., the height of a door.
(d) 3 metres = 10 ft 0 in.
(e) 6 metres = 20 ft. 0 in.
(f) 36 metres = 120 ft. 0 in.

Note that among items (a), (e) and (f) there is a broad exponential relationship and between 20 ft. and 120 ft. there are varied integral extensions employable for defining the dimensions of exterior spaces.

THE SUBSTANCE OF CREATIVE FORGETFULNESS

The most powerful kind of Taoist non-being or intangibility most constructively presents itself in the form of 'creative forgetfulness', in contrast to 'conscious knowledgeability'. The relationship between them is said to be the equal of that which exists between void and mass complement, with the former being constructively infinitive and the latter, ordinarily definitive. According to two great teachers of mine, the late Professor A.M. Friend Jr. and Professor Jean Labatut of Princeton University, 'creative forgetfulness' functions like spring water to refresh our thinking and to refurbish our power of imagination. It appears as if it comes from nowhere, but it goes everywhere.

'Creative forgetfulness' is by no means straight nothingness to begin with. Neither can it emerge by itself as something unique and meaningful. It is the cream of post-comprehension intuition that comes from much hard work in libraries. However, only the catalyst of imagination must ignite many trials and errors in the studio before becoming productive.

With one leaning towards rationalistic comprehension and the other towards romantic innovation, research and studio experimentation together may yet produce a 'scientistic' architecture which, guided by a definite anatomical structure, pursues a flexible posture for the design that will simultaneously suit the contour and context of a site.

The word 'inactivity' in Taosim actually refers to inactiveness in dealing with superficial and unnecessary things. Taoism does not at all look for 'doing nothing'. It teaches the unhappy fact of an inefficacy of words or formalized deeds, and the basic need of physical and spiritual growth that depends on hard work to preserve its potential. The way for the creators of cathedrals to express their love of God and humanity used to be to build persistently. Today, the sweet tediousness of architectural creation happens to be the privilege that hard-working architects enjoy. As Kahlil Gibran would say, their works are what make their love of humanity visible. Personally, I strongly feel that work is also the premise of our faith and the promise of our hope. According to this line of thinking, work indeed is our prayer. Perhaps it could be the salvation of our problematic world after all.

ACKNOWLEDGEMENT

I dedicate this essay to my wife, Jennie Ming Chio Li Chang, for her lifelong support and inspiration.

NOTE

1   See *Tao-te-ching*, Chapter 11.

REFERENCE

Chang, A. (1980) *The Tao of Architecture*, Princeton, NJ: Princeton University Press.

76 The avant-garde in twentieth-century architecture

Robert Harbison

The idea of the artistic radical has been important in the West for centuries. We already find traces of it in Vasari's lives of Giotto and Michelangelo. Between that first step and the idea of a fully fledged avant-garde are a number of stages; next comes the idea of the radical who does not go far enough: a faction among Jacques-Louis David's pupils called him 'Boucher' and 'Pompadour'. They wore rough imitations of Greek dress, lived simply and left no remarkable work.

The convergence of political and artistic energy, and perhaps even their confusion, is often a feature of the avant-garde mentality, so the French Revolution was a crucial spur to Blake's powerful statements of the necessity for permanent revolution in the mental world. His example reminds us of the romantic pedigree of the concept of the avant-garde, which later took misleading shelter under the banner of science.

In the English-speaking world, the very term 'avant garde' remains an awkward import, more at home in France, where brazen antagonism between the artist and his or her (future?) public was part of the stock-in-trade of forward-looking artists from Baudelaire's time onward.

For obvious reasons the idea took a long time reaching architecture. Painters don't need to mobilize institutional support before they can buy canvases and rent studios. Little advance parties of architects, however, are largely cut off from building anything, except for each other. Perhaps there's an even more fundamental contradiction in the notion of an architectural avant-garde: buildings are permanent, and avant-gardes are committed to ceaseless change. In any case, it is clear that the avant-gardist cast of mind came to architecture only when it had thoroughly colonized literature and painting.

The key difference between earlier experimentalism in art and the true avant-garde is that the first is individual and unpoliticized, while the second is collective and propagandistic, promoting itself as the vehicle of historical progress. On the one hand Goya and on the other the Impressionists were sometimes credited with being the first true avant-garde in the visual arts.

Can anyone be sure Goya isn't more radical than Monet? But the later artist's campaign is more self-conscious, part of a programmatic attempt to revise perception, overturning old habits of mind, old aesthetic preferences, and even certain social values. A shift away from clearly defined subject matter is the main engine of the latter.

Architectural avant-gardes sometimes appear only in a later phase of movements which begin in literature or painting. Futurism announced itself in Milan in 1909, but only found architectural adherents in 1914, when the specifically architectural manifesto appeared.

The movement had been city-centred from the beginning, of course, and the first manifesto is full of visionary renderings of speeding vehicles and calls for the demolition of cultural institutions like museums and, presumably, the buildings which hold them. It is full, in other words, of negative energy, most alarming in the famous praise of war and violence.

This has continued to be a prominent function of architectural avant-gardes, to place bombs under cherished features of past architecture. The Futurists called for the demolition of whole classes of structure, while Le Corbusier was prepared to see the obliteration of much of the fabric of Paris in order that his towers should rise in its place. Formally, if not ideologically, much of early Futurism bears Cubist traces; of all the century's movements, Cubism is the archetype of a seeming attack on the subjects and even the physical existence of art.

Another derivative of Cubism, De Stijl, sounds more militant than it looks. The first manifesto of 1918 declared war on the individual and on natural forms in art. After these were suppressed, there remained a vacuum, which was the point. As regards discussion at least, it was a dynamic outcome, and the literary component of avant-gardism is usually crucial. Movements exist in part to make news, which before long leads to the paradoxical result that the public becomes familiar with and even resigned to their presence. Their main means in achieving this is public pronouncements, printed, or better yet, performed. The result is that avant-gardes and their antagonist-publics know better than most artists what they stand for and what their works mean.

The danger is present from the beginning that taking a strong position will lead one to self-parody, and that the more strident one becomes, the less convinced or convincing one becomes too. Such suspicions are raised by Marinetti's endless diatribes, and in recent painting, experimentalism for its own sake has sometimes become the supreme value and the only test. At this point the battlefield has nothing in it but advance units busy outflanking each other, units which contain one or two artists each, but which are like movements because of the dealers, agents and journalists who travel in the producer's train.

Here it is appropriate to note that the single American architect from the heyday of the Continental avant-gardes whom one would most like to include, Frank Lloyd Wright, effectively disowned any such membership. Wright saw himself locked in battle, but entirely alone. He rudely rejects those 'disciples, acolytes and quacks' who might want to adhere and form a movement with him. At the same time he opts for a larger and more permanent organization, Taliesin, than most of his European colleagues, formed on medieval lines. It takes a democracy to reinvent the master and his subservient apprentices.

Cultural avant-gardes in the full sense of the word only occur where a dominant culture possesses a fair degree of reactionary cohesion. Thus in the post-war period many movements ape certain features of earlier avant-gardes, but instead of serious war wage playful theatre. Now, any intending avant-garde lacks an enemy which is single and strong enough, and egotism is exposed more plainly as the basis of its crusade.

Earlier avant-gardes subordinated individuals in the interest of a clear idea. One can gauge the effect of this disguise of the individual presence by comparing two recent and similar phenomena: the monuments of Claes Oldenburg and the projects of the Austrian team Haus Rucker. Both qualify as surrealist architecture, but the descriptive, non-individual name of Haus Rucker lends their work special weight, as if it were a grave and considered act of criticism instead of inspired joking. They are pursuing a programme and building an intellectual edifice, not just following one clever act with another.

So a certain coherence of radical effort combined with strident antagonism to things as they are must come together. Boullée and Ledoux, architectural radicals of the pre-Revolutionary period in France, were dissatisfied with the cultural possibilities of the present, but never formulated this as active antagonism. True avant-gardes aim to turn culture inside out, as the margin takes the place of the centre. The unforeseen end of the process is the moment in which the idea of centre or norm has no more force, and various margins all claim their short-lived victories at once.

The story falls into two main parts – the heyday of the avant-garde from the birth of Cubism to a widespread stilling of artistic dissent prior to the Second World War, and a new outburst of architectural ideology from the 1960s onwards, which can be seen as a diminished aftermath to the first phase. Although the various strands of the avant-garde are diverse, they form a single phenomenon: at a certain point in European cultural history change becomes convulsive, instigated by antagonistic processes which seem at times to threaten civilization's survival. Avant-garde movements are the coherent forms which this disruptive energy takes, and in a wider perspective all tend in the same direction, towards experimentation for its own sake and, inevitably, fragmentation of the work of art, its meaning, and finally of culture itself.

Few commentators would claim a great deal for most of the structures which avant-garde architects actually built. The importance of the movements far transcends completed projects one can point to. Avant-garde thinking has changed permanently the way we understand art and architecture, so that the work of many contemporary designers – from Carlo Scarpa to Frank Gehry, from Robert Venturi to Shin Takimatsu – is unthinkable without early twentieth-century scepticism directed at all aspects of architectural form and function. The energy of such strands of the avant-garde as Surrealism and Constructivism, unleashing respectively the unconscious and the machine, is by no means spent, and the process of cataloguing their descendants has barely begun.

Here follows an outline of the main movements and their relations.

Cubism's effect on architecture was profound, if much filtered. Adolf Loos, an Austrian, gave a highly personal translation into built form, which was made more influential by his striking literary gifts. The Steiner House of 1910 is the early landmark on this path. At that point bold cubic solids externally are matched by sluggish forms in dark, rich substances indoors. Spatially, his house for the Dada poet Tristan Tzara (Paris, 1926) is a breakthrough (see Figures 1 and 2). Tortuous interlocking makes the plan hard to read without sections, which in turn belies the apparent simplicity of the

Figure 1 *Street façade of the Maison Tristan Tzara, Paris, 1926, by Adolf Loos.* (Photograph: *H. Louw*)

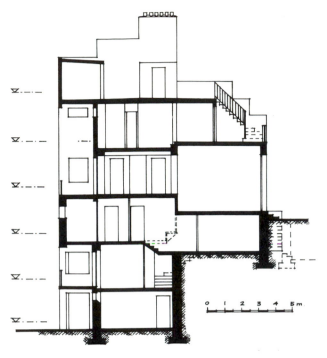

Figure 2 *Section of Maison Tristan Tzara, Paris, 1926, by Adolf Loos.* (Source: *Kulka 1979*)

fantastic quasi-industrial proposals could be built (see Figure 3).

Russian Constructivism is the greatest single descendant of the Italian movement, and probably the strand of avant-garde design from which architects of the 1980s have taken most. Unlike Italy in Marinetti's time, Russia before the Revolution was abnormally receptive to radical cultural imports. The process begins in paint and sculpture and before long eventuates in Tatlin's corner reliefs, which point the way to an architecture splintered, dynamic, light and adventurous in structure.

Russia in the 1920s was one of the great homelands of the avant-garde, the only place where a complete revision of all the constituents of human life seemed possible, spawning a rich variety of proposals for new forms of dress, furniture, dwelling, cultural institution and city. A landmark success was the Vesnin competition proposal for a Palace of Labour in Moscow (1923), which gives a cultural monument the briskness, efficiency and clarity of a factory (see Figure 4). It wasn't built, and within a few years sinister forces had reimposed reactionary classicism in the name of the people.

façade. His later houses in Vienna and Prague carry the principle further and result in complex interpenetrations of abstract volumes.

Futurism is far more important for revolutionary attitudes to cities, machines, and a whole range of related matters than for the reactionary monumentality of most of the projects of Sant'Elia, the best Futurist architect, killed in the First World War before any of his

Figure 3 *La Città Nuova, 1914, drawn by Antonio Sant'Elia.* (Copyright: *Edition Lidiarte*)

Figure 4 *Perspective view of final competition entry for a projected Palace of Labour, Moscow, 1923, by the Vesnin brothers.*

In Holland it all took a milder form. De Stijl is a simplified derivative of Cubism which removes the traces of neo-primitivism evident in both Picasso and Braque at the beginning. Mondrian's paintings and van Doesburg's sugar-cube buildings, which seldom progressed beyond models shown in propagandistic exhibitions, represent this phase. The great monument of the style, by Gerrit Rietveld, a sculptor turned architect, is the Shroeder house in Utrecht. This is a never-equalled pinnacle of painterly architecture, in which structure and space are decomposed to pure line and plane in abstract interaction.

Purism, one of the smallest movements, consisting only of Ozenfant and Le Corbusier, is unusually important because of the towering talent and literary skill of its Swiss component. Corb's pieces collected in *Vers une Architecture*, are, with Loos's and Marinetti's, some of the most effective Modernist propaganda and among the best of all writing about architecture. Purism's argument with Cubism now seems of minor interest. In Le Corbusier the ideology of the machine, dynamic spatial continuities internally, and strong designs on the lives of users are brought together.

A case could be made that Walter Gropius was the most influential of all avant-garde figures in architecture, not through what he built or designed, but as leader of an influential school, the Bauhaus, founded in Weimar in 1919, moved to Dessau in 1925, chased from there in 1932, and extinguished in 1933.

The Bauhaus is now legendary. In its short history it changed prevailing ideas on architectural education, product design, and relations between art and society. It began as a haven of Expressionism, which qualifies in some of its branches as an avant-garde movement, at odds with all the others because a vehicle of spiritualism in art. In Germany this was the strongest strand of avant-garde thinking through the early Weimar years, and no thorough history could leave out Bruno Taut and the alchemico-mystical Glass Chain, which included at various times Hans Scharoun, the Luckhardt brothers, Hermann Finsterlin, and Erich Mendelsohn.

The phase by which the Bauhaus is now most remembered, which welcomed the machine while still relying on intuition in the designer, is the second phase which began around 1923. Like the Russian avant-garde

the Bauhaus was eventually actively crushed by anti-modernist forces.

In some sense that is the natural terminus of the true avant-garde, but in utterances of contemporary architects one often detects the inheritance not far beneath the surface. The anarchist-surrealist strain is carried on in the poems of Coop Himmelblau, and the ultra-rationalist one in Bernard Tschumi's programme for La Villette. Even now, the early twentieth century continues to provide a rich and varied vocabulary of architectural dissent.

REFERENCES

Kulka, H. (1979) *Adolf Loos, Das Werk des Architekten*, Vienna: Löcker Verlag.

Le Corbusier (1923) *Vers une architecture*, Paris: Editions Crès; trans F. Etchells, *Towards a New Architecture*, 1927, London: Architectural Press, reprinted 1970.

FURTHER READING

Two books by Italian historians offer the best general critiques of the idea of the avant garde. For cultural and ideological background (mostly extra-architectural) see Renato Poggioli, *The Theory of the Avant Garde* (1968, Cambridge, Mass.: Harvard University Press). For a powerful neo-Marxist analysis which comes strangely near to a muffled Ruskinian attack on architectural avant gardes for doing capitalism's work, see Manfredo Tafuri, *Architecture and Utopia: Design and Capitalist Development* (1976, Cambridge, Mass.: MIT Press).

There are good recent monographs on almost all the architects mentioned. Tracts and manifestos of the early years are assembled in various places, such as U. Conrads (ed.), *Programmes and Manifestoes on 20th Century Architecture* (1970, London: Lund Humphries), and U. Apollonion, *Futurist Manifestos* (1973, London: Thames & Hudson). Reprints of Moisei Ginzburg's *Style and Epoch* (1924, modern edn 1982, Cambridge, Mass.: MIT Press) and El Lissitsky's *Russia: An Architecture for World Revolution* (1930, modern edn 1970, Lund Humphries) are available, as well as the more familiar polemics of Le Corbusier, especially *Urbanisme* (1925, translated as *The City of Tomorrow*, 1971, London: Architectural Press), *La Ville Radieuse* (1935, translated as *The Radiant City*, 1967, London: Faber), and other works on planning. A pioneering treatment of many of these figures, which remains one of the richest, is Reyner Banham's *Theory and Design in the First Machine Age* (1960, London: Architectural Press).

77 Deutscher Werkbund – the 1914 debate: Hermann Muthesius versus Henry van de Velde

Stanford Anderson

INTRODUCTION

The 1914 debate which shook the foundations of the Deutscher Werkbund had as its main protagonists two architects. Hermann Muthesius, a well-placed Prussian bureaucrat, trained as an architect and central to the development of the Werkbund, posed a set of theses for the future development of this German association of artists, craftspeople and producers. Henry van de Velde, a Belgian, trained as an artist, relatively eccentric to the leadership of the Werkbund, was enlisted as the spokesperson for a group that opposed Muthesius's aims.

Standard interpretations of the debate see Muthesius as the prescient advocate of what the times would enforce: the accommodation of standardization under the conditions of industrial production. Van de Velde stands as the guardian of artistic individualism. Such a characterization of Muthesius's argument reveals at most an aspect of a more general argument about *type*, an argument significantly directed to the cultural environment generally, and thus to architecture. Consequently, van de Velde's opposition must also be seen differently and, indeed, aids in the interpretation of Muthesius's advocacy.

DEUTSCHER WERKBUND

An economic imperative stood behind the founding of the German Werkbund in 1907 (Campbell 1978; Junghanns 1982). For at least three decades, since the admiration of American industrial products at the Philadelphia Centennial Exposition of 1876, German engineers, critics, artists, politicians and producers railed against the 'cheap and nasty' products of the German trades and industry. To make matters worse, cheap industrial production was perceived to have no economic potential for a Germany that had neither privileged access to raw materials nor a captive market as was assured to Britain by its Empire.

After 1900, the political argument of this economic problem emerged in the thought and action of Friedrich Naumann, but the key to its possible solution – and the impetus for the founding of the Werkbund – came from the artists and, especially, architects with whom Naumann associated (Naumann 1908). The architect Hermann Muthesius, the leading authority on the Arts and Crafts movement and the 'free architecture' of England (Muthesius 1904), was only the best informed of many who affirmed the necessity, argued by William Morris, of two interrelated criteria: the satisfaction, if not the joy, of the worker in his or her work, and the coherent relation of process and product. Henry van de Velde – artist, architect and polemicist active in Germany since the late 1890s – learned his respect for Morrisian principles in the avant-garde artistic circles of his native, rapidly industrializing Belgium. For these Continental artists at the beginning of the twentieth century, it was both possible and necessary to extend Morris's principles to processes entailing a division of labour: the work of the artist/designer, the artisan/producer, and even the industrial producer.

The Werkbund was to unite these motives in the concept of *Qualität*. Designs of the highest standard, employing quality materials, produced with the finest artistry and skill, should restore meaningful work, provide products that would be worthy parts of a re-integrated cultural environment, and, through the excellence of these products, allow Germany to compete internationally on the basis of quality rather than quantity. The architect Fritz Schumacher created both the model and the cause for the founding of the Werkbund. At the Third German Arts and Crafts Exhibition (III. Deutsche Kunstgewerbeausstellung) in Dresden, 1906, in the principal section devoted to interior architecture (*Raumkunst*), Schumacher reversed the established policy for representation in such events. Rather than inviting the participation of producers whose association with artists was neither assured nor examined, Schumacher provided the opportunity for selected artist/architects to design entire rooms, or groups of rooms, to be executed by producers of the artists' choosing (Schumacher 1906).

The Dresden exhibition was a critical success, but understandably drew the vigorous criticism of producers and conventional designers who had been neglected within this state-supported event. Muthesius was able to shelter himself and Schumacher's enterprise within the Prussian Ministry of which he, as Advisor on Applied Arts (Referent für das Kunstgewerbe) was a part, but his public advocacy of this time furthered the divisions within the Alliance of German Applied Arts (Fachverband für das Deutsche Kunstgewerbe). At the annual meeting of this association in June 1907, defense of Muthesius led to the withdrawal of the progressive faction: Peter Bruckmann, a silverware producer from Heilbronn, the city from which Naumann was elected to the Reichstag (1907–18); Wolf Dohrn, friend of Naumann and associate of Karl Schmidt of the Deutsche Werkstätten in Dresden; and the noted essayist J.A. Lux (Muthesius 1907).

The stage was now set. A political and cultural initiative was under way; its agents were without an organization. On 5–6 October 1907 at the Four Seasons hotel in Munich, twelve 'artists' and representatives of twelve producing firms met to found the Werkbund. To these two founding categories of members was added that of 'experts' – historians, theoreticians, art critics and others (Junghanns 1982: 144–50). The founding 'artists' were, with one exception, architects. These were architects of note, including Peter Behrens, Theodor Fischer, Josef Hoffman, Joseph Olbrich, Bruno Paul, Richard Riemerschmid, Paul Schultze-Naumburg, and Schumacher. Architects remained dominant in the course of the organization's activities even after the First World War. Member 'artists' came to include graphic artists, craft designers and the like, but few, if any, fine artists – certainly no artists of note. The founding 'producers' included some relatively large enterprises such as the Deutsche Werkstätten in Dresden (later Hellerau, a furniture producer of some scale and rationalized production). The firm, like its co-members, produced works with traditionally close ties to art and the crafts: furniture, fabrics, jewellery and silverware, printers' type, and books. Such firms were, however, later joined by much larger, modern industrial firms such as the vertically integrated electrical products firm, AEG of Berlin.

At the time of the founding of the Werkbund, Muthesius, due to his government position, did not give the keynote speech, but rather Schumacher:

> The time has come when Germany should ... see in [the artist] one of the important powers for the ennobling of work, and thereby to ennoble the entire inner life of the Land and to make the Land victorious in the competition of peoples.... Everything that can be imitated soon loses its value on the international market; only the qualitative values which spring from the inexpressible inner powers of a harmonious culture are inimitable. And consequently there exists in aesthetic power also the highest economic value. After a century devoted to technique and thought, we see the next project which Germany has to fulfil as that of the *reconquest of a harmonious culture*.
>
> In this pioneer work we unite ourselves, not as men who are prideful over what they have already achieved, but rather as men who are proud of what they attempt.
>
> (Schumacher 1907: 330–1)

In the Articles of the Deutscher Werkbund as formulated in July 1908 (Junghanns 1982: 142f), the purpose of the organization was given as 'the elevating of [craft and industrial] work in the collaboration of art, industry and handicraft through education, propaganda and united positions on related issues.'

This statement is deceptively simple. It appears to give sole emphasis to the improved conditions of work with only oblique reference to the broad context of Schumacher's speech, Naumann's politics, and the work of the members. From this statement one may anticipate the usual claim for the importance of the Werkbund: that it was the first organized attempt to construct a viable relation of art to the methods of production within the context of modern industry. Despite the apparent emphasis on process rather than product, perhaps one could even anticipate the signal contribution of Werkbund members, especially Peter Behrens, to industrial design as that field has come to be recognized (Anderson 1968; Buddensieg 1979). Yet the statement of goals and these later claims for the Werkbund simplify both the projected problems and the possible means for their resolution. There were internal complexities and conflict that would erupt in the debate of 1914, differences which still cloud the interpretation of the debate.

A particular peculiarity of the statement of goals is the absence of any reference to architecture – an absence reflected in the standard interpretations of the debate of 1914, and of the Werkbund generally. Yet there was also a privileging of architecture within the Werkbund. The dominance of architects among the founding members and in the course of the Werkbund was noted above. Equally important was the recurrent call for what Schumacher, in his speech at the founding of the Werkbund, termed, with emphasis, the *reconquest of a harmonious culture*. This overarching ambition could not but give an important place to architecture in the Werkbund programme – as was borne out in its exhibitions and publications of the ensuing years (Deutscher Werkbund 1912ff).

THE 1914 DEBATE

The first of the theses Muthesius proposed to the Werkbund read as follows:

> Architecture, and with it the whole area of the Werkbund's activities, is pressing towards standardization, and only through standardization (*Typisierung*) can it recover that universal significance which was characteristic of it in times of harmonious culture.
>
> (Muthesius 1914, trans. Conrads 1970: 28)

The next day van de Velde began his counter-theses with:

> So long as there are still artists in the Werkbund and

so long as they exercise some influence on its destiny, they will protest against every suggestion for the establishment of a canon and for standardization. By his innermost essence the artist is a burning idealist, a free spontaneous creator. Of his own free will he will never subordinate himself to a discipline that imposes upon him a type, a canon. Instinctively he distrusts everything that might sterilize his actions, and everyone who preaches a rule that might prevent him from thinking his thoughts through to their own free end, or that attempts to drive him into a universally valid form, in which he sees only a mask that seeks to make a virtue out of incapacity.

(Muthesius 1914, trans. Conrads 1970: 29)

Described briefly and neutrally: Muthesius, an architect in the service of the government and with strong relations to commerce, encouraged the embrace of *Typisierung*. Van de Velde, an architect trained as an artist and most notable for his distinctive contributions within Art Nouveau, resisted *Typisierung*. In the characteristic interpretation of the 1914 debate (e.g., Campbell 1978: 57), Muthesius's *Typisierung* is understood as 'standardization', which in turn is referenced to the production of objects and has as its norm the establishment of standards for industrial production. Van de Velde is seen as the guardian of artistic individualism. This polarization can be used for or against each of the protagonists: Muthesius may be seen as the voice of a *Realpolitik* advancing the cause of the original Werkbund goals and anticipating the future development of design and industry. Alternatively, he may be seen as serving the interests of business within the Werkbund while endangering its larger artistic and cultural goals. Van de Velde may be seen as recognizing the necessary creative role of the artist in the pursuit of the Werkbund's goals. Alternatively, he may be seen as maintaining a *Jugendstil* idealism which would restore the antagonism between art and industry that had brought the Arts and Crafts movement to an impasse.

However, recall Muthesius's first thesis: 'Architecture, and with it the whole area of the Werkbund's activities ...'. Muthesius thus emphasizes architecture; given the Werkbund's activities, the following clause must give as much attention to crafts as to industrial production. Any interpretation that treats Muthesius's *Typisierung* as standardization in production is problematic: (1) such a demand is not readily applied to architecture even at the end of the twentieth century; it bore no significant relation to the architecture of the Werkbund architects of 1914; (2) standardization bears a negative relation to craft production.

One must then question whether the crucial thrust of Muthesius's theses, his use of *Typus* and *Typisierung*, did invoke standardization as that term was later understood. In both German and English, 'type' has meanings that fit better with the range of Werkbund activities than

does 'standardization'. In 1904, commenting on Gottfried Semper and *Typus*, Cornelius Gurlitt noted this term in the identification of buildings by type of use, then further associated with particular historic styles. Gurlitt also immediately rejected both the ideal and the type as possible sources for work in his own time: 'The solution of the problem is that which modern architecture attempts.... The individualization of the problem, its fulfilment in every detail – it is this which the modern art of building envisions as the ultimate problem' (Gurlitt 1904: 175–6). Thus Gurlitt opposes type and its use in the interpretation of received forms while favouring invention appropriate to contemporary life.

Within architecture, the more classic position (that of Quatremère de Quincy, for example) sees *type* as the uniformity that underlies a corpus of works – e.g., the classical temple. Van de Velde's specific rejection of the 'establishment of a canon', and his insistence on the artist remaining free to think 'his thoughts through to their own free end', suggest that he heard in Muthesius's call, and rejected, both these meanings of type in architecture and 'the whole area of the Werkbund's activities'. Van de Velde went on to express his own belief, also supported in the traditions of architectural discourse, that type should be recognized only a posteriori – after creative solutions were recognized to possess commonalities.

Van de Velde is accused by Campbell and others of intentionally misinterpreting Muthesius. Indeed Anna-Christa Funk's analysis of available correspondence among Walter Gropius, Karl Ernst Osthaus and van de Velde reveals the intensity and personal force of what was a power struggle within the Werkbund (Funk 1978). Yet credence may be given to van de Velde's position for reasons already mentioned. Unlike 'standardization', 'type' – the most obvious interpretation or translation of *Typus* – and 'canon' are concepts that can be applied over the full range of Werkbund activities. It is true that Muthesius's last two theses call for production by large business concerns, but this is stated in such a way as to include rationalized craft production based on types (the Deutsche Werkstätten in Hellerau, for example) as much as serial production based on standardization. One can read 'standardization' into Muthesius's theses, but only in certain of the theses, and as a special case of the more general notion covered by *Typisierung*.

That van de Velde could with reason interpret Muthesius's position as he did is supported by two other crucial sources of information: the buildings by Werkbund architects at the Cologne exhibition at which this debate took place, and Muthesius's speech in the 1914 debate.

The debate took place in the temple-form Festival Hall of the exhibition, a building in which one of the most progressive of the German architects, Peter Behrens, reverted to a direct reliance on type, indeed on

Figure 1 *Festival Hall at the Deutscher Werkbund Exhibition, Cologne, 1914, by Peter Behrens.* (Source: Deutscher Werkbund Jahrbuch *1915*)

Figure 3 *Osram Glass Pavilion at the Deutscher Werkbund Exhibition, 1914, by Bruno Taut.* (Source: Deutscher Werkbund Jahrbuch *1915*)

Figure 2 *Theatre at the Deutscher Werkbund Exhibition, Cologne, 1914, by Henry van de Velde.* (Source: Deutscher Werkbund Jahrbuch *1915*)

Figure 4 *Hamburg-Amerika Line Pavilion at the Deutscher Werkbund Exhibition, Cologne, 1914, by Hermann Muthesius.* (Source: Deutscher Werkbund Jahrbuch *1915*)

the classical canon (see Figure 1). Or one may contrast the work of van de Velde and his circle with that of Muthesius and architects who had sought to fulfil his vision of a Werkbund architecture. Van de Velde designed the Theatre of the exhibition, a building whose innovative stage and well-planned auditorium are wrapped in a simple envelope, bespeaking its ephemeral role and interrupted only by the inventive architectural ornaments of Hermann Obrist (see Figure 2). The most radical building of the Exhibition, the Osram Glass Pavilion, was designed by a member of van de Velde's circle, Bruno Taut (see Figure 3). In contrast, Muthesius designed two pavilions that evoked the then increasingly admired spare forms of the German neo-classicism of a century earlier (see Figure 4). The clearest example of Muthesius's vision of a Werkbund architecture that might restore conventionally accepted norms, and thus a unified urban setting, may be seen in the arcaded shopping street of the Exhibition, by Oswin Hempel (see Figure 5).

In the 1914 Yearbook of the Werkbund, Wilhelm

Figure 5 *Arcaded shopping street at the Deutscher Werkbund Exhibition, Cologne, 1914, by Oswin Hempel.* (Source: Deutscher Werkbund Jahrbuch *1915*)

Ostwald wrote on 'Norms' in a manner that is consonant with Muthesius's position. He claimed that art does not achieve its goal unless there is a resonant recipient who shares the same feelings as are expressed in the work. For Ostwald, art is a thoroughly *social* product; and socialization cannot take place without the establishment of *Normen*, of harmonizing conventions (Ostwald 1914: 77). Even the supposedly conciliatory speech of Muthesius, reversing the argument of Gurlitt cited above, emphasized norms for architecture (Muthesius 1914). For Muthesius, contemporary organic development required transformation from the individualistic to the typical (*Typische*), a transferral which he found particularly characteristic of architecture, and the positive traits of which were revealed in the great periods of architecture. Architecture, for Muthesius, drives towards the typical, scorning the extraordinary and seeking the orderly.

One may, then, understand Muthesius's *Typus* and *Typisierung* as used in architectural theory of his time and as interpreted by van de Velde: *Typisierung* not primarily as standardization imposed by the conditions of modern production, but as conventionalization. Muthesius sought an agreement on style, respectful of precedent even if modestly transformed in relation to new conditions. This was a conservative approach to a goal that Schumacher had advanced at the founding of the Werkbund and which had found wide support also outside the Werkbund: 'the *reconquest of a harmonious culture*'. Van de Velde resisted the enlistment of the Werkbund in such a programme, arguing rather for the necessity of invention and, at most, the recognition of type a posteriori.

The Werkbund debate was cut short by the outbreak of the First World War. When the struggle for control of the Werkbund revived, Gropius, Osthaus, Taut, and Hans Poelzig succeeded under the banner of individualism (Osthaus 1919; Poelzig 1919; Taut 1919). Yet this circle was soon involved in the design of housing estates and then of much else, the modern architecture of the 1920s, that reflected concerns with norms and types. Such works and the writings of Taut and Adolf Behne (Behne 1922) reveal how the so-called individualists could now embrace both artistic innovation and rationalized production in the service of everyday environments. In any case, this was not a fulfilment of Muthesius's programme. Indeed, it remained closer to that of van de Velde, which had never denied that the products of creative effort might yield types.

CONCLUSION

Muthesius's theses proposed a conservative cultural position for all the activities of the Werkbund. This position might, as a special case, incorporate standardization for industry – but even then with types that would be contributive to Muthesius's conservative view of a unified German culture. Even this narrowed view does offer, of course, one conception of industry within cultural production. Van de Velde's theses unabashedly supported artistic individualism and mistrusted the role of commerce. The vehemence of these positions may well reflect the aggravation of the moment, for both van de Velde and Gropius had earlier espoused positive relations to industry. Furthermore, even though van de Velde was more the European and his tactics were different, he too shared the concern of his antagonists to win a new culture through concerted action. If, in the post-war years, the notions of type and standardization reappeared with greater centrality, this was in a new configuration which, if precedents were to be sought, was closer to the van de Velde circle.

Whether before or after the war, there remains a position which denied the assumptions of the 1914 debate – the position of Adolf Loos, to which some of Behne's writings may be allied (Loos 1908; Behne 1917). Loos mistrusted the desire, which he identified as much in the Werkbund as in the earlier Art Nouveau, to achieve a style of the time by artistic imposition, whether conservative or progressive. The Werkbund had been the vehicle for significant debates and the umbrella for particular productions that explored the relations of art, architecture and industry; but the Werkbund debate remained unresolved in its own terms, its premises under question.

REFERENCES

Anderson, S. (1968) 'Peter Behrens and the New Architecture of Germany, 1900–1917', Ph.D. dissertation, Columbia University, New York City.

Behne, A. (1917) 'Kritik des Werkbundes', *Die Tat* 9 (1): 430–8.

—— (1922) 'Kunst, Handwerk, Technik', *Die neue Rundschau* 33 (2): 1021–37; trans. as 'Art, handicraft and technology', 1980, *Oppositions* 22: 96–104.

Buddensieg, T. (1979) *Industriekultur: Peter Behrens und die AEG, 1907–1914*, Berlin: Gebr. Mann.; trans. as *Industriekultur: Peter Behrens and the AEG, 1907–1914*, 1984, Cambridge, Mass.: MIT Press.

Campbell, J. (1978) *The German Werkbund: The Politics of Reform in the Applied Arts*, Princeton, NJ: Princeton University Press.

Conrads, U. (1970) (ed.) *Programs and Manifestoes on 20th-Century Architecture*, Cambridge, Mass.: MIT Press. (Translation of Muthesius' ten theses and van de Velde's counter-theses.)

Deutscher Werkbund (from 1912) *Jahrbuch des Deutschen Werkbundes*, Jena: Diederichs.

Funk, A.C. (1978) *Karl Ernst Osthaus gegen Hermann Muthesius: Der Werkbundstreit 1914 im Spiegel der im Karl Ernst Osthaus Archiv erhaltenen Briefe*, Hagen: Karl Ernst Osthaus Museum.

Gurlitt, C. (1904) 'Die Theorien der Baukunst im XIX Jahrhundert', *Der Bautechniker* 24 (8): 150–3, 174–6.

Junghanns, K. (1982) *Der Deutsche Werkbund: Sein erstes Jahrzehnt*, Berlin: Henschel.

Loos, A. (1908) 'Die Überflüssigen (Deutscher Werkbund)', in Loos, *Trotzdem 1900–1930*, Innsbruck: Brenner, 1931.

Muthesius, H. (1904) *Das englische Haus: Entwicklung, Bedingungen, Anlage, Aufbau, Einrichtung und Innenraum*, 3 vols, Berlin: Ernst Wasmuth, 1904–5; 2nd rev edn, Berlin: Wasmuth, 1908–11.

—— (1907) 'Der Fall Muthesius', *Hohe Warte* 3: 233–48.

—— (1914) *Die Wekbund-Arbeit der Zukunft und Aussprache darüber …*, Jena: Diederichs, 1914. (Muthesius' keynote speech for the Werkbund annual meeting, Cologne, 1914; also includes Fr. Naumann, *Werkbund und Weltwirtschaft*.)

Naumann, F. (1908) *Deutsche Gewerbekunst: Eine Arbeit über die Organisation des deutschen Werkbundes*, Berlin: Buchverlag der Hilfe; reprinted 1964 in F. Naumann, *Werke*, vol. 6, pp. 254–316, Cologne/Opladen: Westdeutscher.

Osthaus, K.E. (1919) 'Deutscher Wekbund', *Das Hohe Ufer* 1 (10): 237–45.

Ostwald, W. (1914) 'Normen', in *Jahrbuch des Deutschen Werkbundes*, Jena: Diederichs.

Poelzig, H. (1919) 'Werkbundaufgaben', *Mitteilungen des Deutschen Werkbundes* 4: 109–24.

Schumacher, F. (1906) 'Die Dresdner Kunstgewerbeausstellung', *Kunstwart* 19 (19): 347–9; (20): 396–400; (21): 458–62.

—— (1907) [Speech at the founding of the Deutscher Werkbund, Munich 1907], *Die Form* 7 (11): 330–1, 1932.

Taut, B. (1919) 'Für den Werkbund!', first published in K. Junghanns 1982: 181–3.

FURTHER READING

Anderson, S. (1980) 'Modern architecture and industry: Peter Behrens, the AEG, and industrial design', *Oppositions* 21: 78–97.

Banham. R. (1960) 'Germany: industry and the Werkbund', ch. 5 of his *Theory and Design in the First Machine Age*, London: Architectural Press.

Berlin, Fachverbände für die wirtschaftlichen Interessen des Kunstgewerbes E.V. (1915) *Der 'Deutsche Werkbund' und seine Ausstellung Köln 1914: Eine Sammlung von Reden und Kritiken vor und nach der 'Tat'*, Berlin.

Burckhardt, L. (ed.) (1980) *The Werkbund: History and Ideology 1907–1933*, Woodbury, NY: Barron.

Dal Co, F. (1990) *Figures of Architecture and Thought: German Architecture Culture 1880–1920*, New York: Rizzoli.

Deutscher Werkbund (1908) *Die Veredlung der Gewerblichen Arbeit in Zusammenwirken von Kunst: Industrie und Handwerk, Verhandlung des Deutschen Werkbundes zu München am 11. und 12. Juli 1908*, Leipzig: R. Voigtländer.

—— (1914) *Deutscher Werkbund Ausstellung Cöln 1914: Offizieller Katalog*, Cologne/Berlin: R. Mosse.

Eckstein, H. (ed.) (1958) *50 Jahre Deutscher Werkbund*, Frankfurt a.M.: Metzmer.

Haug, W.F. (ed.) (1975) *Warenästhetik*, Frankfurt a.M.: Suhrkamp (includes C. Friemert, 'Der "Deutsche Werkbund" als Agentur der Warenästhetik in der Aufstiegsphase der deutschen Imperialismus'); trans. as *Critique of Commodity Aesthetics*, 1986, Minneapolis: University of Minnesota Press.

Heuss, T. (1914) 'Der Werkbund in Cöln', *März* 8 (2): 907–13.

—— (1937) *Friedrich Naumann: Der Mann, das Werk, die Zeit*, Stuttgart/Berlin: Deutsche Verlags/anstalt; 2nd edn 1949, Stuttgart/Tübingen.

Hubrich, H.J. (1981) *Hermann Muthesius; Die Schriften zu Architektur, Kunstgewerbe, Industrie in der 'Neuen Bewegung'*, Berlin: Mann.

Müller, S. (1972) 'Zur Vorgeschichte und Gründungsgeschichte des Deutschen Werkbundes', in J. Frecot and D. Kerbs (eds) *Werkbundarchiv* 1, Berlin: Werkbund Archiv.

Munich, Die Neue Sammlung (1975) *Zwischen Kunst und Industrie: Der Deutsche Werkbund*, Munich: Die Neue Sammlung.

Naumann, F. (1914) *Werkbund und Weltwirtschaft*, Jena: Diederichs.

Posener, J. (1964) *Anfänge des Funktionalismus: Von Arts and Crafts zum Deutschen Werkbund*, Berlin/Frankfurt a.M./Vienna: Ullstein.

Velde, H. van de (1925) *Le Théâtre de l'exposition du 'Werkbund' á Cologne 1914 et la scène tripartite*, Antwerp: J.-E. Buschmann.

—— (1962) *Geschichte meines Lebens*, Munich: Piper; 2nd edn, 1986.

78 Dinocrates and the myth of the megalomaniacal institution of architecture

Werner Oechslin

With a surprisingly flowery and obsequious salutation Ledoux dedicated in 1804 the first of five projected volumes of his work to the Russian Czar, Alexander I. The title of the book, *L'Architecture considérée sous le rapport de l'art, des moeurs et de la législation*, in itself accentuates the social framework which the septentrional Alexander is called upon to make reality:

> Les Scythes attaqués par Alexandre de Macedoine, jusques au milieu des déserts et des rochers qu'ils habitaient, dirent à ce conquérant: Tu n'es donc pas un dieu, puisque tu fais mal aux hommes! Tous les peuples de la terre diront à l'Alexandre du Nord: Vous êtes un homme puisque vous voulez bien accueillir un système social, qui contribuera au bonheur du genre humain.
>
> (Ledoux 1804: 2f.)

The ideal of a new Alexander serving human society is to contrast with the picture of an Alexander who for all his godlike qualities is a despot and a man of fire and sword. Nevertheless, there remains a latent appreciation of the positive side of Alexander, the conqueror and ruler of the world, whose unbounded sovereignty provides the ideal figure of the potential patron. To Czar Alexander, who soon after will be the opponent of Napoleon, another 'new' Alexander on the stage of Europe, Ledoux looks for the realization of his plans.

The high and mighty of this world are in demand – more so than are the distant gods! Hailed as the Grand Mogul or the Emperor of China, or – as in the case of Ledoux – lent gravity by the image of Alexander the Great, aggrandized in myth, they control the fate of great architectural ideas, they stand in consultation above the models. Whether it be Princes of the Church, dressed in bishop's robes and illuminated by the Doves of the Holy Spirit, appraising an urban model, or whether it be, in equally competent pose, businessmen and bankers standing around 'nicely' arranged building bricks, the man who gives employment, the hero, is not just in demand, he is indispensable.[1]

Only the 'House of the Architect' is left entirely to the virtuosity and competence of the designer. In all other cases it is the rule that the bigger the building project and the more extensive the design, the more dependent does everything seem on the favour and authority of the builder. He, the patron and founder, generally holds the model in his hands. The architects present their plans to him in a more or less submissive posture, unless the architectonic idea, like a gift of God, is passed down from on high, as is represented in the picture of David handing over the Temple to Solomon in the description of Solomon's Temple that appeared in Halle in 1718.[2] Whether this takes place in the bosom of the biblical royal family, or whether the kneeling Borromini offers up the remodelled church of St John Lateran,[3] the act of transferring the plans signalizes the long awaited moment of agreement between builder and architect, tokens the imminent realization of great architectural dreams.

There is a legend of which the detailed tradition and its historical reception combine in exemplary fashion the aspects of the relationship between the architect and his employer already intimated. The employer is embodied by Alexander the Great, of whom mention was made at the outset. In the second main character, the architect, however, he meets a respondent whose self-confident bearing suggested the title given by Johann Heinrich Krause (1863), professor in Halle, to his systematic architectoral work: 'Deinokrates oder Hütte, Haus und Palast, Dorf, Stadt und Residenz der alten Welt ... mit Parallelen aus der mittleren und neueren Zeit' ('Deinocrates, or cottage, house and palace, village, town and residency of antiquity ... with parallels drawn from medieval and modern times'); similar to Valéry, who chose the name of an ancient architect, 'Eupalinos', as title for his philosophical reflections on architecture.

The architect in question is one of the best-known architects of antiquity. His name is generally associated with the foundation and construction of the city of Alexandria, although even in ancient times it was a moot point between Strabo and Solinus whether the rebuilding of the temple of Diana in Ephesus, famed as one of the wonders of the world, ought to be ascribed to him, too. 'Dinocrates', the form recorded by Vitruvius, is the most common spelling. Various names are given by the numerous classical authorites, i.e. Diochares and Cheromocarates. In the seventeenth century antiquaries discovered an inscription which, not inappropriately, even recorded the form Democrates (Félibien des Avaux 1687: 40–3).

If we were to call to mind all references to him, up to and including those of Plutarch and Pliny, then a relatively clearly defined picture of the ancient architect would present itself to us. Nevertheless, and solely

First published in *Daidalos* 4, 4 June 1982.

thanks to Vitruvius, he remains a figure of myth and legend. Vitruvius relates the meeting between Dinocrates and his future employer and patron, Alexander, in the preface to his second book. For his part, this story is a pretext to insinuate himself with rhetorical humility into the favour of Augustus. The deeper significance, the doctrine underlying the anecdote, was reserved for the exegesis of the interpreters of Vitruvius. Their diverse interpretations first reveal the extent of the problems inherent in the story.

What then does the legend relate? In the translation of Joseph Gwilt, the following:

> DINOCRATES the architect, relying on the powers of his skill and ingenuity, whilst Alexander was in the midst of his conquests, set out from Macedonia to the army, desirous of gaining the commendation of his sovereign. That his introduction to the royal presence might be facilitated, he obtained letters from his countrymen and relations to men of the first rank and nobility about the king's person; by whom being received, he besought them to take the earliest opportunity of accomplishing his wish. They promised fairly, but were slow in performing; waiting, as they alleged, for a proper occasion. Thinking, however, they deferred this without just grounds, he took his own course for the object he had in view. He was, I should state, a man of tall stature, pleasing countenance, and altogether of dignified appearance. Trusting to the gifts with which nature had thus endowed him, he put off his ordinary clothing, and having anointed himself with oil, crowned his head with a wreath of poplar, slung a lion's skin across his left shoulder, and carrying a large club in this right hand, he sallied forth to the royal tribunal, at a period when the king was dispensing justice. The novelty of his appearance excited the attention of the people; and Alexander soon discovering, with astonishment, the object of their curiosity, ordered the crowd to make way for him, and demanded to know who he was. 'A Macedonian architect', replied Dinocrates, 'who suggests schemes and designs worthy your royal renown. I propose to form Mount Athos into the statue of a man holding a spacious city in his left hand, and in his right a huge cup, into which shall be collected all the streams of the mountain, which shall thence be poured into the sea.'

(Vitruvius, trans. Gwilt 1826: 33–5)

But that is not the end of the story. On the contrary, Alexander makes detailed inquiries and then remarks critically:

> I admire the outline of your scheme, and am well pleased with it: but I am of opinion he would be much to blame who planted a colony on such a spot. For as an infant is nourished by the milk of its mother, depending thereon for its progress to maturity, so a city depends on the fertility of the country surrounding it for its riches, its strength in population, and not less for its defence against an enemy. Though your plan might be carried into execution, yet I think it impolitic. I nevertheless request your attendance on me, that I may otherwise avail myself of your ingenuity.

(Vitruvius, trans. Gwilt 1826: 33–5).

Thus although the episode ultimately turns out well for Dinocrates, objections are made to his brilliance, both physical and architectural, and these objections are characteristic. As a potential employer, Alexander finds fault with the adaptation to the material exigencies of reality. On the one hand, Vitruvius describes the spectacular event of the presentation of the project and illustrates how the artist may attract attention, how in fact he gains publicity by force through his conspicuous behaviour – in a way that even nowadays is known to be not ineffective. On the other hand, the extraordinary originality of the project is central to the story, and thus the project *qua* project is in principle accepted and placed prospectively alongside the wonders of the world, is handed down as an ideal possibility of monumental architecture. Finally, the story as related by Vitruvius contains the reservation inspired by the question of utility and practicability, and which requires the corrective and complementary intervention of the employer.

The accentuation and evaluation of these three main motives of the legend of Dinocrates open up a perspective in which the problems raised above receive all manner of different solutions. Wolfgang Lotz (1937–40) has already demonstrated that in the very first phase of the study of Vitruvius in fifteenth-century Italy, diametrically opposed interpretations were already being advanced. For Francesco di Giorgio the reference to the statue of Alexander cut into the mountain gives occasion to recall the doctrine, expounded elsewhere by Vitruvius, of the analogy between architecture and the human form. In conformity with this idea, and in a synthetic vision of all attributes that is characteristic for the quattrocento, he draws in a reconstruction of the text of Vitruvius a figure of a youth in classical counterpoise, just such a one as he elsewhere uses for the comparison of the ground plan of churches and the human form, and equips it with the lion's skin, but with the town model and bowl instead of the club of Hercules.[4] Combined in one image there thus appear the abstract scheme of an Alexander hewn out of Mount Athos and Dinocrates who with stately step and in his marvellous nudity bears the model. Hercules, Alexander, Dinocrates, thus runs the imaginary sequence of the figures fused together in the picture, whereby unanimity between builder and architect is again suggested.

In the pictorial presentation Francesco di Giorgio adheres strictly to the then conventional form of donor's

Figure 1 *Dinocrates with the model of the ideal town (including water supply) planned for Alexander, by Francesco di Giorgio Martini. (Source: di Giorgio Martini 1967, Plate 210; Cod. Magliabechiano II.I. 141, fol. 27 v., Florence, Biblioteca Nazionale.)*

portrait with town model (see Figure 1), such as used by Giovanni Bellini in the predella with St Terence of the altar-piece created for Pesaro. Not only must a great deal of time elapse before the naturalistic conception of a giant figure cut into the mountain is attained, but it is also necessary that there be the immediate comparison with the visual reconstructions of classical monumental architecture, in themselves increased to colossal proportions.[5] Francesco di Giorgio's drawing, however, shows in clear contrast with the Christian figure of Bellini's donor, the nakedness of the beautifully proportioned body. One feels reminded of the antique bronze nudes *post* Donatello.

Should this be related to the heightened self-awareness of the humanist architect? At least, interpretations that run in this direction are now available. Buonaccorso Ghiberti, in a complete reversal of the account of Vitruvius, lets Dinocrates come forward with the critical arguments and – a logical consequence – he himself refuses to execute his plans. In the work of Filarete, another aspect of the builder–architect relationship is brought to the fore, that which is expressed in the remark attributed to Alexander that such a grand scheme deserves a suit-

able reward. In the background there is still the ideal image of Alexander, the wise ruler who draws on doughty generals for his wars and philosophers for his administration, because, in the words of Leonardo Fiaravanti (1624), what was gained by force of arms is preserved by the counsel of wise men – and the humanist architect is of their number![6]

The view put forward by Leonbattista Alberti renounces such harmony. He places his main emphasis not only on the criticism by Alexander of the lack of usefulness of the scheme and of the remissness of the architect in the matter of victuals. His attack is directed against the superfluous projects of potentates in their entirety, and he is thus a precursor of scepticism towards all things monumental, towards memorial ostentation and everything that seems unduly conspicuous. For someone who had at heart the fundamental universality and pre-eminence of architecture, and thus the universal competence of the architect for the whole planning process, the Dinocrates episode was able to reinforce this further interpretation of Vitruvianism.

In 1556 Daniel Barbaro recommended such a systematic reading, set on a sound philological foundation. Like Francesco di Giorgio before him, he directs his attention to the project itself and subjects to closer scrutiny the words spoken by Dinocrates on presenting this work to Alexander:[6] 'ad te cogitationes et formas adfero' – 'I bring you plans and designs'. Francesco di Giorgio had understood by that 'disegno' (drawing); just as Rode later translated it with 'plans and drawings'. Barbaro's translation is abstract, 'Pensieri & forme' ('ideas and forms'), and closes with the astonishing statement: 'vuol dire fabbrica & discorso, la cosa significata, & quella che significa l'opera, & la ragione dalle qual cose nasce l'Architecttura' (Barbaro 1556: 41–2).[7] The 'suggestions' that Dinocrates has brought with him are thus linked to the concepts 'fabrica & discorso', by means of which Vitruvius defines architecture as a science that embraces everything.[8] The ideal conception of architecture is accordingly revealed in the harmonious agreement between theory and practice. Dinocrates' endeavours are equated with this theoretical postulate. His project represents – in model form – architecture as such! By way of diversion, Barbaro adds to the unavoidable criticism of the lack of victuals the praise of the cities that do 'function', above all Venice!

If the dialectical dealings with theory and practice as conceived by Barbaro were perhaps too high-flown, the apportioning of the problems between architect and employer was all the more down to earth. Thus André Félibien construes the parable of Dinocrates in his *Entretiens* (1666: 31–5) as an indication to subject suggestions made by architects to a more thorough inspection, in order to be one step ahead of the 'vaines promesses' and 'fausses apparences', false promises and deceptive appearances.[9] Appropriately, the criticism is expressed for the benefit of the French king who at the time was embroiled in the polemics between Bernini, Perrault and Colbert over the building of the east façade of the Louvre.

Fischer von Erlach (1721) (see Figure 2) makes a similar attempt to circumscribe the competences of the practising architect. For him, the essence to be extracted from Alexander's judgement was that Dinocrates was more skilful as an architect than as a politician. The French version of the text is even more emphatic: 'Il regarda Dinocrate pour un grand architecte & pour un mauvais économe'. Although, according to Vitruvius, the architect should be responsible for the adjustment to climate, to the nature of the soil and the economic supply situation, both Félibien and Fischer von Erlach, as a precaution, leave the control of these overlapping questions to the builder.

In the treatment of Dinocrates by Giovanni Battista Doni (1667) the state of affairs presented by Vitruvius is yet again reversed. His situation is analogous to that of the parable as a result of his also having an idea to propagate for which he is in search of a patron to make its realization possible. The subject of his appeal is Pope Urban VIII, the 'new Alexander'. Doni submits to him, in his *De restituenda salubritate agri romani*, a monumental project of a quite different kind: the fertilization of extensive tracts of barren land. We find there an allusion to Mount Athos being favoured by a fruitful climate; where monasteries now stood, there once stood whole cities, as if the plan of Dinocrates had in fact been put into practice! But here, too, there then follows the criticism of the lack of victuals. He adds the remark that only the ignorant rabble would allow itself to be impressed by such monstrous notions, whereas the wise – even when faced with the Pyramids – would enjoin themselves to pass a cautious judgement.

Yet this criticism was by no means always accepted. More often than not the fascination of the idea prevailed. Even Goethe was willing to consider the story of the monument in rock dedicated to Alexander 'not altogether improbable' (Körte 1937: 289). Gottlieb von Scheyb, who published under the pseudonym Köremon, was more forthright:

> It now becomes perfectly comprehensible that if the great architect Dinocrates had – as he was ready and willing to do – formed the portrait of Alexander out of Mount Athos, it would have been possible without any supernatural tricks or hocus-pocus. Had Alexander given his permission and procured all the resources for it, as was done in Egypt when the Pyramids were being built, on which many hundreds of thousands laboured, then would perhaps even now on the coast of Macedon, instead of Mount Athos, Alexander in effigy and in his full seated figure still receive the admiration of mankind.
>
> (Köreman 1770: 109)

Figure 2 *Monumental representation of the Vitruvian myth of Dinocrates.* (Source: *Fischer von Erlach 1721, Plate XVIII: 'Der Macedonische Berg Athos in Riesengestalt'*)

With this realistic appraisal the foundation is indeed laid for the future monumental elaborations of the idea of Dinocrates, right up to the portraits of the American presidents cut into the side of Mount Rushmore. Fischer von Erlach, who a moment before was reproving Dinocrates for his lack of economic circumspection, submits unperturbed to the fascination of elaborating graphically the Athos idea. The criticism disappears into a footnote to the advantage of monumental architecture. It is suggested to him from two quarters: by the ancient wonders of the world where unsurpassable grandeur and spectacular invention predominate, and by the wonders of nature which exemplarily provide an 'architectonic' spectacle. Consequently, Fischer von Erlach combines under the grand general heading of his *Entwurf einer historischen Architektur* (*Outline of historical architecture*, 1721) the ancient wonders of the world, from the Egyptian Pyramids to the Colossus of Rhodes, and the natural spectacle offered the wondering observer by the cataracts of the Nile.[10] Just as the wonders of the world are monumental architecture *par excellence*, so the all-embracing metaphor Nature is called upon to underpin the grandiose spectacle. Others have also made the link between nature and art, but Fischer von Erlach was the first to integrate the conception of Dinocrates – in this sense and with the connection between building and Nature peculiar to the story – in the canon of the wonders of the world.[11]

Mount Athos was in any case regarded as a special natural phenomenon. Celebrated in song by Homer and Theocritus, described by Thucydides, Strabo and Pliny, it is deemed worthy of mention by the early travellers in Greece and in the East – Spon, Wheeler, Pocock. When news of wondrous manifestations in China reached Europe via the Jesuit, Martini, and when people heard of the gigantic idol, 'Fe', carved into the mountainside near Tunchuen in the province of Fokien, then the scholars may well have felt themselves reminded of the legend of Dinocrates reported by Vitruvius. Athanasius Kircher links to the idol the question as to whether the Chinese mountain was in fact formed by the hand of man ('Artificis manu exculptus') or rather by the skill of Nature ('an Naturae industria ita effigiatus'). If the first prove true, then the idol should in the light of its surprising size be included among the wonders of the world. Yet since no mention is made of the size, he considers it more likely to be a natural phenomenon of which he then proceeds to quote examples of similar cases, such as in Sicily (Martini 1655: 69; Kircher 1667: 172–3; Petrucci, 1677: 177–9).

Thus, also according to this line of thought, Nature and architecture are one and the same (Oechslin 1981). Their strange elaborations connect and support each other. The visual conception of Mount Athos sketched by Fischer von Erlach is both natural phenomenon and architectonic monument; it is as much inspired by the architectonic mountain formation as by the archetypal cast of the colossal constructions of the wonders of the

Figure 3 *The project Dinocrates by H. Rapin.* (Source: *Andersen 1913*)

world. It is thus not mere chance that the Dinocrates *Evocation*, as Henri Rapin later called his version (Figure 3), is provided with the pyramidal substructure together with the diagonally erected flights of steps, yet without the monumentality of the brutal rockface being mitigated. From the person of Dinocrates to the monumental visualization at the beginning of this century there thus runs a single tradition which sees the creation of Nature and the man-made artefact architecture as one.

Henri Rapin's portrayal is of especial interest because it is introduced in connection with an 'ideal city', which is directly linked to the architecture of the World Fairs with their mass of showpieces, and specifically to the Chicago Exhibition of 1893. In this project of a World Trade Centre, which he completed together with the architect Ernest M. Hébrard, Hendrik Christian Andersen includes the ideal city of Dinocrates in his introductory remarks devoted to the 'grandes conceptions monumentales' (Andersen 1913: 39–40). Yet again the wonders of the world are pressed into service as models of monumental configuration. Yet again, in the criticism of the inadequate economic foundation, the sore point is touched upon, but otherwise purposely ignored. On the other side, Andersen's unstinting admiration of Alexander as the '*seul maître*' takes pride of place. Before him, the great founder of colonies, all races of antiquity bow down. The employer of the architect here appears endowed with an omnipotence which knows no resistance and which alone can and shall be the guarantor of such tremendous building achievements.

Megalomaniacal thinking of this sort is characteristic for the beginning of this century. Not without reason did Josef Ponten place the very first chapter of his notorious book, *Architektur, die nicht gebaut wurde* (*Architecture that was Never Built*), under the motto 'Dinocrates'. Here the standpoint of someone who would like to escape from pedestrian reality and devote himself in the study of architecture to those works instituted by creative acts of genius is particularly welldefined. Ponten commences,

> As a sort of revenge on the all too human, on the pretty and meagre, my love went out to those architectonic ideas on which the gravity of earth was least burdensome, the freest and boldest, the grandest, to everything contained in the words of Scripture to build a tower reaching up to Heaven, so that the peoples may gaze on it in wonder.
>
> (Ponten 1925: 15)

Hyperbole and the sacred word are stretched to serve architectonic conceptions that are introduced under the sign of the Athos project. And here Ponten employs a precise term: the 'babylonic'. The proposal made by Dinocrates to Alexander is called a 'babylonically-monstrous, orientally-colossal idea'. Once again the historical epithets estrange the concrete project of a city

in favour of a mythically heightened and esoterically exaggerated idea, given still greater emphasis by the reference to Semiramis and her intention of having her image carved into a lofty mountain. Fischer von Erlach would give no credit to this story. In this instance, the story serves as evidence, intensifying the hypertrophy, that the idea of the monumental in architecture is ultimately 'oriental'.

Placed next to such an outright avowal of the 'building fever', the text of Vitruvius and his interpreters of the quattrocento seems almost a piece of social criticism. Whoever refuses to be convinced by the reasonable criticism immanent in the work of Vitruvius is left only with the counter-image, the image of catastrophe, the fall of the Tower of Babel, as a deterrent against monumentality in its all too spectacular form. The conception of the colossus is, indeed, ambivalent. There is a decisive difference between the fairly harmless colossus to be found in the park and garden decoration in Giambologna's Appenino and its imitations and reproductions,[12] and the architectonic colossi of the turn of the century, those of Rieht (1899) (see Figure 4) or

Figure 4 *Otto Rieht: a colossal figure cut from stone, 1896.* (Source: *Rieht 1899*)

Figure 5 *Idyllic portrayal of the Dinocratic image of Alexander by Henri de Valenciennes, 1769, London, Trafalgar Galleries.*

Palanti (n.d.). The purpose of intimidation is written too large in their countenance for them to serve as mere memorial figures or simply to bring into play historical or mythical reminiscences. In like manner, Rapin's gloomy mountain colossus, set in a menacingly barren and rocky landscape, contrasts with that idyllic and poetic portrayal by Henri de Valenciennes (Figure 5) which settles the Dinocratic image of Alexander in harmony with man in a fertile and peaceful Arcadia.[13]

Such differing degrees of significance are often consciously rendered explicit by the artist in the image; the admonitions on the theme of the mighty colossus are uttered! Max Klinger adopts the ingredients of the image of Dinocrates in his allegory of the youth striding blamelessly through life.[14] Here the colossus no longer holds the 'flourishing city' and the 'water reservoir' in its hands, they have been supplanted by the natural catastrophe apostrophized in the volcano and by the hourglass which sets its seal on historic time. At the feet of the colossus lies the representation of the destruction of architecture and Nature: a true contrast to the originally optimistic conception of Dinocrates! The impressive pose of the naked colossus seems also to have left its mark on Franz von Stuck. Even more gloomy than in the work of Klinger, *Lucifer* incarnate, wings aspread, gazes out of the picture, inspired now no longer by Dinocrates but by Rodin's Michelangelesque thinker above the gate of Hell.

Klinger himself uses the colossus elsewhere – supine, with armour, helmet and sword – for the concrete portrayal of the symbol of utter destruction. *War* is the title of this variation of the image of Alexander. In this respect, it is descended from Goya's visionary painting[15] of the 'coloso' – or 'panico' – and from the figure

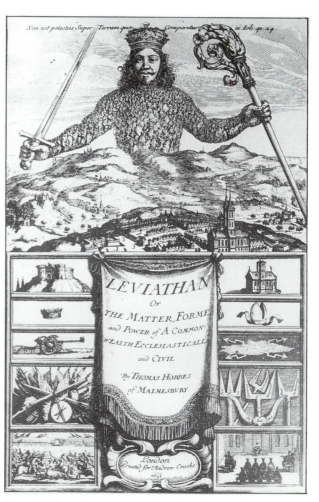

Figure 6 *The colossus, representing the ideology of emperor and state.* (Source: *Hobbes 1651*)

appearing on the title page of Hobbes's *Leviathan* (1651), the ruler of the world equipped with sword and bishop's crook (Figure 6). In Hobbes's tract on ecclesiastical and secular government, the narrative stands under the motto of inviolable authority. 'Non est potestas Super Terram quae Comparetur ei' – 'there is no power on earth comparable to it'. The crowned ruler not only holds the insignia extended over town and country, his body is literally composed of all the people who form the state; corresponding to a metaphor already selected by Francisco de Hollanda for his colossal figure of a warrior.

When confronted with such apocalyptic visions, should one comfort oneself with the irony that seems to cling to the figure of Hercules by Lequeu, nonchalantly stretching itself above the 'Porte de Parisis', invested with the new insignia of 'Liberté'?[16] Or does the superficial adoption of the Dinocrates story by Fischer von Erlach seem, when all is said and done, too naive? Or does one even long to suffer the fate of Encelades, the mightiest of the mythical giants, who after the unsuccessful revolt against the gods was struck by the bolt of Jupiter and buried under Mount Etna? We are here presented with a further counter-image to the symmetrically formed Alexander of Mount Athos, one that is revived in literature in Tasso's *Gerusalemme liberata* (1581) and in the work of Bernardino Baldi (1590), who confidently plays off the strength of the Roman Pantheon against the gigantic power of the colossus. In his *Leviathan*, Hobbes reports of the destruction of the giants on the coming of the Flood. Notwithstanding, and as though nothing had happened, his new political conception is introduced by the colossus gazing over the peaceful countryside.

The liberated imagery of war and destruction seems to be irresistible. The most recent attempt at a 'more human' metaphor for the Dinocratic conception of the exhibition of architecture has been ventured by Charles Simonds in his *Body–landscape–dwelling* (1971), convincing because unadorned (see Figure 7). His proposal – resigned or poetic – adopts the humanistic anthropomorphism of Francesco di Giorgio on the guise of 'body-art'. By miniaturizing the architectural fragments placed on the body he can do without the colossal human figure and thus realizes most closely what Alexander, or rather Vitruvius, had required: the interrelation of man and architecture. In his admonitory intent Simonds does not fall short of the 'Burning Hand' of Baselitz. The gesture that once held the ideal city of Dinocrates and the bowl containing the waters of Mount Athos is unable to extinguish the blaze in the house that has been set on fire.

Figure 7 Body-landscape-dwelling, *New York, 1971, by Charles Simonds.*

NOTES

1 See, for example, the illustration of the new Jerusalem from Fabri 1664, dedicated to Cardinal della Croce.

2 'Der Tempel Salomonis/Nach alle seinen Vorhöfen/ Mauren/Thoren/Hallen heiligen Gefässen ... in einem eigentlichen Modell und materiellen Fürstellung/in dem Waysen-Hause zu Glaucha an Halle ... Anno MDCCXVII. aufgerichtet', Halle, 1718.

3 See the engraving by Giuseppe Belloni and Giuseppe Testana in Rasponi 1656.

4 'Da Alessandra adunque ... fu laudato la similitudine della città al corpo umano' (di Giorgio Martini 1967: 361–2).

5 An early tradition of such a rendering is verified by Agrippa von Nettesheim (1693: 116).

6 Fioravanti (1624: 346 r & v): 'perche col consiglio di huomini savii'si mantiene quello che col valore dell'armi si guadagna'.

7 This statement, which is immediately highly interesting because of the use of the modern sounding 'significata'/ 'significa', is very difficult to translate: 'What is the meaning of construction/practice and discourse/theory, which describe/mean things, and that which the work signified, and the (deeper) base from which architecture originates.'
Vitruvius gives, as the two basic ingredients of (science) architecture, 'fabrica' and 'ratiocinatio', which are usually classified as practice/theory, and which translate something like this: Barbaro – 'fabrica'/'discorso' (construction/discourse); Rode – 'Ausübung'/'Theorie' (practice/

theory); Fensterbusch – 'Handwerk'/'geistige Arbeit' (handicraft/intellectual work).

9 Félibien relates the history as an example of outstanding artistry, but insufficiently studied fancy.

10 The 'completion' of architectural monuments by natural events was repeated elsewhere by Fischer von Erlach as in II, XIV (Stonehenge/'Wundersame Felsen-Bühne' at Salzburg) and III, XV ('Sinesische durch Kunst gemachte Lustberge').

11 For the representation itself he could, of course, refer to the earlier reconstruction of Pietro da Cortonas (Drawing in the British Museum, London). A detailed discussion without a visual reconstruction can be found in the appendix to the history of the Wonders of the World in Caramuei's 'Architectura civil, recta y obligua' of 1678/1681.

12 For Giambologna and related executions see Körte (1937: 297 ff.) and de Caus (1615: Plate 16).

13 Henri de Valenciennes, the reviver of French landscape painting, painted his representation of Dinocrates in 1769 after his return from his third stay in Rome. It clearly forms part of the classical tradition of French landscape painting and can be compared with Poussin's portrait of Polythemus in the Hermitage (see Körte 1937: Plate 23).

14 The paper by Klingers carries the Latin title 'Integer Vitae scelerisque purus' and appeared in 'Vom Tode II Opus XIII'. In addition, a rejected variant (dated 1885) is known.

15 Goya's painting is in the Prado, Madrid, and is dated between 1808 and 1812.

16 Paris, Bibl. Nat. Est., Ha 80, p. 74: 'Porte du Parisis qu'on peut appeler l'Arc du peuple.'

REFERENCES

Agrippa von Nettesheim, H.C. (1693) *De incertitudine & vanitate omnium scientiarum & artium liber* (1530), Frankfurt/Leipzig.

Andersen, H.C. (1913) *Création d'un centre mondial de communication*, Paris.

Baldi, B. (1590) 'Sopra la Rotonda', Sonetti Romani, *Versi e prose*, Venice, p. 285.

Barbaro, D. (1556) *I Dieci Libri dell'Architecttura di M. Vitruvio tradutti et commentati . . .*, Venice.

Caus, S. de (1615) *Les raisons des forces mouvantes, avec diverses machines . . .*, Frankfurt.

Doni, G.B. (1667) *De restituenda salubritate agri romani*, Florence, Introduction and p. 91.

Fabri, G. (1664) *Le Sagre Memorie di Ravenna antica*, Venice.

Félebien des Avaux, J.F. (1687) *Recueil historique de la vie et des ouvrages des plus célèbres architectes*, Paris, 1696 edn.

Félibien, A. (1666) *Entretiens sur les vies et sur les ouvrages des plus excellent peintres anciens et modernes*, Paris.

Fioravanti, L. (1624) *Dello specchio di Scientia universale*, Venice.

Fischer von Erlach, J.B. (1721) *Entwurf Einer Historischen Architektur . . .*, 'Erstes Buch' ('First Book'), Vienna.

Giorgio Martini, F. di (1967) *Trattai di Architettura . . .*, ed. C. Maltese, Milan.

Hobbes, T. (1651) *Leviathan or The Matter, Forme & Power of a Common-Wealth ecclesiasticall and civill*, London: Andrew Crooke.

Kircher, A. (1667) *China Illustrata*, Amsterdam.

Köremon, (1770) *Natur and Kunst in Gemälden, Bildhauereyen, Gebäuden und Kupferstichen, zum Unterricht . . .*, II, Leipzig/Vienna.

Körte, W. (1937) 'Deinokrates und die barocke Phantasie', *Die Antike* XIII: 289.

Krause, J.H. (1863) *Deinokrates oder Hütter, Haus und Palast, Dorf, Stadt und Residenz der alten Welt . . . mit Parallelen aus der mittleren und neueren Zeit*, Jena.

Ledoux, C.N. (1804) 'A Sa Majesté l'Empereur de Toutes les Russies', in *L'Architecture considerée sous le rapport de l'art, des moeurs et de la législation*, 1, Paris.

Lotz, W. (1937/40) 'Eine Deinokratesdarstellung des Francesco di Giorgio', in *Mitteilungen des Kunsthistorischen Institutes in Florenz*, V, pp. 428 sg.

Martini, M. (1655) *Novus Atlas Sinensis*, Amsterdam.

Oeschslin, W. (1981) 'Architecttura e natura; sull'origine e la convertibilità dell'architettura', *Lotus international* 31: 4–19.

Palanti, M. (n.d.) *Architecttura per tutti*, Milan, tav. 164 ('Fonte degli Eroi de Lavoro').

Petrucci, G. (1677) *Prodromo Apologetico alli Studi Chircheriani*, Amsterdam.

Ponten, J. (1925) *Architektur die nicht gebaut wurde*, Stuttgart/Berlin/Leipzig, I.

Rasponi, C. (1656) *De Basilica et Patriarcho Lateranensi Libri quattuor ad Alexandrum VII.*, Rome.

Rieht, O. (1899) *Skizzen, Architektonische und Decorative, Vierte Folge*, Leipzig.

Tasso, T. (1581) *Gerusalemme liberata*, Canto XV, 34.

Vitruvius (1826) *The architecture of Marcus Vitruvius Pollio in ten books*, trans. J. Gwilt, London.

79 Educational objectives in architecture

Nils-Ole Lund

The process of European integration is making headway. An important objective in the attempts to create a large common market is that of enabling labour to move more freely across national borders. As far as the professions are concerned, a prerequisite for free mobility is that the different countries should recognize each other's examinations. Within the architectural profession this happened with the adoption of an EEC directive in 1985. When the directive was adopted it was also decided to set up a committee to advise the Commission in Brussels on the improvement of architectural training.

The efforts to achieve harmonization have been followed up with economic programmes aimed at supporting studies at foreign educational institutions and universities. After students and teachers have studied in another country, it is hoped they will maintain the contacts they made during their stay abroad, or just settle and work in the new country.

All this cross-border co-operation and contact has incidentally also resulted in architects recognizing the special characteristics of their own country. When a British architect concludes after many years of internal discussion about the ideal size of an architectural school that it will function best with about 200 students, it is a shock for him or her to discover that an Italian architectural school may accommodate perhaps 10,000 students and that everyone with a school leaving certificate is freely admitted. The wide differences between the European architectural schools mean that the EEC is not trying to standardize them, but only to impose minimum standards.

Without a knowledge of the historical background, it is impossible to understand why the differences are so marked and why the architectural schools vary in content, form, size, and links with other training institutions. This essay is not the place for an exhaustive discussion of all these differences; it will only be possible to indicate a few matters of particular significance. The status and obligations of the professions differ from country to country, which means that their educational requirements vary. The historical period when a system of training started has in many instances determined its character. The architectural discipline contains elements of the humanities, technology and economics. Looked at in another way, the discipline of architecture is a combination of art, craft and technology. In the course of time the idea of which was the most important element has determined the position of architects in the educational system. The oldest educational school in Scandinavia for example, that in

Copenhagen, was attached to an art academy, because the Danish court in the eighteenth century, under French influence, regarded architecture as a mixture of art and craft. But the majority of Scandinavian architectural schools are faculties of technical universities, because they were started at around the turn of the century when the technical aspects of the discipline were regarded as decisive.

In Vienna the three architectural courses are spread over a technical university, an art academy and a crafts school. The varying affiliations of the schools of architecture has of course resulted in differences in subject content and in the examination systems, just as they have affected views about the need for research.

Yet, despite these historically determined differences, there are many points of similarity between the 200-odd European courses in architecture. These points of similarity become clear when they are compared with the traditional university courses in the humanities, law, theology, natural sciences and medicine.

The highly directed teaching, the practice-oriented content and the absence of true scientific character differentiates architectural training courses almost everywhere from the critical and analytical university tradition. In the architectural curriculum the design project has replaced the lectures and private study of the universities as the most important teaching tool. The necessary ancillary disciplines are related to a series of projects which increase in difficulty as the course progresses.

The close contact with the profession and the latter's reality outside the schools have meant that the academic and intellectual climate has been influenced primarily by the formulation of the profession's problems. Generally teachers have both taught and practised. Recent social developments and the partial industrialization of building have now placed a question mark beside a form of education that emphasizes training and is based on professional experience.

In the early post-war years the industrialization and mechanization had just begun. There was a great and obvious need for building and planning, but the technical and economic means did not exist to meet it. Architectural education at that time was based on the premise that the discipline still comprised a unity. The teachers normally ran a small practice alongside their task at the school and there were no great differences between the viewpoints presented to the students and the standards which guided the profession. It was obviously believed at the schools that there were practising architects who did not meet the quality demands laid down by the courses and there were of course people in the profession who regarded the products of the schools as substandard, but the distance between the schools and the profession was not a difference of principle. The profession's underlying value system was not questioned through discussions and debate. It was the power of example that determined what was regarded as good and beautiful. The profession's strong personalities defined the tradition to which other practitioners adhered.

Even though the international architectural situation started to shift during the early post-war period, the conflicts of architectural ideology had only just begun to influence the schools of architecture. There was then still a large degree of unity about aims and means. Nor were there any specialisms in architectural courses at that time. All the students received the same training and all the courses ended with an examination task in the form of an independently worked-out project for a building. The architectural student did not regard his or her studies as a great artistic or intellectual challenge, but treated them as a necessary preparation for a future career as an architect, first as an assistant and, later, as a principal. If one was active in politics generally or on the political side of the profession, these activities were not allowed to interfere with the training. Those who did not have any client contacts had to obtain commissions after they had graduated by participating in competitions or by designing houses for relatives.

The processes and techniques of building were still craft-based and therefore easy to comprehend. The problems of indoor climate control had not yet been discovered and no one thought of energy-saving. All that was needed to start an architect's office was a drawing board and a telephone. No large amount of capital was required. Even if the profession consisted of equal parts of technology and art, there was no sense of a split between the two components. They were united in a craft approach to building: it should be useful, solid and beautiful.

This description of the situation around 1950 is simplified, but applies broadly to the Scandinavian countries in any event.

Forty years later many changes have occurred in architectural schools as well as the profession. The project-based teaching system is broadly the same as it was about 1950, but there are now many more schools and many more students. There is also a greater variation between courses. Many unified courses have been replaced by a more composite form of study, where students can choose different modules or just specialize. At the schools which have progressed furthest in this direction, it is possible to concentrate in the final part of the course on restoration, industrial design, landscape architecture, planning or building. Only a proportion of the teachers work as practising architects, while, on the

other hand, research has now emerged as a profession in its own right.

To a varying extent the schools have become places where the international architectural trends are picked up and interpreted. The old tacit consensus about aims and means has been replaced by debate and discussion. Architectural education is no longer conceived purely as a necessary learning phase. It has acquired an independent function in relation to research and the generation of ideologies. Many examination tasks must be regarded as architectural experiments rather than realistic projects. The old dream that a graduate architect was ready to launch into practice has been replaced by the recognition that an architectural education can only attempt to lay a foundation, pass on some skills and create an attitude.

The large number of students and the trend in the profession towards the formation of large architectural practices mean that only a few graduate architects can expect to become principals. The new architects will be distributed in different positions and only some of them will be able to design houses. Some will be able to exercise a greater influence on the physical environment in an administrative capacity than they would have managed to achieve as practising architects. A good municipal architect or a good departmental head in the ministry of the environment is of greater significance for the country's appearance than an architect in general practice.

The architect has thus followed the current social trends and widened his or her interests over a growing number of fields, but since this has occurred through specialization the breadth of competence has also been reduced. This specialization not only concerns the profession's economic functions but extends into the building process itself, where the financial and management aspects are separated from the project, which is itself broken down into phases.

While the architects are conquering new, non-traditional areas of activity such as communications, design and administration, other disciplines are intruding into the architect's traditional areas of responsibility. In the building industry it is administration and management which are being left to other specialists; in physical planning it is economists, biologists, geographers and sociologists who are taking over.

Reaction to these developments can take several forms and the reactions are visible both in the profession and in the schools. One type of reaction takes the form of a purification process. The discipline has been 'infected' with all kinds of non-architectural matter. Sometimes architects turn their discipline into a political and social tool, at other times a branch of marketing. It is argued that the time has come for the architect to concentrate on what he or she does best, namely, to concentrate on design. No other profession is concerned with designing the physical environment, while there are a whole lot of others which are good at dealing with subjects like law, technology and economics. It must therefore be the architect who should satisfy society's need for expression. It must be the architect who finds meaning behind the confusing image of society and gives visual form to that meaning (or lack of meaning). If the architect succeeds in doing so, his or her work becomes art.

If one supports this viewpoint, a school of architecture becomes a place for experimenting with form. The school becomes a work-place where teachers and students jointly use the period of study to explore architecture's potential in the hope that it is still possible to defend a meaningful and humane architecture in a society where economic and commercial considerations are constantly increasing their influence.

An architectural education which concentrates on architectural means and on historical experience is exclusive. The research that is carried out becomes an exploration of boundary fields, a mixture of art and philosophy. Where this work penetrates deepest, architecture becomes an existential problem. Instead of trying to exert a wide influence, which is the aim of a multi-faceted training, the architect finds strength by in-depth study of the problem of form.

The other straightforward reaction to social trends is to accept their comprehensiveness. Each time a new field appears, the architectural discipline must secure its influence. In a modern society decisions about the design of the physical environment are taken in many different places. It is no good being able to design beautiful and interesting houses if these houses remain isolated monuments in a visual and functional chaos. The architect must accept responsibility not only for the form, but also for the content, and the responsibility extends further to embrace the society's broader needs. A building project is not only concerned with providing the client with a good and sensible house, but also with ensuring that society's resources are used sensibly and that the people who are to use the building are made comfortable. If an architect designs a tool, his or her task is not only to design a saleable product, but also to develop something that is both usable and meaningful.

In order to be able to take account of all these aspects and to work with a wide variety of problem formulations, the architect must be competent in a series of fields, or at least must master them sufficiently to be able to understand and evaluate the arguments and work for the specialists. The architect's self-conception is that of a generalist who defines him- or herself as the person who recapitulates and co-ordinates the work of others in an attempt to find an appropriate form.

On the basis of this argument all physical objects may form the subject of the architect's interest independent of their magnitude and symbolic significance. It is also immaterial whether he or she achieves influence through drawing, administration or writing.

An architectural education which is organized according to this philosophy is inclusive. It is subject to continual change and expansion. New subject areas are established and others are differentiated. Because governments do not allow the length of the study period to be extended, conflicts arise between the general and special elements of the training. If a school wishes, for example, to give architects a special knowledge of restoration and building conservation, it is necessary to teach traditional building techniques and local architectural history. The basic teaching in the first part of the course does not meet this need. Another conflict arises between the traditional teaching of skills and many ancillary disciplines, the number of which is constantly increasing. An attempt is being made to solve this last dilemma by teaching only a 'basic understanding' of the subject instead of detailed knowledge. The danger of this kind of teaching is that it may produce superficiality and that the architect will not be able to work as a specialist in his or her collaboration with people from other disciplines.

Some of these problems could, of course, be solved if the profession and the schools had an effective system of further and post-entry training, but it has proved difficult to establish such a programme in most places.

Despite their differences, the two training models just described have some features in common. Both differ from the professional model where the aim was to enable the graduate to enter the profession directly as a practising architect. Looking at the discipline of architecture as an institution, it is possible to describe the changes that have occurred. The members of an institution share certain values and are more concerned with internal opinions than with points of view coming from outside. The institution is not necessarily a closed and rigid society. Other parties concerned with building affect the institution of architecture and it is subject to constant change, not least because developments in society force it to adapt. It is the common professional values, the profession's ethics and aesthetic, which hold the institution together and form the tradition which it cannot be without.

But the picture is no longer so unambiguous. Architectural education is no longer an apprenticeship during which young architects learn the profession's values in a kind of formation process and where they are not released until they conform to these values.

The traditional institution, where the profession's values were controlled by powerful people who exerted an influence over the schools (the profession and its journals), has been replaced by a different institution with a more complicated structure. The single centre has become several centres. The most important element is still obviously the profession, but it has been split up into employees and employers, single-disciplinary groupings such as planner-architects, house-architects and industrial designers. A second centre consists of journals and museums, and a third of research, which is partly carried out by independent bodies and partly by architectural schools.

The fourth centre comprises the architectural schools. Here it is clear that the schools have increased their independence and have started to become academic institutions which feel themselves responsible for the profession's traditions and values and are therefore critical towards them. Even if they come under pressure from the state and the profession, they are still sufficiently independent to keep alive a theoretical debate by launching experimental projects and by initiating controversial research. Instead of being educational and training institutions, architectural schools have become forums for dialogue and debate. Architects' schools have become schools of architecture. Architectural trends are now being named after the schools which created them. In Finnish architecture, for example, they refer to two main tendencies named after the schools in Oulu and Helsinki.

Whereas other university disciplines struggle to make contact with outside reality – doctors, for example, are aware that they must do much more than teach general medicine – architectural education seems to be moving in the opposite direction. Here an attempt is being made to create a theoretically and intellectually satisfying counterweight to a commercialized practice. Some European architectural courses have progressed so far in this direction that the teachers cling to an academic career where only research matters. Others have managed to maintain a balance between theory and practice, art and building. How this balance is established will be decisive for the future of architectural education.

80   The impact of tourism on the environment

Jane Fawcett

The International Council on Monuments and Sites (ICOMOS) Charter on Cultural Tourism was prepared and endorsed in 1976 by all the leading international tourist authorities, as well as UNESCO, ICOMOS and Europa Nostra, representing the international heritage organizations. It states that:

> Tourism is an irreversible social, human, economic and cultural fact.... In the context of the phenomena of expansion which confront the human race, tourism appears ... likely to exert a most significant influence on man's environment ... and on monuments and sites in particular. In order to remain bearable this influence must be carefully studied, and at all levels be the object of a concerted and effective policy.
>
> (ICOMOS 1976: 1)

It continues:

> Cultural Tourism is that form of tourism whose object is ... the discovery of monuments and sites.... Whatever may be its ... benefits ... it cannot be considered separately from the negative, despoiling or destructive effects which the massive and un-controlled use of monuments and sites entails.... It is the respect of the world cultural and natural heritage which must take precedence over any other con-siderations, however justified these may be from a social, political or economic point of view.
>
> (ibid.: 2)

As a basis for action it states that:

> The World Tourist organisation ... and UNESCO, in the framework of the International Convention for the Protection of the World Cultural and Natural Heritage, adopted in 1972, shall exert all efforts ... to ensure the implementation of the policy which the signatory bodies have defined as the only one able to protect mankind against the effects of tourism's anarchical growth which would result in the denial of its own objectives.
>
> (ibid.: 3)

The Charter ends with a solemn declaration stating that the duty of these authorities is:

> to respect and protect the authenticity and diversity of cultural values in developing regions and countries as in industrialised nations, since the fate of mankind's cultural heritage is of the very same nature everywhere in the face of tourism's likely expansion.
>
> (ibid.: 4)

The Charter also recommends that the bodies represent-ing tourism and the protection of the natural and monumental heritage should integrate cultural assets into the social and economic objectives and planning of the resources of states; also that special training should be set up by tour operators for personnel working in, and travelling to promote, cultural tourism; and that education in the understanding and respect for monu-ments and sites should be promoted in schools and universities. It recommends that specialists should be encouraged to study the effects of pollution by tourism on monuments, and that their skills should be enlisted to advise tourist authorities on the development of tourist plans and programmes.

This would have proved excellent advice, had it been implemented. Unfortunately, international tourism has become one of the largest businesses in the world, and is promoted by governments, by local government, by government-funded organizations, and by the many facets of the tourist trade. Tourism makes the second largest contribution to the UK budget. There is no doubt that the money spent by tourists, not only at monu-ments and sites but also in many of our historic cities, is of the greatest value in helping to maintain certain ele-ments of the heritage, and in providing employment on a wide scale. This fact has received widespread publicity and has been enlisted as an argument by many authorit-ies in their efforts to promote tourism, but little has been said about the irreversible damage being inflicted upon the heritage all over the world by over-use and lack of controls. I write in the context of this Charter as a con-sultant on cultural tourist projects, as a member of the ICOMOS International Committee on Cultural Tourism, and of the equivalent UK Committee, and as former Secretary of ICOMOS UK.

It was evident at the launch of European Year of Tourism 1990 that the promotion of tourism by the Government, by the British Tourist Authority and English Tourist Board, and by local government Tourist Promotion Officers was regarded as an end in itself and as a desirable goal. All the speakers took their tone from the Junior Minister for Tourism, who opened the confer-ence, and all stressed the importance of making UK faci-lities more competitive in order to increase revenue. Little was spoken about the heritage. In official circles the heritage appears to be regarded as a useful magnet to attract income, but not as a finite and infinitely vulnerable resource which, when once destroyed, can never be recreated. This attitude is all the more surprising since the English Tourist Board reports that, out of 330 million visits to tourist attractions in England in 1989, 162 million were to heritage sites; that 50 per cent of foreign tourists visited the UK in 1989 to see heritage sites, museums and galleries, or the performing arts; and that in 1990 there was 25 per cent more interest in staying in historic towns than elsewhere.

The warnings expressed by the ICOMOS Charter are even more relevant today than when it was written. Just as, in development terms, prime sites attract prime buildings, so outstanding historic sites and monuments the world over attract the greatest crowds. However, these sites, whether for development or for tourist promotion, deserve and require the most sensitive and determined controls. Unfortunately, such controls are seldom forthcoming. The average cultural tourist wishes to visit those sites of which he or she has heard, and the tourist trade and the tourist authorities exploit this interest, to the detriment of the sites themselves.

We have now reached the position where many of the World Heritage Sites, which are, by definition, the most outstanding sites in the world, are being subjected to systematic and often irreversible damage from tourists. Furthermore, owing to world-wide promotion, the visitors are destroying not only the fabric of the monument or site but also the experience itself. The sheer weight of numbers (8 million per annum at Notre-Dame, Paris, around 3.5 million per annum at Westminster Abbey, and roughly 2.5 million at Canterbury and St Paul's Cathedrals and the Tower of London) is making tourism unbearable and also destroying much of the world's heritage. With tourism comes the whole paraphernalia of tourist facilities, such as hotels, airports and car parks.

To halt this process, which involves the exploitation of both the tourist and the site, certain questions must be asked: in whose interest is it, and who profits by it? The second is easier to answer than the first. The total income earned by the UK from tourism for 1989 was £19.4 billion. This figure includes profits made by the promoters of tourism, the tourist industry, the airlines and coach operators, by the spin-offs from tourism to the retailing trade, hotels, caterers and shops. It also includes the immense profits made indirectly through tax by central and local government. Of this very little, and often none at all, goes to maintain the sites themselves. Outstanding landscapes, many archaeological sites, cathedrals and churches, to name a few, are subjected to over-use with little or no compensation.

As for whose interests are being served by the promotion of tourism, most authorities and most tour operators would answer that they were catering for the interests of the tourists themselves, and giving them what they want. When one considers the appalling overcrowding and disruption of airports, double booking, and long queues at high season for most of the experiences on offer, this becomes more questionable. The tourist needs, and deserves, more intelligent advice to avoid such congestion, and the heritage, if it is to survive, merits more protection and less exploitation. All this is recommended in the ICOMOS Charter.

Furthermore, it is not only individual sites that have suffered from tourist exploitation, but whole coasts, landscapes and historic urban areas. The once beautiful coasts and islands of the Mediterranean are now littered with hideous and inappropriate hotels and leisure complexes. The Lake District is being 'killed by love' and over-use by walkers and climbers. The Alps are encrusted with ski-lifts and new skiing villages composed of urban flats and hotels, wholly out of keeping with the local vernacular. The Acropolis, Stonehenge, the Taj Mahal, Westminster Abbey, Notre-Dame, St Peter's and the Vatican, Venice, and many other World Heritage Sites are being physically undermined and environmentally negated.

One only has to read many tourist brochures to see the type of hotel development that has extinguished all beauty along some of the loveliest coasts and islands in Europe. Spain, Majorca, Greece, Crete, Italy, Sardinia, France, Cyprus, Turkey, Malta: the list is endless, the damage and destruction final, and nothing of the original character remains. Where once there was a magnificent sandy bay with deep blue water, approaches from hillsides covered in wild flowers, there is now a clutter of ugly, high-rise concrete hotels, approached by a network of concrete roads and parking lots. Who wants a holiday in such an environment? You can find it at home.

There are several ways in which the proliferation of tourists and tourist clutter can be controlled. One is to promote alternatives which might offer different attractions of solitude and peace, lack of stress, subtle experiences and wide empty landscapes. While the search for the sun motivates the bulk of tourists to travel south, many of the most rewarding and refreshing experiences can be obtained by travelling north, where there is little tourist pressure, great empty beaches, magnificent landscapes to walk in, and where fine castles, abbeys, gardens, historic towns and villages lie waiting to be explored. And there is often sun as well. Scandinavia and northern Europe have for many people more to offer than the overcrowded resorts of the south.

Sir John Smith, founder and trustee of the Landmark Trust, which has saved 200 buildings in Britain from destruction, now let for holiday use, says:

> Our aim is to rouse people's interest in their surroundings in the widest sense – their surroundings both in space and time. The environment is not just a film set. History is part of our environment; so is the way people live.... We hope that every day some of our many guests, as they set up house in one or other of our many places, will feel that 'here a man may, without much molestation, be thinking what he

is, whence he came, what he has done, and to what the King has called him.

(Landmark Trust Annual Report)

The problem of making such experiences available and attractive to tourists is largely one of education, as the ICOMOS Charter states. Here the tourist authorities have a big responsibility, and one which, so far, they have been unwilling to tackle.

Another way out of the problem of overcrowding is to offer substitute experiences on the lines of Disneyland in the United States, Madam Tussaud's, London (2.547 million visitors in 1990), or theme parks like Alton Towers, with fun-fairs, cascades and water splashes, overhead rides, swan boats, etc. (2.070 million visitors in 1990), or Blackpool Pleasure Beach (6.5 million visitors in 1988). Country house owners have made successful attempts to divert visitors from the main house by creating alternative occupations: the lion park and boating lake at Longleat House, Wiltshire, the butterfly house, vintage car museum and garden centre at Syon House, Birdland at Harewood, the railway, butterfly house and adventure playground at Blenheim Palace, the safari park at Windsor, and the vintage car museum at Broadlands. These have helped to relieve the houses themselves from intolerable pressure, and, equally important, they have raised revenue to keep the roof on and to carry out vital repairs. The National Trust has pioneered the creation of audio-visual displays and exhibitions, restaurants, shops, picnic sites and adventure playgrounds with the same objective.

It is surprising that the Albert Dock complex, which was saved from demolition a few years ago, in 1989 had 5.1 million visitors, compared with the British Museum, which had 4.769 million in 1990. Many of these come to see the museum of navigation or the Tate Gallery exhibits or the Harbour Master's House, rather than Jesse Hartley's magnificent dock buildings themselves.

To investigate the range of damage inflicted on the heritage by tourists, ICOMOS UK set up an expert Committee on Cultural Tourism. We have enlisted the help of English Heritage, CADW (Welsh Historic Monuments), the National Trust, the Historic Houses Association, and the Building Research Establishment, and initiated research into the rate of damage being sustained by various types of property, including historic houses, open sites, landscape and cathedrals. We organized a seminar on Tourist Wear and Tear in London in May 1989, in which some of these issues were discussed.

Although damage, some of it irreversible, is being inflicted on all heavily visited sites, there are two categories which cause particular concern, since there are few controls available and little or no payment is extracted to offset this damage. The first category is landscapes, particularly historic, created landscapes of the kind found in National Parks and uplands, which contain much of our finest scenery. Damage to footpaths, to rock and tufa surfaces, and to features such as field patterns, walls and archaeological sites is widespread and serious. The increase of recreational activities, especially walking and climbing, has inflicted deep scars on the landscape and has in many cases destroyed the qualities of wilderness which they once possessed. The treatment of these ravaged areas, by the provision of floating platforms over bogs, of steps and handrails to channel the ascents of steep hills, of stone paving to harden badly eroded paths, has been carried out in many of our National Parks including the Lake District, but is extremely expensive. Unfortunately, unlike the American National Parks, which are government property and where an entrance charge is levied, in the UK it has not been possible to make such a charge. With the exception of the National Trust, which has installed voluntary collection boxes at many of its car parks serving open countryside, no method of levying taxes or funds to repair the damage has been found. The Lake District Planning Board is introducing a new bill to offer further protection to the area, but the suggestion of a bed tax, levied on all residential tourists, has been dropped as politically unacceptable. This is unfortunate as such a tax has been successfully introduced elsewhere in Europe. If neither the tourists nor the tourist trade who bring them are prepared to pay, who will? The National Trust, which owns and maintains approximately a quarter of the Lake District, is running an appeal for £8 million to enable it to pay for the maintenance of its 400 farm buildings, and to repair damage to the landscape caused by walkers. In the case of country houses, castles and archaeological sites for which an entry charge is made, the situation is more manageable. Charges can be increased and controls exerted to limit numbers.

Cathedrals and greater churches comprise the second category causing concern. They are, historically and architecturally, among our most important buildings. They were not built for millions of visitors but for the worship of God, and they therefore lack the facilities many tourists expect, such as restaurants, toilets, car park and shops. Their fabric is particularly vulnerable and their layout makes them unsuitable for accommodating large numbers of visitors. The Deans and Chapters are unwilling to impose compulsory entry charges for the house of God, and so they are exploited by tourism and obtain wholly inadequate returns.

In 1978/9 I carried out a survey for the English Tourist Board on Cathedrals and Tourism. My brief was twofold: to investigate what provisions Deans and Chapters were making for the reception of the 20 million visitors they were then receiving, and also to observe what impact these millions were having upon the buildings. The ETB carried out a count of all visitors, and we analysed from the findings of a questionnaire the types and origins of tourists, their interests and requirements, and the amount they contributed, either through voluntary collection boxes or by compulsory payment for access to selected areas such as chapels, towers, exhibitions, etc. It emerged that the average contribution was 2p per person. It was also revealed, through surveys carried out at Canterbury, Salisbury and Winchester, that 93 per cent of visitors to Canterbury went primarily to see the cathedral, and spent £6.8 million in the city, indicating that the preservation of the cathedral is worth at least £5 million a year to the local economy; in Salisbury, tourist spending in the High Street, the main approach to the cathedral, accounted for 21 per cent of the total retail and catering trade of the city, compared with 7 per cent elsewhere, with 860 jobs being in service trades connected with tourism; and at Winchester, 138 coach parties, totalling over 7,000 tourists, visited the cathedral during eleven days in August.

As most cathedral authorities were unwilling to make a compulsory charge for entry, we advised that by introducing more prominent collecting boxes and by quantifying the amount expected from each visitor, the situation could be drastically improved, and so it was. We also recommended that coach parties should be required to book their time of arrival, and to pay. We investigated the siting and stocking of cathedral shops, and persuaded the Design Council to advise deans and chapters on the selection and design of merchandise, particularly guide books. The existence of car parks, restaurants, toilets, exhibitions and signposting was also considered. We held a conference at the Museum of London to enable the area museums services to advise cathedral authorities on the importance of introducing environmental controls and security for cathedral exhibitions and libraries.

Surveys of cathedral closes with land-use assessments were also carried out, to see how the available accommodation was being used, and to consider possible areas for shops, visitor centres, exhibitions and restaurants outside the cathedrals themselves.

Finally, I carried out a survey of damage inflicted by visitors on four of the most heavily visited buildings: Westminster Abbey, St Paul's Cathedral, Canterbury Cathedral and St George's Chapel, Windsor. I was particularly concerned with floor surfaces – grave slabs, carved ledger stones, tiles and brasses – since widespread damage was evident, important inscriptions were being obliterated and inadequate records appeared to exist. Today, ten years later, the position has changed very little. Better facilities for visitors have been introduced, more money is being extracted in return for visits, but the damage continues. With a Research Award from the Royal Institute of British Architects I carried out a further survey on cathedral damage; the final report was produced in March 1991.

As the recognition and protection of historic floors has until recently received very little attention, my surveys were intended to provide a general assessment of the historic floors in all of the most heavily visited cathedrals and greater churches, with a note of the major historic features and their condition. Recommendations were also made, wherever possible, for the immediate protection of the areas most seriously at risk from over-use.

First, all cathedral architects were written to, requesting information on damage inflicted by visitors on historic floors, especially ledger stones, brasses and decorative tiles, and also asking for details of any controls or protective measures that had been introduced. Although cathedral architects were aware of the damage being inflicted, very little had been done to control it.

At the same time, cathedral librarians were requested to send information on existing records and plans of historic floors, with details of inscriptions and armorials on ledger stones and brasses, as well as information about photographs or prints.

The results of these enquiries were extremely worrying. Many cathedrals have inadequate records of floor slabs, inscriptions, locations of ledger stones or brasses, and such records or floor plans as do exist are divided between cathedral libraries, record offices, or architects' or clerks of works' offices. Some have no records at all, and there is no overview of what exists. Without a full record of all inscriptions, including notes on the lettering, heraldry, location and condition, with an archaeological survey, supported by photographs and rubbings, all entered on a floor plan, a historical element of outstanding importance is being irrevocably lost.

The response to the surveys, which have been circulated individually to all cathedrals for comment, has been most encouraging. Several have already agreed to take some action over their historic floors. These include St Paul's, Winchester, Exeter, Canterbury, Norwich, Ely, Wells and Lincoln Cathedrals, and York Minster. At Bristol and Lichfield Cathedrals surveys were already under way, under Dr Warwick Rodwell.

Reports are now awaited from the Building Research Establishment on various aspects of historic floor protection. The Establishment has inserted studs to monitor the rate of deterioration in sample floor areas in Canterbury and St Paul's Cathedrals and Westminster Abbey. The Building Research Establishment has also been asked to advise on protective pads for chairs and moveable furniture, to avoid scratching, methods of moving stands and chairs for special events without damage to floor surfaces, guidelines for protective covering for areas of special historic significance, and types of matting for extracting dust and grit from visitors' feet at entrances.

The Care of Cathedrals Measure (1991) requires each cathedral to compile an inventory of all furnishings, books, manuscripts, plate and other treasures within five years. Historic floors are now to be regarded as a necessary component of these inventories. Sales and thefts, such as happened with four medieval tiles from Winchester Cathedral, should thus be avoided. Thefts are becoming increasingly frequent and while some of the objects are stolen by tourists as souvenirs, many more are stolen professionally and find their way into the sale rooms.

The promise of government grants worth £11 million for cathedrals should help to remove the temptation to sell treasures in order to pay for necessary repairs. The inventories will give much-needed protection to the treasures with which many cathedrals are still endowed.

Arising from the surveys two initiatives are now under way. Cathedral Recording Teams are being set up, under the Surveyor to the Fabric and with my help, to record all inscriptions and armorials on ledger stones and brasses, with condition reports. Their positions will be entered on floor plans, photographs and rubbings will be taken and the records will be deposited in the cathedral libraries and with the Cathedrals Fabric Commission. Surveys have already started at Exeter and Canterbury Cathedrals, and Westminster Abbey. Other teams will be set up wherever possible. These surveys, which will be based on the methods used by the Church Recorders, should in their turn provide some of the data necessary to help make decisions over controls, repairs and the conservation of historic floor surfaces.

Second, the Dean and Chapter of York Minster, the Cathedrals Fabric Commission and ICOMOS UK have set up a working group of experts, including representatives from the Building Research Establishment, the Royal Commission on Historical Monuments and the York Centre for Conservation Studies, to establish guidelines for the recording and treatment of historic cathedral floors. Using York Minster as an example, methods of recording, recutting, reordering and protecting important ledgers, brasses and tiles will be investigated and guidelines circulated to all cathedrals.

It is clear that widespread damage is being inflicted to monuments, floors and other parts of the fabric. It is also clear that, hard as the cathedral authorities sometimes find it to accept, the majority of those inflicting the damage have little interest in the cathedral as the house of God; they often have no interest in the architecture; and they are, in many cases, destroying for each other whatever experience they might have expected by sheer noise and weight of numbers. It is hoped that these initiatives will help cathedrals to find some solutions to a very difficult problem.

To celebrate European Year of Tourism 1990, ICOMOS UK organized a conference on Heritage and Tourism, based at Canterbury, in an attempt to create a dialogue between conservationists, struggling to preserve the heritage, and the tourist authorities, using it as their principle promotion material. The time is long past when the interdependence of heritage and tourism can be ignored. Tourism needs the heritage as a key to draw the crowds. The heritage needs the support of tourism to finance its maintenance. The ICOMOS Charter recognizes the potential of cultural tourism. It is, however, also essential to determine the capacity of individual monuments and sites to accommodate tourists, to agree on measures to prevent the infliction of irreversible damage, to prevent the negation of experience which results from over-use, and to enhance the enjoyment and understanding of the visitor's experience.

These are complex issues. Often those promoting cultural tourism disregard its impact on the heritage and those attempting to conserve the heritage receive no benefit, and often little consideration, from tourism. A dialogue is therefore essential between representatives of heritage and tourism organizations.

Using Canterbury Cathedral – a World Heritage site – as a case study, the conference made comparisons with Notre-Dame, Paris, and Cologne Cathedral. The likely effects of the Channel Tunnel and the Single European Act on tourism in the 1990s on these cathedrals and on other outstanding monuments and sites were examined. All European governments, and many regional authorities, are promoting tourism, and regard the heritage as an important attraction. In a recent debate in the House of Lords, Britain's heritage was identified as the single most important aspect of its overseas appeal. Of the £19.4 billion earned from tourism in the UK in 1989 (£8.5 billion from foreign visitors and £10.9 billion from UK residents), £171 million was spent on visiting historic properties in the UK; under £11 million was donated to cathedrals.

Methods of controlling the physical impact of tourists on sites were considered, and ways in which the European tourist authorities and industry could help to mitigate the damage, both by contributing towards the costs of maintenance, by advising on controls, and by guiding tourists towards lesser-visited sites rather than by promoting those under greatest pressure.

In September 1990 the secretary of State for Employment, Michael Howard, set up a Task Force to examine the present state of tourism in England, and its effect on the environment. Under the Task Force, which was composed of experts in tourism and environmentalists, three working groups were established to examine the position with regard to: Historic Sites, under the chairmanship of Angus Stirling, Director General, the National Trust; Historic Towns, under Lady Cobham of Ragley Hall; and Landscapes, under Michael Dower, Director of the Countryside Commission. I was a member of the first two groups.

While the initiative was potentially valuable, the time allocated for the preparation of reports (two to three months) was wholly inadequate. The consultants commissioned to carry out case studies, Pieda Tourism and Leisure, were forced to rely on outdated material, owing to the time-scale imposed and the lack of available research. Furthermore, their expertise lies in tourism rather than heritage matters, and the balance was therefore unsatisfactory. In addition to this, the working groups were not permitted to make recommendations over grants and finance, on which the future of the heritage depends.

The report, launched on 1 May 1991 and entitled *Tourism and the Environment: Maintaining the Balance,* marked an advance in public recognition of the fact that the determined promotion of tourism, to which both central and local government are committed, poses increasingly serious threats to the environment, and particularly to the heritage, on which tourism so greatly depends.

It is hoped that further research will be undertaken, and more initiatives promoted, both nationally and internationally, to determine the amount of damage being sustained by heritage sites through misuse, and to resolve methods for control of the massive overuse to which all the world's outstanding sites are now subjected. Only in this way can the anarchic growth of tourism be prevented.

Unless we can control the haphazard use of the heritage for tourism purposes, the warnings of the ICOMOS Charter may indeed become a reality, to the detriment of tourism and to the infinite loss of outstanding elements of our historic past. We cannot allow this to occur. There is no future in destroying this beautiful world for the sake of a little transitory pleasure. The heritage is a priceless treasure; it cannot be traded in for profit.

NOTE

This article is based in part on a study paper produced for the Royal Institute of Chartered Surveyors' Diploma course in Building Conservation.

REFERENCE

ICOMOS (1976) *Charter on Cultural Tourism,* Paris: International Council on Monuments and Sites.

SECTION 5.2

Appreciation of architecture

People seem to have a need for liking buildings, for understanding them and for relating to them symbiotically; they find it increasingly difficult to do so in the fragmented, alienating world of the modern city.

However, considerable advances have been made in our knowledge of how the human psyche works, of how society functions and, coupled with a fresh understanding of the need to exist in a balanced relationship with nature, one must remain hopeful that we are once more approaching an era where architecture will be the visible manifestation of what is best in our civilization.

The ten essays in this chapter explore different aspects of the aesthetic and ethical questions underlying the current architectural debate. The authors, drawn from the fields of environmental psychology, philosophy, art history, architectural practice, criticism, teaching and illustration, have been asked to address specific issues relating to perception, evaluation and communication as these are revealed through the medium of architecture. Their findings, individually and collectively, provide many insights into this complex facet of human culture as well as giving sensible pointers to future action.

The inclusion amongst these of a piece from the nineteenth-century critic and writer John Ruskin, under the title 'The enjoyment of architecture', requires some explanation. Rather than getting two authors to write separately on the pleasures of the architectural experience – one from the perspective of the user, another from that of the creator (very few people nowadays seem able to span these two domains articulately) – it was decided to opt for a historic figure whose work not only had broad public appeal in his day, but whose words still have the power to move. Ruskin was an obvious choice.

Although he himself was, rightly, suspicious of the capacity of words and drawings to convey the essential equalities of the physical experience of a building, John Ruskin has yet to find a match as a champion of the cause of architecture as an art form. This extract from his description of St Mark's, Venice – a building he loved deeply – seems to bring all his many talents (and some shortcomings) as a critic of architecture into focus: the absolute belief in the nobility of the architectural act; the unique fusion of poetic sensitivity and analytical deduction skills; the humility when faced with superior creative powers; the uncompromising commitment to architecture as both a spiritual and a sensual experience; and the intolerance of those who did not appreciate such qualities. These memorable passages are not only timeless in themselves, they are also a timely reminder of the potential of great buildings to transcend the boundaries of time and culture.

H.L.

RECOMMENDED READING

Arnheim, R. (1977) *The Dynamics of Architectural Form*, Berkeley: University of California Press.

Attoe, W. (1978) *Architectural and Critical Imagination*, Chichester: John Wiley.

Bonta, J.P. (1979) *Architecture and its Interpretation: A Study of Expressive Systems in Architecture*, London: Lund Humphries.

Collins, P. (1971) *Architectural Judgement*, London: Faber.

Colquhoun, A. (1981) *Essays in Architectural Criticism; Modern Architecture and Historical Change*, Cambridge, Mass.: MIT Press.

Gombrich, E.H. (1984) *The Sense of Order: A Study in the Psychology of Decorative Art*, 2nd edn, Oxford: Phaidon.

Hersey, G. (1988) *The Lost Meaning of Classical Architecture: Speculations on Ornament from Vitruvius to Venturi*, London: MIT Press.

Huxtable, A.L. (1988) *Kicked a Building Lately?*, Berkeley: University of California Press.

Mercer, C. (1976) *Living in Cities: Psychology and the Urban Environment*, Harmondsworth: Penguin.

Oliver, P. (ed.) (1975) *Sign, Shelter and Symbol*, London: Barrie & Jenkins.

Rasmussen, S.E. (1962) *Experiencing Architecture*, 2nd edn, Cambridge, Mass.: MIT Press.

Rowe, C. (1982) *The Mathematics of the Ideal Villa and Other Essays*, London: MIT Press.

Scott, G. (1980) *The Architecture of Humanism*, London: Architectural Press.

Scruton, R. (1979) *The Aesthetics of Architecture*, London: Methuen.

Unrau, J. (1978) *Looking at Architecture with Ruskin*, London: Thames & Hudson.

Watkin, D. (1977) *Morality and Architecture*, Oxford: Oxford University Press.

81 Personal aspects of the architectural experience

David Canter

Any art-form suffers from the central conundrum of how a personal vision can be so expressed that it communicates to an audience with whom the artist may have no direct contact. Somehow the artist must harness arrogance or confidence to reach out from a private set of experiences to make contact in some public form. Architects have an even greater problem in that their creations gain their meanings from the activities that are housed within those creations. An architectural form can never be dealt with solely as multi-storey sculpture. We may be impressed by the scale of an aircraft hangar but it will not have the same significance as a space of the same size that we know to be a cathedral built to the glory of God.

The great conceit of the International Style and its followers was that buildings could be shaped in simple response to the mechanics of their construction. Amongst the many confusions and paradoxes of the argument espoused by Le Corbusier, then even more strongly by Mies van der Rohe and Oscar Niemeyer, was that the structural properties of materials held all the significance out of which designers could craft their buildings. So, although there were some genuflections in the direction of identifying activities for which buildings were to be repositories, the central mood that character-ized 'modern architecture' for most of the twentieth century was that the building form should derive its meanings solely from within the structural and mechan-ical requirements needed to create the edifice. Reference to other forms and structures, derivation of significance beyond this limited kind of architectural 'function', was considered decadent and immoral.

Yet the conundrum of artistic expression can only be resolved by cross-reference to experiences shared between an artist and his or her audience. These refer-ences may be to common aspects of the human con-dition, fear of mortality, the solace of others and the like, or they may be less profound references to socially recognized aspects of shared experience, such as the way power or humility are represented. For architects these references inevitably draw upon the many and varied experiences of buildings and landscapes that are common across and within any society. Paradoxically, in their desire to create a brave, new, democratic, unadul-terated architecture derived from rational, logical anal-ysis of the problems of building construction, followers of the Modern Movement in fact distanced themselves from their users by creating a whole approach to design that grew out of conversations between designers. They deliberately ignored traditions and their vocabularies which would have provided the cross-references to allow effective communication with the full range of people who experience their buildings.

The parallels in other art-forms of an abstract, esoteric approach, eschewed by a general public and strongly inbred, were apparent when the manifestos of modern, twentieth-century architecture were being written. Yet beyond the claims of modernism in painting or music which undoubtedly liberated art and opened up new forms of artistic experience to a wide audience, for those artists who wished to operate within the realms of architecture, the Modern Movement, far from being democratic, actually provided architects with an oppor-tunity to lay a firm claim to control all aspects of building design. The development of mass building techniques, and the flexibility of the new materials, presented the opportunity for people outside the archi-tectural profession to mimic the past in a relatively superficial way, thereby reducing the need for any involvement by a qualified architect. But the radical break with tradition produced by 'modern architecture' gave a prospect for architects to keep tight hold of the reins to a degree that had never been possible before those 'modern' buildings were assigned to them.

The dominance of this approach to design became so total that its central tenets were clearly revealed to be fatally flawed. Not only was a generation of buildings produced that were universally disliked by all except those initiated into the esoteric rites of Modernism, but far from being pure and functionally logical, what emerged was a new, impoverished vocabulary. Apart-ment blocks, offices, schools, hospitals, airport ter-minals, all could be immediately recognized as such, no matter to what culture, climate or details of use they were meant to relate. Eventually this led to modern architecture inadvertently communicating with the broad audience that experienced it, and at last people were able to say that now they understood this art they did not like it. Unfortunately, it is difficult to dispose of this legacy and both the stalwart and whimsical attempts at Post-Modern architecture still act within the confused rhetoric of the International Style.

The confusion is based upon a mixture of approaches to determining the quality of a work of architecture. How is a building to be judged good or bad? What makes any place deserve to be regarded as highly evaluated? There have always been two frameworks for approaching this question, grounded in fundamentally different epistemologies. Traditionally, when all architectural design had its roots in forms that had gone before and evolved organically in relation to known uses, structural solutions and decorative details, buildings were evaluated on the basis of the reactions of those who experienced them. Those reactions were shaped by what were the accepted forms, but none the less the reactions of appropriately sensitive people could be taken as the basis for judging how good or bad a building was. It was because of this that architecture could take its place within the sisterhood of arts.

Implicit within the essentially empirical approach to architecture was a belief that there were principles that could be drawn upon to describe and defend good architecture, but the relationship between empirical experience and abstract principles was a close one. Twentieth-century architecture changed that. A new set of principles were espoused that grew directly out of the acts of architecture and were seen to have a pure abstraction independent of human experience. Le Corbusier's modular was an abstract scale against which to measure buildings, not a vision of design that integrated human actions and aspirations. The struggle of environmental social scientists and other architectural theorists, since the late 1960s, has been to relate the experience of places once again to the abstractions of building layout and form and, in so doing, to enable architecture once again to take its place amid the communicative arts.

With the changing social framework of post-Second World War urban development the attempt to rediscover the way into an architecture that has meaning could now draw directly upon the old verities that the Victorians took for granted. But there was one aspect of the Victorian tradition which did offer a route into a more empirically sound exploration of architecture. This was the idea that a location could in some senses come alive, be recognized as a 'place'.

The sense of place has reappeared in many guises throughout the history of human considerations of the physical setting. The specification in the Bible of a 'Holy of Holies', a place so special that only the high priest could enter it, is a reflection that is found in all cultures of the notion of particular locations being sacred. In present-day societies, even beyond the preservation of the idea in religious buildings, many parallels can be found in which particular places are inbred with heightened emotional meaning. It may be the managing director's office, or the football pitch in front of the home team's goal. The stage of a major opera house or even the operating theatre of a hospital are also likely to generate feelings not far removed from those that anthropologists would recognize as awe at the sanctity of the place.

These extreme reactions serve to illustrate the more general association of locations with a variety of meanings. They also serve to indicate that the significance of a place is enshrined neither in its particular physical form, nor in the particular people who experience it, but rather in an interplay between these two. Indeed, the operating theatre may seem like just another work-place to the surgeon who has spent his or her life working in such settings, and the managing director's office may feel rather humdrum to its occupant, although both these places may strike fear into the casual visitor.

This identification of the meaning of places with those who experience them causes especial difficulties for communications between social scientists and designers. In the extreme position, environmental psychologists may take the stand that reactions to buildings are so dependent on the particular people whose reactions are being considered, and their particular purposes or activities in those locations, that beyond the physical limits of physiological and mechanical endurance any piece of architecture can have any significance, and consequently be evaluated well or badly. With such an extreme perspective it is understandable that some architects may dismiss social science as irrelevant and users as requiring education, and proceed to produce buildings with which other architects can empathize but not necessarily their users.

Even those architects who still wish to respond to the personal experience of those who will live and work in their creations may express dismay at the strongly psychological perspective, complaining that until their buildings are occupied they cannot know exactly who the users or their particular perspectives will be. So how can their idiosyncrasies be taken into account?

One solution to this dilemma has been a number of attempts to equate the principles for design with universal human reactions. Within this framework, for example, long, wide avenues punctuated with large statues and arches, or massive pyramids, or small, dusky interiors, or complex, multi-coloured façades are all believed to have an incontrovertible and profound impact upon the human psyche. Good and especially great architecture, it is agreed, is so successful because of its contact with primordial human reactions. It would follow that architects would only need to master these archetypes to be sure of success.

Unfortunately there are many problems with this argument. How are we to recognize such universals? By their universality? But this would mean that everything that is common in design has, by definition, profound significance! Commonality could just as readily be an artefact of construction possibilities and the limits of mechanics or mathematics, essentially superficial in any psychological sense.

The other major difficulty with the quest for universal archetypes is the very obvious cultural diversity of building forms. The response that there are architectural forms that have a particular salience within a culture, rather than strengthening the ideal of universals, actually challenges the assumption that they draw upon fundamental, primordial aspects of human transactions with places. Instead they point to the need to understand the ways buildings gain their significance through historical, social and psychological processes.

The problem is that, by putting the reactions to architecture back into the realm of cultural perspectives, the prospect of essentially arbitrary reactions to building forms, depending on who is experiencing them where and when, once again looms. The possibilities of socio-cultural paradigms, within which designers can operate, is less anarchic than the strongly individualistic models that some psychologists may propose, whereby the environment is housed within people rather than outside them, but it still begs the question of whether those socio-culturally based reactions do have any basis in fundamental aspects of human experience of places, or whether the physical forms do have some special properties or characteristics that are consistently relevant to the meanings assigned to these creations.

It seems to me that the answer to this question of identifying the consistent psychological significance of built forms, and probably non-built forms as well, must derive from an understanding of the interplay between what is being created and what is being experienced: in other words, the complex overlay of communications that are interchanged between those involved in giving shape to the physical surroundings and those involved in experiencing them. This interchange unfolds around the identification and creation of settings for action and experience – more generally, the making of places.

If a place is regarded as a multi-model interface between those who have contributed to its identification or creation, or both, and those who experience it, then a number of consequences follow for the personal aspect of architecture. But before turning to these it is interesting to note that for the *natural* environment the identification of places takes on a role that is akin to the creative role in built environments. Further, those settings in which people are both creators and users draw upon rather special processes because of the strength of the feedback between the processes of creation and experience. It may well be that a close examination of intensely personal places will illuminate the more general personal aspects that are the focus of this essay.

But let us return to the physical aspects of place that may have universal significance because of their connection to fundamental processes in the experience of places. These aspects are seen as contributing integrally to the meaning of places, because they have roots in the thesis that people inevitably define locations, at points in time, as having a particular set of characteristics and as being suitable for particular actions. This 'theory of place' proposes that there is, therefore, no such thing as an indeterminate 'place'. There may be ambiguous ones, which have varying meanings for various people or which are difficult to interpret, but places are never meaningless.

The theory assumes that there is a constant drive to give places ever more structure and clearer definition, but that this is constantly changing by the very process of acting on places. The action modifies the meaning, which in turn leads to modified action and so on, in the form of a classical dialectic, out of which people from Hegel and beyond have seen change evolving. The design question is, therefore, what are the aspects of physical form that contribute to the definition of places? A set of seven aspects seems to be indicated from many different studies, providing, in effect, a research agenda for developing the architectural implications of a theory of place.

The first and possibly primary aspects are likely to be those that contribute directly to the definition and identification of places. In identifying, bounding, or distinguishing places some indication is inevitably given of what sorts of places they are, and some framework provided within which human experience can take shape. These issues are also therefore to do with the relationships between places. Their identification requires that they be distinguished from one another. Relative properties in context are therefore likely to be more important than any idiosyncratic qualities of the place itself. Distinctness and processes of definition are primary.

1   How is a place separated from others? The idea of boundaries comes in here, but also the very particular significance that the boundaries carry. Are they natural, artificially made with effort, clearly modifiable? What information do the boundaries carry about the distinctness of the area they help to define. How permeable are they? Do they facilitate the interplay of places by visual, acoustic or mechanical means? Or do they separate a setting totally?

2   The second aspect derives from the contact between places: the mode of entrance to a place. How does it give meaning to the setting and the behaviour within it? How distinct is it? What degree of control of permeability does it allow?

3   A third aspect grows out of these first two, emphasizing interpenetration. Contiguous places and their relationships to each other also help to define their neighbours. The forms of articulation between places are therefore important to understand. Open-plan or closed segments thus can be seen as aspects of fundamental psychological significance, not merely relevant to administrative flexibility.

4   Often physical constraints on the connections between places coalesce into a series of experiences that recognizably forms a path. This fourth aspect introduces a strongly dynamic quality into consideration of places and their properties. These defini-

tions of places that come from their relationships also draw attention to more specific qualities of a setting. These are qualities that are aspects of the way the setting would be described itself, although their implications will be modified by the context.

5   A fifth consideration, then, is *scale*; size, height, distance from various key locations are all relevant. The psychological implications here are not solely about relationships to the size of the human frame but also about the resources and isolation that are implicit in large buildings or long distances. At the other end of the scale are aspects long recognized to be associated with intimacy and privacy.

6   There is the thorny question of materials too. A sixth aspect relates to how they carry significance. There are strong cultural processes here relating to technologies, human resources and historical associations, easily forgotten by those who focus entirely on the structural or abstract visual properties of materials. It should not be forgotten that aluminium was once regarded more highly than gold before new industrial processes made it widely available.

7   Finally there are issues of mass and form. These come last, because they take their meaning so much from what is around them. Squares, circles, complex or simple and so on, carry implications, but this issue is a product of what it is part of. Attempts to use forms as mere abstractions are doomed to failure because they will always mean something. Circular windows are rare and likely to be thought of as portholes. Such aspects derive their implications from the context as much as form any associations the forms take themselves.

Set against these variations in the relative attributes of places are the variations in the people who experience them and the actions and purposes that are central to their experiences. In the past, architectural theorists, whether practitioners or not, tend to have emphasized what were referred to earlier as 'sacred' objectives, uplifting, enriching qualities of environments. This is only a small part of the picture. Many objectives are 'profane' in the sense that they are a search for comfort or space in which to carry out an activity rather than any transcendental experience. The majority are probably between these two poles. Wherever these objectives are placed they will be part of the reasons a person has for being in that place. These reasons are almost invariably socially defined. In other words, a person's expectations and aspirations derive from the interpersonal nexus within which they exist. One of the more obvious labels for this nexus is 'role'. It may be organizational or social, but more generally the design interest is in relation to the physical, contextual implications for that role, which may be summarized as 'environmental role'.

This perspective eschews the search for highly personal, individual differences between people when they experience an environment. Broad groupings of similar reactions are predicted for people whose relationship to a place are similar. Differences are only predicted when the central purposes are different. This accords with some rather unusual findings that, for example, prison officers and prisoners react to their prisons in rather similar ways, agreeing on the differences between those prisons. They have a shared set of purposes within those places, otherwise there would be a riot. In contrast, older people and younger people are often found to think about and deal with public parks in very different ways. To these different groups these places are very different, being used for quite different purposes. The design task is to identify the major types of user and shape the place to take account of the perspectives that each will bring to the place.

Putting the aspects of physical characteristics together with the environmental role differences suggests a matrix, or network, of questions about the significance and implications of various aspects of locations to various groups. Complex as the completion of such a two-dimensional matrix is, it still leaves unexplored a third dimension. This is the characteristics that are taken as salient in considering reactions to aspects of places. Here again, the most appropriately wide continuum may well be from aspects of personal experience that may be labelled sacred through to those that are profane. The particular quality they take on, though, is likely to derive from the role of the people. For example, to the physician sterility and ease of use may give an operating theatre its almost sacred qualities, whereas to a patient its impenetrability may make it a place filled with horror. The potential complexity here may turn out to be simpler in practice because of the links between roles and salient reactions. Indeed, it may even be possible to classify roles in terms of their characteristic reactions.

One group of people whose salient reactions are undoubtedly distinct from most others are those who are responsible for creating and shaping places. Their environmental roles are clearly distinct. Yet no role group acts in isolation. Society consists of transactions between people who have different roles. These transactions can lead to changes in perspectives, but they are often also modified by power relationships. In a sense, then, the move from a reliance on *ex cathedra* principles to empirically derived accounts of the experiences of places is a step towards the democratization of design. An objective that Le Corbusier would have endorsed.

FURTHER READING

Canter, D., Krampen, D. and Stea, D. (eds) (1988) *Environmental Perspectives*, Aldershot: Avebury.

Girourard, M. (1990) *The English Town*, New Haven: Yale University Press.

82 Concepts of beauty in architecture

William Charlton

Those who find little to please them in modern architecture sometimes put the blame on the lack of agreement in our society about what architects should aim at and what constitutes architectural beauty. In what follows I shall first point out that a diversity in concepts of beauty is not a peculiarity of modern times but characterizes the whole history of architecture. I shall then ask to what extent it is inevitable and whether it should be deplored or, rather, welcomed.

Several of the greatest classical Greek architects wrote treatises on architecture (see Tatarkiewicz 1970: 48–51, 270–9), and although the texts have not survived it is clear that they located beauty in what they called *summetria*, a word usually translated as 'proportion'. A building will be successful, they thought, if the parts stand in simple arithmetical proportions to each other and to the whole, and especially if there is one magnitude, say half the width of the base of a column, of which all the others are simple multiples. This idea is developed in Vitruvius and remains dominant among professionals at least until the early Byzantine period. But other ideas can be found in writers who are not themselves builders. It was probably an ancient and widely held popular assumption that beauty consists in functional adaptation. This is formulated as an aesthetic theory by Plato (in *Hippias Major* 295) and Xenophon (in *Memorabilia* III. x) and applied by the latter specifically to architecture (in *Memorabilia* III. viii). It might seem at first that the almost equally ancient notion that beauty in art consists in accurate representation could not be applied to architecture. Plato, however, was able to apply it to craftsmanship generally by saying that a craftsman making a bed or a shuttle is trying to make a likeness in perceptible materials of an ideal bed or shuttle apprehended by intellectual intuition (see *Republic* X. 597; *Cratylus* 389). Plotinus, a theorist whose influence on medieval aesthetics has still to be properly measured, not only upholds this theory (in *Enneads* V. viii. 1; I. vi. 2) but also introduces life and illumination as elements in beauty (in *Enneads* VI. vii. 22). Finally it is not without significance that architects in late antiquity were known as engineers;[1] as Gervase Mathew has emphasized, the achievements of men like Anthemius, the architect of Hagia Sophia, were particularly admired for their technical daring (Mathew 1963: 62).

Plato's dialogues show that even in classical Greece gold was thought to be capable of making things beautiful (see, for example, *Hippias Major* 289f). Perhaps partly as a result of the Christianization of Europe and its fertilization by Jewish culture, both in the Byzantine Empire and in Western Europe throughout the middle ages beauty was thought to be imparted to buildings by rich ornamentation in precious metals and precious stones. Isidore of Seville (*c.*570–636) says that *venustas*, pleasantness or charm, in architecture is 'whatever is added to the buildings for the sake of ornament and beauty (*decor*) such as gilded ceilings, precious marble panels and coloured pictures' (pp. 672–5). Suger of St Denis (1081–1151) praises 'the multicoloured beauty of the gems' in his church (Suger, cited in Tatarkiewicz 1970: II, 175).

In medieval thinking, however, gold, jewels and bright colours were never the sole constituents of architectural beauty. It is clear that many architects valued mathematical proportions, especially designs based on the square roots of 2 and 3, and the golden section, for their own sake. Some also used numbers (3, 7, 9, 365, etc.) for the sake of their symbolic meaning. Philosophical theorists held that a thing will be beautiful if its form or essential nature 'shines out' and is evident to 'sight in the service of reason' (Aquinas 1266–73: Ia IIae 27.1 ad 3). For a building, that means that its function and suitability for that function must be manifest. Terms like 'proportion' are in fact a little confusingly employed, not only for mathematical proportions but also for proportion of means to end or part to function.

We find the same multiplicity in post-medieval thinking. Renaissance architects thought that beauty consists primarily in mathematical proportions. According to Alberti, 'The whole force and rule of design consists in a right and exact adapting and joining together of the lines and angles which compose the face of the building (Alberti 1485, vol. I: i). It is a harmonious set of proportions here which constitutes beauty (ibid., vol. VI: ii). Alberti, however, allows value to ornament as something distinct from beauty so defined: ornament is 'a kind of an auxiliary brightness and improvement to beauty.... Beauty is something lovely which is proper and innate ... and ornament something added or fastened on.' Similarly Ripa (1593) distinguishes beauty, which consists in proportion, from *venustas* as 'a condiment of beauty' (quoted in Tatarkiewicz 1970: III, 230). Palladio, while himself brilliantly exploiting the potentialities of the golden section ratio, also saw geometrical forms as symbolic: the circle is the form most fit to show 'the unity and infinity, the uniformity and the justice of God' (Palladio 1570, Book IV: ii).

The pre-eminence of mathematical proportion in architectural aesthetics was broken only in the eighteenth century, and then largely by philosophers.

Hutcheson and Wolff, writing in 1725 and 1732 respectively, defined beauty in terms of the response of the beholder: an object is beautiful if it causes feelings of pleasure in those, or the most discriminating of those, who contemplate it. This was a revolutionary idea. Whereas formerly it had been supposed that beautiful things please because they are beautiful, it was now claimed that they are beautiful because they please. Beauty is no longer a reason for delight; it is constituted by it. The point was emphasized by Hume in 1739: 'Pleasure and pain are not only necessary attendants of beauty and deformity but constitute their very essence' (Hume 1888: 299). Not that it is improper to ask what properties in an object do in fact cause pleasure; on the contrary, that is precisely the business of aesthetics, which writers like Hutcheson and Burke conceived as a branch of empirical science. But the relation between these qualities and pleasure or distaste is purely causal, like that between various kinds of food and health and sickness.

What qualities in a building, then, are pleasure-causing? Hutcheson and Wolff seem to have thought they were those proportions which architects had imagined to be intrinsically beautiful. Wolff says a building is perfect if in its construction 'all things agree with the rules of architecture' (Wolff 1732: s.512).[2] Hume, in contrast, lays emphasis on functional adaptation, or what Hogarth (who followed him in his 1753 *Analysis of Beauty*: Ch. XI) calls 'fitness'. 'That shape which produces strength is beautiful in one animal, and that which is a sign of agility in another' (Hume 1888: 299).

> A man who shows us any house or building takes particular care among other things to point out the convenience of the apartments, the advantages of their situation, and the little room lost in the stairs, antechambers and passages; and indeed 'tis evident the chief part of the beauty consists in these particulars.[3]
>
> (Hume 1888: 363–4)

These remarks might be used to illustrate the medieval theory that beauty is manifestation of essential nature, but it is important to recognize that the thinking behind them is very different. Hume believed that a building's convenience arouses in us by association of ideas the thought of the comfort and happiness of the owner, and this in turn through sympathy causes pleasure in us.

Burke, in his *Philosophical Enquiry into the Original of our Ideas of the Sublime and the Beautiful* (1757), argued against both proportion and fitness. Eighteenth-century aestheticians tended to polarize all varieties of aesthetic merit into beauty and sublimity. Burke defined beauty as 'those qualities which cause love, or some passion similar to it' (Burke 1757: III, i). These he discovered (by a line of thought which might displease present-day feminists) to be smallness, smoothness, gradual varia-

tion and delicacy: qualities not very prominent or even common in architecture. In Burke's opinion architects should and often do aim rather at sublimity than at beauty. Though Kant disagreed with much that Burke said about the sublime and the beautiful he had sympathy with this particular conclusion. No building can be truly beautiful but (if travellers' tales may be believed) the pyramids and St Peter's at Rome have some claim to be called 'sublime' (Kant 1790: s.26).

Ruskin was still writing in the tradition of Burke and Kant when he distinguished beauty in architecture from power. 'The powerful', he says, 'comes from the human mind' whereas beauty 'is imitated from natural forms' such as those of leaves and shells (Ruskin 1849: III. iii). But by 1849 these ideas were old-fashioned; Hegel's voluminous lectures on aesthetics had given a new direction to European thinking. According to Hegel, architecture is the first form in which the Absolute presents itself artistically, and as such it is, and must always remain, essentially symbolic: symbolizing the Absolute, or ultimate reality, is the most architects can ever aspire to (Hegel 1842–1928, Vol. III: i). Hegel's theory rests on an untrustworthy substructure of imperfect historical knowledge and questionable metaphysics, but Pugin contrived to require architecture to be symbolic while maintaining that 'the great test of architectural beauty is the fitness of the design for the purpose for which it was intended' (Pugin 1836: 1). For he held that the purpose of all the details of a Greek temple or Gothic church is to carry 'a mystical import' and serve as 'emblems of the philosophy and mythology' of the nations responsible for them.

Twentieth-century thinking preserves the pluralism of earlier ages. Le Corbusier (1923) desired that buildings should manifest the economy and efficiency with which they meet the needs of their users; Eric Gill (1933) that they should embody the conception of ultimate reality of the whole society in which they are produced; and many architectural theorists locate beauty in a purely formal organization of volumes or spaces, though few now repose much faith in mathematical formulae as a guide to success. Aestheticians in this century have mostly followed Hume more closely in defining beauty in terms of the beholder's state of mind than in enquiring what properties of objects give rise to this state. Many, however, would agree with C.K. Ogden, I.A. Richards and James Wood (Ogden *et al.* 1922: 21, 72–9) that anything is beautiful which conduces to a complex state of attention in which a variety of emotions are not merely sustained but systematized into a condition of harmonious equilibrium; and that would fit almost any theory of architecture that puts emphasis on form or symbolism.

W.B. Gallie has advanced the thesis that the concept of art is what he calls an 'essentially contested concept' (Gallie 1964, ch. 8). Different schools or groups, he says, have competing ideas of what art should be. There is no way of settling the dispute between them, even though all join in acknowledging certain paradigms of artistic success in the past, since each group will claim it contains the true heirs of the authentic tradition. But the existence of the competition is in general beneficial to art; indeed, its vitality is better preserved by it than it would be by the acknowledged victory of any one school. Gallie does not refer specifically to architecture, but the historical review I have just offered might suggest that it is an art to which the notion of an essentially contested concept is particularly applicable.

But before we adopt Gallie's analysis we should consider if we are not drawn to it partly through having been brought up to believe that competitive team games are essential to character-formation and that competition in the economic sphere maximizes happiness for everyone. Societies have surely produced excellent art and architecture where there has been a single un-challenged tradition. A tradition does not need to have its fundamental assumptions and standards constantly under attack in order to remain living and vigorous. Moreover, the principal positive conceptions we have seen of architectural beauty are not mutually exclusive. A building can have mathematical proportions, and symbolism, and functional adaptation. Even the idea that it should be a perceptible copy of an ideal known by intellectual intuition, though it may be philosophically far-fetched, is consistent with other concepts: the ideal could be superlatively well-proportioned mathematically, superlatively fit and so forth. Conflict is inevitable only between those who maintain that certain mathematical proportions in themselves make for beauty and those who, like Burke, deny this.

In recent years Burke has acquired some redoubtable allies, notably Harold Osborne (1952), Roger Scruton (1979) and Mary Mothersill (1984). I do not, however, find their arguments decisive: some rest on philosophical mistakes about experience or evaluation generally, others fail to take into account the peculiar character of our experience of architecture.

Mary Mothersill considers proportions like the golden section ratio in the context of a discussion about whether there can be rules for producing beauty. She tells us that her garage has golden section proportions but is still not aesthetically pleasing. The assumption underlying this piece of autobiography must be that a proportion can constitute an aesthetic merit only if it is by itself sufficient to make what incorporates it an aesthetic success. But when we are judging a course of action by moral, as distinct from aesthetic, criteria we often think that a circumstance makes it good or bad in some specific way, courageous, say, or generous, or unfair or harmful to a friend, yet still remain unsure whether or not the course ought, all things considered, to be pursued. Something can count for or against a course; it can make the course good or bad *pro tanto* or, so far as it goes, without making it good or bad absol-

utely. Similarly, something can be a genuine merit or fault in a building without making it on balance successful or unsuccessful. What a medieval or Renaissance architect would claim for certain proportions is that they make a building *pro tanto* pleasing.

Osborne, at least for much of his life, accepted the so-called 'sense-data' theory of perceptual experience, according to which our senses give us access not to material objects but only to 'impressions' or 'appearances', which depend for their existence and qualities on the person perceiving. He reasoned that even if an architect gives certain proportions to a structure of stones or bricks, that is not what we see, and thanks to various kinds of optical distortion, the 'appearances' we do see will not have the same proportions. Clearly this argument collapses if, as most philosophers would now agree, this theory of perception is false and we see material objects.

Roger Scruton allows that we can be pleased by the proportions of a façade seen from a suitable viewpoint, but questions if we can be sure of the proportions of three-dimensional interiors, especially as we may not have access to the best positions for judging. He also reminds us that people often get pleasure from buildings which in fact contain golden section proportions without having any idea that those proportions are present. I think he underestimates our skill in perceiving three-dimensional shapes. Even when the top of an object is tilted away from our line of vision we are usually aware of it straight off, without any doubt or conjecture, as round or oval, square or oblong. But more important, he overlooks the fact that much of our visual experience is (in the ordinary as distinct from the Freudian sense) unconscious. Most of our activities – driving, cooking, academic study, even conversation – require us to use our eyes, but we are not consciously aware all the time of all the things we keep under observation.

The buildings the architecture of which is most important to us are those in which we live and work. Our eyes play over these buildings for years; unconsciously as well as consciously we get to know them well. It should be conceded to the critics of proportion that we are not often consciously aware of architectural proportions. Consciously we are more likely to be aware of details and ornaments; but these may be easier to pick out and more pleasant to contemplate if they and their elements stand in relations the eye can easily grasp. In point of fact proportions are often at two removes from consciousness. When we use a building we need to be able to identify parts of it as doors and windows. We also (comical as it may sound) instinctively monitor it for safety. We want to be sure it will not collapse on us and perhaps also that it does not contain hidden enemies. Doors, windows and structural features are objects, in general, of unconscious attention; but again that attention will be less irksome, there will be aesthetic relief to it, if the proportions are good.

In short, the proportions of a building contribute to our aesthetic enjoyment at an unconscious level and over a long period. Their importance springs from a profound difference between architecture and other arts like literature, music and representational painting. A poem or a symphony gets our undivided attention for a short time; we do not live with it. Even a landscape painting (unlike a real landscape) is chiefly enjoyed by being looked at consciously from a single, well-chosen point of view. But a building is something which exercises a more or less unnoticed influence over a whole range of activities and states of mind. If it is successful it will give them all an aesthetic quality.

That is why we should expect to find a greater variety of concepts of beauty in architecture than in other arts. John James has argued that successive master-builders each imposed his own set of proportions on the cathedral of Chartres without erasing those of his predecessors, and that this is what gives it its feeling of architectural richness (James 1977–9). But the point is not confined to proportions. A building ought to be able to lighten the work and life of complex human beings in many different ways. It can do this only by satisfying many different conceptions of beauty; conceptions which do not compete with but complement one another, and which, in the most favourable case, are harmonized by a vigorous and mature tradition.

NOTES

1   *Mēchanikoi* or *mēchanopoioi* instead of *oikodomoi*; see, for example, Procopius, *Buildings*, I.i. 50, 71.
2   Cf. Hutcheson 1725: III.vii.
3   Cf. Hume 1888: 576, 584–5.

REFERENCES

Alberti, L.B. (1485) *De Re Aedificatoria*, 10 vols, Florence: N. Laurentii.

Aquinas, T. (1266–73) *Summa Theologiae*, 1950, Rome: Marietti.

Burke, E. (1757) *A Philosophical Enquiry into the Origin of our Ideas of the Sublime and the Beautiful*, London: Dodsley.

Gallie, W.B. (1964) *Philosophy and the Historical Understanding*, London: Chatto & Windus.

Gill, E. (1933) *Beauty Looks after Herself*, London: Sheed & Ward.

Hegel, G.W.F. (1842–1928) *Vorlesungen über die Asthetik*, Berlin: Duncker & Hamblot; trans. T.M. Knox 1965 2 vols, Oxford: Clarendon.

Hogarth, W. (1753) *The Analysis of Beauty*, London: for the author; 1955, Oxford: Clarendon.

Hume, D. (1749) *A Treatise of Human Nature*, London: John Noon; ed. L.A. Selby-Bigge 1888, Oxford, Clarendon.

Hutcheson, F. (1725) *An Inquiry into the Original of our Ideas of Beauty and Virtue*, London.

Isodore of Seville, *Patrologiae Cursus Completus*, ed. J.P. Migne, 1878, Series Latina, Vol. 82, Paris: Garnier.

James, J. (1977–9) *Chartres, les constructeurs*, Chartres: Société Archéologique d'Eure-et-Loir.

Kant, I. (1790) *Kritik der Urteilskraft*, Berlin and Libau: Lagarde & Friederich; reprinted 1963, Hamburg: Felix Meiner.

Le Corbusier (Jeanneret-Gris, C.E.) (1923) *Vers une Architecture*, Paris: G. Cris.

Mathew, G. (1963) *Byzantine Aesthetics*, London: John Murray.

Mothersill, M. (1984) *Beauty Restored*, Oxford: Clarendon.

Ogden, C.K., Richards, I.A. and Woods, J. (1922) *The Foundations of Aesthetics*, London: George Allen & Unwin.

Osborne, H. (1952) *Theory of Beauty*, London: Routledge & Kegan Paul.

Palladio, A. (1570) *I Quattro Libri dell'Architetura*, Venice: Franceschi; trans. 1715 G. Leoni, *The Four Books on Architecture*; facsimile edn 1965, New York: Dover Publications.

Plato, *Opera*, ed. J. Burnet, 1900–03, Vols I–III, Oxford: Clarendon.

Plotinus, *Opera*, ed. P. Henry and H.R. Schwyzer, 1978–83, Oxford: Clarendon.

Procopius, *Works*, ed. Loeb, trans. H.B. Dewing and G. Downey, 1961, London: Heinemann.

Pugin, A.W.N. (1836) *Contrasts between the Architecture of the 15th and 19th Centuries*, London: for the author.

Ripa, C. (1593) *Iconologia*, Rome: Gigliotti.

Ruskin, J. (1849) *The Seven Lamps of Architecture*, London: Smith Elder.

Scruton, R. (1979) *The Aesthetics of Architecture*, London: Methuen.

Tatarkiewicz, W. (1970) *History of Aesthetics*, The Hague: Mouton.

Wolff, C. von (1732) *Psychologia Empirica*, Frankfurt, Renger.

Xenophon, *Opera*, ed. E.C. Marchant, 1900, Vol. II, Oxford: Clarendon.

83 Architecture and morality

Henryk Skolimowski

AN OVERVIEW OF THE SITUATION

Architecture has always operated within a framework pervaded by values, and thus is related to and controlled by a form of morality. The tenets and principles of this morality are usually implicit and not infrequently hidden. But there is no question that a value system controls and co-ordinates the architect's mind. Thus architecture can be seen as the arena for the struggle of values. But not only architecture. Every practical act is a moral act. We may say further that no human activity is neutral. When performed within a given environment and placed in specific social and economic contexts, practical acts are inevitably translated into moral acts. At the very least the acts are pregnant with moral consequences.

In traditional cultures the underlying value system within which the architect acts is rooted in intrinsic values which are often religious in character.

In the twentieth century (at least the early part of the twentieth century) this system of values is based on the technological imperative: what technology makes possible the architect must implement; new technological possibilities become our ethical imperatives. Not to obey technology is to betray progress. To betray progress is considered a moral sin.

It is quite clear that historically architecture has been a conveyor and perpetuator of values. Architects understand this very well with regard to traditional architecture. They can talk eloquently of how the Parthenon expresses and embodies the ethos and values of the Greek culture, or how the Gothic cathedral epitomizes our quest for transcendence and our god-centred values.

However, architects by and large claim to be innocent and unknowing about the values which impregnate modern architecture (or let us be specific – twentieth-century architecture). This innocence is partly a ploy. Architects, in a sense, refuse to see the moral and social consequences of their designs and buildings. They say that if modern architecture is a mess – from the environmental and social point of view – they (the architects) are not responsible: politicians are responsible and society is responsible because they forced architects to design and build in a certain way.

For some reasons, architects have considerable difficulties in seeing and understanding that they have aligned themselves with wrong values (or, shall we say, one-sided technological values) which are anti-human, cold, alienating, geared to industrial efficiency and not to the quality of life. If the architects did not choose these values, they at least allowed themselves to be *used* as perpetrators of these values. Hence the tragedy of modern architecture. Hence the acrimony of present discussions concerning the meaning and value of modern architecture.

When I was a research student at Oxford, in the early 1960s, a lively controversy took place concerning the future of Christ Church Meadows. The 'authorities' wanted to build a bypass through these meadows – another motorway. Christ Church College fiercely objected on aesthetic and historic grounds. In the name of progress Christ Church dons were abused as antediluvian reactionaries. The college, which had a lot of clout, finally prevailed. Now everybody is happy that a monstrosity was not built so close to historic Oxford colleges.

Times have changed. But architects are still stuck in the old technological morals and values. They are still reluctant to see how much damage they have made in the name of progress. Even today, they defend themselves by saying, if we didn't do it, someone else would. Indeed I have heard architects referring to themselves as 'hired guns'. If there is anything morally wrong with architecture, this is certainly wrong.

THE ETHICAL IMPERATIVES FOR OUR TIMES

Let us now look in a more analytical manner at the various ways in which moral responsibility enters architecture. Morality or ethics enters the realm of architecture on at least four different levels. Some of these levels are obvious, some are more subtle and hidden. To each of these levels there corresponds an ethical responsibility which the architect must maintain in order to be a moral agent. Even if the architect does not want to be a moral agent, he or she is one through the consequences of his or her actions. Here are four different moral responsibilities, corresponding to various levels of the architect's action.

1 *Integrity* or professional integrity.
2 *Sensitivity* or the capacity to read in depth the client's needs and desires.
3 A *larger sense of life* to which the architect positively contributes.
4 An *ecological awareness* which is now absolutely crucial for designing with nature and for taking the responsibility for future generations.

Thus, on the first level, morality enters the realm of

architecture in the form of the architect's integrity in his or her daily professional conduct. Architecture is an exceedingly complex craft and there are myriad ways in which the architect's integrity is put to test. The practice is immoral if the architect cuts corners, produces shoddy designs and buildings, while the client expects otherwise. The client is the innocent, while the architect retains power and can subtly manipulate the client in so many ways.

This aspect of morality in architecture is clearly perceived and looked after by professional codes and professional responsibilities. Yet no code can envisage all possible ways the architect can cheat – even if in small, invisible ways. Therefore what is finally at stake is the architect's integrity. Integrity in this context is a moral category. In the simplest way integrity means: we trust this person to do the job well.

On the second level, morality enters the realm of architecture in the form of the architect's sensitivity to the client's brief. This is specifically the architectural domain: to understand the client's brief well, to understand the client's needs and desiderata completely, to design with the eye to the client's benefit. This is a subtle and often deep art – to elicit from the client what his or her deeper needs are. Many architects are quite sensitive in this way, one might even say extraordinarily sensitive. Yet there are some deeper problems here.

How much should the architect listen to the client and attempt to meet the client's needs, wants, whims? All the way through, some would say; after all, the client pays and we are here to serve. But is that right? Is that *morally* right? Are we not bypassing too easily some moral dilemmas?

The problem lies exactly in the very meaning of the term 'serve'. Should we limit the meaning of the idea of 'service' only to the client who pays? Or should we not at the same time consider (while serving the individual client) whether we should also serve a larger client, that is, society and the whole cultural heritage of human kind? This is by no means an abstract question. Let us consider some examples.

What if we find that our client is a bit vulgar, a bit ostentatious, a bit stupid. Do we simply design to accommodate the client's nature? Is that all there is to the architect's sensitivity and responsibility? Just to flatter and please the client regardless of how mediocre (and perhaps vulgar) his or her taste is? What if our client is from a society which is a bit vulgar, quite limited in its vision and a bit stupid? Might it not be the case that the present consumerist society – as a whole – is of this kind, and therefore catering to its tastes and predilections might not be the best way to serve it, that is, if we want to serve it in an enlightened way?

What is vulgar and what is not is open to debate, some would say. Everything is open to debate, if we want to make it so. I rather like Anthony Burgess's definition of vulgarity. The distinguished writer, after twenty-one years of living abroad, returned to Britain for a longer spell of time and found it to be a land of 'New Vulgaria'. Vulgarity, he writes, 'is a kind of implied philosophy which finds virtue in reduction – the reduction of man, a noble animal, to a set of homuncular responses. *Turning humanity into something far less than what it could be is what vulgarity is about'* (Burgess 1989, my italics). This last statement provides us with an admirable working definition of vulgarity. Catering to vulgarity is a moral problem; indeed, it is a moral sin.

The problem, of course, is a philosophical one: whom do we consider the human person to be? Let us hear the poet Goethe on the subject.

> To treat man as he is
> Is to debase him.
> To treat man as he ought to be
> Is to engrace him.
>
> (Goethe 1940: 459)

In these simple but profound words we have a guide to action and a key as to how to treat the client.

I have deliberately enlarged the scope of the discourse concerning the meaning of 'serving the client well', and concerning the meaning of 'sensitivities required to serve the client well', because too often this discourse is too narrowly conceived. The moral dilemmas occur exactly at the point where we realize that our client is not a pre-packaged box of needs which we are merely unpacking, but that our client is a person steeped in the history of human culture and a part of the evolving tapestry of evolution. If our sensitivities fail to appreciate that, then we are catering to an isolated human monad, perhaps even to a one-dimensional individual. Our failure is then a moral failure – to treat the human person according to his or her deepest nature and within the extraordinary richness of human heritage. We should be mindful that no one is an island.

We have now imperceptibly moved from level two (sensitivity to the need of a particular client) to level three – the sense of the largeness of life. In summary, the architect's sensitivity must be subtle enough to comprehend in depth the client's desires. But it must also be universal enough to comprehend in depth the role of the architect in contributing to society, to human history, to the well-being of the species. As we judge past architecture by its enduring qualities, so we shall be judged by future generations.

The enduring quality of past architecture has to do with the way it serves life. Quality of life is the test which architecture, of any period and any style, must pass sooner or later. The quality of life criterion is an elusive one – very difficult to formulate. But not so difficult to assess in the actual experience. 'Quality' itself is very hard to define, as Robert Pirsig has so eloquently shown in his memorable book *Zen and the Art of Motorcycle Maintenance* (1974). We can assess quality, particularly in architecture, only *post hoc*, only a posteriori.

If we find a given environment working, if it generates interactions which we deem to be life-enhancing, then we judge the building or the built environment as a success. The quality-of-life criterion thus meets the tribunal of life in the actual act of living over a period of time.[1] To be a good architect is to listen to the pulse of life and to respond to it. The sense of largeness of life is the appreciation of its quality, of its inexorable and relentless beat of life, in spite of its contradictions.

One of the aspects of the quality of life which architecture must address is to know when to build and when not to build. The tragedy of the technological society is not that it did not create enough great buildings but that it has left behind too many shoddy, useless, offensive buildings. Louis Kahn put the matter with an admirable clarity when he said: 'The right thing badly done is always better than the wrong thing well done' (Kahn 1986). The moral failure of modern architecture was to confuse the excellence of means with the excellence of ends. Quality-of-life architecture does not signify superior technical means for the execution of spurious building.[2]

Thus we come to level four, ecological awareness or ecological stewardship, which is nowadays of vital importance to architectural thinking and practice. This aspect of architecture – the moral responsibility for the shape of the environment – is so vital that all other achievements pale if we destroy the environment or damage it beyond repair. The moral responsibility for the quality of built environments is difficult to assess with regard to particular buildings *Architects share this responsibility jointly. They face the tribunal of life over a period of time.*

When architects were taken to task in Britain by the Prince of Wales (in the late 1980s) for creating inhuman environments, the charge was moral and ecological. And the two are now intimately and inextricably connected. The ecological awareness, the sense of ecological stewardship, must now become a part of the architect's craft and an inherent aspect of the architectural morality.

ON RELATIVISM AND REVERENCE FOR LIFE

There is one more problem that we need to discuss, namely relativism – in architecture and elsewhere. We are often told that we live in a pluralistic society, in the age in which all traditional, especially absolutist, standards have disappeared, and therefore anything goes. Relativism is thus a consequence of abolishing all absolute creeds and values.

From a moral point of view, relativism is not a position but a surrender of moral responsibility. In fact, relativism is a cheap device of confused minds. This may sound harsh. But it may not be far from the truth. Ours is an age of confusion. And relativism thrives amidst confusion. Relativism is, in fact, a pseudo-philosophical stand justifying confusion. In all great periods of history,

when great things were done, people did not hide behind the screen of relativism, for they knew what the standards were and what were the values they wished to realize.

Nor is relativism defensible in our times – particularly with regard to architecture. There is nothing relative (or better still, relativistic) about integrity, about sensitivity,[3] about the sense of the largeness of life, about the meaning of ecological stewardship. All these basic concepts (really moral principles for architects) may be difficult to define. But that is another matter. All important moral concepts are difficult to define. But this difficulty cannot be our escape hatch from responsibility.

One of the most beautiful ethical concepts is that of reverence for life. It is in fact the underlying pillar of my ecological ethics which I have formulated elsewhere.[4] The four principles which I have analysed actually follow from and are justified by the principle of reverence for life. If architects became fully conscious of this principle and tried to implement it in their practice and in their built environments, we would have stopped the violence which we inflict upon nature, and we might have created an architecture worthy of the human being, a noble animal – as Burgess says.

In my earlier writings,[5] I proposed that instead of the totally inadequate principle, 'form follows function', we now use a new one – '*Form Follows Culture*'. I would be inclined to reformulate this to read '*Form Follows Life*', that is, a reverential conception of life.

In summary, architecture is part of the moral order of the human universe. It does not make explicit judgements about how human beings ought to behave. But it is a conveyor and perpetuator of the moral orders of humanity. It contributes to these orders, usually, by implementing values specific to a given society or culture. These specific values concern the ideal of 'good life'. Good life is finally justified in relation to the idea of quality of life. If architecture does not positively contribute to 'good life', to the life of quality, it looses its *raison d'être*.

The architect cannot be a naïve simpleton who assumes that he or she is merely a servant and must do what a client or a social group orders. The architect is a servant. We are all servants. But the architect is a servant in many contexts of which he or she must be aware. The architect is a servant to and a perpetuator of the great traditions of human culture which, by evolving various architectural orders, has enshrined the beauty of the human condition. The architect is a servant to and a preserver of the integrity of ecological habitats, for if ecological habitats are destroyed, and our planet is reduced to a rubbish heap, we can hardly talk about architecture contributing to a 'good life'.

Thus the concept of 'good life' must include the capacity of architecture to celebrate life, to contribute to the elevation of the human condition, to this rare joy and delight which we experience when we contemplate a wonderful piece of architecture, whether big or small and are in awe of the creative potential of the human mind.

Although one does not wish to be moralistic, one should realize that some clear-cut commandments follow from our discourse on the practice of contemporary architecture, which are especially relevant to twenty-first-century architecture. These commandments could be expressed as follows.

1   Thou shalt not violate the sanctity of the Human Person by reducing that person to a thoughtless consumer.
2   Thou shalt not violate the integrity of nature and its cycles by overusing it and reducing it to a mere resource.
3   Thou shalt not waste energy, resources, space or any aspect of this divine universe, for waste is now a moral sin. Ours must be the ethics of frugality – for the sake of future generations.
4   Thou shalt possess an elevated view of the human condition and of the human destiny, for only then can one design in the image of Reverential Human.[6]

As we have said throughout this essay, it is difficult to appraise architecture morally, point by point, building by building. *The moral appraisal of architecture is the tribunal of life in the long run.* For this reason it is a moral prerogative of the architect to possess the sense of the largeness of life. By his or her very mission, the architect contributes to life at large.

To flow with life and to feel its unique pulse is a mandate and a responsibility without which the architect cannot build truly responsibly, or achieve greatness. This sense of the largeness of life cannot be learned from technical books but can be acquired by the contemplation of the great works of architecture and art, and through the contemplation of the beauty of the human condition.

Architecture in the image of reverence for life – which I have advocated in this essay – may be difficult to achieve. But as Baruch Spinoza says, all things rare and beautiful are difficult to attain.

NOTES

1   See Skolimowski 1981, Chapter 4: 'Architecture and eco-philosophy', and my other writings on architecture.
2   See, for example, Skolimowski 1981, Chapter 4.
3   For a philosophical analysis of the idea of 'sensitivity' and its implications see Skolimowski 1985, especially the early chapters.
4   See especially Skolimowski 1984 and 1990.
5   See, for example, Skolimowski 1981, Chapter 4.
6   Seen in the light of these criteria (commandments), Post-Modern architecture – with its bizarre façades and lack of substance – is but a series of immoral doodlings.

REFERENCES

Burgess, A. (1989) 'Voyage to discovery in the New Vulgaria', *Observer*, 6 August.

Goethe, J.W. von (1940) *Wilhelm Meisters Lehrjahre*, Leipzig: Insel Verlag.

Kahn, L.I. (1986) *What Will Be Has Always Been: The Words of Louis I. Kahn*, New York: Rizzoli.

Pirsig, R.M. (1974) *Zen and the Art of Motorcycle Maintenance*, London: Bantam.

Skolimowski (1981) *Eco-philosophy: Designing New Tactics for Living*, London: Marion Boyars.

—— (1984a) *The Theatre of the Mind*, Wheaton, Ill.: Quest Books.

—— (1984b) 'Eco-ethics as the foundation of conservation', *The Environmentalist* 4 (7).

—— (1990) 'Reverence for life', in R. and J. Engel (eds) *Ethics of Environment and Development: Global Challenge and International Response*, London: Belhaven Press.

84 This is good but is it right?

Cesar Pelli

There is nothing quite so pleasurable for me as to visit my buildings when they're finished and occupied. It is like being part of a miracle taking place. Months and even years of caring and dreaming become reality.

Beyond all the expected pleasures, there are the unexpected ones. New vistas, compositions and patterns of sunlight come to life, and they are particularly precious because I do not remember designing them. They are wonderful strokes of luck.

The building is my design, but it is also its own entity separate from me. This allows me – perhaps forces me – to enter into a long dialogue with it in which every premise, every theory is questioned and reconsidered.

The finished building is my severest critic. Every little error glares back at me reprovingly. I never tell of those because I know many of them will remain invisible to less interested onlookers, but I cannot forget them. There are also more important issues that a building brings to my attention. Often good ideas – well executed, theoretically correct, and successful in their intentions – force me to say, 'This is good, but is it right?'

This is a question perhaps unique to the art of architecture. The ethical issues usually come to the surface when aesthetic intentions are in conflict with some of the social roles a building must play. Here is where architecture separates itself almost completely from the other visual arts.

To be good architecture, a building needs to be not only beautiful but responsible and responsive. Some of these responses are rather obvious. That is, a building has to fulfil reasonably well the purposes for which it was built. If it is an art museum, it should provide an environment where paintings and sculptures can be properly exhibited.

We also know that a building is responsible to the place it occupies and makes in a city. It is a great responsibility for any architect to be given a piece of a city to design – however small it may be – and it is clear to me that the obligations of a building to be a good piece of the city are greater than its obligations as an art object or as part of an architect's oeuvre (see Figure 1). That is, the city is more important than the building, and the building is more important than the architect.

When we design a building, we participate in the never-complete, imperfect, collaborative work of art that is a city, perhaps the most important work of art of any

First published in *Architectural Digest*, August 1988: 29–36, under the title 'Pieces of the city'.

Figure 1 *World Financial Center, Battery Park City, New York, 1981–7, by Cesar Pelli and Associates.* (Photograph: *Timothy Hursley*)

culture. The making of good cities requires not just pragmatic responses to context but lyrical, creative acts respectful of the greater purpose.

The often wrenching clash between the inner drives of an architect and the external forces he or she must respect are not a weakness but a permanent source of strength and renewal of the art of architecture. Great cities are the product of this dynamic balance. It has to be dynamic to be art, and it has to be in balance for the necessary harmony of the whole.

I question blind contextualism, because if the art of building yields completely to context or external conditions, we have no renewing, only blandness. On the other hand, if the architect's internal agenda – be it intellectual, aesthetic or ideological – is imposed on the building, a piece of the city may be harmed. Good cities are very resilient and have been able to absorb rather violent attacks on their fabric. Sometimes the intruding object can become a beautiful and vitalizing exception, such as the Guggenheim Museum on Fifth Avenue, but we can see now that there is a limit to the resiliency of our cities.

The Post-Modernist reaction has brought renewed concern for the quality of our cities, but two great enemies are very much alive. They are the concepts of aesthetic ideology and artistic signature.

Architectural ideology, whether it be Modernism, Classicism or Post-Modernism, tells us that there is an aesthetic system that is best in all circumstances. It is clear to me that this is not so, that each circumstance is unique and requires a uniquely calibrated artistic response. The concept of individual artistic signature says that an architect should have a personal style like a painter or sculptor, usually with a consistent system of forms, materials and colours that is then used, with variations, for every building type in every place. Fidelity to an aesthetic ideology, to an individual vision – or, worse still, to both – has been highly applauded and respected. More so, it has been considered an essential quality of a good architect. I believe these attitudes to be damaging to our cities.

The problem is particularly severe today, when every well-known architect is working in cities that range from Fairbanks to Miami, from Hong Kong to Berlin – completely different contexts that should require carefully considered and different architectural responses. If we continue to build signature buildings in every city of the world – and if architects keep on imitating the latest forms and ideas of a few – each city will end up as a collection of disparate individual statements, be they first-rate or second-rate, originals or imitations.

The importance of an artist's individual style is a concept that comes from painting – an art that can detach itself completely from external pressures. Architecture is very different. It is not a three-dimensional, inhabitable painting. An architect rarely chooses a building's site, purpose or size. A collection of an architect's buildings is an absurdity both physically and intellectually. A collection of photographs, drawings and models of buildings can have historical interest but does not in itself have much artistic value.

The architect begins by understanding and responding to these conditions and then must continue to guide a design through a thicket of laws and ordinances. We all need to understand the circumstances, but instead of doing so to figure out what we can get away with, we must do so with respect. I believe that our artistic purpose gains strength from this attitude of respect. Architects have done so for millennia without weakening their artistic achievements.

After every new design of mine becomes a building, I am once again impressed with its uniqueness (see Figure 2). More and more, my designs have been responding to the unique circumstances of purpose and place; more and more I find the greatest excitement in arriving at the

Figure 2 *World Financial Center, Battery Park City, New York, 1981–7, by Cesar Pelli and Associates.* (Photograph: *Timothy Hursley*)

deepest possible understanding of a place – its character, its past – and through that understanding nurturing a fresh, poetic response into a design.

Instead of concentrating on one particular personal style, I find that to be a good architect I need to be more flexible and open. We work today in more places and with more building types than architects ever have. Not only do I collaborate with engineers and consultants and with other architects in my studio, but I also need to collaborate with the architects who preceded me in a city and with those who will come after me.

We should not judge a building by how beautiful it is in isolation, but instead by how much better or worse that particular place – a city or campus, a neighbourhood or landscape – has become by its addition. If the city has not gained by the addition, we should seriously question the design and the building itself, no matter how beautiful and theoretically correct it may be.

Architecture is so complex and multi-rooted that its learning is slow and gradual. I know that I am a much better architect now than I was ten years ago. I can feel that I am in a particularly rich and creative period of my architectural life, and it is obvious to me that if I continue to learn as I have, in another ten years I should be very, very good.

85 Quality in architecture

Birgit Cold

ARCHITECTURE DEFINED

When using the term architecture, we already have a feeling of quality as opposed to talking merely about buildings. Over time there have been different definitions of what architecture is.

The Swedish architect and theorist Elias Cornell defined architecture as 'the aesthetic organization of practical reality' (Cornell 1966: 9). The English Arts and Crafts architect and theorist W. Lethaby wrote in 1891: '... so is building but the vehicle of architecture which is the thought behind form, embodied and realised for the purpose of its manifestation and transmission' (Lethaby 1974: 1–2).

Or, we may say that architecture is the built environment with an 'artistic nerve', that is, with aesthetically stimulating space and form.

Behind these concepts lies the aim to add to the built environment *something* which speaks to our senses, emotions and minds (see Figure 1).

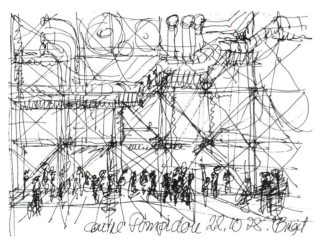

Figure 1 *Centre Pompidou, Paris.*

ARCHITECTURE: CONCEPTIONS, PLACE AND ROLE

Finn Werne, a Swedish architect, writes about 'the invisible architecture', or 'the inner architecture' we all carry with us as dreams and memories.

> These conceptions and pictures and their relations to the visible and outer architecture determine whether we feel at home or not and feel pleasure or not. If there are no relations between the invisible and visible architecture, we become indifferent. To care about the environment is to identify, not only with the neighbourhood and one's own house, but with people and places, with the ancestors and descendants.... The feeling of belonging requires a confirmation in the visible architecture.
>
> (Werne 1987: 203)

These mental pictures, conceptions or mindscape play a consistent part of our emotional and aesthetic evaluation, intellectual interpretation, and the way we use buildings and places.

The English environmental psychologist David Canter argues that the term 'place' is particularly rich in meaning, because it has geographical, architectural and social connotations. This makes it suitable as one of the central concepts for bridging these various disciplines (Canter 1977: 6).

According to Canter (1977: 158), the identification of a place consists of three factors, and the nature of places is the relation between:

1 people's conceptions of
   - what should happen
   - what it should 'look like' or be
   - which behaviour is suitable or expected;
2 the physical attributes, or the architecture, as form, space, materials, colour, furnishing, etc.;
3 the activities.

This interaction is dynamic and changes if one of the parameters changes. People's conceptions are created and changed by what Canter calls the self-fulfilling prophecies. In other words, 'our expectations are a result of patterns of commonly occurring actions, and in turn give rise to actions which fit in with these patterns. This is the reason why conceptual systems, on the one hand are so powerful, and on the other hand are so intertwined with concepts of actions' (Canter 1977: 121).

Canter writes about the important influence that role and status have on conceptions and expectations, which, in their turn, influence the way we experience, interpret and evaluate places. Architects and lay people evaluate differently, partly because it is expected, partly because architects have gained experiences and knowledge which should give a deeper understanding. But there is also a danger of a specialist conformity telling 'the right and the wrong' way of experiencing and evaluating buildings and places (see Figure 2).

ARCHITECTURE: THE ACTIVITY PROCESS

The Danish architect and theorist Jan Gehl has studied the interaction between the physical environment and

Figure 2 *Specialist conformity can tell us 'the right and the wrong' way of evaluating buildings and places.* (Source: *'Normdenken der Experten'*, Carré Bleu)

| | The quality in the built environment | |
	Bad quality	Good quality
The necessary activities	◍	◍
The optional activities	∘	⬤
The following activities (social)	∘	◍

Figure 3 *The process of activities.* (Source: *Gehl 1980*)

process are dependent on an observant mind, and interest in and knowledge about human activity in the built environment.

ARCHITECTURE: THE EXPERIENCE OF QUALITY

The Swedish environmental psychologist Rikard Küller shows in the 'model of man–environment interaction' (Figure 4) that human beings are partly affected by the physical environment (F2) and partly by the social network (F3). He says that, in addition, they are influenced by the activities (F1) in which they engage. This influence, which varies in extent over time (recurrent variation), is modified by their own personal resources, constitution, experiences, etc. (Fn). While the environment activates them in various ways, human beings at the same time endeavour to retain control over their situation by adaptation or compensation (C1–Cn).

What the model indicates is, in part, that activation from various sources must be balanced and adapted to the activities going on in public and semi-public outdoor spaces. He advocates that the quality of the physical environment is dependent on the development of an activity process. The process is described by three steps (see Figure 3).

'The necessary activities' are the dominant determinant for the design, but at the same time 'the optional' and 'following activities' should be considered. We may for example think of designing a pathway: the dimensions for two persons passing each other are chosen (the necessary activity). Places, where it is possible to stop (the optional activity) and sit down in the sun, are designed in a way to help people talk together (the following activity) (Gehl 1980: 9).

All places, indoor and outdoor, are potentials for this process, whether a kitchen or a bathroom, a street or a square. Architects' abilities to imagine this activity

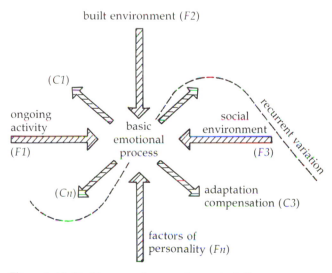

Figure 4 *Model of 'man–environment interaction'.* (Source: *Küller 1976*)

the resources of the individual (Küller 1976; Watzke and Küller 1986: 20). Küller quotes the transactionalist Kilpatric:

> Apparently, the correspondence between percept and object is never absolute. Instead, perception is of functional probabilities, of constructs which emerge from the consequences of past action and serve as directives for furthering the purposes of the organism through action. 'Percept' and 'object' are but two abstracted aspects of this total process and correspondence between the two is simply a function of their being part and parcel of the same thing.
> (Kilpatric 1961: 4, cited in Küller 1976: 1)

As an interpretation we might say that the feeling of quality, or the opposite, arises from the confrontation between object and user. This experience of quality and the quality we attach to the object are two aspects of the same thing. The degree in which quality seems related to the experience, or more the object, may be a question of time, involvement and world view.

In the following, we discuss the quality concept seen from different angles:

1   the *situationally determined quality*, influenced by instant actions and the user's constitution;
2   the *epochally determined quality*, ruled by a set of chosen norms (paradigms);
3   the *historically determined quality*, which apparently rises above situation and norms, and seems to have a long-lasting validity;
4   the *phenomenological view on quality*, where the dialogue is dependent on the sensitivity of the user to the phenomenon – the interplay of existence and meaning.

Situationally determined quality means that the experience of quality originates in the interaction between us and the built environment, in the place where we act.

This is further outlined in Canter's model of 'place experience' (Figure 5). He points out the close relation-

Figure 6 *Sakkerhusene v. Konigsberg*

ship between individual roles and responsibilities people have, and their purpose and goal in being and acting in those places. Roles and goals create a framework, in which the evaluation takes place as an interplay between 'rules of place' and 'cognitive ecology'. 'The rules' are the individual and cultural rules that guide behaviour in places, and 'the cognitive ecology' is people's conceptions and previous experiences of 'what should happen, how, when and with whom'.

Epochally determined quality implies that the experience of quality is linked to or guided by a paradigm belonging to a certain epoch (see Figure 6). We know how styles and fashions flourish and how they die and are neglected by the next generation. Each epoch, style or fashion has its norms and rules.

The observer's sensitivity is then prepared for certain patterns and rules, like an instrument tuned to a special key. If we hear a false sound or an irregularity compared to what we expected, we get disappointed or angry, and the chance of having any experience of quality is nearly always excluded (see Figure 7a). Think of last year's reaction to wide trousers compared with narrow ones, and remember our opposite reactions eighteen years ago. And now, back to wide trousers again, but only for women!

When new ideas emerge and so-called abnormalities have shattered the norms of quality for a period in time, a new epoch or a new paradigm takes over. Again we will 'tune our aerial for a new wavelength'

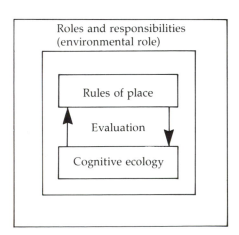

Figure 5 *A system of place experience.* (Source: *Canter 1977*)

(a)

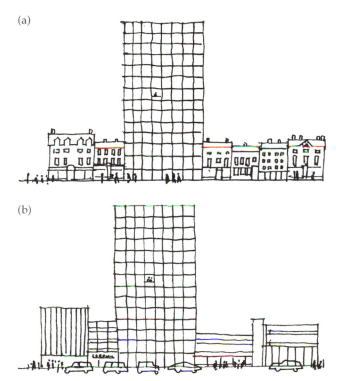

(b)

Figure 7 *(a) An unexpected irregularity can make us disappointed or angry; (b) A new norm is established once new ideas have established themselves over a period of time.*

(see Figure 7b). This process means that we question the context of and disassociate ourselves from the previous architectural paradigm.

Historically determined quality implies that certain objects, buildings and monuments seem to have a long-lasting valid quality or 'eternal quality'. We never ask if the pyramids, the Pantheon or the temples of the Acropolis are of quality. It is beyond dispute, regardless of subjective or interdisciplinary experiences. It seems as if the ancient works of art and architecture, by virtue of their age and monumentally historical identity, are perceived by various cultures as examples of 'eternal quality'. This

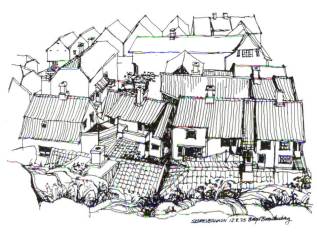

Figure 8 *Anonymous architecture: Skudeneshavn*

quality is often connected with monuments symbolizing power. When we get closer to our time, we notice that the baroque, classicism or Art Nouveau have different sympathizers. It seems as if the closer a style is in time to the ruling paradigm, the more critically it will be evaluated.

But anonymous architecture has also, in the same indisputable way, been given the stamp of quality, especially after being 'discovered' by the Functionalists (see Figure 8). Its values lie in the pure, honest, functional and poetic way of adjusting to the landscape, using local materials and building methods developed through the ages.

This description of 'eternal quality' is of course influenced by present perception and conception of quality. Before romanticism, there was little concern about the quality of the old architectural monuments and the anonymous architecture.

Phenomenologically determined quality may be called 'general quality' if it exists as a concept. We shall consider two of its characteristics: the phenomenological view and the 'law' aspect.

The phenomenological view looks at quality as integrated in or a part of the object's 'being'. It is our job to open up our senses and sharpen our minds to grasp the innate quality.

> The experience of place is not a question of taste. The place is existing as an objective matter, it is like that whether we like it or not, and it reveals its secrets and its richness, if we have open minds and listen to its 'spirit'.
>
> (Norberg-Schulz 1986: 309)

This means that the quality exists in the places, and that we are more or less disposed or motivated to, or capable of, experiencing and evaluating this quality.

From this point of view it may perhaps be easier to understand why historic architecture seems to have 'general quality'. The older a building becomes, the less important the situation, role and status will be in determining the response to it. Our own epoch's norms and rules no longer count so much, and we open up to the architecture and its meaning (see Figure 9).

The belief that certain 'laws' govern a person's experience of quality in any given environment has reappeared regularly in different periods throughout history.

1   During antiquity, Vitruvius; in the Renaissance, Palladio; and in the Modernist phase, Le Corbusier (*Le Modulor*, 1950) – all developed 'laws and principles' in the belief that beauty and harmony are derived from geometrically and mathematically proportioned ratios.

2   Based on contemporary, empirical research, environmental psychologists have proposed a balanced

Figure 9 *Our own epoch's norms no longer apply to old buildings: Piazza San Marco.*

relationship between familiarity and novelty to achieve satisfactory or beautiful architecture.

3   In phenomenology, we find a view of the people–environment relationship which represents the idea that the experience of architecture follows ordered and general laws. The Norwegian architect Thomas Thiis Evensen wants to identify and classify a set of archetypes which contribute to an understanding of the universal content of architecture (Thiis Evensen 1982: xxii).

Architectural theorists and researchers are constantly trying to discover interdisciplinary, objective or universal rules for the relations between human beings and the built environment.

These reflections on the factors which condition quality from situational, to epochal, to 'eternal', and on the general, innate phenomenological quality or the quality governed by 'laws', led me to the conclusion that architectural history, with its various and changing aesthetic expressions and styles, does not offer unambiguous answers to the question 'what is quality?' Rather, history give us a contextual platform from which we may find support and inspiration for the decisions we have to make, whether it is about evaluating, designing, preserving or demolishing buildings. But can we then not define architectural quality at all?

Figure 10 *A new rationalist: Leon Krier's renovation project for Washington, DC.* (Source: *Skude 1988*)

We can and we do. But only as a continuous process, through architectural education and further on in the profession. It must be stressed that *the quality concept cannot be treated as a static, objective, rational or logical concept.*

The *experience* of quality – independent from the philosophical or theoretical treatment of the concept of quality – originates in the confrontation between the individual and the object, building or place. And because of that, it concerns both the characteristics of the individual, the object and the situation.

If we take a closer look at the architecture of different epochs, we find that the same ideas turn up again at intervals. For example, it looks as if we will never be free from antiquity (see Figure 10). The Romans were greatly inspired by the Hellenistic architecture. Their legacy in its turn was transformed during the Renaissance and again in the neo-classical age and is now reinterpreted by the neo-rationalists and to a lesser extent by the Post-Modernists.

The reason why the architecture of the past is perpetually expounded and transformed may be because of its accordance with certain features, conceptions and longings which characterize and therefore feel attractive to each new period of time.

For me, the conclusion to be drawn from these reflections is that we should concentrate more seriously on the authenticity of our own time (see Figure 11) and not just imitate architectural expression in order to solve the

Figure 11 Fehn's pavilion at the Venice Biennale 1983.

current longing for a more significant and aesthetically stimulating architecture.

There are several things we can do, for example we can:

- sharpen our awareness and study the message of time, place and quality in the architecture, and by a contextual understanding we may ourselves get *inspiration to do creative work*;
- train our sensitivity and develop 'a refinement of the senses' in order to experience, try out and create *new cognition*;
- learn about the people–environment relationship to widen our knowledge and understanding of 'the purpose of architecture'.

ARCHITECTURE: THREE VIEWS

To confirm the aesthetic nature of architecture, I want to introduce the views of the American psychologist Daniel Stokols, presented at the International Conference on Environmental Psychology 1988. He identifies three basic approaches to architecture.

1   The minimalist view. The built environment serves as protection against climate and enemies and as a safe setting for social and daily life. 'This perspective assumes that the physical environment exert minimal or negligible influence on the behaviour, health and wellbeing of the users' (Stokols 1988: 30).

2   The instrumental perspective. Architecture serves as an instrument to obtain not only behavioural and economic efficiency, but also an enhanced level of occupants' comfort, safety and well-being. The quality of the architecture comes from its capacity to reach these goals. In this perspective we recognize the ideals of industrial functionalism.

3   The spiritual view. Architecture or 'the socio-physical environment' becomes an end in itself rather than a tool, and emerges as a whole.

Fundamental human values are cultivated, and the

Figure 12 *Todaiji Temple, Nara.*

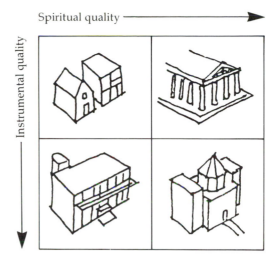

Figure 13 *Matrix of instrumental and spiritual quality.*

human spirit and psyche are enriched. Environmental settings are designed, not only to facilitate the smooth performance of every day activities, but also to provide places to which people are drawn by virtue of their symbolic and affective qualities [see Figure 12].

Recent architectural and social science theories also highlight the symbolic and spiritual facets of environmental design.

The designers are turning away from positivism and functionalism and are becoming increasingly interested in history, culture, myth and meaning. A new sensibility in design is asked for 'in which human activity, human feeling, colour and light together create ordinary human sweetness'.

(Stokols 1988: 31–2)

This third view, which transfers to the architect the responsibility for the creation of quality, requires the power of empathy and understanding of the following:

- users' situation and general human needs;
- conditions of the concept of place, physically, socially and symbolically;
- technical and economical premises on realizing the design concept;
- cultural and artistic nerve needed for creating spiritual architecture.

In other words, the architect is responsible for a practical, theoretical and spiritual interaction between form, function and technique.

As a game and in order to sharpen the view on architectural values, we can make a matrix and by simplifying and systematizing the instrumental and spiritual qualities in buildings we know, we may discuss where to place them and why we place them there (see Figure 13).

And we may go further and make a 'cube of experienced quality'. We then look at the relations between three parameters (see Figure 14):

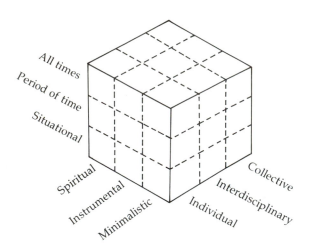

Figure 14 *'Cube' of time–social agreement–level of spirituality.*

1   time – from the present situation, to a period of time (epoch), to 'all times';
2   the level of social agreement – from individual, to interdisciplinary, to collective;
3   the level of quality – from minimalist, to instrumental, to spiritual.

Thus we train our power of empathy, increase our knowledge about architecture and ourselves while having a splendid discussion on the buildings we know, and on whether the term 'aesthetic constant value' exists or not, and, if so, what may eventually characterize this term.

ARCHITECTURE: A PERSONAL VIEW

The interaction, consistency and unity, from details to whole, are concepts of quality we meet in most works of good architecture. Through history these qualities are closely linked to ideal concepts of society, order and permanence. In our time these concepts should not be confused with unambiguous unchangeability or complete harmonic order. The contemporary concepts or interpretations of society should rather be met by a need for establishing mutuality, a complex dialogue and a polyvalence from detail to space, form and environment.

Figure 15 *'Venice on the Thames' – forward to the past: architect John Simpson's neo-classical project, after C. Laubin's oil painting.*

When we are looking at examples of recent architecture, we may find simple and schematic forms locked in an emotionally vacant, neo-classical, often humoristic order. We also find a nostalgic use of decorative motifs that seem to harken back to some forgotten 'age of glory', when kings and emperors commissioned costly works of art – only now they are transformed into modern materials, composites and industrial methods of production (see Figure 15).

In a way one can understand that people, architects and clients search for decorative, symbolic and apparently harmonic expressions in our complex and value-disturbed time. Forty years of insignificant 'box architecture' have also contributed to our hunger for meaningful, expressive and emotional architecture.

I advocate a more searching, 'open and unfinished' architecture, more complex and contradictory, which offers a possibility for the users to participate. It also gives the architect a chance to design more contemporary solutions for a modern way of living, with modern techniques.

When I say 'open and unfinished' in contrast to 'closed and finished', I think of an architecture which in construction, details and design is open for changes and interpretations, but which still keeps its own character. It means an architecture more like a living and growing organism than a fixed and static product.

Figure 16 *University of Trondheim by Hennig Larsen.*

At the same time we need an architecture with a variety of *places*, which may be experienced and used in different ways (see Figure 16).

Whether we like it or not, I believe that in our multicultural society, there should be room for different types of architectural expressions and 'isms'. We are certainly best served by keeping our minds open to different architectural impulses, as long as they are composed and built with *quality*.

And here the argument comes full circle, because we must ask ourselves again: what does 'composed and built with quality' mean?

I will attempt an explanation.

A Norwegian philosopher, Trond Berg Eriksen, recently wrote:

> Quality describes what the thing, the arrangement, the institution really should be – a requirement which they seldom fulfil. It is much easier to see where the quality is missing, or has failed, than where it is present!
>
> (Eriksen 1989: 1)

It may be easier to describe the lack of quality and the absence of 'architectural nerve' than to describe their presence and character. Quality exists and is experienced by virtue of its contrast – lack of quality.

When we are using the term quality, we automatically make a subjective comparison to what we previously have experienced as quality and lack of quality. When Berg Eriksen writes that quality is 'what the thing should be', it may mean that behind this argument there must be an interdisciplinary, culturally based, or even objective agreement about the requirements and expectations, which should be fulfilled by experiencing 'the use of the thing'.

Earlier we have said that the experience of quality is a dynamic process, whereas 'the stamp of quality' is given to certain 'things' in certain periods of time (understood as 'the truth' then and there), while 'other things' have 'eternal quality'.

As an intuitive attempt, I would like to follow up the statement that 'it is much easier to see the lack of quality' by making a series of hypotheses about missing quality. I arrived at the following seven statements without reflecting on whether there should be more or less.

The lack of quality is experienced when:

1   things break down or crack unexpectedly;
2   things grow old in an ugly way;
3   things require an effort we are unable or unwilling to make;
4   things are annoying (not fit for the time or place, perhaps not fit at all) because of their appearance and bare existence;
5   things seem accidentally designed and not properly thought through;
6   things are bad copies;
7   things are pretentious on the surface without having consistency all through.

'Things' might be exchanged by architecture. By starting with the negative aspects, it was easier to formulate the seven positive hypotheses.

Quality is experienced when:

1   architecture can be used for a long span of time;
2   architecture grows old beautifully;
3   architecture is easily legible and simple to use;
4   architecture pleases us in its expression and its bare existence (the pleasure of the right thing in the right place at the right time);
5   architecture seems well considered and properly designed;
6   architecture is original, especial and with its own identity;
7   architecture is consistent all the way through.

These hypotheses tell more about me and my generation of architects than about 'general quality'. Nevertheless, the seven negative and positive hypotheses describe a view of architecture which emphasizes the traditional values, such as durability, authenticity, professionalism and unity, and a functionalist view emphasizing honesty, legibility and functionality (see Figure 17). In addition, we find the need for originality, meaning the need for innovation, novelty and the ability to exceed.

It is not directly evident how these requirements may be combined so that the total result will have the desired quality. But one-sided emphasis on either traditional or innovatory artistic values without a mutual interaction may equally bring unwanted results.

I believe that the interactive battle between traditional and innovatory forces is not a troublesome and annoying one but rather an exciting and stimulating struggle, which goes on continuously and with special intensity during a paradigm shift.

The real fight is about the lack of quality, when neither traditional nor innovatory values are present. It happens when we are copying and repeating former

Figure 17 *Herzberger's De Overloop.*

expressions and forms without keeping the original character, construction and materials, but provide less valuable, less refined or not as long-lasting solutions. It also happens when originality exceeds overwhelmingly, and traditional values are totally neglected.

Vitruvius was 'right' when he said that architecture requires *firmitas*, *utilitas*, and *venustas* – or durability, utility and beauty – to give meaning to artistic and aesthetic quality.

NOTE

All drawings are by the author unless otherwise stated.

REFERENCES

Canter, D. (1977) *The Psychology of Place*, London: Architectural Press.

Cold, B. (1988) *Arkitekturevaluering i teori og praksis*, kompendium, Trondheim: Department of Architecture, Norwegian Institute of Technology.

—— (1989) *Delprogram om evaluering av bygget miljø*, Trondheim: Department of Architecture, Norwegian Institute of Technology.

—— (1989) *Arkitektur og kvalitet*, Trondheim: Department of Architecture, The Norwegian Institute of Technology.

Cornell, E. (1966) *Om rummet och arkitekturens väsen*, Gothenburg: Akademiförlaget.

Eriksen, T.B. (1989) Introduction to *Kvalitet*, special issue of *Samtiden* 2: 1.

Gehl, J. (1980) *Livet mellem husene*, Copenhagen: Arkitektens forlag.

Kilpatric, F.P. (ed.) (1961) *Explorations in Transactional Psychology*, New York: New York University Press.

Küller, R. (ed.) (1976) *The use of space – some physiological and philosophical aspects*, Architectural Psychology Conference paper, Lund: School of Architecture, Lund Institute of Technology.

Le Corbusier (1950) *The Modulor*, London: Faber & Faber.

Lethaby, W. (1974) *Architecture, Mysticism and Myth*, London: Architectural Press.

Norberg-Schulz, C. (1986) *Et sted å være*, Oslo: Gyldendal.

Skude, F. (1988) *Ismerne i det 20. århundrede*, Arkitektur 8, Copenhagen: Byggeriets Studiearkiv.

Stokols, D. (1988) IAPS 10, Proceedings – Vol. 2, *Instrumental and Spiritual Views of People–environment Relations: Current Tensions and Future Challenges*, Delft: Delft University Press.

Thiis Evensen, T. (1982) *Arkitekturens Uttuyksformer*, Oslo: Universitets forlaget.

Werne, F. (1987) *Den Osynliga Arkitekturen*, Gothenburg: Vinge Press.

Watzke, J.R. and Küller, R. (1986) *The Conflict Situations Technique: A Projective Method for Elderly People*, no. 2, Lund: School of Architecture, Lund Institute of Technology.

86 Sign and symbol

John Onians

Signs and symbols have a different character in each area of human activity. The principal determinants of difference are context and medium. In architecture the context is provided by the needs of builders and users. Those who build, from the earliest hut dwellers to present-day developers, seek to shelter and protect, to contain and exclude. Those who use buildings experience being sheltered and protected, contained and excluded. Both builders and users benefit when these needs are not just experienced physically but are communicated. The means of communication is provided by the medium, the physical dispositions of floors, walls and roofs, of supports and apertures, and the properties of materials and surfaces. Any of these features may be used by a builder to express or communicate and be experienced as expressing or communicating by a user. When they are so used or experienced it is possible to talk of them functioning as signs or symbols. Besides having a physical function they express something, stand for something, represent something or mean something, or are perceived as so doing.

It is this close link between physical and expressive properties which gives signs and symbols in architecture their special authority. In literature, for example, or in music, or painting, the medium is much less substantial and expressive properties are clearly predominant. In architecture a wall functions as a real barrier or roof support before it has any expressive overlay, and such overlay is likely as much as anything to confirm that physical function. The link between physical function and expression is kept close by the psychological disposition of both builders and users. The builder who constructs a wall to serve as a barrier or support is likely to want to emphasize whichever role is predominant. The user, uncertain as to how the particular wall is to be understood, will look for signs that resolve the uncertainty. The closest parallels are not with other arts, but with the world of direct human interaction. The relation between builder and user is like that between two people when they meet. Often one person wants to make a particular impression on the other and the other is looking for signs of what that impression will be. A raised fist may both indicate and be understood as a sign of aggression. Open arms may suggest both warmth and the desire to protect and be experienced at so doing. Just as a raised fist really is an instrument of aggression before it is a sign of it, so a wall really does exclude before it expresses exclusion. Buildings have always been put up either to satisfy the needs and aspirations of an individual or group which cannot be satisfied in any other way or else to enlarge on and clarify an existing direct physical relationship between one individual or group and others. The signs and symbols employed in them are inevitably an extension of simpler and more direct ones used by individuals and groups to express themselves and communicate with one another.

The earliest buildings must always have had a value as signs as well as a value as structures. The wall and roof of a primitive hut was always a sign of protection, its inner posts signs of stability, its doorway a sign of openness and its door and threshold signs of controlled access. The sight of a single hut must have evoked feelings of domestic security and the view of a group of huts a sense of social coherence. The bounding fence must always have symbolized safety, the hearth warmth. If seeing and entering one's own settlement brought emotions of relaxation and happiness, seeing and entering that of a rival would provoke uncertainty and fear. Those who prepared the timber and other materials for these structures would have known the significance of what they were doing as much as those who eventually saw and used the finished building. To the extent that such structures were essential for the survival of individual and community, they inevitably became the containers of individual and communal identity. If they were strong and in good condition, they secured such identities. If they were weak or damaged, insecurity threatened.

Architecture thus from the beginning gave meaning to concepts which were fundamental to existence. In many cases hut and settlement did not just communicate the meaning of family or tribe, they constituted them. Such is the importance of architecture for many modern tribal peoples that a particular building type or part of a building may be seen as symbolic of a person in terms of sex or social role, and the early settlements which constituted the first architectural expression are likely to have functioned in a similar way. Certainly from Africa to Oceania the configuration of buildings or groups of buildings was often explicitly understood as modelling relationships, whether amongst people or between people and the supernatural. Well-studied examples are the Dogon villages in which the whole community is arranged to articulate the relative positions of men and women, with the men's house and smithy placed at one end where their analogy with the head in relation to the body expresses their authoritative functions (see Figure 1) (Griaule 1949). The exploitation of the correlation between architecture and the human body as a key to

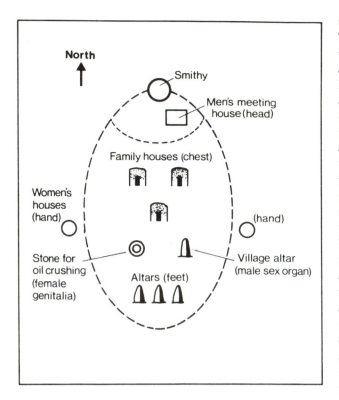

Figure 1 *Diagram of a Dogon village* (Source: *Griaule 1949*)

expressive function is a repeated theme in all cultures and reflects the underlying awareness that the response to buildings is cognate with the response to people.

While it is difficult to extract meaning from the post holes which are the most frequent evidence for early architecture, with the appearance of the first cities better testimony survives in the form of more permanent structures and literary evidence. These document how the expressive power of architecture increased to match the rise in social pressures. Within the dense urban fabric of the cities of Mesopotamia and elsewhere the need to differentiate the roles and statuses of individuals and institutions became ever more urgent. A knowledge of the varied degrees of robustness of different timbers, bricks and stones meant that degrees of strength and durability could also be expressed. Degrees of ornament expressed degrees of wealth. Degrees of complexity of layout were a measure of organizational skills, degrees of accuracy of execution indices of levels of supervision. If a tower represented the ability to dominate and protect, a taller tower could mean greater domination and more towers greater protection. The same was true of taller or thicker walls. A bigger pyramid meant more of almost everything. So did a bigger ziggurat, and greater closeness to heaven and the gods besides.

As buildings became more complicated it was often felt desirable to spell out the meaning of their signs. Erishum I, King of Assyria, built a gate and named the door 'protective goddess', the lock 'Be strong' and the threshold 'Be alert' (Grayson 1972: 12). Solomon's Temple according to the Old Testament was preceded by two columns, one labelled Iachin or 'In him is strength' and the other Boaz or 'He shall establish' (I Kings 7: 21). In areas such as China, where unusually stable social and architectural conditions developed, whole systems of signs and symbols arose. These could be referred to as common knowledge, as when Confucius criticized a fellow townsman for having a house decorated with 'mountain capitals and pondweed kingposts' because these were ornaments associated with higher social status. They could also be codified in books of etiquette such as the *Li Chi*, which says that 'The pillars of the Sons of Heaven are red, those of the feudal princes blackish, those of high officials blue-green and those of the other gentry yellow', or explained by scholars such as the learned commentator on the *Ch'un Ch'iu* who notes that 'the rafters of the shrine of a son of Heaven are to be hewn, rubbed smooth, and polished with a fine stone. Those of the princes are to be hewn and rubbed only, and those of high officials merely hewn' (Sickman and Soper 1971: 366). By the early first millennium the role of architectural signs and symbols was becoming well understood from the China Sea to the Mediterranean. What had previously been an unconscious experience now became consciously exploited by rulers and officials anxious to use all instruments to maintain or modify the social order. Yet it was the unconscious and instinctive nature of people's response to architectural forms which continued to guarantee their power.

In the restlessly competitive world of ancient Greece and Rome, as people sought increasingly to understand the mechanisms of influence and communication on which power and survival were based, responses became more consciously articulated. At one level unconscious reactions were formally recognized and brought to the level of consciousness. Homer compares a well-drilled military formation to a well-built wall (*Iliad* XVI/212–15). Fortification walls become important attributes for cities and the block-work of all walls is treated with a new attention. Euripides makes Iphigeneia dream about her brother Orestes as a column and then interpret her dream as meaning that 'the columns of a house are sons' (*Iphigeneia in Tauris*, line 57). Columns become more important features of architecture than ever before at the same time that a city's young men become more important too. This universalization of the meaning of the column tends to reduce dramatically the representational value of such forms. Representation is replaced by convention.

In Egypt, earlier, some columns had been decorated with palms and papyrus and represented the wealth and fruitfulness of the land, while others had attached Osiris figures and represented the indestructibility of the dead and his tomb. In Greece columns became schematized as fluted vertical supports which, like young men in the community, support house or temple, and, like the best

Figure 2 *The Parthenon, Athens, 447–31 BC.* (Photograph: *J. Onians*)

young men on parade, are uniform in type and regular in their disposition (see Figure 2). In Rome conventions became more important for elements which were already well known. The triangular pediment, for example, became, by virtue of its association with the temple, the insignia of authority, being described as such by Cicero (*De Oratore* 3, 46, 180) and awarded to Julius Caesar as an emblem to put on his house (*Florus* 4, 2). In a more general way, steps and podia became recognized as indices of relative status. For new elements such as the arch, dome and apse, all forms which were easier and cheaper to construct in Roman architecture, new meanings were developed. The arch became associated with the heavens and with conquest, being used with particular emphasis on temple and palace façades and on triumphal and other arches. The dome became recognized as an image of the heavens and thus appropriate to tombs and to the residence.[1] The semicircular niche, probably because it encourages optical concentration while being at the same time cognate with the arch and the dome, became a favourite setting of the emperor and his surrogate as well as of the statues of deities. The architecture-based mnemonic devices of the Roman rhetoricians probably played an important part in strengthening a tendency to use architecture as a system of signs serving as the means of organizing various forms of knowledge.[2]

With the appearance of Christianity, architecture, especially religious architecture, to some extent shifted categories. Building was downgraded along with other worldly material activities and was only rescued by being given a new function as a system of metaphors. Church buildings were increasingly experienced in the terms of the Bible, biblical commentaries, the liturgy, and sermons. The church as a whole was typically adapted from the basilica form which allowed the legal authority of the imperial judicial system to be transferred to God's law and the guarantee of redemption.

The whole building, or just its altar end, might be seen as prefiguring the Heavenly Jerusalem, with its jewelled walls and the Lamb at its centre.[3] The octagonal baptistery was both a tomb and a place of renewal. Jerome said that the only true temple was the soul and so the church might acquire more and larger doors and windows, so that, as Paulinus tells us, Christ might have easier access (Goldschmitt 1940: 307–13). Columns, which were expensive and might otherwise have been the most dangerous tokens of material display, were thought of as apostles, grouped as twelve and placed where they could support the whole building, just as Paul in the Acts claims that the living apostles support the Church (*Galatians* 2: 9). The arch separating nave from altar became an arch of triumph over death (Onians 1988: 59). The experience of religious architecture, by far the most important category for the next thousand years, was shaped by priests and commentators. Buildings were designed to match their interpretations.

The first Christian structures continued to use the architectural forms usual in the Roman empire, but from the Carolingian period onwards there was a further shift. With the decline of cities culture retreated to the monastery and, as the material world collapsed, monks built in their minds a new reality inspired by their reading of the Bible and the church fathers. In a northern Europe poor in real buildings writers like Alcuin of York imagined and gave new meaning to the buildings of the Old Testament, and their biblical commentaries came to form the basis for a whole new interpretation of architecture by writers such as Hrabanus Maurus. Taking up reflections on buildings such as Solomon's Temple, the architectural elements of the encyclopedia of Hrabanus Maurus were all given 'mystical signification'. The door was Christ, columns were apostles or doctors of the church, their bases the Testaments and so on (Hrabanus Maurus: cols 403–5).[4]

Increasingly these and other interpretations affected the new wave of church construction. In terms of the plan, buildings were laid out embodying significant numbers, with threes alluding to the Trinity, eight to the beatitudes, twelves to the apostles and so on. In terms of elevation, since the attribute of the apostles as founders of the church was strength, columns were increasingly replaced by piers. Christ as the 'corner stone' could be particularly well represented by a pier. Later, when the two walls of the church were seen as representing Jews and Gentiles or the clergy and the laity and it became increasingly appropriate that they meet in Christ, the 'cornerstone' or 'keystone', vaults with transverse arches spanned naves and choirs, and intersecting vaults made the two walls meet in a cross with Christ at the centre (Onians 1988: 103). Out of all this emerged the architecture we now call Romanesque, with its carved portals, figured windows, piers and vaults. The only problem with the new magnificent and robust buildings which rose throughout Europe with the revival of economic life was that they were in growing conflict with the traditional Christian values which opposed worldly materialism.

The most articulate exponents of these values were the theologians of the twelfth- and thirteenth-century School of Paris, and it was around Paris that a new architecture was developed which sought to defend itself by minimizing its worldly presence and intensifying its 'mystical signification' (Onians 1988: 112–14). This was the architecture later called Gothic. To minimize its materiality walls were reduced in mass, and piers slimmed to slender vertical supports rising past flimsy sheets of glass to ribbed vaults floating high above. To make even more clear the 'mystical signification' already implicit in the columnar apostles and other statues attached to portals, the semicircular arch tainted with Roman paganism was abandoned. The pointed form with which it was replaced evoked the convergence of branches, and capitals and pinnacles were now covered with fleshy growing leaves, so that what before had been a mass of heavy, dead stone became a flowering embodiment of the living church (Onians 1988: 119–23). The Ste Chapelle in Paris (1246–8), in which the new way of building was most consistently developed, became a model for churches throughout Europe (see Figure 3).

Figure 4 *Tragic scene, showing the setting of noble actions of the upper classes.* (Source: *Serlio 1545*)

The abandonment of Gothic architecture, first in Italy in the fifteenth century and then throughout Europe in the sixteenth, is associated with a shift of economic and political power from the religious to the secular sphere, which in turn shaped several new trends in architectural meaning. In Florence the vitalistic Gothic style became identified with northern Germanic domination, by virtue of its association with hostile Milan, and found itself shunned in favour of the earlier, local Romanesque and ultimately Roman round-arched styles associated with earlier periods of Italian independence. These were now revived as were the associated political institutions. Towers had earlier been symbols of the aspirations for dominance of competing families and now families such as the Medici used the new architectural forms to argue their political ambitions in more complex ways, as we can understand by reading contemporary theorists such as Alberti (1485) and Filarete (1460–4). The materials, proportions and ornaments of columns, doors and windows were used to distinguish the houses of different social classes and different categories of activity within individual building complexes. Rows of identical columns, arches and windows, all framed within a rigorous geometry, indicated a respect for law and order and offered an image of a society in which the new economic and political instabilities were held in check.

Accuracy of layout and detail and a studied correspondence with earlier medieval Tuscan and Roman monuments demonstrated a local and national pride, which inspired, and learning, which impressed. By 1545 Serlio was able to contrast the stable order of an essentially classical tragic scene, the setting of the noble deeds of the upper classes, with a Gothic comic scene, setting of the more uncontrolled actions of the urban middle

Figure 3 *Interior of the Ste Chappelle, Paris, 1246–8.* (Photograph: *Marburg*)

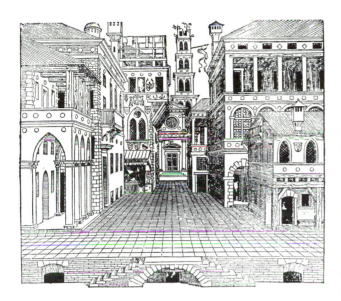

Figure 5 *Comic scene, showing the setting of the uncontrolled actions of the urban middle and lower classes.* (Source: *Serlio 1545*)

and lower classes (see Figures 4 and 5). So positive were the perceived associations of the new classical style of architecture that it soon became established throughout Europe. Kings and princes, national and local governments, recognized it as an essential emblem of power, knowledge and order.

These heavy associations of the now predominant classical architecture inevitably denied the possibility of giving expression to other values and this eventually led to those subsidiary transformations which characterize that seventeenth-century architecture which has come to be defined as baroque. In religious buildings, for example, a heightened spirituality could best be expressed by increased curvilinearity, projection and recession, compression, attenuation and so on, as is first demonstrated in Italy. In the secular world similar features were adapted for use in palaces and government buildings as a means for expressing political power of a more dynamic type, especially in Continental Europe where royal and princely courts held real power into the eighteenth century. In England, by contrast, with the rise of parliament, the avoidance of such curves and a calculated submission to Palladian rules is associated with a recognition that the sacrifice of power by individual members of the aristocracy may increase their collective strength and authority, with benefit to all.

By the mid-eighteenth century the associations of the forms of classical architecture, whether with the Catholic Church or with the English social order, became too limiting for patrons whose preferences had often been developed by personal experiences such as travel or reading. Responding to these aspirations, architects and builders began to exploit other styles which

were seen as the signs of new and private values. Gothic was adapted as 'Gothick', a style more appropriate to an ambience of secret fantasy and intense meditation. Chinese pagodas seemed to express an ancient sympathy with nature. After 1800 the range was further increased. In France Egyptian forms came to be understood as symbolic of death in the cemetery, and in England Islamic forms were introduced to provide an appropriate setting for the wayward lifestyle of the Prince Regent in his Brighton Pavilion. Towers for superiority, pyramids for eternity, domes for pleasure, battlements for protection, colonnades for well-mannered walking; educated owners and visitors alike were ready to have their sensibilities triggered by a wide range of architectural signs (see Wainwright 1990).

It was against this readiness to respond to architectural forms and ornaments as evocative but superficial attire that architects and patrons alike reacted as the nineteenth century advanced. Writers such as Pugin, Ruskin and William Morris were ever more stern in their criticism of such skin-deep appearances which they associated with the corrupting Renaissance revival of classical architecture (see, most recently, Swenarton 1990). For them, Gothic architecture alone had real integrity, its outer forms reflecting not only inner

Figure 6 Unité d'habitation, *Marseilles, 1957–8, by Le Corbusier.*

physical structures but inner spiritual beliefs as well. In France an even more rigorous reaction led by Viollet-le-Duc took the search for integrity so far as to see structural efficiency alone as the sign of aesthetic virtue. Once character and architecture were so closely linked, towards the end of the century other developments followed. In England classical forms were again revived by those who saw them as the best expression of national traits of harmony, order and good manners, while in the United States Louis Sullivan found an appropriate embodiment of the energy and vitality of his new country in surging skyscrapers rippling with organic ornament.

Architecture in the twentieth century has lost none of the types of significance developed earlier, except to some extent in the buildings of the International Movement, whose architects claimed to seek to avoid expressing variations of nation, class, character, etc. and to give instead pre-eminence to universal human functional needs. For Le Corbusier and others concrete and steel offered the optimum means of meeting these requirements. Ornament was banned, as vast projects exploiting sober variations on the simple post and lintel became the required sign of a healthy society (see Figure 6). It was, however, only a matter of time before people came to sense the unhealthiness both of these new societies and of their associated architectures. Individual energies were liberated and personal aspirations tolerated. By the 1980s, architects and patrons rushed to put on again the clothing of arches and vaults, columns and mouldings, which were collectively seen as the sign of a society unashamed of its varied past and vigorous in its diversity. In England there has been a particular effort to associate good building design with good human behaviour. To encourage this the Prince of Wales has formulated a set of Ten Commandments for architects, many of whom once again acknowledge that buildings are ultimately complex instruments for articulating human interaction (see Charles, Prince of Wales 1989). In the 1990s the range of available signs and symbols is greater than it has ever been. It only remains to be seen whether patrons and architects can use them individually with enough sensitivity, and users respond to them with enough alertness, to endow them again with full expressive and communicative power.

NOTES

1   For the meaning of the dome see especially Smith 1956.
2   For ancient memory systems in general see Yates 1966, and for their possible application in Roman art see Onians 1990.
3   For a general discussion of the meaning of medieval church architecture see Krautheimer 1942. For the church and the Heavenly Jerusalem see Rossi and Rovetta 1983.
4   For a detailed interpretation see Onians 1988: 74–81.

REFERENCES

Alberti, L.B. (1485) *De Re Aedificatoria*, trans J. Rykwert, N. Leach and R. Tavernor, *On the Art of Building, in Ten Books*, 1988, Cambridge, Mass. and London: MIT Press.

Charles, Prince of Wales (1989) *A Vision of Britain: A Personal View of Architecture*, London and New York: Doubleday.

Filarete, A. (1460–4) *Trattato d'Architettura*, trans. J. Spencer, 1965, *Treatise on Architecture*, 2 vols, New Haven and London: Yale University Press.

Goldschmitt, R.C. (1940) 'Paulinus' churches at Nola', *Carmen* 28, 11: 307–13.

Grayson, A. (1972) *Assyrian Royal Inscriptions*, Vol. I, Wiesbaden: Harrassowitz.

Griaule, M. (1949) 'L'image du monde au Soudan', *Journal de la société des Africanistes* XIX: 81–8.

Hrabanus Maurus, *De universo*, in J.P. Migne (ed.) (from 1844) *Patrologiae Cursus*, Series Latina, Vol. CXI, cols 9–614, Paris: Garnier.

Krautheimer, R. (1942 'Introduction to an iconography of Medieval architecture', *Journal of the Warburg and Courtauld Institutes* 5: 1–33.

Onians, J. (1988) *Bearers of Meaning: The Classical Orders in Antiquity, the Middle Ages and the Renaissance*, Princeton, NJ: Princeton University Press.

——— (1990) *Quintilian and the Idea of Roman Art*, Oxford: Oxford University Committee for Archaeology.

Rossi, M. and Rovetta, A. (1983) 'Indagine sullo spazio ecclesiale immagine della Gerusalemme celeste', in M.L. Gatti Perrer (ed.) *La Gerusalemme Celeste*, Milan: Università Cattolica Milano.

Serlio, S. (1545) *Regole generali de architettura, Libro Terzo*, Venice.

Sickman, K. and Soper, A. (1971) *The Art and Architecture of China*, Harmondsworth: Penguin.

Smith, B. (1956) *The Dome: A study in the History of Ideas*, Princeton, NJ: Princeton University Press.

Swenarton, M. (1988) *Artisans and Architects: Ruskinian Tradition in Architectural Thought*, London: Macmillan.

Wainwright, C. (1990) *The Romantic Interior: The British Collector at Home 1750–1850*, New Haven and London: Yale University Press.

Yates, F. (1966) *The Art of Memory*, Oxford: Oxford University Press.

FURTHER READING

Bandmann, G. (1951) *Mittelalterliche Architektur als Bedeutungsträager*, Berlin: Gebr. Mann.

Hersey, G. (1988) *The Lost Meaning of Classical Architecture: Speculations on Ornament from Vitruvius to Venturi*, Cambridge, Mass., and London: MIT Press.

Le Corbusier (Jeanneret-Gris, C.E.) (1923) *Vers une Architecture*, Paris: Editions Crès.

Panofsky, E. (1979) *Abbot Suger on the Abbey Church of St Denis and its Art Treasures*, Princeton: NJ: Princeton University Press.

Pugin, A.W.N. (1836) *Contrasts between the Architecture of the*

15th and 19th Centuries, London: Dolman.

Scott, G. (1914) *The Architecture of Humanism,* London: Constable.

Serlio, S. (1619) *Tutte l'Opere di Architettura,* Venice: reprinted 1964, Godstone, Surrey: Gregg.

Smith, E.B. (1956) *The Architectural Symbolism of Imperial Rome,* Princeton: NJ: Princeton University Press.

Viollet-le-Duc, E. (1860) *Entretiens sur l'architecture,* Paris.

Louis Hellman

Drawing on semiotics and current linguistic philosophy, critics in the 1980s evoked a traditional 'language' of architecture as part of the critique of the alleged 'failure' of the Modern Movement. They suggested that, historically, architecture developed its own specific language complete with syntax and a grammar of signs, symbols and meanings.

Many of these symbols and meanings relate to the human body (anthropomorphism). We say buildings 'lie', 'rise up', have 'fronts', 'backs' and 'faces' (façades) with 'silhouettes' or 'profiles' and windows which 'look out'. Historically buildings had tops (heads and hats), middles (body) with 'wings' and bases (feet). Like people they had shape seen from a distance and individual features close to. Modern buildings often look alike from a distance and have no details to relate to. People refer to them as 'faceless', 'inhuman' or 'alien'.

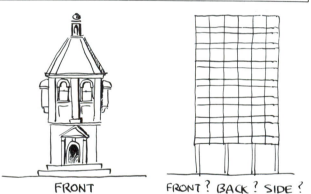

The Modern Movement rejected the old language as outdated and cliché-ridden, and sought to develop a new language based on 'functionalism' and scientific rationalism. Form would result from applying advanced technology to building problems without the need for consciously applied symbolism or aesthetic 'rhetoric'.

In practice the Modernists took as their model buildings which *symbolized* 'efficiency' or 'utility': factories, industrial warehouses and engineering structures. The repetitive, gridded appearance of these buildings became merely a metaphor for scientific rationalism. The buildings expressed the *process* of construction, linear, sequential and additive, as paradigms for machine production or literal rationalization. In other words, Modernism became another style, a machine style, without the truly rational principles it started out from.

The result has been confusion, a communication breakdown between architect and public.

A later source of Modern Movement symbolism was the mechanical machine itself: the aeroplane, the locomotive, the automobile and, particularly, the ocean liner. As machines these were seen to be functional and efficient, and when their appearance was transferred to buildings they in turn seemed to have these characteristics. Early machines often expressed their constituent parts or separated out their functions, for example stairs, flues, ducts and pipes, and buildings followed suit.

Le Corbusier's famous description of the house as 'a machine for living in' reinforces the attempt to break with the language of the past. Since then machine-image euphemisms have been rife in modern architecture. Access balconies become 'decks', plans 'work', elevations are 'articulated', stairs are 'nodes', and so on.

Much of both the aesthetic and actual language of modern architecture also mirrors bureaucratic jargon, cold and ulitarian with no spiritual content. Homes are 'dwelling units', 'low-rise, high-density complexes' or 'point blocks'.

Recent attempts to return to the so-called traditional language of architecture are personified in the 'post-modern' styles: Post-Modernism itself, which grafts old symbols onto modern bodies; pseudo-vernacular, which apes and inflates hand-made traditional buildings for large-scale developments; and reproduction classicism, which clothes supermarkets and computer centres in eighteenth-century garb. This is the architectural equivalent of 'illiteracy'.

Defining architecture in terms of language is inherently limited, and it is no coincidence that it emanates from critics and writers rather than designers. The language of architecture is not static. Modern Movement terms and symbols have been absorbed into the old grammar: 'skyscraper', 'picture window', 'open-plan', 'patio doors', and so on. Airports, office blocks, geodesic domes and other new building types have entered the visual language, and sometimes modern symbols have even replaced archaic ones – a flat-roofed, large-glazed typical school, for example.

The language of architecture is not limited to symbols or signifiers but includes space, time, form, atmosphere, texture, colour, and so on. Using this vocabulary a great architect can create poetry and evoke a spiritual response, whether dealing with a new or old building type, without recourse to mimicking played-out clichés.

88 Expression and interpretation in architecture
Juan Pablo Bonta

Expression and interpretation are aspects of the wider field of meaning in architecture. I shall begin by presenting a simple distinction between expression and interpretation that reflects common parlance, is free from technicalities, and is easy to use. This will be followed by a more exacting model of their relationship, leading to a description of the process of meaning formation and meaning change in architecture.

Architecture *expresses*; architecture is *interpreted*. The distinction between the active and the passive forms of these verbs reveals a significant difference between expression and interpretation. Architecture appears to be playing an active role in the first statement: it expresses certain values or meanings which are received by the passive viewer/user. In the other case, the viewer/user is placed in the role of active interpreter of an essentially passive architecture.

Architecture expresses whatever was embedded into it, so to speak, by the architect, as well as by the other participants in the processes of design and construction. It reflects the social and aesthetic values and the technical judgement of the architect, as well as the skill of the builders, and the largesse of the owners. It reveals the quality of the building's maintenance over time and the habits and behaviour of the users themselves. Ultimately, the content of expression may be extended to include values determined by society at large. Similarly, the interpretation of architecture may be the work of a single person (a critic, a historian, or simply a user); more often, however, interpreters influence each other, so that finally the interpretation may result, as in the case of expression, from an evolving, collective process incorporating an entire social or cultural group.

Both architectural expression and interpretation can be individual or collective, or both; but in the case of expression there is a further possibility, unparalleled in the realm of interpretation: architecture can express values by itself, without the mediation of human agents. Certain qualities of the materials, or the climate, or the passage of time – to mention just a few examples – may add to the expressive content of an architectural work without having been embedded into the fabric by the designer or the users, either consciously or inadvertently. These expressive contents may originate in an unforeseeable chain of events, like the beauty of a sunset or a configuration of waves on the sea. Interpretation, in contrast, cannot occur *ex nihilo*; it necessarily presupposes actions by a human agent – either individual or collective.

Let us use the words *content of architectural expression* to refer to whatever is expressed (or implied) by architecture; likewise, *content of architectural interpretation* is whatever an interpretation infers about architecture. Must these two contents coincide? In other words, does architectural expression determine interpretation, and is the latter expected to be merely a verbal rendering of the former? If these questions were to be answered in the affirmative, an easy validation mechanism could be devised; interpretations would be valid to the extent that they reflect whatever the building expresses.

Tempting as this approach might be, one must nevertheless refrain from endorsing it for a number of reasons – the simplest of which is that the distinction between expression and interpretation would in this case blur to the point of losing all usefulness: the two would become merely different facets of the same process.

Buildings in actual social practice are subject to changing, and often contradictory, interpretations. This can be verified by even a cursory analysis of the architectural literature, which is rich in instances of divergent interpretations of the same building by different critics or historians, or even by the same writer at different points in time. As historians may disagree about the characterization of a building, so jury members may dissent about the worth of a competition entry, and studio critics may differ in their assessment of a student project.

There is no logical inconsistency in admitting the possibility of divergent interpretations of the same work; but if interpretations are expected to be a direct corollary of expression, the issue becomes murky: except for the most extraordinary of circumstances, architecture can hardly express, at the same time, contradictory or changing contents. If coincidence between expression and interpretation is expected, it would follow that of a set of conflicting interpretations only one could be correct, all others necessarily becoming false. Many architectural interpretations in literature and in daily practice are flimsy and could easily be dismissed as flawed; but there are also instances of well-reasoned, cogent interpretations by articulate and respected persons that are at odds with each other, regardless of how one measures reasoning, cogency, articulation and respect. To postulate that only one of them can be correct would be inconsistent with accepted social practices.

If coincidence between the contents of expression and interpretation cannot be taken for granted, both expression and interpretation must play a role in a comprehensive view of meaning in architecture. In fact, any taxonomy of the field must include, at least, the two components.

Interpretations are easier to examine than expressions. Typically, interpretations are conveyed in verbal form – printed and non-printed – in books, journals, magazines, newspapers, lectures, discussions or conversations. Renderings, cartoons and movies may also embody interpretations. But how does one isolate for analysis the content of architectural or artistic expression? Expression cannot be accessed directly, but only through the mediation of interpretations! The question about the coincidence between expression and interpretation necessarily becomes one about matching two interpretations, one of which (usually one's own) being implicitly regarded as the privileged one. Architectural expression, very often, is *my* interpretation of the building; *yours*, on the other hand, is *only* an interpretation. This is, alas, neither defensible or convincing!

Another way to learn about the content of architectural expression would be to ask those directly responsible for it – typically, the architects themselves. There are, however, several shortcomings in taking the word of architects as the ultimate criterion in determining the meaning of their work. First, it could only be done if the architects were alive and available, or if they recorded their thoughts in writing or some other medium. Second, it excludes important legitimate components of expression, such as the effect of maintenance and usage, as well as whatever architecture can express 'by itself'. Third, competent architects may be poor interpreters: they may not know what their work stands for, or they may be incapable of expressing it verbally. Or, conversely, they may be gifted with words, but if they are poor architects they may be incapable of moulding their thoughts into spatial form. To paraphrase a famous dictum of Wimsatt and Beardsley, architecture must be judged like a pudding or a machine: what matters is how it works, not how it was intended to work. Finally, even if the privileged interpretation originates in someone who has played a unique role in the creative process, the content of expression still appears embodied in a (presumably verbal) interpretation.

Let us now explore a somewhat more involved, but ultimately more fruitful, way of describing the relationship between expression and interpretation. The key to this view consists in replacing the notion of *intentionality* for expression. We may often be incapable of penetrating the full range of intentions of an artist or an architect, as noted above; but we do know, at least, that some of the meanings embodied in their work were placed there deliberately, with the purpose of influencing or literally moving us in certain ways – for example, an elaborate door frame to mark an access or an exit. In contrast, other components in the meaning of the work, sometimes no less moving or influential (for example, the results of prolonged use, or a passing quality of light due to the clouds), were not specifically intended or foreseen in the original conception. We may not know for sure what was intended and what was not, but in

terms of the broadest categories, we generally do know. In cases where intentions are unclear, we may question the architects themselves: intentions, unlike expression, belong to the realm of personal subjectivity, and architects' statements about such matters are, in principle, more trustworthy than statements about the meaning of their work. More importantly, interpreters invariably make quick and often unverifiable assumptions about what was and what was not intended in a work and subsequent interpretations are moulded accordingly.

The meaning of architecture can be classified into a series of components according to the answers to two simple questions: (1) was the meaning intentionally embodied in the work by those responsible for it (architect, builders, managers, and so on); and (2) is intentionality recognized by the interpreters? Three out of the four possible combinations of answers typically correspond to types of meaning that are most relevant to design: communication, indication, and intentional indication (see Figure 1).

The statement 'It rains' is a (verbal) signal, intentionally used by someone to communicate something, and recognized by the hearer as being intentional. The sound of rain over the roof, on the other hand, is an index of rain, but not a signal, for it is neither intentionally used to communicate nor is it recognized as being used in that capacity. Indices inform about the 'state-of-the-world'; signals convey 'states-of-mind' (thoughts) of the speaker. Signals may be misread or misunderstood, like indices. In addition, the producers or emitters of signals may be wrong, or they may purposefully try to deceive the interpreters. As indices have no emitters, the possibility of emission error or deceit is not part of the picture in the case of indices.

Generally speaking, interpretations can be validated (1) *intentionally*, by checking them against emitter intentions ('does he or she mean that it is raining?'), (2) *factually*, by checking them against reality ('Is it raining?'), and (3) *socially*, by checking them against the interpretations of other members of the community ('Do others think that this means that it is raining?'). Intentional validation is appropriate only for the communicative component of meaning: success in this area – and in this area only – is measured by the degree of coincidence between intended communication and communication as decoded. Factual validation is generally possible

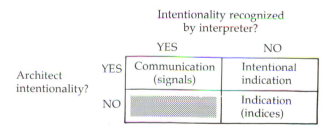

Figure 1 *Components of meaning.*

throughout the entire design gamut ('Is this comfortable-looking chair really comfortable? Is this cathedral-looking structure a cathedral?'), but it rarely applies to the finer points of design meaning: few people would know how to determine whether a beautiful-looking cathedral is really beautiful. Intentional validation isn't often very effective: only scholars could validate intentionally or factually an interpretation of a Gothic cathedral and its statuary; lay people lack access to the pertinent historical and iconographical sources. This is not to imply, however, that they will be uninterested in such a building; they will visit the site in large numbers, participate in guided tours, consult brochures and pamphlets. Also, they will discriminate between acceptable and unacceptable interpretations, validating them socially, preferably by matching them against the interpretations of other tourists. Social validation of architectural interpretations is pervasive: professional, cultural and age groups develop elaborate environmental interpretation systems which are often part of the very cement that holds the group together.

Let us now turn to a simple design example. An architect designing a bar must make sure that the public will recognize the place for what it is. This could be achieved by placing a sign 'BAR' over the entrance; in reading the signal, people would learn what the establishment is, and would realize that the information was conveyed to them *intentionally* by whoever placed the sign – the designer or perhaps the owner. This would be an instance of communication (see Table 1, line 1). Alternatively, users could find out about the nature of the place merely from the sights and sounds obtained from peering through its doors or windows; in this case, no design intention would be apparent, and none would be inferred. The meaning would be the same ('This is a bar'), but it would result from an *indication* conveyed by indices (Table 1, line 2). In one case, patrons are 'told' that this is a bar, in the other case, they merely find it out.

Most designers would shun using labels or signs to make their designs understandable; ideally, users should recognize designed objects for what they are directly, as matters of fact. Design intentions exist, but the semantic operation is most successful if the interpreters remain unaware of intentionality. One can imagine the design of the first Western-type saloon door, with its open areas above and below: perhaps the design intention was to allow for views, sounds and smells to get through, revealing towards the outside the presence of the bar without using communication.[1] Passers-by were to be faced with a matter of fact, even if the reading was made possible because of purposeful design manipulation. This is *intentional indication* – a particularly important component of meaning in architecture and design (Table 1, line 3).

Repeated usage of the saloon door and its popularization through pictures and films will lead to a fundamental change in the nature of its interpretation (see Figure 2). People will no longer need to peep above or below, or listen to the conversation and noises, to recognize the place as a bar; its presence will be *communicated* by the door acting as an architectural signal, comparable to the verbal sign 'BAR'. It will become increasingly less important that actual vision be made possible above the door. As the door becomes conventionalized, its shape may become gradually more schematic or simplified: fewer and fewer of its formal elements may suffice to evoke the meaning of the entire form. When the door becomes a signal it will broadcast that the place is a bar according to a newly established formal vocabulary. As it is the case with any verbal signal, the message could be deceitful or wrong. Interpreters will realize that they are faced not with a 'state-of-the-world', but with a *statement* – 'a state-of-mind' of a store owner or store-front designer (Table 1, line 4).

We are told that hard drinking, crude language and rowdy behaviour were common in Western bars, and no 'ladies' were supposed to be there. When going through

Table 1 The example of the bar door

	Form	Meaning	Component
1	BAR sign	bar	communication
2	open bar	bar	indication
3	saloon door	bar	intentional
4	saloon door	bar	communication
5	saloon door	masculinity	indication
6	same door in sophisticated men's store	masculinity	intentional indication
7	same door	masculinity	communication
8	same door	sophistication	indication
9	same door in fast-food restaurant	sophistication	intentional indication

Figure 2 *A Western saloon and bar door* (Source: *Erdoes 1979*)

the bar doors, patrons knew that they would find, as a matter of fact, a pattern of social interaction seen at the time as typically masculine. This may become the basis for a process of re-semantization, or change of meaning (Table 1, line 5).

Many years later the designer of a sophisticated men's store may discover that she can lure more customers into the shop by exploiting the image of masculinity that by now is associated with the saloon door. Her manipulation of the meaning is intentional, but the trick is most effective if intentionality is not apparent – if the customer truly lives through the fantasy (Table 1, line 6).

If the image is successful, competitors of the store are likely to follow suit; slowly at first, and then more decidedly, sophisticated men's stores will adopt the imagery. Eventually, the new meaning will become conventionalized, losing much of its force (Table 1, line 7). By this time, however, people may expect to see these doors in exclusive stores; if the doors are not there, maybe the store is not all that exclusive. At this stage, the doors have become an indication of sophistication (Table 1, line 8). A new cycle could begin if (say) fast-food restaurants would adopt similar doors, in an attempt to cloak themselves in an aura of exclusivity by building on the emerging meaning.

There is a complex interaction of two types of force here. On the one hand, there is conventionalization of meaning, a process that leads from indication to communication, with indices becoming intentional indices and finally crystallizing into signals. This is a conservative influence impelling stabilization of meaning and, sometimes, decay or simplification in forms. On the other hand, there are forces working towards endowing the same forms with new meanings emerging from the particular context in which they are used. Signals, in this case, become indices, which may eventually provide a support for intentional indices. The successive cycles of conventionalization and re-semantization can follow each other endlessly (see Figure 3). Semantic change and formal evolution throughout architectural history and practice often follow this pattern.

The tri-partite model of Figure 1 can be related to the dual view of expression/interpretation introduced earlier in the essay. The rows of the diagram represent expression: the upper row is the part of expression controlled by the architect, the lower row corresponds to the part conveyed by 'architecture itself'. The columns, in turn, describe the situation from the vantage point of the interpreter: meaning as communication on the left-side column, and meaning as indication on the right-side column. The model reveals that expression and interpretation in architecture often overlap, but do not necessarily coincide.

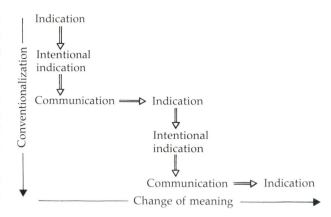

Figure 3 *Pattern of conventionalization and change of meaning.*

NOTE

1   One man's remembrance of his boyhood:

> I always wanted to see the picture of the 'nakkid lady' over the bar and would sneak back and forth in front of them swingin' doors hoping to get a good look, but them doors were working too businesslike, operating on steel springs. You could peak under them and see a lot of boots and spurs lined up by the bar, or you could stand on your tippie-toes and admire a bunch of big hats, but I never got a good look at the nude lady until I was old enough to walk in and buy a drink.
>
> (quoted in Erdoes 1979)

ACKNOWLEDGEMENT

The author gratefully acknowledges Dr Michael Eckersley's editorial suggestions.

REFERENCES

Erdoes, R. (1979) *Saloons of the Old West*, New York: Kopfl.
Wimsatt, W.K. and Beardsley, M.C. (1954) 'The intentional fallacy', in W.K. Wimsatt (ed.) *The Verbal Icon: Studies in the Meaning of Poetry*, Lexington, Ky.: University of Kentucky Press.

FURTHER READING

Bonta, J.P. (1979) *Architecture and its Interpretation. A Study of Expressive Systems in Architecture*, London: Lund Humphries.
——— (1980) 'Notes for a theory of meaning in design', in G. Broadbent, R. Bunt and C. Jencks (eds) *Signs, Symbols, and Architecture*, Chichester and elsewhere: John Wiley.
Buyssens, E. (1970) *La communication et l'articulation linguistique*, Brussels: Presses Universitaires de Bruxelles.

89 The role of the critic

Wayne Attoe

Critics have three classic roles – description, interpretation and judgement – and sometimes assume a fourth and fifth as well. Critics describe buildings and the circumstances associated with their design and construction. Critics interpret buildings, advocating particular ways of understanding architecture. And critics judge buildings by measuring them against selected norms. Critics sometimes move beyond these traditional roles to criticize criticism itself; in doing this they formulate new ways of describing, interpreting and judging architecture. In a fifth role the critic uses the criticism of buildings as a vehicle to accomplish something else, to make a work of art.

These roles are played out in a variety of settings including newspapers, classrooms, professional journals and books, and even the local building inspector's office. While critics historically have focused on individual buildings as subjects for their commentaries, increasingly critics understand that buildings need not – should not – be thought of in isolation, that they must be considered within a broader context. Thus the scope of architecture criticism extends to urban design and city planning, and to product design.

DESCRIPTION

One role of the critic, description, helps us see things we might not otherwise have seen, and tells us things we might not otherwise have known. Some descriptive criticism explains the building itself. Without the critic's help, we might not realize, for example, that the stone exterior of one building is thick and acts structurally to carry the weight of the storeys above, and that in a neighbouring building the stone we see is a thin skin masking a hidden steel frame which is the true, working structural system. Similarly, a building whose visual character seems confused or incomprehensible suddenly can seem reasonable when the critic describes for us the ordering system that underlies it.

Other description explains a building's functioning, for example that surveillance of institutionalized persons is accomplished from a central point from which all doors can be seen, or from a network of substations, or with television cameras. Knowing its functional organization often can help us understand a building's form, and thus lend a greater appreciation for the whole.

A type of descriptive criticism we too seldom encounter is revelation of the processes through which building designs have come about. How different our understanding of two buildings will be when we know

that one was designed by an architect working in an office hundreds of miles away and with infrequent client contact, and that a second building emerged from workshops with a building committee, and that the final design was the architect's amalgamation of that group's ideas. One's impression of buildings cannot but be affected by such information about their generation.

While some description is about building fabric, and other description is about design development and building production, equally illuminating description is about the architect and about the context in which the design was formulated. To appreciate why certain automobile service stations were designed as pagoda-roofed 'Oriental' tea houses, one needs to understand the economic and social context in which the designs were developed (competitive oil companies, increasing automobile ownership), and the educational background of the architect (trained to design in the Beaux-Arts manner of thoughtfully choosing from among a variety of precedents.) The 'Oriental' style was virtually the only precedent which was not already associated with another building type and also was eye-catching. Given the method and circumstances, the choice of this form was almost inevitable (see Figure 1).

The extent and impact of this descriptive role in criticism are influenced by the context in which the criticism appears. Critics writing for newspapers often must use many column-inches to acquaint readers with

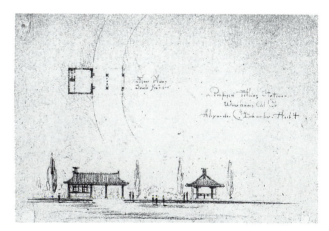

Figure 1 *In 1916, Alexander C. Eschweiler, an architect from Milwaukee, Wisconsin, who had studied at Cornell University, designed a prototype for a chain of 'Oriental'-style service stations erected by the Wadhams Oil Company. The 100 or so stations built in this mode were probably the first instance of distinctive, eye-catching corporate design targeted for the automobile trade.* (Source: *Attoe and Latus 1973*)

Figure 2 *Robert Venturi's interpretation of architectural form as a 'decorated shed' has been illustrated by several critics with this photograph. It makes evident the practice of attaching information about the building's nature and use to an otherwise anonymous structure.*

the bare facts of the building under discussion, for newspapers typically publish few illustrations to accompany criticism, and many readers will not be familiar with the buildings discussed because they are new or in another locale. In scholarly criticism description is often less extensive because critics assume that readers are familiar with the building under discussion. The critic feels relieved of responsibility for extensive descriptive orientation of the reader, and uses the allotted column-inches for other purposes. Still, in other sorts of scholarly discussion description is the *raison d'être* of the piece, for this is where the building is, in effect, documented for posterity. The burden of this role is enormous, for the 'definitive' description of a building – what, when, why, how, who – often becomes the basis for much subsequent interpretation and evaluation of the building.

The importance of and need for descriptive criticism is often overlooked. Because most people do not see what architects see in buildings, the revelation of the building through straightforward description is important and a great responsibility. Straight description is typically not earth-shaking, and seldom makes demands upon critics' creativity or imagination, rather their acuity and objectivity. They must determine what is important to reveal, and must find the words, diagrams or other illustrations which will enable their audience to see and know the building (see Figure 2).

INTERPRETATION

A second role of the critic reveals something quite different. Instead of showing us the building as it is, the critic shows us how it might be interpreted. Metaphorically, the critic throws a veil of interpretation between audience and building through which the building must be seen, and with which the critic contrives a particular vision, a particular way of understanding the building. For many critics this role, interpretation, is more challenging and rewarding than straightforward description, for it demands imagination and strategy. As an advocate for a particular way of understanding a building, the critic must choose convincing similes and metaphors and must present them in a way that easily draws the audience into the particular interpretation advocated. Take a historical example. Consider how our understanding of the classic Greek *agora* changes as the metaphor of interpretation shifts. One critic sees the *agora*, a classical Greek city's commercial, social and political centre, as a stage for rituals, another as the archetypal town centre, another as a collage of only loosely related buildings, and another as a sophisticated system of aesthetic perception. Yet another critic sees each element of the *agora* as a response to the dictates of associated deities. Religious dictate, stage, perceptual system, archetype, collage – these are some of the interpretative veils that critics have employed to understand the *agora*.

Similarly, the designs of the American architect Frank Gehry are characterized, alternatively, as manneristic decadence, as a critique of contemporary culture, as a regional flowering, as a fashion, and as a deconstruction of architectural conventions. It is in this way, through particular metaphorical visions, that most interpretative criticism is formulated.

Often, through repetition and through the convergence of critical opinions, a particular interpretation of a building or architectural complex acquires a canonical quality and starts to be accepted as fact. For example, medieval towns in Europe are widely understood as 'organic' in character, not just interpreted as organic. Similarly, rationality is accepted as a central concern of Modernist architecture, not interpreted as such. Through such a convergence of opinion, interpretation seems to become fact. Eventually, however, subsequent generations of critics can be counted on to remind us that what became canonical is actually conditional, a function of metaphorical interpretation. Typically they do this by proposing an alternative metaphor.

Interpretation can be a powerful tool in the education of architects. When the critic is a teacher who proposes alternative ways of seeing the design problem a student faces, and interprets the student's design solution from a different perspective, revelations occur. The mind is opened to new possibilities, which is a requisite for creativity and problem-solving.

JUDGEMENT

A third role for the critic is judge. A design is measured against a standard and an evaluation is made. That standard might be objective, like the minima and maxima characteristic of building codes which specify with numbers the limits within which designers must work. Yet judgemental criticism can also be quite general when framed as dogma: for example, that buildings should reflect their era, or contrariwise reveal the flawed ideologies of their era; or design should follow time-honoured patterns; or in their construction, form and disposition, buildings should be ecologically responsible; or, 'There should be no features about a building which are not necessary for convenience, or propriety' (Pugin 1841: 1). While absolute in tone, dogma does not lend itself to measurement. This creates problems, for an architect can never know how close to the mark a design comes until the judgement is rendered.

Somewhat more concrete and more readily codified is judgemental criticism based on established building types. A new high-rise, for example, is measured against the tradition of skyscraper designs, their form, structure, interior organization, or impact on urban context, or a combination of these. We see the new instance in relation to its predecessors. An example is San Francisco's 'Downtown Plan' of 1984, which codified critical reaction against flat-topped, 'Manhattan' type high-rise buildings that had been erected there in recent decades. Instead of boxy forms, new high-rise designs were required to emulate an earlier high-rise type, to taper or have a more sculptural top.

Typal criticism is more specific than dogma, yet generic in contrast to the concreteness of measurable criteria. This middle position in terms of specificity makes typal criticism powerful as a guide that is not prescriptive in specific ways, yet carries the authority of a definable tradition.

Often critics in the role of judge do not specify the standard against which they are making their assessments: 'the form is weak'; 'the detailing is ungainly'; 'the concept is *retardataire*'; etc. This is especially true when aesthetic judgements are offered. Probably this failure to identify standards is because critics take them for granted, and because the explication and justification of standards is difficult. It is easier to assume the role of expert, to be someone who by virtue of their position as columnist, scholar or professor is assumed to know and need not justify the standards on which expert judgements are rendered.

CRITICISM OF CRITICISM

A fourth role is somewhat different from describer, interpreter and judge. It is a scrutinizing process in which critics reflect on the methods of criticism and, often, propose alternative techniques, points of view and standards for critical commentary. These discussions can and often do proceed without reference to buildings and places. Instead, they promote or judge critical methods in search of new or better methods for describing, interpreting and judging designs. Formalist, Marxist, structuralist, post-structuralist and deconstructionist criticism are recent examples of critical techniques which cast aside existing ones and promulgated alternative perspectives and missions for the criticism of architecture.

CRITICISM AS ART

In the fifth role the critic turns a discussion of architecture into a vehicle serving quite another purpose, the creation of a work of art. The artistry is evident in compelling photographs, in poetic commentary, in evocative drawings. The role of critic as artist is not exclusive of the other roles, it can be played simultaneously. But the emphasis clearly is on the critical piece as an artefact more than on the architectural object that precipitated it. When the poet Apollinaire shaped words to form an image of the Eiffel Tower, he was making a poem, not writing criticism (see Figure 3).

The role a critic takes or is given will vary with circumstances. Newspaper editors typically want judgements – Is the building good or bad? – and want these judgements ornamented with captivating commentary. By contrast, the editor of scholarly books wants lucid description and convincing interpretation, while the editor of a journal for professional architects typically

Figure 3 *Guillaume Apollinaire's conception of the Eiffel Tower reflects an attitude towards Germans and about poetic form. In his hands architecture became a vehicle to achieve something else.* (Source: *Themerson 1968*)

wants some of each. As might be expected, the aptitudes and inclinations of critics vary with regard to these roles. One person is better suited to cool description, another to impassioned interpretation, another to measured judgement.

Who are the players that assume these roles? In a sense, anyone who speaks about architecture is a critic, for every comment is either descriptive, interpretative, or judgemental, or some combination of these. When we try to be more discriminating and specify who most legitimately plays the role of critic, we confront the problem of credentials. It is sometimes argued that only individuals trained to be architects can criticize buildings responsibly and with understanding, that it takes an insider's knowledge to reveal, interpret and judge a building. Not unexpectedly, others who are not architects contend that it takes an outsider to see what the architect, whose training is largely focused on professional considerations and the business of architecture, cannot see. A third perspective has emerged with particular strength recently, critics whose background is in architecture and whose foreground, so to speak, is in philosophy and social history.

While many critics who write professionally are architects, many others have been trained in art history, or in the broader realm of the humanities. Expectedly, some critics began as journalists who took architecture as their focal subject; with regard to architecture criticism they are self-trained.

Until recently there has been no formalized training for architecture critics. Now there are academic programmes in 'theory and criticism', 'history and criticism' and 'criticism' which offer focused academic work in this subject area. It is too early to determine what impact such formalized training will have on the field of criticism and on architecture and related design professions. Since there are few employment opportunities for architecture critics as such, it is unlikely that these programmes will focus on the training of professional critics, rather they will concentrate on the inculcation of particular values and the exposition of methods and missions for criticism. This kind of exposure and knowledge can enrich and broaden the perspective of someone with professional training in architecture, so we can imagine that this, the post-professional education of architects, is a way in which academic programmes in criticism can have an impact. Degree programmes in criticism also can be a credential for teaching, and it is in this way perhaps more than through conventional published criticism or the advanced education of architects that formalized education in criticism will impact the profession. Critics as teachers more than critics as journalists have a great potential to shape the future of architecture by influencing the development of young architects.

We must assume that most critics want to help shape better buildings for a better world. How to achieve that is a point of contention however, for architecture and the criticism of architecture constantly struggle with polarizing considerations. For example, architecture is both practical and ideological. It can respond to concrete needs and desires, and in this way serve; or it can promulgate theories about new breeds of needs and desires and in this way change people's – and professionals' – aspirations (Ockman 1985). Critics may take either position. Similarly architecture and criticism must choose between the knowns of the past – that which has served us well – and unknowns that might be risky but that might produce better design in the future. Again, critics may take either stance. Finally, critics must decide whether to accept the underlying assumptions of the architect, and use them as the basis of judgement, or question the assumptions as well as the execution of the design ideas.

And when they do take a stand, do critics matter? It matters when they can affect the course of design while decisions are still being made. Too often criticism comes too late. Influential critics are those with foresight and good social and political connections. They have opportunities to affect design prospectively, not respond to it after the fact. Other critics matter when they adopt roles as our conscience. Writers like John Ruskin and Lewis Mumford promulgated values and interpretations that seldom affected specific building projects, but shaped the values of others who did decide what and how to build. Without a doubt teacher/critics matter, too, for they help determine how future architects will see, interpret, and judge architecture, the architect's responsibilities, and the relation of buildings to physical and societal contexts. And yes, even the critics without connections and without the preacher's gift, and without the mentor's role matter. The illuminating, insightful, measured discussion of architecture in any context has the power to reveal architecture to others, and this is no small achievement.

REFERENCES AND FURTHER READING

Books and articles *about* architecture criticism are few. Attoe (1978) identified the methods, settings and techniques of architectural criticism. Through case study analyses, Bonta (1979) exposed some of the processes through which interpretations of architecture are formed.

By contrast, books *of* criticism are so numerous as to defy listing, for virtually everything written about architecture is either descriptive, interpretative or judgemental. Identifying the most influential books and critics is difficult, for influence is not easy to measure.

A few individuals stand out for their contributions to aspects of the field, for example, Ada Louise Huxtable, in journalistic criticism. She was the first recipient of the Pulitzer Prize for architectural criticism. Several books by her are compilations of articles published in the *New York Times.* Charles Jencks has been a prolific interpreter of currents in twentieth-century architecture. His audience has been architects and students, and interested lay people. Peter Reyner Banham exemplified the role of historian/critic in articles and books aimed principally at historians and architects. Alan Colquhoun has been a critic/theorist addressing issues related to theory and practice. Charles W. Moore, known principally as an architect, in fact has produced a substantial body of criticism of interest to architects, educators and students.

Attoe, W. (1978) *Architecture and Critical Imagination*, Chichester: John Wiley & Sons.

Attoe, W. and Latus, M. (1973) 'Buildings as signs: an experiment in Milwaukee', in M. Fishwick and J.M. Neil (eds) *Popular Architecture*, Bowling Green, Ohio: Popular Press.

Bonta, J.P. (1979) *Architecture and Its Interpretation. A Study of Expressive Systems in Architecture*, London: Lund Humphries.

Ockman, J. (ed.) (1985) *Architecture, Criticism, Ideology*, Princeton, NJ: Princeton Architectural Press.

Pugin, A.W.N. (1841) *The True Principles of Pointed or Christian Architecture*, London: John Weale.

Schrammen, J. (1906) *Der große Altar, der obere Markt.* Staatliche Museen zu Berlin, *Die Altertümer von Pergamon*, Vol. 3, pt 1, Berlin: Reimer.

Themerson, S. (1968) *Apollinaire's Lyrical Ideograms*, London: Gaberboccus Press.

Sitte, C. (1965) *City Planning According to Artistic Principles*, trans. G.R. Collins and C.C. Collins, New York: Random House.

90 The enjoyment of architecture: St Mark's, Venice

John Ruskin

Whence to the entrance into St. Mark's Place, called the Bocca di Piazza (mouth of the square), the Venetian character is nearly destroyed, first by the frightful façade of San Moisè, which we will pause at another time to examine, and then by the modernising of the shops as they near the piazza, and the mingling with the lower Venetian populace of lounging groups of English and Austrians. We will push fast through them into the shadow of the pillars at the end of the 'Bocca di Piazza,' and then we forget them all; for between those pillars there opens a great light, and, in the midst of it, as we advance slowly, the vast tower of St. Mark seems to lift visibly forth from the level field of chequered stones; and, on each side, the countless arches prolong themselves into ranged symmetry, as if the rugged and irregular houses that pressed together above us in the dark alley had been struck back into sudden obedience and lovely order, and all their rude casements and broken walls had been transformed into arches charged with goodly sculpture, and fluted shafts of delicate stone [see Figure 1].

Figure 1 *View of St Mark's from the square.* (Source: *Art Resource 2720: 1*)

§ XIV. And well may they fall back, for beyond those troops of ordered arches there rises a vision out of the earth, and all the great square seems to have opened from it in a kind of awe, that we may see it far away; – a multitude of pillars and white domes, clustered into a

Extract from J. Ruskin (1853) *The Stones of Venice*, Vol. 2 of 3 vols, London: Elder Smith; Everyman edn 1907, ed. E. Rhys, London: Dent.

long low pyramid of coloured light; a treasure-heap, it seems, partly of gold, and partly of opal and mother-of-pearl, hollowed beneath into five great vaulted porches, ceiled with fair mosaic, and beset with sculpture of alabaster, clear as amber and delicate as ivory, – sculpture fantastic and involved, of palm leaves and lilies, and grapes and pomegranates, and birds clinging and fluttering among the branches, all twined together into an endless network of buds and plumes; and, in the midst of it, the solemn forms of angels, sceptred, and robed to the feet, and leaning to each other across the gates, their figures indistinct among the gleaming of the golden ground through the leaves beside them, interrupted and dim, like the morning light as it faded back among the branches of Eden, when first its gates were angel-guarded long ago. And round the walls of the porches there are set pillars of variegated stones, jasper and porphyry, and deep-green serpentine spotted with flakes of snow, and marbles, that half refuse and half yield to the sunshine, Cleopatra-like, 'their bluest veins to kiss' – the shadow, as it steals back from them, revealing line after line of azure undulation, as a receding tide leaves the waved sand; their capitals rich with interwoven tracery, rooted knots of herbage, and drifting leaves of acanthus and vine, and mystical signs, all beginning and ending in the Cross; and above them in the broad archivolts, a continuous chain of language and of life – angels, and the signs of heaven, and the labours of men, each in its appointed season upon the earth; and above these, another range of glittering pinnacles, mixed with white arches edged with scarlet flowers, – a confusion of delight, amidst which the breasts of the Greek horses are seen blazing in their breadth of golden strength, and the St. Mark's Lion, lifted on a blue field covered with stars, until at last, as if in ecstasy, the crests of the arches break into a marble foam, and toss themselves far into the blue sky in flashes and wreaths of sculptured spray, as if the breakers on the Lido shore had been frost-bound before they fell, and the sea-nymphs had inlaid them with coral and amethyst.

Between that grim cathedral of England and this, what an interval! There is a type of it in the very birds that haunt them; for, instead of the restless crow, hoarse-voiced and sable-winged, drifting on the bleak upper air, the St. Mark's porches are full of doves, that nestle among the marble foliage, and mingle the soft iridescence of their living plumes, changing at every motion, with the tints, hardly less lovely, that have stood unchanged for seven hundred years.

§ XV. And what effect has this splendour on those who pass beneath it? You may walk from sunrise to sunset, to and fro, before the gateway of St. Mark's, and you will not see an eye lifted to it, nor a countenance brightened by it. Priest and layman, soldier and civilian, rich and poor, pass by it alike regardlessly. Up to the very recesses of the porches, the meanest tradesmen of the city push their counters; nay, the foundations of its pillars are themselves the seats – not 'of them that sell doves' for sacrifice, but of the venders of toys and caricatures. Round the whole square in front of the church there is almost a continuous line of cafés, where the idle Venetians of the middle classes lounge, and read empty journals; in its centre the Austrian bands play during the time of vespers, their martial music jarring with the organ notes, – the march drowning the miserere, and the sullen crowd thickening round them, – a crowd, which, if it had its will, would stiletto every soldier that pipes to it. And in the recesses of the porches, all day long, knots of men of the lowest classes, unemployed and listless, lie basking in the sun like lizards; and unregarded children, – every heavy glance of their young eyes full of desperation and stony depravity, and their throats hoarse with cursing, – gamble, and fight, and snarl, and sleep, hour after hour, clashing their bruised centesimi upon the marble ledges of the church porch. And the images of Christ and His angels look down upon it continually.

That we may not enter the church out of the midst of the horror of this, let us turn aside under the portico which looks towards the sea, and passing round within the two massive pillars brought from St. Jean d'Acre, we shall find the gate of the Baptistery; let us enter there. The heavy door closes behind us instantly, and the light, and the turbulence of the Piazzetta, are together shut out by it.

§ XVI. We are in a low vaulted room; vaulted, not with arches, but with small cupolas starred with gold, and chequered with gloomy figures; in the centre is a bronze font charged with rich bas-reliefs, a small figure of the Baptist standing above it in a single ray of light that glances across the narrow room, dying as it falls from a window high in the wall, and the first thing that it strikes, and the only thing that it strikes brightly, is a tomb. We hardly know if it be a tomb indeed; for it is like a narrow couch set beside the window, low-roofed and curtained, so that it might seem, but that it is some height above the pavement, to have been drawn towards the window, that the sleeper might be wakened early; – only there are two angels who have drawn the curtain back, and are looking down upon him. Let us look also, and thank that gentle light that rests upon his forehead for ever, and dies away upon his breast.

The face is of a man in middle life, but there are two deep furrows right across the forehead, dividing it like

the foundations of a tower: the height of it above is bound by the fillet of the ducal cap. The rest of the features are singularly small and delicate, the lips sharp, perhaps the sharpness of death being added to that of the natural lines; but there is a sweet smile upon them, and a deep serenity upon the whole countenance. The roof of the canopy above has been blue, filled with stars; beneath, in the centre of the tomb on which the figure rests, is a seated figured of the Virgin, and the border of it all around is of flowers and soft leaves, growing rich and deep, as if in a field in summer.

It is the Doge Andrea Dandolo, a man early great among the great of Venice; and early lost. She chose him for her king in his 36th year; he died ten years later, leaving behind him that history to which we owe half of what we know of her former fortunes.

§ XVII. Look round at the room in which he lies. The floor of it is of rich mosaic, encompassed by a low seat of red marble, and its walls are of alabaster, but worn and shattered, and darkly stained with age, almost a ruin, – in places the slabs of marble have fallen away altogether, and the rugged brickwork is seen through the rents, but all beautiful; the ravaging fissures fretting their way among the islands and channelled zones of the alabaster, and the time-stains on its translucent masses darkened into fields of rich golden brown, like the colour of seaweed when the sun strikes on it through deep sea. The light fades away into the recess of the chamber towards the altar, and the eye can hardly trace the lines of the bas-relief behind it of the baptism of Christ: but on the vaulting of the roof the figures are distinct, and there are seen upon it two great circles, one surrounded by the 'Principalities and powers in heavenly places,' of which Milton has expressed the ancient division in the single massy line,

Thrones, Dominations, Princedoms, Virtues, Powers,

and around the other, the Apostles; Christ the centre of both: and upon the walls, again and again repeated, the gaunt figure of the Baptist, in every circumstance of his life and death; and the streams of the Jordan running down between their cloven rocks; the axe laid to the root of a fruitless tree that springs upon their shore. 'Every tree that bringeth not forth good fruit shall be hewn down, and cast into the fire.' Yes, verily: to be baptized with fire, or to be cast therein; it is the choice set before all men. The march-notes still murmur through the grated window, and mingle with the sounding in our ears of the sentence of judgment, which the old Greek has written on that Baptistery wall. Venice has made her choice.

§ XVIII. He who lies under that stony canopy would have taught her another choice, in his day, if she would have listened to him; but he and his counsels have long been forgotten by her, and the dust lies upon his lips.

Through the heavy door whose bronze network closes the place of his rest, let us enter the church itself. It is lost in still deeper twilight, to which the eye must be accustomed for some moments before the form of the building can be traced; and then there opens before us a vast cave, hewn out into the form of a Cross, and divided into shadowy aisles by many pillars. Round the domes of its roof the light enters only through narrow apertures like large stars; and here and there a ray or two from some far away casement wanders into the darkness, and casts a narrow phosphoric stream upon the waves of marble that heave and fall in a thousand colours along the floor. What else there is of light is from torches, or silver lamps, burning ceaselessly in the recesses of the chapels; the roof sheeted with gold, and the polished walls covered with alabaster, give back at every curve and angle some feeble gleaming to the flames; and the glories round the heads of the sculptured saints flash out upon us as we pass them, and sink again into the gloom. Under foot and over head, a continual succession of crowded imagery, one picture passing into another, as in a dream; forms beautiful and terrible mixed together; dragons and serpents, and ravening beasts of prey, and graceful birds that in the midst of them drink from running fountains and feed from vases of crystal; the passions and the pleasures of human life symbolised together, and the mystery of its redemption; for the mazes of interwoven lines and changeful pictures lead always at last to the Cross, lifted and carved in every place and upon every stone; sometimes with the serpent of eternity wrapt round it, sometimes with doves beneath its arms, and sweet herbage growing forth from its feet; but conspicuous most of all on the great rood that crosses the church before the altar, raised in bright blazonry against the shadow of the apse. And although in the recesses of the aisles and chapels, when the mist of the incense hangs heavily, we may see continually a figure traced in faint lines upon their marble, a woman standing with her eyes raised to heaven, and the inscription above her, 'Mother of God,' she is not here the presiding deity. It is the Cross that is first seen, and always, burning in the centre of the temple; and every dome and hollow of its roof has the figure of Christ in the utmost height of it, raised in power, or returning in judgment.

§ XIX. Nor is this interior without effect on the minds of the people. At every hour of the day there are groups collected before the various shrines, and solitary worshippers scattered through the darker places of the church, evidently in prayer both deep and reverent, and, for the most part, profoundly sorrowful. The devotees at the greater number of the renowned shrines of Romanism may be seen murmuring their appointed prayers with wandering eyes and unengaged gestures; but the step of the stranger does not disturb those who kneel on the pavement of St. Mark's; and hardly a moment passes, from early morning to sunset, in which we may not see some half-veiled figure enter beneath the Arabian porch, cast itself into long abasement on the floor of the temple, and then rising slowly with more confirmed step, and with a passionate kiss and clasp of the arms given to the feet of the crucifix, by which the lamps burn always in the northern aisle, leave the church, as if comforted.

§ XX. But we must not hastily conclude from this that the nobler characters of the building have at present any influence in fostering a devotional spirit. There is distress enough in Venice to bring many to their knees, without excitement from external imagery; and whatever there may be in the temper of the worship offered in St. Mark's more than can be accounted for by reference to the unhappy circumstances of the city, is assuredly not owing either to the beauty of its architecture or to the impressiveness of the Scripture histories embodied in its mosaics. That it has a peculiar effect, however slight, on the popular mind, may perhaps be safely conjectured from the number of worshippers which it attracts, while the churches of St. Paul and the Frari, larger in size and more central in position, are left comparatively empty. But this effect is altogether to be ascribed to its richer assemblage of those sources of influence which address themselves to the commonest instincts of the human mind, and which, in all ages and countries, have been more or less employed in the support of superstition. Darkness and mystery; confused recesses of building; artificial light employed in small quantity, but maintained with a constancy which seems to give it a kind of sacredness; preciousness of material easily comprehended by the vulgar eye; close air loaded with a sweet and peculiar odour associated only with religious services, solemn music, and tangible idols or images having popular legends attached to them, – these, the stage properties of superstition, which have been from the beginning of the world, and must be to the end of it, employed by all nations, whether openly savage or nominally civilised, to produce a false awe in minds incapable of apprehending the true nature of the Deity, are assembled in St. Mark's to a degree, as far as I know, unexampled in any other European church. The arts of the Magus and the Brahmin are exhausted in the animation of a paralysed Christianity; and the popular sentiment which these arts excite is to be regarded by us with no more respect than we should have considered ourselves justified in rendering to the devotion of the worshippers at Eleusis, Ellora, or Edfou.

§ XXI. Indeed, these inferior means of exciting religious emotion were employed in the ancient Church as they are at this day, but not employed alone. Torchlight there was, as there is now; but the torchlight illumined Scripture histories on the walls, which every eye traced and every heart comprehended, but which, during my whole residence in Venice, I never saw one Venetian regard for an instant. I never heard from any one the most languid expression of interest in any feature of the church, or perceived the slightest evidence of their understanding the meaning of its architecture; and while, therefore, the English cathedral, though no longer dedicated to the kind of services for which it was intended by its builders, and much at variance in many of its characters with the temper of the people by whom it is now surrounded, retains yet so much of its religious influence that no prominent feature of its architecture can be said to exist altogether in vain, we have in St. Mark's a building apparently still employed in the ceremonies for which it was designed, and yet of which the impressive attributes have altogether ceased to be comprehended by its votaries. The beauty which it possesses is unfelt, the language it uses is forgotten; and in the midst of the city to whose service it has so long been consecrated, and still filled by crowds of the descendants of those to whom it owes its magnificence, it stands, in reality, more desolate than the ruins through which the sheep-walk passes unbroken in our English valleys; and the writing on its marble walls is less regarded and less powerful for the teaching of men, than the letters which the shepherd follows with his finger, where the moss is lightest on the tombs in the desecrated cloister.

§ XXII. It must therefore be altogether without reference to its present usefulness, that we pursue our inquiry into the merits and meaning of the architecture of this marvellous building; and it can only be after we have terminated that inquiry, conducting it carefully on abstract grounds, that we can pronounce with any certainty how far the present neglect of St. Mark's is significative of the decline of the Venetian character, or how far this church is to be considered as the relic of a barbarous age, incapable of attracting the admiration, or influencing the feelings of a civilised community.

The inquiry before us is twofold.... [W]e have first to judge of St. Mark's merely as a piece of architecture, not as a church; secondly, to estimate its fitness for its special duty as a place of worship, and the relation in which it stands, as such, to those Northern cathedrals that still retain so much of the power over the human heart, which the Byzantine domes appear to have lost for ever....

§ XXIV. Now the first broad characteristic of the building, and the root nearly of every other important peculiarity in it, is its confessed *incrustation*. It is the purest example in Italy of the great school of architecture in which the ruling principle is the incrustation of brick with more precious materials; and it is necessary, before we proceed to criticise any one of its arrangements, that the reader should carefully consider the principles which are likely to have influenced, or might legitimately influence, the architects of such a school, as distinguished from those whose designs are to be executed in massive materials.

It is true, that among different nations, and at different times, we may find examples of every sort and degree of incrustation, from the mere setting of the larger and more compact stones by preference at the outside of the wall, to the miserable construction of that modern brick cornice, with its coating of cement, which, but the other day in London, killed its unhappy workmen in its fall. But just as it is perfectly possible to have a clear idea of the opposing characteristics of two different species of plants or animals, though between the two there are varieties which it is difficult to assign either to the one or the other, so the reader may fix decisively in his mind the legitimate characteristics of the incrusted and the massive styles, though between the two there are varieties which confessedly unite the attributes of both. For instance, in many Roman remains, built of blocks of tufa and incrusted with marble, we have a style, which, though truly solid, possesses some of the attributes of incrustation; and in the Cathedral of Florence, built of brick and coated with marble, the marble facing is so firmly and exquisitely set, that the building, though in reality incrusted, assumes the attributes of solidity. But these intermediate examples need not in the least confuse our generally distinct ideas of the two families of buildings: the one in which the substance is alike throughout, and the forms and conditions of the ornament assume or prove that it is so, as in the best Greek buildings, and for the most part in our early Norman and Gothic; and the other, in which the substance is of two kinds, one internal, the other external, and the system of decoration is founded on this duplicity, as pre-eminently in St. Marks.

§ XXV. I have used the word duplicity in no depreciatory sense. In chapter ii. of the 'Seven Lamps,' § 18, I especially guarded this incrusted school from the imputation of insincerity, and I must do so now at greater length. It appears insincere at first to a Northern builder, because, accustomed to build with solid blocks of freestone, he is in the habit of supposing the external superficies of a piece of masonry to be some criterion of its thickness. But, as soon as he gets acquainted with the incrusted style, he will find that the Southern builders had no intention to deceive him. He will see that every slab of facial marble is fastened to the next by a confessed *rivet*, and that the joints of the armour are so visibly and openly accommodated to the contours of the substance within, that he has no more right to complain of treachery than a savage would have, who, for the first time in his life seeing a man in armour, had supposed him to be made of solid steel. Acquaint him with the customs of chivalry, and with the uses of the coat of mail, and he ceases to accuse of dishonesty either the panoply or the knight.

These laws and customs of the St. Mark's architectural chivalry it must be our business to develope.

§ XXVI. First, consider the natural circumstances which give rise to such a style. Suppose a nation of builders, placed far from any quarries of available stone, and having precarious access to the mainland where they exist; compelled therefore either to build entirely with brick, or to import whatever stone they use from great distances, in ships of small tonnage, and for the most part dependent for speed on the oar rather than the sail. The labour and cost of carriage are just as great, whether they import common or precious stone, and therefore the natural tendency would always be to make each shipload as valuable as possible. But in proportion to the preciousness of the stone, is the limitation of its possible supply; limitation not determined merely by cost, but by the physical conditions of the material, for of many marbles pieces above a certain size are not to be had for money. There would also be a tendency in such circumstances to import as much stone as possible ready sculptured, in order to save weight; and therefore, if the traffic of their merchants led them to places where there were ruins of ancient edifices, to ship the available fragments of them home. Out of this supply of marble, partly composed of pieces of so precious a quality that only a few tons of them could be on any terms obtained, and partly of shafts, capitals, and other portions of foreign buildings, the island architect has to fashion, as best he may, the anatomy of his edifice. It is at his choice either to lodge his few blocks of precious marble here and there among his masses of brick, and to cut out of the sculptured fragments such new forms as may be necessary for the observance of fixed proportions in the new building; or else to cut the coloured stones into thin pieces, of extent sufficient to face the whole surface of the walls, and to adopt a method of construction irregular enough to admit the insertion of fragmentary sculptures; rather with a view of displaying their intrinsic beauty, than of setting them to any regular service in the support of the building.

An architect who cared only to display his own skill, and had no respect for the works of others, would assuredly have chosen the former alternative, and would have sawn the old marbles into fragments in order to prevent all interference with his own designs. But an architect who cared for the preservation of noble work, whether his own or others', and more regarded the beauty of his building than his own fame, would have done what those old builders of St. Mark's did for us, and saved every relic with which he was entrusted.

§ XXVII. But these were not the only motives which influenced the Venetians in the adoption of their method of architecture. It might, under all the circumstances above stated, have been a question with other builders, whether to import one shipload of costly jaspers, or twenty of chalk flints; and whether to build a small church faced with porphyry and paved with agate, or to raise a vast cathedral in freestone. But with the Venetians it could not be a question for an instant; they were exiles from ancient and beautiful cities, and had been accustomed to build with their ruins, not less in affection than in admiration: they had thus not only grown familiar with the practice of inserting older fragments in modern buildings, but they owed to that practice a great part of the splendour of their city, and whatever charm of association might aid its change from a Refuge into a Home. The practice which began in the affections of a fugitive nation, was prolonged in the pride of a conquering one; and beside the memorials of departed happiness, were elevated the trophies of returning victory. The ship of war brought home more marble in triumph than the merchant vessel in speculation; and the front of St. Mark's became rather a shrine at which to dedicate the splendour of miscellaneous spoil, than the organised expression of any fixed architectural law, or religious emotion.

§ XXVIII. Thus far, however, the justification of the style of this church depends on circumstances peculiar to the time of its erection, and to the spot where it arose. The merit of its method, considered in the abstract, rests on far broader grounds.

In the fifth chapter of the 'Seven Lamps,' § 14, the reader will find the opinion of a modern architect of some reputation, Mr. Wood, that the chief thing remarkable in this church 'is its extreme ugliness;' and he will find this opinion associated with another, namely, that the works of the Caracci are far preferable to those of the Venetian painters. This second statement of feeling reveals to us one of the principal causes of the first; namely, that Mr. Wood had not any perception of colour, or delight in it. The perception of colour is a gift just as definitely granted to one person, and denied to another, as an ear for music; and the very first requisite for true judgment of St. Mark's, is the perfection of that colour-faculty which few people ever set themselves seriously to find out whether they possess or not. For it is on its value as a piece of perfect and unchangeable colouring, that the claims of this edifice to our respect are finally rested; and a deaf man might as well pretend to pronounce judgment on the merits of a full orchestra, as an architect trained in the composition of form only, to discern the beauty of St. Mark's. It possesses the charm of colour in common with the greater part of the architecture, as well as of the manufactures, of the East; but the Venetians deserve especial note as the only European people who appear to have sympathised to the full with the great instinct of the Eastern races. They indeed were compelled to bring artists form Constantinople to design the mosaics of the vaults of St. Mark's, and to group the colours of its porches; but they rapidly took up and developed, under more masculine conditions, the system of which the Greeks had shown them the example; while the burghers and barons of the North were building their dark streets and grisly castles of oak and sandstone, the merchants of Venice were covering their palaces with porphyry and gold; and at last, when her mighty painters had created for her a colour more priceless than gold or porphyry, even this, the richest of her treasures, she lavished upon walls whose foundations were beaten by the sea; and the strong tide, as it runs beneath the Rialto, is reddened to this day by the reflection of the frescoes of Giorgione.

§ XXIX. If, therefore, the reader does not care for

colour, I must protest against his endeavour to form any judgment whatever of this church of St. Mark's. But, if he both cares for and loves it, let him remember that the school of incrusted architecture is *the only one in which perfect and permanent chromatic decoration is possible*; and let him look upon every piece of jasper and alabaster given to the architect as a cake of very hard colour, of which a certain portion is to be ground down or cut off to paint the walls with. Once understand this thoroughly, and accept the condition that the body and availing strength of the edifice are to be in brick, and that this under muscular power of brickwork is to be clothed with the defence and the brightness of the marble, as the body of an animal is protected and adorned by its scales or its skin, and all the consequent fitnesses and laws of the structure will be easily discernible . . .

§ XLVIII. The due consideration of the principles above stated will enable the traveller to judge with more candour and justice of the architecture of St. Mark's than usually it would have been possible for him to do while under the influence of the prejudices necessitated by familiarity with the very different schools of Northern art. I wish it were in my power to lay also before the general reader some exemplification of the manner in which these strange principles are developed in the lovely building. But exactly in proportion to the nobility of any work, is the difficulty of conveying a just impression of it; and wherever I have occasion to bestow high praise, there it is exactly most dangerous for me to endeavour to illustrate my meaning, except by reference to the work itself. And, in fact, the principal reason why architectural criticism is at this day so far behind all other, is the impossibility of illustrating the best architecture faithfully. Of the various schools of painting, examples are accessible to every one, and reference to the works themselves is found sufficient for all purposes of criticism; but there is nothing like St. Mark's or the Ducal Palace to be referred to in the National Gallery, and no faithful illustration of them is possible on the scale of such a volume as this. And it is exceedingly difficult on any scale. Nothing is so rare in art, as far as my own experience goes, as a fair illustration of architecture; *perfect* illustration of it does not exist. For all good architecture depends upon the adaptation of its chiselling to the effect at a certain distance from the eye; and to render the peculiar confusion in the midst of order, and uncertainty in the midst of decision, and mystery in the midst of trenchant lines, which are the result of distance, together with perfect expression of the peculiarities of the design, requires the skill of the most admirable artist, devoted to the work with the most severe conscientiousness, neither the skill nor the determination having as yet been given to the subject. And in the illustration of details, every building of any pretensions to high architectural rank would require a volume of plates, and those finished with extraordinary care. With respect to the two buildings which are the princi-

pal subjects of the present volume, St. Mark's and the Ducal Palace, I have found it quite impossible to do them the slightest justice by any kind of portraiture; and I abandoned the endeavour in the case of the latter with less regret, because in the new Crystal Palace (as the poetical public insist upon calling it, though it is neither a palace, nor of crystal) there will be placed, I believe, a noble cast of one of its angles. As for St. Mark's, the effort was hopeless from the beginning. For its effect depends not only upon the most delicate sculpture in every part, but, as we have just stated, eminently on its colour also, and that the most subtle, variable, inexpressible colour in the world, – the colour of glass, of transparent alabaster, of polished marble, and lustrous gold. It would be easier to illustrate a crest of Scottish mountain, with its purple heather and pale harebells at their fullest and fairest, or a glade of Jura forest, with its floor of anemone and moss, than a single portico of St. Mark's. The fragment of one of its archivolts [see Figure 2] . . . is not to illustrate the thing itself, but to illustrate the impossibility of illustration.

Figure 2 *The vine. Free, and in service.* (Source: *Ruskin 1853*)

§ XLIX. It is left a fragment, in order to get it on a larger scale; and yet even on this scale it is too small to show the sharp folds and points of the marble vine-leaves with sufficient clearness. The ground of it is gold, the sculpture in the spandrils is not more than an inch and a half deep, rarely so much. It is in fact nothing more than an exquisite sketching of outlines in marble, to about the same depth as in the Elgin frieze; the draperies, however, being filled with close folds, in the manner of the Byzantine pictures, folds especially necessary here, as large masses could not be expressed in the shallow sculpture without becoming insipid; but the disposition of these folds is always most beautiful, and often opposed by broad and simple spaces, like that obtained by the scroll in the hand of the prophet, seen in the plate.

The balls in the archivolt project considerably, and the interstices between their interwoven bands of marble are filled with colours like the illuminations of a manuscript; violet, crimson, blue, gold, and green, alternately: but no green is ever used without an intermixture of blue pieces in the mosaic, nor any blue without a little centre of pale green; sometimes only a single piece of glass a quarter of an inch square, so subtle was the feeling for colour which was thus to be satisfied. The intermediate circles have golden stars set on an azure ground, varied in the same manner; and the small crosses seen in the intervals are alternately blue and subdued scarlet, with two small circles of white set in the golden ground above and beneath them, each only about half an inch across (this work, remember, being on the outside of the building, and twenty feet above the eye), while the blue crosses have each a pale green centre. Of all this exquisitely mingled hue, no plate, however large or expensive, could give any adequate conception; but, if the reader will supply in imagination to the engraving what he supplies to a common woodcut of a group of flowers, the decision of the respective merits of modern and of Byzantine architecture may be allowed to rest on this fragment of St. Mark's alone.

From the vine-leaves of that archivolt, though there is no direct imitation of nature in them, but on the contrary a studious subjection to architectural purpose more particularly to be noticed hereafter, we may yet receive the same kind of pleasure which we have in seeing true vine-leaves and wreathed branches traced upon golden light; its stars upon their azure ground ought to make us remember, as its builder remembered, the stars that ascend and fall in the great arch of the sky: and I believe that stars, and boughs, and leaves, and bright colours are everlastingly lovely, and to be by all men beloved; and, moreover, that church walls grimly seared with squared lines, are not better nor nobler things than these. I believe the man who designed and the men who delighted in that archivolt to have been wise, happy, and holy.

FURTHER READING

Hewison, R. (1978) *Ruskin and Venice*, London: Thames & Hudson.

Unrau, J. (1978) *Looking at Architecture with Ruskin*, London: Thames & Hudson.

PART 6

CASE STUDIES

From the outset we thought it would be attractive to make studies of places to see if, how and to what degree the issues addressed in this book could be seen 'at work'.

We also thought that those issues should not be sought out but rather that each case study should allow its own criteria to emerge from the nature of the place being studied, or the interests of those making the study, or both. If there was to be an element of 'proving the pudding', the detection of flavours was not to be prompted.

'Museu da Minas de São Domingos, Portugal', is a case study of how a young contemporary architect works, what he takes note of when exploring the issues behind a design brief, and the analysis he eventually presents to his clients to help them appreciate his proposed interventions. He makes intensive use of graphics in his exploration of place, people, routes, building traditions and local skills.

'Durham: a town for all seasons' is, in its medieval core, a World Heritage site in the north-east of England. The siting of cathedral and castle is unforgettable to those who have seen it, and Durham itself has a long, rich and fascinating history. It is a good example of a European cathedral-university city and much is known about it. So we thought it an appropriate vehicle for testing the basic themes underpinning basic architectural language.

The first seven essays set the scene through a series of probes – of the place, of the origins of the city, of its people and their traditions and institutions and, of course, of its world-famous cathedral. The case study itself is by five students of architecture at Newcastle University who were working on a short urban study programme: an old city seen through the eyes of young men and women soon to be architects and who will be working well into the twenty-first century. In studying Durham they learned at least some of the ways in which all places may be studied, but they themselves prioritized their reporting.

'People in cities' is a three-part American study. A case study of Portland, Oregon, but introduced by a 'fly on the wall' account of citizen participation (a rich American tradition which is being revitalized and re-harnessed). It is a reminder of planning precedents in the United States and an introduction to the emergence of, and now the significant work of, RUDATS (Regional/Urban Design Assistance Teams). As we said in the introduction to Architectural Space (Section 4.2), the major preoccupation with space towards the end of this century seems to be with urban space, and this American study nicely makes that point.

B.F.

Museu da Minas de São Domingos, Portugal

91 Museu da Minas de São Domingos, Portugal: a study within a study

Giuseppe Intini

THE CASE STUDY: REGIONAL AND URBAN RENEWAL PROPOSALS FOR MINAS DE SÃO DOMINGOS, POMARÃO AND MESQUITA, PORTUGAL

The programme of the project required the physical and social survey of the Portuguese villages, Minas de São Domingos, Pomarão and Mesquita. The study includes an appraisal of the human-made and natural environments plus strategic proposals for regional and urban renewal.

Location

Geographically the three villages are located in the south-east corner of the Alentejo region within the territory administered by the small town of Mertola (see Figure 1). The territory has limited resources, with a topography and climate suited to agriculture and forestry. Its climate, unspoilt areas and tranquil life-style attract seasonal summer tourism. The villages share with the territory inadequate infrastructures and limited services, but have also been subjected to abandonment resulting in urban desolation and dereliction, although their unique and picturesque architectural presence is surrounded by an environment of suggestive beauty.

Background

Early historical references mention Mertola trading with the Phoenicians and Carthaginians, and named by the Romans 'Myrtlis'. It was also described at the beginning of the second century by Ptolemy as *'opidum antiquum et praeclarum'*. The Romans mined various minerals such as pyrite and salts on a large scale, but also made intensive commercial use of the navigable Guadiana river linking Mertola and the Portuguese hinterland with the Mediterranean basin via the ocean.

Figure 1 *View of Mertola.* (Source: *Studio Intini*)

The Roman domination was ended in AD 439 by the Svevos, although it was Arab rule that controlled the region until 1238, when D. Sancho II annexed the region to Portugal.

Mining interests in the area were rekindled in 1857 by the Italian explorer Nicola Biava. The mining rights of the area stretching from Minas de São Domingos to Pomarão were sold to the Belgian company La Sabina, which subcontracted the mining works to the London-based mining company Mason & Barry. Forced by the events of the Portuguese Revolution in 1968, the mines closed. The revolutionaries dismantled the mines' infrastructures including the railway system connecting Minas de São Domingos with Pomarão.

Closure of the mines meant mass emigration. The social and cultural disintegration that built up in those times is now on the political agenda. Hence the efforts of this project, patronized by the local ruling Communist Party, are intended to redress the balance and give permanent job opportunities to the emigrants. In fact the emigrants return annually or periodically to the villages where their families still live – but also because they still rent their cottages with a peppercorn fee in perpetuity.

The villages' architectural and urban presence is also a legacy of the mining activities. Indeed, for the functioning of the mines each village made a specific contribution. At the terminal head of the mines is Minas de São Domingos, which is also the centre of administration and the British management residence. Its edges are delineated by woodland, two lakes and the mining area. The village was inhabited by 3,000 people at its peak but currently houses only 800 people. At the terminal end is Pomarão, situated on the river Guadiana and acting as a port with warehouse facilities and administration.

From a peak population of 600 people only a handful of families now dwell in the village. Both Pomarão and Minas de São Domingos grew, adapted to the mining activities and housed the workforce, whereas Mesquita was already a settlement dating back to Arab domination. The latter is composed of individual farms, outbuildings and farm labourers' cottages, grouped together for defensive reasons.

The hard village life and its meagre rural economy took advantage of the employment opportunities offered by the mines. To reach the workplace the miners crossed the Guadiana river near Pomarão after a walk of 30 minutes to reach the river bank. Although Mesquita always retained its rural and farming activities it also fell victim to mass emigration, which left it empty. With the disappearance of the population, schools and social buildings closed. Their closures left enormous voids in the social and cultural fabric of the villages. Fortunately some of these buildings, empty but in good condition, will provide prime space for tackling the urban renewal programme. It should also be noted that, despite the isolation between the villages because of lack of public transport, thanks to the impetus of the Mertola administration the spirited communities have engaged in archaeological and environmental programmes, instigating new craft and technical workshops while actively sponsoring cultural events, especially during the summer months.

However, it is the housing stock with its permanency and the quality of the surrounding environment that provides opportunities for the villages and, indeed, the whole territory's renewal and prosperity.

DESIGN APPROACH

The design approach is based on the belief that effective architectural solutions are encapsulated in a multiplicity of factors and systems, determined by social, economic, technological and environmental references unique to the project. Hence only a design method based on initiation (intuitive and factual), analysis, synthesis and evaluation (including an understanding and celebration of human factors) can respond to this uniqueness (see Figure 2). This approach considers that art and science have a prominent and determining presence. A creative framework is generated from the contrast between the stimulus of art, emotions, desires, individuality, perception, foresight and celebration, and the impetus of science, analysing the deficiency of knowledge with indifferent, impartial (rarely tolerant) observation of the ideas behind the facts. Hence the initial reactions to the project have been intuitive, followed by analysis to clarify the scope and means of the programme. Synthesis of analysed observations blends the various components, offering a base for humanistic celebration of the strategic design solutions. These processes induce the client and consultant to active participation in a direct and personal dialogue. Parallel to this a dialogue between the historical memory and nature of the site takes place while society's observing and controlling bodies participate.

Precedent and Influences

Architecturally, both Minas de São Domingos and Pomarão show a picturesque application of the English terraced house with planning layouts prepared by the British mining engineers. The uniqueness of the layout is also apparent in the matter-of-fact, Spartan workforce cottages. These consisted of back-to-back cells measuring approximately 4 m. × 4 m. (13 ft. × 18 ft.)

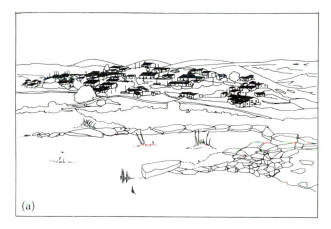

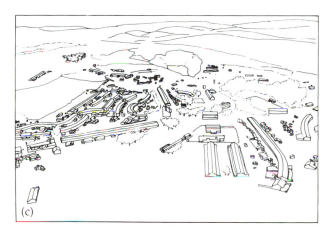

Figure 2 *Strategies were proposed for building fabric, public and private spaces, path and road systems, traffic control, energy generation, water collection, and services infrastructure: (a) Mesquita; (b) Pomarão; (c) Minas de São Domingos. (Source: Studio Intini)*

with two doors (one eventually adapted into a window), and a corner fireplace. Services were not provided and a single cell was usually a family dwelling. In contrast, the administration quarters are villas with private gardens. Indeed, in Minas de São Domingos the residential villas are part of an English park with private access, a tennis court and a cast-iron bandstand manufactured in England.

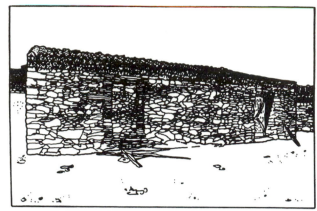

Figure 3 *Quality of environment, Mesquita.* (Source: *Studio Intini*)

Mesquita grew unplanned, and its organic layout presents typical Portuguese vernacular elements such as the external circular oven, stone buildings and dry-stone walls (see Figure 3). The stone-faced buildings were and still are used as stables and stores. Due to cost and availability, metal technology was limited to sporadic applications. In Mesquita even door hinges were made of eucalyptus timber.

However, while architectural typology varies, the construction techniques are common. This consideration is essential in the light of the skills required to undertake the refurbishment of the building stock. The potential for employment and DIY interventions are important considerations towards flexible, suitable and economical design solutions. It should also be stated that it is this construction system that unifies the villages both architecturally and visually.

Construction methods

The construction method consists of hand-made, locally produced clay bricks, Roman tiles and monopitch roof supported by unsawn, barkless eucalyptus tree trunks and bamboo cane ceilings (see Figure 4). Although it is an effective and economical construction, it is essential to improve the thermal and water protection of the roof with the insertion of an insulated protective panel with vapour barrier under the tiles, without the removal of the latter, and to replace the bamboo cane ceiling with

an improved version suited to artisan skills and which makes use of the locally cultivated bamboo. However, housing improvements are not limited to the tasks described above.

Interventions

A manual of plan adaptation, renewal and integration of new housing has been prepared to suggest ways of improving living standards (see Figure 5). To facilitate the tasks the proposed interventions are based on the application of traditional and alternative technologies to harness passive and recyclable energy sources, for instance windmills as electricity generators in Mesquita. Indeed, the potential of solar passive applications is considerable and some of the cottages will be adapted with lean-to buffer solar-catching spaces.

Policy

Parallel to these interventions it is essential to provide the villages with effective infrastructure services such as sewerage, water, telecommunications, electricity and cable systems. The swift completion of these services will help the proposed strategies to fulfil their objectives. These are intended to be flexible and capable of being reinterpreted. Indeed, the only elements of renewal having permanence are the housing stock, including the unsympathetically built outbuildings, and the new programmes of urban interventions which are intended

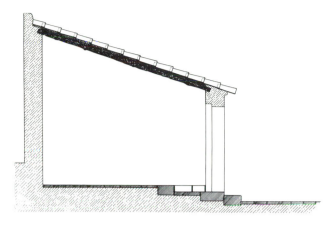

to give civic cohesiveness to each village while providing an immediate impetus towards economic growth. The latter is intended within the terms of co-operation envisaged for the whole territory. In other words each economic asset of the territory will not be duplicated but merely integrated in the whole in order to achieve a spread of activities which will limit internal territorial economic competition.

These objectives are rooted in the need to integrate the existing socio-cultural activities with modern progressive ideals, indeed to preserve and reinforce local cultural values is absolutely necessary to avoid disruption. Continuity and progressive caring intervention would also help to reintegrate young people who, as a social unit, have drifted away. An important task for the whole community is the continuous evaluation and preservation of the existing patrimony. A step towards achieving this is the idea of making the natural terrain and human-made environments a national park, while undertaking a study to reassess the mining areas. A consequence of this strategy is the following project.

PROPOSALS

The new urban interventions are proposals of civic character. Each village will have a piazza, considered as a social and economic space with civic presence with which the population can identify and within which

Figure 4 *Traditional construction method and intervention.* (Source: *Studio Intini*)

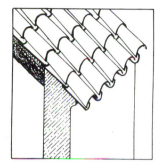

Figure 5 *Housing analysis and intervention.* (Source: *Studio Intini*)

people can interact (see Figure 6). The piazzas will also be rainwater-collecting cisterns (see Figure 7).

Social interaction with visitors, especially in the shape of tourism, has been integrated in the design proposals. For instance, only Pomarão would require large investment in order to prompt a different type of tourism from that envisaged for Mesquita and Minas de

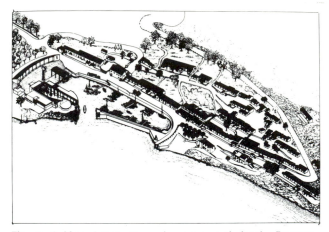

Figure 8 *New intervention of marina and hotel, Pomarão.* (Source: *Studio Intini*)

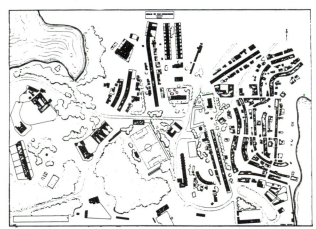

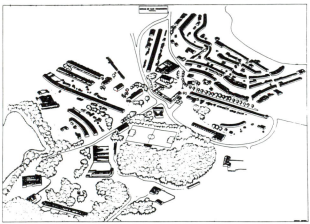

Figure 6 *Existing and proposed piazza, Minas de São Domingos,* (Source: *Studio Intini*)

São Domingos. Mesquita could only sustain tourism of rural character, short stays in rentable cottages, market days and educative interests. Minas de São Domingo would continue as a locality for camping, water sport and relaxation with the addition of educative and archaeological tourism. The tourism generated in Pomarão would be integrated with the intensive inter-national tourism of the Algarve region (see Figure 8). The river Guardiana would be used for excursions, and new mooring facilities associated with a tourist and local centre would contain the intensive international tourism usually disinterested in maintaining local culture or ecological equilibrium. Except for Mesquita the other piazzas will be able to sustain commercial and workshop units. Integral to the piazza designs are sundials and the treatment of piazza surfaces. The design for Mesquita will be based on modern artwork made with Portuguese *azulejas* (ceramic tiles).

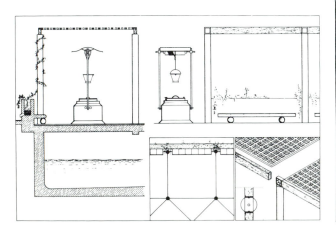

Figure 7 *Detail of cistern under piazza, Mesquita.* (Source: *Studio Intini*)

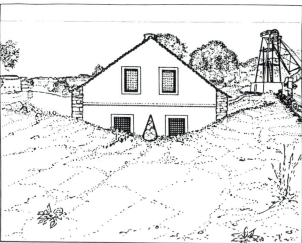

Figure 9 *Elevation of Museu da Minas de São Domingos.* (Source: *Studio Intini*)

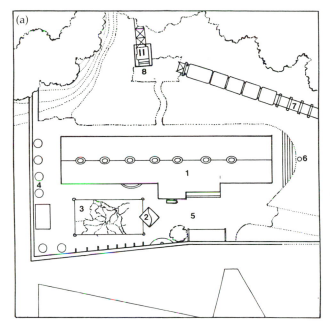

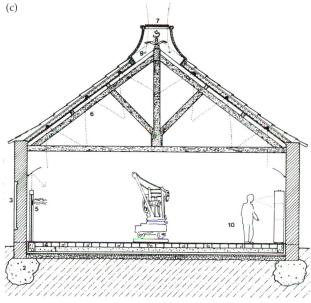

1 Museum
2 Information stand
3 General plan
4 Exhibition arrangement

5 Courtyard
6 Goal
7 Track
8 Mine entrance

1 New floor
2 New foundation
3 Blocked window
4 Cavity
5 Heating system

6 Lighting system
7 Rooflight
8 Ventilation system
9 Natural light
10 Circulation

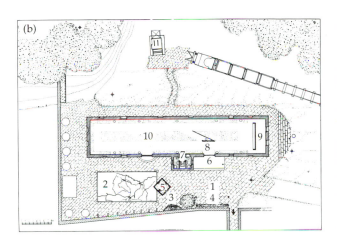

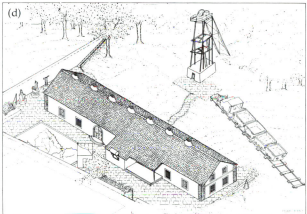

1 Courtyard
2 General plan
3 Fountain
4 Seat
5 Information stand

6 Entrance to museum
7 W.C. and services
8 Reception
9 Office
10 Exhibition area

Figure 10 *A refurbishment proposal. Museu da Minas de São Domingos: (a) site plan; (b) plan; (c) section showing proposal; (d) isometric view.*

Together with these interventions a new use will be found for abandoned buildings and land will be allocated for self-management. Roads will be surfaced with traditional Portuguese cobble-stone systems.

A specific proposal

One of the derelict buildings already the subject of study for new use is a warehouse at the edge of Minas de São Domingos. The building is an ideal location to start archaeological exploration of the mining area, and will be a mining museum (see Figures 9 and 10). Its role will be not merely to display and inform but to act as a catalyst to stimulate research into natural interventions in some of the mining areas, and cultural activities such as film-making, special events and climatic studies. The simple refurbishment of the building is integrated with video information booths scattered around the mining area which will allow the archaeological presence of the area to be interpreted *in situ*.

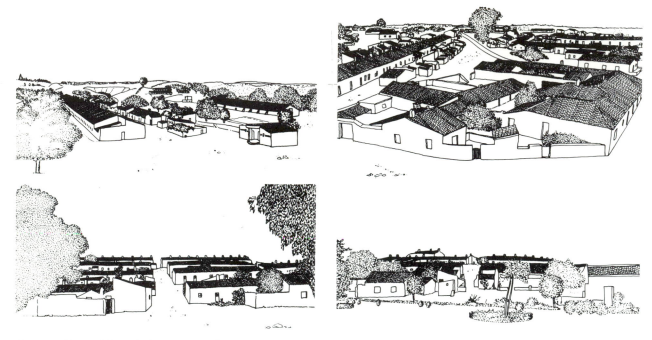

Figure 11 *Views of Minas de São Domingos.* (Source *Studio Intini*)

The project as a whole continues. The strategies have allowed various new ideas and design initiatives to be accommodated. Slowly the task of sewing the community together is happening, simply because when work is planned carefully and realized sensitively, the outcome is invariably beautiful.

Durham: a town for all seasons

92 Durham City: its origins and development

John Tarn

The river Wear, winding slowly to the sea, makes a grand sweep around a rocky plateau, cutting for itself a deep gorge amidst the hills. Water flows on three sides, girding the plateau like a horseshoe, and the only connection to the mainland is by a thin neck of land. To the monks bearing the body of St Cuthbert this seemed a safe resting place, harried from place to place, as they had been, on their journey from Lindisfarne in the turbulent days before the Conquest. The precious relics and the body of the saint reached their final resting place in AD 995, and thereafter Durham became a unique outpost of civilization, readily defended from attack, a place of religious veneration, and thus a monastery of great importance and a seat of government. The Bishops of Durham rapidly rose to power and wealth in the years before the Reformation. Princes both temporal and spiritual, they were entrusted with the government of the County Palatine and within that area they enjoyed the privileges and rights of monarchy, administering justice, receiving taxes and even minting their own coinage; and with the privileges went the responsibilities of keeping the peace and resisting the scourges of the hostile Scottish neighbours.

So the two roles of the bishop found expression from the outset in the twin Norman monuments to their greatness and power. The first was the shrine of the northern saint, the cathedral (see Figure 1); the second was the castle, built to defend the rock and protect the shrine, to be the seat of the bishop and the visible expression of his princely position as the King's direct representative in the north. Since the twelfth century these two buildings, surviving the vicissitudes of eight centuries, have dominated the township which first sheltered on the peninsula and then expanded outwards, in the more peaceful days of the eighteenth and nineteenth centuries on to the 'mainland'.

At the Reformation the Prince Bishop was stripped of his worldly power and the castle then ceased to be the home of a militant bishop, becoming instead the seat of a new university in 1833. The old Norman keep itself was converted seven years later into student rooms by Salvin. Despite these great changes and the decline in importance of the town as a virtual minor capital city, it is today still dominated by that glorious duality, the castle and the cathedral.

Dr Pevsner has described the town as:

> One of the great experiences of Europe to the eyes of those who can appreciate architecture.... The group of Cathedral, Castle and Monastery on the rock can only be compared with Avignon and Prague.
>
> (Pevsner 1953: 77)

The visitor cannot fail to be impressed when arriving either by train or road: from the train the nineteenth century town, with its tight little streets, stretches out below. Beyond are the keep and the galilee, rising out of the trees and obscuring the rock on which they stand. Even at this distance there is no mistaking the massive grandeur and the scale of the old buildings.

No less dramatic are the views given to the pedestrian or the motorist from the town beneath. First he or she emerges at the foot of the western face of the rock to cross the river by Framwelgate Bridge before ascending to the market place.

To the right is the deep Wear valley softly clad in trees on either side and slowly curving out of sight around the peninsula, and high above, again growing out of the trees, are the church and the castle. The vista closes as suddenly as it has opened when the road climbs to the market-place through a tight medieval

Figure 1 *The Cathedral from the north-west.* (Source: *Billings 1843*)

street, pleasant and intimate in scale but now without any architectural merit. Neither does the market-place heighten the experience: a group of nineteenth-century buildings including a church and an equestrian statue, together with the paraphernalia of modernizing civilization. Then up Saddler Street and into Owengate with, first, the alternative route down and over the river to Old Elvet, with the complementary view to that at Framwelgate Bridge, but this time from the other side of the loop with a south-western view of the cathedral. The second diversion would be along North Bailey and into the graceful and reticent backwaters of eighteenth-century Durham; but Owengate presses relentlessly on up the steepening incline and narrowing cobbled streets into Palace Green. All the way the cliffs of building have continued uninterrupted; there have been no hints or vistas out of the confined street, which twists sharply in both directions so that all views are closed within a short distance. The scale of the street is intimate, the buildings small and irregular suggesting a rather large market town, its pattern and shape dictated largely by its site. And so the visitor is totally unprepared for the experience which finally awaits at the top of the last steep incline. Coming quite quickly over the last visual barrier the visitor finds that, first, in front is a flat 'piazza', no hint now of the drama of the rock rising from the river; second, it is still an enclosed space, but this time a regular one, filled with a lawn of collegiate proportions and smoothness, and surrounded on all sides by building.

To the left and right are the typical buildings of a cathedral close, dignified and pleasant without organization or studied grandeur. Behind is the castle, now reduced in scale since only the actual mound on which the keep is standing rises above the level of the plateau. But in front, and filling the whole of the remaining side, is the cathedral, stretched out in almost pure elevation from the tiny galilee, just visible, the twin western towers and the Norman nave, piling up to the Gothic central tower supported on its transepts, and then the Norman choir, terminating in the Nine Altars chapel. So the experience which begins somewhere at the foot of the rock reaches its climax.

This, then, is the greatness of Durham; it is the experience which remains whatever else of the town will fade from memory, for Durham is a piece of natural town planning which no amount of artificial arranging could produce. Yet, apart from the visual satisfaction of the approach to the cathedral, that is not all which contributes to the beauty of the city. The cathedral itself, for example, is the most beautifully proportioned perhaps of all the Norman churches and the one in which it is possible to witness the technical evolution of the Gothic vault. To the south lies the less formal but certainly no less delightful College Green, which is the real close of the cathedral.

If one has left the cathedral by the cloisters and passed into College Green, the route leads out into the South Bailey, where in the classical calm of wholly delightful terraced housing, the cathedral town merges into the university town – which has turned the city into a centre of learning, thus in many and differing ways perpetuating the traditions and glory of the town and monastery in the day of the Prince Bishops. South Bailey terminates in Prebends Bridge, the third of the Durham bridges from which to view the cathedral, and, intrinsically, the most beautiful. From here the town ceases to exist altogether and the view is again of a great church rising from the tree-clad slopes of the rock, which itself seems to grow from the river at its feet.

The evolution of the city did not end with the Georgian housing in the Bailey and the creation of the first provincial university early in the last century. Durham remained the administrative centre of a rapidly developing industrial area, situated, as it was, at the centre of a large coalfield. Like all cities, Durham witnessed the unseemly sprawl of speculative development which took place during the second half of the nineteenth century. But the great industries never came, and growth of the city was comparatively slow and spasmodic. There are no hillsides mapped out for acre upon acre with the grid of byelaw housing interspersed here and there by a mill or a factory belching forth continuous smoke. Nor is there a railway marshalling yard where once the early steam locomotives were serviced and refuelled on the long haul to London or Edinburgh. All this took place elsewhere; the industrial developments took place at Newcastle and on Teesside, the railway yards developed at Darlington and York.

There is much to be thankful for that in this period of expansion when most towns grew at a speed unprecedented in history, and when there was no control over the nature of their development, Durham remained largely untouched by sudden changes due to the industrial revolution. Development was only retarded, however, and the period of growth for Durham came, as Dr Thomas Sharpe (1945: 5–6) points out, after the First World War, and was only halted before it reached full flood by the Second.

The 'city fathers' were then forced to halt all plans for the city and were able to take stock of their unique heritage for the first time, and Dr Sharp was called in towards the end of the war to prepare a development plan. His view was that Durham should develop on a fourfold basis: as a market town, an educational and cultural centre, and a tourist centre. Certain developments, he argued, must take place whether there was a plan or not, and he believed that it was important to decide how the traffic problem was to be solved, where the city should expand and where the major buildings should be sited, otherwise each development would be ill-considered in relation to the whole town concept. Durham remained in Dr Sharp's view the non-industrial town it had always been, but it must assume new importance as an academic and administrative centre for the area, properly equipped to deal with the problems of twentieth-century life. Turning to the interpretation of the plan as architecture, he laid down the following principles for guidance:

> Two principles are suggested as being of special importance in Durham. One is that there should be no attempt to imitate past architectural styles. New building should be in harmony with the old: but this harmony rests in matters like scale, siting and suitability of materials rather than in details of style.... The second principle is applicable to Durham more than to most other towns in England. It is that here, because of the hilly nature of the city the effect of roofline must always be in the mind of the designer.
>
> (Sharp 1945: 81–2)

Nineteen years have passed since these words were written, and the great issues which surround the creation of a new city within the rich historical setting of the past are nowhere nearer tangible reality than they were in 1944. The first major building envisaged in the plan, the Shire Hall, has been built on a site which largely avoids answering the more crucial questions, although in itself a working design which, one feels, fulfils the two precepts of the original plan. The university developments in the past decade have been fraught with tribulation, at least architecturally, especially those which encroached upon the ancient centre; and the greatest task of all – creating an adequate traffic network – has not yet been started.

A great question mark still looms over the whole future of the city. We can but reiterate Dr Sharp's conclusion that, 'given the will, the citizens of Durham have the power to create the city they desire' (ibid.: 93).

DURHAM REVISITED

I wrote that in the summer of 1963. On a sunny November Saturday in 1990, I went back to see what had happened to Durham after twenty-seven years. Of course, during that time I have been back many times and for many differing purposes, but I have never looked at the city with quite that comprehension which I sought in 1963. This time I came by rail, from the south, which is another of those great experiences as the train pulls on to the viaduct just before it reaches the station and there, all at once, is spread out below the whole city. At a first glance and at this distance, the snapshot view is apparently unchanged.

The exit for the foot passenger from the down platform can hardly be described as prepossessing. You emerge from the underpass unceremoniously outside the station and begin an uncertain descent to the town. It soon becomes clear that much, in fact, has changed and much of what is new is at once revealed, beginning, as it turns out, with the least appropriate, too. Mill-

burngate House, built 1965–8, to house the National Savings Bank, lies in full view below and one cannot but agree with Alec Clifton-Taylor when he describes it as 'this assertive lump of hideous concrete' (Clifton-Taylor 1989). A bad and unpropitious start.

But standing on one of the vantage points, just below the station, one can also see that the whole of the new road proposal has been implemented and Thomas Sharp's original ideas are a reality. Two new bridges span the Wear, taking the traffic past the peninsula with new road connections to the east, bringing the necessary city traffic into Elvet or off to the new Durham motorway. To the west, the road connects back into North Road, just below the viaduct, and offers an alternative way out of the city to the north-east. In other words, the proposal which was debated at the 1963 Public Enquiry on the Durham City Through Road Scheme has been implemented more or less exactly as it was designed. That in itself, with hindsight, seems a quite astonishing achievement.

Looking down from my vantage point, the traffic swishes past almost silently and the once under-developed land to the north of Framwelgate Bridge is now fully developed. The road itself appears discreet and, apart from Millburngate House, the extension of the urban grain is, for the most part, appropriate.

So, I pick my way down the hill, across the new road, and make a detour to go through the Millburngate Centre, completed in 1976 to the design of the Building Design Partnership. Inside, by contemporary standards, a modest shopping centre but, clearly, an effective and a popular one. Outside, a successful and appropriately scaled group of buildings, butting up to Framwellgate Bridge and providing a new riverside walk between it and Millburngate Bridge – a positive bonus. The development, which contains housing and car parking as well as a shopping precinct, is a discreet brick and pitched roof design, pre-dating the vernacular disease which affects so many of these projects today, and it well deserved the Civic Trust Award which it received in 1978.

Outside, the familiar street pattern re-emerges. North Road, the old approach to the city, leads to the pedestrianized Framwelgate Bridge. To the south, almost nothing has changed; river, hillside, the towering mass of castle and cathedral are all untouched. George Pace's University Library, which caused such uproar over its original unplanned height, is now reduced and hardly significant. To the north, the view of Millburngate Bridge is acceptable if not beautiful and the riverside elevation on the west bank, largely made up of the Millburngate Centre, is a positive improvement. Only the distant view of Millburngate House reminds us of the less sensitive aspects of the intervening years.

It is now pleasant to stop on the bridge without the successive waves of traffic, controlled at one time by the police officers in the Market Place. For the pedestrian, progress up Silver Street to the Market Place is relaxed, free from fumes and noise and an excuse to linger in what, after all, were pre-vehicular streets. The buildings themselves look better cared for, although the shop-fronts are more anonymous and standardized, and so too are much of their contents. But the texture of the ground with its simple re-paving is in keeping with the character of the city, and is mercifully free of so much of the prettification which characterizes so many conservation areas.

The Market Place itself has benefited from the reduction in traffic and St Nicholas church effectively blocks the view out to the gap created by the new road. In fact, the main arterial road passes at a lower level and the approach to Claypath for the pedestrian is well done. The feeder road breaks the visual continuity, but it seems a reasonable enough price for the relative peace of the town centre. Only traffic going to Palace Green and the Baileys goes up the east side of the Market Place and turns up Fleshergate and on into Saddler Street. You cannot now go down over Elvet Bridge; that part of the town is now reached by a new feeder road from the through road.

I deliberately walked down from the Market Place on the edge of the feeder road to the new roundabout and on into Old Elvet. Looking back, the multi-storey car park behind Boots, on the corner of the Market Place, is an unhappy and over-dominating construction. The County Hotel, which now has a prime site from all directions with excellent access and adequate car parking, has twice expanded in different but equally unconvincing attempts at an appropriate vernacular style. Anyone who has the time, or comes by car, should go up Leazes Road as far as the College of St Hild and St Bede for a view of the great acropolis from an unusual but commanding vantage point. As I crossed into Old Elvet, I realized that the price of this new scheme was the demolition of the Waterloo Hotel, which stood between the bridge and the County Hotel and where on winter afternoons in front of a roaring fire I used to have tea after evensong.

Old Elvet is unchanged, even to the traffic, a mixture of Georgian and strangely incongruous Victorian designs. The university now occupies the old Shire Hall; it is curious to find an old university administered from a building more usually associated with the later civic universities because it is housed in what Clifton-Taylor would doubtless recognize as a building of screaming redness. By contrast, at the top of the hill the old Assize Courts have an unexpectedly serene neo-classical façade by an architect who identified himself with this part of the world – Bonomi. It dates from 1811.

Back at Elvet Bridge, you can pursue a route to Palace Green which was not available in 1963, although it was designed and partially built. Turn into New Elvet where, by the river bank, one of the few sites for inner city expansion by the university has now been filled up. The

development is in a variety of styles, not quite as coherent as Jack Napper proposed in 1962: nerve clearly has at times failed the university authorities, although perhaps not as often as it has done in other places. The Arts Building, the Students' Union and the pedestrian Kingsgate Bridge are all works which would not meet with contemporary approval. What a relief that some of these decisions were taken in a less sycophantic age. The barbaric splendours of the Union Building are perhaps the most surprising and the most appropriate in a city dominated by Norman architecture. The bridge, both as an idea and in its realization is a stroke of genius; I do not share Clifton-Taylor's view that it would have been more appropriate in steel. The contrast, it seems to me, is like the precociousness of the early English beside the Romanesque.

I cross the bridge and go up Bow Lane, along the North Bailey, into the College and through the cloisters. Here, in the historic core, one can feel safe. Or so one thinks! The dark undercroft of the Monks' Dormitory, through which one crept to find the antediluvian toilets, was once filled with grotesque ancient skeletons; now there is a treasury, a restaurant and a gift shop. George Pace's light fittings in the restaurant tell who had a hand in this imaginative resuscitation of a derelict space, and not only does the restaurant deserve its reputation for its food but a few yards away you can contemplate quietly and at first hand the exquisite Celtic beauties of St Cuthbert's pectoral Cross, or the great grotesque original sanctuary knocker.

As for the cathedral itself, the choir is presently full of scaffolding to clean and restore the vault. The intrusion of the great forest of scaffolding poles only increases the majesty of the Norman architecture in the nave and is a reminder of what medieval cathedrals must have looked like for whole generations while they were in building.

One interesting sign of the change in taste has been the repositioning of Gilbert Scott's great pelican lectern in its rightful place in front of the choir screen. Whatever one thinks of his re-ordering of the choir, his sense of design with screen, pulpit and lectern are seen as they were intended, at least for the time being, and that curious neo-classical hutch, which has served as a lectern throughout my lifetime, has been banished for the time being into a corner. I hope it stays there! Liturgical whims have always passed Durham by, additions and fashionable decorations seem not to have a place, the cathedral remains a satisfying mixture of Norman splendour and Bishop Cosin's seventeenth-century black oak.

I had foregone the great experience of climbing up Saddler Street to Palace Green, which I described in 1963 as one of the great experiences of British townscape, but I saw enough to realize that it was unchanged. Instead, I left the Green and made the detour back through the Baileys and down to Prebends Bridge and to the river.

I am always surprised how still it is by the river: you seem so far away from the city which you know lies so close. The university rowing team was on the water, oars dipping rhythmically in and out as coaches barked their criticisms from the bank. More women than men, I noted. The university was on the bank in twos, hand in hand, idly spinning out the walk and, from time to time, younger voices of Durham School at football drifted down from behind the high trees. By now, the light was beginning to go. The river was darkening and, as I came past the old Fulling Mill, the higher trees, still littered with autumn colour, were pierced by the late afternoon sun and the west towers of the cathedral were ablaze, the cool grey stone for once glowing with colour. This is one of the classic views of the cathedral, the seemingly permanent and indestructible building towering high above your head where it has stood for 800 years while below, at your feet, the transient water slips quietly and blackly away.

So, back to the late Saturday afternoon bustle of Silver Street, back over Framwelgate Bridge and on into the unfamiliar new developments and roads that eventually get you up to the station. From the train, as it pulled back on to the viaduct, the cathedral and castle, now palely floodlit in the early night sky, appeared almost suspended in space, ghost-like but definite above the undefined pinpricks of light that make up the city below.

It seemed to me that those who have had the power and the responsibility in the Palatine City of Durham have done their job well, and that one of the great experiences of English architecture and townscape can still be enjoyed by those who have the eyes to see.

REFERENCES

Billings, R.W. (1843) *Architectural Illustrations and Descriptions of the Cathedral Church at Durham*, London.

Clifton-Taylor, A. (1989) 'Durham' (taken from *Another Six Towns*, BBC Books), Bury St. Edmonds: Alastair Press.

Pevsner, N. (1953) *County Durham*, Harmondsworth: Penguin.

Sharp, T. (1945) *Cathedral City: A Plan for Durham*, Durham: Durham Corporation.

Tarn, J.N. (1963) 'Durham City: its origins and development', *Northern Architect* (Journal of the Northern Architectural Association) 12 (Sept./Oct.): 245–6.

93 Durham City: the spirit of the place

Neville Whittaker

Buildings and structures almost invariably become the visual tokens of a place, especially if they are endowed with power of form and purpose. From civic heraldry to local business opportunity the images, the identity and sense of place these tokens convey are adopted to convey the sources of long history and pride in achievement. Of all these visual tokens in use in the north-east of England, that of Durham Cathedral is perhaps the most potent, combining, as it does, permanence, a long history, spiritual aspirations and, perhaps most significantly, technical achievement. Today it sails, like some great ocean liner, over the green backdrop to the city, dwarfing the setting and with magisterial presence presiding over the scene.

Durham City sits above the deep wooded valley of the river Wear and at the focus of a system of small river valleys. The heart of the city is on the narrow peninsula which contains both cathedral and castle and the modern city spreads onto the ring of surrounding hills. This much painted, engraved and drawn ensemble has overshadowed all public perception of the 'city' which grew up around its gates until very recently. Architectural and other guide books say little or nothing – until the recent growth of interest and scholarship – about the town or its buildings.

The *raison d'être* for the City of Durham was the cathedral and any understanding of Durham or its spirit must derive at least from its beginnings. If, in a kind of simplified history in schools fashion, one wished to segment this long history, there are four stages in the development of the City.

DURHAM THE CITADEL

Late in AD 995, a somewhat dishevelled and disheartened band of Christians, led by their bishop, Aldhun, were turning northwards again to Chester-le-Street and Ripon where they had been driven by the invading Norsemen. They carried the miraculously preserved body of their saint, Cuthbert. It was then that the miracle and base of the Durham legend took place as required in all the mystical histories – the coffin grew heavy, stuck fast and resisted all efforts to be moved. The weary group camped and during that night one of the company saw the saint in a vision and was told that Cuthbert wished to lie on the Dun Holm – the hill island – the high wooded peninsula on which the cathedral now stands.

The first church was a modest structure of timber to serve as a shrine for the sacred relics. However, before the itinerant Aldhun died in 1018, a bare twenty-three years after settlement, the first stone church was built and the area fortified.

The site was chosen well. It was easily defended and protected the main north–south route on which it stood. It became the citadel. The bishops were needed by the Norman kings to hold the outposts and borders of the wild north country. They were accorded Palatine powers, a measure of great trust and the let to raise an army.

Even so, the bishop rebelled – but only once, in 1069. That resulted in Norman William harrowing the North and driving the monastic community, together with its restless saint, back into Northumberland, to Lindisfarne. He then sacked the town which had grown up, and built a castle. A Norman bishop was installed and Norman discipline instituted. That was that.

In 1081 William of St Carileph – of Calais – was made bishop and in 1093 he laid the foundation stone of the cathedral we now know. Within a short time the chancel was erected complete with the first ribbed vaulting to the west end of the building. The framework of the cathedral on which later generations only elaborated was built between 1093 and 1133, a bare hundred years after the death of the nomadic Bishop Aldhun.

The bishops wielded autocratic authority. All local power was vested in the Prince Bishops; they had their own local parliament, their own courts, their own coinage and the right to crenelate or fortify buildings. For eight hundred years the history and development of the town was directed to the bishops' interests and in the bishops' hands, governed by monks or bailiffs and their post-reformation prebendary successors. For the first, possibly the last, time the North was governed by the North. Only in 1602 were the burghers of Durham free of the bishop's bailiffs.

Nevertheless, the town of Durham thrived. By the beginning of the seventeenth century the town had spread out from the Market Place, immediately outside the walls of the medieval citadel. There were substantial additions to the streets of Claypath, bridges crossed the river to the area of Elvet to the east and towards the Framwell to the west. Leland describes a handsome and well-built town thus:

> The close itself of the Minstre on the highest part of
> the hille, is well walled and hath diverse faire gates.
> The church self and cloister be very strong and faire.

The castell standeth stately on the north est side of the Minstre and Were runneth under it. The kepe standeth aloft, and is stately builded of viii square fascion and four highes of logginges

(Leland 1549)

There were nineteen prospering merchant companies.

THE COUNTY TOWN OF THE EIGHTEENTH CENTURY

The age of elegance, enlightenment, and a settled lifestyle produced growth and change in the city. Groups and terraces of fine brick houses in the latest styles appeared in the citadel itself, in North and South Baileys and Owengate, across the river in a new South Street and to the east in Old and New Elvet. As the county town, Durham was the focus for society life and a congregating place for the local gentry, many of whom had town houses there. A racecourse and a theatre appeared. Number 44 Saddler Street enjoyed a brief life as a theatre between 1771 and 1791. It was part of Samuel Butler's northern circuit and both Stephen Kemble and his sister Fanny, the redoubtable Mrs Siddons, trod the boards there at the start of their careers. The theatre survives today only in the name of a narrow vennel (path) from the street to the river, Drury Lane, and the remaining Grecian street façade and its paybox.

When Daniel Defoe visited this 'compact neatly contriv'd city' in 1724, he found the church in Durham 'eminent for its wealth; the bishoprick is esteemed the best in England and the prebends and other church livings in the gift of the bishop, and the richest in England. (The clergy lived in 'all the magnificence and splendour imaginable)' (Defoe 1724–6).

Communications improved and staging inns appeared. Main connecting coaches left the inns of Elvet for London, Edinburgh, Newcastle, Lancaster and Leeds, ceasing only in 1850.

THE UNIVERSITY TOWN

Education, and learning, springing from the medieval tradition of scholarship, was to become the next phase of growth and development of the city. There were the resources; Durham had its great ecclesiastical library and there had been the long search for the site of England's third university. There had been various attempts, by Henry VIII and Oliver Cromwell, but it was not until 1833 when Bishop Van Mildert provided the means that the university was finally established. The funding for this was provided from the great revenue of both bishop and chapter, regarded at the time as a national scandal by William Cobbett. An enabling Act was passed whereby the dean and chapter endowed the new foundation and Van Mildert provided his castle in Durham for its use.

For the first century of the university's existence its concerns were chiefly theological but by the mid-century wider interests and scientific developments, in part responding to the growth of industry on nearby Tyneside and Wearside, connected the university with the medical school and later Armstrong's College of the practical sciences in Newcastle upon Tyne. Nevertheless, it remained a small institution and rarely did its numbers exceed 500 until 1924 and the establishment of a science department at Durham. In the years between the two World Wars the numbers grew but so did the imbalance between the two divisions, Durham and Newcastle. By 1945 the Newcastle-based students outnumbered those based at the historic Durham colleges by over three to one. The rapid growth in student numbers thereafter meant that separation in 1963 was inevitable.

The slow growth of the university in the early years meant that it could be contained on the peninsula. As town houses were vacated these were acquired by the university, linked and partitioned, and new colleges and departments were formed. It was neat, compact and contained. Indeed, the results were a tribute to the versatility of terrace houses in that they could be so transformed and continue in satisfactory use.

Following the end of the Second World War and the growth of higher education for all, further new departments and colleges were needed. These new colleges could not be accommodated on the peninsula, although there were some good schemes for site redevelopment and infill. Six new colleges were built across the river, on sites to the south. Architectural style and to a certain extent quality was dependent upon the governing tastes. The earlier colleges were in a plain Neo-Georgian style and it was not until the building of the West Building and Appleby Lecture Theatre in 1950 that serious attempts were made to produce an architecture of the times. The science department had occupied a site alongside the defunct Elvet Colliery. The final change to a new architecture was signalled with the building of Dunelm House, the Students' Union and Staff Club in 1961, on a restricted site flanking the river almost opposite the east end of the cathedral. Dunelm House and the Kingsgate footbridge of 1962 redirected and coordinated the physical planning of a university campus separated by a major river. Thereafter new colleges could spread out in these southerly locations with style and spaciousness and linked by new landscape. A very different campus was to be produced to that of the tightly contained and constricted peninsula.

INDUSTRY AND CHANGE

The fourth stage in the city's development was linked directly with industry, specifically coal and the railway. Durham formed a natural focus for the collieries of the period 1850 to 1950. It was a natural congregating centre, and in 1913 the National Union of Miners headquarters replaced the old Miners' Hall. The city is the host to the Annual Miners' Gala. This annual feast-day gathering used to be attended by vast numbers of men and families marching in (led by the Colliery or Lodge Banner from the local pits) but, alas, it continues as a mere shadow of its former self because of pit closures.

The main railway was slow in progressing north from York. There were other, earlier, local lines and stations serving Durham such as the stations at Gilesgate, and another on a site bordering the racecourse. The present station, opened in 1857, was designed by G.T. Andrews, George Hudson's protégé architect, at the same time as the dramatic railway viaduct. The superb siting of these afforded the most magnificent series of views of the cathedral, castle and city. With these railway works came the building of streets and terraces of artisans' cottages around North Road and the viaduct. Even now with all the changes and improvements to this area the view presents a sight akin to the visions of Gustave Doré. The industrial railway city was a further graft on to the historic core, and the population expanded.

As the twentieth century progressed so Durham's status was to change. The days of the medieval power-house were gone and a declining coal industry meant that even its post-industrial revolution significance was changing. Like many provincial towns and cities it was the product of centuries of growth and accretion, resembling a combination of Barchester and an overgrown pit village.

Older housing areas of the town, like Milburngate, had declined into slums and the occupants were cleared to new, post-garden city estates on the perimeter of the city. Durham received probably more than its fair share of the optimistic but visually disastrous development of the 1960s and early 1970s: the Post Office Savings Bank, the new county Hall, the latter redeemed only by a new attitude and opportunity to create good landscape. There were also the proposed solutions to Durham's growing traffic problems. Much of the development, including the celebrated proposal to site a new power station downstream from the cathedral, fostered the growth and role of groups determined to preserve and conserve the city.

All the while the university was growing and beginning to show the way in which well-considered development and good architecture could be assimilated into the Durham scene.

Even so, Durham was still a small city by any standards. The peninsula, with its major asset of enveloping woodland, was roughly the domain of church and university. The historic core was decaying, there were empty properties, vacant sites and many upper floors were unused. The city was surrounded by large new housing estates both private and public, albeit at a suitable distance not to detract visually from the historic city.

The ancient north–south road ran right through the Market Place where for many years the police controlled traffic from the feeder streets by closed-circuit television. There had been proposed solutions to this dating back to the 1930s, including a new high-level crossing of the river, roundabouts, and so on. Happily, due in major part to the intervention of Thomas Sharp, these were not built.

Sharp's alternative proposal took over thirty years to achieve. A new bypass was built to the west, soon to be superseded by yet one more bypass even further to the west of the city. The most significant change came with the construction of the motorway to the east which, coupled with the new bridges over the river, alleviated traffic pressures on the city centre pro tem. Thomas Sharp presents a gloomy view of the state of Durham City in the late 1930s in his essay 'Britain and the beast'. Even after the Second World War the state and condition of the city had not changed materially.

Developments of the late 1960s and 1970s heralded a new life and attitude to the fabric of the city. Local government reorganization meant that for the first time the city was provided with a range and standard of service which had previously been lacking. The university was growing and demonstrating its attitude to high standards of design. Problems of traffic could be answered and the city was to enter a period of intensive care. The pedestrianization and repaving of the city centre together with a whole range of conservation schemes began to produce appreciable results. At last, earlier attitudes to city centre design – a cold, lifeless, stripped-down vernacular – were abandoned. Durham began to make itself noticed.

Tourism, the blessing and curse of so many historic towns, was also growing. One of the city's major problems had always been the very limited vehicular access to the peninsula. A minibus service was introduced to the cathedral and castle from the bold and fortress-like new multi-storey car park and the coach park. Food and catering, hitherto one of the city's greatest shortcomings, was developing, even within the cathedral precincts – complete with attendant table licence. Alas, with tourism shopping was also changing. The final accolade (or blow, depending on your point of view) was the declaration of the cathedral as a World Heritage Site, along with the Parthenon etc.

Durham was seen as a subject for large-scale development. Difficult sites which had lain empty were now taken up; local authorities were keen to realize on parts of their large land holdings, and even the Diocese brought forth a welter of schemes for hotels, shopping and housing. The 1990s could see Durham change as never before.

Yet Durham over the centuries had always changed and grown. It is by no means a cohesive city. The annular rings of its development are visually evident. It does, however, hold a special place and affection in the north-easterner's heart. People working throughout the north-east are happy to live in the relatively small number of city houses and travel to work. The old animosities between 'town and gown' are still there but the anonymities produced by growth lesson these divisions.

What, then, is the spirit of this disparate city, if, indeed, one can be distilled? Durham engenders a fierce sense of concern and protection. The local Amenity Societies are more active and vocal than almost any others in the north. The District Council has, even though a majority of its members have interests and concerns outside the city, pursued an active rather than a passive role in its planning. Somehow or other,

whether by design or chance, the historic city and its landscape setting has survived. Whether it can continue thus only time will tell.

REFERENCES

Defoe, D. (1724–6) *Tour through the Whole Island of Great Britain*, London; reprinted 1971, ed. P. Rogers, Harmondsworth: Penguin.

Leland, J. (1549) *The Laborious Journey and Search for English Antiquities*, London.

Sharp, T. (1938) 'The North East: hills and hells', in C. Williams Ellis (ed.) *Britain and the Beast*, London: J.M. Dent & Sons.

94 Durham: the city and its landscape

Brian Clouston

The landscape of Durham City is made up of four prime elements – the River Wear, the underlying landform (its geology), its abundance of woodlands and its buildings (see Figure 1). It is the dramatic relationship between the city's landform, created over thousands of years by the erosive power of the river and its woodlands, which gives this northern city its powerful landscape reputation. Durham's historic core, recently given the accolade of being declared a World Heritage Site, heightens the drama of the place.

Why is the landscape of the city so powerful? York and Lincoln have fine cathedrals, as do historic cities elsewhere in our land – Lincoln, Canterbury and Salisbury. Durham is made different by the cathedral's siting, astride the peninsula, the neck of which is plugged by the castle. Viewing both from South Street, across the river gorge, is a stunning visual experience. The castle and cathedral sit on the peninsula, supported by a majestic forest which entirely covers the steep river embankments. At night the cathedral and castle are floodlit and sit sparkling on a dark platform, as if in silhouette. No lights compete in the dark valley below and none disturb the backdrop. One overseas visitor, introduced by me to this view on a misty autumn night, described the scene as orgasmic.

No matter what word or combination of words is used to describe the cityscape, more must be invented to portray the tantalizing nature of the city and its landscape overall. The cathedral, the town and the castle, in combination and in part, appear, disappear and reappear in unexpectedly tantalizing views as one approaches Durham and travels through it. Constant surprise adds to the mystery of the place. Robert Hegg was awestruck in the seventeenth century; others before and after him were, too. We are today.

Durham city is contained by two distinct ridgelines – an outer horseshoe coinciding with the 150 m. (500 ft.) contour and an inner ridge wrapping round the city core. Landform has always dictated routeways to and through the city. Old routeways into the city are of two kinds – ridge routes and valley routes. The processional ways trodden by pilgrims paying homage to St Cuthbert's shrine and the packhorse routes devised cunningly by the drovers to avoid the Prince Bishops' taxes are the most ancient. These are liberally punctuated by the sites and ruins of ancient churches in the case of the pilgrim ways and by pubs in the case of the drovers' roads. Stage-coach routes tended to follow gently graded ridge-lines and valleys which radiated from the city centre.

Much of the nineteenth-century residential expansion of the city followed the line of the older routeways. The advent of motor traffic caused many of these older routeways to be widened. Post-war development overflowed from the prime eastern access routes to the city and spread east towards the river valley from Framwelgate Moor. In the mid-1960s a new through road, with its two new river crossings, was built. This road, together with the newly constructed Gilesgate link road (built on the line of the closed Durham–Sunderland Railway) links the city to the A1(M) trunk road to the east. The new road did much to relieve traffic congestion in the city centre. But until the northern and western bypass roads are completed the city centre will remain under heavy pressure from traffic. It is upon the land lying between this skeleton (of river, peninsula, routeways and steep unbuildable land) that builders throughout the ages gave flesh to the city with structures subordinate in scale to those on the peninsula. The bits left over, those too steep to cultivate and build upon, nature and humans clothed with trees.

THE RIVER WEAR AND DURHAM CITY

The river Wear on its approach to the city flows directly in a gently meandering stream through a wide valley

Figure 1 *The city and its landscape: 'This reverend aged Abby is seated in the heart of the Citty, advanced upon the shoulders of an high Hill, and encompassed again with higher Hills, that he that hath seene the situation of this City, hath seene the Map of Sion, and may save a journey to the Jerusalem. Shee is girded almost rownd with the renoued River of Weer, in which, as in a Glasse of Crystial, shee might once have beheld the beauty, but nowe the ruine of her Walls. To this sumptuous Church, was the last and great Translation of St. Cuthbert.' (Robert Hegg (1626) The Legend of St Cuthbert).*

confined to the east and west by woodland. Here the valley is in agricultural use and is bounded at its edge by commercial woodland, mostly broad-leaved plantations: notably Great High Wood and Hollingside Wood to the west and Shincliffe Woods to the east. The prime concentrations of woodland are to be found on steep riverbank land and on hilltops.

At Shincliffe Bridge the river flows beneath the A177 trunk road, a major traffic artery linking the city to the village of Bowburn and the A1(M) beyond. The stream then turns almost due west at Old Durham. At this point it is flanked to the north by Pelaw Woods and the Gilesgate spur. It is at this point, only half a mile from its centre, that travellers of the valley route become aware of the historic core of the city, with the cathedral and castle dominating its centre. Coming upon the city by this river route, travellers, their wits mellowed by the pastoral valley landscape, are unaware of the splendour about to open up before them.

Similarly, road travellers, coming into the city from the east and passing through the road cutting which divides Mount Joy and Whinney Hill, are not immediately aware of the architectural splendour the city is about to provide. When revealed, views of the peninsula and its sumptuous church are both stunning and surprising.

In many of the great cities of Europe, such as Bergen, St Petersburg, Amsterdam and Paris, people live beside or overlooking their river, even at their city's core. Durham is different. The nearest riverside housing to the city centre on the river route from the south and east is a group of six recently built houses west of Baths Bridge. Student housing flanks the river west of New Elvet. Housing built on the peninsula, now mostly in university ownership or in office use, enjoys views over the wooded river valley but not of the river itself. The handful of houses on South Street again overlook the valley: they enjoy the best views in the city of the cathedral and castle but provide no views of the river. Mid-1960s housing north of Framwelgate Bridge, at the Sands, is set well back from the stream and has valley, rather than river, views.

So the mighty stream responsible for creating the city's landform and therefore its woodlands has been ignored by generations of house builders. The majority have turned their back on the Wear and built high above the course of the river.

Framwelgate Village, which existed until the early 1960s, was a notorious community comprising what were then considered to be slum houses, but nowadays would be cherished as desirable town cottages. It was cleared to rid the city of a nuisance and allow room for the building of the through road. This community was the only one which could claim to be a riverside village in the true sense, with houses properly at the river's edge. Sadly the village is no more. Short-sighted planners, public health inspectors following the book, and

highway engineers looking for an easy road alignment saw to that. Gone with the village is the Bluebell Inn, an old packhorse pub and in its day one of the most renowned hostelries in the county.

THE WOODLANDS OF DURHAM CITY

Woodlands in the city are mostly to be found on steeply sloping land on the river and valley sides. Some are recorded on ancient maps. Others, particularly those below the cathedral and castle, are surprisingly of comparatively recent origin. Prints made in the sixteenth century show the steep banks of the peninsula naked of trees. It must be remembered that the cathedral was at times as much a 'castle against the Scots' as a place of pilgrimage and worship. As such it was necessary to keep the steep slopes clear of vegetation to ensure defending troops enjoyed a clear view of their target invaders. On less steep slopes gardens were cultivated to provide produce for those occupying habitations within the defensible cordon drawn by the river and the medieval bridges called Elvet and Framwelgate.

When the threat of invasion from the north subsided, after the union with Scotland, the steeper slopes of the peninsula were allowed to become covered with trees. In time these self-sown plantations were brought under management by the authority responsible for management of these areas, the Dean and Chapter of Durham Cathedral. During the early 1960s the Dean and Chapter commissioned a distinguished amenity forester, the Hon. Orde Powlett, to prepare and monitor a management plan for the peninsula woodlands.

Their action was timely. Neglect up to that time had allowed these important woodlands to become dominated by the invasive and ubiquitous sycamore to the detriment of the woodland balance overall, and the health of its under-storey in particular.

Thirty years on the woodlands are a fine example of amenity woodland management and contain an abundance of healthy young trees ready to replace those which become mature and require felling.

Elsewhere in the city the responsible authorities, the University of Durham, the County Council and a number of private owners, manage their woodlands with care, responsibility and to a long-term plan. During the 1960s a number of important new woodlands were planted by the County Council on their Aykley Heads estate and on land bounding the new through road.

Sadly the enlightened policy of planting new woodlands within the city lapsed following local government reorganization in 1974. The current City Council's wilful neglect of its own woodland estate reflects badly on an authority claiming overall responsibility for the city's planning and the protection and conservation of its fabric. This dereliction is striking in a city so generously endowed with well-maintained woodland in the ownership of others. Perhaps the only workable solution, guaranteed to ensure the correct management in perpetuity of Durham City's urban forest, would be for those tracts currently in the ownership of neglectful managers (the City Council and Hospital Authority to name but two) to be dedicated to a Durham City Woodland Trust. Private and public owners without the means (or, in the case of the City Council, without the wits) to manage their estate responsibly could divest themselves of that responsibility to the Trust. If such timely action is not taken valuable woodland in Wharton Park and Pelaw Woods will in time disappear, just as the small wood below the railway station disappeared. No one in the city foresaw the ravages of Dutch elm disease in that case.

Opportunities remain for large-scale new woodlands to be planted within the strategic 'green wedges' kept free from development, and which form an important part of the city's landscape.

Until the city gives primacy to the long-term protection of woodland and green spaces and agrees upon the release of land on its fringes, pressure will remain to build on open space in the city. The current 'head in the sand' stance by the Council does the city landscape no good whatsoever. Little or no planting is taking place. In other words, no investment in the future of the city's landscape is happening. Neglect of strategic woodlands by the Council will mean the gradual erosion of that woodland – wilful damage which will take years to repair.

DURHAM – THE FUTURE

I have now lived in Durham for thirty years. For part of that time I worked with the County Council, which up to 1974 was the responsible authority for planning the city. In that role the county authority was responsible for drawing up planning policy governing the growth of the city, a conservation policy for the historic core – including important regulations regarding the height of new buildings – and policy for the management of existing and new woodlands.

It was the county authority who persuaded the university and the Dean and Chapter to adopt management plans for their woodland estate. The authority led by example in planting large tracts of new woodland within its administrative campus estate at Aykley Heads and on land administered by its highways department.

The benefits of these sensible policies are evident in the overall landscape of the city.

Of all the elements in our landscape, it is trees which have the greatest capacity to bring nature into the city. Yet the presence of trees is often seen to be accidental and taken for granted. Care and forward planning is essential to ensure that trees survive in the hostile environment of a city. Virtually all of Durham's woodlands, excepting those planted by the County Council in the 1960s, are an inheritance from the eighteenth and nineteenth centuries. It is this inheritance which needs to be maintained if the character of the city is to be kept.

The river and its riparian edge will change little; the landform of the city changes imperceptibly over time. Little to hurt the drama of the cities built fabric will happen provided established policies are observed and are strictly enforced. Durham City's green mantle is vulnerable to the ravages of time, to disease and the neglect of its owners. Yet these woodlands are Durham's finest inheritance, next only to the cathedral and castle, and its finest investment in securing a future for Durham's landscape.

The seeds of the eighteenth-century landscape movement, which was to green the more affluent parts of the town, were sown in Britain's country estates, where the inspiration of poet and painter was translated into reality through architecture and landscape design.

Alexander Pope wrote:

> Consult the Genius of the Place in all;
> That tells the waters or to rise, or fall;
> Or help the ambitious hill the heavens to scale,
> Or scoops in arching theatres the vale;
> Calls in the Country, catches opening glades,
> Joins willing woods, and varies shade from shades
> Now breaks, or now directs, the intruding lines
> Paint as you plant, and as you work design.
>
> (Pope 1731)

Fine words, fine advice. Advice which should be taken by the City Council. A new landscape plan is needed for Durham City. The last was only part implemented and that was over twenty years ago. Durham's place among the landscape cities of the world depends on it.

REFERENCE

Pope, A. (1731) 'An epistle to Lord Burlington',

95 The city as a stage – Durham Miners' Gala

Diana Brown

First associations with Durham City are the cathedral, the castle and the university, but the name is synonymous with that of the miners. The city forms the focus for miners of the Durham coalfield, and for one day each year the city has been the stage for the 'Big Meeting' or what is now called the Durham Miners' Gala (see Figure 1).

The Gala began over one hundred years ago as a demonstration by the miners – an emotional plea which penetrated the heart of the city.

The nineteenth century was the great age of coal. There was a large natural increase in the demand for coal for domestic purposes as well as for export. However, the underlying cause was the development and growth of steam power. The rapid expansion of the Northern Coalfield was largely facilitated by the extension of the railways; this enabled coal to be distributed more easily and economically. As the Tyne basin experienced more difficulty from the exhaustion of the High Main seam and the increased rate of flooding, it was now possible to turn to areas more remote from the river and the coast and so effectively open up the Northern Coalfield with new pits and villages.

From 1800 the output of coal from the Northern Coalfield rapidly increased; in 1810 the total output was 4.5 million tons and by 1900 it was 45 million tons, a quarter of the national output. The number of miners employed in the region also increased rapidly from 10,000 in 1810 to 60,000 in 1860 and 223,000 in 1912 (Raistrick 1952: 24).

Contemporary reports argue that the miner enjoyed a higher wage than most other comparable groups, but it was a hard life and the accident level was high. By the middle of the nineteenth century, miners in the north-east of England worked under an annual bond which was a legal contract between workers and owners. Theoretically, this contract was mutually beneficial, for, in areas of acute labour shortage, it guaranteed that a master had workmen who were bound to him from one hiring fair to the next, and it also sought to protect the men, ensuring continuity of employment. In practice it gave the employers far-reaching powers; the miner was subject to fines and conditions imposed entirely at the owner's discretion, without redress of any kind, and breaking the agreement meant imprisonment.

The Great Northern Coalfield had the distinction of being the only coalfield in England and Wales where the colliery owners provided the miners' houses, as they say, 'free'. The precedent for this system was established in 1794; the date is from a bond between the proprietor of the West Denton Colliery and one James Row, workman (Simpson 1900: 29).

The collier of the Great Northern Coalfield had other advantages; household coal was either 'free' or very inexpensive. From the Bond of 1843:

> Each person for whom the owners shall provide a dwelling house as part of his wages, shall be provided with fire coal, paying the owners 3d. per week for leading the same.
>
> (Fynes 1971: 292)

There are many accounts of miners enjoying a high standard of comfort and expenditure not found with other labourers. The miner and his family were known for having huge fires burning day and night at a time when other labourers lacked enough fuel to cook a hot meal. It was stated by Leifchild that:

> They may be said to pay nothing for coals, consequently, they keep up fires large enough to roast an ox. Pleasant things are these immense fires on a cold night after the needful ablutions.
>
> (Leifchild 1853, Part II: 192)

Figure 1 *The 'Big Meeting': Durham Miners' Gala.* (Photograph: *courtesy of Beamish Museum*)

Reports of white bread and cakes 'made of the finest white flour', the daily diet of mutton, beef, bacon and eggs, and the holiday feasts of great abundance, are all indications of well-being (Leifchild 1853: 199). The sentiment that colliers don't look for another day was well known, and there are many indications of pitmen eating meat three times daily on the week following pay day, and being left to want until the next pay day.

But it was a hard life, the accident level was high. In 1852, about five men in every thousand employed underground were killed in accidents (Hall 1978: 69; Foster 1895: 107–8) and the toll of non-fatal injuries was probably an even greater cause of economic hardship.

On average 174 men out of every thousand employed in the pits suffered injuries that threw them out of work for periods of more than one week (Benson 1976: 93). The average incapacity lasted for four weeks. Such statistics indicate that few men could hope to avoid some incapacitation during their working life (Hall 1978: 70).

The degree of economic hardship caused by fatal and non-fatal accidents depended upon the compensation and effectiveness of the relief; some coal owners regularly assisted families of those killed in pit disasters. For example, after the Rainton Plain pit disaster of 1823, Lord Londonderry in Durham paid out the sum of £2,000 over a period of twenty years to the relatives of those killed, and in 1844 donated £100 to the families of the ninety-five killed in the Haswell disaster. This was the equivalent of about two weeks' wages per family (Hall 1978: 71; Taylor 1974: 245–6). He also took the initiative in organizing relief funds which offered the miner and his family several shillings per week in the event of an accident (Hall 1978: 71; Welbourne 1923: 72).

A more common form of relief found in the northeast was the payment of so-called 'smart money'. Since at least the beginning of the nineteenth century it had been a custom for some employers to pay out 5 shillings per week to the families of men who had been injured or killed in the pits. It had also been common for some owners to allow the widow of a man who had been killed to remain in her rent-free house (Hall 1978: 71; Benson 1973: 228, 241–2). The degree of responsibility felt towards workers varied greatly from owner to owner. Some refused to pay 'smart money' if the accident was due to the carelessness of the miner himself, and others evicted widows left as a result of a colliery accident.

Tenancy of a colliery dwelling was conditional upon the tenants working at the pit. A man leaving to take up employment with another coal company was evicted from his colliery house, and when labour was in short supply, coal owners competed with each other for men.

The colliery houses were then used as an incentive to induce men, especially those with large families of sons, to work at a particular colliery. Conversely, mass evictions from colliery houses was a common form of reprisal used by owners against miners on strike.

'The Bond' was a cause of continuing dissatisfaction, and at the completion of the yearly bond in 1844, the aggrieved miners resolved to seek better conditions and pay. Every colliery in Northumberland and Durham was laid idle. The strike lasted five months and wholesale evictions of men, women and children took place:

> it being distinctly understood that the dwelling-houses provided for any of the persons hereby hired or engaged are to form part of the wages of such persons; and on the expiration of such hiring in case any of them shall quit or be legally discharged from the employment hereby agreed upon, he or they shall at the end of 14 days thereafter quit such dwelling-house or dwelling-houses, and in case of neglect or refusal, such owners shall be at liberty, and he or they, and their agents and servants are hereby authorized and empowered to enter into and upon such dwelling-houses, and remove and turn out of possession such workman or workmen, and all his and their families, furniture, and effects, without having recourse to any legal proceedings.
>
> (Fynes 1971: 295)

By the end of the strike there was misery and destitution in the mining communities, and the men returned to work compelled by sheer necessity to accept the conditions of the owners. Unable to make headway in wage negotiations, improvement of working conditions became the target. This was brought sharply into focus by an explosion on 15 August 1848 at Murton, in which fifteen men and boys were killed (Galloway 1971: 11, 52). After this disaster, and following the 1852 Seaham explosion, the Institute of Mining and Mechanical Engineers was formed, aiming to improve safety in coal mines (Raistrick 1952: 25).

The social history of the mining communities was bound together with the formation of the mineworkers' unions. By the early 1860s Durham was the only mining area without a union, but after an influx of miners from other regions, the Durham Miners' Association was formed in 1869 (Fynes 1971: 259). On 12 August 1871 the first Durham Miners' Gala took place (Garside 1971: 296). This gathering was a direct result of a resolution that the Durham Miners' Association Council should take into consideration the desirability of holding a general meeting of miners in the central district (Dowding 1983: 10). The idea was that of William Crawford, the earliest president and later secretary of the Durham Miners' Association. His intention was to use the city as a platform to spread the word about the Durham Miners' Association to the mining communities of the Durham Coalfield. To win the struggle for better working conditions, he needed to communicate with the miners and foster their loyalty and brotherhood. In Durham City the stage was set.

A banner with the message 'A fair day's wage for a

fair day's work' was seen by about two thousand people at this first 'Big Meeting' (Mead 1983: 11). To add interest, the rally of the mine 'lodges' was augmented by a band contest and a sports meeting. The Gala was held in Durham City's Wharton Park near the railway station. By the following year the setting had been changed to where it has remained, the Durham Racecourse. On this occasion, miners from 180 collieries marched in front of 20,000 to 30,000 miners (Mead 1983: 11). The Gala has continued with a virtually unchanged format: the parade of the lodges bearing their banners through the streets of Durham City, the politicians receiving the parade from the balcony of the Royal County Hotel, followed by the political speeches held from the platforms of the racecourse, and the fairground holiday atmosphere at the end of the day. By 1897 Durham City's recognition of the Gala was signalled by the introduction of a special miners' service in the cathedral (Mead 1983: 11).

Durham City, the geographical centre to the Durham Coalfield, was surrounded by colliery villages. The miners who were from the collieries near to the city – Ushaw Moor, Bear Park, Sherburn, Kelloe and Bowburn – would march from their villages to the 'Big Meeting'. They would gather at their Institute or Mechanics' Hall in the early hours of the morning and march to Durham to 'get their reets' (Dowding 1983: 18). Those who lived further afield would assemble in their village, getting the banner out and the band prepared to travel by bus. Others, like those in the village of Chopwell, travelled by train; they congregated beside the pit at six o'clock in the morning and marched through the village behind the band and their banner, processing to High Westwood Station picking people up all along the way.

Trains arrived at Durham Station throughout the day and each 'lodge' took its turn to join the procession, marching from the elevated station down the hill, through the narrow streets and over the bridges to the racecourse. Everyone connected with the village would fall in behind the band when their turn came. The procession in Durham started at about eight o'clock, and some years the throng of people would continue for five hours. They marched through the streets to the Market Place, where many would stop for refreshment. Many Durham City traders took advantage of good trading on the day, but great pressures were imposed on the fabric of the city. Although in the early years this political carnival was a peaceful, well-ordered celebration, the street play of the masses resulted in damage to windows and doors. As a precautionary measure shop windows were boarded up, and in recent years violence has made this a necessity.

The highlight of the procession was reached at the Royal County Hotel where, standing on the first-floor balconies facing the widest part of the street, were the miners' leaders and the Labour MPs. These were the leaders of the Labour movement and people who had been invited to speak, and below the balconies the miners gathered to see in person some nationally important figureheads and politicians. The official speeches took place from the platforms on the racecourse and, after these, the 'Big Meeting' became more of a picnic or fairground. It was a meeting place for friends and relatives who would only meet at the annual Gala Day.

At three o'clock the cathedral opened its doors to the miners for a special service. Every year two or three bands were selected to play in the cathedral; these marched up to the cathedral followed by their banners and their village communities. The banners were paraded right up to the high altar, all contributing to the cold power of the cathedral and the solemnity of the service.

By the afternoon the political party on the racecourse drew to a close and the march home began. The banners, not quite so orderly as coming in, swayed this way and that after their good day out.

As the drama unfolds, so, over the years, Durham City has been the backcloth for a variety of performances. Changes in the coalfield have meant that the number of collieries represented at any one Gala has varied. There were seventy-two represented at the first Gala (Garside 1971: 296), which rose to a maximum of three-hundred-and-fifty in 1919. Even in 1956 it was estimated that 300,000 people attended the Gala (Turner 1967: 384). At Durham Gala's Centenary in 1983 (Galas were not held during the First and Second World Wars) the banners of Durham's remaining twelve working pits were supplemented by more than twice that number from former pits.

On Gala Day the crowds fill the narrow winding city streets from Framwelgate to Elvet. Each working colliery parades, proudly bearing its banner and marching behind its band. The banners from those early days of spreading the message to the crowds still depict scenes of the miners' struggles. Some bear portraits of former leaders, others pictures of aged miners' homes; all glow with the richness of their colours – red, blue and gold – but all depict a sense of unity. The design of the Wearmouth banner is particularly worthy of mention. The Lodge had a dispute over the terms of the bond. The banner commemorates the test case at Sunderland Court when four miners were charged, under the Masters and Servants Act (1823), with breaking the bond. The bond was legally cancelled and the men had the right to withdraw their labour without punishment. Under the courtroom scene depicted on the Wearmouth banner were the words: 'Come, let us reason together' (Dowding 1983: 12). The banners were borne by men whose names had been pulled out of the hat, to carry the banner either 'into' or 'out of' the city. The banners were heavy and difficult to carry, particularly in windy conditions; six men were required, two to carry the stout timber poles, and two front and rear carrying the tasselled rigging. Directly under the banners marched the Lodge officials.

The banners, like great sails filled in the wind, added to the spirit and movement of the crowds as they flowed through the streets towards the river and the racecourse. Some of the old banners were so large that they would barely pass through the narrow city streets. At the field the banners encircled the speakers' platform, providing a rich backcloth to the drama of the politicians' forum.

The banners commemorated generations of miners and contributed to the emotions of Gala day. From its political beginnings it grew into a light-hearted family occasion, but joy and sorrow go hand in hand. The banners were the mechanism for reminding the assembled crowds of the miners' hardships. Banners were draped in black crepe to signify a year when death had struck. In 1951, in contrast to the usual proud, noisy thronging masses, the crowd stood sombrely as the banners of Easington and Eppleton, completely covered in black drapes, were borne silently through the crowded streets (Dowding 1983: 13). Two major pit disasters had claimed a total of ninety-two lives in the year. The Easington and Eppleton mining communities went to the Durham Gala in force to pay their respects to the dead.

Another emotional Gala was that of 1969 which marked the centenary of the Durham Miners' Association. With the Gala in decline, thirty antique banners were brought out of storage and borne through the streets by 160 redundant miners (Dowding 1983: 14).

At no moment in the Gala is the sense of brotherhood more profoundly experienced than when the bands play 'Gresford', the miners' hymn of remembrance for those who have died in the pits. There were a variety of bands: military bands, pipe bands, Scottish bands and an American jazz band. If a village did not have its own colliery band, then they would hire one. When the bands played they contributed to the history of the place and the people, of the suffering and the kinship – it made Gala Day into a memorable occasion.

As the pits have closed one by one, so the Miners' Gala has diminished in its significance. The scale and the grandeur have gone, but the setting and emotions remain. All that's left are the banners to remind one of the struggle of the miners. The banners carefully stored, rekindle memories of names, places and events. The strength of Durham City, its respect for the political struggle, the dignity of the cathedral and, above all, the dynamism of the city structure, are a forum close to the art of theatre, for the speeches, processions, the bands, banners and the miners.

REFERENCES

Benson, J. (1973) 'The compensation of English coal miners and their dependents for industrial accidents 1860–1897', unpublished Ph.D. thesis, University of Leeds.

—— (1976) 'The establishment of the West Riding of Yorkshire Miners Permanent Relief Fund', in J. Benson and R.G. Neville (eds) *Studies in Yorkshire Coal Industry*, Manchester: Manchester University Press.

Dowding, W. (1983) 'The big meeting', Centenary Gala Souvenir Programme, Saturday, 16 July, National Union of Mineworkers, Durham Area.

Foster, C. Le N. (1895) *First Annual General Report upon the Mineral Industry for 1894*, London: Eyre & Spottiswoode.

—— 'The English coalmining community 1840–1914', unpublished thesis submitted to the Faculty of the University of North Carolina at Chapel Hill in partial fulfilment of the requirements for the degree of MA in the Department of History.

Fynes, R. (1971) *The Miners of Northumberland and Durham*, Sunderland: SR Publishers.

Galloway, R.L. (1971) *Annals of Coal Mining and the Coal Trade*, 2 vols, Newton Abbot: David & Charles.

Garside, W.R. (1971) *The Durham Miners 1910–1960*, London: George Allen & Unwin.

Liefchild, J.R. (1853) *Our Coal and Our Coal-Pits, the People in Them and the Scenes Around Them by a Traveller Underground*, in 2 parts, London: Longmans, Green & Co.

Master and Servants Act, 1823, amended in 1867.

Mead, H. (1983) 'A host of hearts', *Northern Echo*, July: 11.

Raistrick, A. (1952) *The Development of the Tyne Coal Basin*, paper read before the North of England Institute of Mechanical Engineers at Newcastle upon Tyne, 22 September: 24.

Simpson, J.B. (1900) *Capital and Labour in Coal Mining During the Past Two Hundred Years*, Newcastle upon Tyne: Robinson.

Taylor, A.J. (1974) 'The Third Lord Londonderry and the Coal Trade', *Durham University Journal* (June): 245–6.

Turner, G. (1967) *The North Country*, London: Eyre & Spottiswoode.

Welbourne, E. (1923) *The Miners' Unions of Northumberland and Durham*, London: Cambridge University Press.

96 Durham and the Church: fabricating the gospel

Peter Baelz

When I was Dean of Durham I was often asked what my job involved. On one occasion I replied that I was caretaker of the most wonderful building in the world. Perhaps this was something of an exaggeration. Opinions may differ. But it was certainly not far from the truth, and as a catch-phrase it clearly caught the imagination. I have often used it since whenever I wanted to give an immediate and impressionistic account of the responsibilities which, with other members of the Chapter, a dean of Durham carries.

Durham Cathedral means different things to different people. It depends on one's interests and perspective. Sometimes the telephone would ring in the Vergers' vestry and a voice would enquire: 'Is that the Traveller's Rest?' In fact it was not the local hostelry, although the telephone numbers were deceptively similar. However, it was rather a happy description, I thought. The image of travel, or pilgrimage, is close to the heart of the Christian understanding of life; and the image of a resting place comes straight out of the Fourth Gospel: 'In my Father's house are many mansions [lit. resting-places]' (John 14.1).

Or again the telephone would ring, and another voice would enquire: 'Is that the Cathedral Service Station?' The literal and prosaic answer was 'Sorry, no: we don't sell petrol here.' Once again, however, I could not help thinking that, in its own way, this too was an apt description. After all, what is a cathedral for if not, in some real sense of the word, 'servicing' pilgrims along life's way? The services it offers, for example in restaurant and library, are many and various, in addition to the liturgical services of the church itself.

I could go on suggesting an almost endless series of images of what Durham Cathedral is and does, such as a Mighty Fortress[1] or a Window of Transcendence.[2] The point I wish to emphasize, however, is the one that I have already made, namely, that the cathedral presents a different experience to different people according to their differing interests and perspectives. They are not 'seeing' the same thing.

Consider the cathedral just as a building. To the engineer it represents a technological solution to a technological problem. How was everything lifted into place when the only mechanical device to assist was a winch and pulley? Who was it who first thought of pointing the arches in order to spread the immense load of the wide stone vaults? And the ribbed vaulting – had it the practical function of strengthening the structure,

The interplay of light and shade. (Photograph: *Ian Haines*)

or was its original intention to lead the eye gently up and across and around the vault rather than rudely confront it with a sheer mass of undifferentiated stonework?

Or think of it as a piece of economic history. Where was the stone taken from? How many men at work did it need to complete the main part of the building in only forty years, between 1093 and 1133? Were they conscripted or did they volunteer? How much were they paid? Where did they live? What happened to them when the work was finished? Such questions are, to my mind, of absorbing interest, not least because Northumbria was only sparsely populated at the time when the cathedral was being built.

Or look at its role in social and political history. Think of the part it played in the wars with the Scots or in the government of the Palatinate, its position of eminence and power in an environment of struggle and hardship – north-easterners have been said to have no special love for Dean and Chapter but a very special love for 'Cuthbert's Church' – or its links with the university which in 1832, at a time of political reform, it helped to establish. A book of remembrance, presented by Vaux Brewery, now forms part of the Miners' Memorial and records the many names of those who have lost their

Feretory, choir and nave from the Great East window. (Photograph: *Ian Haines*)

lives in the pits since 1945. A stained glass window, designed and executed by Mark Angus, entitled *Daily Bread* and representing the interplay between the divine and the human economies, marks the centenary of Marks & Spencer.

However, I propose to leave these and other perspectives on one side and to reflect instead on the cathedral as gospel, or good news. Hence the point of my chosen title, 'Fabricating the gospel' – expressing the gospel in the material fabrics of the architect and the builder.

As gospel the building suffers from two major handicaps. First and foremost, it has to be emphasized that 'Church is people, not buildings'.[3] When in the 1970s I was a professor of theology at Oxford I can remember proclaiming that the Church must learn to travel light into the twenty-first century, unencumbered by a surfeit of bricks and mortar. However, the Almighty has a 'wicked' sense of humour, and in the 1980s I was appointed Dean of Durham, to be in charge of one of the most substantial ecclesiastical buildings in the country. Suddenly I found myself having to sing to a different tune, since the idea of letting the cathedral go to rack and ruin was hardly on! Keeping in mind the fact that Church is and always will be people rather than buildings, what, I asked myself, could a building like Durham Cathedral contribute to their understanding of and response to the gospel? If it is to be something more than an edifice in which people gather together to do things that they could equally well do in tents, can it somehow or other itself become a symbolic expression of the gospel?

The second handicap is that the cathedral is redolent of the past. It is classified as an ancient building. Conse-

quently it is thought to belong to ancient history. Moreover, everything that goes on in it – the words spoken, the music sung, the clothes worn – all tend to reinforce the impression that it is backward-looking. And in a sense it is. It is steeped in tradition. Nor is there anything wrong about that, so long as it is also forward-looking, a community of hope as well as of memory. A living tradition must be questioning, searching and alert to development and change; otherwise it becomes fossilized and ineffectual. In an ancient cathedral like Durham there is a constant struggle to present the gospel as a present reality and a live option, a struggle to communicate the faith that God is God of the here and now and of the future as well as God of the past, and that the Spirit which made Jesus the person he was is still able to make of us the persons we are called to be.

Once we have recognized and come to terms with these handicaps, can we then go on to suggest how the cathedral itself may share in the communication of the gospel? Can we detect for the building itself a language and ministry of its own, distinct though not separate from the ministry of those who live and work and worship in it? Can it too share in a ministry of evangelism?

In an article entitled 'Tell it slant', John Tinsley, then bishop of Bristol, made a case for communicating the Christian gospel 'indirectly'. Quoting Emily Dickinson,

Tell the truth but tell it slant
Success in circuit lies

and W.H. Auden,

Truth in any serious sense
Like Orthodoxy, is a reticence

he argued that Christian truth, which by its very nature must engage the imagination and heart of the believer as well as the intellect, is often best conveyed in what at first may seem a roundabout manner. He referred to the Danish philosopher-theologian, Søren Kierkegaard (1813–55), who had made the following comment on Paul's suggestion that followers of Jesus should be 'deceivers, and yet true':

What does it mean, 'to deceive'? It means that one does not begin *directly* with the matter one wants to communicate, but begins by accepting the other man's illusion as good money. So one does not begin thus: I am a Christian; you are not a Christian. Nor does one begin thus: It is Christianity I am proclaiming; and you are living in purely aesthetic categories. No, one begins thus: Let us talk about aesthetics.

(Kierkegaard 1848: 40–1)

This idea of *indirect communication* may, I suggest, offer an escape from a dilemma which sometimes worries those who have the care of cathedrals. I can illustrate the dilemma in this way. Some years ago the Deans and

Provosts, acting corporately, submitted to the Environmental Committee for Historic Buildings and Ancient Monuments a considered reply to that committee's recommendation that there should continue to be no financial support for cathedrals by the state. The substance of their reply is irrelevant; but it included the sentence: 'It is the pastoral task of a cathedral to turn tourists into visitors, visitors into guests, guests into pilgrims and pilgrims into worshippers' (House of Commons Environment Committee 1988, Annex 3: xxv). One cathedral chapter took great exception to this and wrote in a note of dissent: 'We would react most strongly to any attempt to turn us into anything, were we visiting a cathedral, and we believe that the importance of these buildings is that each visitor will make of them what he or she wishes' (House of Commons Environment Committee 1988, Annex 4: xxvii).

This demurrer strikes a chord. None of us wants to be 'turned' by anyone else into anything other than he or she is. It smacks too much of manipulation. On the other hand a cathedral is, willy-nilly, a statement of faith and as such deserves to be heard for what *it* is.

So we caretakers find ourselves halting uneasily between two opinions. On the one hand, we accept the fact that our cathedrals are buildings of special architectural interest, and that those who visit them should be allowed to enjoy them simply as buildings. It is not for us to impose on our guests, who may be of any faith or none, the claims of the Christian gospel. That would he bad manners. It would probably also be counterproductive! On the other hand, we feel that, if we are to be true to the faith to which we are committed, not as some private opinion or pastime but as the ground and goal of all that exists, a faith, moreover, to which the cathedrals themselves are a standing witness, then we should be prepared, in one way or another, to explain to our visitors, whoever and whatever they are, the gracious but persistent claims to life and truth which the gospel makes upon them as well as upon us.

Neither approach seems altogether satisfactory. An attempt at direct evangelism is often as dubious as a determination not to evangelize at all. The latter is certainly more polite, but it is hardly prophetic. The former may perhaps be more prophetic, but, lacking sensitivity and proportion, it can prove a stumbling-block to authentic faith.

What is called for, I suggest, is a kind of *indirect* evangelism. This arises initially out of the conviction that a cathedral is a statement, or parable, of faith and so exercises a ministry in its own right. Its architecture will often resonate with the architecture of the human spirit. There is, for example, in every human being a fundamental need both for stability and for freedom. A cathedral can convey, without the use of the spoken word, a sense of such stability, while at the same time making room for individuals to discover and be themselves. In this way it becomes a symbol and sacrament of God's own creativity; for in creating a world of space and time, a world of which he is himself the unchanging centre, its strength and stay, God presents his creatures with the challenge and opportunity of finding – or, indeed, of losing – themselves.

Again, to take another example, the upward thrust of pillars, spreading outwards into a web of gently curving and interlacing arches, can evoke in the human spirit, more likely than not at the subconscious level, a combined sense of direction and nurture – of a God of purpose and a God of sustenance, Being Itself in whom action and passion are joined in harmonious unity.

Such a process of indirect communication and evangelism is clearly and succinctly portrayed in a prize-winning poem by Anne Castling (1983), submitted in a competition to write a kind of 'spiritual' guide to Durham Cathedral, and entitled 'Coming and Going':

> Standing here in the quiet nave
> Coming in out of the busy world
> Suddenly moved to push the door
> Into the sanctuary,
> I wait now in the dimness,
> Unsure of where to look or how to see,
> Getting my bearings,
> Knowing I should do this and this –
> But, for myself, uncertain.
>
> Sitting now in a side chapel
> Feeling a growing sense of awe
> Ready to look beyond my hesitation
> Up to the roof beam,
> I catch my breath in wonder
> At stone upon stone climbing to far off heaven,
> Suddenly overwhelmed,
> Knowing that ordinary folk
> Could aim so high and certain.
>
> Kneeling at length on the worn stone
> Wanting to feel myself in touch
> Suddenly glad of symmetry and light
> In far perspective,
> I seek my own direction
> Moved by a faith that dared to build in stone,
> Getting my bearings
> Knowing I might do this and this –
> Now, for myself, more certain.

A conversation is already under way. Sometimes, however, the cathedral's own ministry needs to be assisted and enriched by what I call the 'diaconal ministry' of a guide and interpreter. When visitors come in, they may be blinded and deafened by the anxieties and concerns they bring with them. They may feel 'unsure of where to look or how to see'. Or they may distance themselves from the building as mere observers rather than experience it as partners in dialogue, giving it the chance to make its own presence felt and appreciated. (The use of a camera to record instead of the use the eyes to see can all too easily become a kind of spiritual voyeurism.) But we must be circumspect. Our job is not to speak in place of the cathedral, but to enable it to speak for itself. We must try to effect an introduction – and then move out of the way. This means meeting visitors where they are, with the needs and interests that they have, and encouraging them, bit by bit, without bullying or condescension, to recognize, understand and appreciate the cathedral's own symbolic language. The whole process could be likened to the placing of stepping-stones. There is no compulsion to cross from one side of the river to the other; but stepping-stones make the crossing possible. And if someone is attracted by the half-sensed prospect of what lies on the other side, stepping-stones may enable that person to cross over and take a closer look. In some such way as this a person may be drawn towards the reality of the Transcendent, to which, in their own distinctive idioms, art, architecture and religion all point.

The tactics of indirect evangelism are many and varied. If, as I have already suggested, evangelism can be a continuing and developing conversation rather than a doctrinaire pronouncement, then the conversation must be allowed to proceed in its own way and at its own pace. In this conversation the main participant will be the cathedral itself, both as a piece of architecture and as a statement of faith. The spirit of the place, the *genius loci*, must be allowed to speak for itself. There are few so deaf that they will hear nothing of what the spirit has to say. But an interpreter may help. The provision of information is important. But here special care needs to be exercised. The right sort and amount of information will help visitors find their way around and make them feel less like strangers. Too much information, on the other hand, will only confound them and may turn them into just that kind of distanced observer that we do not wish them to be. Information must never be allowed to take the place of experience.

Even more significant than the information we provide is the care we convey, care for our visitors and care for our cathedral. We care enough for them both to make us want to effect an introduction between them. If the cathedral is really a house of God and a home for strangers, then to be made to feel at home in it is one step towards being made to feel at home with God. Because we are all children of God, objects of his creative care, coming to God is a 'coming home'. In T.S. Eliot's often cited words,

> ... the end of all our exploring
> Will be to arrive where we started
> And know the place for the first time.
>
> (*Little Gidding*, 1942)

The tactical moves we can make are numerous, and we all have our own favourite gambits. However, without some guiding theological strategy we can all too easily swing backwards and forwards between doing too little and doing too much. In either case we are likely to feel inadequate and guilty. And that is a splendid recipe for doing the wrong thing for the wrong reason!

The strategy of indirect evangelism is based on the indirect evangelism of God himself. He is present where people are, but their eyes need to be opened to the light of truth and love if they are to discern the presence of the Holy in their midst. So our indirect communication with our visitors begins where they are and with the immediate concerns they have. If they want the loos, then we tell them where the loos are. If they have lost their kids, then we help them to find them. If they are interested in the cathedral's history, then we show them the lists of bishops and deans, and perhaps I tell them the story of the newly appointed bishop, David Jenkins, and the stonemason who was carving Bishop David's name on the stone face: when I had introduced them and they had shaken hands, the stonemason exclaimed, 'Thank God it wasn't that Montefiore; I could never have got his name on one line!' Or, again, if they are interested in the cathedral's architecture, then we talk about stonework and tracery, space, volume and perspective.

Underlying all such encounters and conversations is the conviction that these immediate interests and concerns are part of our common humanity and may become stepping-stones to other connected and 'deeper' concerns. We ourselves may call these deeper concerns worship, or prayer, or reflection, or exploration – or, indeed, something else. But, we believe, these are our visitors' deep concerns too, whether they recognize them or not. They too need to celebrate, to get things off their chests, to have a new look at themselves and the lives they are living, to probe the heights and breadths and depths and to discover new resources of love and hope. It is not for us to dictate the direction or force the pace of their seeking. But in our desire to share with them something of the transcendent glory that has grasped us, and to receive from them something of the same glory that belongs to them, we can enter into a conversation that will lead – God knows where. And if God knows where, and 'our times are in his hand', perhaps we may leave to him the outcome.

NOTES

1   Cf. Martin Luther's hymn, written in 1529, the first line of which is 'Eine feste Burg ist unser Gott'.
2   Cf. the poem by George Herbert (1593–1633) entitled *The Windows*, the first verse of which is:

> Lord, how can man preach thy eternal word?
>   He is a brittle, crazy glass;
> Yet in thy temple thou dost him afford
>   This glorious and transcendent place
>   To be a window, through thy grace.

3   The New Testament word for 'church' (*ecclesia*) refers to

the 'people of God' rather than to the temple or synagogue.

4   'My times are in thy hand' (Psalm 31.15).

REFERENCES

House of Commons Environment Committee (1988) *Historic Buildings and Ancient Monuments: Observations on the First Report of the Committee in Session 1986–87* (HC 146), Chair Sir Hugh Rossi, London: HMSO; Annex 3: Response by Deans and Provosts of English Cathedrals; Annex 4: Response by the Dean and Chapter of Ely Cathedral.

Kierkegaard, S. (1848) *The Point of View for My Work as an Author*, published posthumously 1859, Copenhagen; trans. with introduction and notes by W. Lowrie, 1939. London: Oxford University Press.

97 The last late Romanesque

Adrian Napper

For many writers of the nineteenth and early twentieth centuries, the great Gothic cathedrals of northern Europe represented an ideal. Christian faith and scientific rationalism were perfectly combined to produce an architecture of unsurpassed quality:

> It is impossible to explain in words the content of perfect Gothic art. It is frank, clear, gay; it is passionate, mystical, and tender; it is energetic, clear, sharp, strong, and healthy.
>
> The ideals of the time of energy and order produced a manner of building of high intensity, all waste tissue was thrown off, and the stonework was gathered up into energetic functional members. These ribs and shafts are all at bow-string tension. A mason will tap a pillar to make its stress audible; we may think of a cathedral as so 'high strung' that if struck it would give a musical note.
>
> (Lethaby 1955: 154–5)

What was particularly appealing to these writers was the triumph of progress. A story would be told of continuous development, of a way of building that, through a systematic application of rational development, had reached an apotheosis, most clearly seen in the great thirteenth-century cathedrals of the Ile de France: Paris, Bourges, Chartres, Amiens and Beauvais.

The line could be traced from the Romans and their development of the round arch which had enabled architecture to progress in scale and complexity and to enclose larger and larger spaces. From the round arch and basilican form of the Romans to the Gothic space was continuous progress, so that the Romanesque period becomes one of transition and Durham Cathedral can be seen simply as an intermediate point in that journey. Even from this perspective of narrative history, Durham is undoubtedly of major significance, but this must not be allowed to obscure the fact that in its own right it is architecture of the very highest quality. This quality should not be forgotten and although this essay may appear to concentrate on those developments in the art of building in stone which are most clearly to be seen at Durham, it will also try to highlight the architectural qualities that go hand in hand with the technical development, the creation of free-flowing space and the relation of social forces to the creation of major civic buildings.

GOTHIC STRUCTURE

For most people the pointed arch and the flying buttress are the clearest icons of Gothic architecture. At Durham there are both pointed arches and round arches so, clearly, it marks a period of transition. All accounts indicated that it is the earliest surviving building to have been designed to have a vaulted roof over the main nave. While no flying buttresses are visible, hidden under the aisle roof there are ribs which are clearly functioning as flying buttresses. What can be seen at Durham is the new spacial quality that architecture achieved through adoption of the pointed arch. While it is easy for anyone to recognizes the change from the round to the pointed arch, what is less apparent is the change from 'wall construction' to 'frame construction', liberating architecture and allowing the Gothic period to create revolutionary experiences of light and space.

Geometry

Geometry was the first area of construction that was liberated by the adoption of the pointed arch. The geometry of the semicircular arch is, by its basic nature, restrictive. One dimension, the radius, fixes both the span and the height of the arch. Combinations of semicircular arches are very difficult. Taking a very simple example, a square on plan with two diagonals can be easily formed using semicircular arches on the four sides and across the diagonals (see Figure 1). Since, however, the diagonals have a longer span than the sides, then the apex of the diagonal arch must be higher than the apex of the side arch. This is of little consequence for an individual square, but putting a number of these together has a very significant effect on the space created.

In the long nave of the traditional English cathedrals, this phenomenon becomes particularly significant. The oblong space is required for the processional functions but can easily be uncomfortably divided up by a succession of cross arches, particularly if the main ridge line is higher than the apex of the transverse arch. Various distortions of the round arch were tried. At Durham a compromise solution consists of a mixture of round and pointed arches. The space is magnificent and has a reassurance that is rarely matched by later Gothic churches. The pointed arch also gave the opportunity for a more complex arrangement of the plan, particularly the relation between the position of the column and the ribs in the roof. At Durham there is the opportunity to witness the consequence of a miscalculation of this in the addition to the West End built between 1242 and 1274. Standing in the south side aisle looking up at the roof one can see a rib that has clearly lost its way, and in

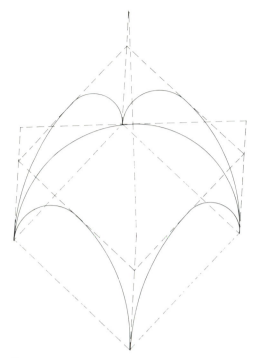

Figure 1 *Round arches on a square.*

an endearing manner wanders uncertainly through the ordered geometry of its peers. It demonstrates vividly how the apparently effortless order has had to be worked out with the greatest care, though by whom and by what means it was done is unclear. There is no documentary evidence that throws light on constructional techniques for any Romanesque or Early Gothic building. One can only assume that large models were made to resolve the overall geometry and also to determine the special shape of each stone in the huge three-dimensional jigsaw.

The frame

Intimately connected with these developments in geometrical sophistication was the emergence of the 'frame' as a constructional system. 'Frame' in this context is used to denote a system whereby the construction is organized into separate parts. The primary structural framework has the task of carrying loads down into the ground. Between the frame are elements of construction which do not have a primary role of transferring load. These may be masonry walls or curved masonry surfaces in roofs or glass set in delicate tracery. Such a system is in contrast to a conventional wall construction where the walling element has to do several jobs, including the structural one of carrying load.

The distinction is less clear when spanning elements like walls and roofs are considered. A masonry vault is certainly not a frame construction but most arrangements of timber would be frames, largely because the morphology of timber produces linear elements. This distinction between 'frame' and what is generally called

'load-bearing' construction is significant for all architecture, not just Gothic. The construction lessons that were developed in the construction of the Gothic cathedrals are still applied to major buildings today. 'Buildability' was an unattractive word coined in the 1980s to describe how easy or difficult it might be to construct a particular building. The 'buildability' of the stone framework enabled the resources of the Middle Ages to construct religious buildings many times larger and, more particularly, many times higher than any previous buildings. Simply lifting the material up in the air required time and energy. If the quantity could be reduced the task became correspondingly easier. Also it was necessary to support the masonry in place until all elements of the system were assembled. This required a forest of temporary timber props. The Gothic system of erecting a framework of relatively light stone ribs supported on columns could, bay by bay, be made stable. Where the roof vaulting is just filling between ribs it can be correspondingly lighter and so temporarily supported off the ribs during construction. Similarly, the surface between the ribs and columns could be filled with secondary frameworks, which in turn were filled with glass. The great space could then be filled with light.

The high vault at Durham, constructed between 1093 and 1133, was probably the prototype that proved the system possible, both in the structural sense that it stood up and could successfully support the weight of the building and the pressure of the wind, but also that it could be constructed in an acceptable length of time using the resources available in a region on the outer fringes of the Christian world. Today major buildings are supported by frames usually of structural steel or reinforced concrete, and the same reasoning applies. It is quicker and easier first of all to erect a frame that is stable and then fill in between the elements with walls, floors and roofs.

Stability

Another reason for building a frame is to ensure the stability of the structure. The first job of a structure is to carry the forces generated by gravity down into the ground. Columns and walls, being vertical, are in the same plane as the force of gravity and carry weight very efficiently. Other forces also act on structures – most critically wind, which acts horizontally. Walls and columns are very much less efficient carrying wind loads, and as they get higher they have to be correspondingly thicker in order to withstand the sideways pressure. Any inaccuracy in construction or inadequacy of foundation will encourage high walls to topple over. Individual walls can be made more stable by thickening generally or thickening at particular points and making buttresses. This all requires space and material, and with columns acting alone they just have to get thicker as they get taller. When, however, wall and columns are linked together to make three-dimensional systems, the stability of the whole system supports every individual member, so a further advantage of a proper frame is that it is much more stable.

In the medieval churches the major space, either the nave or the choir, is a single-storey volume. Early Romanesque examples follow the Roman basilica pattern with side walls connected by a timber roof. While the timber will offer some stability to the wall, it relies on friction at the seating. When, however, the side walls become a row of columns and the tops of the columns are joined across by ribs, the whole system immediately becomes more stable. Side aisles double the side support and again increase the stability. But a problem remains. Since the connecting ribs are made from individual blocks of stone, they are held together by gravity pulling them down. This generates compression forces that have to be resolved by the outward thrusting of the foot of the arch. Such a thrust is no more appreciated by the top of the wall or column than the horizontal wind force, so it too has to be carried down into the ground by some form of buttressing that transfers the load from high level. This could be a thickening of the wall, support from the side wall or the ultimate expression, the flying buttresses. At Durham the restraint is hidden below the roof of the side aisle and then expressed by wall buttresses. Flying buttresses perform the same task but again are constructed as open frameworks which reflect the internal structure and have similar constructional advantages.

At Durham the fatness of the columns is a lasting image for the visitor. In other Norman churches, however, the fat, round columns read as a row with one behind the other denying any space between them. But at Durham the fat, round columns are alternated with even larger columns which are taller and shafted. The lower round columns exist in their own space which joins the nave and the side aisles. The major shafted column soars up to the roof to be connected across to their partner by a substantial rib. Thus the ordering of the structure of the nave unifies the space. In precursors, such as Ely, the wooden ceiling has no continuity with the supporting masonry. They are two elements, each discrete, neither acknowledging the other. The internal frame, first seen at Durham, defines a unified space which has the potential to expand beyond the central heart. The openness of light flooding in through great windows was yet to come, but at Durham there is high-level light from small clerestory windows.

From a distance the form of Durham in its unique setting is superb. Closer to, the external expression is unremarkable. The plain walling, pierced by small, round-headed windows, with modest buttresses, is the only suggestion of the frame contained within. It was not until the advent of the fully developed flying buttress that the total unity of space and structure was achieved and the internal geometry could be deduced from the external expression.

CONTEXT OF DURHAM

The essays in this book have been arranged so as to emphasize how many and varied are the influences on architecture. The physical presence of Durham Cathedral is so strong that it is easy to overlook the social and political forces that created it, particularly since they occurred at a time and a place which offer very little historical evidence other than the building itself. Some general observations are, however, worth making. Romanesque architecture in England is synonymous with the architecture of the Norman Conquest, though its effect could be seen before 1066 at Edward the Confessor's church at Westminster. In the twenty-seven years between the Conquest and the start of construction at Durham, twelve other cathedrals and abbeys were begun.

These were all located in the south and in the Midlands, where the Norman base was relatively secure. The north of England was a different matter. For several centuries the Kingdom of Northumbria, stretching from the Humber to the Forth, had been harried by Danes. Following the Battle of Carham in 1018, the area north of the Tweed became Scotland. The Conqueror's border was guarded by the New Castle on the Tyne only 15 miles (25 km.) north of Durham. It was all unsettled territory. Indeed, after the monks removed St Cuthbert's bones from Lindisfarne, they spent two hundred years looking for an appropriately secure resting place. The towering rock above the incised meander of the river Wear was secure and dominating. The remains of Bede were brought there in 1022.

The new cathedral of 1093 had therefore to fulfil a number of roles. First, Norman authority had to be consolidated, and in this the Benedictine monks were just as important as the army. The Bishop of Durham was always a Prince Bishop, the King's secular as well as spiritual representative.

The use of the tomb of the Saxons' most popular saint as the site of the Normans' symbol of authority as a means of winning over the locals must surely have been influenced by *realpolitik*, or perhaps it was so clearly the best site that it was worth while venerating the Saxon saint. In such a time and place the need for a secure building was paramount. One so massive and dominating would certainly establish the authority of the newcomers. One that demonstrated that a high nave and choir could be built in stone-ribbed vaults was a step on the way to the ultimate achievements of the High Gothic. All together they produce one of the great architectural masterpieces of Western civilization.

REFERENCE

Lethaby, W.R. (1955) *Architecture: An Introduction to the History and Theory of the Art of Building*, London: Oxford University Press.

98 The rib vaults of Durham Cathedral

John James

In the history of medieval architecture the cathedral of Durham played a crucial and vital role. It was at Durham that, as far as we know, the first rib vaults were constructed. Before Durham, vaults followed the pattern the ancient Romans had bequeathed, being what we call barrel or groin. They consisted of solid masses of masonry and mortar that covered the interior spaces in forms like semicircular tunnels cut through the earth. These are called barrel vaults.

Churches are designed in bays. Each bay is bounded by the outside wall of the building and its corners are marked by columns and piers. If the barrel vault runs in one direction joining bay to bay from, say, the entrance of the church to the altar, it creates a space that seems to carry you along with it, hurrying your walk towards your goal. But where barrel vaults also cut across each bay they intersect, and at the join a crease is formed called a groin.

The groin is the origin of the rib, though not for the reason people usually think. When you look up at a vault the ribs that cross over from one pier to the next seem, to our eyes, to be like structural beams that support the stone ceilings. They seem like the ribs of our chest, holding open the spaces of the interior.

Now, it is true that within thirty years of the first ribs being used builders had begun to realize that they could have a structural function. Some time in the 1130s they learned to put the ribs up first and to fill in the spaces between, called the cells, later on. They also learned that the cells could be made a lot thinner, as they could rely on the ribs for support. They also came to realize that when joined with lime mortar the ribs could be relied upon to hold the vault together even when the foundations moved and cracks appeared in the walls. All that was pretty daring, but gradually over the years experience showed them how stable and light rib vaulting could become.

However, at the beginning, around 1100, the rib was not structural. It was a decorative motif or, more precisely, a constructional device rather than a structural one.

Groin vaults were not easy to design where the bays were not square. As you can imagine, the barrel over the smaller bay would not be large enough to meet the crown of the barrel over the larger, as the radius of its semicircular form was too small. There were many solutions to this problem, such as raising the smaller on a few courses of vertical walling, or stilts, until the two crowns were level, or flattening the curve of the taller vault. The outcome was often quite unattractive, as the groin would not be straight when seen from below, but snaked from one side to the other.

Few groin vaults were made of ashlar, but rather of rubble with a plaster finish. It is not, from a practical point of view, easy to finish the plaster neatly along the groin. The material is soft, the position for the workmen fatiguing, and the lighting is invariably inadequate. Few groin vaults were finished with the precision and neatness found in the adjoining piers.

It was a back-to-front problem, and not easy for the masons to solve. The groin was the last step in the erection process, but the first to be noticed by the passer-by. The masons were erecting formwork from above, but later, after the formwork had been stripped away, they wanted to look up from below and see the crease between the barrels straight and true. What the rib did was to give builders a way to place this crease in the early stage of construction exactly where they wanted it, rather than waiting until the end. It was, in its simplest, just a cover-mould such as you might place around a door to tidy up the junction between the frame and the plaster wall.

The rib also resolved another problem in vaulting. Groin vaults are very solid. They are like foundations in the sky. Above what you see, they consist of masses of stone and mortar that fill all the space above the cells to the crown. They are incredibly heavy and solid – so when seen in section these vaults seem more like excavation than erection. As medieval mortar was slow to dry, especially in damp areas like the north of England, the whole weight of the vault had to be supported on formwork until it had begun to set.

They were erected layer by layer, and tied into the walls as they went, until the entire volume above the formwork had been filled. Much more stonework was needed to fill over the vault the closer they came to the summit. The huge vaults over the nave at Durham are totally massive. Walking over them is like being on the pavement below, as all you see is solid and level stonework. The rib, as its possibilities were realized, provided a solution to this problem of weight – and without which the great glass cathedrals of Chartres and Beauvais, with their tall and slender supports, would not have been possible.

The rib neatly completed a difficult junction between opposed curved surfaces. It was a builder's constructional device applied to a traditional and proven vaulting technique. The proof of this is very interesting, and is found at Durham.

In some of the aisle vaults the ribs, when you look up

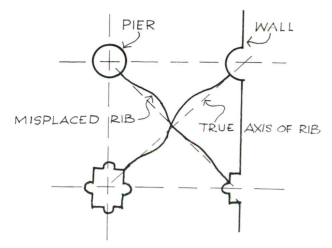

Figure 1 *Durham Cathedral, nave aisle vault showing, slightly exaggeratedly, the serpentine misplacement of the ribs. Drawn by the author.*

at them from underneath, are serpentine in plan rather than straight, and the ribs do not meet the boss at 90° (see Figure 1). The boss is the stone at the intersection of the ribs at the apex of the vault. These misalignments do not occur because the bays have different widths, for they are square: the ribs could have followed straight lines.

The cause can be read in the boss. Since the ribs are not straight, they do not butt against the boss at the angle they would have had the ribs been straight. Though the plane on which they meet is shifted a few degrees off true, the sides of the boss meet the ends of the ribs without any gaps. This is because the sides were cut to suit the actual inclinations the four ribs made to the apex, even though they were twisted. The boss was therefore cut and placed *after* the ribs had been misaligned.

We would presume that the ribs were meant to have been straight, and that they became twisted during erection so that by the time the boss was placed they were incapable of being realigned. This would have happened only if the ribs had been laid up with the rest of the vault and locked into place with the adjoining masonry. If the cells had been built with the ribs rather than afterwards (as was later practice), it would not have been possible to adjust the ribs afterwards and, by the time they reached the apex, the boss would have had to be specially cut to fit. In other words, the ribs were built into the vault as the cells were being erected, layer by layer, and not as separate structural elements. They were, in fact, just added into groin vaults without any change to the *method* of construction.

There is something else about these bosses, an observation that is of the greatest importance in understanding the history of medieval vaulting. It is not generally observable in the aisles, as the bays are square, or nearly so, but it can be seen clearly in the high vaults

of the nave, where the bays are rectangular, being wider than they are long.

The junctions between the boss and the rib have been cut parallel to the sides of the flanking ribs, and not true to the rib it supports (see Figure 2a). This is not how an arch is constructed. If the ribs had been built before the cells these arches would have collapsed long before the rest of the vaults could have been built, simply because the voussoirs of the arch would have slipped off the sides of the boss. It is only the mass filling of the vault that holds them in place. This is why we say that the rib was not at this time conceived as part of the structure, but was only a cover mould. That is, during all three decades that the cathedral was being built, from the aisle vaults to those in the nave, no one recognized that the rib could have had a structural purpose.

There is one exception. Right at the end, in one of the last vaults erected, there is evidence that the rib may have been seen as a structural arch. It is in the sixth bay of the nave: there all the joints around the boss are cut true to the voissoirs (see Figure 2b). The sides of the boss are cut like a proper keystone, true to the lie of the ribs it supports. Was this when the master first realized that the rib could act as an arch, and should therefore be built like one? Was this the beginning of the process which led to an understanding that as the rib was an arch it could be erected separately from the rest of the vault? If so, this realization could be dated to the early 1130s, one generation after the rib was first introduced.

It would not have taken long after that for the

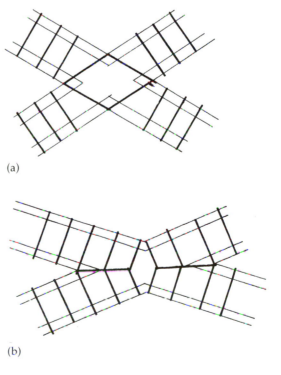

(a)

(b)

Figure 2 *(a) Aisle and most of nave vault bosses; (b) Vault boss to sixth bay of the nave. Drawn by the author.*

masters to have recognized that the ribs should be built first, and that what lay in between was capable of being supported during construction on these ribs, once they were secure and their mortar joints had had time to set. The lighter this layer was, the better, so the thin shell-like cell was born, and with it the essential structural innovation of the style we call Gothic.

In the choir the situation in the high vaults was a little different. Each bay in the nave has two ribs that cross at one boss, separating the four cells. This is why they are called four-part. Six-part vaults are more complex, with three ribs intersecting on a larger boss and separating six cells. They are usually thought to have been much later as they were more difficult to construct. But we shall see that this was not the case. Though located on the northernmost outskirts of the civilized medieval world, Durham again led the way. For six-part vaults were erected over the choir some twenty years before the four-part over the nave.

Writing in 1899, the architect John Bilson remarked that 'there can be no question of a six-part vault here, for the date is much too early for this kind of vaulting' (Bilson 1899: 312; see also James 1984; Bilson 1922). Such statements are always interesting, for it is too often forgotten that our ideas of dating come from very few significant documents. For example, all dating of French Gothic during the crucial and highly inventive period between the choir of Saint-Denis and La Sainte-Chapelle, that is between 1140 and 1240, rests on firm dates for odd parts of only fourteen buildings (see James 1989: 44–9). Except for the cathedral of Chartres (see James 1979–81), no building can be dated as a whole. In this, Durham is the English equivalent of Chartres, as it too (as we shall see) has firmly documented starting and completing dates.

I have the feeling that Bilson's comment was an after-thought, for his drawing suggests the opposite: Figure 3 illustrates the north side of the choir and shows, in dotted lines, the little columns installed for the vaults that are there today, vaults that were built around 1235. They replaced earlier vaults that had either collapsed or become so distressed they had to be replaced.

Bilson shows the edge of the stonework that had supported the cells of the earlier vaults. As the new vaults were set higher than the earlier ones there was a gap between the top of the wall and the under-side of the new cells, which was filled with ashlar that does not match the old masonry. The shape of this supporting edge shows that these vaults must have been six-part. It is extraordinary that, right at the beginning of rib vault construction, the masons designed such a complex vaulting system for the larger spaces (see Figure 4).

Bilson's elevation, which is confirmed when you get up close to the walling under the vaults, shows that the curve of the original vaults is exposed over the major piers, but is not exposed over the minor piers. This indicates that the outline of the cell of the twelfth-century vault must have been irregular, following a shallow curve on the left and set vertically or stilted on the right. If the original had been a four-part vault placed symmetrically across the bay then the outline of the cells would have followed the same curve against the wall on both sides. This is the situation in the nave.

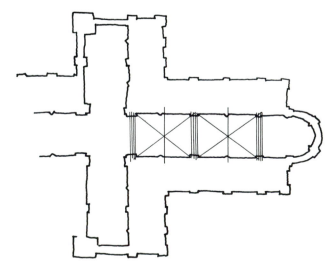

Figure 3 *Durham Cathedral, elevation of north side of choir bay.* (Source: *Bilson 1899*)

Figure 4 *Durham Cathedral, plan of choir showing the arrangement of six-part vaulting. Drawn by the author.*

However, this lopsided geometry is produced by only one kind of vault, a six-part one. I cannot help thinking that Bilson was aware of this, for his drawing so clearly shows this condition. Had he been talked out of it?

If you draw what this vault would have looked like, you will see that the diagonally placed ribs would have had to span a much greater distance than the transverse arches between the walls, and that to fit the ribs underneath the great beams that supported the roof, the ribs would have had to be flattened. Where the arc of the transverse arch could have been set out from a centre placed level with the top of the impost, the centre for the ribs was placed well below the impost. This meant that at the springing the rib did not rise vertically from the impost, but at a noticeable inclination that would bring the boss to the same height as the transverse arch.

A flattened arch is not as secure as a fully curved one. it will tend to sag in the middle more easily. This may be why the vault had to be replaced 120 years later.

It may seem rather strange that the builders would set out rib vaults over the largest span in the building to such an uncertain geometry. But, in a recent survey conducted by the author, 63 per cent of English rib vaults completed before 1140 have a similar geometry. It was the most popular form in this country.

There were two sources of the rib in Christian Europe, and they appeared probably simultaneously: in Moorish Spain and northern England. They formed two separate traditions, whereby there are level summits in the north and domical crowns set well above the surrounding walls in the south. English vault surfaces evolved from the barrel vault, Spanish from the dome. This was natural, as both used ribs to decorate the forms they were accustomed to building; intersecting Roman-style tunnel vaults in England, and Byzantine-style domical vaults in Spain.

As a result of fitting ribs into traditional vault forms, English ribs were round and flattened, while Moorish were often pointed as their domes were more conical than circular. These two concepts moved into France, presumably travelling with the builders who were trained in them. The English system was exported into Normandy, and then into the Paris Basin where the famous vaults of the Saint-Denis choir may have been constructed by an English builder. At the same time another system was carried up to the Loire valley, and thence into Normandy where 38 per cent of vaults before 1140 are domical, the remainder being English in form.

Just as the first motor cars were horse-drawn vehicles with motors added, so the first rib vaults were groin vaults with ribs added. It was not until the 1930s that the definitive form of the car was evolved, which has remained basically unchanged to our own day. Similarly, it was not until just before 1140 that the real nature of the rib vault was sufficiently well understood for its final structural form to be determined. In each case, a generation was needed to slough off the chrysalis of the old form, and to permit the new to emerge.

This is why we can often determine the training ground of the masters building rib vaults on the Continent, for each form bespeaks their origin. It adds further evidence to what we already know of the great distances they would travel in search of work and patronage.

As the transition from rib-as-cover-mould to rib-as-structural-member became clear, the masters began to visualize the loads being concentrated at the piers rather than along the whole length of the walls. This encouraged the masters to design for thrusts being supported at localized piers rather than being uniformly distributed. Yet it is unlikely that many understood, even intuitively, how these forces acted: a very difficult subject, as can be seen in the many articles by art historians and engineers that attempt to comprehend the same issues.

The greater the puzzle, the more their attention would have been drawn towards the pier, and the more they would have tried to resolve the problem of thrusts. Action would have followed the thought, so in this context it is not surprising that containing the thrusts at the pier dominated their thinking until the flying buttress was invented to the south-east of Paris around 1160. Similarly, it is not surprising that the rest of the wall between the piers was increasingly ignored in their structural 'equations' and was thus easily opened up and replaced by glass.

Medieval buildings of this period were not constructed in one campaign, nor was the work directed by the one master. The engagement of masters depended more on funding and weather than it does today. During the past twenty years it has become apparent that masters came and went, sometimes annually, and that detailed planning changed with each new master. Today we are so careful to pre-design every aspect of a building before letting the contractor on to the site that the stochastic medieval employment system seems a bit chaotic. But no English church of this period, nor any of the 1,500 churches built in the Paris Basin during the next hundred years (the region and period that comprise the author's main area of study), was constructed in one campaign under the control of one master. Durham is no exception in this.

In the first bay of the nave there is a change in both the design and the stone being used. Where the first piers to the west of the crossing are built of a dull brown medium-grained sandstone of even colour and texture, the adjacent piers are different in sizes, the drums are covered with chevrons, and the stone comes from another quarry with a variegated greyish-green colour that is fine-grained to the point of waxiness (see Figure 5). The joint can be followed up the face of the wall of the arcade arches until it meets the floor of the tribune. Here the joint moves eastwards to include the first pier. The dimensions and layout of the other tribune piers are

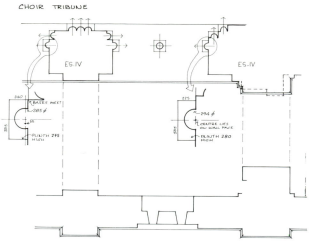

Figure 5 *Durham Cathedral, north nave, first two bays, with the joint marked, drawn by the author.*

Figure 7 *Durham Cathedral, plan of south side of choir tribune, easternmost piers, drawn by the author.*

also different from the eastern piers. The brown stones are free of masons' marks, whereas nearly every third grey stone has a mark. The same combination of stones, dimensions and marks occurs in the choir, showing that these two bays of the nave were probably built with the choir. Figure 6 shows what the eastern bays of the building may have looked like around 1104.

There are six or seven courses of this grey stone, and above that the stone changes again to an orange hue, also with mason's marks, but none of these marks are like those found on the grey stone. The capitals under the choir vaults were carved in this third stone, and with them the ribs for the six-part vaults. The changes in the dimensions and in the shapes of the pier shows that different templates were produced for the workmen employed on each layer. Control of templates, choice of quarries, and the selection of working men seem to go together so that when one changed so did all the others. All this suggests that different masters and different teams of cutters were involved: three masters working out of three different quarries contributed to the construction of three sections that lie between the bases of the tribune shafts and the start of the high vaults.

When you examine the piers each master constructed

in the tribune level, you realize that each approached the design of the high vaults in their own way. The first master, building in brown stone, set in the faces of the choir tribune piers from the face of the arcade wall underneath, and on that ledge supported additional shafts, one on either side of the compound piers and three over the drums (see Figure 7; see also Figure 3). I presume that those alongside the compound piers were to support the diagonal ribs (3) in Figure 8, and that the three intermediate shafts were for two ribs and one transverse arch (2), perhaps with the same section as the rib shafts.

Around the corner, in the transepts, the central shaft on the minor pier was left out. This shaft would have supported the present vault, which does not have a transverse arch: (4) in Figure 8. This arch was probably

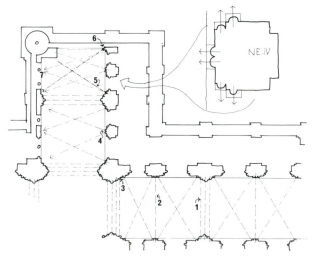

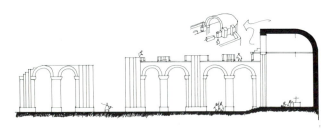

Figure 6 *Durham Cathedral, section of choir and crossing, looking north, c. 1104, drawn by the author.*

Figure 8 *Durham Cathedral, plan of north choir and transept at tribune level, drawn by the author.*

omitted because the transept bay is some 1,400 mm. (4 ft. 7 in.) narrower than the bays in the choir, and the master may have thought that the more acutely inclined ribs would have left too little space between them for another arch to be inserted.

But on the opposite, western side of the transept, in the tribune piers laid out by the second master using the grey stone, the plan was radically changed. This master omitted all supports for rib shafts! The only shafts are those that continue up from the floor. Figure 9 shows the elevation of his wall that covers a narrow access passage.

The first opening reflects the void of the tribune that runs westwards into the nave; the second is a pair of openings placed with little apparent relationship to anything else; while the third matches the windows and is flanked by two smaller openings like the previous pair. None of these relates to the high vaults which, higher up, had to be supported on corbels. The arrangement reflects a horizontally designed elevation rather than a vertically designed one, as if it were to have had a wooden roof.

Therefore, the master who laid out the eastern tribune wanted a four-rib vault as in Figure 8. This was abandoned by his successor in favour of a wooden unvaulted roof.

This second master was in time succeeded by a third, using stone from a different quarry, cut by different carvers. This man altered the design again by reinstating the rib vault scheme, but this time to the six-part proposal shown in Figure 4. So, these changes in masters at the tribune level not only affected the type of stone used and the sizes of the shafts, but the very core of the design itself. In three campaigns the ceiling was changed from four-part stone rib vaults to exposed timber to six-part stone.

The same changes in detailing can be found in the lower parts of the cathedral. There is ample evidence to indicate that the workers were changed often, as were the templates, the technical methods for jointing the

stonework, and the type of the stone used. One example can be verified by anyone walking around the aisles: look carefully at the arrangement of the stones that make up the intersecting arches over the wall dado arcades. Without describing these changes here, the layout of the stones in these arches has been handled in five different ways. As each occupies a distinct part of the building, they indicate that a different set of templates was produced for every group of carvers, and therefore that different masters may have been involved.

This may have been the first time these intersecting arches were used in England. There is one detail which raises a fascinating question: in the choir there are thin paired shafts under the arches which are made from single vertical stones set the full height of the shafts, and let into the ashlar of the walling. Nowhere else in the building do we find this detail. Indeed, I know of no other examples in England.

We know that the Bishop of Durham went to Spain, and possibly to Toledo, just before work started on the cathedral. In that city he could have seen just this detail

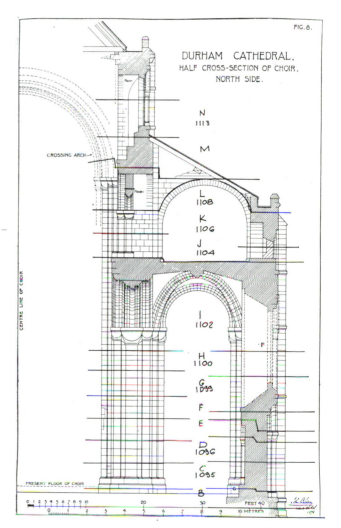

Figure 10 *Durham Cathedral section of choir, north side, showing suggested campaigns and their dates.* (Source: *Bilson 1899*)

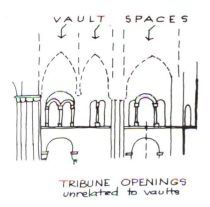

Figure 9 *Durham Cathedral, elevation of north transept tribune, west side, drawn by the author.*

in a number of contemporary buildings. Yet it is not reasonable to expect a bishop, who would have been more concerned with administration and politics than building details, to notice how the shafts had been cut and organized. That is something a builder may have noticed, but not a lay person. Does this suggest that the Bishop took a mason with him to Spain? Or perhaps that a Spanish mason helped at Durham? Rib vaults had been recently installed under an octagonal domed vault in Toledo, suggesting that this mason may have seen Moorish ribs too. Whoever may have brought those details from Spain did not stay long on the cathedral site, for these single-length dado shafts only occur in the eastern aisle walls.

There were at least sixteen campaigns in the choir (see Figure 10), and at least twenty in the west. As a contemporary chronicler wrote, building work proceeded 'modo intentius modo remissius' (Simeon of Durham *c*.1104–7, Vol. 1: 139), which, being freely translated, might be said to read 'by fits and starts'.

For some time the western walls more or less kept pace with those in the choir, so that at the time the window sills in the choir aisles were being placed the foundations were being finished under the western nave doors. Then further work on the west seems to have been abandoned, perhaps while King and Chapter were at loggerheads over the appointment of a new bishop. During this time the monks concentrated on the choir and transept. Work to the west of the joint in Figure 5 does not seem to have recommenced until after the choir had been vaulted, around 1114.

Durham is the only English Norman church whose starting and finishing dates are known, so the sequence of work is important. The dates for the cathedral are based on three documents. The first is Simeon of Durham's *Historia Dunelmensis Ecclesiae*, written about 1104–7, which states that the first trenches were begun on 29 July 1093, and that the first stone was ceremoniously laid on Thursday, 11 August of that year (ibid., Vol. I: 128–68; Vol. II: 220–36).

The second is the continuation of Simeon's history by an anonymous author writing not long afterwards. The writer relates that when Bishop Flambard arrived in 1099 the building work 'had been made as far as the nave' (ibid., Vol. I: 140). The author records the magnificent ceremony that accompanied the translation of Saint Cuthbert's relics to the shrine in the choir in 1104, and states that the nave was completed between 1128 and 1133.

The third document is William of Malmesbury's *De Gestis Pontificum Anglorum*, written some decades later. He recounts the miracle that occurred when Saint Cuthbert's remains were about to be transferred: 'Everything was ready for the translation of the body into the new choir, the choir of the monks, the altar and the tomb. They were only waiting for the wooden materials which were supporting the recent vault of the presby-

tery to be gently removed' when the centering fell down (William of Malmesbury *c*.1123: 275–6). Fortunately, it did not damage the vaults, as the striking of centering is a tricky operation which, if not done carefully, could distort freshly built vaults.

It has been assumed that William was referring to the high vaults, but that is not necessarily so. He was not there at the time, and relied on what he was told for his description. He writes of the vault over the *presbyterium*, which means the most easterly part of the choir, and may have been referring only to the semi-dome over the apse, which is where Cuthbert's tomb lay. This is shown in Figure 6.

What, then, can we make of his words that 'everything was ready'? Can it mean 'everything' in the building, or 'everything' for the liturgic ritual? For the building Malmesbury was being imprecise, for 'everything' was manifestly not 'ready': the centering was still in the way.

Indeed, when we consider that from 1096 onwards the bishop's income had been diverted to the King's needs, and that the monks had to complete the work from their own resources, we should not expect them to have built in the quickest manner. To have constructed the whole of the eastern end with the crossing, the first bays of the nave and the bulk of the transepts in eleven years under such restricted financial conditions would have been too extraordinary an achievement. I am therefore persuaded that the vault referred to by Malmesbury was a semi-dome over the apse.

To summarize: the texts provide just four crucial facts – that the building was begun in 1093, that the nave was under way by 1099 and was completed before 1133, and that high-vault centering was in place somewhere in the east by the middle of 1104.

Of the thirty building campaigns revealed by analysis of the stonework, and which occupied the forty years of construction, the first nine or ten campaigns to the apse vaults can be dated to 1093–1104. Similarly, the last three or four can be dated to 1128–33, and probably included the nave vaults. In between, we can estimate the dates for each part by relating the total number of campaigns to the available years. If they are each assumed to have taken about a year, then the rib vaults at Durham could be dated more or less like this:

eastern aisles	1101–3
apse semi-dome	1103–4
choir springing	1108
choir finished	1113
north transept	1113–18
south transept	1115–20
western aisles	1115–18
nave springing	1125
nave vaults	1128–33.

The earliest chevron mouldings are those over the

western doors from about 1108. The next set of chevrons appeared in the nave aisles about 1115. Was it by carving chevrons on the transept high-vault arches and picking them out as separate decorative items that the masters were stimulated to think of the ribs as arches that were distinct from the mass of the vault?

This realization quite clearly took a long time, for masons had traditionally conceived the vault as a homogeneous lump of masonry, integral with the filling over it, that had to be locked into the adjoining walls. To break this up into its parts, and to conceive of the rib as an arch and to see that the plastered soffit was not just the under-side of a mass but a shell supported on the ribs, required an utterly new point of view.

Can we find out who decided to use ribs? Was it the clergy or the builder? The changes at tribune level described earlier when four-part ribs were intended in one campaign, none in the next and six-part in the third, suggest that it was the builder's decision rather than the client's. As the rib was seen as no more than a cover mould, it may have had no greater significance in the clergy's thoughts than whether a roll or a splay was to be used around the door frame. The decision to use ribs, or even their arrangement, seems to have been the master's personal and private affair. I doubt he thought that ribs were the major innovation that we see today: that was to come later.

REFERENCES

Bilson, J. (1899) 'The beginnings of Gothic architecture', *Journal of the Royal Institute of British Architects* 6 (March): 259–349.

—— (1922) 'Durham cathedral: the chronology of its vaults', *Archaeological Journal* 89: 101–60.

James, J. (1979–81) *The Contractors of Chartres*, 2 vols, Wyong: Mandorla Publications; Woodbridge, Suffolk: Boydell Press.

—— (1984) 'The rib vaults of Durham cathedral', *Gesta* 22 (2): 135–45.

—— (1989) *The Template-Makers of the Paris Basin: Toichological Techniques for Identifying the Pioneers of the Gothic Movement with an Examination of Art Historical Methodology*, Leura: West Grinstead Publications; Woodbridge, Suffolk: Boydell Press.

Simeon of Durham (*c*.1104–7) *Symeonis Monachi Opera Omnia*, ed. T. Arnold, Rolls Series No. 75, 2 vols, 1882, 1885, London.

William of Malmesbury (*c*.1123) *Willelmi Malmesbiriesis Monachi de Gestis Pontificum Anglorum*, ed. N.E.S.A. Hamilton, Rolls Series No. 52, 1870, London.

99 The nature of Durham

Tobias Davidson, David Ellis, Georgia Gilbertson, Jennifer Jeffries and Ng Wai Keen

PROLOGUE

There is a central quality which is the root criterion of life and spirit in a man, a town, a building, or a wilderness. This quality is objective and precise but it cannot be named.

(Alexander 1979: ix)

To name something is to assume a degree of control over it, to lay it open to the distortions of language. For instance, 'Durham is unique', 'Durham is rather dull'. It is also to create the illusion that we understand the named thing. We all know what a car is, but can we identify a single quality which is the exclusive preserve of cars, which distinguishes 'cars' from 'non-cars'? Naming something is not so much evidence of a complete understanding of the named thing as a recognition that there is a family of qualities which we want somehow to hold down and contain. The name provides an axis around which the myth of the object can be explored.

'This quality ... cannot be named.' It can be named and has been named. In this case, the name is Durham. It cannot, however, be paraphrased. To paraphrase something is to diminish it. 'This quality is objective', meaning that it is 'out there', to be picked up, scrutinized, recorded and finally discarded, but that we can never fully understand it. Instead, we can only hope to reveal something of the whole through an appraisal of its component parts.

And this is what we have tried to do. Assembling our thoughts, it became clear that they fell into two categories.

The first had a top, bottom and perhaps something in the middle. At the top was an essence, a cosmological diagram, at the bottom the physiognomy of a cobbled stone. The top does not necessarily carry more weight than the bottom. They are both aspects of the same thing, Durham, but we chose to place them at either end of the spectrum and tread the path in between. Assembling the first part was rather like walking down a road, and, despite the many enticing side streets, getting to the end without having to turn off.

The second was made up of observations which could be represented as points on a plane, to be picked up and discarded at will, a patchwork quilt of many colours and textures. Putting together the second part was like riding up and down in the lift of a large department store and enjoying what each floor had to offer at random.

PART ONE: FROM COSMOS TO MICROCOSM

We began with attempts to understand the potency of Durham's topography and its capacity to yield a series of structures which have always said as much as people need to know about themselves. A description of routes and their spatial qualities gave us a kind of washing line on which to hang our dirty laundry, or rather a firm foundation on which we could each build according to our particular preoccupations. Then, fractal-like, we homed in on smaller and smaller scales, each snapshot a microcosm of Durham.

COSMOLOGY

What is it that invests Durham with its sacred qualities and makes it such an enduring religious centre? On investigating the typology of sacred sites it became clear that Durham's topography possesses some of the qualities Mircea Eliade (1961) identifies as central to many primitive religious settlements.

Durham: cosmic mountain

Chaos and cosmos

One of the outstanding characteristics of traditional societies is the opposition that they assume between their inhabited territory and the unknown and indeterminate space that surrounds it. The form is the world (more precisely our world), the cosmos; everything outside it is no longer a cosmos but a sort of 'other world', a foreign, chaotic space peopled by ghosts, demons, 'foreigners' (who are assimilated to demons and souls of the dead).

(Eliade 1961: 29)

The centre of the world

To settle in a territory is equivalent to consecrating it; ... to organise a space is to repeat the paradigmatic work of the gods.... Whether the space appears in the form of a sacred precinct, a ceremonial house, a city, a world, we everywhere find the symbolism of the Centre of the World.... An example that has the advantage of immediately showing not only the consistency but also the complexity of this type of symbolism [is] the cosmic mountain.... The mountain occurs among the images that express the connection between heaven and earth; hence it is believed to be at the centre of the world ... and marks the highest point in the world; consequently, the territory that surrounds it and constitutes 'our world' is held to be the highest among countries. This is stated in Hebrew tradition: Palestine, being the highest in the land, was not submerged by the flood.

(Eliade 1961: 32–8)

PERCEPTUAL HISTORY

Our fundamental ideas about the world are constantly changing and, with them, the meaning we attach to our surroundings. In the following section we tried to show that the cathedral and castle are part of such a powerful symbolic arrangement, that they appear to have the capacity always to be at the forefront of the dialogue concerning the central issues of our time, and, very often, encapsulate the most important ideas about ourselves.

A sacred place

A community of monks dedicated to the safeguarding of the body of St Cuthbert settle on a rocky plateau. The protective walls exclude a hostile world. The egalitarianism of the community is confirmed by the lack of vertical hierarchy in the settlement (see Figures 1 and 2).

Figure 1 *Egalitarianism of the community is confirmed by lack of vertical hierarchy.*

Figure 2 *Protective walls exclude a hostile world.*

A centre of power

Durham's strategic potential is recognized by William I and it is subsumed into a wider political framework. In 1083 Bishop William of Calais removes the secular community outside the city walls and founds a Benedictine monastery in its place. The community is divided.

The split between the religious and the secular community is reinforced by the topography which embodies anthropomorphic associations of up/spirit/sky and down/body/earth. The cathedral becomes a symbol of the Church's growing power (see Figures 3 and 4).

Figure 3 *The split between religious and secular community is reinforced by the topography.*

Figure 4 *The cathedral becomes a symbol of the Church's growing power.*

A romantic image

Enlightenment philosophers propose for the first time that religion is a human construct. It is thought that people can conquer nature through an understanding of its laws. The cathedral no longer represents a recreation of the divine world; nor is it feared as a symbol of a power that the Church no longer exercises. Instead, it becomes a celebration of humanity's tenacity, a building dedicated not to the glory of God but to the glory of Humans. It towers above the landscape, triumphant over nature.

A further product of the enlightenment is an appreciation of the picturesque. This coincides with the planting of trees on the bank. The cathedral's romantic silhouette soars above the trees, an image synonymous with nostalgia for a mythical golden past. The river is no longer a hostile barrier but nature tamed and welcomed into the city (see Figures 5 and 6).

Figure 5 *The cathedral's silhouette soars above the trees.*

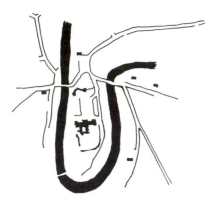

Figure 6 *The river symbolizes nature tamed and welcomed into the city.*

A seat of learning

The black rumble of progress, set in motion by the industrial revolution is felt over much of the north of England. Durham, however, is spared factories, warehouses and goods yards. Like these most overt manifestations of change, the railway passes Durham, never quite engaging with it. The train flirts with the city, promising a new world that never arrives.

New life is generated not by industry but by the founding of the university, which takes over the castle. Where once they represented the mighty twin powers of Church and State, the castle and cathedral are at odds with each other. Religion and education compete for the exclusive rights to Truth. They are rival standard bearers in the war of science on tradition.

Figure 7 *The industrial revolution passes the city by; the castle is taken over by the university, and rivalry begins with the cathedral.*

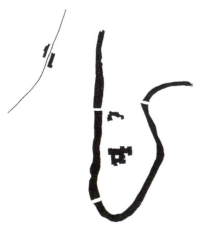

Figure 8 *The industrial revolution passes the city by; the church consolidates its sphere of influence.*

In the face of radical social change, the majority cling to old values with the result that the Church is able to consolidate its sphere of influence; but the cathedral is not immune to changing attitudes. It is at the same time pompous and noble: pompous to the progressives for whom it is a symbol of all that contrives to obscure the truth; noble to reactionaries for whom it is a valiant defender of the faith in the midst of profanity. Meanwhile, the castle has left behind its associations with oppression. It is now an expression of faith in the power of education to liberate the individual (see Figures 7 and 8).

A walled city (again)

The ring road forms a new city wall. The city wall once protected a community of monks from outsiders. It now protects outsiders (students, tourists) from the local community. Once again, the resident community has been banished outside the city walls from where it can watch the unfolding of a new drama; no longer the Church and commerce in delicate equilibrium, but a triangular battle of interests between university, tourist industry and market town (see Figures 9 and 10).

In the meantime, the cathedral has been spread thinly around the globe on picture postcards. Perhaps the belief sustained by some peoples, that the camera steals the soul, should be taken seriously.

Figure 9 *The ring road forms a new city wall.*

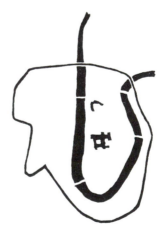

Figure 10 *The new wall protects outsiders (students, tourists) from the local community.*

The future (a cynical postscript)

The cathedral and castle appear to have readily lent themselves to changing interpretations through the ages. It is possible to conceive of Durham Cathedral being turned into the ultimate themed shopping experience, like a sponge absorbing the latest religion – or would its sacred qualities always resist the ultimate profanity?

JOURNEYS: SYMBOLIC QUALITIES

In this section we tried to investigate the way in which journeys and the events in them have the capacity to reinforce the existential meaning we attach to the world. Through an interpretation of the most salient features of these journeys, it became clear that the power of the archetypal arrangement at Durham is such that, despite the apparent displacement of religion from the centre of the Western way of life, the Durham peninsula will always embody the most fundamental distinctions between sacred and profane space.

Student's journey from the campus to the university via Prebends Bridge

The cathedral is Durham's most powerful and enduring symbol. Its proximity to the university and sheer bulk is such that the student cannot avoid orientating him- or herself towards it when approaching the university. It is therefore more than probable that the cathedral will become inseparable from the university in the student's mind.

Setting out from the university campus, the student's first view of the cathedral is across a school playing field. This visual relationship establishes education as an overriding image for Durham – the cathedral presiding over a centre of learning. Moreover, in the journey from the playing field to the cathedral, the student is constantly re-enacting the progress from school to university, providing a constant affirmation of his or her life's structure (see Figure 11).

Figure 11 *Student's journey no. 1: symbolic qualities.*

The journey also confirms the student's separation from the city. The gorge is clearly defined as a result of the abrupt termination of the playing field at its edge. This sets the cathedral and hence the university apart from the city, both physically and symbolically. They occupy a special place, a higher place. Crossing Prebends Bridge (first built as a private route for the clergy and still retaining an air of seclusion), students are perhaps reminded that they too are part of an elite. A prep school on the College Green brings further recollections of the privileged educational lineage that many Durham students will have followed.

Throughout this journey, whether it be along North Bailey or directly up to the college, the cathedral appears to oversee the student's progress and to make the student aware of his or her part in a long tradition of men and women aspiring to the highest intellectual ideas.

Student's journey from the campus to the university via Kingsgate Bridge

Setting out from the university campus, the cathedral is approached tangentially via St Oswald's church. The overriding feature of the journey is the experience of the gradually changing visual relationship between these two places of worship (see Figure 12). At first, St Oswald's is seen at close proximity with the cathedral in the background. Such is the simplicity and unpretentiousness of the church, the cathedral is overbearing in contrast. One is very much reminded of the uncompromising political power that was once centred there.

Continuing the journey past progressively more distinguished town houses, a space leading to Kingsgate Bridge opens up on the left revealing the east end of the cathedral. The position of a university building adjacent to the bridge designates the bridge as predominantly a student route. By side-stepping the historic pilgrims' route and thereby seeming to favour expedience before ritual, the students' convenience before urban hierarchy, the Kingsgate Bridge has the effect of undermining the authority of the cathedral.

The cathedral's scale is brought down by the welcoming domestic buildings in front (see Figure 13). Looking back from the bridge, St Oswald's can be seen perched on the top of the outer bank above a mass of trees. This reinforces the sense that one is leaving the town behind to enter a special zone, a zone which is the almost exclusive domain of students. The dominance of

Figure 12 *Student's journey no. 2: a gradually changing visual relationship between two places of worship.*

Figure 13 *Student's journey no. 2: domestic buildings reduce the cathedral's scale.*

the university on the 'island' bears witness to the displacement of religion by education as a disseminator of social values (though, of course, education's influence is small compared with politics and the media). Education and religion share no common agenda. The university therefore continues to develop largely indifferent to the cathedral's presence. Perhaps the cathedral's visual dominance is now seen as a quirk of history and no longer reflects the position that religion occupies in society today. However, on leaving Bow Lane and experiencing the sudden revelation of the cathedral's immense form, there is a sense that the university is trespassing on religion's territory and cannot totally displace it.

Pilgrim's journey from the railway station to the peninsula

Like a voyeur condemned to being a mere onlooker and never a participant, the modern pilgrim first confronts Durham from behind the screen of a train window. Separated from the city by this glass barrier and enclosed in the train's artificial environment, it is as if the traveller is witnessing a scene fixed in time. The cathedral and castle loom high on the horizon, presiding over the cowering market town, impervious and indifferent to change.

Leaving the station the pilgrim descends to the modern city wall, the ring road. As the river contains expansion on the 'island', so the ring road defines an inanimate city within, forced to gratify the pilgrim's expectations of a city frozen in its golden past. Con-

tinuing the journey towards Framwellgate Bridge, the pilgrim's goal is glimpsed intermittently behind a new, faceless shopping centre.

Once on the 'island', the pilgrim is squeezed into a winding tunnel which apparently conspires to lead all pilgrims away from their objective. On either side, very different attractions beckon, but the familiarity of the shop-fronts merely confirms the expectation that the particular is always surrounded by the general, that banality feeds off the unique. The pilgrim passes the high street shops, moving on to the commercial centre, the market place and its banks; then round and up the hill and past less commercial shops, 'Earthcare' and the university bookshops, marking the transition between the city and the university.

Although there is no definite threshold, the pilgrim experiences a metamorphosis from faceless shopper to faceless tourist in the heart of the university. Approaching the summit, Palace Green unfolds and expands revealing the flat silhouetted bulk of the cathedral. The pilgrim has almost arrived. The scale of the close merely accentuates the immense size of the cathedral. The closer one is, the smaller one becomes. Entering the cathedral, the pilgrim senses that this has been a symbolic journey, a confirmation of an archetypal order – that we continue to aspire to the 'higher' and its anthromorphic associations with spirit and mind (and more traditionally with heaven), but we must pass through the 'lower', the functions of necessity and their traditional connection with the earth.

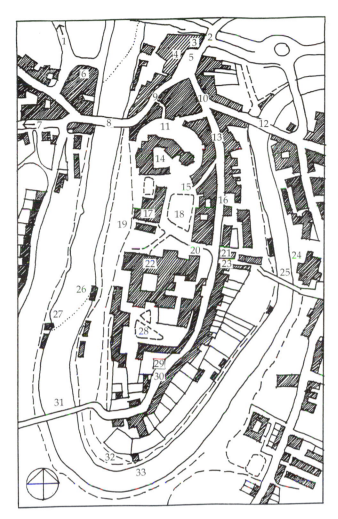

1 Railway Station
2 Claypath
3 St Nicholas
4 Covered market
5 Market-place
6 Milburngate Shopping Centre
7 Bus station
8 Framwelgate Bridge
9 Silver Street
10 Fleshergate
11 Moatside Lane
12 Elvet Bridge
13 Saddler Street
14 Castle
15 Owengate
16 North Bailey
17 Palace Green Library

18 Palace Green
19 Windy Gap
20 Duncow Lane
21 St Mary Le Bow
22 Cathedral
23 Bow Lane
24 Students' Union
   (Dunelm House)
25 Kingsgate Bridge
26 Old Fulling Mill
27 Weir
28 Cathedral Close
29 St Mary-the-Less
30 South Bailey
31 Prebends Bridge
32 Tree-trunk sculpture
33 Temple of Love

Figure 14 *Four major routes through the City of Durham.*

ROUTES: SPATIAL ANALYSIS

> ... to lay out paths, first place goals at natural points of interest. Then connect the goals to one another to form the paths.
>
> (Alexander *et al.* 1977: No. 120, 587–8).

Aspects of the character of Durham can be discerned by analysis of its spaces and the paths that connect them.

We identified four major routes, which enabled us to make observations on the part they play within the complex fabric of Durham (see Figure 14).

Romantic route

Elvet Bridge to Framwelgate Bridge (Figure 15)

Aerial views of the city of Durham show a belt of trees wrapping around the promontory and separating it from the river. These trees have not always existed. Drawings of *c*.1595 show produce for the city growing on the banks. Today, we have a landscaped area, perhaps comparable to a park in the picturesque tradition. The belt of green is punctuated at intervals by lifelines, linking the town to the settlements on the opposite banks (see Figure 16). At each of these points there are public paths linking the bridges at high level and the river. In between these major access points are semi-private links between the river and private gardens, or the cathedral, for example.

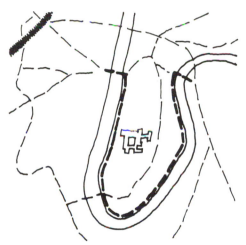

Figure 15 *The first route: Elvet Bridge to Framwelgate Bridge.*

Figure 16 *The town is linked at intervals to settlements on the opposite bank.*

Figure 17 *The river path is a place of contemplation.*

The walk down by the river is different in character and atmosphere from any other area in Durham. It does not lead anywhere in particular, but it does link two major bridges, although these are joined much more efficiently via the Market Place. It is a place for contemplation and thought. A place to walk the dog. A place to take your lover (see Figure 17).

At intervals along the bank of Durham's riverside are situated concentrations of activity. Sometimes these are buildings, sometimes spaces, but more often they are accidents of nature. Along the bank from Elvet bridge are the university boat sheds, which provide backdrops for vigorous activity at all times of the day. Further along there is the 'love' temple and past that again the wood sculpture representing the Last Supper. Nearer, towards the cathedral, there is the Fulling Mill. Despite this, the overriding characteristic of this circuit is the quietness, peace and beauty, quite unexpected in a city centre.

Student route

University campus to Cathedral Close via Prebends Bridge (Figure 18)

The route crossing Prebends Bridge is used extensively by students going from the western colleges of the university campus to those on the peninsula. One of the

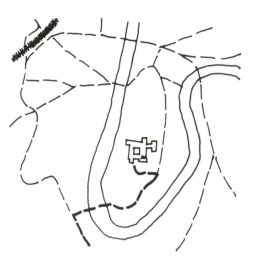

Figure 18 *The second route: university campus to Cathedral Close via Prebends Bridge.*

first glimpses of the cathedral can be seen between two innocuous semi-detached houses. Do the students, however, notice the cathedral, Durham's World Heritage site, after the first term, or does it blend into the scenery? The houses mark the boundary between the public domain of the road and the semi-public feeling of the approach to Prebends Bridge. Wide and popular with tourists, it has convenient niches for viewing the chocolate-box view of the cathedral. It is a rather grand gesture for a backwater entrance. On either side paths lead down to the river.

Once over the bridge, the only gateway still standing indicates the way (Figure 19). We are curious as to where it will lead us. The gateway distinguishes between the semi-public domain of the riverside and the semi-private feeling of the university campus. It is at

Figure 19 *A gateway marks both the route and the boundary between riverside and university campus.*

Figure 20 *The church of St Mary-the-Less.*

Figure 21 *The arched gateway linking North Bailey and Cathedral Close.*

this point that we feel as though we are truly entering a historic walled city.

Once through the gateway, we notice the domestic scale of the narrow street. The dominant house standing alone on the left-hand side contrasts with the frontage on the right-hand side of the street. These are flush and consist of mixtures of sizes, heights, styles and textures. Both sides of accommodation along South Bailey belong to the university, and so at certain times of the day it is not unlike an internal central corridor. Along its length, one catches glimpses of the private courtyards of the colleges.

On rounding the corner we see the road widening to accommodate the church of St Mary-the-Less (Figure 20). Narrow at first, the road opens out. This is dictated by the historic line of South Bailey and the orientation of the church. The road is unevenly balanced with a uniform frontage on the right and garden walls and outbuildings on the left. To reach the church is our immediate aim: to discover the space in which it sits.

The church sits on a raised pedestal giving a formal character to the space over which it presides. Because there are few cars using this space and the academic buildings front on to it, the street has a peaceful atmosphere. The right-hand-side buildings form a common street frontage enclosing the church. This contrasts with the left-hand side, which consists of a series of small outbuildings. It is at this stage that the cathedral reveals itself and we can reorientate ourselves. The way out of the space appears once again to lead away from the cathedral, which does not appear large from this angle.

The route narrows, defining the space we have left, and we again lose sight of the cathedral. There is a noticeable contrast in texture between the floor, walls and roofs.

Progressing along North Bailey, the street becomes more defined as there are now buildings on both sides of it. The solid nature of these buildings, characterized by

their lack of openings, makes the long street feel dark and harsh. Which way do we proceed? No activity can be seen and there is nothing to aim for at the end of the street. Through the arch on the left we see something new – a different building type and formation. The arch is a gateway defining the space between the semi-private North Bailey and the semi-public Cathedral Close (see Figure 21).

The Cathedral Close (Figure 22) becomes part of the tourist route and, as such, is one of the major public squares in Durham. Dominated by the cathedral, it is also protected by it, as the city was in times gone by. The close has an atmosphere of peace and tranquility, unlike the busy Palace Green, no doubt because of the

Figure 22 *The Cathedral Close, one of Durham's major public squares.*

lack of traffic. We enter only if we want to. It is evocative of English village greens as we like to imagine them. Although equal in size to the Palace Green, a more intimate space is created since it is almost totally enclosed by private residences up to three storeys in height. The centre is divided into three areas of lawn and is strewn with trees, a water pump and a water tower, giving the area interest and life.

Student route

University campus to peninsula via Kingsgate Bridge (Figure 23)

From the university we first view the cathedral across playing fields, evoking Constable's paintings of Salisbury Cathedral. But we are remote from the cathedral, a silhouette in the distance, linked to us by the peninsula's tradition of learning. We notice the cathedral when needed – it is a landmark by which we orientate ourselves.

As we move away from the university our visual relationship with the cathedral changes, but it does not appear to be any closer as we move almost parallel with the river. Our concentration is now centred on the road as the built fabric grows around us. We lose sight of the cathedral unless we search it out between the houses. We are now in the public realm, spiritually distant from it. The buildings are domestic in scale, varying in style, form and texture. Further along the road there is a change in the buildings fronting the street, as the road drops dramatically and the houses appear to stop. We expect something (see Figure 24).

As we reach the brow of the hill, we notice two things: the start of retail units in the settlement of Elvet and a brutally modern structure: the Students' Union building (Figure 25). This serves to demarcate the start of the route used almost entirely by students. Although

Figure 24 *The road drops dramatically and the houses appear to stop.*

a public bridge, it has the feeling of being in the private domain.

The entrance to the bridge is alongside the Union building, presenting a spectacular view of the east end of the cathedral (see Figure 26). Unexpectedly, the bridge crosses the river at an angle, creating a continually changing view of it. Unlike the other bridges, Kingsgate bridge is most definitely a route and not a meeting place.

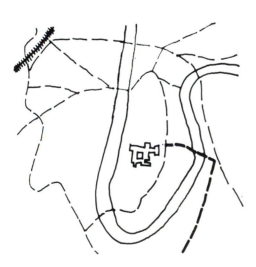

Figure 23 *The third route: university campus to the peninsula via Kingsgate Bridge.*

Figure 25 *The Students' Union building.*

Figure 26 *The entrance to Kingsgate Bridge presents a spectacular view of the east end of the cathedral.*

The steps at the far end create a sense of anticipation of what is to come. Ascending them, we can stop in a small space formed by the rear of a group of buildings and the entrance to the rear of one of the colleges. A view is seen up to the cathedral through a narrow alley (Figure 27), which brings us on to the North Bailey, where we are confronted by the east face of the ca-thedral, the scale of which is quite small from this angle. Turning left or right will bring us to the university colleges.

Tourist route

Railway station to cathedral via Framwelgate Bridge, Market Place, Owengate, Palace Green and the Sanctuary Knocker (Figure 28)

Seen from the railway station, Durham presents its most potent image, setting the scene for what is to come. This experience in Durham is different from that of other English cathedral towns, where our first view is of the urban fabric, with the towers and spires emerging from it. The dominant mass of the cathedral and castle looms over the huddle of smaller buildings, their roofs step-ping down the slope in sympathy with the topography (see Figure 29).

Descending towards the cathedral and castle, we cross the A167 ring road before entering the city centre. As we do so, we lose our sense of direction as we follow the increasing bustle into a shopping street. The build-ings surrounding us are new in appearance, with a variety of forms and sizes, but lacking in scale, texture and interest. Sharing the road, we now travel along with buses and service vehicles, and seem to be entering Framwelgate Bridge from a back entrance. As the build-ings encloses us, we lose sight of the cathedral and our eventual goal.

Figure 27 *A view of the cathedral from a narrow alley approaching North Bailey.*

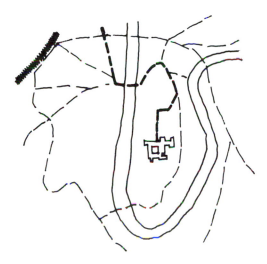

Figure 28 *The fourth route: railway station to cathedral via Framwelgate Bridge, Market Place, Owengate, Palace Green and the Sanctuary Knocker.*

Figure 29 *Seen from the railway station, the cathedral and castle loom over the smaller buildings.*

We head for where we assume the cathedral to be, seeing an entrance between two nondescript buildings. As we continue, the castle and cathedral appear in all their drama, focusing our minds.

As we pass through this entrance, we cross Framwelgate Bridge, the modern gateway to the city. This is emphasized by the close proximity of the buildings on either side of the bridge and the change of floorscape accompanying the pedestrianization of this street. Once again the cathedral and castle castle are within our view, but only if we are looking ... On either side we note subtle entrances leading down to river level. The road

Figure 30 *The castle seems to have no obvious routes leading to it.*

Figure 31 *Silver Street narrows as it progresses.*

Figure 32 *Market Place seen from the brow of Silver Street.*

ahead leads round to the left, away from the castle, which has no obvious routes leading to it (Figure 30). The form and scale of these buildings are subservient to that of the castle. We are drawn round the corner by our curiosity as to what might be there, and by our quest to reach the cathedral. As we do so, the road narrows as we progress up Silver Street (Figure 31), our eyes are drawn upwards to an opening – a square? This is obviously a major shopping street, the retail units being small in width at the bottom of the slope, increasing to two or three units in width towards the top. Façades step in and out and create varied, if not distinguished, architecture. The floorscape is based on historical precedent and creates movement and direction, both up and down.

As we reach the brow of Silver Street, the Market Place reveals itself (see Figure 32). A space that seems as though it should be setting the pace for something slower, it lacks intimacy owing to a stream of vehicles dividing the square into two unequal parts. There is also an unfortunate gap diagonally opposite. This newly enlarged entrance opens up the square, reducing the presence of the north side of the church of St Nicholas. Now pedestrianized, Durham's historic centre of retail and commerce is made up of buildings of all ages and styles. A number are prominent due to their width, exceeding historic plot sizes. The floorscape, which is twenty years old, is a mixture of paving, cobbles and tarmac, defining separate areas. Only by turning around do we see the way out, the façades of the square sweeping round out of sight up Fleshergate.

This route leads us to a fork (Figure 33). Which way? On closer inspection we see a signpost marking the corner, telling us which way to go. The left-hand fork slopes downwards, its sides crowded with shops. The right-hand fork slopes upwards and is plainer and more

narrow. This junction is a place of activity – a place to meet, stop and chat, but also it marks a change in function of the town.

Once past this junction, the atmosphere subtly changes. The shops start to peter out and those that remain change in character. They become less commercial, either relating to tourism, or to the university. Here

Figure 33 *A fork in Fleshergate.*

the buildings still retain their four-storey limit, but, as our eyes start to wander up the hill, up Saddler Street, the road curves to the right while the buildings' roofline remains constant. Towards the brow of the hill, the buildings are only two storeys high, and appear to be older and more varied in character.

Once again we face a decision as the road forks. Straight ahead, the North Bailey, does not seem to contain much of interest, except perhaps a small church tower. To the right, however, a change in floorscape, from tarmac to cobbles, indicates a change in the use and activity as we see our first glimpse of the cathedral since Framwelgate Bridge. The buildings on either side are of little interest compared to what we see through the gap. We are encouraged to press on towards our goal, with high expectations of the cathedral, bathed in light, contrasted against the dark narrow lane that frames our view.

As we progress up Owengate, the road begins to widen and Palace Green itself opens up before us, a wide expanse of virgin green lawn, protected by 'do not walk on the grass' signs and surrounded by car-parking and small buildings belonging to the university and the church (see Figure 34). If we care to look behind us, we see the castle protected by a large gateway, through which we are not encouraged to enter, as it contains the university halls of residence. It is at this point that we now see the cathedral in its entirety (see Figure 35). We experience this revelation in the space of a few steps.

The Palace Green is part of a tradition of space-making around English cathedrals not found in most European counterparts. However, unlike more successful precincts, this space is bare and lifeless. This is due to a number of causes. Because of the low elevations of the surrounding buildings and their inconsistent nature,

Figure 35 *Palace Green, part of a tradition of space-making around English cathedrals.*

the space has little feeling of enclosure and intimacy; and there are no routes through it (as at Winchester and Salisbury, for example), which makes it impossible to utilize. The individual's physical and psychological separation from this green space, and indeed the cathedral, is emphasized by the sea of cars which surrounds the square, and prevent it from being read as a whole.

THRESHOLDS

The point where a path crosses a boundary marks the transition between two separate realms. It is often celebrated with decorative arches and gateways. The threshold becomes a place imbued with meaning and importance. Yet this place is not always apparent: passing from one realm into another can be experienced almost subconsciously as the nature of our environment changes around us.

Direction and topography change as we ascend the cobbled, narrowing lane which leads to the cathedral. It creates a feeling of leaving the city and entering into a calmer, but as yet only glimpsed, world. On emerging from this enclosure we are suddenly struck by a sense of light and space in which we feel suddenly lost. The massive cathedral stands silently, filling up the sky; immediately visible is the elaborate North Door (Figure 36). Now we have a direction and a goal and our path is made simple and straight. Decorative stonework surrounds make the door visually prominent. Two towers and the gable give it impact, while tiers of elaborate arches and slender columns draw us in. Such intricacy has the effect of dissolving the powerful solidity of the cathedral walls – so we enter . . .

The cathedral itself, like the city, is built up of many distinct realms. Each one is sacred and has its place within an age-old tradition of hierarchy. As the most holy places are approached, the traveller passes through a series of arches and exquisite screens which become increasingly diaphanous and delicate. They cause us to slow down and contemplate the sanctity of the place we are nearing.

Figure 34 *Palace Green at the end of Owengate.*

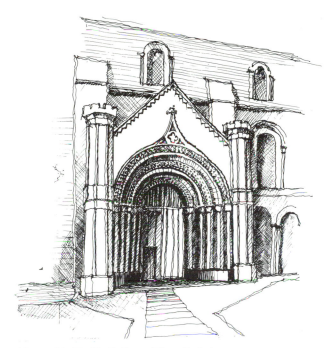

Figure 36 *The North Door of the cathedral.*

Figure 37 *Castellated gate-house in the inner castle courtyard.*

The inner castle courtyard is also reached by crossing several boundaries: a strong opening within a stone wall leads across an open green to a castellated gate-house. The fortress-like quality of this formidable building is emphasized by its castellation. It is hard to tell what lies beyond the dark, tunnelled opening. This is definitely an entrance through which only select people can pass (see Figure 37).

Beyond the cathedral is the Cathedral Close. This was examined in the spatial analysis of the tourist route; it is different in character from Palace Green in that it is less formal, more enclosed and private. The cathedral buildings themselves act as the transitional element between the two spaces: the threshold.

On walking through the cathedral towards the South Door the feeling of enclosure is very strong; the vaulted roof towers overhead and the huge walls are seldom punctuated and their solidity is never compromised. The cloisters form an extension to the cathedral space: within it we are aware of the outside, we feel the breeze and can look out upon an open green. Opposite we see the building which encloses the courtyard; its stone tracery forms a subtle boundary which is neither open nor closed. The two spaces become part of one another. Light and shade give a dynamic quality to the arcaded walkway, creating an outside space inside. Here again, there is a sequence of arches emphasizing the private nature of the quiet close. They are even locked at 10.30 p.m.!

Along the Old Bailey we are now in the realms of the everyday, and yet the small scale of the buildings and the narrow street gives the distinct feeling of being in a hidden world, and the shops, traffic and noise seem far off.

A bend in the road leads us past a picturesque nine-teenth-century church, some allotments and student housing. We are gradually travelling downhill and feel as if we are leaving the town. Prebends Arch marks the end of the street (see Figure 38). It stands at the boundary between the city and the dense woodland and river which bounds it.

Suddenly, the tarmac of the quiet street becomes a sloping gravel path, and the soft light and dark colours of nature replace the solidity of the buildings. Prebends Bridge (Figure 39) is now the gateway sailing over the river Wear, linking the city and the riverside. The

Figure 38 *Prebends Arch marks the boundary between city and dense woodland on the river's edge.*

Figure 39 *Prebends Bridge crosses the river Wear, linking city and riverside.*

colours and treatment of the threshold reveal much about the people whose private domain lies behind. The entrance is an expression of individuality, it can welcome, impress or protect. It is the boundary between public and private, we have to cross it; what is beyond?

We all need to escape from time to time, whether it is from the hustle of the city or the claustrophobic office

Figure 40 *A place of quiet beauty, though the sounds of the city can always be heard, faintly.*

atmosphere. The river and its wooded banks offer relief from the noisy, crowded town. It can be forgotten as we walk or sit in this place of quiet beauty. However, there is never the feeling of isolation because people moving across bridges and the sounds of the city can always be seen and heard, yet only faintly (Figure 40).

TEXTURES AND MATERIALS

Durham sandstone

It was not just Durham's fortress-like topography that made it the perfect place for Cuthbert's monastic community to settle. They also had a site which was rich in minerals. The peninsula of Durham was the centre of a large area of coal measures, providing an immense source of wealth and employment for the region. The coal measures were to be found in a variety of sandstones, which not only provided the soft curves of the surrounding landscape, but also served as a durable building material. These porous stones were used in the building of Durham's castle and cathedral, and their soft honey colour dominates much of the more modest architecture of the city.

The reaction of these sandstones to light means that from the north the cathedral appears dull in colour and has an almost grim solidity (see Figure 41). From the south, however, it has a more golden colour and an apparently smooth texture (see Figure 42). The sandstone lacks radiance and appears a dour greyish-buff in dull weather, but in sunshine it is a warm yellow. At night, the cathedral is flooded with pure white light, giving it a glacial quality, and contrasting with the soft, yellow-lit castle.

Figure 41 *Seen from the north, the sandstone of the cathedral has an almost grim solidity.*

Figure 42 *The sandstone of the cathedral seems smooth and golden coloured when seen from the south.*

The stone from the cathedral and castle has been attributed to small local quarries: Kepier, Baxterwood and Littleburn, downstream of Durham. One can assume that the river Wear provided the means of transport for the boulders. The stone from the cloisters is thought to have been from Esh quarry. That of the monastic buildings came from the Sacrist's quarry, just south of Prebends Bridge. Recent restoration work on the cathedral has been carried out using Dunhouse grit-stone. This stone occurs west and south of the coal measures. It has a similar colour and texture as the sand-stone, but it is more fissile, that is, it is capable of being split or cracked along the grain, and therefore can provide heavy slabs for roofs.

The Durham stones exhibit a variety of different responses to weathering. The University Library stone has organic characteristics; like dry, old bones, it is worn, greying and rough. In the Dean's Garden Wall, the weathering process has given the stone a quality similar to skin, warm, and varying in colour. And at Elvet Bridge the stone is flaking, dry and peeling.

Floorscape

> Buildings, rich in texture and colour, stand on the floor. If the floor is a smooth and flat expanse of greyish tarmac, then the buildings will remain separate because the floor fails to intrigue the eye in the same way that the buildings do. One of the most powerful agents for unifying and joining the town is the floor.
>
> (Cullen 1971: 53)

At the time of the building of the new ring road and accompanying pedestrianization, it was decided that those streets now reserved for pedestrian use should be returned to an earlier floor pattern. This consists of two tracks of smooth paving for cart tracks, with the remainder of the street cobbled to provide grip for horses and pedestrians (see Figure 43). One might justifiably imagine that this fashionable, heritage-conscious move was straight kitsch, but in fact it is very successful. The cart tracks give the streets a strong linearity and sense of purpose. They also have the effect of breaking up the scale of the street into a tripartite arrangement which recalls the divisions of vehicles and pedestrians.

As Gordon Cullen observes, a street that has a floor and walls of a similar texture gives pedestrians a strong sense of containment within a unified entity. On picturing a street in this way one is reminded of John Outram, who equates streets with dried-up river beds (Outram 1988). The river's clear hierarchy, with its time-less cycle of water passing from spring to ocean, is analogous with the pilgrim's route and its constant stream of travellers. It is therefore a shame that the cobbled pattern breaks down at the market square to facilitate parking, breaking a journey that began at Framwelgate Bridge.

The cobbled street

Each stone set is unique. It is created from a natural process – years and layers of forces. It is placed on the road, trampled by horses' hooves, cartwheels, lorries and feet. The surface becomes moulded by time and experience: chipping, smoothening and cleaving. Every stone has its own individual face, sandwiched next to its

Figure 43 *Early streets had two smooth bands of paving for carts, and cobbles to provide grip for horses or pedestrians.*

neighbour, which, although similar, is never identical. The gathering of moss and weeds in the cracks is a testimony to the passage of time.

PART TWO: PATTERNS AND DURHAM

This section attempts to look at Durham through the eyes of patterns. Christopher Alexander's books have been very useful in helping us to focus on different aspects of Durham which we might otherwise have ignored (Alexander 1979; Alexander *et al.* 1977).

Some of the following are merely observations, some are elaborations, others are examples of the applicability of Alexander's ideas in Durham. All of them are subjective. As it will, we hope, become evident, Durham is a complex combination of patterns that enrich each other.

PATTERNS AND FORM

Identifiable neighbourhood
Neighbourhood boundaries

The river, roads and green belt act as boundaries to define very, very clearly, 'DURHAM'. The Durham peninsula is set apart, a district topographical feature that cries out for settlement on it. A *genius loci* then, is it not (see Figure 44)?

Web of public transport
Ring roads

The ring roads help relieve traffic congestion in the heart of Durham. Simultaneously, they define 'Greater Durham' (see Figure 45). Is there a change of image with a change of speed? The peninsula is removed one step from 'civilization' – life-saving really. Durham becomes a slower, by-passed town. And why is the railway station there? Perhaps Durham is too important a city to ignore. More to the point, there is not enough space for goods yards and such. (And who wants to build two

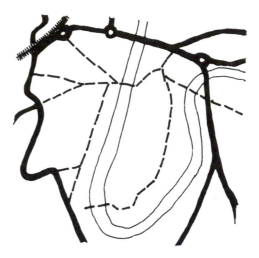

Figure 45 *The web of transport defines 'Greater Durham'.*

bridges over the Wear?) In any case, Durham remains well-connected, but doesn't have an airport. Why not?

The four-storey limit
Cascade of roofs

The buildings in Durham tend to follow the topography. The tallest building, the cathedral, stands on the plateau at the crown of the hill. All the other buildings defer to the primacy of the Church. Following the slope of the hill, the built form accentuates the contours of the site, especially if seen from afar.

The 'four-storey' limit probably resulted from the limitations of available building methods. However, there appears to be an instinctive feeling for scale: the tight site along the Baileys leads to three-storey buildings, whilst the Market Place is ringed by taller buildings of four or more floors.

Market of many shops

The old covered market remains. It is slightly tacky and touristy, but like the Grainger Market in Newcastle it makes a valuable contribution to the fabric of Durham.

Nine per cent parking

Parking in Durham is restricted and very, very expensive. This is necessary if Durham is to avoid becoming choked with cars. Alternative centres may grow up around the parking areas. (Home is where the car park is.) Pedestrians do not need to share the narrow streets with vehicles – a nasty experience if you are in a hurry. Parking solutions are not ideal – the market square is cut into two by the car park.

Web of shopping
Shopping street

Shopping and mercantile activities are secular in nature. Religion occupies the foremost stratum, followed by defence and academia (see Figure 46).

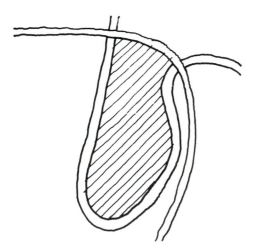

Figure 44 *Boundaries: the Durham peninsula – a genius loci.*

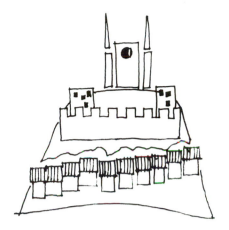

Figure 46 *The web of shopping: shopping street.*

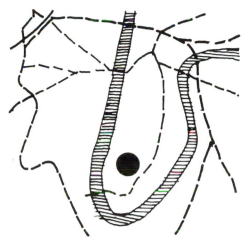

Figure 48 *Sacred site: the cathedral is Durham's* raison d'être.

Banks and other major stores (Boots, Marks & Spencer, etc.) occupy the area around the Market Place as the scale allows for larger, more impressive, buildings. Along Silver Street, there is a varied mix of shops (with an overabundance of shoe shops, perhaps). Surely it is expensive to set up a shop here? We anticipate an increase in specialist and 'yuppie' shops; probably in the newly renovated premises along Saddler Street. There are art galleries and photo-supply shops (a sure sign of tourism!). More specialized and academic needs are met by the Scout/Guide and the university bookshop. Estate agents are located further 'up-strata' on North Bailey. Indeed, shops disappear after Owengate. (Even before then, the fronts begin to get smaller, finally becoming residential up the Baileys.) Perhaps religious disapproval has all but banned pubs from the peninsula. Shopping spills out from the bridges, and a web of shops line the streets leading into the town centre (see Figure 47).

Sacred site
Holy ground

The cathedral is the *raison d'être* of Durham (see Figure

48). Without it we might as well go to York. It was once most sacred, courtesy of the incorruptible Cuthbert and the faithful Bede. Their relics have drawn generations of venerating pilgrims, and this has helped to spread Durham's influence. It is hard to sense the sacredness now. It has been replaced by respect – normal human respect for the dead and a stirring sense of awesomeness within the building itself (which, I suspect, transcends cultures and religion – observe the group of Japanese tourists). The sanctity of the cathedral is muted now, but still commands an undeniable influence on the town. There is no escape.

Activity nodes

The cathedral and the market place were major activity nodes in the medieval town, the cathedral being the purpose of pilgrimage, of learning and of worship, the market place the centre for commercial transactions. With the growth of the town and the decline of the church, new activity nodes developed along the major paths – for example, the shopping centre by Milburn

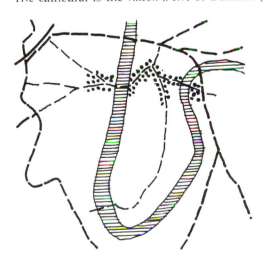

Figure 47 *The web of shopping: shops spill from the bridges into the city centre.*

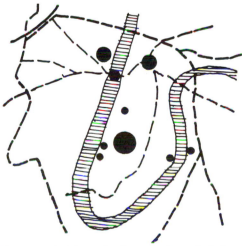

Figure 49 *Activity node: formerly the cathedral and the market place, now new nodes develop along the main paths.*

Gate. The university's presence also resulted in a new set of activities – library, staff/student centre and the various boating houses (see Figure 49).

Shopping is, on the whole, an outdoor activity in Durham. The traditional high street shopping which was rescued from the threat of cars is now being supplemented by larger shops and shopping centres. The result is obviously successful, judging by the amount of people who surge up and down Silver Street.

Perhaps people are prepared to walk further from car-parks to do their shopping in the 'traditional' way. The entire Silver Street/Market Place/Elvet route is a series of nodes linked by bridges which are well-used as a result.

Access to water
Accessible green
Quiet backs

It has been observed that Durham is a city operating on two levels: the level of the street and the level of the water. You cannot escape from water in Durham, given that it is almost surrounded by the Wear. The common perception of a green, leafy Durham is perpetrated by the lush vegetation (in summer) by the river banks.

The green and the river are easily accessible by the paths that connect the two levels of Durham. The river is also used by rowers, whose calming splash-splash is rather incongruous with the low hum of the ever-present traffic somewhere beyond. Nevertheless, one can forget Durham (and not even see the cathedral from down here) and, judging by the tracks, the river is well frequented, too. It is a quiet side to Durham punctuated by the occasional boat house, Fulling Mill, a delightful tree-trunk sculpture and a Greek temple. Such places are necessary to any city, complementing and enriching the urban landscape.

Life cycles

For what sort of people is this historic core? Surely it caters for a rather selective slice of society: the young adults and the tourists. There are no crèches, no primary schools, no old folks' home (and no cinema). Durham is not a town for disabled people, either. The cobbled streets must be very uncomfortable for wheelchairs; the steeply rising Silver Street would be quite a challenge too. Were it not for 'Greater Durham', probably historic Durham would soon no longer be a viable or a vital town. It is too narrowly focused already. During weekends and university holidays, the town is lifeless.

Promenade

To see and to be seen . . .
Where else but on the bridge (see Figure 50)!
The re-routing of the A1 has left Durham with two very wide footbridges. The width (and rough cobbling) of the Framwelgate and Elvet Bridges encourages slowing of pace. People are inclined to stop and stare, to

Figure 50 *Seeing and being seen on the bridges.*

busk, to sell Christmas wrapping paper, to sell gas lighters ('two for a pooound!') without inhibiting the flow of human traffic.

University as a market-place

Durham University is by no means an 'open' university where anyone with any qualification can take or give a course. Being England's third-oldest university, it has its own tradition to uphold. The decision to establish a collegiate system has left the university with a loose and open campus. Academic library buildings are scattered about Durham, but the result is akin to a market-place, where the cross-fertilization of ideas is possible.

The university took over the castle buildings, which soon became inadequate as the university began to grow. Now the university is probably the largest employer in Durham. In fact, the university has taken over the town to such a degree (gradually buying up all the available property along Baileys) that Durham is perceived as a university town. Such a perception is probably indelible, much to the collective despair of some sections of Durham society. It would be interesting to see if this duality (town and gown) could be developed in Durham's interests.

Degree of publicness

Historic Durham is loosely divided into town and university at the Owengate level. It would seem obvious that 'town' is public, and open to all, and that 'gown' is private with restricted access, but this is not so. In reality, there is a mixture, a spillover.

The very public green riverside feels secluded and semi-private. Some sections are quite lonely, and it is quite possible to avoid people.

There are many inviting public alleyways which, at the same time, feel tantilizingly un-public. One can never be quite sure. Along the Baileys, there is the same air of privacy that one gets in a suburban road. Ironically, the Palace Green, the largest of the public spaces, is forbidding by virtue of its unusability and unfriendly 'keep off the grass' signs. In contrast, the Close, which is private, is more welcoming as the public is allowed to wander through. Overall then, the Durham peninsula is a fairly homogeneous semi-public/private space which, in effect, sets it apart from the area outside the city core.

Work community

The Market Place has a communal feeling and a certain sense of grandeur to it. It has a good mix of offices, shops, eating places and public space. It is perhaps hampered by the inevitable (but regulated) car-parking. It must have been even nicer once . . .

Network of paths
Main gateways

Even before the re-routing of the highway, the road network in Durham was simple: one road crossing the neck of the peninsula, another running down the length, with a diversion up to the cathedral (echoing Edinburgh's Royal Mile). The roads serve the upper/city level of Durham. On the lower level, a riverside walkway encircles the peninsula. A third system of routes completes the network by linking these two levels. These links are varied: beaten tracks, well-worn steps, gaps between buildings, etc. Most are subtle and easily overlooked, containing an air of mystery about them.

Durham's complete reliance on bridges has led to them becoming notional gateways. The old walled city had genuine gateways (the last remaining one at the end of the South Bailey). The removal of these gateways has reduced the sensation of entry into the city. The most noticeable gap, of course, is at Gilesgate, next to St Nicholas's church. This has destroyed the sense of enclosure as space 'leaks' out now. At Owengate, the removal of the old North Gate has erased the boundary into the cathedral and castle zone.

So what takes the place of gateways now? At Framwellgate and Elvet, the boathouses take on this role. The pedestrianization of these bridges and their subsequent cobbling help define entry into Durham. The old gateways had the effect of compressing space at the boundary to a larger space (something that can still be experienced coming into the castle). The change in floor materials at Owengate acts as a threshold to the cathedral. The road curves and narrows ever so slightly, compressing space before the climax of the Palace Green.

High places

To climb up and to survey the world is identified by Christopher Alexander as a fundamental human instinct (Alexander *et al.* 1977: 316), but perhaps the castle was built more from a need to watch enemies than for the views it afforded. Yes, the cathedral's towers point us to heaven, but surely no one (save a bell-ringing monk or two) was allowed to climb them.

We can climb up the tower now (for a small fee), a lung-wrenching, head-swirling, spiralling journey which ends in a most welcome view of County Durham. Soak it in, fill your mind with the image of the city, your city now. You are the king, the bishop, ruler of all you survey. The world is at your feet. Look! There is your house, your hotel, your red car. Trace the route you have come from. Shiver in the cold. Snuggle up to your friend and gaze into a future, your future . . . Everything is all right; everything is fine up here. Everything is so small now. Then it's time to leave, time to go down, down, down to the ground and to the real world.

But don't go just yet, don't be in a hurry to leave. Glance around once more and imprint the view and these moments into your memory, your inward eye . . .

Then smuggle it home with you.

Courtyards
Small public squares
Something roughly in the middle

Durham has a number of public squares, the liveliest of which is the market square. The space is bounded by shops, and although unfortunately split in two by the car park, it has a compact nature, seating provisions, telephones and a focal equestrian statue vaguely in the centre. It is like an eddy created by streams of people that feed in and out of it (see Figure 51).

Contrast this with the large and sterile Palace Green. This is a dead, 'dullsville' sort of place, a result perhaps of the overwhelming scale. The surrounding buildings are low (to 'show off' the cathedral) and hence do not provide a semblance of enclosure. There are no trees or anything remotely of interest in the emptiness. The Green's purpose is to show off the cathedral in all its impassive glory, but it is too bland a view. (It is interesting that all five of us failed to take a colour print of this view; nor do the books we have had on hand include it.

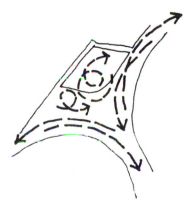

Figure 51 *Eddies in the market square.*

Then, of course, its size must make it difficult to photograph.)

The cloisters within the cathedral are empty now. There must once have been the sound of monks, scurrying about their business. Now there is the occasional dull click of a camera.

The green space enclosed is empty, but not sterile, saved by the great trunk of Cuthbert (see Figure 52). This point of interest saves the court from boredom, drawing people around to it. Likewise, the pump in Cathedral Close, 'roughly in the middle', enriches the sense of enclosure of the tree-scattered lawn.

Building fronts
Family of entrances
Street windows

In all this sameness.
In all this variety, we never feel lost.

(Alexander *et al.* 1977: 145)

Enough said.

Life and death

The character of nature cannot rise without the presence of consciousness of death.

(Alexander 1979)

'Quality' is undefinable, rough, with a blurred edge, nothing totally exact or fixed. Nothing could (or should) last forever.

Death and life. Death with life. Continual, gradual process of disintegration and regeneration. That is how cities work – layer over layer over time.

Think of archaeologists and their work. They chip away strata of time. Think of that building down Silver

Figure 52 *St Cuthbert's statue on Palace Green.*

Street, stripped to its half-timber and brick skin, stripped of seventeenth-, eighteenth- and nineteenth-century additions. What is 'original' anyway?

Durham is an onion, a sum of its layers. Peel it away and nothing remains . . .

A city will live as long as it is allowed to change. We are not advocating a 'slash and burn' architecture. Then again, surely total preservation and fossilization eventually cripple and petrify any city, however good the original intention is?

Part of Durham's charm is to be found in the layers that have built up over time; a jumble of textures along South Bailey; the tantalizing idea that medieval façades lie below those of the severe nineteenth century; the mix of activities, a newly fitted-out W.H. Smith next to an old covered market; the art gallery across a gym, above a bakery, next to a bank . . .

And all this could wither away . . .

Whatever nurtures a city, strangles it too

(Jonathan Raban, *Soft City*).

Durham is a city grown up on the banks of the river, born of the church, weaned on political opportunism and enriched by the work of many generations. A cluster of servant buildings below the twinned towers and powers of Church and State across a common green.

Can that which gave it life, take it away too? Possibly. Think . . .

Think of the Wear, protecting the infant town. Think how it must have held off intruders; then think of it constricting Durham, restricting its growth outwards.

Think of the church, of how the cathedral now so dominates the town, the 'cathedral city'. Forever typecast, forever stereotyped.

Think of how the university stepped in just as the Church and State began to wane. How it must have promised new life, injected energy at first; and now, it has grown to such an extent, buying up properties through the city, Durham is almost as much a university town (and a 'nice' one at that) as a cathedral city.

A place for a summer's walk, a day-trip city from London. Live there? It's unimaginable, somehow.

A one-use town is a recipe for boredom. Part of the problem lies in the fact that Durham is too easily categorized. (London, for instance, could hardly be called a one-liner.) Perhaps, if alternative hearts around Old Elvet or at Milburngate are developed, there will be scope for some growth.

PATTERNS AND EVENTS

The more living patterns there are in a thing – a room, a building, or a town – the more it comes to life as an entirety, the more it glows, the more it has this self-maintaining fire, which is the quality without a name.

(Alexander 1979: 123)

Figure 53 *Durham still maintains its vitality.*

Urban growth and architectural detail in a city appear to be under the influence of the planner-designer, but once a community has taken hold, the community itself can, and must, control the life of the city. Historically, this has been easy to see, although perhaps the Prince Bishops may have taken on the role of city planners. Today it is less apparent who controls the life and growth of the city.

The broad mix of people who use the city of Durham, including (or even especially) the tourists, is what helps to encourage the vitality of the city. Durham has characteristics which the visitor can identify as being common to many European cities or towns: the cathedral, the castle, the market square, the river, the narrow streets, rooftops and alleys. These trigger off a series of responses. Certain things are supposed to happen in these places, and the familiarity of locations helps to give people clues as to how to behave.

The Market Place, for example, is a place to meet people, to use the telephones, as well as being a place to shop. The castle is not just a place for the tourists to visit, but is also a venue for banquets and functions, and is constantly used by students. The cathedral has moved on from merely being a centre of religious activity to being a place for jazz concerts, and is a spectacular glowing display when it is floodlit at night. Green spaces by the river banks provide a place for retreat and alternative activities from those encouraged by the hard landscape of the city.

Common occurrences and everyday incidents can be 'events', but they cannot sustain a city. Even if someone is merely performing a routine activity, such as brewing fresh coffee or listening to a favourite piece of music, it can nevertheless give pleasure to the passer-by. These are harmless and enjoyable activities, but sometimes routine can also breed apathy, antisocial behaviour and even violence.

A city must have goals or dreams, events where people can unleash themselves in socially sanctioned activities. Traditionally, the market square would have provided the perfect set for street theatre, strange visitors and travelling merchants exchanging stories. Sadly, the modern market has become predictable, tacky, and exactly like any other in Britain.

Apart from tourism, Durham is sustained by sporting and cultural events. Cricket and hockey have recently put Durham on the sporting map. In addition to these, the city is host to a series of congresses, rallies, marches and conferences in the summer months. The biggest of these is the Miners' Rally. 'Durham's Big Day' occurs every July. Miners and their wives gather together behind lodge banners to process along the streets, ending their journey at the sports ground, where they listen to a series of political speakers and union leaders.

Durham, for all its faults, is a more than suitable venue for these events. The expansive green spaces outside the peninsula are perfect for large numbers of people to gather and rub shoulders. They are not far from the city centre, with its wide pedestrian streets and narrow alleys which are ideal for processions and parades.

It is occasions such as the Miners' Rally, bringing large numbers of local people together, which maintain Durham's vitality (see Figure 53). Cambridge, for example, has been stifled by academia. Life outside the colleges has become dull. Fortunately for Durham, it is not solely reliant on its university, but on a broad spectrum of individuals and activities that serves to unite the city and continues kindling its 'self-maintaining fire'.

EPILOGUE

> Durham isn't very lively,
> Fairly pretty,
> Faded glory,
> A gently, gently, petrifying,
> Gentrifying
> Castle Town, Cathedral City.
>
> The curving Wear,
> flowing near,
> Has stopped both Scot
> And marshalling-yard blot.
> It still sustains a pulsing heart;
> Four arteries,
> Now filled with less religious blood.
>
> Railway station,
> Tourist information,
> Christmas shopping,
> Easter swotting.

Breathing within this iron lung;
Survival assured,
But future obscured.

Patterns change
And so too this 'quality-with-no-name'.
And what remains
Gradually grows older
(And 'nicer' . . .?).

(Ng Wai Keen)

REFERENCES

Alexander, C. (1979) *The Timeless Way of Building*, New York: Oxford University Press.

Alexander, C., Ishikawa, S. and Silverstein, M. (1977) *A Pattern Language: Towns, Buildings, Construction*, New York: Oxford University Press.

Cullen, G. (1971) *The Concise Townscape*, London: Architectural Press.

Eliade, M. (1961) *The Sacred and the Profane: The Nature of Religion*, trans. W.R. Trask, New York: Harper & Brothers.

Outram, J. (1988) 'Bracken', *Architectural Review* 183 (January): 44–8.

Raban, J. (1975) *Soft City*, London: Fontana.

FURTHER READING

Clack, P. (1985) *The Book of Durham City*, Buckingham: Barracuda Books.

Pevsner, N. (1983) *The Buildings of England: County Durham*, Harmondsworth: Penguin.

Portland, Oregon

100 People in cities – with a case study of Portland, Oregon

David Lewis, Alan Simpson and Charles Zucker

We need – more urgently than architectural utopias, ingenious traffic disposal systems, or ecological programmes – to comprehend the nature of citizenship, to make a serious imaginative assessment of that special relationship between the self and the city; its unique plasticity, its privacy and freedom.

(Jonathan Raban, *Soft City*, 1974: 250)

PEOPLE IN CITIES: THE AMERICAN INSTITUTE OF ARCHITECTS URBAN DESIGN ASSISTANCE TEAM (UDAT) PROGRAMME

In 1989 the American Institute of Architects (AIA) concluded a study of twenty-seven trends that could shape the future of American architecture and cities. When asked what the architect's single greatest contribution to the twenty-first century would be, a large percentage of the 200 nationally renowned experts examining these trends said 'designing liveable communities'.

Today, many communities are engulfed in change and are rethinking public policies that shape their physical growth and development. But the public process that helps a community create its 'vision' of the future, that is shared by the community at large, is not always clearly understood.

American communities evolve through a process some call 'design by negotiation'. That process requires the participation of competing interest groups, citizen coalitions, and public agencies – public scrutiny is viewed as a community design imperative. If architects are to play a leading role in designing communities of distinction under this democratic system, they must be prepared to help at the local level with technical assistance and 'user-friendly' technical information.

Unique among the design disciplines, urban design deals three-dimensionally with environmental interrelationships at a scale far larger than architecture and thus enables decision-makers to think more comprehensively, more carefully, about a community as a whole. Urban design involves several disciplines, such as economics, sociology, engineering, political science, and transportation, working in close co-operation. It provides us with the conceptual ability to develop and implement plans that cross the traditional boundaries that often subdivide a community or region. Urban design gives us tools to visualize – in advance – the results of our plans and to analyse how they will achieve a community's vision of itself.

Over the past twenty-five years more than 100 communities across the United States have benefited from the AIA Urban Design Assistance Team programme. The technique is slowly being introduced into Europe, in Britain and Russia. 'People in cities' will review the UDAT methodology, refer in general to numerous examples of the programme, and will concentrate on one major case study, Portland, Oregon.

PLANNING WITH PEOPLE: A STORY BY DAVID LEWIS[1]

Our story begins with a town meeting. Three hundred and fifty people are crammed into a small church hall. They sit in rows on uncomfortable wooden chairs. No one has to tell them that their city and neighbourhoods are in trouble. The boarded-up shops on Main Street, the peeling paint and sagging porches of the houses in the older neighbourhoods, the closed-down mills up-river, brooding and smokeless, the unemployed in food lines, and the exodus of young families to Texas, Alaska and California in search of other futures, tell them that.

What decade are we in? The 1890s? The Great Depression?

Where is this city? In the Northeast? The Midwest?

Located below the escarpments of hills rich in coal seams, for a century it has been a one-industry town: iron and steel (see Figure 1). But today foreign steel is cheaper than domestic steel. The challenge of the future is to find a new economic base. The mayor has appointed an Economic Revitalization Committee (ERC) of twenty-one men and women – lawyers, bankers,

Figure 1 *Located beneath the escarpments of coal-rich hills, the city was for a century a one-industry town: iron and steel.* (Source: *Batchelor and Lewis 1986*)

merchants and trade union officials. The ERC in turn has called in professional help and has taken a step back in time. It has convened a town meeting to open up for public debate the crisis facing the city.

Many decades have gone by since the last town meeting was held in the city. There was a time when town meetings were quite usual and any issue in the public interest could be debated. In fact town meetings are one of the oldest of the US democratic traditions, dating back to the earliest urban settlements in New England. But as government became more bureaucratic and regulatory, town meetings became less frequent, until they died out altogether. The revival of the tradition at this critical moment for the city has been enthusiastically publicized by the local newspapers and television station, and the mayor has been applauded for his initiative. Banners have been strung across each end of Main Street and the organizers have driven through every residential street with loudspeakers.

The meeting

A cable television camera beams the proceedings into hundreds of sitting rooms in the metropolitan area, so that people who cannot make it to the meeting this hot summer evening can be part of what is going on. And a telephone hook-up put together by a local popular disc jockey, with complicated wires trailing all over the place and speakers propped up on window sills, encourages citizens to 'phone ideas into the church hall and to hear the response their inputs generate.

Planners, architects, economists and other professionals appointed by the ERC are on hand to explain the technical aspects of the crisis. The mayor and council are there to hear the debate. After all, it is important for them to understand the mood and priorities of the people when they come to make the crucial political decisions that lie ahead. The debate begins by being intensely focused. The consultant economist speaks. He uses charts to put the depressing events facing this city into the setting of the national recession. The crisis here is symptomatic, he says, of the crisis facing many other cities in the Northeast and Midwest, including giants like Detroit, Pittsburgh, Cleveland and Chicago. Coming closer to home, he explains how high-sulphur coal has become progressively more expensive to process and how importing cheaper foreign steel fits into the picture of US international trade.

The two steel mills up-river closed three months ago, and no one knows if they will open again. Another mill down-river is on half-time. All three are obsolete and need huge investments of new capital if ever they are to come back. The city's only department store went bankrupt two weeks ago. It is on the main square opposite the domed court-house and back-to-back with the market-house.

But the city cannot rely on traditional sources of public funding. Categorical grants to aid cities have been cut from the national budget. New local resources have to be found to replace them if trends are to be reversed.

Old timer

The people listen respectfully. They find the economist's speech to be cold comfort. An old man gets up and begins to talk. He is not used to speaking in public. But he doesn't talk about urban economics. Nor does he talk about the steel mills. This is odd because everyone knows that the old man has worked all his life in the furnaces. Instead of addressing the issues that the economist talks about – the decline of industry and the erosion of employment – the old man begins talking about the town, the way it used to be when he was a boy. The economist senses that already with the very first speaker the meeting is drifting off the point and tries to intervene. Another man leaps up and says angrily, 'Hey fellow, this is our meeting. You sit down and listen. Let the gentleman say what he has to say.' The old-timer continues.

He tells about his youth, about the time when the market-house, and the church beside it, and shops around the square with shopkeepers' families living in apartments over the shops, were the centre of his community long before there was a department store; about how his grandmother made the dark breads with molasses in them that his mother in her sky-blue dress and long white apron sold on market days; about how people would row their skiffs up-river to bring vegetables and meats and cheeses, and buy weekly supplies; about how his father and uncle on his mother's side worked the coal barges; and about how the cobbled streets rang with the metallic clatter of steelworkers' boots and the hooves of horses and the crunch of wagon wheels as bales of wires and machinery parts were transported to the railhead from a dozen workshops and fabricators long since put out of business by the centralization of the big mills.

Historical society woman

An earnest young woman picks up where the old man left off. She is a member of the local historical society. She tells the meeting that before the department store came there were indeed small shops all around the square, just as the old gentleman has said. The department store, she says, was part of a national chain. But the parent company was too cheap to put up a new building. So instead it hollowed out the interior walls of the old shops, and covered their façades with curtain wall to make it look like a new building. 'I think those old façades are still there,' she says.

The telephone rings. Someone is calling in from outside. The voice crackles from the loudspeaker like dried sticks: 'Yes, indeed, those old façades are still there! I was a carpenter in the construction crew that put the curtain wall up.' 'Maybe,' says the historical society young lady, 'now that the department store is out of business, we can find a way of taking that cheap curtain wall down and putting our main square back.' A row of older people sitting together clap vigorously.

A black mother

A black woman rises to her feet. She is obviously uncomfortable about speaking in public and in front of a television camera. But what she has to say is as eloquent with images as the old-timer's speech had been.

She speaks about a part of the city simply called Westside, the residential streets that used to exist near the big mill up-river. 'The streets were brick and lined on each side by shade trees and clapboard houses with front steps and porches where families could sit on summer evenings, talking with passers-by and keeping an eye on the children's street games. Yes, most of the houses were poor and every spring the river would flood, and the pollution from the tall chimneys of the mill was strong, especially in the autumn when the fog clung to the river. But the houses were owned by the families that lived in them, and were painted white or blue. There were corner stores and local churches, and as you walked up the street in the evening you knew from the smells what everybody was cooking for dinner.

'Then along came the city planners and they said the district was blighted. They told us the floods make the place unhealthy. None of us knew that before. So all the families were evicted and dispersed. Many were too old and poor and tired to start again. They didn't get much for their homes, so they went into public housing. That's what our family had to do. But there we can't own our houses. And income restrictions are imposed on us. If our kids work hard and get through college, they can't live in our community because they earn too much. Poverty and segregation and failure are built into our personal lives.

'The only structures in our old neighbourhood that were not knocked down were three of the churches [see Figure 2]. They are still standing there among the weeds. Every Sunday people come from all over the city to those churches. We call ourselves the absentee community. The architects had big plans for Westside. They were going to build a levee along the river to keep the floods back. And there were to be new houses all strung together, townhouses they called them, and apartments with shops in some of them, and a park along the levee. Everything depended on the levee. Then the federal government cut the national budget for flood control. So nothing was ever done. The model of what the architects wanted to build is still up there in City Hall. We can't live in a model. Not that we would want to live in what they designed for us anyway. No one ever asked us what we wanted. They just went ahead and designed what they thought we ought to have. You see, we don't want to live in apartments or town houses that look like brick boxes with flat roofs. We like to have individual houses with porches, with our own gardens

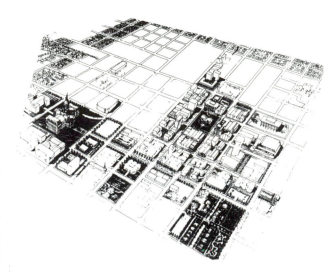

Figure 2 *Three churches were the only structures in the old neighbourhood that were left standing.* (Source: *Batchelor and Lewis 1986*)

at the back. And we didn't ever want those levees that could close us off from the river. We don't mind the floods. We have lived with them all our lives. We were born with them. They only come for a few days in the spring. And our houses and porches were raised up anyway, with front steps and back steps. But no one asked us.'

Common factors

The speech is greeted with general applause. Other speakers follow. Calls on the telephone hook-up come in. The architects have pinned up huge sheets of paper on the walls and are recording with broad flow pens the things the citizens say. Commonalities begin to emerge. At the core of almost everyone's remarks is a resentment against far-away government and big institutions, and against decisions being made without citizens' input. The big mills have knocked out the small fabricators and distributors. The big department store chain has covered up a sequence of small shops which had the shop-keepers' families living in the upper floors. Two regional shopping centres located north and south of the city have drained the commercial strength of the old down-town. Westway has been demolished to make way for government-sponsored housing that was never built. In each case the small textures of individual ownerships and initiatives have been corroded and replaced by remoteness and centralization, and when the national economy went into recession the big elements lacked the nimbleness to respond.

But the market-house survives. It is being joyously rediscovered. At its stalls you can still buy home-made breads and sausages, the sauerkrauts and pasta that reflect the ethnic heritage of this pluralist city, and the produce of small farmers is piled on the counters as though it is spilled each dawn from an unseen cornucopia.

Insights

As the architects write on the large sheets of paper they find themselves seeing the city with insights that are new and exciting to them. They perceive an urban tradition different from the traditions they had learned about in the universities or were promoted in the architectural journals. Indeed, they are seeing the city not from the outside, in terms of its form, but from the inside, in terms of its life. Most of the people in the meeting know nothing of classical history and the sources of eclecticism, and contemporary architecture with its sheer skins of glass, aluminium and pre-cast concrete is perceived as cold in its aesthetics and remote from their everyday lives, a technological language reflecting the power of big money and big institutions.

Two speakers, one of whom is a young pharmacist who operates a drug store on Main Street, even apologize for what they call their lack of education. They like the architects personally and don't want to insult them by saying that they would rather see nothing happen than have more of the ailing downtown razed to make way for modern office and apartment building of the kind that have already gone up here and there in the city, set back and surrounded by asphalt parking areas and blighting the historic sequences and texture of the streets.

But the architects begin to see it differently. All architecture is interventionist. However, the body language of intervention betrays the sensitivity, or lack of it, of clients and designers to local contexts. They suddenly see themselves as symptomatic of the many gaps the meeting has revealed – the gap between bureacratic agencies and the public, between centralized corporations and local initiatives, between contemporary architectural practice and inherited urban form.

At this point the ERC chairman calls for a brief intermission. There are coffee, soft drinks and other refreshments on a long table at the back of the hall. This gives everyone a chance to greet one another and to talk informally, and also to look at some of the maps the architects have pinned up around the room, before the meeting starts up again.

Grids

It is important to know that this city is in basic respects a typical Middletown, USA. It has a population of 85,000. Its unvarying grid of streets collides with the river on the west side where the mills are, and the escarpments of coal-bearing hills to the north and east. To the south the grid simply joins the chequerboard geometry of farmlands as the land opens up to the plains of the Midwest corn belt (See Figure 3).

To fly over the United States from coast to coast, over mountains, lakes, rivers and deserts, is to cross a con-

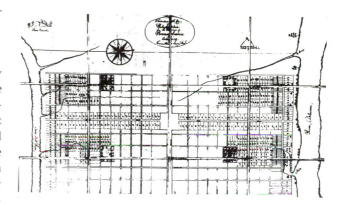

Figure 3 *The unvarying street grid of a typical Middletown, USA.* (Source: *Batchelor and Lewis 1986*)

tinent of majestic size and power. But it is over these agricultural plains of the Midwest that one is aware not only of nature's power but of humanity's dimensions. The plains are subdivided by rectangular grids as exact as graph paper. Within the grids are farm buildings, neat clusters of small white cubes far below, each cluster equidistantly spaced from the next, a white farmhouse, two or three white barns, and a grain tower, built around a square farmyard. And the grids extend for hundreds of miles. Hundreds of miles of equivalence. Looking down on these neat farmlands from an airliner it is not hard to visualize how endless the sky and vast the continent must have seemed to the early explorers and migrants as they inched and hewed their way over the mountains and across the rough scrublands and plains. But once orthogonal geometries had been applied to the open continent by the surveyors and engineers of the eighteenth and nineteenth centuries, huge territories from the Ohio to the Rockies were mapped and became measurable and comprehensible. The geometries, in a word, provided under the endless sky a precision of place and an identity of human scale.

In the history of urbanism nothing quite parallels what happened in the United States in the territorial expansion of the eighteenth and nineteenth centuries. Literally hundreds of new towns were laid out. Often they took their geometry from the rural grids, as the city did. After all, that was the quickest and simplest thing to do. Subdivide the rural grid into streets and subdivide the blocks into building lots. And just as the rural grids continue straight on, regardless of whatever rivers or lakes or hills might lie in their path, urban grids also become meshes thrown across every kind of topography, from the flat land or plains to the extreme topographies of hillsides and valleys. You can see the grid entering the city and continuing through it and out on the other side. Downtown streets and blocks are the same widths and sizes as they are in the residential neighbourhoods. Civic squares are simply unbuilt blocks with a courthouse in the middle and with steps and paving or with trees and lawns within the grid. Grid streets go right on by them. Even when rivers pass through cities with ribbons of parkland along their banks, the grid picks up and continues on the other side until it becomes the rural grid once again.

The architects have brought to the meeting an 1842 map of the city that they have borrowed from the public library. It is yellow with age and ragged at the edges like a dry leaf in winter. The streets are all there and so are the civic spaces. The blocks are subdivided into lots. But the map is so early, there are still very few buildings: just a few tightly knit sequences at the city centre, and the rest an armature, lines on paper, waiting to be filled out.

How did the city get filled out (Figure 4)? All across America one of the most extraordinary events in human history occurred in the second half of the nineteenth century. Tens of thousand of immigrants poured in from all corners of the earth, from the old nations of Europe, but also from the Far East and Latin America, joining those who were already here from Britain, France and Africa, some drawn by the promise of a new life, by jobs in the mills, on the railroads and on the land, in a new nation dedicated to an optimistic dream of democracy and opportunity, others brought by oppression in their own countries of origin, yet others the children of slavery. So they came from many cultures and religions, speaking many tongues, bringing with them vivid echoes of homeland traditions. And cities, like this one, were laid out ready to receive them, with unvarying blocks, lots and set-back lines, and a piece of land for every family to build on. Pattern books of standard house plans and specifications, in accord with standard lot sizes and street frontage requirements, provide basic building boxes, which in turn became vehicles for the richest variety of options, hips, mansards, dormers,

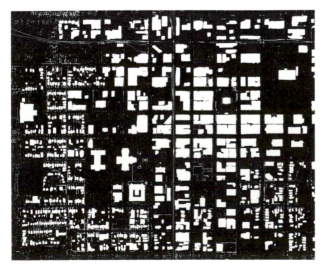

Figure 4 *The street grid filled in during the extraordinary mass immigration of the second half of the nineteenth century.* (Source: *Batchelor and Lewis 1986*)

turrets, cornices, brackets, pediments, bays, doorways, stained glass and rails; a grammar, syntax and vocabulary for the most richly textured language of urban streets in the world, a common urban language in which every family speaks on its façade to say who it is, yet through which it bears a formal and equivalent relationship to the whole.

Looking at maps pinned up on the wall, the citizens instantly recognize where they live. The architects listen in fascination to what people say as they describe to each other their block, their neighbours, and their family's relationship to shops, schools, churches and the city centre; and the architects become aware that what they are hearing is not at all the boredom of the equivalent grid, but its success as an armature that provided holistic interrelationships of extraordinary variety. And as they think about that they see that the grid is really only equivalent when it is seen on a map. In reality the way the network of streets lies over the contours and runs to river, hills and plain gives every block and every vista an individuality to which the densities, uses, and architectures of the city respond.

A young man speaks

When the town meeting resumes the chairman of the ERC says, 'Where do we go from here?' And a young man who has not spoken before gets up and tells the meeting how he and his wife left New York City three years ago and chose deliberately to settle in this city because it was small. 'True, we have problems here, problems that are symptoms of yet far larger problems affecting not just our city but many other cities as well, problems that are national in scale, and although they affect us deeply we cannot solve them on our own. But we have a lot of things we can do if we set our minds to it, and a lot of resources to draw on. The first thing that happened to my wife and me when we came was that our neighbours gave a block party to greet us. We quickly discovered how friendly the whole city is. Everyone knows everyone else. We can get together, as we have done this evening. We can form action groups to get the things done that we know we can do for ourselves.

'We have a city in a beautiful setting, among the hills and beside a beautiful river. Have we ever advertised our hills, with their woodlands and fruit farms? And look at our river, with its uncared-for river banks strewn with garbage: have we ever thought what a marvellous riverside park that could be? Then we have block after block of historic architecture. But we have felled our street trees and permitted historic commercial buildings to be covered with cheap curtain wall and plastic signs.

'We have heard in this meeting about the market-houses. Yet have we thought how symbolic they are of the ethnic heritages that are living in all of us, and that make our culture so rich? Where in the city do we have a place for food festivals, ethnic dances, theatre, jazz or bluegrass? We complain that our public agencies are not responsive to the voices of the citizens, but we forget that our officials are citizens too.

'The budgets they spend for our streets, schools, parks and housing are our own tax money. And one of the things we can do right now is develop a plan of action for Westside that is truly responsive, simply by starting to work with those citizens who refer to themselves as the absentee community.

'So let us begin with the things we can do. We can create a historic district, and restore our historic architecture on a building-by-building basis, which has always been our tradition. We can replace our street trees, and develop a riverside park. We may not be able to start up the steel mills again without investment on a national scale, but we are certainly far more likely to find a developer for the department store property who will put our old façades back, if we let the world know that this city has the determination to pull itself up by its bootstraps, and that it has a plan composed of action-oriented increments in which the citizens are directly involved.'

The young man's speech is greeted with a standing ovation. The chairman immediately suggests that the people form smaller groups on a voluntary basis. The architects, planners and the economist split up and work with each group far into the night – one group on historic architecture, another on parks and street-scapes, yet another on public and private investment partnerships: and so the planning begins.

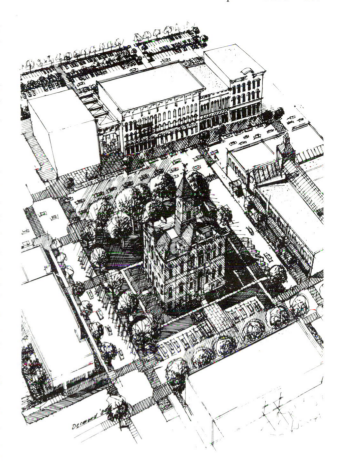

Figure 5 *The city is our most intricate art-form, our richest self-expression.* (Source: *Batchelor and Lewis 1986*)

URBAN DESIGN: A DEVELOPING TRADITION

> The building of cities is one of man's greatest achievements. The form of his cities always has been and always will be a pitiless indicator of the state of his civilisation.
>
> (Edmund N Bacon, *Design of Cities*, 1967: 13).

The city as art and amenity beyond shelter

If cities are the mirrors of their citizens, they are also our most intricate art-form, our richest self-expression (see Figure 5). City-making is the only art-form in which every citizen continually takes part, and it is the only art-form that never reaches a conclusion, short of total destruction.

Night and day people the world over are working on their cities in myriad ways. We knock things down, build things up, change this, change that. With every demolition the city suffers partial death; with every new construction it undergoes a partial rebirth. Each day we are challenged by the city, by what to destroy and what to conserve, by how to remedy obsolescence, by which new need gains priority over other needs; every day we

worry about competition and investment, we scheme and draw, we negotiate and make commitments.

Architects and planners like to think that the city can and should in some way be brought to book: that its form can succumb to reason. Several of the great architects of this century – notably Le Corbusier, Frank Lloyd Wright and Mies van der Rohe – designed utopian visions of how the city should be. We should sigh with relief that they never had the opportunity to build their visions. Clean, spacious, rational, their cities are essentially inhumane and static in time, without evolution; and to operate them, government would have to be dictatorial, and locked into a perpetually receding past.

Cities are not like that. They are organisms that are always changing in space and time (see Figure 6). Not everything involves planners and architects. Indeed, when you get down to it, very little does. Countless agendas are going on simultaneously every day. Even as you are reading these words, developers are dreaming and scheming about strategies to seize new opportunity, and make investments that will permanently alter the city; economists are interpreting the impacts of statistical projections; bankers are meeting with lawyers; and political strategies are being designed – all affecting the lives of citizens.

Figure 6 *The city is an organism that is always changing in space and time.* (Source: *Batchelor and Lewis 1986*)

Some actions being planned at this very moment are perhaps quite large: a new highway, for example, plunging into the historic core of the city. But not all large actions are physical. A change in zoning law, or an escalation in the national interest rates diverting the anticipated core of capital investment, will alter the macro-forms of cities as permanently as large-scale construction. Other actions are quite small and easily overlooked: painting a porch, making a garden, planting street trees along the sidewalk of a neighbourhood street. Yet the cumulative affect of small actions such as these are as important in their own way, possibly even more important, than the highway. They are the direct hands-on utterance of the city's quality and the pride of its citizens.

If all this *appears* to be complex and chaotic, and beyond the control of one person, or even one group of people, the short answer has to be that it *is*. But once again, let us draw a sigh of relief. From time to time, control in cities is seized by a powerful political group or a network of vested financial interests; the pendulum swings away from democracy; and to the degree that this happens the city no longer belongs to the citizens. But inevitably the pendulum swings back again. And when it does, we are always astonished to find that the apparent complexity of cities is well within the comprehension of ordinary citizens, provided they are openly enfranchised and informed.

In the past twenty years we have witnessed innumerable revolts by citizens against pyramidical concentrations of political, economic and design power. Some of these, such as in Eastern Europe, have engulfed nations; other are confined to cities, towns or even neighbourhoods. Enfranchising citizens in determining the future of the communities they live in has been a tradition in several countries for centuries. The United States provides perhaps some of the clearest models of how 'democracy' in action can affect urban design, from the macro-form of urban regions to the detailed quality of

streets and squares. These models of democracy are there for us to look at, evaluate, and redesign to meet our contemporary needs.

In the seventeenth century, communities of settlers in New England, no doubt reacting to the feudalism they had left behind in Europe, governed themselves by means of 'town meetings' as described in our short story, a tradition that continues to this day in towns in Maine, New Hampshire, Vermont and Massachussetts. The principle was simple. Any citizen could bring up any matter that he or she held to be in the public interest, and it would be debated and voted on by the community as a whole. Gradually the definition of citizen became related to local taxes, particularly property taxes, for then citizens had a direct investment in their community through the taxes they paid, and had the right to a say in how public money would be spent. It was in support of this tradition that Thomas Jefferson, a hundred years later, wrote the following words at the end of the eighteenth century:

> I know of no safe despository of the ultimate powers of society but the people themselves; and if we think them not enlightened enough to exercise their control with a wholesome discretion, the remedy is not to take it from them, but to inform their discretion.
> (quoted in Bachelor and Lewis 1986)

And the rights of citizens to be heard, and to have a direct voice in government at all levels from local to national, were entrenched in the United States constitution.

The new world city

It is quite possible to see the grids, on which most American cities are based, as metaphors for democracy. If you look closely at the plans of cities all across the country, you will find that the grid subdivides cities into equal blocks, and each block is subdivided into equal lots, on which individual buildings are built. And if we look at the zoning laws that govern land uses and building permits, we will find rules that control setbacks, heights, sideyards, and percentages of building coverage; and providing you respect these regulations, you can build in whatever style you want to. Consequently, when you look at American cities you are struck by the incredible range and richness of architectural surface and gesture, and in the residential areas you are struck by the continuities of front lawns and backyard open spaces.

Carrying the physical metaphor back to the American notion of democracy, we see that every property owner is encouraged to treat his or her building as a body language of self-expression and individuality, within a geometry of democratic equivalence in which every citizen is an individual, yet is equal in government and before the law. Flying across the United States, you look down on the agricultural grid stretching north and south, east and west, like a giant sheet of graph paper as far as the eye can see, and within this macro-grid one sees at intervals the micro-grids of towns and cities, reminding us that all across the land everyone's front door is related to everyone else's front door, town and country, within a powerful and simple geometry.

However, democracy will languish if we do not continually refurbish it. Lord Acton was right: power corrupts. Special interests, unchallenged, even in a democracy, will exercise power to the limits that we permit them. One of the most important examples in this century of the refurbishment of democracy was the Civil Rights movement. Martin Luther King was not a revolutionary. Quite the contrary. His effort was once again to make democracy work in a contemporary setting for all people, black and white, young and old, poor as well as rich, and to open up democratic procedures to outsiders as well as to those within the established halls of power. His great Civil Rights marches, in which he gathered up men and women from all walks of life, reminded us, through the power of the images on our television screens every news hour, that our cities and urban societies are wholes, and that within their holism the poorest alleyway, where the homeless seek shelter in abandoned buildings and where drug addicts shoot up in doorways strewn with the broken bottles of cheap liquor, is ineluctably connected to the boardrooms of banks and corporations.

It is commonplace to think that, because of the speed and magnitude of change, the complexity of the city is beyond the comprehension, and therefore beyond the discretion, of citizens in exercising control of the policies that affect their lives. The following are examples of very recent escalations of complexity in the United States: the population of Florida grew by 37.1 per cent between 1960 and 1970, and between 1980 and 1995 it is anticipated to increase by another 40 per cent. In California regional growth around San Diego has averaged 1,000 new inhabitants per week for the past fifteen years.

The metropolitan region of Los Angeles has grown faster than any other in the industralized world. With 3.4 million people within the jurisdictional boundaries of the city and 12.5 million in the burgeoning metropolitan areas, the region's annual gross of $240 billion in manufactured goods and services is ahead of entire countries like Australia and Spain, and its port handles almost 40 per cent of the volume of the entire United States. But Los Angeles also attracts the poor and the unskilled. The region has the highest immigration rate in the nation, resulting in rapidly changing demographics. In 1970 Hispanics represented 14 per cent of the metropolitan population; by the year 2000, Hispanics are likely to be the majority ethnic group, making up 50 per cent of all people, in spite of a huge growth in other ethnic groups as well. The city has every problem of segregation, homelessness, poverty, slums and crime. The region as a whole is in desperate need of affordable housing for low

and moderate income levels. Projections indicate that half a million new residential units will be required in the next twenty years; while – just to keep level with growth – 10,000 new units of housing per year are needed, starting now, for families in the low and moderate income ranges.

Statistics of this kind are no more than headlines: they do not reveal the detail of the city; nor do they reveal the changes in macro-form that crises of this kind bring. The macro-form of the Los Angeles region, like many other metropolitan areas in the United States, has changed from having a dominant downtown to being a multi-nodal region. The expressways that were designed to bring commuters into the city have turned out to be centripetal rather than centrifugal. Developments that began as shopping malls have grown into full-blown town centres. For example, two malls, South Coast Plaza in Costa Mesa and Fashion Island in Newport Beach, opened in the 1970s with modest two-storey office buildings around them. But the population of Orange County grew almost two and a half times, from 898,000 in 1970 to 1,932,000 in 1980, a rate of growth that continues unabated. Today each of these malls is surrounded by over 2 million sq. ft. (190,000 sq. m.) of office space. Charles Lockwood and Christopher Leinberger write:

> Words like city and suburb are becoming meaningless in Los Angeles, because they imply a metropolitan area that has followed the traditional development pattern, in which a dominant high-density business centre is surrounded by a dependent and mostly residential periphery. Searching for a more appropriate terminology, some of Southern California's urban experts now describe Los Angeles as a series of 'constellations' forming a 'galaxy'.
>
> The metropolitan area is coalescing into approximately eighteen 'urban village' cores, which are business, retail, housing and environmental focal points in the low-density cityscape. Some of these cores, like Pasadena and Westwood, are decades-old communities that have grown into regional hubs. Others ... have emerged out of bean fields or suburban sprawl. The metropolitan area's largest urban-village core is, of course, downtown Los Angeles, which finally gained a big-city skyline during the recent office building boom.
>
> (Lockwood and Leinberger n.d.)

This transformation of the macro-form of the 2,000 sq. mile (5,000 sq. km.) metropolitan region of Los Angeles from its mononuclear past into a loose federation or hegemony of centres, linked by highways and by a new rapid transit system, is simultaneously occurring in several other metropolitan areas in the United States. In another article the same authors write:

> Few cities have been transformed by the urban-

village phenomenon as rapidly as Atlanta, whose metropolitan region has a population of 2.2 million, having gained 90,000 residents last year and 78,000 the previous year. In 1980 downtown Atlanta was the metropolitan region's unchallenged centre for all kinds of office employment. Although urban-village cores were emerging around shopping malls at the intersections of major highways, office space was limited. And neither in the appearance of the buildings nor in the quality of the tenants were the fledgling urban-village cores any match for the downtown high-rises . . .

By 1985 (just 5 years later) this pecking order had changed completely. Downtown Atlanta had gained 4.3 million sq. feet of new office space, but the Perimeter Centre at the I-285/Georgia 400 intersection, due north of downtown, had gained 7.6 million, and Cumberland Galleria, at the I-285/I-75 intersection, northeast of downtown, 10.6 million. Many of the new buildings were gleaming, architecturally distinguished highrises of the kind that once had been built only downtown. If the present trend continues, the amounts of office space in both the perimeter centre and the Cumberland/Galleria urban-village cores will easily surpass the amount in downtown Atlanta by 1990.

(Lockwood and Leinberger 1987)

Without going into further detail, suffice it to say that the same general phenomenon is occurring in Dallas, Chicago, Washington DC and other major metropolitan areas, including even those older industrial centres of the Northeast such as Cleveland, Pittsburgh, and Buffalo, whose metropolitan population is static or diminishing, and yet whose old urban form is similarly fragmenting into a hegemony of urban cores on sites that until recently were green fields on the periphery.

The results are potentially extremely dangerous. These new peripheral 'urban villages' are for the most part concentrations of shopping, recreation, and offices serving higher income suburban residential areas. They are predominantly occupied by middle and higher income whites, college educated and young, who have moved outwards from the city to escape from the poor and the segregated, taking with them their capacity to pay city taxes. The effect is a deepening crisis for the centre city, which becomes increasingly the location of poverty, drugs and violence, unemployment and homelessness, accompanied by a diminishing tax base and increasing physical obsolescence.

However, the situation at the same time presents opportunities to approach these complex problems on a series of different scales simultaneously. The largest of these scales is of course the region – and the challenge of seeing it holistically. And the smallest scale is the residential block within an urban or suburban neighbourhood. In between lies that crucial scale of the core

and its service, the 'urban village' within the 'galaxy' with its population equivalent to that of a medium-sized town, 50,000–100,000. This is most certainly a scale at which citizens can participate in 'hands-on' planning and urban design processes aimed at identifying the future of the urban village and its role within the regional matrix.

A new focus on localism and participation: citizen empowerment

And so, because of the magnitude and speed of change, are metropolitan areas like these so complex that they are beyond the comprehension of their citizens? Recently in Los Angeles the American Institute of Architects set up a pilot series of interdisciplinary teams to work with six communities at this intermediate scale. Called the Los Angeles Design Action Planning Teams (LA/DAPTs), each was composed of planners and urban designers, economists, developers, politicians, specialists in transportation, architects and environmentalists; and the purpose was to conduct public hearings concerning the goals and issues of each community, and to explore them in workshop settings, leading to not only a greater public understanding but also to consensus on a series of concrete recommendations. Each team produced a fully illustrated report containing responses to a variety of social and residential challenges, core centres, and linkages between cores within the region. These reports then formed the basis for a conference at the full regional scale, as a component of a national Vision for America initiative.

In a cogent way, these LA/DAPTs are a contemporary version of the New England town meeting. They fulfil – in a modern metropolis of unforeseeable dimension – Jefferson's dictum of informing the public discretion, so that recommendations and public consensus may be arrived at in open public meetings, and in the light of the fullest possible public disclosure, accompanied by open discussion from all points of view.

What were the recommendations? They responded to every aspect of policy, from the political and economic to the environmental; and the presence on each team of specialists in salient disciplines enabled the exploration of alternatives to proceed at the most informed intellectual level. The six LA/DAPTs conducted so far represent, of course, only a fraction of the region. Nevertheless several of the recommendations have already moved forward toward implementation, including amendments to the regional rapid transit system to open up linkages with the centre city as well as between the new cores within the galaxy, integrated housing, sites for industries to employ lower and moderate income workers as well as the skilled, and the redesign of core areas to provide precincts for new small businesses.

The importance of the LA/DAPTs is that they are the first initiative to respond to the 'galaxy' form that metropolitan areas are assuming, by conducting a sequence of open hearings and workshops community by community, thus developing a detailed composite of recommendations throughout the huge and complex region. The idea is based on an earlier initiative by the American Institute of Architects, the Regional/Urban Design Assistance Team programme, or R/UDAT, which began in 1967. The founders of this programme saw urban design as essentially an activity that had two main aspects to it. The first was that contemporary urban problems are multi-faceted, and require the inputs of several disciplines. The second was that no one knows the detail and the aspirations of communities better than the inhabitants themselves, and that in every community there exists, in the people who live there, an extraordinary wealth of knowledge and creativity to tap into (see Figure 7).

In just over two decades, more than 120 cities and towns in the United States have hosted teams composed of some of the nation's finest professionals in their fields: economists, sociologists, planners, engineers, lawyers, bankers, environmentalists and architects. Here is a brief account of what happens.

First of all, a R/UDAT is never foisted on any community. Every R/UDAT is invited. During the months before the R/UDAT the city is visited by members of the AIA's R/UDAT Task Group and the team chairperson, who conducts informational meetings to understand the issues, and ensure that relevant background documents are collected and available for team members. A critical outcome of these preliminary visits is that they enable the R/UDAT Task Group to select and invite the finest interdisciplinary talents available from across the nation to address the specific issues that have surfaced.

The all-volunteer team of specialists is then selected and briefed with the background materials which spell out key local issues and provide essential technical information. The team is joined by up to twenty students from nearby schools of architecture, urban design and planning. The host community reimburses all expenses. No fees are paid; indeed, to ensure their objectivity, no team member, or the firm or university he or she might belong to, is permitted to accept any commission for work that results from the R/UDAT's recommendations.

The team's four-day visit generally begins with a physical inspection of the study areas by foot, bus, boat or helicopter. Members confer in a succession of meetings with representatives of the city establishment – mayor and council, planning officials and zoning boards, the Chamber of Commerce, banking and development interests, and community leaders. They study background documents. On the second day there is a town meeting, the first of two. The town meeting, which may last all day, with a morning devoted to plenary sessions and the afternoon to workshops on specific issues, is open to all interested citizens, and its purpose is to hear from individuals and non-establishment groups, neighbourhood organizations, block clubs, and ethnic and minority representatives. Some citizens who have been heard at this first town meeting or at the meetings with the city establishment may be asked back for more detailed one-on-one discussions (Figure 8).

At workshop discussions following the town meeting, team members synthesize what they have learned and hammer out their theoretical approaches to the recommendations they will make. They will also make an outline of the report and allocate tasks among themselves for its production.

The bulk of the production work takes place in 24-hour non-stop work session starting at dawn on the third day. To begin with the team meets to set up the comprehensive interrelationship of their recommendations. Then each team member works on his or her own, or in small groups, in spells of two hours or so, interrupted by team meetings to compare progress and discuss the details of the recommendations that are beginning to emerge. As the day enters night, report writing begins and three-dimensional drawings by the urban designers and architects explore the impacts on the physical environment of recommendations and

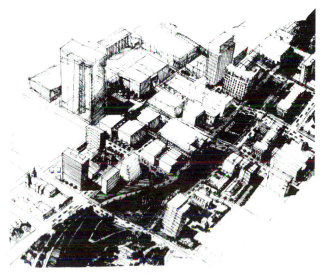

Figure 7 *Contemporary urban problems are multi-faceted, and no one knows the aspirations of a community better than the inhabitants themselves.* (Source: *Batchelor and Lewis 1986*)

Figure 8 *The RUDAT team generally makes a four-day visit, starting with a physical inspection of study areas.* (Source: *Batchelor and Lewis 1986*)

priorities in economics, social issues, and planning. By dawn of the fourth day a 60- to 100-page report is sent to the printers, and the tired team members at last go to bed. That evening, the second open town meeting is held at which the team members present their recommendations, using slides and the report which has come back from the printers in the nick of time.

To appreciate the innovation the R/UDAT initiative represented some twenty-five years ago, we have to cast our minds back to the top-downwards attitude of the architectural profession at that time. Architects and local government officials 'knew what was best', and no local communities had any say. But the 1960s was the decade when the Civil Rights movement was issuing its call for a return to democracy. Those who were shut out insisted on being enfranchised and heard. R/UDAT was the first initiative to respond.

What R/UDAT demonstrated was that urban design is essentially an interdisciplinary activity. Complex situations in cities need a working forum in which the finest specialists in the many aspects of any given problem-solving process are brought together with the citizens whose priorities and insights have to be listened to. Urban design became a method of exploring in three-dimensional graphics the impact on the built environment of alternative courses of action as they emerged from these discussions. Millions of dollars of development have been generated in over a hundred American cities as a result of the adoption of R/UDAT recommendations.

The impact on private practice, and also on the way architecture and urban design are taught in American universities, has been profound. R/UDATs themselves are merely potent four-day demonstrations. But the teams have always included prominent architects and educators. From small beginnings a quarter of a century ago, the application of the principles of interdisciplinary teams and of citizen enfranchisement to urban design practice has thus become widespread. There are no major cities in the United States that do not now have urban designers on their planning agency staffs, and most public planning and urban design contracts insist on citizen participation in the course of the work.

As a result, many of the major architectural practices have urban design arms that conduct their work side by side with economists, sociologists, historians, engineers, lawyers and other professionals who are subcontracted for specific aspects, and the process is set out along a time-line that may stretch for several months, and that includes open workshops with citizens structured to elicit consensus and accountability every step of the way. And in many universities, contextual processes set up as 'urban laboratories' are now built into the curricula of urban design and architectural education. Consequently a whole generation of architects sensitive to contextual accountability is now emerging. It is doubtful whether the clock can be turned back.

URBAN DESIGN IN ACTION PORTLAND, OREGON: THE LAST PLACE IN THE DOWNTOWN PLAN.

I have seen a lot of scenery in life, but I have seen nothing so tempting as a home for man than this Oregon country . . . you have a basis here for civilization on its highest scale, and I am going to ask you a question which you may not like. Are you good enough to have this country in your possession? Have you got enough intelligence, imagination and cooperation among you to make the best use of these opportunities?

(Mumford 1938)

If the AIA UDAT process could be compressed into one basic principle – that the measure of a successful city rests with its people, the strength of their attachment to a place and their ability to join forces in the ongoing process of regeneration and improvement or city-making – then Portland, Oregon, offers a perfect example.

In both the fact and in the spirit Portland evokes an easy-going self-confidence that is rooted in its visible history of accomplishment. There is in Portland a unique 'sense of place' that comes not only from the exceptional look and feel of its downtown – its compact size, the tree lined busy streets, and attention paid to every detail and ornament – but from the way in which the people take pride in making their city liveable.

Portlanders seem to understand the current and potential value the city holds for them, and the time it takes to make changes. As one prominent city developer said at a public meeting in 1983, 'city growth is an ongoing thing to be measured in decades; politicians, by necessity, hold a two-to-four year vision; it takes committed citizenery, business and investment interests and strong community leadership to make changes over the long haul'.

Historical development of Portland city plans

Of two major land claims filed in 1845, establishing Portland's downtown core, the one recorded by Captain John Couch identified and established patterns for future development. Convinced that Portland would make an ideal port on the Williamette river, Couch located a shipping and mercantile business in the far north end of downtown, then only woods and pasture land, and now known as the North Downtown Area. Couch subdivided the land in 1865 using a street pattern oriented to true north, contrasting with the magnetic north orientation of the adjacent downtown business district. This simple shift in geometry, perpendicular streets intersecting diagonal streets, created a strong new avenue (West Burnside) which became a symbolic dividing line between the Central Business District and the North Downtown Area.

Although various plans and policies were prepared

over the years to better connect the two downtown areas, Couch's subdivision had set the course of industrial and transportation development in the North Downtown area which would continue through the 1970s. In 1912 Edward H. Bennett produced the *Greater Portland Plan* which introduced Portland to the 'City Beautiful' era with plans for wide boulevards and improved access to the downtown area 'through the transportation hub north of downtown'; in 1943 Robert Moses produced the Portland Improvement Plan which re-emphasized the support role the North Downtown Area played for the Central Business District; and in 1972 citizens working with the City Planning Department produced the *Downtown Plan*, which created a bold vision for revitalizing the Central Business District, with considerably less attention by now being paid to the North Downtown Area. The new plan set its sights on an economic and urban design image of the Central Business District, which has by 1991 been almost completely implemented as originally conceived. Whilst each successive plan did provide some limited guidance for the North Downtown Area, the primary objectives of

each plan were nevertheless to build upon and improve the economic and physical qualities of the Central Business District (see Figure 9).

By the early 1980s the Downtown Plan had been virtually completed. New office buildings and hotels changed the skyline; plans for a new central civic space were completed, and a riverfront park was created through the demolition of an expressway that had separated the Central Business District from the riverfront. Few development sites remained within the Central Business District, but the city continued to express its need to grow.

The need

From 1972 through to 1982, as the Central Business District flourished under the Downtown Plan, the North Downtown Area continued its downward spiral toward functional obsolescence (see Figure 10). Major changes in the nation's economy were taking place during this period, particularly within industrial and transportation sectors, and Portland too was feeling the effects of this process.

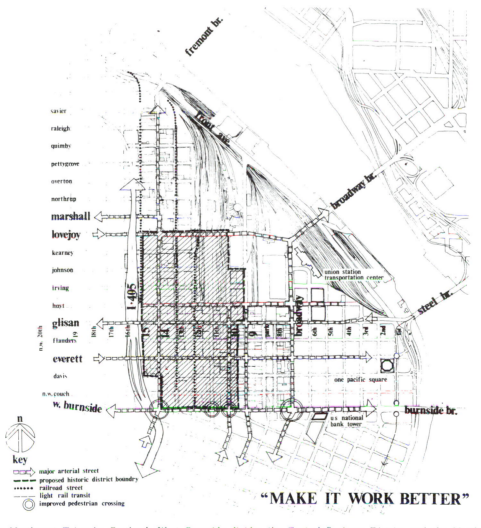

Figure 9 *The Northwest Triangle, Portland; West Burnside divides the Central Business District and the North Downtown Area.* (Source: *AIA RUDAT 1983*)

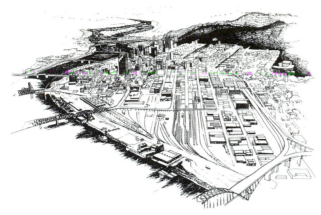

Figure 10 *Existing conditions in the Northwest Triangle, 1983.* (Source: *AIA RUDAT 1983*)

The need for railroad and river frontage multi-storey masonry warehouse buildings on narrow streets within an historic downtown core, was replaced with a need for

access to trunk routes, generous single-storey ware-house space, and market outlets in new suburban in-dustrial and retail centres. Even though the North Downtown remained an active wholesale and retail centre, the public's image of the place worsened as more and more buildings were vacated and businesses moved to outlying suburban locations. The area came to be perceived as a dangerous place known only for its derelict buildings, boarding houses, homelessness, crime and dark, uninviting streets.

The stark contrast between the Central Business District and the North Downtown Area was brought sharply into focus by several events in the early 1980s. The first was the construction of the American Bank building on Burnside Avenue, the tallest building in Portland at the time. From the top floor executive suites, occupants could see a bustling downtown to the south, and weed strewn railroad yards and run-down boarding houses to the north.

The second event was demonstrated through the

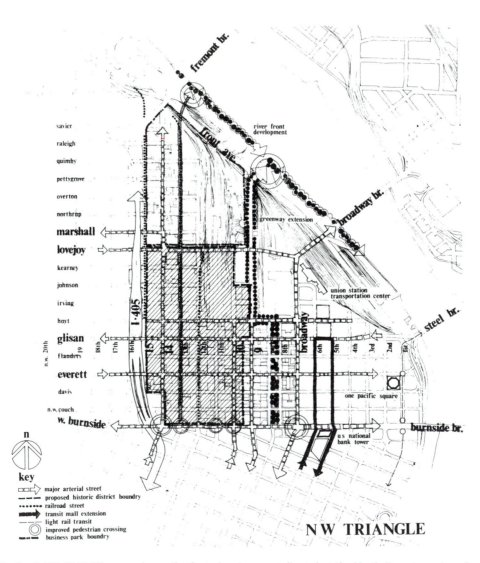

Figure 11 *The Portland AIA RUDAT proposal was the first planning event directed at the North Downtown Area for over 100 years.* (Source: *AIA RUDAT 1983*)

difficulty encountered by the Oregon School of Design in getting special consideration for a zoning change in order to allow the School to move into one of the area's many vacant warehouses; the willingness of developers and new tenancies to move into the area was being inhibited by prevailing zoning laws, the area was not ready for development.

A third significant event was expressed through the need to address problems created by the area's homeless population. In 1981 a citizen advisory committee, together with the Department of Planning, produced the *North of Burnside Land Use Plan*, which dealt with low-income housing and social services, size limitations on new development, creation of the Transportation Centre, and improved pedestrian ways, among other issues. Whilst this plan was important, it dealt with only a small portion of the area and did not capture the public imagination in the way the 1972 plan had done for the Central Business District, or indeed in the way Captain Couch's vision set the ground rules for development in 1865.

If the North Downtown Area was to prosper it needed a new guiding vision, one that would take up where the 1972 plan left off, and in the process develop the vision initiated through the plan of 1865.

The programme

In March 1982 the new president of the Portland Chapter of the American Institute of Architects proposed that, in commemoration of the tenth anniversary of the *Downtown Plan*, the Portland Chapter invite a R/UDAT to visit Portland, meet with its citizens and leaders, and prepare a report of recommendations for the future. This would be the first planning event that specifically addressed the North Downtown Area in over a hundred years (see Figures 11 and 12).

The Portland AIA president recognized the need for an open, public planning process if a new vision for the area were to take hold. He also understood the need for strong visual images towards recommendations that people could readily appreciate, the multi-dimensional social, economic and physical development issues that required a team approach, and the need to utilize a process that would help local organizations and leaders to inspire action and rally for needed improvements.

The Portland AIA Chapter formed a thirteen-member local 'steering committee' to guide the process. The committee was made up of members of the Bureau of Planning, City Council members, local investors and developers, citizen groups, architects and urban designers. A project executive director was enlisted to manage the overall process, who, together with the steering committee, spent some nine months preparing for and carrying out the R/UDAT programme.

An application to the national AIA was prepared by the steering group; a research sub-committee was created to produce a briefing document describing the growth and demise of the North Downtown Area; a sub-

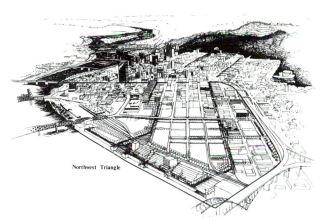

Figure 12 *Proposed business park and historic preservation district, Northwest Triangle.* (Source: *AIA RUDAT 1983*)

committee of area business representatives was formed and a fund-raising programme collected some $20,000, which contributed towards total estimated costs, including volunteers and donated services, of over $180,000. Students were enlisted along with business people, city officials, professionals, and citizens to participate in the process.

At the national AIA level, the Portland proposal for assistance was evaluated, and several reconnaissance visits by national R/UDAT committee members were scheduled to advise the local steering committee on pitfalls to be avoided and opportunities to be seized in setting up the R/UDAT event. This process allowed the national AIA to work with the Portland AIA Chapter to acheive a level of 'readiness' for the intense R/UDAT process and to lay the groundwork and plan for the follow-up on recommendations.

After approval of all aspects of the pre-R/UDAT work by the national AIA R/UDAT committee a letter of commitment was delivered to the Portland AIA notifying them that a team of volunteer professionals would be selected and visit the city on a date to be agreed for a period of four days.

A workroom site was found to accommodate over forty professionals and set up on the ground floor of the Portland School of Design with folding chairs, a large public meeting space, drafting tables, word-processing area, and food area. The Portland AIA R/UDAT programme was in place.

The process

On Thursday, 6 March 1983, an eight-member team selected by the national AIA arrived in Portland. The team included two urban designers, two architects, a regional economist, a preservationist, a transportation planner and a social scientist. Backed by a support team of twelve local professionals and students from the University of Oregon and the Oregon School of Design, the team began by touring the area.

The local steering committee asked that the team

address three main issues in assisting current owners, tenants, city planning agencies, developers and citizens to better understand the value of the North Downtown Area, to initiate discussions about the area's future, and to recommend short- and long-term actions for both public agencies and private groups.

In the first twenty-four hours, the team interviewed over sixty public officials, developers, property owners, tenants and representatives of community organizations. The support team began to produce base maps and research specific issues requested by the professional team.

Working in small, issue-based groups, the team discussed and tested ideas and assumptions. By late Friday evening the team realized that they had to re-define their original assumptions and verify the method and scope of the study; the problems needed greater clarity; there were no urgent or pressing issues requiring immediate action. This absence of a crisis atmosphere represented a challenge and a potential to the R/UDAT team; they needed to 'unearth' the area of missed opportunity and focus attention on what could be, creating a new future, a new reality, rather than attempt to correct conditions which had led to the area's demise. The preservation of the existing, and often historic, building stock was seen to be important since it created a special image and a competitive position when compared to other discrete areas within the city or the region; and while the area was obviously in transition, it became clear that the existing building stock lent itself to multiple uses which could add vitality and investment opportunities to the city.

The R/UDAT process is essentially small group 'brainstorming' sessions during which different team members test hypotheses and urban design concepts at numerous spatial scales, and reassemble to debate differing viewpoints. By Sunday afternoon several dominant themes began to emerge as the team con-tinued to 'sort and order' ideas. The process was punc-tuated only by group dinners. These welcome breaks allowed the R/UDAT and local steering committee members to share ideas and test concepts from the resi-dent communities' perspectives.

By Monday morning a photo-ready typeset and illustrated copy of the final report was sent to the printer, who returned 500 copies of the 50-page docu-ment to a public meeting by 5.00 p.m. that evening. The report was entitled *The Last Place in the Downtown Plan.*

The Response

The Last Place in the Downtown Plan offered Portland a new and optimistic view of the North Downtown Area as a whole – a greenway system linked riverfront devel-opment with development of the street-grid blocks, and a new historic district recognized the re-use potential of the nineteenth-century warehouse buildings along 13th Street (see Figures 13 and 14) – and the establishment of

an area-wide business and community organization.

Specifically the R/UDAT recommended:

• the establishment of a North Downtown Area Association to bring a coalition of business owners, property owners, developers, residents and city officials together to decide upon the area's future (see Figure 15);

• the extension of the Williamette Greenway con-necting the South and North Park blocks into a continuous Portland riverfront;

• the development of the riverfront through a mix of commercial, office and retail activity between the Fremont and Broadway bridges (see Figure 16);

• the completion of the inventory of historically and architecturally significant building, the establish-ment of a mixed-use preservation district, and the creation of a fifty-block historic area for guiding

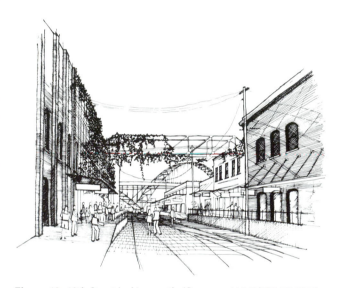

Figure 13 *13th Street looking north.* (Source: *AIA R/UDAT 1983*)

Figure 14 *13th Street looking south: a typical infill.* (Source: *AIA R/UDAT 1983*)

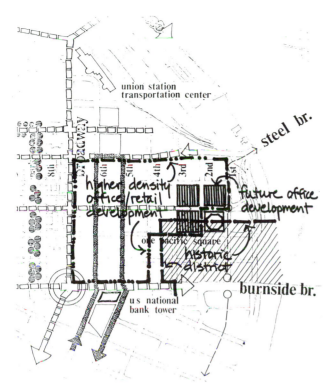

Figure 15 *Burnside office/retail area.* (Source: *AIA R/UDAT 1983*)

North Downtown Area and including recommendations on the future land-use character of six sub-areas, sensitive redevelopment along the riverfront, new transportation facilities, and historic resources proposals.

The newly formed community and business associations kept pressure on the city and citizens to address the new value they had begun to see in their area by holding seminars which informed and debated emerging concepts in creative and adaptive re-use of existing structures and historic preservation. New and adventurous investment in the area became visible, especially within the 'public realm' or the 'street environment' through new landscaping, soft and hard, new paving, seating and street lighting, providing the area with an enriched character and quality, which in turn attracted interest from investors and developers who began to see a new confidence emerging, in both the area and its long-term future. In 1986 a Property Owners Association was formed primarily to establish the North West Thirteenth Avenue Historic District, by 1990 a powerful and pro-active group leading in collaboration with the City Planning Department the North West Historic District improvement programme (see Figure 17).

The City authorities became active in the area independently through major environmental improvement works to Front Avenue along the riverfront, facilitating development and the continuation of the river

adaptive re-use and new construction that would house a mixture of professional, service, distribution, and arts activities;

- the development of the Union Station rail centre and the relocation of the Bus Station to create a transportation terminus;
- the establishment of a twenty-block business park in the railyards;
- and the creation of new neighbourhood support services for residents and transients.

The follow-up

Although not formally or officially adopted by the City of Portland, the R/UDAT study proved to be a highly effective catalyst, creating a turning-point in the history and development of the North Downtown Area, and serving as a basis for every subsequent study that would take place from 1983 to 1992. It stimulated community and business interest and imagination in the area, which has lead to some impressive follow-on programmes and projects directly and indirectly connected with the R/UDAT initiative.

Almost immediately, several investors and developers with interest in the area used the R/UDAT study to establish the North West Triangle Business Association to work with the City; and R/UDAT recommendations prompted the preparation of the *North West Triangle Report*, a R/UDAT follow-up policy document adopted by the City Council in 1985, focusing on the

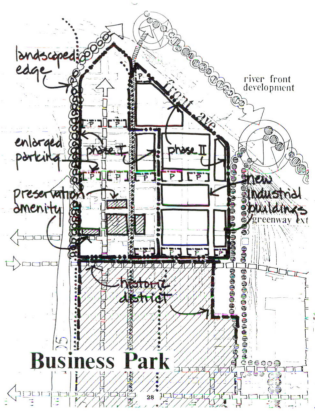

Figure 16 *The riverfront development and business park.* (Source: *AIA R/UDAT 1983*)

'greenway'. In 1987 they took a significant risk in acquiring Union Station as a development opportunity, ahead of the private sector, and it is now a major civic amenity and public attraction.

Individual developers now use the R/UDAT study regularly to interest investors in the area's potential through the conversion of factory loft buildings for apartments, small business accommodation, and studios for designers and artists, whilst the R/UDAT recommendations on transportation and infrastructure improvements are being actively pursued through collaborations between the city authorities and community and business interests (see Figure 18).

By 1988 it was clear that the R/UDAT programme and recommendations had provided the initiative for a number of development projects, urban design proposals, and the establishment of numerous advocacy groups within the area, and that a substantial update in the form of another plan was needed to co-ordinate and build upon these earlier successes. In 1988 the Portland *Central City Plan* was produced. This latest in the succession of plans directed at the city's Downtown and North Downtown has now created the opportunity for the use of a 40-acre (16-hectare) tract of the Railroad Yards to be used for housing, identifying the area as suitable for

residential development: the North Downtown now prepares to house its own live-in community, in one of America's most 'liveable' cities (see Figure 19).

In February 1990 the City of Portland released the *North Downtown Development Programme*, which now lists the variety of projects leading towards the revitalization of the area, ranging through transportation and infrastructure improvements, street and public realm enhancement projects, historic structures, housing, and economic development. The document is a testament to planning and urban design in the City of Portland, and to the energy of the city, and its citizens and business and community interests, in seeking to implement those plans. The report states simply: 'the *Last Place in the Downtown Plan* R/UDAT study and report stimulated considerable interest in the North Downtown Area, which led to the establishment of several area organizations, and has inspired further in-depth studies by the Planning Bureau. It also set the stage for the Thirteenth Avenue Historic District designation and subsequent initiatives' (*North Downtown Development Programme* 1990).

The late 1980s have witnessed the slow introduction of R/UDAT techniques, in community and urban planning, into Europe, most notably in Britain – in

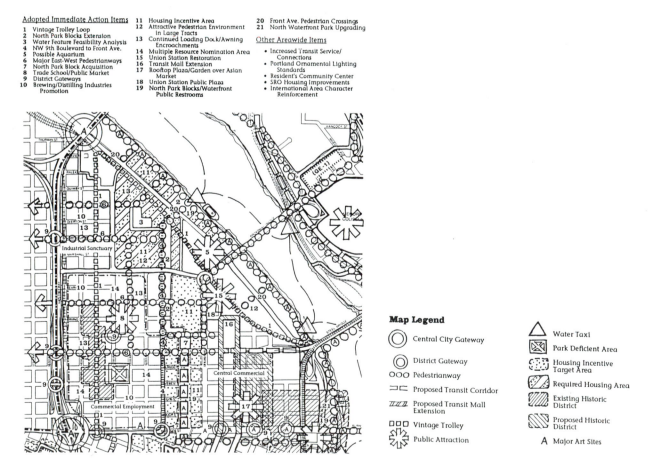

Adopted Immediate Action Items
1 Vintage Trolley Loop
2 North Park Blocks Extension
3 Water Feature Feasibility Analysis
4 NW 9th Boulevard to Front Ave.
5 Possible Aquarium
6 Major East-West Pedestrianways
7 North Park Block Acquisition
8 Trade School/Public Market
9 District Gateways
10 Brewing/Distilling Industries Promotion

11 Housing Incentive Area
12 Attractive Pedestrian Environment in Large Tracts
13 Continued Loading Dock/Awning Encroachments
14 Multiple Resource Nomination Area
15 Union Station Restoration
16 Transit Mall Extension
17 Rooftop Plaza/Garden over Asian Market
18 Union Station Public Plaza
19 North Park Blocks/Waterfront Public Restrooms

20 Front Ave. Pedestrian Crossings
21 North Waterfront Park Upgrading

Other Areawide Items
• Increased Transit Service/ Connections
• Portland Ornamental Lighting Standards
• Resident's Community Center
• SRO Housing Improvements
• International Area Character Reinforcement

Map Legend

◎ Central City Gateway
○ District Gateway
○○○ Pedestrianway
⊐⊏ Proposed Transit Corridor
⊿⊿⊿ Proposed Transit Mall Extension
□□□ Vintage Trolley
✳ Public Attraction

△ Water Taxi
⊠ Park Deficient Area
▦ Housing Incentive Target Area
▨ Required Housing Area
▨ Existing Historic District
▨ Proposed Historic District
A Major Art Sites

Figure 17 *Central city plan.* (Source: *Thirteenth Avenue Urban Design Plan 1990*)

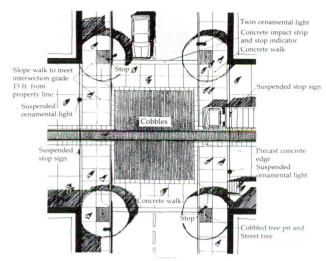

Figure 18 *Proposed intersection improvements.* (Source: *Thirteenth Avenue Urban Design Plan 1990*)

Figure 19 *A schematic view of 13th Street looking south.* (Source: *Thirteenth Avenue Urban Design Plan 1990*)

London and Newcastle upon Tyne – and in the early 1990s in Russia – in Moscow and Perslavl Zalesky. R/UDAT programmes in Europe have been a response, both by community and professional teams, to the clear successes that have taken place in the United States, and specific R/UDAT projects have been advised by those with direct experience of the AIA programme. The need, and the opportunity, exists in Europe for a R/UDAT programme to be developed through the 1990s; what is so far lacking is the procedural and organizational structures, like those offered by the AIA, through which such a programme might be promoted and implemented.

NOTE

1   David Lewis's story was first published in *Spatio e Società* 22, June 1983.

REFERENCES

AIA Regional/Urban Design Assistance Team (1983) *The Last Place in the Downtown Plan*, Portland, Oreg.: American Institute of Architects.

Bacon, E.N. (1967) *Design of Cities*, New York: Penguin.

Batchelor, P. and Lewis, D. (eds) (1986) *Urban Design in Action*, Raleigh, NC: AIA/Student Publication of the School of Design at North Carolina State University.

Bennett, E.H. (1912) *Greater Portland Plan*, Portland, Oreg.: Bureau of Planning, City of Portland.

Central City Plan (1988) Portland, Oreg.: Bureau of Planning, City of Portland.

Downtown Plan (1972) Portland, Oreg.: Bureau of Planning, City of Portland.

Lockwood, C. and Leinberger, C. (1987) 'How business is reshaping America',

——— (n.d.) 'Los Angeles comes of age',

Mumford, L. (1938) 'Address to the Portland Club',

North Downtown Development Program (1990) Portland, Oreg.: Bureau of Planning, City of Portland.

North of Burnside Plan (1981) Portland, Oreg.: Bureau of Planning, City of Portland.

Northwest Triangle Plan (1985) Portland, Oreg.: Bureau of Planning, City of Portland.

Raban, J. (1974) *Soft City*, London: Collins Harvill.

Thirteenth Avenue Urban Design Plan (1990) Portland, Oreg.: Bureau of Planning, City of Portland.

Contributors

Chris Abel is senior lecturer in architecture at the University of Nottingham. He graduated from the Architectural Association School of Architecture in 1968 and has taught architecture at universities in many parts of the world, including North and South America, the Far East and the Middle East. He has written numerous publications on the theory and criticism of architecture in both the developed and developing world. His books include *Transformations* (Roberts Press, Malta, 1987) and *Renault Centre: Norman Foster* (Architecture Design and Technology Press, 1991).

James S. Ackerman is Arthur Kingsley Porter Professor of Fine Arts, Emeritus, at Harvard University. He is the author of books on Michelangelo and Palladio, and, most recently, the villa. He was Slade Professor at Cambridge in 1970. He is a Fellow of the American Academy in Rome and is Corresponding Fellow of the British Academy.

Robert Adam is a director of Winchester Design Architects, an architectural practice in the south of England. He is a practising classicist who applies the principles of classical architecture to a wide range of building types, drawing on the enormously varied history of classicism, and embracing Romanesque and even proto-Gothic architecture. He gained a scholarship to the British School at Rome in 1973. His designs have received awards in Britain and the USA and have appeared in major national and international exhibitions. He is the author of *Classical Architecture: A Complete Handbook* (Viking, 1990).

Bruce Allsopp was, until retirement, Reader in Architectural History at the University of Newcastle upon Tyne, and a Fellow of the Royal Institute of British Architects. He is a founder member of the Society of Architectural Historians of Great Britain, and was Chairman from 1959 to 1965. He has exhibited widely as a water-colour artist and is registered as a typographer and book designer in the Art Workers' Guild, of which he was Master in 1970. He was chairman of the Independent Publishers' Guild (1971–3) and president of the Federation of Northern Art Societies (1980–3). His published work includes more than fifty books – with many now in translations – mostly on architecture, art and social philosophy, as well as seven novels. In 1962 he founded Oriel Press Ltd, of which he remained chairman and managing director after becoming a director of Routledge & Kegan Paul Books Ltd.

Stanford Anderson is Head of the Department of Architecture at the Massachusetts Institute of Technology in Cambridge, Massachusetts. He holds a professional degree in architecture from the University of California at Berkeley, and a Ph.D. in history of art from Columbia University, New York. He is the editor of, and a contributor to, *On Streets: Streets as Elements of Urban Structure* (MIT Press, 1986). He has published extensively on architectural theory, early modern architecture in northern Europe, American architecture and urbanism, and historiography.

Jorge Anzorena is a lecturer in the Department of Philosophical Anthropology at Sophia University, Tokyo. He has a Ph.D. in engineering from the Department of Architecture at Tokyo University. He is the representative in Asia of SELAVIP (Servicio Latino-Americano-Asiatico de Vivienda Popular), the Latin American/Asian People's Housing Service.

Jay Appleton is an Emeritus Professor of Geography in the University of Hull, where he spent most of his working life, with shorter appointments in Australia, New Zealand and North America. He holds degrees of the Universities of Oxford, Durham (King's College, Newcastle) and Hull. His special interests lay in historical and urban geography and transport, but increasingly in the aesthetic aspects of landscape. He is a Fellow of the Royal Geographical Society and the Royal Society of Arts, an Honorary Associate of the Landscape Institute and an Honorary Life Member of the Landscape Research Group, of which he was twice Chairman.

Peter Aspinall is currently Faculty Research Co-ordinator and Reader in the Faculty of Environmental Studies at Heriot-Watt University, Edinburgh. After studying psychology, he worked on aspects of visual function and perception in areas of psychology and medicine. Subsequently, he joined the Architecture, Landscape Architecture, and Planning Schools of the Faculty of Environmental Studies.

Wayne Attoe is Professor at the School of Architecture, Louisiana State University. After studying English and art history at Cornell University, and architecture at the University of California at Berkeley, he began teaching. Later he studied architecture criticism through the Union Institute. He has taught at Louisiana State University, the University of Texas at Austin, and the University of Wisconsin-Milwaukee. His books include

Architecture and Critical Imagination (Wiley, 1978); *Skylines: Understanding and Molding Urban Silhouettes* (Wiley, 1981); *American Urban Architecture: Catalysts in the Design of Cities* (with Donn Logan) (University of California Press, 1989); and, as editor, *Transit, Land Use and Urban Form* (University of Texas Press, 1988) and *The Architecture of Ricardo Legorreta* (University of Texas Press, 1990).

Peter Baelz studied classics and theology at Cambridge University. He was ordained in 1947, and spent the first part of his ministry as a parish priest, mostly in Bournville, Birmingham. In 1960 he returned to Cambridge as Dean of Jesus College and lectured in the philosophy of religion. In 1972 he moved to Oxford to become a Canon of Christ Church and Regius Professor of Moral and Pastoral Theology. In 1980 he was appointed Dean of Durham Cathedral. He retired in 1988.

Geoffrey Baker has taught architectural design, history and theory at universities in Britain and North America. His books include: *Le Corbusier: An Analysis of Form* (Academy Editions, 1989), *Design Strategies in Architecture: An Approach to the Analysis of Form* (Chapman & Hall, 1989) and *Le Corbusier: A Study of Creativity* (Chapman & Hall, 1993). He has written articles specializing in the analysis of significant work by leading contemporary architects and is currently Distinguished Visiting Professor at the University of North Carolina at Charlotte.

Andrew Ballantyne MA, Ph.D., RIBA, is a Lecturer in Architectural History and Theory at the University of Newcastle upon Tyne. He has published in *Architectural History*, *Apollo*, The *Times Literary Supplement*, the *British Journal of Aesthetics* and elsewhere. His central concern is with the ways in which architecture is and has been understood, from the eighteenth century of the Picturesque (the subject of his doctoral study) to Byzantine concepts of the house, via a concern for current practices in the design of architecture.

Micha Bandini was born in Rome, Italy, and graduated from Rome University in Architecture in 1974. Since 1979 she has been teaching on the Architectural Association Postgraduate Programme in History and Theory. She is currently the Head of the Department of Architecture and Interior Design at the University of North London. She has lectured extensively in Europe and the USA.

Juan Pablo Bonta is Professor of Architecture at the University of Maryland at College Park. He is a member of the International Committee of Architectural Critics. He was formerly Professor of Architecture at the University of Buenos Aires. His books include *An Anatomy of Architectural Interpretation* (1975, English, Spanish, French, Russian); *Architecture and its Interpret-ation* (1977 Spanish; 1979 English; 1981 Italian; 1982 German); and *American Architects and Texts: A Study of the Names cited in the Architectural Literature* (in preparation, MIT Press).

Diana Brown graduated as an architect in 1969. On completion of a postgraduate planning course she worked in Durham County Planning Department and developed an interest in mining cottages and villages. In 1977 she was appointed as a lecturer in the Department of Architecture at the University of Newcastle upon Tyne, and registered shortly afterwards for a part-time Ph.D. on colliery cottages. After its completion, her research interests widened to include the Durham Miners' Gala and a study of Pit Head Bath Architecture.

Ronald Brunskill, OBE, has retired as Reader in Architecture at the University of Manchester, but remains active in the building conservation field. He is a Commissioner of English Heritage (and Chairman of its Historic Buildings and Areas and Cathedrals and Churches Advisory Committees), Vice-Chairman of the Royal Commission on the Ancient and Historical Monuments of Wales, Chairman of the Ancient Monuments Society and of Friends of Friendless Churches, and a member of the Cathedrals Fabric Commission of England. He is the author of *Vernacular Architecture of the Lake Counties* (Faber, 1974), *Timber Buildings of Britain* (Gollancz, 1985), *Illustrated Handbook of Vernacular Architecture* (3rd edn, Faber, 1987), *Traditional Farm Buildings of Britain* (2nd edn, Gollancz, 1987) and *Brick Building in Britain* (Gollancz, 1990), as well as many articles in learned journals.

Pieter De Bruyne (1931–87) was born in Aalst, near Brussels. He graduated in 1953 as an interior designer in the Hoger Instituut St Lucas Schaarbeek in Brussels, and taught furniture and interior design there from 1955 until his death. After graduating, he won several competitions. It was not long before his work was being exhibited all over the world, and he secured an international reputation for innovative furniture design. His designs were characterized by pure geometry, primary colours, high polish finishing and technical perfection. He was the initiator of a whole movement in which furniture became part of modern art, as sculpture to be displayed freestanding in space. His inspiration was fed by yearly study tours all over the world, from which he returned bearing numerous drawings he had made of furniture from the past. He was fascinated by the pure geometry, harmony and proportions of Ancient Egyptian furniture, which he thought to be the key of perfection. The book he was preparing on that subject remained unfinished at the time of his death.

Stuart Cameron graduated in sociology from the University of Exeter. He worked as a town planner in local government before becoming a lecturer in the Department of Town and Country Planning at the University of Newcastle upon Tyne. He is the Director of the Diploma in Housing Policy and Management, with research and teaching interests in housing and in urban regeneration.

David Canter is Professor of Psychology and Head of the Department of Psychology at the University of Surrey. He is an honorary member of the Japanese Institute of Architects. His works include *Architectural Psychology* (1970), *Psychology for Architects* (1974), *Psychology of Place* (1977), *Environmental Perspectives* (as joint editor) (Avebury, 1988) and *New Directions in Environmental Participation* (as joint editor) (1988).

Sir Hugh Casson is an architect, broadcaster, artist and patron of the arts. He was Professor of Environmental Design at the Royal College of Art, 1953–75, and Provost there 1980–6. He has been a member of the Royal Mint Advisory Committee since 1972, and was President of the Royal Academy of Arts, 1976–84. He set up private practice as an architect in 1937 with the late Christopher Nicholson, and was a Senior Partner in Casson Conder & Partners, 1946–8. He was Director of Architecture for the Festival of Britain, 1948–51, Trustee of the British Museum (Natural History), 1976–86, and of the National Portrait Gallery, 1976–84, and has been awarded numerous honours and honorary degrees world-wide. He is a regular contributor as both author and illustrator to the technical and lay press. His recent publications include *Hugh Casson's Oxford* (Phaidon Press, 1988), *Japan Observed* (Bellew Publishing Co., 1991), *Hugh Casson's Cambridge* (Phaidon Press, 1992) and *Hugh Casson's Tower of London* (Herbert Press, 1992).

Amos Ih-Tiao Chang was trained as a civil engineer in China and as an architect in the United States. He is also a self-educated philosopher and is a member of the International Society for Chinese Philosophy. He received his MFA professional degree with honour (Damato Prize for best design of the year upon graduation) in 1949 from Princeton University, and the first Ph.D. in Architecture, also from Princeton, in 1951, after which he taught design there for a year. His doctoral dissertation on the theme of 'Intangibility' was published by Princeton University Press in 1956, and was reissued, with slight revision, under the new title of *The Tao of Architecture* in 1980. Chang spent fifteen years practising architecture on his own in Thailand, Singapore and Laos, before becoming an educator at Kansas State University in 1967. He became a Professor Emeritus in 1987.

Sabine Chardonnet qualified as an architect in Paris and holds a doctorate in 'Urbanisme' from the University of Paris. From 1978 to 1981 she was attached to the Centre de Recherche d'Urbanisme (CRU) and published reports on Strasbourg, Aix en Provence, Amiens and Paris. Since then she has been teaching architecture and urban design at schools of architecture in Normandy and Paris (currently Paris Villemin). She is a founder member and President of the ACEA (a council planning and research association) at St Cloud, and Council Member of the EAAE (European Association for Architectural Education).

William Charlton is a Senior Lecturer in Philosophy at Edinburgh University. A graduate of Oxford, he has taught at the universities of Glasgow, Dublin (Trinity College) and Newcastle upon Tyne, and is at present chairman of the Philosophy Department of Edinburgh. His books include *Aesthetics: An Introduction* (Hutchinson, 1970) and *The Analytic Ambition* (Blackwell, 1991), and he has contributed many articles to the *British Journal of Aesthetics*.

Brian Clouston trained as a horticulturalist at the Royal Botanic Garden, Edinburgh. His landscape training was gained at Durham University in the early 1960s. He joined the Planning Department of Durham County Council and contributed to the drawing up of many of the planning policies for Durham City, particularly those to do with the provision of new woodland, landscape conservation and the location of new building. In 1965, Clouston started his own landscape practice, concentrating on land reclamation in northern England, and inner city rehabilitation in Glasgow and Liverpool.

Birgit Cold is Professor of Architectural Design, the Faculty of Architecture at the Norwegian Institute of Technology, University of Trondheim. She has her own practice in Trondheim, started with partners Tore Brantenberg and Edvard Hiorthoy in 1964. The practice is based on awards in architectural competitions in the field of social housing. As an academic, Birgit Cold's teaching, lecturing and research have concentrated on the evaluation of quality in architecture. She taught architecture at Trondheim from 1963 and undertook ten years of research for the Foundation for Scientific and Industrial Research, University of Trondheim, 1973–83. She was a council member of the Norwegian Research Council for Applied Social Science, 1986–8, and of the Council for Social Science Research, 1982–4. She is a board member of the University Senate of Trondheim, the Norwegian Academy of Technical Sciences, the European Association of Architectural Education, the Centre of Technology and Human Values, and the Swedish Council for Building Research, Scientific Advisory Board. During 1987 she was a member of the board of the Norwegian Building Research Institute. Her research has been published in a number of journals, both within and outside Norway.

Suzanne H. Crowhurst Lennard is the Executive Director of the International Making Cities Livable Council (IMCL), editor of the *Making Cities Livable Newsletter*, and Organizer of IMCL Conferences. She is a consultant to cities in the USA and in Europe, in both the public and private sectors. She obtained a B.Arch. (Hons) from Bristol University, and an RWA Diploma from the Royal West of England Academy of Architecture, Bristol, and a Ph.D. (Arch.) from the University of California, Berkeley. Dr Crowhurst Lennard has received awards from the Graham Foundation for Advanced Studies in the Fine Arts, and the New York State Council of the Arts. While teaching at the University of California, she collaborated in the user-centred approach to teaching architectural design. She is author (with Henry L. Lennard) of *Public Life in Urban Places* (Gondolier Press, 1984) and *Livable Cities: Social and Design Principles for the Future of the City* (Gondolier Press, 1987), and the author of *Explorations in the Meaning of Architecture* (Gondolier Press, 1979).

James Stevens Curl is Professor of Architectural History at the Department of Architecture, De Montfort University, Leicester. He is a qualified architect and town planner and holds a doctorate from London University. He is a Fellow of the Society of Antiquaries of London, and a Liveryman of the Worshipful Company of Chartered Architects. He is the author of many books, including *Victorian Architecture* (David & Charles, 1990), *The Art and Architecture of Freemasonry* (Batsford, 1991), which won the Sir Banister Fletcher Award for Best Book of 1991 published in the UK, *Classical Architecture* (Batsford, 1992), *Georgian Architecture* (David & Charles, 1993) and the *Encyclopaedia of Architectural Terms* (Donhead Publishing, 1993). He has also recently contributed to *The Rattle of the North: An Anthology of Ulster Prose* (edited by Patricia Craig, Blackstaff, 1992) and to the *International Dictionary of Architects and Architecture* (St James Press, 1993).

Miles Danby is Professor Emeritus of Architecture, University of Newcastle upon Tyne, and was formerly Director of the Project Office and Centre for Architectural Research and Development Overseas. He was Head of the Department of Architecture at the University of Science and Technology, Kumasi, Ghana, 1963–5, and Professor of Architecture and Head of Department at the University of Khartoum, Sudan, 1965–70. He has also worked in professional practice in Ghana, Saudi Arabia, Spain, Sudan, and the UK. Miles Danby has written numerous articles, papers and reviews, and his books include *Grammar of Architectural Design* (Oxford University Press, 1963) and *Moorish Style* (Phaidon Press, in preparation).

Tobias Davidson, at the time of the case study, was a student on the Bachelor of Architecture course at the University of Newcastle upon Tyne.

Roger Day is a lecturer at the University of Portsmouth's School of Architecture, where his main research interests are in the role of information technology in architectural design. He is joint co-ordinator of the current initiative by the Science and Engineering Research Council to encourage and support research in the applications of information technology to the construction and transport industries.

Mark Dudek qualified as an architect in 1981. He spent three years working and travelling in Germany before returning to London to establish his own practice in 1984. He now divides his time between his Shoreditch office and the School of Architecture at Brighton University, where he is a Senior Lecturer in the Diploma School.

Stuart Durant studied architecture for a time at the Architectural Association during the Brutalist period. He then abandoned architecture for television design. In the 1970s he began teaching Design and Architectural History at Kingston Polytechnic, now Kingston University, where he has remained. He has written on Voysey and Viollet-le-Duc and has published *Ornament: A Survey of Decoration since 1830* (Macdonald, 1986) which has been translated into French, Spanish and Japanese. He has recently completed monographs on Christopher Dresser and Ferdinand Dutert's Palace of Machines at the Exposition Universelle, 1889. He was the originator of the *International Design Yearbook,* and is planning a detailed manual of architectural ornament.

David Ellis, at the time of the case study, was a student on the Bachelor of Architecture course at the University of Newcastle upon Tyne.

Tom Ellis was an architect and partner in the firm of Lyons, Israel, Ellis and Gray. He died in 1988.

Ben Farmer is a Professor of Architecture and Pro-Vice-Chancellor at the University of Newcastle upon Tyne, having previously been Dean of the Faculty of Social and Environmental Sciences. He has taught in six Schools of Architecture in three countries, and is Subject Adviser in Architecture to the Higher Education Funding Council for England and Research Assessor in the Built Environment. He is an Architectural Adviser to the Arts Council, and has many years of experience on the Boards of Architectural Education of the Royal Institute of British Architects (RIBA), the Architects' Registration Council of the UK, and the Council for National Academic Awards. He is a past Chairman of the RIBA Northern Regional Council, which reflects his commitment to the integration of Education and Practice. Professor Farmer has wide international experience as an external examiner and as a senior consultant and advisor to academic institutions. His research interests are architectural education and architectural theory, on which he has published widely.

Jane Fawcett studied Art History at the University of London, under Sir Nikolaus Pevsner and Sir John Summerson. She studied Building Conservation at the Architectural Association, and has been Tutor and Lecturer to the Graduate Diploma course in conservation there since 1977. She was Secretary of the Victorian Society 1963–76, and of the International Council on Monuments and Sites, ICOMOS UK, 1983–92. She was Architectural Consultant to the Yorkshire Dales National Park, when she revised the Statutory Lists of Historic Buildings for English Heritage; and to the English Tourist Board for whom she produced a report, *Cathedrals and Tourism,* 1979. She was a member of working parties on tourism and the environment for the Department of Employment and the English Tourist Board whose report *Tourism and the Environment: Maintaining Balance* was published in 1991. She has been awarded the MBE and Honorary Fellowship of RIBA for services to conservation. Her publications include *Seven Victorian Architects* (Thames & Hudson, 1977); and *The Village in History* (co-author; Weidenfeld & Nicholson/National Trust, 1988).

Sir Norman Foster studied at University of Manchester School of Architecture and at Yale University School of Architecture. He has worked in private practices in the USA and in the UK and has also taught at universities in both countries. A selection of his major projects includes: IBM Pilot Head Office, Hampshire, 1970; Sainsbury Centre for Visual Arts, University of East Anglia; head office for Willis Faber and Dumas, Ipswich, 1979 (first Trustees' Medal, RIBA, 1990); and the winning design in international competition for the new Hong Kong Bank headquarters, Hong Kong, 1979. Other projects include Century Tower, Tokyo, 1987, and Kings Cross London Master Plan, 1988. He has been awarded the Royal Gold Medal for Architecture, in 1983, and the Financial Times Award for outstanding Industrial Architecture and Commendations, several times, and has also gained many European awards.

Michel Foucault (1926–84) was a philosopher and historian of ideas, and was Professor of History of Systems of Thought at the Collège de France, Paris. He wrote a series of very influential and provocative books including *Histoire de la folie* (1961), translated as *Madness and Civilization* (1971); *Les Mots et les choses* (1966), translated as *The Order of Things* (1970); *L'Archéologie du savoir* (1969), translated as *The Archaeology of Knowledge* (1972); and *Histoire de la sexualité* (1976), translated as *The History of Sexuality* (1984).

Peter Fowler is Professor of Archaeology at the University of Newcastle upon Tyne. He was formerly at the University of Bristol, 1965–79, and has twice served on the staff of the Royal Commission on Historic Monuments (England). He is the author of over a dozen books, including *Who Owns Stonehenge* (jointly, Batsford, 1990); *Images of Prehistory* (with M. Sharp, Cambridge University Press, 1990); *The Past in Contemporary Society* (Routledge, 1992); and *Heritage and Tourism in the 'Global Village'* (with P. Boniface, Routledge, 1993). His main academic interests lie in the history and archaeology of farming and landscape, and in the relationships of the present with the past. He is actively involved in numerous bodies, including the National Trust (Council, Executive and Properties Committees; chairman, Archaeology Panel), and is an archaeological consultant to, among others, the Forestry Committee.

Kenneth Frampton is an architect and leading architectural critic. He is currently Professor of Architecture at the Graduate School of Architecture, Planning and Preservation, Columbia University, New York. His books include *Modern Architecture, 1851–1945* (2 vols, Rizzoli, 1984), *The Architecture of Hiromi Fujii* (Rizzoli, 1987), *Richard Meier, Architect* (with Joseph Rykwert, 2 vols, Rizzoli, 1991), and *Modern Architecture: A Critical History* (Thames & Hudson, 1980, 1992).

Dietrich Garbrecht holds degrees in architecture (University of Braunschweig), urban design (University of Stuttgart) and city planning (Massachusetts Institute of Technology). He was one of the first to publish on the behaviour and movement of pedestrians in interaction with urban space, and to claim an appropriate place for walking in urban transport policy and planning. Garbrecht has been a practising designer and planner, has lectured in many countries, and has been a freelance consultant since 1978. His work is characterized by an integration of aesthetics and usability. He is a member of professional institutes in Germany, the United States and Switzerland. In 1982 he was awarded he Germany Cities Foundation Award for the promotion of urban knowledge for his book *Gehen – Ein Plädoyer für das Leben in der Stadt* (Walking – A Plea for Living in Cities) (Beltz Verlag, 1981).

Mark Gelernter obtained his B.Arch. from Montana State University, and his Ph.D. in Architecture from the Bartlett School of Architecture and Planning, University College London. He is Associate Professor, Director of Undergraduate Studies and Co-ordinator of the Architecture Option at the College of Environmental Design, University of Colorado at Boulder. He drew all the new illustrations (and corrected many of the existing ones) in Sir Banister Fletcher's *A History of Architecture* (19th edn, ed. John Musgrove, Butterworth, 1987). He is currently working on a book entitled *Sources of Architectural Form: The Problem of Creation and Knowledge in Western Design Theory.*

Georgia Gilbertson, at the time of the case study, student, Bachelor of Architecture course, University of Newcastle upon Tyne.

David Gosling is Professor of Urban Design and Director of the Center for Urban Design at the College of Design, Architecture, Art, and Planning, University of Cincinatti, and is also State of Ohio Eminent Scholar in Urban Design. From 1973 to 1989 he was Professor of Architecture, Head of Department and Dean at Sheffield University. He previously worked as Deputy Chief Architect at Runcorn New Town, 1965–8, and Chief Architect at Irvine New Town, 1968–73, and was Editor of the Irvine New Town Plan, 1970. He is co-author of *Design and Planning of Retail Systems* (1976, 1984) and of *Concepts of Urban Design* (1984), and was Associate Editor of the *Third World Planning Review*, 1979–91.

Stephen Grabow is Professor of Architecture at the School of Architecture and Urban Design, University of Kansas. The recipient of numerous research and scholarly awards, including the Kousaku-Sha Citation (Tokyo) for the Japanese translation of his book *Christopher Alexander: The Search for a New Paradigm in Architecture* (Routledge, 1983) he was recently a Fulbright Fellow at the Royal Danish Academy of Fine Arts in Copenhagen. He is currently studying the principle of 'isomorphic correspondence' in architecture, art and science, for a book to be entitled *Affinities of Form*.

Barrie B. Greenbie is Professor Emeritus of Landscape Architecture and Regional Planning at the University of Massachusetts, Amherst. A half-century of professional life has included art, drama, architecture and city planning. He has an undergraduate degree in Drama from the University of Miami, Florida, and a Ph.D. in Urban and Regional Planning from the University of Wisconsin, Madison. He has five patents on architectural frames and devices, and his books include: *Spaces: Dimensions of the Human Landscape* (Yale University Press, 1981) and *Space and Spirit in Modern Japan* (Yale University Press, 1988).

Steven Groák is an architect and chartered builder, with a background in engineering and economics. He has taught in several UK schools of architecture and building, as well as teaching and lecturing in the USA, Sweden and Japan. For many years he was Joint Editor of *Habitat International*, an international journal of planning and building. He has made a special study of the work of Alvar Aalto, including much of the work on the relevant *Architectural Monograph* (Academy Editions, 1978). He is currently working for Ove Arup & Partners in London, UK, and has recently written *The Idea of Building* (Spon, 1992).

Ramon Gutierrez was born in Argentina in 1939. He was Professor of the History of Architecture at the Universities of Buenos Aires, Mar del Plata and Nordeste from 1967 to 1990. He has held a number of other posts, including Principal Researcher for the National Research Council of Argentina; Consultant on Unesco's Cultural Development Program for the preservation of Architectural Patrimony; and Director of the magazine *Documents of National and American Architecture*. Ramon Gutierrez is the author of more than fifty books, many of them on the subject of architecture and urban planning in Latin America.

Joseph Gutmann is Emeritus Professor of Art History at Wayne State University, and Adjunct Curator Emeritus at the Detroit Institute of Arts. He holds advanced degrees from New York University–Institute of Fine Arts, and is an ordained rabbi from Hebrew Union College–Jewish Institute of Religion, Cincinatti, from which he received a Ph.D. in 1960 and an honorary Doctor of Divinity degree in 1984. He has been a visiting professor of Art History at Antioch College, the University of Cincinnati, the University of Michigan, the University of Windsor, Canada, and the Spertus College of Judaica. He has also served as rabbi of Temple Beth-El in Birmingham, Michigan, and Congregation Solel in Brighton, Michigan. He is the author of eighteen books, including *The Temple of Solomon* (Scholars Press, 1976), *The Image and the Word* (Scholars Press, 1977), *Hebrew Manuscript Painting* (Braziller, 1978), *Jewish Ceremonial Art* (Yoseloff, 1984) and *The Jewish Life Cycle* (Brill, 1987). He has contributed over 200 learned articles to leading scholarly journals and encyclopedias and writes a monthly column, *Gutmann on Art*, for the *National Jewish Post and Opinion*.

Robert Harbison was born in Baltimore, USA and obtained a Ph.D. from Cornell University. He has lectured widely on architecture, at the Museum of Modern Art, New York, the University of Toronto, Stanford University, Cornell University, and the Architectural Association, London. Robert Harbison is the author of *Eccentric Spaces* (Knopf, 1977; Secker & Warburg, 1989), *Deliberate Regression* (Knopf, 1980), *Pharaoh's Dream* (Secker & Warburg, 1988), *The Built, the Unbuilt and the Unbuildable: In Pursuit of Architectural Meaning* (Thames & Hudson/MIT, 1991), *Creatures from the Mind of the Engineer: The Architecture of Santiago Calatrava* (London Architectural Press, 1992) and *The Shell Guide to English Parish Churches* (Deutsch, 1992).

Patsy Healey is Director of the Centre for Research in European Urban Environments, Department of Town and Country Planning, University of Newcastle Upon Tyne. She has qualifications in geography and planning, and is an expert on the theory and practice of the British planning system. Her published works include: *Local Plans in British Land Use Planning* (Pergamon, 1985); *The*

Political Economy of Land (Gower, 1985); *Land Use Planning and the Mediation of Urban Change* (Cambridge University Press, 1987) and *Rebuilding the City* (Spon, 1992).

Tom Heath was for many years a principal of McConnel, Smith & Johnson, Architects. From 1980 to 1989 he was the editor of *Architecture Australia*, the official journal of the Royal Australian Institute of Architects. He is a member of the International Committee of Architecture Critics. He is the author of two books, *Method in Architecture* (John Wiley & Sons, 1984) and *What, if Anything is an Architect* (Architecture Media Australia, 1991). He is currently University Research Professor of Design at the Queensland University of Technology.

Louis Hellman studied architecture at universities in London and Paris; B.Arch., 1962. He was cartoonist for the *Architect's Journal* since 1967. His 'archi-têtes' series of architect caricatures was first published in the *Architectural Review* in 1984. He has also published in the *Observer*, the *Sunday Times*, the *Guardian*, *Private Eye*, the *New Statesman* and numerous other periodicals. The 'Hellmanisms', a series of comic verses in the form of buildings, have been published weekly in *Building Design* since 1987. Louis Hellman has published four books, including *Architecture for Beginners* (Unwin Publishers/ Writers' and Readers' Publishing Group, 1986). In 1974 he made an animated film for BBC2 entitled *Boom*. He has lectured throughout the UK and also in USA, Australia and Singapore.

Giuseppe Intini is an architectural consultant; he founded Studio Intini in 1984 in Italy and England. The studio provides services in architecture, urban and regional planning and industrial design. The approach is humanistic and scientific, and has close links with artistic creative reference. The studio's recent projects include the expansion of the University of Perpignan, France, which was awarded the Prix du Ministère de l'Equipment, du Logement, des Transports et de l'Espace. Giuseppe Intini is also lecturer and design tutor at the Department of Architecture, University of Liverpool.

John James was for thirteen years an architect in private practice in Sydney. He then spent five years studying the Cathedral of Chartres to identify the nine masters who had created it. From this came a two-volume monograph, *The Contractors of Chartres* (Mandorla Publications, 2 vols, 1979–81), and the more popular, *The Master Masons of Chartres* (West Grinstead Publishing, 1991). In 1978 he presented a paper entitled 'The rib vaults of Durham Cathedral', to the Society of Architectural Historians of Great Britain. This was subsequently published in *Gesta* in 1984, and forms the basis of the article published in the present work. In 1980 he spent four years visiting the 3,500 churches in the Paris area.

identifying the 1,425 that still contained work from the Early Gothic period. After he obtained his Ph.D. in 1988, he published *The Template-Makers of the Paris Basin* (West Grinstead Publishing, 1989), which summarizes the results of his work since 1980.

Jennifer Jeffries, at the time of the case study, student, Bachelor of Architecture course, University of Newcastle upon Tyne

Hala Kardash is an architect, and research associate of the General Organization for Housing, Planning and Building Research in Cairo, Egypt. She has a Ph.D. (1993) from the University of Newcastle upon Tyne, Centre for Architectural Research and Development Overseas. Her research pays specific attention to public housing projects and resident-led adaptation and transformation of the original physical plan and house form.

Ng Wai Keen, at the time of the case study, student, Bachelor of Architecture course, University of Newcastle upon Tyne. He was on a one-year exchange from the School of Architecture, National University, Singapore.

Abdul Aziz Aba Al-Khail graduated from the Ecole Nationale Supérieure des Beaux-Arts, Paris, in 1972, with a State Diploma in Architecture. He studied at the Sorbonne where he obtained a Diploma in the History of Arts, a Certificate in French Linguistics and degrees in Sociology and Anthropology. He is a Lecturer at the University of Arabia Studies of Architecture and in the University of Theology and Islamic Law in Riyadh. He prepares programmes for the French Programme in *Riyad's Broadcast*.

Fazlur R. Khan (1929–82), one of America's leading structural engineers, was born in Dacca. He received a B.Eng. from the University of Dacca in 1950, and lectured there for two years before emigrating to the United States. He was awarded a Ph.D. in Structural Engineering from the University of Illinois at Urbana in 1955. He joined the Chicago office of Skidmore, Owins and Merrill in 1955, and was a general partner of the firm from 1970 until his death. In 1966 he was appointed Adjunct Professor of Architecture at the Illinois Institute of Technology, and was the recipient of numerous awards and honorary degrees. During the 1960s Khan and his colleague Myron Goldsmith advanced several new theories about the construction of very tall buildings. These studies were instrumental in the construction of buildings such as the Sears Tower in Chicago, at 1,454 feet the world's tallest building.

Anthony D. King is Professor of Art History and of Sociology, State University of New York at Binghamton. He is the author of *Colonial Urban Development* (Routledge, 1976), *The Bungalow* (Routledge, 1984), *Urbanism,*

Colonialism and the World Economy (Routledge, 1990) and *Global Cities* (Routledge, 1990), and the editor of *Buildings and Society* (Routledge, 1980) and *Culture, Globalization and the world-system* (Macmillan, 1991).

Lucien Kroll graduated from the national school of architecture (La Cambre) in Belgium in 1951. He has been Professor of Architecture at the Universities of Brussels and Grenoble, and has been a visiting professor at several universities in Europe and the United States. He has become well known for an architecture that closely involves the people for whom it is intended. He has worked on architectural projects across the spectrum, such as the quarters of the medical faculty at the Catholic University of Louvain, various projects in Rwanda, including the Palace of the President of the Republic in Kigali, and houses in Cergy-Pointoise, Alençon and Laroche-Clermault, France. Lucien Kroll has published over 500 articles, and his book *Composants* has been translated into several languages. His work has been the subject of television documentaries, and he has contributed to numerous exhibitions and conferences world-wide. He is a Member of the French Academy of Architecture.

Hans van der Laan (1904–91) studied architecture in the 1920s at the Technische Hogeschool in Delft before entering the Benedictine order, in which he was ordained as a priest in 1934. His earliest work as an architect dates from 1938, but the most significant is the monastery at Vaals begun in 1938 and completed in 1989. In the 1970s and 1980s, Van der Laan built two convents at Waasmunster in Belgium. He came from a family of architects and he taught courses at the architecture school of s'Hertogensbosch that were organized by his brother, Nico. These ideas are expressed in *Architectonic Space* (1977); there is a translation of this work by Richard Padovan, (1983). In 1985 another work, *The Form-Play of Liturgy*, was published but this has not yet been translated. He has also written of the relationship between architecture and clothing.

Robert Lawlor is an American who has been living in Australia for the past twelve years. He has a B.Sc. (State University of New York) and an MA (Pratt Institute NY). A former painter and sculptor, his works have been displayed in the Walter F. Crysler Museum, the Brooklyn Museum and the Pratt Institute, and in various private collections. His published works include *Sacred Geometry, It's Philosophy and Practice* (Crossroads/Thames & Hudson, 1982), *Geometry and Architecture* (1980) and *Homage to Pythagoras* (1981) (both co-written with Keith Critchlow, and published by Lindisfarne Press), *Earth Honouring – The New Male Sexuality* (Park Street Press, Australian edn Millenium Books, 1991), and *Voices of the First Day: Awakening in the Aboriginal Dreamtime* (Inner Traditions International, 1992).

Henry L. Lennard has directed programmes at Columbia University, and at the University of California in San Francisco, where he was Professor of Sociology in Psychiatry, and Director of the Family Study Station. Dr Lennard has also held Professorships at the University of Colorado and New York University. He is Guest Professor at the University of Ulm, Germany. He was educated at the Wasa Gymnasium, Vienna, and obtained a Ph.D. from Columbia University, New York. Dr Lennard has received grants and awards from the National Institute of Mental Health (Career Investigator), the Robert Wood Johnson Foundation, the Commonwealth Fund, the Grant Foundation and the National Science Foundation, among others. His published works include: *Public Life in Urban Places* (as co-author; Gondolier Press, 1984); *The Psychiatric Hospital* (Human Sciences Press, 1986); *Livable Cities: Social and Design Principles for the Future of the City* (as co-author; Gondolier Press, 1987). Dr Lennard is Chairman of the Advisory Board of the International Making Cities Livable Council, and Associate Editor of *Family Systems Medicine* and the *Making Cities Livable Newsletter*.

David Lewis is Professor of Architecture and Urban Design at Carnegie Mellon University Pittsburgh, Pennsylvania; and Chairman of UDA Architects Pittsburgh, Pennsylvania. He received the American Institute of Architects (AIA) National Kemper Award in 1988 and is the author of several books on art, architecture, and urban design. David Lewis was William Henry Bishop Professor at Yale University, 1974–6, and Founder, with Jonathan Barnett and Ann Ferebee, of the International Institute for Urban Design.

Derek Linstrum, Dipl.Arch., Ph.D., FSA, RIBA, trained as an architect and worked in Local Authority offices from 1947 to 1966. He has been a Senior Lecturer at Leeds School of Architecture (1966–71), Radcliffe Reader in Architectural History and Conservation at the University of York (1971–92), and Hoffman Wood Professor of Architecture, University of Leeds (1991–3). He founded and directed postgraduate studies in conservation at York, and has travelled and lectured extensively all over the world. His publications include *Sir Jeffry Wyatville: Architect to the King* (The Clarendon Press, 1972) and *West Yorkshire Architects and Architecture* (Lund Humphries, 1978), and he has contributed many articles and papers to professional and academic journals.

Evelyn Lip obtained her Ph.D. and her Masters in Architecture at Singapore, and has diplomas from universities in the UK and Malaysia in architecture, interior design and building design. She is a specialist on Feng Shui and is a Chinese brush painter and mural artist. She is the author of almost forty books, the most recent of which include: *Chinese Temple Architecture in Singapore* (Singapore University Press, 1983); *Chinese Customs and Festivals* (Macmillan, 1984); *Notes on Things Chinese* (Graham Brash, 1988) and *Feng Shui for Business* (Times Books International, 1989). Evelyn Lip is a Consultant on various aspects of Chinese architecture for major projects in Singapore and Malaysia. She is also a Senior Lecturer in Architecture at the National University of Singapore.

Hentie Louw is a Senior Lecturer at the Department of Architecture at the University of Newcastle upon Tyne. He was born and educated in the Republic of South Africa. After qualifying as an architect at the University of Pretoria he worked in Germany and England while continuing to study architectural history. He obtained his Ph.D. from Oxford University, after gaining a masters degree at Newcastle University. He has published articles on aspects of postmedieval Construction history in Northern Europe. He has actively promoted the development of architectural education in Europe for many years through the European Association for Architectural Education, of which he is currently Vice-President.

David Lowenthal is Emeritus Professor of Geography, University College, London, and currently acts as a consultant on heritage matters. His books include *Our Past Before Us: Why Do We Save It?* (with Marcus Binney, Temple Smith, 1981); *The Past is a Foreign Country* (Cambridge University Press, 1985); *The Politics of the Past* (with Peter Gathercole, Unwin Hyman, 1989); and *Heritage* (Viking/Penguin, forthcoming).

Denis De Lucca was born in Malta in 1952. He was educated at the University of Malta, from where he graduated as an architect in 1975. He is the Head of the Department of Architecture and Urban Design and Dean of the Faculty of Architecture and Civil Engineering at the University of Malta. He has carried out extensive research work on various aspects of architecture in the central Mediterranean area, and has participated in and presented papers at several international conferences.

Nils-Ole Lund is Professor of Architecture at the School of Architecture, Aarhus in Denmark. He qualified with a Diploma in Architecture from the Academy of Fine Arts in Copenhagen. He was Head of School at Aarhus from 1972 to 1985, and was President of the European Association for Architectural Education from 1987 to 1991. His publications include *Teoridannelser i arkitekturen* (Arkitektens Forlag, 1970) and *Nordisk arkitektur* (Arkitektens Forlag, 1991).

Marcel Maarek was born in Tunisia. He is Lecturer in Logic and Typology at the Université de Paris VIII. He is officially responsible for the mathematical entries in the *Larousse Encyclopedia*.

Charles McKean is Secretary and Treasurer, and Chief Executive, of the Royal Incorporation of Architects in Scotland (RIAS), a position he has held since 1979. He is an Honorary Fellow of the RIBA and an Honorary Member of the Saltire Society. In his RIAS capacity he established its Technical Services wing, its Professional Indemnity Insurance Company, its Publishing House, and its exhibition programme. Between 1977 and 1983 he was an award-winning architectural correspondent for *The Times*. He has contributed to journals ranging from *History Today* to the Series of Illustrated Architectural Guides to Scotland, of which he wrote the volumes on Edinburgh, Dundee, the District of Moray, and Banff and Buchan. His other publications include the *The Scottish Thirties: An Architectural Introduction* (Scottish Academic Press, 1987) and *Edinburgh: Portrait of a City* (Century, 1991).

Ali Madani Pour is an architect and urban designer with experience in Iran and the UK. He has published several pieces on urban design and has recently completed a Ph.D. on urban morphology, which explored actors and agencies in the development process. Since 1991, he has been a lecturer in the Department of Town and Country Planning, University of Newcastle upon Tyne.

Michael Manser qualified as an architect in 1954 and is a founder member of the British architectural practice, Manser Associates of London. The firm's work has gained several distinctions and has been published widely in international architectural magazines. Michael Manser contributes regularly to television programmes, newspapers and magazines. He was President of RIBA, 1983–5, and is currently a Council Member of the Royal Society of Arts and an Honorary Fellow of the Royal Canadian Institution of Architects.

Robert Mark is Professor of Architecture and Civil Engineering at the School of Architecture, Princeton University. He is the author of *Experiments in Gothic Structure* (MIT Press, 1983) and *Light, Wind and Structure: Mystery of the Master Builders*, (MIT Press, 1990).

Thomas A. Markus is an architect, and Emeritus Professor at the University of Strathclyde. He has had twenty-five years' experience in university teaching and research, twenty of those as Professor of Building Science at Strathclyde. He has been a visiting teacher in universities in western and eastern Europe, America, Malaysia, Nigeria and Saudi Arabia. He spent eight years in the glass industry, conducting research and development work on glass, windows and the environment. He has written numerous papers, and his books include: *Order in Space and Society: Scottish Architectural Form in the Eighteenth and Nineteenth Centuries* (as editor, Mainstream Publishing Company, 1982); *Visions of Perfection: Architecture and Utopian Thought* (Third Eye

Centre, 1985); and *Buildings and Power: Freedom and Control in the Origin of Modern Building Types* (Routledge, 1993).

John Martin is a civil engineer and is Chairman of the Ove Arup Partnership, London. He joined the firm as a structural engineer in 1957, attracted by its interest in architecture. Later he started and led what became known as building engineering, establishing multi-disciplinary groups of mechanical, electrical and structural engineers working closely together to make a fundamental contribution to good building design. Since then he has been concerned with a wide variety of the firm's activities in civil, industrial and building engineering, and its specialist support activities. Design, and the development of design skills, remain his principal interests.

Charles W. Moore obtained a B.Arch. at the University of Michigan, and an MFA and a Ph.D. at Princeton University. Since 1984 he has held the O'Neil Ford Centennial Chair in Architecture at the School of Architecture in the University of Texas. Charles Moore has also held professorships at the Universities of California and at Yale University. He was Assistant Professor at the University of Utah and at Princeton University and was Visiting Professor of Architecture at Harvard Graduate School of Design. He is professionally associated with the Urban Innovations Group of Los Angeles and with Centerbrook Architects, Essex. He is the author of several notable books, including *Body, Memory and Architecture* (Yale University Press, 1978) and *The Poetics of Gardens* (MIT Press, 1989), and was an AIA Gold Medallist (1991).

Ian Murphy is a practising architect and leader of the Degree Course in Architecture at the University of Westminster. He has considerable experience in both the private and public sectors of the profession, and has been a visiting critic and lecturer at many schools of architecture in the UK, Europe and the USA.

Adrian Napper has been Director of the School of Architecture, Edinburgh College of Art/Heriot-Watt University since 1990. After graduating in Civil Engineering, he worked for some years in practice both as a design engineer for a consultant and as a site engineer for various building contractors. Since the late 1960s he has been lecturing in the design of structures in University Schools of Architecture. For many years he ran a small consulting engineering practice which was concerned with a wide range of building types.

Herman Neuckermans graduated at the Katholieke Universiteit Leuven as an engineer-architect in 1967, and was awarded a Ph.D. in 1976 with a thesis on design methodology and CAAD. He practised as an architect from 1967 till 1974, and has been full professor at the KU Leuven since 1981, teaching basic design, architectural theory and design methodology. His research interests focus on design theory and computer aided design in architecture.

Patrick Nuttgens, CBE, MA, Ph.D., ARIBA, was educated at Edinburgh College of Art and Edinburgh University. After conducting research on the vernacular architecture of the north-east of Scotland, he taught at Edinburgh University and then at the University of York. In 1970 he became Director of Leeds Polytechnic, and after retiring he became an Honorary Professor of York. Patrick Nuttgens is the author of a number of books on architecture and planning, including: *The Landscape of Ideas* (Faber, 1972); the *Mitchell Beazley Pocket Guide to World Architecture* (1980); *The Story of Architecture* (Phaidon Press, 1983) and the *Understanding Modern Architecture* (Unwin Hyman, 1988). On the subject of education he has contributed to many journals, provided a regular weekly column for The *Times Higher Education Supplement*, and written *What Should We Teach and How Should We Teach It?* (Wildwood House, 1988). He has been a broadcaster on television and radio, producing films on subjects such as the Arts and Crafts Movement, modern architecture, Sir Edward Lutyens and Cuthbert Brodrick, as well as a major series on social housing entitled *The Home Front*. He is president of York Georgian Society and chairman of the Yorkshire Historic Churches Trust and York Theatre Royal.

Taner Oc is a Senior Lecturer in Planning at the Institute of Planning Studies and former Vice-Dean of the Faculty of Law and Social Sciences, University of Nottingham. His current research and recent publications examine ethnic minorities and planning, and safer city centres for women. He has taught at the Middle East Technical University, Queen's University of Belfast and George Washington University. He has qualifications in architecture, planning and social sciences. He is a member of the International Society of City and Regional Planners. He edited, with Sylvia Trench, *Current Issues in Planning* (Gower, 1990).

Werner Oechslin is Professor of Art History and Architecture at the Eidgenössische Technische Hochschule in Zurich, where he has been Director of the Institute for History and Theory of Architecture since 1986. He has lectured in many universities and architectural schools in Europe and America. In 1987, he was a guest professor at Harvard University. His research concentrates on diverse areas from Italian architecture (Roman and Piedmontese in particular) to Neoclassical and Modernity. His publications include contributions to the field of ephemeral architecture and contemporary architectural and cultural issues. Werner Oechslin has participated in a number of exhibitions such as the first critical documentation of the IBA-Neubau at the Martin-Gropius-Bau in Berlin, 1984. In 1985 he was on the jury of the Venice Biennale. He has been a coeditor of *Daidalos* (Berlin) since it began in 1981 and is a member of the directorial board of *Lotus International*.

John Onians is Professor of History of Art at the University of East Anglia, Norwich. His publications include *Art and Thought in the Hellenistic Age: The Greek World View 350–50 BC* (London 1979) and *Bearers of Meaning: The Classical Orders in Antiquity, the Middle Ages and the Renaissance* (Princeton University Press, 1988, winner of the 1988 Banister Fletcher Prize). Professor Onians was founding editor of the journal *Art History*.

Juhani Pallasmaa has been engaged in architectural, product and graphic design, and town planning since 1963. He is currently Professor of Architecture at the Helsinki University of Technology and runs an architectural practice in Helsinki. He has held a number of academic and professional positions, including Eero Saarinen Visiting Professor at Yale University (1993); State Artist Professor (1983–8); Director of the Museum of Finnish Architecture (1978–3); Associate Professor at the Haile Selassie I University, Addis Ababa (1972–4); Director of the Exhibition Department of the Museum of Finnish Architecture (1968–72, 1974–83) and Rector of the College of Crafts and Design (1970–2). Juhani Pallasmaa has designed over thirty exhibitions of Finnish architecture, planning and visual arts, shown in thirty countries. He has published numerous articles and has given many lectures abroad, on environmental psychology and the theory of architecture and the arts.

Cesar Pelli was born in Argentina, where he obtained a Diploma in Architecture from the University of Tucuman. He won a scholarship to study at the University of Illinois, where he gained a Masters in Architecture. For the following ten years he worked for Eero Saarinen as Project Designer and was involved in projects such as the JFK Airport and Morse and Stiles Colleges at Yale University. From 1964 to 1968 Cesar Pelli was Director of Design at DMJM, Los Angeles, and then became a Partner in Design Gruen Associates, also Los Angeles. With both firms he designed several award winning projects, including the American Embassy in Tokyo. In 1977 he became Dean at the Yale School of Architecture, and also founded his own firm with Fred Clarke and Diana Balmori. Since then, Cesar Pelli's work has been widely published and exhibited, with two books and several issues of professional journals dedicated to his designs and theories. He is a Fellow of the American Institute of Architects and a Trustee of the Wadsworth Atheneum. He is also a member of the American Academy and Institute of Arts and Letters, the National Academy of Design, the Board of Governors of the magazine *Perspecta*, and the Editorial Board of *On View*. He was the recipient of the Arnold M. Brunner Memorial Prize, and was the first architect to receive a Connecticut State Arts Award.

Dimitri Philippides graduated from the School of Architecture, National Technical University (NTU) of Athens in 1962, and received an Arch.D. degree from the School of Architecture, University of Michigan, in 1973. Since 1975 he has taught at the NTU where he is an Assistant Professor in the Department of Urban and Regional Planning. He has contributed numerous articles to Greek and foreign publications, on traditional and modern Greek architecture and planning. He translated Amos Rapoport's *House Form and Culture* into Greek (Architektonika Themata, 1976); published *Neoelliniki Architektoniki* (Modern Greek Architecture) (Melissa, 1984); *Gia Tin Elliniki Poli* (On Modern Greek Physical Planning) (Themelio, 1990), *Eikosi Theseis Gia Tin Poleodomia* (Twenty Theses on Planning) (Stigmi, 1990), and *To Skyrodema stin Elliniki Architektoniki tou Eikostou Aiona* (The Use of Concrete in Twentieth-Century Architecture in Greece (1992). As an editor, he supervised the first six volumes of *Greek Traditional Architecture* (Melissa, 1980–8). As guest-editor, he has also contributed to three issues of the annual publication *Architecture in Greece*.

Henry Plummer was educated at the School of Architecture and Planning, Massachusetts Institute of Technology, from where he qualified as an architect in 1975. He taught at MIT School before joining Warner-Burns-Toan-Lunde, Architects and Planners office, as Architectural Designer in 1977. Since 1981 he has been the Associate Professor at the School of Architecture, University of Illinois at Urbana-Champaign.

Tom Porter is a Colour Consultant and Senior Lecturer at Oxford School of Architecture. He is co-editor of *Colour for Architecture* (Studio Vista and Van Nostrand Reinhold, 1976) and author of *How Architects Visualise* (Studio Vista and Van Nostrand Reinhold, 1979), *Colour Outside* (Architectural Press and Whitney Library of Design, 1982) and *Graphic Design Techniques for Architectural Drawing* (Hamlyn-Amazon and Van Nostrand Reinhold, 1990). He is co-author of the four-volume series *Manual of Graphic Techniques* (Charles Scribner's Sons and Butterworth, 1988), *Designer Primer* (Charles Scribner's Sons and Butterworth, 1989) and *The Colour Eye* (BBC Books, 1990), the latter accompanying the BBC Television series of the same name.

James Powell is Lucas Professor of Design Systems, Head of the Department of Manufacturing and Engineering Systems, and Deputy Dean of Technology at Brunel – the University of West London. Trained as a building, environmental and human scientist, he worked for over twenty years, both in industry and academia, as an environmental engineer, becoming Head of the Portsmouth School of Architecture before moving to his present post. His pioneering research into the use of multi-media in architectural design information transfer has resulted in major national and European awards for learning, innovation and excellence. At Brunel he was able to extend his research studies in technology transfer and pursue the new research area of 'construction as a manufacturing process'. He has written four books and published over eighty academic papers. He is currently SERC's IT Applications Coordinator for Construction and Chairman of its Education and Training Committee.

Paul Rabinow is Professor of Anthropology at the University of California at Berkeley. His books include *Michel Foucault: Beyond Structuralism and Hermeneutics* (Harvester Press, 1983) and *French Modern: Norms and Forms of the Social Environment* (MIT Press, 1989).

Svetlozar Raev is a freelance architectural critic living in Cologne, Germany. He is a former scientific colleague of Gottfried Böhm when the latter held the Chair for Industrial and Urban Planning at the Rheinisch-Westfälische Technische Hochschule, Aachen, 1964–85. Svetlozar Raev's publications include *Gottfried Böhm, Bauten and Projekte (1950–80)* (1980)

Bill Risebero teaches architecture and planning at the University of East London. He has worked for thirty years as an architect and planner, on housing and community buildings and on local planning projects, mostly in inner London. His books are published in Britain and the United States, and in numerous translations, and include: *The Story of Western Architecture* (1985), *Modern Architecture and Design: An Alternative History* (1990); and *Fantastic Form: Architecture and Planning Today* (1992), all published by Herbert Press. He has visited the Soviet Union and has made a special study of Constructivism.

John Ruskin (1819–1900) was one of the most influential architectural writers ever, although he himself was not an architect. His impact on nineteenth and early twentieth century architectural thinking was immense, both in terms of aesthetic appreciation and social reform. His moralistic approach, however, found little favour during the 'scientific' middle decades of this century. The collapse of international modernism in turn brought about a revival of interest in Ruskin's ideas and a new appreciation for his qualities as a critic and visionary. His two most important books on architecture are *The Seven Lamps of Architecture* (1849) and *The Stones of Venice* (3 vols, 1851–3); both titles are still in print.

Jennifer Scarce is Curator of Eastern Cultures in the National Museums of Scotland, and specializes in the Islamic world. Her work has taken her to Iran, Turkey, Romania and the Arab gulf. Her most recent publications include *The Evolving Culture of Kuwait; Women's Costume of the Near and Middle East* (Unwin Hyman, 1987); a chapter on tilework in *The Arts of Persia* (edited by R.W. Ferrier, Yale University Press, 1989), and a chapter on arts of the eighteenth to twentieth centuries in *The Cambridge History of Iran*, Vol. 7: *From Nadir Shah to the Islamic Republic* (edited by Peter Avery, Galvin Hambly and Charles Melville, Cambridge University Press, 1991). She has also published a study on the Romanian carpet industry. Her current research interests include textile and costume traditions of the Ottoman Turkish Empire, Islamic cultural influences in Eastern Europe and tilework decoration of nineteenth-century Iran.

Alan Simpson is Senior Lecturer in Urban Design at the Bartlett School of Architecture and Planning, University College London (UCL), and Director of Urban Design Associates, Newcastle upon Tyne. He received the American Institute of Architects (AIA) Diploma for services to the AIA Regional/Urban Design Assistance Team (R/UDAT) programme in the United States. He has lectured on urban design and planning in Europe and the United States, and is Founder, with Roger Tillotson, of the Urban Futures Programme in the UK.

Henryk Skolimowski holds the Chair of Ecological Philosophy at the Katedra Filozofii Ekologicnej, Łódź, Poland. He was previously Professor of Philosophy at the College of Engineering Program in Humanities, University of Michigan. He has published over 300 articles, and fifteen books, including *Living Philosophy: Eco-philosophy as a Tree of Life* (Penguin/Arkana, 1992).

Werner Szambien is Head of Research at the National Centre for Scientific Studies (CNRS), Paris. He obtained his Ph.D. from Freie University in Berlin. His publications include: *Jean-Nicolas-Louis Durand, 1760–1834* (Picard, 1984); *Symétrie, Goût, Caractère* (Picard, 1986); *Les Projets de l'An II* (Ecole nationale supérieure des Beaux-Arts, 1986); *Le Muśe d'Architecture* (Picard, 1988), *Karl Friedrich Schinkel* (Hazan, 1989) and *De la rue des Colonnes à la rue de Rivoli* (Délégation à l'action artistique de la ville de Paris, 1992). Most of the rest of his work focuses on international neoclassicism (mainly in France and Germany) and the theory of architecture.

John Tarn took up the Roscoe Chair of Architecture at the University of Liverpool in 1973. He has also been Professor of Architecture at Nottingham, and prior to that he taught at the University of Sheffield. He was a Pro-Vice-Chancellor at Liverpool 1988–91, and was appointed Acting Vice-Chancellor for the session 1991–2. Professor Tarn sits on a number of prestigious outside bodies, including the Council of RIBA, and he has been Chairman of the Architects' Registration Council of the UK. He is currently Chairman of the Planning Control

Committee of the Peak District National Park. His overseas involvements have included membership of the Liaison Committee of Architects in Europe, acting as one of the British members of the EC Advisory Committee for the Architects' Directive, and acting as Advisor to the Indian Registration Council, the Chinese Society of Architects and the Chinese University in Hong Kong. He is an honorary consultant on conservation and tourism to the Chinese city of Chengde. John Tarn is a Fellow of RIBA, the Royal Society of Arts, the Royal Historical Society and the Society of Antiquaries. He was appointed OBE in 1992. He is the author of three books, has contributed to another four, and has written more than twenty-five papers.

Steven Tiesdell is a Lecturer in Planning (Urban Design) at the Institute of Planning Studies, University of Nottingham. He has qualifications in architecture and planning, and has research interests in the housing theories of the Modern Movement, urban design and urban regeneration.

Hartmut H. Topp is Professor for Transportation, Planning and Traffic Engineering in the Department of Architecture, Regional and Environmental Planning, and Civil Engineering at the University of Kaiserslautern in Germany. He was a consulting partner before he joined the University in 1981 and now continues his consultancy with Retzko & Topp in Darmstadt and Düsseldorf. The main topics of his current research work are traffic safety in urban areas, layout and *woonerf* concepts, environmental capacity of urban roads, urban parking strategies and their impact on modal-split.

Cornelis J.M. van de Ven has been an architect in private practice in Eindhoven, the Netherlands, since 1978. He studied at the Academy of Architecture in Rotterdam and also for four years in the United States, receiving a Masters Degree in Architecture from Louis I. Kahn's Studio and a Ph.D. (Arch.) in 1974, both from the University of Pennsylvania, Philadelphia. He has written extensively on architecture and theory in architecture, and his books include *Space in Architecture* (van Gorcum, 1977, 1980, 1987), which was translated into several languages, *Building in Barcelona* (Van Gennep, 1980) and *Museum Architecture* (1989). His work has been published in various national magazines and he has received numerous architectural prizes.

Neville Whittaker is an architect, consultant, writer and part-time lecturer at the University of Newcastle upon Tyne. He is the author of books on the buildings and towns of the north of England. He now works with Civic and National Trusts and is actively involved in the preservation of historic buildings. His understanding of Durham is based on a lifetime's association with the city and on working there for twenty-five years.

Michael Wigginton was educated at the University of Cambridge School of Architecture, and then joined the practice of Skidmore Owings & Merrill in New York. He subsequently joined Yorke Rosenberg Mardall in London where he worked until 1985 as a Senior Associate. In 1986 he became joint principal of Richard Horden Associates. Since 1987 the practice has won several major architectural competitions. Michael Wigginton has written many articles on the relationship between design and technology, and is the author of *Glass in Architecture* (Phaidon, 1993). He sits on the Publications Committee of the Royal Institute of British Architects, and his teaching and lecture programme extends across Europe and the USA. He is also an architect consultant to the 'Fenestration 2000' programme, established by Pilkington Brothers, and the Departments of Energy in the UK and the USA.

Nicholas Wilkinson is an architect, and lecturer at the Centre for Architectural Research and Development Overseas, University of Newcastle upon Tyne. He has travelled extensively on lecture tours and research missions in the People's Republic of China, the Middle East and Latin America. His field of work concerns quality in the built environment, with specific reference to the mechanisms of control and decision-making available to lay people and the professionals. He is founder and Editor-in-Chief of the journal *Open House International*, a refereed international quarterly on housing and urban development ideas, theories and practice.

Jakub Wujek studied at Gdańsk Technical University, Poland and in 1967 began in practice with Arch. Zdzislaw Lipski. He took part in forty-two competitions and was a prize winner of twenty-two. From 1967 to 1976 he designed exhibitions for the Museum of Modern Art in Łódź. He taught at the Higher School of Art and Design in Łódź from 1974 to 1978. He gained a Ph.D. in 1981 and then began to teach at the Institute of Architecture in Łódź. Jakub Wujek is the author of about sixty theoretical papers and the book *Myths and Utopias of 20th Century Architecture* (Arkaoly-Warsaw, 1983). He frequently participates in international conferences and seminars and, as an invited speaker, has visited education establishments in Poland and abroad. He is a member of the Polish Architectural Association (SARP); the Polish Urban Design Association (TUP); and the Comité International des Critiques d'Architecture (CICA).

David Yeomans teaches technology at the University of Manchester School of Architecture. He has a degree in engineering, and has taught structural design and carried out research into the history of timber structures. His books are *The Architect and the Carpenter* (RIBA) and *The Trussed Roof: Its History and Development* (Scolar Press). He was for a time Chief Education Officer at the

Timber Research and Development Association, and is currently involved with research on methods of repair and restoration of timber structures.

Charles Zucker is Senior Director at the American Institute of Architects (AIA) Community Assistance Initiative; and was Deputy Director of the Design Arts Programme of the National Endowment for the Arts, 1978–85. He was also a Faculty Member of the School of Architecture and Environmental Design at the City College of New York, 1969–75.

Index